Accounting 1
Fourth Edition

Accounting 1
Fourth Edition

G.E. Syme B. Com., C.A.
Eastview Secondary School

Prentice-Hall Canada Inc.,
Scarborough   Ontario

Canadian Cataloguing in Publication Data

Syme, G.E.
  Accounting 1

4th ed.
For use in secondary schools.
Includes index.
ISBN 0-13-002593-3

1. Accounting. I. Title

HF5635.S98 1988   657'.042   C88-093296-1

Also Available:
Supplementary Material: Workbook A: Chapters 1-11
Workbook B: Chapters 12-16
Teacher's Key for Workbook A
Teacher's Key for Workbook B
Teacher's Guide

© 1970, 1976, 1982, 1988 by Prentice-Hall Canada Inc., Scarborough, Ontario
All rights reserved. No part of this book may be reproduced in
any form without permission in writing from the publishers.

PRENTICE-HALL, INC., Englewood Cliffs, New Jersey
PRENTICE-HALL INTERNATIONAL, INC., London
PRENTICE-HALL OF AUSTRALIA, PTY., LTD., Sydney
PRENTICE-HALL OF INDIA, PVT., LTD., New Delhi
PRENTICE-HALL OF JAPAN, INC., Tokyo
PRENTICE-HALL OF SOUTHEAST ASIA (PTE.) LTD., Singapore
EDITORA PRENTICE-HALL DO BRASIL, LTDA., Rio de Janeiro
PRENTICE-HALL HISPANOAMERICANA, S.A., Mexico

ISBN 0-13-002593-3

Project Editor: Mary O'Neill
Production Editor: Ian Chunn
Manufacturing: Irene Maunder/Pamela Russell
Design: Robert Garbutt Productions

1 2 3 4 5 6 JD 93 92 91 90 89 88

Typesetting by Q Composition

Printed and bound in Canada by John Deyell Company

To my wife Dale

Accounting 1 could not have been realized without your patience, understanding, caring, and devotion to family.

Policy Statement

Prentice-Hall Canada Inc., Secondary School Division, and the author of *Accounting 1 Fourth Edition* are committed to the publication of instructional materials that are as bias-free as possible. This text was evaluated for bias prior to publication.

The author and publisher of this book also recognize the importance of appropriate reading levels and have therefore made every effort to ensure the highest degree of readability in the text. The content has been selected, organized, and written at a level suitable to the intended audience. Standard readability tests have been applied at several stages in the text's preparation to ensure an appropriate reading level.

Research indicates, however, that readability is affected by much more than word or sentence length; factors such as presentation, format and design, none of which are considered in the usual readability tests, also greatly influence the ease with which students read a book. These and many additional features have been carefully prepared to ensure maximum student comprehension. The section on Readability (page xvii of the Preface) describes those features. Further information is in the Introduction to the *Teacher's Guide*.

Contents

Acknowledgements xi

Preface xiii

1 Accounting and Business 1

1.1 What Is Accounting? 1
1.2 Characteristics of Business 2
1.3 Why Study Accounting? 3
1.4 The Nature of Accounting 5
1.5 Becoming an Accountant 8

2 The Balance Sheet 14

2.1 Financial Position 14
2.2 The Balance Sheet 18
2.3 Claims Against the Assets 26
2.4 Generally Accepted Accounting Principles 28
2.5 Computerized Accounting: The Accounting Spreadsheet 31

3 Analyzing Changes in Financial Position 43

3.1 Business Transactions 43
3.2 Equation Analysis Sheet 44
3.3 Summary of Steps in Analyzing a Transaction 53
3.4 Introduction to Source Documents 54
3.5 Computerized Accounting: Recording Transactions on the Spreadsheet 57

4 The Simple Ledger 68

4.1 Ledger Accounts   68
4.2 Debit and Credit Theory   73
4.3 Account Balances   83
4.4 The Trial Balance   86

5 The Income Statement and Revenue, Expense, and Drawings   103

5.1 The Income Statement   103
5.2 Expanding the Ledger   109
5.3 Completing the Ledger   116
5.4 Computerized Accounting: The Income Statement   122

6 Source Documents   134

6.1 Source Documents   134
6.2 Sales Tax   149
6.3 Computerized Accounting: The Accounting Package—The Computer Menu   154

7 Journalizing and Posting   169

7.1 Accounting versus Bookkeeping   169
7.2 The Journal   172
7.3 Posting   178
7.4 Trial Balance Out of Balance   188
7.5 Computerized Accounting: The Accounting Package—Data Entry   196

8 Subsidiary Ledger Accounting   211

8.1 Subsidiary Ledger Theory   212
8.2 Subsidiary Ledger Systems   217
8.3 Customer's Statement of Account   229
8.4 Computerized Accounting: Subsidiary Ledgers   235

9 The Simple Work Sheet and Classified Financial Statements   249

9.1 The Six-Column Work Sheet   249
9.2 Classified Financial Statements   256
9.3 The Work Sheet and the Financial Statements   259
9.4 Computerized Accounting: The Six-Column Work Sheet   269

10 Adjusting Entries/The Eight-Column Work Sheet   282

10.1 Accountability   282
10.2 Adjusting Entries for Prepaid Expenses and for Late Purchase Invoices   285
10.3 Adjusting for Depreciation   296
10.4 Financial Statements Showing the Effect of Adjustments   308
10.5 Computerized Accounting: Adjusting Entries   313

11 Completing the Accounting Cycle   329

11.1 Adjusting and Closing Entries—Objectives   329
11.2 Journalizing and Posting the Adjusting and Closing Entries   334

12 Accounting for a Merchandising Business   361

12.1 The Merchandising Business   361
12.2 Accounting Procedures for a Merchandising Business   369
12.3 Work Sheet for a Merchandising Business   373
12.4 Merchandise Returns and Allowances   382
12.5 Computerized Accounting: Accounting for a Merchandising Business   392

13 Specialized Journals   411

13.1 The Synoptic Journal   411
13.2 The Five-Journal System   432
13.3 Cash Discounts   442

Summary Exercise
Travel Trailers   470

14 Cash Control and Banking   476

14.1 Petty Cash Fund   476
14.2 Personal Banking   482
14.3 Bank Credit Cards   488
14.4 Banking for a Business   496
14.5 Accounting Controls   510

Supplementary Exercise
Green Thumb Garden Centre   539

15 Analyzing Financial Statements   563

15.1 Users of Financial Statements   563
15.2 Comparing Financial Data   564
15.3 Key Ratios and Statistics   576
15.4 Computerized Accounting: Trend Analysis and Key Ratios and Statistics   590

16 Payroll Accounting   613

16.1 Gross Pay   613
16.2 Payroll Deductions and Net Pay   620
16.3 Recording the Payroll   641
16.4 Payment to Employees   648
16.5 Basic Payroll Records   653
16.6 Computerized Accounting: The Payroll Package   656

Appendix — GAAPs   673

Glossary   677

Index   687

Acknowledgements

Over the years *Accounting 1* has benefited from contributions of many people who gave of their ideas and suggestions freely. I am indebted to these people for helping make *Accounting 1* a better book. The Fourth Edition began with the efforts of a number of teachers who reviewed the Third Edition and provided much constructive criticism. I am grateful for their help.

The vast experience and talent of Bill Riggs, Commercial Director of Sutton District High School, is evident in the Teacher's Guide that accompanies the text. Bill is the principal author of the Teacher's Guide and is also responsible for the career profiles found at the end of each chapter in the text.

Douglas Dover, a bright young student now at the University of Waterloo, took on the difficult task of working out solutions to the mountain of exercise material. His work was essential to proving the accuracy of the exercises and for the development of the companion workbooks.

In the important area of computers in accounting, the expertise was provided by Jim McNight of Port Credit Secondary School in Mississauga, and Lennox Borel, Commercial Director at Lester B. Pearson Collegiate Institute in Scarborough. Their experience and knowledge of computers was essential to the development of the computer sections found throughout the text.

Barbara Victil of the Bank of Nova Scotia in Barrie assisted me with the many details associated with banking. She also read the completed chapter to ensure its accuracy.

I would also like to pay special thanks to those at Prentice-Hall who have been involved in the production of this textbook. Steve Lane guided the project from the beginning, taking part in its planning and development and maintaining its high quality throughout. I greatly appreciate the care and attention taken by project editor Mary O'Neill and production editor Ian Chunn, who structured the rough manuscript into a finished text. Christopher Blackburn provided the clear, comprehensive index that follows the text. Once again Bob Garbutt's handsome and lucid design helps greatly to make the whole text highly readable. I wish to commend Joe Chin for his untiring efforts in coordinating the art and design of this project, supervising the work of a number of people, including the energetic Suzanne Boehler. Finally, Irene Maunder, Pamela Russell and Rand Paterson handled the technical aspects of production with efficiency and enthusiasm.

To all of them I extend my appreciation and gratitude.

G.E.S.

Preface

Accounting 1 Fourth Edition is an introductory accounting text for academic students. The book covers the complete accounting cycle as well as accounting for a merchandising business, specialized journals, cash control and banking, financial statement analysis, and payroll accounting. In addition to explaining the how of accounting (accounting procedures), the book places an emphasis on the why of accounting (accounting theory) and teaches students to critically analyze transactions and financial statements.

The author realizes that teachers will want to adjust the sequence of topics of their programs to fit their students' needs. However, the author has a preferred sequence which is reflected in the text.

The Fourth Edition opens with an introductory chapter intended for the many first year accounting students who have not taken a previous business course, and who consequently have little or no knowledge of business procedures. Chapter 1 discusses a number of aspects of business and accounting. Students learn about the nature of business, types of businesses, the relationship between accounting and business, and accountancy as a career or profession.

Chapters 2 to 5 teach the concepts of accounting in a simple, informal way using a service business. In these four chapters, students are introduced to the balance sheet and the elements of financial position (assets, liabilities, and owner's equity), the effect of transactions on financial position, the concept of a simple ledger and the rules for recording transactions therein, and expanding the ledger to include the income statement (revenue, expense, and drawings accounts).

Source documents are briefly introduced in Chapter 3. They are studied at this point so that students can see that business transactions originate from business documents. Then, in Chapter 6, the topic of source documents is covered fully. A number of source documents are identified and explained in detail.

Chapter 7 deals with the concepts of the journal and posting while Chapter 8 covers subsidiary ledger accounting. Chapters 9-11 explain the end-of-period work done by an accountant.

The work sheet, classified statements, adjusting entries, and the closing process are included. Consequently, the students have been introduced to the complete accounting cycle by the end of Chapter 11.

Chapter 12 expands the theory and practice of accounting to include a merchandising business. All types of transactions involving merchandise are covered. Chapter 13 shows the advantages of specialized journals.

The final three chapters of the book centre on particular aspects of accounting. Chapter 14 deals with cash and banking and introduces the concept of the bank credit card. Chapter 15 presents the usefulness and analysis of financial reports. Finally, Chapter 16 covers payroll.

Flexibility

Accounting is a cumulative subject and thus the topics in the text are presented logically and systematically. Nonetheless, *Accounting 1 Fourth Edition* is flexible enough for teachers to make some adjustments to the order of the chapters.

Chapter 1 can be covered very rapidly in class, or left out entirely depending on the students' accounting background. Chapters 2 through 13 cover the core of accounting in a logical progression and should probably be taught in sequence. The last three chapters can be studied in any order following the completion of Chapter 13.

Changes for the Fourth Edition

Before beginning work on this edition, the author and publisher asked many teachers and students for suggestions as to how *Accounting 1* could be improved. The Fourth Edition has been prepared with the same fundamental goals as were the first three editions. At the urging of teachers, the new edition retains the following features which have made *Accounting 1* so successful:

- an abundance of exercises and a good progression of difficulty for the assignment material
- clear presentation of subject matter
- logical organization

However, a comparison of this text and the earlier editions shows that there has been a number of significant changes for the Fourth Edition.

1. Content Coverage

- *Accounting for Your Money* (Ch. 2 in the Third Edition) is no longer in a separate chapter. Personal banking is covered in Chapter 14, *Cash Control and Banking*.
- *The Journal* (Ch. 6) and Posting (Ch. 7) are no longer two separate chapters. They are now Chapter 7, *Journalizing and Posting*.
- *The Income Statement* (Ch. 8) has been moved ahead of the new Chapter 7 (*Journalizing and Posting*) and is now Chapter 5.
- *Closing Entries* (Ch. 10) is no longer a separate chapter. The topic has been combined with a discussion of adjusting entries in Chapter 11, *Completing the Accounting Cycle*.

- *Source Documents* (Ch. 11) has been moved forward to become Chapter 6. In addition, source documents are presented more frequently in reading sections and in exercises throughout the text.
- *Subsidiary Ledger Accounting* (Ch. 12) has been moved ahead of a discussion of the simple worksheet and classified financial statements, and is now Chapter 8.
- *The Synoptic Journal* (Ch. 14) and the *Five Journal System* (Ch. 15) have been combined into Chapter 13, *Specialized Journals*.
- The chapter on *Cash Register Accounting* (Ch. 16) has been dropped, and relevant content is now included in Chapter 14, *Cash Control and Banking*.
- The chapter on *Accounting Controls* (Ch. 17) has been dropped, but relevant content is included in Chapter 14.
- The topic of adjusting entries (previously part of Chapter 19) has been moved forward and is now dealt with in Chapter 10, *Adjusting Entries/The Eight-Column Work Sheet*.
- The topic of accounting and the computer (previously Chapter 24) has been integrated throughout the Fourth Edition instead of being treated in a separate chapter. A section on the topic of computer applications is included in chapters where it is relevant.
- The accounting cycle is introduced earlier in the new edition and given more emphasis. Chapter 1 introduces the concept of accounting as a cyclical set of procedures so that students are later able to identify where each new accounting stage fits in the accounting cycle.

2. Greater Emphasis on Theory and Analysis

Increasingly, accounting guidelines are stressing that students should be given opportunities to develop the ability to think critically, arrive at decisions using reason and initiative, apply problem-solving models to relevant situations, and develop an understanding of the uses and significance of accounting information and reports. In response to these curriculum developments, *Accounting 1 Fourth Edition* puts much greater emphasis on the theory of accounting and on the development of analytical skills. Consequently, the following changes have taken place for the new edition:

- Additional exercises have been added to develop students' analytical skills involving transactions and financial statements.
- Narrative sections have been rewritten to give greater emphasis to the why of accounting (the underlying theory) while still dealing with the how of accounting (accounting routines).
- The number of case studies has been increased in each chapter to provide students with more practice in analysing authentic-type accounting transactions. Each chapter now contains between 3 and 5 case studies.
- Generally Accepted Accounting Principles (GAAPs) have been added where applicable throughout the text.

3. Improved Chapter Organization

Each chapter is divided into major sections. Within each section, the narrative is further divided into headings and subheadings to help students follow the develoment of a particular topic more easily. Content questions and exercises occur at the end of each section. In addition, there are questions and exercises at the end of each chapter.

4. More Questions and Exercises

Accounting 1 Fourth Edition contains more assignment material than in previous editions:

a) *Section Review Questions* accompany each chapter section. These are recall questions which help students review the content of the section.

b) *Section Exercises* accompany each chapter section. These check comprehension of the concepts taught, and provide practice in any newly-learned accounting routines.

c) *Chapter Exercises* are found at the end of each chapter. These integrate knowledge from all sections of a chapter, while building on skills learned in earlier chapters. Chapter exercises are divided into three categories:

- *Using Your Knowledge* exercises are skill-oriented. These provide students with practice in various accounting routines, such as transaction analysis and error detection.
- *Comprehensive Exercises* are at the comprehension and application levels. This material gives students opportunities to put their knowledge of accounting principles into practice, such as setting up books for a business.
- *For Further Thought* exercises challenge students to combine their accounting knowledge with common sense, and knowledge of "real-world" business practice. These exercises are ideal for group work and discussion.

d) *Case Studies* present real problems in accounting and challenge students to think critically.

e) The *Summary Exercise* and *Supplementary Exercise* are business simulation projects which integrate knowledge from several chapters.

5. Coverage of Accounting and the Computer Integrated Throughout the Text

The subject of computerized accounting is presented in various chapters where applicable. Topics covered include the accounting spreadsheet, the income statement, data entry, subsidiary ledgers, the six-column work sheet, adjusting entries, accounting for a merchandising business, trend analysis, and payroll. These computer sections are accompanied by non-hardware specific exercises. The computer sections are appropriate for either a hands-on, or a concepts-only approach.

6. Improved Career Profiles

The career profiles have been given a more professional orientation in keeping with the likely career objectives of academic students. Greater stress is placed on continuing education and the incorporation of computer studies. In addition, Discussion questions accompany each profile. These questions involve a variety of assignments including oral reports, research, written reports, and class discussions.

7. Increased Emphasis on Group Work, Oral and Writing Skills

Accounting 1 Fourth Edition provides students with opportunities to practice their oral and writing skills as well as to participate in group work. These types of assignments are part of the "For Further Thought" exercises, the case studies, and the career profiles.

8. Updating

The new edition has been updated to reflect changes in professional titles, prices, and equipment used in the accounting process.

Readability

Accounting 1 Fourth Edition offers thorough explanations in a simple, straightforward writing style. This clear presentation assists individualized instruction as it allows students to work on their own or to catch up on missed work.

The author and publisher of this book also recognize the importance of appropriate reading levels and have therefore made every effort to ensure the highest possible degree of readability in the text. The content has been selected, organized, and written at a level suitable for the intended audience. Standard readability tests have been applied at several stages in the text's preparation to ensure an appropriate reading level.

Readability tests, however, can provide only a rough indication of a book's reading level. Research indicates that readability is affected by much more than the number of syllables in a word and/or the length of sentences. Design, format, and motivating content are considered just as important in helping students read. Thus, the following features were incorporated into the content and design of *Accounting 1 Fourth Edition* to further enhance readability and understanding.

1. The text consists of 16 chapters. Each chapter, in turn, is divided into major sections.
2. Chapter sections are listed at the beginning of each chapter. This organizes the chapter at a glance and shows the students how the chapter will develop.
3. Narratives are divided into short segments using a consistent system of headings and subheadings. Thus students are able to make a distinction between the various levels of headings and their relative importance.

4. Review questions occur at the end of every section of a chapter. These are recall questions which help students review the content of the section.
5. Exercises accompany each chapter section. These check comprehension of the concepts taught, and provide practice in any newly-learned accounting routines.
6. Each chapter concludes with a listing of the main concepts and key terms to assist the students during review.
7. Each chapter concludes with a set of assignment material:
    - *Using Your Knowledge* exercises are skill-oriented. These provide students with practice in various accounting routines, such as transaction analysis and error detection.
    - *Comprehensive Exercises* are at the comprehension and application levels. This material gives students opportunities to put their knowledge of accounting principles into practice, such as setting up the books for a business.
    - *For Further Thought* exercises challenge students to combine their accounting knowledge with common sense, and a knowledge of "real-world" business practice. These exercises are ideal for group work and discussion.
    - *Case Studies* present real problems in accounting and challenge students to think critically.
8. The book employs an attractive design to appeal to students and encourage the use of the text. It features an uncluttered, single-column format. In addition, generous use is made of headings, subheadings, and second colour.
9. The printed word is reinforced with over 400 illustrations and charts.
10. Terms are printed in colour and defined in context when first introduced. These terms are then listed at the end of the chapter and defined in the glossary at the end of the text.
11. Short descriptions of accounting careers are included in all chapters as a means to make the material more meaningful to students.
12. The book includes a glossary of terms and a comprehensive index to help students find and use important accounting terms and information.

Student Workbooks

As before, there are two companion workbooks to accompany the text. The workbooks supply all the business papers and accounting forms required to complete the exercises given in the student text. Furthermore, the workbooks feature some additional exercises not included in the text.

Teacher's Keys

There are two Teacher's Keys to accompany the text. Teacher's Key A covers Chapters 1 to 11, and Teacher's Key B Chapters 12 to 16. These Keys supply complete step-by-step solutions for all the workbook exercises, as well as suggested answers for the review questions, case studies, and questions accompanying the careers.

Teacher's Guide

Accounting 1 Fourth Edition is further supplemented by a comprehensive Teacher's Guide. For each chapter, the guide offers:

- An *Overview* which presents introductory comments on the chapter as a whole.
- *Objectives*, written according to behavioural principles and intended to assist teachers when preparing student objectives for their own particular class.
- A *Suggested Chapter Schedule*, designed to guide teachers in terms of how much time to spend on the chapter.
- *Teaching Notes*, including an explanation of the purpose of the chapter and an indication of what students are expected to learn from the material. Notes will also deal with computer applications, and ideas about how to utilize outside resources to supplement the text.
- *Comments on the Exercises*, which point out the purpose of the exercise and indicate the common pitfalls and other mistakes students might make when completing the exercise.
- *Teaching Masters*, included in order to illustrate the major principles of accounting covered in the chapter. Teachers have permission to copy these masters or to use them for making transparencies.
- Two *Tests*: for the Fourth Edition, the tests feature less emphasis on objective questions and more on subjective, essay-type material.

It is impossible to overstate the value for today's students of a basic knowledge of accounting. For those who enter the business world, accounting skills can unlock the door to rewarding careers. But even for those who do not enter business, an understanding of basic accounting concepts can help in such areas as the management of personal finances or the unravelling of an increasingly complex world economic picture.

To help students understand the value of accounting knowledge, I have tried to stress practical accounting applications whenever possible. And to help ensure that the students' introduction to the subject is rewarding, I have tried to capture their interest with a stimulating assortment of concepts, problems, and issues. Students embarking on the study of accounting are taking the first steps toward promising futures. It is my hope that for these students, and for their teachers, *Accounting 1* will provide an invaluable resource and guide.

G.E.S.

Accounting 1

Fourth Edition

1 Accounting and Business

1.1 What Is Accounting?
1.2 Characteristics of Business
1.3 Why Study Accounting?
1.4 The Nature of Accounting
1.5 Becoming an Accountant

As a student just beginning the study of accounting, you would naturally like to know exactly what accounting is. There is no simple definition. Accounting is a system with many aspects. Some aspects are simple, others are complex. It takes several years of serious study and practice to become a professional accountant.

1.1 What Is Accounting?

There are five main activities involved in accounting. These are:
1. the gathering of financial information about the activities of a business or other organization;
2. the preparing and collecting of permanent records. Records provide evidence of purchase, proof of payment, details of payroll, and so on. They also serve as the basis for dealings with other companies;
3. the rearranging, summarizing, and classifying of financial information into a more useable form;
4. the preparing of information reports and summaries:
   a. to help management reach decisions;
   b. to serve the needs of groups outside the business, such as bankers and investors;
   c. to measure the profitability of the business;
5. the establishing of controls to promote accuracy and honesty among employees. As businesses grow, owners can no longer look after everything alone. They have to hire others to help them. As soon as outside employees are hired, accounting controls become essential.

Accounting—An Information System

A good accounting system provides the answers to many questions. For example, owners and managers might seek answers to questions such as the following:
- Is the business earning enough profit?
- Are the selling prices of the products high enough?
- How much does ABC Company owe the business?
- How much does the business owe to XYZ Company?
- How much, in total, is owed by customers?
- Which customers' accounts are overdue?
- How much money is there in the bank account?
- How much is the bank loan?
- How much is being paid in bank interest?
- What is the value of all of the goods for sale?
- Do any of the goods for sale need to be restocked?
- How much was spent on gasoline for the company trucks?
- To whom was cheque No. 502 issued?
- How much does it cost to produce product X?
- How much did John Smith earn last year?

Outside persons, companies, or organizations might seek answers to the following questions:
- Should I lend money to this business? (a banker)
- Should I buy into this business? (a potential investor)
- Should I sell this business? (an owner)
- Is the business well run? (an absentee owner)
- Is the company growing satisfactorily? (an absentee owner)
- Can the business afford to pay more to its employees? (a labour union)
- Is the business paying the proper amount of income tax? (the government)

1.2 Characteristics of Business

The Nature of Business

There are businesses of all types throughout the country. Businesses are the economic framework upon which our society is built. But what is a business? Generally, a business involves the manufacture and/or sale of goods or services in order to earn a profit.

Most businesses fall within one of the following three main categories:

1. The Service Business

A **service business** sells a service to the public; it does not make or sell a product. To picture a service business, think of a bowling alley, a transport company, a rock group, or a medical clinic.

2. The Merchandising Business

A **merchandising business** buys goods and resells them at a higher price for a profit. To picture a merchandising business, think of a hardware store, a marina, a department store, or a record store.

3. The Manufacturing Business

A **manufacturing business** buys raw materials, converts them into a new product, and sells these products to earn a profit. To picture a manufacturing business, think of a construction company, a paper mill, or a steel plant. Although a farm is not a manufacturing company in the strict sense, it is closely related. It is known as a producing business because it produces milk, grain, and other foods.

Forms of Business Ownership

There are three main forms of business ownership. On a walk down any commercial street, you can see examples of each one.

1. You might notice a sign that reads "J. Wouk, Carpenter." This sign indicates that J. Wouk is in business for himself and that he works alone. This type of business is known as a **sole-proprietorship**. The owner is a sole proprietor.
2. You might come across a sign that reads "Fogle, Silver, and Zimmerman, Accountants." This sign suggests that three persons share in the ownership and operation of an accounting business. A business of this type, involving more than one owner, is known as a **partnership**.
3. You might find a sign that reads "Red River Homes Limited." This sign tells you that the business is a limited company or a corporation. A **limited company** or **corporation** is a special form of business that is owned by a number of persons called shareholders. Almost all large business operations are corporations, and some have several thousand shareholders.

1.3 Why Study Accounting?

A knowledge of accounting can be very useful in several ways.

Accounting as a Job

Those of you who decide to enter the business world will find employment more easily if you have a background in accounting. A large number of jobs require accounting and clerical skills. There are different levels of accounting occupations. The higher the level, the more training and experience is required, and the higher the salary offered.

Owning Your Own Business

Many people want to own their own business. Those who achieve this goal soon find themselves faced with accounting tasks. They must do their banking. They must keep track of the amounts owed by their customers. They must keep accounting records for the government. They must produce an income statement for income tax purposes. They may have to prepare payrolls and make payroll deductions. Clearly, a knowledge of accounting is helpful in the small business sector—the fastest-growing segment of our economy.

Accounting in Daily Life

Even if you do not work in the field of accounting, you will still benefit from having a working knowledge of the subject. People with an accounting background know the language of business as well as accounting concepts. They are better able to understand financial matters and to handle their personal business affairs. Also, by knowing what business is all about, they are in a better position to take advantage of business opportunities.

Professional Accountancy

Some of you may choose professional accounting as a career. By completing the requirements of one of the professional bodies of accountants, you can become a Chartered Accountant, a Certified General Accountant, or a Certified Management Accountant. Qualified professional accountants often hold senior management positions and have the right to practise as public accountants.

A **public accountant** is one who serves the general public for a fee in the same way a doctor or a lawyer does. The main type of work done by public accountants is auditing. **Auditing** is the examination and testing of the books, records, and procedures of a business in order to be able to express an opinion about its financial statements. Public accountants also work as management consultants and tax advisors.

Professional accountants may choose industrial or institutional accounting rather than public accounting. *Industrial accountants* work for large companies such as IBM or Stelco. *Institutional accountants* work for the government, banks, large insurance companies and similar organizations.

Complexity of Business

There are many laws laid down by the government concerning fair business practices, income taxes, and so on. They have become so numerous and complex that only experts can thoroughly understand them. Fully qualified accountants know these laws. The increasing complexity of government regulations is the major reason why accounting is one of the fastest-growing of all professions.

1.4 The Nature of Accounting

A typical accounting department has several employees. They can be seen operating business machines, speaking on telephones, engaging in discussion, working with pen and paper, and so on. At first sight, it is difficult to see any differences among the types of work being done. But different activities are being performed.

The accounting department of a business includes a wide variety of functions. In a small business, one or two people may do all the necessary accounting work. In a large business, several people may be needed to carry out the many accounting tasks.

The following section examines some of these accounting tasks and the people performing them for a typical business.

Specific Accounting Tasks

The *credit manager* is Samuel Kwong. One of his responsibilities is to decide whether or not to let new customers buy the company's goods or services on credit. He is responsible for all aspects of accounts receivable (that is, money owing from customers). Sam makes sure that customers' accounts are recorded accurately and collected promptly. If an account becomes overdue, it is Sam who must encourage the customer to pay. Since the company has a large number of customers, Sam is a very busy person.

Sam has a secondary school diploma and has worked for his present employer for six years. Two years ago he enrolled in a program to become a qualified accountant. It will take three more years for him to complete the program. He is gaining valuable experience in his present position, but he realizes that he may have to change companies to improve his status.

The *cash receipts clerk* is Frank Liscombe. Among his duties, Frank opens, sorts, and distributes the mail. Any money received in the mail must be listed for record-keeping purposes. Then it is organized properly for deposit in the bank. Frank is responsible for making the bank deposit each day.

Frank recently graduated from high school, where he concentrated on business subjects. Although his marks were good, he has no desire to go to college at this time. He is quite happy at his present job. Working for a year or two will give him a chance to think about his future.

The *supervisor of payroll* is Janet Doucette. She and her staff prepare the company's weekly payroll. Janet has an important position. The company has a large number of employees, and they depend on Janet to have their cheques ready on time.

Janet has held several different accounting jobs since she left school fifteen years ago. She has no formal training but over the years has acquired a great deal of expert knowledge concerning payroll accounting. She enjoys the challenge of being in charge of the payroll department.

The *accounts payable supervisor* is Susan Kusyk. Susan's position is also an important one. As bills are received from suppliers, they are sent to Susan's department.

There, certain steps are taken to make sure that the bills are made out correctly and are proper charges against the business. Bills are not paid until Susan gives the final approval.

Although she is not a qualified accountant, Susan is a college graduate and has taken a number of accounting courses. Her goal is to complete one of the professional accounting courses. She knows that she will improve her career options if she becomes a qualified accountant.

The *chief accountant and office manager* is Dave Duncan. He is in charge of the accounting department. As the senior person, Dave must ensure that the accounting system and procedures are in place and that the system is running smoothly and efficiently.

Dave is a chartered accountant. He is the only one in the office who understands the entire system. If something goes wrong, Dave can be counted on to work it out. In addition to his many regular duties, Dave is part of the management team. He spends a lot of time preparing data and reports for management and attending management meetings.

Accounting Work in General

The accounting department of a business is expected to perform many activities. These belong in one of three categories:

1. Routine Daily Activities

These are activities that occur in the same way nearly every day of the year. They include processing bills, preparing cheques, daily banking, recording transactions, preparing business papers, and so on.

2. Periodic Accounting Activities

These are activities that occur at regular intervals. Pay cheques are made ready every week or two. The bank accounts are checked every month. The financial reports are prepared every year. Also, the income tax return is prepared every year as required by government regulation.

3. Miscellaneous Activities

Some accounting activities cannot be predicted. For example, if an accounting employee resigns, the position must be filled quickly. An advertisement is prepared, interviews conducted, and a selection made. Or, a bank manager may call, expressing concern over the size of the bank loan. A visit to the bank to discuss the matter may become necessary. Or, a salesperson may call about a new machine that will reduce office costs. Time may be taken to see a demonstration of the equipment.

The Accounting Cycle

Accounting is thought of as occurring in cycles. Accounting activities are performed in relation to equal periods of time known as fiscal periods. The usual length for a fiscal period is one year. The **accounting cycle** can be thought of as the recurring set of accounting procedures carried out during each fiscal period. These accounting activities are carried out repeatedly, period after period. Figure 1.1 shows the recurring nature of accounting activity.

The accounting cycle really consists of two separate cycles. Figure 1.1 shows these with an inner and an outer ring. Some of the activities shown on the outer ring occur every day. Others occur only once a month. The activities on the inner ring normally occur once a year and are based on data provided by the activities of the outer ring.

It must be understood, however, that each cycle is built upon the cumulative results of previous cycles. The business does not have a fresh start each fiscal period.

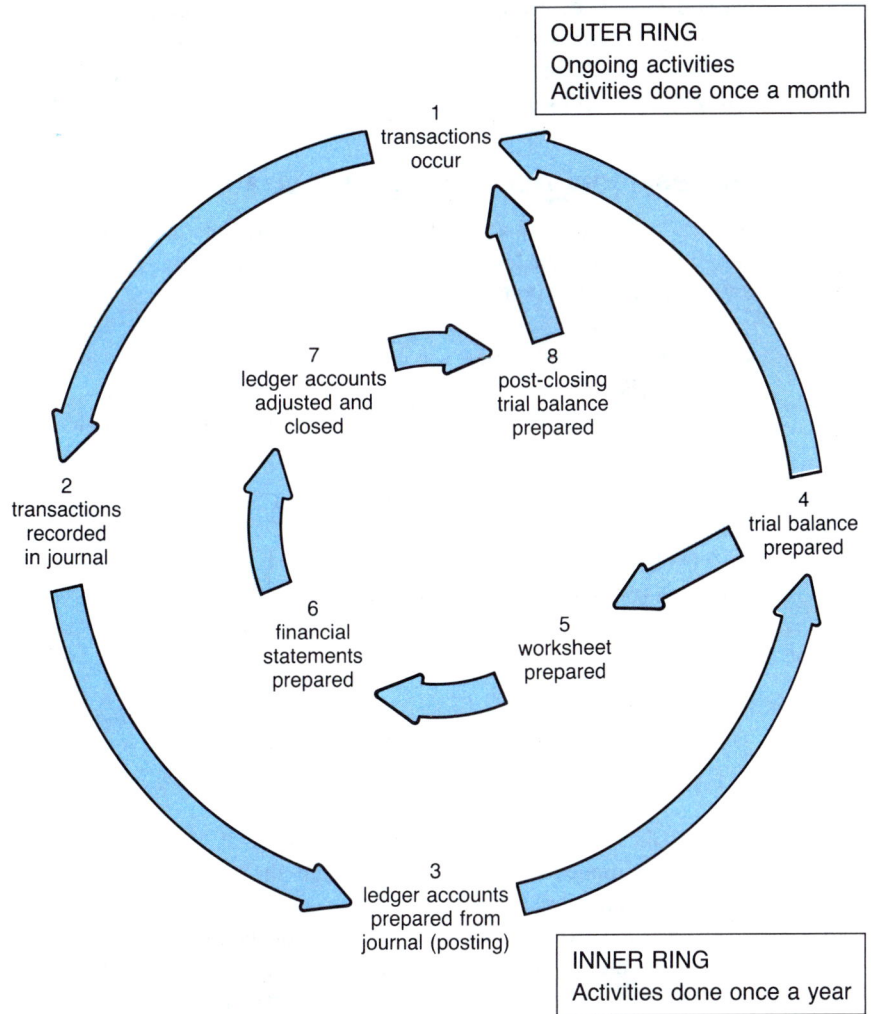

Figure 1.1 The accounting cycle.

1.5 Becoming an Accountant

A great many accounting jobs exist in our society. Some are minor positions with small firms and require basic accounting skills only. Others are high-level positions requiring exceptional competence and training. Between these two extremes, there lies a vast range of accounting occupations in business. To fill these positions are many persons with different backgrounds and abilities, all calling themselves accountants. Some may have little or no formal training. Others may have studied at an advanced level for a number of years.

Accountants get their formal training either in high school, at college or university, or from a professional organization. In addition to formal studies in accounting, on-the-job experience is important. You are not really prepared to do professional accountancy until you have practical experience along with your formal training.

Most colleges and universities offer diplomas or degree courses in business. The study of accounting is included as part of the curriculum of these courses.

Professional Accounting Organizations

To be a fully qualified accountant you must complete the course prescribed by one of the three national professional accounting organizations. The names of these organizations and their national addresses are:

Canadian Certified General Accountants' Association
740–1176 West Georgia Street
Vancouver, B.C.   Professional designation:
V6E 4A2   CGA (Certified General Accountant)

The Society of Management Accountants of Canada
154 Main Street East
M.P.O. Box 2150   Professional designation:
Hamilton, Ontario   CMA (Certified Management
L8N 4A5   Accountant)

Canadian Institute of Chartered Accountants
150 Bloor Street West
Toronto, Ontario   Professional designation:
M5S 2Y2   CA (Chartered Accountant)

Each of these national associations has provincial associations working within provincial requirements. The members of all three of these organizations are highly respected professional accountants.

At one time the accountancy profession was dominated by men. However, women have been entering the profession in increasing numbers. On four occasions in recent years women have won the Institute of Chartered Accountants' Gold Medal for obtaining the highest marks across Canada. Women now make up a significant proportion of all persons in the accounting profession, and the percentage of women entering the profession is increasing annually.

Training to be a CA

The Institute of Chartered Accountants is the senior association in Canada. It is the oldest and largest body of professional accountants in the country. The Institute of Chartered Accountants is the only one that requires its members to have a university degree and to have practical experience in "public accounting" before graduation. Nearly half of the institute's members, far more than either of the other organizations', are employed as public accountants. In some regions, the law provides that only members of the institute be allowed to express an opinion on financial statements.

To become a chartered accountant, a candidate must first obtain a university degree including certain prescribed courses. The candidate must then complete a program of advanced professional study laid down by the Institute of Chartered Accountants. He or she must also serve a term of practical employment as a public accountant, and pass a final examination.

It usually takes five years after enrolment to become a chartered accountant.

Training to be a CGA or CMA

The CGA and CMA programs are similar in a number of ways. To enrol in either of the two courses, you must be a high school graduate. The programs usually take five years to complete. However, the time can be shorter or longer depending on the individual. People usually work full time in accounting occupations while taking these courses. Full-time work is not compulsory, but both associations require that a candidate have practical experience before graduating. Both associations also offer lecture courses at universities and colleges across Canada. To fully qualify, a student must meet all the course requirements and pass a final examination that is the same across Canada.

The principal difference between the CGA and the CMA programs is one of emphasis. The CMA program concentrates on developing management accountants who are expected to work in industry at the management level. The CGA program allows for specialization in different areas (auditing, for example) in the final year. CGAs work in all areas of accounting.

Computers in Accounting

The computer is ideal for use in an accounting environment. In accounting, there is a lot of recording, sorting, calculating, summarizing, storing, and working with numbers. The computer is good at all these activities. In addition, the computer can handle large quantities of data, and can produce data on video screen or by printout. Further, the computer is fast and can provide information for management quickly.

Modern accounting offices use many different accounting packages (sets of programs that work together). Anyone intent on becoming an accountant will study computer courses as part of the curriculum. You will be shown the relationship between accounting and the computer as you progress through this text.

CHAPTER HIGHLIGHTS

Now that you have completed Chapter 1, you should:

1. have a broad understanding of the objectives of accounting;
2. know the three main kinds of businesses and the three forms of business ownership;
3. know the benefits to be gained by having a background in accounting;
4. know what is meant by "professional accountant" and "public accountant";
5. know the type of work performed in an accounting department;
6. understand what is meant by the accounting cycle;
7. know the different ways you can become an accountant;
8. know the three national accounting organizations and the requirements for admission to their programs.

ACCOUNTING TERMS

accounting cycle
auditing
corporation
limited company
manufacturing business
merchandising business
partnership
public accountant
public accounting
service business
sole-proprietorship

CHAPTER QUESTIONS

1. Give an example of a question for which the accounting system can provide the answer.
2. Name two groups who use information provided by the accounting system.
3. Briefly describe the five aspects of an accounting system.
4. In general, what is a business?
5. Define a service business.
6. Define a merchandising business.
7. Define a manufacturing business.
8. What is a sole-proprietorship?
9. What is a partnership?
10. What is a corporation?
11. Why is a knowledge of accounting helpful to someone looking for a job?
12. In what ways is accounting useful to persons who own their own business?
13. How is a knowledge of accounting useful to the ordinary person?
14. What is meant by professional accountancy?
15. What is a public accountant?

16. What is meant by auditing?
17. What is meant by industrial accounting?
18. What is meant by institutional accounting?
19. Why is accounting one of the fastest-growing professions?
20. What type of work does the credit manager do?
21. Why is payroll supervisor an important position?
22. What are the responsibilities of the accounts payable supervisor?
23. Why is the chief accountant included as part of the management team?
24. Name a daily accounting activity.
25. Name a periodic accounting activity.
26. Describe what is meant by the accounting cycle.
27. Why do colleges and universities include accounting courses in many of their programs?
28. Name the three national professional accounting associations.
29. Which of the above three organizations is considered to be the senior body?
30. Name two requirements of the Institute of Chartered Accountants that are not requirements of the other associations.
31. On average, how long does it take after enrolment to become a chartered accountant?
32. Explain why computer studies are now part of the curriculum of accounting courses.
33. Give two characteristics of the computer that make it ideal for use in accounting.

CAREER
David Steel / Student in Accounts

David Steel says that as a kid growing up in Conception Bay, Newfoundland, he liked nothing better than a winter storm because it meant a day off school. To his surprise, when David studied accounting in high school, he found his courses interesting and enjoyable. He decided to continue his study of accounting and become a chartered accountant.

David is now a student in accounts, working toward a professional degree as a chartered accountant in the Co-operative Educational Program at Memorial University in St. John's. This program brings together the theory and practice of accounting. Students spend four months taking classes and then four months gaining practical experience by working for a chartered accountant.

During the four-year program, David will complete nine courses in accounting: two in taxation, one in auditing, two in economics, two in computer science, and four in business-related areas such as law and finance. At the end of the program, David will graduate with an Honours Bachelor of Commerce degree. He then must write the examination for chartered accountants, which actually involves four examinations, each four hours long.

To gain his practical experience, David works with McPherson, Scott and Co., a firm of chartered accountants in St. John's. The company has a wide range of clients, including car dealerships, charities, small man-

ufacturers and trust companies. Some of these companies have manual accounting systems, while others have computerized systems. As a result, David is exposed to a variety of accounting procedures.

This year, David is spending most of his time examining the accounting controls over cash to ensure accuracy and honesty. He advises clients when controls have to be strengthened.

David reviews and analyzes books of accounts to ensure that financial statements are presented fairly. He also helps one of the firm's chartered accountants to complete tax returns. Finally, David performs general bookkeeping for his clients; this includes journalizing, posting, banking, accounts receivable and payroll. This on-the-job training provides

David with the opportunity to experience and learn word processing, the use of electronic spreadsheets, data management, and communications.

According to the terms of David's program, the firm of chartered accountants is responsible for supervising him in all assignments. The accountants also submit a student evaluation to the university; this will be reviewed by David and the accountants together. David's student evaluation will be made available to employers who are considering hiring him.

If David succeeds in becoming a chartered accountant, he will have several career choices. He may decide to take a position in industry as an executive officer, or he may want to start his own accounting practice or join an accounting firm. At present, David intends to work for a corporation when he graduates.

David highly recommends the Co-operative Educational Program to all those who wish to advance their business careers. The combination of study and practical application means that graduates of the program are well equipped to meet the challenges of today's competitive business world.

Discussion

1. Explain what is meant by the term "student in accounts."
2. List some of the duties David performs during the auditing process.
3. The phrase "the financial statements are presented fairly" sets out an important concept in accounting and auditing. In your opinion what do you think this expression means?
4. Discuss the career options open to David when he becomes a chartered accountant.
5. If you were in David's position and were to become a chartered accountant, what career option would you choose and why?
6. Write a report on the Co-operative Educational Program in business offered at the University of Waterloo in Ontario, including in your report the names of other Canadian universities that offer similar programs and the qualifications required to enrol. You can check the school guidance office and the library for this kind of information.

2 The Balance Sheet

2.1 Financial Position
2.2 The Balance Sheet
2.3 Claims Against the Assets
2.4 Generally Accepted Accounting Principles
2.5 Computerized Accounting: The Accounting Spreadsheet

Businesses need good accounting systems in order to produce reports, summaries, and records of day-to-day financial information. One of the most important uses of this information is to show the financial position of an individual or a business.

2.1 Financial Position

The concept of financial position is simple. The following steps outline how the financial position of a business is determined:

1. List the things the business owns that are worth money; these are called **assets**. They do not have to be fully paid for. Give a dollar value to each item and total the list.
2. List and total the debts of the business; these are called **liabilities**.
3. Calculate the difference between the total assets and the total liabilities. This difference is known as the **owner's capital** or **owner's equity**. A less common term is **net worth**.

The **financial position** of a business may be thought of as the status of the business, as represented by the assets, the liabilities, and the owner's equity.

Example:
Let us follow the three-step procedure given above to work out the financial position of A to Z Rent-Alls on September 30, 19––. A to Z Rent-Alls is owned by J. Salas.

Step 1. List the assets of the business; give a dollar value to each item and total the list.

For A to Z Rent-Alls the assets are as follows:

Cash on hand	$ 40.20
Bank balance	710.00
Debt receivable—W. Boa	131.50
Debt receivable—T. Burns	350.00
Rental equipment	75 364.70
Delivery truck	19 965.00
Land	48 000.00
Buildings	95 000.00
Total assets	$239 561.40

Step 2. List and total the debts of the business.
For A to Z Rent-Alls, the liabilities are as follows:

Debt payable—Arrow Supply	$ 1 950.40
Debt payable—Best Repairs	1 250.00
Bank loan	15 000.00
Mortgage payable	65 200.00
Total liabilities	$83 400.40

Step 3. Calculate the difference between total assets and total liabilities.
The calculation is as follows:

Total assets	$239 561.40
Total liabilities	83 400.40
Difference	$156 161.00

The difference of $156 161.00 is J. Salas's investment in the business. It is known as the owner's capital, or equity.

The Fundamental Accounting Equation

Capital or equity is always worked out in the same way. Capital or equity is found by subtracting total liabilities from total assets. This relationship is always true and can be written in the form of an equation.

This **fundamental accounting equation** may be stated in two ways:

$$A - L = OE \quad \text{(Assets} - \text{Liabilities} = \text{Owner's Equity)}$$

or

$$A = L + OE \quad \text{(Assets} = \text{Liabilities} + \text{Owner's Equity)}$$

Now let us use the figures for A to Z Rent-Alls to see the fundamental accounting equation at work.

$$A - L = OE$$
$$\$239\,561.40 - \$83\,400.40 = \$156\,161.00$$

or

$$A = L + OE$$
$$\$239\,561.40 = \$83\,400.40 + \$156\,161.00$$

The fundamental accounting equation is an extremely important concept in the study of accounting. As you will soon see, it is the basis for all accounting theory.

Accounts Receivable and Accounts Payable

Customers often buy goods or services from a business with the understanding that they will pay for them later. These customers then owe money to the business. They are in debt to the business. The business is right to include the debts owed to it as one of its assets. These debts are known as **accounts receivable** (sometimes abbreviated A/R or A.R.). Each of the customers that owes money to the business is one of its **debtors**. A debtor is anyone who owes money to the business.

In turn, a business often purchases goods and services from its suppliers with the understanding that payment will be made later. The business is in debt to its suppliers. The business is right to include these debts on the balance sheet in the liability section. Debts owed by the business are referred to as **accounts payable** (sometimes abbreviated A/P or A.P.). Each of the suppliers owed money by the business is one of its **creditors**. A creditor is anyone to whom the business owes money.

Section Review Questions

1. Explain how to calculate a person's financial position.
2. Karen Lipka has assets of $150 000 and liabilities of $75 000. What is her equity?
3. If a business has an equity of $125 000 and liabilities of $75 000, how much are the assets worth?
4. Define asset.
5. Define liability.
6. Define equity.
7. What is another term that means the same thing as equity?
8. What are accounts receivable?
9. What are accounts payable?
10. What is the term used to describe any supplier to whom the business owes money?
11. What is the term used to describe any company or person who owes money to a business?

Section Exercises

1. **List eight assets that a small business might own.**

2. **List three liabilities that a small business might owe.**

3. **Classify each of the following as an asset or a liability:**

   Office Furniture
   An amount owed to H. Krueger, a creditor
   Land
   Supplies
   Bank Loan
   Buildings
   An unpaid heating bill

   An amount owed by R. Jonas, a debtor
   Mortgage Payable
   Trucks
   A Canada savings bond
   An account receivable
   An account payable

4. **If the total assets of a business are $37 486.49 and the total liabilities are $11 547.80, calculate the owner's equity.**

5. **On December 31, 19–1, A. Lower's accounting equation was as follows:**
   Assets ($150 000) − Liabilities ($70 000) = Equity ($80 000)
   If during 19–2, the assets increased by $70 000 and the liabilities decreased by $20 000, calculate the owner's equity at December 31, 19–2.

6. **If during 19–6 the equity increases by $52 000, and the assets increase by $26 000, what change has occurred to the liabilities?**

7. **If total assets increase by $10 000, and the equity increases by $5 000, what change has occurred in the liabilities?**

8. **If the liabilities increase by $15 000, and the equity decreases by $5 000, what change has occurred in the assets?**

9. **Paul Silva's assets and liabilities are listed below in alphabetical order.**

   Bank loan, $4 000; Building, $140 000; Cash, $1 435; City Service (a debtor), $960; Emerson Electric Ltd. (a creditor), $1 200; Equipment, $23 750; Francis and Company (a debtor), $350; Frank's Service Station (a creditor), $375; Mortgage on building, $76 000; Supplies, $370.

   1. List the assets in one column and total them.
   2. List the liabilities in another column and total them.
   3. Calculate Paul Silva's equity.

10. Claude Pineau, a factory worker in Hull, Quebec, asks you to help him find out how much he is worth. From a discussion with him you find out the following facts.

   a. His bank balance is $754.
   b. He owns a home valued at $82 500 which has a mortgage on it of $12 500.
   c. He owns furniture and household equipment valued at $16 000.
   d. He owns a summer property valued at $65 000 which he bought with money borrowed from the bank. Since the time of purchase he has paid back $20 000 of the loan.
   e. He has unpaid bills amounting to $1 560.
   f. He owes his father-in-law, M. Dupuis, the sum of $10 000 which he borrowed interest-free several years ago at the time he bought his home.

   List Claude Pineau's assets in one column, his liabilities in another, and calculate his net worth.

2.2 The Balance Sheet

The formal way of presenting financial position is by means of a balance sheet. The balance sheet of A to Z Rent-Alls is shown in Figure 2.1. A **balance sheet** is a statement showing the financial position of a business, person, or other organization on a certain date.

```
                    A to Z Rent-Alls
                    Balance Sheet
                    September 30, 19—

Assets                              Liabilities
Cash on Hand              40 20    Assets
Bank Balance             710 —      - Arrow Supply      1950 40
Accounts Receivables                - Best Repairs      1250 —
  - W. Boa               131 50    Bank Loan           15000 —
  - J. Burns             350 —     Mortgage Payable    65200 —
Rental Equipment       75364 70    Total Liabilities   83400 40
Delivery Truck          1965 —      Owner's Equity
Land                    4800 —     J. Salas, Capital  156161 —
Buildings               9500 —
Total Assets          239561 40   Total Liabilities and Equity  239561 40
```

Figure 2.1 The balance sheet of a small business, A to Z Rent-Alls.

Section 2.2   19

Preparing a Balance Sheet

The steps in preparing a simple balance sheet are shown in the following illustrations. The figures for A to Z Rent-Alls are used in the example.

1. Write in the statement heading on columnar paper as shown in Figure 2.2.

   WHO: The name of the business → *A to Z Rent-Alls*

   Balance Sheet ← WHAT: The name of the statement

   September 30, 19—

   WHEN: The date of the statement

Figure 2.2 The heading on a balance sheet.

2. Write in the assets on the left side as shown in Figure 2.3.

Sub-heading

A to Z Rent-Alls
Balance Sheet
September 30, 19—

Assets		
Cash on Hand	40 20	
Bank Balance	710 —	
Accounts Receivable		
— W. Boa	131 50	⎫ Amounts in money column
— J. Burns	350 —	⎭
Rental Equipment	75 364 70	
Delivery Truck	19 965 —	
Land	48 000 —	
Buildings	95 000 —	← Single ruled line before the total
Total Assets	239 561 40	← The total of the assets

Figure 2.3 The assets listed on a balance sheet.

3. Write in the liabilities on the right side as shown in Figure 2.4.

A to Z Rent-Alls				
Balance Sheet				
September 30, 19—				
Assets			Liabilities (Sub-heading)	
Cash on Hand	40 20		Accounts Payable	
Bank Balance	710 —		— Arrow Supply	1950 40
Accounts Receivable			— Best Repairs	1250 —
—W. Boa	131 50		Bank Loan	15000 —
—J. Burns	350 —		Mortgage Payable	65200 —
Rental Equipment	75364 70		Total Liabilities	83400 40
Delivery Truck	1965 —		Single ruled line before the total	
Land	48000 —			
Buildings	95000 —		The total of the liabilities	
Total Assets	239561 40			

Figure 2.4 The liabilities listed on a balance sheet.

4. Beneath the liabilities write in the owner's equity figure as shown in Figure 2.5. As you know, this is the difference between the total assets and the total liabilities.

A to Z Rent-Alls				
Balance Sheet				
September 30, 19—				
Assets			Liabilities (Sub-heading)	
Cash on Hand	40 20		Accounts Payable	
Bank Balance	710 —		— Arrow Supply	1950 40
Accounts Receivable			— Best Repairs	1250 —
—W. Boa	131 50		Bank Loan	15000 —
—J. Burns	350 —		Mortgage Payable	65200 —
Rental Equipment	75364 70		Total Liabilities	83400 40
Delivery Truck	1965 —		Owner's Equity	
Land	48000 —		J. Salas, Capital	156161 —
Buildings	95000 —		The name of the owner and the word "capital"	
Total Assets	239561 40			

Figure 2.5 The equity recorded on a balance sheet.

5. Complete the balance sheet by writing in the final total on the right side. Finish it off with double ruled lines beneath the two final totals as shown in Figure 2.6.

The statement heading tells: Who? What? When?

Accounts Receivable: Debts owing from customers, usually in alphabetical order

Assets are listed in the order of their liquidity, or how easily they can be turned into cash.
Cash is listed first, bank balance is second, then accounts receivable, and so on.

Accounts Payable: Debts owing to suppliers, usually in alphabetical order.

Liabilities are listed in the order in which they must be paid.

The owner's name goes in the equity section.

The final totals are on the same line and double underlined.
Single ruled lines before totals.
Two final totals must agree.

A to Z Rent-Alls
Balance Sheet
September 30, 19—

Assets		Liabilities	
Cash on Hand	40 20	Accounts Payable	
Bank Balance	7 10 —	— Arrow Supply	1 950 40
Accounts Receivable		— Best Repairs	1 250 —
— W. Boa	1 31 50	Bank Loan	15 000 —
— J. Burns	3 50 —	Mortgage Payable	65 200 —
Rental Equipment	75 364 70	Total Liabilities	83 400 40
Delivery Truck	19 965 —	Owner's Equity	
Land	48 000 —	J. Salas, Capital	156 161 —
Buildings	45 000 —		
Total Assets	239 561 40	Total Liabilities and Equity	239 561 40

Figure 2.6 Important features of a balance sheet for a business.

Important Features of the Balance Sheet

1. A three-line heading is used.
   The heading tells:
   WHO? —the name of the business, organization, or individual (if the business does not have a name);
   WHAT? —the name of the financial statement: in this case, balance sheet;
   WHEN? —the date on which the financial position is determined.

2. The assets are listed on the left side of the balance sheet and the liabilities and the owner's equity are listed on the right side.

3. The assets are listed in the order of their liquidity. **Liquidity** means the ease with which the assets can be converted into cash. Cash and bank balance, being the most liquid, are listed first. Accounts receivable are listed next because they are usually collected within thirty days. Supplies and long-lasting assets such as land, buildings, and equipment are listed later because normally they are not converted into cash.

4. The liabilities are listed in the order in which they would normally be paid.

5. The details of any item are fully disclosed on a balance sheet. For example, on the balance sheet of A to Z Rent-Alls, shown above, the used delivery truck is shown in the Assets section at its value of $19 965. The amount that is owed on the truck, $15 000 to the bank, is shown in the Liabilities section. This is more informative than to show the truck at $4 965, which is how much of it the business really owns.

6. The two final totals, one for each side of the balance sheet, are recorded on the same line and double underlined.

7. The owner of a business will have assets and liabilities that are strictly personal and do not belong on the balance sheet of the business. Examples are: the family home, the family boat, and the amount owed on the family car. It is important to remember to keep business assets and liabilities separate from personal ones.

Basic Recordkeeping Practices

When to Abbreviate

Avoid using abbreviations on financial statements such as balance sheets except when listing a business name that includes an abbreviation. For example, General Bakeries Limited is the full name of a business; therefore, the word Limited should not be abbreviated. However, in the case of Canadian Electric Co., the abbreviation for "Company" is used because it is part of the formal name of the business.

Use of Columnar Paper

It is important for an accounting student to learn to use columnar paper. When columnar paper is used, notice how the figures are placed carefully in the columns. This is to help the accountant total the columns correctly. Observe also that dollar signs, periods, and commas are not used when recording amounts of money in columns.

When using columnar paper, even-dollar amounts may be shown by placing a dash in the cents column. Thus, in the following illustration, 12— is used instead of 12.00. The two zeros are used on typed reports, and are preferred by some on a financial statement such as the balance sheet.

Use of Ruled Lines

If a column of figures is to be totalled (added or subtracted), a single line is drawn beneath the column and the total is placed beneath this single line as shown below:

```
131 10
 14 11
  3 05
176 26
```

If a total happens to be a final total, such as the last amounts on the balance sheet, a double ruled line is drawn immediately beneath the total as shown below:

```
 14 62
194 75
 30 —
 12 65
252 02
```

On most balance sheets, in order to place the two final totals on the same line, it is necessary to leave one or more blank lines between the figures in a column and the column total. When this is done, the single ruled line is placed close to the "total" figure and not immediately beneath the figures in the column. The following examples show this.

```
 46 10          46 10
 92 05          92 05
 19 64          19 64
137 88         137 88


295 67         295 67
incorrect       correct
```

Neatness

It is most important that an accountant's work be neat and perfectly legible. This is necessary so that no one misinterprets the writing or the numbers. Although the work should never be untidy, it is not necessary that it be beautiful—only neat and legible.

From the very beginning you should make it a habit to strive for neatness, accuracy, and clarity in all of your exercises. Be sure to use your ruler to make ruled lines beneath headings and in the columns.

Chapter 2

Section Review Questions

1. What is a balance sheet?
2. When does the name of the owner of a business appear in the heading of a balance sheet?
3. On which side of a balance sheet are the assets listed? the liabilities?
4. How is an automobile that is not fully paid-for listed on a balance sheet?
5. What four items may be omitted when listing figures on columnar paper?
6. On which side of a balance sheet does a creditor appear?
7. What is meant by a single ruled line drawn beneath a column of figures?
8. Why is it important for an accountant's work to be neat?
9. When is a double ruled line drawn beneath a total?
10. When can short forms or abbreviations be used on financial statements?
11. Give two forms of the fundamental accounting equation.
12. Which is the most liquid asset?
13. In what order are liabilities listed on a balance sheet?
14. In what order are assets listed on a balance sheet?

Section Exercises

1. Kate Kramer is the owner and operator of The Kramer Company located in Revelstoke, B.C. On September 30, 19--, The Kramer Company had the following assets and liabilities. Prepare the September 30 balance sheet for The Kramer Company.

Assets	
Cash on Hand	$ 106
Bank Balance	1 530
J. Crothers (debtor)	1 100
R. Zack (debtor)	370
Supplies	1 200
Furniture and Equipment	14 700
Delivery Equipment	20 100
Liabilities	
Anglo Supply Co. (creditor)	740
C.P. Gregg (creditor)	3 000
Bank Loan	10 000

2. The New Western Company in Brandon, Man., owned by Guy Albrecht, had the following assets and liabilities on March 31, 19--. Prepare a balance sheet for the company, as of that date.

Bank	$ 1 896
Tasty Beverages (debtor)	750
Food Haven (debtor)	400
Metro Mall (debtor)	1 235
Supplies	850
Furniture and Equipment	75 840
Land	50 000
Building	140 000
Trucks	35 000
Household Finance Company (creditor)	19 345
General Trading Company (creditor)	2 356
Lightning Electronics (creditor)	3 378
Bank Loan	10 000
Mortgage Payable	75 000

3. **Michael Travis, the owner of Travis and Company located in Moncton, N.B., gave the following list of assets and liabilities to a public accountant and asked him to prepare a balance sheet as of March 31, 19--. Prepare the balance sheet as if you were the public accountant.**

Amounts owed to Travis and Company:

—G. Fordham	$ 1 042.16
—W. Gaines	743.86
—D. Samuelson	1 346.95

Amounts owed by Travis and Company to suppliers:

—Raymond and Company	125.00
—Gem Finance Co.	1 236.45
—Empire Insurance Co.	150.00
—Beacon Company	1 567.25
—General Supply Co.	15 540.00
Office Supplies	326.40
Building	135 000.00
Bank Balance	4 946.03
Land	46 000.00
Office Equipment	11 960.00
Shop Equipment	3 535.00
Delivery Equipment	14 240.00
Bank Loan	25 000.00
Mortgage Payable	52 000.00

4. **Workbook Exercise: Finding errors on a balance sheet.**

2.3 Claims Against the Assets

Consider these questions: Who owns the assets of a business? If a business closes down, to whom do the assets belong? The answer to these questions is that the assets belong to those persons who provided the funds that were used to acquire the assets.

A balance sheet shows who has a claim against the assets of a business. The balance sheet of Paramount Design, owned by Janet Korey, shows clearly who has a claim against the assets of her business.

Paramount Design Balance Sheet December 31, 19—			
Assets		**Liabilities**	
Cash	1 407 10	Bank Loan	9 000 —
Accounts Receivable		Accounts Payable	
— R. Mason	350 —	— Oakes Supply	750 —
— H. Morgan	1 706 —	— Modern Art Store	1 905 —
Supplies	1 250 —		11 655 —
Furniture	9 700 —	**Owner's Equity**	
Equipment	10 000 —	Janet Korey, Capital	32 108 10
Automobile	19 350 —		
	43 763 10		43 763 10

Claims of the creditors.
Claim of the owner.

Figure 2.7 The balance sheet of Paramount Design showing the claims against the assets.

As shown on the left side of the balance sheet, Janet's business assets are $43 763.10. The right side of the balance sheet shows that these assets, or the funds to obtain them, were provided by: the bank, $9 000; the other creditors, $750 and $1 905; and Janet herself, $32 108.10.

Expressed in another way:

$$\underbrace{\$43\ 763.10}_{\text{Assets}} = \underbrace{\$9\ 000 + \$750 + \$1\ 905}_{\substack{\text{Creditors' claims} \\ \text{against the assets}}} + \underbrace{\$32\ 108.10}_{\substack{\text{Owner's claim} \\ \text{against the assets}}}$$

Creditors' Claims First

If for any reason a business is closed down, the claims of the creditors are settled first, and then the claim of the owner. This means that the owner has to accept any losses that might occur from selling off any assets. On the other hand, the owner benefits from any profits that might occur. The owner always gets what is left after the claims of the creditors have been paid.

Suppose that Janet Korey closed down the business, and in the process suffered a loss of $7 200 when selling off the assets. The equation shown above would not remain the same but would appear as follows:

$$\underbrace{\$36\ 563.10}_{\substack{\text{Assets} \\ \text{(now all cash)} \\ \text{down \$7 200}}} = \underbrace{\$9\ 000 + \$750 + \$1\ 905}_{\substack{\text{Creditors' claims} \\ \text{remain the} \\ \text{same}}} + \underbrace{\$24\ 908.10}_{\substack{\text{Owner's} \\ \text{claim down} \\ \$7\ 200}}$$

Section Review Questions

1. Who has a claim against the assets of a business?
2. How can you quickly find out who has a claim against the assets of a business?
3. Who has first claim against the assets of a business?
4. Who benefits or suffers from gains or losses of closing down a business?

Section Exercises

1. Joseph Litz is the owner of Bayliner Boat Charters, a business in Truro, N.S., that has six sailboats for hire. Mr. Litz has been able to make a comfortable living from renting out these boats during the sailing season.

    The balance sheet of Bayliner Boat Charters is shown below.

    BAYLINER BOAT CHARTERS
    BALANCE SHEET
    OCTOBER 31, 19--

Assets			Liabilities	
Bank	$	900	Bank Loan	$ 18 000
Accounts Receivable		1 050	Accounts Payable	3 740
Supplies		1 250	Mortgage Payable	80 000
Equipment		4 390		$101 740
Boats		32 850	Owner's Equity	
Property		175 000	J. Litz, Capital	113 700
		$215 440		$215 440

    Mr. Litz is past retirement age and is finding the business more than he can comfortably handle. He has attempted to sell it intact, but was unsuccessful. He has decided, therefore, to sell the assets for cash and pay off the claims of the creditors. In this way he can get his equity out of the business.

    Mr. Litz hires a liquidator to help him. Through this person's services, the accounts receivable are collected in full. The supplies are sold for $500; the equipment is sold for $2 000; the boats are sold for $20 350; and the property is sold for $180 000. The liquidator charges $1 500.

Prepare a detailed calculation showing how much Mr. Litz will receive as a result of his claim against the assets.

2. Carla Mann is the owner of Carla's Interior Design in Yorkton, Saskatchewan. A new firm has come to town and Carla has accepted a position with them. Carla is closing down her own business and is in the process of selling the assets.

Just before she accepted her new position, the balance sheet of Carla's Interior Design was as follows:

CARLA'S INTERIOR DESIGN
BALANCE SHEET
JUNE 30, 19--

Assets		*Liabilities*	
Cash	$ 1 500	Bank Loan	$ 9 500
Accounts Receivable	7 870	Accounts Payable	1 250
Supplies	1 520		$10 750
Equipment	3 740	*Owner's Equity*	
Automobile	17 500	Carla Mann, Capital	21 380
	$32 130		$32 130

Carla was successful in selling the supplies for $1 200 cash and the equipment for $2 200 cash. She was also able to collect in cash all of the accounts receivable except for $870 which was considered to be uncollectable.

1. **Prepare a simple balance sheet on July 31, after disposing of the three assets mentioned above.**
2. **Suggest the simplest way to dispose of the remaining assets and thus complete the closing of the business.**

2.4 Generally Accepted Accounting Principles

The Canadian Institute of Chartered Accountants (CICA) is the leading professional organization in Canadian accounting. This organization establishes the principles and procedures that are the standards for all accountants. The complete body of accounting knowledge and opinion is contained in the *CICA Handbook* which is updated regularly.

Accountants follow what are known as GAAPs. **GAAPs** are generally accepted accounting principles, concepts, and conventions. Some of these GAAPs are found in the *CICA Handbook*; others have become common practice through use over a period of years. Three GAAPs are introduced below. Other GAAPs are introduced at appropriate times throughout the text. A list of GAAPs is given in the appendix on page 673.

GAAP—The Business Entity Concept

The **business entity concept** provides that the accounting for a business or organization be kept separate from the personal affairs of its owner, or from any other business or organization. This means that the owner of a business should not place any personal assets on the business balance sheet. The balance sheet of the business must reflect the financial position of the business alone. Also, when transactions of the business are recorded, any personal expenditures of the owner are charged to the owner and are not allowed to affect the operating results of the business.

The balance sheet of A to Z Rent-Alls in Figure 2.1 on page 18 complies with the business entity concept. The balance sheet reflects the affairs of the business only. No personal assets or liabilities are included.

GAAP—The Continuing Concern Concept

The **continuing concern concept** (also known as the Going Concern Concept) assumes that a business will continue to operate, unless it is known that such is not the case. The dollar values associated with a business that is alive and well are straightforward. For example, a supply of envelopes with the company's name printed on them would be valued at their cost price. This would not be the case if the company were going out of business. In that case, the envelopes would be difficult to sell because the company's name is on them. When a company is going out of business, the values of the assets usually suffer because they have to be sold under unfavourable circumstances. The values of such assets often cannot be determined until they are actually sold.

GAAP—The Principle of Conservatism

The **principle of conservatism** provides that accounting for a business should be fair and reasonable. Accountants are required in their work to make evaluations and estimates, to deliver opinions, and to select procedures. They should do so in a way that neither overstates nor understates the affairs of the business or the results of operation.

Section Review Questions

1. Name the dominant accounting organization in Canada.
2. Over the years what has the above organization established?
3. In what publication are most of the rules of accounting found?
4. What does GAAP stand for?
5. Explain what is meant by the business entity concept.
6. Explain what is meant by the continuing concern concept.
7. Explain what is meant by the principle of conservatism.

Section Exercises

1. **This exercise also appears in your workbook.**
   Kevin Kaghee is the owner of Central Paving Company in Charlottetown, P.E.I. His personal and business assets and liabilities are listed below.
   1. Separate the list below into the two columns provided.
   2. Calculate the total assets and the total liabilities in each column.
   3. Calculate Kevin Kaghee's personal net worth and his equity in Central Paving Company.

Assets	Amount	Business	Personal
Accounts Receivable	$ 27 460		
Boat and Motor	16 520		
Business Bank Balance	1 852		
Business Automobiles	48 054		
Furniture and Appliances	6 528		
Government Bonds of Owner	20 000		
House and Lot	99 600		
Office Furniture and Equipment	18 324		
Office Supplies	3 545		
Owner's Automobiles	18 657		
Paving Materials	55 326		
Personal Bank Balance	1 258		
Plant Property and Buildings	125 358		
Summer Cottage	65 874		
Trucks and Equipment	285 657		
Total Assets			
Liabilities			
Accounts Payable	3 500		
Business Bank Loan	56 000		
Mortgage on Plant Property	75 000		
Mortgage on House and Lot	60 000		
Mortgage on Summer Cottage	22 300		
Owed to Finance Co.—Business Equipment	136 522		
Total Liabilities			
Owner's equity			

2. **Answer the following questions in your workbook.**
   1. A customer who owes $500 to the business has recently died. The lawyers for the customer have indicated to the business that there is only a one in four chance of the debt being paid.
      a. Should the amount be included on the balance sheet of the business?
      b. Which GAAP(s) affect this situation? Explain.
   2. A contracting company is involved in a dispute over its bill to a customer. The bill for $500 000 was recently reduced to $400 000 by a decision of the courts. The company is now appealing the decision.
      a. Which amount should be taken into the accounts (recognized)?
      b. Which GAAP(s) affect this situation? Explain.
   3. Six months ago you closed out your business. Now, a person has expressed an interest in acquiring the business. The potential buyer requests a current balance sheet, but you provide her with the one that was prepared just prior to closing.
      a. Will the balance sheet be accepted by the buyer and her accountant?
      b. Which GAAP(s) affect this situation? Explain.
   4. Martha Higgins is currently trying to borrow some money from the bank. She has listed her personal automobile ($25 000) on the business balance sheet to make the statement look more attractive to the banker.
      a. Is this a reasonable thing to do?
      b. Which GAAP(s) affect this situation? Explain.
   5. The manager of a business has heard that the business might be sold and that he might lose his job as a result. When preparing a balance sheet for the owner, the manager values everything as low as possible in order to discourage the prospective buyer. He claims that this practice is allowed by the principle of conservatism.
      a. Is the manager correct in his claim?
      b. Which GAAP(s) affect this situation? Explain.
   6. A figure of $25 000 for computerized office equipment appears on a company balance sheet. Recently, better quality equipment has been developed and put on the market. However, the existing equipment still does an adequate job for the company, and the company has no intention of replacing it.
      a. Should the equipment figure be eliminated because it represents obsolete equipment?
      b. Which GAAP(s) affect this situation? Explain.

2.5 Computerized Accounting: The Accounting Spreadsheet

The Accounting Spreadsheet

You probably know about computer software which is purchased for use on a computer. In data processing, the word "spreadsheet" refers to software that can be programmed to do a number of accounting–related tasks.

The first step in using a spreadsheet is to load the software into the computer's memory. On the computer's screen this will produce a grid like the one shown in Figure 2.8.

Figure 2.8 A spreadsheet as it might appear on the screen.

Each rectangle in the grid is known as a "cell." The cells are identified as A1, A2, B5, C8, and so on. Spreadsheets vary in size but are always larger than the screen. You cannot see all of the grid at one time. However, you can see any part of the grid by moving it back and forth, or up and down, on the screen. This is done with the cursor keys or another device.

Information can be entered on the screen through the keyboard. The cursor is moved to the desired cell and the information is keyed in. This information is visible on the screen. For any screen cell the programmer can

- leave the call blank;
- enter a label, which is a string of letters or characters, such as a column heading;
- enter a numerical value.

The programmer can also enter "hidden" formulas which do not appear on the screen but which are linked to the cells by the computer. Hidden formulas are used to make calculations as in the example below, for the final output of the spreadsheet program. There can be one hidden formula for each cell. Any hidden formula can be seen by calling it up on a "status" line which appears above the grid on the screen.

When a program is prepared and tested, it can be stored on a disk. It can be called up and used at any time.

Example

Shown below is a spreadsheet program designed to produce some statistics for a sales department. When the program is loaded into the computer, the screen appears as in Figure 2.9.

```
  |     |      A          |   B   |      C       |      D       |     E        |      F
  |-----|-----------------|-------|--------------|--------------|--------------|----------------
  |  1  |                 |       |              |              |              |
  |  2  | XYZ SALES ANALYSIS     |              |              |              |
  |  3  |                 |       |   PRODUCT    |   PRODUCT    |   PRODUCT    |   TOTAL BY
  |  4  | SALESPERSON     |       |      A       |      B       |      C       |   SALESPERSON
  |  5  | ANDERSON A.     |       |              |              |              |
  |  6  | BROWN C.        |       |              |              |              |
  |  7  | DAVIS G.        |       |              |              |              |
  |  8  | GREEN B.        |       |              |              |              |
  |  9  | HARRISON F.     |       |              |              |              |
  | 10  |                 |       |              |              |              |
  | 11  | TOTALS BY PRODUCT      |              |              |              |
```

Figure 2.9 The spreadsheet for a sales analysis as it appears on the screen.

But what you see on the screen is not the complete program. There are hidden formulas that you cannot see on the grid. Figure 2.10 shows the complete program with the hidden formulas in faint print.

```
  |     |      A          |   B   |      C       |      D       |     E        |      F
  |-----|-----------------|-------|--------------|--------------|--------------|----------------
  |  1  |                 |       |              |              |              |
  |  2  | XYZ SALES ANALYSIS     |              |              |              |
  |  3  |                 |       |   PRODUCT    |   PRODUCT    |   PRODUCT    | TOTALS BY
  |  4  | SALESPERSON     |       |      A       |      B       |      C       | SALESPERSON
  |  5  | ANDERSON A.     |       |              |              |              | SUM(C5:E5)
  |  6  | BROWN C.        |       |              |              |              | SUM(C6:E6)
  |  7  | DAVIS G.        |       |              |              |              | SUM(C7:E7)
  |  8  | GREEN B.        |       |              |              |              | SUM(C8:E8)
  |  9  | HARRISON F.     |       |              |              |              | SUM(C9:E9)
  | 10  |                 |       |              |              |              |
  | 11  | TOTALS BY PRODUCT      | SUM(C5:C9)   | SUM(D5:D9)   | SUM(E5:E9)   | SUM(F5:F9)
```

↑ Means the sum of the figures entered in cells C5 to C9.

Figure 2.10 The spreadsheet for a sales analysis showing the hidden formulas associated with certain screen cells.

To use this program, simply key in the individual sales figures while the "calculator key" is turned off. When all the figures are entered turn on the calculator key. Then, all the vertical and horizontal totals are calculated automatically. The final output appears on the screen as shown in Figure 2.11 below.

```
!----!----------------!----------------!----------------!----------------!----------------!------------
!    !       A        !       B        !       C        !       D        !       E        !       F
!----!----------------!----------------!----------------!----------------!----------------!------------
! 1  !                !                !                !                !                !
! 2  !XYZ SALES ANALYSIS               !                !                !                !
! 3  !                !                !    PRODUCT     !    PRODUCT     !    PRODUCT     !TOTALS BY
! 4  !SALESPERSON     !                !       A        !       B        !       C        !SALESPERSON
! 5  !ANDERSON A.     !                !      152       !      198       !      225       !      575
! 6  !BROWN C.        !                !      175       !      485       !      200       !      860
! 7  !DAVIS S.        !                !      201       !      210       !      196       !      607
! 8  !GREEN B.        !                !      158       !      165       !      186       !      509
! 9  !HARRISON F.     !                !      356       !      290       !      310       !      956
!10  !                !                !                !                !                !
!11  !TOTALS BY PRODUCT                !     1042       !     1348       !     1117       !     3507
```

                                               Raw data   Automatic totals

Figure 2.11 The spreadsheet for a sales analysis in its final form. The raw data has been entered on the keyboard. The totals were calculated automatically.

A copy of the output can be obtained using the printer. The column and row identifiers will not be shown on the printout.

A major advantage of the spreadsheet software is that it can handle error corrections and changes in data. For example, suppose that one of the sales figures were entered incorrectly. By merely correcting the one figure on the screen, all the calculations can be redone in a matter of seconds.

A simple balance sheet can be prepared using a spreadsheet program. Hidden formulas are necessary to calculate the total assets, the total liabilities, and the owner's equity. All other information is in the form of labels or numerical values. If a name happens to be larger than one cell, two cells are used, or the name can be abbreviated.

Computer Review Questions

1. What is a spreadsheet in data processing?
2. What is the first step in using a spreadsheet?
3. What is the name given to any position on the grid?
4. You cannot see all of the grid at one time. What do you do to see a part of the grid that is not presently on the screen?
5. How is a label put on the grid?
6. How is a value put on the grid?
7. In addition to labels and numeric values, what else is associated with a spreadsheet?
8. What can be done with a spreadsheet program once it is completed and tested?
9. When a spreadsheet program is loaded into the computer, what action must the user take to make use of it?
10. What hidden formulas would be used to prepare a balance sheet using a spreadsheet?
11. What is shown in the cell D7 of the spreadsheet in Figure 2.11?
12. In Figure 2.11, if you were to change one of the sales figures, what would happen on the screen?

Computer Exercises

1. Prepare a spreadsheet program for the balance sheet of A to Z Rent-Alls in Figure 2.1. Obtain help from your teacher or by reading the spreadsheet manual for your computer. When your program is completed, save it on disk.

2. Load the program from question 1 above. Modify the data to include the following changes:
   1. add an account receivable for C. Orr, $1 500;
   2. increase the cash on hand by $500;
   3. reduce the bank loan by $10 000.

   What are the new figures for: a. total assets?

   b. total liabilities?

   c. owner's equity?

CHAPTER HIGHLIGHTS

Now that you have completed Chapter 2, you should:

1. understand what is meant by the financial position of a person or a business;
2. know the meaning of accounts receivable and accounts payable;
3. be able to prepare a simple balance sheet in proper form for a business or an individual;
4. understand the fundamental accounting equation;
5. understand the meaning of claims against the assets;
6. be able to use basic recordkeeping practices;
7. understand the concept of liquidity;
8. know three generally accepted accounting principles: the business entity concept, the continuing concern concept, and the principle of conservatism.

ACCOUNTING TERMS

accounts payable	fundamental accounting equation
accounts receivable	GAAP
asset	generally accepted accounting principle
balance sheet	going concern concept
business entity concept	liability
capital	liquidity
continuing concern concept	net worth
creditor	owner's equity
debtor	principle of conservatism
financial position	

CHAPTER EXERCISES

Using Your Knowledge

1. **This multiple choice exercise on the balance sheet and accounting theory also appears in your workbook. For each of the following questions, write in your notebook the letter that represents the best possible answer.**

    1. The financial position of a business is
        a. the difference between total assets and total liabilities.
        b. represented by the assets, the liabilities, and the capital.
        c. the same as the net worth of the business.

    2. If the total assets increase by $10 000 and the total liabilities decrease by $10 000, the capital will
        a. increase by $20 000.
        b. be unchanged.
        c. decrease by $20 000.

    3. Which one of the following is not true?
        a. A − C = L
        b. A − L = C
        c. A + L = C
        d. A = L + C

    4. A balance sheet shows
        a. all of the owner's assets and liabilities.
        b. a financial picture of the business on a certain date.
        c. the progress of the business over a period of time.

    5. Which one of the following is not true?
        a. The heading of a balance sheet shows the date as of which it was prepared.
        b. Assets are listed in the order of their liquidity.
        c. Accounts receivable are considered to be a liquid asset.
        d. Personal assets have no place on the business balance sheet.
        e. A truck which cost $10 000 and for which $6 000 is owed is listed on the balance sheet at $4 000.

    6. Abbreviations may be used on financial statements
        a. when it is necessary to crowd things to conserve space.
        b. to save time in preparing the statements.
        c. in a company name if the abbreviation is a formal part of the name.

    7. Which one of the following is least true? Columnar paper helps the accountant
        a. to add columns more accurately.
        b. to make records easier to read.
        c. to make the records more attractive.
        d. to make recordkeeping go more quickly.

8. Which one of the following is not true?
   a. Ruled lines are used to underline headings.
   b. Ruled lines are used to indicate that columns of numbers are to be totaled.
   c. Ruled lines are necessary to separate sections of the balance sheet.
   d. Ruled lines are doubled to indicate a final total.

9. Before a business is closed down, the equation for it is:
   Assets ($125 000) = Liabilities ($37 000) + Equity ($88 000)
   If assets of $70 000 are sold for $20 000, assets of $50 000 are sold for $90 000, and the remaining assets stay the same, the equation will become
   a. $55 000 = $37 000 + $18 000.
   b. $115 000 = $37 000 + $78 000.
   c. $75 000 = $37 000 + $38 000.
   d. $135 000 = $47 000 + $88 000.
   e. $115 000 = $27 000 + $88 000.

10. Which one of the following is not true?
    a. In the liability section on a balance sheet, accounts payable are listed first.
    b. On a balance sheet there are three main totals.
    c. On a balance sheet the owner's name only appears in the heading.
    d. On a balance sheet the final totals are always on the same line.

For Further Thought

2. **Briefly answer the following questions.**
   1. The balance sheet is thought of as being a "snapshot" of the business. Explain this statement.
   2. Assets and liabilities can be thought of as things that can be touched. For example, you can go into the parking lot and touch the automobile. The equity is not like this. Explain.
   3. Give reasons why businesspersons sell on credit when there is a chance that they will not be able to collect the debt.
   4. Work out another acceptable definition of a balance sheet besides the one given in the textbook.
   5. In three words, tell what information is contained in the heading of a balance sheet.
   6. Supplies are considered to be a more liquid asset than land. In a going concern, neither asset is expected to be sold for cash. Give an explanation for this.
   7. If a bank were to lend funds to a business, the bank would become a secured creditor. What does this mean? How does the bank accomplish it? Why do other creditors not do the same?
   8. The *CICA Handbook* is published in loose-leaf form so that it can be easily updated. Explain how this updating is done.
   9. Given what you know so far, explain how the earnings of a business could be determined from its balance sheets if you knew how much the owner had withdrawn.
   10. There is a saying in accounting: "Anticipate no profits and account for all possible losses." Which GAAP does this saying correspond to?

CASE STUDIES

Case 1 A Balance Sheet Interpretation

Shown below is the balance sheet of S. Magbool.

S. MAGBOOL
BALANCE SHEET
JANUARY 31, 19--

Assets		Liabilities	
Cash	$ 6 000	Accounts Payable	$ 35 000
Accounts Receivable	14 000	Mortgage Payable	60 000
Land	40 000		$95 000
Buildings	95 000	*Owner's Equity*	
Equipment	25 000	S. Magbool, Capital	85 000
	$180 000		$180 000

Question

1. Based on the limited information given, would you say that Magbool has any kind of a financial problem? Explain.

Case 2 Can We Borrow?

On December 31, 19--, you present your balance sheet, shown below, to the manager of the local bank, with the hope of obtaining a small bank loan. During your conversation with the manager, certain facts are brought out.

a. About $8 000 owing from customers is considerably overdue.
b. A yearly mortgage payment of $4 000 is due next March 1.
c. All creditors' accounts are due within 30 days.
d. The average earnings of the business for the past five years have been very good.

BALANCE SHEET
DECEMBER 31, 19--

Assets		Liabilities	
Cash	$ 5 000	Accounts Payable	$17 000
Accounts Receivable	25 000	Mortgage Payable	35 000
Land	10 000		$52 000
Equipment	20 000		
Building	30 000	Capital	38 000
	$90 000		$90 000

Questions

1. Would the bank manager grant the loan?
2. What concerns might the manager have?

Case 3 Considering the Purchase of a Business

Your friends Joseph and Janice Dubois have recently inherited some money and want to use it to purchase a business of their own. They have come to you for advice regarding the possible purchase of a sand and gravel business. They learned about the sale of the sand and gravel business through an advertisement in the newspaper.

The business is being sold by K. Vako who has owned it for twenty years and wants a change because of failing health. The business has been profitable over the years, earning an average of $50 000 per year over the last ten years.

The following balance sheet has been prepared by Mr. Vako personally.

VAKO SAND AND GRAVEL
BALANCE SHEET
DECEMBER 31, 19–6

Assets			Liabilities	
Bank	$	500	Bank Loan	$ 30 000
Accounts Receivable		17 400	Accounts Payable	22 740
Supplies		1 100	Mortgage Payable	50 000
Land		40 700		$102 740
Buildings		38 000		
Equipment		67 600	*Owner's Equity*	
Gravel Deposits		200 000	K. Vako, Capital	262 560
		$365 300		$365 300

Mr. Vako is asking $250 000 for the business. This seems to be a very good price. It is less than his capital figure as shown on the balance sheet.

Work in a small group to help Joseph and Janice decide if they should buy the sand and gravel business. Prepare a list of questions that need to be answered and be ready to present your list to the class. To help you, a first question is already given below.

1. What condition is the equipment in and is it really worth $67 600?

Case 4 Placing a Value on Assets

Hilda Lahti is the owner of Custom-Made Products in Prince George, British Columbia. Originally, Custom-Made Products was a machine shop that produced custom work of many kinds. In the last few years the company has developed and patented a line of scaffolding equipment for contractors and builders. The scaffolding equipment produced by the company is better than that of its competitors. As a result, the company has had great success with the new product. At the same time, the custom machine shop division of the business has been doing poorly. There is a lot of competition from other machine shops in the community. In the last year the company earned $135 000. $110 000 of this was from the sale of scaffolding equipment and only $25 000 from the machine shop.

Recently, Hilda has decided to make a major change in the company operations. In particular, she has decided to get out of machine shop work. She intends to concentrate the entire energies of the company on expanding the markets for scaffolding, and developing new products of this type. The change in policy has been made official and the customers of the company have been notified.

The most recent balance sheet of the company, prepared for the company's bank, shows the following:

Assets	
Cash	$ 1 500
Accounts Receivable	20 540
Supplies	1 821
Land and Building	102 500
Machinery and Equipment	205 365
Automotive Equipment	65 385
Total Assets	$397 111
Liabilities	
Bank Loan	$105 000
Accounts Payable	11 850
Mortgage Payable	85 000
Total Liabilities	$201 850
Owner's Equity	$195 261

The bank manager who receives the above balance sheet notices that no adjustment has been made to reflect the company's decision to quit custom machine shop work. Inquiries reveal that the company has $155 000 of specialized machine shop equipment. This figure is included in the Machinery and Equipment figure of $205 365 on the balance sheet. It is generally agreed that the market for this type of equipment is quite poor. The company's equipment is outdated, and most other machine shops have already acquired modern computerized equipment.

Questions

1. Why would the bank manager be concerned about repayment of the bank loan?
2. What additional information is available to the bank manager to help in evaluating the company's loan?
3. What needs to be done regarding the above balance sheet?
4. Assuming that a buyer for the machine shop equipment is found at a price of $35 000, what changes should be made on the balance sheet?
5. Prepare a simple balance sheet to show the changes.
6. What GAAP influenced you in your thinking?

CAREER
Samuel Essex / Sole Proprietor

In high school, Samuel Essex of Vernon, British Columbia, took a number of business couses, including accounting. After graduation, he was hired as a bookkeeper for a branch office of the Trane Service Agency, an international corporation. Samuel worked with cash receipts, accounts receivable and accounts payable.

After two years, Samuel decided to leave and start his own business. Following months of preparation, he opened Sam's Fabric Shoppe in a rented store on Vernon's main street. The business has been extremely successful. Samuel sells a high-quality selection of fabrics, wool, and needlepoint supplies. He enjoys the independence, variety, and contact with people that owning one's own store provides.

As the sole proprietor of a small business, Samuel does all his own accounting; his training and experience in this area have proven invaluable. Although he is very busy, Samuel enrolled in a correspondence introductory accounting course at the university. This course acquainted him with some very important accounting principles: the business entity concept, the continuing concern concept, and the principle of conservatism.

Today in his own business, Samuel's accounting duties include keeping track of accounts receivable and accounts payable and reconciling his monthly bank statement. He also has to make sure that the correct amount of sales tax is sent to the provincial government. Further, he must be certain to have enough stock on hand to meet the demands of his customers.

Samuel has recently approached his local bank for a loan of $10 000. He wants to purchase a microcomputer with a double disk drive, a printer and a software package for his general ledger and his merchandise inventory. This will enable him to manage a larger stock. By buying in larger quantities, Samuel hopes to take advantage of suppliers' discounts and increase his inventory. The loan manager, following standard procedure, has asked Samuel to produce a balance sheet for his business. Samuel's balance sheet contains the following assets, liabilities and owner's equity:

SAM'S FABRIC SHOPPE
BALANCE SHEET
JUNE 30, 19--

Assets		*Liabilities*	
Cash on Hand	$ 50.00	Accounts Payable	
Bank Balance	3 000.00	Northcab Silk Co.	$ 1 800.00
Accounts Receivable		H.A. Kidd Co.	2 200.00
Bodley & Son	350.00		$ 4 000.00
Lukes	200.00		
Merchandise Inventory	17 000.00		
Supplies	1 400.00	Owner's Equity	
Furniture & Fixtures	13 000.00	Samuel Essex, Capital	42 000.00
Office Equipment	11 000.00		
	$46 000.00		$46 000.00

Having prepared the balance sheet, Samuel now sees that not all the assets belong to him. If the loan is granted, then the claims against the assets of Sam's Fabric Shoppe will total $13 000. Nonetheless, Samuel is determined to expand his business. He feels that the risk is justified by the prospect of increased success for his business, made possible through the use of new microcomputer equipment.

Discussion

1. List some advantages and disadvantages of being a sole proprietor.
2. Discuss the types of merchandise inventory and supplies Samuel would have in his store.
3. How have Samuel's accounting courses helped him operate his business successfully?
4. Discuss how Samuel would use the microcomputer equipment in his business.
5. Examine Samuel's balance sheet. Can you see any reason why the bank manager might not grant the loan of $10 000?
6. What additional information might the bank manager want in order to grant this loan?
7. If Samuel were denied the loan from the bank, discuss other approaches he could take in order to obtain the $10 000 for the purchase of the computer equipment he is interested in.

3 Analyzing Changes in Financial Position

3.1 Business Transactions
3.2 Equation Analysis Sheet
3.3 Summary of Steps in Analyzing a Transaction
3.4 Introduction to Source Documents
3.5 Computerized Accounting: Recording Transactions on the Spreadsheet

3.1 Business Transactions

On any given day in a business many events occur that cause the financial position of the business to change. Each of these events is called a business transaction. A **business transaction** may be defined as a financial event that causes a change in financial position.

For example, suppose the business buys a new truck for which it pays $20 000 cash. This event is a transaction because it causes the financial position of the business to change. There would be an increase in the Trucks account of $20 000. There would be a decrease in the Cash account of $20 000.

Or, suppose that the business owes $7 000 to City Finance and makes a payment of $1 000 against the debt. This event is also a transaction causing the financial position to change. The amount owed to City Finance will be reduced by $1 000. The cash on hand will be reduced by $1 000.

On the other hand, suppose that the city plumbing inspector inspects the building and leaves a letter suggesting some improvements. This is not a business transaction because no assets or liabilities have changed as a result of the activity.

Section Review Questions

1. What is a transaction?
2. Explain the following sentence: "Transactions are the raw materials of accounting."
3. Give an example of a transaction.
4. Give an example of a non-transaction.

Section Exercises

1. **Given that a transaction is a financial event that requires changing the statement of financial position, decide whether or not each of the following is a transaction. The business is Best Consultants of Calgary, Alberta.**

   1. $800 is paid by the business to Mercury Finance to reduce the amount owed to them.
   2. The owner, P. Dufour, withdraws $500 from the business for her own personal use.
   3. A new employee is needed in the payroll department. P. Dufour interviews Stan Martin for the job.
   4. A $700 consulting service is provided for R. Bertoli on credit.
   5. The business pays the rent for the month, $500.
   6. The employee in question 3 above is hired to start work next Monday at $300 per week.
   7. The business purchases a new computer for cash at the price of $3 000.
   8. The computer in question 7 above is defective and is replaced at no cost to the business.

2. **Workbook Exercise: Additional practice in transaction selection.**

3.2 Equation Analysis Sheet

Your next step in the study of accounting is to learn how the various business transactions affect and change the financial position. To begin with, look at the balance sheet of Metropolitan Movers of Burnaby, B.C. (Figure 3.1).

METROPOLITAN MOVERS
BALANCE SHEET
—DATE—

Assets		Liabilities	
Cash	$13 500	Accounts Payable	
Accounts Receivable		Central Supply	$ 1 750
B. Cava	1 300	Loan Payable	
K. Lincoln	2 500	Mercury Finance	18 370
Equipment	11 500	Total Liabilities	$20 120
Trucks	24 500	Owner's Equity	
		J. Hofner, Capital	33 180
Total Assets	$53 300	Total Liabilities and Equity	$53 300

Figure 3.1 The balance sheet of Metropolitan Movers.

The balance sheet of Metropolitan Movers shows the value of the assets, liabilities, and capital on a particular date. As business transactions occur, the values of assets, liabilities, and capital change. The balance sheet is not a suitable type of record on which to record these changes. Therefore, let us arrange the balance sheet items in a different manner. We will transfer the assets, liabilities, and capital from the balance sheet to an equation analysis sheet. This sheet is ideal for studying and recording changes in financial position. In Figure 3.2 you can see the balance sheet items for Metropolitan Movers entered on an equation analysis sheet. Note that this arrangement is in the form of the fundamental accounting equation.

	ASSETS					LIABILITIES		OWNER'S EQUITY
	Cash	A/R B. Cava	A/R X. Lincoln	Equipment	Trucks	A/P Central Supply	Loan Pay'l Mercury Finance	J. Hofner Capital
Beginning Balance	13 500	1 300	2 500	11 500	24 500	1 750	18 370	33 180
			53 300			=	20 120 +	33 180

Figure 3.2 Equation analysis sheet for Metropolitan Movers.

Updating the Equation Analysis Sheet

Let us now examine how transactions affect financial position.

Transaction 1. $1 200 cash is paid to Mercury Finance.

After this payment is made, the financial position shown in Figure 3.2 will no longer be correct. Two changes are necessary: Cash must be reduced by $1 200, and the amount owed to Mercury Finance must also be reduced by $1 200. These changes are recorded on the equation analysis sheet shown in Figure 3.3.

	ASSETS					LIABILITIES		OWNER'S EQUITY
	Cash	A/R B. Cava	A/R X. Lincoln	Equipment	Trucks	A/P Central Supply	Loan Pay'l Mercury Finance	J. Hofner Capital
Beginning balances	13 500	1 300	2 500	11 500	24 500	1 750	18 370	33 180
Transaction 1	-1 200						-1 200	
New balances	12 300	1 300	2 500	11 500	24 500	1 750	17 170	33 180
			52 100			=	18 920 +	33 180

Figure 3.3 Equation analysis sheet after transaction 1.

In analyzing transaction 1, observe that:

1. The amounts for Cash and Mercury Finance are updated: Cash is decreased by $1 200 and the debt owed to Mercury Finance is decreased by $1 200.
2. The amounts for the other items remain unchanged.
3. After the changes are recorded and the new totals determined, the equation is still in balance.

Chapter 3

Transaction 2. K. Lincoln, who owes Metropolitan Movers $2 500, pays $1 100 in part payment of the debt.

Can you figure out the changes to be made on the equation analysis sheet? Try to do this mentally before looking ahead at Figure 3.4.

	ASSETS					LIABILITIES			OWNER'S EQUITY
	Cash	A/R B. Cava	A/R K. Lincoln	Equipment	Trucks	A/P Central Supply	Loan Pay'l Mercury Finance	J. Hofner Capital
Beginning balances	13 500	1 300	2 500	11 500	24 500	1 750	18 370	33 180
Transaction 1	−1 200						−1 200	
New balances	12 300	1 300	2 500	11 500	24 500	1 750	17 170	33 180
Transaction 2	+1 100		−1 100					
New balances	13 400	1 300	1 400	11 500	24 500	1 750	17 170	33 180
			52 100			=	18 920 +	33 180

Figure 3.4 Equation analysis sheet after transaction 2.

In analyzing transaction 2, observe that:
1. The figure for Cash is increased by the amount received, $1 100.
2. The figure for K. Lincoln is decreased by $1 100. $1 400 is still owing on the debt.
3. After the changes are recorded, the equation is still in balance.

Transaction 3. Equipment costing $1 950 is purchased for cash.

Again, try to make the changes mentally before looking at the entries recorded in Figure 3.5.

	ASSETS					LIABILITIES			OWNER'S EQUITY
	Cash	A/R B. Cava	A/R K. Lincoln	Equipment	Trucks	A/P Central Supply	Loan Pay'l Mercury Finance	J. Hofner Capital
Beginning balances	13 500	1 300	2 500	11 500	24 500	1 750	18 370	33 180
Transaction 1	−1 200						−1 200	
New balances	12 300	1 300	2 500	11 500	24 500	1 750	17 170	33 180
Transaction 2	+1 100		−1 100					
New balances	13 400	1 300	1 400	11 500	24 500	1 750	17 170	33 180
Transaction 3	−1 950			+1 950				
New balances	11 450	1 300	1 400	13 450	24 500	1 750	17 170	33 180
			52 100			=	18 920 +	33 180

In analyzing transaction 3 observe that:
1. Cash is decreased by the amount paid, $1 950.
2. Equipment is increased by the cost of the equipment acquired, $1 950.
3. After the changes are recorded, the equation is still in balance.

Transaction 4. **A new pick-up truck is purchased at a cost of $18 000. Metropolitan Movers pays $10 000 cash and arranges a loan from Mercury Finance to cover the balance of the purchase price.** (Note: This is considered to be a single transaction. Mercury Finance will pay $8 000 directly to the truck dealer who will be paid in full.)

Again try to work out the changes mentally before looking at the equation analysis sheet in Figure 3.6.

	ASSETS					LIABILITIES		OWNER'S EQUITY
	Cash	A/R		Equipment	Trucks	A/P	Loan Pay'l	J. Hofner
		B. Cava	K. Lincoln			Central Supply	Mercury Finance	Capital
Beginning balances	13 500	1 300	2 500	11 500	24 500	1 750	18 370	33 180
Transactions	-1 200						-1 200	
New balances	12 300	1 300	2 500	11 500	24 500	1 750	17 170	33 180
Transaction 2	+1 100		-1 100					
New balances	13 400	1 300	1 400	11 500	24 500	1 750	17 170	33 180
Transaction 3	-1 950			+1 950				
New balances	11 450	1 300	1 400	13 450	24 500	1 750	17 170	33 180
Transaction 4	-10 000				+18 000		+8 000	
New balances	1 450	1 300	1 400	13 450	42 500	1 750	25 170	33 180
			60 100			=	26 920 +	33 180

Figure 3.6 Equation analysis sheet after transaction 4.

In analyzing transaction 4 observe that:
1. Cash is decreased by the amount paid out, $10 000.
2. Trucks is increased by the cost of the new truck, $18 000.
3. The liability to Mercury Finance is increased by the additional amount borrowed, $8 000.
4. After the changes are recorded, the equation is still in balance.

Chapter 3

Transaction 5. Metropolitan Movers completes a storage service for B. Cava at a price of $1 500. A bill is sent to Cava to indicate the additional amount that Cava owes.

Work out the changes necessary and compare them with the equation analysis sheet in Figure 3.7.

	ASSETS					LIABILITIES			OWNER'S EQUITY
	Cash	A/R		Equipment	Trucks	A/P Central Supply	Loan Pay'l Mercury Finance	J. Hofner Capital
		B. Cava	X. Lincoln					
Beginning balances	13 500	1 300		2 500	11 500	24 500	1 750	18 370	33 180
Transaction 1	−1 200						−1 200	
New balances	12 300	1 300		2 500	11 500	24 500	1 750	17 170	33 180
Transaction 2	+1 100			−1 100					
New balances	13 400	1 300		1 400	11 500	24 500	1 750	17 170	33 180
Transaction 3	−1 950				+1 950				
New balances	11 450	1 300		1 400	13 450	24 500	1 750	17 170	33 180
Transaction 4	−10 000					+18 000		+8 000	
New balances	1 450	1 300		1 400	13 450	42 500	1 750	25 170	33 180
Transaction 5		+1 500							+1 500
New balances	1 450	2 800		1 400	13 450	42 500	1 750	25 170	34 680
	61 600						26 920 +	34 680

Figure 3.7 Equation analysis sheet after transaction 5.

Transaction 5 is not as simple to understand as the previous four. But "understanding" is vital to becoming a good accountant. Transaction 5 may be explained as follows:

1. Cava owes $1 500 more to Metropolitan Movers and therefore the figure for Cava is increased by $1 500.
2. No other asset or liability is affected.
3. J. Hofner's Capital is increased by $1 500.

There are two ways to explain this increase in capital. First, remember that Metropolitan Movers is in the business of providing a service to earn profit. When the service to Cava is completed, and Cava legally owes the $1 500, a gain has been made. Metropolitan Movers is then better off by the amount of this gain. This is recorded by increasing the capital of the owner, J. Hofner.

Second, the increase in capital can be shown by arithmetic. Remember that capital is the difference between the total assets and the total liabilities.

	ASSETS	LIABILITIES	CAPITAL
After transaction 5	$61 600 −	$26 920 =	$34 680
Before transaction 5	$60 100 −	$26 920 =	$33 180
		Increase in capital =	$ 1 500

Clearly, there is an increase in capital of $1 500, which must be recorded on the equation analysis sheet.

Transaction 6. J. Hofner, the owner, withdraws $500 for personal use.

Work out the necessary changes and then check your work against the equation analysis sheet in Figure 3.8.

	ASSETS					LIABILITIES		OWNER'S EQUITY
	Cash	A/R B. Cava	A/R K. Lincoln	Equipment	Trucks	A/P Central Supply	Loan Pay'l Mercury Finance	J. Hofner Capital
Beginning balances	13 500	1 300	2 500	11 500	24 500	1 750	18 370	33 180
Transaction 1	− 1 200						−1 200	
New balances	12 300	1 300	2 500	11 500	24 500	1 750	17 170	33 180
Transaction 2	+ 1 100		−1 100					
New balances	13 400	1 300	1 400	11 500	24 500	1 750	17 170	33 180
Transaction 3	− 1 950			+1 950				
New balances	11 450	1 300	1 400	13 450	24 500	1 750	17 170	33 180
Transaction 4	−10 000				+18 000		+8 000	
New balances	1 450	1 300	1 400	13 450	42 500	1 750	25 170	33 180
Transaction 5		+1 500						+1 500
New balances	1 450	2 800	1 400	13 450	42 500	1 750	25 170	34 680
Transaction 6	− 500							− 500
New balances	950	2 800	1 400	13 450	42 500	1 750	25 170	34 180
		61 100				=	26 920 +	34 180

Figure 3.8 Equation analysis sheet after transaction 6.

In analyzing transaction 6 observe that:
1. Cash is decreased by $500, the amount withdrawn.
2. No other asset or liability is affected.
3. Capital is decreased by $500. After changing the cash figure, the difference between total assets and total liabilities is $34 180. This is $500 less than it was immediately before the transaction.
4. After the changes are recorded, the equation is still in balance.

Chapter 3

Transaction 7. One of the trucks requires an engine adjustment costing $75. The repair is paid for in cash when the truck is picked up.

Work out the necessary changes and then check your work against the equation analysis sheet in Figure 3.9.

		ASSETS				LIABILITIES		OWNER'S EQUITY
Beginning balances	Cash	A/R B. Cava	A/R K. Lincoln	Equipment	Trucks	A/P Central Supply	Loan Pay'l Mercury Finance	J. Hofner Capital
Beginning balances	13 500	1 300	2 500	11 500	24 500	1 750	18 370	33 180
Transaction 1	-1 200						-1 200	
New balances	12 300	1 300	2 500	11 500	24 500	1 750	17 170	33 180
Transaction 2	+1 100		-1 100					
New balances	13 400	1 300	1 400	11 500	24 500	1 750	17 170	33 180
Transaction 3	-1 950			+1 950				
New balances	11 450	1 300	1 400	13 450	24 500	1 750	17 170	33 180
Transaction 4	-10 000				+18 000		+8 000	
New balances	1 450	1 300	1 400	13 450	42 500	1 750	25 170	33 180
Transaction 5		+1 500						+1 500
New balances	1 450	2 800	1 400	13 450	42 500	1 750	25 170	34 680
Transaction 6	-500							-500
New balances	950	2 800	1 400	13 450	42 500	1 750	25 170	34 180
Transaction 7	-75							-75
New balances	875	2 800	1 400	13 450	42 500	1 750	25 170	34 105
			61 025			=	26 920 +	34 105

Figure 3.9 Equation analysis sheet after transaction 7.

In analyzing transaction 7 observe that:

1. Cash is decreased by $75, the amount paid for the repair.
2. No other asset or liability is affected. The value of the truck on the equation analysis sheet is not increased because of the repair.
3. Capital is decreased by $75. After changing the cash figure, the difference between total assets and total liabilities is $34 105. This is $75 less than it was immediately before the transaction.
4. After the changes are recorded, the equation is still in balance.

Updating the Balance Sheet

The figures for an updated balance sheet for Metropolitan Movers are taken from the last line of the equation analysis sheet. Figure 3.10 shows the new balance sheet.

METROPOLITAN MOVERS
BALANCE SHEET
—DATE—

Assets		Liabilities	
Cash	$ 875	Accounts Payable	
Accounts Receivable		Central Supply	$ 1 750
B. Cava	2 800	Mercury Finance	25 170
K. Lincoln	1 400	Total Liabilities	$26 920
Equipment	13 450	Owner's Equity	
Trucks	42 500	J. Hofner, Capital	34 105
Total Assets	$61 025	Total Liabilities and Equity	$61 025

Figure 3.10 The updated balance sheet of Metropolitan Movers.

Section Review Questions

1. Name the form used in this chapter for analyzing transactions.
2. Explain how this form is related to the balance sheet.
3. Explain the mathematical way of telling if capital has increased after a business transaction.
4. How do you know if you balanced a transaction on an equation analysis sheet?
5. For what type of transaction does only one item change?

Section Exercises

1. **The opening financial position is shown here for Sheila's Interior Decorating, owned by Sheila Kostiuk. In your workbook, or on columnar paper, record in the correct columns the changes required for the transactions below. After each transaction, calculate the new totals and make sure that the equation balances.**

	Cash	Accounts Receivable D. Murray	Supplies	Office Furniture	Truck	Accounts Payable Ace Supply / Pine Motors	S. Kostiuk Capital
Opening Balances	1 000	50					1 050

Transactions

1. Stationery and supplies are purchased from Ace Supply, $75 on credit. They will be paid for within 30 days.

2. A new desk for the office costing $450 is purchased for cash.
3. D. Murray, a debtor, pays her debt in full.
4. A $100 service is performed for a customer who pays immediately in cash.
5. A used truck costing $6 500 is purchased from Pine Motors. A down payment of $500 is made. It is agreed that the remainder of the purchase price will be paid within three months.
6. $75 is paid to Ace Supply, a creditor.
7. The owner, Sheila Kostiuk, withdraws $100 from the business for her own use.

2. The balance sheet of Triangle Real Estate, at the close of business on September 30, 19--, is as follows:

TRIANGLE REAL ESTATE
BALANCE SHEET
SEPTEMBER 30, 19--

Assets			Liabilities	
Cash		$ 216	Account Payable	
Accounts Receivable			Acme Supply	$ 1 562
P. Adams	375			
J. Hahn	150		Owner's Equity	
N. Swartz	200		J. Morse, Capital	25 521
Supplies		4 175		
Equipment		21 967		
		$27 083		$27 083

1. Record the above balance sheet figures on the equation analysis sheet provided in your workbook.
2. Analyze the transactions of October 1, listed below, and record the necessary changes on the equation analysis sheet. After each transaction, ensure that the equation is still in balance.
3. After completing transaction 5, prepare a new balance sheet.

Transactions of October 1

1. $100 cash is received from N. Swartz in part payment of the amount owed by him.
2. $200 cash is paid to Acme Supply in part payment of the debt owed to them.
3. Supplies costing $95 are purchased for cash from the Standish Company.
4. Triangle Real Estate sells a home for A.J. Buhler. For this service, Triangle Real Estate receives a commission of $4 700 cash.
5. A new desk is purchased from Ideal Furniture for $950 cash.

3. Alliance Appliance Service, in Renforth, Ont., owned by Wayne Dalli, has the following assets and liabilities at the close of business on October 20, 19--.

Assets		Liabilities	
Cash	$ 1 395	Bank Loan	$ 5 000
Accounts Receivable		Mortgage Payable	52 700
N. Chang	100		
P. O'Neil	527		
Equipment	8 316		
Delivery Truck	19 750		
Land	40 000		
Building	80 000		

1. Record the above items on an equation analysis sheet. Do not forget to calculate and include the capital figure.
2. Analyze the transactions of October 21, listed below, and record the necessary changes on the equation analysis sheet.
3. After completing transaction 5, calculate the new totals and ensure that the equation is still in balance. Then, prepare a new balance sheet.

Transactions of October 21

1. The owner, in need of money for his personal use, draws $500 cash out of the business.
2. P. O'Neil pays her debt of $527.
3. A repair service is performed for a customer. The customer pays the full amount of the bill in cash, $90.
4. A new electrical tester is purchased and paid for in cash, $410.
5. The regular monthly mortgage payment is made, $900 in cash.

4. **Workbook Exercise:** Additional practice in using an equation analysis sheet.

3.3 Summary of Steps in Analyzing a Transaction

You have seen how each of six transactions made it necessary to change the record of the financial position. You are now ready to study the concept of financial change in general.

The following suggestions will help you in analyzing transactions:

1. Try to be logical and to use good common sense when thinking about the transaction.
2. Carefully analyze the information given for any transaction. Your first objective is to make all the necessary changes in any of the assets, the liabilities, or both.
3. Your second objective is to see if the capital has changed. Recalculate the assets total and the liabilities total and calculate the difference between the two totals. Then compare this figure with the capital figure immediately before the transaction.

    Eventually, you will just know whether or not capital has changed. Generally, if a business is better off after a transaction, capital has increased. If a business is worse off after a transaction, capital has decreased.
4. Make certain that at least two of the individual items (any of the assets, liabilities,

or the capital) have changed. It is possible for several items to change, *but never only one*.

5. Make sure that the equation is still in balance.

Developing Good Work Habits

The first step in the accounting process is to analyze a transaction to determine the financial changes that result from it. You must recognize the importance of performing this step correctly. Accounting must be accurate. Therefore, you must be accurate.

You must also realize that the possible number of different transactions is very large. Do not think of trying to memorize all of the changes for all of the transactions. If you tried to rely on memory alone, you could not become a truly good accountant. Good accountants use their memory, of course, but they also rely on common sense, clear thinking, and a thorough understanding of accounting theory.

Section Review Questions

1. In working out the changes caused by a transaction, what is the first objective? What is the second objective?
2. What do good accountants rely on besides their memory?
3. Why must accounting be done accurately?
4. What is a good clue as to whether capital has increased or decreased?

3.4 Introduction to Source Documents

Most of the activity within a business creates business papers or documents. These are necessary for a variety of reasons such as proof of purchase, proof of payment, reference, and so on. The papers move from person to person and from department to department.

Much of the activity mentioned above requires the making of accounting entries. Some of the transactions are initiated within the accounting department: the writing of a cheque, for example. Other transactions are initiated elsewhere in the organization, for example, the purchasing of goods. The accounting department must be informed of transactions regardless of where they originate. The accounting department must learn of any business activity that requires the making of an accounting entry. This is done by means of business papers, called source documents. They are called source documents because they are the source of the data used by the accounting department to make the accounting entries. A *source document* is a business paper, such as an invoice, that is the original record of a transaction and that provides the information needed when accounting for the transaction.

Examples of source documents include hydro bills, telephone bills, cheque copies, receipts, cash register summaries, and credit card statements. In Chapter 6, a full discussion is devoted to source documents, with illustrations. For now, remember: 1) accounting entries are made from business papers known as source documents, and 2) source documents are kept on file for reference purposes and as proof of transactions.

GAAP—The Objectivity Principle

This is a generally accepted accounting principle related to source documents. The **objectivity principle** states that accounting will be recorded on the basis of objective evidence. Objective evidence means that different people looking at the evidence will arrive at the same values for the transaction. Simply put, this means that accounting entries will be based on fact, and not on personal opinion or feelings.

The source document for a transaction is almost always the best objective evidence available. The source document shows the amount agreed to by the buyer and the seller, who are usually independent and unrelated to each other.

Income tax auditors and others may want to ask questions about a business. Source documents are kept on file so such questions may be easily answered.

Section Review Questions

1. Give reasons why business papers are created within a business.
2. Where in the business do business papers originate?
3. What must happen to any business paper for which an accounting entry is necessary?
4. What are these business papers called?
5. State and explain the accounting principle of objectivity.
6. Give some examples of source documents.
7. What happens to source documents after the accounting entries have been completed?

Section Exercises

1. **Examine the source document below and answer the questions that follow, using what you know so far.**

```
CAMPBELL                    Suite 40  100 University Avenue,
& ASSOCIATES                Toronto, Ontario M5J 2K4

                            Smokey Valley Ski Club
                            R.R. #1, Stratford, Ont.
July 22, 19-0               N5A 6S5
─────────────────────────────────────────────────────
Our fee for professional services rendered,
auditing the records of the club for the
year ended April 15, 19-0, preparing therefrom
financial statements as at that date, and
reporting thereon:

                                         $ 600.00
                                         ────────
```

A professional bill received by Smokey Valley Ski Club. This bill came from a firm of chartered accountants and shows the charge for auditing the club's records and preparing its financial statements.

Chapter 3

1. Who issued the bill?
2. Who received the bill?
3. When was the bill issued?
4. Does the bill say when payment is due?
5. In your opinion, what accounting changes will be made by the receiver?
6. For what service was this bill issued?

2. Examine the source document below and answer the questions that follow, using what you know so far.

```
                                        Box 500, Orillia, Ontario   L3V 6K7

           THE DAVEY COMPANY
                   TROPHIES    GIFTWARE    ENGRAVERS

 Sold to:  Smokey Valley Ski Club
           R.R. #1
           Stratford, Ont. N5A 6S5
 Date   Dec. 5, 19-0
```

PURCH. ORDER NO.	FED. SALES TAX	PROV. SALES TAX	DELIVERY DATE	TERMS	SHIP VIA
6506		10.36	12/5	30 days	CPX

35	Name tags		148.00
		Tax	10.36
			158.36

A purchase invoice received by Smokey Valley Ski Club. This document came from a small service business and shows the charge made for name tags worn by the members.

1. Who issued the bill?
2. Who received the bill?
3. When was the bill issued?
4. When were the goods delivered?

Section 3.4   57

5. When is this bill due for payment?
6. Why was this bill issued?
7. In your opinion, what accounting changes will be made by the purchaser?
8. Was this a cash sale transaction?

3. Examine the source document below and answer the questions that follow.

SMOKEY VALLEY SKI CLUB
R.R. #1, Stratford, Ont. N5A 6S5

015

Nov. 12   19 --

PAY TO THE ORDER OF   Mid-West Ski Lifts and Equipment $ 10 000.00

Ten Thousand -------------------------- xx DOLLARS

THE COMMERCIAL BANK

Smokey Valley Ski Club
per *A. Hart*
     R. Schwartz

⑈015⑈ ⑆11962⑈509⑈   7427⑈0⑈

---

1. What kind of source document is it?
2. Who issued the source document?
3. Who received the source document?
4. What do you think this source document is paying for?
5. As a result of this source document, which of the following is most likely to be true for the Smokey Valley Ski Club?
   a. An asset and a liability will both increase.
   b. An asset and a liability will both decrease.
   c. An asset will increase and another asset will decrease.
   d. An asset and equity will both decrease.

3.5 Computerized Accounting: Recording Transactions on the Spreadsheet

Recording Transactions on the Spreadsheet

When numerical data is entered on a spreadsheet, calculations and totals can be done automatically. These are done using formulas that you create yourself, as shown in the previous chapter. The same is true when any changes are made to any of the numerical data on the spreadsheet. Its ability to make automatic calculations is the most valuable feature of a computer spreadsheet.

The computer spreadsheet is ideal for analyzing changes in financial position on an equation analysis sheet. It can show the adjusted column totals automatically after each transaction is recorded. It can also be used to show that the total assets are equal to the total liabilities plus the owner's equity.

You will not find it difficult to prepare a spreadsheet program for an equation analysis sheet. Use the data in Figure 3.1 to begin with. Leave seven lines for the transactions and one line for the column totals. Blank lines between the transactions, as shown below, will improve the presentation. As you record changes caused by the transactions, use the negative sign with each amount representing a decrease. The column totals will be automatically adjusted after each transaction is recorded.

When developing your program you will find that the same formula is used again and again to produce the column totals. You can repeat the formulas if you wish. But there is an alternative that you should consider. There is a "replicate" command that allows you to copy a specific formula into a number of cells. You can read about this in the manual for your spreadsheet, or you can get help from your teacher.

Your objective is to design a program that will produce output such as that shown below in Figure 3.11

	A	B	C	D	E	F	G	H
1								
2						A/P	A/P	
3		A/R	A/R	EQUIP-		CENTRAL	MERCURY	J. HOFNER
4	CASH	CAVA	LINCOLN	MENT	TRUCKS	SUPPLY	FINANCE	CAPITAL
5								
6	13 500	1 300	2 500	11 500	24 500	1 750	18 370	33 180
7								
8	-1 200						-1 200	
9								
10	1 100		-1 100					
20	13 400	1 300	1 400	11 500	24 500	1 750	17 170	33 180
21								
22								

Figure 3.11 A spreadsheet for an equation analysis sheet.

Be sure to save your program for future use.

In your exercises you will likely encounter spreadsheets that are wider than the screen. This is not a problem until you want to print the results on paper. Check your printer to see if it can use paper that is wider than standard size. Or, check your printer manual to see if it can print in a compressed mode that allows for more than 80 characters per line. Another alternative is to print the spreadsheet in two parts, the left part first and the right part second. Discuss these options with your teacher.

Computer Review Questions

1. What is the most valuable feature of a spreadsheet?
2. Why is the computer spreadsheet ideal for use with an equation analysis sheet?
3. How should decreases be shown on the spreadsheet for this chapter?
4. Explain what replication means.
5. What are the three options available for printing out a spreadsheet that is wider than the screen?

Computer Exercises

1. On the spreadsheet you have prepared, complete the seven transactions for Metropolitan Movers given in the text.
2. a. Load the spreadsheet program from Exercise 1.
   b. Modify it to complete the Comprehensive Exercise (Merrymen Window Washing) at the end of the chapter.
   c. Continue the exercise using some transactions of your own choice.

CHAPTER HIGHLIGHTS

Now that you have completed Chapter 3, you should:

1. understand the factors that create changes in financial position;
2. be able to define "business transaction";
3. be able to work out the changes created in any of the assets, liabilities, or capital for any simple transaction;
4. be able to record a series of transactions on an equation analysis sheet;
5. be able to prepare a balance sheet from an equation analysis sheet;
6. be able to state the five steps in analyzing a business transaction;
7. know the purpose of source documents;
8. understand the objectivity principle.

ACCOUNTING TERMS

business transaction
objectivity principle

CHAPTER EXERCISES

Using Your Knowledge

1. Shown below is an equation analysis sheet for the business of Brad Provost, a painter and decorator in Sydney, N.S.

   Examine the entries made on this sheet. Then prepare a list of five transactions that would have caused the changes in the financial position indicated by the entries.

	ASSETS				LIABILITIES			OWNER'S EQUITY
	Cash	Accounts Receivable		Supplies	Equipment	Bank Loan	Accounts Payable		B. Provost Capital
		C. Sully	F. Vanwees				P.M. Co.	Norpaints	
	400	135		250	1500	8500	500	300	9985
1.	+250			-250					
2.				+150				+150	
3.	+300								+300
4.		+115							+115
5.	-300						-300		
	650	250		0	1650	8500	500	0	150	10400

2. Shown below is an equation analysis sheet for the business of Brian Lee, an architect.

   After studying this sheet, prepare a list of five transactions that would have caused the changes in financial position as shown.

	ASSETS					LIABILITIES		OWNER'S EQUITY
	Cash	Acc. Rec'l	Supplies	Equipment	Auto	Bank Loan	Acc. Pay'l High Finance	B. Lee, Cap'l
		L. Swan						
	500		1300	7000	17000	4000	5000	16800
1.	+500	+1300						+1800
2.	+1500				-7000		-5000	-500
3.	-1000				+20000	+19000		
4.	-150							-150
5.			-50					-50
	1350	1300	1250	7000	30000	23000	0	17900

3. At December 31, 19–1, Dowse Corporation had assets totaling $85 000. At December 31, 19–2, the assets totaled $115 000. During the same period, liabilities increased by $35 000. If the equity at the end of the first year amounted to $60 000, what was the amount of the owner's equity December 31 of the second year? Show how you arrive at your answer.

4. Describe four transactions that would cause the owner's equity to decrease.

5. Describe two transactions that would cause the owner's equity to increase.

6. Workbook Exercise: Completing a schedule showing changes in total assets, total liabilities, and owner's equity for a series of transactions.

Comprehensive Exercise

7. Merrymen Window Washing is a business owned and operated by Carl Savich in Timmins, Ontario. On November 30, 19––, at the end of the day, the financial position of the business is as shown on the following balance sheet.

MERRYMEN WINDOW WASHING
BALANCE SHEET
NOVEMBER 30, 19––

Assets		Liabilities	
Cash	$ 2 750	Accounts Payable	
Accounts Receivable		Cleanall Co.	$ 124
T. Brock	420	Hipp Co.	475
D. Pederson	75	Loan Payable	
Supplies	880	Simplex Finance	8 560
Truck	15 050		$ 9 159
Equipment	12 947	Owner's Equity	
		C. Savich, Capital	22 963
	$32 122		$32 122

1. Set up the balance sheet items on an equation analysis sheet. Leave a blank column for a new account payable.
2. Analyze the transactions of December 1, listed below, and record the necessary changes on the equation analysis sheet.
3. After completing the transactions, calculate the new totals, ensure that the equation is still in balance, and prepare a new balance sheet.

Transactions of December 1

1. The regular monthly instalment payment of $800 is paid to Simplex Finance.
2. $400 of supplies is purchased from Hipp Co. but not paid for.
3. $200 cash is received from T. Brock in part payment of his debt.
4. A new hoist is purchased from N.R.C. Co. for $2 125. A cash down payment of $300 is made. The balance of the purchase price is to be paid at a later date.

5. The old hoist, included in the Equipment figure at $550, is sold for $100 cash.
6. A $500 window washing service is performed for D. Pederson. Pederson pays $575, for this service and to pay off the amount owed.
7. The truck was in a serious collision and is a write-off. The insurance company agrees to pay $14 500. Of this $14 500, Simplex Finance receives the amount owed to them against the truck, and Merrymen Window Washing receives the rest.
8. A new truck costing $23 000 is purchased. An $8 000 down payment is made. The balance is financed through Simplex Finance.
9. The amount owed to Hipp Co. is paid in full.
10. $50 of supplies are taken on a job and used up.

For Further Thought

8. Briefly answer the following questions.

1. Assume that your assets include a truck worth $7 000. Assume further that the truck represented by the $7 000 has recently been wrecked in an accident and that you are negotiating with your insurance company for a settlement. What financial changes (if any) will be recorded at this time?

    Your insurance company settles with you for the above accident and you receive the settlement cheque of $5 000. What financial changes (if any) will be recorded?

2. One of your customers slips on the ice of your walkway and is injured. You receive a letter from the customer's lawyer to the effect that the customer is suing for $10 000. What financial changes (if any) will be recorded at this time?

3. In your opinion, what is the difference between an account payable and a loan payable?

4. Explain why it is impossible for a balance sheet to be out of balance and to be correct.

5. Explain why it is impossible for only a single item to change as a result of a business transaction.

6. Examine the simple chart below on which the scale is in $100s.

```
                    TOTAL LIABILITIES       CAPITAL              TOTAL ASSETS
                            L                 C = ?                    A
    |__|__|__|__|__|__|__|__|__|__|__|__|__|__|__|__|__|__|__|__|__|__|__|__|__|
    0  1  2  3  4  5  6  7  8  9 10 11 12 13 14 15 16 17 18 19 20 21 22 23 24 25
```

a. What is the figure for total assets?
b. What is the figure for total liabilities?
c. Calculate the capital. How is it represented on the chart?

Assume that a new desk is purchased for $200 cash.

    d. Mentally, calculate the new figure for total assets.

    e. Mentally, calculate the new figure for total liabilities.

    f. Mentally, place these new figures on the chart. Will the capital figure change and, if yes, by how much? How does the chart show this?

7. Examine the chart below on which the scale is in $100s.

```
          L           C = ?            A
          ↓                            ↓
|----|----|----|----|----|----|----|----|----|----|----|----|----|----|----|----|----|----|----|----|----|----|----|----|----|
0  1  2  3  4  5  6  7  8  9 10 11 12 13 14 15 16 17 18 19 20 21 22 23 24 25
```

    a. What is the figure for total assets?

    b. What is the figure for total liabilities?

    c. Calculate the capital. How is it represented on the chart?

Assume that there is a loss by water damage of supplies worth $300 and that there is no insurance coverage on the supplies.

    d. Mentally, calculate the new figure for total assets.

    e. Mentally, calculate the new figure for total liabilities.

    f. Mentally, place these new figures on the chart. Will the capital figure change and, if yes, by how much? How does the chart show this?

8. Explain why an equation analysis sheet is better than a balance sheet for recording accounting changes.

9. Name a source document that would not originate in the accounting office.

10. You are given fifty shares of Compuco by an aunt who has died. The share certificates show a face value of $10 each. Explain how you would arrive at a true value for the shares.

11. Describe what is meant by the term "at arm's length."

12. Describe what might happen if there were no "principle of objectivity" in accounting.

CASE STUDIES

Case 1 Is Money Better?

Hannah and Tina are school friends of yours at Vanier High School in Clark's Harbour, N.S. The two girls happen to be discussing their personal fortunes at the moment. Hannah is feeling rich because she has $2 000 in a personal bank account. A distant aunt who died recently left her the money.

64 Chapter 3

Tina feels pretty well-off, too. She has less money but she also has some valuable possessions that were left to her by her grandmother. For reasons that she cannot explain, she feels that she is just as well-off as Hannah.

You get into the conversation at lunch break. You suggest to the two girls that they each prepare a personal balance sheet. You explain how to go about it and how to use the estimated replacement value for non-cash items. The balance sheets, you say, will show who is better-off financially.

The girls prepare their balance sheets according to your directions and come up with the following:

HANNAH'S BALANCE SHEET SEPTEMBER 30		TINA'S BALANCE SHEET SEPTEMBER 30	
Assets		*Assets*	
Bank balance	$2 000	Bank balance	$ 10
Clothes	1 500	Stereo set	500
		Jewellery	1 000
		IBM shares	1 100
		Clothes	1 200
Total	$3 500	Total	$3 810
Liabilities and Equity		*Liabilities and Equity*	
Debts owing	nil	Debts owing	$200
Hannah's Capital	3 500	Tina's Capital	3 610
Total	$3 500	Total	$3 810

When the two girls get together to compare balance sheets, they still cannot agree. Hannah thinks that she is better off because she has more cash and clothes. Tina disagrees because she has greater capital.

Discuss these balance sheets with Hannah and Tina. Explain to them how to measure a person's equity.

Case 2 *Can You Spend the Equity?*

Raj Singh is a young man who has just inherited a business from his father who was killed in an accident. Raj has little business experience but is anxious to learn and willing to work hard.

The business has not been operating very profitably lately because it badly needs to replace out-dated equipment. This will cost $35 000.

The latest balance sheet of the business shows the following:

Assets		Liabilities	
Cash	$ 3 000	Accounts Payable	$ 5 000
Accounts Receivable	17 000	Bank Loan	30 000
Land	30 000	Mortgage Payable	50 000
Building	50 000		$85 000
Equipment	20 000	Owner's Equity	35 000
	$120 000		$120 000

After examining the balance sheet, Raj believes that he sees the solution to the problem. He wants to use the equity to purchase the new equipment. The accountant hastens to point out to Raj that this is not possible. Raj demands an explanation.

Question
1. What explanation will the accountant give?

Case 3 Checking Out a New Customer

Arthur Field, the owner of New Age Manufacturing, comes to you to arrange for the buying on credit of materials for his business. He advises you that the orders will amount to approximately one-half million dollars a year. This amount of new business could have a very beneficial effect on your company. You would even have to expand your own facilities to take advantage of it. You tell Mr. Field that you need time to consider the proposal.

Your banker advises you to find out as much as you can about New Age Manufacturing. You go to a credit investigation bureau. They provide you with the following balance sheet totals for New Age Manufacturing.

Assets	$450 000
Liabilities	445 000
Equity	5 000

Questions
1. What dangers are there in dealing with New Age Manufacturing?
2. Would you do business with Mr. Field?

CAREER
Melissa Porchuk / Student

Melissa Porchuk is now in her final year at Swift Current Comprehensive High School in Swift Current, Saskatchewan. Her future plans are to obtain a Bachelor of Commerce degree at the University of Regina and then to enroll in the Institute of Chartered Accountants program.

During her last two years in high school, Melissa has been studying accounting and computer concepts to prepare herself for a responsible position in the business world. She has enjoyed her accounting courses and her grades have been very good in this area.

Because she had taken accounting courses, Melissa was able to get a summer job in the accounting department of Agri-Co Freight Company, which specializes in the shipping of wheat and other locally produced grains.

During her first summer months at Agri-Co Freight, Melissa was responsible for checking the calculations on all sales invoices and preparing daily sheets of these invoices. She received payments from customers and recorded them in the customers' accounts. In addition, Melissa was responsible for checking the accuracy of various source documents for payment, such as telephone bills, purchase invoices, hydro bills, and tax bills.

During her second summer with Agri-Co Freight, the company changed from a manual system to a computer system for accounts receivable. Melissa studied computer systems in high school, and was very excited about the change. She continued to handle all customers' accounts, coded all sales invoices for computer entry, prepared cheque remittance forms to enter these payments in the computer, and completed all weekly and monthly accounts receivable balances for the computer.

Each month, Melissa received a computer printout of the accounts receivable and presented the total to the company controller for verification. She also issued monthly computer-produced customer statements.

Because she has controlled the paper flow of a wide variety of tasks within an accounting office, Melissa realizes that being organized, neat and accurate are extremely important.

Her accounting courses and work experience provide Melissa with a good base for further study. She finds it easier to concentrate on the concepts of accounting because she has already mastered the practical aspects.

Melissa is very pleased with the work she has done for Agri-Co Freight during the summer months. Her employers are so impressed with her work they would like her to return during the summer while she studies at university. They want her to accept a highly responsible position with the company once she has completed her education.

Discussion

1. List five business transactions Melissa handles in her daily accounting routine.
2. Melissa is responsible for many source documents in her job. Name the source documents in Melissa's profile that would cause the Capital account to increase.
3. Explain how Melissa would code the sales invoices for entry in the computer.
4. Do you think "legible record-keeping" is necessary today, since most records are produced by computer?
5. One of Melissa's responsibilities is to check the accuracy of various source documents before payment. Explain how you would check the accuracy of telephone bills, purchase invoices, hydro bills and tax bills before these bills are paid.
6. Give examples of objective evidence that are illustrated in Melissa's career profile.

4 The Simple Ledger

4.1 Ledger Accounts
4.2 Debit and Credit Theory
4.3 Account Balances
4.4 Trial Balance

The purpose of Chapter 3 was to show you the effect that transactions have on financial position. In Chapter 3, you practised analyzing transactions and keeping a financial position up-to-date. The method used, the equation analysis sheet, was a very simple one. However, that method is not satisfactory when working with a complete business operation.

In an active business, many transactions occur each day. To be able to handle them all, accountants use a more complete system, based on the concepts of the previous chapter. While the system is more complex, it is also more efficient and orderly, and it is universally accepted. As you will learn, it is a very effective system.

4.1 Ledger Accounts

In this chapter you will be learning the system used to maintain an up-to-date financial position. For this purpose, accountants long ago developed the account and the ledger.

An **account** is a page specially designed to record the changes in one component part of the financial position. There is one account for each different item affecting the financial position.

All the accounts together are called the ledger. A **ledger** is a group or file of accounts.

Section 4.1   69

a. Card ledger (courtesy of Luckett Loose Leaf, Ltd.).

b. Loose-leaf ledger (courtesy of Luckett Loose Leaf, Ltd.).

c. Magnetic tape (courtesy of IBM Canada Ltd.).

d. Diskette.

Figure 4.1 Four forms of the ledger.

A ledger can be prepared in different ways (see Figure 4.1). The accounts can be prepared on cards to form a card ledger. They may be prepared on loose-leaf paper to form a loose-leaf ledger. Or, the accounts may be recorded on a magnetic tape or magnetic disk to be used in a computerized system. All the methods are still in use, but computerized systems are becoming more and more common as computers and computer software improve.

Let us begin our study of ledger accounts by referring to the records of Pacific Trucking owned by Byron Rissien of Prince Albert, B.C. The balance sheet of this business is shown in Figure 4.2.

Chapter 4

	PACIFIC TRUCKING BALANCE SHEET JUNE 30, 19--		
Assets		*Liabilities*	
Cash	$ 3 265	Bank Loan	$18 000
Accounts Receivable		Accounts Payable	
W. Caruso	150	Dini Bros.	1 516
R. Van Loon	620	Packham Supply	3 946
Supplies	2 465		$23 462
Trucks	55 075	*Owner's Equity*	
Equipment	22 174	B. Rissien, Capital	60 287
	$83 749		$83 749

Figure 4.2 The balance sheet of Pacific Trucking.

The data from this balance sheet is used to set up the separate pages, called accounts. Pacific Trucking will have ten accounts, one account for each item on the balance sheet. These accounts are Cash, Account Receivable—R. Van Loon, Account Receivable—W. Caruso, Supplies, Trucks, Equipment, Bank Loan, Account Payable—Packham Supply, Account Payable—Dini Bros., and B. Rissien, Capital. All these accounts together form the ledger for Pacific Trucking.

ASSETS	=	LIABILITIES	+	OWNER'S EQUITY
Cash 3265	Supplies 2465	Bank Loan 18000		B. Rissien, Capital 60287
Account Receivable W. Caruso 150	Trucks 55075	Account Payable Dini Bros. 1516		
Account Receivable R. Van Loon 620	Equipment 22174	Account Payable Packham Supply 3946		

Figure 4.3 The simple ledger accounts of Pacific Trucking.

Figure 4.3 shows the information from the balance sheet of Pacific Trucking presented as accounts in a ledger. These accounts are called T-accounts because, as you can see, each one looks like a T. The T-account is a simple kind of account, used mainly to explain accounting theory. The formal account, the one actually used in business, will be introduced in a later chapter.

Important Features of Ledger Accounts

Using the above ledger as a guide, let us look at three important features of all ledger accounts.

1. Each individual balance sheet item is given its own specially divided page with the name of the item at the top. Each of these pages is called an account. In Figure 4.3, there are ten accounts. You must learn to call them the Cash account, the R. Van Loon account, the Packham Supply account, the Bank Loan account, and so on.
2. The dollar figure for each item is recorded in the account on the first line. It is especially important to record the dollar figure on the correct side of the account. For any item, the correct side is the side on which the item would appear on a simple balance sheet. Observe that for each of the asset accounts, the dollar amount is placed on the left side of the account page. For each of the liability accounts and the capital account, the dollar amount is placed on the right side of the account page.
3. The ledger and the balance sheet both show financial position, although in different ways. If you have a ledger, a balance sheet can be prepared from it. If you have a balance sheet, a ledger can be prepared from it.

Section Review Questions

1. How many accounts are there in a ledger?
2. Name the different forms a ledger can take.
3. How were ledgers prepared fifty years ago?
4. The accounting records are commonly referred to as the "books." Why would this name be used?
5. Why are computerized accounting systems becoming very common?
6. Why are the beginning amounts for a ledger usually taken from a balance sheet?
7. What is the principal use of T-accounts?
8. Explain where the dollar amounts are placed in the accounts when setting up the beginning amounts in a ledger.

Section Exercises

1. The balance sheet for Stevens Woodworking is shown below.

STEVENS WOODWORKING
BALANCE SHEET
–DATE–

Assets		Liabilities	
Cash	$ 2 000	Bank Loan	$ 20 000
Accounts Receivable		Account Payable	
A. Marks	375	Gem Lumber	2 500
C. Prentice	1 150	Mortgage Payable	55 000
Land	30 000		$ 77 500
Building	45 000		
Equipment	27 800	Owner's Equity	
Truck	14 500	T. Stevens, Capital	43 325
	$120 825		$120 825

Set up the ledger for Stevens Woodworking in the T-accounts provided in your workbook.

2. The balance sheet of Dr. Pauline Inaba is shown below.

DR. PAULINE INABA
BALANCE SHEET
–DATE–

Assets		Liabilities	
Cash	$ 500	Accounts Payable	
Accounts Receivable		A.B. Associates	$ 1 200
P. Auul	350	Medico Supply	2 300
S. Wouke	1 250		$ 3 500
Supplies	3 900		
Furniture and Equipment	18 320	Owner's Equity	
Automobile	21 040	Pauline Inaba, Capital	41 860
	$45 360		$45 360

Set up the ledger of Dr. Inaba in the T-accounts provided in your workbook.

3. Shown below is the ledger of Lilly Wall who operates an interior design business. The asset and liability account balances are given.

Cash	Accounts Receivable	Supplies
500.00	2 100.00	1 545.00

Equipment	Accounts Payable	Bank Loan
2 800.00	950.00	2 000.00

Lilly Wall, Capital
?

Show the fundamental accounting equation for Lilly Wall.

4.2 Debit and Credit Theory

In your work so far you have learned that the idea of "left side" and "right side" is important in accounting. This is especially true when using ledger accounts. The theory of accounting using ledger accounts is based entirely on the understanding that there are two distinct sides to every account page.

The two sides of an account page are described in the same way by accountants everywhere. **Debit** is the word associated with the left side of an account. **Credit** is the word associated with the right side of an account. There is no deeper meaning; debit means "left," credit means "right."

Remember that the two new terms apply to every account, as shown below.

Any Account	
left side	right side
DEBIT	CREDIT
(short form DR or Dr)	(short form CR or Cr)

These two new words—debit and credit—are probably the two most important words in the accountant's vocabulary. Let us now begin to use these two new accounting terms. Looking back at the simple ledger in Figure 4.3 you will notice that the values of the assets were placed on the left side—the debit side—of their accounts. The values of the liabilities and of the capital were placed on the right side—the credit side—of their accounts. You may correctly conclude from this that assets are accounts with debit values and that liabilities and capital are accounts with credit values.

The Rules of Debit and Credit

Now that you are familiar with the simple ledger and the terms debit and credit, you are ready to learn how changes are recorded in the accounts. There is a simple set of rules for recording changes in accounts. These rules are summarized in the chart below:

THE RULES OF DEBIT AND CREDIT

	To record INCREASES	To record DECREASES
In ASSET accounts	Record the amount of the increase on the DEBIT side of the account.	Record the amount of the decrease on the CREDIT side of the account.
In LIABILITY and CAPITAL accounts	Record the amount of the increase on the CREDIT side of the account.	Record the amount of the decrease on the DEBIT side of the account.

Applying the Rules of Debit and Credit

To give you practice in using the new rules of debit and credit, a number of transactions of Pacific Trucking are analyzed below. In applying these rules to the transactions, you should try to do the analyses before reading the explanations. You must master the technique of analyzing transactions if you want to be a skilled accountant.

Transaction 1. **$200 of supplies is purchased from Packham Supply, to be paid for later.**

Analysis To correctly analyze a transaction it is helpful in the initial stages to use a "transaction analysis sheet." This sheet, shown below, provides a place to organize your thoughts about the transaction. Proceed according to the following steps:

1. In column (1), write down the names of the accounts that are affected by the transaction. In this example:

(1) Account Names	(2) Account Classification: Asset, Liability, or Capital	(3) Increase (+) or Decrease (−)	(4) Debit or Credit	(5) Amount
Supplies				
Packham Supply				

2. In column (2), write down whether each of these accounts is an asset, a liability, or the capital. In this example:

(1) Account Names	(2) Account Classification: Asset, Liability, or Capital	(3) Increase (+) or Decrease (−)	(4) Debit or Credit	(5) Amount
Supplies	Asset			
Packham Supply	Liability			

3. In column (3), write down whether the accounts are to be increased or decreased. In this example:

(1) Account Names	(2) Account Classification: Asset, Liability, or Capital	(3) Increase (+) or Decrease (−)	(4) Debit or Credit	(5) Amount
Supplies	Asset	+		
Packham Supply	Liability	+		

4. In column (4), write down whether the accounts are to be debited or credited. Apply the rules given in the previous section. In this example: to increase an asset you debit the account; to increase a liability you credit the account.

(1) Account Names	(2) Account Classification: Asset, Liability, or Capital	(3) Increase (+) or Decrease (−)	(4) Debit or Credit	(5) Amount
Supplies	Asset	+	DR	
Packham Supply	Liability	+	CR	

5. In column (5), write in the amounts by which the accounts are increased or decreased. In this example:

(1) Account Names	(2) Account Classification: Asset, Liability, or Capital	(3) Increase (+) or Decrease (−)	(4) Debit or Credit	(5) Amount
Supplies	Asset	+	DR	200 —
Packham Supply	Liability	+	CR	200 —

This final step completes what is known as the accounting entry for the transaction. An **accounting entry** may be defined as all of the changes in the accounts caused by one business transaction, expressed in terms of debits and credits. An accountant would express the accounting entry for transaction 1 in the following way: debit Supplies and credit Packham Supply, $200. An accountant would write down the accounting entry as follows:

	DR	CR
Supplies	$200	
Packham Supply		$200

Notice that the debited account and amount come first. The credited account and amount come second, and are indented.

After the accounting entry is recorded in the accounts, the accounts appear as shown below:

Supplies
2 465
200

Account Payable Packham Supply
3946
200

Transaction 2. **$500 is paid to Dini Bros. in part payment of the amount owed to them.**

Analysis This transaction is recorded on a transaction analysis sheet as follows:

(1) Account Names	(2) Account Classification: Asset, Liability, or Capital	(3) Increase (+) or Decrease (−)	(4) Debit or Credit	(5) Amount
Dini Bros.	Liability	−	DR	500 −
Cash	Asset	−	CR	500 −

An accountant would express this accounting entry as follows: debit Dini Bros. and credit Cash, $500. It would be written as follows:

	DR	CR
Dini Bros.	$500	
Cash		$500

After the accounting entry is recorded, the accounts appear as shown below:

Cash
3265 | 500

Account Payable Dini Bros.
500 | 1516

Section 4.2

Transaction 3. **$200 cash is received from R. Van Loon in part payment of her debt.**

Analysis The accounting entry for this transaction is worked out on the transaction analysis sheet as follows:

(1) Account Names	(2) Account Classification: Asset, Liability, or Capital	(3) Increase (+) or Decrease (−)	(4) Debit or Credit	(5) Amount
Cash	Asset	+	DR	200 —
R. Van Loon	Asset	−	CR	200 —

Read the accounting entry as follows: debit cash and credit R. Van Loon, $200. Write the accounting entry as shown below.

	DR	CR
Cash	$200	
R. Van Loon		$200

After the changes are recorded, the accounts appear as follows:

```
         Cash                 Account Receivable
                                  R. Van Loon
   3 265 | 500                  620 | 200
     200 |
```

Transaction 4. **A delivery service is provided for a customer at a price of $400. The customer pays cash at the time the service is completed.**

Analysis The accounting entry for this transaction is worked out on the transaction analysis sheet as follows:

(1) Account Names	(2) Account Classification: Asset, Liability, or Capital	(3) Increase (+) or Decrease (−)	(4) Debit or Credit	(5) Amount
Cash	Asset	+	DR	400 —
B. Rissien, Capital	Capital	+	CR	400 —

Read this accounting entry: debit Cash and credit B. Rissien, Capital, $400. Write the accounting entry as follows:

	DR	CR
Cash	$400	
B. Rissien, Capital		$400

After the accounting entry is recorded in the accounts, they will appear as shown below:

```
        Cash                    B. Rissien, Capital
   3 265  | 500                            | 60 287
     200  |                                |    400
     400  |
```

Transaction 5. A used truck costing $8 000 is purchased from Dini Bros. A cash down payment of $2 500 is made at the time of the purchase and the balance is to be paid at a later date.

Analysis This transaction affects three accounts. The accounting entry for the transaction is worked out as follows:

(1) Account Names	(2) Account Classification: Asset, Liability, or Capital	(3) Increase (+) or Decrease (−)	(4) Debit or Credit	(5) Amount
Trucks	Asset	+	DR	8 000 —
Cash	Asset	−	CR	2 500 —
Dini Bros.	Liability	+	CR	5 500 —

Read this accounting entry: debit Trucks, $8 000; credit Cash, $2 500; and credit Dini Bros., $5 500. Write the accounting entry as follows:

	DR	CR
Trucks	$8 000	
Cash		$2 500
Dini Bros.		$5 500

After the accounting entry is recorded in the accounts, the accounts will appear as follows:

```
        Cash                   Trucks         Account Payable
                                                 Dini Bros.
   3 265  |  500            55 075  |           500 | 1 516
     200  | 2 500            8 000  |               | 5 500
     400  |
```

Section 4.2

Transaction 6. A delivery is completed for R. Van Loon at a price of $350. Van Loon does not pay for the service at the time it is provided but agrees to pay within sixty days.

Analysis The accounting entry for this transaction is worked out on the transaction analysis sheet as follows:

(1) Account Names	(2) Account Classification: Asset, Liability, or Capital	(3) Increase (+) or Decrease (−)	(4) Debit or Credit	(5) Amount
R. Van Loon	asset	+	DR	350 −
B. Rissien, Capital	Capital	+	CR	350 −

Read this accounting entry: debit R. Van Loon and credit B. Rissien, Capital, $350. Write the accounting entry as follows:

	DR	CR
R. Van Loon	$350	
B. Rissien, Capital		$350

After the accounting entry is recorded in the accounts, they will appear as shown below:

```
  Account Receivable              B. Rissien, Capital
    R. Van Loon
  620  | 200                           | 60287
  350  |                                |   400
                                        |   350
```

Transaction 7. One of the lifting machines (part of Equipment) breaks down. **$650 cash is spent on repairing the machine.**
(A common mistake made by beginners with this type of transaction is to increase the Equipment account. To help you avoid this mistake, here is a clue: the owner is worse off financially because the machine had to be repaired.)

Analysis This transaction is worked out on the transaction analysis sheet as follows:

(1) Account Names	(2) Account Classification: Asset, Liability, or Capital	(3) Increase (+) or Decrease (−)	(4) Debit or Credit	(5) Amount
Cash	asset	−	CR	650 −
B. Rissien, Capital	Capital	−	DR	650 −

Read this accounting entry: debit B. Rissien, Capital and credit Cash, $650. Write the accounting entry as follows:

	DR	CR
B. Rissien, Capital	$650	
Cash		$650

After the accounting entry is recorded, the accounts will appear as follows:

```
        Cash                    B. Rissien, Capital
  3265 │  500                      650 │ 60 287
   200 │ 2500                          │    400
   400 │  650                          │    350
```

Double-Entry System of Accounting

Whenever a transaction occurs, changes must be made in the accounts. For any transaction, all of the account changes together are known as the accounting entry.

In this chapter, so far, there have been seven transactions which required seven accounting entries. These seven accounting entries are summarized in Figure 4.4.

Transaction	Accounts	Debit Amount	Credit Amount
1	Supplies Packham Supply	$200	$200
2	Dini Bros. Cash	$500	$500
3	Cash R. Van Loon	$200	$200
4	Cash B. Rissien, Capital	$400	$400

5	Trucks
	    Cash
	    Dini Bros.
		$8 000	$2 500
			5 500

6	R. Van Loon B. Rissien, Capital	$350	$350
7	B. Rissien Capital Cash	$650	$650

Figure 4.4 Seven accounting entries for Pacific Trucking.

If you have been observant, you will have noticed something about these seven transactions that is very special. Each of the above seven transactions balances within itself. The total of the debit amounts equals the total of the credit amounts. This is basic to the whole accounting process and will be true for every possible transaction. If you ever find an accounting entry that does not balance within itself, you can be certain that the entry is not correct. On the other hand, a balanced entry is not necessarily a correct entry. If it is balanced, that means that the entry probably is correct. If an entry does not balance, there is no chance that it is correct.

Now you can understand why the system you have been working with is known as the double-entry system of accounting. In the **double-entry system of accounting**, every transaction is recorded in the accounts as a debit (or debits) and as a credit (or credits) so that the total of the debit entries equals the total of the credit entries. The double-entry system of accounting is in general use throughout the business world.

Section Review Questions

1. Explain the meaning of the words "debit" and "credit."
2. Explain the system that is used when setting up the beginning financial position in a ledger.
3. For what accounts does an increase mean "debit"?
4. For what accounts does a decrease mean "debit"?
5. For what accounts does an increase mean "credit"?
6. For what accounts does a decrease mean "credit"?
7. What is a transaction analysis sheet used for?
8. What is an accounting entry?
9. What special condition should be true of every accounting entry?
10. What condition is true for an accounting entry that does not balance?
11. What condition is true for an accounting entry that does balance?
12. Explain the meaning of the double-entry system of accounting.

Section Exercises

1. **Complete the following in your notebook by writing in the words "increase" or "decrease" in the rectangles provided.**

ASSETS		=	LIABILITIES		+	OWNER'S EQUITY	
Debit	Credit		Debit	Credit		Debit	Credit

2. Flora Monday is the owner-operator of a fitness clinic. The ledger used in her business contains the following accounts:

> Cash
> Accounts Receivable (several)
> Supplies
> Furniture
> Equipment
> Automobile
> Accounts Payable (several)
> Flora Monday, Capital

Listed below are transactions of Flora's business. Examine these transactions and record your analysis on the transaction analysis sheet provided in your workbook and shown below. To help you understand how the transaction analysis sheet works, the first transaction has been done for you. Be sure that each entry balances within itself.

Transactions

1. $300 cash is received from J. Parker, one of the accounts receivable.
2. $200 of supplies is purchased for cash.
3. Little Bros., one of the accounts payable, is paid $100.
4. The owner withdraws $250 for her personal use.
5. A piece of new equipment costing $500 is purchased from Champion Sports. $125 cash is paid at the time of purchase with the balance of $375 to be paid within 30 days.
6. A new customer signs up for a fitness course. The $300 fee is paid in cash.

Transaction Analysis Sheet

Trans-action No.	Account Names	Account Classification: Asset, Liability, or Owner's Equity	Increase (+) or Decrease (−)	Debit or Credit	Amount
1.	Cash	asset	+	DR	300 —
	Acct Receivable J. Parker	asset	−	CR	300 —

3. **Workbook Exercise:** Additional practice in using a transaction analysis sheet.

4. **Workbook Exercise:** Completing a chart showing the accounts debited and the accounts credited for a series of transactions.

4.3 Account Balances

In the ledger of Pacific Trucking there are ten accounts (see Figure 4.3). The following information is stored in each account:

1. the name of the account, which is written at the top;
2. the dollar value of the account;
3. the account indicator, which tells whether the value of the account is a debit or a credit.

Calculating the Balance of an Account

To calculate the balance of a T-account, two steps are performed. These two steps are shown in Figure 4.5, using accounts from the ledger of Pacific Trucking.

Figure 4.5 Calculating the balance of a T-account.

1. Add separately the two sides of the account. Use tiny pencil figures to write down these two subtotals, one beneath the last item on each side. These tiny totals are called **pin totals** or **pencil footings**.
2. a. Subtract the smaller total from the larger total.
   b. Write the result beside or beneath the larger of the two pin totals from Step 1. Circle this final amount.

The circled amount is the dollar value of the account. The side on which it is recorded indicates which type of balance it is, debit or credit. Together the two pieces of information represent the account balance. The **account balance** gives the dollar value of an account and shows whether it is a debit or credit value.

Interpreting the Balance of an Account

It is not enough simply to find the account balances. You must now learn to interpret the information stored in the accounts. They must mean something to you. Look at the accounts in Figure 4.5 and see what you can learn from them.

It should be clear what the account balances are. The Cash account has a balance of $215 and it is a debit balance because it is entered on the left side. Similarly, the R. Van Loon account has a balance of $770, debit, and the Dini Bros. account has a balance of $6 516, credit.

So far you are familiar with three types of accounts: assets, liabilities, and the capital. At this stage, all accounts fall into one of these categories. You already know that assets have debit balances and that liabilities and capital have credit balances.

It follows therefore that:

a. the Cash account is an asset because it has a debit balance.
b. the R. Van Loon account is an asset (an account receivable) because it has a debit balance.
c. the Dini Bros. account is a liability (an account payable) because it has a credit balance, and is not the capital account.

Exceptional Account Balances

Occasionally, an account that would normally have a debit balance ends up as a credit account, and vice versa. Opposite balances like this are not necessarily the result of mistakes, although that possibility should certainly be checked out. There may be a good reason for an account to end up with a balance opposite to its normal one.

For example, suppose that Jack Evans, a customer, owes us $50. Suppose also that he sends a cheque for $55 in payment. His account will end up with a credit balance of $5, even though he is a customer and normally has a debit balance. The account balance is correct. It shows that the business owes Jack Evans $5. The account is temporarily a liability account.

A similar situation can affect the Bank account. For instance, if we were to spend more out of the bank account than we have in it (the bank would have to agree to this), we would end up with a credit balance in the Bank account. What does this credit balance mean? It means that the Bank account is temporarily in a liability position and that we are in debt to the bank.

Other transactions can bring about exceptional balances as well. Consider the following:

- you overpay an account payable;
- a customer with no account balance returns unsatisfactory merchandise for credit;
- you return goods for credit to a supplier with whom you have no account balance.

Exceptional balances do not last long. Ordinary business activity usually causes them to return to normal quickly.

Section Review Questions

1. What three pieces of information does an account contain?
2. Explain the two steps in calculating the balance of a T-account.
3. How do you know which type of balance (debit or credit) an account has?
4. What kind of account has a debit balance?
5. What kind of account has a credit balance?
6. What does it mean if an account has an exceptional balance?
7. Give two examples of situations that result in an exceptional balance.

Section Exercises

1. The selected accounts below appear in your workbook. Calculate their balances. Remember to make your pencil footings in tiny figures, and to circle the balance on the correct side of the account.

Cash		Account Receivable H. Devrie		Account Payable P. Helka		R. Smart, Capital	
250	190	25	175	30	75	150	3 140
1 210	48	150		45	40		
360	512	70			175		
29		35					

    1. What does the debit balance in the H. Devrie account mean?
    2. What does the credit balance in the P. Helka account mean?

2. The following three accounts have exceptional balances. Examine them and answer the questions that follow.

Bank		Account Receivable P. Chu		Account Payable J. Reicher	
	500		100	300	

    1. For each account explain what is unusual about the balance.
    2. For each account give a possible cause of the exceptional balance.

3. A number of phrases appear below. To the right there are two columns, one headed "Debit" and the other headed "Credit." In your workbook, indicate

whether each phrase is best represented by the word "debit" or by the word "credit" by placing a check mark in the appropriate column.

	Debit	Credit

1. The left side of an account.
2. The balance of an account receivable.
3. The balance of a supplier's account.
4. A decrease in a liability.
5. An exceptional balance in the Bank account.
6. The balance in the Equipment account.
7. The right side of an account.
8. The balance in the Bank Loan account.
9. An exceptional balance in an accounts payable account.
10. The larger side of a liability account.
11. A creditor's account.
12. A customer's account.
13. An increase in an asset.
14. A debtor's account.

4.4 The Trial Balance

When setting up a ledger, as in Figure 4.3, the information for the accounts is usually obtained from a balance sheet. This way, the ledger begins in a balanced position. The total of the accounts with debit balances equals the total of the accounts with credit balances.

The changes caused by business transactions are recorded in the ledger. These changes are all in the form of balanced accounting entries. As a result, the ledger should be balanced after each full accounting entry. Just as a balance sheet must balance, a ledger must also balance.

Periodically, it is necessary to check the accuracy of the ledger. This is done by means of a "trial balance." The taking off of a trial balance is a simple procedure to find out if the ledger is in balance. A **trial balance** is a listing of the account balances in a ledger. It is used to see if the dollar value of the accounts with debit balances is equal to the dollar value of the accounts with credit balances. To do this you simply add up all the debit balances, add up all the credit balances, and see if the two totals are the same. If they agree, the ledger is said to be **in balance**. If they do not agree, the ledger is said to be **out of balance**. The whole process, called **taking off a trial balance**, is usually done at the end of each month.

The completed ledger for Pacific Trucking is shown in Figure 4.6. Let us now see if it is in balance.

ASSETS

LIABILITIES AND CAPITAL

Cash		Supplies		Bank Loan		B. Rissien, Capital	
3 265	500	2 465			18 000	650	60 287
200	2 500	200					400
650	650	2 665					350
3 865	3 650	(2665)				650	61 037
(215)							(60 387)

Account Receivable R. Van Loon		Trucks		Account Payable Packham Supply	
620	200	55 075			3 946
350		8 000			200
970	200	63 075			4 146
(770)		(63 075)			(4 146)

Account Receivable W. Caruso		Equipment		Account Payable Dini Bros.	
150		22 174		500	1 516
					5 500
				500	7 016
					(6 516)

Figure 4.6 The completed ledger of Pacific Trucking.

Methods of Taking Off a Trial Balance

To take off a trial balance proceed as follows:
1. List all the accounts and their balances.
2. Place the debit balances in a debit column and the credit balances in a credit column.
3. Add up the two columns.
4. See if the two column totals are the same. Only if the two column totals are the same can you consider your ledger work to be correct.
5. Write a heading at the top. A heading is necessary on the trial balance. It must show the name of the individual or business, the title "Trial Balance," and the date.

The completed trial balance for the above ledger is shown in Figure 4.7.

Heading: Who? What? When?

Pacific Trucking
Trial Balance
July 2, 19—

ACCOUNTS	Debits	Credits
Cash	215	
Accounts Receivable — W. Caruso	150	
— R. Van Loon	770	
Supplies	2665	
Trucks	63075	
Equipment	22174	
Bank Loan		18000
Accounts Payable — Packham Supply		4146
— Dini Bros.		6516
B. Rissien, Capital		60387
	89049	89049

Accounts listed in ledger order.
Account balances listed in correct columns.
Column totals should agree.

Figure 4.7 The trial balance for the ledger of Pacific Trucking.

Another way of taking off a trial balance is by using a printing calculator. This is a more convenient method and so is used very commonly.

The procedure is as follows:

1. Clear the machine by pressing the total button.
2. Enter the balances in the machine in ledger order.
   Make sure to enter the: **debits** as +'s,
                                credits as —'s.
3. Take off a total by depressing the total button. If your ledger work is correct, the sum of the +'s entered will be equal to the sum of the —'s entered. Therefore, the total should be 0.00.

The adding machine method of taking off a trial balance is illustrated in Figure 4.8. Be certain that you understand the principle involved. Your work is arithmetically correct if you get zero for your tape total. Your ledger is out of balance if you do not get zero for your tape total. If this happens, you must begin a search for the error or errors.

*Pacific Trucking
Trial Balance
July 2, 19—*

        0 • T ← Heading is handwritten on paper tape.

        0 • T ← Clear the machine to start.

    2 1 5 • +
    7 7 0 • +
    1 5 0 • + ← Debit balances are entered as +'s.
  2 6 6 5 • +
6 3 0 7 5 • +
2 2 1 7 4 • +
1 8 0 0 0 • − ← Credit balances are entered as −'s.
  4 1 4 6 • −
  6 5 1 6 • −
6 0 3 8 7 • −
        0 • T ← Final total should be nil. This is known as a zero proof.

Figure 4.8 Trial balance done on a printing calculator.

Importance of the Trial Balance

It is important to an accountant to have the ledger in balance. The work is not accurate if the ledger is not in balance. A ledger out of balance is a certain sign that at least one error has been made in the accounts.

A good accountant does not rest until all errors are found and corrected. Moreover, the accountant must test the ledger fairly often. It is standard practice to take off a trial balance every month. Regardless of the method used, a trial balance should be kept on file for a year, or at the least until after the visit of the official auditors.

Trial Balance Out of Balance

Trial balances do not work out on the first attempt most of the time. When this happens, it means that at least one error has been made in the accounting process. It is the accountant's job to find and correct these errors. The errors may have been caused by faulty addition, by entering an item on the wrong side, and so on. Even if the ledger is in balance, it might still have errors in it. A ledger that is in balance proves only that it is mechanically or mathematically correct. The accountant may have made incorrect entries, but they were balanced ones. Errors such as these are often the most difficult to find.

It takes a methodical approach to locate accounting errors because they are often quite difficult to detect. Skill in finding errors is a great advantage to an accountant.

For now, there is a four-step procedure to follow if you find a ledger that does not balance. This method is expanded in a later chapter (see page 188). The four steps are:

1. re-add the trial balance columns;
2. check the figures from the ledger against those of the trial balance. Make sure that none are missing, none are on the wrong side, and none are for the wrong amount;
3. re-calculate the account balances;
4. check that there is a balanced accounting entry in the accounts for each transaction.

You may be lucky enough to balance the ledger without having to go through all these steps. In this event, your task is finished and you can file your trial balance.

On the other hand, you may have completed all the steps and still not have balanced the ledger. When this happens, it means that you have erred. You will have to go through the steps again, this time working more carefully. If all the steps are done correctly, the errors will be found, and the ledger will be balanced.

Section Review Questions

1. Give a mathematical explanation of why a ledger should always balance.
2. Describe the procedure for balancing a ledger.
3. Describe how one takes off a trial balance when using a printing calculator.
4. Why is it important to balance the ledger?
5. How often should the ledger be tested by balancing it?
6. What happens to a completed trial balance?
7. For how long is a trial balance kept on file?
8. What does it mean if you complete the procedure for balancing a ledger and the ledger is still not in balance?

Section Exercises

1. **Mr. J. Strom is the owner of a hardware store in Lethbridge, Alta. At the end of the year he attempted to prepare a trial balance of the accounts in the general**

ledger as shown below. The balances themselves are correct. But Mr. Strom has no knowledge of double-entry bookkeeping and so he has made many errors in listing the balances. Find the errors and prepare a corrected trial balance.

J. STROM
TRIAL BALANCE
DECEMBER 31, 19--

	Debit	*Credit*
Cash	$ 3 000	
Land	50 000	
Accounts Receivable		$ 10 940
Supplies	3 400	
Office Equipment	15 350	
Automobile		21 200
Building	140 000	
Accounts Payable	5 160	
Bank Loan		52 000
J. Strom, Capital		108 230
Mortgage Payable		78 500
	$216 910	$270 870

2. The accounts and balances of Ceco Co. are arranged below in alphabetical order. Prepare a trial balance of Ceco Co. with the accounts arranged in normal ledger order. Remember to write in the three-part heading. Date the trial balance June 30 of this year.

Accounts and Balances	
Automobile	$22 500
Account Payable—Jondahl Co.	1 350
Account Payable—P. Swartz	4 250
Account Receivable—M. Legris	3 500
Account Receivable—W. Nishi	850
Bank Loan	10 000
C. Oke, Capital	27 471
Cash	7 000
Equipment	7 296
Supplies	1 925

3. Workbook Exercise: Finding out why a simplified ledger does not balance.

4. Workbook Exercise: Finding out why a simplified ledger does not balance.

CHAPTER HIGHLIGHTS

Now that you have completed Chapter 4, you should:

1. know what an account is and what a ledger is;
2. know the rules of debit and credit as they apply to assets, liabilities, and capital;
3. be able to record transactions in T-accounts and calculate an account balance;
4. know what the balance in a T-account means;
5. understand the concept of double-entry accounting;
6. be able to take off a trial balance using both the handwritten method and the machine method;
7. understand the importance of the trial balance;
8. be able to locate and correct errors in T-accounts.

ACCOUNTING TERMS

account
account balance
accounting entry
credit
debit
double-entry system of accounting
in balance
ledger
out of balance
pencil footings
pin totals
taking off a trial balance
trial balance

CHAPTER EXERCISES

Using Your Knowledge

1. Indicate whether each of the following statements is true or false by entering a "T" or an "F" in the space indicated in your workbook. Explain the reason for each "F" response in the space provided.

1. A number of individual balance sheet items may appear on one account page, as long as they are shown separately.
2. Many accountants use the equation analysis sheet instead of the ledger.
3. There is a page in the ledger for the total assets figure.
4. T-accounts are ideal for small businesses.
5. The first dollar amount recorded in an account is placed on the same side as it appears on a simple balance sheet.
6. In Latin, debit means "left" and credit means "right."
7. There is no account for capital because it can always be found by subtracting the total assets from the total liabilities.
8. A transaction analysis sheet is a permanent accounting record.
9. For every transaction, there is always one debit amount and one credit amount which are equal.
10. A balanced accounting entry is a correct accounting entry.
11. The balance of an account that is not zero must be either a debit or a credit.
12. The J.R. Dahl account in the ledger of C. Jacob is either an account payable or an account receivable.
13. Eric Lai's account has a credit balance. This means that he purchased our services on credit.
14. An exceptional balance merely means that it is opposite to what it would be normally.
15. A customer is given a refund because of unsatisfactory service. The account of this customer would then have an exceptional balance.
16. A ledger contains an exceptional balance. A trial balance cannot be taken until the exceptional item is transferred to another part of the ledger.
17. A trial balance that is in balance proves that there are no errors in the accounts.
18. A trial balance is taken using a printing calculator. When the total key is pressed, the figure 89.00 comes up. This is the amount of the error.
19. The business buys supplies and pays cash. The accounting entry made in the accounts is Dr Cash and Cr Supplies. This causes the ledger to be out of balance.
20. A correct trial balance needs to be kept only until the next one is taken.

2. **Workbook Exercise: Determining transactions from entries made in a T-account ledger.**

3. **Workbook Exercise: Determining transactions from entries made in a T-account ledger.**

4. **The trial balance prepared by your company at the end of the month did not balance. In reviewing the entries for the month, the accountant noticed that one of the transactions was recorded as a debit to Furniture & Fixtures, $500, and**

a debit to Cash, $500. Answer the following questions and explain your answer for each.

1. Was the Cash account overstated, understated, or correctly stated on the trial balance? If overstated or understated, show by how much.
2. Was the total of the debit column of the trial balance overstated, understated, or correctly stated? If overstated or understated, show by how much.
3. Was the total of the credit column of the trial balance overstated, understated, or correctly stated? If overstated or understated, show by how much.

5. The accountant for M. Finney, owner of a janitorial service business, prepared a trial balance at the end of December. When Mr. Finney examined the trial balance, he noticed that the S. Pearson Co. had a debit balance of $375. Mr. Finney remembered depositing a cheque received from Pearson for that amount. He wants to know why a debit balance still exists on the records. Give three different explanations of how this could happen.

6. State whether the following errors would cause a trial balance to be out of balance and by how much. Explain why or why not.

    1. The entry to record the purchase of delivery equipment was omitted from the Delivery Equipment account, $150.
    2. A new desk was purchased for cash. Cash was credited but Office Supplies was debited instead of Office Equipment. The cost of the desk was $400.
    3. Cash of $100 was received from a client for services performed. Cash was debited for $100 and Capital was credited for $10.
    4. Cash of $500 was borrowed from the bank. Cash was credited for $500 and Bank Loan was debited $500.

7. Examine the source document opposite and answer the questions below.

    Questions
    1. Who issued the fees form?
    2. Who received the fees form?
    3. Why was the form issued?
    4. Who filled in the details on the form?
    5. In your opinion, when is the deadline for paying this bill?
    6. It states that a cheque is enclosed. Is it necessary that the amount of the cheque agree with the summary?
    7. In your opinion, what accounting entry will be made by Louis Tusek?
    8. Based on what you know so far, what accounting entry will be made by the Smokey Valley Ski Club?
    9. Was this a cash transaction?

ANNUAL FEES FORM

SMOKEY VALLEY SKI CLUB

Name: *Louis Tusek*   Phone Home: 325-6410
Address: *15 Cam Street* (Street)   Phone Bus: 325-4987
Orillia (City)

List all family members who will be skiing:

Name	Age Dec. 1	Annual fee
Louis	35	250.00
Teresa	32	200.00
Ginger	12	125.00
Dene	8	125.00
Roger	6	125.00
	TOTAL FEE	825.00

I (the undersigned) hereby agree to comply with and be governed by the By-Laws, Rules and Regulations of the Club now or hereafter in force or as amended from time to time and I agree to be responsible for any debts incurred by members of my family.

Dated this *15th* day of *November* 19 ___
Signature *Louis Tusek*
I enclose my cheque for $ *825.00*

SMOKEY VALLEY SKI CLUB   R.R. #1, Stratford, Ont. N5A 6S5

A fees form for a member of the Smokey Valley Ski Club. This form, together with a cheque, shows the annual payment for this member's family. The cheque is made out to the ski club and is deposited in the bank.

Comprehensive Exercises

8. A. Hoysted is a sign painter and truck letterer. Her business has the following assets and liabilities:

Assets		Liabilities	
Cash	$ 2 216	Bank Loan	$ 6 500
Accounts Receivable		Accounts Payable	
G. Anderson	357	Consumers' Supply	1 375
N. Ostrowski	402	Nu-Style Furniture	2 951
Office Supplies	2 980	Loan Payable	11 980
Painting Supplies	4 120		
Office Furniture	5 090		
Automobile	20 000		

1. Set up A. Hoysted's financial position in T-accounts. Include the equity account.

2. For the transactions listed below record the accounting entries in T-accounts. If it is helpful for you, use a transaction analysis sheet.

Transactions
1. Received $200 cash from a customer for painting a sign.
2. Paid $500 to Consumers' Supply.
3. Received $402 cash from N. Ostrowski.
4. Sold an extra office desk (which is included in the Office Furniture figure at $450) to G. Brand at a price of $250. Brand paid $100 cash and owed the balance.
5. Reduced the bank loan by $1 000.
6. Paid the regular monthly loan payment, $500.
7. Paid the balance owing to Consumers' Supply.

3. Calculate the account balances and balance the ledger by taking off a trial balance.

---

9. Rainbow Real Estate is a business owned by Cathy Rogers. The assets and liabilities of the business are as follows:

Assets		Liabilities	
Cash	$ 1 056	Bank Loan	$19 000
Accounts Receivable		Account Payable	
D. Murray	1 351	Tuck Corporation	1 520
A. Niemi	2 516		
Office Supplies	1 115		
Furniture and Equipment	11 916		
Properties Owned	18 042		
Automobile	27 965		

The financial position of Rainbow Real Estate is set up in T-accounts in the workbook. Use a transaction analysis sheet if necessary. Calculate and record the balances in the accounts and take off a trial balance.

Transactions

1. Received $516 cash from A. Niemi.
2. Sold a home for V. Morris. For this service, Morris owes $4 150 to Rainbow Real Estate.
3. Paid $95 cash for office supplies.
4. Received $20 000 cash for sale of a property. (The property is included in the Properties Owned figure at $5 000.)
5. Paid $15 000 cash to the bank to reduce the amount of the bank loan.
6. Paid $520 cash to Tuck Corporation.
7. Paid $40 cash for a new headlight for the automobile.
8. Received $800 cash from D. Murray.
9. The owner withdrew $500 cash for her personal use.
10. Received $2 000 cash from V. Morris.
11. Paid the balance of the debt to Tuck Corporation in cash.
12. Purchased a new office desk at a cost of $600 from Pioneer Furniture but did not pay cash for it.
13. Sold a home for A. McIntosh. McIntosh paid Rainbow Real Estate $5 100 cash for the service.

For Further Thought

10. Briefly answer the following questions.

1. What size of business is likely to have a loose-leaf ledger?
2. In a handwritten ledger one can see the figures. How do you think the amounts are stored in a computerized system?
3. A ledger account does not have the word "asset," "liability," or "equity" recorded on it. How can you tell if the account is an asset, a liability, or equity?
4. Assets, liabilities, and equity can each be thought of as having a natural side. What is the natural side for an asset? a liability? equity?
5. The formal account, designed for handwritten records, has two distinct sides—the debit side and the credit side. Do you think that account data takes this form when it is stored in the computer? Explain.
6. Accountants have a special way of expressing amounts when they talk to each other. For example, the amount $2 315.12 would not normally be expressed as two thousand, three hundred and fifteen dollars and twelve cents. Try to guess how an accountant would express this amount.
7. Try to express the following as an accountant would.
   a. $51 326.26
   b. $7.50
   c. $750.00
   d. $3 145.00
   e. $31.45

Chapter 4

8. Explain why the rules of debit and credit are identical for liabilities and equity.
9. Explain why you do not debit Automobiles when you pay to get a fender straightened out on your automobile.
10. Is the statement "For every debit there is a credit" perfectly true? Explain.
11. What is the purpose of pin totals? Why are they written in pencil? Is it all right to erase them at any time?
12. What assumption would you make if an account balance were given to you without your having been told if it is a debit or credit balance?
13. Suppose that you, an outsider to the business, were told that Sarah Jones had an account balance of $350. Can you tell if Sarah Jones is a debtor or a creditor?
14. What is an exceptional account balance? Would a better word be "unusual"? "opposite"? "abnormal"?
15. The method of taking off a trial balance using a printing calculator is referred to as the "zero proof method." Explain why this is so.

CASE STUDIES

Case 1 Property Value on a Balance Sheet

You are a loan officer with the Reliable Trust Company in Dryden, Ont. On March 30, 19-- a young businessman, Gary Inch, comes to you in the hope of borrowing $75 000 for a business venture. When you inquire about his personal financial status, he presents you with the balance sheet shown below.

GARY INCH
BALANCE SHEET
MARCH 20, 19--

Assets		Liabilities	
Cash	$ 2 000	Accounts Payable	$ 5 300
Accounts Receivable	1 500	Mortgage Payable	30 000
Furniture	9 000		$35 300
Supplies	1 300		
Truck	17 000	Owner's Equity	
Building Lot	75 000	Gary Inch, Capital	70 500
	$105 800		$105 800

When examining this statement, you become concerned about the item Building Lot for $75 000. You have lived in Dryden for several years and you know that there are not many properties in town that are worth that much money.

Gary informs you that he bought the property one month ago for $30 000 and that he borrowed the entire sum from his father. This is shown properly on the statement as Mortgage Payable.

Your conversation with Gary indicates that he truly believes that the property will increase in value in the near future and that he has listed it at the amount he expects to sell it for. When you find out the location of the property, you realize that it is a piece of land that took over two years to sell.

Questions

1. What is your opinion about listing the property at $75 000?
2. What would you say to Gary about this particular item?
3. Would you lend Gary the money based only on the financial data given to you? Explain.

Case 2   *A Sale of Two Companies*

Shown below, side by side, are the balance sheets of two different companies as of the same date.

	Company A	Company B
Assets		
Cash	$ 71 500	$ 700
Accounts Receivable	3 000	59 500
Supplies	1 300	2 500
Equipment	15 600	27 400
Land and Building	24 000	145 000
Total	$115 400	$235 100
Liabilities and Equity		
Accounts Payable	$ 7 800	$ 15 900
Loan Payable	15 000	30 000
Mortgage Payable	42 000	108 000
Owner's Equity	50 600	81 200
Total	$115 400	$235 100

Assume that each of these two companies has suddenly been forced out of business and must liquidate its assets and pay off its debts. Which company would you prefer to own? Give reasons.

Case 3 Analyzing the Progress of a Business

Shown below in comparative form are the account balances of Metro Haulage Company for the years 19–3, 19–4, 19–5, and 19–6. The net income figures for 19–4 and 19–5 are also shown.

	19–3	19–4	19–5	19–6
Assets				
Cash	$ 500	$ 500	$ 500	$ 500
Accounts Receivable	10 000	11 000	12 000	12 000
Supplies	1 000	1 000	1 100	1 100
Land and Building		100 000	100 000	100 000
Equipment	4 000	5 000	5 000	10 000
Trucks	25 000	25 000	50 000	50 000
Total Assets	$40 500	$142 500	$168 600	$173 600
Liabilities and Equity				
Accounts Payable	$ 5 500	$ 6 000	$ 6 000	$10 000
Bank Loan	10 000	10 000	25 000	
Mortgage Payable		80 000	75 000	70 000
Owner's Equity	25 000	46 500	62 600	93 600
Total Liabilities and Equity	$40 500	$142 500	$168 600	$173 600
Net Income (Profit)		$35 000	$40 000	

Questions

1. In 19–4:
   a. In detail, explain the increase in the total assets.
   b. What were the sources of the funds that were used to acquire the above assets?
   c. How much money did the owner take out of the business?
2. In 19–5:
   a. In detail, explain the increase in the total assets.
   b. In addition to the assets in a), what else were funds needed for?
   c. What were the sources of funds used to pay for a) and b) above?
   d. How much money did the owner take out of the business?
3. In 19–6:
   a. By how much did the total assets increase?
   b. For what else was money needed in 19–6?
   c. Where did the money come from to pay for a) and b) above?
   d. Calculate the profit of the company if the owner took $19 000 out of the business.

CAREER
Tony Constantino / Co-operative Education Student

Tony Constantino is 18 years old and is in his last year at the Windsor School of Commerce. With the help of the director of business studies at his school, Tony is now participating in a co-operative education program. In the morning, he attends classes in English, mathematics, science and law. In the afternoon from 1:30 to 4:30 each day, he works in the accounting department of Tiara Construction Ltd. With the assistance of his accounting teacher, Mr. Mills, and the management accountant of the company, Tony will earn two accounting credits for the work he performs. He has already earned one credit in accounting by covering all the major topics you will cover this year.

Until he started work at Tiara, Tony had never used a computer. However, he had read about the use of the computer in his accounting course and welcomed the chance to compare a manual and a computerized accounting system.

All of Tiara's ledger accounts are stored permanently on a file in the computer. In addition, all customer accounts of other businesses are recorded in a file. Other files that Tony will come in contact with during this year will be an inventory file and a payroll file.

The computer, when instructed by a coded message, will automatically complete many of the steps in the accounting cycle. Still, Tony is thankful that he mastered the rules for analyzing transactions to understand which accounts should be debited and which credited. He soon learned that a computer cannot make such decisions when entries are keyed-in from source documents. Computer use demands an understanding of the complete accounting cycle.

From his talks with the accountant, Tony realizes that automated record-keeping will, in time, do more and more of the clerical tasks that are routine. This means that the accountant of the future will be someone who does less mechanical work, and more analyzing and reporting. Improved skill in communicating will be an important key for success in future accounting careers.

Tony expects to enroll in business administration at the University of Western Ontario in September, majoring in accounting and electronics. He hopes to become a CMA and eventually to work for a large company as a management consultant. The accounting he has already learned, both in the classroom and in the accounting department of Tiara Construction Ltd., means that Tony is off to a good start. He knows, though, that before he can consider himself a professional accountant, much diligent work and study lie ahead for him.

Discussion

1. What are some of the advantages of taking part in a co-operative education program in accounting?
2. Why is it important for Tony to have mastered the analysis of transactions when he uses the computer to input information?
3. a. List the steps in the accounting cycle you have learned so far.
   b. "Computer use demands an understanding of the complete accounting cycle." Explain.
   c. Explain how the computer automatically completes many of the steps in the accounting cycle.
4. What are some of the businesses in your community that would welcome a co-operative education student in accounting?
5. In addition to the kinds of information mentioned in the career profile, what other accounting information may be stored permanently on a file?
6. Explain why skill in communication will be important for future accountants.

5 The Income Statement and Revenue, Expense, and Drawings

5.1 The Income Statement
5.2 Expanding the Ledger
5.3 Completing the Ledger
5.4 Computerized Accounting: The Income Statement

You are now ready to learn about a second financial statement—the income statement. You will also learn how to gather the data to prepare this new financial statement.

5.1 The Income Statement

An income statement is a very important financial statement. It tells the owners how the business is doing: that is, whether or not it is profitable. The owners will be keenly interested in this information because their livelihoods and the continuation of their business depend on profitability.

An income statement is illustrated below in Figure 5.1. You can see in the illustration that an income statement contains some items that are new to you. You will see for the first time an item called revenue and another item called expense. Revenue is an increase in equity resulting from the receipts from the sale of goods or services. Expense is a decrease in equity resulting from the costs of the goods or services used to produce the revenue. In simple terms, revenues may be thought of as the receipts from the sales made by the business, and expenses as the costs of running the business.

If the total revenues are greater than the total expenses then a net income (profit) has been earned. **Net income** is the difference between total revenues and total expenses, if the revenues are greater than the expenses. If the total expenses are greater than the total revenues then a loss has been suffered. **Net loss** is the difference between total revenues and total expenses, if the expenses are greater than the revenues.

By definition an **income statement** is a financial statement that summarizes the items of revenue and expense, and shows the net income or net loss of a business, for a given period of time.

Chapter 5

Revenue
An increase in equity resulting from the proceeds of the sale of goods or services. Two types of revenue are shown.

Expense
A decrease in equity resulting from the cost of the goods or services used to produce the revenue.

Expenses are shown in detail.

```
              CHERUB AIR SERVICE
               INCOME STATEMENT
            YEAR ENDED DECEMBER 31, 19—
```

Revenue		
Charter Flights		$174 327
Flying Lessons		78 604
Total Revenue		$252 931
Operating Expenses		
Advertising	$	503
Bank Interest and Charges		2 756
Building Maintenance		1 102
Depreciation—Aircraft		46 702
Depreciation—Equipment		3 071
Depreciation—Truck		2 042
Gasoline and Oil		35 962
Insurance		1 746
Licences		1 505
Light, Heat, and Water		2 017
Miscellaneous Expenses		312
Rent		12 000
Repairs on Aircraft		15 072
Telephone		1 416
Wages		40 764
Total Expenses		$166 970
Net Income		$ 85 961

Net income is not cash.

Heading tells:
1. Name of business.
2. Name of statement.
3. Accounting period for which the figures have been accumulated.

This is the way to arrange the figures if only one column is used.

Net Income
The difference between total revenues and total expenses, if the revenues are greater than the expenses. In this case:

Revenues	$252 931
Expenses	− 166 970
Net Income	$ 85 961

Net income is also known as net profit.

Net Loss
Occurs if the expenses are greater than the revenues.

Figure 5.1(a) An income statement for a service business, one that sells a service but not goods. A single-column presentation is shown.

CHERUB AIR SERVICE
INCOME STATEMENT
YEAR ENDED DECEMBER 31, 19--

Revenue
Charter Flights	$174 327	
Flying Lessons	78 604	
Total Revenue		$252 931

Operating Expenses
Advertising	$ 503	
Bank Interest and Charges	2 756	
Building Maintenance	1 102	
Depreciation—Aircraft	46 702	
Depreciation—Equipment	3 071	
Depreciation—Truck	2 042	
Gasoline and Oil	35 962	
Insurance	1 746	
Licences	1 505	
Light, Heat, and Water	2 017	
Miscellaneous Expenses	312	
Rent	12 000	
Repairs on Aircraft	15 072	
Telephone	1 416	
Wages	40 764	
Total Expenses		166 970
Net Income		$ 85 961

Figure 5.1(b) The income statement for Cherub Air Service showing a two-column presentation.

The Income Statement Put to Use

By Owners and Managers

The income statement is a very useful tool. It tells the owners or managers if their business is earning a profit and how much the profit is. The income statement is helpful to them in forming company goals and policies, and in making business decisions.

A business will not survive long if it does not earn a profit. All of the figures making up the profit or loss may be seen on the income statement. The figures for the current year may be compared with those for the prior year or years. Unfavourable trends or problems may be seen quickly and can then be corrected. Successful businesspeople make good use of the information on the income statement.

By Bankers

Bankers will want to see the financial statements of any business to which they lend money. Bankers need to know if the borrower will be able to repay the loan. Financial statements help inform bankers about the condition of a business.

By Income Tax Authorities

Every business is required by law to prepare an income statement once each year. The net income figure of a business (if it is not a corporation) must be included on the owner's income tax return. The income statement must be sent to the government along with the owner's income tax return.

The Fiscal Period

Now that you have learned about net income, it is time to introduce another new concept in accounting. Net income is measured over a specific length of time, called the fiscal period, or the accounting period. The **fiscal period** (also the **accounting period**) is the period of time over which earnings are measured. All fiscal periods for a business are of the same length.

The earnings figure of a business does not mean anything if you do not know how long it took to produce those earnings. You would not be informed if all you knew about the net income of a business was that it amounted to $4 000. You would not be very favourably impressed if it took one year to earn that amount. However, if the $4 000 were earned in only one week, you would probably be quite impressed.

In business today, the fiscal period is usually one year. The fiscal year does not have to be the same as the calendar year. It just has to run for twelve consecutive months. For example, a fiscal year could begin on July 1 and end on June 30 of the following year.

Half-yearly, quarterly, or monthly fiscal periods are used by some businesses. Managers can keep a close watch over their business by using short fiscal periods. Even when fiscal periods shorter than one year are used, it is still necessary to produce an annual income statement for income tax purposes.

The Bank Account

Businesspeople rely heavily on the banking system. It is the least expensive and most convenient way to make payments. Also, bank accounts are safe. It should be clear to you that the handling of large quantities of cash is unsafe.

The most important reason that businesses use banking services is the convenience of making payments. It is much easier to send a cheque to someone than it is to deliver cash in person. This is especially true if the buyer and the seller are dealing with each other over a long distance. It is common practice to make all but very small payments by cheque. The charges for bank services are quite reasonable.

As a result, you can expect to see an account called Bank in the ledger rather than one called Cash. When money is received or paid out, it is the Bank account, not Cash, that is increased or decreased.

The words "bank" and "cash" are often used interchangeably. When an item is bought for cash, it is paid for at the time it is purchased. However, the payment is often made by cheque, and not by actual cash.

Cash and banking are discussed fully in Chapter 14.

GAAP—The Time Period Concept

The **time period concept** provides that accounting take place over specific time periods known as fiscal periods. These fiscal periods are of equal length, and are used when measuring the financial progress of a business.

Section Review Questions

1. What does the income statement tell, as compared with the balance sheet?
2. Why will the owners be keenly interested in the income statement?
3. The income statement is made up primarily of two new items. Name them.
4. Explain how a profit comes about.
5. Explain how a loss is suffered.
6. Explain what a service business does.
7. Name three groups of people who make use of income statements.
8. How does management make use of the income statement?
9. How do bankers make use of the income statement?
10. Why is it necessary to provide a copy of the income statement to the tax department?
11. Explain the concept of the fiscal period.
12. Aside from the name of the statement, how does the income statement differ from the balance sheet?
13. What is the name of the generally accepted accounting principle connected with the fiscal period?
14. Does a business normally keep its funds in the form of cash, or in a bank account?

Chapter 5

15. Does a business normally have a Cash account or a Bank account in its ledger?
16. You buy an item for cash. Explain how this is possible if you actually paid by cheque.

Section Exercises

1. From the following information for the month ended November 30, 19--, prepare an income statement for Atlas Associates. Use two money columns.

    Fees Earned, $31 700; Salaries Expense, $13 400; Rent Expense, $6 000; General Expense, $1 200; Advertising Expense, $600; Car Expense, $3 700; Light and Heat Expense, $3 500.

2. From the following trial balance prepare an income statement for Booreman Enterprises after a six month period ended June 30, 19--. Use the single money column form. Include revenue and expenses only.

    BOOREMAN ENTERPRISES
    TRIAL BALANCE
    JUNE 30, 19--

Bank	$ 1 800	
Accounts Receivable	22 315	
Supplies	1 300	
Equipment	28 247	
Automobiles	31 110	
Bank Loan		$ 15 000
Accounts Payable		8 316
C. Booreman, Capital		54 624
C. Booreman, Drawings	26 400	
Revenue from Fees		92 750
Bank Charges	512	
Car Expenses	12 302	
Light, Heat, and Water	4 315	
Miscellaneous Expense	904	
Rent Expense	6 000	
Telephone	1 175	
Wages	34 310	
	$170 690	$170 690

3. Workbook Exercise: Preparing an income statement using the two-column form.

4. There are a number of errors in the income statement below for Mayfare Plumbing, owned by James Fare.

    1. Identify the errors and list them in the space provided in your workbook.
    2. Calculate the correct net income.

```
                    INCOME STATEMENT
                       JAMES FARE
                    DECEMBER 31, 19–5
Revenue
    Sales and Service                                    127 416.00

Operating Expenses
    Advertising                          1 150.50
    Bank Charges                         1 750.00
    Depreciation of Automobile           4 296.--
    Gas and Oil                          4 935.--
    Light, Heat, and Power               3 975.12
    Materials Used                      15 906.--
    Miscellaneous                          257.00
    Telephone                              250.00
    Wages                               18 076.09

    Total Expenses                                        55 095.71

    Net Profit                                            72 320.29,
```

5. You happen to see a copy of a company's income statement for the half-year ended March 31, 19–3. You wonder, "What is this company's annual fiscal period?"
   What are the two possible annual fiscal periods for this company?

5.2 Expanding the Ledger

The ledgers that you have worked with so far have had a single equity account—the capital account. Any changes in the equity of a business were recorded in that one account. Now you must become familiar with a ledger that has a number of accounts in an equity section. These new accounts in the equity section are used to gather the figures that go on the income statement. An illustration of an expanded ledger is shown in Figure 5.2. Observe that the accounts are numbered. You will see how these numbers are used as you progress through the text.

The illustration shows clearly that the owner's equity section of the ledger contains the following accounts:

1. a capital account. This account is used for the capital balance at the beginning of the fiscal period (plus new capital from the owner, if any).
2. a revenue account. In some businesses there may be more than one revenue account.
3. a number of expense accounts.
4. a drawings account.

The new accounts in the equity section are discussed in detail below.

Revenue

Revenue is an increase in equity resulting from the proceeds of the sale of goods or services. Consider the following transaction:

> Eve Boa, a lawyer, draws up a legal agreement for a client and for her services is paid a fee of $250 in cash.

This transaction increases both Bank and equity by the amount of $250. Before, you would have debited Bank and credited E. Boa, Capital. Now, you will debit Bank as before. But an increase in equity from business operations is *revenue* and must be credited to the Fees Revenue account. The accounting entry is:

	DR	CR
Bank	$250	
Fees Revenue		$250

Think along the following lines:
1. revenue represents an increase in equity;
2. an increase in equity requires a credit entry;
3. therefore, the Fees Revenue account is credited.

All similar transactions affecting fees revenue will be credited to the Fees Revenue account. The account will have a credit balance. The account balance will be the total fees earned for the fiscal period to date.

Usually, a business has only one revenue account and it is given an appropriate name. For example, a loan company earns its revenue in the form of interest. Its revenue account would likely be called Interest Revenue. A real estate company would have a revenue account called Commissions Earned. Suitable names for the revenue accounts of other types of businesses might be Rental Revenue, Fees Earned, Royalties, and so on.

GAAP—The Revenue Recognition Convention

The **revenue recognition convention** provides that revenue be taken into the accounts (recognized) at the time the transaction is completed. Usually, this just means recording revenue when the bill for it is sent to the customer. If it is a cash transaction, the revenue is recorded when the sale is completed and the cash received.

It is not always quite so simple. Think of the building of a large project such as a dam. It takes a construction company a number of years to complete such a project. The company does not wait until the project is entirely completed before it sends its bill. Periodically, it bills for the amount of work completed and receives payments as the work progresses. Revenue is taken into the accounts on this periodic basis.

It is important to take revenue into the accounts properly. If this is not done, the earnings statements of the company will be incorrect and the readers of the financial statements misinformed.

Bank	105	A/P Sooter Store	205	E. Boa, Capital	305
2 439			4 400		21 878

A/R H. Geroux	110	A/P OK Supply	210	E. Boa, Drawings	310
1 420			1 200	3 950	

A/R J. Magill	115	Bank Loan	215	Fees Revenue	405
757			940		23 660

A/R E. Parsons	120			Advertising Expense	505
1 395				1 321	

Supplies	125			Car Expenses	510
2 316				2 615	

Office Equipment	130			Rent Expense	515
7 550				1 300	

Automobile	135			Sundry Expense	520
16 800				385	

				Wages Expense	525
				9 830	

TOTAL ASSETS	=	TOTAL LIABILITIES	+	OWNER'S EQUITY
$32 677		$6 540		$26 137

Equity Section Summary

There are four types of accounts in the equity section.

1. The Capital account: shows the equity figure at the beginning of the fiscal period, plus new capital from the owner, if any.

   The following three are used to show changes in capital from one period to the next.

2. Revenues: Increases in equity resulting from the proceeds of the sale of goods or services. A revenue account normally has a credit balance.

3. Expenses: Decreases in equity resulting from the costs of the materials or services used to produce the revenue. An expense account normally has a debit balance.

4. Drawings: Decreases in equity resulting from the owner's personal withdrawals. The Drawings account normally has a debit balance. Drawings is not a factor when calculating net income or loss.

Figure 5.2 The expanded ledger of Eve Boa, a lawyer.

Expense

Expense is a decrease in equity resulting from the costs of the materials and services used to produce the revenue. Consider the following transaction:

> Eve Boa pays her secretary the regular weekly wage of $400 in cash.

This transaction requires that both Bank and equity be decreased by $400. The decrease to Bank is handled as before, by a credit to that account. But a decrease in equity from business operations is an *expense*. It must be debited to an expense account. In this example, the Wages Expense account is debited. The accounting entry is:

	DR	CR
Wages Expense	$400	
Bank		$400

Think along the following lines:
1. expense represents a decrease in equity;
2. a decrease in equity requires a debit entry;
3. therefore, the Wages Expense account is debited.

The Wages Expense account, or any expense account for that matter, will normally receive debit entries. All wages will be accumulated in the one account. It will have a debit balance that is the total of the wages for the period to date.

There are many transactions that involve expenses. For example:

> Eve Boa receives the monthly furnace oil bill for $195 from Municipal Oil. The bill is not paid immediately.

The accounting entry for this transaction is:

	DR	CR
Heat Expense	$195	
A/P—Municipal Oil		$195

In any business, there are a number of expense accounts, each one representing a specific sort of decrease in equity. The name of the account tells the nature of the decrease. Typical expense accounts are: Rent Expense, Delivery Expense, Insurance Expense, Bank Charges, and Postage. Observe that the word "expense" is not always included in the account title.

GAAP—The Matching Principle

The matching principle is an extension of the revenue recognition convention, which we looked at earlier. The **matching principle** states that each expense item related to revenue earned must be recorded in the same fiscal period as the revenue it helped to earn. If this is not done, the financial statements will not measure the results of operations fairly.

For example, consider Karen Lepsoe who borrowed $20 000 to buy property for the purpose of reselling it at a profit. Six months later she sold the property for $28 000. On the surface it appears that a profit of $8 000 was made. But this fails to take into account the expenses associated with the transaction. The real profit from the transaction is calculated as follows:

Selling price of property		$28 000	
Deduct: Cost of property	$20 000		Costs and
Legal fees	400		expenses
Property taxes	350		matched
Bank interest	1 200		against
Realtor's commission	1 120		revenue.
Total costs and expenses		23 070	
Net profit		$ 4 930	

The matching principle will be considered more fully when we discuss "adjustments" in a later chapter. Adjustments are necessary for a proper determination of the figures for the financial statements.

Drawings

Drawings is a decrease in equity resulting from the withdrawal of assets from the business by the owner for personal use. The Drawings account may be thought of as the owner's personal withdrawal account. Decreases in equity entered in the Drawings account are *not* expenses. They are charged to the owner through the Drawings account.

Cash is the most common item withdrawn by an owner for personal use. For example:

> Eve Boa, the owner of the business, withdraws $300 to pay for personal expenses.

This transaction requires that equity and Bank both be decreased by $300. The decrease to Bank is handled in the usual way, as a credit to that account. But this particular decrease in equity is not an expense and must be charged to the owner. The correct accounting entry to record the transaction is:

	DR	CR
E. Boa, Drawings	$300	
Bank		$300

The Drawings account is also affected when the owner buys something for personal use but has the business pay for it. The owner may wish to take advantage of a special price that is offered to businesses but not to individuals. Or it may simply be that this form of payment is more convenient. In any event, when recording the transaction, the debit must be to Drawings.

For example, assume that Eve Boa purchases a new coffee-maker through the business for personal use. A bill for $85 for the coffee-maker arrives in the office from Baystore. The $85 is not an expense of the business. It must be charged to Eve Boa. The accounting entry to record the bill is:

	DR	CR
E. Boa, Drawings	$85	
Accounts Payable—Baystore		$85

All entries affecting Drawings follow the rules of debit and credit. Drawings represents a decrease in equity, and decreases in equity require debit entries. Therefore, the Drawings account normally receives debit entries. All drawings will be gathered in this one account and it will have a debit balance.

Some other transactions that affect the Drawings account are:
- the owner takes assets other than cash out of the business for personal use. These could be something like a typewriter, a table, or merchandise.
- the owner might collect a debt from a customer and keep the money for personal use. The accounting clerks would have to be told of this.

Section Review Questions

1. What new accounts are there in the equity section of the ledger?
2. What is the purpose of the Capital account in the expanded ledger?
3. What is the source of data for the income statement?
4. Define revenue.
5. Define expense.
6. Define drawings.
7. Which accounts in the equity section affect the calculation of net income?
8. Give three examples of transactions that affect drawings.
9. Explain the revenue recognition convention.
10. Explain the matching principle.

Section Exercises

1. **A business has the beginning financial position recorded in the schedule below and in your workbook. Ten simple transactions are listed to the left. Work out the revised totals for assets, liabilities, and owner's equity after each transaction. Enter these totals in your workbook. Complete the last two columns of the chart by recording: a) the amount of change in equity (if any), and b) whether the change in equity represents revenue, expense, or drawings.**

	Total Assets	Total Liabilities	Owner's Equity	Change in Equity	Revenue? Expense? Drawings?
Starting position	10 000	6 000	4 000		
Transactions					
1. Purchased $400 of supplies and paid cash.					
2. Reduced bank loan by $1 000.					
3. Received $800 cash from a debtor.					
4. Sold services for $900 cash.					
5. Sold services on credit, $1 500.					
6. Paid hydro for month just ended, $125.					
7. Owner withdrew $750 cash for personal use.					
8. Paid employee's wages, $600.					
9. Purchased truck on credit, $20 000.					
10. Owner took supplies for personal use, $250.					

2. Eric Inahaba is in business for himself as a groundskeeper and gardener in Hamilton, Ont. He cuts grass, weeds gardens, and trims trees and shrubs for a number of customers on a regular basis. The following accounts are in Eric Inahaba's ledger:

    101 Bank
    110 Account Receivable—G. Hung
    111 Account Receivable—F. Sawchuk
    112 Account Receivable—W. Scott
    120 Equipment
    130 Chemical Supplies
    140 Truck
    201 Bank Loan
    210 Account Payable—Banner News
    211 Account Payable—Pesticide Products
    212 Account Payable—Pro Hardware
    301 E. Inahaba, Capital
    302 E. Inahaba, Drawings
    401 Revenue
    501 Advertising Expense
    502 Miscellaneous Expense
    503 Telephone Expense
    504 Truck Expense

Chapter 5

In your workbook record the accounting entries for the following transactions in the customary form used by accountants.

Transactions
July
- 2   Received a bill from Pesticide Products regarding the purchase of $125 worth of insecticide on account.
- 5   Received a bill from Pro Hardware for $150 for the purchase of a new ladder on account.
- 6   Issued a cheque for $100 to W. Decorte for part-time wages.
- 10   Received $50 from a customer for services performed for cash.
- 13   Issued a bill to G. Hung for $100 for services sold on account.
- 13   Received a bill from the *Banner News* regarding a $50 advertisement placed in the newspaper on account.
- 16   Received a memo from E. Inahaba, the owner, stating that he had received $100 from a cash customer. The money was not put in the bank as usual but was kept by Mr. Inahaba and put into his pocket. Mr. Inahaba paid $40 of this money for gasoline for the truck and kept the rest for his personal use.
- 19   Received a notice from the bank stating that $240 had been taken by them from the business's bank account to pay for interest charges on the bank loan.

3. Workbook Exercise: Additional practice in recording accounting entries.

5.3 Completing the Ledger

Chart of Accounts

It is customary to number the accounts in the ledger. These numbers are used for identification and reference, particularly in computerized systems. The numbering system used in this text is the common three-digit one shown below. You will use these numbers in later chapters.

Assets	100–199
Liabilities	200–299
Capital / Drawings	300–399
Revenues	400–499
Expenses	500–599

A **chart of accounts** is a list of the ledger accounts and their numbers arranged in ledger order. Most businesses have copies of their chart of accounts available for their employees, and for outsiders such as auditors. Eve Boa's chart of accounts is shown in Figure 5.3. It is taken from the ledger in Figure 5.2. Notice the gaps left in case new accounts need to be inserted.

	E. BOA		
	CHART OF ACCOUNTS		
Assets		*Equity*	
Bank	No. 105	E. Boa, Capital	No. 305
Accounts Receivable		E. Boa, Drawings	310
H. Geroux	110	Fees Revenue	405
J. Magill	115	Advertising Expense	505
E. Parsons	120	Car Expense	510
Supplies	125	Rent Expense	515
Office Equipment	130	Sundry Expense	520
Automobile	135	Wages Expense	525
Liabilities			
Accounts Payable			
Sooter Store	205		
OK Supply	210		
Bank Loan	215		

Figure 5.3 E. Boa, chart of accounts.

Debit and Credit in the Expanded Ledger

The ledger is now expanded to include revenues, expenses, and drawings. Thus, the rules of debit and credit must now include these new items. The complete rules of debit and credit are as follows:

ACCOUNT	TO INCREASE	TO DECREASE
Assets	Debit	Credit
Liabilities	Credit	Debit
Capital	Credit	Debit
Revenue	Credit	Debit
Expense	Debit	Credit
Drawings	Debit	Credit

Debit and Credit Balances

An accountant needs to understand thoroughly the account balances in a ledger. At this stage it is not very difficult to tell whether an account is an asset or an expense, a liability or revenue. But it will not always be simple. Remember these rules:

1. Accounts with debit balances are either assets, expenses, or drawings.
2. Accounts with credit balances are either liabilities, capital, or revenue.

Trial Balance Procedure Unchanged

The new types of account do not change the trial balance procedure. Simply total the accounts with debit balances, total the accounts with credit balances, and see that the two totals agree. This is illustrated in Figure 5.4 with the trial balance of Eve Boa's ledger (Figure 5.2).

No.	Account	Debit	Credit
105	Bank	2439 –	
	Accounts Receivable		
110	H. Geroux	1420 –	
115	J. Magill	757 –	
120	E. Parsons	1395 –	
125	Supplies	2316 –	
130	Office Equipment	7550 –	
135	Automobile	16 800 –	
	Accounts Payable		
205	Sooter Store		4400 –
210	O.K. Supply		1200 –
215	Bank Loan		940 –
305	E. Boa, Capital		21 878 –
310	E. Boa, Drawings	3950 –	
405	Fees Revenue		23 660 –
505	Advertising Expense	1321 –	
510	Car Expense	2615 –	
515	Rent Expense	1300 –	
520	Sundry Expense	385 –	
525	Wages Expense	9830 –	
		52 078 –	52 078 –

E. Boa
Trial Balance
... date ...

Figure 5.4 Trial balance of E. Boa's ledger.

Buying and Selling on Credit

Businesses with good reputations are able to buy goods on short-term credit. This is a convenient way to do business and is an accepted practice in general use. The purchaser is able to delay payment for a short period of time, usually thirty days. The buyer thus has time to inspect or test the goods thoroughly before paying for them, and can refuse to pay for the goods if they are not satisfactory.

The buying and selling of goods on short-term credit is quite common in our society. Therefore, expect to see this type of transaction frequently in your exercises.

On Account

The term "on account" is used extensively in modern business. It is an essential part of business vocabulary. The term is used in four specific ways:

1. Suppose an item is purchased on credit. This means that it is not paid for at the time of purchase. This is a purchase on account. A **purchase on account** is a purchase that is not paid for at the time the purchase is made.
2. Suppose an item is sold on credit; that is, it is not paid for at the time it is sold. This is a sale on account. A **sale on account** is a sale for which the money is not received at the time the sale is made.
3. Suppose money is paid out to a creditor to decrease the balance owed to the creditor. This is a payment on account. A **payment on account** is money paid to a creditor to reduce the amount owed to that creditor.
4. Suppose money is received from a debtor company to reduce the amount owed to us. This is a receipt on account. A **receipt on account** is money received from a debtor to reduce the amount owed by that debtor.

Section Review Questions

1. What is a chart of accounts?
2. Who uses a chart of accounts?
3. Describe the account numbering system used in this text.
4. Prepare a chart of rules of debit and credit in their final form.
5. What types of account balances are normally found in an asset account? a liability account? a revenue account? an expense account? the drawings account? the capital account?
6. Why do businesses prefer to make purchases on credit?
7. The term "on account" is used in four ways. What are these four ways?
8. What must have happened previously, before you can receive money on account from a customer?

Section Exercises

1. **Using the table below, complete the exercise that follows in your workbook.**

   1. Asset debit
   2. Asset credit
   3. Liability debit
   4. Liability credit
   5. Capital debit
   6. Capital credit
   7. Drawings debit
   8. Drawings credit
   9. Revenue debit
   10. Revenue credit
   11. Expense debit
   12. Expense credit

Chapter 5

A series of transactions is given below. Show the effect of the accounting entry for each transaction. The first transaction is done for you.

1. Purchase a new car on account.
2. Receive payment on account from a customer.
3. Owner withdraws cash for personal use.
4. Owner starts a new business by investing cash.
5. The car is repaired and paid for in cash immediately.
6. Perform a service for a customer for cash.
7. Perform a service for a customer on account.
8. Purchase supplies for cash.
9. Receive a bill for gas and oil for the car.
10. Pay a creditor on account.
11. Some supplies are ruined and thrown out.

1	4

2. The ledger of Emily Stokaluk is given below as at March 31, 19––.

Bank	Accounts Receivable	Supplies
10 100	8 300	950

Land	Building	Equipment
35 000	110 000	22 000

Automobiles	Accounts Payable	Bank Loan
24 000	2 800	10 000

Mortgage Payable	E. Stokaluk, Capital	E. Stokaluk, Drawings
75 000	52 088	15 000

Fees Earned	Interest Earned	Advertising
132 500	1 000	1 200

Bank Charges	Building Maintenance	Gas and Oil
350	420	1 800

Light and Heat	Miscellaneous Expense	Repairs to Car
1 640	128	850

Wages
41 650

1. Prepare a trial balance in your workbook.
2. Prepare a chart of accounts based on the numbering system used in the text.

---

3. The ledger accounts of Karen's Air Service are shown below in alphabetical order.

   Accounts Payable
   Accounts Receivable
   Advertising Expense
   Airplanes
   Automobiles
   Bank
   Bank Charges
   Building
   Building Repairs
   Equipment
   General Expense
   Insurance Expense

   Kathy Koy, Capital
   Kathy Koy, Drawings
   Land
   Legal Expense
   Mortgage Payable
   Revenue—Freight
   Revenue—Passengers
   Salaries
   Supplies
   Supplies Used
   Telephone
   Wages

   1. Rearrange these accounts into the usual ledger order.
   2. Prepare a chart of accounts using the textbook numbering system as a guide.

---

4. Shown below and in your workbook is a chart of the rules of debit and credit. Complete the chart in your workbook by writing the words "increase" or "decrease" in the appropriate spaces.

   A = L + OE

Assets		Liabilities		Capital		Revenue	
DEBIT	CREDIT	DEBIT	CREDIT	DEBIT	CREDIT	DEBIT	CREDIT

Drawings		Expense	
DEBIT	CREDIT	DEBIT	CREDIT

5.4 Computerized Accounting: The Income Statement

Computer Exercises

1. Prepare a spreadsheet program for an income statement such as the one in Figure 5.1(b). Enter the figures for Cherub Air Service.
2. What formula did you use to calculate the total expenses?
3. What formula did you use to calculate the net income?
4. Make the following changes to the data and observe how changes in other locations on the spreadsheet are made automatically.
   1. Revenue from flying lessons: $96 205.20;
   2. Advertising: $2 500;
   3. Wages: $42 102.

5. Enter the following formulas in your program and observe the results.
   1. Advertising is set at 1 per cent of revenue;
   2. Wages are set at 15 per cent of revenue.
   Be sure to save your program.

   Cherub Air Service is considering hiring a new pilot. The company believes that this will increase both kinds of revenue by 45 per cent. However, it is assumed that the following expenses will each increase by 25 per cent: Gasoline and Oil, Insurance, and Repairs on Aircraft. Also, the new pilot will earn wages of $45 000.

   Write a new program to reflect the proposed changes. You might consider placing the percentage changes in cells by themselves. In this way, the calculation for each new account balance will be:

   | The cell that contains the percentage | × | The account balance | + | The account balance |

   For example, assume that the percentage change of .25 is located in cell J30 and the account balance for Gasoline and Oil is located in E20. The Gasoline and Oil figure for the new income statement would be:

   | J30 | × | E20 | + | E20 |

   Give your opinion on whether the owner should go ahead with the proposal or not. Explain your reasoning.

CHAPTER HIGHLIGHTS

Now that you have completed Chapter 5, you should:

1. understand net income and net loss and be able to calculate both;
2. be able to prepare a basic income statement from supplied figures;
3. understand the importance of the income statement to owners, managers, and other interested parties;
4. understand that the data for the income statement is accumulated in special accounts in the equity section of the ledger;
5. be able to define revenue, expense, and drawings;
6. be able to make simple analyses and comparisons from given financial data;
7. be able to use the term "on account" in the four customary ways;
8. know the reason why businesses prefer to buy on credit;
9. know the reasons why businesses use bank accounts;
10. know three new generally accepted accounting principles: the time period concept, the revenue recognition concept, and the matching principle.

ACCOUNTING TERMS

accounting period
chart of accounts
drawings
expense
fiscal period
income statement
matching principle
net income

net loss
payment on account
purchase on account
receipt on account
revenue
revenue recognition convention
sale on account
time period concept

CHAPTER EXERCISES

Using Your Knowledge

1. **For each of the accounts listed, indicate whether it would normally have a debit or credit balance.**

   Supplies; Advertising Expense; A. Bryce, Drawings; G. Wright, a creditor; Rent Expense; Fees Earned; Bank Loan; W. Magill, a debtor; A. Bryce, Capital; Mortgage Payable; Automobile.

2. Mrs. E. Foreman owns and operates a small florist shop in Gander, Nfld. She deposits all cash received in the bank and makes all payments by cheque. At the end of the last fiscal period, the Bank account showed a credit balance of $1 350 after all balances were found to be correct.

   1. Assuming no errors, how is it possible for the Bank, an asset account, to have a credit balance?
   2. How should this item be shown on the balance sheet?
   3. If, during the fiscal period, the revenues exceeded the expenses by $2 000 and the drawings amounted to $2 600, what is the net income figure for the period?

3. The income statement of Bianco Company is shown below.

   BIANCO COMPANY
   INCOME STATEMENT
   YEAR ENDED DECEMBER 31, 19--

Revenue		$47 416
Expenses		
Car Expense	$ 1 732	
Rent	3 500	
Utilities	1 075	
Wages	23 072	29 379
Net income		$18 037

   Two errors were found in the books after the above statement was prepared:
   a. A bill for $750 for automobile repairs had been incorrectly debited to automobiles.
   b. $5 000 of owner's drawings had been incorrectly debited to Wages.
   Prepare a corrected income statement.

4. The account balances in the ledger of Pamela Garside, a sculptor, are shown below in the T-accounts.

Bank	A.R. - P. Adler	A.R. - A. Jackson	Equipment
1 745	50	70	5 000

Supplies	Automobiles	A.P.- Century Finance	A.P.- B & B. Stone
610	7 900	5 500	110

P. Garside, Capital	P. Garside, Drawings	Revenue	Car Expense
5 625	200	11 920	500

Light, Heat, Water	Rent	Wages	
280	300	6 500	

Pamela's auditor discovered the following errors when checking the records:
a. $150 of cash revenue was credited incorrectly to the Capital account.
b. $500 of the owner's drawings was debited incorrectly to the Wages account.
c. $400 of automobile expense was debited incorrectly to the Automobiles account.
d. $110 of equipment was incorrectly debited to Car Expense.

1. In your workbook, write out the accounting entries necessary to correct the above errors.
2. The net income figure prior to the auditor's discoveries was determined to be $4 340. What will the corrected income figure be?

5. With the expanded ledger, the accounting equation now appears as shown below. In your workbook, complete the schedule by filling in the rectangles with the correct figures.

	Assets	=	Liabilities	+	Beginning Capital	+	Revenues	−	Expenses	−	Drawings
End of Year 1	100	=	20	+	70	+	60	−	45	−	5
Year 2	120	=	30	+		+	90	−	60	−	
Year 3	130	=		+		+	105	−	80	−	20
Year 4		=	30	+		+	110	−	95	−	10

6. A partially completed summary of financial data is given below. The data pertains to the fundamental accounting equation for Hugh Miller over a period of two years.

	Assets	Liabilities	Equity
End of 19–1		$27 400	
End of 19–2			$19 300

In your workbook fill in the missing figures, given that:
1. revenues for 19–2 are $42 000;
2. expenses for 19–2 are $22 000;
3. drawings for 19–2 are $18 000;
4. the assets decreased by $5 000 from the end of 19–1 to the end of 19–2.

Comprehensive Exercise

7. The accounts required for this exercise are provided for you in the workbook. Also, there is ruled paper for you to write down the accounting entries for the transactions in the accountant's customary manner.

N.A. James
Chart of Accounts

101 Bank
110 Account Receivable—Jenkins and Co.
120 Office Supplies
125 Office Equipment
130 Automobile
210 Account Payable—Office Supply Company
301 N.A. James, Capital
302 N.A. James, Drawings
401 Fees Earned
505 Advertising Expense
510 Car Expense
515 Donations Expense
520 Miscellaneous Expense
525 Rent Expense

N.A. James, a public accountant, decided to begin a business of his own on October 1, 19--. At that time he invested in the business a bank balance of $5 000 and an automobile of $18 000.

1. Work out the accounting entry for the above. Write down the accounting entry, and then record it in the T-accounts.

2. For each of the transactions listed below, write down the accounting entry and then record it in the T-accounts.

Note on the Handling of Supplies in Exercises

It is common practice in accounting to allow the Supplies account to become incorrect during the accounting period, and to make it correct at the end of the accounting period. This is a technique used by accountants for convenience.

In your accounting entries:

- When supplies are purchased, make the following accounting entry.

	DR	CR
Supplies	$$$$	
Bank, or creditor		$$$$

- When supplies are used up in the business, make no accounting entry.

The technique for updating the Supplies account is treated in Chapter 10.

Transactions

1. Purchased $300 of office supplies for cash. Issued a cheque in payment.
2. Issued a cheque for $50 for an advertisement in a local newspaper.
3. Received a bill from Office Supply Company in regard to the purchase of a desk, a chair, and a filing cabinet at a total cost of $1 100 on account.
4. Mr. James was hired by a client, Jenkins and Co. At the conclusion of the work, Mr. James charged Jenkins and Co. $900 and issued a bill for this service performed on account.
5. B. Masters, a client, paid $100 in cash for a bookkeeping service. W. Shields, another client, paid $75 in cash for having her tax return prepared. The total of $175 was deposited in the bank.
6. A cheque for $100 was sent as a donation to the Salvation Army.
7. A cheque for $300 was received from Jenkins and Co. on account.
8. A cheque was issued to Office Supply Company in full payment of the balance of its account.
9. Paid Louis's Service Station $120 for gasoline and repairs to the business automobile. A cheque was issued right away.
10. Performed an accounting service for T. Wu and received $200 cash in full payment. The owner, N.A. James, did not deposit this money in the bank, but kept it for his personal use.
11. Issued a cheque for $750 in payment of the rent for the month of October.
12. Purchased $120 of office supplies from Woolworth's. The purchase was paid for by cheque.
13. Issued a cheque for $50 for an advertisement in a local newspaper.
14. Issued a bill for $600 to Jenkins and Co. for accounting services performed on account.
15. Issued a cheque for $70 for postage stamps. (Note: Stamps are not considered to be supplies.)
16. Issued a cheque for $500 to the owner for his personal use.

3. Balance the ledger by means of a trial balance.

4. Prepare an income statement for the period, which is the month of October, 19--.

For Further Thought

8. **Briefly answer the following questions.**
   1. In earlier chapters there was no income statement to show the net income of a business. How can the owner calculate net income without producing an income statement?
   2. John earns $8 000 and Gary earns $10 000. Who has the better earnings? Explain.
   3. The rules say that a credit entry is required to increase equity. Explain why an expense account, which is part of the equity, requires a debit entry to increase it.

4. Explain why there are usually only one, or two, revenue accounts, but a number of expense accounts.
5. Expense accounts can be presented on the financial statement in three possible ways:
   a. alphabetically;
   b. in descending order by the size of the account balance;
   c. in no particular order.
   Which do you prefer? Explain the reason for your choice.
6. Which way would you organize the expense accounts in the ledger? Explain the reason for your choice.
7. Some companies have to provide financial statements for the general public. The financial statements prepared for management would not be the ones given out to the general public.
   a. What would some of the differences be?
   b. Give some reasons why different statements are prepared.
8. What information from the financial statements would a banker for a business be particularly interested in?
9. A company may have fiscal periods of any length as long as it also produces a financial statement annually. Why does a company have to produce an annual statement?
10. Suppose that you were handed a ledger and asked to determine the equity. Describe two ways that this can be done.
11. Give appropriate names for the revenue account for the following businesses:
    a. a doctor;
    b. a loan company;
    c. a real estate company;
    d. a dry cleaning company;
    e. a photographer;
    f. a hairdresser.
12. You now know seven GAAPs. Name them.
13. A business could be quite profitable and yet could have money problems. Give one reason why this might happen.
14. The text states that accounts with credit balances are either liabilities, equity, or revenue. Still, it is possible for the Bank account to have a credit balance. Explain this apparent inconsistency.
15. Give three reasons why businesses prefer to make their purchases on credit.

CASE STUDIES

Case 1 Analyzing an Income Statement Covering Two Years

Shown below is an income statement for Professional Engineering and Consulting showing the figures for 19–7 and 19–6. Study these income statements, and answer the questions that follow.

PROFESSIONAL ENGINEERING AND CONSULTING
INCOME STATEMENT
YEAR ENDED JUNE 30, 19-7 and 19-6

	19-7	*19-6*
Revenues		
Consulting	$ 62 250	$ 60 402
Construction	202 365	290 201
Designing	35 250	36 603
	$299 865	$387 206
Operating Expenses		
Advertising	$ 3 520	$ 3 400
Automobiles Expense	25 025	16 350
Bank Charges	15 850	1 200
Building Expenses	4 200	3 700
Equipment Maintenance	1 525	1 750
Insurance	5 014	2 000
Light, Heat, and Water	3 124	3 107
Miscellaneous Expense	312	250
Property Taxes	1 215	950
Telephone	1 507	704
Wages	102 301	78 201
Total Expenses	$163 593	$111 612
Net Income	$136 272	$275 594

Questions

Part A

1. Comment on the change in the total revenues.
2. Comment on the change in the total expenses.
3. Comment on the change in the net incomes.

Part B

The owner, C. Haywood, is quite concerned about the dramatic decrease in net income from 19-6 to 19-7. Prepare a brief report explaining the four most significant factors in the drop in profit. A useful technique for you to attempt at this time is the making of percentage comparisons.

Case 2 Studying Results of Operation

Shown below are the results of operation for Dr. Tanis Tamo for a five-year period.

DOCTOR TANIS TAMO
OPERATING RESULTS (in thousands)

	19–1	19–2	19–3	19–4	19–5
Revenue					
Fees Earned	$143	$160	$184	$214	$239
Expenses					
Car Expenses	$20	$22	$23	$25	$27
Insurance	8	8	9	12	13
Light & Heat	15	16	17	20	22
Office Expenses	11	11	13	17	18
Rent	12	12	12	15	18
Telephone	5	5	6	7	8
Wages	20	22	28	30	33
Total Expenses	$91	$96	$108	$126	$139
Net Income	$52	$64	$76	$88	$100

Questions

1. On the graph paper in your workbook draw a five-year graph of a) the revenue, and b) the total expenses.
2. Are total expenses increasing as fast as revenue over the five years?
3. Which expense has the greatest percentage increase?
4. Which expense has the least percentage increase?
5. Revenues are expected to rise by only 2 per cent in 19–6. This is because the workload is near its maximum. Doctor Tamo is anxious to increase her net income in 19–6 to $110 thousand. How can this possibly be done? Give specific suggestions.

Case 3 Perspective on Financial Statements

Neil Poje of Nolalu, Ontario has an oil distribution business. The business has a $100 000 bank loan with a local bank. Following normal practice, the bank manager has requested a copy of the financial statements of the business for the latest year. Neil has provided her with audited financial statements. In simplified form, these statements are as follows:

POJE FUELS
BALANCE SHEET
JUNE 30, 19--

Assets

Cash	$ 5 000
Accounts Receivable	14 000
Inventory of Oil	70 000
Other Assets	150 000
Total Assets	$239 000

Liabilities and Equity

Bank Loan	$100 000
Accounts Payable	30 000
Total Liabilities	$130 000
Owner's Equity	109 000
Total Liabilities and Equity	$239 000

POJE FUELS
INCOME STATEMENT
YEAR ENDED JUNE 30, 19--

Revenues	$250 000
Cost of Oil	150 000
Gross Profit	$100 000
Expenses	65 000
Net Income	$ 35 000

The bank manager is concerned about this particular loan because of uncertainty in the oil industry.

Questions

1. In your opinion, what specific statement items will the bank manager be most interested in?
2. What other analyses will she likely make?
3. What concerns might Neil Poje have in regard to his own business?

Case 4 *A Fair Billing Procedure?*

The field of energy conservation has become an important one. Allan Timura has gained prominence in his community by specializing in this interesting field. The quality of his knowledge and ideas is unquestioned and there is a large demand for his services. He is a busy man.

Allan knows the value of his work and charges a high fee for his services. At the present time the rate for his services is $200 an hour. He charges all of his working days to his clients.

Not all of Allan's time, however, is spent working directly for his clients. He frequently takes time to work on a few projects of his own, or to visit his stockbroker regarding his investments. He charges this time to his clients.

When questioned about his billing practice, Allan defends it. He believes that, regardless of what he is actually doing, his mind is at work for his clients. He claims that his own projects are used to experiment and test ideas that ultimately benefit his clients. Also, he claims, his projects relax him and prevent him from becoming tired or stale, keeping him sharp for his clients.

Question

1. Is Allan's billing procedure a fair one? Are his arguments sound? Discuss.

CAREER
Robert Hunt, CMA / Intermediate Accountant

Robert Hunt was born in Lennoxville, Québec, where his family lived until just after he finished high school. Robert enjoyed his accounting courses in high school to such a degree he decided to pursue an accounting career. His family moved to Sherbrooke, Québec, and thereafter, Robert went to work as a payroll clerk with C.P. Clare Ltd., a firm that manufactures computer parts and printers. As a payroll clerk, he calculated the hours worked by employees, calculated employee bonuses, and prepared various reports for the cost accountant. Since most of the company's business is done in French, it is fortunate for Robert that he is fully bilingual.

Robert soon decided to obtain a

professional degree in accounting. He enrolled in the Certified Management Accountants (CMA) program and began taking courses at night, while working full time during the day. After a few years of study, Robert earned the right to use the letters CMA after his name.

Robert was quickly promoted to junior accountant. In this position, he controlled accounts receivable and accounts payable, prepared bank reconciliation statements, and kept track of the company's cash payments.

He presently works as an intermediate accountant for two of the companies controlled by Vitesse Transport Limitée, a firm that transports freight. He reports directly to the management accountant. His major duty is preparing two monthly financial statements: the income statement and the balance sheet. To prepare these statements, Robert must reconcile four different bank accounts each month. He must also maintain control of all fixed assets of the business and prepare the monthly trial balance of the general ledger. In addition to these duties, Robert makes sure that the company's taxes are paid. Finally, he prepares Statistics Canada reports for government use, providing a list of the company's major expenditures and other statistical information.

Robert's career in accounting is progressing well. If he continues his hard work and keeps himself informed through further study of generally accepted accounting principles, he should rise quickly to a key accounting position.

Discussion

1. What are some of the accounting duties Robert performs?
2. Write a report on the Certified Management Accountants program. Include the following information in your report:
   - educational requirements;
   - business communications requirements;
   - fees;
   - number of courses to earn the CMA designation;
   - courses that are studied.
3. What generally accepted accounting principles are important to Robert when he prepares his financial statements?
4. Outline some of the duties of a cost accountant. What are some of the reports Robert would prepare for the cost accountant?
5. What do you think would be some of the advantages of being bilingual if you were to enter the business world in the future?
6. How does Robert maintain control over all the fixed assets of Vitesse Transport Limitée?
7. Why does a business such as Vitesse Transport Limitée have four different bank accounts?

6 Source Documents

6.1 Source Documents
6.2 Sales Tax
6.3 Computerized Accounting:
     The Accounting Package—The Computer Menu

6.1 Source Documents

The topic of source documents was briefly introduced in Chapter 3. In this chapter, source documents will be studied in detail.

A number of business transactions are started outside the accounting department. These are transactions initiated not by accounting personnel, but by the owner, salespeople, department heads, managers, and other authorized people.

How does the accounting department find out about all transactions? They are informed of them by means of business papers which are sent to them. These business papers are called source documents. A **source document** is a business paper which shows the nature of a transaction and provides all the information needed to account for it properly. The accounting department uses the source documents as the basis for recording the accounting entries. Almost every accounting entry is based on a source document.

For some transactions there are no conventional source documents. The owner withdrawing money for personal use is an example. In such a case, the accounting entry must be supported by some other business paper or record. In this instance, a memorandum from the owner would be sufficient. In other cases, the supporting documents might be:

- detailed calculations prepared by the accounting department;
- a previous source document, such as a long-term rental agreement, which covers a series of transactions.

A company is required to keep source documents on file. They will be used within the office for reference purposes, locating errors, and so on. As well, source documents provide the factual evidence to verify transactions of the business. They provide the proof that the accounting records have been prepared accurately and honestly.

Several basic source documents will be explained and illustrated in the next few pages. They are considered to be basic source documents because they are used in the most common business transactions. A company called Masthead Marine, owned by

David Scott of Vancouver, B.C., is used to illustrate these source documents. Masthead Marine is in the business of selling boats, marine equipment, and boat parts and supplies.

Cash Sales Slip

A *cash sales slip* is a business form showing the details of a transaction in which goods or services are sold to a customer for cash. Usually, there is an original and two copies. The features of a cash sales slip and the uses for the copies are shown in Figure 6.1.

Figure 6.1 Cash sales slip representing a sale of goods or services for cash.

Accounting Entry for a Cash Sales Slip

The accounting copy goes to the accounting department as the source document for the accounting entry. For this sales slip, the accounting entry is:

	DR	CR
Bank	$35.90	
Sales (Revenue)		$35.90

A similar entry will be made for all cash sales slips.

Sales Invoice

Many businesses do not deal with the general public and therefore normally do not have cash sales. Businesses of this type make nearly all their sales on account. For each sale on account, a sales invoice is issued to the customer. A **sales invoice** is a business form showing the details of a transaction in which goods or services are sold on account. Usually there is an original and several copies. The features of a sales invoice and the uses for the copies are shown in Figure 6.2.

In any sales transaction, the party that sells is known as the "vendor" and the party that buys is known as the "purchaser." In this case Masthead Marine is the vendor and S. & S. Boatworks is the purchaser.

Figure 6.2 A sales invoice representing a sale of goods or services on account.

Accounting Entry for a Sales Invoice

The accounting copy goes to the accounting department as the source document for the accounting entry to record the sale. For this sales invoice the accounting entry is:

	DR	CR
Account Receivable—S. & S. Boatworks	$835.70	
Sales (Revenue)		$835.70

A similar accounting entry will be made for all sales invoices.

Dual Purpose Sales Slip

Some businesses dealing with the general public do business both for cash and on account. There is a business form that will handle both types of transaction. This is the dual purpose sales slip. A **dual purpose sales slip** is a business form showing the details of a transaction in which goods or services are sold either for cash or on account. There is a place on the form where the sales person checks off the type of transaction—cash, or charge. An example of a dual purpose sales slip is shown in Figure 6.3.

Except for these two boxes, this form is identical to the cash sales slip examined earlier.

Figure 6.3 Dual purpose sales slip.

Accounting Entry for a Dual Purpose Sales Slip

The accounting entry for the source document shown above is:

	DR	CR
Account Receivable—B. Harper	$65.00	
Sales (Revenue)		$65.00

If the cash box had been checkmarked, the accounting entry would have been:

	DR	CR
Bank	$65.00	
Sales (Revenue)		$65.00

Purchase Invoice

Masthead Marine is not always the vendor company. Often, it makes purchases from other companies. Then, it is the purchaser company. When Masthead Marine makes a purchase on account from a supplier, the company supplying the goods issues a sales invoice to Masthead Marine. When the vendor's invoice arrives at the office of Masthead Marine, it becomes a purchase invoice. A **purchase invoice** is a business form representing a purchase of goods or services on account. It is the name used in the office of the purchaser to differentiate between its own sales invoices and those of its suppliers.

Two examples of purchase invoices are shown in Figures 6.4 and 6.5.

- The name of the vendor. The company is to be credited to an account payable.
- The invoice date
- Shows how long Masthead Marine has to make the payment.
- Provides complete information regarding the service performed and the parts needed to make the repair.
- The total amount of the bill

This is only a reference number, not a control number, from the viewpoint of Masthead Marine.

Figure 6.4 A purchase invoice for repairs to a lift truck.

Section 6.1 **139**

```
                                    The name of the vendor.
                                    The company to be
                                    credited in an account
                                    payable.

  Phone      COLEMAN BOATS    INVOICE NO.
  842 0107                       236 ───── For reference purposes
                99 Wharf Road
               Vancouver, B.C.
  Sold to:        V7B 1P3
  Masthead Marine         Date March 6, 19-- ── The invoice date
  Box 298, Station 8
  Vancouver, B.C.         Terms Net 60 ───── Shows how long Masthead
  V7C 8P7                                     Marine has to make
  Quantity Part No. Description  Price  Amount  payment
     10      124   Coleman Kevlar              A complete description of
                    Canoes, 16' 675.00 6 750.00 the goods purchased


                         Total         6 750.00 ── The total amount of the bill
```

Figure 6.5 A purchase invoice for merchandise for resale.

Accounting Entries for Purchase Invoices

Masthead Marine buys a variety of goods and services from numerous suppliers. No single accounting entry will do for all the different items purchased. The account debited will depend on what particular goods or services are purchased. The account credited will always be the same—accounts payable.

The accounting entry for the purchase invoice in Figure 6.4 is:

	DR	CR
Equipment Repairs	$241.50	
Account Payable—General Engineering		$241.50

The accounting entry for the purchase invoice in Figure 6.5 is:

	DR	CR
Merchandise Inventory	$6 750.00	
Account Payable—Coleman Boats		$6 750.00

The above two entries show clearly:
- the account debited depends on the nature of the goods or services purchased;
- the account credited is always an account payable.

Cheque Copies

It has already been established that all payments are normally paid by cheque. The cheques themselves are sent out in the mail. A **cheque copy** is a document supporting the accounting entry for a payment by cheque.

Cheques may be issued for any number of things: cash purchases, wages, owner's withdrawals, payments on account, and so on. Most cheques are issued to pay for things previously bought on account and which are supported by purchase invoices on file. The purchase invoices being paid for are summarized on the tear-off portion of the cheque. This is shown in Figure 6.6.

A payment might be for a cash purchase, that is, something being paid for at the time of the purchase. In such a case, the cheque copy itself is not sufficient proof that the payment is proper. A purchase invoice is also needed to support the accounting entry for a cash purchase.

For some payments, no supporting voucher is needed. For owner's withdrawals, the cashed cheque endorsed by the owner is sufficient proof of proper payment. For wages, the company's payroll records are the proof of proper payment.

Figure 6.6 A cheque representing a payment made by the company. The accounting department copy of this cheque is the source document for the payment.

Accounting Entry for a Cheque Copy

The accounting department copy is sent to the accounting department where it is used as the source document for the transaction. The debit part of the accounting entry depends on the nature of the transaction. The credit part of the accounting entry is always to Bank. For this particular cheque copy the accounting entry is:

	DR	CR
Account Payable—Sterling Spars	$1 802.90	
Bank		$1 802.90

Cash Receipts List

Each day, in business, some cheques or cash are usually received from customers. These are referred to as the "cash receipts." The cheques themselves cannot be kept to support the accounting entries. The cheques must be deposited in the bank. Therefore, before making the deposit a listing of the cash receipts is prepared by the mail clerk or another employee.

The **cash receipts list** is a business paper representing the money coming in from customers. The cash receipts list is the source document for the cash receipts accounting entries. This listing shows the names of the customers, the dollar amounts, and what the amounts are for in each case. To help prepare this form the clerk uses the information on the tear-off portions of cheques received, or remittance advices sent along with the cheques. A **remittance advice** is a form accompanying the cheque explaining the payment. Sometimes it is no more than a copy of the invoice.

A cash receipts list is shown in Figure 6.7.

```
Masthead Marine

Cash Receipts List          March 9, 19--


A. Baldwin           Inv. 6829              $  375.02
F. Perri             Inv. 7010                 965.50
Pier 10 Marina       Inv. 6419    $426.10
                     Inv. 6731     375.62      801.72
                                            $2 142.24

         Total
Prepared by Jan Marshall
```

- The transaction date
- The details of the cheques received
- The total amount received
- The copy goes into a permanent reference file kept by the person who prepares the listing.

Figure 6.7 A cash receipts list.

Accounting Entry for a Cash Receipts List

The original list goes to the accounting department as the source document for the accounting entry. For the cash receipts list above, the accounting entry is:

	DR	CR
Bank	$2 142.24	
Account Receivable—A. Baldwin		$375.02
Account Receivable—F. Perri		$965.50
Account Receivable—Pier 10 Marina		$801.72

Bank Advices

There are times when the bank initiates a change in the bank account of a business. The bank informs the business of such a transaction by means of a bank advice or bank memo. A **bank debit advice** is a bank document informing the business of a decrease made in the business's bank account. A **bank credit advice** is a bank document informing the business of an increase made in the business's bank account.

In Figure 6.8, the Commercial Bank has sent a bank debit advice to Masthead Marine telling them that their account was charged interest on a bank loan.

Tells whether the account has been debited or credited

Date of the entry

An explanation for the entry

Amount of the entry

Figure 6.8 A bank advice.

Accounting Entry for a Bank Advice

The bank advice goes to the accounting department as the source document for the accounting entry. In this case the entry is:

	DR	CR
Bank Charges and Interest	$113.50	
Bank		$113.50

If the form had been a credit advice, the Bank account would have been debited and an appropriate account credited.

Summary of Source Documents and Related Accounting Entries

Source Document	Transaction Description	Accounting Entries Account Debited	Accounting Entries Account Credited
Cash sales slip	A sale of goods or services for cash	Bank	Sales (Revenue)
Sales invoice Charge sales slip	A sale of goods or services on account	Accounts Receivable	Sales (Revenue)
Purchase invoice	A purchase of goods or services on account	1. An expense account such as Advertising 2. An asset account such as Supplies or Merchandise Inventory	Accounts Payable
Cheque copy	1. Paying an account payable *2. Cash purchase of an asset *3. Cash payment for an expense 4. Owner draws out money for personal use	1. A liability account such as Accounts Payable 2. An asset account such as Automobiles 3. An expense account such as Car Expense 4. The Drawings account	Bank
Cash receipts list	The cheques received from customers on account	Bank	Accounts Receivable
Bank debit advice	A decrease in the bank account initiated by the bank	Bank Interest or Bank Charges	Bank

*Must be accompanied by a purchase invoice

Additional Supporting Documents and Vouchers

In addition to the source documents listed above you may encounter the following:
- cash register slips;
- receipts, such as those for donations, or for postage;
- hydro bills, telephone bills;
- credit card or charge account statements;
- insurance endorsement certificates;

- written memos from the owner;
- bank statements;
- Visa or Mastercard statements;
- cash register internal tapes.

Number of Copies of Source Documents

There is no fixed required number of copies of business documents. Each business develops its own system to suit its own needs and preferences. Some owners and managers prefer a simple system, others a more elaborate one. The number of copies of any particular business document depends primarily on how elaborate the system is. Generally, the more elaborate the system, the greater the number of copies required to satisfy it.

GAAP—The Cost Principle

The **cost principle** states that the accounting for purchases must be at their cost price. In almost all cases, this is the figure that appears on the source document for the transaction. There is no place for guesswork or wishful thinking when accounting for purchases.

The value recorded in the accounts for an asset is not changed later if the market value for the asset changes. It would take an entirely new transaction based on new objective evidence to change the original value of an asset.

There are times when the above type of objective evidence is not available. In those instances, the transaction is recorded at fair market value, which must be determined by some independent means.

Section Review Questions

1. Not all transactions requiring accounting entries are initiated by the accounting staff. Explain.
2. How does the accounting department find out about all transactions?
3. What is a source document?
4. What is the principal use of source documents in the accounting department?
5. Give an example of a transaction for which there is no conventional source document.
6. Who else, besides the accounting department, may have reason to use the source documents on file?
7. What is the purpose of a cash sales slip?

8. Why is the cash sales slip regarded as being less formal than the sales invoice?
9. Explain the essential difference between a sales invoice and a cash sales slip.
10. Explain who the "vendor" is.
11. Explain how the to use the dual-purpose sales slip.
12. What is a purchase invoice?
13. Explain why all accounting entries for purchase invoices are not the same.
14. Why is a cheque not used as a source document?
15. What is the most common type of transaction for which a cheque is issued?
16. What supporting documents are needed for a cash purchase?
17. What is the supporting evidence for a payroll cheque?
18. Explain what cash receipts are.
19. Why is it necessary to prepare a cash receipts listing?
20. From what two sources does the clerk obtain the data to prepare the cash receipts listing?
21. Why do banks issue bank advices?
22. A bank debit memo requires a credit entry in the bank account of the business. Explain.
23. State the cost principle.
24. Why is an invoice regarded as an ideal source document?

Section Exercises

1. Answer the following questions related to the source document below.

    1. What business document is it?
    2. What is the purpose of the document?
    3. Where does the information come from to prepare the list?
    4. Why is a list prepared?
    5. In the listing what does "on account" mean compared to "Invoice 4502"?
    6. Give the accounting entry that would be made as a result of the listing.
    7. Who is G. Smalley?

	SAYERS AND ASSOCIATES	
	CASH RECEIPTS LIST	MARCH 14, 19--
Degagne Machine Shop	on account	$ 500.00
Kivella Bake Shop	Inv. 4502	315.43
Molner Paints	Inv. 3909	214.60
Robitaille Taxi	on account	200.00
G. Smalley	Total	$1 230.03

2. Answer the following questions related to the source document below.

1. What business document is it?
2. What is the purpose of the document?
3. Who is the issuer of the document?
4. Explain the purposes of the document number.
5. Give the accounting entry that would be made by the issuer of the document.

DAVIDSON TREE EXPERTS
Horseshoe Valley
Ontario, L4M 4Y8
Phone 321-8765

DATE: March 10, 19 __
NAME: F. Vailliant
ADDRESS: Craighurst

QUANTITY	DESCRIPTION	PRICE	AMOUNT
6	pruning of mature trees, removing dead wood	30	180 —
2	cut down and remove mature trees	75	150 —
		TAX	
RECEIVED ABOVE IN GOOD ORDER F. Vailliant		TOTAL	330 —

CASH SALES SLIP 2651

3. Answer the following questions related to the source document below.

1. What business document is it?
2. Who is the sender of the document? Who is the receiver?
3. To which business is this document the equivalent of a sales invoice? To which business is it a purchase invoice?
4. Give the accounting entry that would be made by the sender of the document.
5. Give the accounting entry that would be made by the receiver of the document.

IN ACCOUNT WITH

Our file No. 3862

KNUTSEN AND TREBLEY
BARRISTERS, SOLICITORS

5200 Dufferin Street
Fredericton, New Brunswick
E3B 4A7

TO Hansen and Company,
Fredericton, New Brunswick,
E3B 5B7

Re: Hansen and Company v. Lorimer Bros.
Motor Vehicle Accident

To our fee for all services herein, including office consultations, receiving instructions and advising, obtaining police accident report and interviewing witnesses, attending to issuing Writ of Summons and arranging service thereof, correspondence and negotiations with solicitors for defendant and completion of settlement, obtaining payment of settlement proceeds and reporting to you, in all $450.00

Paid to issue Writ of Summons	$17.00	
Paid bailiff to serve Writ	21.50	
Paid police for accident report	10.00	48.50
Total fees and disbursements		$498.50

This is our account set and subscribed this 17th day of March, 19--. Per

P. Knutsen

Chapter 6

4. The document below arrives at your place of business by mail. Answer the following questions concerning it.

   1. What business document is it?
   2. Who do you work for?
   3. Why was this document sent to your company?
   4. What does the broken line on the document represent?
   5. Explain the information beneath the broken line.
   6. Give the accounting entry that would be made in the books of your company to record the source document.
   7. What happens to the upper part of this document?

```
┌──────────────────────────────────────────────────────────────────────────┐
│   CARBIDE TOOLS LIMITED      4000 Essex Drive                            │
│                              Vancouver, B.C.            No. 1101         │
│                              V7R 8S8                                     │
│                                                    May 10      19 __     │
│   PAY TO THE     Presto-Can Company                                      │
│   ORDER OF                                         $   1 368.30          │
│                                                                    30    │
│   One Thousand, Three Hundred and Sixty-Eight-----------------   ─── DOLLARS
│                                                                   100    │
│                                                                          │
│         THE COMMERCIAL BANK                                              │
│         CITY HARBOUR BRANCH                                              │
│         VANCOUVER, B.C.                      Marianne Mayo               │
│                                              CARBIDE TOOLS LIMITED       │
│                                                                          │
│         ⑈030800 3⑈04⑈:  004⑈:  ⑈030800 3⑈                              │
├─ ─ ─ ─ ─ ─ ─ ─ ─ ─ ─ ─ ─ ─ ─ ─ ─ ─ ─ ─ ─ ─ ─ ─ ─ ─ ─ ─ ─ ─ ─ ─ ─ ─ ─ ──┤
│   IN PAYMENT OF THE FOLLOWING                                            │
│           Invoice          Date           Amount                         │
│           #6149        April 16        $   217.02                        │
│           #7002        April 30            400.12                        │
│           #7109        May 7                751.16                       │
│                        Total            $1 368.30                        │
│   CARBIDE TOOLS LIMITED                                         1101     │
└──────────────────────────────────────────────────────────────────────────┘
```

5. Answer the following questions related to the source document below.

   1. What business document is it?
   2. In whose books of account is an accounting entry now necessary as a result of this source document?
   3. Give the accounting entry that would be made as a result of the source document.

6.2 Sales Tax

Sales tax is one way the federal and provincial governments raise funds. There is a lot of detailed regulation associated with sales tax: which items are taxed, which items are not, what forms are necessary, and so on. A business involved in the selling of goods or services needs someone in the office to be familiar with sales tax regulations. Government offices are set up in many communities to provide the necessary forms, regulations, and assistance.

This text will not deal with sales tax in a detailed way. Sales tax will be explained in simple terms only, to provide a view of the basic concepts and procedures.

Retail Sales Tax

A retail sales tax is charged by most provincial governments. A **retail sales tax** is a percentage tax based on and added to the price of goods sold to a customer. The rates of tax vary from province to province and are established by the provincial governments. It is usual in Canada to tax the final consumer only. A sale from a wholesaler to a retailer would not be taxed.

Accounting for Sales Tax

The Purchaser

The purchaser of goods or services does no accounting for sales tax. The purchaser simply accounts for the transaction at the final figure on the sales slip, or invoice. This final figure includes the sales tax.

The Seller

The seller is charged with the responsibility of administering the sales tax. The seller is obliged to do the following:

1. calculate the tax and add it on to the normal price of the goods;
2. collect the tax from the customer;
3. accumulate the sales tax charged to the customers in a special liability account, called Sales Tax Payable;
4. pay the accumulated sales tax over to the government periodically. In some cases sales tax will be paid to the government before it is collected from the customer.

Sales Tax on a Cash Sale The simplest transaction involving sales tax is the "cash sale." The seller determines the amount of the tax, adds it to the price, and collects the total from the customer. The cash sales slips used so far have not included sales tax. Now that we know about sales tax, this item will be included on the cash sales slips. Examine the cash sales slip in Figure 6.9.

Figure 6.9 A cash sales slip on which a sales tax has been added.

Keep in mind that sales tax must be paid to the government periodically. It therefore represents a liability payable to the government and is accumulated in the Sales Tax Payable account. For the above sales slip, the accounting entry is:

	DR	CR
Bank	$212.93	
Sales		$199.00
Sales Tax Payable		$ 13.93

Sales Tax on a Charge Sale   Sales tax is also added to a sale on account represented by a sales invoice. In Figure 6.10, a sales invoice is shown that includes a five per cent sales tax. With a charge sale the seller does not collect the tax at the time of the sale, but must wait until the customer pays his or her account. This is usually within thirty days.

Figure 6.10   Sales invoice on which a sales tax has been added.

The accounting entry for the above sales invoice is:

	DR	CR
Account Receivable—Marathon Recreation	$337.84	
Sales		$321.75
Sales Tax Payable		16.09

Remitting Sales Tax

Sales tax is collected for a month and then is paid over to the government. In most regions, the sales tax collected in any one month is to be paid to the government by the fifteenth of the following month. Taxes collected in January are to be paid by the fifteenth of February, and so on. From time to time, government auditors pay visits to businesses to check the accuracy of records, collections, and payments.

Assume that a total of $415.23 was recorded in the Sales Tax Payable account in the month of January. The T-account would appear as follows:

```
         Sales Tax Payable
                | Jan.    415.23
```

The account represents a liability owed by the business to the government. When the balance is paid, the accounting entry to record the payment is:

	DR	CR
Sales Tax Payable	$415.23	
Bank		$415.23

The payment will clear the January balance. In the meantime, the sales tax items for February will be gathering in the account.

Section Review Questions

1. Why do governments apply a sales tax on goods and services?
2. Where does one go to find out about sales tax rules and regulations?
3. What special accounting for sales tax is done by the purchaser of goods that have a tax added?
4. What four things is the seller of goods and services required to do regarding sales tax?
5. A cash sale of $100 is made. A sales tax of seven per cent is applied. How much does the customer pay?
6. What kind of account is the Sales Tax Payable?
7. How often is sales tax remitted to the government?
8. Explain how a business person may be required to pay sales tax to the government before it has been collected from the customer.

Section 6.2   153

Section Exercises

1.
   1. Calculate the sales tax for each of the following if the rate of tax is five per cent.
   2. Calculate the total amount to be paid by the customer for each of the following.
   3. Give the accounting entry for each transaction in the books of the vendor.

   Transactions

   1. A cash sale of goods at a price of $75.
   2. A cash sale of goods at a price of $120.
   3. A charge sale of goods at a price of $58.60.
   4. A charge sale of goods at a price of $98.00.
   5. A sale of goods at a price of $130 with a down payment of $50.

2. The invoice below was issued to Island Marina by Masthead Marine.
   1. Give the accounting entry to be made in the books of the vendor.
   2. Give the accounting entry to be made in the books of the purchaser, if the account to be debited is Merchandise Inventory.

   MASTHEAD MARINE
   ECHO BAY
   VANCOUVER, B.C.
   P.O. Box 298
   Station 8
   V7C 8P7
   Phone 842-9999

   SOLD TO: Island Marina
   4000 Island Highway
   Campbell River, B.C.
   V9W 2J4

   DATE: July 3, 19--
   TERMS: Net 30 days

QUANTITY	PART NO.	DESCRIPTION	PRICE	AMOUNT
6	77-1139	Saturn off-shore compasses	$ 95.00	$ 570.00
2	03-3295	LG2 dual log indicator	299.00	598.00
				$1 168.00
		5% sales tax		58.40
				$1 226.40

   SALES INVOICE   NO. 3267

3. Jack Pritchard paid $330.96, including five per cent sales tax, for some furniture.
   1. **Calculate the price of the goods before the sales tax is added.**

2. Calculate the sales tax on the goods.
3. Prove your work.

4. Examine the account below and answer the questions that follow.

ACCOUNT Sales Tax Payable					No. 22
DATE	PARTICULARS	PR	DEBIT	CREDIT	Dr/Cr	BALANCE
19— Feb. 1	Forwarded	—			Cr	476 30
15		CP80	476 30			
28		SJ61		242 95		
28		CR57		316 20	Cr	559 15
Mar. 15		CP82	559 15			
31		SJ64		251 86		
31		CR59		302 19	Cr	554 05

1. How much sales tax was accumulated in January?
2. How much sales tax was accumulated in February?
3. What does the account balance represent?
4. How much sales tax was accumulated in March?
5. When will the sales tax accumulated in March be paid?
6. Give the accounting entry that will be made for the transaction of April 15.

5. On February 28, 19—, Moore's Marina sold the merchandise shown below to Valerie Miniaci of Bear Island, Alberta. The sale was made on account.

        2   Grumman canoes   @ $925.00 each
        4   Paddles   @ $ 82.00 a pair

In your workbook write up the above sale on a dual-purpose sales slip. Sales tax at five per cent is to be added.

6.3 Computerized Accounting: The Accounting Package—The Computer Menu

The Accounting Package

The accounting department is responsible for performing a number of routine accounting procedures. These routine procedures can still be done manually by clerical employees. Today, however, more and more businesses prefer to use computers. Businesses that do their accounting by computer use accounting software purchased from a manufacturer or a dealer. The accounting package includes a number of related programs designed to do several accounting tasks. The programs are stored on disks and kept on file until required.

In addition to the accounting package, the business must have a computer system that will run the software. This usually means a computer with a fairly large main memory, two disk drives, a screen, and a printer. It is important to note that software designed for one make of computer may not run on other computers.

The Computer Menu

The first step in using an accounting package is to load the software into the computer. Once loaded, the computer takes over by guiding the user with helpful displays and prompting messages. This is referred to as being "user-friendly."

When you run your accounting software, the main menu is one of the first things appearing on the screen. The main menu is a list of options provided in the package. It requires the user to choose one of the options. A typical main menu from an accounting package appears below in Figure 6.11.

```
           ACCOUNTING APPLICATIONS

    CHOOSE ONE OF THE FOLLOWING OPTIONS BY NUMBER.

              1. GENERAL LEDGER

              2. ACCOUNTS RECEIVABLE

              3. ACCOUNTS PAYABLE

              4. PAYROLL

              5. INVENTORY

    YOUR CHOICE
```

Figure 6.11 A main menu.

When you enter the number of your choice, another menu (a sub-menu) appears on the screen. Suppose you were to choose number 1 from the main menu above. A sub-menu such as the one shown in Figure 6.12 below would then appear on the screen.

```
SELECT ONE OF THE FOLLOWING OPTIONS BY LETTER.

A. INITIAL TRIAL BALANCE      E. ENDING TRIAL BALANCE

B. JOURNALIZE TRANSACTIONS    F. INCOME STATEMENT

C. GENERAL JOURNAL            G. BALANCE SHEET

D. GENERAL LEDGER             X. QUIT

   YOUR CHOICE
```

Figure 6.12 A sub-menu.

When the user responds by entering a letter, the system continues to help the user by displaying prompting messages. Suppose the letter E were chosen from the above menu. A prompting message like the one shown in Figure 6.13 below would appear.

```
             TRIAL BALANCE

   SELECT 'S' OR 'P' AS INDICATED BELOW.

            S. SCREEN DISPLAY?

            P. PRINTOUT?

   YOUR CHOICE
```

Figure 6.13 Prompting messages displayed on the screen.

Obviously, the user can choose to have the ending trial balance displayed on the screen or printed out on the printer.

There are many different accounting packages available on the market. Each one has its own particular format and commands. When an accounting package is obtained, the user has to take the time to become thoroughly familiar with it. For your work in the classroom, read the manual for your software, or seek guidance from your teacher.

Computer Review Questions

1. Where does one acquire the software to perform accounting?
2. What is included in the "accounting package"?
3. In what physical form does the accounting package come?
4. There is one very important consideration when buying an accounting package. Explain.
5. What are the usual components of a computer system capable of performing accounting?
6. What is the first step in running accounting software?
7. How is software made "user-friendly"?
8. What does the term "menu" mean as applied to computers?
9. How does the businessperson who acquires an accounting package become familiar with it?

Computer Exercises

1. Indicate which of the following statements are not true by placing an "F" in the space provided to the right in your workbook. Assume that there are no faults in the programming or the computer system.

    a. Some persons still prefer to do accounting by hand because they are afraid of the computer.
    b. Most businesses are using computers to do accounting because the computers are less expensive than they used to be.
    c. Most businesses program their own accounting packages.
    d. When you run your accounting software, you will see a menu on the screen.
    e. A computer menu requires the user to make a choice.
    f. There are many different accounting packages on the market.
    g. There will be a manual to accompany your accounting package.

2. This exercise appears in your workbook.

    For each of the following statements fill in the blank(s) with the number corresponding to the most appropriate word or phrase from the list given below.

1. The accounting department is responsible for performing a number of _____ .
2. Routine accounting tasks can still be done _____ .
3. The accounting package includes a number of _____ designed to do specific accounting tasks. These _____ are stored on _____ .
4. The computer system required to perform accounting will usually include a computer with a fairly large memory, a _____ , _____ , and a _____ .
5. Step one in running an accounting package is to _____ the software.
6. One of the things that the user will see on the screen is the _____ .
7. The use of helpful displays and prompting messages is a factor in being _____ .
8. The main menu is a list of _____ provided in the package.
9. A menu requires the user to make a _____ .
10. Each individual accounting package has its own particular _____ and _____ .

List of Words and Phrases

1. accounting procedures
2. choice
3. commands
4. disks
5. format
6. load
7. manually
8. menu
9. options
10. printer
11. programs
12. screen
13. two disk drives
14. user-friendly

CHAPTER HIGHLIGHTS

Now that you have completed Chapter 6, you should:

1. be able to recognize a number of basic source documents and know their uses:
2. know the accounting entries for a variety of source documents;
3. know of the supporting proofs for accounting entries that do not have source documents;
4. understand that source documents are part of an overall accounting system for controlling and recording accounting transactions;
5. understand the cost principle and the objectivity principle in recording transactions;
6. know the purpose of sales tax imposed by governments;
7. be able to calculate sales tax and record sales tax on source documents;
8. know the accounting entries for source documents containing sales tax;
9. know the accounting entry for remitting sales tax to the government.

ACCOUNTING TERMS

bank credit advice	cheque copy	remittance advice
bank debit advice	cost principle	retail sales tax
cash receipts list	dual purpose sales slip	sales invoice
cash sales slip	purchase invoice	source document

CHAPTER EXERCISES

Using Your Knowledge

1. Identify the source document or documents that would support the following transactions:

   a. Debt paid on account
   b. Supplies purchased for cash
   c. Service performed on account
   d. Money withdrawn by owner
   e. Bank loan reduced
   f. Donation paid by cash
   g. Receipt from customer on account
   h. Supplies purchased on account
   i. Sale made on account
   j. Service performed for cash
   k. Bank interest charged
   l. Hydro bill paid by cash

2. The following exercise also appears in your workbook. Complete the following summary.

Nature of Transaction	Source Document or Documents	Account Debited	Account Credited
Payment on Account			
Sale on Account			
Bank Service Charge			
Cash Payment of Phone Bill			
Cash Received on Account			
Purchase of Equipment on Account			
Cash sale			

Chapter 6

3. The following exercise also appears in your workbook. In the chart below, to the left, are listed a number of source documents. To the right is a list of numbered transactions. You are to match the transactions with the source documents by writing in the transaction number beside the source document to which it relates. Some transactions affect more than one source document. In these cases write in the transaction number beside each source document affected.

Source Document	Transaction Number		Transactions
Bank Credit Memo			1. Owner withdraws money.
Bank Debit Memo			2. Purchase of equipment on account.
Cheque Copy			3. Payment on account.
Cash Sales Slip			4. Cash sale.
Sales Invoice			5. Cash payment for donation.
Purchase Invoice			6. Purchase of office supplies by cash.
Receipt Invoice			7. Sale on account.
Cash Receipts List			8. Cheques received from customers on account.
Owner's Written Memo			9. Increase bank loan.
Sales Slip Received			10. Owner invests additional money in the business.
Bank Statement			11. Bank service charge.

4. Indicate whether each of the following statements is true or false by placing a "T" or "F" in the space indicated in your workbook. Explain the reason for each "F" response in the space provided.

   1. Anyone in the business can initiate an accounting transaction.
   2. Every accounting entry is based on a source document.
   3. The only purpose of source documents is to provide the basis for an accounting entry.
   4. A business that sells to its customers on a cash basis would not normally use a sales invoice.
   5. The accounting entry for all cash sales slips is essentially the same.
   6. Sales invoices are used by businesses that make most of their sales on account.

7. For every sales invoice there is a debit to an account receivable.
8. Dual-purpose sales slips are the choice of businesses that sell for cash and also on account.
9. Every sales invoice is also a purchase invoice.
10. The debit entry for every purchase invoice is always the same.
11. The supporting document for a payment on account is the tear-off portion of a cheque.
12. The credit entry for every cheque copy payment is always the same.
13. Cheques received are considered to be cash received.
14. The bank has no right to make deductions from the accounts of its customers.
15. We debit Bank when we receive a bank debit memo.
16. The cost principle states that every acquisition of assets is to be recorded at their cost price.
17. The best objective evidence of a purchase is a purchase invoice received at "arm's length."
18. Only provincial governments are allowed to levy sales taxes.
19. The purchaser of goods or services is required to make accounting entries for sales tax.
20. The Sales Tax account is an expense account.

Comprehensive Exercises

5. Champion Rent-All, a business in Parry Sound, Ont., rents out tools and equipment. The accounts for the business are as follows:

Bank	Rental Revenue
Accounts Receivable	Bank Charges
Supplies	Delivery Expense
Rental Tools and Equipment	Light, Heat, and Water
Truck	Miscellaneous Expense
Sales Tax Payable	Rent
Accounts Payable	Telephone
Frank N. Mazur, Capital	Wages
Frank N. Mazur, Drawings	

In the space provided in your workbook, write up the accounting entries for the following transactions.

Transactions

1. *Cash Sales Slip*
   No. 409, to W. Franklin, $52.50 plus 5% sales tax of $2.63; total $55.13.
2. *Charge Sales Slip*
   No. 410, to G. Fairbridge, $87.50 plus 5% sales tax of $4.38; total $91.88.
3. *Purchase Invoice*
   From Vulcan Machinery, No. 3062 for one hydraulic jack, a rental tool, $315.

Chapter 6

4. *Cheque Copy*
   No. 1475, to Fair Supply Company, $215.90 on account.
5. *Cash Sales Slip*
   No. 411, to R. Gullett, $115.10 plus 5% sales tax of $5.76; total $120.86.
6. *Cash Receipt*
   From P. Mathers, $402.20 on account.
7. *Cheque Copy*
   No. 1476, to Municipal Hydro, for cash payment of hydro bill, $172.
8. *Cheque Copy*
   No. 1477, to R. Klein, $512 for wages.
9. *Cash Sales Slip*
   No. 412, to A. Heisse, $90 plus 5% sales tax of $4.50; total $94.50.
10. *Cheque Copy*
    No. 1478, to the owner, Frank Mazur, for his personal use, $350.
11. *Credit Card Statement*
    From Husky Oil Company, $209 for gas and oil used in the delivery truck.
12. *Bank Debit Memo*
    For bank service charge, $42.50.
13. *Cheque Copy*
    No. 1479, to R. Klein, $512 for wages.

---

6. Janet Nuttall is in business as a commercial artist in Winnipeg, Man. The accounts for her business are shown below:

   Bank
   Accounts Receivable
   Art Supplies
   Equipment
   Automobile
   Accounts Payable
   Sales Tax Payable

   Janet Nuttall, Capital
   Janet Nuttall, Drawings
   Fees Revenue
   Car Expenses
   Electricity Expense
   Miscellaneous Expense
   Rent Expense
   Telephone Expense

   In the space provided in the workbook, write up the accounting entries for the following transactions. Add seven per cent on all sales transactions.

   ### Transactions

   1. *Sales Invoice*
      No. 192, to Mountain Distributors, $175.
   2. *Sales Invoice*
      No. 193, to Old Fort Trading Co., $300.
   3. *Cheque Copy*
      No. 316, to Central Garage for the cash payment for repairs to the business automobile, $115.

4. *Cheque Copy*
   No. 317, to Twin City Hydro for the cash payment of the monthly hydro bill, $65.
5. *Purchase Invoice*
   From C. & C. Equipment, No. 1401, for one large metal drawing table, $475.
6. *Cheque Copy*
   No. 318, to Dejavu Art Supply for the cash payment for artist's supplies, $85.
7. *Cheque Copy*
   No. 319, to the owner for her personal use, $350.
8. *Sales Invoice*
   No. 194, to Display Design Company, $255.
9. *Cash Receipt*
   From Victor Schilling, $150 on account
10. *Cheque Copy*
    No. 320, to C. & C. Equipment, $475 on account.
11. *Sales Invoice*
    No. 195, to Scoville Sales, $235.
12. *Cheque Copy*
    No. 321, to Fleming Properties, for the monthly rent, $375.
13. *Purchase Invoice*
    From Lougherys Limited, No. 634, for drafting and artist's equipment, $215.
14. *Cheque Copy*
    No. 322, to Twin City Telephone, for cash payment of the monthly telephone bill, $28.50.
15. *Credit Card Statement*
    From Imperial Oil, for the gas and oil used in the automobile, $71.40.
16. *Cash Receipt*
    From Old Fort Trading Co., $300 on account.

7. **Comment briefly on each of the following. Be prepared to present your comments to the class.**

   1. In a period of rising prices, the assets on the balance sheet will be understated. Therefore, the balance sheet is misleading.
   2. Joan Nordquist purchased the property next to her business at a price of $50 000. The property was acquired for a much-needed expansion to the business premises. One week later, Joan received an independent offer to purchase the property for $75 000 but turned it down. However, she instructed her accountant to increase the value of the property in the accounts to $75 000. It is her opinion that a new value for the property was established by the offer to purchase.
   3. Fred Hebert purchased a new piece of equipment for his business. The normal selling price of this equipment was $22 000. Fred was given a special price of $18 000 because he was a close friend of the dealer. Fred was undecided as to the value the equipment should be recorded at in the accounts.

4. A company ran out of cash even though it was a consistently good money-maker. How could this happen?
5. The Colossimo Company ordered a new van at a cost of $23 000 on March 19. It was agreed that Colossimo Company would not take delivery of the van until July 31. Colossimo Company does not know if it should record the transaction now.
6. Sarah Tolp inherited a used automobile upon the death of a relative. She brought it into her business. She instructed the accountant to record the car at a value of $25 000 but provided no business papers to support that figure.

For Further Thought

8. Briefly answer the following questions.

    1. Name three jobs in a secondary school that carry the right to make purchases.
    2. Explain the term "source document."
    3. Give an example other than owner's drawings of a transaction for which there would be no normal source document.
    4. In the Truck account there is a debit entry for a new truck in the amount of $25 000. You suspect that this figure is wrong. You find that the source document for the transaction is missing from the files when you look for it. How could you verify the amount?
    5. Cash sales slips are pre-numbered as a control feature. What would you tell your employees to do about cash sales slips that were spoiled and had to be redone?
    6. Explain how an invoice can be both a "sales invoice" and a "purchase invoice."
    7. Cash sales slips are usually loaded into a metal container for ease in preparation. What happens to the copies immediately after they are prepared?
    8. Why can the invoice numbers on purchase invoices not be used for control purposes?
    9. The person who receives the mail, makes out the cash receipts list, and deposits the receipts in the bank is not normally an employee in the accounting department. Explain why.
    10. The rule states that assets are debited when they are increased. However, the bank issues a "debit" memo when it decreases the bank account. Explain.
    11. Once the cost of an asset is recorded in the accounts, it is not normally changed regardless of its market value. Give some reasons for this rule.
    12. Sales tax added on to an invoice in March has to be paid by April 15. However, the invoice in question may not be collected until May. Express an opinion on this.

CASE STUDIES

Case 1 Acquiring Assets in a Package Deal

Ted Cyr is the owner of a large contracting company in Thomson, Manitoba. A competitor of Cyr's went bankrupt and his equipment was liquidated at a public auction. One particular "lot" of equipment attracted Cyr's attention. The lot included: one bulldozer, two dump trucks, one crane, one pavement roller, and a property on which there was a sizeable construction building and one large sand pit. Cyr acquired all of these as one package, for a bid of $275 000.

Cyr is a businessman who keeps proper books and records and complies with all accounting standards and conventions. He intends to set up the newly acquired assets properly in the accounts. He is not sure how to do this because they were acquired as a package. He is certain at least that the equipment and the land should be set up in separate accounts.

Cyr hires you, a public accountant, to prepare the accounting entries to record the new assets. Explain how you could accomplish this.

Case 2 Is a Profit Always a Profit?

In 19–2 Marjorie Maepea, a dealer of small sailboats in Summerside, Prince Edward Island, had a profitable year. She ended the 19–2 period with an extra $25 000 in cash available and was looking for a good investment opportunity. For some time she considered using the money to purchase a larger sailboat, to see if there was a market in Summerside for larger boats. In particular she looked at a ten-metre Tarzen selling for $25 000, but finally decided against buying it. Eventually she purchased a nearby piece of commercial property for which she paid $25 000.

At the end of 19–5 the land purchased in 19–2 was sold for $40 000. Marjorie felt good about the deal. The profit of $15 000 looked good on the books. Marjorie once more had lots of cash available to pursue other business ventures. She again considered the move to larger boats and looked at the Tarzen 10, which was virtually unchanged from 19–2. She was surprised to learn that the 19–5 price of a Tarzen 10 was $40 000.

Questions
(Note: Ignore factors other that those above.)

1. Is Marjorie any better off in 19–5 than she was in 19–2?
2. Has Marjorie really made a profit?
3. Should Marjorie have to pay income tax on the book profit of $15 000?

Case 3 *Profit Before Sentiment?*

John Pemberton had worked for T.W. Jones as chief accountant for six months. He was proud of the efficiency and enthusiasm shown by his staff.

One day, John was visibly upset after returning from a meeting with Mr. Jones. At the meeting, Mr. Jones had suggested that John dismiss the two senior employees in his department and bring in two young employees at the bottom of the salary scale. This would save the company several thousand dollars a year. "There is no room for sentiment in the business world," Mr. Jones had said.

John knew that his department would survive without the senior employees. There were intermediate-level employees in the department who were waiting for an opportunity to move up to bigger responsibilities. There would be a slight inconvenience but not much more.

John considered the proposal for some time and could not feel comfortable with it. Both of the senior employees were older men, aged 55 and 60 respectively. John knew that it would not be easy for these men to find employment at the salary level they now enjoyed. Unfortunately, there was no union in the company to protect the rights of these men. John was also concerned about his own future. If he did not go along with the scheme, his employer would consider him 'soft' and his job might be endangered.

Questions

1. Is Mr. Jones's scheme a good one from a strictly business point of view?
2. Is Mr. Jones's scheme legal?
3. Does John have the right to consider his own future ahead of the future of others?
4. What do you think John should do?

CAREER
Barbara Blaney, CA / Public Acountant

Barbara Blaney was born in Sydney, Australia. Her parents moved to Halifax when she was only three years old, so Barbara feels like a true Nova Scotian.

After high school, Barbara immediately enrolled at Dalhousie University to work towards a Bachelor of Commerce degree. When she graduated, Barbara had intended to go straight into the job market. Unfortunately, unemployment was high at the time. Barbara applied for a student loan and went back to Dalhousie to study for a Master of Business Administration degree with a concentration in accounting and information systems.

Upon graduation, Barbara articled for her C.A. designation with Clarkson, Gordon & Co., in their Halifax office. Because she held an M.B.A. degree, the Institute of Chartered Accountants granted Barbara advanced standing in many of the courses a C.A. student must take. With this advantage, she was able to complete all the requirements and pass the examinations for her C.A. designation in less than two years.

Barbara now had to make a decision. Based on her academic qualifications, she had many offers of employment, from chartered accountants, private industry and from government. Her other choice was to set up her own accounting practice.

Barbara decided she would prefer to be her own boss. She set up her practice in a small town outside of Halifax. She hired a clerk-typist to handle the clerical work and two accounting clerks to help her handle the routine accounting functions. With a small business loan, she purchased a computerized accounting system. It consisted of two microcomputers, two disk drives, a printer, and software which could handle ledgers, payroll, inventory, and accounts receivable and payable.

Barbara visited the various small businesses in the community and convinced them to let her handle all their bookkeeping on the computer. For some of her clients, Barbara found it necessary to design sales invoices similar to those illustrated in this chapter. To have each business keep track of cheques received from customers, she set up a List of Cash Receipts form. She insisted that all businesses have numbered cheques and that the copies of purchase invoices be attached to each cheque copy as proof of payment.

Now, Barbara visits her clients each week and collects all their source documents to take them back to the office. Using these source documents as input, her accounting clerks key the information into the computer using the permanent file for each business. The computer gives her a printout of the trial balances, income statements, and balance sheets.

Because the computer handles so much of the routine work, Barbara is able to spend more time in developing appropriate planning and forecasting activities. She is called upon to prepare income tax returns for her clients and also to make suggestions about how to save the businesses money. She is also requested to provide management services. She advises businesses about all aspects of sales, purchasing, accounting systems and data processing.

Barbara is extremely pleased with her decision to set up her own accounting practice. She enjoys being her own boss and derives a great deal of satisfaction from making her own decisions. After a few difficult years in the beginning, Barbara's practice is now financially successful. This allows her to spend more time enjoying her favourite leisure activities, travelling and fishing.

Discussion

1. What source documents did Barbara have her clients set up to control cash?
2. Discuss the advantages and disadvantages of setting up your own accounting practice.
3. Write a report on the Chartered Accountancy program. In your report, include the following information:
   - educational requirements;
   - experience requirements;
   - advanced standing;
   - number of courses to earn the CA designation;
   - courses that are studied.
4. Identify and explain the use of the source documents you recognize in Barbara's profile.
5. Write a report on the Master of Business Administration degree at a university of your choice. Find out the qualifications needed to enrol, the number of courses required for graduation, length of time the program takes to complete, and the average needed for graduation.
6. If you were in Barbara's position as a CA, how would you convince businesses to let you handle their bookkeeping systems?
7. Why does Barbara have the businesses attach copies of all purchase invoices to the cheque copies?
8. What are the various duties Barbara performs for her clients as a public accountant?
9. What are the advantages for Barbara of setting up her accounting practice in a small town rather than in Halifax?

7 Journalizing and Posting

7.1 Accounting versus Bookkeeping
7.2 The Journal
7.3 Posting
7.4 Trial Balance Out of Balance
**7.5 Computerized Accounting:
       The Accounting Package—Data Entry**

You have now learned a number of important accounting concepts. In particular, you have learned about the balance sheet and the income statement, transactions, the ledger, and source documents. So far, your learning has been theoretical in nature. In this chapter you will see some of the practical applications of these concepts in accounting.

7.1 Accounting versus Bookkeeping

Most people today still confuse "accounting" and "bookkeeping." But accounting and bookkeeping are different.

The Bookkeeper   The work of a bookkeeper is clerical in nature and for the most part concerned with routine matters. A bookkeeper works under the supervision of an accountant. The term "bookkeeper" is gradually being replaced by the term "accounting clerk." Some of the jobs that a bookkeeper does are:
1. ensuring that transactions are right and proper and that the necessary supporting documents are present and correct;
2. recording the accounting entries in the books of account and balancing the ledger as necessary;
3. making the payroll calculations and preparing the payroll cheques and other payroll records;
4. carrying out all necessary banking transactions.

The Accountant The work of an accountant, on the other hand, is far broader in scope and requires more education and experience. A professional accountant is usually responsible for maintaining the entire accounting system. Some of the things an accountant is concerned with are:

1. developing a system to ensure that correct data are entered into the system;
2. ensuring that generally accepted accounting standards are met;
3. interpreting the data produced by the accounting system;
4. preparing reports based on the data output from the system;
5. participating in management meetings and assisting in making business decisions;
6. supervising the work of all accounting employees.

A qualified accountant has a high-level position. The top people in many large corporations are qualified accountants.

Bookkeeping—Manually or by Computer

For centuries, all bookkeeping activity was handwritten. There was no other way of maintaining accounting records. There was a handwritten book of accounting entries. The ledger was a handwritten book of accounts. The accounting records came to be known as "the books," as they still are today.

The use of computers for bookkeeping is increasing steadily. There are two reasons for this. First, computer hardware is reasonably priced and of sound quality. Second, accounting applications programs are reliable and easy to use. It is likely that all bookkeeping will be done by computers in the near future.

However, there are still three important reasons for not ignoring handwritten methods of bookkeeping:

1. Many small businesses and organizations still do their bookkeeping by hand.
2. Manual methods are ideal for studying accounting. The learner gains a better understanding of the accounting process and the benefits of electronic processing.
3. Your accounting education would not be complete without a knowledge of the handwritten method.

Section Review Questions

1. Describe briefly the nature of a bookkeeper's work.
2. Who supervises the work of a bookkeeper?
3. What term is replacing the word "bookkeeper"?

4. Describe two specific tasks of an accounting clerk.
5. Describe the scope of an accountant's work.
6. What is a "professional" accountant?
7. Describe two specific tasks of an accountant.
8. What is "manual" bookkeeping?
9. Explain how accounting records came to be called "the books."
10. Give two reasons for the increased use of computers in bookkeeping.
11. What do you see as the future for manual bookkeeping?
12. Why can we not ignore handwritten methods of bookkeeping?

Section Exercise

1. **This exercise appears in your workbook.**
    1. Which of the following does not fit?
        a. An accounting clerk verifies source documents.
        b. An accounting clerk ensures that the ledger balances.
        c. An accounting clerk works neatly to guard against errors.
        d. An accounting clerk studies tax bulletins to keep up-to-date.
    2. Which of the following does not fit?
        a. An accounting clerk works out accounting entries.
        b. An accounting clerk, together with the owner, compares this year's and last year's income statements.
        c. An accounting clerk records accounting entries in the books.
        d. An accounting clerk inquires about a suspected error made by the bank.
    3. Which of the following does not fit?
        a. An accountant is a professional person.
        b. An accountant has a broad knowledge of "accounting."
        c. An accountant ensures the accuracy of the payroll deductions.
        d. An accountant discusses the business's "cash flow" with the owners.
    4. Which of the following does not fit?
        a. An accountant talks about the final qualifying exams.
        b. An accountant investigates the credit rating of a new customer.
        c. An accountant is promoted to vice-president.
        d. An accountant is ill; a meeting with the bank manager has to be cancelled.
    5. Which of the following does not fit?
        a. Computers are reasonably priced.
        b. Computers never break down.
        c. Computers produce better profit figures.
        d. Computer programs are not yet reliable.

6. Which of the following does not fit?
  a. Handwritten accounting records are a thing of the past.
  b. The use of computers in accounting is on the increase.
  c. Manual methods are common in the classroom.
  d. In a computerized accounting system, the ''books'' are no longer books.

7.2 The Journal

The ledger accounts alone do not satisfy all the needs of accounting. Each accounting entry is split up when it is recorded in the ledger. The data for each accounting entry is recorded in two or more accounts. As transactions mount up, the bits and pieces of the accounting entries become scattered throughout the ledger. The details for any one transaction become difficult to put back together. Yet this is often necessary. It is for this reason that accountants use another book called a ''journal.''

A **journal** is a book in which the accounting entries for all transactions are recorded individually in the order of their occurrence. A journal provides an important daily record of all transactions.

A **journal entry** is the complete accounting entry for a transaction, in the form it is written in the journal. **Journalizing** is the process of recording accounting entries in the journal.

The journal is known as a **book of original entry** because each balanced accounting entry is recorded there first. The basic process of recording transactions first in the journal and then in the ledger is shown by the chart in Figure 7.1 below.

Transactions occur. → Transactions are recorded in a journal in order by date. → The accounting entries are transferred to the ledger accounts.

Figure 7.1 The first three steps in the accounting cycle.

The Two-Column General Journal

There are several different types of journals used in accounting. First, we will study the simplest one—the two-column general journal. A **two-column general journal** is a simple journal with two money columns, one for the debit amounts and one for the credit amounts. Figure 7.2 shows a sample page of a two-column general journal. Observe that columns are also provided for the date, particulars, and posting reference (P.R.). The Posting Reference column, often called the Folio (Fo.) column, is used to cross-reference the journal to the ledger. Cross-referencing is explained later, on page 182.

Section 7.2   **173**

		GENERAL JOURNAL			PAGE 16	
DATE		PARTICULARS	P.R.	DEBIT	CREDIT	
19— Nov.	9	Supplies	108	135 —		
		Bank	101		136 —	
		Letterhead and envelopes;				
		Cheque # 40				
	12	Equipment	120	900 —		
		Supplies	108	400 —		
		Accs. Payl - Olivetti	210		1100 —	
		Bank	101		200 —	
		IBM typewriter; ribbons and				
		stationery; cheque #41				
	28	Accs. Payl - Woodwards	214	750 —		
		Bank	101		750 —	
		Partial Payment; cheque #42				
Dec.	3	Accs. Recl - W. Hill	112	300 —		
		Revenue	401		300 —	
		Service on account				
	17	Bank	101	5000 —		
		Bank Loan	201		5000 —	
		Increase in bank loan				

General Journal Facts

Pages numbered consecutively

Each accounting entry balances

Blank line between transactions

A "compound entry" affects more than two accounts

Abbreviations permitted

Include source document number, — Explained on page 172.

Simple brief explanations

Figure 7.2   A page from a two-column general journal.

Recording the Date

The following is the customary procedure for recording the date in the date column of a journal.

1. The year is entered in small figures on the first line of each page. The year is not repeated for each entry. A new year is entered at the point on the page where it occurs.
2. The month is entered on the first line of each page. The month is not repeated for each entry. A new month is entered at the point where it occurs.
3. The day is entered on the first line of each journal entry. The day is repeated no matter how many transactions occur on any given day.

Steps in Recording a Journal Entry

There are four steps in recording a general journal entry. These are as follows:

1. Enter the date in the date column.

DATE	PARTICULARS	P.R.	DEBIT	CREDIT
19—				
12				

GENERAL JOURNAL — PAGE 16

2. Enter the names of the accounts to be debited at the left margin of the Particulars column. Enter the debit amounts in the Debit money column.

12	Equipment		900—	
	Supplies		400—	

3. Enter the names of the accounts to be credited. They are indented about 2.5 cm in the Particulars column. Enter the credit amounts in the Credit column.

12	Equipment		900—	
	Supplies		400—	
	Accs Payl—Olivetti			1100—
	Bank			200—

4. Write a brief explanation for the entry beginning at the left margin of the Particulars column on the line beneath the last credit item.

12	Equipment		900—	
	Supplies		400—	
	Accs Payl—Olivetti			1100—
	Bank			200—
	IBM typewriter; ribbons and stationery; cheque #41.			

Usefulness of the General Journal

The chief purpose of the general journal is to provide a continuous record of the accounting entries in the order in which they occur. But this is not its only use.

The accounting clerk works out the accounting entries from the source documents and records them in the journal. The clerk can then see the work in an organized way. This is the time to check that each entry balances, and generally that everything is in order. A job done well at this stage reduces errors and prevents problems from occurring later.

The journal is also useful for reference purposes. It is often necessary to refer back to the journal to verify a transaction. This is particularly the case when balancing the ledger.

The Opening Entry

Every accounting entry is recorded first in the journal. This is done even for the very first accounting entry, the one that sets up the financial position from a balance sheet. The journal entry that starts the books off, or "opens" them, is known as the **opening entry**.

The opening entry for Shirley Cassar's photography business can be seen in Figure 7.3. The figures for this accounting entry came from a balance sheet prepared at the time.

Oct. 30	Bank	1400 —	
	Supplies	2425 —	
	Equipment	8715 —	
	Automobile	19 550 —	
	Shirley Cassar, Capital		32 090 —
	Opening financial position		
	of Shirley Cassar		

Figure 7.3 The opening entry for a small business.

Section Review Questions

1. Explain what is meant by "each accounting entry is split up when it is recorded in the ledger."
2. Why is a second book, the journal, necessary in accounting?
3. Define "journal."
4. Give another name for "journal entry."
5. What is meant by "journalizing"?
6. Why is a journal known as a "book of original entry"?
7. Describe the appearance of a two-column general journal.
8. What is another name for "posting reference"?
9. In the two-column general journal, how do you tell where one journal entry ends and another one begins?
10. Are abbreviations permitted in the journal?

11. Answer the following questions about the two-column general journal:
    a. Where is the year always entered?
    b. When do you re-enter the year?
    c. Where is the month always entered?
    d. When do you re-enter the month?
    e. What is the rule for recording the day of a transaction?
12. Which accounts are recorded first when recording a journal entry?
13. Which accounts are indented when recording a journal entry?
14. Describe how explanations are recorded in the journal.
15. Describe what is meant by the opening entry.
16. What else does the journal provide besides a daily list of accounting entries?

Section Exercises

1. **Workbook Exercise:** Journalizing accounting entries from source documents.

2. Described below are source documents for Wayne Siebert, a professional photographer in Kelowna, B.C. Journalize the accounting entries for these transactions in a two-column general journal using the following accounts:

   Accounts—Bank
   Accounts Receivable—various debtors
   Photo Supplies
   Accounts Payable—various creditors
   Sales Tax Payable
   W. Seibert, Capital
   W. Seibert, Drawings
   Fees Earned
   Automobile Expense
   Bank Charges

   Transactions

   November
   4   *Sales Invoice*
       —No. 571 for $275 plus sales tax of $13.75 to R. Chevrier for photo services completed on account.
   6   *Purchase Invoice*
       —Received from Black's Photo in the amount of $265 for photo supplies received in good condition.
   9   *Purchase Invoice*
       —Received from Texaco Oil in the amount of $165 for gasoline used in the company car.
   10 *Cheque Copy*
       —No. 652 for $325 issued to the owner for his personal use.
   12 *Cash Sales Slip*
       —No. 214 for $145 plus sales tax of $7.25 for photography work performed for cash.

15 *Bank Debit Memo*
   —From Commercial Bank in the amount of $35.50 for bank service charges.
20 *Memorandum*
   —From the owner stating that he had taken $75 of photo supplies for his personal work at home.
22 *Cash Receipt*
   —Received $412 from H. Walker on account.
25 *Cheque Copy*
   —No. 653 paying for the supplies purchased above on November 6.
28 *Purchase Invoice*
   —Received from Oakley Motors in the amount of $750 for body repairs done on the business automobile.

3. **The general journal shown below contains a number of errors. Study the given journal and prepare a list describing these errors.**

DATE	PARTICULARS	P.R.	DEBIT	CREDIT
Feb 3	Bank		200-	
	Account Receivable – P. Simms			200-
	Partial payment from customer.			
Feb 7	Bank			50-
	Supplies		50-	
	Pencils, pens and papers purchased from Reingolds.			
Feb 10	Bank		90-	
	M. Farris, Capital		60-	
	Equipment			250-
	Sold equipment ($250) for $90 cash.			
Feb 22	Account Payable – General Finance		315-	
Feb 22	Bank			315-
	Account Receivable – N. Proulx		125-	
	M. Farris, Capital			125-
	Service performed for cash.			
Mar 3	Supplies			20-
	Accounts Payable – Reingolds		20-	
	Purchased folders on credit.			

4. **A number of journal entries are shown below without dates or explanations. These entries are for a beauty shop operated by Kelly Marshall in Kapuskasing, Ont.**

   Examine these entries and i) prepare a list of transactions that could have caused them; ii) indicate the source document for each transaction.

Bank	25	
Kelly Marshall, Capital		25
Supplies	30	
Bank		30
Kelly Marshall, Capital	200	
Bank		200
Jan Vasko—Account receivable	20	
Kelly Marshall, Capital		20
Supplies	70	
Fain Bros.—Account payable		70

5. **Rob Czank begins business with the following assets and liabilities: Cash, $1 200; Office Equipment, $3 900; Land, $42 500; Building, $85 900; Account Payable to Diamond Equipment, $350; Mortgage on Building, $32 560.**

   After calculating the equity figure, record the opening entry for Rob Czank on August 1, 19-- in a two-column general journal.

7.3 Posting

You have now been introduced to the journal and the ledger, the two important books in the accounting process. You are now ready to learn to use these books "formally," just as accountants do.

The Balance Column Account

So far we have only considered the simple two-sided ledger account, showing debits on one side and credits on the other. However, a second style of ledger account, known as the balance column account, is actually more useful and convenient. The **balance column account** has three money columns, one for the debit amounts, one for the credit amounts, and one for the balance. It is the most commonly used account. The T-account and the balance column account are compared in Figure 7.4.

Bank

```
        5000  |   350
         700  |  1750
         200  |   960
         450  |
  (3290) 6350 |  3060
```

T-ACCOUNT

The journal page number is shown.

The type of balance is indicated.

ACCOUNT *Bank* NO. 101

DATE		PARTICULARS	P.R.	DEBIT	CREDIT	DR.CR.	BALANCE
19— July	14	The date of each entry is shown.	J4	5000 —		DR	5000 —
	17		J4	700 —		DR	5700 —
	18	Particulars column not used until later on.	J5		350 —	DR	5350 —
	18		J5		1750 —	DR	3600 —
	21		J6	200 —		DR	3800 —
	23	Each entry has its own line.	J7	450 —		DR	4250 —
	24		J7		960 —	DR	3290 —

STANDARD ACCOUNT

Debit and credit columns form the core of the account.

The balance may be shown after each entry.

Figure 7.4 Comparison of entries made in a T-account (top) and in a standard balance column account.

Notes:
1. The word "entry" has different meanings in accounting. It may mean the full accounting entry with which you are already familiar. Or, as is intended in this instance, it may mean just one part of the full accounting entry.
2. An error commonly made by beginners is to use the DR/CR column to show whether an entry was made in the debit column or the credit column. There is no need to show this because the kind of entry made can be seen at a glance.

   The purpose of the DR/CR column is to show the kind of balance that the account has. In Figure 7.4, you can see that the Bank account has a Debit balance of $3 290.

Opening an Account

An accounting entry often affects an item for which there is no account in the ledger. When this happens, it is necessary to open an account. **Opening an account** means to prepare an account page and to place it in its proper place in the ledger.

To open an account, proceed as follows:

1. Obtain an unused account page.
2. Write the name for the new account at the top of the page. The account name is known as the **account title**.
3. Write in the account number.
4. Insert the new account in its proper place in the ledger.

Formal Posting

In the previous section you learned that each accounting entry is first recorded in the journal. It is then transferred, or "posted," to the ledger. **Posting** is the process of transferring information from the journal to the ledger. Every individual amount recorded in the journal must be posted separately. The six-step procedure for posting is described in the next section, and illustrated in Figure 7.5.

Six Steps in Posting

For each individual amount entered in the journal, you must perform the following six steps. Five of these steps are performed in the ledger; one of the steps is performed in the journal.

In the Ledger

1. Turn to the proper account in the ledger.
2. Record the date. Use the next unused line in the account.
3. Record the page number of the journal (where the transaction is journalized) into the (P.R.) posting reference column of the account. Prefix this number with the letter J; for example, J14. As you will see later, several journals are used in accounting. Therefore, you must use a code to tell you which journal is being referred to.
4. Record the amount. Debit amounts are entered in the debit columns of the accounts. Credit amounts are entered in the credit columns of the accounts.
5. Calculate and enter the new account balance in the balance column. Indicate whether it is a debit or a credit balance.

In the Journal

6. Record the account number to which the posting was made. Enter this in the posting reference column on the same line as the amount being posted.

Section 7.3   **181**

GENERAL JOURNAL

Date	Particulars	P.R.	Debit	Credit
19— Aug 14	Office Furniture	110	425 —	
	Bank	101		150 —
	Acc. Payable – Office Supply	212		275 —

(The journal entry being posted)

LEDGER ACCOUNTS

Bank   No. 101

Date	Particulars	P.R.	Debit	Credit	DR. CR.	Balance
19— Aug 3	Forwarded	—			Dr	704 15
9		J13	502 —		Dr	1206 15
14		J14		150 —	Dr	1056 15

Office Furniture   No. 110

Date	Particulars	P.R.	Debit	Credit	DR. CR.	Balance
19— Feb 2		J6	507 06		Dr	507 06
Apr 16		J9	370 —		Dr	877 06
Aug 14		J14	425 —		Dr	1302 16

Accounts Payable – Office Supply   No. 212

Date	Particulars	P.R.	Debit	Credit	DR. CR.	Balance
19— May 3		J10		386 —	Cr	386 —
June 15		J10	386 —			0
Aug 14		J14		275 —	Cr	275 —

(The ledger accounts affected)

Figure 7.5 Six steps in the formal posting of a journal entry.

Cross-Referencing

Steps 3 and 6 of the foregoing posting sequence perform what is known as cross referencing. Expressed in simple terms, **cross-referencing** is the recording of the journal page number in the account, and the recording of the account number in the journal. Cross-referencing is illustrated in Figure 7.6.

GENERAL JOURNAL				Page 37
DATE	PARTICULARS	PR	DEBIT	CREDIT
19— Nov. 18	Buildings	120	2 475 —	
	P. Sloan, Capital	301	300 —	
	Bank			2 775 —
	Purchase of materials to add to buildings; some materials taken by owner.			

The fact that no number has been recorded here means that the entry has not yet been posted.

Figure 7.6 Cross-referencing.

Section 7.3

LEDGER ACCOUNTS

Bank — No. 101

DATE	PARTICULARS	PR	DEBIT	CREDIT	Dr/Cr	BALANCE
19- Nov. 15	Forwarded	—			Dr	3 027 50
17		J36	412 90		Dr	3 440 40

Buildings — No. 120

DATE	PARTICULARS	PR	DEBIT	CREDIT	Dr/Cr	BALANCE
19- Jan. 3		J30	18 432 —		Dr	18 432 —
Mar. 10		J32	2 170 —		Dr	20 602 —
Nov. 18		J37	2 475 —		Dr	23 077 —

P. Sloan, Capital — No. 301

DATE	PARTICULARS	PR	DEBIT	CREDIT	Dr/Cr	BALANCE
19- Nov. 10	Forwarded	—			Cr	20 250 —
15		J34	250 —		Cr	20 000 —
18		J37	300 —		Cr	19 700 —

Correcting Errors in the Books

Over the years professional accountants have made it a rule not to erase. Erasures in the books might arouse the suspicions of the auditors, the official examiners of the books and records. Therefore, other methods are used for making corrections.

Errors Found Immediately

It is simple to correct an error that is found right away. Simply stroke neatly through the incorrect figures or letters and write in the correct ones immediately above. Figures 7.7 and 7.8 show this type of correction. An accounting clerk should learn to write small so that errors can be corrected easily.

GENERAL JOURNAL				
Date	Particulars	P.R.	Debit	Credit
Jun 16	Cash		50 —	
	~~B. Martin~~ A. Ascot			50 —
	Payment of account balance			

Figure 7.7 Correcting a name in the journal.

ACCOUNT						No. 5
Date	Particulars	P.R.	Debit	Credit	DR. CR.	Balance
19— Feb 5		J3	64 10		Dr	64 10
8		J6	131 75 ~~141 85~~		Dr	195 85 ~~205 95~~

Figure 7.8 Correcting an amount in an account.

Errors Found Later

The accounting department may not learn of an error until after quite some time has passed. In many cases, the error can be corrected by means of an accounting entry. For example, consider the following situation:

On July 5, an accounting clerk noticed that an invoice for $752 was debited to the wrong account. The invoice was clearly for supplies but had been debited to the Equipment account. The error was made on January 17, almost six months earlier.

The two accounts involved appear as shown in Figure 7.9:

Supplies

Date	Partcs	Dr	Cr	Balance
Jan 1	Forwarded			150- Dr
Feb 12		370-		520- Dr
20		110-		630- Dr
Mar 30		50-		680- Dr
Apr 19		225-		905- Dr
May 12		70-		975- Dr
28		125-		1100- Dr
Jun 25		45-		1145- Dr

Equipment

Date	Partcs	Dr	Cr	Balance
Jan 1	Forwarded			7350- Dr
Jan 17		752-		8102- Dr
Jun 5		1100-		9202- Dr

Figure 7.9 The two accounts affected by an incorrect posting.

The best way to correct an error of this type is with a correcting journal entry. A **correcting journal entry** is an accounting entry that rectifies the effect of an error. In the above case, the entry is needed to cancel the $752 in the Equipment account and set it up in the Supplies account. This journal entry is:

	DR	CR
Supplies	$752.00	
Equipment		$752.00
To correct posting error made on January 17th.		

This method makes it unnecessary to squeeze $752 in the Supplies account, to stroke through and change several dollar amounts, and to change several trial balances.

After correction, the two accounts appear as shown in Figure 7.10.

Supplies

Date	Partcs	Dr	Cr	Balance
Jan 1	Forwarded			150- Dr
Feb 12		370-		520- Dr
20		110-		630- Dr
Mar 30		50-		680- Dr
Apr 19		225-		905- Dr
May 12		70-		975- Dr
28		125-		1100- Dr
Jun 25		45-		1145- Dr
Jul 5		752-		1897- Dr

Equipment

Date	Partcs	Dr	Cr	Balance
Jan 1	Forwarded			7350- Dr
Jan 17		752-		8102- Dr
Jun 5		1100-		9202- Dr
Jul 5			752-	8450- Dr

Figure 7.10 The two accounts after correction.

Forwarding Procedure

When an account page is full, the account must be continued on a new page. The information on the last line of the completed page is forwarded to a new page. **Forwarding** is the process of continuing an account or journal on a new page by carrying forward all relevant information from the completed page. The process of forwarding is illustrated in Figure 7.11.

ACCOUNT J. J. Barker					No. 4	
DATE	PARTICULARS	PR	DEBIT	CREDIT	Dr/Cr	BALANCE
19— Feb 7		J1	150 62		Dr	150 62
9		J3	374 50		Dr	525 12
11		J5		150 62	Dr	374 50
12		J5	216 51		Dr	591 01
16		J8	75 62		Dr	666 63
18		J9		374 50	Dr	292 13
19		J9	583 62		Dr	875 75
21 Forwarded		J10		292 13	Dr	583 62

ACCOUNT J. J. Barker					No. 4	
DATE	PARTICULARS	PR	DEBIT	CREDIT	Dr/Cr	BALANCE
19— Feb 21 Forwarded					Dr	583 62

Figure 7.11 The finished account page after being forwarded (a.) and the new account page with the balance brought forward (b.).

The Accounting Cycle

The total set of accounting procedures that must be carried out during each fiscal period is known as the "accounting cycle." You first encountered the accounting cycle in Chapter 1. The steps in the accounting cycle are introduced gradually throughout the text. Figure 7.12 shows the four steps in the accounting cycle that have been studied so far.

Transactions occur. Source documents. → Accounting entries recorded in journal. → Journal entries posted to the ledger accounts. → Ledger balanced by means of trial balance. → More to come

Figure 7.12 The first four steps in the accounting cycle.

Section Review Questions

1. Name the two important books in the accounting process.
2. Name the simple account that shows debit amounts on one side and credit amounts on the other.
3. Name the style of account used most commonly.
4. Why is this style of account most useful?
5. Describe the steps in opening an account.
6. Where are accounting entries first recorded?
7. What is "posting"?
8. Give the five steps in posting that are performed in the ledger.
9. Give the one step in posting that is performed in the journal.
10. Describe "cross-referencing."
11. Describe the procedure for making a simple correction in the accounts or journal.
12. Describe the procedure for making a correction of an error found after some time has passed.
13. What is "forwarding"?
14. Name the first four steps in the accounting cycle.

Section Exercises

1. The partially completed account shown below also appears in your workbook. Complete the balance column by calculating and entering the balance after each entry. Be sure to indicate each time whether the balance is debit or credit.

188   Chapter 7

DEBIT	CREDIT	Dr Cr	BALANCE
			No. 21
1000 -			
	300 -		
	235 -		
100 -			
	600 -		
	215 -		
700 -			
120 -			
	302 -		
	417 -		
	914 -		
1500 -			

2. **Workbook Exercise: Posting transactions.**

3. **Workbook Exercise: Posting transactions.**

4. **Workbook Exercise: Forwarding an account balance.**

7.4 Trial Balance Out of Balance

As you have already learned, sometimes the trial balance does not balance. It is your job as bookkeeper or accountant to find and correct the errors. Skill in finding errors is important to an accountant.

Figure 7.13 shows the five steps to be followed when a trial balance does not balance. Often, the error or errors will be detected before all the steps are carried out. However, if you finish the five steps and the account still does not balance, then you did not do them correctly. You will have to go through the sequence again, this time working with more care.

Section 7.4   **189**

BALANCING THE GENERAL LEDGER

Figure 7.13 Flowchart of the procedure for balancing the general ledger.

Sequence of Balancing Steps

1. Re-add trial balance columns.
2. Check transfer of account balances from ledger to trial balance.
3. Re-add accounts from point of previous balance. Double-check account indicator (i.e. DR or CR).
4. Check postings from point of previous balance.
   Watch for:
   - incorrect amounts,
   - amounts not posted,
   - amounts posted twice,
   - amounts posted in wrong column.
5. Check to see that each individual journal entry balances (from point of previous balance).

Short Cuts in Detecting a Single Error

It may take a lot of time to go through the routine described in Figure 7.13. Experienced accountants try to avoid this whenever they can. They usually try one of four quick tests first.

The initial step in any of the quick tests is to calculate by how much the trial balance is out. Then any of the following tests may be applied:

1. An error in addition has likely been made if the trial balance difference is a multiple of ten such as ten cents, one dollar, and so on. Therefore, steps 1 and 3 of the error routine should be performed first.

2. Scrutinize both the ledger and the journal looking for any amount that is equal to the trial balance difference. Whenever you find such an amount, verify it to make sure that it has been handled correctly.

3. If the trial balance difference is an even amount, divide it by two. Then search (1) the trial balance, and (2) the ledger accounts for this amount. If an equivalent amount is found, check it carefully. In particular, look to see if a debit amount has been posted or transferred as a credit, or vice versa. An error of this type always produces a trial balance difference equal to twice the amount of the error.

   For example, consider the simplified trial balance shown below. It contains a single error. The $30 item listed as a credit should have been listed as a debit.

   ```
              TRIAL BALANCE
              110
               40
                              30 ←——— Error
                              55
                             200
               50
               25
              ___            ___
              225            285
                              ↑
                              └─── Trial balance difference $60
   ```

   Notice that the difference between the totals is $60, twice the amount of the error.

4. Divide the trial balance difference by 9. If it divides evenly, it is likely that a transposition error has occurred. A **transposition error** is a mistake caused by the interchanging of digits when transferring figures from one place to another. A transposition error has occurred when, for example, $35.60 is posted as $36.50, or when $1 200 is transferred as $120. Such errors always produce a trial balance difference that is exactly divisible by 9. When this happens, steps 2 and 4 of the checking sequence should be performed first.

Section Review Questions

1. Why is skill in locating errors important to an accountant?
2. Give the five-step procedure to be followed when a trial balance does not balance.
3. What has to be done if the five-step procedure is completed, but the ledger is still not balanced?
4. What must be done before applying any of the short-cut tests?
5. What kind of error does a trial balance difference of $10 suggest?
6. In regard to the error in question **5** above, what steps would be followed first?
7. If the trial balance difference is not an even amount, which of the short-cut tests can be eliminated?
8. Explain what happens mathematically when an amount is posted to the wrong side of an account.
9. What is a transposition error?

Section Exercises

1. **Workbook Exercise:** Locate and correct errors in a given journal, ledger, and trial balance.

2. **Workbook Exercise:** Locate and correct errors in a given journal, ledger, and trial balance.

3. The four mini-exercises below will give you practice at using the short-cut techniques for locating errors when a trial balance does not balance. Each exercise has one error in it which you are to find. For each mini-exercise, go through the sequence of steps outlined below. Once you locate the error you need not continue with the subsequent steps.

   Short-Cut Steps to Locating an Error
   a. Write down the trial balance difference.
   b. Is it a round amount like $1, or $10, or $100? If no, go to step **c**. If yes, then re-add the trial balance and re-add the accounts in the ledger.
   c. Search the journal, ledger, and trial balance for an entry equal to the trial balance difference. Check any such entries to ensure that a posting was not missed or posted twice, or an account balance was not missed or listed twice.
   d. Does the trial balance difference figure divide evenly by 9? If no, go to step **e**. If yes, check for a transposition error in transferring account balances onto the trial balance or in posting from the journal to the ledger.
   e. Is the trial balance difference an even amount? If yes, divide the amount by two and write down the result. Then, search the records for this amount. Check any entry for this amount to ensure that the entry was not posted to the wrong side of an account, or an account balance was not listed on the wrong side of the trial balance.

Chapter 7

1. Why does it not balance?

JOURNAL

PARTICULARS	DR	CR
Bank	4500	
Equipment	3600	
Capital		8100
Supplies	73	
Accounts Payable		73
Expense	47	
Bank		47
Bank	195	
Revenue		195
Drawings	100	
Bank		100
Accounts Receivable	63	
Revenue		63
Supplies	38	
Bank		38

LEDGER

Bank
4500	47
195	100
	38
(4510) 4695	185

Accounts Receivable
| 63 | |

Supplies
73	
38	
111	

Equipment
| 3600 | |

Accounts Payable
| | 73 |

Capital
| | 8100 |

Drawings
| 100 | |

Revenue
	159
	63
	222

Expense
| 47 | |

TRIAL BALANCE

DR	CR
4510	73
63	8100
111	222
3600	
100	
47	
8431	8395

2. Why does it not balance?

JOURNAL

PARTICULARS	DR	CR
Bank	3 000	
Equipment	2 000	
Capital		5 000
Supplies	490	
Bank		490
Accounts Receivable	155	
Revenue		155
Expense	56	
Bank		56
Expense	72	
Accounts Payable		72
Bank	312	
Revenue		312
Drawings	97	
Bank		97

LEDGER

Bank
3 000	490
312	56
	97
(2669) 3 312	643

Accounts Receivable
| 155 | |

Supplies
| 490 | |

Equipment
| 2 000 | |

Accounts Payable
| | 72 |

Capital
| | 5 000 |

Drawings
| 97 | |

Revenue
	155
	312
	467

Expense
| 56 | |

TRIAL BALANCE

DR	CR
2669	72
155	5000
490	467
2000	
97	
56	
5467	5539

Chapter 7

3. Why does it not balance?

JOURNAL

PARTICULARS	DR	CR
Bank	2 500	
Equipment	7 000	
Capital		9 500
Accounts Receivable	371	
Revenue		371
Bank	269	
Revenue		269
Supplies	53	
Accounts Payable		53
Drawings	127	
Bank		127
Expense	86	
Bank		86
Expense	49	
Accounts Payable		49

LEDGER

Bank	
2 500	127
269	86
(2 556) 2 769	213

Supplies	
53	

Accounts Payable	
	53
	49
	102

Drawings	
127	

Expense	
86	
49	
135	

Accounts Receivable	
371	

Equipment	
7000	

Capital	
	9 500

Revenue	
	371
	269
	540

TRIAL BALANCE

DR	CR
2556	102
371	9500
53	540
7000	
127	
135	
10242	10142

Section 7.4

4. Why does it not balance?

JOURNAL

PARTICULARS	DR	CR
Bank	4 000	
Equipment	3 000	
Capital		7 000
Supplies	216	
Accounts Payable		216
Accounts Receivable	321	
Revenue		321
Expense	73	
Bank		73
Expense	34	
Accounts Payable		34
Drawings	41	
Bank		41
Bank	150	
Accounts Receivable		150

LEDGER

Bank
4000	73
150	41
(4036) 4150	114

Accounts Receivable
| 321 | 150 |
| (171) | |

Supplies
| 216 | |

Equipment
| 3000 | |

Accounts Payable
	216
	34
	250

Capital
| | 7000 |

Drawings
| 41 | |

Revenue
| | 321 |

Expense
73	
34	
107	

TRIAL BALANCE

DR	CR
4036	250
171	7000
216	41
3000	321
107	
7530	7612

7.5 Computerized Accounting: The Accounting Package—Data Entry

The Accounting Package—Data Entry

Input The accounting staff is responsible for analyzing the source documents and working out the accounting entries. The entry of data into the computer is done by account numbers. Therefore, the job is performed by someone who is thoroughly familiar with the chart of accounts. The computer has the chart of accounts stored in its memory and can translate any account number into an account name immediately.

Before they are entered into the computer, business transactions are written up on a data input form like the one shown in Figure 7.14.

TRANSACTION NUMBER	DATE (M,D)	DEBIT NUMBER	DEBIT AMOUNT	CREDIT NUMBER	CREDIT AMOUNT	EXPLANATION CODE
29	4,28	110	80 25	501	75 -	
				220	5 25	16
30	4,28	100	500 -	120	500 -	5
31	4,28	530	40 -	100	40 -	17

DATA INPUT FORM FOR April 28 (DAY)   PAGE 46

Figure 7.14 A coding sheet for recording accounting entries.

A data entry clerk keys in the data from the data input form using an "input" device. The most common input device is the keyboard. Before this can be done, however, the accounting software must be "loaded and running."

In the previous chapter you saw a menu illustrated in Figure 6.12. Option B of this menu sets up the computer for processing transactions and will display a series of prompts on the screen to assist the user.

The sequence of prompts will be approximately as described below. Each rectangle (-▢-) indicates a request for specific information to be entered at that point.

Each time information is keyed in, the "return" or "enter" key is pressed. Each "return" moves the flashing "cursor" to the next screen location for receiving data.

1. Enter the transaction date (m,d) -▢-

2. Enter ACCOUNT DEBITED ▢   **Enter AMOUNT DEBITED** ▢

> Step 2 will be repeated until the return is pressed without any data entered. This allows for more than one debit entry. When a return without data is made, the computer moves to step 3.

3. Enter ACCOUNT CREDITED ▢   **Enter AMOUNT CREDITED** ▢

> Step 3 will also be repeated until the return is pressed without data. This allows for more than one credit entry. A return without data in step 3 indicates that all debits and credits are entered. At this time the computer checks the mathematical equality of debits and credits. If the debits do not equal the credits, an error message is displayed. This gives the data entry clerk an opportunity to make corrections at step 4.

4. Enter explanation code number ▢

> The explanation codes are picked up from a list provided in the manual by the program designer. The entry of the explanation code indicates the completion of the transaction.

5. If accounting entry is correct, press RETURN key ▢

    If you wish to REDO this transaction, press R ▢

> The pressing of the R key at this point will abort the data entered on the screen and return the user to step 1. The pressing of the return key causes the computer to take the transaction data into its memory for further processing.

Chapter 7

6. More transactions (Y/N)?

> A "Y" response at step 6 causes the computer to return to step 1 for another transaction. An "N" response causes the computer to return to the sub-menu. The user can then choose another option or quit processing.

All seven of the above steps can be seen on the screen just before step 6 is completed. At that time the display on the screen will be like that shown in Figure 7.15.

```
Enter the transaction date (m,d)   4,1
Enter ACCOUNT DEBITED    1 BANK        Enter AMOUNT DEBITED    500
Enter ACCOUNT DEBITED
Enter ACCOUNT CREDITED   63 CAPITAL    Enter AMOUNT CREDITED   500
Enter ACCOUNT CREDITED
Enter explanation code number    1  Opening entry
More transactions (Y/N)?
```

Figure 7.15   Prompting messages on the computer screen.

In a computerized accounting environment, the entering of correct data into the system is clearly a very important function. Keep in mind, however, that the computer is only as good as the people preparing and entering the transaction data. If the data is incorrect, the computer will produce incorrect results. This is referred to as "Garbage In, Garbage Out." Clearly, the data entry clerks have important responsibilities.

Output   Once the data is entered, the power of the computer can be utilized. The computer can perform routine bookkeeping tasks quickly and flawlessly. A variety of bookkeeping records, reports, and statements are immediately available through the simple selection of an option from a menu.

Computer Review Questions

1. The person preparing transactions for entry into the computer must be thoroughly familiar with the chart of accounts. Why?
2. What is the first step in preparing transactions for entry into the computer?
3. Name one "input" device.
4. What must be done to the computer before the transaction can be entered?
5. How does the computer assist the person entering transaction details?
6. Entering debit accounts and amounts is done in step 2 of the textbook sequence. What does the user do to move ahead to step 3?
7. At what point does the computer check the equality of debits and credits?
8. If the debits do not equal the credits, what does the computer do?
9. What tells the computer that the transaction is completely entered?
10. Explain the meaning of "Garbage In, Garbage Out."
11. Name five records or reports that can be produced after the transactions are entered.

Computer Exercise

Any textbook exercise involving journalizing, posting, balancing, and so on can be done using an accounting package and a compatible computer system. When doing such exercises, remember two things:

1. The account numbers in the textbook exercise must be changed to agree with the numbering system used in the software. Get the numbers from the manual. It is easy to do. Your teacher will help you.
2. The transaction explanations must be entered by code. You will have to obtain the list from the manual.

1. Do exercise 7 (page 202) of this chapter on the computer. Compare the results with your handwritten solution. Use one account for all accounts receivable and one account for all accounts payable.

CHAPTER HIGHLIGHTS

Now that you have completed Chapter 7, you should:

1. know, in general, the difference between the work done by a bookkeeper and that done by an accountant;
2. understand why manual bookkeeping methods are still used;
3. be able to journalize, post, and balance correctly;
4. be able to work out an "opening entry" from a balance sheet and to "open" an account;
5. understand why both a journal and a ledger are used in the accounting process;
6. be able to use a balance column account correctly and with ease;
7. understand the purpose of cross-referencing;

8. know how to forward the balance of an account to a new page;
9. know the first four steps in the accounting cycle;
10. know how to make corrections in the journal and in the accounts, and how to make correcting journal entries;
11. be able to use correctly the short cuts in locating trial balance errors.

ACCOUNTING TERMS

account title
balance column account
book of original entry
correcting journal entry
cross-referencing
forwarding
journal

journal entry
journalizing
opening an account
opening entry
posting
transposition error
two-column general journal

CHAPTER EXERCISES

Using Your Knowledge

1. Indicate whether each of the following statements is true or false by placing a "T" or an "F" in the space indicated in your workbook. Explain the reason for each "F" response in the space provided.

    1. Bookkeeping and accounting mean the same thing.
    2. The "books of account" are the books that accountants study from.
    3. Computers have not taken over the bookkeeping function entirely. Therefore, there is still a good reason for knowing the handwritten method.
    4. A journal is like a diary of accounting entries.
    5. When a bookkeeper thinks of an accounting entry, he thinks "debit" first.
    6. The chief advantage of the three-column account is that there is room for the account balance.
    7. Both sides of an account page (front and back) are used for the same item, for example, Bank.
    8. Entering the journal page number in the account is the sixth step in the posting process.
    9. The step described in **8** above is performed in the journal.
    10. The process of setting up an account is known as "forwarding."
    11. The fourth step in the accounting cycle, as we know it, is the taking off of a trial balance.
    12. It is not possible for the ledger to be out of balance and also to be correct.
    13. If the trial balance difference is an even amount, the error could not be a transposition error.

14. If the trial balance difference is zero, the ledger is in balance.
15. Posting a debit item incorrectly as a credit produces a trial balance credit total that is smaller than the debit total by twice the amount of the error.
16. Only very rarely does a transaction affect only one account.
17. Ledger accounts are arranged alphabetically in order to find them more easily.
18. The presence of the account number in the journal indicates that the posting of an item has been completed.

2. Complete the chart in the workbook about the effect of errors on a trial balance.

Error Situations	Trial Balance Will Not Balance — Debits greater than Credits by ($$)	Trial Balance Will Not Balance — Credits greater than Debits by ($$)	Trial balance will balance but will not be correct
1. An entire journal entry is posted as $400 instead of $100.			
2. A debit of $200 is posted twice.			
3. A debit of $150 is posted as a credit.			
4. The Bank account is over-added by $80.			
5. The Drawings account balance of $5 500 is missed when preparing the trial balance.			
6. The Revenue account balance of $72 000 is listed on the trial balance as a debit.			
7. An entire general journal entry for $325 is not posted.			
8. An entire general journal entry for $50 is posted in reverse.			
9. A $40 debit is not posted.			
10. A $500 credit is posted as $50.			
11. A debit of $60 to Bank was posted to a customer's account.			
12. A $40 debit is posted as $400.			

3. An accounting clerk has prepared his trial balance as of June 30, 19--, and determines that total debits equal total credits. He breathes a sigh of relief and informs his boss that his ledger is in balance and that therefore the accounts are correct. His boss, a chartered accountant, tells him that this is not necessarily the case. She asks him to prepare a list of all the possible errors that could occur and yet not cause the trial balance to be out of balance.

   Prepare this list as if you were the accounting clerk.

4. An employee working on his first trial balance discovers that the Furniture and Equipment account has a credit balance of $5 000 and a customer's account has a credit balance of $200. Has the accountant made a mistake in his records or is this situation possible? Explain.

5. You have been employed by Wilson Building Supplies as an accounting clerk. Your main duty is to record journal entries daily and post to the general ledger. Your procedure in posting is to post the entries by account order. For example, you first go through all your journal entries and post all Bank entries. You then proceed to the second account, and so on. Explain the advantage of this method.

6. Dean Perry posts from the journal to the ledger at the end of each week. Because he prepares a balance sheet once a year, he believes it is necessary to prepare a trial balance only once a year. What are the disadvantages of taking a trial balance only once a year?

Comprehensive Exercise

7. The accounts required for this exercise are shown in the chart of accounts below. If you are not using the workbook for this exercise, allow 18 lines for the Bank account.

   GENERAL ENGINEERING
   CHART OF ACCOUNTS

101 Bank	301 Pat Schelling, Capital
111 A/R L. Pero	302 Pat Schelling, Drawings
113 A/R K. Puna	401 Service Revenue
115 A/R Spectrum Co.	505 Automobiles Expense
117 A/R W.J. Thomson	510 Bank Charges
120 Supplies	515 General Expense
125 Equipment	520 Rent Expense
130 Automobiles	525 Telephone Expense
201 Bank Loan	530 Wages Expense
211 A/P Imperial Garage	
213 A/P Home Hardware	
220 Sales Tax Payable	

Pat Schelling, a millwright, began a business called General Engineering. His beginning financial position is shown in the following balance sheet:

GENERAL ENGINEERING
BALANCE SHEET
AUGUST 31, 19--

Assets		Liabilities	
Bank	$ 2 000	Bank Loan	$20 000
Supplies	1 450		
Equipment	14 732	*Owner's Equity*	
Automobiles	28 957	P. Schelling, Capital	27 139
	$47 139		$47 139

1. **Journalize the opening entry and post it in the accounts.**
2. **Journalize and post the transactions for September shown below.**

Transactions

September

1   *Cheque Copy*
    —To Rosewell Investments in the amount of $900 for the rent for the month.

3   *Purchase Invoice*
    —From Home Hardware for $235 regarding supplies purchased on account.

5   *Sales Invoices*
    —To W.J. Thomson, $3 500 plus $245 sales tax, for services rendered on account.
    —To L. Pero, $2 000 plus $140 sales tax, for services rendered on account.

9   *Cash Sales Slip*
    —Sold a piece of equipment for $500 cash (assume no sales tax). This piece of equipment had originally cost $1 200 and was included in the Equipment account at that figure. (Note: although a sale has been made, this transaction does not affect the revenue account which is used only for the normal revenue of the business.)

10 *Sales Invoice*
    —To Spectrum Co., $800 plus $56 sales tax, for services rendered on account.

11 *Cheque Copy*
    —To the owner for his personal use, $500.

12 *Cheque Copy*
    —To Home Hardware on account, $235.

15 *Purchase Invoice*
    —Received from Imperial Garage charging for gasoline and oil used in the company automobiles, $342.

16 *Cheque Copy*
    —Issued to the Marketplace for the cash purchase of supplies, $165. A bill for the supplies was attached to the cheque copy.

18 *Cash Receipt*
    —Received a cheque from W.J. Thomson in full payment of the account balance.

18 *Cheque Copy*
—To the owner repaying him for out-of-pocket expenses: Postage, $32; Parking, $40; and Gas and Oil for business purposes, $78; total $150.

19 *Bank Debit Memo*
—Received a memorandum from the bank stating that $250 had been deducted from the business bank account for bank interest and bank service charges.

19 *Cheque Copy*
—To an employee for wages, $575.

19 *Sales Invoice*
—To K. Puna, $600 plus $42 sales tax, for services rendered on account.

22 *Memorandum*
—From the owner, stating that the bank had acted on his instructions to reduce the bank loan by $2 000.

24 *Cheque Copy*
—To Bell Telephone for $58 in payment of the telephone bill which was attached.

25 *Cash Receipt*
—Received a cheque from L. Pero for $1 000 on account.

26 *Sales Invoice*
—To W.J. Thomson, $400 plus $28 sales tax, for services rendered on account.

26 *Cheque Copy*
—To the owner for his personal use, $450.

29 *Memorandum*
—From the owner stating that: 1) he had paid $190 out of his own pocket for supplies used for business purposes, and, 2) his Drawings account is to be credited for the above amount.

30 *Cheque Copies*
—To an employee for wages, $570.
To Imperial Garage paying $342 on account.

30 *Purchase Invoice*
—From Imperial Garage charging for gasoline and oil used in the company automobiles, $312.

3. Balance the ledger by means of a trial balance.
4. Prepare an income statement for the month of September.
5. Prepare a simple balance sheet as at September 30. Remember that Equity = Assets − Liabilities.

For Further Thought

8. Briefly answer the following questions.

1. People who work in accounting departments usually describe themselves as "accountants" regardless of how well qualified they are. Give your opinion of this practice, with reasons.

2. Is the person in charge of the "payroll" of a large business an important employee? Explain.
3. Not long ago, you earned your accountant's qualification while employed by Superior Tire Manufacturing Company. You have recently taken a new position with the General Life Insurance Company. Your new position presents you with many difficulties directly related to the accounting function. Explain how this could be possible.
4. Name three different types of businesses that might use manual accounting methods.
5. The computer helps the accountant to journalize correctly. How does it do this?
6. Your teacher asks you to give the accounting entry for the purchase of supplies for cash. You begin your response, "Credit Bank and————." Your teacher stops you, believing that you are incorrect. Why would the teacher think so?
7. The accounts shown in your workbook are usually only a few lines long. In actual practice they are a full page long. When setting up your ledger, would you put one account on the front side of the page, and a different account on the back? Support your answer with good reasons.
8. When cross-referencing, some accountants just use check marks. What are the advantages and disadvantages of this technique?
9. An accounting error that is found after quite some time would be corrected by a journal entry. Why would this method be used instead of stroking out incorrect figures and writing in the correct ones?
10. A posting intended for Smith's account in the accounts receivable ledger was incorrectly made to Smythe's account. How would this error be detected?
11. Many students prefer to look at the solutions manual when they have an exercise that does not balance. Why is this a bad habit?
12. If your ledger does not balance by $5 and you have been unable to find the error after a four-day search, is it all right simply to change one of the accounts to force it into balance? Justify your opinion.

CASE STUDIES

Case 1   "To Fire or Not to Fire?"

Sylvia Lomax is a recently qualified chartered accountant. Her first position after graduation has been chief accountant with Mayflower Movers of Saskatoon, Saskatchewan. Shortly after taking this position, she placed an advertisement in local newspapers for an experienced bookkeeper. She hired Steve Sheba, one of several applicants for the job.

Steve's first task in his new position was to take off a trial balance. This task usually took about half a day to complete. Steve began work on the trial balance in the afternoon of his first day on the job. At the end of the day the ledger was not yet balanced. Again at the end of the second day the ledger was not yet balanced.

Sylvia waited patiently for two more days for the task to be completed. When it was still not done at the day's end, she became concerned about Steve Sheba.

Questions

1. Are all ledgers the same to a bookkeeper?
2. Has Sylvia allowed enough time for Steve to have balanced the ledger?
3. Is Sylvia right to be concerned about Steve?
4. Who is at fault here: Steve, or Sylvia? Give reasons for your choice.
5. What should Sylvia do to correct this situation?

Case 2 *Frustration for the Auditor*

Pera Painting, of Montréal, Québec, has applied to the bank for a loan. The bank manager has some doubts about this customer. The owner of Pera Painting is Warren Dean, an aggressive young man with a reputation in the community for fast living. The records that Dean has submitted to the bank indicate that the business is quite profitable. However, Dean's recordkeeping techniques are unusual, and the bank manager is unsure about their accuracy. The bank manager asks Noel Des Roches, a public accountant, to audit the books.

Noel soon learns about Dean's methods. While at high school, Dean took an accounting course. Now he does his own bookkeeping. In order to save time, Dean does not use a journal but records all accounting entries directly in the accounts. In addition, he keeps a file of all business papers. He claims that he has never had a problem in backchecking on a transaction.

Noel finds it a slow process trying to figure out which debits correspond to which credits in the ledger. He always seems to need Dean to explain things to him and Dean is usually out on a job. On the third day, Noel finds that he cannot proceed further until Dean explains some puzzling entries. Unfortunately, Dean is not available, having left for a week's skiing in Europe.

Shown below are the unverified entries in the accounts. (These are not all of the accounts and entries of the business, but only the ones that Noel has not yet figured out.)

Bank	Acc Rec'l – P. Watt	Materials	Property
5 000	5 000	5 000	5 000	10 000	
	10 000				

Automobile	Acc Pay'l – C.P. Paints	City Loan Co.	
10 000		5 000		5 000	

Questions

1. From an office clerk, Noel learns the following:
   a. Dean bought either a car or an investment property from a customer. There was some talk of offsetting the customer's account balance against the cost price.
   b. Dean has a habit of taking some of the files home with him. Since there are no files or banking records in the office pertaining to the car or the property, Noel assumes that Dean has taken them home. Because Dean lives alone, these records are unavailable.

   Prepare a list of transactions that would explain the entries in the accounts.

2. Eventually, Noel realizes that he can't finish the audit until Dean returns from Europe, and reports this to the bank manager. The bank manager asks Noel to write up a report for Dean. Noel is to explain the difficulties he has encountered with Dean's records and how these difficulties can be avoided by using conventional accounting procedures.

   Write this report as if you were Noel Des Roches.

Case 3 Is Bank Accounting Different?

Accounting is one of Susan Lott's favourite subjects at school. She often talks at the dinner table about what she has learned in class that day. Susan's brother Ed has no formal accounting training, but is a junior clerk at a bank and is involved in bank accounting. One evening, Ed questions Susan's explanation of debit and credit theory. Ed claims that a customer's bank account is increased by means of a credit and decreased by means of a debit, and he produces a bank statement to prove it. Susan admits that her brother is right, and the next day Susan brings the issue up in her accounting class. As she suspected, her accounting teacher has a logical explanation.

Question

1. Write out a brief explanation of this issue as if you were the teacher.

Case 4 Does Automated Accounting Use Standard Theory?

Andy, another relative of Susan Lott, works as a clerk in the data processing and computer centre of a large corporation in Montréal. He claims that accounting is no longer done as Susan is learning it. Susan has now spent several months studying accounting. She is upset at Andy's suggestion that she is learning outmoded techniques.

Questions

1. Is there a different theory of accounting when it is computerized?
2. Even though accounting systems may use different journals and ledgers, do they use different theories of accounting?

CAREER
Jane Clarke / Office Manager

When Jane Clarke was a student in Peterborough, Ontario, she never imagined that one day she might work in the field of accounting. Jane took a general course of study in high school and was not really sure what kind of a career she would pursue.

After Jane graduated from high school, she spent three years working as a dental assistant. She enjoyed the variety of responsibilities that this position offered. Essentially, Jane's job was to ensure that the dental practice ran as smoothly and efficiently as possible. She saw that dental equipment and supplies were well maintained. She also acted as receptionist, putting patients at ease in the waiting room. She kept the patients' files and the dentist's appointment book up-to-date, and sent out notices to remind patients of their appointments.

As her boss's confidence in her grew, Jane was also trusted with the bookkeeping. She kept a cash receipts book and a two-column general journal, sent out statements to the patients at the end of each month, and, as each cheque was received, matched it with the appropriate bill, endorsed it, and listed it for deposit. Jane made sure that every bill not paid in cash was listed as an account receivable. (Do you recall the revenue recognition accounting principle in Chapter 5?) She also kept track of accounts payable, checked purchase invoices against the goods that were received, and issued cheques periodically to creditors.

Jane performed various additional bookkeeping jobs for the dental practice. She purchased supplies and stamps and carefully kept track of these purchases in the journal. She made any necessary correcting entries in the two-column general journal. Each month, Jane also prepared the bank reconciliation statement.

However, Jane found that in order to advance in her career, she would have to increase her knowledge of accounting. After three years, she decided to leave work and return to school. She recently completed a three-year business administration diploma with majors in accounting and computer systems at Sir Sandford Fleming College in Peterborough.

Soon after completing her program, Jane became a junior accountant for Jacobi Television, a small chain of television and radio stores. Jane quickly impressed her employer with her maturity, responsibility, and initiative. She was promoted to office manager for the company, the position she holds now.

Jane believes that in the future, companies will need the skills of the management accountant. In particular, forecasting and budgeting skills will become more important. Because she wanted to improve her ability in these areas, Jane enrolled in the Certified General Accounting (CGA) program. She has now completed four of the five levels for her CGA designation. She looks forward to completing the program and becoming a full-fledged accountant.

As office manager, Jane supervises all office and clerical staff and acts as a liaison between employees and management. She advises the owner on financial matters and employee relations, and also performs a number of specific accounting functions.

Some of Jane's duties are related to accounts receivable. She keeps track of printouts of customers' accounts and makes sure that the computerized monthly statements to customers are sent out. Jane also works with accounts payable. She approves purchase invoices for payment and determines the accounts to be debited for these invoices, such as Supplies or Office Equipment, before they are input into the computer.

As Jacobi Television's office manager, Jane has complete control over the journal and the general ledger. Both the general ledger computer file and all back-up files are her responsibility. A printout of all transactions for each day is given to her to manually check the accuracy of the information.

Finally, Jane handles a number of banking duties. She approves cheques for deposit, endorses cheques and reconciles the bank statement each month.

Jane is delighted with her accounting career. She finds the variety stimulating and enjoys the responsibility. She looks forward with confidence to future success as an accountant.

Discussion

1. What duties did Jane perform in the dentist's office?
2. What source documents did Jane probably handle in this business?
3. What are the books of account handled by Jane in her position as office manager at Jacobi Television?
4. Describe some of Jane's accounting functions for Jacobi Television.
5. Why do you think it was necessary for Jane to obtain formal training in accounting?
6. What is meant by "back-up files"?

7. Write a report on the Certified General Accountants program. Include the following information in your report:
   - educational requirements;
   - experience requirements;
   - business communication requirements;
   - fees;
   - number of levels of courses;
   - number of courses to earn the CGA designation;
   - a description of accounting courses that are studied.
8. Prepare a report on the three-year Business Administration Diploma course at a community college of your choice. Find out the qualifications needed to enrol, the number of courses required for graduation, how many accounting courses must be taken, and the average needed for graduation.
9. In her career, Jane has performed both bookkeeping and accounting functions. Set up three columns. In the first column, list Jane's bookkeeping functions; in the second column, list her accounting functions; in the third column, place a check mark opposite the functions that you have now learned.

8 Subsidiary Ledger Accounting

8.1 Subsidiary Ledger Theory
8.2 Subsidiary Ledger Systems
8.3 Customer's Statement of Account
8.4 Computerized Accounting: Subsidiary Ledgers

A growing business quickly reaches the point where additional people are needed to carry out all of the accounting and office duties. At the same time, the owner of the business will be trying to keep costs down by hiring the least expensive employees. The least expensive employees are those whose skills, training, and experience are at an early stage of development.

A system has evolved that permits most office duties to be handled by junior employees under the supervision of a few senior persons. This system uses "subsidiary ledgers" and "control accounts" to divide duties in a business office.

As a business grows, its ledger grows too, but in a special way. The increase in the ledger comes mostly from the accounts of customers and creditors. The other ledger accounts seldom increase in number; they only increase in the size of their balances.

Figure 8.1 illustrates the growth of a ledger. Notice that the number of accounts for customers and creditors increases, while the number of other accounts remains about the same.

Figure 8.1 The growth of a ledger.

Chapter 8

Some large businesses, Bell Canada for example, have ledgers that contain thousands of customers' accounts.

8.1 Subsidiary Ledger Theory

In a mature business the office work is organized so that most of it is done by junior personnel under the guidance of a few senior persons. The bookkeeping for customers' and creditors' accounts is ideally suited to a division of work. It makes good business sense to separate these accounts from the rest of the ledger. Then they can be looked after independently by accounting clerks.

To begin the study of subsidiary ledgers, examine the T-account ledger in Figure 8.2. This is a typical ledger except that the number of customers' and creditors' accounts is very small.

Bank 101	Acc. Rec'l J. Martin 105	Acc. Rec'l R. Sloan 106
2 516 –	965 –	420 –

Acc. Rec'l G. Adler 107	Acc. Rec'l F. Flood 108	Off. Equip. 120
335 –	274 –	9 016 –

Auto 130	Acc. Pay'l Superior Co. 205	Acc. Pay'l Little Co. 206
14 200	275 –	126 –

Acc. Pay'l Royal Co. 207	Acc. Pay'l Metro Co. 208	A. Bell, Cap. 301
425 –	335 –	26 430

A. Bell, Drgs 302	Revenue 401	Car Expense 501
4 200	10 742	2 216

Office Exp. 505	Rent 510	Wages 515
875 –	800 –	2 516

Figure 8.2 A simple ledger.

From this ledger extract all of the accounts of customers, and all those of creditors, and set them aside in two separate groups. This is shown in Figure 8.3. In each new group, take out the account numbers and arrange the accounts in alphabetical order. Place the customers' and creditors' addresses on the account pages.

By definition, a group of accounts is a ledger. Therefore, each of the two new groups of accounts is a ledger. The accounting system now contains three ledgers.

Figure 8.3 Partially developed three-ledger system.

The ledger of customers' accounts is known as the accounts receivable ledger. The **accounts receivable ledger** is a book or file containing all of the accounts of customers. The accounts in this ledger normally have debit balances.

The ledger of creditors' accounts is known as the accounts payable ledger. The **accounts payable ledger** is a book or file containing all of the accounts of ordinary creditors. The accounts in this ledger normally have credit balances.

It is necessary for each ledger to have its own identity now that there are three ledgers in the system. For this reason, the main ledger is called the general ledger. The **general ledger** is the main ledger of a business containing accounts for assets, liabilities, equity, revenues, and expenses.

The change-over to the three-ledger system is not yet completed. Certain accounts were removed from the general ledger in Figure 8.3. Therefore, it no longer balances within itself. It cannot be left in this condition. Balancing the general ledger is fundamental to the whole process of accounting.

The next step, therefore, is to open two new accounts in the general ledger to replace all of those accounts that were removed from it. The two new accounts are called Accounts Receivable and Accounts Payable. They are shown in Figure 8.4.

Notice that the Accounts Receivable account is given a debit balance of $1 994. This amount replaces all of the customers' accounts that were removed. Observe also that the Accounts Payable account is given a credit balance of $1 161. This amount replaces all of the creditors' accounts that were removed. The final state of the three-ledger system is shown in Figure 8.4.

a. General ledger (in balance).

b. Accounts receivable ledger. A subsidiary ledger (equal in value to its control account).

c. Accounts payable ledger. A subsidiary ledger (equal in value to its control account).

Figure 8.4 The simple three-ledger system.

Subsidiary Ledgers

We now have two new ledgers in our accounting system. These are the accounts receivable ledger and the accounts payable ledger. Each of these two new ledgers is called a subsidiary ledger. A **subsidiary ledger** is a separate ledger that contains a number of accounts of a similar type such as accounts receivable. The accounts in a subsidiary ledger make up the detailed data for one related account in the general ledger.

Further, we now have two new accounts in the general ledger. These are the Accounts Receivable account and the Accounts Payable account. Each of these two new accounts is called a control account. A **control account** is a general ledger account which represents the sum of the balances in a related subsidiary ledger.

Now that subsidiary ledgers have been introduced into the accounting system, they must be included in the monthly "balancing" process. A subsidiary ledger must agree with its control account. The account balances in a subsidiary ledger must be totaled, and that total must agree with the balance of the control account. If it does not, errors exist and must be found and corrected.

Balance Sheet Presentation

In the three-ledger system, the financial statements should not be prepared until the three ledgers have all been balanced. Only then can you feel confident that the figures are correct.

When you now prepare a balance sheet, you will not list the individual customers' or creditors' accounts. Instead, you will enter the balances of the control accounts. In this way, the statements will show the total owed by all customers and the total owed to all ordinary creditors. Figure 8.5 shows accounts receivable and accounts payable as they appear on a simple balance sheet.

```
                    DR. P.R. HAYASHI
                    BALANCE SHEET
                    MARCH 31, 19-3
                        Assets
Bank                                         $  1 650.21
Accounts Receivable                            17 086.14
Supplies                                          902.35
Equipment                                      10 500.00
Automobile                                     19 302.00
                                              $49 440.70

                      Liabilities
Accounts Payable                              $  4 072.16
Bank Loan                                       10 000.00
                                              $14 072.16

                    Owner's Equity
P.R. Hayashi, Capital                         $35 368.54
                                              $49 440.70
```

Figure 8.5 Balance sheet for a doctor using the three-ledger system.

Section Review Questions

1. Why does a business have both junior and senior employees?
2. What type of accounts increase most in a growing business?
3. What happens to the other accounts (usually)?
4. In a mature office, which type of employee will you find more of—junior or senior?
5. Which type of employee looks after the accounts receivable accounts in a typical office?
6. The customers' accounts are considered to be a ledger when they are separated from the main ledger. Explain why.
7. Give the formal name of the customers' ledger.

8. Give the formal name of the ordinary creditors' ledger.
9. What type of balance do the accounts of the creditors usually have?
10. What is the formal name of the main ledger?
11. What type of accounts are found in the main ledger?
12. Give the names of the two accounts in the main ledger that replace the accounts of customers and trade creditors.
13. There are three aspects to the balancing process in a three-ledger system. Describe the three aspects.
14. What is a "subsidiary ledger"?
15. What is a "control account"?
16. The accounts receivable ledger normally has only accounts with debit balances. How then is it possible to balance this ledger?
17. How are the customers' accounts now presented on a balance sheet?

Section Exercises

1. The trial balance of Proctor's Pet Store in Weyburn, Sask., is shown below.

PROCTOR'S PET STORE
TRIAL BALANCE
JUNE 30, 19--

Bank	$ 1 150	
Accounts Receivable		
P. Shewchuk	350	
J. Britt	920	
C. Powell	1 500	
D. Zecca	500	
W. Pritz	2 900	
Supplies	1 550	
Equipment	15 037	
Accounts Payable		
Cleaners' Supply House		$ 900
Wendall's Store		250
Arnwell Animal Hospital		1 500
Tracy Proctor, Capital		18 122
Tracy Proctor, Drawings	11 000	
Revenue		29 435
Light and Heat Expense	2 475	
Miscellaneous Expense	316	
Rent Expense	12 000	
Telephone Expense	509	
	$50 207	$50 207

1. Calculate the value of the accounts receivable accounts.
2. Calculate the value of the accounts payable accounts.
3. T. Proctor changes over to a three-ledger system of accounting, with subsidiary ledgers and control accounts. Perform the following:
   a. Show the general ledger trial balance.

b. Show the accounts receivable subsidiary ledger trial balance and make sure it agrees with the general ledger control account.

c. Show the accounts payable subsidiary ledger trial balance and make sure it agrees with the general ledger control account.

2. Hans Schmidt operates a repair shop in Thessalon, Ont. On December 31, 19-- the trial balance for the business included the following accounts of customers and suppliers.

Customers		Trade Suppliers	
Aho Armas	$ 95.20 Dr	Biltmore Plumbing	$ 215.00 Cr
Bilous Stan	526.00 Dr	Fleming Door Frames	85.00 Cr
Cobb John	1 552.00 Dr	Goodrich Rubber	352.00 Cr
Dealice Guido	956.30 Cr	Hlady Aluminum	1 565.00 Cr
Franzmann Sheila	1 230.00 Dr	Host Rent-a-Car	295.10 Cr
Hickey George	29.60 Dr	Ideal Woodcraft	75.00 Dr
James Leslie	3 750.00 Dr	Imperial Trailers	335.60 Cr
Mutz J.	642.00 Dr	KBM Supply	1 525.00 Cr
Robbenhaur M.	1 200.80 Dr	Urbanski Tile	743.25 Cr
Torma Mike	175.10 Cr		
Wen William	478.30 Dr		

Answer the following questions.

1. What should the balance be in the Accounts Receivable control account?
2. What should the balance be in the Accounts Payable control account?
3. Give the most likely explanation for the credit balances in the list of customers' accounts.
4. Give the most likely explanation for the debit balance in the list of suppliers' accounts.
5. Would it be proper to transfer the two credit balances from the receivables to the payables, and the one debit balance from the payables to the receivables? Give some points for and against such an action.
6. Suppose that the transfer suggested above was made. What would the balances be in the control accounts?
7. What figure(s) should appear on the balance sheet for accounts receivable? Explain your answer.

8.2 Subsidiary Ledger Systems

Bookkeeping for Accounts Receivable

The flowcharts in figures 8.6 and 8.7 show the clerical procedures needed to look after accounts receivable. A thorough examination of these flowcharts will show you how to maintain the accounts receivable ledger.

Chapter 8

SALES INVOICE
CUSTOMER
ACCOUNTS RECEIVABLE

Note:
The two source documents that affect accounts receivable are:
1. Sales invoices
2. Cash receipts daily summary

One copy of each source document goes to Accounts Receivable Clerk.

CASH RECEIPTS DAILY SUMMARY
A/R

Accounts Receivable Clerk
A) Debits a customer's account for every sales invoice. (Daily)
B) Credits a customer's account for every receipt on account. (Daily)

Source documents are initialled when posted. Invoice numbers are entered in the accounts in the "Particulars" Column.

ACCOUNTS RECEIVABLE CLERK
Work Station
Action

ACCOUNTS RECEIVABLE SUBSIDIARY LEDGER

The total of subsidiary ledger accounts must be agreed with the control account monthly.

A — Filed Alphabetically
D — Filed By Date

Figure 8.6 Accounts Receivable System Work of the Accounts Receivable Clerk.

Section 8.2   219

Note:
The two source documents that affect accounts receivable are:
1. Sales invoices
2. Cash receipts daily summary

One copy of each source document goes to General Ledger Clerk.

General Ledger Clerk

A) Receives a copy of all source documents requiring an accounting entry.
B) Journalizes the accounting entries.

For Sales invoices:
　DR Accounts Receivable
　　CR Revenue
　　CR Sales Tax Payable

For Cash receipts on account:
　DR Bank
　　CR Accounts Receivable

Work Station

Action

Action

Filed Numerically

Filed by date

Monthly, the balance of the Accounts Receivable control account must be agreed with the subsidiary ledger total.

Figure 8.7 Accounts Receivable System   Work of the General Ledger Clerk.

The highlights of the flowcharts are:

1. There are two source documents that affect accounts receivable. These are: a. *sales invoices*, and
   b. *cash receipts daily summary*.
2. There are a number of copies of each of the source documents.
3. A copy of each source document is forwarded to the accounts receivable clerk.
4. A different copy of each of the two source documents is forwarded to the general ledger clerk.
5. The work of the accounts receivable clerk requires:
   a. *for each sales invoice*—a debit entry to a customer's account;
   b. *for each receipt on account*—a credit entry to a customer's account.
6. The work of the general ledger clerk requires an accounting entry for every source document.
   a. *For each sales invoice*, the accounting entry is:

	DR	CR
Accounts Receivable	$$$$	
Sales (Revenue)		$$$$
Sales Tax Payable		$$$$

   b. *For each receipt on account*, the accounting entry is:

	DR	CR
Bank	$$$$	
Accounts Receivable		$$$$

7. The subsidiary ledger is updated daily and balanced with its control account monthly.

Balancing the Ledgers

There are three ledgers to balance in a three-ledger system. The procedure for balancing the general ledger remains the same. However, the subsidiary ledgers must also be balanced. This is usually done by the subsidiary ledger clerk as follows.

Each subsidiary ledger must be balanced with its control account as shown in Figure 8.8. The procedure is simple. First make sure that the subsidiary ledger and the control account are posted to the same point in time. Then:

1. total all of the account balances in the subsidiary ledger;
2. match the total against the balance of the control account in the general ledger.

If the two totals agree then the subsidiary ledger is in balance. If the two do not agree, then the subsidiary ledger is not in balance. The latter condition indicates that there are errors to be found and corrected somewhere in the ledgers.

Schedule of Accounts Receivable
May 31, 19--

A. Adams	$ 50
B. Brown	100
C. Hussein	30
S. Smith	25
T. Thomas	175
W. Wand	35
Total	$415

General Ledger
Trial Balance
May 31, 19--

	DR	CR
Bank	$ 200	
Accounts Receivable	415	
Supplies	140	
Capital		$ 845
Drawings	400	
Revenue		1 210
Advertising	125	
Utilities	325	
Wages	450	
	$2 055	$2 055

Figure 8.8 Balancing the subsidiary ledger with the control account.

Accounting Controls

The three-ledger system forms part of the overall system of "internal control."

The accounting clerk who maintains the subsidiary ledger does so independently. This person has no access to cash and no involvement with any other accounting records that affect accounts receivable.

The general ledger clerk who prepares the accounting entries from the source documents works independently. This person does not initiate any source documents.

The general ledger and the two subsidiary ledgers are all maintained independently of each other. When they are brought into balance with each other at the end of each month, it serves to prove that the work of the employees involved is both accurate and honest.

Bookkeeping for Accounts Payable

The previous section explained the procedures for maintaining the accounts receivable. The accounts payable can be handled by a very similar set of procedures.

The highlights of a system for accounts payable are:

1. There are two source documents that affect accounts payable. These are: a. *purchase invoices* (see Note 1 below), and
    b. *cheque copies—on account only* (see Note 2 below).

2. The accounts payable subsidiary ledger is maintained by the accounts payable clerk.

3. The general ledger is maintained by the general ledger clerk.

4. The work of the accounts payable clerk requires:
    a. *for each purchase invoice*—a credit entry to a creditor's account;
    b. *for each cheque copy (on account)*—a debit entry to a creditor's account.

5. The work of the general ledger clerk requires the making of accounting entries for each source document.
    a. *For each purchase invoice*, the accounting entry is:

	DR	CR
An asset or an expense*	$$$$	
Accounts Payable		$$$$

    * The account affected depends on what was purchased.

    b. *For each cheque copy on account*, the accounting entry is:

	DR	CR
Accounts Payable	$$$$	
Bank		$$$$

6. The subsidiary ledger is balanced with the control account monthly.

Note 1. Each purchase invoice goes through a rigorous series of verifying checks before being recorded in the accounts. It is important to ensure that: a) the goods or services were actually ordered, b) the goods or services are the right ones and were received in good conditon, c) the price on the invoice is the agreed price, and d) there are no errors or omissions on the invoice.

Note 2. Not all cheques issued affect accounts payable. For example, a cheque issued to the owner for personal use, or a cheque for a cash purchase of supplies, does not affect accounts payable.

Non-Routine Entries to Subsidiary Ledgers

You have seen that accounting systems are designed so that the information flows to the office clerks by means of business source documents. However, there are some transactions for which there are no regular source documents. Such transactions do not fit into the regular accounting routine.

For example, suppose that Naomi Kuper, the owner of a business, collects an overdue $200 account in full from a customer, B. Marr. Ms. Kuper happens to be short of cash at the time. She keeps the money for her personal use instead of turning it into the business.

First, Ms. Kuper would inform the accounting department of the transaction. She has no wish to deceive anyone. The accountant would make the following accounting entry in the journal:

	DR	CR
N. Kuper Drawings	$200	
Accounts Receivable		$200

To record the collection by N. Kuper of the account of B. Marr. Funds were kept by N. Kuper for her personal use.

There is no regular source document for this type of transaction. Without the source document, the accounts receivable clerk will not learn about the transaction in the usual way. The accountant understands this, and will make the entry in the subsidiary ledger personally, or will inform the clerk by means of a written memo. The accountant must attend to this promptly because the subsidiary ledger must be kept up-to-date.

Keeping Subsidiary Ledgers Up-to-Date

Customers' and creditors' accounts should be kept as up-to-date as possible. Customers' accounts are usually posted daily. But there is normally a slight delay in posting creditors' accounts because it takes time to complete the verification of the purchase invoices.

It is no longer necessary to keep the general ledger right up-to-date. The posting of the general ledger can be left until the end of the month now that the customers' and creditors' accounts are kept separately. At that time, the posting is done more efficiently, in one concentrated effort.

It is standard practice to balance all three ledgers once a month, after all postings have been completed.

It is possible to keep track of the daily bank balance in various ways without having to keep the general ledger Bank account up-to-date.

Locating Errors When a Subsidiary Ledger Does Not Balance

When a subsidiary ledger does not balance, a search for the errors must be made. In looking for errors, remember that for every amount entered in a subsidiary ledger there must be an equivalent amount entered in the control account, and vice versa.

In your search for errors, there is no need to go back in the accounts beyond the current month. The ledgers are balanced at the end of every month and the trial balances are kept on file as proof. If errors exist in the accounts, they must have been made after the last balancing was done.

Section Review Questions

1. What are the two source documents that affect accounts receivable?
2. How do the clerks who look after the different ledgers learn about the transactions?
3. Describe the work done by the accounts receivable clerk.
4. Describe the work done by the general ledger clerk.
5. Why is the accounts receivable ledger updated daily?
6. Normally, a subsidiary ledger will not balance with its control account if both ledgers are not posted up to the same point in time. Explain.
7. What has to be done if a subsidiary ledger does not balance with its control? Whose responsibility is it?
8. Describe how to take off a subsidiary ledger trial balance.
9. There is a "control" aspect to the system of subsidiary ledgers and control accounts. Describe this.
10. What are the two source documents that affect accounts payable?
11. Why is the accounts payable ledger not perfectly up-to-date?
12. Why is it necessary to keep the accounts receivable accounts up-to-date but not the general ledger accounts?
13. What is the advantage of posting once a month in the general ledger?
14. If an error exists in the accounts it will have occurred since the last balancing. Explain.

Section Exercises

1. Study the flowcharts in Figures 8.6 and 8.7 and answer the following questions.
    1. How many copies of sales invoices are shown?
    2. How many copies of cash receipts daily summaries are shown?
    3. How many copies of each of the above are forwarded to accounting personnel?
    4. What eventually happens to all of the copies of the source documents that are received in the accounting department?
    5. What happens to the original of sales invoices?
    6. What do the solid lines with arrows indicate?
    7. Describe the work done by the subsidiary ledger clerk.
    8. Describe the work done by the general ledger clerk.
    9. What do broken lines with arrows indicate?
    10. How often are the subsidiary ledgers balanced?

2. Develop two flowcharts that represent the accounts payable system. These two charts should be similar to the two charts in the textbook representing the accounts receivable system.

3. Workbook Exercise: Complete a chart showing the effect of source documents on subsidiary ledgers and the general ledger.

4. Your office duties with the Quick Distributing Co. include those of accounts receivable clerk. You are to post daily to the customers' accounts from the business documents that you receive.

   On the morning of each working day, the following business documents arrive on your desk:

   a. Copies of all sales invoices issued on the previous working day by the Sales Department.

   b. A listing of the day's cash receipts, prepared first thing each morning by the clerk who opens the mail.

   1. Set up the accounts receivable ledger as of June 30, 19--, from the following detailed trial balance. If you are using the workbook, the ledger is set up for you.

   QUICK DISTRIBUTING CO.
   ACCOUNTS RECEIVABLE TRIAL BALANCE
   JUNE 30, 19--

Adam Bros., 12 Mountain Avenue	Inv. No. 480	$ 67.20	
	507	94.20	$ 161.40
Cozo & Son, 620 Main Street	512		75.65
A.G. Farmer, 120A Blackwell Ave.	514		315.62
S.P. Handy, Ltd., 75 Porter Ave.	484	216.25	
	511	200.22	416.47
R. Mortimer, 60 Hawley Crescent	470	516.25	
	496	621.90	
	505	608.36	1 746.51
Renforth Sales, 192 Dale Place	510		137.62
Vista Limited, 2001 Central Ave.	515		50.00
			$2 903.27

   2. Post to the customers' accounts from the following business papers. In the particulars column enter invoice numbers.

Transactions

July

2 *Invoices*
   —No. 516, Adams Bros., $59.24.
   —No. 517, Renforth Sales, $145.50.
   Cash Receipts
   —A.G. Farmer, No. 514, $315.62.
   —S.P. Handy, Ltd., No. 484, $216.25.

3 *Invoice*
   —No. 518, Cozo & Son, $75.85.
   Cash Receipts
   —Nil

Chapter 8

4 *Invoices*
—No. 519, A.G. Farmer, $217.90.
—No. 520, The Williams Company, 417 Lake Street $150.00.
Cash Receipts
—Adams Bros., No. 480, $67.20.
—R. Mortimer, No. 470 & No. 496, $1 138.15.

5 *Invoices*
—No. 521, Vista Limited, $94.95.
—No. 522, S.P. Handy, Ltd., $104.16.
—No. 523, R. Mortimer, $56.00.
Cash Receipt
—Renforth Sales, No. 510, $137.62.

6 *Invoices*
—No. 524, Adams Bros., $167.07.
—No. 525, The Williams Company, $75.00.
Cash Receipts
—Cozo & Son, No. 512, $75.65.
—Vista Limited, No. 515, $50.00.

3. Take off a trial balance of the subsidiary ledger as of July 6 and balance the subsidiary ledger with the control account. The senior accountant has arrived at a control figure of $2 048.45.

---

5. On September 30, 19‒‒, the detailed accounts payable trial balance of Magnetic Controls Company was as follows:

MAGNETIC CONTROLS COMPANY
ACCOUNTS PAYABLE TRIAL BALANCE
SEPTEMBER 30, 19‒‒

Daiton Enterprises	106 Fleet Street, Barbary	516		$ 430.74
Gordon & Associates	7400 King Street, Oak City	B7407		216.92
Henderson Associates	Box 65, Welton	16421	$ 507.00	
		16907	615.00	1 122.00
Kohler, R.M.	141 Nixon Avenue, Barbary	615		104.70
North State Packaging	1500 Middle Road, Lennox	901		74.87
Orenson & Company	560 The Eastway, Dayson	1604	$1 046.26	
		1809	516.15	1 562.41
Riggs, J.B.	75 Baxter Road, Estwing	74621		502.00
Smithers, P.R.	106 Farr Street, Wibbling	74		57.05
Union Advertising	7900 Primeau Avenue, Marks County	16352	$ 436.21	
		17201	702.16	
		17306	518.90	1 657.27
				$5 727.96

1. Set up the accounts payable ledger of Magnetic Controls Company. If you are using the workbook the ledger is already set up for you.

2. From the business documents listed below, perform the duties of the accounts payable clerk by posting to the accounts payable ledger. Record source document numbers in subsidiary ledger accounts.

Transactions

October

1 *Purchase Invoices*
   —Smithers, P.R., No. 104, $151.89.
   —North State Packaging, No. 1046, $57.25.
   Cheque Copies
   —No. 65720, Union Advertising, on account, $800.
   —No. 65721, Henderson Associates, Inv. 16421, $507.

2 *Purchase Invoices*
   —Wrouse & Reid, 14 Kay Street, Saxton, No. 597G, $316.29.
   —Union Advertising, No. 18002, $505.
   —Orenson & Company, No. 1856, $216.
   Cheque Copies
   —No. 65722, Daiton Enterprises, Inv. 516, $430.74.
   —No. 65723, Orenson & Company, on account, $500.

5 *Purchase Invoices*
   —Gordon & Associates, No. B7502, $315.20.
   —Kohler, R. M., No. 719, $174.90.
   —Riggs, J. B., No. 74998, $472.47.
   Cheque Copies
   —No. 65734, North State Packaging, Inv. 901, $74.87.
   —No. 65735, Union Advertising, balance of Inv. 17201, $338.37.

6 *Purchase Invoices*
   —Daiton Enterprises, No. 702, $375.62.
   —Henderson Associates, No. 17436, $1 746.21.
   Cheque Copy
   —No. 65739, Gordon & Associates, Inv. B7407, $216.92.

7 *Purchase Invoices*
   —Henderson Associates, No. 17807, $65.25.
   —Kohler, R. M., No. 792, $107.64.
   —Wrouse & Reid, No. 602B, $392.61.
   Cheque Copies
   —No. 65744, Henderson Associates, Inv. 16907, $615.
   —No. 65745, Orenson & Company, balance of Inv. 1604, $546.26.
   —No. 65746, Wrouse & Reid, Inv. 597G, $316.29.
   —No. 65747, Smithers, P. R., Inv. 74, $57.05.

3. Take off an accounts payable ledger trial balance and see that it agrees with the balance of the control account. The correct control account figure is $6 221.79.

6. The simplified general ledger and subsidiary ledgers of Blue Bell Company are given below in T-accounts. These accounts are set up for you in the workbook. If you are not using the workbook, you will have to set up the ledger on blank paper making room for the accounting entries to come.

General Ledger

Bank	Accounts Receivable	Supplies
500	1 700	70

Equipment	Automobiles	Bank Loan
4 000	10 000	1 000

Accounts Payable	C. Chen, Capital	C. Chen, Drawings
1 450	14 550	200

Revenue	Advertising Expense	General Expense
12 400	500	130

Light and Heat	Rent Expense	Wages Expense
1 500	1 800	9 000

Accounts Receivable Ledger

Aube	Crozier	Elyk
300	200	150

Isola	Perrier	Tams
500	300	250

Accounts Payable Ledger

Ace Co.	Delta Co.	Galaxy Co.
225	150	75

Meteor Co.	Sun Co.	Venus Co.
300	400	300

Required:
1. Ensure that the subsidiary ledgers are in balance with their respective control accounts to start with.
2. Perform the duties of the accounts receivable clerk. Select from the source documents shown below those that affect the accounts receivable and post them directly to the T-accounts in the subsidiary ledger.
3. Perform the duties of the accounts payable clerk. Select from the source documents shown below those that affect the accounts payable and post them directly to the T-accounts in the subsidiary ledger.
4. Perform the duties of the general ledger clerk. Work out the accounting entries for the source documents shown below, journalize them in a two-column general journal, and post to the T-accounts in the general ledger. Ignore dates, explanations, and sales tax.

Source Documents

No.	Document	Name	Amount	Explanation
1.	Sales invoice	Crozier	$220	Sale on account
2.	Purchase invoice	Ace Co.	150	Advertising
3.	Cash receipt	Elyk	150	On account
4.	Sales invoice	Perrier	175	Sale on account
5.	Purchase invoice	Sun Co.	130	Supplies
6.	Cash receipt	Isola	300	On account
7.	Sales invoice	Tams	40	Sale on account
8.	Cheque copy	Sun Co.	400	On account
9.	Purchase invoice	Meteor Co.	350	Light and heat
10.	Cash receipt	Perrier	300	On account
11.	Cheque copy	Ace Co.	225	On account
12.	Cheque copy	Venus Co.	300	On account
13.	Cash sales slip	Winters	175	Cash sale
14.	Cheque copy	Chen	320	Drawings

5. Balance the three ledgers.

7. **Workbook Exercise:** Journalizing and balancing in a simple three-ledger system.

8.3 Customer's Statement of Account

You have seen that a business keeps detailed records of the accounts of its customers. A business needs to notify its customers about the status of their accounts if it expects to be paid promptly. Businesses do this by sending statements of account regularly to their customers. A **statement of account** is a record of a customer's account for a period of time, usually one month. It gives the customer a history of the account for the month, and the balance owing at the end of the month. The statement of account is used as a gentle request for payment.

The method of preparing statements of account depends on how much automation there is in the accounting system.

Manual Accounting System

The following method is used in a manual system of accounting.

1. The customer's accounts are kept in a subsidiary ledger in the way that you have seen. Each customer is given an account page on which all transactions of the customer are recorded. The entries continue on the account page until it is filled. Then the account balance is forwarded to a new page and the process continues.
2. A statement of account is prepared on a separate form and sent to each customer at the end of each month. The statement of account starts with the last balance shown on the previous statement. It then shows the transactions for the ensuing month and ends with the balance at the end of that month. Figure 8.9 shows a manual statement of account.

Figure 8.9 The ledger account and the statement of account for the month of June for H. Atkins.

Automated Accounting System

The manual system for producing customers's statements is too slow and time-consuming for a business with a large number of customers. A business with many credit customers requires a system that uses electronic equipment.

Figure 8.10 A series of machine-printed statements for A. Klein.

In a computerized accounting system the customers' accounts are maintained as shown below in Figure 8.10.

1. A new ledger sheet is set up in the subsidiary ledger each month for each customer. The ending balance on the old ledger sheet is forwarded to become the beginning balance on the new (current) sheet. The old sheet is then filed away. As Figure 8.10 shows, each customer's account is made up of a number of monthly ledger sheets that follow one another in a series.
2. The transactions for the current month are recorded in the usual manner except that the entries are machine printed and calculated.
3. The ledger sheets are not created on a daily basis. Instead, the computer stores all of the data for all of the customers for the entire month in its memory banks. At the end of the month, it produces all of the customers' accounts and monthly statements in a single operation that may take only a few hours. An individual customer's account can be examined at any time simply by calling it up on the computer screen.
4. If the ledger sheets are prepared in duplicate, the copy is used as the customer's statement of account. The customer receives an exact copy of his account when this system is used. Banks use this method to produce bank statements for chequing accounts and business current accounts.

The computer can easily be programmed to produce two originals at little additional time or expense. This saves having to use messy carbon paper.

Figure 8.11 shows a computer-produced statement sent to a customer from a national department store. It is easy to show a great deal of information on computer-produced statements.

Figure 8.11 Computer-produced statement of account of a national department store.

Statements of Account and the Customer

You have seen that a business produces a statement of account for each customer each month. Let us now examine this important document from the customer's point of view.

A statement of account should always be checked by the customer for errors. Although the degree of accuracy in business recordkeeping is remarkably high, errors and oversights do occur. The customer should keep a file of statements of account and of the bills for purchases and returns made. Along with adequate banking records, these enable the customer to check each statement of account as it arrives. All errors should be reported to the suppliers.

Section Review Questions

1. Why does a business notify its customers about the status of their accounts?
2. What is a "statement of account"?
3. Describe what a statement of account looks like if a manual system is used.
4. Explain how manual accounts differ physically from automated accounts.
5. In a computerized system, can customers' accounts be kept up-to-date if they are not printed out each day? Explain.
6. Describe what a statement of account looks like if a computerized system is used.
7. How can the use of messy carbon paper be avoided?
8. What should the person or company do when it receives a statement of account?

Section Exercises

1. From the account of Richard Kott, shown below, prepare the statement of account for the month of April on the form provided in the workbook.

ACCOUNT R. Kott, 30 Beechwood Crescent, Baton Place, Manitoba No.						
DATE		PARTICULARS	PR	DEBIT	CREDIT	Dr/Cr	BALANCE
19- Feb.	28	Balance Forwarded	—			Dr	431 20
Mar.	12	# 3162		75 70		Dr	506 90
	18	on account			300 —	Dr	206 90
	26	# 3230		174 60		Dr	381 50
	31	# 3319		296 50		Dr	678 00
Apr.	5	on account			131 20	Dr	546 80
	12	# 3457		96 40		Dr	643 20
	19	# 3516		219 50		Dr	862 70
	24	on account			500 —	Dr	362 70
	28	# 3680		315 20		Dr	677 90
May	2	# 3775		61 30		Dr	739 20
	15	on account			46 80	Dr	692 40

2. Michele Penna received the statement of account shown below.

Lake Street
Thunder Bay
Ont. P9Z 1R3

Phone
326 1900

Lakeside Supply

In Account With
Michele Penna
1402 Archibald Street
Thunder Bay, P9Z 4Y6

Date	Reference	Charges	Credits	Balance
Mar 31	Balance Forward			372.16
Apr 9	#3126	115.70		
14	Payment Received		200.00	
17	#3296	131.50		
20	#3384	274.35		
23	#3410	164.53		
27	#3592	15.16		873.40

2% Interest on Overdue Accounts

Michele keeps complete records of her dealings with other businesses. An examination of her files reveals the following:

a. A check mark on Lakeside Supply's statement of account for March showed that the balance of $372.16 had been found to be correct.

b. Four bills of sale from Lakeside Supply showed that the purchases during the month were as follows:

April 9 No. 3126 $115.70
      14 No. 3296   131.50
      23 No. 3410   164.53
      27 No. 3592   15.16

c. The cheque register entries showed that two payments had been made to Lakeside Supply during the month as follows:

April 10 No. 376 $200.00
      30 No. 390   172.16

1. What discrepancies are there between Michele's records and the company's?

2. Give probable reasons for these discrepancies.

3. Suggest what Michele should do regarding these discrepancies.

---

3. The Metropolitan Telephone Company follows the practice of sending monthly statements to its nearly one million customers. However, the accounting department has found it difficult to achieve the company's goal of sending out statements within one week of the month's end.

Suggest an alternative approach to statement preparation that might be acceptable to the company.

8.4 Computerized Accounting: Subsidiary Ledgers

Subsidiary Ledgers

One of the many benefits of the accounting package is the automatic updating of the subsidiary ledgers and their balancing with the control accounts. The raw data is fed in; the computer does the rest.

The usual technique is to give each customer and supplier an individual number. The customer's or the supplier's number is entered along with other data if the transaction affects accounts receivable or accounts payable. The presence of these numbers causes the computer to follow a subroutine that updates the subsidiary ledgers and automatically balances them with their respective control accounts.

A simple spreadsheet model for subsidiary ledger accounting is given below in Figure 8.12.

Chapter 8

```
         A              B           C           D           E              F
 1
 2      #1             #2          #3          #4         #21            #31
 3                  ACCOUNTS                             ACCOUNTS
 4     CASH        RECEIVABLE    SUPPLIES    EQUIPMENT   PAYABLE         CAPITAL
 5     1000           1700         500         5000       1820            6380
 6
 7                  Hidden                               Hidden         Hidden
 8                  Formula                              Formula        Formula
 9                  B22                                  E22            SUM (A5:D5) – E5
10
11
12
13
14
15
16
17  ACCOUNTS RECEIVABLE                      ACCOUNTS PAYABLE
18  ADAMS              300                   JONES CO.        720
19  CARTER             400                   QUICK CO.       1000
20  PETERS             700                   SAX CO.          100
21  ZIM                300
22  TOTAL             1700                   TOTAL           1820
23
24
              Hidden                                   Hidden
              Formula                                  Formula
              SUM (B18:B21)                            SUM (E18:E20)
```

Figure 8.12 A spreadsheet model for subsidiary ledgers.

In the model shown above observe the following:
1. a simple ledger is given across the top of the spreadsheet;
2. the details of the subsidiary ledgers are given in other (unused) areas of the spreadsheet;
3. there are five hidden formulas in the program;
4. the model begins with the ledger in balance and the subsidiary ledgers in agreement with their respective control accounts.

The model allows you to change the account balance of any individual debtor's or creditor's account and to see the respective control account changed automatically. The capital account is updated as well. You can also change the balance of the Cash, Supplies, or Equipment and the Capital balance will be recalculated automatically. It is good practice to have the computer *do the calculations twice*. This ensures that no calculation is based on cells containing "old" data.

Computer Review Questions

1. What is the source of the data for entry to the data input form?
2. What does the computer replace in an accounting environment?
3. What triggers the subroutine in accounts receivable accounting?
4. In the textbook model, what is given across the top of the spreadsheet?
5. Explain the formula pointing to the Capital figure.
6. Explain the formula pointing to the accounts receivable subsidiary total.
7. If a customer's account balance is changed in the model, explain what else happens automatically.
8. If the Cash balance is changed, what else changes automatically?
9. Explain why calculations should be done twice to ensure correct results.

Computer Exercises

1. Set up a spreadsheet program similar to the one given in the text for Rainbow Real Estate from Chapter 4. This is exercise 9 at the end of that chapter. If you program the computer to calculate the Capital automatically, some of the transactions will require only one change. Transaction 2 is like this. Simply add V. Morris's debt to the list of debtors and the control account and the Capital account will be adjusted automatically.

2. You can do a number of textbook exercises on a model similar to the one shown in the text. However, your model may be much larger than the simple textbook example. Exercise 6 in Section 8.2 (page 228) is a good example. The exercise as it stands requires the work of three employees. On the computer model only one employee, the data entry clerk, is needed.

    Because the exercise includes revenue and expense accounts and a Drawings account, the Capital account should not be programmed to balance automatically after each transaction. Each transaction will require at least two changes on the spreadsheet. But all of the changes will not be entered on the top line. Some will be entered in the subsidiary ledgers.

CHAPTER HIGHLIGHTS

Now that you have completed Chapter 8, you should:

1. know what a subsidiary ledger is and what a control account is;
2. understand the theory of the three-ledger system of accounting;
3. know how accounts receivable and accounts payable are presented on a balance sheet;
4. understand a simple accounting system for accounts receivable and for accounts payable;

5. know the source documents and the accounting entries that affect accounts receivable and accounts payable;
6. know how to handle non-routine transactions that affect subsidiary ledgers;
7. be able to locate errors in a subsidiary ledger that is out of balance;
8. understand the accounting control features of the three-ledger system;
9. know how a customer's statement of account is prepared manually and by computer.

ACCOUNTING TERMS

accounts payable ledger
accounts receivable ledger
control account

general ledger
statement of account
subsidiary ledger

CHAPTER EXERCISES

Using Your Knowledge

1. **This exercise appears in your workbook. For each statement below place a "T" (for true) or an "F" (for false) in the spaces provided. For each problem, one, two, three, or four of the parts may be correct. Assume that the system described in the chapter is used.**

    1. An entire journal entry, for a $500 purchase invoice for supplies, is not recorded. As a result,
        a. The general ledger still balances.
        b. Two accounts in the general ledger have incorrect balances.
        c. The accounts payable ledger does not agree with its control account.
        d. The total in the accounts payable ledger is $500 more than the balance in the control account.
    2. A cheque for $400 received from a customer is posted to the customer's account as a credit of $40. As a result,
        a. The general ledger does not balance.
        b. The accounts receivable ledger does not agree with its control account.
        c. The total of the accounts receivable ledger is greater than the balance in the control account.
        d. The accounts receivable ledger equals the control account but contains one or more errors.
    3. $208 cash received from a customer is recorded correctly in the journal and ledger but is credited to the customer's account as $280. To correct this error the accountant should:
        a. Credit the customer's account $72.
        b. Debit the customer's account $72.

c. Debit the control account $72.
  d. Credit the control account $72.
4. A sales transaction for $800 is entered in the general journal as follows:

   Revenue $800
       Accounts Receivable $800

   As a result of this entry:
   a. The general ledger trial balance does not balance.
   b. The accounts receivable ledger disagrees with the control account by $800.
   c. The balance in the revenue account is incorrect by $800.
   d. The balance in the revenue account is incorrect by $1 600.
5. A purchase invoice for $250 is posted in the accounts payable ledger as a debit. As a result,
   a. The accounts payable ledger does not equal the control account.
   b. The difference between the accounts payable ledger and the control account is $250.
   c. The difference between the accounts payable ledger and the control account is $500.
   d. The general ledger balances.
6. A debit of $1 200 is not posted to a customer's account in the accounts receivable ledger. As a result,
   a. The Revenue account and the Accounts Receivable account are both incorrect.
   b. The general ledger remains in balance.
   c. The balance of the control account is greater than the total of the accounts receivable ledger by $1 200.
   d. The balance of the control account is smaller than the total of the accounts receivable ledger by $1 200.

---

2. **Analyzing the Effect of Errors**

   At the end of June, the accountant for Marcus Company finds that the total in the accounts receivable subsidiary ledger does not agree with the balance in the control account. The subsidiary ledger total is $13 125 and the control figure is $13 500.

   The accountant's investigation reveals five errors. Complete a schedule to show the effect of correcting each of the following errors. Be sure to arrive at the correct accounts receivable figure.

   Errors

   1. A sales invoice for $300, recorded correctly in the control account, was not posted to the subsidiary ledger.
   2. A sales invoice for $325, recorded correctly in the control account, was posted twice in error to the customer's account in the subsidiary ledger.
   3. A cash receipt for $100, recorded properly in the subsidiary ledger, was omitted from the control account.

4. A cash receipt for $75, recorded correctly in the control account, was posted to the wrong side of the customer's account in the subsidiary ledger.
5. An invoice for $500, posted correctly in the control account, was posted as $50 in the subsidiary ledger.

---

3. At the end of May, 19--, Ken Nakamoto found that the accounts receivable ledger and its control account were out of balance. His efforts to balance the ledger uncovered the errors set out below.

Errors

1. A sales invoice for $600 was posted in the subsidiary ledger as $660.
2. A cash receipt on account for $300 was not posted in the subsidiary ledger.
3. A sales invoice for $500 was missed entirely by the general ledger clerk.
4. The debit entry pertaining to a sales invoice for $800 was posted in the general ledger as a credit.
5. A sales invoice for $550 was not posted in the subsidiary ledger.
6. A sales invoice for $750 was missed entirely, by both the subsidiary ledger clerk and the general ledger clerk.
7. A cash receipt on account for $280 was not posted in the subsidiary ledger.

**Required: Given that the subsidiary ledger figure (before balancing) is $32 456,
a. determine the correct total for the subsidiary ledger and the control account;
b. calculate the control figure before any corrections were made.**

---

4. In your workbook complete the chart shown below by placing check marks in the appropriate boxes.

Source Document	In the Subsidiary Ledger						In the General Ledger											
	Which subsidiary ledger is affected?		Will the account be increased or decreased?		Will the account be debited or credited?		The accounting entry will be											
							Bank		Accounts Receivable		Accounts Payable		Asset or Expense		Revenue	
	A/R	A/P	In-crease	De-crease	Dr	Cr	Dr	Cr	Dr	Cr	Dr	Cr	Dr	Cr	Dr	Cr
purchase invoice																
cash receipt on account																
sales invoice																
cheque copy on account																

5. **Workbook Exercise: Challenge**—completing a chart analyzing the effect of errors in a three-ledger system.

Comprehensive Exercise

6. Rachel Bragg is a public accountant in Dartmouth, N.S. On March 31, 19--, her general ledger trial balance is as follows:

R. BRAGG
GENERAL LEDGER TRIAL BALANCE
MARCH 31, 19--

No. 101 Bank	$ 1 850.00	
105 Accounts Receivable	7 220.00	
110 Supplies	2 750.00	
115 Office Equipment	18 400.00	
120 Automobile	24 700.00	
205 Accounts Payable		$ 6 449.70
301 R. Bragg, Capital		47 374.15
302 R. Bragg, Drawings	12 000.00	
401 Fees Income		31 650.00
505 Car Expenses	3 295.60	
510 Light and Heat	950.20	
515 Miscellaneous Expense	375.40	
520 Rent	3 000.00	
525 Telephone	516.15	
530 Wages	10 416.50	
	$85 473.85	$85 473.85

1. Set up the general ledger accounts as of March 31, 19--. (Two workbook ledger accounts are required for Bank.) If you are using the workbook the ledger is already set up for you.

2. Set up the accounts receivable ledger as of March 31, 19--. Observe that the total of the four accounts is equal to the balance of the control account in the general ledger. If you are using the workbook the ledger is already set up for you.

   The accounts receivable ledger on March 31, 19--, contains the following accounts:

Blue Cab Company	16 Fox Street	Inv. No. 74	$1 920.00
Champion Store	175 Main Street	75	750.00
Oasis Restaurant	325 Second Street	76	1 550.00
Village Restaurant	400 Main Street	77	3 000.00
			$7 220.00

3. Set up the accounts payable ledger as of March 31, 19--. Observe that the total of the four accounts is equal to the balance of the control account in the

general ledger. If you are using the workbook the ledger is already set up for you.

The accounts payable ledger on March 31, 19--, contains the following accounts:

M. Ball, Consultant	430 Red Road, Bigtown	$1 700.00
R. & R. Supply	151 King Street	2 740.00
Stirling Company	46 River Road	759.50
Tom's Garage	705 Victoria Street	1 250.20
		$6 449.70

4. Each day you are to perform the duties of both the accounts receivable clerk and the accounts payable clerk. From the list of business transactions shown below, you are to post daily to any customers' or creditors' accounts affected. Although it will be necessary for you to post directly from the list of transactions, try to imagine that you are posting directly from the source documents themselves. Also, remember that not all business transactions affect the accounts of customers and creditors.

Transactions

April

1 *Cheque Copy*
—No. 105, to P. Walters, $1 000, monthly rent.

3 *Sales Invoice*
—No. 78, to Blue Cab Company, $800.

5 *Cash Receipt*
—From Oasis Restaurant, $1 000, on account.

8 *Purchase Invoice*
—From Tom's Garage, $295, gasoline and oil.

9. *Cheque Copy*
—No. 106, R. & R. Supply, $740, an account.

12 *Sales Invoices*
—No. 79, to Champion Store, $500.
—No. 80, to Village Restaurant, $1 000.

15 *Cheque Copy*
—No. 107, to Municipal Telephone, $75.50, telephone for month.

15 *Cash Receipt*
—From Blue Cab Company, $1 920, on account.

19 *Sales Invoice*
—No. 81, to Oasis Restaurant, $390.

22 *Purchase Invoice*
—From Stirling Company, $210, for supplies.

24 *Cheque Copies*
—No. 108, to M. Ball, $1 000, on account.
—No. 109, to Stirling Company, $759.50, on account.
30 *Cheque Copies*
—No. 110, to Municipal Hydro, $90, electricity for month.
—No. 111, to R. Carter, $300, part-time wages for month.

5. **Each day you are to perform the duties of the junior accountant. Journalize each of the above transactions in the two-column general journal. Do not post to the general ledger accounts until the end of April.**

6. **As the junior accountant, you are to post the general journal to the general ledger at the end of the month. Then you are to take off a general ledger trial balance. It is your responsibility to see that the ledger balances.**

7. **As the accounts receivable clerk, you are to take off a trial balance of the accounts receivable ledger as of April 30, 19––. It is your responsibility to see that the accounts receivable ledger balances with the control account.**

8. **As the accounts payable clerk, you are to take off a trial balance of the accounts payable ledger as of April 30, 19––. It is your responsibility to see that the accounts payable ledger balances with the control account.**

For Further Thought

7. **Briefly answer the following questions.**

   1. What do the terms ''division of labour'' and ''specialization'' have to do with accounts receivable?
   2. Subsidiary ledgers are looked after by junior persons. Explain why.
   3. Why are subsidiary ledger accounts usually arranged alphabetically?
   4. Do all creditors' accounts go in the accounts payable ledger? Explain.
   5. Can there be other ''control'' accounts besides accounts receivable and accounts payable?
   6. Is it enough to show just the total of accounts receivable on the balance sheet? Explain.
   7. Assume that the accounting department receives only one copy of each sales invoice and cash receipts daily summary. How could all of the accounting be done using such a system?
   8. Subsidiary ledger clerks do not make ''balanced'' accounting entries. Explain.
   9. Where will the errors be found if the subsidiary ledger does not agree with its control account? In the general ledger? In the subsidiary ledger? In both?
   10. What prevents the accounts receivable clerk from obtaining the money from a customer, pocketing it, and crediting the customer's account?
   11. In a computerized system the general ledger is not one continuous record. Explain.

12. You are instructed by the owner that a certain customer has died and that her account will not be collectable. What should be done with the account? What accounting entry or entries should be made?
13. The general ledger clerk receives a copy of every source document. The subsidiary ledger clerks receive copies of some source documents only. Explain why this is so.
14. Neither the general ledger nor the subsidiary ledgers contain any errors. Yet the subsidiary ledgers do not balance with their respective control accounts. Explain how this is possible.
15. Explain why it is not necessary to keep the general ledger up-to-date on a daily basis.

CASE STUDIES

Case 1 Overcoming a Lack of Control over Accounts Receivable

When Brian Barnes went to work as the chief accountant for Durante Paving Company, he quickly noticed that the system of handling accounts receivable was quite different from any system that he had encountered before. The system was theoretically simple and worked as follows:

a. The production department issued sales invoices and sent them to the accounting department. The accounting department, after making the appropriate accounting entries, filed these invoices in an "unpaid invoices" file, arranged alphabetically by customer.
b. As payments were received from customers, the appropriate invoices were withdrawn from the unpaid file, stamped PAID, and filed in a "paid invoices" file.
c. The file of unpaid invoices represented the accounts receivable subsidiary ledger of the company.

Each month, the accounting department prepared a detailed list of the unpaid invoices for the owner. When the owner, Mr. Durante, looked over this list, he always found errors in it, such as an item on the list that he knew had been paid, or an item listed twice and showing slightly different amounts. Mr. Durante was annoyed by these errors, and often accused the accounting department of incompetence. Barnes was also concerned because, since joining the company, he hadn't once been able to balance the subsidiary ledger with the general ledger control account. Barnes launched an investigation to find and overcome the weaknesses in the system. He found no fault with his own staff members who performed their duties correctly. But he did find a serious problem with the "unpaid invoices" file. Other employees, particularly engineers and production foremen, were continually using the file, inserting and removing invoices without notifying the accounting department. These employees claimed that they needed the invoices for reference when discussing charges with customers, renegotiating a price, and so on. The engineering department did not keep its own file of invoices on special prenumbered forms. The invoices were typed up on ordinary letterhead paper.

Questions

1. The production engineers and foremen misused the "unpaid invoices" file. Give examples of specific occurrences that would create errors in the accounts receivable.
2. Suggest changes to the system that would allow the accounting department to gain control over the accounts receivable.
3. After fixing the accounting system, Barnes sees the owner, Mr. Durante, remove an invoice from the file without notifying the accounting department. How should Barnes handle this problem?

Case 2 *Is the Policy Good or Bad?*

Joan Webster, the owner of a small business, decides that she should "look after Number One," as she puts it.

Webster has a thorough system of recordkeeping for accounts receivable. She makes certain that every debt is collected on time, and her collection record is extremely good. However, Webster has an entirely different attitude toward accounts payable. "Why," she asks, "should I keep records of how much I owe to others? Let them keep track of how much I owe them. And, if they don't do a thorough job of it, maybe I'll get away without paying for something." She believes that other businesses should control their accounts receivable as she controls hers.

As a result of this policy, Webster's procedure for handling incoming purchase invoices is very casual. After the purchase invoices are received and checked, they are placed in a pile on an office desk. The pile represents the accounts payable of the business, but no accounting entries are made to record them.

The purchase invoices stay in the pile on the desk until a request for payment is made. Then Webster removes the particular invoice in question and authorizes its payment. When the cheque in payment is issued, the purchase invoice is then accounted for as if it were a cash purchase of goods or services. The purchase invoice is filed with the cheque copy.

Questions

1. Is Webster's policy a reasonable one? Explain.
2. Would Webster's accounts be useful in providing information for management decisions?
3. When financial statements are prepared, how should the pile of unpaid bills be handled?

Case 3   Evaluating the Creditworthiness of Two Companies

The simplified financial statements for two different companies appear below:

	Company A	Company B
Balance Sheet Data		
December 31, 19--		
Assets		
Bank	$ 1 000	$ 2 000
Accounts Receivable	30 000	8 000
Other Assets	80 000	74 000
Total	$111 000	$84 000
Liabilities and Equity		
Bank Loan	$ 25 000	—
Accounts Payable	5 000	$ 5 000
Owner's Equity	81 000	79 000
Total	$111 000	$84 000
Income Statement Data		
Year Ended December 31, 19--		
Revenue	$90 000	$80 000
Expenses		
Bank Interest	$ 5 000	—
Other Expenses	50 000	$43 000
Total Expenses	$55 000	$43 000
Net Income	$35 000	$37 000

Required:

You receive a loan application for $50 000 from each of the above companies to finance an expansion program. Analyze the above data and write a report on the creditworthiness of each of the two companies. In your report, address the following:
1. the percentage of accounts receivable compared to revenue;
2. how company A has financed its accounts receivable;
3. the effect issue 2 above has had on the net income;
4. the danger of the large accounts receivable figure being caused by overdue and uncollectable accounts;
5. whether or not you would grant the loans, and under what conditions.

CAREER
Carol Smalley / Accounts Payable Supervisor

While Carol Smalley was attending R. H. King Collegiate in Scarborough, Ontario, she particularly enjoyed the accounting courses she took as part of a business and commerce program. This background helped her to get a job as a cashier with State Farm Insurance upon graduation. After less than a year in this position, she was promoted to commissions clerk.

Since then, Carol's accounting career has been wide and varied. From State Farm Insurance, Carol moved into International Business Machines as an accounts payable clerk. Her responsibilities there included organizing the invoices for payment, insuring that discounts for early payment were made, and matching invoices to packing slips and purchase orders so that payment could be approved by the general manager.

After a year and a half with IBM, Carol left her job to start a family. Then after a four-year absence from the work force, she joined Prentice-Hall Canada Inc., a publishing company. She began by working in the customer service department and later moved to the accounts receivable department as a collection clerk. Eventually, after three years as an accounts payable processor, Carol was promoted to accounting operations administrator.

In this position, Carol gained invaluable experience in setting up accounting systems on a personal computer. Her main responsibility during this time was to set up a fixed asset system in which all furniture and equipment, corporate computers, microcomputers and distribution and production equipment were listed by serial number and cost value. In this way, they could much more easily be reconciled with the general ledger. She also learned a great deal about Prentice-Hall's procedure for handling royalties (payments paid to authors) and travel and entertainment expenses. With her knowledge in this area, Carol wrote the company's Procedures Manual on the handling of royalty expenses.

Recently, Carol was promoted once again. She is now accounts payable supervisor, responsible for overseeing five other employees. The accounts payable department looks after payment of all expenses, including inventory and royalties. Carol oversees the input and processing of all payables expenses.

Although a great deal of Carol's present skills were learned on the job, she feels that her high school accounting courses gave her a firm foundation. They taught her not only basic accounting concepts and procedures, but also the importance of organization, accuracy, and thoroughness.

Discussion

1. What are the accounting jobs Carol has held since graduating from high school?
2. How have Carol's accounting courses helped her in her career?
3. List the information that is placed on a computer data form.
4. What were Carol's duties as an accounts payable clerk while employed at IBM?
5. List all the source documents Carol has handled in her various accounting positions.
6. Why would an audit accountant who can work with computers be one of the most sought-after types of accountants?
7. Investigate computer systems and programming courses included in community college and university accounting programs.

9 The Simple Work Sheet and Classified Financial Statements

9.1 The Six-Column Work Sheet
9.2 Classified Financial Statements
9.3 The Work Sheet and the Financial Statements
9.4 Computerized Accounting: The Six-Column Work Sheet

In the preceding chapters you learned about the system for recording transactions in the books of account. Next, you will learn the technique used by accountants to prepare the balance sheet and the income statement.

Financial statements are prepared from the information provided by the ledger accounts. They are prepared at the end of the fiscal period, and whenever else they may be required. The preparation of financial statements is normally work of an advanced nature done by senior people.

9.1 The Six-Column Work Sheet

Accountants use a business form called a work sheet to help prepare the financial statements. A **work sheet** is an informal business paper prepared in pencil on columnar bookkeeping paper, used to organize and plan the information for the financial statements. The work sheet is usually prepared in pencil so that changes may be made easily.

In reality, accountants use an eight-column work sheet, on which they include "adjustments." You will study the eight-column work sheet and adjustments in the next chapter. The six-column work sheet is used at this time in order to present the new concepts as simply as possible.

The steps in preparing a work sheet are detailed below.

1. Write in the heading on work sheet paper. Examine the heading in Figure 9.1 carefully. Observe the precise way that the fiscal period is described.

ACCOUNTS	TRIAL BALANCE		INCOME STATEMENT		BALANCE SHEET	
	DR	CR	DR	CR	DR	CR

Inter-City Rent Alls Work Sheet Year Ended December 31, 19-

2. Record the trial balance as shown in Figure 9.2. It is essential that the trial balance columns be correct before you continue. There is no hope of producing a correct work sheet if the trial balance does not balance. Figure 9.2 shows how this is done.

Inter-City Rent Alls Work Sheet Year Ended December 31, 19-

ACCOUNTS	TRIAL BALANCE		INCOME STATEMENT		BALANCE SHEET	
	DR	CR	DR	CR	DR	CR
Bank	3 457 15					
Accounts Receivable	1 940 250					
Supplies	1 240 -					
Equipment	20 400 -					
Automobiles	32 936 57					
Accounts Payable		5 296 10				
Sales Tax Payable		561 11				
Bank Loan		10 000 -				
R. Tessier, Capital		50 000 -				
R. Tessier, Drawings	24 000 -					
Sales		95 907 -				
Advertising Expense	756 -					
Bank Charges Expense	1 742 -					
Car Expenses	6 575 80					
Miscellaneous Expense	175 -					
Rent Expense	12 000 -					
Telephone Expense	1 200 -					
Utilities Expense	1 370 -					
Wages Expense	36 509 19					
	161 764 21	161 764 21				

Figure 9.2 Recording the trial balance on a work sheet.

3. Extend each of the amounts from the trial balance columns into one of the four columns to the right, as in Figure 9.3. The process is simple and logical. Revenue and expense items are extended into the Income Statement columns. These are the items that make up the net income or net loss. All other items—assets, liabilities, capital, and drawings—are extended into the Balance Sheet columns. Observe that the drawings are not a net income item and are not transferred to the Income Statement section.

Be careful to transfer amounts accurately, and to record debit amounts in debit columns and credit amounts in credit columns. Be sure, too, that no single amount is transferred to two places and that no item is missed.

Inter-City Rent Alls Work Sheet Year Ended December 31, 19--

ACCOUNTS	TRIAL BALANCE DR	TRIAL BALANCE CR	INCOME STATEMENT DR	INCOME STATEMENT CR	BALANCE SHEET DR	BALANCE SHEET CR
Bank	3457 15				3457 15	
Accounts Receivable	1940 250				1940 250	
Supplies	1240 -				1240 -	
Equipment	20400 -				20400 -	
Automobiles	32936 57				32936 57	
Accounts Payable		5296 10				5296 10
Sales Tax Payable		561 11				561 11
Bank Loan		10000 -				10000 -
R. Tessier, Capital		50000 -				50000 -
R. Tessier, Drawings	24000 -				24000 -	
Sales		95907 -		95907 -		
Advertising Expense	756 -		756 -			
Bank Charges Expense	1742 -		1742 -			
Car Expenses	6575 80		6575 80			
Miscellaneous Expense	175 -		175 -			
Rent Expense	12000 -		12000 -			
Telephone Expense	1200 -		1200 -			
Utilities Expense	1370 -		1370 -			
Wages Expense	36509 19		36509 19			
	161764 21	161764 21				

Figure 9.3 Extending the amounts on a work sheet.

4. Balance the work sheet, as shown in Figure 9.4. There are three steps in balancing the work sheet.
    a. Total each of the four right-hand money columns and write in the totals.
    b. Calculate the difference between the two Income Statement columns (in our example $35 579.01), then the difference between the two Balance Sheet columns (again $35 579.01), and see that the two differences are equal.

    If they are not the same, the work sheet does not balance. It is mathematically impossible for the work sheet to be correct if it does not balance. Therefore, you should not proceed to the preparation of the financial statements until all errors have been found and corrected.
    c. Record the above information on the work sheet in a neat and orderly fashion as shown in Figure 9.4.

| Inter-City Rent Alls Work Sheet Year Ended December 31, 19-- ||||||
| ACCOUNTS | TRIAL BALANCE || INCOME STATEMENT || BALANCE SHEET |
	DR	CR	DR	CR	DR	CR
Bank	3 457 15				3 457 15	
Accounts Receivable	19 402 50				19 402 50	
Supplies	1 240 -				1 240 -	
Equipment	20 400 -				20 400 -	
Automobiles	32 936 57				32 936 57	
Accounts Payable		5 296 10				5 296 10
Sales Tax Payable		561 11				561 11
Bank Loan		10 000 -				10 000 -
R. Tessier, Capital		50 000 -				50 000 -
R. Tessier, Drawings	24 000 -				24 000 -	
Sales		95 907 -		95 907 -		
Advertising Expense	756 -		756 -			
Bank Charges Expense	1 742 -		1 742 -			
Car Expenses	6 575 80		6 575 80			
Miscellaneous Expense	175 -		175 -			
Rent Expense	12 000 -		12 000 -			
Telephone Expense	1 200 -		1 200 -			
Utilities Expense	1 370 -		1 370 -			
Wages Expense	36 509 19		36 509 19			
	161 764 21	161 764 21				
Net Income			60 327 99	95 907 -	101 436 22	65 857 21
			35 579 01			35 579 01
		Balancing figure	95 907 -	95 907 -	101 436 22	101 436 22

Figure 9.4 Balancing the work sheet (net income situation).

Net Income or Net Loss

The balancing figure on the work sheet tells the amount of the net income or net loss for the fiscal period. A look at the Income Statement columns tells which of the two it is. A net income has been earned if the total revenues (credit column) are greater than the total expenses (debit column). A net loss has been incurred if the total expenses (debit column) are greater than the total revenues (credit column).

Finalizing the work sheet for a loss situation is done slightly differently than for a profit situation. The balancing figure is placed in the outer two of the last four columns when there is a profit. A balancing figure of $35 579.01 is shown in Figure 9.4. The balancing figure is placed in the inner two of the last four columns when there is a loss. A balancing figure of $356.07 is shown in Figure 9.5.

Figure 9.5 Balancing the work sheet (net loss situation).

Section Review Questions

1. When are financial statements prepared?
2. Who, in the accounting department, usually prepares financial statements?
3. Name and describe the form used by accountants to help them prepare the financial statements.
4. How many steps does the text show for completing a work sheet?
5. Explain an important aspect of step 2 in completing a work sheet.
6. Which items are extended to the Balance Sheet columns?
7. How do you know if the work sheet balances?
8. Why is it important to balance the work sheet?
9. Why is the Drawings account not extended to the Income Statement section?
10. Describe briefly the way to balance a work sheet.
11. How do you tell whether the business has made a profit or suffered a loss?

Section Exercises

1. For each account listed below, indicate whether it would be extended to Income Statement Debit, Income Statement Credit, Balance Sheet Debit, or Balance Sheet Credit. (A chart for this exercise is provided in the workbook.)

    Accounts Payable
    Miscellaneous Expense
    Revenue
    Advertising
    Wages
    Mortgage Payable
    Light and Heat
    Equipment
    G. Rojek, Capital
    Delivery Expense

    Bank Loan
    Accounts Receivable
    Automobile
    Bank
    G. Rojek, Drawings
    Sales
    Bank Charges
    Rent
    Supplies
    Trucks

2. From the simplified data shown below, complete a work sheet for N. Foreman and Company for the month ended April 30, 19––. (Profit situations.)

    TRIAL BALANCE APRIL 30, 19––

Bank	$ 750.20	
Accounts Receivable	15 375.10	
Supplies	1 250.00	
Equipment	18 500.00	
Automobiles	29 375.00	
Bank Loan		$30 000.00
Accounts Payable		5 331.00
N. Foreman, Capital		25 000.00
N. Foreman, Drawings	3 000.00	
Fees Revenue		18 200.00
Bank Charges	250.00	
Car Expenses	1 750.00	
Miscellaneous Expense	512.20	
Light and Heat	746.00	
Rent	1 100.00	
Telephone	276.50	
Wages	5 646.00	
	$78 531.00	$78 531.00

3. **Workbook Exercise:** Additional practice at completing a work sheet.

4. The work sheet below contains a number of errors. Locate the errors, make the necessary corrections, and balance the work sheet. A work sheet has been provided in the workbook.

Work Sheet — The Arthur Company — Month Ended Oct. 31, 19—

Accounts	Trial Balance Dr.	Trial Balance Cr.	Income Statement Dr.	Income Statement Cr.	Balance Sheet Dr.	Balance Sheet Cr.
Bank	1722 16				1722 16	
Acc. Rec'l – J. Young	323 –				332 –	
Acc. Rec'l – M. Watson	72 –				72 –	
Acc. Rec'l – H. Chan	116 –				116 –	
Supplies	1255 –				1255 –	
Office Equipment	5863 –				5863 –	
Automobiles	13200 –				1320 –	
Acc. Pay'l – O.K. Supply		421 72				421 72
Acc. Pay'l – City Hydro		116 42				116 42
Acc. Pay'l – Slick Oil Co.		331 19				331 19
Bank Loan		10000 –				10000 –
P. Arthur, Capital		10504 82				10504 82
P. Arthur, Drawings	1000 –			1000 –		
Revenue		4903 17		4903 17		
Advertising	465 12		465 12			
Automobile Expenses	270 –				270 –	
Bank Charges	56 40		56 40			
Miscellaneous Exp.	113 74		113 74			
Rent	400 –		400 –			
Salaries	1280 –		1280 –		1280 –	
Telephone	25 60		25 60			
Utilities	115 30					
	26277 32	26277 32	2340 86	5903 17	12230 16	21074 15
Net Income			3562 31			8843 99
			5903 17	5903 17	12230 16	29918 14

9.2 Classified Financial Statements

Balance Sheet—Account Form and Report Form

The balance sheets in this chapter look different from those you learned about earlier. Those balance sheets were shown in account form. The **account form of balance sheet** is one on which the information is presented in a side-by-side, or horizontal, format.

In this chapter you will study a style of balance sheet known as the report form. The **report form of balance sheet** is one on which the information is presented in a one above the other, or vertical, format. The two styles are contrasted in Figure 9.6. The report form of balance is common because it uses standard-sized paper.

Figure 9.6 The balance sheet in the account form (left) and in the report form (right).

Classified Balance Sheet

Financial statements that are classified are introduced in this chapter. A **classified financial statement** is one in which the data is grouped according to major categories. A sample classified balance sheet is shown in Figure 9.7. Observe the overall appearance of this balance sheet carefully. Be sure to relate the marginal notes to the sample statement. In particular, note the meanings of the terms "current assets," "plant and equipment," "current liabilities," and "long-term liabilities." You will learn more about classified statements as you progress through the text.

Section 9.2   257

PEOPLES' SECURITY COMPANY
BALANCE SHEET
DECEMBER 31, 19--

ASSETS

Current Assets
Bank	$ 1 750	
Accounts Receivable	35 879	
Supplies	1 350	$ 38 979

Fixed Assets
Land	$40 000	
Building	55 000	
Equipment	15 070	
Automobiles	33 350	143 420
		$182 399

LIABILITIES AND OWNER'S EQUITY

Current Liabilities
Accounts Payable	$ 9 450	
Bank Loan	25 000	
Sales Tax Payable	752	
Mortgage Instalment (current)	850	$ 36 052

Long-term Liability
Mortgage Payable	80 000

J. Otto, Capital
Balance January 1		$50 287
Net Income	$38 560	
Drawings	22 500	
Increase in Equity		16 060
Balance December 31		66 347
		$182 399

Current Assets — Unrestricted cash or other assets that will be converted into cash within one year and assets that will be used up within one year

Plant and Equipment or Fixed Assets — Long-term assets held for their usefulness in producing goods or services

Current Liabilities — Short-term debts, payment of which is expected to occur within one year

Long-term Liabilities — Debts of the business that are not due within one year

Capital — Total assets minus total liabilities
This section is organized to show clearly the beginning balance, the increase or decrease through profit or loss, the decrease through owner's withdrawals, and the ending balance.

Inner columns are used to list individual items building up to a subtotal.

The two balancing totals.

Figure 9.7 The classified balance sheet of Peoples' Security Company.

Classified Income Statement

Preparing simple classified income statements is something that you have already been doing. The items on the income statement have been grouped as revenues and expenses. Later in the text, you will learn how to make additional classifications on the income statement. You may look ahead to see such a statement on page 447.

Section Review Questions

1. In what style were the balance sheets of the early chapters prepared?
2. Describe the account form of the balance sheet.

3. Describe the report form of the balance sheet.
4. Give the accountancy meaning of the word "classified."
5. Name the two asset classifications on the simple balance sheet in Figure 9.7.
6. Give another accepted name for "Plant and Equipment."
7. Name the two liability classifications on the simple balance sheet in Figure 9.7.
8. Describe how the capital is presented on the new form of balance sheet.
9. Describe how the columns are used in the preparation of a classified balance sheet.
10. What are the two classifications on the simple income statement?

Section Exercises

1. Classify the accounts given below into one of the categories named at the right.

Accounts	Categories
Accounts Payable	Current Assets
Accounts Receivable	Plant and Equipment
Advertising	Current Liabilities
Bank Charges	Long-term Liabilities
Bank Loan	Owner's Equity
Bank	Revenue
Buildings	
Commissions Earned	
Delivery Expense	
F. Ryback, Capital	
F. Ryback, Drawings	
General Expense	
Insurance Expense	
Mortgage Payable (Current Instalment)	
Mortgage Payable (Non-current)	
Postage	
Rent	
Supplies	
Telephone	
Wages	

2. Shown below is the unclassified balance sheet for The Boat Repair Centre, owned by Anna Rodriguez of Kenora, Ont.

1. Give the total of the current assets.
2. Give the total of the fixed assets.
3. Give the total of the current liabilities.
4. Give the total of the long-term liabilities.
5. Explain why there is an increase in capital.
6. Explain why the equity section begins on October 1 and ends on September 30.
7. What is the amount of the total mortgage payable?

THE BOAT REPAIR CENTRE
BALANCE SHEET
SEPTEMBER 30, 19–4

Assets
Bank		$ 2 125.00
Accounts Receivable		15 256.36
Office Supplies		1 500.00
Repair Supplies and Materials		15 236.00
Land		36 000.00
Building		48 000.00
Equipment		16 250.00
Truck		22 356.90
		$156 724.26

Liabilities
Accounts Payable		$ 5 216.35
Bank Loan		10 000.00
Mortgage Instalment due within one year		2 000.00
Mortgage Payable		48 000.00
		$ 65 216.35

Owner's Equity
A. Rodriguez, Capital			
Balance October 1, 19–3		$80 356.00	
Net Income	$35 615.20		
Drawings	24 463.29		
Increase in Capital		11 151.91	
Balance September 30, 19–4			91 507.91
			$156 724.26

9.3 The Work Sheet and the Financial Statements

Owners and business executives rarely look at the raw data of actual financial records. They rely on the accounting department to maintain the records properly and to process the data into more meaningful form. The owners and executives want to see finished accounting reports and financial statements. It is up to the accounting department to produce first-class reports and statements.

A completed work sheet contains all of the information needed to prepare the balance sheet and the income statement. Develop the habit of looking only to the work sheet for this information. It is the best, and sometimes the only, source of the information. This will be especially true after the introduction of adjustments in the next chapter.

Figures 9.8, 9.9, and 9.10 show how the balance sheet and the income statement of Inter-City Rent Alls are prepared directly from information on the work sheet.

Chapter 9

Inter-City Rent Alls		Year Ended December 31, 19__		
ACCOUNTS	INCOME STATEMENT DR	INCOME STATEMENT CR	BALANCE SHEET DR	BALANCE SHEET CR
Bank			3457 15	
Accounts Receivable			19402 50	
Supplies			1240 —	
Equipment			20400 —	
Automobiles			32936 57	
Accounts Payable				5296 10
Sales Tax Payable				561 11
Bank Loan				10000 —
R. Tessier, Capital				50000 —
R. Tessier, Drawings			24000 —	
Sales		95907 —		
Advertising Expense	756 —			
Bank Charges Expense	1742 —			
Car Expenses	6575 80			
Miscellaneous Expense	175			
Rent Expense	12000 —			
Telephone Expense	1200 —			
Utilities Expense	1370 —			
Wages Expense	36509 19			
	60327 99	95907 —	101436 22	65857 21
Net Income	35579 01			35579 01
	95907 —	95907 —	101436 22	101436 22

All of the figures for the Income Statement come from these two columns of the work sheet.

Figure 9.8 A partial work sheet for Inter-City Rent Alls giving the information for the financial statements in Figure 9.9 and Figure 9.10.

Inter-City Rent Alls
Balance Sheet
December 31, 19__

Assets

Current Assets		
Bank	3457 15	
Accounts Receivable	19402 50	
Supplies	1240 —	24099 65
Plant and Equipment		
Equipment	20400 —	
Automobiles	32936 57	53336 57
		77436 22

Liabilities and Owner's Equity

Current Liabilities		
Accounts Payable	5296 10	
Sales Tax Payable	561 11	
Bank Loan	10000 —	15857 21
R. Tessier, Capital		
Balance January 1		50000 —
Net Income	35579 01	
Drawings	24000 —	
Increase in Capital		11579 01
Balance December 31		61579 01
		77436 22

All of the figures for the Balance Sheet come from these two columns of the work sheet.

Figure 9.9 The balance sheet, prepared from the amounts in the "Balance Sheet" columns of the work sheet.

Inter-City Rent Alls
Income Statement
Year Ended December 31, 19—

Revenue		
Sales		95907 —
Operating Expenses		
Advertising	756 —	
Bank Charges	1742 —	
Car Expense	6575 80	
Miscellaneous Expense	175 —	
Rent	12000 —	
Telephone	1200 —	
Utilities	1370 —	
Wages	36509 19	60327 99
Net Income		35579 01

Figure 9.10 The income statement, prepared from the amounts in the "Income Statement" columns of the work sheet.

Building the Equity Section of a Balance Sheet

Figure 9.11 gives three examples of the equity section of a balance sheet, and shows how the information for them is derived from the work sheet.

Case 1. Net income greater than drawings.

Work sheet R. Wall	Mo ended June 30, 19–
	Balance Sheet
Accounts	Dr.	Cr.
Bank	1 507 10	
R. Wall, Capital		12 276 53
R. Wall, Drawings	1 500 –	
	21 680 35	19 971 28
Net Income		1 709 07
	21 680 35	21 680 35

Case 2. Drawings greater than net income.

Work Sheet T. Smith	Yr ended Dec. 31, 19–
	Balance Sheet
Accounts	Dr.	Cr.
Bank	1 951 75	
T. Smith, Capital		20 376 64
T. Smith, Drawings	15 376 70	
	94 209 15	83 615 12
Net Income		10 594 03
	94 209 15	94 209 15

Case 3. A loss.

Work Sheet S. Brown	3 Mos Ended Sept. 30, 19–
	Balance Sheet
Accounts	Dr.	Cr.
Bank	671 12	
S. Brown, Capital		31 216 40
S. Brown, Drawings	19 400 –	
	92 071 40	97 219 02
Net Loss	5 147 62	
	97 219 02	97 219 02

Figure 9.11 Equity items are transferred from the work sheet (*left*) to the balance sheets (*right*) for three different situations.

Section 9.3   263

R. Wall, Capital

Balance June 1			12276 53
Net Income	1709 07		
Drawings	1500 —		
Increase in Capital		209 07	
Balance June 30			12485 60

T. Smith, Capital

Balance January 1			20376 64
Net Income	10594 03		
Drawings	15376 70		
Decrease in Capital		4782 67	
Balance December 31			15593 97

S. Brown, Capital

Balance July 1			3121 40
Net Loss	5147 62		
Drawings	19400 —		
Decrease in Capital		4547 62	
Balance December 31			6668 78

Understanding the Equity Section of the Balance Sheet

The three equity sections from the previous page are examined again below from a different viewpoint. Figure 9.12 tells us that in each case, the equity section starts with the capital figure at the beginning of the fiscal period, shows the changes in capital during the period, and finishes with the capital at the end of the period.

Case 1.

Net income greater than drawings results in an increase in capital.

```
R. Wall, Capital
  Balance June 1                    1227 63      ← Beginning date / Beginning capital
  Net Income         1709 07
  Drawings           1500 —
  Increase in Capital              209 07        ← Ending capital
  Balance June 30                           12485 60  ← Ending date
```

The dates show the fiscal period to be for one month.

Case 2.

Drawings greater than net income results in a decrease in capital.

```
T. Smith, Capital
  Balance January 1                 20376 64    ← Beginning date / Beginning capital
  Net Income        10594 03
  Drawings          15376 70
  Decrease in Capital              4782 67      ← Ending capital
  Balance December 31                       15593 97  ← Ending date
```

The dates show the fiscal period to be for one year.

Case 3.

A loss results in a decrease in capital.

```
S. Brown, Capital
  Balance, July 1                   31216 40    ← Beginning date / Beginning capital
  Net Loss           5147 62
  Drawings          19400 —
  Decrease in Capital              24547 62     ← Ending capital
  Balance December 31                       6668 78   ← Ending date
```

The dates show the fiscal period to be for **six** months.

Figure 9.12 Three equity sections showing how equity changes in a fiscal period.

Typed or Printed Financial Statements

In the business world, financial reports are usually typewritten or printed. However, as a student you will find it more convenient to prepare your statements in handwritten form.

Shown below in Figure 9.13 is a typical typewritten balance sheet. Observe in particular the way in which dollar signs are used.

```
                    EASTERN COMPANY
                     BALANCE SHEET
                     MARCH 31, 19--

                         ASSETS

Current Assets
  Bank                              $  2 560.50
  Accounts Receivable                  35 258.25
  Supplies                              2 540.00    $ 40 358.75

Plant and Equipment
  Land                              $75 000.00
  Building                          150 250.00
  Furniture and Fixtures             18 568.50
  Delivery Equipment                 42 321.58      286 140.08
                                                   $326 498.83

              LIABILITIES AND OWNER'S EQUITY

Current Liabilities
  Bank Loan                         $50 000.00
  Accounts Payable                    8 503.58       58 503.58

Long-Term Liability
  Mortgage Payable                                  180 000.00

R.C. Safir, Capital
  Balance January 1, 19--            $48 236.85
  Net Income             $86 651.94
  Drawings                46 893.54

  Increase in Capital                 39 758.40

Balance March 31, 19--                              87 995.25
                                                  $326 498.83
```

On typewritten statements, a dollar sign is used with the first figure in every column and the first figure beneath every ruled line in every column.

On formal statements the "cents" part of an even dollar amount is always shown by two ciphers and never by a dash.

Figure 9.13 An example of a typed financial statement.

More on the Accounting Cycle

You have already learned that there is a certain set of procedures to be followed during a fiscal period. Journalizing, posting, and balancing of the ledger are carried out by junior employees. The next two steps involve the preparation of the work sheet and the financial statements. They are carried out by senior people. All the steps together constitute the accounting cycle.

The steps of the accounting cycle studied so far are shown in Figure 9.14 below.

```
                    ┌─────────────────────────┐
                    │   Transactions occur.   │
                    │   Source documents.     │
                    └───────────┬─────────────┘
                                ▼
                    ┌─────────────────────────┐
                    │   Accounting entries    │
                    │   recorded in journal.  │
  Performed by      └───────────┬─────────────┘
    junior                      ▼
   personnel        ┌─────────────────────────┐
                    │  Journal entries posted │
                    │  to the ledger accounts.│
                    └───────────┬─────────────┘
                                ▼
                    ┌─────────────────────────┐
                    │ Ledger balanced by means│
                    │   of a trial balance.   │
                    └───────────┬─────────────┘
                                ▼
                    ┌─────────────────────────┐
                    │  Work sheet prepared.   │
  Performed by      └───────────┬─────────────┘
    senior                      ▼
   personnel        ┌─────────────────────────┐
                    │    Balance sheet and    │
                    │ Income Statement prepared.│
                    └───────────┬─────────────┘
                                ▼
                          More to come
```

Figure 9.14. Steps in the partial accounting cycle.

Section Review Questions

1. Why do managers and owners usually not look at the actual accounting records?
2. What records do the managers and owners look at?
3. Why should an accounting department be concerned about producing first-rate reports and statements?
4. Where is the best place for an accountant to obtain all of the necessary information for the balance sheet and the income statement?
5. The equity section of the balance sheet is made up from three figures on the work sheet. What are these three figures?
6. In regard to question 5 above, what set of conditions produces an increase in equity?
7. Explain the two sets of conditions that produce a decrease in equity.
8. In what two ways, besides the print, do typed financial statements differ from handwritten ones?
9. Give the six steps in the accounting cycle learned so far.

10. Which of the above steps are performed by junior personnel? Which are performed by senior personnel?

Section Exercises

1. **In your workbook, complete the following statements with the most appropriate word or phrase.**

    1. Accounting department personnel work with _____ data. Owners and managers prefer _____ data.
    2. Financial statements and reports are the _____ of the accounting department.
    3. All of the information necessary for the preparation of the financial statements is found on the _____ .
    4. An increase in equity can only occur if there is a _____ that is _____ than the _____ .
    5. There will be a decrease in equity if the _____ are _____ the net income.
    6. There will be a decrease in equity if there is a _____ regardless of the amount of the drawings.
    7. The equity section of a balance sheet shows:
        a. _____ ,
        b. _____ ,
        c. _____ ,
        d. _____ ,
        e. _____ .
    8. A fiscal year that ends on November 30, 19–5 will have begun on _____ .
    9. A fiscal half-year that ends on March 31, 19–4 will have begun on _____ .
    10. On typed financial statements, it is customary to include _____ .

2. **Complete the following schedule by filling in the blanks in the copy provided in your workbook.**

Items	Opening Capital	Net Income or Net Loss (−)	Drawings	Ending Capital
a.	$ 30 000	$15 000	$10 000	$
b.	50 000	−2 000	7 000	
c.	70 000	32 000		75 500
d.		16 000	19 500	33 200
e.	56 000		30 000	40 000
f.	45 000		25 000	15 000
g.	22 000		10 000	28 000
h.		25 000	18 000	42 000
i.	120 000	42 000		112 000

3. Prepare the Equity section of the balance sheet from the data given for each case below.

Owner's name	T. Hunter	S. Robb	W. Head
Fiscal period	Year ended December 31, 19—	Three months ended March 31, 19—	Month ended May 31, 19—
Opening capital	$27 042.62	$19 641.25	$20 196.74
Net income	39 171.04	22 462.67	−3 750.20
Drawings	35 000.00	25 575.00	10 047.17

4. Prepare the income statement and the classified balance sheet from the following completed work sheet.

Work Sheet — Lakeland Insurance Agency — Year Ended Dec. 31, 19—

Accounts	Trial Balance Dr	Trial Balance Cr	Income Statement Dr	Income Statement Cr	Balance Sheet Dr	Balance Sheet Cr
Cash	2704 30				2704 30	
Accounts Receivable	5495 57				5495 57	
Supplies	1767 —				1767 —	
Office Equipment	5437 50				5437 50	
Automobiles	16 438 —				16 438 —	
Accounts Payable		2420 71				2420 71
Bank Loan		10 000 —				10 000 —
Arno Niemi, Capital		14 353 92				14 353 92
Arno Niemi, Drawings	4876 18				4876 18	
Commissions Earned		92 403 50		92 403 50		
Advertising	6130 75		6130 75			
Car Expenses	3640 20		3640 20			
Miscellaneous Expense	216 91		216 91			
Rent	4200 —		4200 —			
Telephone	1270 87		1270 87			
Utilities	1737 70		1737 70			
Wages	21 376 15		21 376 15			
	119 178 13	119 178 13	38 572 58	92 403 50	80 605 55	26 774 63
Net Income			53 830 92			53 830 92
			92 403 50	92 403 50	80 605 55	80 605 55

9.4 Computerized Accounting: The Six-Column Work Sheet

The Six-Column Work Sheet

A work sheet can be viewed as a manual spreadsheet. Looking at a work sheet you will see rows and columns just as on an electronic spreadsheet. But the electronic spreadsheet allows you to enter (or change) trial balance data and to obtain a finished work sheet in seconds.

A simple spreadsheet program to produce the six-column work sheet for P. Simpson is given below in Figure 9.15. The hidden formulas are shown in faint print. The program is designed to:

1. add the trial balance columns. The user must make a visual check to see that the two column totals agree;
2. transfer the trial balance figures to the appropriate columns for the financial statements;
3. total the remaining money columns and complete the work sheet.

	A	B	C	D	E	F	G	H
1	P. SIMPSON	COMPANY	WORK	SHEET			MONTH	ENDED OCT. 31, 19--
2		ACCOUNTS	TRIAL BALANCE		INCOME STATEMENT		BALANCE	SHEET
3			DR.	CR.	DR.	CR.	DR.	CR.
4	BANK						C4	
5	AR/J. MORRISON						C5	
6	AR/N. MARTIN						C6	
7	SUPPLIES						C7	
8	OFFICE EQUIPMENT						C8	
9	AUTOMOBILE						C9	
10	AP/ACE FINANCE							D10
11	AP/GRAND'S ST							D11
12	AP/INDUST SUPPL							D12
13	P. SIMPSON	CAPITAL						D13
14	P. SIMPSON	DRAWINGS					C14	
15	FEES REVENUE					D15		
16	CAR EXPENSES				C16			
17	LIGHT AND HEAT				C17			
18	MISC EXPENSE				C18			
19	RENT				C19			
20	TELEPHONE				C20			
21	WAGES				C21			
22			SUM(C4:C21)	SUM(D4:D21)	SUM(E4:E21)	SUM(F4:F21)	SUM(G4:G21)	SUM(H4:H21)
23					F22-E22			G22-H22
24	NET INCOME	OR LOSS			E22+E23	F22	G22	H22+H23
25								
26								

Figure 9.15 A spreadsheet program to do a six-column work sheet.

To use this program it is merely necessary to enter the trial balance figures while the calculator is turned off. When the figures are all entered, activate the calculator twice. The work sheet will be completed in seconds. Single- or double-ruled lines can be included in the program by using a series of dashes or equal signs. The "replicate" command is useful here to copy formulas over a range of cells.

Be sure to save your program on disk before entering the trial balance data. This makes it easier to use for another application.

Computer Review Questions

1. How does a spreadsheet make the preparation of a work sheet easier?
2. What command do most spreadsheets use for copying a formula over a range of cells?
3. What formulas are used in Figure 9.15 to total the trial balance columns?
4. What figure is shown in cell E23 of the spreadsheet in Figure 9.15?
5. How is the net income or net loss obtained on the spreadsheet?
6. In Figure 9.15, if you were to reduce the figure in cell D15, what would happen on the screen (calculator turned on)?

Computer Exercises

1. Using the program given in the chapter, prepare a work sheet for Exercise 2 on page 254. Save your program on disk when it is completed.

2. Load the program from question 1 above. Modify the program to bring about the following changes:
   a. increase Car Expense by $2 000;
   b. decrease Drawings by $2 000;
   c. add wages of $10 000;
   d. increase Capital by $7 000.

   1. What is the new figure for net income or net loss?
   2. What are the new balance sheet totals?

CHAPTER HIGHLIGHTS

Now that you have completed Chapter 9 you should:

1. be able to prepare a six-column work sheet;
2. understand the purpose of the work sheet;
3. know the two forms of the balance sheet—report form and account form;
4. know the meaning of "classified" with respect to financial statements;
5. be able to prepare a classified balance sheet and income statement;
6. understand that the data for the financial statements comes directly from the work sheet;
7. understand the three variations of the equity section of a balance sheet;
8. know the first six steps in the accounting cycle.

ACCOUNTING TERMS

balance sheet—account form
balance sheet—report form
classified financial statement
current liability
current asset

fixed asset
long-term liability
plant and equipment
work sheet

CHAPTER EXERCISES

Using Your Knowledge

1. Stacey Worrell, an accounting student, has discovered a slight variation in the procedure for balancing a work sheet. Her method is shown below.

Work Sheet — Morton Enterprises — Mo. Ended Dec. 31, 19—

Accounts	Tr. Bal. Dr.	Tr. Bal. Cr.	Inc. St. Dr.	Inc. St. Cr.	Bal. Sht. Dr.	Bal. Sht. Cr.
Bank	12 -				12 -	
Acc. Rec'l - G. Flavelle	8 -				8 -	
Supplies	15 -				15 -	
Equipment	40 -				40 -	
Truck	120 -				120 -	
Acc. Pay'l - Tops Hardware		17 -				17 -
V. Maswich, Capital		141 -				141 -
V. Maswich, Drawings	75 -				75 -	
Revenue		300 -		300 -		
General Expense	10 -		10 -			
Light and Heat	50 -		50 -			
Rent	90 -		90 -			
Telephone	8 -		8 -			
Wages	30 -		30 -			
	458 -	458 -	188 -	300 -		
Net Income			112 -			112 -
			300 -	300 -	270 -	270 -

1. Give your opinion of this method.
2. Explain why the balance sheet columns balance with the $112 net income figure included, but would not if the figure were excluded.

2. The balance in the Capital account of the O.K. Suppliers on January 1, 19--, was $26 000. The balance in this account was $27 500 at the end of the year. Net income for the year was $5 000. Explain why the balance in Capital was not $31 000.

3. For each of the following, check off the most appropriate response in the space provided in your workbook.

1. Financial statements are prepared
    a. once a year.
    b. at the end of the fiscal period.
    c. whenever management requires it.
    d. all of the above.
    e. none of the above.

2. A work sheet
    a. is one of the books of account.
    b. is one of the financial statements.
    c. is used instead of the financial statements.
    d. is all of the above.
    e. is none of the above.

3. Extending amounts on a work sheet means
    a. adding to the amounts because of additional transactions.
    b. placing debit amounts in debit columns and credit amounts in credit columns.
    c. transferring amounts into the Balance Sheet section or the Income Statement section.
    d. all of the above.
    e. none of the above.

4. The process of balancing the work sheet involves
    a. totaling the four right-hand money columns.
    b. calculating the difference between the two money columns in each of the last two sections.
    c. ensuring that the differences in b) above are equal to each other.
    d. all of the above.
    e. none of the above.

5. A work sheet will not balance if
    a. the Telephone Expense amount is extended to the Balance Sheet section Debit column.
    b. the Drawings amount is extended to the Income Statement section Debit column.
    c. the Capital amount is extended to the Balance Sheet section Debit column.
    d. all of the above.
    e. none of the above.

6. You can tell what the net income figure is by
   a. looking at the balancing figure in the Balance Sheet section of the work sheet.
   b. looking at the balancing figure in the Income Statement section of the work sheet.
   c. looking at the equity section of the completed balance sheet.
   d. all of the above.
   e. none of the above.
7. All of the following statements, except one, are either true or not true. Indicate the one which is not clearly right or wrong.
   a. The report form of balance sheet is the only style used in the real business world.
   b. The report form of balance sheet is common because it uses standard-sized paper.
   c. The report form of balance sheet is horizontal in form.
   d. The style of the report form of balance sheet eliminates the need for "balancing" totals.
   e. The report form of balance sheet is more difficult to understand.
8. On a classified balance sheet
   a. automobiles are not included in the Fixed Assets section because their value decreases over time.
   b. a mortgage payable has nothing to do with current liabilities because it represents a long-term debt.
   c. supplies are not included as a current asset because they are not normally converted into cash.
   d. a bank loan is included in long-term liabilities.
   e. the values shown for the fixed assets are not necessarily their true market value.
9. All of the following statements, except one, are either true or not true. Indicate the one which is not clearly right or wrong.
   a. The data in the books of account is considered to be "raw" data.
   b. An accountant is judged on the basis of accounting statements and reports. Therefore, such statements and reports should be first-class in form and content.
   c. All of the data necessary for the financial statements can be found on the work sheet.
   d. An overall decrease in capital can occur in two ways. An overall increase in capital can occur in only one way. Therefore, decreases in capital are more common.
   e. The beginning balance in the equity section of the balance sheet is not always dated January 1.
10. During a fiscal period a business suffered a loss of $12 000, began the period with a capital balance of $20 000, and ended the period with a negative capital balance of $2 000. The drawings for the fiscal period were
    a. $6 000.
    b. $10 000.
    c. $30 000.
    d. $18 000.
    e. $14 000.

Comprehensive Exercises

4. The trial balance of Ying Lo, a lawyer, on June 30, 19–5, after a fiscal period of six months, is as follows:

Bank	$ 516.20	
Accounts Receivable	9 255.50	
Office Supplies	1 525.00	
Office Equipment	10 356.00	
Automobile	19 255.65	
Professional Library	5 363.25	
Accounts Payable		$ 2 858.25
Ying Lo, Capital		34 024.81
Ying Lo, Drawings	20 000.00	
Fees Earned		55 285.00
Car Expenses	4 592.36	
Light and Heat Expense	589.25	
Miscellaneous Expense	1 254.85	
Rent	7 200.00	
Salaries	9 235.00	
Telephone	3 025.00	
	$92 168.06	$92 168.06

Complete a six-column work sheet and prepare the classified financial statements.

5. The trial balance of Star Delivery, owned by Danielle Nowak, on December 31, 19––, after a fiscal period of one year, is as follows:

Bank	$ 1 852.25	
Accounts Receivable	15 325.00	
Office Supplies	1 863.00	
Furniture and Equipment	7 258.36	
Land	45 500.00	
Buildings	52 365.50	
Automobile	9 255.65	
Trucks	36 252.95	
Accounts Payable		$ 3 859.25
Bank Loan		25 000.00
Mortgage Payable		75 000.00
Danielle Nowak, Capital		58 099.98
Danielle Nowak, Drawings	32 000.00	
Revenue		125 254.00
Gas and Oil Expense	26 215.24	
Insurance Expense	2 657.25	
Miscellaneous Expense	1 526.85	
Telephone	965.32	
Truck Repairs	4 240.65	
Utilities Expense	1 575.65	
Wages	48 359.56	
	$287 213.23	$287 213.23

Complete a six-column work sheet and prepare the classified statements. $5 000 of the mortgage payable is due within one year.

For Further Thought

6. **Briefly answer the following questions.**
    1. The subtotals of the Balance Sheet columns of the work sheet do not agree by exactly the amount of the net income. Explain why this is so.
    2. If the Equipment account balance in the Trial Balance section of the worksheet is extended incorrectly to the Income Statement debit column, the work sheet will still balance. Why is this so?
    3. List three errors that would cause a work sheet to be out of balance.
    4. Which form of the balance sheet—report form or account form—gives the better presentation of the financial statement? Give reasons for your answer.
    5. Describe how columns are used efficiently in the preparation of financial statements.
    6. What is probably the most significant observation that can be made from a classified balance sheet?
    7. What can the owner of a business do to ensure that the accounting department does its work properly?
    8. Your friend in the accounting class has difficulty preparing the equity section of the balance sheet. Explain how to do this for all three situations studied in section 9.3.
    9. Is the owner's equity the amount that the owner would get from the sale of the business, or is it merely the amount of capital that the owner has invested in the business?
    10. Explain why it is better to use a work sheet for the preparation of the financial statements, rather than work directly from the ledger.

CASE STUDIES

Case 1 Interpreting Balance Sheets

Firewood Supply is a small business operated on a seasonal basis by Gerry Riel in St. Boniface, Manitoba. Comparative condensed balance sheets for the business for the 19–1 and 19–2 seasons are shown below.

FIREWOOD SUPPLY
BALANCE SHEET
DECEMBER 31, 19–2
(With comparative figures for 19–1)

	19–1	19–2
Assets		
Bank	$ 2 000	$ 3 000
Accounts Receivable	14 000	20 000
Equipment	15 000	15 000
Truck	15 000	29 000
	$46 000	$67 000
Liabilities and Equity		
Accounts Payable	$10 000	$20 000
Bank Loan	14 000	14 000
Owner's Equity	22 000	33 000
	$46 000	$67 000

Questions

1. Calculate the net income if the owner's drawings amounted to $15 000.
2. Explain how the accounts receivable would increase by $6 000.
3. Describe the business's ability to pay its debts.
4. The assets increased from $46 000 to $67 000. Explain in detail where the funds came from to acquire the assets.

Case 2 Financing Student Council Activities

At the beginning of the school year, the Riverview High School student council has inherited a bank balance that was overdrawn by $935. The council has no assets.

The members of the council executive are extremely concerned and have asked you, the treasurer, to examine the records of the council to find out the reasons for the poor financial position. They have also asked you to make recommendations for providing good management in the coming year.

As a result of your investigation you find out that the previous council began its year with a positive bank balance of $200 and an inventory of five hundred fully paid-for T-shirts which had cost $1 each.

The bank book shows that the following transactions took place during the previous year.

Case Studies

	Cheques	Deposits	Balance
Beginning balance			200
Sale of student cards (940 × $2.50)		2 350	2 550
Cost of printing student cards	350		2 200
Grant to drama club	1 000		1 200
Proceeds from dance (Nightmare)		2 000	3 200
Profit on refreshments (Nightmare)		70	3 270
Charge for musicians (Nightmare)	1 500		1 770
Grant to choir	1 000		770
Proceeds from sale of 500 T-shirts		375	1 145
Proceeds from variety show		140	1 285
Grant to athletic department	1 000		285
Proceeds from dance (Brainstorm)		300	585
Charge for musicians (Brainstorm)	1 600		−1 015
Profit on refreshments (Brainstorm)		80	−935

The previous student council had decided to have only top-notch entertainment at dances. Although this meant that the musical groups were expensive, a large profit was expected to be made on every dance. However, the "Brainstorm" dance fizzled because of bad weather and poor scheduling.

The T-shirts were sold at a bargain rate in order to promote school spirit. The three $1 000 grants were normal annual commitments made to the three school organizations.

Questions

1. Rearrange the above data to show the total receipts and the total expenditures for the year just completed and show clearly how the bank balance dropped from $200 to negative $935.
2. Describe the factors which, in your opinion, contributed directly to the poor financial position.
3. Give recommendations for better managing the financial affairs of the student council in the future.
4. Suggest ways to remedy the negative bank balance.

Case 3 Responsibility for Loss?

Sue Zabjek, a history teacher, had 90 students who needed textbooks. The local bookstore had not provided good service in previous years. Therefore, to save money for her students and to avoid delay, Sue decided to buy the textbooks directly from the publisher. Sue clearly stated to her classes that she intended to sell the books at cost with no profit to her. The books arrived with an invoice for $1 350.

Sue's system for selling the books was very informal. As students crowded around her desk, Sue would take money from each one, give out a text, put the money in her drawer, and then repeat the process.

At the end of a week, Sue decided to take stock of her sales. She found that she had $1 050 in her desk. She also had 14 unsold books. By simple arithmetic, Sue calculated that she was missing either $90 or six books.

Before deciding on a course of action, Sue surveyed her classes to learn the status of the texts. Her survey showed that 76 students had their texts and 14 did not.

Questions

1. a. Did the publisher send the correct number of books?
   b. How could the shortage have been caused? Give three possibilities.
   c. Describe measures that Sue could have taken to prevent such an occurrence.

Sue did not believe that she should bear the $90 loss. Therefore, she decided to increase the charge per book by $1 for all 90 students. The increased price of the text was still lower than the bookstore price of $18.50. However, when she announced her decision to her students she met considerable resistance.

A few students refused to pay as a matter of principle, and others began to follow suit. They claimed that the teacher had agreed to sell the texts at cost price and should keep her word. These students did not believe they should be penalized for the teacher's failure to take adequate precautions.

Another student, whose father owned the bookstore, was furious at the price increase. From the beginning she had felt that Sue's plan brought unfair competition against her father. Now she could no longer restrain herself; she registered a formal complaint to the school principal against the teacher. The principal did not like to get involved, but finally agreed to discuss the matter with the teacher.

Questions

2. a. Should a teacher be allowed to bypass local competition in the purchase of textbooks? Give reasons for your answer.
   b. Should Sue Zabjek have to suffer the $90 loss, or is her course of action a reasonable one? Give reasons to support your response.
   c. What should the principal say to Ms. Zabjek?

Case 4 Finding a Solution to a Money Problem

The Harper Valley Ski Club is a small private ski club in Creston, B.C. When the club was first established it was expected to be strictly private with approximately one hundred family memberships. The original members paid about $4 000 for their shares.

However, the current market value for shares sold on the open market is only about $2 000.

Over the years the club has never had an easy time financially, but has managed to avoid serious difficulties. However, in 19–2 the club experienced hardship brought on by two factors. First, the club installed snow-making equipment at a cost of $200 000 the funds for which it borrowed from the bank. Second, bank interest rates rose to 20 per cent.

For the year just ended the financial statements of the club showed the following.

HARPER VALLEY SKI CLUB BALANCE SHEET		
Assets		
Bank	$	1
Accounts Receivable		4 000
Land and Building		150 000
Equipment		500 000
Total		$654 001
Liabilities and Equity		
Bank Loan		$200 000
Accounts Payable		5 000
Capital		449 001
Total		$654 001

HARPER VALLEY SKI CLUB INCOME STATEMENT	
Revenue	
Ski Fees	$300 000
Expenses	
Bank Interest	$40 000
Other Expenses	265 000
Total Expenses	$305 000
Net Loss	$5 000

The financial situation has made many members dissatisfied for the following reasons:
1. there has been an extra assessment on the members to cover the losses;
2. the club has no funds with which to make any of the improvements which were planned. To manage these would take an annual net income of approximately $25 000;
3. the situation is making it difficult for members who wish to leave the club (moving away, etc.) to sell their shares;
4. there is no apparent solution to the problem.

Required: Propose a scheme to solve the club's financial difficulties. The members will not accept an increase in fees.

CAREER
Julie Devji / Accounting Supervisor

When Julie Devji graduated from high school in Chatham, Ontario, she decided to take some time off before beginning a career. She spent the next year travelling through Europe, an experience she says she will never forget. When she returned to Chatham, she felt it was time to get down to business. She had taken accounting in high school, and went to work as a billing clerk for McCoy Chrysler Dodge, a car dealership.

During the next three years, Julie received additional on-the-job training in accounting. When she had finished this training, Julie became the bookkeeper for the dealership. In this job, she took charge of accounts receivable and prepared the payroll for the company's employees.

Julie also enrolled in the Certified General Accounting (CGA) program, which she completed successfully in five years.

job, she took charge of accounts receivable and prepared the payroll for the company's employees.

Julie also enrolled in the Certified General Accounting (CGA) program, which she completed successfully in five years.

Two years ago Julie was promoted to her present position as supervisor of the accounting department. Julie oversees all the company's accounting. She is responsible for seeing that all journal entries are recorded daily and making sure that all postings are made to the general ledger monthly. Every month she prepares the general ledger trial balance and the work sheet. Julie also prepares the company's financial statements, the income statement, and the balance sheet. Because the dealership is a trading business, she must also keep track of its inventory.

Julie reports directly to the owner of the dealership and sends all financial reports to the Canadian head office of Chrysler Corporation. She arranges payment of all gasoline taxes, retail sales tax and payroll taxes. At the end of each year, she prepares the T4 slips for all forty employees. She also contacts customers by telephone regarding overdue accounts, statement billing and customer complaints.

Julie's position offers challenge, variety and responsibility. Her work encompasses all the steps that you have studied to date, including the journal, the ledger, the trial balance, the work sheet, and the financial statements.

Discussion

1. What steps in the accounting cycle does Julie perform?
2. Why is McCoy Chrysler Dodge classified as a trading business? Can this business also be classified as a service business? Explain.
3. What are five current assets and four fixed assets that would appear on the classified balance sheet Julie prepares for McCoy Chrysler Dodge?
4. How many separate revenue accounts would appear on the income statement of McCoy Chrysler Dodge?
5. What type of inventory would Julie keep track of in this business?
6. What uses would McCoy have for a microcomputer in the business? What type of computer software would this business require? What computer programs can be used to change from a manual bookkeeping system to a computerized system?
7. What do you think of Julie's decision to travel in Europe before she settled upon a career?
8. How would you approach a customer, whose account is long overdue, to make payment?

10 Adjusting Entries/ The Eight-Column Work Sheet

10.1 Accountability
10.2 Adjusting Entries for Prepaid Expenses and for Late Purchase Invoices
10.3 Adjusting for Depreciation
10.4 Financial Statements Showing the Effect of Adjustments
10.5 Computerized Accounting: Adjusting Entries

In the previous chapter you learned that accountants use a work sheet to help them prepare the financial statements. You were told that the six-column work sheet was not the one commonly used. Now, you will learn about the eight-column work sheet—the one that accountants do use. You will also learn why "adjusting entries" are made before the financial statements are prepared. Further, you will learn about management's obligation to provide proof of its performance.

10.1 Accountability

Accounting data is used in many ways. Perhaps its most important use is that it provides the information for the financial statements. It is through the financial statements that managers of companies carry out an important function known as accountability. **Accountability** is the company officers' obligation to show how well they have been managing the company. Management must provide evidence of its performance. This is required by law, agreement, or custom.

Users of Financial Statements

There are five groups who are the most common users of financial statements. The groups are:

1. **Managers** Managers probably use the financial statements more than any other group. They carefully study the statements in order to improve results and efficiency, and to eliminate weaknesses. The statements help them make key business decisions.

2. **Owners**   Many owners are not directly involved in managing their companies. They use financial statements to evaluate the performance of the people who run the company for them, as well as to learn about company activities in general.

3. **Creditors**   Creditors, particularly bankers, require financial statements regularly. They use them to stay informed about a company's progress, and its ability to meet its loan obligations. Bankers make sure that they are ready to act swiftly to protect their loans.

4. **Shareholders**   The law requires that shareholders of corporations be provided with financial statements regularly. The shareholders are the real owners of the company and must be made aware of its progress.

5. **Investors and brokers**   Shares of public corporations are traded by stockbrokers through stock exchanges. The employees of stockbrokerage companies, and potential investors, stay informed about the affairs of corporations by reading their financial reports.

Quality of Financial Statements

As was pointed out above, accounting statements are very important to various groups of individuals. Naturally, these groups will expect statements that are accurate, complete, up-to-date, and reliable. It is for this reason that the accounting profession has established the body of accounting standards known as generally accepted accounting principles. These standards play an important part in the accountability process. The reader of financial statements—absentee owner, banker, shareholder, or other—should be able to read the statements with confidence. To make sure that the standards are being met, most companies are required to have an independent audit. An **audit** is a critical review by a public accountant of the internal controls and accounting records of a company. The audit makes it possible to evaluate the fairness of a company's financial statements.

Before you can produce top-notch financial statements, there are additional generally accepted accounting principles that you must learn.

GAAP—The Consistency Principle

The **consistency principle** requires that accountants must use the same methods and procedures from period to period. If they change a method from one period to another they must say so clearly on the financial statements. The readers of financial statements have the right to assume that consistency has been applied unless there is a statement of some change in procedure.

The consistency principle prevents people from manipulating figures on financial statements by changing methods of accounting. For example, consider the case of a contracting company that recognizes revenue when payments are received, not when invoices are issued. If this company were to have a bad year, it would be wrong to make the results look better by including some revenue for invoices issued but not paid for.

GAAP—The Materiality Principle

The **materiality principle** provides that accountants must follow generally accepted accounting principles except when to do so would be expensive, or difficult, and where it makes no real difference if the rules are ignored. If a rule is temporarily ignored, the net income of the company must not be significantly affected, nor should the reader's ability to judge the financial statements be impaired.

For example, suppose that an invoicing error for $50 was discovered by a company that had just received its financial statements from the printer. Assume also that the error affected the net income of approximately $350 000 shown on the financial statements. In this case, no effort would be made to correct the error because the $50 is not significant in relation to the net income figure of $350 000.

GAAP—The Full Disclosure Principle

The **full disclosure principle** provides that all information needed for a full understanding of the company's financial affairs be included in the financial statements. Some items may not affect the ledger accounts directly. These would be included in the form of accompanying notes.

For example, suppose that a chemical company was being sued for millions of dollars by employees claiming that their health was ruined by working for the company which had assured them that no danger existed. Assume also that the company would suffer seriously if it lost the lawsuit. This information must be revealed to the reader of the financial statements by means of an accompanying note.

Other examples of items that might require an accompanying note are tax disputes and company takeovers.

Section Review Questions

1. What are the two additional columns on the work sheet used for?
2. What is probably the most important use for accounting data?
3. What is meant by accountability?
4. Give reasons why managers would require financial statements.
5. Name five groups of individuals who use financial statements.
6. Why would an absentee owner of a business want financial statements for his or her business?
7. Why do bankers insist on financial statements from businesses to which they lend money?
8. Why do corporations provide their shareholders with financial reports?
9. Why do stockbrokers obtain copies of financial reports of public companies?
10. Why are users of financial statements able to rely on them?
11. Give another expression for ''accounting standards.''

12. What is an audit, and what is its purpose?
13. What two things does the auditor seek to do when performing an audit?
14. Explain the consistency principle.
15. Explain the materiality principle.
16. Explain the full disclosure principle.

Section Exercise

1. **Briefly answer the following questions.**

    1. Who is required by law to provide financial statements as evidence of accountability?
    2. Who would be required by agreement to provide financial statements as evidence of accountability?
    3. Are governments accountable to the people in the way that managers are accountable to company shareholders?
    4. Give three ways that management would use data from the financial statements. Do not include normal daily routines.
    5. What can an absentee owner do if he or she is not satisfied with the results of the business as shown on the financial statements?
    6. How else (besides reading the financial reports) could an absentee owner stay informed of company activities?
    7. Banks sometimes take swift action to protect a loan that they believe has gone bad. What action do you think that they would take?
    8. Usually banks obtain "security" before giving a loan. What does this mean?
    9. If a bank loan is secured, why is it sometimes still necessary to take swift action?
    10. What might banks insist on to be sure they are provided with reliable financial statements?
    11. What can a shareholder who is not happy with the progress of a corporation do about it?
    12. Compare what can be done in question 11 above with what can be done in question 5 above.
    13. What does the reader of an unaudited financial statement rely on?
    14. Assume that you lost a large sum of money in a business deal. Assume further that you relied on information from audited financial statements, some of which proved to be incorrect. What might you do about this?

10.2 Adjusting Entries for Prepaid Expenses and for Late Purchase Invoices

The Adjustment Process

Financial statements are used extensively to assist in making business decisions. Therefore, it is important for financial statements to be accurate, up-to-date, and consistent from year to year. The responsibility for these documents rests entirely with the company's accountants. When preparing financial statements, the accountants must ensure that

1. all accounts are brought up-to-date;
2. all late transactions are taken into account;
3. all calculations have been made correctly;
4. all GAAPs have been complied with.

Bringing the account data up-to-date at statement time is known as "making the adjustments." The accounting entries produced by this process are known as the adjusting entries. An **adjusting entry** is one made to assign amounts of revenue or expense to the proper accounting period before finalizing the books for the fiscal period.

Adjusting entries are necessary because the books of account are allowed to become inexact between statement dates. This does not mean inaccurate. Rather, it means that certain things have been left undone. The accounts do not need to be perfectly accurate between statement dates. Time, effort, and money can be saved by leaving some things undone. However, at statement time, the omissions must be put right.

There are numerous situations where it is convenient to allow the accounting records to become inexact during the accounting period. Consider the following example.

> On July 1, Markell Company lends $18 250 to its president John Fumo. He is given a favourable interest rate of six per cent. No date is specified for repayment. Interest on the loan is to be paid annually each July 1. The company has a December 31 year-end.

Technically, Fumo owes the company $3 a day for interest on the loan. This is calculated as follows: $18 250 × 6/100 × 1/365 = $3. Precise accounting would require making the following accounting entry once each day.

	DR	CR
Interest Receivable—John Fumo	$3	
Interest Earned		$3

If it were done this way, 183 such entries would be recorded before the year-end. Clearly, there is little purpose in this. The total interest owed is neither large nor important. It can be computed in a matter of seconds when necessary.

The full amount of the interest due—$549 in this case—will be recorded with one adjusting entry at the year-end.

Adjusting Entries and the Eight-Column Work Sheet

There is a close connection between the adjusting entries and the eight-column work sheet. As the work sheet is being prepared, adjusting entries are worked out and recorded on the work sheet in a section headed Adjustments. The work sheet is balanced and finalized before any adjusting entries are recorded in the accounts. To show how this is done, a work sheet for Cassidy Cartage is started in Figure 10.1. You will be shown how the adjusting entries are recorded on the work sheet as we proceed.

Cassidy Cartage	Work Sheet		Year Ended Dec 31, 19-4			
ACCOUNTS	TRIAL BALANCE		ADJUSTMENTS			
	DR	CR	DR	CR		
Bank	1240 51					
Accounts Receivable	18 475 —					
Supplies	1480 90					
Prepaid Insurance	3 892 —					
Furniture & Equipment	5120 —					
Accumulated Depreciation F.& E.		924 —				
Automotive Equipment	78 000 —					
Accumulated Depreciation Auto. Eq.		23 400 —				
Accounts Payable		3 750 —				
Bank Loan		25 000 —				
P. Marshall, Capital		26 223 42				
P. Marshall, Drawings	42 000 —					
Revenue		213 821 —				
Bank Charges	3 500 —					
Light, Heat & Water	3 750 —					
Miscellaneous Expense	1951 65					
Rent	24 000 —					
Telephone	1 800 —					
Truck Expenses	4 195 116					
Wages	65 957 20					
	293 118 42	293 118 42				

Figure 10.1 The trial balance of Cassidy Cartage recorded on the work sheet.

Adjusting for Supplies Used

Supplies is an account that is allowed to become inexact during the accounting period. It is simply a nuisance to make an accounting entry every time supplies are used, or even once a day. Therefore, such entries are not made. Prompt attention is given to supplies when they are purchased, but not when they are used. As a result, the Supplies account is not correct at the end of the fiscal period. However, the matching principle requires that the account be made correct when financial statements are prepared. This is done by means of an adjusting entry.

Calculating the Amount of the Adjustment for Supplies

The balance in the Supplies account should be equal to the cost of the supplies that are actually on hand, the ones that were not used. Therefore, the first task in working out the supplies adjustment is to take a "physical inventory" of supplies. This involves the preparation of a listing like the one shown in Figure 10.2.

Chapter 10

	Cassidy Cartage Supplies Inventory December 31, 19–4		
Description	Quantity	Cost	Value
Envelopes, #10, white	2 boxes	$29.00	$ 58.00
Envelopes, #8, white	3 boxes	23.50	70.50
Envelopes, manila	37	.25	9.25
Ball pens, blue	15	.22	3.30
Pencils, black, HB	75	.95	71.25
Pencils, red	32	.89	28.48
Pencils, auto .5	3	7.85	23.55
Scotch tape, 1 cm	12	4.50	54.00
Scotch tape, 2 cm	8	6.50	52.00
Paper clips, regular	16 boxes	1.89	30.24
Paper clips, jumbo	5 boxes	3.50	17.50
Gummed labels, #505	3 pkgs	6.50	19.50
Elastic bands	5 boxes	3.59	17.95
		Total	$526.00

Figure 10.2 The supplies inventory listing for Cassidy Cartage.

The Supplies figure on the trial balance for Cassidy Cartage is $1 480.90. The inventory listing shows $526.00. The difference between the two figures, $954.90, is the dollar amount of the supplies used (or spoiled, or stolen). It is the figure used in the adjusting entry.

The Adjusting Entry for Supplies

Two objectives are reached in making the adjusting entry for supplies.
1. The Supplies account is brought into agreement with the true supplies figure shown on the inventory listing.
2. The Supplies Expense account is made to reflect the supplies used during the fiscal period, as required by the matching principle.

The adjusting entry shown below achieves these two objectives.

	DR	CR
Supplies Expense	$954.90	
Supplies		$954.90

The adjusting entry for supplies is not journalized at this time. It is only recorded in the Adjustment section of the work sheet as shown in Figure 10.3.

Observe that the adjusting entry is referenced with a circled numeral ''1.''

Cassidy Cartage	Work Sheet			Year Ended Dec 31, 19-4					
ACCOUNTS	TRIAL BALANCE		ADJUSTMENTS						
	DR	CR	DR	CR					
Bank	1240 51								
Accounts Receivable	1847 5 —								
Supplies	1480 90			① 954 90					
Prepaid Insurance	389 2 —								
Furniture & Equipment	512 0 —								
Accumulated Depreciation F & E		92 4 —							
Automotive Equipment	7800 0 —								
Accumulated Depreciation Auto Eq		2340 0 —							
Accounts Payable		37 5 0 —							
Bank Loan		2500 0 —							
P. Marshall, Capital		2622 3 42							
P. Marshall, Drawings	4200 0 —								
Revenue		21382 1 —							
Bank Charges	350 0 —								
Light, Heat & Water	375 0 —								
Miscellaneous Expense	1951 65								
Rent	2400 0 —								
Telephone	180 0 —								
Truck Expenses	4951 16								
Wages	6595 7 20								
	29311 8 42	29311 8 42							
Supplies Used			① 954 90						

↳ If account name does not appear in trial balance, it must be written in below.

Figure 10.3 The supplies adjustment recorded on the work sheet.

Adjusting for Insurance Used

There are times in business when expense items are paid for in advance. This presents no special problem if the period covered by the expense item (rent, for example) falls entirely within the fiscal period. However, some items (insurance, for example) cover a longer period of time and may affect the following fiscal period as well. Items of this nature are called prepaid expenses and require special accounting treatment at statement time.

A **prepaid expense** is one that is paid for in advance but whose benefits extend into the future. The most common prepaid expense is insurance. When you purchase car insurance, for example, you usually pay in advance for one year's coverage. There are insurance policies of many kinds. Some offer coverage for two, or even three, years.

When prepaid expenses are purchased they are usually debited to a prepaid expense account. For insurance, the account is called Prepaid Insurance. The accounting entry to purchase insurance is

	DR	CR
Prepaid Insurance	$$$$	
Cash, or Accounts Payable		$$$$

As time passes, prepaid insurance gradually decreases in value until it runs out. Let us say that you purchased car insurance for one year on March 1 at a cost of $600. On September 1 the insurance coverage would be half used. It would only have a refund value of $300 (less a service charge). On December 31, the company's year-end, the policy would have two months left to run. This would be valued at $100. The policy would expire on February 28 if not renewed.

During the accounting period, however, no attempt is made to keep the Prepaid Insurance account up-to-date. No accounting entries are made to record the insurance that is used up. Because of this, the balance in the Prepaid Insurance account is not correct during the accounting period.

Calculating the Amount of the Adjustment for Insurance

Again, working with the example of Cassidy Cartage, the trial balance shows a figure of $3 892 for Prepaid Insurance. We know that this balance is wrong. However, we are now in the process of preparing the financial statements. The Prepaid Insurance account must be corrected by means of an adjusting entry.

The balance in the Prepaid Insurance account must be made equal to the total value remaining in all of the insurance policies still in force at the statement date. This figure may be calculated by means of an insurance schedule such as is shown in Figure 10.4 below.

PREPAID INSURANCE SCHEDULE
DECEMBER 31, 19-4

Company	Policy Date	Term	Expiry Date	Premium	Unused Portion	Value Remaining
Acme	Aug 1/-3	2 yrs	Jul 31/-5	$ 816	7/24	$ 238
Fidelity	Aug 1/-3	2 yrs	Jul 31/-5	1 248	7/24	364
Guarantee	Mar 1/-4	1 yr	Feb 28/-5	948	2/12	158
Fireman's	Nov 1/-4	2 yrs	Oct 31/-6	1 152	22/24	1 056
						$1 816

Figure 10.4 A prepaid insurance schedule.

The Prepaid Insurance figure on the trial balance shows $3 892. The Prepaid Insurance Schedule shows $1 816. The difference between the two figures, $2 076, is the dollar amount of the insurance used up. It is the figure used in the adjusting entry.

The Adjusting Entry for Insurance Used

The adjusting entry for prepaid insurance accomplishes two things.
1. The Prepaid Insurance account is brought into agreement with the insurance schedule.
2. The Insurance Expense account is made to reflect the insurance used during the fiscal period, as required by the matching principle.

The accounting entry shown below achieves the two objectives.

	DR	CR
Insurance Expense	$2 076	
Prepaid Insurance		$2 076

The adjusting entry is not journalized at this time. It is entered in the Adjustments section of the work sheet as shown in Figure 10.5.

Cassidy Cartage	Work Sheet		Year Ended Dec 31, 19-4	
ACCOUNTS	TRIAL BALANCE		ADJUSTMENTS	
	DR	CR	DR	CR
Bank	1 240 51			
Accounts Receivable	1 847 5			
Supplies	1 480 90			① 954 90
Prepaid Insurance	3 892 —			② 2 076 —
Furniture & Equipment	5 120 —			
Accumulated Depreciation F. & E.		924 —		
Automotive Equipment	78 000 —			
Accumulated Depreciation Auto. Eq.		23 400 —		
Accounts Payable		3 750 —		
Bank Loan		25 000 —		
P. Marshall, Capital		26 223 42		
P. Marshall, Drawings	4 200 —			
Revenue		21 382 11		
Bank Charges	3 500 —			
Light, Heat & Water	3 760 —			
Miscellaneous Expense	1 951 65			
Rent	2 400 —			
Telephone	1 800 —			
Truck Expenses	4 195 16			
Wages	6 595 20			
	29 311 8 42	29 311 8 42		
Supplies Used			① 954 90	
Insurance Used			② 2 076 —	

Figure 10.5 The insurance adjustment recorded on the work sheet.

Adjusting for Late Purchase Invoices

You have already seen a number of "laws" used by accountants. You can now appreciate that an accountant must be on the watch for items that require special handling when the time comes to prepare financial statements. Among the items to which an accountant gives special attention are late arriving purchase invoices.

Goods and services are often bought toward the end of an accounting period. The bills for these items may not arrive until the subsequent fiscal period. Of course, that is the wrong fiscal period for them. The matching principle states that expenses are to be recognized in the same period as the revenue that they helped to earn. This means that the accounting department must see to it that all items are recorded in their proper accounting period in order to arrive at a proper determination of net income.

The financial statements cannot be completed until two to three weeks after the end of the accounting period. This period of waiting is necessary and sufficient for the late arrival of purchase invoices from suppliers. During this waiting period, the accounting department examines all purchase invoices in order to separate out those that affect the fiscal period just ended. The purchase invoices that are set aside are summarized into an accounting entry to be recorded on the work sheet. Then they are placed back into the system for processing in the usual manner.

Cassidy Cartage — Work Sheet — Year Ended Dec 31, 19-4

Accounts	Trial Balance DR	Trial Balance CR	Adjustments DR	Adjustments CR
Bank	1 240 51			
Accounts Receivable	1 847 5 —			
Supplies	1 480 90			① 954 90
Prepaid Insurance	389 2 —			② 207 6 —
Furniture & Equipment	512 0 —			
Accumulated Depreciation F. & E.		92 4 —		
Automotive Equipment	7 800 0 —			
Accumulated Depreciation Auto. Eq.		2 340 0 —		
Accounts Payable		375 0 —		③ 62 6 —
Bank Loan		2 500 0 —		
P. Marshall, Capital		2 622 3 42		
P. Marshall, Drawings	4 200 0 —			
Revenue		2 138 2 11 —		
Bank Charges	35 0 0 —			
Light, Heat, & Water	37 5 0 —			
Miscellaneous Expense	195 1 65		④ 8 5 —	
Rent	2 400 0 —			
Telephone	180 0 —		⑤ 4 5 —	
Truck Expenses	4 195 1 16		③ 49 6 —	
Wages	6 595 7 20			
	29 311 8 42	29 311 8 42		
Supplies Used			① 954 90	
Insurance Expense			② 207 6 —	

Figure 10.6 The adjustment for late invoices recorded on the work sheet.

For the example of Cassidy Cartage, assume that the three bills shown below represent the "late" purchase invoices belonging to the fiscal period just ended.

Late Purchase Invoices

Telephone	$ 45
Truck repair	496
Typewriter repair	85
Total	$626

These late invoices are summarized into an accounting entry as follows:

	DR	CR
Telephone Expense	$ 45	
Truck Repairs	496	
Miscellaneous Expense	85	
Accounts Payable		$626

This accounting entry is shown on the work sheet for Cassidy Cartage in Figure 10.6. The purchase invoices are then absorbed into the regular accounting system to be checked, recorded, and eventually paid.

Section Review Questions

1. Why are adjusting entries necessary?
2. Why are accounts allowed to become inexact between statement dates?
3. Define "adjusting entry."
4. What accounting entry in regard to supplies is ignored between statement dates?
5. What accounting entry in regard to supplies is not ignored?
6. What GAAP is involved in regard to the adjustment for supplies?
7. What has to be done at the end of the fiscal period before the "supplies used" can be calculated?
8. Give the basic adjusting entry for "supplies used."
9. Where are adjusting entries first recorded?
10. What is a prepaid expense?
11. What is the most common prepaid expense?
12. Name the account that is debited when insurance is paid for in advance.
13. What must be done before the "insurance used" can be calculated?
14. What is the basic adjusting entry for insurance used?
15. Explain what a late purchase invoice is.

Chapter 10

Section Exercises

1. Complete the following schedule in your workbook.

Supplies	Trial Balance Figure	Supplies Closing Inventory Figure	Supplies Expense Figure
1.	$300.00	$100.00	
2.		$175.00	$250.00
3.	$950.00		$740.00

Prepaid Insurance	Trial Balance Figure	Prepaid Insurance Final Calculation	Insurance Expense Figure
1.	$875.00	$325.00	
2.	$925		$315.00
3.		$410.00	$375.00

2. Using the following information, complete the inventory sheet and make the adjusting entry in the T-accounts in your workbook.

Inventory Listing

Inventory Item	Quantity	Unit Price	Value
Rubber bands	3 boxes	$1.50 per box	
Envelopes #8	10 boxes	32.00 per box	
Envelopes #10	4 1/2 boxes	36.00 per box	
Envelopes, manila	2 boxes	28.00 per box	
Typing paper	4M sheets	15.60 per M	
Letterhead	10M sheets	22.50 per M	
Copy paper	4M sheets	10.00 per M	
Carbon paper	2 boxes	6.00 per box	
Paper clips	12 boxes	1.50 per box	
Staples	15 boxes	4.10 per box	
Pencils, regular	4 doz.	5.50 per doz.	
Pencils, red	2 doz.	6.10 per doz.	
		Total	

Supplies
2018.—

Supplies Used

3. During its first year of operation, Force Company purchased the following insurance policy.

	Company	Policy Date	Term	Premium
19–1	Genuine	March 1	2 years	$240

   1. Calculate the prepaid insurance at the end of 19–1.
   2. Calculate the insurance expense for 19–1.
   3. Give the adjusting entry for insurance used in 19–1.

   During its second year of operation, Force Company purchased the following additional insurance policies.

	Company	Policy Date	Term	Premium
19–2	Regal	Sept. 1	1 year	$144
	Standard	Nov. 1	2 years	120

   4. What is the balance in the Prepaid Insurance account at the end of 19–2 before any adjusting entry?
   5. Calculate the value of prepaid insurance at the end of 19–2.
   6. What is the insurance expense for 19–2?
   7. Give the adjusting entry for insurance used in 19–2.
   8. Prove the insurance expense figure for 19–2 by calculating it in another way.

4. During its first two years of operation, Quest Company purchased the following insurance policies.

	Company	Policy Date	Term	Premium
19–1	Surety	March 1	2 years	$240
	Royal	July 1	1 year	120
	State	October 1	2 years	240
19–2	Crown	August 1	2 years	240

   1. How much was spent on insurance in 19–1?
   2. What is the value of the prepaid insurance at the end of 19–1?
   3. What is the insurance expense for 19–1?
   4. Give the adjusting entry for insurance used in 19–1.
   5. What is the balance in the Prepaid Insurance account at the end of 19–2 before any adjusting entry?
   6. Calculate the value of prepaid insurance at the end of 19–2.
   7. What is the insurance expense for 19–2?
   8. Give the adjusting entry for insurance used in 19–2.

5. A businessman's fiscal year-end is September 30. One of his business expenditures is for truck licences.

1. If he spends $240 on truck licences for the calendar year, calculate the value of prepaid licences at the end of his fiscal year.
2. If the balance in the Prepaid Licences account is $300, give the accounting entry to adjust Prepaid Licences.
3. Explain how the balance in Prepaid Licences becomes $300.

6. **Workbook Exercise:** Completing a chart apportioning cost of insurance to a series of accounting periods.

10.3 Adjusting for Depreciation

The Nature of Depreciation

Assets that are bought, not for the purpose of reselling them, but for the purpose of using them to produce revenue, are known as "fixed assets." Assets of this type are also known as "long-lived assets," "capital equipment," and "plant and equipment."

With the exception of land, every fixed asset is expected to be used up in the course of time and activity, and so to decrease or depreciate in value. **Depreciation** is the decrease in value of an asset over time.

The following is an example of how depreciation works. Assume that a person purchases a new truck at a cost of $24 000 in order to begin a delivery business. After operating for five years, the business is closed down. During the course of closing down the business, the truck (now used) is sold for $1 500. Clearly, over the five-year period, the truck cost the business $22 500 ($24 000 − $1 500). Just as clearly, the truck was needed to carry on the business.

To see the true profit picture of the business, the $22 500 cost of the truck cannot be ignored. Theoretically, the $22 500 must be included as an expense of the business at the rate of $4 500 ($22 500/5) for each of the five years. The profit picture of the company over its five-year life might look like this:

	19–1	19–2	19–3	19–4	19–5
Revenues	$57 560	$65 250	$68 354	$65 270	$59 230
Expenses					
Depreciation Truck	$4 500	$4 500	$4 500	$4 500	$4 500
Other Expenses	36 750	38 256	39 954	42 570	45 320
Total Expenses	$41 250	$42 756	$44 454	$47 070	$49 820
Net Income	$16 310	$22 494	$23 900	$18 200	$9 410

The above schedule shows that the $22 500 net cost of the truck has been spread evenly over its five-year life. This is the essence of depreciation. Each year that the company benefited from the truck's use has been charged with $4 500, an equal portion of its cost. Depreciation has nothing to do with showing the value of an asset.

Calculating Depreciation

It is not possible to calculate depreciation exactly until the end of the asset's life. Only then can you say how many years it was used, and what its final worth was. But accountants and business people cannot wait until then. Depreciation must be included on every income statement. So, depreciation must be estimated while the asset is still in use.

Straight-line Depreciation

The simplest way of estimating depreciation is the straight-line method. The **straight-line method of depreciation** is one that divides up the net cost of the asset equally among the years of the asset's life. For this method, the following formula is used:

$$\text{Straight-line depreciation for one year} = \frac{\text{Original cost of asset} - \text{Estimated salvage value}}{\text{Estimated number of periods in the life of the asset}}$$

The following two examples show how the calculation works.

1. Cassidy Cartage purchased $78 000 of automotive equipment on January 1, 19–2. It estimated that the assets would be useful for six years. At the end of that time, the equipment would have a market value of $7 800.
   Applying the formula to this data gives the following calculation:

   $$\text{Estimated annual depreciation} = \frac{\$78\ 000 - \$7\ 800}{6} = \$11\ 700$$

   This gives an estimated annual depreciation figure of $11 700 for Automotive Equipment. The figure is the same each year.

2. Cassidy Cartage purchased $5 120 of Furniture and Equipment on January 1, 19–2. The company estimated that the assets would be useful for ten years at which time they would have a market value of $500.
   Applying the formula to this data gives the following calculation:

   $$\text{Estimated annual depreciation} = \frac{\$5\ 120 - \$500}{10} = \$462$$

This gives an estimated annual depreciation figure of $462 for Furniture and Equipment. The figure is the same each year.

Depreciation for Part Year   The above calculations were for a full year. A further calculation is necessary if the asset is used for only part of a year. This can happen if the asset is purchased or disposed of during the year. It may also happen if the fiscal period being reported on is shorter than one year.

Consider the following example. The Edwards Company purchases a building on May 1, 19–5 for $120 000. The building is expected to be used for thirty years, after which it will be worth $30 000. The Edwards Company prepares quarterly financial statements (that is, it issues statements every three months).

The annual depreciation for the above building is ($120 000 − $30 000)/30, which is $3 000. The quarterly depreciation is $3 000/4 or $750. However, in the first statement period after the purchase of the asset, it had only been in use for two months. Therefore, depreciation for only two months can be charged to this period. This amount is $500.

Declining-Balance Method of Depreciation

There is more than one way of calculating depreciation. The declining-balance method is common because the government of Canada requires it on statements that are submitted for income tax purposes. A company that does not use the declining-balance method must modify the financial statement that it sends to the government.

The **declining-balance method of depreciation** is one in which the annual depreciation is calculated by multiplying the undepreciated (remaining) cost of the asset by a fixed percentage figure. In the first year, the undepreciated cost figure is equal to the purchase price (capital cost). The percentage figures set by the government are shown in the table below.

	GOVERNMENT OF CANADA RATES OF DEPRECIATION	
Class	Description	Rate
3	Buildings of brick, stone, or cement	5%
6	Buildings of frame, log, or stucco	10%
8	Office furniture and equipment	20%
10	Trucks, tractors and automotive equipment	30%
29	Manufacturing and processing equipment	50%

To see how declining-balance depreciation is calculated, assume that a truck is purchased on January 1, 19–1 for $22 000. The table above shows that the rate to be used is 30 per cent.

Year 1

For the 19–1 fiscal year the depreciation = $22 000 × 30% = $6 600.

> Summary: Undepreciated cost before depreciation $22 000
> Depreciation for 19–1 .... <u> 6 600</u>
> Undepreciated cost at end of 19–1 .... $15 400

Year 2

For the 19–2 fiscal year the depreciation = $15 400 × 30% = $4 620.

> Summary: Undepreciated cost before depreciation $15 400
> Depreciation for 19–2 .... <u> 4 620</u>
> Undepreciated cost at end of 19–2 .... $10 780

The annual calculations continue in this way until the asset is disposed of.

Comparison of the Two Methods

The two schedules below show how the depreciation for the above asset would be calculated under the straight-line and the declining-balance methods. Assume the truck was expected to last for eight years and have an ending value of $2 000.

Straight-line method			*Declining-balance Method*		
Year	Depreciation	Undepreciated Cost	Year	Depreciation	Undepreciated Cost
Original cost		$22 000	Original cost		$22 000
1	$2 500	19 500	1	$6 600	15 400
2	2 500	17 000	2	4 620	10 780
3	2 500	14 500	3	3 234	7 546
4	2 500	12 000	4	2 264	5 282
5	2 500	9 500	5	1 585	3 697
6	2 500	7 000	6	1 109	2 588
7	2 500	4 500	7	776	1 812
8	2 500	2 000	8	544	1 268

The straight-line method produces depreciation figures that are the same each year. Over the estimated life of the asset the book value of the asset is gradually reduced until it reaches the estimated terminal value. Only one calculation is necessary.

The declining-balance method produces depreciation figures that are larger in the early years and smaller in the later years. Estimated final value is ignored when using this method. A new calculation is necessary every year.

The Adjusting Entry for Depreciation

The adjusting entry for depreciation has two aims. These are:
1. to reduce the asset account by the amount of the depreciation;
2. to set up the depreciation figure in a depreciation expense account.

However, this is not done in the manner you would expect. This is because the reduction in the asset is not made in the asset account. Rather, it is made in a separate "accumulated depreciation" account known as a contra account. A **contra account** is one that must be considered along with a given asset account in order to show the true book value of the asset account. A contra account is also known as a "valuation" account.

The following sequence of events shows how the accumulated depreciation account is used in conjunction with the asset account. The data in the straight-line table above is used in the example.

a. When the asset is acquired:

Truck	Accumulated Depreciation of Truck
22 000	

Net book value: $22 000

b. After one years depreciation:

Truck	Accumulated Depreciation of Truck
22 000	2 500

Net book value: $19 500

c. After two years depreciation:

Truck	Accumulated Depreciation of Truck
22 000	2 500
	2 500

Net book value: $17 000

d. After three years depreciation:

Truck	Accumulated Depreciation of Truck
22 000	2 500
	2 500
	2 500

Net book value: $14 500

This pattern continues.
The basic adjusting entry to record depreciation is

	DR	CR
Depreciation Expense	$$$$	
Accumulated Depreciation (of Asset)		$$$$

Two adjusting entries are required for Cassidy Cartage because there are two fixed assets on the trial balance. The depreciation figures for these two items were calculated previously. They are: for Automotive Equipment, $11 700; for Furniture and Equipment, $462.

The adjusting entries to record the depreciation for Cassidy Cartage are:

		DR	CR
1.	Depreciation of Automotive Equipment	$11 700	
	Accumulated Depreciation—Automotive Equipment		$11 700
2.	Depreciation of Furniture and Equipment	$462	
	Accumulated Depreciation—Furniture and Equipment		$462

You can see these recorded on the work sheet for Cassidy Cartage in Figure 10.7. You can also see that the two Adjustment columns are totaled and balanced. This is done on an eight-column work sheet after all of the adjustments have been recorded.

Cassidy Cartage — Work Sheet — Year Ended Dec 31, 19-4

Accounts	Trial Balance DR	Trial Balance CR	Adjustments DR	Adjustments CR
Bank	1240 51			
Accounts Receivable	1847 5 —			
Supplies	1480 90			① 954 90
Prepaid Insurance	389 2 —			② 207 6 —
Furniture & Equipment	5120 —			
Accumulated Depreciation F.&E.		924 —		④ 462 —
Automotive Equipment	78000 —			
Accumulated Depreciation Auto Eq.		23400 —		⑤ 11700 —
Accounts Payable		3750 —		③ 626 —
Bank Loan		25000 —		
P. Marshall, Capital		26223 42		
P. Marshall, Drawings	42000 —			
Revenue		213824 —		
Bank Charges	3500 —			
Light, Heat, & Water	3750 —			
Miscellaneous Expense	1951 65		③ 85 —	
Rent	24000 —			
Telephone	1800 —		③ 45 —	
Truck Expenses	41951 16		③ 496 —	
Wages	65957 20			
	293118 42	293118 42		
Supplies Used			① 954 90	
Insurance Expense			② 2076 —	
Depreciation Furn. & Equip.			④ 462 —	
Depreciation Automotive Equip.			⑤ 11700 —	
			15818 90	15818 90

Figure 10.7 The adjusting entries for depreciation recorded on the work sheet, and the Adjustments columns balanced.

Extending the Work Sheet

Each line of the work sheet must be extended to one of the last four columns. Each item is extended as follows:

1. Evaluate the first four columns for the item. This may involve adding or subtracting depending on what is contained in these columns. The process will result in one number together with its debit or credit indicator.
2. Transfer the value found in step 1 above to one of the last four columns of the work sheet. Each item belongs to either the Income Statement columns or the Balance Sheet columns. Debit values are transferred to debit columns and credit values are transferred to credit columns.

Any item on the work sheet may be extended as long as there are no more adjustments that will affect that item. Many accountants wait until all of the adjusting entries are recorded, and then perform all of the extensions at one time.

Figure 10.8 shows all of the items extended on the work sheet for Cassidy Cartage.

Balancing the Work Sheet

The process of balancing the work sheet is identical to that learned in the previous chapter. This involves:

1. totaling each of the last four columns;
2. determining the difference between the two Income Statement columns in this case, ($55 092.09), and the difference between the two Balance Sheet columns (also $55 092.09);
3. ensuring that the two differences in 2. above are the same. If they are not, then the work sheet does not balance, and contains one or more errors. These must be found and corrected before the financial statements are prepared.

Figure 10.8 shows the balanced work sheet for Cassidy Cartage.

Accounts	Trial Balance DR	Trial Balance CR	Adjustments DR	Adjustments CR	Income Statement DR	Income Statement CR	Balance Sheet DR	Balance Sheet CR
Bank	1240 51						1240 51	
Accounts Receivable	18475 —						18475 —	
Supplies	1480 90			① 954 90			526 —	
Prepaid Insurance	3892 —			② 2076 —			1816 —	
Furniture & Equipment	5120 —						5120 —	
Accumulated Depreciation F. & E.		924 —		④ 462 —				1386 —
Automotive Equipment	78000 —						78000 —	
Accumulated Depreciation Auto. Eq.		23400 —		⑤ 11700 —				35100 —
Accounts Payable		3750 —		⑥ 626 —				4376 —
Bank Loan		25000 —						25000 —
P. Marshall, Capital		26223 42						26223 42
P. Marshall, Drawings	42000 —						42000 —	
Revenue		21382 1 —				21382 1 —		
Bank Charges	3500 —				3500 —			
Light, Heat, & Water	3750 —				3750 —			
Miscellaneous Expense	1951 65		③ 85 —		2036 65			
Rent	24000 —				24000 —			
Telephone	1800 —		③ 45 —		1845 —			
Truck Expenses	41951 16		⑥ 496 —		42447 16			
Wages	65957 20				65957 20			
	293118 42	293118 42						
Supplies			① 954 90		954 90			
Insurance Expense			② 2076 —		2076 —			
Depreciation Furn. & Equip.			④ 462 —		462 —			
Depreciation Automotive Equip.			⑤ 11700 —		11700 —			
			15818 90	15818 90	158728 91	213821 —	147177 51	92085 42
Net Income					55092 09			55092 09
					213821 —	213821 —	147177 51	147177 51

Figure 10.8 The extended and balanced work sheet for Cassidy Cartage.

Section Review Questions

1. Define depreciation.
2. What is the essence of depreciation from an accountant's point of view?
3. Why is it not possible to make a precise calculation of depreciation until the end of the asset's useful life?
4. What is the simplest depreciation method?
5. What depreciation method is required by Revenue Canada for income tax purposes?
6. Give the formula for calculating straight-line depreciation.
7. Describe how to calculate declining-balance depreciation.
8. How is depreciation for partial years handled?
9. Give the basic adjusting entry for depreciation.
10. How is a depreciable asset represented in the ledger accounts?
11. What is a contra account?
12. Describe the process of extending the work sheet.

Section Exercises

1. In your workbook, divide up the total expense for each of the following situations among the proper fiscal periods. Assume a company that commenced business on January 1, 19–1 and has a fiscal year-end of December 31.

    1. A truck was purchased on January 1, 19–1 for $18 000. It was expected to last for five full years at the end of which it would have a trade-in value of $3 000. Use the straight-line method of depreciation.

19–1	19–2	19–3	19–4	19–5

    2. A used vehicle was bought on November 1, 19–1 for $5 800. It was expected to last for four full years at the end of which it would have a resale value of $1 000. Use the straight-line method of depreciation.

19–1	19–2	19–3	19–4	19–5

    3. A building was purchased on May 1, 19–2 for the sum of $113 000. It was expected to last for 25 years at which time it would have a resale value of $5 000. Use the straight-line method of depreciation.

19–1	19–2	19–3	19–4	19–5

    4. A new machine was bought on January 1, 19–1 for $54 000. It is depreciated using the declining-balance method at the rate of 20 per cent.

19–1	19–2	19–3	19–4	19–5

5. A new building was bought on July 1, 19–1 for $282 000. It is depreciated using the declining-balance method at the rate of 5 per cent.

19–1	19–2	19–3	19–4	19–5

2. A company purchases equipment costing $100 000 which it expects to last for 7 years and have a salvage value of $5 500.

   1. For the use of management, prepare a depreciation schedule for the first five years of the asset's life showing depreciation calculated on a straight-line basis.
   2. Prepare a depreciation schedule for the first five years of the asset's life showing depreciation calculated on a declining-balance basis at the government rate of 20 per cent.

3. This exercise appears in your workbook.
   The general ledger of Salk Company at the end of its annual fiscal period appears below.
   1. Using the additional information that is provided, record the year-end adjusting entries directly in the T-accounts.
   2. Prepare an adjusted trial balance.

Bank	Accounts Receivable	Supplies
400	8 285	1 900

Prepaid Insurance	Land	Buildings
1 800	50 000	70 000

Accum. Depr.—Buildings	Equipment	Accum. Depr.—Equipment
6 750	96 500	24 000

Accounts Payable	J. Salk, Capital	J. Salk, Drawings
3 200	144 985	30 000

Revenue	Bank Charges	Delivery Expense
140 700	450	1 500

Light and Heat	Miscellaneous Expense	Telephone Expense
1 300	490	390

Wages Expense	Supplies Used	Insurance Expense
56 620		

Depreciation—Buildings	Depreciation—Equipment

Additional Information:

1. Inventory of supplies at the year-end is $850.
2. Unexpired insurance at the year-end is $625.
3. Depreciation is calculated on a straight-line basis. The building is expected to last 40 years, at which time it will be worth $25 000. The equipment is expected to last 15 years, after which it will be worth $6 500.

4. **Workbook Exercise:** Recording adjusting entries directly into T-accounts.

5. The following work sheet also appears in your workbook. It contains a number of errors. Locate the errors, correct them, and balance the work sheet.

Pinnacle Company — Work Sheet — Year Ended December 31, 19—

ACCOUNTS	TRIAL BALANCE DR	TRIAL BALANCE CR	ADJUSTMENTS DR	ADJUSTMENTS CR	INCOME STATEMENT DR	INCOME STATEMENT CR	BALANCE SHEET DR	BALANCE SHEET CR
Bank	3 170 —							
Accounts Receivable	19 473 —							
Supplies	1 850 —			1 200 —			1 850 —	
Prepaid Insurance	4 795 —		3 130 —				7 925 —	
Land	70 000 —							
Building	90 750 —						90 750 —	
Accumulated Depreciation Bldg.		12 943 22		3 890 34				16 833 56
Office Equipment	17 350 —						17 350 —	
Accumulated Depreciation O.E.		8 466 80		1 776 4				10 243 44
Automotive Equipment	38 429 50						38 429 50	
Accumulated Deprec Auto. Eq.		25 248 18		3 954 40				3 954 40
Accounts Payable		7 216 10		3 62				7 216 10
Bank Loan		15 000 —				15 000 —		
Mortgage Payable		100 000 —				100 000 —		
S. Bloom, Capital		62 483 40						62 483 40
S. Bloom, Drawings	25 000 —					25 000 —		
Sales		99 374 10				99 374 10		
Bank Charges	1 640 30				1 640 —			
Car Expenses	7 316 50		157 —		7 473 50			
Light, Heat & Water	6 017 —				6 017 —			
Miscellaneous Expense	1 536 —		95 —		1 631 —			
Property Taxes	2 250 —				2 250 —			
Telephone	1 847 —		110 —		1 957 —			
Wages	39 307 50				39 703 50			
	330 731 80	330 731 80						
Supplies Used			1 200 —					
Insurance Expense			3 130 —					
Deprec. Office Equipment			1 776 4					
Deprec. Auto Equipment			3 954 40					
					58 672 —	239 374 10	156 367 50	100 730 90
					180 702 10			155 636 60
					239 374 10	239 374 10	156 367 50	156 367 50

6. From the trial balance and additional information shown below, complete the work sheet for the year ended September 30, 19–4 for Karen Denby, proprietor of a real estate business.

KAREN DENBY, REAL ESTATE
TRIAL BALANCE
SEPTEMBER 30, 19–4

Bank	$ 3 800	
Accounts Receivable	10 000	
Supplies	500	
Prepaid Insurance	1 000	
Prepaid Licences	400	
Land	50 000	
Building	70 000	
Accumulated Depreciation—Building		$ 5 600
Furniture and Equipment	15 000	
Accumulated Depreciation—Furniture and Equipment		4 000
Automotive Equipment	17 000	
Accumulated Depreciation—Automotive Equipment		6 300
Accounts Payable		400
Bank Loan		100 000
Karen Denby, Capital		40 000
Karen Denby, Drawings	30 000	
Commissions Revenue		96 600
Advertising Expense	4 700	
Bank Charges	8 600	
Car Expenses	8 000	
Commissions Expense	18 000	
Light and Heat Expense	2 200	
Miscellaneous Expense	200	
Postage Expense	600	
Telephone Expense	900	
Wages Expense	12 000	
	$252 900	$252 900

Additional Information:
1. The supplies inventory at September 30 is $200.
2. The prepaid insurance schedule shows a value of $300 for prepaid insurance.
3. The prepaid licences figure in the trial balance represents a licence fee of $200 each for two cars. These fees are for the calendar year.
4. Depreciation is calculated on a straight-line basis.

    The building is expected to have a useful life of 50 years after which its value will be $5 000.

    The furniture and equipment are expected to have a useful life of 15 years after which they will have a value of $900.

    The automobiles are expected to have a useful life of 5 years after which they will have a value of $1 250.

10.4 Financial Statements Showing the Effect of Adjustments

The work sheet is designed to help the accountant organize data needed to prepare the financial statements. In this chapter you have seen how adjusting entries upgrade the data so that the statements are correct and up-to-date.

Remember that the work sheet is the only source of information you need to prepare the statements. All of the figures needed to prepare a balance sheet are found in the

CASSIDY CARTAGE
INCOME STATEMENT
YEAR ENDED DECEMBER 31, 19–4

Revenue		$213 821.00
Expenses		
Bank Charges	$ 3 500.00	
Depreciation—Furniture and Equipment	462.00	
Depreciation—Automotive Equipment	11 700.00	
Insurance Expense	2 076.00	
Light, Heat, and Water	3 750.00	
Miscellaneous Expense	2 036.65	
Rent	24 000.00	
Supplies Used	954.90	
Telephone	1845.00	
Truck Expense	42 447.16	
Wages	65 957.20	158 728.91
Net Income		$ 55 092.09

Figure 10.9 The financial statements for Cassidy Cartage.

Balance Sheet columns of the work sheet. All of the figures needed to prepare an income statement are found in the Income Statement columns of the work sheet. You do not have to look anywhere else.

The financial statements for Cassidy Cartage are given in Figure 10.9. They were prepared from the work sheet in Figure 10.8. Examine these statements carefully; they contain some new items. Four new expenses appear on the income statement. A new section for prepaid expenses appears on the balance sheet. Also, the fixed asset section of the balance sheet is developed to show the net book value of each class of asset.

CASSIDY CARTAGE
BALANCE SHEET
DECEMBER 31, 19-4

Assets

Current Assets
Bank		$ 1 240.51	
Accounts Receivable		18 475.00	$19 715.51

Prepaid Expenses
Supplies		$ 526.00	
Prepaid Insurance		1 816.00	2 342.00

Plant and Equipment
Furniture and Equipment	$ 5 120.00		
Less Accumulated Depreciaton	1 386.00	$ 3 734.00	
Automotive Equipment	$78 000.00		
Less Accumulated Depreciation	35 100.00	42 900.00	46 634.00
			$68 691.51

Liabilities and Owner's Equity

Current Liabilities
Accounts Payable		$ 4 376.00	
Bank Loan		25 000.00	$29 376.00

P. Marshall, Capital
Balance January 1, 19-4		$26 223.42	
Net Income	$55 092.09		
Drawings	42 000.00		
Increase in Equity		13 092.09	
Balance December 31, 19-4			39 315.51
			$68 691.51

Section Review Questions

1. In what ways does the work sheet assist the accountant?
2. What is meant by "upgrading the data"?
3. Where is the information located to prepare the financial statements?
4. What new classification appears on the balance sheet in this chapter?
5. Describe what is different about the presentation of fixed assets.

Section Exercises

1. This exercise also appears in the workbook.
   Classify each of the following items using the abbreviations explained below.

ITEM	ITEM
Accounts Payable	General Expense
Accounts Receivable	Insurance Expense
Accumulated Depreciation—Automobiles	Interest Earned
	Investment in Canada Savings Bonds
Accumulated Depreciation—Building	Legal Expense
	Mortgage Payable (current)
Advertising	Mortgage Payable (non-current)
Audit Fee	Office Expense
Bank	Office Salaries
Bank Charges	Postage
Bank Loan	Prepaid Insurance
Building Repairs	Prepaid Licences
Buildings	Rent
Commissions Earned	Salaries
Delivery Expense	Sales Tax Payable
Depreciation—Automobiles	Supplies
Depreciation—Building	Supplies Used
Fees Earned	Telephone
Frances Freeman, Capital	Wages
Frances Freeman, Drawings	

CLASSIFICATIONS

Current Assets	CA
Prepaid Expenses	PE
Plant and Equipment	PL
Current Liabilities	CL
Long-Term Liabilities	LTL
Owner's Equity	OE
Revenue	Rv
Operating Expenses	Ex

2. A partial work sheet is given below for Muskoka Septic Cleaning. From this work sheet prepare a classified balance sheet and an income statement. The current year's instalment of the mortgage payable amounts to $2 000.

Muskoka Septic Cleaning — Year Ended Dec. 31, 19-5

Accounts	Trial Bal. DR	Income Statement DR	Income Statement CR	Balance Sheet DR	Balance Sheet CR
Bank	7506			7506	
Accounts Receivable	9371 40			9371 40	
Supplies	1105 —			270 —	
Prepaid Insurance	1604			502 —	
Land	40000 —			40000 —	
Building	42120 —			42120 —	
Accum. Deprec. Building					7813 —
Office Equipment	1850 —			1850 —	
Accum. Deprec. Office Equip.					1092 24
Trucks & Equipment	48900 —			48900 —	
Accum. Deprec. Trucks & Equip.					37159 11
Accounts Payable					1997 50
Bank Loan					15000 —
Mortgage Payable					42150 —
Jane Chegano Capital					35639 16
Jane Chegano Drawings	20000 —			20000 —	
Revenue			62046 83		
Bank Charges	2170	2170 —			
Light & Heat	2642	2642 —			
Miscellaneous Expense	31	366 —			
Property Taxes	104	1047 —			
Telephone	91	915 40			
Truck Expenses	1041	10415 25			
Wages	12614	12614 30			
	195720				
Supplies Used		835 —			
Insurance Expense		1102 —			
Depreciation of Building		1805 63			
Depreciation of Office Equip.		189 44			
Depreciation of Trucks		5031 81			
		39133 83	62046 83	163764 01	140851 01
Net Income		22913 —			22913 —
		62046 83	62046 83	163764 01	163764 01

3. Shown below is the adjusted trial balance of ABC Company arranged alphabetically as of December 31, 19–6.

Examine the trial balance carefully and answer the questions that follow. Round off figures to the nearest dollar.

ABC COMPANY
TRIAL BALANCE
DECEMBER 31, 19–6

	DR	CR
Accounts Payable		$ 15 364
Accounts Receivable	$ 18 500	
Accumulated Depreciation—Automotive Equipment		28 321
Accumulated Depreciation—Buildings		14 042
Accumulated Depreciation—Office Equipment		4 930
Advertising Expense	2 750	
Automotive Equipment	37 270	
Bank	1 800	
Bank Charges and Interest	3 250	
Bank Loan		20 000
Buildings	75 700	
Depreciation of Automotive Equipment	3 835	
Depreciation of Building	3 245	
Depreciation of Office Equipment	855	
Drawings	50 000	
Gasoline and Oil Expense	11 437	
Insurance Expense	3 275	
J. Scott, Capital January 1		57 155
Land	50 000	
Light and Heat Expense	12 070	
Miscellaneous Expense	350	
Mortgage Payable		65 000
Office Equipment	8 350	
Prepaid Insurance	2 750	
Revenue		124 276
Supplies	1 075	
Supplies Used	1 250	
Telephone Expense	950	
Wages	40 376	
	$329 088	$329 088

Questions

1. Given that the current portion of the mortgage payable is $2 500, calculate the totals of each classification on the balance sheet.
2. Is this company in a good position to pay its debts? Explain.
3. Does the company have an increase or decrease in capital over the year? How much is the increase or decrease?
4. Given that the fixed assets were all purchased on January 1, and are depreciated

on the declining-balance method at government rates, calculate exactly when they were purchased.
5. Is this a profitable business in terms of the percentage of net income compared to the owner's investment? What is the percentage figure?
6. Calculate the percentage of net income compared to total revenue.
7. In percentage terms, how much of this company is owned by the owner, and how much by the creditors?

10.5 Computerized Accounting: Adjusting Entries

Computer Exercises

1. Given below is the spreadsheet application program for the worksheet of Cassidy Cartage (Figure 10.8). The hidden formulas are given in faint print.

	A	B	C	D	E	F	G	H	I	J	K
1	CASSIDY CARTAGE					WORK	SHEET			YEAR ENDED DEC. 31, 19--	
2		ACCOUNTS		TRIAL BALANCE		ADJUSTMENTS		INCOME STATEMENT		BALANCE SHEET	
3				DR	CR	DR	CR	DR	CR	DR	CR
4	BANK									D4	
5	ACCOUNTS RECEIVABLE									D5	
6	SUPPLIES									D6+F6-G6	
7	PREPAID INSURANCE									D7-G7	
8	FURNITURE AND EQUIPMENT									D8+F8	
9	ACCUMULATED DEPRECIATION FURN & EQUIP										E9+G9
10	AUTOMOTIVE EQUIPMENT									D10+F10	
11	ACCUMULATED DEPRECIATION AUTO EQUIP										E11+G11
12	ACCOUNTS PAYABLE										E12+G12
13	BANK LOAN										E13
14	CAPITAL										E14
15	DRAWINGS									D15+F15	
16	REVENUE								E16		
17	BANK CHARGES							D17+F17			
18	LIGHT, HEAT AND WATER							D18+F18			
19	MISCELLANEOUS EXPENSE							D19+F19			
20	RENT EXPENSE							D20+F20			
21	TELEPHONE EXPENSE							D21+F21			
22	TRUCK EXPENSES							D22+F22			
23	WAGE EXPENSE							D23			
24	TRIAL BALANCE TOTALS			SUM(D4:D23)	SUM(E4:E23)						
25	SUPPLIES USED							F25			
26	INSURANCE EXPENSE							F26			
27	DEPRECIATION BUILDINGS							F27			
28	DEPRECIATION AUTOMOTIVE EQUIPMENT							F28			
29						SUM(F4:F28)	SUM(G4:G28)	SUM(H4:H28)	SUM(I4:I28)	SUM(J4:J28)	SUM(K4:K28)
30	NET INCOME (LOSS-)							I29-H29			J29-K29
31								H29+H30	I29+I30	J29+J30	K29+K30

1. Load your spreadsheet software into the computer. Build the program above into the spreadsheet. Be sure to save this program as is.
2. Load the above applications program into the computer. Enter the trial balance figures and the adjustment figures in the appropriate cells. Make the calculations twice. Print the completed spreadsheet and compare it with the one in the text on page 309.
3. Change some of the figures in the adjustments. Observe the effect of these changes on the work sheet. Be sure to calculate twice.

2. Using the spreadsheet program that you saved from the previous exercise, complete the work sheet for Taurus Trucking with the information given below. Observe the net income figure.

TAURUS TRUCKING
TRIAL BALANCE
FOR YEAR ENDED DECEMBER 31, 19--

	DR	CR
Bank	$ 4 500	
Accounts Receivable	24 356	
Supplies	2 860	
Prepaid Insurance	3 200	
Furniture and Equipment	16 530	
Accumulated Depreciation—Furniture and Equipment		$ 4 800
Automotive Equipment	84 362	
Accumulated Depreciation—Automotive Equipment		32 000
Accounts Payable		4 360
Bank Loan		25 000
Capital		67 198
Drawings	30 000	
Revenue		110 350
Bank Charges	240	
Light, Heat, and Water	2 540	
Miscellaneous Expense	360	
Rent Expense	9 000	
Telephone Expense	1 200	
Truck Expense	10 350	
Wages Expense	54 210	
	$243 708	$243 708

Adjustments
1. Supplies on hand at year-end: $1 520
2. Prepaid Insurance calculation at year-end: $1 250
3. Depreciation on Furniture and Equipment: $1 200
4. Depreciation of Automotive Equipment: $16 000
5. Late arriving bill for Truck Expense: $450

For Further Thought

A trucking service for $5 200 was completed in early January and recorded in January. However, 75 per cent of this work was finished before the year-end. Change the work sheet to reflect the amount of this revenue that applied to the year just ended. Observe how the work sheet changes automatically. Remember to make the calculations twice. What is the revised net income figure?

CHAPTER HIGHLIGHTS

Now that you have completed Chapter 10, you should:

1. understand what is meant by "accountability";
2. know the five most common users of financial statements, and how they make use of them;
3. know what is meant by "quality" financial statements;
4. understand the purpose of an audit;
5. know three additional GAAPs:
   - the consistency principle,
   - the materiality principle,
   - the full disclosure principle;
6. understand fully the adjusting entries for supplies used, insurance used, late invoices, and depreciation;
7. be able to calculate depreciation in two ways, by the straight-line method and the declining-balance method;
8. understand the concept of a "contra" account;
9. be able to complete an eight-column work sheet;
10. understand how the "adjusted" items affect the financial statements.

ACCOUNTING TERMS

accountability
adjusting entry
audit
consistency principle
contra account
declining-balance method of
　depreciation

depreciation
full disclosure principle
materiality principle
prepaid expense
straight-line method of depreciation

CHAPTER EXERCISES

Using Your Knowledge

1. **Use T-accounts to help you through this exercise.**
   Dictating Systems Company of Burlington, Ontario started business on January 1, 19–3. During its first year, it purchased the following insurance policies.

Company	Policy Date	Term	Premium
Atlantic	March 1, 19–3	3 years	$216.00
Pacific	Sept. 1, 19–3	3 years	468.00

   1. What is the balance in the Prepaid Insurance account on December 31, 19–3 before any adjusting entries?
   2. Calculate the correct prepaid insurance figure as at December 31, 19–3.
   3. Give the adjusting entry for the 19–3 year-end.
   4. Prove the insurance expense figure for 19–3.

   During the 19–4 year, Dictating Systems purchased the following insurance policies.

Company	Policy Date	Term	Premium
Indian	June 1, 19–4	1 year	$252.00
Arctic	June 30, 19–4	2 years	360.00

   5. What is the balance in the Prepaid Insurance account on December 31, 19–4 before any adjusting entries?
   6. Calculate the correct prepaid insurance figure as at December 31, 19–4.
   7. Give the adjusting entry for the 19–4 year-end.
   8. Prove the insurance expense figure for 19–4.

   During the 19–5 year, Dictating Systems purchased or renewed insurance policies as follows.

Company	Policy Date	Term	Premium
Superior	Feb. 1, 19–5	2 years	$336
Indian	June 1, 19–5	1 year	264
Huron	Nov. 1, 19–5	3 years	396

   9. What is the balance in the Prepaid Insurance Account on December 31, 19–5 before any adjusting entries?
   10. Calculate the correct prepaid insurance figure as at December 31, 19–5.
   11. Give the adjusting entry for the 19–5 year-end.
   12. Prove the insurance expense figure for 19–5.

2. During the first three years of a company's life, it purchased or renewed insurance policies as shown in the chart below. The company has a December 31 year-end.

Year	Company	Date	Term	Premium
19–1	Ace	February 1	1 year	$120
	Star	April 30	2 years	300
	Galaxy	September 30	1 year	672
19–2	Beneficial	January 31	2 years	288
	Ace	February 1	1 year	132
	Guardian	May 1	1 year	168
	Empire	December 1	2 years	576
19–3	Ace	February 1	1 year	156
	Provincial	July 1	2 years	240
	Dominion	October 1	1 year	168

Complete the following summary in your workbook.

Year	Insurance Expense For Year	Value of Prepaid Insurance at Year-end
19–1		
19–2		
19–3		

3. A company purchases a truck at a cost of $25 000 which it expects to last six years and have a salvage value of $3 500.

   1. **Prepare two depreciation schedules as follows:**
      a. A six-year schedule showing depreciation calculated on a straight-line basis.
      b. A six-year schedule showing depreciation calculated on a declining-balance basis at the government rate of 30 per cent.

   2. Many accountants claim that, when repairs are also considered, the declining-balance method of calculating depreciation provides a more reliable way to charge all operating expenses of a truck against revenue. Is this argument valid? Explain. A chart may be helpful.

4. **Workbook Exercise: Challenge**—completing a chart calculating unexpired insurance at the ends of successive periods.

5. Examine each of the following situations carefully. In each case, decide if an adjusting entry is necessary. If you decide one is not, give an explanation. If you decide one is, give the adjusting entry. Also, state the accounting principles involved in making your decision.

   In each case you are dealing with a company that has a December 31 year-end. You are employed by the company either as an auditor or as an accoutant.

1. The company is a paving company. It keeps on hand (Paving Materials account) a supply of materials which it needs for the type of work it performs. During the course of preparing the work sheet, you are handed $12 500 of "materials used slips" which should have been given to you before December 31. All of these slips pertained to jobs completed before December 31.

2. The company owns a building which has become unnecessary. It rents the building at a monthly renter fee of $1 000. The renter provides twelve post-dated cheques for the rent in advance. During the course of your audit you discover that the rent cheques for the last four months of the year were not deposited. The employee who had attended to this had terminated his employment and the replacement had not known about the rental arrangements. The cheques were found in an envelope in the company safe and were deposited in January.

3. Last March 1, the company that you work for borrowed $20 000 from a close friend of the owner. The agreement was that the principle would be paid back in five years, and that the loan would carry interest at the rate of 15 per cent to be paid annually on March 1. The loan was recorded but no entries were made for the interest.

4. During the course of your audit you discover that the owner of the company has had a $17 500 personal automobile charged to Truck Expense. The automobile was purchased on September 1. The company uses the declining-balance method of depreciation at government rates.

5. While performing the audit of a movie theatre, you uncover the following situation. During November and December the movie house conducted a promotion on the sale of books of theatre tickets. These were intended as gift ideas for the Christmas season. The promotion was a success. $32 500 was taken in and was credited to Ticket Revenue. Your investigation revealed that none of the tickets had been used in the year just ended.

6. During the course of your audit for a lawyer you discover that she had engaged in a barter transaction that was never recorded in the company books. The lawyer had done legal work for a construction company which had built a recreation room for the lawyer in full payment. The contractor, when contacted by you, said that the amount involved was $25 000.

7. The company which you work for has a two-weekly pay system with a one week hold back. In other words, employees are not paid until one week after a pay period is completed. You find out that the total payroll of $27 500 for the two weeks which ended on December 31 was recorded one week later, in the month of January.

8. You are engaged in auditing a major company with a net income in the range of $4 000 000. During the course of your audit you discover that the company neglected to depreciate a $100 000 brick building which had an undepreciated cost of $73 509.19. The company has already had its financial statements printed.

9. The company you are auditing usually records revenue when the jobs are completed. You discover that a job worth $72 000 was recorded on January 5, after the year-end. Your inquiries reveal that the job was entirely completed before the year-end but that it took a few days to get the invoice prepared.

10. During the course of your audit you find that $2 500 of this January's sales were recorded in the books in December last. Your questions reveal that the owner had requested this be done to improve the income statement for the period just ended.

6. **Challenge Exercise:** On December 31, 19–4 the end of a fiscal year, the general ledger trial balance of Dominion Realty is as follows.

DOMINION REALTY
TRIAL BALANCE
DECEMBER 31, 19–4

	DR	CR
Bank	$ 4 012.25	
Accounts Receivable	15 650.00	
Investment—20% Government Bonds	50 000.00	
Supplies	2 850.00	
Prepaid Insurance	2 890.00	
Land	38 950.00	
Buildings	42 250.00	
Accumulated Depreciation—Buildings		$ 10 750.00
Furniture and Equipment	13 350.00	
Accumulated Depreciation—Furniture and Equipment		4 800.00
Automobiles	75 000.00	
Accumulated Depreciation—Automobiles		30 000.00
Accounts Payable		13 356.00
Loan Payable—6%		20 000.00
Mortgage Payable—12%		50 000.00
J. Lampu, Capital		119 020.65
J. Lampu, Drawings	42 000.00	
Commissions Earned		102 560.00
Interest Earned		5 000.00
Advertising	8 525.00	
Bank Charges	325.35	
Building Maintenance	1 257.25	
Car Expenses	17 356.80	
Loan Interest Expense	900.00	
Mortgage Interest Expense		
Light, Heat, and Water	2 856.00	
Miscellaneous Expense	956.00	
Postage	1 356.00	
Property Taxes	1 050.00	
Telephone	2 596.00	
Wages and Salaries	31 356.00	
	$355 486.65	$355 486.65

Using the additional information shown below:
1. **complete an eight-column work sheet;**
2. **prepare a classified balance sheet;**
3. **prepare an income statement.**

Additional Information:
1. Purchase invoices received in January, 19–5 which pertain to goods or services received in 19–4 are for the following:

Building Maintenance	$358.00
Supplies	185.90
Car Expenses	489.00
Advertising	500.00

2. The supplies counted and valued as of December 31, 19–4 are $750.

3. The details of insurance policies in force at December 31, 19–4 are:

Company	Policy Date	Term	Premium
Acme	July 1, 19–3	2 years	$240
Inland	April 1, 19–4	1 year	192
Empire	Dec. 1, 19–3	2 years	432
Imperial	Sept. 1, 19–4	3 years	288

4. Depreciation is calculated on a straight-line basis.
Buildings cost $42 250, are expected to have a useful life of 30 years, and to have a market value of $10 000 at the end of that time.
Furniture and equipment cost $13 350, are expected to have a useful life of 15 years, and to have a market value of $1 350 at the end of that time.
Automobiles cost $75 000, are expected to have a useful life of five years, and to have a resale value of $25 000 at the end of that time.

5. The loan payable of $20 000 bears interest at the rate of 6 per cent per annum. Interest payments of $300 are made at the end of each quarter year. However, the last payment for 19–4 was not made on time.

6. The full amount of the mortgage payable is due in 19–9. However, the interest is payable every December 31. The 19–4 interest was not paid until early in 19–5.

7. The Government of Canada bonds pay interest every June 30 and December 31. The procedure is to clip the proper interest coupon from the bond and to cash it at the bank. This was done properly at June 30 but not at December 31.

Comprehensive Exercise

7. Tom Michaud is in the plastering business under the name of Tom's Plastering. From the following trial balance and additional information, prepare the work sheet and the financial statements for Tom's Plastering for the year ended October 31, 19–1.

TOM'S PLASTERING
TRIAL BALANCE
OCTOBER 31, 19–1

	DR	CR
Bank	$ 1 412.01	
Accounts Receivable	8 025.00	
Supplies	1 416.70	
Small Tools	1 903.00	
Prepaid Insurance	2 107.80	
Equipment	9 500.00	
Accumulated Depreciation—Equipment		$ 3 200.00
Truck	19 500.00	
Accumulated Depreciation—Truck		8 000.00
Accounts Payable		2 407.35
Bank Loan		10 000.00
Tom Michaud, Capital		18 212.28
Tom Michaud, Drawings	35 534.00	
Revenue		120 365.00
Bank Interest and Charges	1 325.15	
Materials Used	25 369.20	
Miscellaneous Expense	756.32	
Rent Expense	6 000.00	
Telephone Expense	864.32	
Truck Expense	8 325.40	
Utilities Expense	4 563.26	
Wages Expense	35 582.47	
	$162 184.63	$162 184.63

Additional Information:

1. Office supplies on hand at October 31 are valued at $360.
2. Unexpired insurance at October 31 is calculated at $510.95.
3. Depreciation is calculated using the straight-line method. All assets were on hand for the entire year.

    The equipment cost $9 500 and was expected to last for ten years. It was estimated that it would be worth $1 500 at that time.

    The truck cost $19 500 and was expected to last for five years. It was estimated that it would be worth $3 500 at that time.

4. Late bills pertaining to the 19–1 year were as follows:

Supplies	$ 56.20
Miscellaneous Expense	26.85
Truck Expense	563.85
Total	$646.90

5. The small tools at October 31 are valued at $350. The tools represented by the difference between the $350 figure and the trial balance figure have been lost, stolen, or used up.
6. Of the $25 369.20 shown on the trial balance under Materials Used, $2 850 is still on hand and unused.

For Further Thought

8. Briefly answer each of the following questions.

1. Accountability does not always refer to financial statements. Give an example of another accountability situation.
2. There are ways to manipulate financial information. Which group of users is in the best position to manipulate financial statements? Explain.
3. Is accountability a factor in a business owned and operated by one person? Explain.
4. What is the principal measure of a banker's performance? Explain.
5. Mrs. Smith is a shareholder in the Coca-Cola Company which has millions of shares outstanding. Mrs. Smith owns 50 shares. As one of the owners, Mrs. Smith receives a financial report. If Mrs. Smith disapproved of certain actions of the company, what could she do about it? What influence would she have?
6. The following is a quotation from the CICA Handbook: "Where assets of the business are pledged as security against liabilities, the nature and, where practicable, the carrying value of such assets should be disclosed." What accounting principle is a factor here? What does the quotation mean?
7. An auditor might confidently give an opinion on the fairness of the financial statements of a company even though only two or three weeks were spent actually auditing the company's books. On what does the auditor rely to sign the statements with confidence?
8. The text states that "inexact" does not mean "inaccurate." Explain.
9. Explain how the value of the first four columns of a work sheet are determined. In your answer cover all the possible debit and credit combinations.
10. Prompt attention is given to supplies when they are purchased but not when they are used. Explain why.
11. How accurate should one be when taking a supplies inventory? Give your reason.
12. How accurate should one be when calculating prepaid insurance? Give your reason.
13. Explain why you would not calculate prepaid insurance every day in order to keep the accounts up-to-date.
14. Invoices for items purchased usually arrive sometime after the goods or services. This is not a problem except at statement time. Explain.
15. Depreciation, to an accountant, does not mean the same thing as it does to the ordinary person. What does it mean to the ordinary person? What factors affect or cause depreciation in the normal sense?
16. Straight-line depreciation requires the making of estimates in advance. How would one obtain reasonably good estimates for an automobile?
17. A company that uses straight-line depreciation is required to modify its statements to reflect declining-balance depreciation for income tax purposes. Does this require keeping two sets of books? Explain.
18. You are about to calculate the declining-balance depreciation from the figures on the work sheet. How do you figure out quickly on what to base the precentage rate?
19. You are told that the net book value of Trucks is $22 500. What does this information not tell you?
20. Give the rule stated previously for extending the items on the work sheet.

CASE STUDIES

Case 1 Avoiding Income Tax

George Uttz, owner of a large business, has attempted an income tax dodge. George has debited Truck Expense rather than Trucks with the $200 000 cost of several new trucks that he has just purchased.

Questions
1. Has George done anything illegal?
2. What does George stand to gain from his intentional error?
3. If the error is not corrected, what will the immediate tax benefit be if George's tax rate is 40 per cent?
4. What other monetary benefit is there besides the saving in income tax?
5. What will the effect be in subsequent years?

Case 2 Comparing Depreciation

John Franks, a businessman, seeks your advice in regard to the depreciation method that he should use in his business. To help you explain the two methods, complete the following table in your workbook.

John's only depreciable asset is automotive equipment costing $100 000, expected to last eight years, and to have a salvage value of $5 000.

Year	Net Income Before Depreciation	Declining-Balance at 30%			Straight-Line			Income Tax Gain (or Loss)
		Depreciation for Year	Net Income for Year	Income Tax at 40%	Depreciation For Year	Net Income For Year	Income Tax at 40%	
1	75 000							
2	75 000							
3	80 000							
4	82 000							
5	85 000							
6	85 000							
7	90 000							
8	90 000							

Questions
1. Under which method is depreciation higher in the earlier years?
2. Which method provides a tax advantage in the early years?
3. What is the net tax advantage or disadvantage after 8 years?
4. What is the net saving in bank interest after 8 years?
5. Why would a businessperson choose the government declining-balance method?
6. Give an advantage or disadvantage of the straight-line method.

Case 3 Banker Beware

You are the manager of a Corner Brook, Newfoundland bank that has loaned $25 000 to Eunice Freeman, the owner of Ace Consulting Services. You have become concerned about the loan. Eunice has not been cooperative about reducing the loan even when she seems to have money available.

Eunice has provided you with the latest financial statements for the year ended December 31, 19–5. You have just placed these beside the statements for the previous year. The two sets of statements, side by side, appear as follows:

Balance Sheet Year 19–4			Balance Sheet Year 19–5	
ASSETS			**ASSETS**	
Cash	$ 9 000		Cash	$ 2 000
			Accounts Receivable	12 000
Equipment	21 000		Equipment	21 000
Total	$30 000		Total	$35 000
LIABILITIES AND EQUITY			**LIABILITIES AND EQUITY**	
Bank Loan	$25 000		Bank Loan	$25 000
Capital	5 000		Capital	10 000
Total	$30 000		Total	$35 000

Income Statement Year Ended December 31, 19–4			Income Statement Year Ended December 31, 19–5	
Revenues	$59 000		Revenues	$51 000
Expenses	24 000		Expenses	26 000
Net Income	$35 000		Net Income	$25 000

Study the above statements as if you were the banker. Then answer the following questions in your workbook.

1. What significant new item appears on the 19–5 statement?
2. Give two specific pieces of data that suggest the company is experiencing financial difficulties.
3. Assume that Eunice has used the cash basis of accounting prior to 19–5. This means that revenue was recognized when (and not until) the cash was received for services rendered. In 19–5, however, the balance sheet includes the item Accounts Receivable in the amount of $12 000. Clearly, Eunice has changed to a system that recognizes revenue when it is billed (accrual basis). Suggest a reason why this was done.
4. Redo the statements for 19–5 to be consistent with prior years.
5. What principle has been violated by Eunice?

6. Eunice comes to you to inform you that the revenue for 19–5 should be greater by $200 because of a bookkeeping error. What effect will this have on your evaluation of her company? What principle is at work here?

Case 4   Meeting the Deadline

Stetsko and Company performs all of its own accounting up to the trial balance stage. Then Lu and Company, a firm of chartered accountants from the big city, prepares the adjusting entries and the financial statements.

You are an auditor with Lu and Company, which has just completed the financial statements for Stetsko. You have just driven 500 miles to deliver these statements for an important business meeting that day, and to begin some other audit work.

When you open your files, you find that your working papers have been tampered with. Most important, the balance sheet, the work sheet, and the list of adjusting entries for Stetsko are missing. Only the income statement is present.

The important meeting is only two hours away. Working only with the client's pre-adjustment trial balance and the income statement, prepare an up-to-date balance sheet in time for the meeting. In addition, prepare a list of the adjusting entries that would have been on the work sheet.

STETSKO AND COMPANY
PRE-ADJUSTED TRIAL BALANCE
JUNE 30, 19--

	DR	CR
Bank	$ 4 172.50	
Accounts Receivable	27 421.00	
Supplies	1 365.00	
Prepaid Insurance	2 280.00	
Furniture and Equipment	12 596.00	
Accumulated Depreciation—Furniture and Equipment		$ 2 500.00
Automotive Equipment	24 800.00	
Accumulated Depreciation—Automotive Equipment		6 500.00
Accounts Payable		6 521.92
Bank Loan		20 000.00
Sales Tax Payable		560.00
I. Stetsko, Capital		25 558.20
I. Stetsko, Drawings	15 000.00	
Sales		58 072.50
Bank Charges	1 132.10	
Automotive Expense	4 547.52	
Miscellaneous Expense	761.50	
Rent	2 600.00	
Telephone	1 712.00	
Wages	21 325.00	
	$119 712.62	$119 712.62

STETSKO AND COMPANY
INCOME STATEMENT
SIX MONTHS ENDED JUNE 30, 19--

Revenue
    Sales $58 072.50

Operating Expenses
Automotive Expense	$ 4 997.52	
Bank Charges	1 132.10	
Depreciation—Furniture and Equipment	500.00	
Depreciation—Automotive Equipment	1 250.00	
Insurance Expense	1 580.00	
Miscellaneous Expense	851.50	
Rent	2 600.00	
Supplies Used	955.00	
Telephone	1 822.00	
Wages	21 325.00	37 013.12
Net Income		$21 059.38

Case 5   *Declining-Balance versus Distance-Used*

The company you work for depreciates its trucks using the declining-balance method at government rates. Your boss suggests to you that this does not fairly charge the cost of the truck to the years of its use. It is her opinion that the cost of the truck should be charged over the years on the basis of actual use, that is, on the basis of kilometers travelled. You agree that it is worth considering and decide to make a comparison.

In your investigation you select one truck that was recently sold and for which you have full and complete records. The truck was bought on January 1, 19–1 at a cost of $35 000, had no major repairs, and lasted until December 31, 19–8 at which time it was sold for $3 500. Your records also show that the truck travelled the distances in the following table.

Year	Distance
19–1	21 468 km
19–2	35 698 km
19–3	42 654 km
19–4	45 965 km
19–5	40 365 km
19–6	35 632 km
19–7	27 526 km
19–8	16 201 km
Total	265 509 km

Prepare two depreciation schedules for the above truck to compare the declining-balance method with the distance-used method. With the distance-used method, the depreciation for the first year is calculated as follows: 21 468/265 509 × (35 000–3 500).

Discuss the merits of your boss's proposal.

CAREER
Paulette Dubois / Management Accountant

Paulette Dubois grew up in Montréal, Québec and graduated with a bachelor's degree in psychology from l'Université de Québec à Montréal in the late 1970s. Instead of pursuing a graduate degree in her specialty, social psychology, she chose to train and work as a secretary before deciding on a permanent career. Paulette accepted a position as secretary to the controller of Domtar Inc., a company that manufactures paper products. Because of her position there and the influence of management accountants in the office, she decided accounting was the career she was looking for.

Paulette obtained a junior position with Morisette et Tremblay, a firm of public accountants, and at the same time enrolled in the Chartered Accountant's (CA) program. Paulette's duties at work included completing customers' tax returns, performing basic accounting functions for small businesses, and preparing the financial statements for clients. She also worked with an auditing team examining accounting procedures for all the firm's clients each year. It was her responsibility to make sure all clients were following generally accepted accounting principles for consistency, materiality and full disclosure on all financial statements.

Three years later, when Paulette received her CA designation, she went to work as an accountant with the Nordberg Company, a manufacturer of mining equipment. In this position, Paulette was responsible for keeping track of customers' credit and for the collection of accounts receivable. Her duties included the preparation of insurance schedules and the calculation of the year-end inventory of equipment and supplies. Paulette reported directly to the general manager.

In search of a more responsible accounting position, Paulette next joined EMCO Ltd., a manufacturer of plumbing supplies, as their management accountant. At the same time, she enrolled in the Society of Management Accountants (CMA) program, which she completed during evenings and weekends over the next two years.

Paulette's responsibilities as management accountant are varied and interesting. She especially likes the fact that her job takes her to many different places. She travels throughout Canada, the United States and England examining the accounting systems of various branches of the company. She is continually called upon to make major decisions for the head office, such as whether to buy new companies or merge with others. She established the data processing system for the Canadian branches of EMCO and ensures that all corporate policies are carried out. As management accountant, Paulette also prepares the yearly work sheet and sees to it that all accounts, such as prepaid insurance, supplies, interest charges, and depreciable fixed assets are adjusted at year-end.

Each year, Paulette sets up schedules of fixed assets to record the year's depreciation expense, using the declining-balance method. She then uses the work sheet to prepare the consolidated financial statements. Paulette passes these statements on to her immediate superior, the company controller, for analysis.

Paulette is pleased she chose accounting as a profession. She finds her work challenging and absorbing and enjoys the people she works with. She feels that the accounting field offers many opportunities for advancement and looks forward to a promising career.

Discussion

1. Why did Paulette choose to enrol in the CMA program when she had already earned a CA designation?
2. What are the duties Paulette has as a Management Accountant at EMCO?
3. **a.** Explain why some businesses use the declining-balance method and other businesses use the straight-line method of depreciation when they record depreciation on their fixed assets.
   b. Which method is approved by Revenue Canada?
4. One of Paulette's major duties is to prepare the consolidated financial statements and send these statements to management. Why might groups other than management be interested in Paulette's statements?
5. Examine a company's notes to its financial statements. Prepare a list of those accounts that required a footnote and explain why it was necessary to make these disclosures.
6 Paulette has many accounts to adjust at year-end, such as Prepaid Insurance, Supplies and Depreciation of Automobiles. Can you think of any additional accounts Paulette might have to adjust at year-end, and why it would be necessary to make such adjustments?

11 Completing the Accounting Cycle

11.1 Adjusting and Closing Entries—Objectives
11.2 Journalizing and Posting the Adjusting and Closing Entries

In the last chapter you saw how the eight-column work sheet is completed and used to prepare the financial statements. This achieved one of the most important purposes of the accounting process. However, accounting is cyclical in nature. Remember the "time period concept." It states that financial reporting, on net income in particular, is done in equal periods of time. The accounts must now be made ready for the next cycle.

11.1 Adjusting and Closing Entries—Objectives

The final stage of the accounting cycle is to prepare the accounts for the next fiscal period. However, two new accounting terms must be introduced first.

Real Accounts and Nominal Accounts

Asset and liability accounts are considered to be real accounts. **Real accounts** are ones whose balances continue into the next fiscal period. Examples of real accounts include Bank, Trucks, and Accounts Payable.

On the other hand, revenue, expense, and drawings accounts are considered to be nominal accounts (also known as temporary equity accounts). **Nominal accounts** are ones whose balances do not continue into the next fiscal period. Nominal accounts are related to the income statement and the income statement deals only with a single fiscal period. Nominal accounts begin each fiscal period with a nil balance.

Closing Out the Nominal Accounts

Once the income statement for a period has been completed, the balances in the nominal accounts are no longer useful. These "old" balances in the nominal accounts must be removed to make the accounts "fresh" for the next accounting period. There must be no balance left in any nominal account to start off a new fiscal period. This process is known as closing the accounts, closing out the accounts, or clearing the accounts. **Closing an account** means to cause it to have no balance. The nominal accounts are closed out at the end of every fiscal period, as shown in section 11.2.

End-of-Period Procedure

There are a number of things to be done at the end of each fiscal period. These are:

1. Journalize and post the adjusting entries. You will recall that some accounts were allowed to become inexact during the fiscal period. These were updated on the work sheet and on the financial statements, but not in the accounts. Now, all of the ledger accounts must be brought up-to-date as well.
2. Journalize and post the closing entries. This prepares the nominal accounts for the next fiscal period. You will be shown how to do this in the next section.
3. Update the Capital account. This happens automatically as a result of performing step 2. As you know, during any fiscal period the total equity of a business is not contained in a single account. It is contained in a number of accounts in the equity section of the ledger. The Capital account shows the equity balance at the beginning of the period. Any changes in equity during the period are contained in revenue, expense, and drawings accounts. But, as one of the last steps in the accounting cycle, the Capital account is made to show the final equity figure.
4. Take off a post-closing trial balance. There is a lot of room for making errors in the process of journalizing and posting the adjusting and closing entries. A trial balance is taken off to ensure that the ledger is still in balance. A **post-closing trial balance** is one that is taken as soon as the closing entries have been posted.

Complete Accounting Cycle

The post-closing trial balance is the final step in the accounting cycle. Figure 11.1 shows the steps in the accounting cycle in its final form.

Section 11.1

performed daily {
- Transactions occur. Source documents.
- Accounting entries recorded in the journal.
} **performed by junior personnel**

performed monthly {
- Journal entries posted to the ledger accounts.
- Ledger balanced by means of a trial balance.
}

performed at the end of each fiscal period {
- Work sheet prepared.
- Income statement and balance sheet prepared.
- Adjusting entries journalized and posted.
- Closing entries journalized and posted.
- Reversing entries journalized and posted.
} **performed by senior personnel**

Figure 11.1 The complete accounting cycle.

Section Review Questions

1. Explain the time period concept.
2. What does the final stage of the accounting cycle involve?
3. What is a "real" account?
4. What is a "nominal" account?
5. What are nominal accounts also called?
6. With what part of the ledger are nominal accounts associated?
7. Why are "old" balances cleared out of the nominal accounts?
8. Explain what is meant by "closing an account."
9. What four things must be done at the end of the accounting period?
10. What steps have been added to the accounting cycle in this chapter?

Section Exercises

1. A list of accounts appears below and in your workbook. Indicate which of these are nominal accounts.

    Accounts

Accounts Payable	Insurance Expense
Accounts Receivable	Land
Advertising	Legal Expense
Automobiles	Mortgage Payable
Bank	Postage
Bank Charges	Rent
Bank Loan	Revenue from Commissions
Building	Salaries
Capital—Sylvia Magill	Sales
Car Expenses	Supplies
Delivery Expense	Telephone
Drawings—Sylvia Magill	Wages
Equipment	

2. A simplified ledger appears below and in your workbook.

Bank	Bank Loan	S Mosar, Capital	S Mosar, Drawings
100	300	740	750

Accounts Receivable	Accounts Payable	Advertising Revenue	Sales Revenue
200	150	1 750	450

Supplies		Bank Charges	Light and Heat
50		20	40

Equipment		Miscellaneous Exp	Printing Expense
1 050		5	500

		Rent	Telephone
		250	25

		Wages	
		400	

1. Calculate the total assets, total liabilities, and the owner's equity. Prove the accuracy of your figures.
2. By stroking out and/or changing figures, show how this ledger would appear if the closing entries were completed.

3. Workbook Exercise: Completing a chart showing the steps in the accounting cycle.

Chapter 11

4. **In your workbook complete each of the following sentences by inserting the number representing the most appropriate word or phrase from the list below.**

   1. Accounting is _____ in nature.
   2. The _____ states that financial reporting is done in equal periods of time.
   3. Asset and liability accounts are considered to be _____ accounts.
   4. _____ are ones that have their balances continue on into the succeeding fiscal period.
   5. Revenue, expense, and drawings accounts are considered to be _____ accounts.
   6. _____ are ones that _____ their balances continue on into the succeeding fiscal period.
   7. Another name for nominal account is _____ .
   8. Nominal accounts begin each fiscal period with _____ .
   9. The process of removing the ''old'' balances from the nominal accounts is known as _____ .
   10. _____ means to cause it to have no balance.
   11. During a fiscal period the Capital account shows _____ .
   12. Changes in equity during a fiscal period are contained in _____ accounts.
   13. At the end of the fiscal period the ledger is brought up-to-date by _____ .
   14. One of the final steps in the accounting cycle is to bring the Capital account _____ and to _____ the nominal accounts.
   15. The final step in the accounting cycle is _____ .

List of Words and Phrases
1. a nil balance
2. close out
3. closing an account
4. closing the accounts
5. cyclical
6. do not have
7. journalizing and posting the adjusting entries
8. nominal
9. nominal accounts
10. real
11. real accounts
12. revenue, expense, and drawings
13. temporary equity account
14. the balance at the beginning of the period
15. the post-closing trial balance
16. time period concept
17. up-to-date

11.2 Journalizing and Posting the Adjusting and Closing Entries

You have just studied the objectives of the adjusting and closing entries. Now you will learn how to achieve those objectives.

The ledger of C. Hua, a lawyer, is used to illustrate the process. Shown below in

Figure 11.2 and Figure 11.3 are the ledger and the work sheet for C. Hua after a fiscal period of one year. Notice the following:
1. the trial balance figures on the work sheet are taken from the ledger;
2. the trial balance figures are pre-adjustment figures;
3. the data for the adjusting and closing entries are outlined. All of the necessary information is available on the work sheet. There is no point in looking in any other place.

Bank	Accounts Payable	C. Hua, Capital	C. Hua, Drawings
750	3 730	23 071	37 000

Accounts Receivable		Fees Earned	Bank Charges
12 900		95 700	110

Supplies		Auto Expense	Miscellaneous Expense
1 800		5 116	375

Prepaid Insurance		Rent Expense	Salaries
3 650		18 000	17 500

Office Equipment		Telephone	Supplies Used
15 000		1 920	1 250

Accumulated Depreciation—Office Equipment		Insurance Used	Depreciation—Office Equipment
6 020			

Automobile		Depreciation—Automobile	Income Summary
24 000			

Accumulated Depreciation—Automobile
9 600

ASSETS ($42 480) − LIABILITIES ($3 730) = EQUITY ($38 750)

Figure 11.2 The ledger of C. Hua, a lawyer, before any adjustments.

C. Hua, Lawyer — Work Sheet — Year Ended December 31, 19—

Accounts	Trial Balance DR	Trial Balance CR	Adjustments DR	Adjustments CR	Income Statement DR	Income Statement CR	Balance Sheet DR	Balance Sheet CR
Bank	750 —						750 —	
Accounts Receivable	12 900 —						12 900 —	
Supplies	1 800 —			1 250 —			550 —	
Prepaid Insurance	3 650 —			2 175 —			1 475 —	
Office Equipment	15 000 —						15 000 —	
Acc. Deprec. Off. Eq.		6 020 —		860 —				6 880 —
Automobile	24 000 —						24 000 —	
Acc. Dep. Auto		9 600 —		3 200 —				12 800 —
Accounts Payable		3 730 —		200 —				3 930 —
C. Hua, Capital		23 071 —						23 071 —
C. Hua, Drawings	37 000 —						37 000 —	
Fees Earned		95 700 —				95 700 —		
Bank Charges	110 —				110 —			
Auto Expense	5 116 —		150 —		5 266 —			
Misc. Expense	375 —		50 —		425 —			
Rent Expense	18 000 —				18 000 —			
Salaries	17 500 —				17 500 —			
Telephone	1 920 —				1 920 —			
	138 121 —	138 121 —						
Supplies Used			1 250 —		1 250 —			
Insurance Used			2 175 —		2 175 —			
Deprec. Off. Eq.			860 —		860 —			
Deprec. Auto			3 200 —		3 200 —			
			7 685 —	7 685 —	50 706 —	95 700 —	91 675 —	46 681 —
Net Income					44 994 —			44 994 —
					95 700 —	95 700 —	91 675 —	91 675 —

Annotations:
- The adjusting entries
- The figures for closing entry #2
- The figures for closing entry #1
- The figure for closing entry #3
- The figure for closing entry #4

Figure 11.3 The completed work sheet for C. Hua, a lawyer.

The person who records the adjusting and closing entries does not have to be the one who prepares the work sheet. There is a particular set of procedures to follow and it works in all cases. It is often necessary for an accountant to make use of the work of others.

Journalizing and Posting the Adjusting Entries

Journalize and post *all and only* those adjusting entries that appear in the Adjustments section of the work sheet. This is no time for discovering new adjustments. The adjustment decision process took place when the work sheet was prepared. Now it is simply a matter of putting these adjustments into the accounts.

This can be done by individual entries as shown in Figure 11.4 below, or in one grand entry as is done by many accountants. The entries are usually dated on the last day of the fiscal period. They are headed "Adjusting Entries" so there is no need for explanations.

Adjusting Entries				
Dec.	31	Supplies Used	1250 —	
		Supplies		1250 —
	31	Insurance Used	2175 —	
		Prepaid Insurance		2175 —
	31	Depreciation Office Equipment	860 —	
		Accumulated Deprec. Office Equip		860 —
	31	Depreciation Automobile	3200 —	
		Accumulated Deprec. Automobile		3200 —

Figure 11.4 The adjusting entries for C. Hua.

After journalizing and posting these adjusting entries, the ledger accounts will be updated. The updated ledger for C. Hua is shown in Figure 11.5.

Chapter 11

Bank	Accounts Payable	C. Hua, Capital	C. Hua, Drawings
750	3 730	23 071	37 000
	200		
	⓪ 3930		

Accounts Receivable		Fees Earned	Bank Charges
12 900		95 700	110

Supplies		Auto Expense	Miscellaneous Expense
1 800	1 250	5 116	375
⓪ 550		150	50
		⓪ 5266	⓪ 425

Prepaid Insurance		Rent Expense	Salaries
3 650	2 175	18 000	17 500
⓪ 1475			

Office Equipment		Telephone	Supplies Used
15 000		1 920	1 250

Accumulated Depreciation— Office Equipment		Insurance Used	Depreciation— Office Equipment
	6 020	2 175	860
	860		
	⓪ 6880		

Automobile		Depreciation— Automobile	Income Summary
24 000		3 200	

Accumulated Depreciation— Automobile			
	9 600		
	3 200		
	⓪ 12800		

ASSETS ($34 995) − LIABILITIES ($3 930) = EQUITY ($31 065)

Figure 11.5 The ledger of C. Hua after posting the adjusting entries.

Journalizing and Posting the Closing Entries

There is no *single* way that closing entries must be recorded. The four-step procedure shown below is a common method. The entries are headed Closing Entries.

Closing Entry No. 1

The first closing entry transfers the balances in the revenue account(s) to a new nominal account called Income Summary. The figures for this closing entry are found in the Income Statement section credit column of the work sheet, as outlined in Figure 11.3.

Since revenues have credit balances, debit entries are needed to close them out. Knowing this will help you work out the first closing entry for C. Hua, which appears below in Figure 11.6.

	Closing Entries		
Dec 31	Fees Earned	9570000	
	Income Summary		9570000

Figure 11.6 The first closing entry for C. Hua.

Closing Entry No. 2

The second closing entry transfers the balances in the expense accounts to the Income Summary account. The figures for this closing entry are found in the Income Statement section debit column of the work sheet as outlined in Figure 11.3. Use all of the figures down to and including the subtotals, and no others.

Since expenses have debit balances, credit entries are needed to close them out. Understanding this will help you work out the second closing entry for C. Hua, which appears below in Figure 11.7.

31	Income Summary	5070600	
	Bank Charges		11000
	Auto Expense		526600
	Miscellaneous Expense		42500
	Rent Expense		1800000
	Salaries		1750000
	Telephone		192000
	Supplies Used		125000
	Insurance Used		217500
	Depreciation Office Equipment		86000
	Depreciation Automobile		320000

Figure 11.7 The second closing entry for C. Hua.

The ledger of C. Hua after the second closing entry is shown below in Figure 11.8.

Bank	Accounts Payable	C. Hua, Capital	C. Hua, Drawings
750	3 730	23 071	37 000
	200		
	(3930)		

Accounts Receivable		Fees Earned	Bank Charges
12 900		95 700 | 95 700	110 | 110
		Ø	Ø

Supplies		Automobile Expense	Miscellaneous Expense
1 800 | 1 250		5 116	375
(550)		150 | 5 266	50 | 425
		Ø	Ø

Prepaid Insurance		Rent Expense	Salaries
3 650 | 2 175		18 000 | 18 000	17 500 | 17 500
(1 475)		Ø	Ø

Office Equipment		Telephone	Supplies Used
15 000		1 920 | 1 920	1 250 | 1 250
		Ø	Ø

Accumulated Depreciation—Office Equipment		Insurance Used	Depreciation—Office Equipment
6 020		2 175 | 2 175	860 | 860
860		Ø	Ø
(6 880)			

Automobile		Depreciation—Automobile	Income Summary
24 000		3 200 | 3 200	50 706 | 95 700
		Ø	(44 994)

Accumulated Depreciation—Automobile
9 600
3 200
(12 800)

ASSETS ($34 995) − LIABILITIES ($3 930) = EQUITY ($31 065)

Figure 11.8 The ledger of C. Hua after posting the first two closing entries.

The equity section of the ledger is considerably changed at this point. All of the revenue and expense accounts now have nil balances. They have been closed out. Only three accounts in the equity section have a balance. Ignoring the accounts with nil balances, the equity section appears as follows.

C. Hua Capital	C. Hua Drawings	Income Summary
23 071	37 000	50 706 | 95 700
		(44 994)

The Income Summary account is new to you. The **Income Summary account** is one in which the revenues and expenses are summarized during the closing entry process. The balance in this account represents either the amount of net income or the amount of net loss. It will be closed out to the owner's capital account.

The Income Summary account for C. Hua now contains the following:
- the total revenues of $95 700 on the credit side;
- the total expenses of $50 706 on the debit side;
- the account balance of $44 994 credit which is the net income figure.

If a loss had been suffered, the debit side of the account would have been greater than the credit side, and the account would have a debit balance.

Closing Entry No. 3

The third closing entry transfers the balance in the Income Summary account to the owner's Capital account. The amount is easily picked up from the work sheet. If the account has a credit balance, it will take a debit entry to close it. If the account has a debit balance, it will take a credit entry to close it. The third closing entry for C. Hua appears below in Figure 11.9.

	31	Income Summary		44 994	
		C. Hua, Capital			44 994

Figure 11.9 The third closing entry for C. Hua.

Closing Entry No. 4

The fourth closing entry transfers the balance of the Drawings account to the Capital account. Again, the figure for this entry is easily picked up from the work sheet. Since the Drawings account always has a debit balance, a credit entry is needed to close it. The fourth closing entry for C. Hua appears below in Figure 11.10.

	31	C. Hua, Capital		37 000	
		C. Hua, Drawings			37 000

Figure 11.10 The fourth closing entry for C. Hua.

The ledger for C. Hua, with all four closing entries posted, appears in Figure 11.11 below. The objectives of the closing entries have been achieved. The Capital account shows the true balance and the nominal accounts are cleared and ready for the next fiscal period.

Bank		Accounts Payable		C. Hua, Capital		C. Hua, Drawings	
750			3 730	37 000	23 071	37 000	37 000
			200		44 994		∅
			(3930)		(31065)		

Accounts Receivable			Fees Earned		Bank Charges	
12 900			95 700	95 700	110	110
				∅		∅

Supplies			Automobile Expense		Miscellaneous Expense	
1 800	1 250		5 116		375	
(550)			150	5 266	50	425
				∅		∅

Prepaid Insurance			Rent Expense		Salaries	
3 650	2 175		18 000	18 000	17 500	17 500
(1475)				∅		∅

Office Equipment		Telephone		Supplies Used	
15 000		1 920	1 920	1 250	1 250
			∅		∅

Accumulated Depreciation—Office Equipment		Insurance Used		Depreciation—Office Equipment	
	6 020	2 175	2 175	860	860
	860		∅		∅
	(6880)				

Automobile		Depreciation—Automobile		Income Summary	
24 000		3 200	3 200	50 706	95 700
			∅	44 994	
					∅

Accumulated Depreciation—Automobile	
	9 600
	3 200
	(12 800)

ASSETS ($34 995) − LIABILITIES ($3 930) = EQUITY ($31 065)

Figure 11.11 The ledger of C. Hua after all four closing entries have been posted.

Closing Entries—Summary

The four closing entries do the following:
1. close out the revenue account(s) to the Income Summary account;
2. close out the expense accounts to the Income Summary account;
3. close out the Income Summary account to the Capital account;
4. close out the Drawings account to the Capital account.

Post-Closing Trial Balance

The accuracy of the ledger must be checked after you have finished journalizing and posting the adjusting and closing entries. This is done by taking off the post-closing trial balance.

The post-closing trial balance for C. Hua's ledger is shown below in Figure 11.12.

C. HUA
POST-CLOSING TRIAL BALANCE
DECEMBER 31, 19--

	DR	CR
Bank	$ 750	
Accounts Receivable	12 900	
Supplies	550	
Prepaid Insurance	1 475	
Office Equipment	15 000	
Accumulated Depreciation—Office Equipment		$ 6 880
Automobile	24 000	
Accumulated Depreciation—Automobile		12 800
Accounts Payable		3 930
C. Hua, Capital		31 065
	$54 675	$54 675

Figure 11.12 The post-closing trial balance for the ledger of C. Hua, a lawyer.

Uses of the Work Sheet

You have already used a work sheet and are aware of its usefulness in preparing the financial statements. However, there are other uses for a work sheet.

A work sheet is beneficial in the following ways:
1. A work sheet provides a method of organizing the figures for the financial statements. It contains all of the up-to-date figures for the statements in one convenient place.
2. A work sheet lets the accountant see the effect of adjusting entries before they are recorded in the accounts. Accountants sometimes have a choice in how to handle an adjustment.
3. A work sheet proves the arithmetic accuracy of the figures before they are used in the financial statements.
4. A work sheet is the source for obtaining all of the information for recording the adjusting and the closing entries.

Section Review Questions

1. Explain exactly which adjusting entries are to be processed at the year-end.
2. What is accomplished by processing the adjusting entries at the year-end?
3. What is the normal source of the information for the closing entries?
4. Explain exactly how to obtain the information for the first closing entry.
5. Explain exactly how to obtain the information for the second closing entry.
6. In what new account are the revenues and expenses summarized?
7. What does the balance in the Income Summary account represent (before it is closed out)?
8. What is the purpose of a post-closing trial balance?
9. Why is a post-closing trial balance briefer than a regular trial balance?
10. Give the four uses of a work sheet.

Section Exercises

1. Shown below is the completed work sheet for Dr. E. Santala of Porcupine, Ontario. In your workbook, journalize the adjusting and closing entries for Dr. Santala.

Dr. E. Santala, Dentist — Work Sheet — Yr. Ended December 31, 19—

Accounts	Trial Balance DR	Trial Balance CR	Adjustments DR	Adjustments CR	Income Statement DR	Income Statement CR	Balance Sheet DR	Balance Sheet CR
Bank	1375 10						1375 10	
Accounts Receivable	3749 0 —						3749 0 —	
Supplies	10350 —			7250 —			3100 —	
Prepaid Insurance	5906 —			4050 —			1856 —	
Equipment	15731 0 —						15731 0 —	
Accum. Deprec. Equipment		9287 583		1288 683				10576 266
Investment - Govt. Bonds	100000 —						100000 —	
Accounts Payable		4365 —						4365 —
E. Santala, Capital		204315 77						204315 77
E. Santala, Drawings	8000 0 —						8000 0 —	
Fees Earned		18037 4 —				18037 4 —		
Interest Earned		7500 —		2500 —		10000 —		
Bank Charges	170 —				170 —			
Light & Heat	2957 —				2957 —			
Miscellaneous Expense	14365 0				14365 0			
Rent	30000 —				30000 —			
Telephone	2759 —				2759 —			
Wages & Salaries	47302 —				47302 —			
	48943 060	48943 060						
Supplies Used			7250 —		7250 —			
Insurance Expense			4050 —		4050 —			
Depreciation Equipment			1288 683		1288 683			
Bond Interest Receivable			2500 —				2500 —	
			26686 83	26686 83	10881 133	19037 4 —	39600 610	31444 343
Net Income					8156 267			8156 267
					19037 400	19037 400	39600 610	39600 610

2. Shown below is the completed work sheet for R. Tompko who operates a barber shop in Revelstoke, British Columbia.

In your workbook:
1. Journalize the adjusting and closing entries in the general journal provided.
2. Post the adjusting and closing entries in the general ledger provided.
3. Take off a post-closing trial balance.

Golden Tresses Hair Stylists — Work Sheet — Year Ended Dec. 31, 19—

Accounts	Trial Balance DR	Trial Balance CR	Adjustments DR	Adjustments CR	Income Statement DR	Income Statement CR	Balance Sheet DR	Balance Sheet CR
Bank	790 —						790 —	
Supplies & Materials	2 755 —		800 —	1 055 —			2 500 —	
Prepaid Insurance	2 450 —			1 625 —			825 —	
Equipment	24 370 —						24 370 —	
Accum. Deprec. Equipment		7 000 —		1 000 —				8 000 —
Accounts Payable		1 075 —		800 —				1 875 —
R. Tompko, Capital		9 922 —						9 922 —
R. Tompko, Drawings	42 000 —						42 000 —	
Revenue		98 370 —				98 370 —		
Advertising	1 200 —				1 200 —			
Bank Charges	96 —				96 —			
Light & Heat Expense	2 104 —				2 104 —			
Materials Used	6 950 —		1 055 —		8 005 —			
Miscellaneous Expense	1 902 —				1 902 —			
Rent	6 000 —				6 000 —			
Wages	25 750 —				25 750 —			
	116 367 —	116 367 —						
Insurance Expense			1 625 —		1 625 —			
Depreciation Equipment			1 000 —		1 000 —			
			4 480 —	4 480 —	47 682 —	98 370 —	70 485 —	19 797 —
Net Income					50 688 —			50 688 —
					98 370 —	98 370 —	70 485 —	70 485 —

3. **Workbook Exercise:** Journalizing and posting adjusting and closing entries from a completed work sheet and taking off a post-closing trial balance.

4. Indicate whether each of the following statements is true or false by placing a "T" or an "F" in the space indicated in your workbook. Explain the reason for each "F" response in the space provided.

   1. Journalizing and posting the adjusting and closing entries is a routine task that can be done by any knowledgeable accounting clerk.
   2. All of the data required to journalize the adjusting and closing entries can be found on the work sheet.

3. It can be assumed that all adjustments have been thought of once the work sheet is completed.
4. The adjusting entries must be journalized and posted to bring the ledger into agreement with the figures for the financial statements.
5. An explanation is needed for each individual adjusting entry being journalized.
6. The adjusting and closing entries in the journal are dated as of the end of the fiscal period.
7. The closing entries can only be processed using the four-step method.
8. The figures for the first closing entry (as described in the textbook) are taken from the Income Statement section, Debit column of the worksheet.
9. Since revenue accounts have debit balances, credit entries are needed to close them out.
10. The second closing entry (as described in the textbook) transfers the balances in the expense accounts to the Income Summary account.
11. When the adjusting entries and the first two closing entries are journalized and posted, all of the accounts in the equity section of the ledger except three will have nil balances.
12. A loss has been suffered if the Income Summary account has a credit balance before it is closed out.
13. The first two entries in the Income Summary account are the same as the subtotals of the Income Statement section of the work sheet.
14. The Income Summary account is not closed out if a loss occurs.
15. A work sheet is not necessary in a computerized system because the mathematical accuracy of the figures is assured.

CHAPTER HIGHLIGHTS

Now that you have completed Chapter 11, you should:

1. understand the difference between a real account and a nominal account;
2. understand the purpose of nominal accounts;
3. understand why nominal accounts must be cleared;
4. know the four stages of the end-of-period accounting process;
5. know the complete accounting cycle;
6. know the four benefits of the work sheet;
7. be able to journalize and post the adjusting entries and the closing entries;
8. understand the purpose of the Income Summary account;
9. know the purpose of the post-closing trial balance.

ACCOUNTING TERMS

closing an account
income summary account
nominal account

post-closing trial balance
real account

CHAPTER EXERCISES

Using Your Knowledge

1. Pest Exterminators of Halifax, Nova Scotia suffered a fire in which many important accounting records were destroyed. You have been hired to assist them in reconstructing their records. Shown below are three items that were not destroyed because the firm's bookkeeper had been preparing them at home. From the data below, prepare the work sheet for Pest Exterminators.

Item 1

PEST EXTERMINATORS
POST-CLOSING TRIAL BALANCE
DECEMBER 31, 19--

	DR	CR
Bank	$ 1 200	
Accounts Receivable	15 350	
Supplies	1 850	
Prepaid Insurance	900	
Land	40 000	
Buildings	50 000	
Accumulated Depreciation—Buildings		$ 17 600
Equipment	11 750	
Accumulated Depreciation—Equipment		5 400
Trucks	34 570	
Accumulated Depreciation—Trucks		12 286
Accounts Payable		6 743
Bank Loan		40 000
Joan Budd Capital		73 591
	$155 620	$155 620

Item 2

	DR	CR
<div align="center">**PEST EXTERMINATORS** **ADJUSTING ENTRIES** **DECEMBER 31, 19--**</div>		
Supplies	176	
Miscellaneous Expense	102	
Truck Expense	250	
Accounts Payable		528
Supplies Used	2 276	
Supplies		2 276
Insurance Used	1 900	
Prepaid Insurance		1 900
Depreciation Buildings	1 600	
Accumulated Depreciation—Buildings		1 600
Depreciation Equipment	600	
Accumulated Depreciation—Equipment		600
Depreciation Trucks	3 072	
Accumulated Depreciation—Trucks		3 072

Item 3

	DR	CR
<div align="center">**PEST EXTERMINATORS** **CLOSING ENTRIES** **DECEMBER 31, 19--**</div>		
Revenue	126 375	
Income Summary		126 375
Income Summary	83 405	
Bank Interest and Charges		5 162
Light and Heat		2 700
Miscellaneous Expense		1 048
Telephone		1 050
Truck Expense		13 291
Wages		50 706
Supplies Used		2 276
Insurance Used		1 900
Depreciation—Building		1 600
Depreciation—Equipment		600
Depreciation—Trucks		3 072
Income Summary	42 970	
Joan Budd, Capital		42 970
Joan Budd Capital	40 000	
Joan Budd, Drawings		40 000

2. **Given the following limited information, prepare the closing entries for O. Como.**

O. COMO BALANCE SHEET NOVEMBER 30, 19--			
Assets			
Bank			$100
Accounts Receivable			300
Supplies			70
			$470
Liabilities			
Accounts Payable			$150
Owner's Equity			
Balance November 1		$170	
Net Income	$650		
Drawings	500		
Increase in Equity		150	
Balance November 30			320
			$470

O. COMO INCOME STATEMENT MONTH ENDED NOVEMBER 30, 19--		
Revenue		$1 800
Expenses		
General Expense	$ 50	
Utilities	100	
Wages	1 000	
		$1 150
Net Income		$650

3. At the end of the fiscal year, the accountant for Canadian Auto Supply Company closed the accounts and prepared the balance sheet and the income statement which showed a net income of $42 372.65. He then submitted the two statements to each of the officers of the company.

   When the treasurer received the statements, she compared them with the statements of the preceding year and was surprised to find that the net income had decreased by approximately $4 000. She suspected that something was wrong.

   Upon making an independent check of the books, she found that during the first month of the year, $1 800 had been paid out for insurance, to cover a period of three years. This entire premium had been charged to Insurance Expense for the year. She also found that $2 500 was charged to Office Supplies for the year, but that $2 200 of this was still on hand at the end of the year.
   1. **What errors would the treasurer point out to the accountant?**
   2. **What is the correct net income for the year, assuming that no other errors have been found?**
   3. **Give the required correcting entries.**

4. John, a student in accounting, comes to you, his teacher, with the following difficulty. After a great deal of time and effort, John has failed to balance the post-closing trial balance, and has become quite frustrated. "Everything was going fine," he states.

"My balance sheet balanced. My income statement agreed. I just can't figure it out."

John's balance sheet, income statement, and post-closing trial balance are given below.

1. **How can you tell quickly which figure(s) on the post-closing trial balance are probably the incorrect ones?**
2. **Which figure(s) are wrong in this trial balance?**
3. **Explain what error or errors John has made.**

BALANCE SHEET

Assets
Bank	$ 1 301	
Accounts Receivable	7 406	
Supplies	385	
Land	21 900	
Buildings	75 382	
Equipment	19 462	
		$125 836

Liabilities
Bank Loan	$12 000	
Accounts Payable	5 726	
Mortgage Payable	52 672	$ 70 398

Owner's Equity
Beginning balance		$71 314	
Net Loss	$ 876		
Drawings	15 000		
Decrease in equity		15 876	
Ending balance			55 438
			$125 836

INCOME STATEMENT

Revenue		$19 462
Expenses		
Advertising	$ 3 902	
Delivery	3 764	
Wages	12 000	
Utilities	672	20 338
Net Loss		$ 876

POST-CLOSING TRIAL BALANCE

Bank	$ 1 301	
Accounts Receivable	7 406	
Supplies	385	
Land	21 900	
Buildings	75 382	
Equipment	19 462	
Bank Loan		$ 12 000
Accounts Payable		5 726
Mortgage Payable		52 672
Owner's Equity		57 190
	$125 836	$127 588

Chapter Exercises

5. **Workbook Exercise: Challenge**—completing work sheets and statements from data for two successive months.

6. **Workbook Exercise: Challenge**—completing transactions by the year from data for two successive years.

Comprehensive Exercise

7. The general ledger trial balance of the Oakville Journal, after a fiscal period of one year, is given below. Additional information is also provided.

OAKVILLE JOURNAL
TRIAL BALANCE
DECEMBER 31, 19–8

	DR	CR
Bank	$ 2 750.00	
Accounts Receivable	15 317.20	
Supplies and Materials	23 795.16	
Prepaid Insurance	4 200.00	
Land	75 000.00	
Buildings	150 000.00	
Accumulated Depreciation—Buildings		$ 45 000.00
Equipment	180 500.00	
Accumulated Depreciation—Equipment		84 800.00
Automotive Equipment	95 325.00	
Accumulated Depreciation—Automotive Equipment		20 000.00
Accounts Payable		9 216.42
Bank Loan		100 000.00
Mortgage Payable—10%; Due in 19–12		110 000.00
R. Lucht, Capital		122 638.91
R. Lucht, Drawings	50 000.00	
Revenue—Advertising		218 946.00
Revenue—Circulation		91 315.00
Bank Interest and Charges	12 150.00	
Building Maintenance	3 220.00	
Car Expense	4 960.50	
Light and Heat	11 350.00	
Miscellaneous Expense	5 940.13	
Mortgage Interest	5 500.00	
Postage	1 240.00	
Office Salaries	34 319.15	
Sales Promotions	2 750.00	
Truck Expense	26 334.19	
Telephone	2 946.00	
Wages	94 319.00	
	$801 916.33	$801 916.33

Part A

From the above trial balance, with the additional information below, do the following in your workbook:
1. Complete the work sheet.
2. Prepare the income statement and the balance sheet for 19–8.
3. Journalize the adjusting and closing entries.
4. Post the adjusting and closing entries in the T-accounts provided.
5. Take off a post-closing trial balance.

Additional Information:
1. The value of materials and supplies at the year-end amounted to $8 013.56.
2. The value of unexpired insurance at the year-end amounted to $1 325.00.
3. The mortgage interest is due each June 30 and December 31. The payment for June 30 was made but the payment for December 31 was not made until sometime in the following January.
4. Depreciation is on a straight-line basis as follows:
    Building: Purchased January 1, 19–1
        Estimated terminal value—$30 000
        Estimated useful life—40 years
    Equipment: Purchased January 1, 19–1
        Estimated terminal value—$21 500
        Estimated useful life—15 years
    Trucks and Automobiles: Purchased January 1, 19–6
        Estimated terminal value—$15 325
        Estimated useful life—8 years
5. Late bills arriving in January, 19–9 which pertain to the 19–8 fiscal period are as follows:

Supplies and Materials	$509.60
Car Expense	200.00
Truck Expense	746.20
Miscellaneous Expense	35.00
Total	$1 490.80

Part B

The above data shows that the Oakville Journal uses the straight-line method of depreciating its fixed assets. However, as has been previously mentioned in the text, the government of Canada requires the declining-balance method of depreciation on statements submitted for income tax purposes. Therefore, the income statement must be changed before being sent to Revenue Canada. Complete the schedule in your workbook showing 1) the depreciation figures calculated using the declining-balance method, and 2) the net income figure reported to Revenue Canada. Observe that this is the eighth year for the building and the equipment and the third year for the automotive equipment. The rates of depreciation are 5 per cent, 20 per cent, and 30 per cent respectively.

For Further Thought

8. Briefly answer the following questions.

1. Explain why the time period concept pertains more to the income statement than to the balance sheet.
2. The Bank account is on-going or continuous in nature. Explain.
3. Is the owner's Capital account a nominal account? Explain.
4. Assume that the nominal accounts are not closed out at the end of a fiscal period. Explain how this affects account data for the next fiscal period.
5. Assume that the accounts are updated and closed out at the end of an accounting period. For how long will the account balances remain accurate?
6. Usually, the owner's Capital account is up-to-date only on the last day of the fiscal period. Why does this not create a problem for the users of the financial data?
7. What would be the best first step toward balancing a post-closing trial balance that did not balance?
8. You are given a completed work sheet prepared by another employee. You are asked to process the adjusting and closing entries. Explain why this will be no problem for you.
9. Suppose that, when you are performing the task in question 8 above, you detect that an adjusting entry was overlooked or forgotten in error. What, if anything, would be done about this?
10. Assume that the first two closing entries have been processed. What does it mean if the Income Summary account has a credit balance? Is the amount of the credit balance significant?

CASE STUDIES

Case 1 A Mix-Up in Year-End Accounting

Brenda James is a self-employed public accountant in Wallenstein, Ontario. She performs a variety of accounting services for a number of clients within a 300 kilometre radius of her office. At the present time she happens to be working in a small town about 120 kilometres from home.

While there, Brenda receives a telephone call from her office regarding a problem with the work of another client in the same town. Before returning home, Brenda pays a visit to this other client, Academy of Music, to provide assistance.

Academy of Music does its own accounting up to the trial balance stage. Brenda does the year-end accounting. She has recently provided Academy of Music with a set of financial statements and a list of adjusting and closing entries for the client to journalize and post. The client takes off the post-closing trial balance.

The accounting clerk for Academy of Music sensed that something was wrong with the list of adjusting and closing entries. He decided not to process them until he talked to Brenda. Brenda has to work with data available in the client's office because all of her working papers are at her office. To prepare to study the situation, she gathers together the following:

A.

ACADEMY OF MUSIC
BALANCE SHEET
DECEMBER 31, 19–2

Assets

Current Assets
Bank		$ 3 750	
Accounts Receivable		18 184	
Supplies		300	
Prepaid Insurance		630	$22 864

Plant and Equipment
Equipment	$24 375		
Less Accumulated Depreciation—			
Equipment	7 000	$17 375	
Automobile	$19 780		
Less Accumulated Depreciation—			
Automobile	9 768	10 012	27 387
Total Assets			$50 251

Liabilities and Owner's Equity

Current Liability
Accounts Payable			$ 5 085

Owner's Equity
Balance January 1		$39 586	
Net Income	$32 580		
Drawings	27 000		
Increase in Capital		5 580	
Balance December 31			45 166
Total Liabilities and Equity			$50 251

B.

ACADEMY OF MUSIC
INCOME STATEMENT
YEAR ENDED DECEMBER 31, 19–2

Revenue
Fees Earned		$95 300

Operating Expenses
Bank Charges	$ 102	
Car Expense	16 222	
Light and Heat	3 825	
Miscellaneous Expense	370	
Rent	6 000	
Telephone	500	
Wages	28 375	
Supplies Used	650	
Insurance Used	1 420	
Depreciation of Equipment	2 000	
Depreciation of Automobile	3 256	62 720
Net Income		$32 580

C.

ACADEMY OF MUSIC
ADJUSTING AND CLOSING ENTRIES
DECEMBER 31, 19–2
(provided by Brenda James)

	DR	CR
Adjusting Entries		
Supplies Used	810	
Supplies		810
Insurance Used	1 080	
Prepaid Insurance		1 080
Depreciation of Equipment	2 000	
Accumulated Depreciation—Equipment		2 000
Depreciation of Automobile	3 256	
Accumulated Depreciation—Automobile		3 256
Car Expense	210	
Miscellaneous Expense	160	
Accounts Payable		370
Closing Entries		
Fees Earned	81 316	
Income Summary		81 316
Income Summary	55 928	
Bank Charges		1 120
Car Expense		13 280
Light and Heat		3 307
Miscellaneous Expense		215
Rent		5 400
Telephone		400
Wages		25 060
Supplies Used		810
Insurance Used		1 080
Depreciation of Equipment		2 000
Depreciation of Automobile		3 256
Income Summary	25 388	
F. Oke, Capital		25 388
F. Oke Capital	20 000	
F. Oke, Drawings		20 000

D.

ACADEMY OF MUSIC
UNADJUSTED GENERAL LEDGER
December 31, 19–2

Bank	Accounts Receivable	Supplies	Prepaid Insurance
3 750	18 184	950	2 050

Equipment	Accum. Dep.—Equipment	Automobile	Accum. Dep.—Automobile
24 375	5 000	19 780	6 512

Accounts Payable	F. Oke, Capital	F. Oke, Drawings	Fees Earned
4 370	39 586	27 000	95 300

Bank Charges	Car Expenses	Light and Heat	Miscellaneous Expense
102	15 707	3 675	370

Rent	Telephone	Wages	Supplies Used
6 000	450	28 375	

Insurance Used	Depreciation—Equipment	Depreciation—Automobile	Income Summary

Questions

1. How can Brenda tell if something is wrong?
2. Is the list of adjusting and closing entries the correct one? Explain.
3. Does the list supplied have anything to do with Academy of Music? Explain.
4. Give the most likely explanation for the error.
5. Work out the adjusting entries from the information that you have available. Start to prepare a new list of adjusting and closing entries.
6. Work out the closing entries and complete the list of adjusting and closing entries.

Case 2 Once a Liability, Always a Liability?

Birch Contracting Company in Nanaimo, B.C., was obliged by law to provide vacation pay to every employee equal in amount to two per cent of the gross pay of the employee. This liability for vacation pay became due and payable on June 1 of each year.

Most of the company's work was seasonal in nature and required a lot of manual labour. Therefore, Birch Contracting employed many migrant workers who stayed for only one season. These workers were often new Canadians who did not know Canadian laws and regulations.

Birch Contracting provided for the necessary vacation pay and the accounting entries were properly recorded in the books. However, the company made no effort to contact former employees when the payment came due. Locating former employees was difficult, time-consuming, and often impossible. Therefore, the company chose to wait until the employees made the contact. Consequently, all former employees who did not contact the company were never paid their vacation pay.

Over a period of years, the liability for vacation pay as shown by the ledger grew to a sizable amount. The company accountant felt that something should be done about the liability, but the owner directed her to leave things as they were.

Questions

1. Is the company policy a reasonable one?
2. Should an unpaid liability be left on the books indefinitely?
3. What two advantages are gained by leaving the unpaid liability on the books indefinitely?
4. How would correct accounting practice deal with the above situation?

Case 3 *Keeping Branch Managers on the Alert*

The 11-UP Company produces a soft drink for sale to the general public. The owner and general manager, W. Bully, operates the head office plant in Toronto, Ont. In addition to the main plant, Bully has set up branch plants in three smaller centres to serve a large region in southern Ontario.

The success of 11-UP is based on its particular flavour. Bully developed the recipe for 11-UP some years ago and he is still the only one who knows the formula. The recipe is locked up in a vault in the office of a trust company.

Bully's branch system is very simple. Bully selects the site, builds the plant, and equips it according to a standard plan. He then hires local people to run the branch operation. At the branches, the product is made by combining a special syrup concentrate with sugar and water. The branches purchase the syrup concentrate from head office for a uniform price. The selling price of the soft drink is also uniform throughout the entire area.

Once a year Bully calls the branch managers to head office for a meeting at which the branch results for the year are discussed and analyzed. Bully calls this meeting his "showdown." The branch managers do not particularly enjoy the proceedings.

Before the annual meeting, the branch offices are required to send their financial reports to head office. A grand summary of the results of all of the branches is then prepared for the meeting. The grand summary for the next annual meeting is shown in Table 11-1.

Table 11-1 Financial Summary of Branch Operations of the 11-UP Company

	LONDON BRANCH		HAMILTON BRANCH		WINDSOR BRANCH	
General Data						
Manager	A. Slaughter		M. Masconi		R. Bogart	
Population of area served	410 000		700 000		330 000	
Number of employees	9		12		8	
Number of trucks	5		8		4	
Profit and Loss Data	in $000s	% of Sales	in $000s	% of Sales	in $000s	% of Sales
Sales	$760	100.0	$1 108	100.0	$620	100.0
Sales per capita	$1.85		$1.58		$1.88	
Controllable Expenses						
Advertising	$ 21	2.8	$ 37	3.4	$ 15	2.4
Sales Promotion	5	.7	6	.5	4	.6
Concentrate	185	24.4	269	24.3	176	28.4
Sugar	20	2.6	30	2.7	19	3.1
Maintenance						
—Equipment	2	.3	5	.4	2	.3
—Trucks	2	.3	9	.8	1	.2
—Plant	1	.1	1	.1	—	.0
Gasoline and Oil	265	34.8	320	28.9	160	25.8
Wages	91	12.0	127	11.5	95	15.3
Electricity	1	.1	1	.1	1	.2
Heating	1	.1	1	.1	1	.2
Bottle Breakage	1	.1	4	.3	—	.0
Non-Controllable Expenses						
Depreciation	80	10.5	87	7.8	85	13.7
Taxes	2	.3	2	.2	3	.5
Manager's Salary	35	4.6	40	3.6	35	5.6
Total Expenses	$712	93.7	$939	84.7	$597	96.3
Net Profit	$ 48	6.3	$169	15.3	$ 23	3.7

Mr. Bully is a thorough manager. He takes the trouble to analyze the financial summary thoroughly, looking for items that are deficient or excessive which may indicate a weakness in branch operations. Mr. Bully's objective is to eliminate weaknesses, such as theft, carelessness, and wastage, in order to maximize profits.

Questions
1. Analyze the statements as if you were Mr. Bully. Prepare a list of four items that seem to be unusual enough to warrant an explanation from the particular manager affected.
2. Provide reasons that could explain the unusual items on your list.

CAREER
Russell Trivett / Controller

Russell Trivett's interest in business affairs goes back to when he was just twelve years old. At that time Russell earned his pocket money by helping his aunt and uncle with their convenience store in his home town, Yellowknife, Northwest Territories. After he graduated from high school, Russell attended the University of Calgary. Seven years later, he had obtained both a Bachelor of Commerce degree and a Master of Business Administration degree.

After graduation, Russell felt there would be plenty of career opportunities for him in Calgary. He articled with Thorne Riddell, Chartered Accountants, in their Calgary office. He studied advanced areas of accounting, taxation, and auditing to earn his CA designation.

He then joined International Carriers Ltd., a public transportation company employing five hundred people, as its management accountant. His major duties were to design and, in some cases, revise the accounting system, set up data processing systems, supervise the maintenance of the accounting records, and prepare the financial statements for senior management.

Russell eventually began to feel a need for new challenges in his career. Because the top accounting positions at International Carriers Ltd. would remain filled for some time, he decided to look elsewhere for advancement.

He left International Carriers Ltd. to become the controller for the Duratex Corporation, a manufacturer of doors and windows. As controller, Russell is the chief accounting officer for the company. He oversees the work of more than sixty employees in the cost department, the payroll department, the accounting department, and the computer department.

Russell supervises the preparation of work sheets and the adjusting and closing entries at year-end. He prepares the classified financial statements and tax returns for the company. He also interprets and analyzes financial statements and other related data for his immediate superior, the vice-president of finance.

Russell plays a key role in the long-term planning and development of the four departments he oversees. He is in charge of the ongoing development of a computer system designed to meet the company's expanding needs as efficiently as possible.

As his career has progressed, Russell has found that those who aspire to top positions in accounting must continue to update their accounting knowledge and skills. Russell has taken several on-the-job courses in management training. He believes accountants should receive intensive training in communication and human relations as well as a basic knowledge of the other functions of business.

For now, he is happy in his position with Duratex. He feels that he may, sometime in the future, return to Yellowknife to set up his own practice.

Discussion

1. Which of Russell's duties as a controller did you study in this chapter?
2. What is the difference between a controller and a treasurer of a company?
3. Compare the career profiles of Paulette Dubois (Chapter 10) and Russell Trivett. Include the number of jobs each has held, their educational backgrounds, and the future aspirations of both.
4. How will the computer drastically alter the nature of Russell's job?
5. What are some of the opportunities in business for individuals with a CA designation?
6. What are the steps in the accounting cycle Russell performs as the controller of Duratex Corporation?
7. Why is it necessary for accountants to receive training in communication and human relations?

12 Accounting for a Merchandising Business

12.1 The Merchandising Business
12.2 Accounting Procedures for a Merchandising Business
12.3 Work Sheet for a Merchandising Business
12.4 Merchandise Returns and Allowances
12.5 Computerized Accounting: Accounting for a Merchandising Business

12.1 The Merchandising Business

So far we have studied only service businesses. These are the businesses that sell services rather than goods. Now, however, you are ready to study accounting for the merchandising or trading business. A **merchandising business** is a business that sells goods rather than a service. A **wholesaler** is a merchandising business that buys goods from manufacturers and sells to retailers. A **retailer** is a merchandising business that buys goods from wholesalers and manufacturers and sells to the general public.

Merchandise Inventory

Businesses which buy goods for the purpose of selling them at a profit are dealing in merchandise. The quantity of merchandise on hand is known as **merchandise inventory** or **stock-in-trade**.

The type of merchandise included in inventory varies from business to business. For instance, the merchandise inventory of a lumber company consists of various types and sizes of wood products. The merchandise inventory of a food retailer consists of a variety of food commodities. The merchandise inventory of an automobile dealer consists of new and used cars as well as replacement parts.

Merchandise Inventory on the Balance Sheet

A merchandising business buys goods to sell to its customers. Therefore, it keeps a stock of goods on hand. This inventory of goods usually has a large dollar value and must be included as an asset on the balance sheet. Merchandise inventory is listed as a current asset because it will normally be sold and converted into cash within one year. It is listed at its cost price, and not its selling price, in accordance with generally accepted accounting principles. An illustration of merchandise inventory on a balance sheet is shown in Figure 12.1 below.

HARDY'S HARDWARE
BALANCE SHEET
JUNE 30, 19--

Assets

Current Assets		
Bank	$ 1 205	
Accounts Receivable	18 305	
Merchandise Inventory (at cost)	42 582	$62 092
Prepaid Expenses		
Supplies	$ 3 526	
Insurance	3 564	7 090
Plant and Equipment		
Store Equipment	$25 658	
Delivery Equipment	18 350	44 008
		$113 190

Figure 12.1 A partial balance showing merchandise inventory as a current asset.

Cost of Goods Sold on the Income Statement

The inventory figure on the balance sheet is only one aspect of accounting for merchandise inventory. The balance sheet figure represents the cost of the inventory that *was not sold*, that is, the inventory still on hand. The cost of the inventory that *was sold*, known as the **cost of goods sold**, is an important cost to be included on the income statement.

An item that is sold for $100 may have cost around $75. This leaves a profit of $25 before deducting for other expenses. Clearly, the cost of any item sold is a very significant expense. The total cost of all of the items sold is usually the biggest expense of a merchandising business. Figure 12.2 below shows a simplified income statement for a merchandising business. Observe that the cost of goods sold figure is considered to be so significant that the statement is prepared in two stages. In the first stage, the cost of goods sold figure is deducted from the sales (revenue) figure to arrive at the gross profit. The **gross profit** is the difference between the selling price and the cost price of the goods sold. It is also seen as the profit figure before deducting any operating expenses.

MASTER TRADING COMPANY
INCOME STATEMENT
YEAR ENDED JUNE 30, 19--

Revenue		
Sales		$201 967
Cost of Goods Sold		117 381
Gross Profit		$ 84 586
Operating Expenses		
Bank Charges	$ 915	
Depreciation of Equipment	1 432	
Depreciation of Automobile	8 376	
Gasoline and Oil	7 532	
Light and Heat	2 072	
Miscellaneous Expense	358	
Rent	4 800	
Telephone	953	
Wages	20 368	$ 46 806
Net Income		$ 37 780

Figure 12.2 Simplified income statement for a trading company showing the cost of goods sold and the gross profit.

Two Aspects of Merchandise Inventory

The chart below gives a picture of two aspects of merchandise inventory. Assume that a business had $120 000 of goods available for sale during a fiscal period, and that $25 000 of these goods were still on hand (unsold) at the end of the period.

```
                    ┌─────────────────────┐
                    │ Total cost of goods │
                    │  available for sale │
                    │during the fiscal period│
                    │      $120 000       │
                    └─────────────────────┘
                              │
                              is
                            either
```

```
┌──────────┐                              ┌──────────┐
│ Not Sold │                              │   Sold   │
│ $25 000  │                              │ $95 000  │
└──────────┘                              └──────────┘
```

Includes goods that are lost, broken, or stolen.

┌──────────────────────┐   ┌──────────────────────┐
│ Represents the goods │   │ Represents the cost │
│ on hand at the end of│   │ of the goods sold and│
│ the accounting period.│   │ goes on the income   │
│ Appears as a current │   │ statement as an expense.│
│ asset on the balance │   │   │
│   sheet.   │   │ The income statement │
└──────────────────────┘   │ cannot be prepared   │
                                          │ without this figure. │
                                          └──────────────────────┘

Perpetual and Periodic Inventory Methods

There are two common methods of accounting for merchandise inventory. These are the perpetual method and the periodic method.

Perpetual Inventory Method

The **perpetual inventory method** is one in which a detailed record of inventory is kept up-to-date on a daily basis. For many businesses it is now essential to know the inventory details daily and to be able to calculate the cost of goods sold figure on short notice. The perpetual inventory method involves additional time, effort, and cost. The extra accounting is done either by additional staff or by means of a business computer. In the past the perpetual method was not generally used because of the added expense. But the perpetual method is becoming more common with the increasing use and lower cost of business computers.

Periodic Inventory Method

The periodic inventory method is a simpler and cheaper way to account for merchandise inventory. The **periodic inventory method** is one in which inventory is detailed and valued only at the end of the fiscal period, which is usually once a year. During the accounting period no attempt is made to keep up-to-date inventory records nor to calculate the cost of goods sold figure.

Over the years, the periodic method has been the most commonly used method. In this chapter, we will focus on the periodic inventory method.

The Inventory Cycle

Merchandise is sold fairly quickly in a successful business. The business has to renew its stock regularly in order to have ample quantities on hand. Merchandise moves in and out of a business in the following pattern.
1. There is the beginning inventory.
2. Merchandise is sold and moves out more or less continually during the accounting period.
3. Inventory is replaced by the purchase of new stock from time to time.
4. At the end of the accounting period, the inventory is approximately equal to the beginning inventory.

This inventory cycle is shown in Table 12.1 below.

Chapter 12

Month	Transaction	Units Purchased	Units Sold	Units On Hand
	Beginning Inventory			1 700
January	Sales		500	1 200
February	Sales		400	800
March	Sales		700	100
	Purchases	1 500		1 600
April	Sales		800	800
May	Sales		300	500
	Purchases	2 100		2 600
June	Sales		900	1 700
July	Sales		500	1 200
August	Sales		350	850
	Purchases	1 000		1 850
September	Sales		650	1 200
October	Sales		200	1 000
November	Sales		400	600
	Purchases	900		1 500
December	Sales		100	1 400
	Totals	5 500	5 800	

- Total Purchases: 5 500
- Total Sales: 5 800
- Ending Inventory: 1 400

Table 12.1 Schedule of inventory movement for one fiscal year.

The data in Table 12.1 may be arranged and summarized in the following form:

	Units
Beginning inventory	1 700
+ Purchases	5 500
= Total goods available for sale	7 200
− Merchandise sold	5 800
= Ending inventory	1 400

The cost price of these units represents the ending inventory and is a current asset on the balance sheet.

The selling price of these units represents the revenue on the income statement.

The cost price of these units represents a deduction from revenue to arrive at the gross profit figure.

Cost of Goods Sold Formula

The inventory pattern summarized above may be expressed in an equation as shown below. This equation is true whether expressed in terms of units or dollars.

Beginning Inventory + Merchandise Purchased − Merchandise Sold = Ending Inventory

A simple mathematical rearrangement of this equation is given below. This is an important accounting formula. It is the means by which businesses that use the periodic inventory method can calculate the cost of goods sold figure at statement time.

$$\text{Cost of Beginning Inventory} + \text{Cost of Merchandise Purchased} - \text{Cost of Ending Inventory} = \text{Cost of Merchandise Sold}$$

The End-of-Period Inventory

When the periodic inventory method is used, the total cost value of the goods on hand is not known. However, this figure is necessary for the preparation of both financial statements. Using the periodic inventory method makes it necessary to take a physical inventory in order to take off financial statements. A **physical inventory** is the procedure by which the unsold goods of a merchandising business are counted and valued (at cost prices). This valuation gives the ending inventory figure. It is an important current asset on the balance sheet. It is also an element in the calculation of the cost of goods sold on the income statement.

Limitation of the Periodic Inventory Method

When the periodic inventory method is used, financial statements cannot be obtained unless a physical inventory is taken. This is a time-consuming procedure that often makes it necessary to close down business operations for a day or two. Why is the periodic method used so extensively despite this limitation? The answer is simple. The periodic method is much less expensive than the perpetual method. This is important for small businesses, such as drugstores and hardware stores, that have to keep track of inventories made up of a large number of different items.

Section Review Questions

1. Describe a service business.
2. Describe a merchandising business.
3. Define the terms "wholesaler" and "retailer."
4. Describe the merchandise inventory of a drugstore.
5. Give another name for merchandise inventory.
6. What has happened to the goods available for sale that are not on hand?
7. Where is merchandise inventory listed on the balance sheet?
8. Explain the significance of the cost of goods sold figure.
9. Explain the meaning of gross profit.

10. Explain the difference between the perpetual inventory method and the periodic inventory method.
11. What types of businesses will use the perpetual inventory method?
12. What types of businesses will use the periodic inventory method?
13. Explain why a small variety store would choose to use the periodic inventory method.
14. Give the four steps in the inventory cycle.
15. Give the cost of goods sold formula.
16. Why is it necessary to take a physical inventory when using the periodic inventory method?

Section Exercises

1. **Workbook Exercise:** Completing a multiple-choice exercise regarding merchandise inventory.

2. For each of the following businesses, state five specific items that would normally be found in the merchandise inventory.
   1. Auto dealer.
   2. Builder's supply dealer.
   3. Furniture and appliance store.
   4. Sports store.
   5. Grocery store.
   6. Hardware store.
   7. Photography store.
   8. Electronics store.
   9. Department store.

3. **Workbook Exercise:** Completing a chart regarding selling prices, cost prices, and gross profits.

4. The chart shown below appears in the workbook.
   1. Complete the chart by filling in the blank spaces.

	Year 1	Year 2	Year 3
Beginning inventory	100 units	units	units
Merchandise purchased	units	900 units	units
Goods available for sale	800 units	units	units
Merchandise sold	units	1 000 units	800 units
Ending inventory	300 units	units	50 units

   2. If the units cost $5 each throughout Year 3, work out the Cost of Goods Sold section of the Income Statement.

5. **Arranged alphabetically below is a list of data as of December 31, 19--, the end of a fiscal year. From this list, prepare the following:**
   1. a simple balance sheet;
   2. a simple income statement.

Accounts Payable	$ 36 250
Accounts Receivable	15 200
Advertising	2 000
Bank	1 500
Bank Charges	2 630
Bank Loan	25 000
Cost of Goods Sold	165 336
Depreciation of Equipment	8 583
Equipment	77 710
Gas and Oil Expense	8 500
Inventory (Ending)	25 300
K. Akroyd, Capital (Beginning)	47 839
K. Akroyd, Drawings	40 000
Light and Heat	6 000
Miscellaneous Expense	1 150
Prepaid Insurance	2 600
Rent	12 000
Sales	303 120
Supplies	1 500
Telephone	1 550
Wages	40 650

12.2 Accounting Procedures for a Merchandising Business

So far you have learned the following facts about the periodic inventory system for a merchandising business.
- The final inventory figure must be included on the balance sheet as a current asset.
- The cost of goods sold figure must be included on the income statement.
- Neither the inventory figure nor the cost of goods sold figure is known during the accounting period.
- The cost of goods sold figure can be calculated by means of the formula developed in the previous section.

Now you will learn about the accounts that are needed for calculating the cost of goods sold figure at the end of the fiscal period.

The Merchandise Inventory Account

Under the periodic inventory method, the merchandise inventory of a business is kept in two accounts. One of these is the Merchandise Inventory account. It shows the inventory figure as of the beginning of the accounting period.

At the fiscal year-end, the inventory is counted and valued at cost price to arrive at the merchandise inventory grand total. The inventory account is adjusted to make it equal to the updated figure, which becomes the beginning inventory figure for the next fiscal period. This periodic inventory adjustment is the only accounting entry made to the Merchandise Inventory account.

You will now find a Merchandise Inventory account appearing in most of your exercises. Remember that the account balance was updated at the end of the preceding fiscal period. For your purposes, the balance of the Merchandise Inventory account represents the beginning inventory for the current period.

The Purchases Account

The merchandise purchased during the fiscal period is collected in an account called Purchases. "Purchases" is a short version of "Purchases of Merchandise for Resale." If merchandise for resale is purchased for cash, the accounting entry (at the cost price) is:

	DR	CR
Purchases	$$$$	
Bank		$$$$

If merchandise for resale is purchased on account, the accounting entry (at the cost price) is:

	DR	CR
Purchases	$$$$	
Accounts Payable		$$$$

Be sure you understand that it is the purchase of merchandise inventory that is being discussed here. Other items purchased are handled in the usual way. For example, if a tire company buys office supplies, then Office Supplies is debited. However, if a tire company buys tires for sale to its customers, then Purchases is debited.

The Sales Account

The revenue account for a merchandising business is called "Sales." If goods are sold for cash, the accounting entry (at the selling price) is:

	DR	CR
Bank	$$$$	
Sales		$$$$

If goods are sold on account, the accounting entry (at the selling price) is:

	DR	CR
Accounts Receivable	$$$$	
Sales		$$$$

When a business sells goods, the physical inventory is reduced. However, no accounting entries are made to record this decrease in inventory. It is easier to allow the inventory to be inexact during the fiscal period and to correct it at the end. You will be shown how to do this later in the chapter.

The Freight-in Account

The **Freight-in account** is used to accumulate transportation charges on incoming goods. These charges are kept separate from transportation charges on outgoing goods which are recorded in as Delivery Expense. Freight-in is accumulated separately because it is a cost related to the goods purchased and must be included in the calculation of the cost of goods sold.

The charges for freight-in or delivery expense are usually found on invoices of trucking companies, railways, or other shipping companies. If a business has its own trucks these charges may be on bills related to the running of the equipment such as bills for gasoline, oil, and repairs.

Duty refers to special charges imposed by the government on certain goods imported from a foreign country. If any duty is being charged, it is handled in the same way as freight-in.

Section Review Questions

1. Why is the final inventory figure included on the balance sheet?
2. How is the cost of goods sold figure determined for inclusion on the income statement?
3. In what two accounts in the general ledger is merchandise inventory recorded?
4. What does the balance in the Merchandise Inventory account represent during the fiscal period?
5. What prices are used to value the merchandise inventory?
6. What is the account title "Purchases" a short version of?
7. Give the accounting entry for the purchase of merchandise for resale on account.
8. Give the accounting entry for the purchase of a delivery truck for cash.
9. What is the revenue account usually called in the ledger of a merchandising company?
10. If the periodic inventory method is used, what accounting step is ignored when a sale is made? Try to give the accounting entry for this step.
11. What charges are recorded in the Freight-in account?

Section Exercises

1. **Journalize the following transactions in a two-column general journal for Excel TV and Stereo:**

   Transactions

   December
   - 1 Received an invoice, No. 435, from Paramount Manufacturing for a shipment of television sets, $3 045.00.
   - 2 Received an invoice, No. B616, from Murray Transport Company for transportation charges on the above shipment of television sets, $435.
   - 3 Received an invoice, No. 7042, from Swiss Stationers for a shipment of office forms and supplies to be used in the business, $236.
   - 4 Issued Sales Invoice, No. 789, to W. Parker for stereo speakers and electronic parts, $417.
   - 5 Issued Cash Sales Slip, No. 143, for the cash sale of merchandise from the store, $92.
   - 6 Received an invoice, No. 902, from Haniko Electric for a shipment of electronic parts, $2 678.

2. **Workbook Exercise: Additional practice in journalizing transactions.**

3. **In your workbook, complete each of the following statements by inserting in the spaces provided the most appropriate word or phrase from the list given below.**

   1. The final inventory figure appears on the _____ and on the _____ .
   2. Neither the _____ nor the _____ is known during the accounting period.
   3. The cost of goods sold figure is _____ using a _____ .
   4. Merchandise inventory is kept in two accounts. These are: _____ and _____ .
   5. The _____ normally shows the merchandise inventory figure as of the _____ .
   6. At the fiscal year-end, the inventory is counted and valued at _____ .
   7. The Merchandise Inventory account is adjusted _____ .
   8. The _____ is the only accounting entry made to the Merchandise Inventory account.
   9. Merchandise purchased during the fiscal period is debited to the _____ .
   10. The ''Purchases'' account is a short form of _____ .
   11. If merchandise is purchased on account, the account debited is _____ .
   12. If a tire company purchases office supplies, the account debited is _____ .
   13. For a merchandising business, the sales account is the _____ .
   14. When a business using the periodic inventory method sells goods, there is no accounting entry to record the _____ .
   15. The Freight-in account is used to accumulate _____ .

Section 12.3   **373**

List of Words and Phrases

at the end of the fiscal period
balance sheet
beginning of the fiscal period
calculated
cost of goods sold figure
cost prices
decrease in inventory
formula
income statement
inventory adjustment

inventory figure
merchandise inventory
merchandise inventory account
office supplies
purchases
purchases account
purchases of merchandise for resale
revenue account
transportation charges on incoming goods

12.3 Work Sheet for a Merchandising Business

There are three new accounts for you to learn to handle on the work sheet and on the statements. These accounts are shown below in T-accounts.

Merchandise Inventory	Purchases	Freight-in
72 074	210 853	5 731

The value (at cost) of the merchandise on hand at the beginning of the fiscal period.

The total cost of all merchandise inventory purchased during the fiscal period.

The total transportation costs of bringing the goods into the business.

As you already know, the figures for the financial statements are obtained from a completed work sheet. Therefore, you must learn to handle these new accounts on the work sheet.

You will see these new accounts on the partial work sheets in Figure 12.3 and Figure 12.4. Study these two illustrations carefully to see how the accounts are dealt with, and why they are handled as they are.

How It Is Done

WORK SHEET	Trident Trading Co.				Year Ended December 31, 19-			
ACCOUNTS	TRIAL BALANCE		ADJUSTMENTS		INCOME STATEMENT		BALANCE SHEET	
	DR	CR	DR	CR	DR	CR	DR	CR
Merchandise Inventory	72074 —				72074 —	83562 —	83562 —	
Freight-in	5731 —				5731 —			
Purchases	210853 —				210853 —			

Beginning inventory is extended to the Income Statement debit column.

Both Purchases and Freight-in are extended to the Income Statement debit column.

Ending inventory, obtained by a physical inventory, is entered in two columns: the Income Statement credit column and the Balance Sheet debit column.

Figure 12.3 Partial work sheet showing how Merchandise Inventory, Purchases, and Freight-in are handled.

Why It Is Done

WORK SHEET	Trident Trading Co.				Year Ended December 31, 19-			
ACCOUNTS	TRIAL BALANCE		ADJUSTMENTS		INCOME STATEMENT		BALANCE SHEET	
	DR	CR	DR	CR	DR	CR	DR	CR
Merchandise Inventory	72074 —				72074 —	83562 —	83562 —	
Freight-in	5731 —				5731 —			
Purchases	210853 —				210853 —			

The elements for the cost of goods sold calculation are found in the Income Statement section.

The ending inventory figure is found in the Balance Sheet section.

Figure 12.4 Partial work sheet showing how the Merchandise Inventory, Purchases, and Freight-in are related to the financial statements.

Income Statement for a Merchandising Business

The three new accounts are highlighted on the full work sheet for Trident Trading Co. shown in Figure 12.5. The income statement developed from this work sheet appears

WORK SHEET	Trident Trading Co.				Year Ended December 31, 19—			
ACCOUNTS	TRIAL BALANCE		ADJUSTMENTS		INCOME STATEMENT		BALANCE SHEET	
	DR	CR	DR	CR	DR	CR	DR	CR
Bank	4072 –						4072 –	
Accounts Receivable	27340 –						27340 –	
Merchandise Inventory	72074 –				72074 –	83562 –	83562 –	
Supplies	2840 –			2560 –			280 –	
Prepaid Insurance	4242 –			2915 –			1327 –	
Equipment	24316 –						24316 –	
Accumulated Depreciation Equip.		11866 –		2490 –				14356 –
Automobiles	37416 –						37416 –	
Accumulated Depreciation Auto.		24582 –		3850 –				28432 –
Accounts Payable		15270 –		565 –				15835 –
Bank Loan		10000 –						10000 –
Sales Tax Payable		2210 –						2210 –
R. Kehoe, Capital		88616 –						88616 –
R. Kehoe, Drawings	40000 –						40000 –	
Sales		377508 –				377508 –		
Advertising	1141 –				1141 –			
Bank Charges	2651 –				2651 –			
Car Expense	4749 –		250 –		4999 –			
Delivery Expense	1377 –				1377 –			
Freight-in	5731 –				5731 –			
Light & Heat	3673 –		315 –		3988 –			
Miscellaneous Expense	1507 –				1507 –			
Purchases	210853 –				210853 –			
Rent	12000 –				12000 –			
Salaries	24000 –				24000 –			
Telephone	1850 –				1850 –			
Wages	48220 –				48220 –			
	530082 –	530082 –						
Supplies Used			2560 –		2560 –			
Insurance Used			2915 –		2915 –			
Depreciation Equipment			2490 –		2490 –			
Depreciation Automobiles			3850 –		3850 –			
			12080 –	12080 –	402206 –	461070 –	218313 –	159449 –
Net Income					58864 –			58864 –
					461070 –	461070 –	218313 –	218313 –

Figure 12.5 The full work sheet for Trident Trading Company.

in Figure 12.6. The Cost of Goods Sold section is a major addition to the income statement. You will have to master this new section in order to prepare an income statement for a merchandising business.

TRIDENT TRADING CO.
INCOME STATEMENT
YEAR ENDED DECEMBER 31, 19--

Revenue		
Sales		$377 508
Cost of Goods Sold		
Merchandise Inventory, January 1	$ 72 074	
Purchases	210 853	
Freight-in	5 731	
Goods Available for Sale	$288 658	
Less: Merchandise Inventory, December 31	83 562	205 096
Gross Profit		$172 412
Operating Expenses		
Advertising	$ 1 141	
Bank Charges	2 651	
Car Expenses	4 999	
Delivery Expense	1 377	
Depreciation—Equipment	2 490	
Depreciation—Automobiles	3 850	
Insurance Used	2 915	
Light and Heat	3 988	
Miscellaneous Expense	1 507	
Rent	12 000	
Salaries	24 000	
Supplies Used	2 560	
Telephone	1 850	
Wages	48 220	113 548
Net Income		$58 864

Figure 12.6 The income statement for Trident Trading Co. showing the cost of goods sold section.

Closing Entries for a Merchandising Business

A very interesting result occurs when the closing entry process, described in Chapter 11, is applied to a merchandising business. The process very neatly cancels out the old inventory figure and sets up the new one. In other words, the closing entry process automatically adjusts the inventory account at the end of the fiscal period.

You can see how this is done by studying the simplified data in Figures 12.7 to 12.9.

WORK SHEET								
ACCOUNTS	TRIAL BALANCE		ADJUSTMENTS		INCOME STATEMENT		BALANCE SHEET	
	DR	CR	DR	CR	DR	CR	DR	CR
Bank	2500 –						2500 –	
Accounts Receivable	12150 –						12150 –	
Merchandise Inventory	15300 –				15300 –	16200 –	16200 –	
B. Lee, Capital		27880 –						27880 –
B. Lee, Drawings	10000 –						10000 –	
Sales		35000 –				35000 –		
Freight-in	2370 –				2370 –			
Purchases	14250 –				14250 –			
Other Expenses	6310 –				6310 –			
	62880 –	62880 –			38230 –	51200 –	40850 –	27880 –
Net Income					12970 –			12970 –
					51200 –	51200 –	40850 –	40850 –

First closing entry includes inventory

Second closing entry includes inventory

Figure 12.7 A simplified work sheet with the figures for the first and second closing entries outlined.

		Closing Entries		
Dec	31	Merchandise Inventory	16200 –	
		Sales	35000 –	
		Income Summary		51200 –
	31	Income Summary	38230 –	
		Merchandise Inventory		15300 –
		Freight-in		2370 –
		Purchases		14250 –
		Other Expenses		6310 –
	31	Income Summary	12970 –	
		B. Lee, Capital		12970 –
	31	B. Lee, Capital	10000 –	
		B. Lee, Drawings		10000 –

Figure 12.8 The four closing entries, derived from the above work sheet.

378 Chapter 12

```
        Bank                  Accounts Receivable        Merchandise Inventory
     2500                       12150                      15300  | 15300
                                                           16200
                                                          (16200)
     B. Lee Capital              B. Lee Drawings              Sales
    10000  | 27880             10000  | 10000             35000  | 35000
            12970
           (30850)
       Freight-in                  Purchases               Other Expenses
     2370  | 2370               14250  | 14250             6310  | 6310

     Income Summary                          TRIAL BALANCE
    38230  | 51200                          DR         CR
    12970                                 2 500      30 850
                                         12 150
                                         16 200
                                         ────────    ────────
                                         30 850      30 850
```

Figure 12.9 The general ledger after completing the closing entries. The account balances before the closing entries are entered in black.

As you can see, the closing entry process has had the following effects:
- it has closed out all of the equity accounts except the Capital;
- it has updated the Capital account. The new balance is $30 850;
- it has adjusted the Merchandise Inventory account. The new balance is $16 200. This balance will remain in the account until the next set of closing entries are recorded.

Section Review Questions

1. Name the three new accounts that appear on the work sheet of a merchandising company.
2. What does the trial balance figure for Merchandise Inventory represent?
3. What does the trial balance figure for Purchases represent?
4. What important function must be carried out before the work sheet can be completed?
5. Explain in detail how to extend the Merchandise Inventory line.
6. Explain how to extend the Purchases line.
7. Explain how to extend the Freight-in line.
8. Where are the figures found for the cost of goods sold section of the income statement?
9. Why is the cost of goods sold section of the income statement so important?
10. Is the closing entry process basically the same as when first introduced?

11. What must one be careful of when recording the first two closing entries?
12. What new result occurs after processing the first two closing entries?
13. Where is the information for the closing entries found?
14. What is the total effect of all of the closing entries?

Section Exercises

1. The partially completed work sheet shown below also appears in the workbook.
    1. Complete the work sheet. The ending inventory figure is $43 700.
    2. Prepare an income statement.
    3. Prepare a balance sheet.
    4. Journalize the closing entries.

Work Sheet — Bok Trading Company — Year Ended Dec. 31, 19—

Accounts	Trial Balance DR	Trial Balance CR	Adjustments DR	Adjustments CR	Income Statement DR	Income Statement CR	Balance Sheet DR	Balance Sheet CR
Bank	500 —							
Accounts Receivable	18 300 —							
Merchandise Inventory	39 600 —							
Supplies	2 500 —			1 200 —				
Prepaid Insurance	1 800 —			1 150 —				
Equipment	27 850 —							
Accumulated Depreciation Equip.		10 000 —		2 500 —				
Accounts Payable		7 400 —		350 —				
Sales Tax Payable		7 200 —						
R. Bok, Capital		52 890 —						
R. Bok, Drawings	10 000 —							
Sales		94 310 —						
Purchases	41 500 —		300 —					
Freight-in	950 —							
Light & Heat	2 750 —							
Miscellaneous Expense	350 —		50 —					
Rent	4 800 —							
Telephone	1 500 —							
Wages	19 400 —							
	171 800 —	171 800 —						
Supplies Expense			1 200 —					
Insurance Expense			1 150 —					
Depreciation Equipment			2 500 —					

2. Shown below is the trial balance for Small Engine Sales and Service at December 31, 19--, the end of an annual fiscal period.

1. **Complete the work sheet using the following additional information:**
   1. Closing inventory of merchandise—$35 651
   2. Closing inventory of supplies—$350
   3. Closing inventory of parts and materials—$4 560
   4. Unexpired insurance at December 31—$600
   5. Late bills—none
   6. Depreciation of equipment is on a straight-line basis. The terminal value of the equipment is estimated at $1 600 and its useful life is estimated at ten years.
   7. Depreciation of the truck is on a straight-line basis. The terminal value of the truck is estimated to be $3 000 and its useful life is estimated at five years.
2. **Prepare an income statement.**
3. **Prepare a balance sheet.**
4. **Journalize the adjusting and closing entries.**

SMALL ENGINE SALES AND SERVICE
TRIAL BALANCE
DECEMBER 31, 19--

	DR	CR
Bank	$ 520	
Accounts Receivable	12 680	
Merchandise Inventory	36 050	
Supplies	1 975	
Parts and Materials	10 350	
Prepaid Insurance	1 150	
Equipment	18 600	
Accumulated Depreciation—Equipment		$ 6 800
Truck	18 000	
Accumulated Depreciation—Truck		6 000
Accounts Payable		5 360
Bank Loan		9 500
Sales Tax Payable		320
H. Rohr, Capital		35 700
H. Rohr, Drawings	25 000	
Revenue—Sales		80 362
Revenue—Service		66 215
Bank Charges	410	
Freight-in	862	
Light and Heat	2 240	
Miscellaneous Expense	650	
Purchases	52 795	
Rent	3 600	
Telephone	1 250	
Truck Expense	5 825	
Wages	18 300	
	$210 257	$210 257

3. Shown below is the completed work sheet for Barbini Stone Products.
   1. Journalize the adjusting and the closing entries in the general journal.
   2. Post the adjusting and closing entries to the T-accounts provided in the workbook.
   3. Take off a post-closing trial balance.

Work Sheet — Barbini Stone Products — Yr. Ended Dec. 31, 19—

Accounts	Trial Balance DR	Trial Balance CR	Adjustments DR	Adjustments CR	Income Statement DR	Income Statement CR	Balance Sheet DR	Balance Sheet CR
Bank	3250—						3250—	
Accounts Receivable	3465010						3465010	
Merchandise Inventory	43700—				43700—	40500—	40500—	
Supplies	340050			2104—			129650	
Prepaid Insurance	2090—			950—			1140—	
Land	35000—						35000—	
Building	95000—						95000—	
Accumulated Depreciation Bldg.		42000—		3500—				45500—
Equipment	53400—						53400—	
Accumulated Depreciation Equip.		18400—		4600—				23000—
Trucks	76000—						76000—	
Accumulated Depreciation Trucks		24000—		12000—				36000—
Accounts Payable		4237540		1135—				4351040
Sales Tax Payable		135480						135480
T. Barbini, Capital		18167905						18167905
T. Barbini, Drawings	36000—						36000—	
Sales		232250—				232250—		
Advertising	2570—		100—		2670—			
Freight-in	3705—		70—		3775—			
Light and Heat	12316—				12316—			
Miscellaneous Expense	1750—		25—		1775—			
Purchases	8070250		940—		8164250			
Telephone	1250—				1250—			
Wages	5727515				5727515			
	54205925	54205925						
Supplies Expense			2104—		2104—			
Insurance Expense			950—		950—			
Depreciation Buildings			3500—		3500—			
Depreciation Equipment			4600—		4600—			
Depreciation Trucks			12000—		12000—			
			24289—	24289—	22755765	272750—	37623660	33104425
Net Income					4519235			4519235
					272750—	272750—	37623660	37623660

12.4 Merchandise Returns and Allowances

When a sale is made on account, the seller issues a sales invoice and makes the appropriate accounting entry. No further action is necessary for most sales transactions except to ensure that the customer pays the account.

In the Books of the Vendor

Occasionally, however, a correction or a cancellation of a sales invoice is necessary. Consider the sales invoice in Figure 12.10.

```
                                                                    P.O. Box 298
        Phone                                                       Station 8
        842-9999              ECHO BAY                              V7C 8P7
                            VANCOUVER, B.C.

                      MASTHEAD MARINE

          Penticton Marina
  SOLD TO  4000 Skaha Lake Road           DATE   April 14, 19--
          Penticton, B.C.
          V2A 6G9                         TERMS  60 days

  ┌──────────┬──────────┬─────────────────────────┬──────────┬──────────┐
  │ QUANTITY │ PART NO. │      DESCRIPTION        │  PRICE   │  AMOUNT  │
  ├──────────┼──────────┼─────────────────────────┼──────────┼──────────┤
  │    2     │ 15-2500  │ Gusher '25' pump        │ $315.00  │ $630.00  │
  │  8 Pacs. │ 48-1020  │ Skyblazer Red Signal    │          │          │
  │          │          │ Flares                  │   18.50  │  148.00  │
  │          │          │                         │          │          │
  │          │          │                  Total  │          │ $778.00  │
  └──────────┴──────────┴─────────────────────────┴──────────┴──────────┘

  SALES INVOICE           CUSTOMER'S COPY                      NO. 8321
```

Figure 12.10 The customer's copy of a sales invoice.

Masthead Marine, the vendor, will make the following accounting entry for this invoice.

	DR	CR
Accounts Receivable	$778.00	
Sales		$778.00

In T-accounts:

Accounts Receivable (Penticton Marina)		Sales
778		778

Correction or Cancellation of a Sales Invoice

The purchaser in this transaction is Penticton Marina. Assume that Penticton Marina learns that the Skyblazer flares are defective. Penticton Marina will notify the seller, Masthead Marine, that the flares are defective and are being returned. Penticton Marina will expect its account to be decreased by Masthead Marine.

Credit Invoice

The standard procedure in this situation is for the seller to issue a credit invoice. A **credit invoice**, or a **credit note**, is a "minus" invoice issued by the vendor to reverse a charge that was previously made on a regular sales invoice. Credit invoices are used to adjust, correct, or cancel a customer's account for any of the following reasons:

- the goods prove to be defective and are returned;
- the goods prove to be less than satisfactory but are kept by the customer. In this case, the customer will be given an allowance (a reduction) off the invoice price;
- an error is made on the sales invoice. In this case, the error will be made right.

In our example, Masthead Marine issues the credit invoice shown below in Figure 12.11.

MASTHEAD MARINE
Phone 842-9999
ECHO BAY
VANCOUVER, B.C.
P.O. Box 298
Station 8
V7C 8P7

SOLD TO: Penticton Marina
4000 Skaha Lake Road
Penticton, B.C.
V2A 6G9

DATE: April 14, 19-
TERMS: 60 days

QUANTITY	PART NO.	DESCRIPTION	PRICE	AMOUNT
8 Pacs	48-1020	Skyblazer Red Signal Flares (defective merchandise)	18.50	148.00
		Total		$148.00

CREDIT INVOICE   CUSTOMER'S COPY   NO. 841

The path of a credit invoice is the same as that of a regular sales invoice.

The word 'credit' is prominently displayed.

The invoice is printed in red or on pink paper.

Figure 12.11 The customer's copy of a credit invoice.

A credit invoice has the opposite effect to a regular sales invoice. As a result, the customer's account will be decreased by being "credited." Masthead Marine will make the following accounting entry for the credit invoice.

	DR	CR
Sales	$148.00	
Accounts Receivable		$148.00

After the credit invoice is processed by Masthead Marine, the effect in the accounts is as follows:

Accounts Receivable (Penticton Marina)		Sales	
778	148	148	778
(630)		(630)	

The balance in Penticton Marina's account has been correctly reduced to $630.

In the Books of the Purchaser

Penticton Marina, the purchaser, will handle the transaction in a similar manner. When the source documents are received, the following accounting entries are made.

When the (purchase) invoice is received:

	DR	CR
Purchases	$778.00	
Accounts Payable		$778.00

In the accounts:

Purchases		Accounts Payable (Masthead Marine)	
778			778

When the credit invoice is received:

	DR	CR
Accounts Payable	$148.00	
Purchases		$148.00

In the accounts:

Purchases		Accounts Payable (Masthead Marine)	
778	148	148	778
(630)			(630)

Cash Refunds

The cash sale is a very common business transaction. But dissatisfaction can occur with cash sales as well as with charge sales. A customer who has paid cash for merchandise which has to be returned will usually receive a refund. A **cash refund** is the return of money to the buyer from the seller when merchandise is returned.

In principle, the accounting for refunds is similar to that for credit invoices. However, when a refund is given:
- no credit invoices are issued. Neither accounts receivable nor accounts payable is affected;
- instead, cash is handed over, or a cheque is issued. The accounting entry to record the transaction affects the Bank account. A refund cheque issued for goods returned requires the following accounting entry.

	DR	CR
Sales	$$$$	
Bank		$$$$

Returns and Allowances Accounts

Some businesses, such as large department stores, want complete information about returns and allowances. They want to know what proportion of their sales were returned by their customers. They also want to know what proportion of their purchases (of merchandise) were returned to their suppliers. Businesses that require this special information get it by accumulating it in special "returns and allowances" accounts.

Sales Returns and Allowances Accounts

Figure 12.12 below contrasts the two different methods of handling returns and allowances for sales.

Where no account for returns and allowances is used

Sales	
560	2 500
395	2 240
720	3 560
	2 152
	3 852
	2 695
	(15 324)

Where a separate account for returns and allowances is used

Sales		Sales Returns and Allowances
	2 500	560
	2 240	395
	3 560	720
	2 152	(1 675)
	3 852	
	2 695	
	(16 999)	

Net book value = 15 324

Figure 12.12 Chart showing the different methods of handling sales returns and allowances.

Take note of the following observations.

- The single account at the left produces an account balance which represents the net sales figure. To obtain the returns and allowances figure, the account would have to be analyzed.
- The two accounts at the right produce two account balances. One represents the total sales figure. The other represents the total returns and allowances figure.

Purchases Returns and Allowances Accounts

The concept is exactly the same for purchases returns and allowances. Figure 12.13 below contrasts the two different methods of handling returns and allowances for purchases.

Where no account for returns and allowances is used	Where a separate account for returns and allowances is used
Purchases	**Purchases** / **Purchases Returns and Allowances**
5 260 | 250	5 260 | | | 250
3 852 | 658	3 852 | | | 658
9 236 | 902	9 236 | | | 902
4 247	4 247 | | | *1 810*
1 757	1 757
3 845	3 845
26 387	*28 197*
	Net book value = 26 387

Figure 12.13 Chart showing the different methods of handling purchases returns and allowances.

The effect here is the same as for sales above. The two accounts provide information not provided by one account alone.

Sample Transactions Using Returns and Allowances Accounts

Sales Returns and Allowances

Transaction 1 Simplex Company sells $500 of goods to A. Moss. An invoice is issued for the sale on November 12, 19--. Sales tax is added at the rate of five per cent.

The accounting entry to be made by Simplex Company is as follows:

	DR	CR
Accounts Receivable—A. Moss	$525.00	
Sales		$500.00
Sales Tax Payable		25.00

Transaction 2 A portion of the goods sold to A. Moss is defective and is returned. Simplex Company issues a credit invoice for $180 plus the sales tax of $9.

The accounting entry to be made by Simplex Company is as follows:

	DR	CR
Sales Returns and Allowances	$180.00	
Sales Tax Payable	9.00	
Accounts Receivable—A. Moss		$189.00

The effect of the above entries in the accounts is shown below:

Accounts Receivable (A. Moss)		Sales Tax Payable		Sales	Sales Returns and Allowances
525	189	9	25	500	180

Net sales = $320

Purchases Returns and Allowances

Transaction 1 On June 12, 19--, Baytown Drug Market receives a shipment of drugs and the sales invoice for them from Drug Wholesale Company in the amount of $1 147.

The accounting entry to be made by Baytown Drug Market is as follows:

	DR	CR
Purchases	$1 147	
Accounts Payable (Drug Wholesale)		$1 147

Transaction 2 On June 14, Baytown Drug Market notices a number of packages in the shipment from Drug Wholesale are damaged. The damaged goods are returned for credit and a credit invoice for $483 is received from Drug Wholesale.

The accounting entry to be made by Baytown Drug Market is as follows:

	DR	CR
Accounts Payable—Drug Wholesale	$438	
Purchases Returns and Allowances		$438

The effect of the above entries in the accounts is shown below:

Purchases		Purchases Returns and Allowances	Accounts Payable (Drug Wholesale)	
1 147		438	438	1 147

Net purchases = $709

Returns and Allowances on the Income Statement

Both sales returns and allowances and purchases returns and allowances appear on the income statement of companies that use them. They are treated as deductions from

TRIDENT TRADING CO.
INCOME STATEMENT
YEAR ENDED DECEMBER 31, 19--

Revenue
Sales		$398 659	
Less Returns and Allowances		21 151	
Net Sales			$377 508

Cost of Goods Sold
Merchandise Inventory, January 1		$ 72 074	
Purchases	$229 209		
Less Returns and Allowances	18 356		
Net Purchases		210 853	
Freight-in		5 731	
Goods Available for Sale		$288 658	
Less: Merchandise Inventory, December 31		83 562	205 096
Gross Profit			$172 412

Operating Expenses
Advertising	$ 1 141	
Bank Charges	2 651	
Car Expense	4 999	
Delivery Expense	1 377	
Depreciation—Equipment	2 490	
Depreciation—Automobiles	3 850	
Insurance Used	2 915	
Light and Heat	3 988	
Miscellaneous Expense	1 507	
Rent	12 000	
Salaries	24 000	
Supplies Used	2 560	
Telephone	1 850	
Wages	48 220	113 548
Net Income		$58 864

Figure 12.14 The income statement of Trident Trading Co. including returns and allowances.

sales and from purchases respectively. Their inclusion on the statement makes it a slightly more difficult statement to prepare. The income statement of Trident Trading Co. (page 376) is shown again in Figure 12.14 as it would appear if returns and allowances accounts were used.

Revised Cost of Goods Sold Formula

To handle all types of business situations, the cost of goods formula is changed slightly. The revised formula shows "Net Cost of Merchandise Purchased." This takes into account the likelihood that there will be some returns and allowances during the period. The formula, in its final form, is as follows:

| Cost of Beginning Inventory | + | Net Cost of Merchandise Purchased | − | Cost of Ending Inventory | = | Cost of Merchandise Sold |

Section Review Questions

1. What form is issued when a sale is made on account?
2. When a sale is made and the customer is satisfied, what is the usual next step?
3. What happens when a customer is dissatisfied?
4. What business form is issued when a customer's account is adjusted downward?
5. Describe a credit invoice.
6. What is another name for a credit invoice?
7. For what three reasons are credit notes issued?
8. For the simplest system studied so far, give the accounting entry for the issuing of a credit invoice.
9. What is a cash refund?
10. For the simplest system studied so far, give the accounting entry for a cash refund for merchandise returned by a customer.
11. Why do some businesses keep "returns and allowances" accounts?
12. Briefly explain the difference between accounting for a business that keeps returns and allowances accounts and one that does not.
13. For the simplest system studied so far, give the accounting entry for a credit note for $100 for goods returned to a supplier.
14. For a system using returns and allowances accounts, give the accounting entry for a credit note for $100 for goods returned to a supplier.
15. Explain how to handle returns and allowances accounts on the income statement.

Section Exercises

1. Examine the two source documents below and answer the questions that follow.

    A.

    ```
    EQUIPMENT RENTAL INVOICE
    BOX 100, HALIFAX, N.S., B3L 2Z4          PHONE 233 6767

    ACADIA
    EQUIPMENT AND SUPPLY
    ```

CONTRACT NO.	DATE SHIPPED	SHIPPED VIA	INVOICE NUMBER
402	Sept. 10	Acadia	D4023
BILLING NO.	**DATE RETURNED**	**RETURNED VIA**	**INVOICE DATE**
36	Sept. 13	Acadia	Sept. 14, 19--

    RENTED TO Cornwallis Construction
    20 Cornwallis Street
    Halifax, Nova Scotia
    B3K 1A1

    TERMS Net 30 days

    SHIPPED TO Same

    OVERDUE ACCOUNTS 2% per month

STOCK NO.	DESCRIPTION	NO. DAYS, WEEKS, MOS.	RATE	AMOUNT
146	Forklift truck	3 days	$100.00	$300.00

    1. From the point of view of Acadia Equipment and Supply, what source document is document A?
    2. From the point of view of Cornwallis Construction, what source document is document A?
    3. What source document is document B?

B.

CREDIT INVOICE

BOX 100, HALIFAX, N.S. B3L 2Z4   PHONE 233 6767

ACADIA
EQUIPMENT AND SUPPLY

CONTRACT NO.	DATE SHIPPED	SHIPPED VIA	INVOICE NUMBER
402	Sept. 12		C1129
BILLING NO.	**DATE RETURNED**	**RETURNED VIA**	**INVOICE DATE**
36	Sept. 13		Sept. 19, 19--

RENTED TO: Cornwallis Construction
2016 Cornwallis Street
Halifax, Nova Scotia
B3K 1A1

SHIPPED TO:

TERMS: Net 30 days

OVERDUE ACCOUNTS: 2% per month

STOCK NO.	DESCRIPTION	NO. DAYS, WEEKS, MOS.	RATE	AMOUNT
146	Credit allowed due to malfunction of forklift truck	$\frac{1}{2}$	$100.00	$50.00

CREDIT

4. Which company is the sender of the documents?
5. Which company is the purchaser?
6. Give the accounting entries for these two documents as if you were the accountant for Acadia Equipment and Supply. Acadia Equipment and Supply does not use returns and allowances accounts.
7. Give the accounting entries for these two documents as if you were the accountant for Cornwallis Construction. Cornwallis Construction does not use returns and allowances accounts.

2. **Journalize the following transactions of Copeland's Furniture Mart. Copeland's Furniture Mart does not use returns and allowances accounts.**

   1. May 31 Cash Sales slip #1060 to A. Rosen for sale of goods $155 plus sales tax of $10.85; total $165.85; payment received in full.
   2. June 4 Cash Refund slip #1075 to A. Rosen for return of goods $155 plus sales tax of $10.85; total $165.85; cash refunded in full.

3. **Workbook Exercise:** Additional practice in journalizing accounting entries from source documents.

4. **From the following partial work sheet prepare the income statement for Tonk Traders to the point where the gross profit is reached.**

Work Sheet   Tonk Traders   Year Ended December 31, 19--

Accounts	Income Statement DR	Income Statement CR
Merchandise Inventory	43 250.40	48 901.25
Sales		102 356.00
Sales Returns and Allowances	4 698.23	
Freight-in	6 235.14	
Purchases	60 258.20	
Purchases Returns and Allowances		9 562.45

12.5 Computerized Accounting: Accounting for a Merchandising Business

Accounting for a Merchandising Business

You have seen that many companies use accounting software packages and that one of the options available is inventory control. Inventory control programs provide up-to-the-minute detailed information regarding merchandise in stock. They are used in particular by large department stores and large general merchandise and auto parts stores.

Businesses that use an inventory control package obtain the following benefits:

- clerks using a terminal are able to find out if any particular piece of merchandise is in stock;
- the company can keep the quantity of every inventory item at its optimum point, with neither too much nor too little on hand. An inventory that is too large is expensive in two ways: the purchase cost is high, and extra storage space must be paid for. This money can be put to better use in other ways. If the inventory is too small, the store might run out of individual items and thus lose sales. A computerized inventory system alerts management when the quantity of any item becomes low and should be reordered;
- the company is able to produce financial statements daily. This is possible because the up-to-date inventory total and the cost of goods sold total are known by the computer at all times. Thus, management is informed daily of the progress of the business and is able to take swift action to solve or avoid problems.

An inventory control system is organized numerically. A unique number is given to each individual inventory item. Given the unique code for any item, the computer can give back any information about the item that is stored in its memory. This includes a complete description of the product and the quantity on hand.

It takes several people to make the system work. As goods are received from suppliers they are added to the inventory by clerks entering data through input devices. When goods are returned, the clerks enter the deductions from inventory.

The more technically complex part of the inventory processing happens in the store. Each cash register is a point-of-sale computer terminal connected to the store's main computer. As items are sold or returned, the cashier enters the code numbers and the quantities of the items through the cash register keyboard or by means of an electronic scanner. The information is transferred directly to the store's central computer, which is programmed to update the detailed inventory. As well, the computer updates the Merchandise Inventory account and the Cost of Goods Sold account in the general ledger.

Most supermarkets are geared to use the Universal Product Code (UPC). The universal product code is represented by the black bars seen on most consumer products.

The UPC does not contain the price of the product but it does precisely identify the product. The UPC is read by a laser scanning device at the checkout counter. Once the product is identified, the system seeks out the price and makes the necessary calculations. If the scanning device refuses to read a particular code, the clerk enters the information through the keyboard. The final outcome is an itemized bill printed out for the customer.

As "smart" as the computer is, it does not automatically know when goods are lost, stolen, or broken. Therefore, a manual check of the inventory is required. This is usually carried out on a random basis throughout the year.

Computer Review Questions

1. What stores, in particular, make use of sophisticated inventory control systems?
2. Give three advantages of using an inventory control system.
3. Explain why a business should maintain as small an inventory as feasible.
4. Explain the problem that can occur if an inventory is too small.
5. What is a point-of-sale terminal?
6. Explain the purpose of a point-of-sale terminal with respect to inventory control.
7. Explain what the Universal Product Code is.
8. Explain how the UPC is used in supermarkets.

CHAPTER HIGHLIGHTS

Now that you have completed Chapter 12, you should:

1. know what is meant by the terms merchandising business, wholesaler, and retailer;
2. know what is meant by merchandise inventory or stock-in-trade;
3. understand that the total cost of goods available for sale during a fiscal period is either 1) on hand, or 2) sold, broken, lost, or stolen;
4. be able to include merchandise inventory correctly on the balance sheet and on the income statement;
5. understand what is meant by gross profit;
6. know the difference between the periodic and the perpetual inventory methods;
7. know the inventory cycle and the cost of goods calculation;
8. know the accounting entries for 1) the purchase and sale of merchandise inventory, 2) freight-in, and 3) duty;
9. understand the accounting entries that affect the Merchandise Inventory account;
10. understand the need to take an end-of-period inventory;
11. be able to prepare a work sheet for a merchandising business;
12. be able to record the closing entries for a merchandising business;
13. understand the concept of merchandise returns and allowances;
14. be able to identify a credit invoice and to make the accounting entries for a credit invoice issued and a credit invoice received;
15. know the accounting entries for a cash refund;
16. understand why some businesses use special accounts for returns and allowances;
17. know the accounting entries for transactions that affect returns and allowances accounts;
18. be able to prepare an income statement that includes returns and allowances accounts.

ACCOUNTING TERMS

cash refund
cost of goods sold
credit invoice
credit note
duty
freight-in
gross profit
merchandise inventory

merchandising business
periodic inventory method
perpetual inventory method
physical inventory
retailer
stock-in-trade
wholesaler

CHAPTER EXERCISES

Using Your Knowledge

1. **In a two-column general journal record the accounting entries for the following selected transactions of Industrial Supply owned by Otto Graf. Industrial Supply does not use returns and allowances accounts. Choose your own account names.**

    Transactions

    May
    1   *Sales Invoice No. 501*
        —To Hewitt Construction for sale of merchandise on account; $656.00 plus 7% sales tax, total $701.92.
    2   *Bank Debit Advice*
        —For interest and bank charges for April; $65.85.
    4   *Cheque Copy No. 1002*
        —Issued to the owner for his personal use; $500.
    5   *Purchase Invoice*
        —Received from Dofasco for merchandise for resale; $1 072.14.
    8   *Credit Invoice*
        —Received from Great Lakes Wood Products; allowance for defective goods; $585.00.
    9   *Sales Invoice No. 502*
        —To Northern Contracting for sale of merchandise on account; $846.00 plus 7% sales tax, total $905.22.

10 *Cheque Copy No. 1003*
    —Issued to the Provincial Treasurer in payment of the sales tax for April; $1 754.34.
11 *Cheque Copy No. 1004*
    —Issued to the Post office for the cash purchase of postage stamps; $160.
12 *Cash Receipt*
    —Received from Arrow Electric on account; $625.95.
15 *Credit Invoice No. 503*
    —Issued to Handy Made Products for unsatisfactory goods returned; $585.00 plus 7% sales tax, total $625.95.
16 *Cheque Copy No. 1005*
    —Issued to Olympia Distributors on account; $755.65.
19 *Cash Sales Slip No. 12520*
    —Issued to T. Maloney for the cash sale of merchandise; $102.50 plus 7% sales tax, total $109.68.
22 *Cheque Copy No. 1006*
    —Issued to Speedy Muffler for the cash purchase of a new muffler system for the truck; $166.92.
24 *Cheque Copy No. 1007*
    —Issued to Bell Canada for the cash payment of the telephone bill for one month; $65.35.
25 *Cash Receipt*
    —Received from Easy Products on account; $1 000.
26 *Purchase Invoice*
    —Received from Pacific Transport for transportation charges on incoming merchandise; $896.50.
29 *Credit Note*
    —Received from Kohler Generators for merchandise returned; $2 850.
31 *Cheque Copy No. 1008*
    —Issued to P. Vanderkam for wages; $950.74.

2. **Workbook Exercise: Journalizing transactions involving returns and allowances accounts.**

3. Indicate whether each of the following statements is true or false by placing a "T" or an "F" in the space indicated in your workbook. Explain the reason for each "F" response in the space provided.
    1. A "wholesaler" is a "merchandiser." Therefore, a "merchandiser" is a "wholesaler."
    2. Some of the goods found in the inventory of a hardware store are also goods found in the inventory of a building supply store.
    3. Merchandise inventory is on the balance sheet under Prepaid Expenses.
    4. The cost of goods sold figure normally includes the cost of goods that are lost, stolen, or broken.

5. The merchandise inventory of a drug store is calculated by counting all of the goods on hand and multiplying by the selling prices marked on the goods.
6. An item that cost $40 and sold for $80 produced a gross profit of fifty per cent of the selling price.
7. The difference between the selling price and the cost price of the goods for a fiscal period is also the net income figure before any operating expenses are deducted.
8. The goods not sold represent the ending inventory.
9. The goods sold at selling prices represent the revenue figure.
10. The perpetual inventory system has not been commonly used because of the amount of work required to keep track of the many individual items in the inventory.
11. A used car business could easily uses the perpetual inventory system because the number of items in its inventory is quite small.
12. XYZ department store uses the periodic inventory method. It must take a physical inventory at least once a year.
13. A perpetual inventory results in a "calculated" inventory figure. The inventory quantities shown on a perpetual inventory listing should be checked by actually inspecting the inventory from time to time. This would make clear whether or not any goods were stolen.
14. If the beginning inventory was 10 000 units and the ending inventory was 12 000 units, the business sold more units than it purchased.
15. The merchandise inventory figure can be found during the fiscal period from the Merchandise Inventory account.
16. The Purchases account is used to accumulate all purchases during the period.
17. When a business that uses the periodic method sells goods, no accounting entry is made to reduce the merchandise inventory. If it were made, the entry would be debit Cost of Goods Sold and credit Merchandise Inventory.
18. The Freight-in account is used to accumulate all transportation charges during the fiscal period.
19. Freight-in is considered to be a cost of the goods acquired.
20. On the work sheet the Purchases figure in the trial balance is extended to the Income Statement section, Debit column.
21. On the work sheet the Merchandise Inventory figure in the trial balance is extended to the Balance Sheet section, Debit column.
22. Both the beginning and the ending inventory figures are shown on the income statement of a merchandising company.
23. The Merchandise Inventory account is automatically adjusted by the closing entries.
24. A credit invoice is issued by the vendor and received by the buyer.
25. The accounting entry for a credit note issued is either:

	DR	CR
Accounts Receivable	$$$$	
Sales		$$$$
or		
Accounts Receivable	$$$$	
Sales Returns and Allowances		$$$$

4. From the partial work sheet shown below:
   1. Prepare an income statement and a balance sheet.
   2. Journalize the closing entries.

Work Sheet — Master Trading Company — Year Ended December 31, 19--

Accounts	Income Statement Dr	Income Statement Cr	Balance Sheet Dr	Balance Sheet Cr
Bank			950.85	
Accounts Receivable			37 372.50	
Merchandise Inventory	45 957.00	43 500.00	43 500.00	
Supplies			1 350.00	
Prepaid Insurance			1 865.00	
Equipment			28 040.00	
Accumulated Depreciation—Equipment				9 216.00
Automobiles			25 350.00	
Accumulated Depreciation—Automobiles				9 000.00
Accounts Payable				26 210.70
Sales Tax Payable				1 027.52
Bank Loan				25 000.00
Grace Strom, Capital				49 175.29
Grace Strom, Drawings			30 000.00	
Sales		216 350.50		
Sales Returns & Allowances	4 092.00			
Purchases	75 316.20			
Purchases Returns & Allowances		7 621.90		
Freight-in	1 592.00			
Advertising	1 585.00			
Bank Charges	2 685.00			
Car Expenses	8 356.00			
Delivery Expense	5 695.21			
General Expense	1 632.25			
Light and Heat	1 875.25			
Rent	12 000.00			
Telephone	1 115.33			
Wages	47 256.32			
Supplies Used	2 563.00			
Insurance Used	2 417.00			
Depreciation—Equipment	1 536.00			
Depreciation—Automobiles	3 000.00			
	218 673.56	267 472.40	168 428.35	119 629.51
Net Income	48 798.84			48 798.84
	267 472.40	267 472.40	168 428.35	168 428.35

5. The following statement shows the results of operation for two successive years.

THE WALTON COMPANY
INCOME STATEMENT
YEARS ENDED DECEMBER 31, 19–8 AND 19–9

	19–8	19–9
Sales	$100 000	$120 000
Cost of Goods Sold		
Opening Inventory	$ 20 000	$ 25 000
Purchases		
Goods Available for Sale	$	$ 63 000
Less Closing Inventory	25 000	
Cost of Goods Sold	$	$
Gross Income	$ 65 000	$
Expenses	$	$ 37 000
Net Income	$ 33 000	$ 42 000

1. In your workbook, fill in the blanks to complete the above statement.
2. Suppose that on December 31, 19–8, the merchandise inventory was miscounted. Instead of $25 000 as shown, it was counted as $21 000.
   a. What effect would this understatement have on the net income figure for 19–8?
   b. What effect would it have on the net income figure for 19–9?
3. What effect, if any, would the above noted error have on the balance sheet for 19–8?

6. Outpost Marine is a company that maintains a perpetual inventory that includes several hundred items. Two of the items listed on the February 28th inventory are:

Item	Code	Quantity on Hand
Schaefer Cheek Blocks	320	23
Barton Cam Cleat	3011	20

1. Shown below are the source documents for inventory items received and inventory items shipped during the month of March. From this list of source documents, select those that pertain to the two items above and calculate the number of each of the two items on hand at the end of March.

Date		Source Document	Stock Number	Quantity
March	1	Shipping Order	320	5
	1	Shipping Order	3011	6
	2	Receiving Report	551	10
	3	Shipping Order	1018	35
	3	Receiving Report	1000	20
	4	Receiving Report	4014	25
	5	Shipping Order	320	15
	8	Receiving Report	6757	5
	8	Shipping Order	3011	10
	10	Receiving Report	1912	25
	11	Receiving Report	4210	20
	11	Shipping Order	1912	15
	12	Shipping Order	1129	100
	15	Receiving Report	3011	35
	18	Receiving Report	112	24
	19	Shipping Order	320	2
	20	Receiving Report	3121	30
	23	Shipping Order	3011	15
	25	Receiving Report	320	25
	30	Shipping Order	320	12
	31	Shipping Order	3011	20
	31	Receiving Report	6745	12

2. If the price of the items purchased on March 25 was $16 each, calculate the value of item #320 for the inventory.

7. The Sutton Hardware Store takes inventory only at the end of the calendar year because of the inconvenience involved. The gross profit of the business is stable and averages forty per cent. On January 31, at the end of the first month of business, the ledger included the following five account balances.

Merchandise Inventory	$ 51 920
Sales	103 850
Purchases	73 950
Freight-in	1 258
Operating Expenses	22 357

1. Use the above information to estimate the closing inventory. Then prepare a condensed income statement for the month of January.

8. The accountant for a small company prepared an income statement which showed a net income figure of $38 525. The company's bank requested an audit of this statement. The following errors were found by the auditor who checked the books and records:

1. The $4 200 cost of installing new equipment had been charged to Repair Expense instead of to Equipment. The new equipment would be depreciated at the rate of $400 a year.
2. A $100 credit to Purchase Returns and Allowances was incorrectly credited to Sales Returns and Allowances.
3. The calculation for depreciation of automobiles was incorrectly overstated by the amount of $1 500.
4. No adjusting entry for supplies was made. The ledger showed a balance for supplies of $2 850; the supplies counted at the year-end amounted to $840.
5. The ending inventory figure used by the company accountant was $32 650 but there were a number of errors in arriving at that figure. The auditor revised the ending inventory figure to be $29 350.

Calculate the net income figure that would appear on the audited income statement.

9. Hiram Retail is a family owned department store in Winnipeg, Manitoba. When the physical inventory was taken at the year-end, an entire department was overlooked. As a result the inventory was understated by $10 000.
Use some hypothetical figures to help you answer the following questions.

   1. How will the inventory understatement affect the cost of goods sold?
   2. How will the inventory understatement affect the gross profit?
   3. How will the inventory understatement affect the net income?
   4. How will the inventory understatement affect the balance sheet?
   5. What would be your answers to questions 1 to 4 if the $10 000 error had been an inventory overstatement?
   6. If you were the manager of a company and were looking for a way to make the profit appear higher, what might you consider doing?
   7. If you were the owner of a company and were considering cheating to save on income tax, what might you consider doing?

For Further Thought

10. Briefly answer the following questions.

    1. Paula Waukey is the owner of a paper products business. Her company makes available a large variety of paper and related products such as paper towels, coffee filters, table covers, disposable coffee cups, and so on. Paula's customers could buy more cheaply by dealing directly with the manufacturers of the products. However, they continue to do business with Paula. Explain why Paula's customers choose to do business with her.

2. A road building company might have several inventories on hand. These could include office supplies, sand, stone, asphalt, and gasoline. Explain the difference between these inventories and merchandise inventory.
3. The text indicates that merchandise that is lost, broken, or stolen, is lumped in with cost of goods sold. Explain the logic of this.
4. Merchandise inventory on hand at the end of the fiscal period is listed on the balance sheet at its cost price. Indirectly, some inventory is listed on the income statement at its selling price. Explain.
5. Give a logical reason for showing the gross profit separately on the income statement.
6. Having a computerized inventory system allows a business to carry a smaller total inventory. Explain why this is possible. What is the advantage of being able to carry a smaller inventory?
7. The text states that the selling prices of goods are marked on the merchandise, but not the cost price. Why is the cost price not marked on the goods?
8. The merchandise sold is listed in two places on the income statement. Explain how this can be.
9. Explain why the closing inventory is valued at its cost price.
10. Explain why freight-in is included in the cost of goods sold calculation.
11. Give a logical reason why a business would close down for a day or two in order to take inventory.
12. Many businesspeople who use the periodic inventory system would rather not bother with inventory taking. However, they do it anyway. Explain why.
13. Explain why inventory count tickets are pre-numbered.
14. Assume that a large department store wants to take a quick inventory with some sacrifice of accuracy, to give it a rough idea of its progress. Try to devise a method of shortening the inventory procedure to give a reasonably close result.
15. The method of handling the merchandise inventory on the work sheet may be thought of as a "manipulation" rather than as an "adjustment." Explain.
16. Which financial statement do you think is of the most interest to a banker? Explain your answer.
17. What do you think is the most common error made by students when doing the closing entries for a merchandising business?
18. Explain how the credit note got its name.
19. In purchase transactions where there are returns and allowances involved, it is normal to wait until all of the source documents are received before making payment. Why would this be done?
20. Some businesses refuse to give a refund for merchandise returned. Explain how they handle this type of transaction.

CASE STUDIES

Case 1 *Analyzing Income Statements*

Shown below are the income statements for two different companies in the furniture business.

INCOME STATEMENTS
YEAR ENDED DECEMBER 31, 19--

	Company A	Company B
Revenue		
Sales	$121 206	$415 072
Cost of Goods Sold	70 704	211 686
Gross Profit	$ 50 502	$203 386
Operating Expenses		
Advertising	—	$ 43 072
Bank Charges	$ 990	5 765
Building Maintenance	140	3 500
Delivery Expense	10 403	35 206
Insurance	509	1 532
Licenses	120	435
Light, Heat, and Water	1 850	5 775
Miscellaneous Expense	119	717
Rent	4 800	12 000
Telephone	275	716
Wages	10 402	40 307
Total Expenses	$ 29 608	$149 025
Net Income	$ 20 894	$ 54 361

Questions

1. Describe your mental picture of these two companies (large or small, high profile or low profile, etc.) giving specific reasons for your impression.
2. B's expenses are much larger than A's, and yet B is able to earn more than twice the net income of A. How is this possible?
3. The relationship between the cost price of the goods and the selling price of the goods is crucial in any business. Consider the following analysis for Company A:
    Sales $121 206—100%
    Cost of Goods Sold $ 70 704— 58%

Company A's goods cost 58% of their selling price.
a. Calculate this same percentage figure for Company B.
b. If the figure for Company B was fifty-eight per cent, the same as for Company A, how much lower would Company B's net income be?

Case 2 Irregularity Disclosed by Income Statement

Mark Trewin is the owner of Spyhill Ski Shop. His accountant has just handed him the financial statements for the year. The income statement is shown below in condensed form.

SPYHILL SKI SHOP
INCOME STATEMENT
YEAR ENDED JUNE 30, 19--

Revenue			
Sales		$110 000	100%
Cost of Goods Sold			
Opening Inventory	$ 36 500		
Purchases	67 000		
	$103 500		
Deduct Closing Inventory	36 000	67 500	61%
Gross Profit		$42 500	39%
Operating Expenses		29 000	27%
Net Income		$ 13 500	12%

Mark is upset by this statement, and suggests to his accountant that an error has been made. His accountant assures him that everything was checked and double-checked because of the low net income figure. No error was found.

Mark is particularly troubled by the gross profit figure. The operating expenses appear to be normal. Mark explains that all of his merchandise is marked up one hundred per cent and that there have been no special sales needed to move the goods. In other words, Mark feels that the gross profit should be at its normal figure of approximately fifty per cent.

Because he has to be away a great deal, Mark relies heavily on his store manager. In past years Jill Zaba was the manager and no problems were encountered. A year ago, Jill left for a better position. This year the store was managed by Jon Yeo. Jon came from out of town and not much is known about him.

Questions
1. Assuming that the sales figure is correct, what should the figure for cost of goods sold have been?
2. What is the most likely reason for the high figure for cost of goods sold?
3. Try to show the cost of goods sold section as it would appear if there had been no irregularity.
4. Suggest how the owner can correct any irregularities.

Case 3 A Scheme to Save Income Tax?

Vince Lyons owns a large and profitable sporting goods business in Regina, Sask. He has recently had a run of bad luck on the stock market, which has left him very short of funds. Unfortunately, he is badly in need of money to pay his income tax which is almost due.

Vince desperately needs a way to reduce the amount of income tax that he will have to pay. After much searching, he comes up with a scheme that he thinks may work. He describes this scheme to his wife, Louisa, to get her reaction.

Vince explains to Louisa that his income tax is based primarily on the net income of the business. He shows her condensed figures for the current year and the projected figures for next year. These are shown below.

	This year's actual figures	Next year's projected figures
Sales	250 000	300 000
Cost of Goods Sold		
Beginning inventory	50 000	60 000
Purchases	147 500	170 000
Goods available for sale	197 500	230 000
Deduct ending inventory	60 000	65 000
	137 500	165 000
Gross Profit	112 500	135 000
Expenses	65 000	75 000
Net Income	47 500	60 000

Vince proposes to understate this year's ending inventory by $20 000, causing the net income tax to be understated by the same amount. This way, Vince expects to reduce his tax bill by $7 000.

Vince does not consider this action to be dishonest. He explains to Louisa that an understatement this year will cause an overstatement the next year. He shows her the figures as they would appear containing the suggested inventory change. As Vince points out, the net income for the two years is still $107 500 whichever way it is calculated. Although he will pay less tax this year, he will make it up by paying more next year. Rather than cheating, he is simply postponing tax payment for a while. According to Vince, he will have no problem paying his taxes next year.

	This year's actual figures (modified)	Next year's projected figures (modified)
Sales	250 000	300 000
Cost of Goods Sold		
Beginning inventory	50 000	40 000
Purchases	147 500	170 000
Goods available for sale	197 500	210 000
Deduct ending inventory	40 000	65 000
	157 500	145 000
Gross Profit	92 500	155 000
Expense	65 000	75 000
Net Income	27 500	80 000

Questions

1. Is Vince correct when he claims that the net income for two years remains the same no matter how it is arrived at?
2. Will Vince be breaking the law?
3. Does the scheme offer a hidden benefit to Vince apart from the $7 000 tax deferral?
4. What dangers do you see in this scheme?

Case 4 Challenge *Understating Inventory on Tax Returns*

Carol Menzies is the owner of Classic Glass and Mirror. In the years 19–1 through 19–5, Carol submitted the following income statements to the income tax department.

SCHEDULE OF REPORTED NET INCOME FOR CLASSIC GLASS AND MIRROR
(in thousands of dollars)

Year	1	2	3	4	5
Sales	200	220	250	280	320
Cost of Goods Sold					
Opening Inventory	40	30	30	40	40
Purchases	90	115	140	160	190
Goods Available	130	145	170	200	230
Less Closing Inventory	30	30	40	40	50
Cost of Goods Sold	100	115	130	160	180
Gross Profit	100	105	120	120	140
Operating Expenses	60	65	70	70	80
Net Income	40	40	50	50	60

The above statements are correct except in one respect. Carol has understated the closing inventory figures in each of the five years. The true ending inventory figures are respectively $40, $50, $70, $80, and $100 (thousands).

The government income tax rates during this period of time are given in the schedule below. Carol has paid her income taxes promptly.

GOVERNMENT INCOME TAX RATES
(in thousands of dollars)

Net Income	Rate
$1– $20	20%
$21– $30	24%
$31– $40	28%
$41– $50	32%
$51– $60	36%
$61– $70	40%
$71– $80	44%
$81– $90	48%
$91–$100	52%
Over $100	56%

Part A

1. Recalculate the net incomes to reflect the correct inventory figures.
2. Record the answers to the following questions.
   a. Record the amount by which the inventory is understated for each of the five years.
   b. Record the amount by which the net income is understated for each of the five years.
   c. Calculate and record the income tax on the reported net income figures for each of the five years.
   d. Calculate and record the (correct) income tax on the revised net income figures for each of the five years.
   e. Calculate and record the saving in income tax for each of the five years.
   f. Assume that the owner used the tax money saved to reduce her bank loan on which interest at twelve per cent was charged. Calculate and record the interest saved in each year. To help you in this calculation, the income tax saved in the first year would accumulate for four years. The interest saved for that year is: ($4 800 × 1.12 × 1.12 × 1.12 × 1.12) − $4 800 = $2 752.89
   g. Calculate and record the accumulated total income tax and interest saved by the end of the fifth year.

Part B

The tax department was tipped off anonymously that Carol Menzies was cheating on her income tax. Carol was paid a surprise visit by the tax auditors who uncovered all of Carol's misrepresentations. The income tax authorities decided:

- to levy a fine of $10 000;
- to leave the tax returns for Years 1 to 4 untouched;
- to record the correct *closing* inventory of $100 000 on the 19–5 income statement and to calculate the tax on the revised 19–5 figure according to the tax table;
- to charge interest on the unpaid taxes at the rate of twelve per cent, the same rate Carol was charged by her bank.

1. Calculate the tax bill facing Carol as a result of the income tax audit.
2. Give possible reasons to explain why Carol misrepresented the inventory in 19–1.
3. Give possible reasons why Carol continued to misrepresent inventories in subsequent years.
4. If the auditors had decided to recalculate each of the net incomes for the five years, the extra expense to Carol would have been less. Explain why.

CAREER
George Ormsby / Auditor

George Ormsby enjoyed the accounting courses he took at his high school in Edmonton, Alberta. After graduation, he enrolled at the University of Alberta to take the Bachelor of Commerce program. George completed his degree in four years, and began working for an accounting firm, Thorne Riddell. While employed with the firm, he continued to study accounting in the evenings and on the weekends. Eventually, he passed his final examinations to become a chartered accountant, and set up practice on his own. His major clients were merchandising businesses.

After a year in his own practice, George joined the firm of McPherson, Scott and Co., as one of six partners. Each partner in the company is responsible for certain aspects of the business. One partner is in charge of a management committee which carries out policy decisions by signing cheques, approving invoices and audit invoices, arranging contracts, and so on. Another partner is in charge of the preparation of adjusting and closing journal entries and the financial statements of the partnership. Another partner is in charge of personnel and a fourth partner specializes in tax problems. George performs a variety of special functions for the firm, such as updating the manual that outlines the firm's accounting, auditing, and office procedures. He also designed and directed the use of general office forms such as sales invoices and credit invoices.

As a licensed public accountant, George audits the books of service and merchandising businesses for the partnership. He prepares financial reports for shareholders of corporations, for lending institutions, and for other individuals with concerns in the business. George reviews the internal control systems of his clients to make sure that transactions are recorded correctly and that assets are protected from loss or theft. His focus is on assets, cash, accounts receivable, and merchandise inventory. He examines his clients' general ledger and journals and assists in their inventory-taking to find the value of their assets. For some clients he advises the set-up of a computerized perpetual inventory system to control the merchandise inventory. He also prepares corporate tax returns for his clients.

George, like most auditors today, has a great deal of data processing knowledge. He constantly reviews the information output by the computer. The computer has now become a valuable aid to him. With it, George is able to provide a monthly service to his clients by keeping some of their records on accounting software systems housed in his office.

One of George's responsibilities is to oversee and advise students who work for the firm. He warns them that although accounting pays well, it can also be very demanding. Good chartered accountants must be willing to meet high professional standards and continuously improve their understanding, particularly in the areas of computer technology, tax regulations, and auditing principles. They must stay informed of changes in their field by regularly reading about new developments.

George believes that the computer will provide both the time and opportunity for accountants to develop their skills in dealing with other people. Strong communication skills will be important for success in future accounting careers.

For George, these are the qualities of a good accountant:
- a good mathematical ability;
- the ability to communicate their findings in plain language;
- accurate work habits, a passion for problem solving, courtesy, integrity and honesty.

George believes that accounting, especially in the field of auditing, is becoming more technical and specialized. He feels, therefore, the more education an accountant has, the better that accountant will be.

Discussion

1. Give ten examples of merchandising businesses in your community.
2. What are the duties George performs for his clients?
3. What skills should a good chartered accountant continuously improve?
4. In George's opinion, what are the qualities of a good accountant? Do you agree?
5. What are some of the auditor's major duties when performing an audit for a client?
6. How has the computer become a valuable aid to the accountant?
7. It is said that one never stops learning, even when school is finished. How has this been true for George Ormsby?
8. As an accountant, George performs many accounting services. One major service is to prepare financial reports for shareholders, lending institutions and other concerned individuals.
   - Why would shareholders want to read these financial statements?
   - Who are "the other concerned individuals"?

13 Specialized Journals

13.1 The Synoptic Journal
13.2 The Five-Journal System
13.3 Cash Discounts

You have gained a fairly complete understanding of the accounting process. You are now ready to study accounting techniques designed to make the accounting process more efficient.

13.1 The Synoptic Journal

In the business world, the two-column general journal is used mainly for non-routine transactions. Routine, or ordinary, transactions are generally recorded in "specialized" journals. The synoptic journal is a specialized journal designed for small businesses with only a few accounting employees.

The **synoptic journal** is a journal with a number of columns to accumulate accounting entries. Most special journals have a number of columns and are known as **multi-columnar journals**.

Journalizing in the Synoptic Journal

An illustration of a synoptic journal is shown below in Figure 13.1. Observe the special money columns for Bank debit, Bank credit, Accounts Receivable debit, Accounts Receivable credit, Accounts Payable debit, Accounts Payable credit, Sales credit, Purchases debit, and Sales Tax Payable credit.

Figure 13.1 A page from a synoptic journal.

411

A synoptic journal need not be identical to the one in the illustration. The headings depend to some extent on the nature of the business. For example, a service business would not need a column for purchases. Also, a synoptic journal may be designed with more columns than shown in the illustration.

The idea of the synoptic journal is to have special columns in which to sort items during the journalizing process. This saves time later when entries are posted. The individual items in the special columns are not posted singly. It is the totals of the special columns that are posted. Only one posting is needed for each special column.

For example, assume that fifty individual amounts have been entered in the Bank debit column of a synoptic journal. It is the total of these fifty amounts, not each separate amount, that is posted. The accounting department saves a good deal of time and effort by posting totals rather than individual amounts.

In theory, one could have a special column for every general ledger account. However, this would make the journal too cumbersome to be practicable. In practice, special columns are set up only for items that occur frequently. A general section is provided for other items.

Journalizing in the synoptic journal is easy. Obtain a sheet of "synoptic" paper and try the following sample entries for Consumers' Trading Company.

Transaction 1
May 4: Cash Sales Ticket No. 57: Sale of $256.00 of merchandise for cash; tax of $17.92; total, $273.92.

You should have no trouble working out the accounting entry for this transaction as follows:

	DR	CR
Bank	$273.92	
Sales		$256.00
Sales Tax Payable		17.92

In the synoptic journal this accounting entry would be recorded as follows:

Transaction 2
May 5: Sales Invoice No. 65: Issued to Paul Rogan; sale of $412.00 of merchandise on account; sales tax of $28.84; total, $440.84.

The accounting entry for this transaction is:

	DR	CR
Accounts Receivable (P. Rogan)	$440.84	
Sales		$412.00
Sales Tax Payable		28.84

In the synoptic journal this entry follows the previous entry in the manner shown below. Observe that no explanations are necessary for routine transactions. Also, remember that the postings to the subsidiary ledgers are made directly from source documents.

SYNOPTIC JOURNAL							MONTH OF May 19--					PAGE 41	
DATE	CUSTOMER SUPPLIER	REF NO.	BANK DR	BANK CR	ACCOUNTS RECEIVABLE DR	ACCOUNTS RECEIVABLE CR	ACCOUNTS PAYABLE DR	ACCOUNTS PAYABLE CR	SALES OR INCOME CR	PURCHASES DR	SALES TAX PAYABLE CR	OTHER ACCOUNTS ACCOUNT	PR DR CR
May 4	Cash Sale	57	273 92						256 -	179 2			
5	P. Rogan	165				440 84			412 -	288 4			

Transaction 3   May 6: Purchase Invoice: Received from Empire Wholesale for merchandise purchased on account; $816.00.

The accounting entry for this transaction is:

	DR	CR
Purchases	$816.00	
Accounts Payable (Empire Wholesale)		$816.00

In the synoptic journal the entry is recorded as shown below.

SYNOPTIC JOURNAL							MONTH OF May 19--					PAGE 41	
DATE	CUSTOMER SUPPLIER	REF NO.	BANK DR	BANK CR	ACCOUNTS RECEIVABLE DR	ACCOUNTS RECEIVABLE CR	ACCOUNTS PAYABLE DR	ACCOUNTS PAYABLE CR	SALES OR INCOME CR	PURCHASES DR	SALES TAX PAYABLE CR	OTHER ACCOUNTS ACCOUNT	PR DR CR
May 4	Cash Sale	57	273 92						256 -	179 2			
5	P. Rogan	165				440 84			412 -	288 4			
6	Empire Wholesale							816 -		816 -			

Transaction 4   May 7: Purchase Invoice and Cheque Copy No. 74: For the cash purchase of supplies from Deluxe Stationers; $235.40.

The accounting entry for this transaction is:

	DR	CR
Supplies	$235.40	
Bank		$235.40

In the synoptic journal the entry is recorded as shown below.

SYNOPTIC JOURNAL							MONTH OF May 19--					PAGE 41	
DATE	CUSTOMER SUPPLIER	REF NO.	BANK DR	BANK CR	ACCOUNTS RECEIVABLE DR	ACCOUNTS RECEIVABLE CR	ACCOUNTS PAYABLE DR	ACCOUNTS PAYABLE CR	SALES OR INCOME CR	PURCHASES DR	SALES TAX PAYABLE CR	OTHER ACCOUNTS ACCOUNT	PR DR CR
May 4	Cash Sale	57	273 92						256 -	179 2			
5	P. Rogan	165				440 84			412 -	288 4			
6	Empire Wholesale							816 -		816 -			
7	Deluxe Stationers	74		235 40								Supplies	235 40

The purchase of supplies does not happen frequently. Therefore, there is no special column for Supplies and the item is entered in the Other Accounts section.

Chapter 13

Transaction 5 May 7: Cheque Copy No. 75: Paid the rent for the month to Arrow Realty, $800.

The accounting entry for the transaction is:

	DR	CR
Rent	$800.00	
Bank		$800.00

In the synoptic journal, the accounting entry is recorded as shown below.

DATE	CUSTOMER SUPPLIER	REF NO.	BANK DR	BANK CR	ACCOUNTS RECEIVABLE DR	ACCOUNTS RECEIVABLE CR	ACCOUNTS PAYABLE DR	ACCOUNTS PAYABLE CR	SALES OR INCOME CR	PURCHASES DR	SALES TAX PAYABLE CR	OTHER ACCOUNTS ACCOUNT	PR	DR	CR
19— May 4	Cash Sale	57	273 92						256 —		17 92				
5	P. Rogan	165			440 84				412 —		28 84				
6	Empire Wholesale							816 —		816 —					
7	Deluxe Stationers	74		235 40								Supplies		235 40	
7	Arrow Realty	75		800 —								Rent		800 —	

    Rent Expense is recorded in the Other Accounts section because it is an infrequently occurring item.

Additional Transactions

A number of additional transactions of a routine nature are listed below. Try to journalize them on your own before comparing your work with the synoptic journal entries in Figure 13.2.

May
- 10 *Cheque Copy No. 76*
    Issued to A. Baldwin on account; $173.50.
- 10 *Cheque Copy No. 77*
    Issued to G. English & Co. on account; $500.00.
- 11 *Cash Receipt*
    Received from R. Mayotte on account; $352.00.
- 11 *Cash Receipt*
    Received from P. Fuhr on account; $620.00.

13 *Cheque Copy No. 78*
Issued to M. Cham in payment of wages; $585.00.
13 *Cheque Copy No. 79*
Issued to D. Adams in payment of wages; $650.00.
14 *Sales Invoice No. 166*
Issued to M. Delgaty for merchandise sold on account; $196.00 plus $13.72 sales tax; total $209.72.
14 *Sales Invoice No. 167*
Issued to Carl Holm for merchandise sold on account; $240.00 plus $16.80 sales tax; total $256.80.
17 *Purchase Invoice*
Received from Continental Railway for freight charges on incoming merchandise; $436.50.
18 *Purchase Invoice*
Received from Budget Oil for gasoline and oil used in the delivery truck; $262.54.
19 *Cheque Copy No. 80*
Issued to P. Kerr, the owner, for personal use; $800.00.
20 *Cheque Copy No. 81 together with Purchase Invoice*
Issued to Ideal Supply in payment of merchandise purchased for cash; $475.00.
21 *Purchase Invoice*
Received from Circle Supply for supplies purchased on account; $267.50.
21 *Purchase Invoice*
Received from Deluxe Stationers for the purchase on account of a new office desk at a cost of $1 053.95 and supplies at a cost of $224.70; total $1 278.65.
24 *Memorandum from Owner*
To the effect that the company has borrowed $5 000 from the bank effective immediately.
26 *Cheque Copy No. 82*
Issued to Empire Wholesale on account; $400.00.
26 *Purchase Invoice*
Received from Prairie Manufacturing for the purchase of merchandise on account; $750.00.
26 *Cash Receipt*
Received from R. Stoddard on account; $300.00.
27 *Cheque Copy No. 83*
Issued to M. Cham for wages; $585.00.
27 *Cheque Copy No. 84*
Issued to D. Adams for wages; $650.00.
31 *Sales Invoice No. 168*
Issued to Purity Company for the sale of merchandise on account; $540.00 plus $37.80 sales tax; total $577.80.

Chapter 13

SYNOPTIC JOURNAL

DATE		CUSTOMER/SUPPLIER	REF. NO.	BANK DR	BANK CR	ACCOUNTS RECEIVABLE DR	ACCOUNTS RECEIVABLE CR
19— May	4	Cash Sale	57	273 92			
	5	P. Rogan	165			440 84	
	6	Empire Wholesale					
	7	Deluxe Stationers	74		235 40		
	7	Arrow Realty	75		800 —		
	10	A. Baldwin	76		173 50		
	10	English & Co.	77		500 —		
	11	R. Mayotte		352 —			352 —
	11	P. Fuhr		620 —			620 —
	13	M. Cham	78		585 —		
	13	D. Adamo	79		650 —		
	14	M. Delgaty	166			209 72	
	14	Carl Holm	167			256 80	
	17	Continental Railway					
	18	Budget Oil					
	19	P. Kerr	80		800 —		
	20	Ideal Supply	81		475 —		
	21	Circle Supply					
	21	Deluxe Stationers					
	24	Continental Bank		5000 —			
	26	Empire Wholesale	82		400 —		
	26	Prairie Manufacturing					
	26	R. Stoddard		300 —			300 —
	27	M. Cham	83		585 —		
	27	D. Adams	84		650 —		
	31	Purity Company	168			571 80	
				6545 92	5853 90	1485 16	1272 00

Figure 13.2 Synoptic journal with entries for one month.

Section 13.1 **417**

MONTH OF _May_ 19___ PAGE _41_

ACCOUNTS PAYABLE DR	ACCOUNTS PAYABLE CR	SALES OR INCOME CR	PURCHASES DR	SALES TAX PAYABLE CR	OTHER ACCOUNTS ACCOUNT	P.R.	DR	CR
		256 —		17 92				
		412 —		28 84				
	816 —		816 —					
					Supplies		235 40	
					Rent		800 —	
173 50								
500 —								
					Wages		585 —	
					Wages		650 —	
		196 —		13 72				
		240 —		16 80				
	436 50				Freight-in		436 50	
	262 54				Delivery Exp.		262 54	
					Drawings		800 —	
			475 —					
	267 50				Supplies		267 50	
	1278 65			224 70	Office Equip.		1053 95	
					Bank Loan			5000 —
400 —								
		750 —		750 —				
					Wages		585 —	
					Wages		650 —	
		540 —		37 80				
1073 50	3811 19	1644 00	2265 70	115 08			6325 89	5000 00

Balancing the synoptic journal

```
Debits     0 •  T
6 5 4 5 • 9 2  +
1 4 8 5 • 1 6  +
1 0 7 3 • 5 0  +
2 2 6 5 • 7 0  +
6 3 2 5 • 8 9  +

1 7 6 9 6 • 1 7  T
- - - - - - - - - - - -
```

```
Credits    0 •  T
5 8 5 3 • 9 0  +
1 2 7 2 • 0 0  +
3 8 1 1 • 1 9  +
1 6 4 4 • 0 0  +
  1 1 5 • 0 8  +
5 0 0 0 • 0 0  +

1 7 6 9 6 • 1 7  T
- - - - - - - - - - -
```

Balancing the Columnar Journal

At the bottom of every journal page, and at the end of every month, a procedure called cross balancing is performed on the synoptic journal, or on any columnar journal. **Cross balancing** is the process of checking the grand total of all the debit columns against the grand total of all of the credit columns to make sure that the two grand totals agree. The steps in cross balancing a columnar journal are described below. Refer to Figure 13.2 as you study these steps.

1. Immediately beneath the last entry on the page, and in ink, draw a single ruled line across all money columns of the journal.
2. Separately, total (foot) each money column and write in the total in small pencil figures just beneath the single ruled line. You will recall that these tiny pencil figures are known as pencil footings or pin totals.
3. Using a printing calculator, separately add all the pin totals of the debit columns and all the pin totals of the credit columns. Include all columns of the journal. These two sums should yield the same grand total. The journal is in balance if the two sums are the same. The journal is out of balance if the two sums are not the same. A journal out of balance indicates that at least one error has been made in its preparation. You may not proceed to the posting of the journal until all errors have been located and corrected.
4. When the journal is balanced, write in the column totals in ink immediately beneath the pin totals.
5. In ink, draw a double ruled line across all money columns immediately beneath the inked-in column totals.

Forwarding in the Columnar Journal

A new journal page is started at the beginning of each month. Also, during the month, a new page must be started whenever a page is filled up. When a new page is started during the month, it is customary to start it off with the balanced totals from the bottom of the previous page. The totals at the end of one page are "forwarded" to the next page. This procedure is illustrated in Figure 13.3.

Section 13.1   419

A SYNOPTIC PAGE JUST COMPLETED

SYNOPTIC JOURNAL										MONTH OF June 19—		Page 30	
DATE	PARTICULARS	BANK DR	BANK CR	ACCS REC'L DR	ACCS REC'L CR	ACCS PAY'L DR	ACCS PAY'L CR	SALES CR	PCH'S DR	S. TAX PAY'L CR	OTHER ACCOUNTS ACCOUNT	PR / DR	CR
Jun 3	G. Peltier			11				10		1			
26	R. Buie	55						50		5			
26	T. Jacobs		20			20							
26	T. C. Realty		100								Rent	100	
27	Gen'l Supply					120			120				
28	C. Wang	15			15								
29	P. Sax		12						12				
30	R. Sloan			55				50		5			
	Forwarded	850	790	410	505	370	420	850	790	85		280	50

Totals on the last line of the old page become the starting figures for the new page. In this way totals are accumulated for the entire month.

Starting line of new page has same date as last line of old page.

THE NEW PAGE BEING STARTED

SYNOPTIC JOURNAL										MONTH OF June 19—		Page 31	
DATE	PARTICULARS	BANK DR	BANK CR	ACCS REC'L DR	ACCS REC'L CR	ACCS PAY'L DR	ACCS PAY'L CR	SALES CR	PCH'S DR	S. TAX PAY'L CR	OTHER ACCOUNTS ACCOUNT	PR / DR	CR
Jun 30	Forwarded	850	790	410	505	370	420	850	790	85		280	50

"Forwarded" is written.

Chapter 13

SYNOPTIC JOURNAL									MONTH OF June, 19 –			Page 30	
DATE	PARTICULARS	BANK		ACCS REC'L		ACCS PAY'L		SALES	PCH'S	OTHER ACCOUNTS			
		DR.	CR.	DR.	CR.	DR.	CR.	CR.	DR.	ACCOUNT	PR.	DR.	CR.
Jun. 3	Y. Peltier			10				10					
7	R. Buie	65						65					
8	S. Katz		50							Rent Exp.		50	
10	J. Jones		7			7							
12	W. Bye							15	15				
14	S. Black	9			9								
16	J. Thompson			12				12					
18	V. Jackson		14			14							
20	A. Adams						30	30					
21	B. Yon	4				4							
23	M. Carter	6						6					
25	D. Davidson			11				11					
30	S. Sloan		8							Car Exp.		8	
		84	79	33	13	21	45	104	45			58	

Bank
84 | 79

Accs Rec'd
33 | 13

Accs Pay'l
21 | 45

Capital

Drawings

Mdse Inventory

Equipment

Bank Loan

Sales
| 104

Purchases
45 |

Car Expense
8 |

Rent Expense
50 |

Figure 13.4 Posting the synoptic journal (simplified).

Posting the Synoptic Journal

Let us recall some facts about posting in general before discussing how to post the synoptic journal. First, posting to the general ledger is done once a month. Therefore, the synoptic journal is posted once a month because it is posted to the general ledger. Second, posting to the subsidiary ledgers is done directly from source documents. The subsidiary ledger posting is done daily by an accounting clerk not involved with the general ledger.

Posting the synoptic journal requires a different procedure because it is a multi-columnar journal. The basic procedure is illustrated in Figure 13.4, using a simplified example. Study the example carefully, and observe that:

- the synoptic journal is balanced before posting is begun;
- for each of the "special" columns, the column totals are posted rather than the individual amounts within the columns. By posting only the totals, a great deal of time is saved;
- the Other Accounts section lists items that are generally unrelated. Therefore, the individual amounts contained within the columns in this section have to be posted separately. Posting the Other Accounts section of the synoptic journal is very similar to posting from a two-column general journal.

Formal Technique for Posting the Synoptic Journal

Figure 13.5 below shows an example of formal posting from the synoptic journal. Observe the following details:

- the entries in the accounts are dated with the last day of the month;

- "Sn" or "SN" and the journal page number are used in the accounts when cross-referencing;

- the following rules apply when cross-referencing in the journal:
   a. the account number is entered in brackets immediately beneath the column total being posted;
   b. for items in the Other Accounts section, the account number is entered in the Posting Reference column beside the amount being posted;

- the account balances are not calculated until all the postings are completed.

The synoptic journal after being posted entirely, with the posting reference numbers entered, appears as shown in Figure 13.6.

SYNOPTIC JOURNAL (Partial)

SYNOPTIC JOURNAL							
DATE	PARTICULARS	CHQ NO.	BANK DR.	BANK CR.	ACCOUNTS REC'L DR.	ACCOUNTS REC'L CR.	
19— May 4	Cash Sale		56 —				
5	Paul Boxer				112 —		
6	Empire Wholesale						
7	Deluxe Stationers	74		37 20			
7	Arrow Realty	75		400 —			
31	Purity Company				96 —		
			1 627 —	2 550 90	627 —	571 —	
			1 627 —	2 550 90	628 —	571 —	
			(1)	(1)			

GENERAL LEDGER (Two accounts only)

Account **Bank** No. 1

Date	Particulars	P.R.	Debit	Credit	DR. CR.	Balance
19— Mar. 31	Balance brought forward	—			DR	1 351 40
Apr. 30		Sn 41	1 630 20			
30		Sn 41		1 264 19	DR	1 717 41
May 31		Sn 42	1 627 —			
31		Sn 42		2 550 90		

Figure 13.5 Formal posting from the synoptic journal. The illustration shows only three postings involving two ledger accounts.

Section 13.1   423

MONTH OF May 19 — Page 42

ACCOUNTS PAY'L			SALES	PURCH'S	Supplies	OTHER ACCOUNTS			
DR.	CR.	NO.	CR.	DR.	Dr	ACCOUNT	P.R.	DR.	CR.
		57	56 —						
		165	112 —						
	316 —			316 —					
					37 20				
						Rent Expense	58	400 —	

			168	96 —						
319	70	1 094 22		684 —	776 —	153 20			2 396 22	1 000 —
319	70	1 094 22		684 —	776 —	153 20			2 396 22	1 000 —

Account Rent Expense   No. 58

Date	Particulars	P.R.	Debit	Credit	DR. CR.	Balance
19— Apr. 30	Balance brought forward	—			DR	800 —
May 31		Jn42	400 —			

SYNOPTIC JOURNAL

DATE	PARTICULARS	CHQ. NO.	BANK DR.	BANK CR.	ACCOUNTS REC'L DR.	ACCOUNTS REC'L CR.
19— May 4	Cash Sale		56 —			
5	Paul Boyer				112 —	
6	Empire Wholesale					
7	Deluxe Stationers	74		37 20		
7	Arrow Realty	75		400 —		
10	A. Baldwin	76		73 50		
10	G. English & Co.	77		46 20		
11	R. Smith		96 —			96 —
11	F. Jones		375 —			375 —
13	M. Field	78		312 —		
13	R. French	79		285 —		
14	M. Birch				250 —	
14	Y. Ash				170 —	
17	Continental Railway					
18	Budget Oil					
19	G. Ripley	80		300 —		
20	Ideal Supply	81		300 —		
21	Circle Supplies					
21	Deluxe Stationers					
24	Crescent Bank		1 000 —			
26	Empire Wholesale	82		200 —		
26	Prairie Mfg.					
26	R. Stoddard		100 —			100 —
27	M. Field	83		312 —		
27	R. French	84		285 —		
31	Purity Company				96 —	
			1 627 —	2 550 90	628 —	571 —
			1 627 —	2 550 90	628 —	571 —
			(1)	(1)	(2)	(2)

Figure 13.6 Synoptic journal showing posting references.

Section 13.1

MONTH OF May 19— Page 42

ACCOUNTS PAY'L DR.	ACCOUNTS PAY'L CR.	NO.	SALES CR.	PURCH'S DR.	Supplies Dr	OTHER ACCOUNTS ACCOUNT	PR.	DR.	CR.
		57	56 —						
		165	112 —						
	316 —			316 —					
					37 20				
						Rent Expense	56	400 —	
73 50									
46 20									
						Wages Expense	58	312 —	
						Wages Expense	58	285 —	
		166	250 —						
		167	170 —						
	87 50					Freight-in	55	87 50	
	64 72					Delivery Exp.	53	64 72	
						Ripley Drugs	32	300 —	
				300 —					
	46 —				46 —				
	420 —				70 —	Office Equip	9	350 —	
						Bank Loan	22		1 000 —
200 —									
	160 —			160 —					
						Wages Exp.	58	312 —	
						Wages Exp.	58	285 —	
		168	96 —						
319 70	1 094 22		684 —	776 —	153 20			2 396 22	1 000 —
319 70	1 094 22		684 —	776 —	153 20				
(21)	(21)		(41)	(51)	(4)				

Two-Journal System

Generally, accounting offices make use of both the synoptic journal and the two-column general journal. The synoptic journal is used by a junior employee to record the routine transactions of the business. The two-column general journal is used by a senior accounting person to record entries of a non-routine, and usually more complex, nature.

In a two-journal system each journal is prepared independently of the other. At the end of every month, each of the journals is posted separately to the general ledger. If the general ledger does not balance, the search for errors must include both journals. The chart below illustrates the process.

TWO-LEDGER SYSTEM

```
Routine                                              Non-routine
transactions    ┌─────────┐      ┌──────────┐       transactions
recorded        │Synoptic │      │Two-column│       recorded
by              │Journal  │      │ General  │       by
junior          └─────────┘      │ Journal  │       senior
accounting                       └──────────┘       accounting
clerk                                                clerk
                    │                 │
                 (Posted)          (Posted)
                    │                 │
                    └────┬────────────┘
                    ┌─────────┐
                    │ General │
                    │ Ledger  │
                    └─────────┘
```

Variations in Journalizing in the Synoptic Journal

1. Debit entries may be entered in Credit columns and credit entries may be entered in Debit columns, but they must be circled, or written in red. This special treatment of an entry indicates that its effect in the column is the opposite to that specified in the column heading. When the column is totaled, the circled item must be subtracted to give the proper total. A refund or a credit invoice would be handled in this way.

2. Most accounting entries require only one line in the synoptic journal. However, there are times when two or more lines may be required. This occurs when at least

two of the accounts affected by the transaction need to be entered in the Other Accounts section of the journal.

These two variations are illustrated below in Figure 13.7.

SYNOPTIC JOURNAL											MONTH OF August 19___			PAGE 96
DATE	CUSTOMER SUPPLIER	REF. NO.	BANK		ACCOUNTS RECEIVABLE		ACCOUNTS PAYABLE		SALES OR INCOME CR	PURCHASES DR	SALES TAX PAYABLE CR	OTHER ACCOUNTS		
			DR	CR	DR	CR	DR	CR				ACCOUNT	PR	DR	CR
Aug 4	M. Hicks (Refund)	1262		16371					(153-)		(1071)			
9	Midwest Oil									568 17		Light & Heat		230 05
												Car Expense		338 12

Figure 13.7 Variations in recording in the synoptic journal.

Section Review Questions

1. The two-column general journal is mostly used for what type of transaction?
2. For what type of transaction are the specialized journals used?
3. Define "multi-columnar" journal.
4. Why does each line of the synoptic journal usually balance?
5. Explain how the synoptic journal saves time when entries are posted.
6. For which items are special columns set up in the synoptic journal?
7. Explain how to balance a synoptic journal.
8. Explain how to forward the synoptic journal.
9. Explain how to cross-reference in the synoptic journal.
10. Why is a general journal usually used along with a synoptic journal?
11. Describe how to record a debit entry in a credit column. How is the entry handled when the columns are being totaled?
12. Explain why some accounting entries require more than one line in the synoptic journal.

Section Exercises

1. **Indicate whether each of the following statements is true or false by entering a "T" or an "F" in the space indicated in your workbook. Explain the reason for each "F" response in the space provided.**

    1. A non-routine transaction is one that is out of the ordinary.
    2. The synoptic journal is ideally suited to a large company.
    3. A synoptic journal is a multi-columnar journal.
    4. In the synoptic journal there would be a special column for Sales Tax Payable because it is a frequently occurring item.
    5. The headings in a synoptic journal are always the same as those shown in the textbook.

6. The main advantage of the synoptic journal is time saved in journalizing transactions.
7. An advantage of the synoptic journal is that it is not necessary to balance the accounting entry for every transaction.
8. The synoptic journal is balanced at the end of every month and at the end of every page.
9. The accuracy of the synoptic journal is checked by cross balancing.
10. The synoptic journal should be cross balanced before the final totals are inked in and the journal ruled off.
11. It is customary to forward the totals from one page of the synoptic journal to the next.
12. The total of the Other Accounts debit section is posted as a debit to the general ledger.
13. The postings from the synoptic journal are dated the last day of the month.
14. No cross-referencing is necessary when using a synoptic journal.
15. A two-journal system provides a different route for non-routine transactions.
16. A debit amount can be entered in a credit column if it is circled.
17. Every entry in the synoptic journal takes only one line.

2. **On page 19 of the synoptic journal of Donway Distributing, record the transactions listed below for the month of August, 19--. Add sales tax of seven per cent on all sales of merchandise. Use the following chart of accounts.**

DONWAY DISTRIBUTING
Chart of Accounts
101 Bank
105 Accounts Receivable
110 Merchandise Inventory
115 Supplies
120 Building
121 Accumulated Depreciation—Building
125 Office Equipment
126 Accumulated Depreciation—Office Equipment
201 Accounts Payable
205 Bank Loan
210 Sales Tax Payable
215 Mortgage Payable
305 A. Orlando—Capital
310 A. Orlando—Drawings
405 Sales
505 Purchases
510 Freight-in
515 Advertising
520 Building Maintenance
525 Car Expense

530 Interest and Bank Charges
535 Light and Heat
540 Miscellaneous Expense
545 Telephone
550 Wages

Transactions

August

2   *Cheque Copy No. 702*
    —To D. Macdonald; for painting of the business premises; $856.00.

3   *Sales Invoice No. 210*
    —To N. Rae; sale of goods on account; $184.00 plus sales tax.

3   *Cash Receipt*
    —From Viceroy Homes; on account; $150.00.

5   *Cheque Copy No. 703*
    —To T. Vint; for wages; $290.00.

5   *Cash Sales Slip No. 91*
    —To M. Franci; cash sale of merchandise; $85.00 plus sales tax.

8   *Cheque Copy No. 704*
    —To Cash; for cash purchase of postage stamps; $320.00. (Cashed by an employee who purchased the stamps.)

8   *Sales Invoice No. 211*
    —To Atlas Stores; sale of goods on account; $502 plus sales tax.

9   *Purchase Invoice*
    —From Diamond Wholesalers; merchandise purchased on account; $925.00.

10 *Purchase Invoice*
    —From Continental Railway; for freight charges on incoming goods; $315.00.

11 *Cash Sales Slip No. 92*
    —To J. Vincent; cash sale of merchandise; $150.00 plus sales tax.

12 *Cheque Copy No. 705*
    —To Vance Brothers; on account; $300.00.

12 *Cheque Copy No. 706*
    —To T. Vint; for wages; $290.00.

15 *Cheque Copy No. 707*
    —To *Century News*; for newspaper advertisement; $42.00.

15 *Cheque Copy No. 708*
    —To A. Orlando; for owner's personal use; $300.00.

18 *Cash Sales Slip No. 93*
    —To A. Anderson, cash sale of merchandise; $55.00 plus sales tax.

19 *Cheque Copy No. 709*
—To Merry Manufacturing; on account; $500.00.

19 *Cheque Copy No. 710*
—To T. Vint; for wages; $290.00.

19 *Cash Receipt*
—From J. Regnault; on account; $200.00.

22 *Cheque Copy No. 711*
—To Trade Group; mortgage instalment; $356.75 ($285.20 is debt reduction; $71.55 is interest expense).

22 *Sales Invoice No. 212*
—To T. Schmidt; sale of goods on account; $170.00 plus sales tax.

23 *Purchase Invoice*
—From Deluxe Oil Company; $240.00 ($180.00 for business use; $60.00 for personal use by owner).

24 *Bank Debit Advice*
—From General Bank; for service charge; $42.00.

25 *Cheque Copy No. 712*
—To A. Orlando; for owner's personal use; $500.00.

26 *Cash Sales Slip No. 94*
—To K. Beka; cash sale of merchandise; $110.00 plus sales tax.

26 *Cheque Copy No. 713*
—To T. Vint; for wages; $290.00.

29 *Purchase Invoice*
—From Federated Supply; for the purchase of merchandise; $1 240.00.

30 *Cheque Copy No. 714*
—To Public Utilities Commission; for hydro charges for month; $146.00.

31 *Sales Invoice No. 213*
—To Brian Keep; sale of goods on account; $190.00 plus sales tax.

31 *Cash Receipt*
—From J. Klassen; on account; $400.00.

After recording the transactions do the following:
1. Cross balance and rule the journal.
2. Summarize the postings that would be made to the general ledger. List the information in three columns: Account; Debit Amount; Credit Amount. Show that the postings are balanced by totaling the two money columns.

---

3. This exercise also appears in your workbook.
Shown below, in condensed form, are the synoptic journal and the T-account general ledger of Plastic Products, owned by Jean Webb.

1. Post the synoptic journal to the general ledger. Ignore dates and cross-references. Use check marks to indicate that postings are completed.
2. Take off a general ledger trial balance.

Synoptic Journal

DATE	PARTICULARS	BANK DR	BANK CR	ACCS REC'L DR	ACCS REC'L CR	ACCS PAY'L DR	ACCS PAY'L CR	SALES CR	PCH'S DR	S. TAX PAY'L CR	OTHER ACCOUNTS ACCOUNT	PR	DR	CR
Jun 20	Forwarded	1800	1450	2150	1970	1270	1350	1750	1460	160				
23	Laine	55						50		5				
23	Moors		60								Rent		60	
24	Park			110				100		10				
25	Reid	80			80									
25	Ruel		250					250						
25	Sacerty		20								Telephone		20	
26	Bass							150	150					
26	Clayton							300	300					
27	Delski		40								Wages		40	
27	Eady							90			Car Exp		90	
27	Green		70								Freight		70	
27	Hock	400			400									
30	Klaus		230			230								
30	McCoy	88						80		8				
30	Nagy			77				70		7				
30	Perry			44				40		4				
		2423	2120	2381	2450	1750	1890	2090	1910	194			280	

General Ledger

Bank	Accounts Receivable	Mdse. Inventory	Supplies
70	350	900	100

Equipment	Accum. Depr.—Equipment	Bank Loan	Accounts Payable
2 000	500	1 000	150

Sales Tax Payable	J. Webb, Capital	J. Webb, Drawings	Sales
300	2 520	500	4 500

Purchases	Freight-in	Bank Charges	Car Expenses
2 000	100	40	500

General Expense	Rent	Telephone	Utilities
90	300	50	1 220

Wages
750

4. **Workbook Exercise:** Posting the synoptic journal to a simple ledger.

13.2 The Five-Journal System

The synoptic journal described in the previous section is suitable only for a very small business or organization. The reason is that only one person at a time can work on it. Most businesses soon grow to a point where more than one person needs to be involved

Source Documents

Five Journals

Cash Register Slips, Cash Sales Slips, Bank Credit Memos, Cash Receipts Lists → *All transactions that directly cause an increase in the bank balance.* → **Cash Receipts Journal**

Charge Sales Slips, Sales Invoices, Credit Invoices Issued → *All sales of merchandise on account.* → **Sales Journal**

Cheque Copies, Bank Debit Memos → *All transactions that directly cause a decrease in the bank balance.* → **Cash Payments Journal**

Purchase Invoices, Credit Invoices Received → *All transactions involving the buying of any type of goods or services on account.* → **Purchases Journal**

Other Source Documents → *All transactions that do not fit into the other four journals.* → **General Journal**

POSTING → **General Ledger**

Note: Subsidiary Ledgers maintained independently.

Figure 13.8 Basic structure of the five-journal system.

in the journalizing process. Systems using more than one journal have been developed for this reason. The five-journal system is such a system.

The **five-journal system** is one in which five separate journals are operated at the same time, each journal restricted to a particular type of transaction. The basic structure of the five-journal system is illustrated in Figure 13.8. As you can see, the accounting entries are channelled from the various source documents into the five separate journals. Each journal is restricted to a particular type of transaction. Each of the journals is posted individually to the general ledger. As before, the subsidiary ledgers are posted independently from separate copies of the source documents.

There are two main advantages to using a number of journals. The first is that doing so allows several people to be involved in the journalizing process at the same time. The second is that it makes the accounting system more efficient by allowing specialization of duties among the staff. The five-journal system inevitably leads to the accounting clerks becoming specialists within the system. Large offices may require a specialist for each journal. Smaller offices often find that one person can handle two journals very well. A natural relationship exists between sales and cash receipts. There is also a natural relationship between purchases and cash payments. These pairs make very effective units of work within the accounting department.

Learning to operate the five-journal system is not going to be difficult for you. You will find no difference in the general journal. Also, each of the new "special" journals is a columnar journal similar in concept to the synoptic journal. The real difference lies in the fact that all of the routine transactions do not go into a single journal. Instead, they are channelled into one of four special journals.

Cash Receipts Journal

The **cash receipts journal** is used to record all transactions that directly increase the bank balance. Every accounting entry in the cash receipts journal involves a debit to Bank. The two most common transactions in the cash receipts journal are "cash sales" and "receipts on account."

A partially completed page from a typical cash receipts journal is shown below in Figure 13.9. It was prepared from the source documents listed below.

Transactions

February
- 4   *Cash Sales Slip No. 64*
      Issued to R. Lentz; merchandise $118.00; sales tax $8.26; total $126.26.
      Cash Sales Slip No. 65
      Issued to M. Reid; merchandise $78.25; sales tax $5.48; total $83.73.
- 5   *Cash Receipts*
      Received from T. Song on account; $500.00.
      Received from P. Yurick on account; $160.50.
- 6   *Cash Sales Slip No. 66*
      Issued to G. Ostrum; merchandise $105.00; sales tax $7.35; total $112.35.

Chapter 13

    6   *Cash Receipt*
         Received from K. Pape on account; $106.47.
    7   *Bank Credit Advice*
         Received from Centennial Bank; for interest earned; $725.00.
    8   *Cash Sales Slip No. 67*
         Issued to C. Drew; merchandise $85.25; sales tax $5.97; total $91.22.

Special Considerations

- The cash receipts journal is a columnar journal and follows the rules for all columnar journals.
- Cash sales go in the cash receipts journal. Sales on account go in the sales journal. If a sale is partly for cash and partly on account, it goes into the cash receipts journal.

CASH RECEIPTS JOURNAL   MONTH OF *Feb* 19____   PAGE 16

DATE	PARTICULARS	OTHER ACCOUNTS DR ACCOUNT	P.R.	AMOUNT	SALES TAX PAYABLE CR	SALES CR	ACCOUNTS RECEIVABLE CR	REF. NO.	BANK DR
Feb 4	R. Lentz				8 26	118 —		64	126 26
4	M. Reid				5 48	78 25		65	83 73
5	F. Song						500 —		500 —
5	P. Yurich						160 50		160 50
6	G. Ostrum				7 35	105 —		66	112 35
6	K. Pape						106 47		106 47
7	Centennial Bank	Interest Inc.		725 —					725 —
8	C. Drew				5 97	85 25		67	91 22

Figure 13.9 A partially completed page of a cash receipts journal.

Sales Journal

The **sales journal** is used to record all transactions involving the sale of merchandise on account. Transactions related to sales on account are the only ones entered in the sales journal. The source documents for entries to the sales journal are sales invoices, credit invoices, and charge sales slips.

   A partially completed page from a sales journal is shown below in Figure 13.10. It was prepared from the following transactions.

Transactions

February
    5   *Sales Invoice No. 652*
         Issued to R. Rau; merchandise $59.00; sales tax $4.13; total $63.13.
        Charge Sales Slip No. 125
         Issued to L. Sauve; merchandise $84.50; sales tax $5.92; total $90.42.

6   Credit Invoice No. 653
    Issued to C. Myzk for unsatisfactory merchandise returned; merchandise $145.00; sales tax $10.15; total $155.15.
    Sales Invoice No. 654
    Issued to R. Halfmoon; merchandise $245.85; sales tax $17.21; total $263.06.
7   Charge Sales Slip No. 126
    Issued to H. Didyk; merchandise $110.25; sales tax $7.72; total $117.97.
8   Sales Invoice No. 655
    Issued to A. Han; merchandise $65.00; sales tax $4.55; total $69.55.

Special Considerations

SALES JOURNAL			MONTH OF _____ 19 ___			PAGE ___
DATE	PARTICULARS	REF NO.	SALES TAX PAYABLE CR		SALES CR	ACCOUNTS RECEIVABLE DR
Feb 5	R. Rau	652	4 13		59 —	63 13
5	L. Sauve	125	5 92		84 50	90 42
6	C. Myzk (credit)	653	(10 15)		(145 —)	(155 15)
6	R. Halfmoon	654	17 21		245 85	263 06
7	H. Didyk	126	7 72		110 25	117 97
8	A. Han	655	4 55		65 —	69 55

Figure 13.10   A partially completed page of a sales journal.

Cash Payments Journal

The **cash payments journal** is used to record all transactions that directly decrease the bank balance. Every accounting entry in the cash payments journal results in a credit to Bank. The most common type of transaction recorded in the cash payments journal involves the issuing of a cheque. Cheques may be issued for a number of reasons.

Figure 13.11 below shows a partially completed page of a cash payments journal. The journal was prepared from the following transactions.

Transactions

February

3   Cheque Copies
    No. 72; issued to Collins Bros. on account; $250.00.
    No. 73; issued to Taylor Company on account; $550.00.

4   **Bank Debit Advice**
Received from Centennial Bank; for bank service charges; $54.65.
Cheque Copies
No. 74; issued to B. Sims for wages; $650.21.
No. 75; issued to C. Tett for wages; $702.35.

5   **Cheque Copies**
No. 76; issued to D. Wedow, the owner, for personal use; $1 000.
No. 77; issued to Harbour Trade Centre for the cash purchase of merchandise for resale; $905.65.
No. 78; issued to Kyro's Supply; for the cash purchase of supplies; $323.73.
No. 79; Issued to Superior Engineering; a down payment on the purchase of equipment costing $5 029.00; $1 000.

Special Considerations

- The cash payments journal is sometimes called the cash disbursements journal.
- The cash payments journal follows the rules for columnar journals.
- Purchases for cash go in the cash payments journal. Purchases on account go in the purchases journal. A purchase that is partly paid for by cash goes in the cash payments journal.

CASH PAYMENTS JOURNAL   MONTH OF *Feb* 19____   PAGE *19*

DATE	PARTICULARS	OTHER ACCOUNTS DR			WAGES DR	PURCHASES DR	ACCOUNTS PAYABLE DR	REF. NO.	BANK CR
		ACCOUNT	P.R.	AMOUNT					
Feb 3	Collins Bros.						250 —	72	250 —
3	Taylor Company						550 —	73	550 —
4	Centennial Bank	Bank Charges		54 65					54 65
4	B. Sims				650 21			74	650 21
4	C. Tett				702 35			75	702 35
5	D. Wedow	Drawings		1000 —				76	1000 —
5	Harbour Trading					905 65		77	905 65
5	Kyro's Supply	Supplies		323 73				78	323 73
5	Superior Engin'g	Equipment		5029 —			4029 —	79	1000 —

Figure 13.11   A partially completed page of a cash payments journal.

Purchases Journal

The **purchases journal** is used to record all transactions involving the buying of goods or services on account. Every accounting entry in the purchases journal results in a credit to Accounts Payable. The suppliers' invoices are the source documents for entries in the purchases journal.

A partially completed page of a purchases journal is shown in Figure 13.12. The journal was prepared from the following transactions.

Transactions

February

3   *Purchase Invoice*
    Received from Williams Equipment; for repairs to warehouse equipment; $562.50.

4   *Purchase Invoice*
    Received from Acklands; for warehouse and office supplies; $762.58.
    Purchase Invoice
    Received from Pascoe's; for items charged to miscellaneous expense; $145.36.

5   *Purchase Invoice*
    Received from Reliable Trading; for merchandise for resale; $2 500.00.
    Purchase Invoice
    Received from Mason and Mason; for merchandise for resale; $1 950.00.

6   *Purchase Invoice*
    Received from Grand Trunk Railway; for transportation charges on incoming merchandise; $256.00.
    Purchase Invoice
    Received from Hector Oil Company; for gas and oil used in the company automobiles; $315.62.

Special Considerations

- The purchases journal follows the rules for all columnar journals.
- The accountant for a business may file purchase invoices alphabetically or numerically. Where numeric order is used, a reference number must be placed on every purchase invoice received.

PURCHASES JOURNAL — MONTH OF *Feb* 19___ — PAGE 31

DATE	PARTICULARS	OTHER ACCOUNTS DR ACCOUNT	P.R.	AMOUNT	CAR EXPENSE DR	SUPPLIES DR	PURCHASES DR	REF. NO.	ACCOUNTS PAYABLE R
Feb 3	Williams Equip.	Bldg. Mntnce		562 50					562 50
4	Acklands					762 58			762 58
4	Pascoes	Misc. Exp.		145 36					145 36
5	Reliable Trading						2500 —		2500 —
5	Mason & Mason						1950 —		1950 —
6	Grand Trunk Rwy	Freight-in		256 —					256 —
6	Hector Oil				315 62				315 62

Figure 13.12 A partially completed page of a purchases journal.

Posting in the Five-Journal System

The four special journals must be balanced and ruled before they can be posted at the end of each month. The procedure for balancing a columnar journal was learned in the previous section. Basically, you must add the debit column totals, add the credit column totals, and see that the two sums are the same. If the sums are equal, the journal is ruled and ready for posting.

You have known for some time how to post the general journal. You have just learned how to post a columnar journal. This is almost all that you need to know to post in the five-journal system.

Each journal is posted separately but the order in which they are posted does not matter. No attempt to balance the ledger should be made until all five journals have been posted.

There is no change in the way subsidiary ledgers are handled. They are still posted directly from copies of source documents and are balanced against their control accounts monthly.

Cross-Referencing

When several journals are used it becomes necessary to identify them specifically by means of a code. For example, page seventeen of the general journal is identified as GJ17. Each of the several journals is given its own simple code as follows.

Journal	Code
Cash Receipts	CR
Cash Payments	CP
Sales	S
Purchases	P
General	GJ or J
Synoptic	SN or Sn

The sample account shown below in Figure 13.13 uses the new coded posting references in an account.

ACCOUNT	Accounts Receivable					No. 2	
DATE	PARTICULARS	PR	DEBIT		CREDIT	Dr/Cr	BALANCE
19— Mar. 31	Balance Forwarded	—				Dr	6474 07
31		S67	1304 7 25				
31		C-74			1209 6 40		
31		J19			42 42	Dr	7382 50

Figure 13.13 A ledger account showing the journal codes.

Section Review Questions

1. Why is the synoptic journal suitable only for a small business or organization?
2. Describe the five-journal system.
3. Give the two main advantages of using a number of journals.
4. Describe the types of transactions that go in each of the four special journals.
5. What are the two most common transactions that are entered in a cash receipts journal?
6. How do you handle a sale that is partly on account and partly for cash?
7. Why is a "general" section not needed in the sales journal?
8. Every accounting entry in the cash payments journal has one common element. What is it?
9. Give another name for the cash payments journal.
10. What is the source document for all entries in the purchases journal?
11. In what order are the journals posted in a five-journal system?
12. What codes are used for cross-referencing in the five-journal system?

Section Exercises

1. **A list of transactions appears below. From this list select and record those transactions that would be recorded in the cash payments journal.**

   Transactions

   April
   1. The owner, Patricia Sopinka, increased her equity in the business by depositing her personal cheque for $1 000 in the business bank account.
   2. Issued cheque No. 40 to J. Chekov for the cash purchase of supplies, $155.15.
   3. Issued sales invoice No. 70 to M. Kosir. This was for the sale of merchandise of $180 plus sales tax of seven per cent.
   5. Received a purchase invoice from Sue Brown Manufacturing for the purchase of merchandise, $791.80.
   8. Issued cheque No. 41 to Chong Supply Co. for the cash purchase of merchandise, $342.40.
   9. Received a cheque from Carol Padovik on account, $350.
   10. Issued cheque No. 42 to Municipal Hydro for the cash purchase of electricity for one month, $78.
   12. Received a purchase invoice from District Supply for the purchase of supplies, $450.47.
   15. Issued cheque No. 43 to Sharon Maki Wholesale on account, $750.
   17. Issued sales invoice No. 71 to Carole's Catering. This was for the sale of merchandise of $250 plus sales tax of seven per cent.
   19. Received a debit memo from the bank for service charges for one month, $54.00.
   22. Received a memo from the owner stating that she had collected $200 on account from P. Walker but had used the money for her personal use.

24 Cash sales slip No. 72 was issued for the cash sale of merchandise, $85 plus sales tax of $5.95.
25 Issued cheque No. 44 for the cash payment of the telephone bill for one month $45.
30 Issued cheque No. 45 to Projects Inc. on account, $1 000.

Cross balance the journal.

2. **State in which of the five journals each transaction below would be recorded.**

   Transactions
   1. A cheque is issued to a supplier on account.
   2. A purchase invoice is received from a supplier of merchandise.
   3. A cheque is received on account from a customer.
   4. A cash sale is made to a customer.
   5. A sale on account is made to a customer.
   6. A cheque is issued to the owner for his personal use.
   7. A cheque is issued to pay the wages for the period.
   8. A sales invoice is issued.
   9. A correcting entry is made to transfer a debit amount from the Supplies account to the Miscellaneous Expense account.
   10. A cheque is issued to pay for a cash purchase of merchandise.
   11. A bank debit advice for a service charge is received.
   12. A cheque is issued to a supplier on account.
   13. A cheque is issued to pay for the monthly rent.
   14. A bank debit advice is received with respect to an NSF cheque.
   15. A bank credit advice is received with respect to interest earned.
   16. A new typewriter is purchased and a down payment is required. A cheque is issued.
   17. The owner collects a debt from a customer but keeps the money for his personal use.
   18. The owner spends a sum of money out of his own pocket for business purposes and is reimbursed by means of a cheque.

3. 1. **Journalize the transactions shown below in the five journals of Domino Wholesale Company. The accounts for Domino Wholesale Company are as follows:**

   Bank
   Accounts Receivable
   Merchandise Inventory
   Supplies
   Equipment
   Accounts Payable
   Sales Tax Payable
   Anna Popov, Capital
   Anna Popov, Drawings
   Sales

   Purchases
   Freight-in
   Bank Charges
   Delivery Expense
   General Expense
   Light, Heat, and Water
   Postage Expense
   Rent Expense
   Telephone Expense
   Wages Expense

Section 13.2   **441**

Transactions (**Note:** Seven per cent sales tax to be added to all sales)

Date	Source Document	No.	Name	Explanation	Amount
May 1	Cheque copy	75	Morris and Hannah	Rent for May	$425.00
2	Purchase invoice		Grinnelco	Merchandise	378.00
2	Cash receipt		R. Jones	On account	436.80
4	Cash sales slip	97	A. Racicot	Merchandise sold	70.00
4	Information memo			An error was discovered in the general ledger. An amount of $30 which had been debited to General Expense should have been debited to Supplies.	30.00
5	Cheque copy	76	P. Fobert	Wages	275.00
8	Sales invoice	317	C. Perry	Goods sold	215.00
9	Cash receipt		S. Storey	On account	95.00
9	Purchase invoice		Wonder Mfg.	Supplies	110.25
9	Cheque copy	77	A. Popov	Personal use	300.00
10	Purchase invoice		Pressed Fittings	Merchandise	435.75
10	Sales invoice	318	Mercer Company	Goods sold	190.00
11	Cash receipt		R. Russell	On account	200.00
12	Purchase invoice		Newday Supplies	Supplies	210.00
May 12	Cheque copy	78	General Supply	On account	$125.50
15	Purchase invoice		Baldwin's	Supplies	78.75
15	Sales invoice	319	T. Ward	Goods sold	216.00
16	Credit invoice issued	320	C. Perry	Merchandise returned $70 plus $4.90 tax	74.90
16	Cash receipt		R. Grant	On account	150.00
17	Cash sales slip	98	P. Fuhrman	Goods sold	65.00
17	Sales invoice	321	B. Adler	Goods sold	195.00
18	Cheque copy	79	Provincial Treasurer	Sales tax for prior month	497.07
19	Purchase invoice		Continental Railway	Freight-in	96.40
19	Sales invoice	322	G. Nolan	Goods sold	110.00
19	Information memo			An error was detected in the accounts receivable ledger. An amount of $62 which should have been credited to J. Walker's account was credited in error to M. Walker's account.	62.00
22	Cheque copy	80	Bell Telephone	Telephone	52.70

Date	Source Document	No.	Name	Explanation	Amount
22	Cheque copy	81	Baldwin's	Cash purchase of supplies	26.25
23	Sales invoice	323	W. Phillips	Goods sold	280.00
23	Cash sales slip	99	P. Leonard	Goods sold $190 Down payment $50	190.00 50.00
23	Cash sales slip	100	H. Fogh	Goods sold	370.00
24	Credit invoice received		Grinnelco	For goods returned $55 plus tax	58.85
25	Bank debit memo		Western Bank	Bank service charge	34.70
25	Cheque copy	82	A. Popov	Personal use	300.00
26	Cheque copy	83	O.K. Welding	On account	150.00
29	Cheque copy	84	A. Popov	Repaying owner for expenditures that she made for business purposes. Charge: General Expense 35.00 Supplies 110.00	145.00
29	Bank debit memo		Western Bank	NSF cheque of R. Russell	200.00
30	Cheque copy	85	S. Tybo	Wages	300.00
31	Purchase invoice		Jim's Garage	Gas and oil used in the delivery vehicle, $124.80; in the owner's car, $62.50	187.30

2. Balance and rule each of the five journals.

4. Workbook Exercise: Posting and balancing in a five-journal system (simplified).

13.3 Cash Discounts

You are probably already acquainted with cash discounts. They are usually offered on the bills for utilities in the home, such as the water, hydro, gas, or oil bills.

A **cash discount** is a reduction that may be taken off the amount of a bill if payment is made on or before the discount date stated on the bill. The purpose of a cash discount is to encourage the customer to pay promptly. Many businesses, like utility companies, offer cash discounts to their customers.

Terms of Sale

Every business establishes certain terms of sale with its customers. The phrase **terms of sale** refers to the arrangements made with customers as to when the goods or services are to be paid for and whether a cash discount is offered.

There are various terms of sale. The most common ones are outlined below.

Standard Terms of Sale

1. **C.O.D.** Cash on delivery. The goods must be paid for at the time they are delivered.
2. **On Account** or **Charge**. The full amount of the invoice is due at the time the invoice is received but a brief time, usually 25 days, is given to make payment.
3. **30 Days** or **Net 30**. The full amount of the invoice is due thirty days after the date of the invoice.

   60 Days or **Net 60**. The full amount of the invoice is due sixty days after the date of the invoice.
4. **2/10,N/30**. This is read as "two percent, ten, net thirty" or just "Two, ten, net thirty." If the bill is paid within ten days of the invoice date, a cash discount of two per cent may be taken. Otherwise, the full amount of the invoice is due thirty days after the invoice date.

   1/15,N/60. If the bill is paid within fifteen days of the invoice date, a cash discount of one per cent may be taken. Otherwise, the full amount of the invoice is due sixty days after the invoice date.

The terms of sale often depend on the customer's reputation for reliability in paying. A reliable customer of long standing will probably be granted very favourable terms. A new customer, about whom little is known, may be expected to pay cash on delivery, at least for a short time.

The terms of sale are recorded on the sales invoice as shown in Figure 13.14 below. Every time a sale is made and an invoice is sent out, the customer is reminded of the terms for payment. Also, the terms are usually recorded on the customer's account card, so that the credit manager, the sales manager, and other interested people may refer to them easily.

Accounting for Cash Discounts

Accounting for a cash discount begins at the time a credit sale is made to a customer and an invoice offering a cash discount is issued. Examine the invoice shown in Figure 13.14, for which Masthead Marine is the seller and Nanaimo Marina is the buyer.

```
                                                    P.O. Box 298
                    ECHO BAY                        Station 8
                 VANCOUVER, B.C.                    V7C 8P7
                                                    Phone
          MASTHEAD MARINE                           842-9999

         Nanaimo Marina
  SOLD TO 5000 Departure Bay Road    DATE  June 4, 19--
         Nanaimo, B.C.
         V9T  4B9                    TERMS 2/10, n/30
```

QUANTITY	PART NO.	DESCRIPTION	PRICE	AMOUNT
12	HA 346	Tubular Jam Cleat ½ in	$ 3.85	$ 46.20
6	HA 433	Mast Gate Muscle Box	35.95	215.70
12	HA 4872	Shroud Adjuster	12.50	150.00
		Total		$411.90

SALES INVOICE   CUSTOMER'S COPY   NO. 10094

Figure 13.14 A sales invoice with the terms of sale shown.

In the Books of the Buyer (Nanaimo Marina)

The invoice, when received by Nanaimo Marina, becomes a purchase invoice. For this purchase invoice, the following accounting entry is recorded in the purchases journal.

```
                                              DR        CR
   Purchases                                $411.90
         Accounts Payable (Masthead Marine)           $411.90
```

In the T-accounts the effect is:

```
                                    Accounts Payable
        Purchases                   (Masthead Marine)
       _____                  _____
         411.90                            411.90
```

Someone in the accounting department of Nanaimo Marina will be responsible for checking the purchase invoices to see if any discounts are offered. Where discounts are offered, special treatment is necessary to ensure that payment is made within the discount period.

In this case the cheque is made out for $403.66. This amount is arrived at by deducting the two per cent discount ($8.24) from the amount of the invoice ($411.90). The tear-off portion of the cheque will show that the cheque is in payment of invoice No. 10094, and that a discount of $8.24 has been deducted.

From the cheque copy, the following accounting entry is made in the cash payments journal.

	DR	CR
Accounts Payable (Masthead Marine)	$411.90	
Discounts Earned		$ 8.24
Bank		403.66

The cumulative effect of the two transactions in the T-accounts is:

Purchases	Accounts Payable (Masthead Marine)	Bank	Discounts Earned
$411.90	$411.90 | $411.90	$403.66	8.24

Debt eliminated in full

Bank decreased by $403.66

An income account

In the Books of the Seller (Masthead Marine)

From the data on the sales invoice copy, Masthead Marine makes the following accounting entry in the sales journal.

	DR	CR
Accounts Receivable (Nanaimo Marina)	$411.90	
Sales		$411.90

The effect in the T-accounts is:

Accounts Receivable (Nanaimo Marina)	Sales
411.90	411.90

Upon receiving Nanaimo Marina's cheque for $403.66, Masthead Marine includes the cheque on the Daily List of Cash Receipts. A copy of the listing is forwarded to the accounts receivable clerk for posting to the customer's account in the subsidiary ledger. This clerk checks any discounts taken to see that they are calculated correctly and are within the discount period. The customer's account is credited with the gross amount, in this case $411.90.

From the listing an accounting entry is also recorded in the cash receipts journal as follows:

	DR	CR
Bank	$403.66	
Discounts Allowed	8.24	
Accounts Receivable (Nanaimo Marina)		$411.90

After this accounting entry, the cumulative effect in the accounts is:

Accounts Receivable (Nanaimo Marina)	Sales	Bank	Discounts Allowed
411.90 | $411.90	| 411.90	$403.66 |	8.24 |

Paid in full

Received $403.66

An expense account

Additional Cash Discount Facts

1. Occasionally, a customer takes a late discount. In other words, the customer takes the discount after the discount period has passed.

    Business people try to be reasonable when faced with this situation. There may be postal delays to consider. No business wants a reputation for being cheap. At the same time, a business does not want to be taken advantage of by its customers.

    If a business decides to disallow a late discount, the usual practice is to cash the customer's deficient cheque and to credit the customer's account with the amount of the cheque only, not the gross amount. This will leave a small balance in the account. It is good business to write a polite letter requesting the customer to make up the deficiency.

2. The Discounts Earned account is often referred to as the Discounts off Purchases account. The Discounts Allowed account is often referred to as the Discount off Sales account.

3. Every business will try to take advantage of the cash discounts offered by its suppliers. Therefore, entries to the Discounts Earned account can be expected to occur frequently. These entries will normally require a special column when a columnar journal is used.

4. Not all businesses offer cash discounts to their customers. A business that does not offer cash discounts will not have a Discounts Allowed account.

5. Occasionally, an invoice is received on which there is a cash discount, and sometime before the discount date a portion of the goods is returned or an allowance granted. In a case such as this, the usual procedure is to take the discount on the net cost of the goods, that is, the invoice figure less the credit note amount. Also, the discount date is adjusted to start from the date shown on the credit note.

Cash Discounts on the Income Statement

There is more than one way of handling cash discounts on the income statement. The method selected depends on the amount of the discounts and the preference of the accountant. If the amounts involved are small, they might be combined into another account such as Miscellaneous Expense. A more formal method is shown in Figure 13.15 below. When the formal method is used, Discounts Allowed and Discounts Earned are treated as deductions from Sales and from Purchases respectively.

```
                    TRIDENT TRADING CO.
                     INCOME STATEMENT
                 YEAR ENDED DECEMBER 31, 19--

Revenue
  Sales                                              $403 955
  Less Returns and Allowances        $21 151
       Discounts Allowed               5 296          26 447
  Net Sales                                                       $377 508

Cost of Merchandise Sold
  Inventory, January 1                                $ 72 074
  Purchases                           $233 567
  Less Returns and Allowances  $18 356
       Discounts Earned          4 358   22 714
  Net Purchases                                        210 853
  Freight-in                                             5 731
  Merchandise Available for Sale                      $288 658
  Less: Inventory, December 31                          83 562     205 096
     Gross Profit                                                 $172 412

Operating Expenses
  Advertising                                         $  1 141
  Bank Charges                                           2 651
  Car Expenses                                           4 999
  Delivery Expense                                       1 377
  Depreciation—Equipment                                 2 490
  Depreciation—Automobiles                               3 850
  Insurance Used                                         2 915
  Light and Heat                                         3 988
  Miscellaneous Expense                                  1 507
  Rent                                                  12 000
  Salaries                                              24 000
  Supplies Used                                          2 560
  Telephone                                              1 850
  Wages                                                 48 220     113 548
     Net Income                                                   $ 58 864
```

Figure 13.15 The income statement of Trident Trading Co. including discounts allowed and discounts earned.

Section Review Questions

1. Define "cash discount."
2. Define "terms of sale."
3. Why would a business sell goods C.O.D.?
4. Why would the buying firm accept C.O.D. as the terms of sale?
5. What does the term "Net 30" mean?
6. What does the term "2/10,N/30" mean?
7. Where would the customer see the terms of sale for a transaction?
8. Where could the manager of a business see the terms of sale for any customer?
9. How does a business ensure that cash discounts are taken when available?
10. Which account—Discounts Allowed or Discounts Earned—is associated with a sales transaction?
11. What is another name for Discounts Allowed?
12. What is another name for Discounts Earned?
13. A business may not have an account for Discounts Allowed. Explain why.
14. Assume that there is a sales transaction followed by a sales return, and that there is a discount offered. On what figure is the discount calculated? On what date does the discount period begin?
15. Where does "discounts allowed" appear on the income statement?
16. Where does "discounts earned" appear on the income statement?

Section Exercises

1. Complete the following schedule by calculating the amount of the payment that is necessary in each case. Where credit notes are involved assume that the discount period is adjusted to start from the date on the credit note.

Date of Invoice	Amount of Invoice	Terms of Sale	Amount of Credit Note	Date of Credit Note	Date Payment is Made	Amount of Payment Required
Mar 12	$ 52.50	2/10, n/30	—	—	Mar 20	
May 18	47.25	Net 30	—	—	May 27	
Sep 4	115.50	3/15, n/60	—	—	Oct 10	
Feb 6	1 050.00	1/20, n/60	$126.00	Feb 18	Mar 6	
Oct 19	588.00	2/10, n/30	42.00	Nov 5	Nov 27	
Aug 27	882.00	2/15, n/60	168.00	Sep 7	Sep 10	

2. Complete the following schedule by calculating the date that payment is required to pick up the discount, and the amount of the payment required.

Date of Invoice	Amount of Invoice	Terms of Sale	Amount of Credit Note	Date of Credit Note	Date Payment is Required	Amount of Payment Required
May 14	$147.00	2/10, n/30	–	–		
Apr 15	315.00	3/20, n/60	$42.00	May 1		
Jun 3	220.05	2/10, n/60	78.75	Jun 20		
Nov 20	59.25	2/15, n/60	36.75	Dec 2		

3. 1. a. In two-column general journal form, record the accounting entry for the invoice shown below in the books of Circle Supply.

```
900 Park Street                                    Maple City
              Circle ◯ Supply

SOLD TO: Watson Construction
         1500 Randell Road
         Maple City  X3Y 7N5     INVOICE NUMBER 715
DATE August 3, 19--              TERMS 2/10, n/30
```

Quantity	Description	Unit Price	Amount
10 boxes	#10 Woodscrews	$5.50	$55.00
2	Standard Crowbars	4.10	8.20
			63.20
	5% Sales Tax		3.16
			$66.36

b. On August 12 a cheque in the amount of $65.03 is received from Watson Construction. In two-column general journal form, show the accounting entry to be recorded in the books of Circle Supply.

1. Watson Construction charges the merchandise shown on the above invoice to an account called Small Tools and Supplies. Show the journal entries for the above two transactions that will be made in the books of Watson Construction. Use appropriate dates.

4. 1. a. In the books of Circle Supply, in two-column general journal form, show the accounting entry to be recorded for the invoice below.

Circle Supply
900 Park Street — Maple City

SOLD TO: Jackson and Jackson
Marmora Road
Maple City X3Y 6T8

INVOICE NUMBER 873
DATE September 3, 19--
TERMS 2/10, n/30

Quantity	Description	Unit Price	Amount
100	General Purpose Connectors	$1.00	$100.00
	5% Sales Tax		5.00
			$105.00

b. Some of the goods are found to be inadequate and are returned for credit. The following credit invoice is issued. Show the accounting entry in general journal form to record this credit invoice in the books of Circle Supply. Circle Supply does not use a Returns and Allowances account.

Circle Supply
900 Park Street — Maple City

SOLD TO: Jackson and Jackson
Marmora Road
Maple City X3Y 6T8

CREDIT INVOICE NUMBER 891
DATE September 9, 19--

Quantity	Description	Unit Price	Amount
10	General Purpose Connectors (Ordered on Invoice #873)	$1.00	10.00
	5% Sales Tax		.50
			10.50

c. On September 19, a cheque is received in full payment of the sales invoice, less the credit invoice, less the cash discount. Show the accounting entry in general journal form to record the receipt of this cheque.

2. Record the accounting entries to be made for the above transactions in the books of Jackson and Jackson. Use appropriate dates. The goods affect the Supplies account.

CHAPTER HIGHLIGHTS

Now that you have completed Chapter 13, you should:

1. understand the advantages of a multi-columnar journal;
2. be able to journalize, cross balance, post, and forward in a synoptic journal;
3. know the advantages of the synoptic journal;
4. understand the reason for a two-journal system;
5. know the variations in journalizing in the synoptic journal;
6. understand the advantages of the five-journal system;
7. be able to journalize and post in the five-journal system;
8. understand the purpose of offering a cash discount;
9. know the accounting entries for discounts earned and discounts allowed;
10. know how discounts earned and discounts allowed are presented on the income statement.

ACCOUNTING TERMS

C.O.D.
cash discount
cash payments journal
cash receipts journal
cross balancing
five-journal system

multi-columnar journals
purchases journal
sales journal
synoptic journal
terms of sale

CHAPTER EXERCISES

Using Your Knowledge

1. Indicate whether each of the following statements is true or false by placing a "T" or an "F" in the space indicated in your workbook. Explain the reason for each "F" response in the space provided.

1. The general journal is not normally used if the business has a synoptic journal.
2. There is a special column for every general ledger account in the synoptic journal.
3. The chief disadvantage of the synoptic journal is that you have to post column totals.
4. An accounting entry that takes more than one line cannot be recorded in the synoptic journal.
5. There would be a special column for Rent Expense in the synoptic journal.
6. The synoptic journal is balanced at the end of every page.
7. The date used when formally posting the synoptic journal is the last day of the month.
8. A credit to Sales in the synoptic journal would normally be entered in the Other Accounts credit column.
9. All sales of merchandise are recorded in the sales journal.
10. The cash payments journal is also known as the cash disbursements journal.
11. Additional cash invested in the business by the owner would be recorded in the general journal.
12. A bank debit advice requires an entry in the cash receipts journal.
13. The five-journal system inevitably leads to the clerks becoming specialists within the system.
14. The general ledger would not balance if only four of the five journals were posted.
15. A purchase partly for cash and partly on account would be recorded in the purchases journal.

2. Two columns of a synoptic journal are totaled incorrectly, but the errors offset each other. The total of the Sales column is $2 000 more than it should be, and the total of the Accounts Receivable credit column is $2 000 less than it should be.
   1. What will be the effect on the accounts? On the ledger? On income? On total assets?
   2. How might the errors be detected?

3. Before posting to the general ledger, the equality of the debit and credit column totals in the journals should be proved. Suppose that this was not done, and that the total of a column in the cash receipts journal was incorrectly added by $100.
   1. How would this error first be discovered?
   2. What steps would normally be followed to find the cause of the error?

4. M. Lunney Co. has two bank accounts, one with a balance on deposit of $100 000 and one, for payroll, which is overdrawn by $5 000. The bank charges interest on the $5 000.
   Is the bank's practice fair? Explain.

5. N. Howard conducts a small retail business. At the time of a sale she collects the tax from the customer but makes no attempt to distinguish on her books between the amount of the sale and the amount of the sales tax. In her entries involving cash sales she debits Cash and credits Sales for the total amount.

Chapter Exercises 453

1. If Howard's total sales for the month amount to $52 500, how much sales tax would she remit to the provincial treasurer of the rate if the rate of tax is five per cent? Assume that all sales are taxable.
2. What entry would be made to record the sales tax?

6. Bob Jarvis, the accountant for Wright Brothers, sets up an accounting system to eliminate the accounts receivable and accounts payable ledgers. All invoices owing to creditors and all invoices due from customers are kept in separate file folders until paid. When invoices are paid, they are removed from the customers' and creditors' files and placed in a file for paid invoices. At the end of the month the unpaid files are totaled and these totals agreed with the balances in the control accounts in the general ledger.
   What advantages and disadvantages are there to such a system?

7. Shoe store owner D. Mugami made approximately 300 credit sales and 100 credit purchases each month. Mr. Mugami recorded all these sales and purchases in a general journal. A friend asked him why he did not use a sales journal and a purchases journal. Mr. Mugami replied that he did not understand their use. He believed that they simply divided the work among several people. Since he did his own accounting, he had no need for these special journals.
   Is division of labour the only reason for using special journals? Explain.

8. A review of the accounting records of Nixon Co. disclosed the following errors.
   1. Cash received from H. Latimer for $285.00 was entered correctly in the cash receipts journal, but posted to the accounts receivable ledger as $258.00.
   2. An invoice for forty-five cartons at $1.75 each shipped to Best Drug Store was extended and entered in the sales journal as $87.75.
   3. Cash of $65.00 was entered correctly in the cash receipts journal as received from M. Smith, but was posted in the accounts receivable ledger to the account of M. Smythe.
   4. The footings of the "Purchases" column in the cash payments journal were overstated by $100.
   5. A cheque for $150 payable to G. Graham for legal fees was entered incorrectly in the cash payments journal as $160. The journal has not yet been posted.
   Show how these errors should be corrected, giving journal entries where applicable.

9. 1. Give the accounting entries in general journal form for each of the following source documents as they would be made in the books of Circle Supply. Circle Supply uses Returns and Allowances accounts.

   2. Give the accounting entries in general journal form for each source document as they would be made in the books of Kitchen Cabinetry. The Supplies account is to be charged for the goods.

Invoice 802

Circle Supply
900 Park Street — Maple City

SOLD TO: Kitchen Cabinetry
East Side Road
Maple City   X3Y 4H2

INVOICE NUMBER 802

DATE Aug. 9, 19--   TERMS 2/10, n/30

Quantity	Description	Unit Price	Amount
1 Ctn	#35 Copper Wire	$65.00	$ 65.00
24	Propane Torch Refills	5.95	142.80
			$207.80
	5% sales tax		10.39
			$218.19

Credit Invoice 851

Circle Supply
900 Park Street — Maple City

SOLD TO: Kitchen Cabinetry
East Side Road
Maple City   X3Y 4H2

DATE Aug. 17, 19--

CREDIT INVOICE NUMBER 851

Quantity	Description	Unit Price	Amount
	Credit to correct price on Propane Torch refills		
24	Propane Torch Refills	5.95	$142.80
	Should be		
24	Propane Torch Refills	5.35	128.40
			$14.40
	5% Sales Tax		.72
			$15.12

Check No. 1001

Kitchen Cabinetry
MAPLE CITY

No. 1001
August 26, 19--

PAY TO THE ORDER OF Circle Supply $ 199.01

One Hundred and Ninety-nine-------------------01/100 DOLLARS

CENTENNIAL BANK
MAPLE CITY BRANCH

A. B. Ames
KITCHEN CABINETRY

⑈142⑈004⑈ 054 ⑈03003⑈

IN PAYMENT OF THE FOLLOWING

Invoice #802		$218.19
Credit Invoice #851		15.12
	Net	$203.07
2 percent discount		4.06
		$199.01

KITCHEN CABINETRY

No. 1001

10. Prepare an income statement from the following partial work sheet.

Work Sheet   Superior Trading Company   Year Ended December 31, 19--

Accounts	Income Statement Dr	Income Statement Cr	Balance Sheet Dr	Balance Sheet Cr
Bank				
Accounts Receivable				
Merchandise Inventory	44 323.40	43 750.00		
Supplies				
Prepaid Insurance				
Equipment				
Accumulated Depreciation—Equipment				
Automobiles				
Accumulated Depreciation—Automobiles				
Accounts Payable				
Sales Tax Payable				
Bank Loan				
Grace Strom, Capital				
Grace Strom, Drawings				
Sales		201 245.50		
Sales Returns & Allowances	4 102.00			
Purchases	73 219.20			
Purchases Returns & Allowances		5 625.00		
Freight-in	1 501.00			
Advertising	1 426.00			
Bank Charges	2 247.00			
Car Expenses	8 135.00			
Delivery Expense	5 535.20			
Discounts Allowed	3 525.24			
Discounts Earned		1 023.65		
General Expense	1 505.15			
Light and Heat	1 785.25			
Rent	12 000.00			
Telephone	1 052.25			
Wages	46 056.35			
Supplies Used	2 203.00			
Insurance Used	2 075.00			
Depreciation—Equipment	2 500.00			
Depreciation—Automobiles	4 000.00			
	217 191.04	251 644.15		
Net Income	34 453.11			
	251 644.15	251 644.15		

Comprehensive Exercises

11. F. Dunn is the sole proprietor of Crest Hardware in Iona, N.S. He operates the store with the assistance of his wife and some occasional part-time help. Mrs. Dunn works in the store and is also responsible for all direct aspects of accounting. The financial statements are prepared annually from her records by a professional accountant.

The books of account are very simple and consist of a general ledger, an accounts receivable ledger, an accounts payable ledger, and a synoptic journal. The last page used in the synoptic journal is page 72.

Most of the sales of the business are cash sales or C.O.D. sales. The rate of sales tax is seven per cent. The cash receipts are deposited in the bank on a daily basis. All payments are made by cheque.

The number of accounts in both subsidiary ledgers is very small. Mr. Dunn grants credit to only a few customers and buys his stock from only a few suppliers. Because of the small number of debtors and creditors the subsidiary ledger routine is very simple. All transactions are recorded in the synoptic journal and the postings to the subsidiary ledgers are made directly from the source documents.

The three ledgers of Crest Hardware are set up in the workbook from the following trial balances.

CREST HARDWARE
TRIAL BALANCE
JUNE 30, 19--

Account	Debit	Credit
101 Bank	$ 12 400.00	
105 Accounts Receivable	13 365.25	
110 Merchandise Inventory	46 090.20	
115 Supplies	1 395.00	
120 Store Equipment	20 906.00	
121 Accumulated Depreciation—Store Equipment		$ 12 000.00
130 Delivery Equipment	19 500.00	
131 Accumulated Depreciation—Delivery Equipment		6 000.00
201 Accounts Payable		10 265.35
205 Sales Tax Payable		2 240.00
210 Loan Payable—Federal Finance		8 550.85
301 F. Dunn Capital		71 952.08
302 F. Dunn Drawings	6 000.00	
401 Sales		48 585.50
505 Delivery Expense	5 258.00	
510 Freight-in	956.23	
515 General Expense	2 953.10	
520 Purchases	14 120.00	
525 Rent Expense	2 400.00	
530 Wages Expense	14 250.00	
	$159 593.78	$159 593.78

CREST HARDWARE
ACCOUNTS RECEIVABLE TRIAL BALANCE
JUNE 30, 19--

R. Lai (Invoice 1407)	$ 4 072.15
G. Langford (Invoice 1431)	6 316.20
R. Potts (Invoice 1436)	2 976.90
	$13 365.25

CREST HARDWARE
ACCOUNTS PAYABLE TRIAL BALANCE
JUNE 30, 19--

City Hardware Supply (Their Invoice No. 17421)	$ 6 742.10
Special Steel Products (Their Invoice No. 147A)	3 523.25
	$10 265.35

1. **Record the journal entries in the synoptic journal for the transactions listed below. Post to the subsidiary ledgers on a daily basis. No names are recorded in the synoptic journal for cash sales.**

Transactions

July

2 *Cash Sales Slip* No. 206
—$216.00 plus sales tax.
Sales Invoice
—No. 1475, to R. Lai, $190.00 plus sales tax.
Purchase Invoice
—No. 18021, from City Hardware Supply, $1 264.25, for purchase of merchandise.

3 *Cash Sales Slip* No. 207
—$102.00 plus sales tax.
Cash Receipt
—From R. Lai, $4 072.15 on account.

5 *Cash Sales Slip* No. 208
—$55.00 plus sales tax.

6 *Cash Sales Slip* No. 209
—$350.00 plus sales tax.
Cheque Copy
—No. 316, to R. Niosi, $98, wages for part-time help.

7 *Cash Sales Slip* No. 210
—$140.00 plus sales tax.
Purchase Invoice
—No. 18340, from City Hardware Supply, $2 316.25, for purchase of merchandise.

Cheque Copies
—No. 317, Special Steel Products, $500, on account.
—No. 318, City Hardware Supply, $6 742.10 paying No. 17421.
—No. 319, F. Dunn, $250, drawings.

9 *Cash Sales Slip* No. 211
—$260.00 plus sales tax.

10 *Cash Sales Slip* No. 212
—$75.00 plus sales tax.
Sales Invoice
—No. 1476, to G. Langford, $590 plus sales tax.

12 *Cash Sales Slip* No. 213
—$40.00 plus sales tax.
Purchase Invoice
—No. 192A, Special Steel Products, $375.00 for purchase of merchandise.
Cheque Copy
—No. 320, to J. Sacco, $100 wages for part-time help.

13 *Cash Sales Slip* No. 214
—$250.00 plus sales tax.
Cheque Copy
—No. 321, to Special Steel Products, $3 023.25 balance of 147A.

14 *Cash Sales Slip* No. 215
—$185.00 plus sales tax.
Sales Invoice
—No. 1477, to R. Potts, $311.00 plus sales tax.
Purchase Invoice
—No. 1244, from Clix Oil Company, $275.00 for gasoline and oil used in the delivery truck.
Cheque Copies
—No. 322, F. Dunn, $150, drawings.
—No. 323, to Provincial Treasurer, $2 240.00, paying sales tax for previous month.

16 *Cash Sales Slip* No. 216
—$175.00 plus sales tax.
Cash Receipt
—From G. Langford, $6 316.20 in payment of invoice No. 1431.

17 *Cash Sales Slip* No. 217
—$225.00 plus sales tax.
Purchase Invoice
—No. 344, Joe Jay Transport, $375.15, charges for transportation on incoming merchandise.

19 *Cash Sales Slip* No. 218
—$240.00 plus sales tax.

Cheque Copy
—No. 324, to Oak Investments, $400, for the rent for the month.

20 *Cash Sales Slip* No. 219
—$142.00 plus sales tax.

21 *Cash Sales Slip* No. 220
—$264.00 plus sales tax.
Cheque Copy
—No. 325, to F. Dunn, $250, drawings.

23 *Cash Sales Slip* No. 221
—$89.00 plus sales tax.
Sales Invoice
—No. 1478, to R. Lai, $311.00 plus sales tax.
Cheque Copies
—No. 326, to D. Phin, $75 part-time wages.
—No. 327, to Public Utilities Commission, $176.10 cash payment of electricity and water bills.
—No. 328, to City Telephone Company, $149.00 cash payment of telephone bill.

24 *Cash Sales Slip* No. 222
—$248.00 plus sales tax.
Cash Receipt
—From R. Lai, $203.30, invoice No. 1475.

26 *Cash Sales Slip* No. 223
—$55.00 plus sales tax.
Cheque Copy
—No. 329, to City Hardware Supply, $1 264.25, for invoice No. 18021.

27 *Cash Sales Slip* No. 224
—$80.00 plus sales tax.

28 *Cash Sales Slip* No. 225
—$343.00 plus sales tax.
Cheque Copy
—No. 330, to F. Dunn, $250, drawings.
Purchase Invoice
—No. 18472, from City Hardware Supply, $350.00 for store supplies.

2. **Balance the synoptic journal.**
3. **Post the synoptic journal to the general ledger.**
4. **Balance the general ledger.**
5. **Balance the subsidiary ledgers.**

12. **Workbook Exercise: Journalizing, posting and balancing with five journals and three ledgers.**

13. **Workbook Exercise: Locating and correcting errors in a five-journal system.**

14. Record the following selected transactions of Wholesale Food Distributors in general journal form. In working out your answers, bear in mind the following:

   a. A few of the transactions are dependent on previous ones.
   b. Wholesale Food Distributors maintains separate accounts for Purchases Returns and Allowances and for Sales Returns and Allowances.
   c. The amounts of certain cheques (receipts and expenditures) have been left for you to decide.

Transactions

November

3   *Sales Invoices*
   —No. 962, Palmer's Grocery, $496.26; terms, 2/10,n/30; add five per cent sales tax.
   —No. 963, Grey's Market, $376.14; terms, 2/10,n/30; add five per cent sales tax.
   —No. 964, Alec's Groceteria, $197.26; terms, 2/10,n/30; add five per cent sales tax.

4   *Cheque Copy*
   —No. 404, to D. K. Knight, $100, loan to an employee to help her overcome a personal hardship.

5   *Purchase Invoice*
   —No. 213, from Gordon Canners, $1 260, dated Nov. 2; terms 3/20,n/60, for merchandise purchased.

6   *Bank Debit Note*
   —From City Bank, $75.10, cheque returned NSF from Doyle's Grocery.

7   *Cheque Copy*
   —No. 412, to Outboard Motor Sales, $425; instructions from J.D. Doan, the owner, to pay for a new outboard motor delivered to her cottage for personal use.

8   *Purchase Invoice*
   —No. 5698, from Elmer Canners, $1 050; for merchandise purchased; terms, Net 60 days, dated Nov. 6.

10 *Credit Note Received*
   —No. 445, from Gordon Canners, $147, dated Nov. 9; allowance granted on invoice No. 213 for incorrect goods.

10 *Cheque Copy*
   —No. 443, to Petty Cash, to replenish petty cash as per the following summary of charges:
   Travelling Expense $12.92
   Delivery Expense   40.89
   Building Maintenance   26.14
   Miscellaneous Expense   16.19

11 *Cheque Copy*
   —No. 447, to Jane Brown's, $475, to pay for C.O.D. delivery of a new office desk.

12   *Cash Receipt*
     —Cheque of Grey's Market, paying sales invoice No. 963.
     Credit Note Issued
     —No. 1007, to Palmer's Grocery, $56.70 including five per cent sales tax, for defective merchandise returned; discount period adjusted to begin on November 12.
14   *Credit Note Received*
     —No. 565, from Burlington Fruit Growers Association, $2 332.80, correcting their invoice No. 412, which was issued incorrectly in the amount of $2 592 instead of $259.20. (Note: This is neither a ''return'' nor an ''allowance.'')
18   *Cheque Copy*
     —No. 474, to G. Simcoe, $47.25; cash refund for defective merchandise that had been returned, $45, sales tax, $2.25.
22   *Cash Receipt*
     —Cheque from Palmer's Grocery, paying invoice No. 962 and credit note No. 1007 less discount.
25   *Cheque Copy*
     —No. 491, to Gordon Canners, paying sales invoice No. 213 and credit note No. 445 less discount.
26   *Cheque Copy*
     —No. 497, to Elmer Canners, paying invoice No. 5698.
30   *Cash Receipt*
     —Cheque from Alec's Groceteria, paying sales invoice No. 964.

For Further Thought

15. **Briefly answer the following questions.**
    1. Northern Contracting is a small company with fewer than a dozen employees. The formal accounting of Northern Contracting is performed by a public accountant. The owner and his wife do the clerical routines. Why would the public accountant not be expected to perform the clerical routines? Specifically, name the tasks that the owners would probably have to do themselves.
    2. Pet World and Salon uses a synoptic journal in which no columns for accounts receivable are provided. Give a reason for omitting these columns.
    3. In the synoptic journal, there is no column for Sales debit. A debit entry to sales may be entered in the Sales credit column provided that it is circled. How else could the debit entry to sales be recorded?
    4. After cross balancing the synoptic journal, an accountant found (by good fortune) that one of the totals was incorrect. How then could the journal have cross balanced?
    5. A very small business uses a synoptic journal. This business does not have independent clerks to maintain subsidiary ledgers, nor does it prepare copies of source documents for posting to subsidiary ledgers. Suggest a system of posting to subsidiary ledgers for this business.

6. A company which uses a synoptic journal sold goods to a customer for cash and issued a cash sales slip. When recorded in the synoptic journal, the sales slip was entered in the Accounts Receivable debit column. Would the synoptic journal cross balance? How might the error be detected?
7. You are taking over as the accountant for a small company which has been using only a two-column general journal. You have decided to change to a two-journal system including a synoptic journal. How would you go about selecting the headings for the columns?
8. The accountant for ABC Company was physically disabled and was not able to write small. Inked-in totals beneath pin totals were an impossibility for her. However, she knew only too well the need for testing to see that the journal was in balance before inking in the totals. Suggest an alternative procedure for this accountant.
9. The new bookkeeper for XYZ Company did not know about forwarding the synoptic journal during the month. At the end of May there were five independently balanced pages of the synoptic journal. How would you handle this situation?
10. The owner of a business at one time did the bookkeeping for the business and understood the system perfectly. On one occasion, she came to inform the present bookkeeper that she had collected money from a customer for a cash sale but had pocketed the money. The bookkeeper was temporarily absent and so the owner recorded the transaction herself. In what journal would she record the transaction? How much would the choice of journals matter?
11. An accounting clerk entered a sale on account in the general journal. What difficulties might this action create?
12. The text states that a natural relationship exists between sales and cash receipts. Explain this statement.
13. Assume that five different people look after the five different journals in a five-journal system. Would it be better for each of the five to be involved in the posting or to assign the task to one individual? Explain.
14. There could be more than five journals in an accounting system. Name one other journal that would be a sensible addition to the system.
15. The textbook and workbook do not have many columns in their columnar journals. This is because the sizes of the pages are limited. In real situations more columns would be desirable. In what two ways could an accountant obtain journal pages with more columns?
16. You have just posted the cash payments journal but have not yet done the cash receipts journal. You notice that the Bank account has a credit balance. Is this a problem? Explain.
17. An accounting clerk posts the Discounts Allowed figure of $185 from the cash receipts journal to the debit side of the Discounts Earned account. Will this cause the ledger to be out of balance? Will this produce an incorrect net income figure, and if so, by how much?
18. Some accountants prefer to account for cash discounts on purchases in a way different from that described in the text. When a cash discount is allowed on a purchase, it is calculated immediately and deducted on the invoice in order to

arrive at a net purchase figure. The accounting entry for the transaction is recorded at this net figure. Consequently:
a. For a $100 purchase of merchandise, with a two per cent discount, what will the accounting entry be?
b. If the discount period is ten days and payment is made on time, what will the accounting entry be to record the payment?
c. If payment is not made within the discount period, how much must be paid?
d. Figure out the accounting entry for question **c** above.
e. The accounting entry in question **d** above reveals an important piece of information. What is it? Explain.

CASE STUDIES

Case 1 *No Journal!*

Assume that you have just taken a job with Goodwood Construction as a senior accounting clerk. You are somewhat surprised by the accounting system Goodwood uses, described below. In your previous position you had become accustomed to the traditional five-journal system.

Goodwood does not use a traditional purchases journal or cash payments journal. In fact, Goodwood does not use a journal for these transactions. Here is the system used by Goodwood:

1. when a purchase invoice is received, it is verified in all respects;

2. no entry is made in a journal. Instead, the cheque to pay the purchase invoice is prepared. A simplified example of the type of cheque used is shown below;

cheque →

Date __August 14__ 19 __--__   No. 176

Pay to the order of __General Supply Company__

The sum of __One Thousand, Seven Hundred and Six__ /100 Dollars

$ __1 706.00__   Signature __R. Main__

stub →

Accounting Summary

	Purchases	$1 506.49
	Supplies	157.20
	Car Expenses	42.31
	Total	$1 706.00

3. the original cheque and the cheque copy are forwarded to the accounting department;
4. the cheque itself is filed temporarily until time for payment arrives. Payment is looked after by another employee;
5. the cheque copies are accumulated by the month in a two-hole binder. This file of cheque copies is used for reference purposes during the month;
6. at the end of the month the file of cheque copies becomes the basis for one grand accounting entry for all the cheque copies. The procedure is to go through the file a number of times, each time making an addition of one particular item. For example, all of the purchases might be added the first time through, all of the supplies the second time through, and on the third pass, all of the car expenses. Eventually all the individual charges are subtotaled by account. The grand total of all the individual subtotals, of course, has to balance with the total of all the cheques. It is not an easy process because there is a lot of room for making errors. One grand accounting summary is eventually prepared. An example is shown below.

```
        ACCOUNTING SUMMARY
           CHEQUE COPIES
        MONTH OF AUGUST, 19--

   Purchases              $25 326.12
   Supplies                 2 568.21
   Car Expenses             4 352.78
   —                             $$
   —                             $$
   —                             $$
   —                             $$
   —                             $$
   Total                   $42 158.63

   Total Cheques           $42 158.63
```

The above summary is used as the source document for one accounting entry to record all the cheque copies for the month. The large, compound entry is recorded in the general journal. The entry is made as if all the cheques were paid even though many of them would still be on hand.

Questions
1. Why would a system like this be used?
2. What difficulties or inconveniences can you see in such a system?
3. How should the cheque copies be filed? Is there a need for more than one file?

4. How should the cheques not issued be dealt with at the month end? At statement time?
5. What is your general impression of the system? Would you adopt it? Give reasons.
6. Give a name to this system.

Case 2 *Squeeze Play*

Highway Construction is a firm that builds major roads and highways. Its contracts frequently involve substantial sums of money. Consequently, its accounts receivable and accounts payable are quite sizeable.

Highway Construction obtains large quantities of raw materials, supplies, and services from numerous smaller companies. These are always purchased on credit, and the amounts of money involved are usually considerable. Individual bills of $100 000 or more are not uncommon. At the time of purchase, Highway Construction always agrees to the supplier's terms of sale. These terms usually request payment within thirty days with no discounts.

In road construction, cash inflows are often slow and irregular. As a result, Highway Construction makes no attempt to adhere to the terms laid down by the suppliers. It pays its debts when its own cash position is good. Often, the suppliers have to wait for as long as ninety to a hundred days.

Small suppliers can seldom afford to wait a hundred days for customers to pay large sums of money. Small suppliers have their own debts to pay, and payrolls to meet. Therefore, Lequita Adkins, the chief accountant for Highway Construction, receives many telephone calls urgently requesting immediate payment of overdue accounts.

Lequita is experienced at dealing with these suppliers. Over the years she has worked out a neat scheme for handling their request for payment. First, she expresses surprise that the supplier did not know that Highway Construction always takes 90 days to pay its suppliers. Lequita then goes on to say that the only exception to this policy is if a supplier offers a two per cent cash discount. The supplier is usually desperate for the money and agrees to the two per cent discount, which at the time may seem trivial.

Lequita Adkins claims that she makes money for Highway Construction with this scheme, even if she has to borrow the money at fifteen per cent to make the payment. She says that she can back up the claim with calculations.

Questions
1. Is Lequita Adkins a sharp businessperson? Explain.
2. Is Lequita's policy an ethical one?
3. On a bill for $200 000, how much is a two per cent discount?
4. Is Lequita correct when she states that she makes money for the company with this scheme? Prove your answer with a calculation.

Case 3 Crook or Saint?

R. C. Bews was obsessed with building his business. He had started out by using an inheritance to establish a small paving company. Since then, R. C. had fashioned Bews Construction Limited into one of the major road construction companies in Ontario.

R. C. was a man of mixed temperament. He was often pleasant and kind, but he could be ruthless in business. R. C. could fire an employee without a twinge of conscience. His workers quickly learned not to waste a penny.

If performance is judged by profit alone, R. C. was a good businessperson. Between 19–1 and 19–9, Bews Construction Limited's net income was never lower than $500 000 (before income tax). In two of those years, it was over $1 000 000.

Bews Construction was located in Toronto, Ontario. Metropolitan Toronto is a major city; its population then was over two million. The surrounding area, consisting of a number of counties, had an equivalent population. Four million people drive a lot of cars, and require a great many well-maintained roads and highways. Road and highway construction and maintenance is a function of government. Therefore, the bulk of Bews Construction Limited's business was with city, county, and provincial government departments.

R. C. always tried to foster good relationships with each government employee that he dealt with, whether a major executive or simply a project inspector on the site. R. C. wined and dined these employees, and also made sure that he was in a position to grant them favours. He always made it a point to have extra tickets for the big hockey or baseball game. If a theatre attraction was sold out, R. C. could always find an extra pair of tickets for a grateful executive. He kept a long Christmas list of civic employees. The least important recipients were given bottles of liquor, while the most important received colour television sets. Rarely was a gift refused. During the hot summer months, a very comfortable lakefront cottage, complete with boat and car, was kept fully stocked and available for important officials.

R. C. claimed to be an honest man who expected nothing in return for his generosity. The gifts merely expressed his appreciation for the past friendship and cooperation of the recipient. The gifts also allowed him to share his prosperity with those people who had innocently contributed to the growth and development of his company.

Questions

1. Was R. C. a good businessperson?
2. What is your opinion of his policy of giving favours?
3. Is this policy consistent with his attitude toward his own employees?
4. Do you believe R. C.'s claim that there are no strings attached to his gifts? Discuss.
5. Suggest some advantages that R. C. might gain from his policy.
6. Are there any unfair income tax advantages to the company? To the recipients of the gifts?
7. If you had to express R. C.'s policy in one word, what would it be?

Case 4 Does the Business Come First?

J. C. Macdonald loved cars. He was lucky enough to own a Studebaker dealership, Macdonald Studebaker, during the years when that car enjoyed great popularity. During these peak years, Macdonald Studebaker became a large and very prosperous concern.

J. C. used some of his profits from Macdonald Studebaker to purchase a small specialty machine shop called Specialty Fittings. This company manufactured stainless steel fittings designed to meet the sanitation needs of the dairy and brewery industries.

Although J. C. owned Specialty Fittings outright, he left its management to hired executives. J. C. limited his own involvement to a weekly visit of one or two hours. This way, he could devote most of his time to his first love, the car business.

After a few years the Studebaker became less popular. Macdonald Studebaker made fewer sales and lower profits. Eventually, the business faced bankruptcy. After a series of substantial losses, Macdonald Studebaker had heavy debts and a severe shortage of cash. Meanwhile, the fortunes of Specialty Fittings were on an upswing. Good management and a good product combined to push Specialty Fittings ahead year after year.

J. C. began to draw funds out of Specialty Fittings and to put them into the ailing Macdonald Studebaker. At first this presented no problem to Specialty Fittings. However, as J. C.'s demands for cash persisted, Specialty Fittings also began to experience financial problems.

The accountant for Specialty Fittings, Ken Bond, was seriously upset by J. C.'s actions. Ken believed that J. C. was "pouring good Specialty money down the Studebaker sewer." To curtail J. C.'s withdrawals, Ken began to juggle the accounting records so that Specialty Fittings would seem to have less money than it really had. Ken did not steal the money. He kept it safely tucked away in a secret bank account, out of the reach of J. C. Macdonald.

Eventually, the company's auditors discovered Ken's activities. They had no alternative but to report their findings to J. C. Three hours after learning about the deception, J. C. Macdonald fired Ken Bond.

Questions
1. As a businessperson what was J. C. Macdonald's problem?
2. Did Ken Bond have a moral right to protect the company for which he worked?
3. Was there an alternative approach that Ken Bond could have taken?
4. Should Ken have been fired?
5. Was there an alternative approach that J. C. Macdonald could have taken?

CAREER
Rita Sacello / Vice-President of Finance

During her high school years, Rita Sacello was involved in several school activities; not only was she an active participant in athletics, she was also involved with a junior achievement club. The experience Rita obtained, and the exposure to marketing, finance and accounting the club provided, combined to arouse her interest in the business environment.

After finishing high school, Rita Sacello completed her Bachelor of Arts degree with a major in finance. This program included a number of accounting courses.

After graduation, Rita started working as a bookkeeper for Emerson Electric, a large manufacturer of electric motors. She enjoyed the work so much she decided to study towards a professional accounting degree. She enrolled in the Society of Management Accountant's (CMA) program and completed her courses at night while working full time in the day.

Rita has since worked her way up from bookkeeper to the positions of accountant, credit manager, office manager, controller, accounting manager, and finally to vice-president of finance.

In her position as accountant, Rita controlled all the special journals used: the sales journal, cash receipts journal, purchases journal, cash payments journal, and the general journal. She supervised the postings of these journals to the general ledger and the subsidiary ledgers.

As the controller of the company, Rita gained experience in a wide variety of accounting responsibilities, including cost accounting, pricing, controlling the budget, supervising accounts payable, and controlling the general ledger. She also monitored the company's internal control system and effectively co-ordinated accounting procedures throughout the corporation.

As vice-president of finance, Rita is responsible for every accounting operation and financial decision that occurs in the company. She directs the preparation and analysis of the Income Statement and the Balance Sheet. She co-ordinates the preparation of all budgets and financial forecasts. She designs and administers the company's cash management program and makes sure that the company's assets are effectively managed. She also acts as the company liaison with external auditors.

Rita monitors and updates all the company's accounting systems and internal control measures. Recently, she has been in charge of developing a computerized system to meet the company's accounting needs. She highly recommends learning about computers to anyone entering today's ever-changing business world.

Rita believes that in the 90s companies will need the skills of accountants at all levels of management. She believes that those who enter top managerial positions must be prepared to devote as much time and energy to their careers as the work demands.

Discussion

1. Prepare a research paper on junior achievement clubs in your community.
2. Outline Rita's role as the accountant for Emerson Electric and relate her duties to the accounting systems you learned in this chapter.
3. What are Rita's responsibilities as a corporate controller and vice-president of finance?
4. How do you respond to Rita's comment, "Those who enter top management positions must be prepared to devote as much time and energy to their careers as the work demands"?
5. Prepare a list of the positions that Rita has held, and place check marks after each job that requires a knowledge of accounting skills.
6. Explain briefly the difference between external and internal auditors.

Summary Exercise

Travel Trailers

Travel Trailers is a business owned and operated by Charles Fowler. The business earns its income from the selling and servicing of mobile homes and trailers. All sales and service transactions are subject to a five per cent sales tax.

Travel Trailers is able to treat the sale of every unit as a cash transaction. This is possible because of special arrangements made with an independent finance company. Travel Trailers receives payment in full for every unit sold. For units sold on credit, the finance company pays Travel Trailers and arranges to collect from the customer on an instalment plan.

1. Set up the general ledger of Travel Trailers as of May 31, 19-- from the combined chart of accounts and general ledger trial balance shown opposite (on page 471). If you are using the workbook, the ledger is already set up for you.

2. Set up the accounts receivable ledger of Travel Trailers as of May 31, 19-- from the information shown below. If you are using the workbook, the ledger is already set up for you.

Customer	Address	Invoice	Amount
B. Fraser	15 Gray Street	634	$ 367.50
W. Hoyle	49 First Street	635	78.75
A. Newman	250 Fort Road	629	262.50
Schell Brothers	96 Garrison Avenue	633	1 060.50
N. Thompson	20 Wilson Avenue	630	624.75
L. Walker	4 Dennis Avenue	631	89.25
			$2 483.25

TRAVEL TRAILERS
GENERAL LEDGER TRIAL BALANCE
MAY 31, 19--

101 Bank	$ 11 751.75	
110 Accounts Receivable	2 483.25	
115 Merchandise Inventory	125 423.00	
120 Supplies	1 151.00	
125 Prepaid Insurance	2 650.00	
130 Equipment	28 472.00	
135 Accumulated Depreciation, Equipment		$ 7 341.60
140 Delivery Truck	22 000.00	
145 Accumulated Depreciation, Delivery Truck		8 000.00
201 Accounts Payable		19 987.00
205 Bank Loan		120 000.00
210 Sales Tax Payable		1 694.24
305 C. Fowler, Capital		22 418.71
310 C. Fowler, Drawings	15 000.00	
405 Sales		189 423.51
410 Discounts Earned		1 034.20
505 Purchases	96 581.75	
510 Freight-in	1 174.72	
515 Bank Charges and Interest	4 516.50	
520 Insurance Expense		
525 Depreciation, Delivery Truck		
530 Depreciation, Equipment		
535 Light and Heat	4 350.40	
540 Miscellaneous Expense	994.58	
545 Rent	6 250.00	
550 Supplies Expense		
555 Telephone	1 376.20	
560 Wages	45 724.11	
	$369 899.26	$369 899.26

3. **Set up the accounts payable ledger of Travel Trailers as of May 31, 19-- from the following information. If you are using the workbook, the ledger is already set up for you.**

Supplier	Address	Reference	Amount
Double-G Industries	Manortown	420	$10 575.00
Maynard's Cartage	49 Larry Lane		nil
Modern Mobile Homes	West City	2213	2 100.00
National Hardware	64 Venture Street	2309	2 787.00
Parker Manufacturing	10 Bergen Street		nil
Windsor Manufacturing	Windsor	404	4 525.00
			$19 987.00

Summary Exercise

4. Travel Trailers uses five journals in its accounting system as shown below.

Sales Journal — Page 19

Date	Particulars	Ref. No.	Sales Tax Payable CR	Sales CR	Acc's Rec'l DR

Purchases Journal — Page 74

Date	Particulars	Other Accounts DR			Freight-in DR	Supplies DR	Pchs's DR	Ref. No.	Accs Pay'l CR
		Account	PR	Amount					

Cash Receipts Journal — Page 37

Date	Particulars	Other Accounts Cr			Acc's Rec'l CR	Sales Tax Payable CR	Sales CR	Ref. No.	Bank DR
		Account	PR	Amount					

Cash Payments Journal — Page 84

Date	Particulars	Other Accounts DR			Wages DR	Drawing DR	Accs Pay'l DR	Ref. No.	Bank CR
		Account	PR	Amount					

General Journal — Page 5

Date	Particulars	PR	Debit	Credit

Journalize the following transactions for June. Use the journal page numbers shown. Post to the subsidiary ledgers daily directly from the source documents. Terms of sale are Net 30 unless noted otherwise.

Transactions

June

1 Sales Invoice
   —No. 636, to A. Newman, for repairs to trailer; $590 plus sales tax.
   Cheque Copy
   —No. 755, to General Real Estate, for the rent for June; $1 250.

2 Sales Invoice
   —No. 637, to L. Walker, for trailer parts; $900 plus sales tax.
   Cheque Copy
   —No. 756, to Double-G Industries, on account; $5 000.

3 Purchase Invoices
   —From Parker Manufacturing, No. 40, for supplies; $247.80; terms 2/10,N/30.
   —From Double-G Industries, No. 472, for trailer parts; $1 551.20.

4 Cash Receipts List
   —From W. Hoyle, on account; $78.75.
   —From Federated Finance Company, No. 7042, for the sale of a trailer; selling price, $12 700; sales tax $635; total $13 335.
   Bank Debit Advice
   —From Central Bank, for interest on bank loan for May; $1 200.

5 *Cheque Copies*
   —No. 757, to C. Fowler, for personal use; $1 000.
   —No. 758, made out to Cash, for the wages for the week; $2 178.50.
   Sales Invoice
   —No. 638, to N. Thompson, for trailer repairs and parts; $1 370 plus sales tax.
8 *Cheque Copy*
   —No. 759, to J.C. Pat Supply, for the cash purchase of supplies, $243.50, and miscellaneous expense, $135.25; total $378.75.
   Memorandum
   —Correction required: $56.20 of Miscellaneous Expense had been debited in error to Freight-in.
9 *Cash Receipts List*
   —From A. Newman, on account; $262.50.
   Purchase Invoices
   —From Windsor Manufacturing, No. 452, for trailer parts; $1 452.00.
   —From Maynard's Cartage, No. 64, for transportation charges on incoming merchandise; $217.50; terms 2/10, N/30.
10 *Bank Debit Advice*
   —From Central Bank, to reduce the bank loan; $10 000.
   Sales Invoice
   —No. 639, to B. Fraser, for trailer parts; $450 plus sales tax.
   Cash Receipts List
   —From Federated Finance Company, No. 7043, for the sale of a trailer; selling price, $14 500; sales tax, $725; total $15 225.
   Credit Note Issued
   —No. 27, to A. Newman, for unsatisfactory goods returned; $125 plus sales tax.
   Cheque Copies
   —No. 760, to Modern Mobile Homes, for payment in full of account; $2 100.
   —No. 761, to Double-G Industries, on account; $5 000.
   Purchase Invoice
   —From Windsor Manufacturing, No. 481 for a new trailer; $14 500.
11 *Sales Invoice*
   —No. 640, to Schell Brothers, for trailer parts and service; $1 575 plus sales tax.
   Cheque Copy
   —No. 762, to C. Fowler, owner's personal use; $500.
12 *Cash Receipts List*
   —From Schell Brothers, on account; $1 500.
   —From B. Fraser, on account, $367.50.
   —From N. Thompson, on account; $500.
   Cheque Copies
   —No. 763, made out to Cash, for the wages for the week; $2 042.75.
   —No. 764, to Parker Manufacturing, paying invoice No. 40 less the two per cent discount; $242.84.

15 *Cash Receipts List*
—From Federated Finance Company, No. 7044, for the sale of a trailer; selling price, $10 200; sales tax $510; total $10 710.
Cheque Copies
—No. 765, to Provincial Treasurer, paying sales tax for May; $1 694.24.
—No. 766, to Windsor Manufacturing, on account; $15 000.

16 *Purchase Invoices*
—From Maynard's Cartage, No. 82, for transportation charges on incoming goods; $182.50; terms 2/10, N/30.
—From National Hardware, No. 2412, for trailer parts; $259.
—From Double-G Industries, No. 515, for a new trailer; $17 680.
—From Windsor Manufacturing, No. 499, for trailer parts; $283.50.

17 *Sales Invoice*
—No. 641, to W. Hoyle, for trailer servicing; $110 plus sales tax.
Cheque Copy and Sales Slip
—No. 767, to Emerald Store, for the cash purchase of miscellaneous expense items; $140.50.

18 *Cheque Copies*
—No. 768, to C. Fowler, owner's personal use; $1 200.
—No. 769, to National Hardware, on account; $2 787.
—No. 770, to Maynard's Cartage, paying invoice No. 64 less the two per cent discount; $213.15.

19 *Credit Note Received*
—From Double-G Industries, No. 520, price adjustment on invoice No. 515; $1 050.
Purchase Invoice
—From National Hardware, No. 2480, for trailer parts; $409.50.
Cheque Copy
—No. 771, made out to Cash, for the wages for the week; $2 040.

22 *Sales Invoice*
—No. 642, to L. Walker, for trailer parts and service; $290 plus sales tax.
Purchase Invoice
—From Parker Manufacturing, No. 68, for trailer parts; $358.80; terms 2/10, N/30.
Memorandum
—The owner had collected $89.25 from L. Walker (for invoice No. 631) but had kept the money for personal use.

24 *Cash Receipts List*
—From Federated Finance Company, No. 7045, for the sale of a trailer; selling price, $11 500; sales tax, $575; total $12 075.

25 *Cheque Copies*
—No. 772, to C. Fowler, for personal use; $350.
—No. 773, to Maynard's Cartage, paying invoice No. 82 less the two per cent discount; $178.85.

Bank Debit Advice
—From Central Bank, to reduce the bank loan; $5 000.

26 *Sales Invoice*
—No. 643, to A. Newman, for trailer repairs; $236 plus sales tax.
Cheque Copies
—No. 774, to Windsor Manufacturing, on account; $1 760.50.
—No. 775, made out to Cash, for the wages for the week; $2 452.00.
—No. 776, to City Hydro, for hydro for the month; $495.80.
—No. 777, to Bell Telephone, for telephone for the month; $202.00.

29 *Cash Receipts List*
—From B. Fraser, on account; $472.50.
—From Schell Brothers, on account; $1 214.25.
Purchase Invoice
—From National Hardware, No. 2561, for supplies; $930.

30 *Sales Invoice*
—No. 644, to W. Hoyle, for trailer servicing; $230 plus sales tax.

5. **Balance the special journals.**

6. **Post the five journals to the general ledger.**

7. **Balance the general ledger as of June 30.**

8. **Balance the subsidiary ledgers as of June 30.**

9. **Prepare an eight-column work sheet using the additional information below:**
   1. Supplies on hand at June 30, $1 300.
   2. Prepaid Insurance as of June 30, $1 599.
   3. Depreciation of Equipment: straight-line over ten years with an estimated terminal value of $4 000.
   4. Depreciation of Delivery Truck: straight-line over five years with an estimated terminal value of $2 000.
   5. Late purchase invoices: Purchases $740.
                             Miscellaneous Expense   102.
   6. Merchandise Inventory at June 30, $136 120.

10. **Prepare an income statement (six-month fiscal period) and a balance sheet as of June 30.**

11. **Journalize and post the adjusting entries and closing entries.**

12. **Take off a post-closing trial balance.**

14 Cash Control and Banking

14.1 Petty Cash Fund
14.2 Personal Banking
14.3 Bank Credit Cards
14.4 Banking for a Business
14.5 Accounting Controls

The word "cash" can be used in both a narrow and a broad sense. In its narrow sense, cash means dollar bills and coins. In its broad sense, cash also includes cheques, bank balances, and other items such as credit card vouchers or money orders—anything that can be deposited in a bank account.

Cash in this broad sense is vital to a business. The principal objective of a business is to earn a profit. This profit must eventually be converted into cash. A business needs cash to pay its bills, to meet its expenses, to reward its owners, and so on.

A quantity of cash is generally kept on hand in the office. However, a business keeps most of its cash in the safety of a bank account.

14.1 Petty Cash Fund

The most common method of making payment for expenditures is by cheque. However, it is not always convenient to issue a cheque, and payment in cash is often expected. Consider the following transactions.

- The custodian needs some electrical fuses. During her lunch hour she purchases with her own money some electrical fuses from the hardware store. She then submits the cash register slip to the accounting department so that she may be repaid.
- Two salaried employees are asked to work overtime in order to complete a special job. They are each given $12 for supper money.
- A parcel is delivered by an express company for which express charges of $12.50 must be paid immediately.

The usual way to pay for small expenditures of this type is with cash from a petty cash fund. A **petty cash fund** is a small quantity of cash, usually no more than $200, that is kept in the office for small expenditures.

Establishing a Petty Cash Fund

To establish a petty cash fund, a small sum ($100 to $200) is withdrawn from the bank account and put in the care of someone in the office. More precisely, a cheque is issued (usually made out to Petty Cash) and given to the person selected to be in charge of the petty cash. This person cashes the cheque and brings the money (in the form of small bills and coins) back to the office to be kept in a metal cash box (with lock). Outside of office hours the petty cash box is kept in the company safe. This is known as the imprest system. The **imprest method of petty cash** is a system for handling small expenditures in which a certain amount of cash is entrusted to an individual.

The accounting entry to establish a petty cash fund is shown by the following example.

Transaction It is decided to establish a petty cash fund of $100. A cheque in the amount of $100 is made out to Petty Cash and is given to the person chosen to keep the petty cash. The cheque is cashed and the money put in a petty cash box.

The accounting entry to establish the petty cash fund is the following:

	DR	CR
Petty Cash	$100	
Bank		$100

When this accounting entry is posted, the petty cash box will contain $100 in cash and will be in agreement with the Petty Cash account.

Operating the Petty Cash Fund

The keeper of the petty cash fund is authorized to make small payments out of the fund as necessary. Every amount paid out of the fund must be replaced by a bill for the expenditure (submitted by the person receiving the money). If a bill is not available, the recipient of the money must fill out a petty cash voucher such as the one shown in Figure 14.1. A **petty cash voucher** is a form that is filled out when money is paid out of the petty cash fund and no bill for the expenditure is available.

Figure 14.1 A petty cash voucher.

The bill or petty cash voucher is then placed in the box. A supply of unused petty cash vouchers (also known as petty cash slips) is kept with the petty cash fund.

At any time, the total of the bills, vouchers, and cash in the petty cash box should be equal to the amount of the petty cash fund. The keeper of the fund is responsible for seeing that this is so.

Accounting for this aspect of petty cash is easy because no accounting entries are made. It is one of those accounting situations in which it is convenient to allow the records to become temporarily incorrect.

Replenishing the Petty Cash Fund

The cash in the petty cash box decreases as bills and vouchers are paid. A point is reached when there may not be enough cash in the fund to pay for the next bill or voucher to be presented. To prevent this, a lower limit is usually placed on the fund. When the lower limit for the petty cash fund is reached, the fund must be replenished. **Replenishing petty cash** is the procedure by which the petty cash fund is renewed when it reaches an already-determined lower limit.

To show the accounting for replenishing petty cash, let us work with a petty cash fund of $100 having a lower limit of $10. Assume that the contents of the petty cash box are:

Cash	$ 7.15
Bills and vouchers	92.85
Total	$100.00

Assume further that the bills and vouchers contained in the petty cash box are the following:

No.	Account Charged	Amount
1	Miscellaneous Expense	$12.59
2	Postage	10.00
3	Miscellaneous Expense	13.75
4	Building Maintenance	11.56
5	Donations	5.00
6	Building Maintenance	4.75
7	Truck Expense	15.15
8	Miscellaneous Expense	5.30
9	Postage	5.70
10	Supplies	9.05
		$92.85

The petty cash fund must be replenished because the petty cash box contains less cash than the lower limit of $10. The steps to be followed are:

1. the keeper of the fund prepares a summary of the charges from the bills and vouchers in the box. There is no definite form in which the summary must be prepared. The summary might be drawn up like the one in Figure 14.2. The bills and vouchers from which the summary is prepared are attached to the summary;

```
                    Petty Cash Fund
                  Summary of Charges
                    October 2, 19—

           Building Maintenance           16 31
           Donations                       5 —
           Miscellaneous Expense          31 64
           Postage                        15 70
           Supplies                        9 05
           Truck Expense                  15 15
                                          92 85
```

Figure 14.2 A summary of charges from a petty cash fund.

2. the petty cashier submits the summary, together with the bills and vouchers, to the person or department that issues cheques;

3. a cheque, usually made out to Petty Cash, for an amount equal to the total on the summary (in this case $92.85) is obtained in exchange for the vouchers. The summary and the supporting documents are accepted as the source document for the cheque;

4. the cheque is cashed by the petty cashier and the money is added to the total ($7.15) in the petty cash box. The fund has been restored to its original amount of $100. The petty cash fund is then ready to begin another cycle;

5. an accounting entry must be made for the petty cash replenishing cheque. In our example, the accounting entry is:

	DR	CR
Building Maintenance	$16.31	
Donations	5.00	
Miscellaneous Expense	31.64	
Postage	15.70	
Supplies	9.05	
Truck Expense	15.15	
Bank		$92.85
	Debits taken from summary.	Credit taken from cheque.

We have seen that only two accounting entries are involved in the recording of petty cash transactions:

1. the entry to establish the fund. A similar entry is used to increase the fund;

2. the entry to replenish the fund.

Section Review Questions

1. What does "cash" mean in its narrow sense?
2. What does "cash" mean in its broad sense?
3. Where does a business keep most of its cash?
4. What is the commonest method of making payment for expenditures?
5. What is the purpose of a petty cash fund?
6. When is a petty cash voucher used?
7. Describe the contents of the petty cash box.
8. How can the contents of the petty cash box be checked for correctness?
9. When is the petty cash fund replenished?
10. What happens to the vouchers in the petty cash box?

Section Exercises

1. On January 15, Mary Markel issues a cheque in the amount of $200 to establish a petty cash fund. Give the accounting entry in general journal form to establish the petty cash fund.

2. On February 20, Seneca Sales Company issues a cheque to increase the petty cash fund from $100 to $150. Give the accounting entry in general journal form to increase the petty cash fund.

3. On March 16, 19--, after a bill of $12.16 is paid, the contents of a petty cash fund with a lower limit of $10 are as follows:

Cash	$7.68
Bills and Vouchers	
Supplies	10.00
Miscellaneous Expense	6.04
Miscellaneous Expense	1.25
Sales Promotion	8.50
Building Maintenance	10.50
C. Parkes, Drawings	12.00
Car Expense	8.17
Postage	8.50
Miscellaneous Expense	2.05
Postage	9.00
Miscellaneous Expense	4.15
Building Maintenance	12.16

1. Prepare the summary of charges necessary to replenish the fund.

2. In general journal form, write out the accounting entry necessary to replenish the fund.

4. On June 10, 19--, a petty cash fund with a lower limit of $12 is in the following condition:

Cash	$8.25
Bills and Vouchers	
Delivery Expense	15.00
Wages	10.00
Office Expense	15.02
Supplies	10.75
Advertising	12.00
Supplies	11.79
Advertising	15.00
Wages	12.50
Office Expense	12.14
P. Martin, Drawings	10.00
Office Expense	4.20
Office Expense	2.00
Supplies	11.35

1. **Prepare the summary of charges necessary to replenish the fund.**
2. **In general journal form, write out the required accounting entry to replenish the fund.**

5. **Indicate whether each of the following statements is true or false by placing a "T" or an "F" in the space indicated in your workbook. Explain the reason for each "F" response in the space provided.**

   1. The Petty Cash account in the general ledger must never change.
   2. A petty cash voucher must be prepared for every payment out of the fund.
   3. The petty cash fund is used for the purpose of cutting down on the number of cheques issued.
   4. The accounting entry to replenish the petty cash fund is made by the keeper of the fund.
   5. The petty cash box is locked and put away in a safe place outside business hours.
   6. The keeper of the petty cash fund must never borrow from it.
   7. The petty cash summary is organized by general ledger accounts.
   8. A payment out of petty cash can only be charged to an expense account or an asset account.
   9. The keeper of the fund is expected to make up any shortage in the petty cash fund.
   10. If an auditor were to check the petty cash fund, the procedure would be to total all of the cash and vouchers in the box and check this total against the balance in the Petty Cash account.

14.2 Personal Banking

Banks provide essential services for both businesses and individuals. Our modern economy would grind to a halt if the services of banks were suddenly withdrawn.

The principle services provided by banks are:
- the safekeeping of money;
- the processing of cheques and bank credit card vouchers, facilitating the "electronic transfer of funds" between people and/or businesses;
- the lending of money to businesses and individuals;
- the processing of "bank" credit card transactions (discussed in detail in a later section);
- the handling of foreign currencies.

Basic Personal Bank Accounts

Banks provide pamphlets which explain the various types of accounts, interest rates, and service charges. The banks are able to meet the special needs of all customers by having a variety of accounts. There is a surprisingly large variety of types of bank accounts available to the general public. The three most common bank account types are summarized below. Details were provided by the Bank of Nova Scotia. Other types of accounts provide combinations of the features described below.

PERSONAL BANK ACCOUNTS—SUMMARY

Pure Savings Account	*Daily Interest Savings Account*	*Personal Chequing Account*
Interest is added to the balance twice a year. This interest is calculated on the minimum monthly balances for the period. There is no interest if the minimum balance is less than $50 for the period.	Interest is added to the balance, calculated on the daily closing balance. The interest rate is slightly lower than for a pure savings account.	No interest is added.
No cheques are allowed.	No cheques are allowed.	30 cents is charged for each cheque.
Withdrawals are free.	Two free withdrawals or transfers each month; thereafter, there is a $1 charge for each transaction.	30 cents is charged for each withdrawal.
A passbook record of the account is provided.	A passbook record of the account is provided.	A bank statement is provided each month. All cashed cheques are returned to the depositor.

Section 14.2   483

A bank statement for a personal chequing account is shown in Figure 14.3.

Scotiabank
THE BANK OF NOVA SCOTIA

85092
GEORGIAN MALL
726-3690

MR ALFRED JARRY
330 VICTORIA STREET
REGINA, SASKATCHEWAN
S4R 1J8

ACCOUNT NUMBER

9674-32

STATEMENT OF: SCOTIA CHEQUING ACCOUNT
FROM: FEB. 21, 19--   TO: MAR. 21, 19--   PAGE: 1

DESCRIPTION	DEBITS	CREDITS	DATE M D	BALANCE
BALANCE FORWARD			02 21	36 18
DEPOSIT		2192.26	02 22	2553.44
CHEQUE 46	29.99			
CHEQUE 73	600.00			
CHEQUE 72	136.00		02 25	1787.45
CHEQUE 74	182.00		02 28	1605.45
CHEQUE 48	58.19			
CHEQUE 75	70.00			
CHEQUE 101	29.00		03 01	1448.26
TRANSFER FROM 0474320		200.00		
CHEQUE 50	172.37			
CHEQUE 47	134.02		03 05	3141.87
CHEQUE 103	40.53			
CHEQUE 102	20.00		03 06	3081.34
CHEQUE 77	2000.00		03 07	1081.34
CHEQUE 76	158.51		03 08	922.83
CHEQUE 106	42.79			
CHEQUE 105	96.00		03 11	784.04
CHEQUE 49	15.97		03 14	768.07
CHEQUE	150.00		03 15	618.07
CHEQUE 107	22.00		03 19	596.07
SERVICE CHARGE	5.36		03 21	590.71

NO. OF DEBITS	TOTAL AMOUNT – DEBITS	NO. OF CREDITS	TOTAL AMOUNT – CREDITS	NO. OF ENCLOSURES	MORE ITEMS ON PAGE
19	3,962.73	2	4,192.26	18	

PLEASE EXAMINE THIS STATEMENT PROMPTLY – REPORT ERRORS OR OMISSIONS TO THE BANK WITHIN 30 DAYS OF RECEIPT OF THE STATEMENT

Figure 14.3 A bank statement for a personal chequing account.

Opening an Account

You must open a bank account before you can enjoy the privileges of banking. To do this:

- visit the bank;
- complete the required bank forms with the help of a bank employee. One of these will be a "signature" card;
- put a sum of money on deposit. A **bank deposit** is an amount of money placed in a bank account.

Deposits to the account or withdrawals from the account may be made in the bank during banking hours and by electronic teller at any time. Cheques may be issued on some types of bank accounts.

For each bank transaction a bank form must be prepared. This form becomes the source document for the transaction. The three most common bank forms are the deposit slip, the withdrawal slip, and the cheque.

Keeping Personal Bank Records

It is a good practice to keep a detailed record of your transactions and bank balance. There are three good reasons for this:

1. you will know your true bank balance at any time. This helps you avoid the embarrassment of writing cheques when there is no money in the account. Writing cheques that "bounce" is not good for your reputation and could damage your credit rating. It is difficult to borrow money if your credit rating is poor;
2. you can easily check back on any particular payment, or analyze your payments for income tax or other purposes;
3. you will have a means of checking the accuracy of the bank's record. This is useful if there is any discrepancy between the bank's record and your own.

The simplest form of personal record is the three-column booklet which banks usually hand out free of charge.

NSF Cheque

A cheque is not cash. It is merely a slip of paper on which a formal promise to pay is written. When you accept a cheque you gamble that the cheque will be good. Most of the time cheques are good, but often enough they are not, and individuals and business people must be very cautious.

If you accept a cheque from someone, it will probably pass through these stages:

1. you will either cash the cheque or deposit it in your bank account. In either case the bank will require that you endorse the cheque by signing it on the reverse side. By endorsing the cheque you are legally contracting to guarantee the cheque should anything go wrong with it. Endorsement is discussed on page 505;
2. the bank gives you cash or credits your account with the amount of the cheque;

3. your bank forwards the cheque through the bank clearinghouse to the bank of the person who issued the cheque;
4. the issuer's bank attempts to deduct the amount of the cheque from the issuer's bank account. The deduction will be made if the balance in the account is large enough to cover the cheque.

If the Funds are Insufficient

5. If the balance is not large enough, the bank stamps the cheque "Not Sufficient Funds" (NSF) and sends it back to your bank. The cheque has now been "dishonoured"; in common speech, it has "bounced." An **NSF cheque** is one that was not cashed when presented to the issuer's bank because there were not sufficient funds in the issuer's bank account to cover the amount of the cheque;
6. the dishonoured cheque is then returned to your bank. Your bank will immediately deduct the amount of the worthless cheque from your account. Remember, you have already received the money or had your account increased, and you did agree to guarantee the cheque;
7. there is a service charge of about $10 charged to the issuer of a dishonoured cheque. The innocent party also has to pay a small charge;
8. now, you attempt to contact the person who gave you the worthless cheque, in order to recover your money. This may not be easy;
9. if the cheque above was one received by a business, an accounting entry would have been made through the cash receipts journal when the cheque was first received. For example, the entry might have been:

		DR	CR
Bank		$150.00	
	Accounts Receivable		$150.00
	(R. Walters)		

Once it is known that the cheque has bounced, this entry will have to be reversed by an exactly opposite entry recorded in the cash payments journal. The entry will be:

	DR	CR
Accounts Receivable	$150.00	
(R. Walters)		
Bank		$150.00

Certified Cheque

To avoid the nuisance of a bounced cheque, as well as the possible loss of money, you can insist on any cheque offered to you being certified. A **certified cheque** is one for which the bank takes the funds out of the issuer's account in advance, and puts them in a special account to honour the cheque when it is presented.

It is the person who issues the cheque who takes it to his or her bank to be certified.

The funds are removed from the bank account at that time, the cheque is boldly marked "CERTIFIED" with a special stamp and returned to the issuer. There is a small bank charge for the service. The person to whom the cheque is issued can clearly see that it is certified and can be confident that it will not bounce.

You should ask for cash or a certified cheque when you are dealing with a stranger and when the amount of money involved is large. This might be the case if you were selling a used car by means of a newspaper advertisement.

Post-Dated Cheque

There are times when it is appropriate to write a post-dated cheque. A **post-dated cheque** is one that is dated for some time in the future. For example, a cheque written on January 15 but dated for March 1 is a post-dated cheque.

The usual reason for issuing post-dated cheques is to meet a series of payments such as for a mortgage. Usually, at the beginning of each year, twelve cheques, dated January 1, February 1, and so on, are given to the mortgage-holder. The mortgage-holder can then cash one of the cheques on the first day of each month.

You might also choose to write a post-dated cheque to pay off a personal loan. This gives the appearance of having made the payment, but in fact payment is delayed until a future date, pay day, for example. You then have time to get money into your bank account.

Section Review Questions

1. What are the five main services provided by banks?
2. Name the three most common types of personal bank accounts.
3. On which type of bank account is interest added?
4. Which type of bank account gives the highest rate of interest?
5. For which type of bank account is a bank statement provided?
6. Which type of bank account is best for writing cheques?
7. Name the three most common bank forms used with personal bank accounts.
8. Describe the simplest form of personal bank record.
9. What is an NSF cheque?
10. What is the simplest way to endorse a cheque?
11. What is meant by the word "bounced" in connection with banking?
12. Why does the bank have the right to take the amount of an NSF cheque out of the depositor's account?
13. What is a certified cheque?
14. Why would a person request a certified cheque?
15. What is a post-dated cheque?
16. Why would a person issue a post-dated cheque?

Section Exercises

1. **Indicate whether each of the following statements is true or false by placing a "T" or an "F" in the space indicated in your workbook. Explain the reason for each "F" response in the space provided.**

    1. A pure savings account is designed for the person who makes very few withdrawals.
    2. You are not allowed to write cheques on a pure savings account. Therefore, you can only get money out of a pure savings account by closing out the account.
    3. The interest rate on a daily interest savings account is always about one-half a point higher than it is on a pure savings account.
    4. A passbook record of a savings account can only be updated at the bank.
    5. The personal chequing account is not intended to be used for saving money.
    6. There is no limit to the number of cheques that can be written on a personal chequing account.
    7. The bank requires a depositor to sign a signature card because a signature card is a form of receipt.
    8. A personal bank record is not really necessary because the bank keeps a record of your account.
    9. If Joan Arnott's bank balance as shown by the bank is $352, she can write a cheque for that much money with no fear of its bouncing.
    10. A cheque is considered to be cash, but it is not assured cash until it has been cleared by the banking system.
    11. The purpose of endorsing a cheque is so the bank can compare the endorsement with the signature card.
    12. When you deposit a cheque the bank gives you immediate credit for the amount even though the cheque might bounce.
    13. You visit your sister-in-law's bank to cash a cheque for $100 that she has given to you. The bank informs you that there is only $90 in your sister-in-law's account and gives you the $90.
    14. You should request cash or a certified cheque when you sell a used car to a stranger.
    15. On March 15, 19–1, a bank would not cash a cheque dated March 20, 19–1.

2. Pugh & Co. made a cash sale to H. Vernon for $55 plus $2.75 sales tax for a total of $57.75. Vernon gave a cheque in payment. A few days after depositing the cheque in the bank, Pugh & Co. was notified by its bank that Vernon's cheque was NSF.

    1. **What entries would Pugh & Co. record at the time of making the sale?**
    2. **What entries would record the fact that the cheque is NSF?**

3. Pugh & Co. sold goods on account to H. Vetiri. The goods were priced at $107, the sales tax was $5.35, and the total was $112.35. The next month, Pugh & Co. received a cheque from Vetiri for $112.35 and deposited it in the bank. A few days later, the company was informed that the cheque had bounced. Discussion with Mrs. Vetiri

disclosed that she was temporarily short of funds and would pay the bill in the near future.

1. What entries would be made by Pugh & Co. at the time of the sale?
2. What entries would be made by Pugh & Co. upon receipt of Vetiri's cheque?
3. What entries would record the fact that the cheque is NSF?

4. Krista Lamer is an employee of a chartered bank. One day at lunch she and her friend, Judy Babych, began to discuss finances, banking, interest rates, and so on. During the conversation, Krista learned that Judy had only one bank account, a chequing-savings account, and that the balance in this account was usually about $10 000. Judy thought that the chequing-savings account was ideal for her because she could write all the cheques that she wanted and still earn interest on the balance.

Krista knew that by a simple change in bank accounts Judy could earn more bank interest.

What would Krista advise Judy to do? Give reasons for your answer.

14.3 Bank Credit Cards

Credit cards are used so much in our society that we can visualize a society without money—a cashless society. Credit cards are available for department stores such as Sears and Eaton's, oil companies such as Petro-Canada and Texaco, and other large retail outlets such as Canadian Tire. We are so used to credit cards that many individuals and merchants would be badly affected if their use were ever discontinued.

Most smaller retail outlets do not offer their own individualized credit cards. For them the alternative is Visa or Mastercard. These are credit cards sponsored by the major chartered banks. With bank credit cards consumers can make purchases on short-

Figure 14.4 A Visa card.

term credit at any retail outlet that accepts the bank's credit cards. The illustrations used in the text are supplied by the Bank of Nova Scotia, one of the sponsoring banks of the Visa card. The concepts involved are the same or similar for any bank credit card.

Obtaining a Bank Credit Card

It is not difficult to obtain a bank credit card if you have a good credit record. Simply visit the local branch office of the bank and obtain an application form. Complete the form and either leave it with the branch or mail it to the credit card centre. Within a few days the credit card will arrive in the mail. A Visa card is illustrated opposite in Figure 14.4.

Features of Bank Credit Cards

Presented below are some common features of bank credit cards.
- For the consumer, there are no initial costs of obtaining a credit card.
- There is small annual fee charged to the merchant who contracts to use the service.
- The consumer is usually given an initial credit limit of $1 500. This may be increased by making a special application to the credit card centre.
- There may be a transaction fee of fifteen cents per transaction up to a maximum of $1 per month.
- A statement of account is sent to the consumer each month. The consumer is given twenty-one days from the statement date to make payment. If payment is made within that time, no interest is charged. If payment is overdue, interest at a high rate will be charged. Interest rates vary depending on economic conditions.
- Bank credit cards may be used to obtain a cash advance which is essentially a bank loan. Interest on a cash advance is charged daily and begins right away.
- The credit card centre acts as a clearinghouse for merchants' transactions from all of the sponsoring banks. With its powerful computerized equipment, the centre is able to sort out the thousands of transactions by customer and by bank branch, and prepare all the necessary monthly statements and other summaries.
- The interest rate, credit limit, outstanding balance, minimum payment, and credit limit are all shown on the monthly statement to the customer.

Advantages of Bank Credit Cards

Their wide acceptance indicates that there are strong reasons for the popularity of bank credit cards. The most important reasons are:

1. the cards can be used in most retail outlets;
2. the consumer does not have to carry large sums of money;
3. the consumer can obtain a quick cash advance by visiting a branch office of the bank;
4. the consumer can purchase necessities, or take advantage of special sales, at a time when the money is not otherwise available;

5. the consumer's credit rating is established with a merchant when the credit card is presented. The merchant is assured of being paid provided that:
   a. the store clerk checks the good standing of the card;
   b. for any purchase over the floor limit (usually $75), the clerk phones the credit card centre to make sure that the customer's credit limit is not exceeded.

Disadvantages of Bank Credit Cards

There are difficulties with bank credit cards as well as advantages. Two of these are:

1. many consumers cannot control their spending. They get into trouble with the credit card centre by overspending and being unable to make the required payments. Their problem is made worse by the high interest rate charged on overdue accounts. Furthermore, they may come to depend on credit buying for their survival;
2. interest is charged on overdue accounts at a fairly high rate. It might be better for the consumer to seek an ordinary bank loan which normally carries a lower interest rate.

Accounting for Bank Credit Card Transactions

The steps in credit card transactions are outlined below.

1. The first step in a bank credit card transaction occurs when the customer makes a purchase, or returns goods, in a store that accepts the customer's credit card. The store clerk will:
   a. write up the sale on a credit card sales slip or "credit" voucher;
   b. run the sales slip through the imprinting device using the customer's credit card as shown in Figure 14.5. This prints the customer's name and identification number and the merchant's name and identification number on the sales slip.

Figure 14.5 A completed Visa sales slip.

c. give one copy of the sales slip to the customer and keep two for the store. One of these will be forwarded to the bank along with the bank deposit.
2. The merchant will probably have a number of bank credit card transactions each day. The sales slips for these transactions must be kept in a safe place during the day.
3. During or at the end of the day, the credit card slips are prepared for inclusion in the bank deposit. This involves:
   a. summarizing all of the slips for the day to obtain daily totals;
   b. writing in the totals from part a. onto a Merchant Deposit Summary as shown below in Figure 14.6;

Figure 14.6 Visa merchant deposit summary slip.

c. placing the credit card slips and the summary into a special envelope provided by the bank;
d. recording the gross amount from the summary slip on the bank deposit slip. You will see how this is done on page 506.
4. When preparing the accounting entries for the day, the credit card slips must be included. In theory, the accounting entry is:

	DR	CR
Bank	$$$$	
Sales		$$$$
Sales Tax Payable		$$$$
Credit card slips for the day		

The Role of the Bank and the Credit Card Centre

When the merchant makes a bank deposit, the bank credits the account with the total value of the deposit. This includes the credit card slips. Thus, the merchant receives quick payment in full by the bank for all of the credit card sales made during the day. The branch then forwards all of the credit card slips for all of its customers to the credit card centre each day.

In turn,

- the credit card centre takes over the responsibility and the difficulties of collecting from the consumers. There are always some customers who do not pay on time or cannot pay at all;
- with its powerful computerized equipment, the centre acts as a clearinghouse for all of the slips from all of the bank branches.

Naturally, the bank does not provide the credit card service free of charge. The banks earn revenue from the service by applying three types of service charges.

1. The transaction fees, and interest on advances and overdue balances.
2. The annual fees charged to the merchants.
3. The discounts taken off the credit card slips deposited by the merchants. This is agreed to by the merchant and the credit card centre. The merchant does not really get full value for the gross amount of the credit card slips. The bank calculates a percentage of all of the slips for the month and deducts this amount from the merchant's account. The merchant first sees the amount of the deduction on his bank statement. The necessary accounting entry for this deduction is as follows:

	DR	CR
Credit Card Discount Expense*	$$$$	
Bank		$$$$

*(or, simply, Bank Charges)

The discount rate for each merchant is based on volume of sales. The discount schedule in Figure 14.7 shows that the rates have ranged from a low of two per cent to a high of five and a half per cent. Every six months the merchant's sales figures are reviewed by Visa and an adjustment in the rate is made if it is warranted.

Scotiabank
THE BANK OF NOVA SCOTIA

VISA
MEMBER DISCOUNT SCHEDULE

*Average Monthly Volume	Average Draft Size			
	Under $30.00	$30.00 – 49.99	$50.00 – 99.99	$100.00 and Over
	%	%	%	%
$ 1– $ 999	5.50	4.25	3.25	3.25
1,000– 2,499	4.75	4.00	3.25	2.75
2,500– 4,999	4.50	3.75	3.00	2.75
5,000– 12,499	4.25	3.50	2.75	2.50
12,500– 19,999	4.00	3.25	2.50	2.25
20,000– 29,999	3.75	3.00	2.25	2.25
30,000– 49,999	3.50	2.75	2.25	2.00
50,000– 74,999	3.25	2.75	2.00	2.00
75,000– 149,999	3.00	2.50	2.00	2.00
150,000– 299,999	2.50	2.25	2.00	2.00
300,000– and over	2.00	2.00	2.00	2.00

*Average Monthly Volume is calculated March 31 and September 30 of each year based on preceding 12 months' sales. Rate change if warranted to be implemented May 1 and November 1 and will apply to the future six month period (See over for further particulars).

Figure 14.7 Visa merchant discount schedule.

Section Review Questions

1. Which types of companies were the first to offer credit cards?
2. Which types of stores use major bank credit cards?
3. What could prevent you from obtaining a bank credit card?
4. Describe how long customers have to make payment on their accounts.
5. What is a consequence of a consumer not paying on time?
6. A consumer can make a purchase on credit using a bank credit card. What other type of transaction can be effected using a bank credit card?
7. Who keeps track of all the transactions of all the consumers?
8. Give five advantages of a bank credit card.
9. Give two disadvantages of a bank credit card.
10. The merchant who includes bank credit card slips in the bank deposit does not get full credit for them. Explain.
11. Explain what is meant by the discount rate and review of the discount rate.

Section Exercises

1. **Indicate whether each of the following statements is true or false by placing a "T" or an "F" in the space indicated in your workbook. Explain the reason for each "F" response in the space provided.**

    1. Small retail outlets do not offer their own individualized credit cards because they prefer not to sell on credit.
    2. Carrying a bank credit card is like having plastic money.
    3. Anyone can obtain a bank credit card.
    4. The consumer pays a small initial service charge to obtain a bank credit card.
    5. The maximum credit limit for a bank credit card is $1 500.
    6. There is a fee of fifteen cents for every transaction.
    7. It is possible to use a bank credit card regularly without having to pay interest.
    8. It is cheaper to obtain money by a bank credit card cash advance than to get a regular bank loan.
    9. The charge for interest on a bank credit card cash advance begins on the statement day.
    10. A great many retail outlets do not accept bank credit cards. This is the cards' chief disadvantage.
    11. Under normal circumstances a consumer establishes a credit rating by presenting a bank credit card.
    12. The use of credit cards slows things down at the cash register.
    13. During or at the end of the day, the bank credit card slips are included in the bank deposit.
    14. The credit card centre comes back to the merchant for payment if the consumer does not pay.
    15. The major banks provide bank credit card services to help merchants make more sales.
    16. The two common bank credit cards are Visa and Mastercard.

Chapter 14

17. Bank credit card services would probably not have become widely available without the development of the computer.
18. A bank credit card cannot be used by anyone but its rightful owner. Therefore, there is no reason to worry if the card is lost.
19. The merchant never has to worry about collecting his money if a customer offers a credit card in payment.
20. When accounting for the day's bank credit card sales, the debit is to Accounts Receivable (credit card centre).

2. Shown below are two Visa vouchers. Study these two vouchers, then answer the questions that follow.

   A.

   B.

Questions
1. What type of transaction does voucher A represent?
2. What type of transaction does voucher B represent?
3. Are these vouchers related? Explain your reasoning.

4. Who receives either the original or a copy of these vouchers?
5. Give the name of the merchant.
6. Give the name of the customer.
7. When does the merchant get paid for voucher A?
8. If the statement date is October 31, what will be the due date for the two vouchers?
9. How will voucher B be handled when making up the bank deposit of October 30?
10. What is the value of the net sales for the two vouchers including sales tax?
11. How much will the merchant be charged for these two vouchers if the discount rate is 2.75 per cent? How will the merchant pay the discount?
12. How much money will the merchant realize from these two vouchers?

3. A Visa statement for Robin Goodfellow appears below. Examine this statement, then answer the questions that follow.

Scotiabank VISA
THE BANK OF NOVA SCOTIA
THIS IS YOUR MONTHLY VISA STATEMENT
KEEP THIS FOR YOUR RECORD

CHARGEX ACCOUNT NO: 4537 015 824 672
CUSTOMER'S NAME: ROBIN GOODFELLOW
PAGE: 1

DATE	REFERENCE NUMBER	DEBITS/CREDITS (-)	PARTICULARS		
JAN15	001	18.03	KELSEYS ROAD HOUSE	THUNDER BAY	ON
JAN15	002	448.33	REMBER'S FURN WAREHOUSE	THUNDERBAY	ON
JAN17	003	52.43	BEV PORTERS SPORTWEAR	THUNDER BAY	ON
JAN22	004	53.55	RAMADA INN	SAULT STE MARON	
JAN28	005	100.00-	PAYMENT - THANK YOU		
FEB02	006	26.58	PICKFAIR SEAFOOD REST	THORNHILL	ON
FEB05	007	23.53-	ZELLERS BARRIE	211BARRIE	ON
FEB05	008	195.27	J J JACKSONS FASHIONS	BARRIE	ON
FEB19	009	.75	TRANSACTION FEE		

DATE OF LAST STATEMENT	BALANCE ON LAST STATEMENT	+ INTEREST	+ TOTAL DEBITS THIS MONTH	− TOTAL CREDITS THIS MONTH	= NEW BALANCE
21JAN87	351.95	5.19	794.94	123.53	$ 1028.55

BALANCE ON LAST STATEMENT CONSISTS OF:

PURCHASES**	CASH ADVANCES	INTEREST
348.72	.00	3.23

NEW BALANCE CONSISTS OF:

PURCHASES**	CASH ADVANCES	INTEREST
1023.36	.00	5.19

**ANY BILLED SERVICE AND TRANSACTION CHARGES ARE INCLUDED IN THIS AMOUNT

THIS MONTH'S PAYMENT	51.00
OVERDUE PAYMENTS PLEASE PAY NOW	.00
AMOUNT OVERLIMIT	.00
MINIMUM PAYMENT DUE	51.00

SEE REVERSE FOR IMPORTANT INFORMATION ABOUT YOUR STATEMENT

CREDIT LIMIT	1500.00

STATEMENT DATE: FEB 19 87
DUE DATE THIS MONTH'S PAYMENT: MAR 12 87
027306
AMOUNT PAID:

TEAR OFF HERE AND RETURN LOWER PORTION WITH YOUR PAYMENT · REGISTERED TRADE MARK OF BNS · BNS REGISTERED USER OF MARKS

1. What is the statement date?
2. What is the due date shown on the statement?
3. What is Robin Goodfellow's account balance as of the statement date?
4. How many purchases were made during the statement period?
5. What is the value of the purchases made during the statement period?
6. How many payments were made during the statement period?
7. What is the amount of the payments made during the statement period?
8. What is the minimum amount that is due?
9. What percentage of the outstanding balance is the minimum amount?
10. Visa payments can be made at your local bank branch. How else can they be paid?
11. What is this customer's credit limit?
12. How much interest was charged during the statement period?

14.4 Banking for a Business

A large part of business banking has to do with "cash receipts." The cash receipts of a business represent the money taken in from business operations. These funds must be carefully controlled and deposited in the bank promptly.

Daily Cash Receipts

The cash receipts of a business are usually received in one of the following three ways.

1. Mail Receipts

It is customary for a business that sells on credit to receive payment from its customers by way of cheques through the mail. Each business day the clerk in charge of the mail separates out any cheques received and prepares a listing of them. They are then given up for deposit to the bank. You previously saw this cash receipts list in Chapter 6. The mail clerk is usually someone who does not work in the accounting department. Using an independent person in this way is a control technique that helps to ensure that the funds received will be handled and recorded properly. The usual accounting entry is:

	DR	CR
Bank	$$$$	
Accounts Receivable		$$$$

2. Over-the-Counter Sales

Some small businesses sell only a few goods over the counter, and place the money received in a drawer or cash box. It is customary for a business of this type to use dual-purpose sales slips. A sales slip, and a forms register in which to keep sales slips, are illustrated below in Figure 14.8. The slips are pre-numbered to ensure that all slips can be accounted for. This is a simple but effective accounting control technique. Cash sales, charge sales, refunds, returns for credit, and receipts on account can all be processed using the dual-purpose sales slips.

Figure 14.8 A dual-purpose sales slip and a forms register machine.

Proving the Cash For each transaction a copy of the sales slip is kept in the lower section of the register. At the end of every business day a control procedure known as **proving the cash** or balancing the cash is carried out. The sales slips for the day are analyzed and a summary prepared such as the one shown below in Figure 14.9.

Figure 14.9 A daily sales summary for a dual-purpose sales slip system.

The cash on hand by actual count at the end of every business day should be equal to the net cash sales figure on the summary. If it is not, there is a cash shortage or a cash overage as shown.

The summary, slips, and cash are forwarded to the accounting department for further processing. The accounting entry for the above summary is as follows:

	DR	CR
Accounts Receivable	$2 556.66	
Bank	4 149.30	
Cash Short or Over	10.00	
Accounts Receivable		$ 500.00
Sales		5 809.31
Sales Tax Payable		406.65

3. Cash Register Receipts

Today, most retail businesses are equipped with one of two types of sophisticated cash register. One type is the point of sale terminal. A **point of sale terminal** is an electronic cash register that is connected to a central computer, which is the heart of a sophisticated information system. The other type is the stand-alone electronic cash register which is not connected to a computer. Cash registers, today, can continually interact with a computer to provide up-to-the minute information for the use of both management and store personnel. For example:

- Jerry Henry purchases a new drill using his charge card. The transaction is processed through a cash register. Immediately, Jerry's account and the inventory figure for drills are updated.
- Sylvia Murphy visits a department store to settle the balance of her overdue account. A clerk, using a computer terminal, calls up the details of Sylvia's account. Sylvia pays the balance of her account.
- Jim Star visits a department store to purchase a bicycle tire but cannot find the size he needs on the floor. He asks a store clerk if that size is available. The clerk, through a computer terminal, calls up the inventory status of the item and is able to tell Jim that the store does have the size in stock.

Even stand-alone cash registers have many valuable features. Today's operator may never have to make a mental or manual calculation. Price, sales tax, discount, and change computations can all be handled automatically, eliminating any possibility of error. As well, a number of accumulators are at work as transactions occur, building up totals to be printed out later. A typical stand-alone cash register is illustrated in Figure 14.10.

Change Fund (Float)   The **change fund** or **float** is a small quantity of money, usually between fifty and one hundred dollars, in small bills and coins. This fund is used to make change for customers. It is placed in the cash drawer of the cash register at the beginning of each business day. At the close of the day, small bills and coins equalling the amount of the float are taken from the cash register drawer and put safely away. This is the float for the next business day.

Document Printer
A device that prints the details of any transaction on the bill of sale or other document. Money received, money paid out, gift certificates, and so on are validated when the transaction details are printed on them by the company's own cash register. Also, the device can be set up to refuse to record a transaction unless a document is inserted in the opening of the slip printer.

Swivel Display Window
A window in which the details of the transactions are displayed for the customer. The customer acts as an auditor of the transaction, making sure that the operator records amounts correctly.

Detailed Audit Tape
A continuous paper-tape record of every entry in the order of occurrence. The machine assigns a reference number for each transaction which is printed on all related documents. This makes it easier to check back on any particular transaction.

Customer's Take-Home Receipt
A detailed machine-printed paper record of the transaction for the customer.

Operator's Display and Prompting Window
A display window that (1) provides a readout of the transaction details so that the operator may visually check them and (2) tells the operator what function has to be performed next on the machine.

Keyboard
The keys used by the operator to enter the transaction details, and to cause the data to be permanently recorded.

Cash Drawer
A sectioned drawer that provides a safe and convenient place for the cash.

Four-Position Control Lock
A locking device that controls different machine functions. The daily totals cannot be accessed except with a special key which is under the control of a supervisory person.

NCR 2140
ELECTRONIC CASH REGISTER

Figure 14.10 A typical stand-alone electronic cash register. Courtesy National Cash Register of Canada Limited.

The float is created in the first place by issuing and cashing a cheque made out to Cash. The accounting entry for the transaction is:

	DR	CR
Cash Float	$$$$	
Bank		$$$$

Detailed Audit Tape   Cash registers are used for transactions other than just cash sales. Charge sales, Visa sales, receipts on account, credit notes, and payments for small expenditures (known as "paid outs") can all be processed using a cash register. A duplicate sales slip, or similar document, is required for all transactions except cash sales. A copy of the sales slip is kept in the cash drawer. A cash register refund slip is illustrated in Figure 14.11.

Figure 14.11   A cash register voucher for a refund transaction.

As transactions occur during the day, the details are stored inside the cash register on a paper tape known as the detailed audit tape or the audit strip. The **audit strip** is a continuous record of all transactions made during the day. It is the equivalent of a series of customers' take-home receipts all joined together. Each transaction is given an individual reference number by the machine, in consecutive order, for convenience in back-checking on any particular transaction.

The daily totals are shown on the audit strip in Figure 14.12. Remember that a special key must be inserted in the control lock before the machine will release the totals. This key is kept under the control of a supervisor. The daily totals are needed to prove the cash and to work out the accounting entry for the day. A detailed audit tape, with explanations of the various codes, is illustrated in Figure 14.12.

Figure 14.12 A cash register detailed audit tape (simplified).

Chapter 14

Proving the Cash In a cash register environment the cash is proved at the end of every business day. A modern cash register can produce most of the figures required on a daily balancing form (in this text called the Cash Proof and Accounting Summary). At the end of the day a blank form is inserted into the document printing device on the machine and the day's totals are machine-printed under the control of a supervisor. A completed form is shown in Figure 14.13.

CASH PROOF AND ACCOUNTING SUMMARY

DATE *March 18*, 19 —

CASH REGISTER TOTALS	TO LINE NO.	TOTALS
Cash Sales less Refunds (Incl. Tax)	—	861.35
Visa Sales less Visa Returns (Incl. Tax)	2	1 633.36
Charge Sales (Incl. Tax)	3	316.72
Received on Account	8	1 200.00
Returns for Credit (Incl. Tax)	9	133.75
Paid Outs	—	75.00
Sales Less Returns	10	2 502.50
Sales Tax (Net)	11	175.18

CASH PROOF

Total Cash Received Less Paid Outs	—	1 986.35
Cash By Actual Count	1	1 975.35
Cash Short	7	11.00
Cash Over	12	

PAID OUTS BREAKDOWN

Account *Supplies*	4	40.00
Account *Miscellaneous Expense*	5	35.00
Account	6	
Total Paid Outs		75.00

ACCOUNTING ENTRY

LINE NO.	ACCOUNTS	DR	CR
1	Cash 1 975 35		
2	Visa 1 633 36 → Total to Bank →	3 608 71	
3	Accounts Rec'l (Charge Sales)	316 72	
4	Asset or Expense *Supplies*	40 —	
5	Asset or Expense *Misc. Expense*	35 —	
6	Asset or Expense		
7	Cash Short or Over	11 —	
8	Accounts Rec'l (Rec'd on A/c)		1 200 —
9	Accounts Rec'l (Ret'd for Cr.)		133 75
10	Sales		2 502 50
11	Sales Tax Payable		175 18
12	Cash Short or Over		
	BALANCING TOTALS	4 011 43	4 011 43

CASHIER'S SIGNATURE *Keith Hernandez*

Figure 14.13 The Cash Proof and Accounting Summary form.

A copy of the machine-produced Cash Proof and Accounting Summary form is retained by the cashier. The cashier then follows the procedure outlined below.

1. The cash and the vouchers are removed from the cash drawer and separated from each other.
2. The cash is proved as follows:
   a. The float is removed and placed in safekeeping for the next business day.
   b. The remaining cash is counted carefully. The total is written in on the line for Cash in Drawer by Actual Count on the balancing form. This amount should agree with the machine-produced figure immediately above it for Net Cash Received. If these two figures do not agree, the difference represents either a cash shortage or a cash overage. It is recorded on the line that reads Cash Short or the line that reads Cash Over. In Figure 14.13 a shortage of eleven dollars is recorded.
3. Specific voucher groups are totaled and agreed with their corresponding summary figures. This is done in several categories.
   a. Bank credit card sales slips are agreed with the summary figure of $1 633.36.
   b. The charge sales slips of the business itself are agreed with the summary figure of $316.72.
   c. "Received on account" slips are agreed with the summary figure of $1 200.
   d. "Returns for credit" slips are agreed with the summary figure of $133.75.
   e. "Paid out" bills are agreed with the summary figure of $75.
4. The paid out bills are analyzed and broken down by ledger account. The details are entered on the summary form. The example shows $40.00 for Supplies and $35.00 for Miscellaneous Expense.
5. The Accounting Summary section of the form is completed from the data above it. This section shows the accounting entry for the day's receipts. The figures with a line number to their left are transferred down to the appropriate line number in the Accounting Summary section. When all appropriate figures are transferred, the accounting summary section should balance. If it does not, the form has not been completed correctly and must be checked over until the error or errors are found.
6. The cash, vouchers, and the daily balance form are forwarded to the accounting department. The accounting department will see that the money is deposited promptly in the bank, and make the appropriate accounting entries in the cash receipts journal as shown in Figure 14.14.

Cash Receipts Journal — Month of March, 19—

Date	Particulars	Other Accounts Cr. Account	P.R.	Amount	Sales Tax Payable Cr.	Sales Credit	Acc's Rec'l Dr	Cr	Bank Dr
12	Cash Summary	Supplies		40 —	175 18	2 502 50	316 72	1 200 —	3 608 71
		Misc. Exp.		35 —				133 75	
		Cash Short							
		or Over		11 —					

Figure 14.14 The daily cash register accounting summary recorded in the cash receipts journal.

Cash Short or Over

Businesses that deal with the general public for cash are subject to cash shortages and cash overages. Some businesses hold their clerks responsible for shortages and overages. That is, the clerks may keep any overages, but must make up any shortages out of their own pockets. No shortages or overages are recorded in the books when this policy is adopted.

Other firms accept the shortages and overages as part of doing business. Any shortages or overages must be recorded in a Cash Short or Over account. Any shortages are entered as debits to the account. Any overages are recorded as credits to the account.

At any particular time, the balance in the account represents either a shortage (expense, debit) or an overage (income, credit) depending on the type of balance in the account. It is usual for the account to end up with a debit balance. This is because customers who have been given too little change are more likely to complain than those who have been given too much change.

The Current Bank Account

With regard to business bank accounts, there is usually more work involved for the bank's employees than for those of the business itself. For example, checking the coins and currency in a business's deposit can be quite time-consuming. People in business are expected to use a type of bank account known as the current account. A **current bank account** is one designed especially for the use of business people. The principal features of a current bank account are outlined below. There may be slight variations of these features from one bank chain to another.

- No interest is added.
- There is one free deposit, electronic funds transfer, or cheque per monthly statement period for each full $400 of minimum monthly credit balance.
- Thereafter, there is a small charge for each deposit, electronic funds transfer, or cheque processed per monthly statement period.
- There is a small minimum charge each monthly statement period.
- A bank statement is provided each month.
- The paid cheques are returned to the depositor each month along with the bank statement.
- Books of duplicate deposit slips are provided free of charge.

Preparing the Business Deposit

During the business day, the day's receipts are prepared for deposit. It is best to make the deposit as soon as possible to avoid having a large amount of money on the premises However, the nature of some businesses makes it impossible to complete this task until after banking hours. For them, the deposit must be made using the night depository service.

The person preparing the deposit must keep the following in mind:

1. bills must be sorted by denomination for ease of counting;
2. coins are to be placed in coin wrappers when there are sufficient quantities of coin;
3. banks require that the depositor endorse (that is, guarantee) each cheque by signing it on the reverse side. Businesses endorse all cheques ''For Deposit Only'' as shown in Figure 14.15. Usually, a business has an approved rubber stamp with which to make the endorsements. The endorsement shown in Figure 14.15 is a restrictive endorsement. A **restrictive endorsement** is one that places conditions in regard to the cashing or depositing of the cheque. In the illustration nothing could happen to this cheque except that it be deposited in the account of Tech Industries Limited. If the cheque was lost or stolen, it could not be cashed. If a cheque is endorsed in blank, that is, with just a signature, it could possibly be cashed by anyone who happened to possess it;

Figure 14.15 A restrictive endorsement on the back of a cheque.

4. the completed deposit slip must agree with the cash proofs and the accounting entries;
5. a duplicate deposit slip, stamped by the bank, must be obtained as the company's receipt for the deposit. The bank retains the original. If a night depository is used, the bank will mail out the receipted duplicate deposit slip. A completed deposit slip is shown in Figure 14.16.

Chapter 14

Figure 14.16 A completed deposit slip for a business.

Section Review Questions

1. Name the three most common types of cash receipts of a business.
2. What is the usual reason a business would receive "mail" receipts?
3. What business form is commonly used by a business that sells goods over the counter?
4. Describe the basic process of proving the cash for a business that sells goods over the counter.
5. Cash registers today can be more than just cash registers. Explain.

6. What is meant by a stand-alone cash register?
7. Name several features of a typical stand-alone cash register.
8. Describe what the "float" is.
9. What types of transactions can be processed using a cash register?
10. Describe the two principal features of a detailed audit tape.
11. Give the name of the cash register balancing form used in this text.
12. The cash register summary totals are printed out on the detailed audit tape at the end of the day. Where else can they be printed?
13. Why are there cash overages or cash shortages?
14. Which is the more common—cash overage or cash shortage? Explain.
15. Who uses a current bank account?
16. Which personal bank account is similar to the current bank account?
17. When preparing a business deposit, what must be done with the coins?
18. How is a cheque endorsed for a business deposit?
19. What is meant by a "restrictive" endorsement?

Section Exercises

1. Using the information given below, perform the following:

    1. Complete the sales summary and cash proof on the sheet provided in your workbook. The business does not accept Visa or Mastercard.
    2. Write out the accounting entry for the day's transactions from the details on the summary sheet.

    Vouchers

Voucher	Transaction	Sale	Tax	Total
No. 57	Cash sale	$315.00	$22.05	$337.05
No. 58	Charge sale	206.00	14.42	220.42
No. 59	Cash sale	392.00	27.44	419.44
No. 60	Cash refund	102.00	7.14	109.14
No. 61	Cash sale	740.00	51.80	791.80
No. 62	Charge sale	315.00	22.05	337.05
No. 63	Charge sale	216.00	15.12	231.12
No. 64	Cash sale	375.00	26.25	401.25
No. 65	Cash refund	208.00	14.56	222.56
No. 66	Credit note	58.00	4.06	62.06
No. 67	Cash sale	374.00	26.18	400.18
No. 68	Credit note	216.00	15.12	231.12

    Cash in Drawer, after Removing Change Fund

    Bills $1 × 56   Coins 1¢ × 937
           $2 × 19   5¢ × 251
           $5 × 29   10¢ × 311
           $10 × 80   25¢ × 652
           $20 × 23
           $50 × 6

2. Using the information shown below, perform the following:

   1. On the daily balance form provided in the workbook, fill in the totals that would be machine-printed by the cash register on February 28, 19——.
   2. Complete the remainder of the form.
   3. Show that the vouchers agree with the appropriate summary figures.

   Additional Information

   a. *Cash Register Daily Totals*

   $1 325.73 CASL
      843.16 VISA
      295.00 RECD
       40.00 P.O.
      525.37 CHRG
       87.74 CRDT
      170.52 TAX
   2 436.00 MDS
   1 580.73 CASH

   b. *Cash on Hand, Including $50 Float*

Bills	$20 × 46	
	$10 × 40	
	$5 × 31	
	$2 × 28	
	$1 × 21	
Coin	1¢ × 263	
	5¢ × 130	
	10¢ × 166	
	25¢ × 192	

   c. *Vouchers on Hand*

   Sales slip No. 75, credit note for $48.15.
   Sales slip No. 76, charge sale for $124.12.
   Sales slip No. 77, Visa sale for $273.92.
   Sales slip No. 78, received on account, $75.
   Sales slip No. 79, Visa sale for $181.90.
   Sales slip No. 80, Visa sale for $218.28.
   Sales slip No. 81, received on account, $125.
   Sales slip No. 82, charge sale for $401.25.
   Supplier's bill, for postage, $16.00.
   Sales slip No. 83, Visa sale for $78.11.
   Sales slip No. 84, credit note for $39.59.

Sales slip No. 85, received on account, $95.
Sales slip No. 86, Visa sale for $90.95.
Supplier's bill, for supplies, $24.00.

3. **Workbook Exercise:** End-of-day balancing procedure in a cash register environment.

4. Assume that the Cash Short or Over account is posted daily as in the account below. Examine the account and answer the following questions.

Cash Short or Over

Date	Particulars	P.R.	Debit	Credit	DR/CR	Balance
19— July 3			10 —			
4			2 —			
7				5 —		
10			20 —			
11				1 —		
12			5 —			
14				50		
17				1 50		
18			2 —			
20			1 —			
24			10 —			
25				75		
26			3 —			
27			10 —			
28			5 —			
31			1 —		Dr	60 25

1. On how many days was there a cash shortage?
2. On how many days was there a cash overage?
3. Is the net result for the month an overage or a shortage?
4. Does this account as it stands represent an expense or an income?

5. At the end of a business day, Joanne Adamson is responsible for preparing the night deposit for Marks and Associates. The deposit is to be made up from the currency and Visa slips shown below.

1. Prepare the deposit on the form provided in the workbook for June 10, 19—. Use account no. 756210.
2. Agree the deposit with the accounting entry figure of $8 978.29.

Currency

    Bills $1 × 57
              $2 × 85
              $5 × 42
              $10 × 78
              $20 × 101
              $50 × 22
              $100 × 8

    Coin   1¢ × 151
              5¢ × 86
              10¢ × 158
              25¢ × 141

Visa Slips

James	$109.14
Carter	83.46
Paracy	483.64
DeCorte	102.72
Hill	24.61
Melnyk	630.23
Thrower	85.60

Cheques

Thompson	$362.73
Meyer	55.64
Bogard	911.64
Geyer	155.50
Metsopoulis	228.98
Morris	189.95
Savela	334.91
Webb	25.68

14.5 Accounting Controls

Every business establishes some kind of accounting system or set of procedures. The owner of a business should make the time and effort to establish a good system, one that has strong "internal control."

Internal Control

An accounting system that promotes employee honesty, accuracy, and efficiency is considered to have good internal control. **Internal control** is the set of accounting procedures established to protect the assets from theft and waste, ensure accurate accounting data, encourage efficiency, and adhere to company policies.

No internal control is necessary in a small business where the owner functions alone. But as the business grows and employees are hired, accounting controls become a factor in managing the business. Where there are a large number of employees, a good system of internal control is essential. A business should not take chances about its employees' honesty and dedication. It should take whatever steps it can to protect itself.

A good system of internal control can be quite involved and highly detailed. Some fundamental rules of good internal control are:

1. in the processing and preparation of accounting records and documents, the system should be designed, where possible, so that the work of one person must agree with the work of another person whose work is done independently;
2. the person who records transactions or prepares accounting records should not also be the one to control or handle the assets physically;
3. all assets should be kept in a safe place. The presence of two authorized persons should be required before access to negotiable assets is allowed. (Negotiable assets are those that can be easily converted into cash);
4. powers of approval and authorization should be restricted to a few key employees;
5. periodically, an audit by an independent public accountant should be carried out to ensure that the accounting system is being followed correctly, and to improve the system if weaknesses are found;
6. responsibilities should be firmly established. It should be easy to tell who is responsible for errors or missing assets.

Procedures for the Control of Cash

Internal control affects all aspects of a business but is especially needed for cash. Cash is the single item most likely to be stolen outright by employees. Cash is the item most likely to be embezzled, that is, stolen secretly, with the help of falsified accounting records. Cash has no special marks to identify it, and is easily exchanged for other goods or services.

The following are internal control measures specially designed to protect the cash of a business.

1. *Separate duties.* In general, the people who handle the cash should not be the same ones who keep the records for the cash. For example, the person who opens the mail and prepares the daily list of mail receipts should not be a member of the accounting department. If this procedure is followed, a theft can only take place if two or more employees decide to act together. (This is known as collusion.) A mail clerk who acted alone would be caught easily. Suppose, for instance, that the mail clerk managed to cash a customer's cheque for personal use. The customer's account would not be credited with the amount of the cheque and there would eventually be a complaint. An investigation would point to the mail clerk who had access to the cheque.

2. *Deposit funds daily.* The total cash receipts for the day should be deposited by the end of that day. In this way the amount of cash in the office is kept to a minimum. Theft is both prevented and discouraged. A night depository system is provided by banks for the benefit of businesses who take in cash outside of banking hours.

3. *Deposit funds intact.* All of the cash receipts of each business day should be deposited intact. Cash received during the day should not be available for making payments or for borrowing by employees. The only exception to this rule is for cash register "pay outs" which are controlled by the cash register audit strip.

4. *Make all payments by cheque.* Except for petty cash expenditures, all payments should be supported by documents and follow a rigid set of approvals. Payment should never be by cash, only by cheque. When all payments are made by cheque and all cash receipts are deposited intact, the records prepared by the company correspond to the records prepared by the bank. It is then possible to compare the one against the other. This control technique, known as the bank reconciliation, is described in the next section.

5. *Mark cheques "For Deposit Only."* Mark all cheques received "For Deposit Only." Each cheque can only be credited to the business's bank account and cannot be cashed in any other way.

6. *Prepare deposit slips in duplicate.* The deposit slip shows the details of the deposit, and is useful if any question arises regarding the deposit. A duplicate of the deposit slip should be stamped by the teller and retained by the business as a receipt for the deposit.

7. *Use cash registers in retail stores.* Cash registers should be used in retail outlets of any size and the cash receipts should be balanced every day. The audit strip and the balancing form become the source documents for the entries to the accounting system.

8. *Reconcile bank accounts monthly.* As was mentioned above, the company's and the bank's records can be compared or "reconciled." If a company has more than one bank account, each one should be reconciled monthly.

Bank Reconciliation

Since both the bank and the business keep a record of the same funds, you might expect the month-end balance shown by the bank statement to agree with the month-end balance shown by the general ledger Bank account. This rarely happens.

Usually, the bank statement balance differs from the Bank account balance in the general ledger. How then can the accounting department be certain that either record is correct? The accuracy of both balances is proven by a process known as the bank reconciliation. A **bank reconciliation** is a routine procedure to determine why the balance on deposit in the bank does not agree with the balance on deposit as shown by the books of the company. The procedure involves a thorough investigation of the two sets of records and ends only after all the causes of the difference are uncovered. The process is completed by the preparation of a bank reconciliation statement. A **bank reconciliation statement** is a statement showing the causes for the difference between the bank balance as shown by the bank and the bank balance as shown in the general ledger of the depositor. An example of a bank reconciliation statement is shown in Figure 14.17.

Boxwell and Company
Bank Reconciliation Statement
March 31, 19—

Bank's Record			Company's Record		
Balance per statement		1204 90	Balance per ledger		1157 76
Add Late Deposit		300 51	Deduct: Error in recording cheque #697 for postage.		
		1505 41	Was recorded as $25.60		
Deduct Outstanding Cheqs.			Should have been 26.50		
#702	$60.00		Difference .90		90
#705	72.40				1156 86
#709	51.90				
#710	175.00				
#711	2.75	362 05	Deduct: Bank service charge not recorded in company books.		13 50
True balance		1143 36	True balance		1143 36

Figure 14.17 A bank reconciliation statement.

Steps in Reconciling a Bank Account

The steps in reconciling a bank account are outlined below.

1. Have the following records available:
    a. the bank statement and related vouchers received from the bank;

b. the bank reconciliation statement for the previous month;
c. the general ledger Bank account;
d. the cash receipts journal;
e. the cash payments;
f. the general journal.

2. Write the heading Bank Reconciliation Statement and the date on a sheet of paper. Then divide the page down the middle. Write the heading "Company's Record" on one side. Write the heading "Bank's Record" on the other side.

3. Enter the ending balance from the bank statement on the side of the page headed Bank's Record. Enter the ending balance from the general ledger Bank account on the side of the page headed Company's Record.

4. Search for and identify all of the "discrepancy items," that is, the items causing the two balances to differ. This is the most difficult and the most important part of the reconciliation. It involves an item-by-item comparison of the bank's record with the business's record. The search is for items that are not recorded equally in both sets of records. Locating the discrepancy items involves a well-organized and skilful search. The techniques for doing this are explained below.

5. Record the discrepancy items on the reconciliation statement, adding or subtracting them as necessary until the two balances are shown to be equal. This step is also explained below. The reconciliation is not complete until a balance is reached.

Locating the Discrepancy Items The following suggestions will be helpful to you in searching out the discrepancy items.

a. When comparing the two sets of records, it is never necessary to go back in the records beyond one month. The previous reconciliation statement will show any differences that originated before then.

b. The bank's record must be compared item by item with the business's record. When individual items are found to correspond exactly, they are marked in some way with a coloured pen or pencil. After the comparison is completed, the items without coloured marks beside them represent the discrepancy items.

c. The most common discrepancy item is the quantity of uncashed cheques commonly known as the outstanding cheques. An **outstanding cheque** is a cheque that is issued and recorded by the company, but not cashed by the bank, during the period covered by the bank statement. When a cheque is issued by a business, it is recorded promptly in the books of the business, but it is not recorded in the records of the bank until it is presented to them for payment. In many cases, this may be after several days or even weeks have passed.

d. Another common discrepancy item is the late deposit. A **late deposit** is a deposit that is made and recorded in the books of the business on the last day (usually) of the period covered by the bank statement, but which does not appear on the bank statement because of a processing delay. The late deposit usually appears as the first item on the bank statement for the following period.

e. Several other discrepancy items may occur. For example, a bank employee or a company employee might make an error, such as recording an incorrect amount.

Another example might be a bank service charge that the company had not yet learned of.

f. When comparing the records, it is important to deal with items from the previous reconciliation statement. Most of those items will cease to be discrepancy items during the current month. However, there are usually some that do not get cleared up in the current month and must be carried forward to the new reconciliation statement. For example, consider a cheque that was outstanding on the reconciliation statement for April 30. This cheque would be still outstanding as of May 31 if it was not cashed during the month of May. It would have to go on the reconciliation statement for May 31. On the other hand, if the cheque was cashed during the month of May, it would no longer be an outstanding cheque and would be marked off as being cleared.

Recording the Discrepancy Items Discrepancy items are recorded on the bank reconciliaton statement.

a. All discrepancy items must be included. It is customary to group items of a similar nature, such as outstanding cheques.
b. Each item is recorded on one side of the reconciliation statement only, either on the bank side or on the company side. Always choose the side for which the item has not shown up as of the reconciliation date. For example, an outstanding cheque would be recorded on the bank's side because it represents an item not seen by the bank. Similarly, a bank service charge would be recorded on the company's side because it represents an item not seen in the company's records.
c. Each item represents either an increase or a decrease to the balance. Common sense should tell you which it is. Just decide what effect the item has on the bank balance and act accordingly. For example, cheques and service charges represent decreases to the bank balance and are therefore treated as deductions. Similarly, deposits increase the bank balance and are therefore treated as additions.
d. The two final totals on the reconciliation statement will be the same if all discrepancy items are found and entered properly. If the totals are not equal, the process must be repeated until a balance is reached.

Bringing the Accounts Up-to-Date

The discrepancy items on the company's side of the reconciliation statement are the reasons why the Bank account is not currently up-to-date. These particular items must be journalized and posted to bring the Bank account up-to-date. For the reconciliation statement in Figure 14.17 the following two journal entries are necessary.

	DR	CR
Mar. 31 Miscellaneous Expense	$ .90	
Bank		$ .90
To correct error on cheque #697		
31 Bank Charges	13.50	
Bank		13.50
To record bank charges for March		

Personal Bank Reconciliation

Individuals, as well as businesses, should reconcile their bank accounts regularly. One cannot be certain of the accuracy of personal bank records unless they are reconciled. A reconciliation for a personal account is simpler than one for a business. Usually, there are fewer transactions, and only the one personal record (the personal record book) to compare with the bank statement. Still, it is a task requiring care and perseverence.

Section Review Questions

1. Define "internal control."
2. Why is internal control not necessary for a one-person business?
3. When does internal control become necessary?
4. Describe what is meant by "separation of duties" with respect to internal control.
5. What is the purpose of having an independent audit?
6. Why should responsibilities be firmly established?
7. Why is cash control extremely important?
8. Explain what is meant by the phrase, "depositing funds intact."
9. What is a bank reconciliation?
10. Why is a bank reconciliation necessary?
11. What is a discrepancy item?
12. What is an outstanding cheque?
13. What is a late deposit?
14. What does it mean to bring the accounts up-to-date, with respect to a bank reconciliation?

Section Exercises

1. **Analyze each of the following mini-cases and prepare a brief report taking into consideration the following possibilities:**
   —Is there dishonesty or theft?
   —Is there income tax evasion?
   —Are there poor hiring practices?
   —Who benefits? the owner? the employee?
   —Who loses? the owner? the general public?
   —Identify weaknesses in internal control.
   —Identify or speculate upon internal control strengths.
   —State what steps could be taken to improve the system.

   1. The Doggie Salon is a very small family operation in the business of washing and grooming dogs. The work is done for cash and the money is collected when the dog is picked up. There is no paper work. The owner pockets the cash.

2. Joan Ormsby works for City Car Rental. On most weekends Joan arranges for her friend Peter to have the use of one of the cars free of charge.

3. Phil Baker is negotiating with a contractor to have his driveway paved. After a price is unofficially agreed upon, Phil tells the contractor that the job is hers if she is willing to take cash under the table at a fifteen per cent discount. The contractor agrees because she needs the work.

4. Mary Gozzard drives a delivery van for Excel Electrical Supply. She is allowed to take the van home at night so that she can make deliveries on her way to and from work. Mary usually manages to slip some materials for herself into the van. She drops these off at her home where she either uses them herself or sells them to others.

5. Myra Metz is the owner of a jewellery store. She does not like to be in the store all the time and uses part-time workers to help out in the store. There is a large turnover of the staff. The store is barely profitable and Myra senses that a lot of merchandise goes missing.

6. Karen Ion has a position of authority with the Exact Company. She arranges for a major repair to be performed on her home and for the repair bill to be sent to her employer. Karen intercepts the bill when it arrives, approves it for payment, and has it processed through the company.

7. Fran Boyko has a responsible position with Apex Company. She arranges with a supplier of goods to the company to charge a higher than normal price for them. Fran later approves these inflated bills for payment. Fran receives a percentage.

8. Darren Park is an executive with Supreme Products. He sets up a fictitious company which he owns outright. Through this company Darren sends phony invoices to Supreme Products. Later, he approves the phony bills for payment. The money paid to the phony company ends up in Darren Park's pocket.

9. Syd Gerrard takes a job as a doorman for a theatre. He tells his friends that he will be able to let them in free. However, he finds that this is not easily done.

10. Herb Morris is employed as a gasoline attendant. His friends come to the station when he is there trying to get free gasoline. Herb says that he cannot give out free gas without getting caught.

11. Super Sand and Gravel is engaged by Crown Road Builders to deliver loads of stone to the site of a road building project. The stone costs $500 a load. Jim Cox, foreman at the site, signs for each load as it is delivered. The signed slips form the basis for the invoice sent by Super Sand and Gravel to Crown Road Builders. Jim Cox has a friend who is building a house not far from the job site. The house needs a lot of stone for the large driveway, basement, and garage. Jim diverts a number of loads from the job site to the home of his friend, and signs for them as if they had been delivered to the project. Jim is rewarded by his friend for the favour.

12. Valley Forest is a ski resort with an extensive network of cross-country ski trails. The fee for cross-country skiing is six dollars a day, paid at the main chalet. Many

people do not bother to pay for the cross-country skiing but merely drive to remote sections of the course and enter and exit freely.

13. A friend of yours works as a waitress in a local restaurant. One evening you are dining at the restaurant at a time when your friend is on duty. You suggest to her that it would be nice if you could have a free dinner. Your friend replies that she would be sure to be caught.
14. All of the trucks of General Construction get their gasoline from company pumps. Some of the drivers work out a scheme in which their personal cars are parked in locations where it is easy to stop by and syphon gas into them.
15. Joanne Lake is the accounts receivable clerk for a large company. On many occasions customers come personally to the company to pay their accounts in cash. Joanne, who is often short of money, keeps the cash for her own use with the intention of paying it back later. She is far behind in paying back the money.
16. Stephanie Chabot is a roofing contractor. She has a hired crew that does all of the roofing. Stephanie makes the contacts and does the estimating. She never loses any materials. Her workers find it impossible to work for anyone else on the sly, without Stephanie's knowledge.
17. K. K. Brown's company owns a lot of heavy construction equipment. When making a half million dollar purchase of new units, K. K. insists that the invoices be made to look like a purchase of spare parts. K. K. can then write the equipment off immediately instead of depreciating it over a period of time.
18. Eric and Thelma together own a butcher shop and grocery store. Whenever they need food for their family, they just take it home out of the store. There is no bookkeeping involved.
19. Mario Tremblay is a carpenter. He is building a new bathroom in his home and requires some plumbing work. Andrew Carmichael is a plumber. He is building an addition onto his house and needs some carpentry work. The two men agree to exchange services free of charge.
20. Canair is a large airplane manufacturer. The building of aircraft requires many special tools which the employees are not expected to own. Within the plant is a central tool area (crib) in which tools of all kinds are stored. Employees who need special tools are expected to obtain them from the tool crib. In return, they sign a receipt (chit) which is kept on file in the tool crib. When a tool is returned, the chit is given back to the employee. The staff operating the crib do no other work. The chits on file in the crib are reviewed periodically to make sure that tools are returned. Any employee who quits or is dismissed does not get paid until the outstanding chits are settled.

2. The following are the personal chequing account record and the bank statement for the account of Paul Swartz for the month of June. Paul Swartz's bank reconciliation statement for May is also shown.

Section 14.5   519

1. From these records, reconcile the bank account of Paul Swartz as of June 30.
2. State what entry or entries are necessary to bring the personal record to the true bank balance.

   A. Paul Swartz's previous reconciliation.

```
                    Paul Swartz
                 Bank Reconciliation
                    May 31, 19—

   Personal Record              Bank Statement

Latest Balance  1 200.75   Latest Balance  1 450.75
                           Deduct:
                           Outstanding cheques
                            #44   100 —
                            #45   150 —      250 —

True Balance   1 200.75    True Balance   1 200.75
```

   B. Paul Swartz's personal record.

CHEQUE NO.	DATE	CHEQUE ISSUED TO	AMOUNT OF CHEQUE	V	AMOUNT OF DEPOSIT	BALANCE FORWARD
	19—					1 200 75
46	Jun 2	Rowlands Garage	237 50			963 25
47	4	Joanne's Clothes	92 50			870 75
48	9	Provincial Treasurer	9 —			861 75
49	15	Rockway Gardens	7 73			854 02
50	20	The Examiner	5 50			848 52
51	20	Daily Times	6 30			842 22
	27	Salary			740 —	1 682 22
52	30	Marigold Apartments	275 —			1 407 22

C. Bank statement sent to Paul Swartz.

GENERAL BANK

STATEMENT OF ACCOUNT WITH **PAUL SWARTZ**

CHEQUES	DEPOSITS	DATE	BALANCE
Balance forward		May 31	1 450.75
100.00		June 1	1 350.75
150.00		June 4	1 200.75
237.50		June 9	963.25
92.50	9.00	June 16	861.75
7.73		June 20	854.02
	740.00	June 27	1 594.02
5.50		June 30	1 588.52
S.C. 1.75		June 30	1 586.77

S.C. Service Charge

3. **Workbook Exercise: Additional bank reconciliation exercise.**

4. Answer the following questions about J. C. Water's bank reconciliation statement as shown below:

J. C. WATERS
BANK RECONCILIATION STATEMENT
MARCH 31, 19--

Balance per bank statement		$2 046.75
Add late deposit, March 31		271.50
		$2 318.25
Less outstanding cheques		
#418	$ 62.80	
#522	103.40	
#523	41.90	208.10
True balance		$2 110.15
Balance per Cash account		$2 186.85
Less bank charges	$ 5.40	
NSF cheque—Walker	71.30	76.70
True balance		$2 110.15

1. Does the $2 046.75 represent the bank balance at the beginning or at the end of the month?

2. Why do you think the March 31 deposit was not included in the bank balance?

3. How does Waters know that there are three cheques outstanding? Why are they subtracted?

4. Is $2 186.85 the cash balance at the beginning or at the end of the month?

5. What is an NSF cheque? Why is it subtracted from the balance per books?

6. A certified cheque for $200 payable to R. Smit is still outstanding. Why is it not part of the outstanding cheques on the bank reconciliation statement?

CHAPTER HIGHLIGHTS

Now that you have completed Chapter 14, you should:

1. know the purpose of a petty cash fund;
2. know how to establish, operate, and replenish a petty cash fund;
3. know the accounting entries for establishing and for replenishing a petty cash fund;
4. know the basic services, accounts, documents, and statements of chartered banks;
5. know what is meant by NSF cheque, certified cheque, and post-dated cheque;
6. know the advantages, disadvantages, and procedures related to bank credit cards;
7. be able to do the accounting for bank credit card transactions;
8. appreciate the place of cash registers in a modern computerized system;
9. understand the purpose of, and be able to interpret, the detailed audit strip;
10. be able to prove the cash and prepare the bank deposit and related accounting summaries;
11. be able to account for cash short or over;
12. know the features of a current bank account;
13. understand the meaning of internal control;
14. know the specific control features associated with cash;
15. be able to reconcile a bank account for a business or an individual;
16. be able to perform the accounting entries that result from a bank reconciliation.

ACCOUNTING TERMS

audit strip	internal control
bank deposit	late deposit
bank reconciliation	NSF cheque
bank reconciliation statement	outstanding cheque
cash short or over	personal chequing account
certified cheque	petty cash fund
change fund	petty cash voucher
current bank account	point-of-sale terminal
daily interest savings account	post-dated cheque
detailed audit tape	proving the cash
float	pure savings account
imprest method for petty cash	replenishing petty cash

CHAPTER EXERCISES

Using Your Knowledge

1. You are the keeper of the petty cash fund for Graphic Art Supplies. Since the fund is very low, you are in the process of preparing the petty cash summary to be used to obtain the replenishing cheque.

    Below left is a listing of the vouchers in the petty cash box, giving a description of the nature of the payment for each. Below right is the chart of accounts for Graphic Art Supplies.

    Prepare the petty cash summary for the purpose of obtaining the replenishing cheque.

PETTY CASH VOUCHERS

1.	Owner's parking receipt	$ 9.00
2.	Paint for building	13.50
3.	New broom for janitor	12.75
4.	Typewriter ribbons	8.35
5.	Supper money for employee	7.50
6.	Postage stamps	15.00
7.	New window pane	20.00
8.	Telegram charge	10.50
9.	Donation to Boy Scouts	10.00
10.	Payment to student for cleaning up the grounds	10.50
11.	Mileage to employee for using personal car for business	17.50
12.	Coffee and doughnuts brought in for a business meeting	24.35
13.	Dog licence for watchdog	10.00
14.	Parking receipt of owner	7.00
15.	Supper money for employee	7.50
16.	Postage for parcel delivery	15.00

CHART OF ACCOUNTS

1 Bank
2 Accounts Receivable
3 Merchandise Inventory
4 Supplies
5 Equipment
6 Automobile
20 Bank loan
21 Accounts Payable
30 Judi Mavar, Capital
31 Judi Mavar, Drawings
40 Sales
50 Purchases
51 Freight-in
52 Advertising
53 Bank Charges
54 Building Maintenance
55 Car Expense
56 Delivery Expense
57 Donations Expense
58 Light and Heat Expense
59 Miscellaneous Expense
60 Telephone Expense
61 Wages Expense

2. This exercise also appears in your workbook.

From the audit strip given below:
1. Compute the summary totals that would be produced by the machine.
2. Work out the accounting entry for the above totals if the Paid Out is for supplies.

```
           137.00  MDS
             9.59  TAX
           146.59  TOTL
           150.00  CASH
CASL 166     3.41  CHNG


           175.00  MDS
VISA 167   187.25  TOTL


           100.00  RECD
RECD 168   100.00  TOTL


           356.25  MDS
            24.94  TAX
VISA 169   381.19  TOTL


           REFUND
           128.00- MDS
             8.96- TAX
           136.98- TOTL
CASL 170   136.98- CASH


            50.00  P.O.
P.O. 171    50.00  TOTL


           150.00  MDS
            10.50  TAX
           160.50  TOTL
           170.00  CASH
CASL 172     9.50  CHNG


            70.00  MDS
             4.90  TAX
CHRG 173    74.90  TOTL
```

```
                SUMMARY
CASL 174  ____•____ (CASH SALES INCL. TAX)
RECD 175  ____•____ (VISA SALES INCL. TAX)
P.O. 176  ____•____ (PAID OUTS)
CHRG 177  ____•____ (CHRG SALES INCL. TAX)
RECD 178  ____•____ (RECEIVED ON ACCOUNT)
CRDT 179  ____•____ (RETURN FOR CREDIT)
TAX  180  ____•____ (NET SALES TAX)
MDS  181  ____•____ (SALES LESS RETURNS)
CASH 182  ____•____ (NET CASH RECEIVED)
```

3. **Workbook Exercise: Completing a chart about bank reconciliations.**

4. **Shown below are all of the records that you will need to reconcile the current bank account of Proctor & Kemp at July 31, 19--.**
   (Note: Normally the bank returns all of the "paid" cheques to the business along with the bank statement. This cannot be done in a textbook. Instead, on the bank statement in brackets beside each amount in the Cheques column is either an explanation of the charge or the cheque number.)

   A. Bank reconciliation statement for the previous month's end, shown below.

<u>Proctor & Kemp</u>
<u>Bank Reconciliation Statement</u>
<u>June 30, 19-</u>

Balance per Bank Statement	1406.03	Balance per General Ledger	773.28
Add: Late Deposit	551.00	Deduct: Bank Charge not entered in books of company	
	1957.03	(1) Service charge $16.50	
Deduct: Outstanding Cheques		(2) Loan Interest 33.50	50.00
#83 $5.10			
780 71.03			
828 400.00			
846 96.02			
852 123.50			
860 15.00			
871 16.01			
873 17.50			
881 33.60			
886 121.47			
889 60.00			
890 170.00			
891 31.94			
892 27.61			
894 13.82			
898 12.50			
899 18.65	1233.75		
True Balance	723.28	True Balance	723.28

B. "Amount of Deposits" column of cash receipts journal for July, page 14.

$$
\begin{aligned}
\$\ \ 262.75& \\
312.70& \\
274.19& \\
161.40& \\
700.20& \\
265.92& \\
400.61& \\
396.21& \\
\underline{316.40}& \\
\underline{\$3\ 090.38}&
\end{aligned}
$$

C. July general journal entry affecting "Bank", page 9.

Bank	5.10	
Miscellaneous Income		5.10
To cancel outstanding cheque		
No. 83 issued June 19--		

D. Excerpts from cash payments journal for July, page 18.

Explanation	Chq. No.	Bank Credit
	900	$ 100.00
	901	171.31
	902	142.19
Loan Interest, June		33.50
Service Charge, June		16.50
	903	16.41
	904	17.50
	905	10.00
	906	12.40
	907	19.61
	908	31.40
	909	76.39
	910	65.20
	911	500.00
	912	216.75
	914	8.21
	915	2.60
	916	9.40
	917	50.00
	918	50.00
	919	33.19
	920	29.33
	921	65.00
	922	25.00
	923	25.00
	924	419.63
	925	372.60
	926	900.00
		$3 419.12

E. Partial general ledger Bank account.

BANK					No. 1	
Date	Particulars	P.R.	Debit	Credit	Balance	DR CR
19– June 30					773.28	DR
July 31		CR14	3090.38			
July 31		CP18		3419.12		
July 31		J9		5.10	449.64	DR

F. July bank statement.

Cheques				Deposits	Date	Balance
					June 30	1 406.03
18.65	(899)	31.94	(891)	551.00	July 2	1 906.44
121.47	(886)				3	1 784.97
100.00	(900)	96.02	(846)	262.75	5	1 851.70
12.50	(898)				5	1 839.20
71.03	(780)	27.61	(892)		6	1 740.56
142.19	(902)				6	1 598.37
400.00	(828)			312.70	8	1 511.07
15.00	(860)	13.82	(894)		9	1 482.25
16.01	(871)	171.31	(901)		10	1 294.93
17.50	(904)				10	1 277.43
10.00	(905)			274.19	11	1 541.62
500.00	(911)				12	1 041.61
33.60	(N.S.F. cheque of R.C. Jones)			161.40	15	1 169.42
50.00	(913)				16	1 119.42
170.00	(890)	12.40	(906)		17	937.02
76.39	(909)				19	860.63
31.40	(908)			700.20	22	1 529.43
9.40	(916)	19.61	(907)		23	1 500.42
2.60	(915)				23	1 497.82
				265.92	25	1 763.74
33.19	(919)			400.61	26	2 131.16
17.50	(873)				27	2 113.66
50.00	(917)			396.21	30	2 459.87
25.00	(922)	419.63	(924)		31	2 015.24
165.00	(Promissory Note paid to J. Timko)				31	1 850.24
29.00	(Interest on Loan)				31	1 821.24
12.60	(Service Charge)				31	1 808.64

Reconcile the bank account and make the necessary accounting entries in the books of the company. Cheque no. 913 is for supplies.

5. **Workbook Exercise:** Additional bank reconciliation exercise.

6. **Workbook Exercise:** Additional bank reconciliation exercise.

Comprehensive Exercise

7. For each of the following groups, indicate which statement is NOT true by recording the appropriate letter in the space indicated in your workbook.

1. a. Cash means dollar bills and coins only.
   b. The principal objective of a business is to earn a profit.
   c. The usual method of establishing a petty cash fund is to issue a cheque made out to Petty Cash.
   d. The imprest system of petty cash involves entrusting the cash to an individual.
   e. The vouchers and the cash in the petty cash box should add up to the balance of the Petty Cash account.

2. a. The cheque made out to Petty Cash is usually handed over to the person responsible for the petty cash fund.
   b. Outside of office hours the petty cash box is usually kept in the company safe.
   c. For every expenditure out of the petty cash fund there must be a bill or sales slip from a store.
   d. When a payment is being made out of the petty cash fund, no accounting entries are made immediately.
   e. The petty cash fund must be replenished when the amount of cash in the box gets low.

3. a. The first step to replenishing the petty cash fund is to prepare a summary of the vouchers in the petty cash box.
   b. The petty cashier submits the summary of charges, together with the bills and vouchers, in order to obtain a cheque.
   c. The summary and the vouchers together are accepted as the source document for the replenishing cheque.
   d. The accounting entry to record the replenishing cheque is: debit Petty Cash; credit Bank.
   e. The accounting entry to replenish the petty cash fund is one of the two accounting entries that affect petty cash.

4. a. Banks provide essential services for both businesses and individuals.
   b. The processing of cheques and bank credit card vouchers is known as the electronic transfer of funds.
   c. Banks are able to meet the needs of most customers by having a variety of accounts and services.
   d. The interest rate for a daily interest savings account is higher than it is for a pure savings account.
   e. You must put some money in a bank account to "open" it.

5. a. The bank statement given to the customer once a month is identical to the bank's own record.
   b. Except for breakdowns, electronic tellers may be used at any time.
   c. It is difficult to borrow money if your credit rating is poor.

d. Writing cheques that bounce can be damaging to your credit rating.

   e. The true bank balance is the one shown by the bank's record.

6. a. Placing only your signature on the back of a cheque made out to you is an "open" endorsement.

   b. Banks require the payee (the person to whom the cheque is issued) to guarantee the cheque by signing it on the back.

   c. If the balance in the issuer's account is not large enough to cover the amount of a cheque, the bank will dishonour it.

   d. A cheque that has not bounced is a dishonoured cheque.

   e. The bank has the right to take the amount of a dishonoured cheque out of your account without contacting you.

7. a. The accounting entry to record a dishonoured cheque is the exact opposite of the accounting entry that was made when the cheque was deposited.

   b. You must phone the bank to find out if a cheque that you received is certified.

   c. You can be sure of a cheque not bouncing if it is certified.

   d. The funds to pay a certified cheque are taken out of the bank account at the time the cheque is certified.

   e. A post-dated cheque is one that is dated for some time in the future.

8. a. The usual reason for issuing a post-dated cheque is to meet a series of payments such as for a mortgage.

   b. A certified cheque is marked GUARANTEED by the bank.

   c. A cheque written on January 15 but dated for March 1 is a post-dated cheque.

   d. You should ask for a certified cheque when you are dealing with a stranger and when the amount of money is large.

   e. The bank does not cash cheques bearing a future date.

9. a. Bank credit cards can be obtained from large department stores and similar chains.

   b. Most smaller retail outlets do not offer their own individualized credit cards.

   c. Visa and Mastercard are bank credit cards sponsored by major banks.

   d. The consumer is usually given twenty-one days from the statement date to make payment.

   e. Bank credit cards may be used to obtain a cash advance.

10. a. The bank credit card system depends on computerized equipment to make it work.

   b. The consumer's credit rating is established with a merchant when the credit card is presented.

   c. For some purchases it is better to take an ordinary bank loan than to use the bank credit card.

   d. Credit card slips are deposited in the bank just as if they were cheques from customers.

   e. The consumer pays all of the charges made by the banks for the bank credit card system.

11. a. A listing of cheques received in the mail is prepared because the cheques have to be deposited in the bank.
    b. The listing of the cheques in part **a** is prepared by a member of the accounting department who knows the system.
    c. Sales slips are pre-numbered so that all slips can be accounted for.
    d. In a business where there are "cash" receipts, it is necessary to prove the cash at the end of each day.
    e. There is a greater chance for a cash shortage than there is for a cash overage.

12. a. A point-of-sale terminal is a stand-alone electronic cash register.
    b. A "float" is a small sum of money set aside to be used as a starting fund for the cash register each day.
    c. The detailed audit tape is locked inside the cash register.
    d. At the end of each day the cash register can be made to produce summary totals for the day.
    e. A modern cash register can itself produce most of the figures needed to prove the cash.

13. a. At the end of each day the cash, vouchers, and daily balance form are forwarded to the accounting department.
    b. A cash shortage is entered as a debit to an expense account.
    c. A current bank account is one designed especially for the use of businesses.
    d. With a current account the paid cheques are returned to the depositor at the end of each month.
    e. Cash is said to be proved when there is no shortage or overage.

14. a. Businesses endorse all cheques "FOR DEPOSIT ONLY."
    b. All cheques for deposit must be endorsed.
    c. For businesses, deposit slips are prepared in duplicate.
    d. Every business requires internal control to ensure accuracy and honesty.
    e. The person who records transactions or prepares accounting records should not also be the one to control or handle the assets physically.

15. a. Cash is the single item most likely to be stolen.
    b. The total cash receipts for the day should be deposited on that day and intact.
    c. Since both the bank and the business keep a record of the same funds, the two balances should always agree unless an error has been made.
    d. Every bank account should be reconciled once a month.
    e. An outstanding cheque is a cheque that is issued and recorded by the company but not cashed by the bank.

For Further Thought

8. Briefly answer the following questions.

1. You have a pure savings account in a local bank which pays interest every six months on the minimum balance for the six months. Except for one day, on which

your balance dipped to $49, you have maintained a balance in your account of $3 500 for the latest six-month period. On what balance will you be paid interest? Comment on this.

2. For emergency use only you acquired a card that permits you to use the automatic tellers for your bank. You have never had to use the service until now, when you find yourself out of town and without money. However, you cannot remember your personal identification number which is necessary to operate the machines. When seeking help from a nearby bank branch, you are told that there is no way for them to help you get your number. Comment on this predicament.

3. You do not keep a personal record of your bank transactions. Instead, you rely entirely on the bank's record. Why is this a poor practice?

4. A company that is not able to pay its bills can be forced into bankruptcy. The XYZ Company was forced into bankruptcy although it had consistently made substantial profits. Explain how this is possible.

5. ABC Company is a small business that sells over the counter, mostly for cash. The company does not use a petty cash fund, but takes money out of the general cash receipts to pay for any small expenditures. Why is this a poor practice?

6. PQ company has a petty cash fund but it is not under any one employee's specific control. Why is this undesirable?

7. The auditor of a company, when checking the petty cash fund, finds that the total of the cash and vouchers is $25 less than the balance shown by the Petty Cash fund. Explain how this could happen. What should the auditor do about it?

8. The auditor of a company, when checking the petty cash fund, finds a number of employees' I.O.U.s in the fund. However, the fund totals correctly with the I.O.U.s included. What course of action should the auditor take?

9. You are the custodian of the petty cash fund. An employee presents you with a legitimate bill to be paid from the fund, but there is not enough cash in the fund to pay it. What will you do?

10. XYZ Company has a petty cash fund of $300. On December 31, the company's year-end, the fund contained $22.50 in cash, the rest in vouchers. What should be done about this?

11. A major commercial bank offers a special category for large deposits. This is a daily interest savings account that offers its highest interest rate but requires maintaining a minimum balance of $5 000. How can the bank make money with this plan?

12. You accepted a cheque for a debt from a friend because you knew with certainty that sufficient funds were in the bank to cover it. However, there were not sufficient funds in the account when you presented the cheque for payment five days later. How could this be possible?

13. You accept a cheque drawn on a bank in a nearby town. You drive to the nearby town to cash the cheque right away. The bank there will not cash the cheque for you but does certify it. Why would they follow this procedure?

14. A post-dated cheque is sent to your business in the mail to pay a bill but you do not notice that the cheque is post-dated. When you attempt to deposit the cheque the bank refuses it. Explain your feelings.
15. Frank and Edna are discussing their credit card spending. Frank claims that the transaction fees are quite reasonable and that there are no interest charges if the account is paid promptly. Edna points out that, despite this, they *are* paying a lot for interest each month. Explain how this can be the case.
16. You are about to write a cheque for $4 500 to pay for a new computer. While you are waiting, another customer pays for an identical purchase with a Visa card. You know that the merchant will only receive about $4 365 for the Visa sale because of the Visa discount. You change your mind and offer the merchant a cheque for $4 365. Will the merchant accept your offer? Comment on this.
17. Assume that Bill Wallingford, a local businessperson, neither rolls coins nor arranges currency by denomination when he is making up his daily deposit. Assuming that the bank accepts Bill's deposit in this state, what effect will it have on the bank teller and the people in the line-up behind Bill?
18. A cheque made out to Timothy Waukey is endorsed by Timothy as follows: ''Pay to the order of Jack Keeshig only.'' What kind of endorsement is this? What can happen to this cheque?
19. Jack Morgan works in the warehouse of North-American Auto Supply. He regularly steals merchandise in order to add to his wages. How will Jack benefit from the stolen merchandise? What difficulties will Jack encounter in disposing of the goods?
20. You are the accountant for a large business with a great deal of banking activity. When you receive the monthly bank statement you observe that it has the same balance as the general ledger account. Should you reconcile the bank in this case? Explain.

CASE STUDIES

Case 1   *Service Charges: Are They Always Fair?*

Sarah Hurtig and her husband Irwin have two bank accounts: a savings account and a chequing account. Each of the two accounts is a joint account, meaning that either of the partners can independently use the accounts in all respects.

The two partners keep a personal record of each account and do attempt to keep them up-to-date. However, it is not always easy to do this, particularly with the chequing account, which gets a lot of use. Both partners cannot have the personal register at the same time, which would let them make the appropriate updating entries. Still, each one often needs to write a cheque at a time when the other partner has the register. When this happens, the one without the register tries to remember to make a note of the cheque or cheques written. These notes are supposed to be used to bring the register up-to-date as quickly as possible.

In theory this sounds simple enough, but it does not always work in practice. During one particular Christmas rush neither Sarah nor Irwin took the register at a time when both were writing lots of cheques. And, because they were either tired or busy or distracted, they failed to update the register for several days. Each assumed that there was plenty of money in the account.

However, on this occasion, the balance in the chequing account was overspent and the account was "overdrawn." This means that the balance in the account became a minus balance. In effect, this is a bank loan. In such a case, the bank takes action to cover the overdraft. It looks to see if there are any funds available in other accounts owned by the same depositor. If there are, it transfers sufficient funds to cover the overdraft allowing the cheque to be honoured. The Hurtigs had a healthy balance in their savings account and the transfer was made. The bank charged $3.50 for the service.

Unfortunately, in this case, the Hurtigs had written several cheques and each one put the account into a new overdraft position. Each time, the bank followed the same procedure including the $3.50 service charge. Since there were 14 such cheques, the total charge was $49.00.

The Hurtigs did not learn of the overdraft situation until they received their bank statement in the mail. When they saw what had happened, they were annoyed.

Questions
1. In your opinion, why were the Hurtigs annoyed?
2. In your opinion, were the Hurtigs justified in being annoyed? Explain.
3. Why do you think the bank acted in the manner it did?
4. What can the Hurtigs do to ensure that their personal register is kept up-to-date in the future? Explain.

Case 2   Is Ignorance Bliss?

Garn Mennell, a student, started up a summer business as a small contractor. Garn was regarded as being "handy with tools" and was proficient at building decks, garages, and so on; he could also do a nice job of re-roofing houses.

The funds with which to start his business came from the following sources: a newly acquired inheritance of $5 000, a low interest loan of $10 000 from his brother, and a $3 000 non-interest bearing loan from a chartered bank (part of a government program to help youth employment). With these funds Garn purchased a used truck for $7 000, ladders and equipment for $1 000, and other tools for $500. The remaining funds were placed in a business bank account.

Garn was quite good at attending to the numerous details associated with starting up a new business. As well, Garn did a thorough job of looking after the banking records and of obtaining and filing vouchers for all expenditures. He also designed first-rate estimating sheets and contracts to help him in pricing and ensuring a solid legal base for each job. However, Garn had absolutely no knowledge of accounting, and he completely neglected this aspect of running the business.

During the first season of business, Garn was able to get a number of jobs, but not enough to keep him busy all the time. He bought construction materials on credit and was able to pay his trade debts when they became due. At the end of the season he had no trade debts, had repaid the bank loan, and had paid back one-half of the principal (but no interest) on the loan from his brother. He was satisfied that things were going well. He had lots of spending money, was enjoying himself thoroughly, and had a truck to drive around. As well, he took pleasure in owning his own business, and could hold his head high among his friends.

The second season was much the same as the first except that jobs were fewer. Although Garn's work was of good quality, he was not very good at acquiring new business. He felt awkward about knocking on doors looking for work and relied on newspaper advertisements and the yellow pages. As a consequence, Garn had fewer contracts and was able to enjoy more free time as well as his status as a businessman. Towards the end of the season, however, he began to suspect that all was not well. He was beginning to experience difficulty in paying his trade bills on time and this made him uneasy. At the end of the season, he was concerned enough to ask the help of a family friend who was an accountant. The first suggestion he received was to make a list of the assets and liabilities of the business, which he did. The list showed the following:

Assets		Liabilities	
Bank balance	$150	Bank Loan	$2 000
Truck (Market Value)	5 500	Loan from brother	5 000
Total	$5 650	2 years interest	950
		Trade debts	2 000
		Total	$9 950

For two seasons Garn had been confident that he was operating a profitable business. He was absolutely certain that he had made a profit on every individual job. But now he was shaken by the picture presented by the list of assets and liabilities.

Questions

1. How much cash did Garn have in the bank to begin with, after purchasing the major assets?
2. What is Garn's present equity figure?
3. Is it possible to determine Garn's profit or loss? Explain.
4. Is it possible to determine how much money Garn withdrew for personal use? Explain.
5. How could the above situation develop without Garn's being aware of it?
6. Outline briefly the reasons for Garn's predicament.
7. What is meant by "spending capital"?
8. What is the best course of action for Garn to take now?

Case 3 The Good Life on Plastic Money

Kevin and Jean Ross grew up during the age of credit cards. It is not surprising then, that they have lots of them. Kevin, in particular, likes to show off his wallet full of credit cards. They include: Sears, The Bay, Eaton's, Canadian Tire, Visa, Mastercard, Imperial Oil, Texaco, Petro-Can, American Express, Air Canada, and En Route.

Kevin and Jean saw no reason to worry about using credit cards. They were both university graduates with high-paying jobs and lots of common sense and ability. But they also liked the good life and denied themselves very little. They bought an expensive house with fine furnishings. They ate out two or three times a week. They loved to travel and took at least one overseas vacation a year.

When they were in their twenties and living in an apartment, their lifestyle was easy to maintain. They found no difficulty in making payments on time and avoided any interest charges.

When they were in their thirties (with two children) and had moved into their nice home, their use of credit cards had changed. They seemed to have lost sight of the "account balance" amount and could only see the figure for the "minimum payment required." In most cases, this was the amount that they paid.

Now, Kevin and Jean are in their forties. To their surprise, they are often having difficulty paying even the minimum payment required. Several times now, they have received letters from creditors requesting them to reduce the balance of their account. Without really understanding it all, Kevin and Jean have realized that they are in a financial hole and need help. For assistance, they turn to the Metropolitan Credit Counselling Service.

Questions
1. Explain the chain of circumstances that led up to the situation that Kevin and Jean find themselves in.
2. In your opinion, how common is Kevin's and Jean's situation? Explain.
3. When credit limits are established, designed to keep spending within reason, how can a situation like Kevin's and Jean's develop?
4. What will the advice of the credit counselling service probably be? Explain fully.
5. Will Kevin and Jean be able to continue their lifestyle?

Case 4 Is Opportunity Knocking?

Frances Wywrot, a widow, is physically handicapped and has stopped working. Her only source of income is from $200 000 of long-term government bonds. These bonds were purchased from her own savings and from life insurance proceeds that she received when her husband died. The bonds are not guaranteed, provide for interest at twelve per cent, and have a market value of $96 for each $100 of face value.

In recent years Frances has found it increasingly difficult to maintain a decent standard of living. She has let it be known among her friends that she is looking for ways to increase her income.

A local entrepreneur who is building apartment buildings approaches Frances with a business proposal. The entrepreneur claims that Frances will receive a twenty-five per cent return on an investment in apartment buildings if she can put up a minimum of $120 000 cash. There is no guarantee, but a severe shortage of apartment units does exist in the community and the risk is considered to be minimal.

Frances is seriously considering the proposal and comes to you for advice. She is fearful of disposing of the bonds because the income from them is assured. Nevertheless, she feels that she must do something in order to improve her lot. She is considering the following three options:

i. sell all of the bonds, and invest the entire proceeds;
ii. sell $125 000 of the bonds to produce the minimum investment of $120 000 cash, and keep $75 000 in bonds;
iii. keep all of the bonds, and borrow $120 000 from the bank to invest.

Using the additional information given below, work out the net income from each of the three proposals over a two-year period. Advise Frances on the option that she should choose.

1. Income tax is calculated according to the following schedule:
   - on income between $20 001 and $30 000, thirty-two per cent;
   - on income between $30 001 and $40 000, thirty-six per cent;
   - on income over $40 000, forty per cent.

   Ignore any special income tax exemptions and conditions.
2. Personal capital losses are not chargeable as an expense of the project.
3. Bank interest is chargeable as an expense of the project. The current rate of bank interest is fifteen per cent.

Case 5   *Bank Credit Cards for all Businesses?*

Jack Graves has a painting business in Pointe Claire, Québec. Over the past year, business for Jack has been slow and he has not been fully employed. He is looking for ways to increase his business and discusses his problem with Michelle Lavoie, a friend who has a retail clothing store.

Michelle tells Jack that she had had a similar problem which she corrected by arranging to use bank credit cards. Once she started to accept bank credit cards, her sales increased by about fifteen per cent. In addition, she was able to discontinue selling on credit and no longer had to bother about collecting accounts receivable. Bad debts were entirely eliminated. Michelle considered herself to be much better off despite being charged for the service.

Jack is considering the use of bank credit cards for his business.

Discuss Jack's situation using the following questions as a guide.

1. What types of businesses are more likely to benefit from the use of bank credit cards than others?
2. Is the use of bank credit cards likely to help all types of business?
3. Would the bank accept Jack's business for credit card use? Explain.
4. If Jack could obtain bank card use, would his business benefit much? Explain.

CAREER
David Nagashima / Regional Manager

David Nagashima was first exposed to accounting in his high school classes at Campbellton High School in Campbellton, New Brunswick.

In 1975, after graduating with a Bachelor of Commerce degree from the University of New Brunswick, he started his banking career as a management trainee with Canada Trust. During this period, David gained experience in all the offices of the company's accounting system. He learned, for example, how to process loans, keep ledgers, handle many types of bank accounts, calculate interest and exchange foreign currency.

As his career progressed, David joined the Canadian Imperial Bank of Commerce as an account executive and service product manager. He was promoted to senior product manager, and his duties included developing personal lines of credit and marketing the services offered by the bank. As part of this marketing, he prepared radio advertisements to promote the bank's services; keeping abreast of the competition was important. David was also responsible for preparing the advertising budget and presided over regular meetings on budget estimates.

Seeking broader horizons, David went to the Bank of Montreal where his first job was project manager responsible for personal loans at the bank's fully automated branch (with computerized bank statements). David's specific tasks were to recommend interest rates on loans, report rates to senior executives, stage conferences to promote better ways to market loans, and, again, be responsible for budget estimates and budget submissions. He was then given responsibility for opening and subsequently managing a Bank of Montreal in a shopping mall. Later still, his responsibilities as bank manager for consumer marketing in New Brunswick included giving direct market assistance to a hundred and fifty branches. David decided whether or not to open, close, or relocate branches; he also monitored each bank's trends in profits, loans, deposits, and revenues and expenses.

Because of the nature of the banking industry, David understood that he might be called on to change locations at any time.

David is now regional manager responsible for profitability, customer relations and corporate liaison for fourteen branches of the Bank of

Montreal in the Campbellton area of New Brunswick. As regional manager, his duties include the hiring of branch managers and the preparation of budgets which must be approved by the regional vice-president. The qualities David looks for in applicants for branch manager are maturity, problem-solving ability, a marketing background and accounting and computer experience. David also analyzes the profits of each bank in the region and recommends ways to increase profits and cut costs. In his position as regional manager, David is involved in community relations work. He speaks to service groups and schools, organizes activities in the community, and appears on television and radio shows to discuss various banking topics. David realizes the importance of communication skills.

Because he knew that practical experience was valuable, David worked his way up through the branch banking system. He enjoyed branch banking affairs so much that he has remained in this field rather than seeking a role in head office.

David is now thirty-two years old, and his hope is to become a vice-president in charge of eleven bank areas.

Discussion

1. Make a chart illustrating David's education and career advancements. In the first column, list David's past positions, what he does now, and what he hopes to do in the future. In the next column, place a check mark after each job that requires a basic knowledge of accounting skills. In a third column, next to the appropriate positions list the educational programs David has completed and those he will have to complete to attain his career goals.
2. What are the qualities David looks for when he is hiring a branch manager?
3. Prepare an advertisement for the "Canadian Northern Bank" setting out reasons why your bank can provide better service than your competitors.
4. What do you regard as a "significant cash shortage"? How would David help his staff keep cash discrepancies to a minimum?
5. What is meant by the branch banking system in Canada?
6. Using the business section of the newspaper, make a chart showing each of the following for a period of one month:
   a. interest notes on loans
   b. mortgage rates
   c. interest rates on deposits
   Use the figures from three banks and three trust companies of your choice.
7. Prepare a report on the four-year Bachelor of Commerce degree at a university of your choice. Find out the qualifications needed to enrol, the number of courses required for graduation, how many accounting courses must be taken, what other business courses are offered, and the average needed for graduation.

Supplementary Exercise

Green Thumb Garden Centre

Introductory Information

The Green Thumb Garden Centre is a business owned and operated by Mr. G. O. Emms. It is a seasonal business which the owner closes down each year during the winter months. During the season that the business is open, the business is operated seven days a week.

The Green Thumb Garden Centre sells a variety of trees and shrubs and all of the common garden and landscaping materials. All goods and services are subject to a seven per cent government sales tax.

Mr. Emms employs a number of workers. Most of these are hired on a part-time basis as they are needed. Once each week, Mr. Emms withdraws from the bank (by means of a cheque made out to Cash) sufficient cash to pay the employees.

Most of the sales of the business are on a cash or Visa basis. As a result, the accounting system of the business is geared toward the cash register. There are only a few charge customers. All sales transactions and receipts from customers are processed through the cash register.

The system uses the three special journals that follow:

Purchases Journal

						Page 77	
Date	Name	Other Accounts Dr.	Truck Expense Dr.	Soil Prep. & Mtce. Dr.	Equipment Expense Dr.	Purchases Dr.	Accounts Payable Cr.

Cash Payments Journal

							Page 47	
Date	Name	Other Accounts Dr.	Wages Dr.	G.O.E. Drawings Dr.	Soil Prep. & Mtce. Dr.	Discounts Earned Cr.	Accounts Payable Dr.	Bank Cr.

Cash Receipts Journal

							Page 65	
Date	Name	Other Accounts Cr.	Cash Short & Over Dr.	Discounts Allowed Dr.	Sales Tax Payable Cr.	Sales Cr.	Accounts Receivable Cr.	Bank Dr.

539

Supplementary Exercise

At the close of each day's business, a cash register balancing procedure is performed and an accounting summary is prepared. A bank deposit is made each day by using a night depository service.

Small expense items are not paid for out of the cash register funds. Mr. Emms maintains a petty cash fund of $100 for this purpose.

The business uses the periodic inventory system.

The three ledgers of the Green Thumb Garden Centre as of May 31, 19-- are set up in the workbook and the trial balances are shown below. The workbook also contains the cash receipts journal (page 65), the cash payments journal (page 47), and the purchases journal (page 77).

GREEN THUMB GARDEN CENTRE
GENERAL LEDGER TRIAL BALANCE
MAY 31, 19--

No.	Accounts	DR	CR
105	Petty Cash	$100.00	
110	Bank	3 527.24	
115	Accounts Receivable	1 925.18	
120	Merchandise Inventory	75 746.53	
125	Supplies	595.00	
130	Land	48 000.00	
135	Buildings	65 500.00	
140	Accumulated Depreciation, Buildings		$9 000.00
145	Trucks and Tractors	40 500.00	
150	Accumulated Depreciation, Trucks & Tractors		14 400.00
205	Bank Loan		20.000.00
210	Accounts Payable		7 861.87
215	Sales Tax Payable		2 195.45
220	Mortgage Payable		45 500.00
305	G. O. Emms, Capital		153 015.91
310	G. O. Emms, Drawings	15 654.60	
405	Sales		45 042.19
505	Bank Charges	547.53	
510	Building Repairs	146.51	
515	Cash Short and Over	10.50	
520	Discounts Allowed	95.75	
525	Discounts Earned		54.70
530	Equipment Expense	506.86	
535	Freight-in	856.60	
540	Light, Heat, & Power	1 306.75	
545	Miscellaneous Expense	192.45	
550	Purchases	30 001.05	
555	Soil Preparation and Maintenance	4 858.25	
560	Telephone	519.42	
565	Trucks Expense	2 104.40	
570	Wages	4 375.50	
		$297 070.12	$297 070.12

GREEN THUMB GARDEN CENTRE
ACCOUNTS RECEIVABLE TRIAL BALANCE
MAY 31, 19--

Customer	Usual Terms	Invoice Date	Invoice Number	Amount
F. Carson & Sons	2/10,n/30	May 30	408	$541.80
C. Swinton	2/10,n/30	May 26	407	1 094.63
Varga Brothers	2/10,n/30	May 24	402	288.75
				$1 925.18

GREEN THUMB GARDEN CENTRE
ACCOUNTS PAYABLE TRIAL BALANCE
MAY 31, 19--

Supplier	Terms	Inv. No.	Inv. Date	Inv. Amount	Account Balance
Acorn Seed	2/15,n/30	654	May 18	$147.00	
		672	May 21	317.10	$464.10
Clay Ceramic Co.	Net 45	1701	Apr 24		540.75
Canada Products	Net 30	B160	May 4	58.80	
		B188	May 12	98.91	
		B249	May 30	35.91	193.62
Kemp Haulage	1/10,n/30	747	May 23	52.50	
		754	May 23	52.50	
		760	May 23	52.50	
		772	May 27	52.50	
		795	May 31	78.75	288.75
M. & M. Chemicals	Net 60	1046	Apr 9		1 932.00
Poplar Finance	Per contract				2 560.00
Sylvester Concrete	Net 30	446	May 5		783.51
Triangle Sod	Net 30	374	May 22		1 099.14
					$7 861.87

1. **Journalize the transactions listed below. Post daily to the subsidiary ledgers, directly from the source documents.**

Transactions

June 1 *Cash Register Summary*

LINE NO.	ACCOUNTS	DR	CR
1	Cash 169 20		
2	Visa 331 70	500 90	
3	Accounts Rec'l (Charge Sales)		
4	Asset or Expense		
5	Asset or Expense		
6	Asset or Expense		
7	Cash Short or Over	2 —	
8	Accounts Rec'l (Rec'd on A/c)		
9	Accounts Rec'l (Ret'd for Cr.)		
10	Sales		470 —
11	Sales Tax Payable		32 90
12	Cash Short or Over		
	BALANCING TOTALS	502 90	502 90

CASHIER'S SIGNATURE *C. Deng*

Purchase Invoice
—From Canada Products, No. B261, $372.75, dated May 31, terms Net 30, for fertilizer for resale.

June 2 *Cash Register Summary*

LINE NO.	ACCOUNTS	DR	CR
1	Cash 443 47		
2	Visa 331 70	775 17	
3	Accounts Rec'l (Charge Sales)		
4	Asset or Expense *Discounts Allowed*	5 78	
5	Asset or Expense		
6	Asset or Expense		
7	Cash Short or Over		
8	Accounts Rec'l (Rec'd on A/c)		288 75
9	Accounts Rec'l (Ret'd for Cr.)		
10	Sales		460 —
11	Sales Tax Payable		32 20
12	Cash Short or Over		
	BALANCING TOTALS	780 95	780 95

CASHIER'S SIGNATURE *C. Deng*

"Received" Voucher
—Voucher No. 416 made out to Varga Brothers for $282.97 in payment of invoice No. 402, less the two per cent discount.

Supplementary Exercise

Purchase Invoice

—From Triangle Sod, No. 406, $312.90, dated June 1, terms Net 30, for sod for resale.

Cheque Copies

—No. 661, to Acorn Seed Company, $?, paying invoice 654 less the two per cent discount.

—No. 662, to Kemp Haulage, $?, paying invoices 747, 754, and 760 less the one per cent discount.

June 3 *Cash Register Summary*

LINE NO.	ACCOUNTS	DR	CR
1	Cash 276 06	573 52	
2	Visa 297 46		
3	Accounts Rec'l (Charge Sales)		
4	Asset or Expense		
5	Asset or Expense		
6	Asset or Expense		
7	Cash Short or Over		
8	Accounts Rec'l (Rec'd on A/c)		
9	Accounts Rec'l (Ret'd for Cr.)		
10	Sales		536 —
11	Sales Tax Payable		37 52
12	Cash Short or Over		
	BALANCING TOTALS	573 52	573 52

CASHIER'S SIGNATURE   C. May

Cheque Copy

—No. 663, to Petty Cash, $?, to reimburse the petty cash fund for the following petty cash expenditures:

PETTY CASH SUMMARY
JUNE 3, 19--

Building Repairs	$14.10
Equipment Expense	2.50
Soil Preparation and Maintenance	35.50
Truck Expense	17.70
Miscellaneous Expense	26.75

Supplementary Exercise

June 4   *Cash Register Summary*

LINE NO.	ACCOUNTS	DR	CR
1	Cash 53 50	353 10	
2	Visa 299 60	337 05	
3	Accounts Rec'l (Charge Sales)		
4	Asset or Expense		
5	Asset or Expense		
6	Asset or Expense		
7	Cash Short or Over		
8	Accounts Rec'l (Rec'd on A/c)		
9	Accounts Rec'l (Ret'd for Cr.)		
10	Sales		645 —
11	Sales Tax Payable		45 15
12	Cash Short or Over		
	BALANCING TOTALS	690 15	690 15

CASHIER'S SIGNATURE   *C. May*

"Charge" Voucher

—Voucher No. 417 made out to Varga Brothers for the sale of merchandise, $315.00 plus seven per cent sales tax, terms 2/10,n/30, total $337.05.

Purchase Invoices

—From Clay Ceramic Co., No. 1916, $1 003.80, dated June 3, terms Net 45, for flower pots and ornamental garden items for resale.

—From M. & M. Chemicals, No. 1193, $784.00, dated June 3, terms Net 60, for insecticides for resale.

Cheque Copies

—No. 664, to Sylvester Concrete, $?, paying invoice No. 446.

—No. 665, to Public Utilities Commission, $44.85, for electricity for the month of May. (Cheque No. 665 was issued as soon as this bill was received.)

Bank Statement and Vouchers

—The bank statement and related vouchers and paid cheques for May arrived from the bank. Included in the vouchers was a debit note for bank charges in the amount of $41.50 for May. This was the first notice of these charges.

At this time, the following reconciliation statement was prepared. You will need this statement in order to prepare a reconciliation statement at the end of June.

Supplementary Exercise

Green Thumb Garden Centre
Bank Reconciliation Statement
May 31, 19—

Balance per Bk. Statement		3 406 15	Balance per General Ledger	3 527 24
Add: Outstanding Deposit		516 31	Deduct: Bank Interest and Service Charge	41 50
		3 922 46		
Deduct: Outstanding Cheques				
#641	$74.00			
#650	36.50			
#654	29.12			
#655	116.26			
#657	37.40			
#658	42.15			
#659	95.14			
#660	6.15	436 72		
True Balance		3 485 74	True Balance	3 485 74

June 5   *Cash Register Summary*

ACCOUNTING ENTRY

LINE NO.	ACCOUNTS	DR	CR
1	Cash 1 292 44	1 731 14	
2	Visa 438 70		
3	Accounts Rec'l (Charge Sales)		
4	Asset or Expense *Discounts Allowed*	21 89	
5	Asset or Expense		
6	Asset or Expense		
7	Cash Short or Over	5 —	
8	Accounts Rec'l (Rec'd on A/c)		1 094 63
9	Accounts Rec'l (Ret'd for Cr.)		
10	Sales		620 —
11	Sales Tax Payable		43 40
12	Cash Short or Over		
	BALANCING TOTALS	1 758 03	1 758 03

CASHIER'S SIGNATURE   *C. Deng*

"Received" Voucher
—Voucher No. 418, made out to C. Swinton for $1 072.74 in payment of invoice No. 407 less the two per cent cash discount.

Supplementary Exercise

Cheque Copies

—No. 666, to Cash, $604.16, for wages for the week.

—No. 667, to G. O. Emms, $440.00, for personal drawings of the owner.

—No. 668, to Acorn Seed Company, $?, paying invoice No. 672 less the two per cent cash discount.

June 6 *Cash Register Summary*

LINE NO.	ACCOUNTS	DR	CR
1	Cash *347 75*		
2	Visa *165 85*	513 60	
3	Accounts Rec'l (Charge Sales)	552 19	
4	Asset or Expense		
5	Asset or Expense		
6	Asset or Expense		
7	Cash Short or Over		
8	Accounts Rec'l (Rec'd on A/c)		
9	Accounts Rec'l (Ret'd for Cr.)		
10	Sales		996 07
11	Sales Tax Payable		69 72
12	Cash Short or Over		
	BALANCING TOTALS	1 065 79	1 065 79

CASHIER'S SIGNATURE *C. Deng*

"Charge" Voucher

—Voucher No. 419, made out to C. Swinton, $516.07 plus seven per cent sales tax, for sale of merchandise, terms 2/10,n/30, total $552.19.

Purchase Invoices

—From Equipment Repair and Supply, No. 21, $157.50, dated June 5, terms Net 30, for repairs to equipment.

—From Canada Products, No. B295, $997.50, dated June 4, terms Net 30, for fertilizers and chemicals to be charged as follows: Purchases, $871.50; Soil Preparation and Maintenance, $126.00.

Cheque Copies

—No. 669, to Clay Ceramic Co., $540.75, paying invoice No. 1701.

—No. 670, to Kemp Haulage, $?, paying invoice No. 772 less the one per cent cash discount.

—No. 671, to Canada Products, $58.80, paying invoice No. B160.

June 7   *Cash Register Summary*

LINE NO.	ACCOUNTS	DR	CR
1	Cash 481 50		
2	Visa 508 25	989 75	
3	Accounts Rec'l (Charge Sales)		
4	Asset or Expense		
5	Asset or Expense		
6	Asset or Expense		
7	Cash Short or Over		
8	Accounts Rec'l (Rec'd on A/c)		
9	Accounts Rec'l (Ret'd for Cr.)		
10	Sales		925 —
11	Sales Tax Payable		64 75
12	Cash Short or Over		
	BALANCING TOTALS	989 75	989 75

CASHIER'S SIGNATURE   *C. Deng*

Cheque Copy
—No. 672, to Public Utilities Commission, $97.50, cash payment of water bill (charged to Soil Preparation and Maintenance).

June 8   *Cash Register Summary*

LINE NO.	ACCOUNTS	DR	CR
1	Cash 648 66		
2	Visa 80 25	728 91	
3	Accounts Rec'l (Charge Sales)		
4	Asset or Expense *Discounts Allowed*	10 84	
5	Asset or Expense		
6	Asset or Expense		
7	Cash Short or Over		
8	Accounts Rec'l (Rec'd on A/c)		541 80
9	Accounts Rec'l (Ret'd for Cr.)		
10	Sales		185 —
11	Sales Tax Payable		12 95
12	Cash Short or Over		
	BALANCING TOTALS	739 75	739 75

CASHIER'S SIGNATURE   *C. Deng*

"Received" *Voucher*
—Voucher No. 420 made out to F. Carson & Sons for $530.96 in payment of invoice No. 408 less the two per cent cash discount.

Cheque Copies
—No. 673, to M. & M. Chemicals, $1 932.00, paying invoice No. 1046.
—No. 674, to Poplar Finance, $275.00, regular monthly payment on truck.

Supplementary Exercise

June 9 *Cash Register Summary*

LINE NO.	ACCOUNTS	DR	CR
1	Cash 119 84		
2	Visa 230 05	349 89	
3	Accounts Rec'l (Charge Sales)		
4	Asset or Expense		
5	Asset or Expense		
6	Asset or Expense		
7	Cash Short or Over		
8	Accounts Rec'l (Rec'd on A/c)		
9	Accounts Rec'l (Ret'd for Cr.)		
10	Sales		327 —
11	Sales Tax Payable		22 89
12	Cash Short or Over		
	BALANCING TOTALS	349 89	349 89

CASHIER'S SIGNATURE *C. Deng*

Purchase Invoices

—From City Gas & Oil, No. 1651, $135.68, dated June 8, terms Net 30, for gasoline and oil used in the trucks and equipment as follows: Trucks, $94.67; Equipment, $41.01.

—From Kemp Haulage, No. 822, $231.00, dated June 7, terms 1/10, n/30, for topsoil for resale.

June 10 *Cash Register Summary*

LINE NO.	ACCOUNTS	DR	CR
1	Cash 225 77		
2	Visa 53 50	279 27	
3	Accounts Rec'l (Charge Sales)		
4	Asset or Expense		
5	Asset or Expense		
6	Asset or Expense		
7	Cash Short or Over		
8	Accounts Rec'l (Rec'd on A/c)		
9	Accounts Rec'l (Ret'd for Cr.)		
10	Sales		261 —
11	Sales Tax Payable		18 27
12	Cash Short or Over		
	BALANCING TOTALS	279 27	279 27

CASHIER'S SIGNATURE *C. May*

Cheque Copies
—No. 675, to Northwestern Telephone Company, $45.20, cash payment of telephone bill.
—No. 676, to Kemp Haulage, $?, paying invoice No. 795 less the one per cent cash discount.

June 11 *Cash Register Summary*

LINE NO.	ACCOUNTS	DR	CR
1	Cash 26 75		
2	Visa 267 50	294 25	
3	Accounts Rec'l (Charge Sales)		
4	Asset or Expense		
5	Asset or Expense		
6	Asset or Expense		
7	Cash Short or Over		
8	Accounts Rec'l (Rec'd on A/c)		
9	Accounts Rec'l (Ret'd for Cr.)		
10	Sales		275 —
11	Sales Tax Payable		19 25
12	Cash Short or Over		
	BALANCING TOTALS	294 25	294 25

CASHIER'S SIGNATURE *C. May*

Purchase Invoice
—From M. & M. Chemicals, No. 1221, $781.90, dated June 10, terms Net 60, to be charged to Soil Preparation and Maintenance.

Cheque Copy
—No. 677, to Canada Products, $98.91, paying invoice No. B188.

Supplementary Exercise

June 12 *Cash Register Summary*

LINE NO.	ACCOUNTS	ACCOUNTING ENTRY DR	CR
1	Cash 102 —	198 30	
2	Visa 96 30		
3	Accounts Rec'l (Charge Sales)	283 55	
4	Asset or Expense		
5	Asset or Expense		
6	Asset or Expense		
7	Cash Short or Over	5 —	
8	Accounts Rec'l (Rec'd on A/c)		
9	Accounts Rec'l (Ret'd for Cr.)		
10	Sales		455 —
11	Sales Tax Payable		31 85
12	Cash Short or Over		
	BALANCING TOTALS	486 85	486 85

CASHIER'S SIGNATURE *C. Deng*

"Charge" Voucher

—Voucher No. 421 made out F. Carson & Sons for the sale of merchandise, terms 2/10,n/30, $265.00 plus seven per cent sales tax, total $283.55.

Cheque Copies

—No. 678, to Cash, $705.19, for the wages for the week.
—No. 679, to G. O. Emms, $350.00, for owner's personal drawings.
—No. 680, to Foster Bros., $44.21, for the cash purchase of miscellaneous items to be charged to Miscellaneous Expense.

June 13 *Cash Register Summary*

LINE NO.	ACCOUNTS	ACCOUNTING ENTRY DR	CR
1	Cash 150 50	637 35	
2	Visa 486 85		
3	Accounts Rec'l (Charge Sales)		
4	Asset or Expense		
5	Asset or Expense		
6	Asset or Expense		
7	Cash Short or Over	10 —	
8	Accounts Rec'l (Rec'd on A/c)		
9	Accounts Rec'l (Ret'd for Cr.)		
10	Sales		605 —
11	Sales Tax Payable		42 35
12	Cash Short or Over		
	BALANCING TOTALS	647 35	647 35

CASHIER'S SIGNATURE *C. Deng*

Purchase Invoice

—From Acorn Seed Company, No. 756, $82.43, dated June 12, terms 2/15,n/30, for the purchase of merchandise for resale.

June 14   *Cash Register Summary*

LINE NO.	ACCOUNTS	DR	CR
1	Cash 779 71		
2	Visa 192 60	972 31	
3	Accounts Rec'l (Charge Sales)		
4	Asset or Expense *Discounts allowed*	6 74	
5	Asset or Expense		
6	Asset or Expense		
7	Cash Short or Over		
8	Accounts Rec'l (Rec'd on A/c)		337 05
9	Accounts Rec'l (Ret'd for Cr.)		
10	Sales		600 —
11	Sales Tax Payable		42 —
12	Cash Short or Over		
	BALANCING TOTALS	979 05	979 05

CASHIER'S SIGNATURE   *C. Deng*

"Received" Voucher

—Voucher No. 422 made out to Varga Brothers, $330.31, in payment of invoice No. 417 less the two per cent cash discount.

Purchase Invoice

—From Triangle Sod, No. 452, $787.50, dated June 12, terms Net 30, for the purchase of sod for resale.

Bank Debit Advice

—This debit note from Central Bank stated that $2 000 had been deducted from the business bank account for the purpose of reducing the bank loan. Mr. Emms had instructed the bank to make the deduction.

June 15 *Cash Register Summary*

LINE NO.	ACCOUNTS	DR	CR
1	Cash 331 70	433 35	
2	Visa 101 65		
3	Accounts Rec'l (Charge Sales)		
4	Asset or Expense		
5	Asset or Expense		
6	Asset or Expense		
7	Cash Short or Over		
8	Accounts Rec'l (Rec'd on A/c)		
9	Accounts Rec'l (Ret'd for Cr.)		
10	Sales		405 —
11	Sales Tax Payable		28 35
12	Cash Short or Over		
	BALANCING TOTALS	433 35	433 35

CASHIER'S SIGNATURE *C. Deng*

Cheque Copies
—No. 681, to Provincial Treasurer, $?, paying the sales tax for the previous month.
—No. 682, to Proud Insurance Company, $378.50, paying the regular monthly mortgage payment.

June 16 *Cash Register Summary*

LINE NO.	ACCOUNTS	DR	CR
1	Cash 203 30	535 —	
2	Visa 331 70		
3	Accounts Rec'l (Charge Sales)		
4	Asset or Expense		
5	Asset or Expense		
6	Asset or Expense		
7	Cash Short or Over		
8	Accounts Rec'l (Rec'd on A/c)		
9	Accounts Rec'l (Ret'd for Cr.)		
10	Sales		500 —
11	Sales Tax Payable		35
12	Cash Short or Over		
	BALANCING TOTALS	535 —	535 —

CASHIER'S SIGNATURE *C. Deng*

Cheque Copies
—No. 683, to Central Supply, $89.38, for the cash purchase of supplies.
—No. 684, to Mainline Express, $105.85, for the cash payment of express charges to be charged to Freight-in.

June 17 *Cash Register Summary*

LINE NO.	ACCOUNTS	DR	CR
1	Cash 760 50		
2	Visa 374 50	1135 —	
3	Accounts Rec'l (Charge Sales)		
4	Asset or Expense *Discounts allowed*	11 04	
5	Asset or Expense		
6	Asset or Expense		
7	Cash Short or Over		
8	Accounts Rec'l (Rec'd on A/c)		552 19
9	Accounts Rec'l (Ret'd for Cr.)		
10	Sales		555 —
11	Sales Tax Payable		38 85
12	Cash Short or Over		
	BALANCING TOTALS	1146 04	1146 04

CASHIER'S SIGNATURE C. May

"Received" Voucher
—Voucher No. 423 made out to C. Swinton for $541.15 in payment of invoice No. 419 less the two per cent cash discount. Although the payment arrived after the discount date, it was decided to allow the discount.

Purchase Invoices
—From Equipment Repair and Supply, No. 40, $201.60, dated June 15, terms Net 30, for truck repairs.
—From Kemp Haulage, No. 856, $211.05, dated June 16, terms 1/10,n/30, for topsoil and fertilizer to improve the condition of the soil on the business's property, to be charged to Soil Preparation and Maintenance.

Cheque Copy
—No. 685, to Kemp Haulage, $?, paying invoice No. 822 less the cash discount.

Supplementary Exercise

June 18 *Cash Register Summary*

LINE NO.	ACCOUNTS	DR	CR
1	Cash 144 45	476 15	
2	Visa 331 70		
3	Accounts Rec'l (Charge Sales)	428 —	
4	Asset or Expense		
5	Asset or Expense		
6	Asset or Expense		
7	Cash Short or Over		
8	Accounts Rec'l (Rec'd on A/c)		
9	Accounts Rec'l (Ret'd for Cr.)		
10	Sales		845 —
11	Sales Tax Payable		59 15
12	Cash Short or Over		
	BALANCING TOTALS	904 15	904 15

CASHIER'S SIGNATURE *C. May*

"Charge" Voucher

—Voucher No. 424 made out to Varga Brothers for the sale of merchandise, terms 2/10,n/30, $400.00 plus seven per cent sales tax, total $428.00.

Cheque Copy

—No. 686, to The Business House, $35.75, for the cash purchase of items to be charged to Miscellaneous Expense.

June 19 *Cash Register Summary*

LINE NO.	ACCOUNTS	DR	CR
1	Cash		
2	Visa 330 63	330 63	
3	Accounts Rec'l (Charge Sales)		
4	Asset or Expense		
5	Asset or Expense		
6	Asset or Expense		
7	Cash Short or Over		
8	Accounts Rec'l (Rec'd on A/c)		
9	Accounts Rec'l (Ret'd for Cr.)		
10	Sales		309 —
11	Sales Tax Payable		21 63
12	Cash Short or Over		
	BALANCING TOTALS	330 63	330 63

CASHIER'S SIGNATURE *C. Deng*

Purchase Invoice

—From Sylvester Concrete, No. 491, $1 236.25, dated June 17, terms Net 30, for patio stones for resale.

Cheque Copies

—No. 687, to Cash, $567.25, for the wages for the week.

—No. 688, to G. O. Emms, $400.00, for owner's personal drawings.

June 20   *Cash Register Summary*

LINE NO.	ACCOUNTS	DR	CR
1	Cash 160 50	502 90	
2	Visa 342 40		
3	Accounts Rec'l (Charge Sales)		
4	Asset or Expense		
5	Asset or Expense		
6	Asset or Expense		
7	Cash Short or Over		
8	Accounts Rec'l (Rec'd on A/c)		
9	Accounts Rec'l (Ret'd for Cr.)		53 50
10	Sales		420 —
11	Sales Tax Payable		29 40
12	Cash Short or Over		
	BALANCING TOTALS	502 90	502 90

CASHIER'S SIGNATURE   *C. Deng*

"Credit Note" Voucher

—Voucher No. 425 made out to Varga Brothers for the return of unsatisfactory merchandise, $50.00 plus seven per cent sales tax, total $53.50.

Purchase Invoice

—From Triangle Sod, No. 474, $558.08, dated June 19, terms Net 30, for purchase of sod for resale.

June 21 *Cash Register Summary*

LINE NO.	ACCOUNTS	DR	CR
1	Cash 428|14		
2	Visa 421|58	849|72	
3	Accounts Rec'l (Charge Sales)		
4	Asset or Expense		
5	Asset or Expense		
6	Asset or Expense		
7	Cash Short or Over		2|—
8	Accounts Rec'l (Rec'd on A/c)		
9	Accounts Rec'l (Ret'd for Cr.)		
10	Sales		796|—
11	Sales Tax Payable		55|72
12	Cash Short or Over		
	BALANCING TOTALS	851|72	851|72

CASHIER'S SIGNATURE   C. Deng

Cheque Copies

—No. 689, to Petty Cash, $?, to replenish the petty cash fund for the following expenditures:

PETTY CASH SUMMARY
JUNE 21, 19—

Soil Preparation and Maintenance	$26.15
Truck Expense	36.75
Miscellaneous Expense	35.01

—No. 690, to Triangle Sod, paying invoice No. 374.

June 22   *Cash Register Summary*

LINE NO.	ACCOUNTS	DR	CR
1	Cash 397 72	638 47	
2	Visa 240 75		
3	Accounts Rec'l (Charge Sales)	2 200 56	
4	Asset or Expense *Discounts Allowed*	5 67	
5	Asset or Expense		
6	Asset or Expense		
7	Cash Short or Over		
8	Accounts Rec'l (Rec'd on A/c)		283 55
9	Accounts Rec'l (Ret'd for Cr.)		
10	Sales		2 393 60
11	Sales Tax Payable		167 55
12	Cash Short or Over		
	BALANCING TOTALS	2 844 70	2 844 70

CASHIER'S SIGNATURE   *C. Deng*

"Charge" Voucher
—Voucher No. 426 made out to C. Swinton for the sale of merchandise, terms
2/10,n/30, $2 156.60 plus seven per cent sales tax, total $2 200.56.
"Received" Voucher
—Voucher No. 427 made out to F. Carson & Sons for $277.88 paying invoice No. 421 less the two per cent cash discount.

June 23 *Cash Register Summary*

LINE NO.	ACCOUNTS	ACCOUNTING ENTRY	DR	CR
1	Cash 42 80		579 94	
2	Visa 537 14			
3	Accounts Rec'l (Charge Sales)			
4	Asset or Expense			
5	Asset or Expense			
6	Asset or Expense			
7	Cash Short or Over			
8	Accounts Rec'l (Rec'd on A/c)			
9	Accounts Rec'l (Ret'd for Cr.)			
10	Sales			542 —
11	Sales Tax Payable			37 94
12	Cash Short or Over			
	BALANCING TOTALS		579 94	579 94
CASHIER'S SIGNATURE	C. Deng			

June 24 *Cash Register Summary*

LINE NO.	ACCOUNTS	ACCOUNTING ENTRY	DR	CR
1	Cash 208 15		491 70	
2	Visa 283 55			
3	Accounts Rec'l (Charge Sales)			
4	Asset or Expense			
5	Asset or Expense			
6	Asset or Expense			
7	Cash Short or Over		50	
8	Accounts Rec'l (Rec'd on A/c)			
9	Accounts Rec'l (Ret'd for Cr.)			
10	Sales			460 —
11	Sales Tax Payable			32 20
12	Cash Short or Over			
	BALANCING TOTALS		492 20	492 20
CASHIER'S SIGNATURE	C. May			

Purchase Invoices

—From Acorn Seed Company, No. 801, $813.75, dated June 23, terms 2/15,n/30, for merchandise for resale.

—From Clay Ceramic Co., No. 2016, $136.50, dated June 22, terms Net 45, for merchandise for resale.

June 25 *Cash Register Summary*

LINE NO.	ACCOUNTS	DR	CR
1	Cash 98 44	398 04	
2	Visa 299 60		
3	Accounts Rec'l (Charge Sales)		
4	Asset or Expense		
5	Asset or Expense		
6	Asset or Expense		
7	Cash Short or Over		
8	Accounts Rec'l (Rec'd on A/c)		
9	Accounts Rec'l (Ret'd for Cr.)		
10	Sales		372 —
11	Sales Tax Payable		26 04
12	Cash Short or Over		
	BALANCING TOTALS	398 04	398 04
CASHIER'S SIGNATURE	C. May		

Cheque Copy
—No. 691, to Poplar Finance Co., $182.00, for regular finance payment on tractor.

June 26 *Cash Register Summary*

LINE NO.	ACCOUNTS	DR	CR
1	Cash 188 25	418 30	
2	Visa 230 05		
3	Accounts Rec'l (Charge Sales)		
4	Asset or Expense		
5	Asset or Expense		
6	Asset or Expense		
7	Cash Short or Over		
8	Accounts Rec'l (Rec'd on A/c)		
9	Accounts Rec'l (Ret'd for Cr.)		
10	Sales		390 —
11	Sales Tax Payable		27 30
12	Cash Short or Over		1 —
	BALANCING TOTALS	418 30	418 30
CASHIER'S SIGNATURE	C. Deng		

Cheque Copies
—No. 692, to Acorn Seed Co., $?, paying invoice No. 756 less the two per cent cash discount.
—No. 693, to Cash, $505.60, for the wages for the week.
—No. 694, to G. O. Emms, $400.00, for the owner's personal drawings.

Supplementary Exercise

June 27 *Cash Register Summary*

LINE NO.	ACCOUNTS	ACCOUNTING ENTRY DR	CR
1	Cash 768 26		
2	Visa 454 75	1223 01	
3	Accounts Rec'l (Charge Sales)		
4	Asset or Expense *Discounts Allowed*	7 49	
5	Asset or Expense		
6	Asset or Expense		
7	Cash Short or Over		
8	Accounts Rec'l (Rec'd on A/c)		374 50
9	Accounts Rec'l (Ret'd for Cr.)		
10	Sales		800 —
11	Sales Tax Payable		56 —
12	Cash Short or Over		
	BALANCING TOTALS	1230 50	1230 50

CASHIER'S SIGNATURE *C. Deng*

"Received" Voucher
—Voucher No. 428 made out to Varga Brothers for $419.44 in payment of Voucher No. 424 less the two per cent cash discount.

Purchase Invoice
—From Canada Products, No. B340, $330.75, dated June 25, terms Net 30, for merchandise for resale.

June 28 *Cash Register Summary*

LINE NO.	ACCOUNTS	ACCOUNTING ENTRY DR	CR
1	Cash 146 59		
2	Visa 354 17	500 76	
3	Accounts Rec'l (Charge Sales)		
4	Asset or Expense		
5	Asset or Expense		
6	Asset or Expense		
7	Cash Short or Over		
8	Accounts Rec'l (Rec'd on A/c)		
9	Accounts Rec'l (Ret'd for Cr.)		
10	Sales		468 —
11	Sales Tax Payable		32 76
12	Cash Short or Over		
	BALANCING TOTALS	500 76	500 76

CASHIER'S SIGNATURE *C. Deng*

June 29 *Cash Register Summary*

LINE NO.	ACCOUNTS	DR	CR
1	Cash 242 89		
2	Visa 218 28	461 17	
3	Accounts Rec'l (Charge Sales)		
4	Asset or Expense		
5	Asset or Expense		
6	Asset or Expense		
7	Cash Short or Over		
8	Accounts Rec'l (Rec'd on A/c)		
9	Accounts Rec'l (Ret'd for Cr.)		
10	Sales		431 —
11	Sales Tax Payable		30 17
12	Cash Short or Over		
	BALANCING TOTALS	461 17	461 17

CASHIER'S SIGNATURE *C. Deng*

Cheque Copies
—No. 695, to Canada Products, $35.91, paying invoice No. B249.
—No. 696, to First-Rate Repair Service, $233.10, cash payment to be charged to Equipment Expense.

Credit Note Received
—From Triangle Sod, No. 509, $183.75, with respect to defective goods shipped on invoice No. 474.

June 30 *Cash Register Summary*

LINE NO.	ACCOUNTS	DR	CR
1	Cash 26 75		
2	Visa 444 05	470 80	
3	Accounts Rec'l (Charge Sales)		
4	Asset or Expense		
5	Asset or Expense		
6	Asset or Expense		
7	Cash Short or Over		
8	Accounts Rec'l (Rec'd on A/c)		
9	Accounts Rec'l (Ret'd for Cr.)		
10	Sales		440 —
11	Sales Tax Payable		30 80
12	Cash Short or Over		
	BALANCING TOTALS	470 80	470 80

CASHIER'S SIGNATURE *C. Deng*

Supplementary Exercise

2. Balance the journals and post to the general ledger.
3. Balance the general ledger, and the two subsidiary ledgers.
4. On June 3, the bank statement and related vouchers for June arrive in the mail. The bank statement is shown below. Reconcile the bank account for Green Thumb Garden Centre as of June 30.

THE CENTRAL BANK

In Account With: **Green Thumb Garden Centre, Concord Highway**

Cheques and Debits				Deposits	Date	Balance
			Balance Brought Forward		May 31	3 406.15
(#650)	36.50	(#660)	6.15	516.31	June 1	3 879.81
(#659)	95.14			500.90	June 2	4 285.57
(#661)	144.06			775.17	June 3	4 916.68
				573.52	June 4	5 490.20
(#662)	155.92	(#663)	96.55	353.10		
(#665)	44.85				June 5	5 545.98
(#657)	37.40			1 731.14		
				513.60		
				989.75	June 8	8 743.07
(#666)	604.16			728.91	June 9	8 867.82
				349.89	June 10	9 217.71
(#667)	440.00	(#668)	310.76	279.27	June 11	8 746.22
(DM)	2 000.00	(Loan Reduction)		294.25	June 12	7 040.47
(#658)	42.15	(#669)	540.75	198.30		
(#681)	2 195.45			637.35		
				972.31	June 15	6 070.08
				433.35	June 16	6 503.43
(#641)	74.00	(#670)	51.97	535.00	June 17	6 912.46
(#671)	58.80	(#677)	98.91	1 135.00	June 18	7 889.75
(#682)	378.50	(#685)	228.69	476.15	June 19	7 758.71
(#655)	116.26	(#686)	35.75	330.63		
				502.90		
				849.72	June 22	9 289.95
(#673)	1 932.00	(#684)	105.85	638.47	June 23	7 890.57
(#675)	45.20	(#678)	705.19	579.94	June 24	7 720.12
(#679)	350.00	(#687)	567.25	491.70	June 25	7 294.57
(#676)	77.96			398.04	June 26	7 614.65
(#654)	29.12			418.30		
				1 223.01		
				500.76	June 29	9 727.60
(#688)	450.00	(#691)	182.00	461.17		
(#690)	1 099.14					
(DM)	210.00	(Bank Interest)			June 30	8 247.63

15 Analyzing Financial Statements

15.1 Users of Financial Statements
15.2 Comparing Financial Statements
15.3 Key Ratios and Statistics
15.4 Computerized Accounting: Trend Analysis and Key Ratios and Statistics

The set of financial statements for a company shows its financial position simply and clearly. However, financial statements alone do not satisfy the needs of all readers. Many people are interested in special information which goes beyond that found on standard financial statements.

15.1 Users of Financial Statements

Financial statements may be used by many different persons, groups, companies, and agencies. Those interested fall into two groups.

Insiders

The **insiders** of a company are its owners and its executive and management group. The management of a company studies the financial statements most thoroughly. They apply a number of tests to the data and use the data to make special calculations. They are looking for danger signals and unfavourable trends. They want to get rid of the company's weak points and encourage its strengths. The management group has a lot at stake. Their careers usually depend on the continued success of their company.

At one time managers had to wait until the end of an accounting period to obtain much of the information they needed. This has all changed in the age of the computer. It is possible now to obtain most information as soon as it is needed. Managers must pay attention to results on a daily basis, or run the risk of losing out to a competitor who does.

The owners of a company are keenly interested in the progress of the business. In many cases they depend on the income from the business for their livelihood. Profits are usually related to the quality of the management. Profitability, therefore, will be a major factor in deciding if a change in management is advisable.

In other cases, the owners view the company strictly as an investment, and evaluate its performance in comparison with other investment possibilities.

Outsiders

The **outsiders** of a company include bankers and other creditors, prospective investors, shareholders, and government agencies such as Revenue Canada.

Bankers, when asked to lend money to a business, normally request financial statements covering several years of operation. Bankers analyze these statements to evaluate the borrower's ability to repay the loan. In particular, they look at two things. One of these is the company's ability to make a profit. The other is the worth and marketability of the company's assets in case they have to be sold to repay the loan.

Investors and prospective investors in a company are interested in the trend of the company's earnings. Investors are always looking for companies that are growing and profitable. They are also anxious to sell any interest they have in companies that seem to be heading for trouble.

Section Review Questions

1. Why do standard financial statements not satisfy the needs of all readers?
2. Name the two major groups who are interested in financial statements.
3. Who are the "insiders"?
4. Who are the "outsiders"?
5. Which group of people studies the financial statements most thoroughly?
6. In general terms, what is the group in question 5 above looking for?
7. Describe two uses to which the owners put the financial statements.
8. What does a banker look for in the financial statements of a company to which the bank has just lent money?
9. Why are investors interested in a company's financial statements?

15.2 Comparing Financial Data

There are many techniques of analysis to help one evaluate a company. A number of these are discussed below.

Comparative Financial Statements

A common technique for analyzing financial data is to compare financial statements over two years or a number of years. A **comparative financial statement** is one that presents the figures for successive years side by side in columns. Comparative financial statements are illustrated below for Apollo Company in Figures 15.1 and 15.2. Highlighted items are explained later.

The comparative balance sheet in Figure 15.1 shows the book values of the individual balance sheet items in the first and second columns. The dollar increases or decreases are shown in the third column. The percentage increases or decreases are shown in

APOLLO COMPANY
COMPARATIVE BALANCE SHEET
DECEMBER 31, 19-2 and 19-1

	19-2	19-1	Increase or Decrease	% Change
ASSETS				
Current Assets				
Bank	$ 7 220	$ 4 000	$ 3 220	80.5
Accounts Receivable	42 100	17 500	24 600	140.6
Merchandise Inventory	45 300	22 600	22 700	100.4
Prepaid Expenses	2 050	2 100	−50	−2.4
	$ 96 670	$ 46 200	$50 400	109.2
Plant and Equipment (Net)				
Land	$ 40 000	$ 40 000	—	—
Buildings	57 500	60 000	−$2 500	−4.2
General Equipment	41 750	47 500	−5 750	−12.1
Automotive Equipment	49 900	61 900	−12 000	−19.4
	$189 150	$209 400	−$20 250	−9.7
Total Assets	$285 820	$255 600	$30 220	11.8
LIABILITIES AND OWNER'S EQUITY				
Current Liabilities				
Bank Loan	$ 20 000	$ 10 000	$10 000	100.0
Accounts Payable	36 700	19 050	17 650	92.7
	$ 56 700	$ 29 050	$27 650	95.2
P. Kovacs, Capital				
Balance January 1	$226 550	$215 374	$11 176	5.2
Add Net Income	57 370	56 176	1 194	2.1
	$283 920	$271 550	$12 370	4.6
Less Drawings	54 800	45 000	9 800	21.8
Balance December 31	$229 120	$226 550	$ 2 570	1.1
Total Liabilities and Equity	$285 820	$255 600	$30 220	11.8

Figure 15.1 A comparative balance sheet for Apollo Company.

the fourth column. This format is used again for the comparative income statement in Figure 15.2 below.

When analyzing comparative financial statements, one looks first for items showing unusual change. These could signal difficult situations. Items showing unusual change are investigated to find out if corrective action is needed.

APOLLO COMPANY
COMPARATIVE INCOME STATEMENT
YEARS ENDED DECEMBER 31, 19–2 and 19–1

	19–2	19–1	Increase or Decrease	% Change
Revenue				
Net Sales	$333 723	$319 802	$13 921	4.4
Cost of Goods Sold				
Inventory, January 1	$ 22 600	$ 20 400	$ 2 200	10.8
Net Purchases	200 318	173 619	26 699	15.4
Goods Available for Sale	$222 918	$194 019	$28 899	14.9
Less Inventory, December 31	45 300	22 600	22 700	100.4
Cost of Goods Sold	$177 618	$171 419	$ 6 199	3.6
Gross Profit	$156 105	$148 383	$ 7 722	5.2
Operating Expenses				
Advertising	$ 5 500	$ 5 750	–$250	–4.3
Car Expense	18 010	17 450	560	3.2
Depreciation—Building	2 500	2 500		
Depreciation—Office Equipment	5 750	5 750		
Depreciation—Automotive Equipment	12 000	12 000		—
Insurance	1 050	1 350	–300	–22.2
Interest and Bank Charges	2 800	1 400	1 400	100.0
Miscellaneous Expense	310	300	10	3.3
Light, Heat, and Power	1 340	1 210	130	10.7
Supplies Used	1 400	1 475	–75	–5.1
Telephone	1 475	1 462	13	.9
Wages and Salaries	46 600	41 560	5 040	12.1
	$ 98 735	$ 92 207	$ 6 528	7.1
Net Income	$ 57 370	$ 56 176	$ 1 194	2.1

Figure 15.2 A comparative income statement for Apollo Company.

There are times when no change is also considered a bad thing. For example, suppose management advertises heavily in an effort to increase sales substantially. In this case, no change in sales would be a serious disappointment and a major concern.

Changes that are favourable are naturally encouraged and applied in other areas. Changes that are unfavourable receive special attention in order to correct or eliminate them. Sometimes the solution involves changing the people in management. At other times it is necessary to change the way things are done.

You can see from the comparative financial statements of Apollo Company that some items require investigation. These items have been highlighted for you and are discussed below.

Accounts Receivable Accounts receivable are almost two and a half times as large in 19–2 as they were in 19–1. Any large increase in accounts receivable is seen as unfavourable. No comparable sales increase has occurred that might help to explain the situation. Answers to the following questions must be found quickly. Has there been an ill-advised change in credit-granting policy? Do the accounts receivable include any large uncollectable accounts? Does the collection policy of the company need to be strengthened? Is the credit manager doing a satisfactory job?

Sales Sales have increased modestly. The danger is that perhaps the increase is only the result of higher prices due to inflation. Perhaps there has been no increase in the number of units sold. If not, why not? Usually, a company strives to increase its sales every year.

Purchases and Closing Inventory Both purchases and closing inventory are considerably larger than in the previous year. In particular, the inventory has more than doubled—a disturbing increase. It takes money to keep a large stock on hand. It is a general rule in business to keep inventories as low as possible. In this case, the large increase demands an explanation. The increase might be acceptable if it were the result of large-scale buying to take advantage of special low prices. The increase would be a major concern to management if it were the result of any of the following: overbuying; buying at excessively high prices; maintaining too large an inventory; or having a lot of unsalable goods on hand.

Accounts Payable and Bank Loan Any increase in debt is seen as undesirable. The need for credit means that the company is short of its own funds. Large accounts payable are worrisome because the funds to pay them off must be earned. In this case, the increase is probably related to the increase in the merchandise inventory. Still, it will be a concern to management.

Insurance At a time when insurance prices are rising, why has there been a decrease in insurance expense? A premium reduction or a well thought-out cutback in coverage would be acceptable. However, allowing insurance policies to lapse because of inattention would be cause for alarm.

Bank Interest This item has doubled, but is explained by the fact that the bank loan has doubled.

Wages Wages have increased by $5 040. In a period of rising prices, some increase in wages is to be expected. Several factors may explain the increase. Perhaps there has been a recent wage settlement, or perhaps the employees are working below their potential. Perhaps there are more employees than necessary, or it may be that the employees are working more overtime than necessary. Immediate action is necessary if the increase is caused by poor supervision.

Net Income Net income has increased only slightly. Managers and owners always look for a healthy increase in net income. A small increase may suggest the need for a more aggressive management style. It could also mean that the company should look for new opportunities.

Common-Size Financial Statements

There are many occasions when someone, usually an investor, wishes to compare the financial statements of two different companies. The task can be difficult because the dollar size of the two companies may be quite different.

Common-Size Income Statement

To begin the study of common-size financial statements, examine the income statement data shown in Figure 15.3.

COMPARATIVE FINANCIAL DATA FOR COMPANY A AND COMPANY B		
	Company A	Company B
Sales	$72 051	$232 508
Cost of Goods Sold		
Opening Inventory	$ 6 600	$ 26 500
Purchases	39 830	113 005
Cost of Goods Available	$46 430	$139 505
Less Closing Inventory	6 800	27 900
Cost of Goods Sold	$39 630	$111 605
Gross Profit	$32 421	$120 903
Operating Expenses		
Advertising	$ 1 500	$ 2 500
Depreciation	2 875	7 200
Interest	5 010	28 500
Wages	13 402	55 370
Other	1 528	2 153
Total Expenses	$24 315	$ 95 723
Net Income	$ 8 106	$ 25 180

Figure 15.3 A financial comparison of two different companies.

It is not easy to compare these two companies just by looking at the dollar figures. It is easier if the figures are converted to percentages. This can be done so that the two companies appear to be the same size. In the case of an income statement, each item is converted to a percentage figure using the sales figure as the base. The sales figure is set at 100 per cent. All of the other figures in the same column are calculated as a percentage of that sales figure. For example, the gross profit percentage figure for company A is calculated this way:

$$\frac{32\ 421}{72\ 051} \times 100 = 45$$

All of the other percentages are calculated using the same base of $72 051. Figure 15.4 shows the previous illustration modified by the addition of the percentages.

COMMON-SIZE INCOME STATEMENT
COMPANY A AND COMPANY B
YEAR ENDED DECEMBER 31, 19--

	Company A $	Company A %	Company B $	Company B %
Sales	$72 051	100.0	$232 508	100.0
Cost of Goods Sold				
Opening Inventory	$ 6 600	9.1	$ 26 500	11.4
Purchases	39 830	55.3	113 005	48.6
Cost of Goods Available	$46 430	64.4	$139 505	60.0
Less Closing Inventory	6 800	9.4	27 900	12.0
Cost of Goods Sold	$39 630	55.0	$111 605	48.0
Gross Profit	$32 421	45.0	$120 903	52.0
Operating Expenses				
Advertising	$ 1 500	2.1	$ 2 500	1.1
Depreciation	2 875	4.0	7 200	3.1
Interest	5 010	6.9	28 500	12.3
Wages	13 402	18.6	55 370	23.8
Other	1 528	2.1	2 153	.9
Total Expenses	$24 315	33.7	$ 95 723	41.2
Net Income	$ 8 106	11.3	$ 25 180	10.8

Figure 15.4 A common-size income statement.

Including the percentages makes it appear as if the companies are the same size. This is why such statements are called common-size financial statements. A **common-size financial statement** is one that includes the figures for two companies in percentage terms. These percentages are calculated to give the reader the impression that the two companies are the same size. This makes it easier to compare the two companies. This technique is also used frequently to compare the same company over a period of two or more years.

The percentage analysis reveals information not easily seen with a straight comparison of dollar figures. For example, in Figure 15.4:

- Company B earns a seven per cent higher gross profit, yet produces a half a per cent lower net income;
- Company B has much higher interest charges and wages than Company A;
- neither company has a very good profit figure when compared to the sales figure.

Common-Size Balance Sheet

You have seen that the base figure for a common-size income statement is the sales figure. For a common-size balance sheet the base figure for making the calculations is the total assets figure. Figure 15.5 below shows a common-size balance sheet.

COMMON-SIZE BALANCE SHEET
COMPANY P AND COMPANY Q
DECEMBER 31, 19--

	Company P $	%	Company Q $	%
ASSETS				
Current Assets				
Bank	$ 5 000	2.2	$ 3 000	.3
Accounts Receivable	22 400	9.9	74 270	8.0
Merchandise Inventory	27 550	12.2	101 350	10.9
Total Current Assets	$ 54 950	24.3	$178 620	19.2
Plant and Equipment				
Land	$ 49 000	21.6	$150 000	16.2
Buildings	70 000	30.9	275 000	29.6
Equipment	52 500	23.2	325 000	35.0
Total Plant and Equipment	$171 500	75.7	$750 000	80.6
Total Assets	$226 450	100.0	$928 620	100.0
LIABILITIES AND OWNER'S EQUITY				
Current Liabilities				
Accounts Payable	$ 19 200	8.5	$ 94 300	10.1
Bank Loan	—	—	100 000	10.8
Total Current Liabilities	$ 19 200	8.5	$194 000	20.9
Owner's Equity				
Capital, January 1	$198 750	87.5	$721 950	77.7
Add Net Income	60 500	26.7	57 370	6.2
	$259 250	114.5	$779 320	83.9
Deduct Drawings	52 000	23.0	45 000	4.8
Capital, December 31	$207 250	91.5	$734 320	79.1
Total Liabilities and Equity	$226 450	100.0	$928 620	100.0

Figure 15.5 A common-size balance sheet.

The most significant fact revealed by this common-size statement is the difference in percentage of earning power. Based on its assets, Company P earns 26.7 per cent whereas Company Q earns only 6.2 per cent.

Trend Analysis

Another technique used for examining financial statements is the trend analysis. A **trend analysis** presents financial data in percentages, for a number of successive periods, so that tendencies can be seen that are not evident when looking at the dollar figures alone. Trend analyses are usually presented horizontally and are not used to compare different companies. They are used to work out trends and projections for the future of a given company.

In a trend analysis, the first period is selected as the base period. The dollar amounts for the base period are given the value of 100 per cent. The figures for subsequent periods are then expressed as percentages of the base period. Figures 15.6 and 15.7 show how this is done. Two steps are involved.

1. Selected data are presented in dollars for a number of periods as shown in Figure 15.6.

WESTWIND COMPANY LIMITED
COMPARATIVE INCOME STATEMENT SELECTED DATA
19–1 to 19–5

	Year 1	Year 2	Year 3	Year 4	Year 5
Sales	$65 000	$67 700	$70 900	$74 750	$78 000
Cost of Goods Sold	32 100	33 000	34 000	35 000	35 600
Gross Profit	$32 900	$34 700	$36 900	$39 750	$42 400
Operating Expenses	20 700	22 350	23 200	25 250	28 000
Net Income	$12 200	$12 350	$13 700	$14 500	$14 400

Figure 15.6 A schedule of income statement data for a five-year period.

2. The dollar amounts are converted to percentages using the first year's figures as the base value. The resulting trend analysis is shown in Figure 15.7.

WESTWIND COMPANY LIMITED
COMPARATIVE INCOME STATEMENT SELECTED DATA
IN PERCENTAGES FROM 19–1 to 19–5

	Year 1	Year 2	Year 3	Year 4	Year 5
Sales	100	104	109	115	120
Cost of Goods Sold	100	103	106	109	111
Gross Profit	100	105	112	121	129
Operating Expenses	100	108	112	122	135
Net Income	100	101	112	119	118

Figure 15.7 A trend analysis of income statement data for a five-year period.

This trend analysis clearly shows tendencies not evident from looking at the dollar amounts alone.

- Sales have experienced a steady and satisfactory rate of increase.
- Cost of goods sold has risen steadily, but the rise has not been as steep as for sales.
- The excess of sales over cost of goods sold has resulted in an exceptional climb in the rate of gross profit.
- Operating expenses have risen more steeply than any other item, particularly in the fifth year.
- Net income has not kept pace with gross profit. In the most recent year, net income actually declined.

From this trend analysis, it can be concluded that Westwind Company Limited has experienced a steady rate of growth. It has been able to improve its rate of gross profit over the five-year period. An important factor has been its ability to control the cost of goods sold. However, it has not shown the same ability to control its operating expenses. As a result, net income, although showing a healthy increase over the five-year period, fell during the fifth year.

Section Review Questions

1. Describe a comparative financial statement.
2. What must the reader of comparative financial statements make sure of?
3. What is the principal purpose of a comparative financial statement?
4. Why is an item that shows extraordinary change looked at carefully?
5. There are times when no change is considered a bad sign. Explain.
6. What course of action is followed if an item is deemed to show unfavourable change?
7. What is the principal purpose of common-size financial statements?
8. Explain the name "common-size financial statements."
9. What is the usual base figure for a common-size income statement?
10. What is the usual base figure for a common-size balance sheet?
11. A common-size analysis reveals information not readily seen from a straight comparison of dollar figures. Explain.
12. What is the purpose of a trend analysis?
13. Why is a trend analysis usually shown in percentage terms?
14. What is the base figure for a trend analysis?

Section Exercises

1. Shown below are the condensed financial statements for Rose Company and Lily Company.

    1. In your workbook, convert these figures to common-size form.

COMPARATIVE BALANCE SHEETS
ROSE COMPANY AND LILY COMPANY
DECEMBER 31, 19–6

	Rose Company	Lily Company
ASSETS		
Bank	$ 41 474	$ 34 971
Accounts Receivable	44 371	24 008
Merchandise Inventory	106 780	42 464
Plant & Equipment	183 538	26 725
Automobiles	25 675	8 390
Total Assets	$401 838	$136 558
LIABILITIES AND EQUITY		
Accounts Payable	$ 86 480	$ 13 940
Bank Loan	50 000	
Mortgage Payable	120 000	
Total Liabilities	$256 480	$ 13 940
Owner's Equity		
Beginning Capital	$114 728	$118 539
Net Income	105 630	29 079
	$220 358	$147 618
Drawings	75 000	25 000
Ending Capital	$145 358	$122 618
Total Liabilities and Equity	$401 838	$136 558

COMPARATIVE INCOME STATEMENTS
ROSE COMPANY AND LILY COMPANY
YEAR ENDED DECEMBER 31, 19–6

	Rose Company	Lily Company
Sales	$767 830	$332 879
Cost of Goods Sold		
Beginning Inventory	$ 98 200	$ 44 224
Purchases	561 280	208 740
Cost of Goods Available	$659 480	$252 964
Less Ending Inventory	106 780	42 464
Cost of Goods Sold	$552 700	$210 500
Gross Profit	$215 130	$122 379
Operating Expenses		
Bank Interest	$ 7 000	$ 1 000
Mortgage Interest	11 250	
Depreciation—Equipment	5 500	6 600
Depreciation—Automobiles	10 000	3 500
Rent		24 000
Wages	35 750	47 500
Other Expenses	40 000	10 700
Total Expenses	$109 500	$ 93 300
Net Income	$105 630	$ 29 079

2. Answer the following questions.
   a. Lily Company has the higher gross profit but the lower net income. Explain why this is so.
   b. Comment on the difference in the equity of the two companies. Explain the effect of this on the income statements.

---

2. Shown below is the partially completed comparative balance sheet for Playfair Company.

   1. Complete the statement for Playfair Company in your workbook.

   2. Identify the four most significant changes. For each, say whether the change has been good or bad.

PLAYFAIR COMPANY
COMPARATIVE BALANCE SHEET
DECEMBER 31, 19–4 AND 19–3

	19–4	19–3	Increase or Decrease(–)	% Change
ASSETS				
Current Assets				
Bank	$ 9 090	$ 5 500	_____	•
Accounts Receivable	65 220	35 700	_____	•
Merchandise Inventory	67 096	42 100	_____	•
Prepaid Expenses	3 540	3 500	_____	•
Total Current Assets	$144 946	$ 86 800	_____	•
Fixed Assets				
Land	$ 50 000	$ 50 000	_____	•
Buildings (Net)	135 000	138 000	_____	•
Equipment (Net)	141 000	160 000	_____	•
Automobiles (Net)	25 000	30 000	_____	•
Total Fixed Assets	$351 000	$378 000	_____	•
Total Assets	$495 946	$464 800	_____	•
LIABILITIES AND OWNER'S EQUITY				
Current Liabilities				
Accounts Payable	$ 97 936	$ 52 750	_____	•
Bank Loan	50 000	50 000	_____	•
Total Current Liabilities	$147 936	$102 750	_____	•
Long-Term Liability				
Mortgage Payable	$ 70 000	$ 75 000	_____	•
Total Liabilities	$217 936	$177 750	_____	•
T. Jennings, Capital				
Capital, January 1	$287 050	$277 700	_____	•
Net Income	90 960	84 350	_____	•
	$378 010	$362 050	_____	•
Drawings	100 000	75 000	_____	•
Capital, December 31	$278 010	$287 050	_____	•
Total Liabilities & Equity	$495 946	$464 800	_____	•

3. This exercise also appears in your workbook. The current assets and the current liabilities of Goodenough Company for a five-year period are shown below.

GOODENOUGH COMPANY

	Year 1	Year 2	Year 3	Year 4	Year 5
a. Current Assets	$50 702	$51 716	$53 237	$55 265	$57 800
b. Current Liabilities	$30 406	$31 014	$31 622	$32 534	$33 447
a. minus b. Working Capital					

1. Complete the above schedule by calculating the working capital for the five-year period.
2. Prepare a percentage trend analysis from the above schedule in the space indicated below.

GOODENOUGH COMPANY
WORKING CAPITAL TREND ANALYSIS

	Year 1	Year 2	Year 3	Year 4	Year 5
Current Assets					
Current Liabilities					
Working Capital					

4. The income statement for Gorry and Associates is given below.
   1. Prepare a percentage trend analysis.
   2. Comment on each line of the analysis in terms of performance and meaning.

GORRY AND ASSOCIATES
INCOME STATEMENT DATA
19–1 to 19–5

	Year 1	Year 2	Year 3	Year 4	Year 5
Sales	$120 000	$121 200	$124 800	$125 950	$128 500
Cost of Goods Sold	65 000	66 300	67 600	68 250	70 200
Gross Profit	$ 55 000	$ 54 900	$ 57 200	$ 57 700	$ 58 300
Operating Expenses	30 000	30 600	31 500	32 700	33 600
Net Income	$ 25 000	$ 24 300	$ 25 700	$ 25 000	$ 24 700

15.3 Key Ratios and Statistics

A number of ratios and statistics may be worked out to make the analysis of financial statements more meaningful. Some simple calculations can be made in regard to specific aspects of the statements. The ratios and numbers should not be studied in isolation but should be used alongside other pertinent facts and information. In particular, one should try to compare them with figures for the industry as a whole.

Accounting ratios may be divided into two distinct types:
1. liquidity or solvency ratios
2. profitability percentages.

Several specific ratios are calculated below for Apollo Company. The statements appear on pages 565 and 566. The calculations are made for two successive years in each case, but this is not a requirement.

Liquidity or Solvency Ratios

Liquidity ratios or **solvency ratios** are used to help assess the ability of a company to pay its debts.

Current Ratio or Working Capital Ratio

The formula:

$$\text{current ratio} = \frac{\text{total current assets}}{\text{total current liabilities}}$$

The data:

	19–2	19–1
Total Current Assets	$96 670	$46 200
Total Current Liabilities	$56 700	$29 050

The computations:

	19–2	19–1
current ratio =	$\frac{96\ 670}{56\ 700}$	$\frac{46\ 200}{29\ 200}$

The results:

	19–2	19–1
current ratio =	1.7	1.6

Interpretation The **current ratio** measures a business's ability to pay its debts in the normal course of business operations. This is an important consideration because a business that is unable to pay its debts can be closed down by its creditors.

The general standards for interpreting current ratios are shown in the following table.

Current Ratio	Interpretation
2.5	very good
2.0	good
1.5	fair
1.0	poor*
less than 1.0	precarious

*Except in regard to certain specialized industries such as public utilities.

Apollo Company's current ratio is not good. Its ability to pay its debts on time is not assured. The company should seek to improve this ratio.

The current ratio is also referred to as the working capital ratio. The **working capital** of a business is found by subtracting the total current liabilities from the total current assets. The working capital for Apollo Company for the second year is $96 670 − $56 700 = $39 970.

Quick Ratio or Acid-Test Ratio

The formula:

$$\text{quick ratio} = \frac{\text{total current assets (less inventory and prepaid expenses)}}{\text{total current liabilities}}$$

The data:

	19–2	19–1
Current Assets		
Bank	$ 7 200	$ 4 000
Accounts Receivable	42 100	17 500
Merchandise Inventory	45 300	22 600
Prepaid Expenses	2 050	2 100
Total Current Assets	$96 670	$46 200
Current Liabilities	$56 700	$29 050

The computations:

	19–2	19–1
quick ratio =	$\dfrac{\$96\ 670 - \$47\ 350}{\$56\ 700}$	$\dfrac{\$46\ 200 - \$24\ 700}{\$29\ 050}$

The results:

	19–2	19–1
quick ratio =	.87	.74

Interpretation The calculation of the quick ratio includes only quick assets, those that can be converted into cash quickly. Therefore, the **quick ratio** measures a business's ability to pay its debts within a short period of time, say two months. It would be used by someone who was concerned about the business's ability to continue operating. A quick ratio figure of less than one is undesirable, but not uncommon.

Collection Period

The formula:

$$\text{collection period} = \frac{\text{accounts receivable}}{\text{average charge sales per day}}$$

The data:

	19–2	19–1
Accounts Receivable	$ 42 100	$ 17 500
Sales*	$333 732	$319 802

*Assume that all sales are charge sales.

The computations:

	19–2	19–1
collection period =	$\dfrac{42\ 100}{333\ 723/365}$	$\dfrac{17\ 500}{319\ 802/365}$

The results:

	19–2	19–1
collection period (in days) =	46	20

Interpretation The **collection period** figure gives an indication of the number of days it takes the business to collect an account receivable. The lower the number, the better it is. The meaning of the figure depends on the business's usual terms of sale and its discount policy. A general rule of thumb is that the figure should be less than one and a half times the usual credit period. If a discount is offered, the figure should be lower.

Apollo Company's collection period figure for 19–1 is exceptionally low. The figure for 19–2 is more normal.

Inventory Turnover

The formula:

$$\text{inventory turnover} = \frac{\text{cost of goods sold}}{\text{average merchandise inventory}}$$

The data:

	19–2	19–1
Cost of Goods Sold	$177 618	$171 419
Beginning Inventory	$ 22 600	$ 20 400
Ending Inventory	$ 45 300	$ 22 600

The computations:

	19–2	19–1
inventory turnover =	$\dfrac{177\ 618}{\dfrac{22\ 600 + 45\ 300}{2}}$	$\dfrac{171\ 419}{\dfrac{20\ 400 + 22\ 600}{2}}$

The results:

	19–2	19–1
inventory turnover =	5.2	8.0

Interpretation The **inventory turnover** figure represents the number of times a business has been able to sell and replace its inventory in one year. An inventory turnover of 8.0 means that the business has been able to sell and replace its goods eight times a year or every month and a half. To be most useful, this figure must be compared with other years, or with other companies in the same line of business. Not all lines of business have the same rate of turnover.

Apollo Company shows a marked decrease in the turnover figure from its first year to its second. This is a further indication of the inventory problem discussed earlier.

Debt/Equity Ratios

The formulas:

$$\text{debt ratio} = \frac{\text{total liabilities}}{\text{total assets}}$$

$$\text{equity ratio} = \frac{\text{total equity}}{\text{total assets}}$$

The data:

	19–2	19–1
Total Liabilities	$ 56 700	$ 29 050
Total Equity	$229 120	$226 550
Total Assets	$285 820	$255 600

The computations:

	19–2	19–1
debt ratio =	$\dfrac{56\ 700}{285\ 820}$	$\dfrac{29\ 050}{255\ 600}$

$$\text{equity ratio} = \frac{229\ 120}{285\ 820} \quad (19\text{–}2) \qquad \frac{226\ 550}{255\ 600} \quad (19\text{–}1)$$

The results:

	19–2	19–1
debt ratio =	19.8%	11.4%
equity ratio =	80.2%	88.6%

Interpretation The **debt ratio** shows the proportion of the total assets that has been acquired using borrowed money. The **equity ratio** shows the proportion of the total assets that has been acquired using the owner's money. The two percentages are complementary, which means that they add up to 100.

Creditors and prospective creditors are interested in these two ratios. They like to see a high proportion of owner's money in a business. Owners with a high stake in the business are strongly committed to its success.

Creditors of Apollo Company would undoubtedly view the ratios favourably. Were the two figures reversed, so that the owners had the small eleven to twenty per cent share in the business, creditors would view the situation quite differently.

Times Interest Earned Ratio

The formula:

$$\text{times interest earned} = \frac{\text{net income}}{\text{interest expense}}$$

The data:

	19–2	19–1
Net Income	$57 370	$56 176
Interest Expense	$ 2 800	$ 1 400

The computation:

$$\text{times interest earned} = \frac{57\ 370}{2\ 800} \quad (19\text{–}2) \qquad \frac{56\ 176}{1\ 400} \quad (19\text{–}1)$$

The results:

	19–2	19–1
times interest earned =	20.5	40.1

Interpretation The **times interest earned ratio** measures the company's ability to cover its interest expense. The figures for Apollo Company are extremely favourable. This indicates that Apollo Company can handle its interest charges very easily. However, a company that had a low figure, for example five, would have to express some concern over interest charges. The higher the ratio the better. Creditors would be very cautious in dealing with a company with a low figure.

Profitability Percentages

Profitability percentages are used to evaluate a company's ability to make a profit. The profit figure is compared to other years, other companies, and other investment possibilities.

Rate of Return on Net Sales

The formula:

$$\text{rate of return on net sales} = \frac{\text{net income}}{\text{net sales}} \times 100$$

The data:

	19–2	19–1
Net Income	$ 57 370	$ 56 176
Net Sales	$333 723	$319 802

The computation:

19–2

$$\text{rate of return} = \frac{57\ 370}{333\ 732} \times 100$$

19–1

$$\frac{56\ 176}{319\ 802} \times 100$$

The results:

	19–2	19–1
rate of return =	17.2%	17.6%

Interpretation The **rate of return on net sales** measures the dollars that remain after all expenses are deducted from net sales. Comparing this figure with other years gives an indication of a company's progress. In Apollo Company's case, the rate of return has dropped slightly. This would be a disappointment, but the rate seems quite healthy at 17.2 per cent.

One should be sure to look at the rate of return figure as well as the net income figure in dollars. As shown by the schedule below, it is possible to have an increase in net income dollars and yet have a drop in the net income percentage.

	Year 1	Year 2
Sales	$500 000	$525 000
Net Income	$ 50 000	$ 50 500
Net Income %	10.0%	9.6%

Rate of Return on Owner's Equity

The formula:

$$\text{return on owner's equity} = \frac{\text{net income}}{\text{owner's average equity}} \times 100$$

The data:

	19–2	19–1
Net Income	$57 370	$56 176
Beginning Capital	$226 550	$215 374
Ending Capital	$229 120	$226 550

The computation:

$$\text{return on owner's equity} = \underbrace{\frac{57\,370}{\frac{226\,550 + 229\,120}{2}} \times 100}_{19-2} \quad \underbrace{\frac{56\,176}{\frac{215\,374 + 226\,550}{2}} \times 100}_{19-1}$$

The results:

	19–2	19–1
return on owner's equity =	25.2%	25.4%

Interpretation The **return on owner's equity** measures how well the business is doing compared to the owner's investment in it. The owner can compare this figure with other investment opportunities. In particular, the owner would be interested in knowing how much the equity could earn in interest if it could be loaned out. However, the capital of a business cannot just be taken out. A buyer must be found first. In other words, the capital invested in a business is not always available to be invested in other ways.

The owner of Apollo Company would be quite happy with the above return on investment figures. They are a great deal higher than current interest rates.

Section Review Questions

1. What is a ratio or statistic as applied in accounting?
2. Ratios should not be analyzed in isolation. Explain.
3. What are the two distinct types of ratios?
4. What can we learn from a liquidity or solvency ratio?
5. What can we learn from a profitability ratio?
6. How is the current ratio calculated?
7. Explain the difference between the current ratio and the quick ratio.
8. What is working capital?
9. What does the current ratio measure?
10. What does the quick ratio measure?
11. What is the formula for the collection period statistic?
12. What does the collection period statistic mean?
13. How is the inventory turnover calculated?
14. What does the inventory turnover figure mean?
15. Explain the reason for the difference between the turnover figure for a fruit market and the figure for a gift store.
16. What does it mean to say the debt ratio and the equity ratio are complementary?
17. What do the debt/equity ratios tell the reader?
18. How is the times interest earned statistic calculated?
19. Does the rate of return on net sales figure need to be compared with other figures or is it meaningful on its own?
20. How can one use the rate of return on owner's equity statistic?

Section Exercises

1. The balance sheet and income statement for Saturn Sales Company are shown below. Assume all sales are made on account.

SATURN SALES COMPANY
BALANCE SHEET
DECEMBER 31, 19–5

ASSETS

Current Assets
Bank	$ 3 400	
Accounts Receivable	33 070	
Merchandise Inventory	27 400	$ 63 870

Prepaid Expenses
Supplies		1 500

Plant and Equipment
Land	$ 50 000	
Buildings	125 000	
Equipment	69 000	244 000
Total Assets		$309 370

LIABILITIES AND EQUITY
Current Liabilities
  Bank Loan $ 25 000
  Accounts Payable   17 970 $ 42 970

Long-Term Liability
  Mortgage Payable   65 700

Owner's Equity
  P. Shawn, Capital, January 1 $194 895
  Net Income $30 805
  Withdrawals   25 000
  Increase in Capital   5 805
  P. Shawn, Capital, December 31   200 700
    Total Liabilities and Equity $309 370

SATURN SALES COMPANY
INCOME STATEMENT
YEAR ENDED DECEMBER 31, 19–5

Revenue
  Sales $343 342

Cost of Goods Sold
  Merchandise Inventory, January 1 $ 26 500
  Purchases   226 500
  Merchandise Available for Sale $253 000
  Less: Merchandise Inventory, December 31   27 400   225 600
    Gross Profit $117 742

Operating Expenses
  Interest Expense $ 8 256
  Depreciation of Building   6 250
  Depreciation of Equipment   6 900
  Power   2 800
  Miscellaneous Expense   350
  Telephone   425
  Car Expense   4 940
  Wages   57 016   86 937
    Net Income $ 30 805

Calculate the following to one decimal place. Give your opinion as to whether each ratio is poor, fair, good, *etc.*
1. Current ratio.
2. Quick ratio.
3. Collection period.

4. Inventory turnover.
5. Net income percentage.
6. Rate of return on owner's investment.
7. Debt ratio.
8. Equity ratio.
9. Times interest earned.

2. **The following data applies to Calvino Company.**
   a. The collection period is 36.5.
   b. The current ratio is 1.3.
   c. The net income percentage is 12.5.
   d. The debt ratio is 15.

Use this data to fill in the missing information on the partially completed financial statements in your workbook.

INCOME STATEMENT
YEAR ENDED DECEMBER 31, 19–8

Revenue
Sales $170 000

Cost of Goods Sold
  Opening Inventory
  Purchases $128 500
  Goods Available for Sale
  Closing Inventory   _____
  Cost of Goods Sold $129 000

Gross Profit $ _____

Operating Expenses $ _____

Net Income $ _____

BALANCE SHEET
DECEMBER 31, 19–8

ASSETS

Current Assets
Bank $ 3 700
Accounts Receivable
Merchandise Inventory 10 500

Total Current Assets $_____

Plant and Equipment
Land $ 35 000
Buildings and Equipment _____

Total Plant and Equipment $_____

Total Assets $_____

LIABILITIES AND OWNER'S EQUITY

Current Liabilities
Bank Loan $ 15 000
Accounts Payable _____

Total Current Liabilities $_____

Owner's Equity
Beginning Capital $134 750
Add: Net Income _____

Deduct: Drawings $_____

Ending Capital $_____

Total Liabilities and Owner's Equity $_____

3. Shown below side by side are the simplified financial statements of Pluto Company and Neptune Company. These two companies are in the same line of business. Pluto Company is considering expanding its business by purchasing Neptune Company. Neptune Company has been having financial difficulties recently. Assume that all sales are on account.

BALANCE SHEETS, DECEMBER 31, 19--

	PLUTO	NEPTUNE
Assets		
Bank	$ 5 000	$ 10 000
Accounts Receivable	80 000	72 000
Merchandise Inventory	52 000	40 000
Supplies	1 800	2 500
Land	70 000	
Buildings	125 000	
Equipment	85 000	142 000
Automobiles	62 000	92 000
Total Assets	$480 800	$358 500
Liabilities		
Bank Loan	$ 30 000	$ 90 000
Accounts Payable	32 000	30 000
Mortgage Payable	60 000	
Total Liabilities	$122 000	$120 000
Owner's Equity		
Beginning Capital	$320 300	$226 700
Net Income	$142 630	$ 52 000
Drawings	104 130	40 200
Increase in Capital	$ 38 500	$ 11 800
Ending Capital	$358 800	$238 500
Total Liabilities and Equity	$480 800	$358 500

INCOME STATEMENTS
YEAR ENDED DECEMBER 31, 19--

	PLUTO	NEPTUNE
Sales	$921 630	$570 000
Cost of Goods Sold		
Beginning Inventory	$ 48 000	$ 42 000
Purchases	609 000	304 100
Goods Available for Sale	$657 000	$346 100
Less: Ending Inventory	52 000	40 000
Cost of Goods Sold	$605 000	$306 100
Gross Profit	$316 630	$263 900
Operating Expenses		
Depreciation	$ 33 500	$ 55 000
Gas and Oil	42 600	47 200
Interest	15 000	20 000
Power	7 500	6 000
Miscellaneous	1 900	1 500
Rent		24 000
Telephone	1 500	1 200
Wages	72 000	57 000
Total Expenses	$174 000	$211 900
Net Income	$142 630	$ 52 000

1. Work out all of the key ratios and statistics for the two companies.
2. Decide whether Pluto Company should buy Neptune Company. Give reasons for your decision.

15.4 Computerized Accounting: Trend Analysis and Key Ratios and Statistics

Computer Exercises

1. Given below is a spreadsheet application program for a trend analysis. The data is taken from Figure 15.6 for Westwind Company Limited. The program is designed so that the top section will show the dollar amounts and the bottom section will show the percentages. The hidden formulas are given in faint print.

	A	B	C	D	E	F	G
1	WESTWIND COMPANY LIMITED						
2	COMPARATIVE	INCOME STATEMENT					
3	19-1 TO 19-5						
4							
5			19-1	19-2	19-3	19-4	19-5
6	SALES						
7	COST OF GOODS SOLD						← For raw data
8	GROSS PROFIT						
9	OPERATING EXPENSES						
10	NET INCOME						
11							
12			19-1	19-2	19-3	19-4	19-5
13	SALES		100	D6/C6*100	E6/C6*100	F6/C6*100	G6/C6*100
14	COST OF GOODS SOLD		100	D7/C7*100	E7/C7*100	F7/C7*100	G7/C7*100
15	GROSS PROFIT		100	D8/C8*100	E8/C8*100	F8/C8*100	G8/C8*100
16	OPERATING EXPENSES		100	D9/C9*100	E9/C9*100	F9/C9*100	G9/C9*100
17	NET INCOME		100	D10/C10*100	E10/C10*100	F10/C10*100	G10/C10*100
18							
19							
20							

   a. Load your spreadsheet software into the computer. Then build the above program into the spreadsheet. Read the manual or find out from your teacher how to eliminate the decimal fractions. Save the program so that it can be used for other applications.

   b. With the calculator turned off, enter the raw data from Figure 15.6 into the screen. When finished, turn the calculator on. Compare the results with Figure 15.7. Print out the results if you wish.

   c. Change some of the raw data in the example and observe the results on the screen.

   d. Use the program from this exercise to do exercise 4 on page 576.

2. The computer spreadsheet is exceptionally good for calculating accounting ratios and statistics. You will see this if you complete the following exercise.

   1. Use the program outlined below as a guide to preparing a program on the accounting spreadsheet. Do all calculations to two decimal places. Save the program as shown so that it can be reused. The hidden formulas are shown in faint print.

	A	B	C	D
1	FINANCIAL STATEMENT ANALYSIS			
2				
3	RAW DATA		YEAR 1	YEAR 2
4	TOTAL CURRENT ASSETS			
5	TOTAL QUICK ASSETS			
6	TOTAL CURRENT LIABILITIES			
7	TOTAL ACCOUNTS RECEIVABLE			
8	TOTAL CHARGE SALES			
9	BEGINNING INVENTORY			
10	ENDING INVENTORY		For raw data	For raw data
11	COST OF GOODS SOLD			
12	TOTAL ASSETS			
13	TOTAL LIABILITIES			
14	BEGINNING EQUITY			
15	ENDING EQUITY			
16	NET INCOME			
17	INTEREST EXPENSE			
18	NET SALES			
19				
20	KEY RATIOS AND STATISTICS			
21	WORKING CAPITAL		C4-C6	D4-D6
22	CURRENT RATIO		C4/C6	D4/D6
23	QUICK RATIO		C5/C6	D5/D6
24	COLLECTION PERIOD		C7/C8*365	D7/D8*365
25	INVENTORY TURNOVER		C11/(C9+C10)*2	D11/(D9+D10)*2
26	DEBT RATIO		C13/C12*100	D13/D12*100
27	EQUITY RATIO		C15/C12*100	D15/D12*100
28	TIMES INTEREST EARNED RATIO		C16/C17	D16/D17
29	RATE OF RETURN ON NET SALES		C16/C18*100	D16/D18*100
30	RATE OF RETURN ON OWNER'S EQUITY		C16/(C14-C15)*200	D16/(D14+D15)*200

   2. Load the above program into the computer. In the space for the raw data, enter the data from the financial statements for Apollo Company which appear on pages 565 and 566. After the computer makes the calculations, compare your results with the calculations made with this data throughout the chapter.

   3. Use this program to work out the ratios for question 1 following Section 15.2 on page 573.

3. Given below is a spreadsheet program to produce common-size statements. The program is based on the data in Figure 15.5 on page 570. The hidden formulas are given in faint print. Prepare the program and save it before entering any raw data.

	A	B	C	D	E	F
1	COMMON-SIZE BALANCE SHEET					
2	COMPANY P AND COMPANY Q					
3	DECEMBER 31, 19--					
4						
5	ASSETS		$	%	$	%
6	CURRENT ASSETS					
7	BANK			C7/C16*100		E7/E16*100
8	ACCOUNTS RECEIVABLE			C8/C16*100		E8/E16*100
9	MERCHANDISE INVENTORY			C9/C16*100		E9/E16*100
10	TOTAL CURRENT ASSETS		Raw data	C10/C16*100	Raw data	E10/E16*100
11	PLANT AND EQUIPMENT			C11/C16*100		E11/E16*100
12	LAND			C12/C16*100		E12/E16*100
13	BUILDINGS			C13/C16*100		E13/E16*100
14	EQUIPMENT			C14/C16*100		E14/E16*100
15	TOTAL PLANT & EQUIPMENT			C15/C16*100		E15/E16*100
16	TOTAL ASSETS			100.00		100.00
17	LIABILITIES AND EQUITY		$	%	$	%
18	CURRENT LIABILITIES			C18/C16*100		E18/E16*100
19	ACCOUNTS PAYABLE			C19/C16*100		E19/E16*100
20	BANK LOAN			C20/C16*100		E20/E16*100
21	TOTAL CURRENT LIABS			C21/C16*100		E21/E16*100
22	OWNER'S EQUITY		Raw data	C22/C16*100	Raw data	E22/E16*100
23	CAPITAL, JANUARY 1			C23/C16*100		E23/E16*100
24	NET INCOME			C24/C16*100		E24/E16*100
25	DRAWINGS			C25/C16*100		E25/E16*100
26	CAPITAL, DECEMBER 31			C26/C16*100		E26/E16*100
27	TOTAL LIABS AND EQUITY			C27/C16*100		E27/E26*100
28				100.00		100.00

1. Enter the data from the balance sheets for Companies P and Q in the spaces reserved for raw data. After the computer makes the calculations, compare the results with those in the textbook.

2. Use the above program as a guide in order to do the first part of question 1 for Rose Company and Lily Company on page 573.

3. Prepare a spreadsheet program to do the second part of the above question.

CHAPTER HIGHLIGHTS

Now that you have completed Chapter 15, you should:

1. know who analyzes financial statements and for what reasons;
2. be able to prepare and interpret comparative financial statements;
3. be able to prepare and interpret common-size financial statements;
4. be able to prepare and interpret trend analyses;
5. be able to calculate and interpret the following liquidity ratios and statistics: current ratio; quick ratio; collection period; inventory turnover; debt/equity ratios; times interest earned ratio;
6. be able to calculate and interpret the following profitability percentages: rate of return on net sales; rate of return on owner's equity.

ACCOUNTING TERMS

accounts receivable turnover
acid-test ratio
collection period
common-size financial statement
comparative financial statement
current ratio
debt ratio
equity ratio
insiders
inventory turnover
liquidity ratio
outsiders
profitability percentage
quick ratio
rate of return on net sales percentage
rate of return on owner's equity
solvency ratio
times interest earned ratio
trend analysis
working capital
working capital ratio

CHAPTER EXERCISES

Using Your Knowledge

1. The condensed financial statements of Magnus Company for the years 19-5 and 19-6 are shown below. This exercise also appears in your workbook.

MAGNUS COMPANY
COMPARATIVE BALANCE SHEET
DECEMBER 31, 19-5 and 19-6

	19-5	19-6	Net Change
ASSETS			
Bank	$ 13 000	$ 960	$
Accounts Receivable	29 500	35 200	
Merchandise Inventory	37 450	38 950	
Prepaid Expenses	3 700	2 600	
Land	64 500	64 500	
Buildings	90 000	166 500	
Equipment	75 000	146 400	
Automobiles	30 000	21 000	
	$343 150	$476 110	$
LIABILITIES AND EQUITY			
Bank Loan	$ 40 000	$200 000	$
Accounts Payable	26 500	18 700	
Mortgage Payable	125 300	112 770	
Owner's Equity	151 350	144 640	
	$343 150	$476 110	$

MAGNUS COMPANY
COMPARATIVE INCOME STATEMENT
YEARS ENDED DECEMBER 31, 19-5 AND 19-6

	19-5 Amount	Percent	19-6 Amount	Percent
Sales	$289 500	•	$309 120	•
Costs of Goods Sold	142 750	•	155 700	•
Gross Profit	$146 750	•	$153 420	•
Operating Expenses				
Advertising	$ 1 500	•	$ 1 500	•
Car Expense	4 000	•	4 050	•
Depreciation of Building	4 250	•	8 500	•
Depreciation of Equipment	18 000	•	29 280	•
Depreciation of Automobiles	9 000	•	9 000	•
Power	3 500	•	3 950	•
Interest and Bank Charges	16 530	•	36 530	•
Supplies Used	1 000	•	1 100	•
Wages	36 700	•	38 900	•
Total Operating Expenses	$ 94 480	•	$132 810	•
Net Income	$ 52 270	•	$ 20 610	•

1. Complete the Net Change column of the comparative balance sheet.
2. Complete the Percent columns of the comparative income statement.

3. Answer the following questions related to the income statement:
   a. By how many dollars have sales increased?
   b. By how many dollars has net income decreased?
   c. Do the percentages indicate that the profit decline is caused by the cost of goods sold or the operating expenses?
   d. State the three operating expenses that show the greatest increases.
4. State the three balance sheet items that show the greatest increases.
5. From the above data write a brief explanation describing the factors that caused the profit decline. Explain also, with reasons, whether you believe this condition is permanent.

---

2. The following is the partially completed common-size comparative income statement for two companies in the same line of business. You are preparing this analysis with a view to making an investment in one of the two companies. This exercise appears in your workbook.

COMMON-SIZE COMPARATIVE INCOME STATEMENT
YEAR ENDED DECEMBER 31, 19-3

	Dollars		Percentage of Sales	
	Co. A	Co. B	Co. A	Co. B
Sales	$200 000	$150 000	•	•
Cost of Goods Sold				
Opening Inventory	$ 50 000	$ 25 000	•	•
Purchases	123 000	81 200	•	•
Goods Available for Sale	$173 000	$106 200	•	•
Less Closing Inventory	57 000	24 000	•	•
Cost of Goods Sold	$116 000	$ 82 200	•	•
Gross Profit	$ 84 000	$ 67 800	•	•
Operating Expenses				
Advertising	$ 5 000	$ 4 000	•	•
Bank Interest	900	10 000	•	•
Depreciation Building	10 000	—	•	•
Depreciation Equipment	4 500	3 000	•	•
General Expense	1 900	1 500	•	•
Insurance	500	400	•	•
Postage	750	350	•	•
Property Tax	2 000	—	•	•
Rent	—	18 000	•	•
Telephone	450	300	•	•
Wages	13 740	9 500	•	•
Total Expenses	$ 39 740	$ 47 050	•	•
Net Income	$ 44 260	$ 20 750	•	•

1. **Complete the common-size income statement. (Calculations to one decimal place.)**

2. **Answer the following questions:**
   a. Which company has the larger net income?
   b. Which company has the larger percentage net income?
   c. Which company has the larger investment in inventory?
   d. Which company has the larger gross income percentage?
   e. Which company does not own its own building?
   f. What are the three clues to question **e.**?
   g. If the owners' equities are $80 000 for Company A, and $30 000 for Company B, calculate the respective returns on owners' investment.
   h. Which company gives the greater return on owners' investment?
   i. Which company has the greater interest-bearing debt?
   j. How much is Company B disadvantaged by not owning its own building?
   k. Listed below are factors that favour Company A or Company B. For each one, indicate the company favoured.

	Favours Co. A	Favours Co. B
i. Greater net income.		
ii. Higher gross income percentage.		
iii. Greater return on owners' investment.		
iv. More established, owns own building.		
v. Lower inventory.		
vi. Lower expense.		
vii. Greater potential to reduce expenses.		
viii. Greater share of market (sales).		
ix. Fewer interest-bearing debts.		

   l. In which company would you choose to invest? Give reasons.

3. **The following data applies to Sparta Company.**
   a. The inventory turnover figure is 8.5.
   b. The collection period figure is 40.
   c. The rate of return on average equity is 25%.

   Use this data to fill in the missing figures on the partially completed financial statements that appear in your workbook.

SPARTA COMPANY
INCOME STATEMENT
YEAR ENDED DECEMBER 31, 19–3

Sales		$ _____
Cost of Goods Sold		
Beginning Inventory	$ _____	
Purchases	_____	
Goods available for sale	$ _____	
Less Ending Inventory	21 000	
Cost of Goods Sold		$170 000
Gross Profit		$ _____
Operating Expenses		$114 375
Net Income		$ _____

SPARTA COMPANY
BALANCE SHEET
DECEMBER 31, 19–3

ASSETS

Current Assets

Bank	$ _____
Accounts Receivable	35 000
Merchandise Inventory	21 000
Total Current Assets	$ _____

Fixed Assets

Land	$ 50 000
Plant and Equipment	_____
Total Fixed Assets	$120 000
Total Assets	$ _____

LIABILITIES AND EQUITY

Current Liabilities

Accounts Payable	$ _____
Bank Loan	20 000
Total Current Liabilities	$ 32 000

Owner's Equity

Beginning Capital	$130 000
Net Income	_____
	$ _____
Drawings	_____
Ending Capital	$ _____
Total Liabilities and Equity	$ _____

Comprehensive Exercises

4. Certain financial data pertaining to Anson Company are given below. Assume that all sales are on account.

ITEM 1

STATEMENT OF OWNER'S EQUITY
YEAR ENDED DECEMBER 31, 19–8

Beginning Balance	$542 000
Add: Net Income from Operations	83 000
Profit on Sale of Land	200 000
	$825 000
Deduct: Drawings for Year	50 000
Ending Balance	$775 000

ITEM 2

ANSON COMPANY
INCOME STATEMENT
YEAR ENDED DECEMBER 31, 19–8

Revenue		$700 000
Cost of Goods Sold		475 000
Gross Profit		$225 000
Expenses		
Operating Expenses (except depreciation)		120 000
Profit Before Depreciation		$105 000
Depreciation		
Buildings	$ 4 000	
Equipment	18 000	$22 000
Net Income		$ 83 000

---

1. In your workbook, complete the Net Change column of the balance sheet.

2. Answer the following questions:
   a. What caused the decrease in Buildings?
   b. What caused the decrease in Equipment?
   c. What caused the decrease in Land?
   d. Does Anson Company sell on credit? Explain.
   e. How much did the company make on the sale of the land?
   f. For how much was the land sold?

ITEM 3

ANSON COMPANY
COMPARATIVE BALANCE SHEET
YEARS ENDED DECEMBER 31, 19–7 AND 19–8

	19–7	19–8	Net Change
ASSETS			
Current Assets			
Bank	$ 4 000	$509 000	$
Merchandise Inventory	50 000	50 000	
	$ 54 000	$559 000	$
Fixed Assets			
Land	$380 000	$ 80 000	$
Buildings	80 000	76 000	
Equipment	90 000	72 000	
	$550 000	$228 000	$
Total Assets	$604 000	$787 000	$
LIABILITIES AND EQUITY			
Current Liabilities			
Bank Loan	$ 20 000	—	$
Accounts Payable	42 000	$ 12 000	
	$ 62 000	$ 12 000	$
Owner's Equity			
R. Anson, Capital	$542 000	$775 000	$
Total Liabilities and Equity	$604 000	$787 000	$

g. The bank balance increased by $505 000. Prepare a schedule that shows the increases to bank and the decreases to bank that resulted in the net increase of $505 000.

    Increases 1.
              2.

                          Total Increases _____

    Decreases 1.
               2.
               3.

                          Total Decreases _____
                          Net Increase   _____

5. You are given the following limited information about a company by a client.

Sales (approximate)	$300 000
Long-term debt	nil
Current ratio	1.7
Quick ratio	.8
Collection period	63 days
Inventory turnover	2.9
Debt ratio	.56
Times interest earned	11.2
Net income as a percentage of equity	7.6

Discuss the meanings of these ratios and statistics in a small group. Prepare a report about the company and be ready to present the results of your discussion to the class.

6. On the financial statements of Phoenix Company an inventory turnover figure of 9.1 is shown. This is based on the following information.

Cost of goods sold	$100 000
Beginning inventory	$ 10 000
Ending inventory	$ 12 000

The calculation made by the company is:

$$\frac{100\ 000}{\frac{10\ 000 + 12\ 000}{2}} = 9.1$$

You feel that the average inventory is really much higher. You show that the inventories shown on an end-of-month basis are:

January	$ 10 000
February	11 000
March	13 000
April	15 000
May	17 000
June	20 000
July	22 000
August	23 000
September	20 000
October	15 000
November	14 000
December	12 000
Total	$192 000

The total of $192 000 divided by 12 gives a figure of $16 000. Using this figure in the calculation produces an inventory turnover figure of 6.3.

Is the $16 000 figure the real average inventory? Is the 6.3 the real inventory turnover figure? Explain.

For Further Thought

7. Briefly answer the following questions.

1. Bankers, when approached for a loan, will look primarily at two aspects of a company. What are these?
2. When comparing financial statements from year to year, it is important that the data be prepared consistently. Why? Give an example.
3. Company A's sales figure showed a ten per cent drop which was considered unfavourable. Company B's sales figure showed no change. Explain whether Company B's status is favourable or not.
4. Why is it advisable to keep inventories as low as possible? Give reasons.
5. Do you agree that common-size statements make two companies appear to be of the same size? Explain.
6. Would a trend analysis be suitable for a display on a chart? Explain.
7. A company with a high inventory turnover is able to operate on a low per-item profit margin. A company with a low inventory turnover cannot survive on a low margin. Explain why.
8. A company with an equity ratio of eight per cent is seeking to purchase goods from you on credit. Explain the danger of dealing with this company. What could you do to protect yourself?
9. A company with a high debt ratio probably also has a low figure for times interest earned. Why?
10. Your banker is concerned about your current ratio which is calculated based on the following data.

Current Assets	
Bank	$ 150
Accounts Receivable	9 052
Merchandise Inventory	22 540
Prepaid Expenses	800
Marketable Securities—at cost	80 000
	$112 542
Current Liabilities	
Accounts Payable	$ 75 256
Bank Loan	100 000
	$175 256

Why is the banker concerned about this current ratio? You are able to show that the marketable securities have a market value of $125 000. How does this change the picture?

11. The collection period of a company is gradually increasing. What could be causing this? Give two possibilities.

12. The assets of a company are based on their cost prices and therefore many of the assets are undervalued in terms of current market prices. If the assets are undervalued, so is the equity because the two are mathematically related. How does this affect the debt/equity ratio? the rate of return on owner's equity?

13. It becomes necessary for you to evaluate two companies very quickly. You decide to use only five ratios. Which five ratios would you select and why?

14. If you were allowed to use only one ratio to evaluate a company, which one would you use? Explain your choice.

15. The current ratio for your company is calculated as follows:

$$\frac{152\,630}{82\,603} = 1.8$$

The auditor of your company discovers that $42 000 of obsolete merchandise is included in the inventory figure. How should this be handled? How will it affect the current ratio?

CASE STUDIES

Case 1 Owning Your Own Business: A Blessing or a Curse?

Part A

Ausma Ozolins is a high school teacher earning over $40 000 a year. Recently, she inherited $50 000 on the death of a relative. Her husband, George Ozolins, has worked in the payroll department of a large corporation for a number of years. His present salary is $28 000. He sees no hope of promotion because he is not a qualified accountant. Ausma and George consider investment opportunities for the inherited money. Eventually, they decide that they want to open a men's clothing shop. In this way, they hope to do better than just earn interest and provide a way for George to improve his earnings.

They learn of a men's clothing store for sale in a popular shopping center and begin negotiations with the owner. The owner provides them with a set of audited financial statements to help them evaluate the business. These statements are shown below.

COMPARATIVE BALANCE SHEET

	19–3	19–4	19–5
ASSETS			
Current Assets			
Bank	$ 3 000	$ 6 300	$ 11 400
Inventory	35 000	45 000	42 000
Supplies	2 000	1 900	2 000
Total Current Assets	$ 40 000	$ 53 200	$ 55 400
Fixed Assets			
Store Equipment	$ 80 000	$ 72 000	$ 64 000
Total Assets	$120 000	$125 200	$119 400
LIABILITIES AND EQUITY			
Current Liability			
Accounts Payable	$ 20 000	$ 22 450	$ 21 450
Long Term Liability			
Personal Loan (12%)	$ 60 000	$ 60 000	$ 45 000
Owner's Equity			
Beginning Capital	$ 48 000	$ 40 000	$ 42 750
Net Income	52 000	57 750	65 200
	$ 90 000	$ 97 750	$107 950
Drawings	50 000	55 000	55 000
Ending Capital	$ 40 000	$ 42 750	$ 52 950
Total Liabilities and Equity	$120 000	$125 200	$119 400

COMPARATIVE INCOME STATEMENT

	19–4	19–5
Revenue		
Sales	$245 000	$260 000
Cost of Goods Sold		
Beginning Inventory	$ 35 000	$ 45 000
Purchases and Freight	150 000	142 000
Cost of Goods Available	$185 000	$187 000
Less Closing Inventory	45 000	42 000
Cost of Goods Sold	$140 000	$145 000
Gross Profit	$105 000	$115 000
Operating Expenses		
Advertising	$ 3 500	$ 4 000
Depreciation—Equipment	8 000	8 000
Interest	7 200	7 200
Miscellaneous	2 100	2 900
Rent ($5000 + 1% of Sales)	7 450	7 600
Utilities	4 000	4 100
Wages	15 000	16 000
Total Expenses	$ 47 250	$ 49 800
Net Income	$ 57 750	$ 65 200

1. The Ozolins are not skilled in Accounting. They hire you, a qualified accountant, to assist them in evaluating the financial statements. Study the above statements and work out ratios for 19–4 and 19–5. Look for significant trends, and make a statement about the strengths and weaknesses of the business.

Part B (Challenge)

The Ozolins decide to buy the business. They pay book value for the store. They also agree to pay off the personal loan of $45 000. They have the cash to purchase the owner's equity. But they have to take out a bank loan, at 15%, to pay off the personal loan. The Ozolins put up their house as security for the bank loan.

It is decided between them that George will leave his present job in order to manage the store, and Ausma will continue with her teaching and help out in the store.

The results of their first full year of operation are shown by the financial statements below.

OZOLINS MEN'S WEAR
BALANCE SHEET
DECEMBER 31, 19–6

ASSETS

Current Assets
Bank	$ 1 000
Accounts Receivable	25 000
Inventory	64 000
Supplies	1 400
Total Current Assets	$ 91 400

Fixed Assets
Store Equipment	$ 56 000
Total Assets	$147 400

LIABILITIES AND EQUITY

Current Liabilities
Accounts Payable	$ 30 100
Bank Loan	45 000
Total Current Liabilities	$ 75 100

Owner's Equity
Beginning Capital	$ 52 950
Net Income	39 350
	$ 92 300
Drawings	20 000
Ending Capital	$ 72 300
Total Liabilities and Equity	$147 400

OZOLINS MEN'S WEAR
INCOME STATEMENT
YEAR ENDED DECEMBER 31, 19–6

Revenue
Sales	$230 000

Cost of Goods Sold
Beginning Inventory	$ 42 000
Purchases and Freight	160 000
Cost of Goods Available	$202 000
Less Closing Inventory	64 000
Cost of Goods Sold	$138 000
Gross Profit	$ 92 000

Operating Expenses
Advertising	$ 1 000
Bad Debts	15 000
Depreciation—Equipment	8 000
Interest	6 750
Miscellaneous	2 400
Rent ($5000 + 1% of Sales)	7 300
Utilities	4 200
Wages	8 000
Total Expenses	$ 52 650
Net Income	$ 39 350

2. The Ozolins come to you again for assistance. It is your task to size up the financial situation accurately and to be in a position to answer any questions that they may have. To help you in this respect: a) complete the comparative financial statements for 19–5 and 19–6; b) work out any accounting ratios to help you. (Charge sales were $75 000.)

3. Prepare some brief notes to help you in your discussion with the Ozolins. Be prepared to answer questions regarding the following:
   a. net income
   b. inventory
   c. bad debts
   d. favourable or unfavourable trends
   e. favourable or unfavourable ratios

4. Be prepared to recommend a course of action for the Ozolins. Decide whether they should sell or continue in business. Give reasons for your recommendations.

Case 2 Is the Manager Competent?

Bill Mallon has owned and operated a retail business for several years. Last year he retired and hired Sue Ans as the new manager at an annual salary of $30 000. Sue promised to expand the business and to increase profits. Mr. Mallon left on a world cruise for a year, and Sue was given a free hand to run the business.

Upon his return, Mr. Mallon is eager to see how the business has done under Sue Ans's management. He anxiously compares the most recent statement, reflecting Sue's work, with the statement of the previous year, when he was manager. At first glance, Mr. Mallon is disappointed with the results. He must now decide whether to retain Sue as manager or seek someone else.

Income statements for the two most recent years appear below, as well as additional data. Analyze this information and answer the questions that follow.

MALLON ENTERPRISES
INCOME STATEMENT

	19–1 (Mallon)	19–2 (Ans)
Sales	$315 000	$480 000
Cost of Goods Sold		
Opening Inventory	$ 80 000	$ 85 000
Purchases	195 000	285 000
Goods Available for Sale	$275 000	$370 000
Less Closing Inventory	85 000	55 000
Cost of Goods Sold	$190 000	$315 000
Gross Profit	$125 000	$165 000
Operating Expenses		
Advertising	$ 2 000	$ 7 000
Bad Debts	300	2 500
Bank Interest	10 000	5 000
Car Expense	3 000	3 100
Depreciation of Car	1 500	1 500
Delivery Expense	9 000	8 000
Depreciation of Delivery Truck	3 600	—
Light and Heat	1 700	2 000
Miscellaneous Expense	300	350
Rent	13 000	16 500
Telephone	400	500
Wages and Salaries	24 500	55 000
Loss on Sale of Truck		2 000
Total Expenses	$ 69 300	$103 450
Net Income	$ 55 700	$ 61 550

Additional Information:
The following policy changes were made by Sue Ans:
a. More money was spent on advertising in an attempt to increase sales.
b. Credit was granted more freely in an attempt to increase sales.
c. The size of the inventory was reduced, but not the number or the variety of products.
d. The delivery equipment was sold and an outside trucking firm was hired to make the deliveries.
e. Neither the plant nor the facilities were expanded.

1. Complete a comparative income statement.

2. Calculate all of the ratios for which the necessary figures are available.

3. Answer the following questions.
    1. What two factors are the probable cause of the increase in sales?
    2. Identify a direct monetary gain caused by the reduction in inventory.
    3. Did a monetary saving result from the change in the method of delivery?
    4. If you answered "yes" to question 3 above, how much was the saving?
    5. Why did wages and salaries increase so much?

4. Prepare a list of the expense items over which Sue Ans had no control.

5. Acting as if you were Sue Ans, convince Mr. Mallon that you managed the business competently in his absence. Back up your claim with appropriate figures and calculations.

Case 3   To Lend or Not to Lend

Part A
In the city of Kempenfelt, population 150 000, Gary Maw owns the most popular store for stereo and electronic equipment. Gary's store is extremely modest, but the location is ideal. There is good access to Gary's store from anywhere in the city. Gary has built up an excellent reputation for quality merchandise, low prices, and excellent service.

Gary Maw's improving financial position is shown by the following comparative financial statements.

COMPARATIVE BALANCE SHEET

	19–5	19–6	19–7	19–8
ASSETS				
Cash	$ 3 040	$ 1 814	$ 8 680	$ 6 180
Accounts Receivable	37 820	39 000	45 500	49 600
Merchandise Inventory	22 200	23 400	25 600	35 000
Prepaid Expenses	1 042	1 092	1 012	1 052
Store Equipment	11 950	9 950	8 350	7 150
Total Assets	$76 052	$ 75 256	$ 89 142	$ 98 982
LIABILITIES AND EQUITY				
Bank Loan	$20 000	$ 20 000	$ 30 000	$ 30 000
Accounts Payable	24 794	26 198	24 684	31 074
Owner's Equity	31 258	29 058	34 458	37 908
Total Liabilities and Equity	$76 052	$ 75 256	$ 89 142	$ 98 982

COMPARATIVE INCOME STATEMENT

	19–6	19–7	19–8
Sales	$180 000	$210 000	$240 000
Cost of Goods Sold	89 200	100 000	121 550
Gross Profit	$ 90 800	$110 000	$118 450
Operating Expenses			
Depreciation	$ 2 000	$ 1 600	$ 1 200
Other Expenses	40 000	48 000	53 800
Total Expenses	$ 42 000	$ 49 600	$ 55 000
Net Income	$ 48 800	$ 60 400	$ 63 450
Drawings	$ 50 000	$ 55 000	$ 60 000

1. **Complete a schedule of key ratios for 19–6, 19–7, and 19–8. Assume that one-half of all sales are credit sales.**

2. **Provide a general statement about this business, giving your opinion of its profitability, efficiency, weaknesses, and so on.**

Part B

Gary Maw has learned recently that a national chain of electronics and stereo specialists is opening a branch store within a year in a large new downtown mall. To meet this competition, Gary believes that he will have to restructure his store to provide greater room, variety, and convenience in more modern surroundings.

Gary intends to acquire the empty property next door to his store and to build a modern store with plenty of parking. He has found out the following facts.
1. The property will cost $80 000 and the building $170 000, for a total of $250 000.
2. The bank rate is twelve per cent.
3. Current mortgage rates are nine per cent and a mortgage loan in the amount of $210 000 is available if he decides to go ahead.
4. $10 000 of additional equipment will be needed.

Gary has no outside savings. He realizes that he will have to obtain an additional bank loan of $50 000. He knows that he will have to reduce his drawings by about half until the new store is firmly established and profitable. He is determined to become much more aggressive in collecting accounts receivable. He intends to do some serious research into advertising.

Gary has arranged to visit his bank manager to discuss the necessary bank loan. Gary brings an estimated income statement for 19–9 as if the expansion had taken place on January 1, 19–9. He knows that the bank manager will want to see such a statement. The statements are as follows.

ESTIMATED FINANCIAL STATEMENTS, 19–9

1. **BALANCE SHEET**

ASSETS	
Cash	$ 39 210
Accounts Receivable	34 800
Merchandise Inventory	38 635
Prepaid Expenses	1 152
Land	80 000
Building (net)	161 500
Store Equipment (net)	13 720
Total Assets	$369 017
LIABILITIES AND EQUITY	
Bank Loan	$ 80 000
Accounts Payable	40 439
Mortgage Payable	205 000
Owner's Equity	43 578
Total Liabilities & Equity	$369 017

2. **INCOME STATEMENT**

Sales		$264 000
Cost of Goods Sold		132 000
Gross Profit		$132 000
Operating Expenses		
Depreciation—Equipment	$ 3 430	
Depreciation—Building	8 500	
Mortgage Interest	18 900	
Bank Interest	9 600	
Other Expenses	65 900	
Total Expenses		$106 330
Net Income		$ 25 670

3. **Assume that you are the bank manager. State whether or not you would grant the loan. Give reasons for your decision. To help you make this decision, work out accounting ratios. (Assume that credit sales make up one-half of the sales figure.)**

CAREER
Kim Brady / Financial Analyst

Encouraged by an older brother who is a public accountant, Kim Brady enrolled in the Certified General Accounting (CGA) program while still at high school in Vancouver, British Columbia. She graduated from high school with an average of eighty per cent and won several academic awards.

The following year, Kim enrolled in Business Administration at Simon Fraser University, and during her four-year honours program she again earned high marks. She was able to obtain ten course exemptions for her CGA program. After she graduated, Kim had to complete only six of the sixteen courses to earn her CGA title.

Kim's first employer was Barry Demers, a Certified Management Accountant (CMA). Kim worked as a senior accounting clerk, keeping the clients' books and performing all accounting work up to the taking of the trial balance for the general ledger. While working for Demers, Kim completed her six remaining courses and became a Certified General Accountant.

Kim now works as a financial analyst for Sterling Drugs, a leading manufacturer of drugs and household items which employs more than three hundred people. Kim's is a highly responsible position. She analyzes all the figures on the income statement and the balance sheet and presents her findings to management. She examines current ratios and quick ratios and conducts trend analyses for a number of successive periods. She continually monitors and analyzes the profit figures and investigates any figures that vary from those of the previous month or previous year. This process is called "analytical analysis" and is used by external auditors when comparing current account balances with those of the previous year.

Further analysis of the financial statements leads Kim to compare budgeted expenses with actual costs and to review accounts to see if they are out of line. She prepares monthly journal entries and makes adjustments for expenses from previous and for future accounting periods. She also supervises the preparation of fixed asset schedules, manufacturing costs, and inventory costs.

At Sterling Drugs, Kim is responsible for analysing four distinct financial topics: costs, budgets, financial analysis systems, and plant and payroll accounting.

In the area of financial analysis and planning, Kim uses the computer to simulate different situations. She is then able to provide management with a chance to see potential trouble spots and evaluate the probable results of proposed activities. She calls this process "model building." Some examples of the models Kim provides for management include short-range forecasts, new product analyses, ratios analyses by sales area and product line, cash flow analyses, budgeting, profit and loss analyses and financial ratio analyses.

Kim firmly believes that the future of accounting and financial analysis will centre on the computer. Because of her interest in computer programming, Kim attends many company-sponsored training programs to further her knowledge and skills in this important field.

Discussion

1. What is meant by "analytical analysis"?
2. a. How was Kim able to earn ten course exemptions in her CGA program?
   b. What is the minimum mark she had to achieve in each of her university courses in order to receive this exemption?
3. Describe Kim's duties as a financial analyst for Sterling Drugs and relate these duties to the material learned in this chapter.
4. What is the purpose of a budget?
5. How do you think Kim's accounting courses helped her to achieve her present position as a financial analyst?
6. How does Kim employ the computer as a management tool for analysis?

16 Payroll Accounting

16.1 Gross Pay
16.2 Payroll Deductions and Net Pay
16.3 Recording the Payroll
16.4 Payment to Employees
16.5 Basic Payroll Records
16.6 Computerized Accounting: The Payroll Package

The term **payroll** refers to that part of the accounting process that deals with salaries, wages, and commissions paid to employees. Payroll may seem simple to the worker who receives money in return for his time and effort. It is, however, a complex process,
and the person in charge of it has a great deal of responsibility. The paymaster must be well-informed about numerous government rules, regulations, and other related matters.

Both federal and provincial governments have passed important legislation that greatly affects payroll procedures. Examples include the Income Tax Act, the Unemployment Insurance Act, the Canada Pension Plan Act, and various provincial hospitalization acts. These acts set out regulations that employers, by law, must follow. The regulations are many and often complex, and take a great deal of study. Revenue Canada supplies booklets outlining all of the federal rules and regulations.

The most basic requirements to be followed by an employer are:

1. to make appropriate deductions from the earnings of its employees in accordance with the regulations;
2. to know what income and other benefits (such as use of automobile, travel allowances, *etc*.) are taxable;
3. to keep abreast of changes in the regulations;
4. to keep detailed payroll records as required and to permit verification of these records when asked to do so;
5. to remit to the government, or other agencies, the amounts withheld from the employees, together with the employer's own contribution where required.

16.1 Gross Pay

Gross pay is the amount of an employee's earnings before any deductions are made from it. There are three different methods of determining gross pay: salaries, wages, and commissions.

Salaries

Salaries are paid to office workers, teachers, supervisors, executives, and many civil servants. A **salary** is a fixed sum of money paid to an employee on a regular basis over a given period of time (usually one year). A person on salary is allowed a certain number of sick days without any loss of pay.

Consider the case of Harold Evans, who is employed by Nor-Can Grocers Limited, a food wholesaler. Mr. Evans receives an annual salary of $25 700 and is paid every two weeks, or bi-weekly. (There are twenty-six bi-weekly pay periods in a year.) His pay for each bi-weekly pay period is calculated as follows:

$$\frac{\overset{\text{annual salary}}{\$25\ 700}}{\underset{\substack{\text{number of pay periods} \\ \text{per year}}}{26}} = \$988.46 \quad \begin{cases} \text{each} \\ \text{bi-weekly} \\ \text{period} \end{cases}$$

Wages

Wages are payments to workers for their labour, on an hourly, daily, or weekly basis, or by the piece. Payment by the piece means that the workers are paid according to the quantity of goods they produce (piecework). Some businesses pay a certain minimum hourly rate plus a piecework bonus for quantities produced over and above a stated amount per day or week.

Time Clocks and Timecards

Timecards are often used by workers who are paid by the hour. A **timecard** is a card on which a time clock records the times that the employee starts and finishes work

Figure 16.1 A time recorder. Courtesy of Simplex International Time Equipment Company Ltd.

each day. Timecards are used by the payroll department to calculate the total hours worked by each employee for each pay period. A time clock is illustrated in Figure 16.1.

When a timecard is inserted into a time clock, the mechanism of the clock automatically imprints the time at which the employee is entering or leaving work. This is normally referred to as "punching in" and "punching out." Time clocks are normally located near the employees' entrance to the plant, and placed so that they can be seen by a foreman or supervisor to prevent improper use. A timecard for a one-week period is shown in Figure 16.2. The times are automatically printed by the clock in one of six columns: Morning In, Morning Out, Afternoon In, Afternoon Out, Extra In, Extra Out.

Time Card

Week Ended September 14   19 --

Social Ins. No. 603 456 667

Name Burns, Joseph

Day	Morning In	Morning Out	Afternoon In	Afternoon Out	Extra In	Extra Out	Total Hours
M	7:58	12:01	12:59	5:01			8
T	7:56	12:01	12:58	5:02			8
W	8:03	12:00	12:58	5:01			7¾
T	7:58	12:01	12:59	5:01			8
F	7:59	12:01	12:57	5:00	5:57	7:02	8/1
S	7:59	12:02					/4
S							

	Hours	Rate	Earnings
Regular Time	39 ¾	12.00	477.00
Overtime	5	18.00	90.00
Gross Pay			567.00

Figure 16.2 A completed time card.

Completing the Timecard

At the end of each pay period the payroll department completes the timecards, such as the one shown in Figure 16.2, for all employees. For each card, a payroll clerk must perform the steps outlined below.

1. Calculate the number of hours worked each day. Regular hours and overtime hours are shown separately.
2. Total the number of regular hours.
3. Total the number of overtime hours.
4. Complete the bottom section of the card. There is space provided to multiply the regular hours by the regular rate, and the overtime hours by the overtime rate. Then the regular earnings and the overtime earnings are added together to obtain the gross earnings for the employee.

> **Notes**
>
> For the calculations in this text, the rules below are used. The actual rules used in business will vary from company to company.
>
> a. The regular work week consists of a five-day week of eight hours per day for a total of forty hours. Any time worked after 5:00 P.M., or on Saturday or Sunday, is considered overtime.
> b. Employees who are late arriving for work are penalized as follows:
>   • Fifteen minutes, if they are late by one to fifteen minutes,
>   • Thirty minutes, if they are late by sixteen to thirty minutes, and so on.
> c. The rate of pay for overtime is one and a half times the regular rate.

Commissions

Commissions are paid to salespersons and sales agents. A **commission** is an agreed-upon percentage of the dollar value of sales made by the employee. In most cases, however, a basic salary is paid in addition to the commission to provide the employee with at least a minimum income during difficult periods.

Consider the case of Rod Ferguson, a salesman for Nor-Can Grocers Limited who receives $250 per week and a commission equal to one-half of one per cent of the net sales made by him. During the last two weeks Mr. Ferguson sold $59 000 worth of merchandise.

Rod Ferguson's pay is calculated as follows:

Basic salary (two weeks × $250)	=	$500
Commission (1/2 × 1% × $59 000)	=	295
Total earnings for two weeks	=	$795

Section Review Questions

1. Define payroll.
2. Why does the person in charge of payroll have a responsible position?
3. Name three government Acts that affect payroll.
4. How does one obtain the details of government regulations regarding payroll?
5. Describe the five most basic payroll requirements imposed on an employer.
6. What is gross pay?
7. What is a salary?
8. What are wages?
9. Explain the purpose of the timecard.
10. Explain the rule to be used in this textbook in regard to overtime hours.
11. Explain the rule to be used in this textbook in regard to late arrival for work.
12. What is the overtime rate to be used in this text?
13. What are commissions?
14. Why would someone on commission also get a salary?

Section Exercises

(Note: Use the rules set out on page 616 for all exercises.)

1. **Complete the following schedule in your workbook.**

Annual Salary	Payroll Period	Gross Pay Per Period
$39 000	Weekly	
	Weekly	$800
$22 750	Bi-weekly	
	Bi-weekly	$1 250
$36 000	Semi-monthly	
	Semi-monthly	$1 800
$30 000	Monthly	
	Monthly	$3 200

2. Phyllis Marshall earns a salary of $35 000 per year. In the workbook calculate the gross pay she would receive under each of the payroll periods given.

Payroll Period	Gross Pay
a. Weekly	
b. Bi-weekly	
c. Semi-monthly	
d. Monthly	

3. Complete the following schedule in your workbook.

Total Hours	Regular Rate	Regular Hours	Overtime Hours	Regular Pay	Overtime Pay	Gross Pay
46	$11.50					
43	$14.50					
44 1/2	$12.00					
54	$21.00					
47 1/4	$13.75					

4. Grace Fung works in a factory assembling radio components. She is paid $50 a day ($25 for a half day) plus $4 for each component that she completes. In the workbook, calculate Grace's gross pay for one week based on the production figures given.

Day	Number of Units Completed	Salary	Piecework Earnings	Gross Pay
Monday	10			
Tuesday	9			
Wednesday (1/2)	5			
Thursday	11			
Friday	10			
TOTALS				

5. The timecards for two employees are given below and in your workbook.

Time Card

Week Ended   July 23   19 --
Social Ins. No. 642 393 438
Name   Frank Windsor

Day	Morning In	Morning Out	Afternoon In	Afternoon Out	Extra In	Extra Out	Total Hours
M	7:58	12:01	12:58	5:01			
T	8:07	12:00	12:57	5:02			
W	7:56	12:03	12:59	5:00			
T	7:59	12:02	1:01	5:03			
F	7:57	12:02	12:59	5:01			
S							
S							

	Hours	Rate	Earnings
Regular Time		14.00	
Overtime			
Gross Pay			

Time Card

Week Ended   July 23   19 --
Social Ins. No. 643 461 217
Name   Ray Peterson

Day	Morning In	Morning Out	Afternoon In	Afternoon Out	Extra In	Extra Out	Total Hours
M	7:58	12:01	1:00	5:02			
T	7:59	12:00	12:58	5:01	5:59	8:55	
W	7:57	12:01	12:59	5:02			
T	7:56	12:01	12:58	5:03			
F	7:59	12:01	12:59	5:01			
S	7:58	12:01					
S							

	Hours	Rate	Earnings
Regular Time		12.20	
Overtime			
Gross Pay			

1. Determine and write in the total number of regular hours and overtime hours worked each day for each employee.
2. Calculate and write in the regular and the overtime earnings for each employee.
3. Calculate and write in the gross pay for each employee.

6. The Greenfield Real Estate Company pays its salespeople a basic salary of $325 per month plus a two per cent commission on their sales. In your workbook, complete the schedule shown below.

Sales Person	Sales for Month	Salary	Commission	Gross Earnings
Mary Hunt	$90 000			
Anna Mocha	$122 000			
Bob Rennie	$75 000			
Fay Savard	$316 000			
Paul Thors	$50 000			
Gloria Unich	$70 000			
Gladys Wilson	$26 000			

16.2 Payroll Deductions and Net Pay

You are probably aware of the factors involved in the preparation of a paycheque. Employees are hired with the understanding that they will be paid a certain amount per hour, week, or year. However, certain deductions are made before the employee is actually paid.

As we have seen, Harold Evans receives an annual salary of $25 700 payable every two weeks in equal portions of $988.46. This amount is his "gross pay." When Evans receives his cheque, however, it is made out for only $688.50. Harold Evans was not shortchanged the difference of $299.96. The $299.96 is the total amount deducted from his pay. The amount that Harold Evans receives, $688.50, is his net pay. The **net pay** is the amount of pay remaining after all deductions have been made.

The payroll equation is:

GROSS PAY minus DEDUCTIONS equals NET PAY

For Harold Evans:

$988.46   minus $299.96   equals $688.50

Payroll Journal

The calculations that are necessary in order to arrive at the net pay for Harold Evans are recorded in a special journal. The **payroll journal**, or **payroll register**, is a columnar journal designed especially for recording payroll calculations and figures. The payroll journal used by Nor-Can Grocers Ltd. is shown in Figure 16.3.

| Employee | Net Claim Code | Earnings ||| C.P.P. | U.I. Premium | R.P.P. | Income Tax || Health Ins. | Union Dues | Group Life | Total Ded'ns | Net Pay |
		Regular	Extra	Gross				Taxable Earnings	Ded'n					
Harold Evans		988 46		988 46										

PAYROLL JOURNAL — For the 2 Weeks ended May 24, 19__

Figure 16.3 A payroll journal form with gross pay recorded.

Social Insurance Number

An employer is required to withhold certain amounts from an employee's pay. These deductions include Canada Pension Plan or Quebec Pension Plan contributions, personal income taxes, and unemployment insurance premiums. Naturally, care must be taken to ensure that employees are credited properly for their contributions. For this purpose, the federal government requires all employees to have a social insurance number, recorded on a social insurance card.

The social insurance number system is Canada's method of permanently identifying every citizen of the country. It is the number used by the government to direct information correctly to an individual's account or file. The federal government will not pay out any benefits unless the claimant has a social insurance number. The social insurance card for Harold Evans with its nine-digit number is shown in Figure 16.4.

Figure 16.4 A social insurance card.

Canada Pension Plan Deduction

The federal government instituted a pension plan for Canadian workers which became effective January 1, 1966. This plan is called the Quebec Pension Plan in Quebec, and the Canada Pension Plan (C.P.P.) in the rest of the country.

The Canada Pension Plan booklet (1987) provides many details about the plan. In particular it states:

> Employers must deduct the required Canada Pension Plan contribution from the remuneration of every employee
> - who is eighteen years of age and has not reached seventy years of age, and
> - who is employed in pensionable employment during the year, and
> - who is not receiving a Canada or a Quebec Pension Plan retirement or disability pension.

Employee Contributions

The simplest way of determining C.P.P. deductions is by using the tables provided in the government booklet. A page from this booklet is included at the end of this section. The booklet contains a set of deduction tables for every possible payroll period. Each set of tables gives a series of possible earning figures and their corresponding pension contributions.

To determine the deduction for an employee, look down the column headed "Remuneration" until you find the range containing the employee's gross pay figure. Observe the C.P.P. deduction figure to the immediate right. This is shown in Figure 16.5 below for Harold Evans, whose gross pay is $988.46.

Remuneration Rémunération		C.P.P. R.P.C.
From-*de*	To-*à*	
985.88 -	986.42	16.02
986.43 -	986.98	16.03
986.99 -	987.53	16.04
987.54 -	988.09	16.05
988.10 -	988.64	16.06
988.65 -	989.20	16.07
989.21 -	989.76	16.08
989.77 -	990.31	16.09
990.32 -	990.87	16.10

Figure 16.5 A section from the C.P.P. tables showing the deduction figure for Harold Evans.

The C.P.P. deduction for Harold Evans is $16.06. It is recorded in the C.P.P. column of the payroll journal opposite Harold Evans's name. This is shown below in Figure 16.6.

PAYROLL JOURNAL							For the 2 Weeks				ended May 24		19 —
		Earnings					Deductions						
Employee	Net Claim Code	Regular	Extra	Gross	C.P.P.	U.I. Premium	R.P.P.	Income Tax		Health Ins.	Union Dues	Group Life	Total Ded'ns	Net Pay
								Taxable Earnings	Ded'n					
Harold Evans		988 46		988 46	16 06									

Figure 16.6 Payroll journal with C.P.P. deduction recorded.

(Note: There is a maximum limit on the amount to be paid in one year. In 1986 the amount was $419.40. It is the employer's responsibility to keep track of the total deducted for every employee. Once the maximum figure is reached, no further deductions will be made in that calendar year.)

Employer's Contribution

The employer is required to contribute to the C.P.P. fund as well as the employee. You will be shown how this is handled in a later section.

Unemployment Insurance Deduction

In Canada, employed workers pay a portion of their earnings into an unemployment insurance fund. These payments are in the form of deductions made by the employer from the employees' pay cheques. If a worker who has made sufficient contributions to the fund becomes unemployed while willing and able to accept employment, that worker is entitled to receive payments out of the fund.

Employee Contributions

The unemployment insurance premium deductions are found in the same government booklet as the C.P.P. contributions. The tables read in the same way as for the C.P.P., but there are two important differences:

1. There is only one set of U.I. deduction tables, to be used for all payroll periods.
2. There is a maximum deduction figure for each different payroll period. You can see this in the sample pages of tables placed at the end of this section. The maximum deductions for each of the various pay periods are given at the bottom of each page and are also highlighted within the tables themselves.

Harold Evans's deduction figure is highlighted in Figure 16.7 below. Observe that the maximum deduction for bi-weekly payrolls is $23.27.

Remuneration Rémunération		U.I. Premium Prime d'a.-c.	Remuneration Rémunération		U.I. Premium Prime d'a.-c.	Fro
From-de	To-à		From-de	To-à		
984.47 -	984.89	23.14	1015.11 -	1015.53	23.86	104
984.90 -	985.31	23.15	1015.54 -	1015.95	23.87	104
985.32 -	985.74	23.16	1015.96 -	1016.38	23.88	104
985.75 -	986.17	23.17	1016.39 -	1016.80	23.89	104
986.18 -	986.59	23.18	1016.81 -	1017.23	23.90	104
986.60 -	987.02	23.19	1017.24 -	1017.65	23.91	104
987.03 -	987.44	23.20	1017.66 -	1018.08	23.92	104
987.45 -	987.87	23.21	1018.09 -	1018.51	23.93	104
987.88 -	988.29	23.22	1018.52 -	1018.93	23.94	104
988.30 -	988.72	23.23	1018.94 -	1019.36	23.95	104
988.73 -	989.14	23.24	1019.37 -	1019.78	23.96	105
989.15 -	989.57	23.25	1019.79 -	1020.21	23.97	105
989.58 -	989.99	23.26	1020.22 -	1020.63	23.98	105
990.00 -	990.42	23.27	1020.64 -	1021.06	23.99	105
990.43 -	990.85	23.28	1021.07 -	1021.48	24.00	105
990.86 -	991.27	23.29	1021.49 -	1021.91	24.01	105
991.28 -	991.70	23.30	1021.92 -	1022.34	24.02	105
991.71 -	992.12	23.31	1022.35 -	1022.76	24.03	105

Maximum Premium Deduction for a Pay Period of the stated frequency.
Déduction maximale de prime pour une période de paie d'une durée donnée.

Weekly - Hebdomadaire	11.63
Bi-Weekly - Deux semaines	23.27
Semi-Monthly - Bi-mensuel	25.20
Monthly - Mensuellement	50.41

Figure 16.7 A section of the unemployment insurance tables showing the deduction for Harold Evans.

The unemployment insurance deduction for Harold Evans is $23.23. This deduction is recorded in the U.I. column of the payroll journal as shown below in Figure 16.8.

Figure 16.8 Payroll journal with U.I. deduction recorded.

Employer's Contribution

The employer is also required to contribute to the unemployment insurance fund. The employer's contribution is 1.4 times that contributed by the employees. You will see how this is handled in a later section.

Registered Pension Plan Deduction

Employees are often enrolled in private "registered" pension plans through their places of employment. A **registered pension plan (R.P.P.)** or a **registered retirement savings plan (R.R.S.P.)** is a private pension plan approved by the government for income tax purposes. The amount of premium (to an allowed maximum) paid into a registered plan may be used by the employees as a deduction when calculating their income taxes.

Usually, both the employee and the employer contribute an amount which is a set percentage of the employee's gross pay. Nor-Can Grocers Ltd. has a registered pension plan. Both the employees and the employer contribute to the plan at the rate of five per cent of gross pay.

The deduction for Harold Evans is five per cent of $988.46, which is $49.42. This is recorded in the R.P.P. column of the payroll journal as shown in Figure 16.9. The company contributes an equal amount. You will see how this is handled later.

Employee	Net Claim Code	Earnings Regular	Extra	Gross	C.P.P.	U.I. Premium	R.P.P.	Income Tax Taxable Earnings	Ded'n	Health Ins.	Union Dues	Group Life	Total Ded'ns	Net Pay
Harold Evans		988 46		988 46	16 06	23 23	49 42							

PAYROLL JOURNAL — For the 2 Weeks ended May 24, 19—

Figure 16.9 Payroll journal with R.P.P. deduction recorded.

Income Tax Deduction

According to Canadian income tax laws, employers are required to make a deduction from the earnings of each employee for personal income tax. The amount to be deducted is based on two factors:

1. the total of the employee's personal exemptions;
2. the amount of the employee's taxable earnings.

Personal Exemption

Every employee is required to fill out a Tax Exemption Return form known as the TD1. A completed TD1 form for Harold Evans is shown in Figure 16.10. This form is used to determine the employee's total personal exemption. The **total personal exemption** is the amount that a person may earn in a year without being taxed. The amount varies depending on the employee's marital status, the number of dependent children, and other factors including family allowance benefits. This form is completed by every employee once a year, or when an employee changes jobs or begins a new job.

Figure 16.10a An employee's TD1 form, front.

Claim for Exemptions — *Exemptions demandées*

1. **Basic Personal Exemption** — *Exemption personnelle de base* ▶ $ 4,180
2. **Claim only one of these two exemptions** — *Demandez une seule des deux exemptions suivantes:*
   2.1 **If Married and Supporting Spouse** — *Si vous êtes marié(e) et soutien de votre conjoint*
   - ☐ whose net income while married will not exceed / *dont le revenu net dans l'année, pendant le mariage, ne dépassera pas* | $520   Claim — *Demandez* $3,660
   - ☐ whose net income while married will exceed / *dont le revenu net dans l'année, pendant le mariage, dépassera* | $520 but not / *sans dépasser* $4,180

   Less spouse's net income — *Moins le revenu du conjoint* $2,500

   Claim — *Demandez* $ 1,680 ▶ $ 1680 —

   2.2 **If single, divorced, separated or widow(er), and supporting dependant**
   Si vous êtes célibataire, divorcé(e), séparé(e) ou veuf(veuve), et soutien d'une personne à charge
   See Note 1 — *Voir la note 1*
   - ☐ (iii) whose net income will not exceed / *dont le revenu net pour l'année ne dépassera pas* | $520   Claim — *Demandez* $3,660
   - ☐ (iv) whose net income will exceed / *dont le revenu net pour l'année dépassera* | $520 but not / *sans dépasser* $4,180

   Less: dependant's net income — *Moins le revenu net de la personne à votre charge* $

   Claim — *Demandez* $

   * Name and relationship to you
   Nom et lien de parenté avec vous

3. **Exemption for Dependant Children** — *Exemption pour enfants à charge*
   See Note 2, give details and claim according to — *Voir la note 2 Donnez les précisions demandées et demandez l'exemption selon les conditions suivantes*
   (i) under age 18 at December 31st and net income will not exceed $2,760, claim $710. If net income exceeds $2,760 but not $4,180, claim $710 minus one-half the amount in excess of $2,760.
   moins de 18 ans le 31 décembre. Si son revenu net ne dépassera pas 2760$ demandez 710$ Si son revenu net se situera entre 2760$ et 4180$; demandez 710$ moins la moitié de la fraction qui dépasse 2760$
   (ii) age 18 or over at December 31st and net income will not exceed $1,340, claim $1,420. If net income exceeds $4,180 claim $1,420 minus one half the amount in excess of $1,340.
   18 ans ou plus le 31 décembre Si son revenu net ne dépassera pas 1,340$; demandez 1420$ Si son revenu net se situera entre 1,340$ et 4180$; demandez 1420$ moins la moitié de la fraction qui dépasse 1340$
   (iii) age 18 or over at December 31st and mentally or physically infirm and net income will not exceed $2,740 claim $1,440. If net income exceeds $2,740 but not $4,180 claim $1,440 minus the amount in excess of $2,740.
   ou 18 ans ou plus le 31 décembre, mais l'enfant souffre d'une incapacité physique ou mentale. Si son revenu net ne dépassera pas 2740$; demandez 1440$ si son revenu net se situera entre 2740$ et 4180$; demandez 1440$ moins la fraction qui dépasse 2740$

Name of child (Attach list if space is insufficient) — *Nom de l'enfant (Faute d'espace annexez une liste)*	Estimated annual net income — *Revenu net annuel estimatif*	Date of birth — *Date de naissance* Day/*Jour* Month/*Mois* Year/*Année*	If over 21, state school attended or whether mentally or physically infirm. *Si elle a plus de 21 ans, indiquez l'école fréquentée et dites-si elle souffre d'une incapacité physique ou mentale*	
DAVID	—	17 OCT 77		▶ $ 710 —
CATHERINE	—	3 OCT 79		▶ $ 710 —
				▶ $

4. **Other Exemptions** — *Autres exemptions*
   (i) Parents, Grandparents, Brothers, Sisters, Aunts or Uncles Resident in Canada (including in-laws)
   Père, mère, grands-parents, frères, sœurs, tantes et oncles résidant au Canada (et ceux du conjoint)
   See note 3 and give details. — *Voir la note 3 et donnez les précisions demandées*

Name and address of dependant *Nom et adresse de la personne à charge* (Attach list if space is insufficient) *(Faute d'espace annexez une liste)*	Dependant — *Personne à charge* Net income *Revenu net* / Year of birth *Année de naissance*	Estimated cost to you of support of dependant — *Montant estimatif pour l'entretien de la personne à charge*	If over 21, state school attended or whether mentally or physically infirm *Si elle a plus de 21 ans, indiquez l'école fréquentée ou dites si elle souffre d'une incapacité physique ou mentale*	
				▶ $

   (ii) **Age Exemptions** — *Exemptions en raison d'âge*
   If you are 65 years of age or over — *Si vous avez 65 ans ou plus*   Claim — *Demandez* $2,610 ▶ $
   If your spouse is 65 years of age or over you may claim any unused balance of the exemption: amount (maximum $2,610) — *Si votre conjoint a 65 ans ou plus, vous pouvez demander la fraction inutilisée de son exemption jusqu'à concurrence de 2610$*   Unused Balance / *Fraction inutilisée* ▶ $

   (iii) **Disability Exemptions** — *Exemptions pour invalidité*
   For persons blind or lame, or confined to a bed or wheelchair for a substantial period each day throughout any 12 month period beginning in the year, for yourself — *Pour les personnes aveugles à un moment quelconque de l'année et pour celles qui doivent garder le lit ou demeurer dans un fauteuil roulant une grande partie de la journée, tous les jours, pendant une période d'au moins 12 mois commençant dans l'année - pour vous-même*   Claim — *Demandez* $2,610 ▶ $
   You may claim any unused balance of the disability exemption, maximum $2,610 to which your spouse child, grandchild or supported individual is entitled See note 1 — *Vous pouvez demander la fraction inutilisée de l'exemption pour invalidité à laquelle ont droit votre conjoint, vos enfants, petits-enfants ou personnes à votre charge. Voir la note 1*   Unused Balance / *Fraction inutilisée* ▶ $

5. **Pension Income or Qualified Pension Income Exemption** — *Exemption relative au revenu de pensions ou au revenu de pensions admissible*
   If you are 60 years of age or over and have qualified pension income or are 65 years of age or over and have pension income, or if under age 60 and no contribution has been made to a registered retirement savings plan or registered pension plan from a qualified pension income, claim the lesser of $1,000 or the amount received
   Si vous avez 60 ans ou plus et avez un revenu de pensions ou si vous avez 65 ans ou plus et avez un revenu de pensions ou si vous avez moins de 60 ans et n'avez fait aucune contribution provenant d'un revenu de pensions admissible dans un régime enregistré d'épargne-retraite ou un régime enregistré de pensions, demandez le montant de la pension reçu jusqu'à concurrence de 1000$ ▶ $

6. **Student Exemptions** — *Exemption pour les étudiants*
   (i) Claim $50 for each month in the year you will be a student in full-time attendance at the following: a university or college or an institution offering job retraining courses — *Demandez 50$ pour chaque mois de l'année où vous fréquentez à plein temps une université, un collège ou un établissement dispensant des cours de rééducation professionnelle.*   ▶ $
   (ii) Claim your tuition fees less the total amount of all scholarships, fellowships or bursaries exceeding $500 which you will receive during the calendar year — *Demandez vos frais de scolarité moins la fraction supérieure à 500$ du total de toutes les bourses d'études, de perfectionnement (fellowships) ou d'entretien que vous recevrez au cours de l'année civile*   ▶ $

7. **Total** add items 1 to 6 — *Total Additionnez les montants 1 à 6* ▶ $ 7280 —
8. **Deduct: Taxable Family Allowance Payments** (To be received in year for children claimed above.)
   Soustraire: les allocations familiales imposables (A recevoir au cours de l'année pour les enfants nommés ci-dessus) ▶ $ 757 92
9. **Net Claim** — (Will not be less than $4,180. Enter this amount on reverse side)
   Demande nette — (Ne doit pas être inférieure à 4,180$ Inscrivez ce montant au verso) ▶ $ 6522 08

Notes
1 - Claim exemptions for a relative (a) dependent on you or you and one or more other persons; and (b) residing with you, in a dwelling maintained by you or by you and other persons to whom the dependant is related (Claim only if there is agreement that no other person claims for the same dependant or for the same desidence)
2 - Claim exemption for a dependent son, daughter, grandchild, niece or nephew under 21, or over, if in full-time attendance at school, college, university or infirm. Claim only for a niece or nephew if (a) you have complete custody and control, and (b) the child resides in Canada Do not claim here for a child claimed in item 2.2
3 - No claim can be made here for a dependant over age 21 who is not mentally or physically infirm unless it is a brother or sister in full time attendance at a school or university, or a dependant already claimed in item 2.2. The maximum that can be claimed here is the relevant maximum specified in item 3 and if any other person contributes to the support of the dependant, the aggregated claim of both persons cannot exceed that maximum

Notes
1 - Demandez une exemption pour un parent a) à votre charge ou à votre charge et à celle d'une ou de plusieurs autres personnes, et b) résidant avec vous dans un logement tenu par vous ou par vous et par d'autres personnes apparentées à la personne à charge (**Ne** demandez cette exemption **que** s'il est entendu que personne d'autre ne la demandera pour la même personne à charge ou pour le même logement.)
2 - Demandez une exemption pour un fils, fille, petit-enfant, neveu ou nièce de moins de 21 ans à votre charge, ou âge de 21 ans ou plus s'il fréquente à plein temps l'école, le collège, l'université, ou s'il est infirme. Un neveu ou nièce ne peut être à votre charge que a) si vous en avez la garde et la responsabilité entière, et b) si l'enfant réside au C— Ne faites pas ce de demande pour un enfant nommée au numéro 2.2
3 - Aucun montant ne peut être demandé ici pour une personne à charge de 21 ans, qui ne souffre pas d'une incapacité physique ou mentale (sauf un frère ou qui fréquente à plein temps l'école ou l'université), ou pour une personne à au numéro 2.2 Le montant que puisse être demandé ici est le maximum au numéro 3 et si une autre personne contribue à l'entretien de la pe— somme des demandes des deux personnes à l'égard de cette dernie— ce maximum

Figure 16.10b An employee's TD1 form, back.

Figure 16.10 shows that Harold Evans has a total personal exemption figure of $6 522.08 and, consequently, a net claim code of 5. The net claim code figure is used when referring to the income tax deduction tables.

Taxable Earnings

The **taxable earnings** of an employee are the gross pay less the following three deductions:

1. contributions to the Canada Pension Plan;
2. contributions to unemployment insurance;
3. contributions to a registered pension plan.

The calculation necessary to obtain the taxable earnings figure can be seen below, as it is worked out for Harold Evans.

Gross pay		$988.46
Less: C.P.P. contribution	$16.06	
U.I. contribution	23.23	
Registered pension plan contribution	49.42	
Total of contributions		88.71
Taxable earnings		$899.75

The taxable earnings figure for Harold Evans is recorded in the payroll journal as shown in Figure 16.11.

Figure 16.11 Payroll journal showing taxable income.

Employee Contributions

As they do for the Canada Pension Plan and unemployment insurance, Revenue Canada, Taxation provides a booklet of tables for personal income taxes. A page from the section of the booklet dealing with bi-weekly pay periods is given at the end of this section. The shaded column along the left side shows the bi-weekly pay brackets. Along the top are thirteen column headings representing the net claim codes.

Section 16.2   **629**

The correct deduction figure for income tax is found where the appropriate "pay bracket" line intersects with the correct "net claim code" column. Harold Evans's taxable earnings fall within the range 891.00–900.99. His net claim code is 5. Figure 16.12 shows that the figure at the intersection of this row and column is $164.25.

BI-WEEKLY PAY Use appropriate bracket — PAIE DE DEUX SEMAINES Utilisez le palier approprié	IF THE EMPLOYEE'S "NET CLAIM CODE" ON FORM TD1 IS – SI LE -CODE DE DEMA							
	1	**2**	**3**	**4**	**5**	**6**	**7**	
	DEDUCT FROM EACH PAY — RETENE.							
801.00 – 810.99	165.80	161.30	153.20	145.25	136.70	129.70	125.55	11
811.00 – 820.99	168.85	164.35	156.25	148.30	139.75	132.75	128.45	12
821.00 – 830.99	171.90	167.45	159.30	151.35	142.85	135.85	131.45	12
831.00 – 840.99	174.95	170.50	162.35	154.40	145.90	138.90	134.55	12
841.00 – 850.99	178.00	173.55	165.45	157.50	148.95	141.95	137.60	13
851.00 – 860.99	181.10	176.60	168.50	160.55	152.00	145.00	140.65	13
861.00 – 870.99	184.15	179.65	171.55	163.60	155.05	148.05	143.70	13
871.00 – 880.99	187.20	182.75	174.60	166.65	158.15	151.15	146.75	14
881.00 – 890.99	190.25	185.80	177.65	169.70	161.20	154.20	149.85	14
891.00 – 900.99	193.75	188.85	180.75	172.80	164.25	157.25	152.90	14
901.00 – 910.99	197.30	192.15	183.80	175.85	167.30	160.30	155.95	14
911.00 – 920.99	200.80	195.65	186.85	178.90	170.35	163.35	159.00	15
921.00 – 930.99	204.30	199.20	189.90	181.95	173.45	166.45	162.05	15
931.00 – 940.99	207.85	202.70	193.35	185.00	176.50	169.50	165.15	15
941.00 – 960.99	213.10	207.95	198.65	189.60	181.10	174.10	169.70	16
961.00 – 980.99	220.15	215.00	205.65	196.55	187.20	180.20	175.85	16
981.00 – 1000.99	227.20	222.05	212.70	203.55	193.75	186.30	181.95	17
1001.00 – 1020.99	234.25	229.10	219.75	210.60	200.80	192.75	188.10	18
1021.00 – 1040.99	241.25	236.10	226.80	217.65	207.85	199.80	194.80	18

Figure 16.12 A section of the income tax deductions booklet showing the deduction for Harold Evans.

The deduction of $164.25 for Harold Evans is recorded in the payroll journal as shown below in Figure 16.13. An employee's income tax is paid entirely by the employee.

PAYROLL JOURNAL					For the 2 Weeks		ended May 24	19 —				
	Net Claim Code	Earnings			Deductions						Total Ded'ns	Net Pay
Employee		Regular	Extra	Gross	C.P.P.	U.I. Premium	R.P.P.	Income Tax || Health Ins.	Union Dues	Group Life		
								Taxable Earnings	Ded'n						
Harold Evans	5	988 46		988 46	16 06	23 23	49 42	899 75	164 25					

Figure 16.13 Payroll journal with income tax deduction recorded.

Health Insurance Deduction

Most provinces operate a universal health insurance program. The basic plan generally covers both doctors' fees and hospital expenses. Employers are authorized to deduct from the employees' pay the amount of the premiums as set out by the provincial governments. The premium for a single person is less than that for a married person or one who has dependent children. The rates to be used in this text are:

BI-WEEKLY HEALTH INSURANCE RATES	
1. Single person	$24.00
2. Married person	$48.00

In recent years, health insurance plans have developed that provide additional benefits not included in the basic health plans operated by the provinces. Such programs as extended health care and dental health care are now quite common.

Employers often pay a portion, or in some cases the entire cost, of the premium for the health care programs for their employees. In this text, assume that the employer pays seventy-five per cent of the cost.

For Harold Evans, who is married, the bi-weekly premium is $48.00. His employer pays three-quarters of this amount, or $36.00. Harold Evans pays one-quarter, or $12.00. Figure 16.14 shows this amount recorded properly in the payroll journal.

Employee	Net Claim Code	Regular	Extra	Gross	C.P.P.	U.I. Premium	R.P.P.	Taxable Earnings	Ded'n	Health Ins.	Union Dues	Group Life	Total Ded'ns	Net Pay
Harold Evans	5	988 46		988 46	16 06	23 23		949 42	899 75	164 25	12 00				

PAYROLL JOURNAL — For the 2 Weeks ended May 24, 19—

Figure 16.14 Payroll journal with health insurance deduction recorded.

Union Dues Deduction

The employees of many businesses are organized in labour unions. Dues to the union are often deducted by the employer and paid periodically to the union. This obligation of the employer is usually part of the contract negotiated between the employer and the employees' union.

The amount that is deducted from the employees' pay is set by the union. The union to which Harold Evans belongs requires a deduction of $10.00 each pay period from every union member. Figure 16.15 shows this amount recorded correctly in the payroll journal.

Figure 16.15 Payroll journal with union dues deduction recorded.

Group Life Insurance Deduction

Some firms make it possible for their employees to enrol in a group life insurance plan. Premiums for this plan are handled as payroll deductions. Premiums are negotiated between the insurance company and the employees' group or the company. Usually, the premium depends on the amount of insurance coverage selected.

For the purposes of this text the insurance premium rate is as shown below. The maximum coverage is $100 000. The employees pay the full premium.

GROUP LIFE INSURANCE PREMIUM RATE
$0.50 for each $1 000 of coverage

Harold Evans has $50 000 of group life insurance coverage. His premium is $0.50 × 50 = $25.00. Figure 16.16 shows this amount recorded correctly in the payroll journal.

Figure 16.16 Payroll journal with group life deduction recorded.

Other Deductions

Other deductions may be made from an employee's earnings if authority is granted by the employee. They are handled in a manner similar to those deductions already discussed. Some of these other deductions include extended health care, a dental plan, the United Way, Canada Savings Bonds, and disability insurance.

Calculating Net Pay

At this point, the last deduction has been made for Harold Evans. There are two steps remaining. First, the deductions are totaled and the total is entered in the column headed Total Deductions. Second, the total deductions figure ($299.96) is subtracted from the gross pay figure ($988.46) giving the net pay figure ($688.50). This is entered in the Net Pay column. These two final amounts are shown entered in the payroll journal in Figure 16.17.

Employee	Net Claim Code	Earnings Regular	Extra	Gross	C.P.P.	U.I. Premium	R.P.P.	Income Tax Taxable Earnings	Ded'n	Health Ins.	Union Dues	Group Life	Total Ded'ns	Net Pay
Harold Evans	5	988 46		988 46	16 06	23 23	49 42	899 75	164 25	12 00	10 00	25 00	299 96	688 50

For the 2 Weeks ended May 24, 19—

Figure 16.17 Payroll journal showing total deductions and net pay.

Completing the Payroll Journal

The procedure that has been discussed and illustrated for Harold Evans is repeated for each of the employees in the company. One line of the payroll journal is used for each employee. All the payroll details for every employee are entered in the journal. The final step in preparing the payroll journal is adding all the money columns and cross balancing the journal. The completed payroll journal for Nor-Can Grocers Ltd. is shown in Figure 16.18.

Employee	Net Claim Code	Regular	Extra	Gross	C.P.P.	U.I. Premium	R.P.P.	Taxable Earnings	Ded'n	Health Ins.	Union Dues	Group Life	Total Ded'ns	Net Pay
Harold Evans	5	988 46		988 46	16 06	23 23		49 42	899 75	164 25	12 00	10 00	25 00	299 96	688 50
Ronald Baker	3	961 54		961 54	15 58	22 60		48 08	875 28	174 60	12 00	10 00	10 00	292 86	668 68
Bob Funston	8	769 23		769 23	12 12	18 08		38 46	700 57	87 20	12 00	10 00	50 00	227 86	541 37
Les Williams	4	1000 00		1000 00	16 22	23 27		50 00	910 51	175 85	6 00	10 00	20 00	301 34	698 66
Dennis Murray	5	961 54		961 54	15 58	22 60		48 08	875 28	174 60	12 00	10 00	50 00	332 86	628 68
		4680 77		4680 77	75 56	109 78		234 04	4261 39	776 50	54 00	50 00	155 00	1454 88	3225 89

PAYROLL JOURNAL   For the 2 Weeks ended May 24, 19—

Figure 16.18 A completed payroll journal.

Proving the Accuracy of the Payroll Journal

There are three steps taken to prove the accuracy of the payroll journal. Ensure that:
1. the Regular Earnings column + the Extra Earnings column = the Gross Earnings column;
2. the sum of all of the deductions columns = the Total Deductions column;
3. the Gross Earnings column − the Total Deductions column = the Net Pay column.

CANADA PENSION PLAN CONTRIBUTIONS — COTISATIONS AU RÉGIME DE PENSIONS DU CANADA

BI-WEEKLY PAY PERIOD — *PÉRIODE DE PAIE DE DEUX SEMAINES*

895.88 — 2132.53

Remuneration / Rémunération From-*de* — To-*à*	C.P.P. R.P.C.	Remuneration / Rémunération From-*de* — To-*à*	C.P.P. R.P.C.	Remuneration / Rémunération From-*de* — To-*à*	C.P.P. R.P.C.	Remuneration / Rémunération From-*de* — To-*à*	C.P.P. R.P.C.
895.88 – 896.42	14.40	935.88 – 936.42	15.12	975.88 – 976.42	15.84	1412.54 – 1422.53	23.78
896.43 – 896.98	14.41	936.43 – 936.98	15.13	976.43 – 976.98	15.85	1422.54 – 1432.53	23.96
896.99 – 897.53	14.42	936.99 – 937.53	15.14	976.99 – 977.53	15.86	1432.54 – 1442.53	24.14
897.54 – 898.09	14.43	937.54 – 938.09	15.15	977.54 – 978.09	15.87	1442.54 – 1452.53	24.32
898.10 – 898.64	14.44	938.10 – 938.64	15.16	978.10 – 978.64	15.88	1452.54 – 1462.53	24.50
898.65 – 899.20	14.45	938.65 – 939.20	15.17	978.65 – 979.20	15.89	1462.54 – 1472.53	24.68
899.21 – 899.76	14.46	939.21 – 939.76	15.18	979.21 – 979.76	15.90	1472.54 – 1482.53	24.86
899.77 – 900.31	14.47	939.77 – 940.31	15.19	979.77 – 980.31	15.91	1482.54 – 1492.53	25.04
900.32 – 900.87	14.48	940.32 – 940.87	15.20	980.32 – 980.87	15.92	1492.54 – 1502.53	25.22
900.88 – 901.42	14.49	940.88 – 941.42	15.21	980.88 – 981.42	15.93	1502.54 – 1512.53	25.40
901.43 – 901.98	14.50	941.43 – 941.98	15.22	981.43 – 981.98	15.94	1512.54 – 1522.53	25.58
901.99 – 902.53	14.51	941.99 – 942.53	15.23	981.99 – 982.53	15.95	1522.54 – 1532.53	25.76
902.54 – 903.09	14.52	942.54 – 943.09	15.24	982.54 – 983.09	15.96	1532.54 – 1542.53	25.94
903.10 – 903.64	14.53	943.10 – 943.64	15.25	983.10 – 983.64	15.97	1542.54 – 1552.53	26.12
903.65 – 904.20	14.54	943.65 – 944.20	15.26	983.65 – 984.20	15.98	1552.54 – 1562.53	26.30
904.21 – 904.76	14.55	944.21 – 944.76	15.27	984.21 – 984.76	15.99	1562.54 – 1572.53	26.48
904.77 – 905.31	14.56	944.77 – 945.31	15.28	984.77 – 985.31	16.00	1572.54 – 1582.53	26.66
905.32 – 905.87	14.57	945.32 – 945.87	15.29	985.32 – 985.87	16.01	1582.54 – 1592.53	26.84
905.88 – 906.42	14.58	945.88 – 946.42	15.30	985.88 – 986.42	16.02	1592.54 – 1602.53	27.02
906.43 – 906.98	14.59	946.43 – 946.98	15.31	986.43 – 986.98	16.03	1602.54 – 1612.53	27.20
906.99 – 907.53	14.60	946.99 – 947.53	15.32	986.99 – 987.53	16.04	1612.54 – 1622.53	27.38
907.54 – 908.09	14.61	947.54 – 948.09	15.33	987.54 – 988.09	16.05	1622.54 – 1632.53	27.56
908.10 – 908.64	14.62	948.10 – 948.64	15.34	988.10 – 988.64	16.06	1632.54 – 1642.53	27.74
908.65 – 909.20	14.63	948.65 – 949.20	15.35	988.65 – 989.20	16.07	1642.54 – 1652.53	27.92
909.21 – 909.76	14.64	949.21 – 949.76	15.36	989.21 – 989.76	16.08	1652.54 – 1662.53	28.10
909.77 – 910.31	14.65	949.77 – 950.31	15.37	989.77 – 990.31	16.09	1662.54 – 1672.53	28.28
910.32 – 910.87	14.66	950.32 – 950.87	15.38	990.32 – 990.87	16.10	1672.54 – 1682.53	28.46
910.88 – 911.42	14.67	950.88 – 951.42	15.39	990.88 – 991.42	16.11	1682.54 – 1692.53	28.64
911.43 – 911.98	14.68	951.43 – 951.98	15.40	991.43 – 991.98	16.12	1692.54 – 1702.53	28.82
911.99 – 912.53	14.69	951.99 – 952.53	15.41	991.99 – 992.53	16.13	1702.54 – 1712.53	29.00
912.54 – 913.09	14.70	952.54 – 953.09	15.42	992.54 – 1002.53	16.22	1712.54 – 1722.53	29.18
913.10 – 913.64	14.71	953.10 – 953.64	15.43	1002.54 – 1012.53	16.40	1722.54 – 1732.53	29.36
913.65 – 914.20	14.72	953.65 – 954.20	15.44	1012.54 – 1022.53	16.58	1732.54 – 1742.53	29.54
914.21 – 914.76	14.73	954.21 – 954.76	15.45	1022.54 – 1032.53	16.76	1742.54 – 1752.53	29.72
914.77 – 915.31	14.74	954.77 – 955.31	15.46	1032.54 – 1042.53	16.94	1752.54 – 1762.53	29.90
915.32 – 915.87	14.75	955.32 – 955.87	15.47	1042.54 – 1052.53	17.12	1762.54 – 1772.53	30.08
915.88 – 916.42	14.76	955.88 – 956.42	15.48	1052.54 – 1062.53	17.30	1772.54 – 1782.53	30.26
916.43 – 916.98	14.77	956.43 – 956.98	15.49	1062.54 – 1072.53	17.48	1782.54 – 1792.53	30.44
916.99 – 917.53	14.78	956.99 – 957.53	15.50	1072.54 – 1082.53	17.66	1792.54 – 1802.53	30.62
917.54 – 918.09	14.79	957.54 – 958.09	15.51	1082.54 – 1092.53	17.84	1802.54 – 1812.53	30.80
918.10 – 918.64	14.80	958.10 – 958.64	15.52	1092.54 – 1102.53	18.02	1812.54 – 1822.53	30.98
918.65 – 919.20	14.81	958.65 – 959.20	15.53	1102.54 – 1112.53	18.20	1822.54 – 1832.53	31.16
919.21 – 919.76	14.82	959.21 – 959.76	15.54	1112.54 – 1122.53	18.38	1832.54 – 1842.53	31.34
919.77 – 920.31	14.83	959.77 – 960.31	15.55	1122.54 – 1132.53	18.56	1842.54 – 1852.53	31.52
920.32 – 920.87	14.84	960.32 – 960.87	15.56	1132.54 – 1142.53	18.74	1852.54 – 1862.53	31.70
920.88 – 921.42	14.85	960.88 – 961.42	15.57	1142.54 – 1152.53	18.92	1862.54 – 1872.53	31.88
921.43 – 921.98	14.86	961.43 – 961.98	15.58	1152.54 – 1162.53	19.10	1872.54 – 1882.53	32.06
921.99 – 922.53	14.87	961.99 – 962.53	15.59	1162.54 – 1172.53	19.28	1882.54 – 1892.53	32.24
922.54 – 923.09	14.88	962.54 – 963.09	15.60	1172.54 – 1182.53	19.46	1892.54 – 1902.53	32.42
923.10 – 923.64	14.89	963.10 – 963.64	15.61	1182.54 – 1192.53	19.64	1902.54 – 1912.53	32.60
923.65 – 924.20	14.90	963.65 – 964.20	15.62	1192.54 – 1202.53	19.82	1912.54 – 1922.53	32.78
924.21 – 924.76	14.91	964.21 – 964.76	15.63	1202.54 – 1212.53	20.00	1922.54 – 1932.53	32.96
924.77 – 925.31	14.92	964.77 – 965.31	15.64	1212.54 – 1222.53	20.18	1932.54 – 1942.53	33.14
925.32 – 925.87	14.93	965.32 – 965.87	15.65	1222.54 – 1232.53	20.36	1942.54 – 1952.53	33.32
925.88 – 926.42	14.94	965.88 – 966.42	15.66	1232.54 – 1242.53	20.54	1952.54 – 1962.53	33.50
926.43 – 926.98	14.95	966.43 – 966.98	15.67	1242.54 – 1252.53	20.72	1962.54 – 1972.53	33.68
926.99 – 927.53	14.96	966.99 – 967.53	15.68	1252.54 – 1262.53	20.90	1972.54 – 1982.53	33.86
927.54 – 928.09	14.97	967.54 – 968.09	15.69	1262.54 – 1272.53	21.08	1982.54 – 1992.53	34.04
928.10 – 928.64	14.98	968.10 – 968.64	15.70	1272.54 – 1282.53	21.26	1992.54 – 2002.53	34.22
928.65 – 929.20	14.99	968.65 – 969.20	15.71	1282.54 – 1292.53	21.44	2002.54 – 2012.53	34.40
929.21 – 929.76	15.00	969.21 – 969.76	15.72	1292.54 – 1302.53	21.62	2012.54 – 2022.53	34.58
929.77 – 930.31	15.01	969.77 – 970.31	15.73	1302.54 – 1312.53	21.80	2022.54 – 2032.53	34.76
930.32 – 930.87	15.02	970.32 – 970.87	15.74	1312.54 – 1322.53	21.98	2032.54 – 2042.53	34.94
930.88 – 931.42	15.03	970.88 – 971.42	15.75	1322.54 – 1332.53	22.16	2042.54 – 2052.53	35.12
931.43 – 931.98	15.04	971.43 – 971.98	15.76	1332.54 – 1342.53	22.34	2052.54 – 2062.53	35.30
931.99 – 932.53	15.05	971.99 – 972.53	15.77	1342.54 – 1352.53	22.52	2062.54 – 2072.53	35.48
932.54 – 933.09	15.06	972.54 – 973.09	15.78	1352.54 – 1362.53	22.70	2072.54 – 2082.53	35.66
933.10 – 933.64	15.07	973.10 – 973.64	15.79	1362.54 – 1372.53	22.88	2082.54 – 2092.53	35.84
933.65 – 934.20	15.08	973.65 – 974.20	15.80	1372.54 – 1382.53	23.06	2092.54 – 2102.53	36.02
934.21 – 934.76	15.09	974.21 – 974.76	15.81	1382.54 – 1392.53	23.24	2102.54 – 2112.53	36.20
934.77 – 935.31	15.10	974.77 – 975.31	15.82	1392.54 – 1402.53	23.42	2112.54 – 2122.53	36.38
935.32 – 935.87	15.11	975.32 – 975.87	15.83	1402.54 – 1412.53	23.60	2122.54 – 2132.53	36.56

Table 16.1 Canada Pension Plan contributions schedule.

UNEMPLOYMENT INSURANCE PREMIUMS / PRIMES D'ASSURANCE-CHÔMAGE

For minimum and maximum insurable earnings amounts for various pay periods see Schedule II. For the maximum premium deduction for various pay periods see bottom of page.

Les montants minimum et maximum des gains assurables pour diverses périodes de paie figurent en annexe II. La déduction maximale de primes pour diverses périodes de paie figure au bas de la présente page.

Remuneration / Rémunération From-de – To-à	U.I. Premium Prime d'a.-c.	Remuneration / Rémunération From-de – To-à	U.I. Premium Prime d'a.-c.	Remuneration / Rémunération From-de – To-à	U.I. Premium Prime d'a.-c.	Remuneration / Rémunération From-de – To-à	U.I. Premium Prime d'a.-c.
858.09 – 858.51	20.17	888.73 – 889.14	20.89	919.37 – 919.78	21.61	950.00 – 950.42	22.33
858.52 – 858.93	20.18	889.15 – 889.57	20.90	919.79 – 920.21	21.62	950.43 – 950.85	22.34
858.94 – 859.36	20.19	889.58 – 889.99	20.91	920.22 – 920.63	21.63	950.86 – 951.27	22.35
859.37 – 859.78	20.20	890.00 – 890.42	20.92	920.64 – 921.06	21.64	951.28 – 951.70	22.36
859.79 – 860.21	20.21	890.43 – 890.85	20.93	921.07 – 921.48	21.65	951.71 – 952.12	22.37
860.22 – 860.63	20.22	890.86 – 891.27	20.94	921.49 – 921.91	21.66	952.13 – 952.55	22.38
860.64 – 861.06	20.23	891.28 – 891.70	20.95	921.92 – 922.34	21.67	952.56 – 952.97	22.39
861.07 – 861.48	20.24	891.71 – 892.12	20.96	922.35 – 922.75	21.68	952.98 – 953.40	22.40
861.49 – 861.91	20.25	892.13 – 892.55	20.97	922.77 – 923.19	21.69	953.41 – 953.82	22.41
861.92 – 862.34	20.26	892.56 – 892.97	20.98	923.20 – 923.61	21.70	953.83 – 954.25	22.42
862.35 – 862.76	20.27	892.98 – 893.40	20.99	923.62 – 924.04	21.71	954.26 – 954.68	22.43
862.77 – 863.19	20.28	893.41 – 893.82	21.00	924.05 – 924.46	21.72	954.69 – 955.10	22.44
863.20 – 863.61	20.29	893.83 – 894.25	21.01	924.47 – 924.89	21.73	955.11 – 955.53	22.45
863.62 – 864.04	20.30	894.26 – 894.68	21.02	924.90 – 925.31	21.74	955.54 – 955.95	22.46
864.05 – 864.46	20.31	894.69 – 895.10	21.03	925.32 – 925.74	21.75	955.96 – 956.38	22.47
864.47 – 864.89	20.32	895.11 – 895.53	21.04	925.75 – 926.17	21.76	956.39 – 956.80	22.48
864.90 – 865.31	20.33	895.54 – 895.95	21.05	926.18 – 926.59	21.77	956.81 – 957.23	22.49
865.32 – 865.74	20.34	895.96 – 896.38	21.06	926.60 – 927.02	21.78	957.24 – 957.65	22.50
865.75 – 866.17	20.35	896.39 – 896.80	21.07	927.03 – 927.44	21.79	957.66 – 958.08	22.51
866.18 – 866.59	20.36	896.81 – 897.23	21.08	927.45 – 927.87	21.80	958.09 – 958.51	22.52
866.60 – 867.02	20.37	897.24 – 897.65	21.09	927.88 – 928.29	21.81	958.52 – 958.93	22.53
867.03 – 867.44	20.38	897.66 – 898.08	21.10	928.30 – 928.72	21.82	958.94 – 959.36	22.54
867.45 – 867.87	20.39	898.09 – 898.51	21.11	928.73 – 929.14	21.83	959.37 – 959.78	22.55
867.88 – 868.29	20.40	898.52 – 898.93	21.12	929.15 – 929.57	21.84	959.79 – 960.21	22.56
868.30 – 868.72	20.41	898.94 – 899.36	21.13	929.58 – 929.99	21.85	960.22 – 960.63	22.57
868.73 – 869.14	20.42	899.37 – 899.78	21.14	930.00 – 930.42	21.86	960.64 – 961.06	22.58
869.15 – 869.57	20.43	899.79 – 900.21	21.15	930.43 – 930.85	21.87	961.07 – 961.48	22.59
869.58 – 869.99	20.44	900.22 – 900.63	21.16	930.86 – 931.27	21.88	961.49 – 961.91	22.60
870.00 – 870.42	20.45	900.64 – 901.06	21.17	931.28 – 931.70	21.89	961.92 – 962.34	22.61
870.43 – 870.85	20.46	901.07 – 901.48	21.18	931.71 – 932.12	21.90	962.35 – 962.76	22.62
870.86 – 871.27	20.47	901.49 – 901.91	21.19	932.13 – 932.55	21.91	962.77 – 963.19	22.63
871.28 – 871.70	20.48	901.92 – 902.34	21.20	932.56 – 932.97	21.92	963.20 – 963.61	22.64
871.71 – 872.12	20.49	902.35 – 902.76	21.21	932.98 – 933.40	21.93	963.62 – 964.04	22.65
872.13 – 872.55	20.50	902.77 – 903.19	21.22	933.41 – 933.82	21.94	964.05 – 964.46	22.66
872.56 – 872.97	20.51	903.20 – 903.61	21.23	933.83 – 934.25	21.95	964.47 – 964.89	22.67
872.98 – 873.40	20.52	903.62 – 904.04	21.24	934.26 – 934.68	21.96	964.90 – 965.31	22.68
873.41 – 873.82	20.53	904.05 – 904.46	21.25	934.69 – 935.10	21.97	965.32 – 965.74	22.69
873.83 – 874.25	20.54	904.47 – 904.89	21.26	935.11 – 935.53	21.98	965.75 – 966.17	22.70
874.26 – 874.68	20.55	904.90 – 905.31	21.27	935.54 – 935.95	21.99	966.18 – 966.59	22.71
874.69 – 875.10	20.56	905.32 – 905.74	21.28	935.96 – 936.38	22.00	966.60 – 967.02	22.72
875.11 – 875.53	20.57	905.75 – 906.17	21.29	936.39 – 936.80	22.01	967.03 – 967.44	22.73
875.54 – 875.95	20.58	906.18 – 906.59	21.30	936.81 – 937.23	22.02	967.45 – 967.87	22.74
875.96 – 876.38	20.59	906.60 – 907.02	21.31	937.24 – 937.65	22.03	967.88 – 968.29	22.75
876.39 – 876.80	20.60	907.03 – 907.44	21.32	937.66 – 938.08	22.04	968.30 – 968.72	22.76
876.81 – 877.23	20.61	907.45 – 907.87	21.33	938.09 – 938.51	22.05	968.73 – 969.14	22.77
877.24 – 877.65	20.62	907.88 – 908.29	21.34	938.52 – 938.93	22.06	969.15 – 969.57	22.78
877.66 – 878.08	20.63	908.30 – 908.72	21.35	938.94 – 939.36	22.07	969.58 – 969.99	22.79
878.09 – 878.51	20.64	908.73 – 909.14	21.36	939.37 – 939.78	22.08	970.00 – 970.42	22.80
878.52 – 878.93	20.65	909.15 – 909.57	21.37	939.79 – 940.21	22.09	970.43 – 970.85	22.81
878.94 – 879.36	20.66	909.58 – 909.99	21.38	940.22 – 940.63	22.10	970.86 – 971.27	22.82
879.37 – 879.78	20.67	910.00 – 910.42	21.39	940.64 – 941.06	22.11	971.28 – 971.70	22.83
879.79 – 880.21	20.68	910.43 – 910.85	21.40	941.07 – 941.48	22.12	971.71 – 972.12	22.84
880.22 – 880.63	20.69	910.86 – 911.27	21.41	941.49 – 941.91	22.13	972.13 – 972.55	22.85
880.64 – 881.06	20.70	911.28 – 911.70	21.42	941.92 – 942.34	22.14	972.56 – 972.97	22.86
881.07 – 881.48	20.71	911.71 – 912.12	21.43	942.35 – 942.76	22.15	972.98 – 973.40	22.87
881.49 – 881.91	20.72	912.13 – 912.55	21.44	942.77 – 943.19	22.16	973.41 – 973.82	22.88
881.92 – 882.34	20.73	912.56 – 912.97	21.45	943.20 – 943.61	22.17	973.83 – 974.25	22.89
882.35 – 882.76	20.74	912.98 – 913.40	21.46	943.62 – 944.04	22.18	974.26 – 974.68	22.90
882.77 – 883.19	20.75	913.41 – 913.82	21.47	944.05 – 944.46	22.19	974.69 – 975.10	22.91
883.20 – 883.61	20.76	913.83 – 914.25	21.48	944.47 – 944.89	22.20	975.11 – 975.53	22.92
883.62 – 884.04	20.77	914.26 – 914.68	21.49	944.90 – 945.31	22.21	975.54 – 975.95	22.93
884.05 – 884.46	20.78	914.69 – 915.10	21.50	945.32 – 945.74	22.22	975.96 – 976.38	22.94
884.47 – 884.89	20.79	915.11 – 915.53	21.51	945.75 – 946.17	22.23	976.39 – 976.80	22.95
884.90 – 885.31	20.80	915.54 – 915.95	21.52	946.18 – 946.59	22.24	976.81 – 977.23	22.96
885.32 – 885.74	20.81	915.96 – 916.38	21.53	946.60 – 947.02	22.25	977.24 – 977.65	22.97
885.75 – 886.17	20.82	916.39 – 916.80	21.54	947.03 – 947.44	22.26	977.66 – 978.08	22.98
886.18 – 886.59	20.83	916.81 – 917.23	21.55	947.45 – 947.87	22.27	978.09 – 978.51	22.99
886.60 – 887.02	20.84	917.24 – 917.65	21.56	947.88 – 948.29	22.28	978.52 – 978.93	23.00
887.03 – 887.44	20.85	917.66 – 918.08	21.57	948.30 – 948.72	22.29	978.94 – 979.36	23.01
887.45 – 887.87	20.86	918.09 – 918.51	21.58	948.73 – 949.14	22.30	979.37 – 979.78	23.02
887.88 – 888.29	20.87	918.52 – 918.93	21.59	949.15 – 949.57	22.31	979.79 – 980.21	23.03
888.30 – 888.72	20.88	918.94 – 919.36	21.60	949.58 – 949.99	22.32	980.22 – 980.63	23.04

Maximum Premium Deduction for a Pay Period of the stated frequency. Déduction maximale de prime pour une période de paie d'une durée donnée.		
Weekly – Hebdomadaire	11.63	
Bi-Weekly – Deux semaines	23.27	10 pp per year – 10 pp par année 60.49
Semi-Monthly – Bi-mensuel	25.20	13 pp per year – 13 pp par année 46.53
Monthly – Mensuellement	50.41	22 pp per year – 22 pp par année 27.50

Courtesy of Revenue Canada Taxation
Reproduced with permission of the Minister of Supply and Services Canada

Table 16.2a Unemployment insurance premiums schedule.

UNEMPLOYMENT INSURANCE PREMIUMS / PRIMES D'ASSURANCE-CHÔMAGE

For minimum and maximum insurable earnings amounts for various pay periods see Schedule II. For the maximum premium deduction for various pay periods see bottom of page.

Les montants minimum et maximum des gains assurables pour diverses périodes de paie figurent en annexe II. La déduction maximale de primes pour diverses périodes de paie figure au bas de la présente page.

Remuneration Rémunération From-de — To-à	U.I. Premium Prime d'a.-c.	Remuneration Rémunération From-de — To-à	U.I. Premium Prime d'a.-c.	Remuneration Rémunération From-de — To-à	U.I. Premium Prime d'a.-c.	Remuneration Rémunération From-de — To-à	U.I. Premium Prime d'a.-c.
980.64 – 981.06	23.05	1011.28 – 1011.70	23.77	1041.92 – 1042.34	24.49	1072.56 – 1072.97	25.21
981.07 – 981.48	23.06	1011.71 – 1012.12	23.78	1042.35 – 1042.76	24.50	1072.98 – 1073.40	25.22
981.49 – 981.91	23.07	1012.13 – 1012.55	23.79	1042.77 – 1043.19	24.51	1073.41 – 1073.82	25.23
981.92 – 982.34	23.08	1012.56 – 1012.97	23.80	1043.20 – 1043.61	24.52	1073.83 – 1074.25	25.24
982.35 – 982.75	23.09	1012.98 – 1013.40	23.81	1043.62 – 1044.04	24.53	1074.26 – 1074.68	25.25
982.77 – 983.19	23.10	1013.41 – 1013.82	23.82	1044.05 – 1044.46	24.54	1074.69 – 1075.10	25.26
983.20 – 983.61	23.11	1013.83 – 1014.25	23.83	1044.47 – 1044.89	24.55	1075.11 – 1075.53	25.27
983.62 – 984.04	23.12	1014.26 – 1014.68	23.84	1044.90 – 1045.31	24.56	1075.54 – 1075.95	25.28
984.05 – 984.46	23.13	1014.69 – 1015.10	23.85	1045.32 – 1045.74	24.57	1075.96 – 1076.38	25.29
984.47 – 984.89	23.14	1015.11 – 1015.53	23.86	1045.75 – 1046.17	24.58	1076.39 – 1076.80	25.30
984.90 – 985.31	23.15	1015.54 – 1015.95	23.87	1046.18 – 1046.59	24.59	1076.81 – 1077.23	25.31
985.32 – 985.74	23.16	1015.96 – 1016.38	23.88	1046.60 – 1047.02	24.60	1077.24 – 1077.65	25.32
985.75 – 986.17	23.17	1016.39 – 1016.80	23.89	1047.03 – 1047.44	24.61	1077.66 – 1078.08	25.33
986.18 – 986.59	23.18	1016.81 – 1017.23	23.90	1047.45 – 1047.87	24.62	1078.09 – 1078.51	25.34
986.60 – 987.02	23.19	1017.24 – 1017.65	23.91	1047.88 – 1048.29	24.63	1078.52 – 1078.93	25.35
987.03 – 987.44	23.20	1017.66 – 1018.09	23.92	1048.30 – 1048.72	24.64	1078.94 – 1079.36	25.36
987.45 – 987.87	23.21	1018.09 – 1018.51	23.93	1048.73 – 1049.14	24.65	1079.37 – 1079.78	25.37
987.88 – 988.29	23.22	1018.52 – 1018.93	23.94	1049.15 – 1049.57	24.66	1079.79 – 1080.21	25.38
988.30 – 988.72	23.23	1018.94 – 1019.36	23.95	1049.58 – 1049.99	24.67	1080.22 – 1080.63	25.39
988.73 – 989.14	23.24	1019.37 – 1019.78	23.96	1050.00 – 1050.42	24.68	1080.64 – 1081.06	25.40
989.15 – 989.57	23.25	1019.79 – 1020.21	23.97	1050.43 – 1050.85	24.69	1081.07 – 1081.48	25.41
989.58 – 989.99	23.26	1020.22 – 1020.63	23.98	1050.86 – 1051.27	24.70	1081.49 – 1081.91	25.42
990.00 – 990.42	23.27	1020.64 – 1021.06	23.99	1051.28 – 1051.70	24.71	1081.92 – 1082.34	25.43
990.43 – 990.85	23.28	1021.07 – 1021.48	24.00	1051.71 – 1052.12	24.72	1082.35 – 1082.76	25.44
990.86 – 991.27	23.29	1021.49 – 1021.91	24.01	1052.13 – 1052.55	24.73	1082.77 – 1083.19	25.45
991.28 – 991.70	23.30	1021.92 – 1022.34	24.02	1052.56 – 1052.97	24.74	1083.20 – 1083.61	25.46
991.71 – 992.12	23.31	1022.35 – 1022.76	24.03	1052.98 – 1053.40	24.75	1083.62 – 1084.04	25.47
992.13 – 992.55	23.32	1022.77 – 1023.19	24.04	1053.41 – 1053.82	24.76	1084.05 – 1084.46	25.48
992.56 – 992.97	23.33	1023.20 – 1023.61	24.05	1053.83 – 1054.25	24.77	1084.47 – 1084.89	25.49
992.98 – 993.40	23.34	1023.62 – 1024.04	24.06	1054.26 – 1054.68	24.78	1084.90 – 1085.31	25.50
993.41 – 993.82	23.35	1024.05 – 1024.46	24.07	1054.69 – 1055.10	24.79	1085.32 – 1085.74	25.51
993.83 – 994.25	23.36	1024.47 – 1024.89	24.08	1055.11 – 1055.53	24.80	1085.75 – 1086.17	25.52
994.26 – 994.68	23.37	1024.90 – 1025.31	24.09	1055.54 – 1055.95	24.81	1086.18 – 1086.59	25.53
994.69 – 995.10	23.38	1025.32 – 1025.74	24.10	1055.96 – 1056.38	24.82	1086.60 – 1087.02	25.54
995.11 – 995.53	23.39	1025.75 – 1026.17	24.11	1056.39 – 1056.80	24.83	1087.03 – 1087.44	25.55
995.54 – 995.95	23.40	1026.18 – 1026.59	24.12	1056.81 – 1057.23	24.84	1087.45 – 1087.87	25.56
995.96 – 996.38	23.41	1026.60 – 1027.02	24.13	1057.24 – 1057.65	24.85	1087.88 – 1088.29	25.57
996.39 – 996.80	23.42	1027.03 – 1027.44	24.14	1057.66 – 1058.08	24.86	1088.30 – 1088.72	25.58
996.81 – 997.23	23.43	1027.45 – 1027.87	24.15	1058.09 – 1058.51	24.87	1088.73 – 1089.14	25.59
997.24 – 997.65	23.44	1027.88 – 1028.29	24.16	1058.52 – 1058.93	24.88	1089.15 – 1089.57	25.60
997.66 – 998.08	23.45	1028.30 – 1028.72	24.17	1058.94 – 1059.36	24.89	1089.58 – 1089.99	25.61
998.09 – 998.51	23.46	1028.73 – 1029.14	24.18	1059.37 – 1059.78	24.90	1090.00 – 1090.42	25.62
998.52 – 998.93	23.47	1029.15 – 1029.57	24.19	1059.79 – 1060.21	24.91	1090.43 – 1090.85	25.63
998.94 – 999.36	23.48	1029.58 – 1029.99	24.20	1060.22 – 1060.63	24.92	1090.86 – 1091.27	25.64
999.37 – 999.78	23.49	1030.00 – 1030.42	24.21	1060.64 – 1061.06	24.93	1091.28 – 1091.70	25.65
999.79 – 1000.21	23.50	1030.43 – 1030.85	24.22	1061.07 – 1061.48	24.94	1091.71 – 1092.12	25.66
1000.22 – 1000.63	23.51	1030.86 – 1031.27	24.23	1061.49 – 1061.91	24.95	1092.13 – 1092.55	25.67
1000.64 – 1001.06	23.52	1031.28 – 1031.70	24.24	1061.92 – 1062.34	24.96	1092.56 – 1092.97	25.68
1001.07 – 1001.48	23.53	1031.71 – 1032.12	24.25	1062.35 – 1062.76	24.97	1092.98 – 1093.40	25.69
1001.49 – 1001.91	23.54	1032.13 – 1032.55	24.26	1062.77 – 1063.19	24.98	1093.41 – 1093.82	25.70
1001.92 – 1002.34	23.55	1032.56 – 1032.97	24.27	1063.20 – 1063.61	24.99	1093.83 – 1094.25	25.71
1002.35 – 1002.76	23.56	1032.98 – 1033.40	24.28	1063.62 – 1064.04	25.00	1094.26 – 1094.68	25.72
1002.77 – 1003.19	23.57	1033.41 – 1033.82	24.29	1064.05 – 1064.46	25.01	1094.69 – 1095.10	25.73
1003.20 – 1003.61	23.58	1033.83 – 1034.25	24.30	1064.47 – 1064.89	25.02	1095.11 – 1095.53	25.74
1003.62 – 1004.04	23.59	1034.26 – 1034.68	24.31	1064.90 – 1065.31	25.03	1095.54 – 1095.95	25.75
1004.05 – 1004.46	23.60	1034.69 – 1035.10	24.32	1065.32 – 1065.74	25.04	1095.96 – 1096.38	25.76
1004.47 – 1004.89	23.61	1035.11 – 1035.53	24.33	1065.75 – 1066.17	25.05	1096.39 – 1096.80	25.77
1004.90 – 1005.31	23.62	1035.54 – 1035.95	24.34	1066.18 – 1066.59	25.06	1096.81 – 1097.23	25.78
1005.32 – 1005.74	23.63	1035.96 – 1036.38	24.35	1066.60 – 1067.02	25.07	1097.24 – 1097.65	25.79
1005.75 – 1006.17	23.64	1036.39 – 1036.80	24.36	1067.03 – 1067.44	25.08	1097.66 – 1098.08	25.80
1006.18 – 1006.59	23.65	1036.81 – 1037.23	24.37	1067.45 – 1067.87	25.09	1098.09 – 1098.51	25.81
1006.60 – 1007.02	23.66	1037.24 – 1037.65	24.38	1067.88 – 1068.29	25.10	1098.52 – 1098.93	25.82
1007.03 – 1007.44	23.67	1037.66 – 1038.08	24.39	1068.30 – 1068.72	25.11	1098.94 – 1099.36	25.83
1007.45 – 1007.87	23.68	1038.09 – 1038.51	24.40	1068.73 – 1069.14	25.12	1099.37 – 1099.78	25.84
1007.88 – 1008.29	23.69	1038.52 – 1038.93	24.41	1069.15 – 1069.57	25.13	1099.79 – 1100.21	25.85
1008.30 – 1008.72	23.70	1038.94 – 1039.36	24.42	1069.58 – 1069.99	25.14	1100.22 – 1100.63	25.86
1008.73 – 1009.14	23.71	1039.37 – 1039.78	24.43	1070.00 – 1070.42	25.15	1100.64 – 1101.06	25.87
1009.15 – 1009.57	23.72	1039.79 – 1040.21	24.44	1070.43 – 1070.85	25.16	1101.07 – 1101.48	25.88
1009.58 – 1009.99	23.73	1040.22 – 1040.63	24.45	1070.86 – 1071.27	25.17	1101.49 – 1101.91	25.89
1010.00 – 1010.42	23.74	1040.64 – 1041.06	24.46	1071.28 – 1071.70	25.18	1101.92 – 1102.34	25.90
1010.43 – 1010.85	23.75	1041.07 – 1041.48	24.47	1071.71 – 1072.12	25.19	1102.35 – 1102.76	25.91
1010.86 – 1011.27	23.76	1041.49 – 1041.91	24.48	1072.13 – 1072.55	25.20	1102.77 – 1103.19	25.92

Maximum Premium Deduction for a Pay Period of the stated frequency.
Déduction maximale de prime pour une période de paie d'une durée donnée.

Weekly – Hebdomadaire	11.63
Bi-Weekly – Deux semaines	23.27
Semi-Monthly – Bi-mensuel	25.20
Monthly – Mensuellement	50.41
10 pp per year – 10 pp par année	60.49
13 pp per year – 13 pp par année	46.53
22 pp per year – 22 pp par année	27.50

Courtesy of Revenue Canada Taxation
Reproduced with permission of the Minister of Supply and Services Canada

Table 16.2 b Unemployment insurance premiums schedule.

ONTARIO
BI-WEEKLY TAX DEDUCTIONS
Basis — 26 Pay Periods per Year

ONTARIO
RETENUES D'IMPÔT DE DEUX SEMAINES
Base — 26 périodes de paie par année

TABLE 3

IF THE EMPLOYEE'S "NET CLAIM CODE" ON FORM TD1 IS — SI LE «CODE DE DEMANDE NETTE» DE L'EMPLOYÉ SELON LA FORMULE TD1 EST DE

BI-WEEKLY PAY / PAIE DE DEUX SEMAINES	1	2	3	4	5	6	7	8	9	10	11	12	13	See note on page 4 / Column A
	DEDUCT FROM EACH PAY — RETENEZ SUR CHAQUE PAIE													
$591.00 – 600.99	102.90	98.70	90.95	83.40	75.30	68.75	64.80	58.80	50.45	41.65	32.95	24.55	17.25	7.30
601.00 – 610.99	105.65	101.60	93.85	86.30	78.20	71.55	67.60	61.55	53.25	44.35	35.55	27.15	19.85	7.30
611.00 – 620.99	108.75	104.50	96.75	89.25	81.10	74.45	70.35	64.30	56.00	47.10	38.15	29.75	22.45	7.30
621.00 – 630.99	111.65	107.40	99.70	92.15	84.05	77.40	73.25	67.05	58.75	49.85	40.75	32.35	25.05	7.30
631.00 – 640.99	114.55	110.30	102.60	95.05	86.95	80.30	76.15	69.80	61.50	52.60	43.35	34.95	27.65	7.30
641.00 – 650.99	117.45	113.20	105.50	97.95	89.85	83.20	75.05	72.70	64.25	55.35	46.15	37.55	30.25	7.30
651.00 – 660.99	120.35	116.10	108.40	100.85	92.75	86.10	81.95	75.60	67.00	58.10	48.90	40.15	32.85	7.30
661.00 – 670.99	123.25	119.00	111.30	103.75	95.65	89.00	84.85	78.50	69.75	60.85	51.65	42.75	35.45	7.35
671.00 – 680.99	126.20	121.95	114.20	106.65	98.55	91.90	87.75	81.40	72.60	63.60	54.40	45.50	38.05	7.45
681.00 – 690.99	129.05	124.85	117.10	109.60	101.45	94.80	90.70	84.30	75.55	66.35	57.15	48.25	40.65	7.60
691.00 – 700.99	132.10	127.75	120.05	112.50	104.40	97.75	93.60	87.20	78.45	69.10	59.90	51.00	43.25	7.75
701.00 – 710.99	135.20	130.70	122.95	115.40	107.30	100.65	96.50	90.10	81.35	71.95	62.65	53.75	46.00	7.75
711.00 – 720.99	138.30	133.75	125.85	118.30	110.20	103.55	99.40	93.05	84.25	74.85	65.40	56.50	48.60	7.75
721.00 – 730.99	141.30	136.85	128.75	121.20	113.10	106.45	102.30	95.95	87.15	77.75	68.15	59.25	51.55	7.75
731.00 – 740.99	144.35	139.90	131.75	124.10	116.00	109.35	105.20	98.85	90.05	80.65	70.95	62.00	54.30	7.75
741.00 – 750.99	147.40	142.95	134.85	127.00	118.90	112.25	108.10	101.75	92.95	83.60	73.85	64.75	57.05	7.75
751.00 – 760.99	150.50	146.00	137.90	129.95	121.80	115.15	111.05	104.65	95.90	86.50	76.75	67.50	59.80	7.75
761.00 – 770.99	153.55	149.05	140.95	132.00	124.75	118.05	113.95	107.55	98.80	89.40	79.65	70.30	62.55	7.75
771.00 – 780.99	156.60	152.15	144.00	136.05	127.65	121.00	116.85	110.45	101.70	92.30	82.60	73.20	65.30	7.90
781.00 – 790.99	159.65	155.20	147.05	139.10	130.60	123.90	119.75	113.40	104.60	95.20	85.50	76.10	68.05	8.05
791.00 – 800.99	162.70	158.25	150.15	142.20	133.65	126.80	122.65	116.30	107.50	98.10	88.40	79.00	70.85	8.15
801.00 – 810.99	165.80	161.30	153.20	145.25	136.70	129.70	125.55	119.20	110.40	101.00	91.30	81.90	73.75	8.15
811.00 – 820.99	168.85	164.35	156.25	148.30	139.75	132.85	128.45	122.10	113.30	103.95	94.20	84.80	76.65	8.15
821.00 – 830.99	171.90	167.45	159.30	151.85	142.85	135.85	131.45	125.00	116.25	106.85	97.10	87.70	79.55	8.15
831.00 – 840.99	174.95	170.50	162.35	154.40	145.90	138.90	134.55	127.90	119.15	109.75	100.00	90.65	82.45	8.20
841.00 – 850.99	178.00	173.55	165.45	157.50	148.95	141.95	137.60	130.90	122.05	112.65	102.90	93.55	85.35	8.20
851.00 – 860.99	181.10	176.60	168.50	160.55	152.00	145.05	140.65	133.95	124.95	115.55	105.85	96.45	88.30	8.20
861.00 – 870.99	184.15	179.65	171.55	163.60	155.05	148.05	143.70	137.00	127.85	118.45	108.75	99.35	91.20	8.20
871.00 – 880.99	187.20	182.75	174.60	166.65	158.15	151.15	146.75	140.05	130.85	121.35	111.65	102.25	94.10	8.20
881.00 – 890.99	190.25	185.80	177.65	169.70	161.20	154.20	149.85	143.15	133.90	124.30	114.55	105.15	97.00	8.20
891.00 – 900.99	193.75	188.85	180.75	172.80	164.25	157.25	152.90	146.25	136.95	127.20	117.45	108.05	99.90	8.20
901.00 – 910.99	197.30	192.15	183.80	175.85	167.85	160.30	155.95	149.25	140.00	130.15	120.35	110.95	102.80	8.20
911.00 – 920.99	200.80	195.65	186.85	178.50	170.35	163.35	159.00	152.30	143.05	133.20	123.25	113.90	105.70	8.20
921.00 – 930.99	204.30	199.20	189.90	181.95	173.45	166.45	162.05	155.35	146.15	136.25	126.20	116.80	108.65	8.20
931.00 – 940.99	207.85	202.70	193.35	185.00	176.55	169.50	165.15	158.45	149.20	139.30	129.05	119.70	111.55	8.20
941.00 – 950.99	213.10	207.95	198.65	189.60	181.10	174.10	169.70	163.00	153.80	143.90	133.65	124.05	115.90	8.20
951.00 – 980.99	220.15	215.00	205.65	196.55	187.20	180.20	175.85	169.15	159.90	150.00	139.75	129.90	121.70	8.20
981.00 – 1000.99	227.20	222.05	212.70	203.55	193.75	186.30	181.95	175.25	166.00	156.15	145.90	136.00	127.50	8.20
1001.00 – 1020.99	234.25	229.05	219.75	210.60	200.80	192.75	188.10	181.40	172.15	162.25	152.00	142.25	133.65	8.50
1021.00 – 1040.99	241.25	236.10	226.80	217.65	207.85	199.80	194.80	187.50	178.25	168.35	158.15	148.25	139.65	8.80

Table 16.3 Bi-weekly tax deductions schedule.

Section Review Questions

1. What is "gross pay"?
2. What is "net pay"?
3. What is the payroll equation?
4. Where are the payroll calculations made?
5. Explain the purpose of the social insurance number.
6. At what age does a person begin to contribute to the Canada Pension Plan?
7. What is the simplest way to determine the deductions for the C.P.P.?
8. Explain how to find the deduction figure for the C.P.P.
9. Explain how to find the deduction figure for unemployment insurance.
10. Where does a person see what the maximum deduction figure is for unemployment insurance?
11. What is an R.R.S.P.?
12. Explain why it is more difficult to determine the deduction for income tax than it is for the Canada Pension Plan.
13. Where does one encounter the "total personal exemption" figure?
14. Where is the net claim code used?
15. On what two things does the income tax deduction depend?
16. What is a TD1 form?
17. Explain how taxable earnings are determined.
18. Explain how to read the income tax deduction tables.
19. Explain how to complete the payroll journal.
20. Describe three balances that can be performed to test the accuracy of the payroll journal.

Section Exercises

1. 1. In your workbook, complete the schedule that appears below. Use Tables 16.1, 16.2, and 16.3 where necessary.

Employee	Bi-weekly Gross Pay	C.P.P. Deduction	U.I. Deduction	R.P.P.(5%) Deduction
F. Mazur	$896			
C. Koch	$910			
P. Parsons	$1 101			
G. Vittelli	$1 050			
Y. Van Del	$940			

Section 16.2

2. For G. Vittelli, how many deductions for C.P.P. will be made during the year? What will be the amount of the final deduction?

2. 1. Complete the following schedule in the workbook. The payroll period is bi-weekly.

Net Claim Code	Gross Earnings	C.P.P. Deduction	U.I. Deduction	R.P.P. Deduction 6%	Taxable Earnings	Income Tax Deduction	Net Amount After Tax
10	904.70						
8	964.30						
5	1070.10						
1	933.16						
2	975.00						
TOTALS							

2. Balance the above schedule.

3. In your workbook, complete the line shown below. J. Bell is single, does not belong to a union, and has $100 000 of group life insurance coverage. The rate of R.P.P. contribution is five per cent. The employer pays three-quarters of the health insurance and one-half of the group life.

PAYROLL JOURNAL For the 2 Weeks ended June 10 19__

Employee	Net Claim Code	Earnings - Regular	Extra	Gross	C.P.P.	U.I. Premium	R.P.P.	Income Tax - Taxable Earnings	Ded'n	Health Ins.	Union Dues	Group Life	Total Ded'ns	Net Pay
J. Bell	8	900—		700—										

4. Complete each of the following statements by inserting in your workbook the number corresponding to the appropriate word or phrase from the list below.

   a. An amount kept back from an employee's gross pay is known as a _____ .
   b. The amount of pay remaining after all deductions have been made is known as _____ .
   c. Payroll calculations are summarized in a book known as the _____ .
   d. Keeping back an amount from an employee's pay is called _____ it.

e. Certain payroll deductions are made on behalf of the federal government. The _____ system is used to keep track of all these deductions for all of the citizens of the country.

f. The deductions in question **e.** above are for _____ , _____ , and _____ .

g. To assist employers in making the deductions in question **f.** above, the government provides _____ .

h. The Canada Pension Plan deduction and the Unemployment Insurance deduction are based on the _____ figure.

i. For the Canada Pension Plan, there is a _____ figure after which no further deductions will be made for the year.

j. Employers, as well as employees, must _____ to the Canada Pension Plan and Unemployment Insurance funds.

k. A payroll made every two weeks is known as a _____ payroll.

l. $25.20 is the maximum unemployment insurance deduction for a _____ payroll period.

m. A private pension plan that is approved by the government is known as a _____ pension plan.

n. An employee fills out a TD1 form in order to determine the _____ figure.

o. The _____ number is based on the figure arrived at in question **n.** above.

p. The deduction for income tax is not based on gross earnings. It is based on (estimated) _____ earnings.

q. The figure in question **p.** above is found by making three deductions from the gross pay figure. These three deductions are required by _____ .

r. Most provinces operate a _____ .

s. The payroll journal is a _____ journal and therefore must be _____ .

List of Words and Phrases
1. bi-weekly
2. Canada Pension Plan
3. columnar
4. contribute
5. cross balanced
6. deduction tables
7. gross pay
8. health insurance plan
9. income tax
10. maximum
11. net claim code
12. net pay
13. payroll deduction
14. payroll journal
15. registered
16. Revenue Canada
17. semi-monthly
18. social insurance number
19. taxable
20. total exemptions
21. unemployment insurance
22. withholding

16.3 Recording the Payroll

Once the payroll journal has been prepared and balanced, the payroll is recorded in the books of accounts. The following aspects of payroll must be considered:

1. the totals from the payroll journal;
2. the *employer's* contribution to the Canada Pension Plan;
3. the *employer's* contribution to the unemployment insurance fund;
4. the *employer's* contribution to the registered pension plan (if any);
5. the *employer's* contribution to health insurance (if any).

The accounting entries to record each of the above five aspects of payroll are explained below.

The Accounting Entries

1. The Totals from the Payroll Journal

Figure 16.19 below shows totals taken from the payroll journal recorded in the form of a general journal entry.

DATE	PARTICULARS	P.R.	DEBIT	CREDIT	
19— May 24	Salaries Expense		4 680 77		The gross pay
	Canada Pension Plan Payable			75 56	
	Unemployment Ins. Payable			109 78	Each of the credit items is a column total and represents a liability to be paid in the near future.
	Reg'd Pension Plan Payable			234 04	
	Employees Income Tax Payable			776 50	
	Health Insurance Payable			54 00	
	Union Dues Payable			50 00	
	Group Life Insurance Payable			155 00	
	Payroll Payable			3 225 89	
	To record payroll totals for May 24, 19—				

GENERAL JOURNAL   PAGE 43

Figure 16.19 Totals from the payroll journal recorded in the general journal.

2. The Employer's Contribution to the Canada Pension Plan

The government booklet about the Canada Pension Plan states, "Every employer is required to make a contribution on behalf of employees equal to the contributions deducted from them." The payroll journal for Nor-Can Grocers Ltd. shows that the employees contributed $75.56 through payroll deductions. The employer must contribute an equal amount. Figure 16.20 below shows the accounting entry for this recorded in the general journal. Observe the two aspects of this accounting entry:

1. there is an expense because the business has to pay out of its own pocket;

2. there is a liability because the business owes the money. It has not been paid yet.

May	24	Canada Pension Plan Expense		75 56	
		Canada Pension Plan Payable			75 56
		Employer's C.P.P. contribution			

Figure 16.20 General journal entry to record employer's C.P.P. contribution.

3. The Employer's Contribution to Unemployment Insurance

The government booklet on Unemployment Insurance states, "Calculate the employer's premium at 1.4 times the employee's premium." The payroll journal for Nor-Can Grocers Ltd. shows that the employees contributed $109.78 through payroll deductions. The employer must contribute this amount multiplied by 1.4; that is, $109.78 × 1.4 = $153.69. Figure 16.21 below shows the accounting entry for this recorded in the general journal. Note the two aspects: the expense, and the liability.

May	24	Unemployment Insurance Expense		153 69	
		Unemployment Ins. Payable			153 69
		Employer's U.I. contributions			

Figure 16.21 General journal entry to record employer's U.I. contribution.

4. The Employer's Contribution to the Registered Pension Plan

The agreement between Nor-Can Grocers Ltd. and its employees states that both the employees and the employer shall contribute equally to the registered pension plan.

The payroll journal for Nor-Can Grocers Ltd. shows that the employees paid $234.04 to the registered pension plan through payroll deductions. The employer, therefore, is liable for an equal amount. Figure 16.22 shows the accounting entry for this recorded in the general journal.

May	24	Registered Pension Plan Expense		234 04	
		Reg'd Pension Plan Payable			234 04
		Employer's R.P.P. contribution			

Figure 16.22 General journal entry for employer's R.P.P. contribution.

5. The Employer's Contribution to Health Insurance

Nor-Can Grocers Ltd. and its employees agreed that the employer pays three-quarters and the employees pay one-quarter of the cost of health insurance. Thus, the employer pays three times as much as the employees. The payroll journal for Nor-Can Grocers Ltd. shows that the employees paid $54.00 for health insurance through payroll deductions. Therefore, the employer must pay 3 × $54.00 = $162.00. Figure 16.23 below shows the accounting entry for this recorded in the general journal.

May	24	Health Insurance Expense		162 00	
		Health Insurance Payable			162 00
		Employer's health insurance contribution			

Figure 16.23 General journal entry for employer's health insurance contribution.

The Effect in the Accounts

Each of the five accounting entries in the previous section is posted to the accounts in the general ledger. Figure 16.24 below shows the effect of these five accounting entries in the accounts involved.

LIABILITY ACCOUNTS   Explanations

Canada Pension Plan Payable

	75.56	← Employees' contribution
	75.56	← Employer's contribution
Balance	151.12	← Total owed for C.P.P.

Unemployment Insurance Payable

	109.78	← Employees' contribution
	153.69	← Employer's contribution
Balance	263.47	← Total owed for U.I.

Registered Pension Plan Payable

	234.04	← Employees' contribution
	234.04	← Employer's contribution
Balance	468.08	← Total owed for R.P.P.

Employees' Income Tax Payable

| | 776.50 | ← Employees' contribution |
| Balance | 776.50 | ← Amount owed for employees' income tax |

Health Insurance Payable

	54.00	← Employees' contribution
	162.00	← Employer's contribution
Balance	216.00	← Total owed for health insurance

Union Dues Payable

| | 50.00 | ← Employees' contribution |
| Balance | 50.00 | ← Amount owed for union dues |

Group Life Insurance Payable

| | 155.00 | ← Employees' contribution |
| Balance | 155.00 | ← Amount owed for group life insurance |

Payroll Payable

| | 3 225.89 | ← The net pay figure |
| Balance | 3 225.89 | ← Amount owed to employees |

```
EXPENSE ACCOUNTS                          Explanations
     Salaries Expense
4 680.77 ◄─────────┐
                   │
                   │
  Canadian Pension Plan Expense
  75.56 ◄──────────┤
                   │                       Cost
                   │                       to the
  Unemployment Insurance Expense           company
  153.69 ◄─────────┤                       for
                   │                       employee
                   │                       benefits
  Registered Pension Plan Expense
  234.04 ◄─────────┤
                   │
                   │
    Health Insurance Expense
  162.00 ◄─────────┘
```

Figure 16.24 General ledger accounts with payroll entries recorded.

Payment of Payroll Liabilities

To the Federal Government

The amounts withheld from employees in any month for the federal government are to be paid by the fifteenth day of the following month. For example, deductions made in August are due by September the fifteenth, and so on. This regulation applies to the Canada Pension Plan, unemployment insurance, and personal income taxes. Cheques sent to the government of Canada are made out to the Receiver General for Canada.

A special two-part form, PD7AR (Tax Deduction—Canada Pension Plan—Unemployment Insurance Remittance Return), accompanies the payment. The upper portion is submitted along with the cheque. The lower portion is retained for the employer's own records. The payment may be made at a branch of a bank or sent to the appropriate taxation center.

To determine the amount of the cheque, add the balances for the month just ended for the accounts shown below. Assume the amounts shown are the month-end balances.

Canada Pension Plan Payable	$ 307.21
Unemployment Insurance Payable	528.02
Employees' Income Tax Payable	1 509.30
Total	$2 344.53

One cheque is drawn for the combined amount of $2 344.53, and is paid to the government. The accounting entry to record the payment is:

	DR	CR
Canada Pension Plan Payable	$ 307.21	
Unemployment Insurance Payable	528.02	
Employees' Income Tax Payable	1 509.30	
Bank		$2 344.53

To Other Institutions or Agencies

Other liabilities arising from payroll deductions are dealt with in much the same way. The amount is determined from the accounts. A cheque to the appropriate agency is prepared and issued. The accounting entry, as shown below, eliminates the liability from the accounts.

	DR	CR
Liability Account	$$$$	
Bank		$$$$

Section Review Questions

1. Give five aspects of payroll that require accounting entries.
2. Not all of the columns in the payroll journal are used to work out the accounting entry. Explain why.
3. How much C.P.P. does the employer have to pay, relative to the employees?
4. How much U.I. does the employer have to pay, relative to the employees?
5. If the deduction from employees for U.I. is $100, how much will the employer have to pay?
6. Explain why there are liability accounts involved in payroll.
7. Explain why there is more than one expense account involved in payroll.
8. To whom is the cheque to the federal government made out?
9. Explain how the amount of the cheque to the federal government is calculated.
10. What form is prepared to accompany the above cheque?
11. In what two ways can one pay the federal government?
12. When is the cheque to the government due?

Section Exercises

1. The illustration below shows the final column totals from the payroll of Hudson Fisheries for the semi-monthly pay period ended October 15.

Section 16.3

PAYROLL JOURNAL														For the ½ Month ended Oct. 15 19—
Employee	Net Claim Code	Earnings			C.P.P.	U.I. Premium	R.P.P.	Deductions		Health Ins.	Union Dues	Group Life	Total Ded'ns	Net Pay
		Regular	Extra	Gross				Income Tax Taxable Earnings	Ded'n					
TOTALS		4982 50	1612 95	6595 45	116 35	67 34	329 77	6081 99	1277 22	40 50	84 —	158 50	2073 68	4521 77

1. Given that the employer matches the employees' contributions for R.P.P. and pays seventy-five per cent of the health insurance, prepare the general journal entries to record this payroll.
2. Post the journal entries for the above payroll to the T-accounts provided in the workbook.
3. Journalize and post the accounting entry to pay the employees.
4. Given that the payroll for the next period is identical to the one above, post the second payroll for October to the T-accounts (all entries).
5. Journalize and post the accounting entry to pay the employees.
6. Answer the following questions.
   a. How much is owed to the federal government for the month of October?
   b. How much is owed to the health insurance agency for the month of October?
   c. Give the accounting entry for the payment in question a. above.
   d. Give the accounting entry for the payment in question b. above.

2. **Workbook Exercise:** Answering questions with regard to payroll accounts.

3. Briefly answer each of the following questions.

   1. The first pay period in February ends on the fourteenth. One of the payroll journal entries is the following:

	DR	CR
C.P.P. Expense	$184.00	
C.P.P. Payable		$184.00

      How much was deducted from the employees' pay for the Canada Pension Fund?

   2. In this same pay period the journal entry for unemployment insurance is the following:

	DR	CR
U.I. Expense	$212.80	
U.I. Payable		$212.80

      How much was deducted from the employees' pay for unemployment insurance?

3. Assume that the payroll data for the second pay period in February is the same as the first. What will be the balances at the end of the month in each of the following accounts?

    a. Unemployment Insurance Expense
    b. Unemployment Insurance Payable
    c. Canada Pension Fund Expense
    d. Canada Pension Fund Payable

4. For the second payroll in February one of the journal entries was the following:

	DR	CR
Health Insurance Expense	$288.00	
Health Insurance Payable		$288.00

    a. What was the amount of the employees' contribution for health insurance for the month if the insurance plan is as described in the text?
    b. What will be the balances at the end of the month in each of the following accounts?

        Health Insurance Expense
        Health Insurance Payable

5. Using the group life insurance rates given in the text, calculate the insurance coverage for an employee from whom a payroll deduction of $37.50 was made in the second pay period.

16.4 Payment to Employees

Paying by Cash

There are still a few small companies which pay their employees with cash. When employees are paid in cash, it is necessary to have the right number of bills and coins to fill the envelopes. The first step in obtaining these is to prepare a currency requisition form such as that shown in Figure 16.25.

The completed currency requisition form is given to the bank together with a cheque made out for the total amount of the payroll. In return, the company receives cash in the denominations shown on the form and equalling the amount of the cheque. The accounting entry to record the cheque is:

	DR	CR
Payroll Payable	$$$$$	
Bank		$$$$$

The effect of this entry is to eliminate the liability in the Payroll Payable account.

The currency requisition form is also used when preparing the pay envelopes. The pay envelopes are filled with the bills and coins indicated on the form. Included with

PAYROLL CURRENCY REQUISITION						PAY PERIOD ENDED May 24 19—			
EMPLOYEE	NET PAY	$20	$10	$5	$1	25¢	10¢	5¢	1¢
Harold Evans	688 50	34		1	3	2			
Debra Falk	668 68	33		1	3	2	1	1	3
Sue Olinik	541 37	27			1	1	1		2
Joe Savard	698 66	34	1	1	3	2	1	1	1
Eric Vacher	628 68	31		1	3	2	1	1	3
NUMBER OF COINS OR BILLS		159	1	4	13	9	4	3	9
DOLLAR VALUE	3225 89	3180	10	20	13	2.25	.40	.15	.09

Figure 16.25 A completed payroll currency requisition form.

each pay envelope is a statement showing the employee's earnings, deductions, and net pay. This statement may be a separate statement or may be printed on the outside of the envelope. The employee's signature is obtained at the time of renumeration as proof of payment.

Paying by Cheque

Many businesses, especially firms with a large number of employees, prefer to pay by cheque rather than by cash. This eliminates the problem of having large sums of money around. Also, the cancelled cheques serve as evidence that the employees did receive their pay.

The cheques for the employees may be drawn from the company's regular bank account or from a special payroll bank account established for payroll cheques only.

Regular Bank Account

A separate cheque, drawn on the regular bank account, is issued to each employee. The accounting entry for each cheque, when recorded in the cash payments journal, is:

	DR	CR
Payroll Payable	$$$$	
Bank		$$$$

The sum of all of the individual payroll cheques issued will be equal to the total of the Net Pay column of the payroll journal. Since each cheque results in a debit to the Payroll Payable account, they will effectively eliminate the credit balance in this liability account.

Special Payroll Bank Account

To allow the payroll department to operate independently and to issue its own payroll cheques, many businesses set up a separate payroll bank account.

Under this method, only one cheque is drawn on the regular bank account each pay period for the amount of the total net pay. In the cash payments journal the accounting entry to record the cheque is:

	DR	CR
Payroll Payable	$$$$	
Bank		$$$$

This cheque is given to the payroll department. It is cashed by depositing it in the special payroll bank account. This provides the funds for the payroll department to meet its obligations for one pay period.

The payroll department then issues its own payroll cheques to the employees. No accounting entries are required for these payroll cheques. When they are all cashed, the balance in the payroll bank account will be reduced to zero.

However, some employees are slow to cash their cheques. Often, before all of the cheques are cashed, a new payroll cycle begins by the deposit for the next payroll. Thus the payroll bank account might never actually reach the stage where it has a zero balance.

Section Review Questions

1. What are two uses for the currency requisition form?
2. Explain how the currency requisition form is balanced.
3. When paying employees by cash, what is it important to obtain in return?
4. Why do most businesses prefer to pay their employees by cheque?
5. Most businesses who pay their employees by cheque prefer to set up a special "payroll" bank account. Why would they prefer this method?
6. No accounting entries are required for "payroll" cheques issued. Explain why.

Section Exercises

1. **Workbook Exercise: Preparing a currency requisition form.**

2. **Shown below and in your workbook are certain records of Central Supply House. These records pertain to the company's payroll bank account.**

   A. The reconciliaton statement for the payroll bank account as at February 28, 19--

   CENTRAL SUPPLY HOUSE
   BANK RECONCILIATION
   PAYROLL ACCOUNT
   FEBRUARY 29, 19--

Balance per bank statement		$3 269.42
Deduct outstanding cheques		
#1201	$502.16	
#1210	372.42	
#1237	906.16	
#1242	726.42	
#1243	316.20	
#1244	446.06	3 269.42
True bank balance		nil

   B. Payroll cheques issued during the month of March.

PAY PERIOD ENDED MARCH 14, 19--		PAY PERIOD ENDED MARCH 28, 19--	
No.	Amount	No.	Amount
1245	$530.72	1258	$512.36
1246	602.17	1259	614.50
1247	741.02	1260	854.23
1248	600.00	1261	745.19
1249	375.16	1262	725.32
1250	475.02	1263	651.32
1251	550.12	1264	845.71
1252	615.18	1265	245.16
1253	705.19	1266	258.94
1254	695.00	1267	865.34
1255	712.99	1268	258.78
1256	232.16	1269	896.54
1257	312.13	1270	358.56
Total	$7 146.86	Total	$7 831.95

C. Payroll account bank statement for the month of March 19--.

Cheques and Charges		Deposits	Date	Balance
CENTRAL BANK Downtown Centre Winnipeg, Manitoba In account with: Central Supply House				
Balance Forward				$3 269.42
(#1210) 372.42	(#1237) 906.16		Mar 3	
(#1242) 726.42	(#1201) 502.16		Mar 3	$ 762.29
(#1244) 446.06			Mar 6	$ 316.20
		7 146.86	Mar 14	$7 463.06
(#1245) 530.72	(#1248) 600.00		Mar 15	
(#1246) 602.17	(#1249) 375.16		Mar 15	
(#1247) 741.02	(#1251) 550.12		Mar 15	$4 063.87
(#1253) 705.19	(#1254) 695.00		Mar 16	
(#1255) 712.99			Mar 16	$1 950.69
(#1243) 316.20			Mar 21	$1 634.49
(#1256) 232.16			Mar 25	$1 402.33
(#1250) 475.02		7 831.95	Mar 28	$8 759.26
(#1258) 512.36	(#1259) 614.50		Mar 31	
(#1262) 725.32	(#1265) 245.16		Mar 31	
(#1267) 865.34	(#1269) 896.54		Mar 31	$4 900.04

Prepare a bank reconciliation statement for the above as of March 31, 19--.

3. A simplified payroll is given below.

Employee	Gross Pay	CPP	UI	RPP	Tax	Union	Net Pay
Mary Aduono	500	10	12	50	56	6	366
Beth Demitrio	550	11	13	55	60	6	405
Joan Pasquale	480	9	11	48	50	6	356
Bruno Wyotick	540	10	12	54	62	6	376
	2070	40	48	227	228	24	1503

Briefly answer each of the following questions regarding the above payroll.
1. How much would be deducted from the bank to cover this payroll if it were paid in cash?
2. Give the accounting entry to record the payment of this payroll if it were paid in cash.
3. Give the accounting entry to record the payment of this payroll if it were paid by cheques drawn on a special payroll bank account.
4. Why is a cheque for payroll drawn on the general bank account if the payroll is paid for by means of special payroll cheques?
5. What is the amount of the cheque in question 4 above?

16.5 Basic Payroll Records

You are aware by now of the importance of written records in the accounting process. There are a number of important records produced by the payroll department. Three of these are:

1. the payroll journal;
2. the payroll cheque, or payroll cash statement;
3. the employee's earnings record.

Payroll Journal

You are familiar with the payroll journal. It is shown in Figure 16.3. It is prepared for each pay period and is used to accumulate all of the figures for each pay period.

The Payroll Journal as a Book of Original Entry

So far, the payroll journal has been used as a summary sheet. As a result, it has been necessary to journalize the totals from the payroll journal into the general journal.

Some business firms use the payroll journal as a book of original entry. Certain column totals are posted directly from the payroll journal to the general ledger. When this system is used, it is still necessary to process payroll entries 2, 3, 4, and 5 as described in section 16.3, Recording the Payroll. These entries record the employer's share of employee benefits. There is no standard way of handling this. The method used is left to the discretion of the accountant.

Payroll Cheques or Payroll Cash Statements

Most businesses pay their employees by cheque. Attached to each cheque is a tear-off portion that shows the employee's gross pay, the various deductions, and the net pay. A payroll cheque is shown in Figure 16.26.

Businesses that prefer to pay their employees by cash use a payroll cash statement. It serves the same purpose as the voucher portion of the payroll cheque. It indicates the earnings, the various deductions, and the net pay. When payment is made by cash, a signature must be obtained from each employee.

Figure 16.26 A payroll cheque for Harold Evans.

Employee's Earnings Record

The employer must keep track of many details with respect to each employee's earnings. The **employee's earnings record** form is used to accumulate payroll details pay by pay individually by employee. This form is illustrated in Figure 16.27.

At the end of the calendar year, the column totals of the employee's earnings record provide the information necessary for the T4 slips. A **T4 slip** must be prepared for every employee, and represents a summary of the employee's earnings and deductions for one year. This form is required for income tax purposes. Copies of the T4 slips are sent to Revenue Canada, and given to the employees.

A T4 slip is shown below in Figure 16.28.

Figure 16.27 An employee's earnings record form.

Figure 16.28 A T4 slip for Harold Evans.

Section Review Questions

1. Name the three important payroll records discussed in this section.
2. Explain how the payroll journal can be used as a book of original entry.
3. How do employees who are paid in cash learn of the details of their pay?
4. How do employees who are paid by cheque learn of the details of their pay?
5. What is an employee's earnings record?
6. What is the purpose of the employee's earnings record?
7. What is the purpose of the T4 slip?
8. Three parties obtain copies of the T4 slip. Who are they?

Section Exercises

1. Mary Watson started work with the Empire Company on January 1 at a salary of $1 000 for every two weeks. Mary received two $100 pay raises during the year. The first took place after twenty weeks. The second took place after forty weeks. Part of Mary's employee's earnings record card is shown below.

DATE	EMPLOYEE	NET CLAIM CODE	REG	EXTRA	GROSS	C.P.P.	U.I.	R.P.P.	TAX	INSCE.	UNION DUES	GROUP LIFE	RED SHIELD	TOTAL DEDUC'S	NET PAY
Jan 14	Mary Watson	4	1000 —		1000 —	16 22	23 27	50 —	175 85	12 —	8 —	30 —	5 —	320 34	679 66
Jun 3	Mary Watson	4	1100 —		1100 —	18 02	23 27	55 —	210 60	12 —	8 —	30 —	5 —	361 89	738 11
Oct 21	Mary Watson	4	1200 —		1200 —	19 82	23 27	60 —	238 75	12 —	8 —	30 —	5 —	396 84	803 16

1. Calculate the following yearly totals for Mary Watson:
   a. gross pay;
   b. Canada Pension Plan;
   c. unemployment insurance;
   d. registered pension plan;
   e. income tax.
2. For which pay period was the last C.P.P. deduction for the year made? What was the amount of this last deduction?
3. Why did the deduction for unemployment insurance not increase during the year?

2. Given below is the employee's earnings record for Carol Mann for the period from January 1 to December 31, 19--.

NAME	Carol Mann		S.I.N. 723 852 487				
Date	Gross Pay	CPP	UI	RPP	Inc Tax	Other	Net Pay
Jan 31	3 500.00	59.17	50.41	175.00	790.60	125.56	2 299.26
Feb 28	3 500.00	59.17	50.41	175.00	790.60	125.56	2 299.26
Mar 31	3 500.00	59.17	50.41	175.00	790.60	125.56	2 299.26
Apr 30	3 500.00	59.17	50.41	175.00	790.60	125.56	2 299.26
May 31	3 500.00	59.17	50.41	175.00	790.60	125.56	2 299.26
Jun 31	3 500.00	59.17	50.41	175.00	790.60	125.56	2 299.26
Jul 31	3 500.00	59.17	50.41	175.00	790.60	125.56	2 299.26
Aug 31	3 500.00	5.21	50.41	175.00	806.40	125.56	2 337.42
Sep 30	4 000.00		50.41	200.00	964.40	125.56	2 659.63
Oct 31	4 000.00		50.41	200.00	964.40	125.56	2 659.63
Nov 30	4 000.00		50.41	200.00	790.60	125.56	2 299.26
Dec 31	4 000.00		50.41	200.00	790.60	125.56	2 299.26

1. From this record determine the figures that would be entered on the T4 slip in the following boxes:
   - Box C   Employment Income Before Deductions
   - Box D   Employee's Pension Contribution Canada Plan
   - Box E   U.I. Premium
   - Box F   Registered Pension Plan Contribution
   - Box G   Income Tax Deducted
2. Explain why the CPP deductions were changed starting in the month of August.

16.6   Computerized Accounting: The Payroll Package

The Payroll Package

More and more businesses are using accounting packages to perform routine procedures. Until recently, these were all done manually by clerical employees. There are several software packages on the market to handle payroll. These packages can do all of the accounting and recordkeeping for payroll. In addition, they are programmed for updating payroll deduction tables annually.

There are certain general procedures that are common to all payroll packages. Every package will begin with a master menu that shows the options available. A typical master menu appears in Figure 16.29 below.

```
            MASTER MENU

    1.   Maintain employee file

    2.   Time sheet entry and edit

    3.   Payroll cheque preparation

    4.   Reporting menu

    5.   File housekeeping
```

Figure 16.29 A payroll master menu.

An option from the menu can be selected by pressing the appropriate key. This brings a sub-menu onto the screen. For example, if you selected option 1 from the master menu, the sub-menu shown in Figure 16.30 below would appear.

```
          EMPLOYEE FILE MENU

    1.   Add, change, or delete employees

    2.   Display employee list

    3.   Print employee information

    4.   Return to master menu
```

Figure 16.30 A payroll sub-menu.

Payroll packages are designed to include error messages that help the user correct simple errors. There are "help" screens which can be called up if needed. There is also a detailed reference manual for more serious problems.

Employee data and payroll data should be written up on data input forms before actually using the payroll package. Samples of payroll data input forms are shown below in Figure 16.31 and 16.32.

Figure 16.31 An employee file data input form.

The input form in Figure 16.31 above is used to create the employee master file. This file is called up and used by the computer for the preparation of every individual payroll.

Figure 16.32 A payroll data input form.

The input form in Figure 16.32 above is prepared once for each pay period. A clerk enters this data into a computer file on disk. This file is merged with the employee master file when the individual pay amounts are calculated.

Most payroll programs will generate the following:

1. payroll journal;
2. payroll cheques;
3. a list of all personnel information;
4. employee earnings records;
5. T4 slips;
6. record of employment forms.

Computer Review Questions

1. Name one feature that is common to all payroll packages.
2. What happens when you select an option from the master menu?
3. How can you resolve problems that occur when using a payroll package?
4. What must you do before actually using a computer payroll package?
5. What data input form is used to prepare the master payroll file?
6. What reports and forms can be generated by a payroll package?

Computer Exercise

1. a. Using the payroll package that you have available, prepare the payroll for exercise 1 in the Using Your Knowledge section of the Chapter Exercises on page 660.
   b. Print out an employee list for the above.

CHAPTER HIGHLIGHTS

Now that you have completed Chapter 16, you should:

1. understand the nature of accounting for payroll;
2. know the three most common methods of paying employees and how to make the calculations for each method;
3. be able to determine common payroll deductions and read government tables of deductions for income tax, unemployment insurance, and the Canada Pension Plan;
4. understand the purpose of the TD1 form;
5. know how to determine the employer's contribution for unemployment insurance, Canada Pension Plan, and other employee benefits;
6. know how to prepare basic payroll records: the payroll, the payroll cheque or cash statement, and the employee's earnings record;
7. know the accounting entries to record a complete payroll;

8. understand that employees' deductions out of payroll, and the employer's obligatory contributions, are to be remitted to the appropriate government department or other organization;
9. understand how the T4 slip is prepared from the employee earnings record.

ACCOUNTING TERMS

commission
employee's earnings record
gross pay
net pay
payroll
payroll journal
payroll register
registered pension plan

registered retirement savings plan
salary
taxable earnings
timecard
total personal exemption
T4 slip
wages

CHAPTER EXERCISES

Using Your Knowledge

1. **A blank payroll journal for this exercise appears in the workbook.**

   1. **Prepare the payroll journal from the data given below for the two weeks ending August 12, 19‑‑. Use rates and rules as given in the text if not stated otherwise.**

      a.

Employee	Hours Worked Wk. 1	Hours Worked Wk. 2	Net Claim Code	Hourly Rate	Health Insurance Coverage	Life Insurance Coverage
Axelson A.	40	48	9	$ 9.90	Family	$ 50 000
Jones P.	40	40	1	13.00	Single	100 000
Koehler M.	40	40	3	12.00	Family	50 000
Peterson S.	46	46	5	11.00	Family	100 000
Sauve R.	40	40	4	12.50	Single	75 000

      b. Each employee is enrolled in the registered pension plan with contributions set at four per cent of the gross pay. The employer matches the employees' contributions.
      c. Union dues are set at $8.00 for each employee per pay period.

   2. **Total the columns of the payroll journal and perform the steps to ensure its accuracy.**
   3. **Journalize the accounting entries to record the five aspects of the payroll and to pay the employees by means of one cheque to the payroll bank account.**

2. **Workbook Exercise:** Additional payroll calculation exercise.

3. A blank payroll journal for this exercise appears in the workbook.

   1. Prepare the payroll journal from the data given below for the two weeks ending January 20, 19––. Use rates and rules as given in the text except where stated otherwise.
      A. Each of the employees listed below is employed by E-Z Trading Company. They are paid every two weeks. Those in the warehouse are paid on an hourly basis. The sales people are paid a salary plus commission.

      For the warehouse workers, a regular work week is forty hours. They belong to the IAM union and pay union dues of $10 each pay period. Overtime is paid at the rate of time and half.

      The salespeople are paid a basic salary of $350 per pay period. They also receive a commission of two per cent of their sales for the period. Salespeople do not belong to the union.

Employee	Net Claim Code	Hours	Hourly Rate	Net Sales	Health Insurance Status	Group Insurance Coverage
Bower I.	4	80	$11.50		Single	$100 000
Durand D.	6	84	$11.00		Married	$100 000
Hansen W.	8	87	$10.00		Married	$50 000
Kuchma E.	2	86	$12.00		Single	$75 000
Milani M.	5			$27 500	Married	$100 000
Nyman G.	3			$37 000	Married	$90 000
Sutherland T.	9			$32 500	Married	$80 000

      B. The rate of contribution to the registered pension plan for employees is five per cent of gross pay. The employer contributes one and a half times the amount paid by the employees.
      C. The employer pays two-thirds of the health insurance costs.
      D. Group life insurance is paid for entirely by the employees at the rate of 35 cents for each $1 000 of coverage.

   2. Complete and balance the payroll journal.

   3. Journalize the accounting entries to record the five aspects of the payroll and to pay the employees by means of one cheque made out to the payroll bank account. Wages and salaries are kept in separate accounts.

Comprehensive Exercises

4. Karen Paquette of Cornwall, Ontario has been in business for several years. Given below are selected ledger accounts for her business. Shown in these accounts are all of the accounting entries affecting payroll for the month of February.

Bank		C.P.P. Payable		Wages Expense	
8 225		740	190	10 000	
3 050			190	10 500	
8 680			200		
750			200		
2 010					

U.I. Payable		C.P.P. Expense	
920	210	190	
	294	200	
	230		
	322		

R.P.P. Payable		U.I. Expense	
2 010	500	294	
	500	322	
	505		
	505		

Income Tax Payable		R.P.P. Expense	
1 390	750	500	
	760	505	

Hospital Insurance Payable		Hospital Insurance Expense	
750	125	250	
	250	250	
	125		
	250		

Payroll Payable	
8 225	8 225
8 680	8 600

Answer the following questions regarding the above accounting entries.

1. What is the total cost related to payroll for the month of February?
2. Explain the credit entry of $3 050 in the bank account.
3. What is the length of the payroll period?
4. Explain the debit entry of $750 in the Hospital Insurance Payable account.
5. What fraction of the total cost of hospital insurance does the company pay?
6. To what extent does the employer contribute to the employees' pension fund?
7. How often is payment made by the company for hospital insurance?
8. Give the amount of the cheque that will be sent to the federal government in March.

5. **Shown below are the summary figures for the first four payrolls for Precision Company. These are followed by additional information.**

Payroll Summaries

Pay Date	Gross Pay	C.P.P.	U.I.	R.P.P.	Income Tax	Health	Union	Net Pay
Jan 14	5 700	98	101	285	560	75	50	4 531
Jan 28	5 400	90	97	270	520	75	50	4 298
Feb 11	5 800	99	103	290	570	75	50	4 613
Feb 25	5 900	100	105	295	580	75	50	4 695

Additional Information
1. Use the rules set out in the chapter. Round off to the nearest dollar where necessary.
2. Payment for health insurance is made on the fifteenth of the following month.
3. Payments for R.P.P. and Union are made at the end of every second month.
4. Assume that the bank balance always has sufficient funds on hand to make the payments.
5. The accounts needed for this exercise are those shown below. They are set up for you in the workbook.

Bank	Payroll Payable
Canada Pension Plan Payable	Wages Expense
Unemployment Insurance Payable	Canada Pension Plan Expense
Registered Pension Plan Payable	Unemployment Insurance Expense
Employees' Income Tax Payable	Registered Pension Plan Expense
Health Insurance Payable	Health Insurance Expense
Union Dues Payable	

1. Record all accounting entries for these four payrolls for the period from January 1 to March 15. Record these entries directly into the T-accounts in your workbook without using a journal. Record the entries in their correct order.

2. Calculate the total expense of these four payrolls. Show that this total expense figure is equal to the total paid out in cash.

For Further Thought
1. **Briefly answer each of the following questions.**

   1. In the government booklet for the Canada Pension Plan there is a summary of types of employment and benefits that are subject to C.P.P. contributions. What steps would you take to resolve a doubt you had about a certain kind of employment?
   2. Explain why a contractor pays by the hour and not with a salary.
   3. Give one definite advantage of being paid by the hour.
   4. Think of some examples of jobs that would pay for piecework.

5. What measures are usually enough to prevent workers from punching a friend's timecard as well as their own?
6. Usually, there is at least a one-week delay in paying employees. What do you think is the reason for this?
7. For what reason would an employee be paid double time and a half?
8. From the employee's point of view, are payroll deductions all negative things? Explain.
9. Explain the purpose of a pension.
10. With insurance in general, the greater the risk you are, the more you pay. For example, if you have a number of speeding convictions, your car insurance premium increases. In some cases, your insurance might be cancelled. In view of the above, is it right to regard unemployment insurance as "insurance"? Explain.
11. At one time, people whose employment was considered to be assured (teachers, for example) did not have to pay into the unemployment insurance fund. Give two reasons why that situation changed so that now almost everyone pays.
12. On the deduction tables for unemployment insurance in the text, two maximums appear on the second of the two pages. Explain what they are and why they are so close.
13. The unemployment insurance booklet states that the premium rate for employees is 2.35 per cent. The employer pays 1.4 times that paid by the employee. What is the employer's rate?
14. Why do you think there are registered pension plans when there is already the Canada Pension Plan?
15. Income taxes are deducted from each pay during the year on an estimated basis. How does the government eventually get the right amount from each person?
16. A province operates a universal health insurance program but does not fund it by payroll deduction premiums. How would it pay for the program? Give an advantage and a disadvantage of this method?
17. Explain what is meant by extended health care.
18. Management and unions are often adversaries. Why would management agree to deduct union dues for the benefit of a union which it considers to be an opponent?
19. For the sake of simplicity, the text shows the accounting for payroll performed using five entries. Some accountants, using the payroll journal as a book of original entry, manage to have only one accounting entry for each payroll. Figure out how to do this.
20. Where are the figures found for calculating the amount of the cheque to be sent to the Receiver General on March 15?
21. Explain why the true balance of a payroll bank account is theoretically zero.
22. Is it possible to have an overdraft in the payroll bank account? Explain.
23. Matt Cook's T4 slip indicates that his employer has withheld $5 260 for income tax from his earnings for the year. When Matt prepares his income tax return, he discovers that the total tax he has to pay is only $4 830. How can this happen?
24. Syd Templeman has just received a $200 dollar raise—from $900 to $1 100 every two weeks. Syd has family coverage for health insurance and $100 000 of life insurance. He does not belong to a union. Using the rates and policies from the text, calculate how much larger Syd's take-home pay will be if his net claim code is 4.

25. Maxwell Company's payroll is due to be paid this afternoon. The payroll amounts to $22 565 but Maxwell Company has only $14 275 in its general bank account. Should Maxwell Company be concerned about this, and to what degree? Explain. What steps should Maxwell Company be taking in regard to this situation?

CASE STUDIES

Case 1 Comparing Wage Increases

The following salaries and wages are paid by the Magic Tape Company.

Employee		Salary or Wage
General Manager: P. Sanderson		$180 000
Plant Workers:	M. Bailey	18 000
	B. Dorst	19 000
	N. Gehrals	28 000
	V. Ripley	35 000

The owner of this company, P. Epps, grants a ten per cent pay raise to the plant employees to cover a ten per cent rise in the cost of living. Sanderson, the general manager, argues that what applies to the plant employees also applies to him, and he puts in a request for a ten per cent pay increase.

Questions
1. Comment on Sanderson's request, using some simple calculations or figures.
2. Are percentages a fair way to compare earnings?

Case 2 Wage Increase—How Much Can Be Offered?

You are the proprietor of Brite Cleaners. The following data is extracted from your most recent income statement.

Revenue:	Cleaning	$134 900
	Storage	5 974
	Tailoring	30 500
		$171 374
Expenses:	Rent	$ 4 800
	Delivery	2 930
	Wages	104 300
	Supplies used	3 250
	General expense	1 975
	Depreciation	7 560
	Power	4 250
		$129 065
	Net Income	$ 42 309

The employees have requested a twenty per cent increase in wages.

Questions

1. Assuming that no other expense is affected, how much would the wage increase cost the company?
2. Can you grant this request and still make a profit, based on the above statements?
3. How much would the net income be if the increase were granted?
4. You want to make at least $30 000 per year from the business, and you expect an increase of $5 000 in revenue for the coming year. Calculate the maximum increase that you can grant to your employees, expressed in dollars and as a percentage. Assume there is no increase in other expenses.

Case 3   *Dummy Employees on the Payroll*

Armco is a very large developer of homes in the Toronto area. At the present time, the company is engaged in the building of several large subdivisions in five different locations. The company has several hundred field workers on its payroll.

Because they work on the sites, the field workers rarely have occasion to visit the head office. Also, there is considerable turnover of staff in this industry. Consequently, to the payroll department, the field workers are just names, not faces.

The field workers are paid by the hour but do not punch a time clock. Their hours are kept on individual time sheets by the supervisors on the various jobs. Once a week, the supervisors bring the time sheets to head office and give them directly to Pat Pasco, the paymaster.

Pat Pasco is technically a very good paymaster. She has a lot of experience and knows all there is to know about payroll. She keeps absolute control over everything that happens in her department and sees to it that the department is run smoothly and efficiently.

The time sheets received by Pat from the foremen are turned over to payroll clerks to be processed. However, before handing them over, Pat slips in a couple of phony timesheets. These phony timesheets show fictitious names, addresses, social insurance numbers, and so on. The payroll department processes the phony sheets along with all of the legitimate ones. When the payroll is completed and the cheques ready, they are all given to Pat for her signature.

Pat signs the cheques and forwards them to the supervisors who in turn distribute them to the workers. Of course, the two phony cheques are removed by Pat for herself. Pat is smart enough to have established a way of cashing the cheques, adjusting the payments to the government, and so on. She also sees to it that from time to time the phony employees leave and new ones begin working for Armco. She seems to have all the bases covered.

Questions

1. In your opinion, is this scheme possible? Give reasons why you think so.
2. If you answered "Yes" to question 1, how long do you think the scheme could go undetected? In your opinion, how might it be detected?

Case 4 A Profit-Sharing Proposal

A.
You are the accountant for Sayers & Company, a successful and growing company. The company has just completed its sixth fiscal year of operation. Its income statement for 19–6 is shown below in abbreviated form.

```
                    SAYERS & COMPANY
                    INCOME STATEMENT
                YEAR ENDED DECEMBER 31, 19–6
                     (Figures in Thousands)
```

Revenue		$2 000
Operating Expenses		
Wages	$ 400	
Other Expenses	1 280	1 680
Net Income		$ 320

The company is presently involved in wage negotiations with its union. There have been persistent difficulties between the union and the company resulting in one strike and several other disruptions. At the present time, the union is demanding a ten per cent wage increase retroactive to the 19–6 year.

The owner is frustrated by the unpleasantness of union versus management confrontations. He hopes to eliminate them by introducing a plan which ties employees' incomes to company profits. He makes the following proposal to the employees.

Item 1. The employees will terminate their connection with the union.
Item 2. There will be no more wage negotiations.
Item 3. The total wages figure for every fiscal year will be fixed at sixty per cent of the "income before wages" figure (net income plus wages).
Item 4. The plan will be retroactive to 19–6.
Item 5. The plan is expected to foster harmony, increase productivity, and keep the number of employees to a minimum. It is to the employees' benefit to keep their numbers low.

Questions

1. From the above income statement, calculate the wages as a percentage of "income before wages."
2. Prepare a revised income statement for 19–6 based on the owner's profit-sharing formula.
3. Calculate the percentage wage increase that would occur immediately if the owner's plan were accepted.
4. Explain the employer's claim that it is to the employees' benefit to keep their numbers down.

B.
As part of the discussions with the employees the owner reveals the company's projections for the next three years. These are as follows.

	19–7	19–8	19–9
Revenue	2 100	2 200	2 500
Other Expenses (excluding wages)	1 320	1 400	1 580

5. Using the above data, prepare a schedule showing the projected income statements in comparative form for the years 19–6 through 19–9.
6. Prepare the above income statements in trend analysis form.
7. Based on the projected data, show the wage increases from year to year using the traditional method of calculating wage increases.
8. Decide whether or not the employees should accept the profit-sharing plan. Give reasons for your decision.

C.
Assume that the employees did accept the owner's profit-sharing proposal. Also, assume that years 19–7, 19–8, and 19–9 have been concluded and that the actual figures for these years is now known. Some of these figures are shown below.

	19–6	19–7	19–8	19–9
Revenue	2 000	2 150	2 280	2 350
Other Expenses	1 280	1 320	1 390	1 400

9. Complete a comparative schedule of income statements based on the actual data.
10. Compare this data with the projected data worked out previously. Give your opinion as to whether the profit-sharing plan has been successful or not. Consider both the employees' and the employer's point of view. Perform whatever analysis is necessary. Back up your opinion with facts.

Case 5   Employee's Wages—How Much?

The Cycle and Sports Centre is the foremost repair centre for bicycles in the community. There is never a shortage of repair work, and there is always a large backlog of repair work waiting to be done. The Centre depends on this repair work for a substantial portion of its revenue.

One summer, the business hires George Sumac, a university student, to repair bicycles on a part-time basis. George suggests that he and the owners split the repair bills on a fifty-fifty basis. This will not include any charges for the bicycle parts that the store supplies. The owners, a father and a son, agree to the suggestion.

This arrangement works fine in the first season. George turns out to be an exceptional worker. He repairs bicycles quickly and thoroughly. Customers rarely complain about his work. As George becomes more experienced, however, he begins to turn out a greater volume of repair work. The more work that George turns out, the more he earns in wages. George earns $14 000 in his second year, and $17 000 in his third.

The owners, particularly the father, become increasingly concerned. They are not used to paying part-time workers $17 000 in a season.

The owners meet with George to discuss the situation. The father insists that George is overpaid and will have to take a smaller percentage. George argues that he actually works on a piecework basis. He may earn good money, but his work merits it. The more he earns, the more the company earns as well.

The father is unable to accept George's arguments. George refuses to take a cut and gives up his job.

Questions
1. Is the father justified in his claim that the amount paid for part-time work is excessive?
2. Is George right to refuse to take a cut in pay?
3. What will the owners have to do now that George is gone?
4. What factors are the store owners ignoring?
5. Can the store make more money without George's services?

CAREER
Thu Vinh Lan / Senior Payroll Supervisor

Thu Vinh Lan arrived in Canada with his family when he was eleven years old. While in high school, he decided that a business education would improve his chances of a successful career in his new country. Thu began preparing for a business career by taking a number of accounting courses. After graduating from high school, he continued this preparation by completing a three-year business administration diploma at a local community college.

After college, Thu worked for a General Motors dealership. There, his duties included the control of the general ledger and the preparation of the financial statements.

For the past five years, Thu has been employed by Suburban Metal Industries, a medium-sized manufacturing company, as the senior payroll supervisor.

Each week, Thu prepares the payroll for salaried personnel. On each employee's master sheet, he records days worked, vacation pay, rate changes, hospitalization charges, sick leave, changes in personal income tax exemptions, and so on. All this information is then summarized and fed into the computer so that salary cheques can be issued. Two other payroll clerks, under Thu's supervision, prepare the payroll in an identical manner for employees who are paid hourly wages.

Thu is responsible for a payroll of 220 employees who work on salary. In addition, he prepares the confidential payrolls for the executive officers of the company at the head and regional offices. Thu also calculates the commissions earned by the salespeople and sales agents, and supervises the typing and mailing of the commission statements.

Each month, he arranges payroll deductions for the Canada Pension Plan, unemployment insurance, income tax, union dues, hospitalization and the company pension plan. At the end of each month, Thu determines the total wages, salaries and commissions paid during the month and sends these figures to the accounting department for entry in the general journal. Finally, at the end of each year, he sees that T4 slips are typed and sent to all employees.

In the computerized payroll system for Suburban Metal Industries, the entries for pay and deductions are based on the employee's classification, such as mechanic, assembly line or maintenance worker, and so on. For each employee, the number of regular and overtime hours is keyed into the computer. This input is automatically sorted by means of employee number and department. The computer prints out the total amount of the cheques issued so that Thu can transfer the proper amount of money to the special payroll account.

As supervisor of payroll, Thu co-ordinated the changeover from a manual to a computerized payroll system, and redesigned his department to take full advantage of the computer. This was a great challenge for him, and he considers today an exciting time to be an accountant.

Discussion

1. List the information that Thu records on each employee's master sheet. Is this sheet similar to an employee's earnings record?
2. What is the purpose of a special payroll account?
3. Why are the payroll records for the executive officers of a company usually confidential?
4. Describe and state the importance of a T4 slip.
5. As senior payroll supervisor, Thu has the responsibility over all the payroll accounts. Prepare a payroll chart of accounts for Suburban Metal Industries and classify each account. Your chart should contain at least ten accounts.

Appendix— GAAPs

Generally Accepted Accounting Principles, Concepts, and Conventions

The Business Entity Concept

The business entity concept provides that the accounting for a business or organization be kept separate from the personal affairs of its owner, or from any other business or organization. This means that the owner of a business should not place any personal assets on the business balance sheet. The balance sheet of the business must reflect the financial position of the business alone. Also, when transactions of the business are recorded, any personal expenditures of the owner are charged to the owner and are not allowed to affect the operating results of the business.

The Continuing Concern Concept (Also, the Going Concern Concept)

The continuing concern concept assumes that a business will continue to operate, unless it is known that such is not the case. The values of the assets belonging to a business that is alive and well are straightforward. For example, a supply of envelopes with the company's name printed on them would be valued at their cost. This would not be the case if the company were going out of business. In that case, the envelopes would be difficult to sell because the company's name is on them. When a company is going out of business, the values of the assets usually suffer because they have to be sold under unfavourable circumstances. The values of such assets often cannot be detemined until they are actually sold.

The Principle of Conservatism

The principle of conservatism provides that accounting for a business should be fair and reasonable. Accountants are required in their work to make evaluations and estimates, to deliver opinions, and to select procedures. They should do so in a way that neither overstates nor understates the affairs of the business or the results of operation.

The Objectivity Principle

The objectivity principle states that accounting will be recorded on the basis of objective evidence. Objective evidence means that different people looking at the evidence will arrive at the same values for the transaction. Simply put, this means that accounting entries will be based on fact and not on personal opinion or feelings.

The source document for a transaction is almost always the best objective evidence available. The source document shows the amount agreed to by the buyer and the seller, who are usually independent and unrelated to each other.

The Time Period Concept

The time period concept provides that accounting take place over specific time periods known as fiscal periods. These fiscal periods are of equal length, and are used when measuring the financial progress of a business.

The Revenue Recognition Convention

The revenue recognition convention provides that revenue be taken into the accounts (recognized) at the time the transaction is completed. Usually, this just means recording revenue when the bill for it is sent to the customer. If it is a cash transaction, the revenue is recorded when the sale is completed and the cash received.

It is not always quite so simple. Think of the building of a large project such as a dam. It takes a construction company a number of years to complete such a project. The company does not wait until the project is entirely completed before it sends its bill. Periodically, it bills for the amount of work completed and receives payments as the work progresses. Revenue is taken into the accounts on this periodic basis.

It is important to take revenue into the accounts properly. If this is not done, the earnings statements of the company will be incorrect and the readers of the financial statements misinformed.

The Matching Principle

The matching principle is an extension of the revenue recognition convention. The matching principle states that each expense item related to revenue earned must be recorded in the same accounting period as the revenue it helped to earn. If this is not done, the financial statements will not measure the results of operations fairly.

The Cost Principle

The cost principle states that the accounting for purchases must be at their cost price. This is the figure that appears on the source document for the transaction in almost all cases. There is no place for guesswork or wishful thinking when accounting for purchases.

The value recorded in the accounts for an asset is not changed later if the market value of the asset changes. It would take an entirely new transaction based on new objective evidence to change the original value of an asset.

There are times when the above type of objective evidence is not available. For example, a building could be received as a gift. In such a case, the transaction would be recorded at fair market value which must be determined by some independent means.

The Consistency Principle

The consistency principle requires accountants to apply the same methods and procedures from period to period. When they change a method from one period to another they must explain the change clearly on the financial statements. The readers of financial statements have the right to assume that consistency has been applied if there is no statement to the contrary.

The consistency principle prevents people from changing methods for the sole purpose of manipulating figures on the financial statements.

The Materiality Principle

The materiality principle requires accountants to use generally accepted accounting principles except when to do so would be expensive or difficult, and where it makes no real difference if the rules are ignored. If a rule is temporarily ignored, the net income of the company must not be significantly affected, nor should the reader's ability to judge the financial statements be impaired.

The Full Disclosure Principle

The full disclosure principle states that any and all information that affects the full understanding of a company's financial statements must be included with the financial statements. Some items may not affect the ledger accounts directly. These would be included in the form of accompanying notes. Examples of such items are: outstanding lawsuits, tax disputes, and company takeovers.

Glossary

A

Account A specially ruled page used to record financial changes. There is one account for each different item affecting the financial position. All of the accounts together form the ledger.

Account balance The value of an account showing the dollar amount and an indication as to whether it is a debit or a credit value.

Account form of balance sheet A balance sheet which presents the information in a horizontal format, the assets being shown to the left and the liabilities and equity being shown to the right. *Contrast* Report form of balance sheet.

Accountability The obligation of management (or other group or person) to supply evidence, usually periodic, of its action or performance as required by custom, regulation, or agreement.

Accounting cycle The total set of accounting procedures that must be carried out during each fiscal period.

Accounting entry All the changes in the accounts caused by one business transaction, expressed in terms of debits and credits. For each accounting entry, the total of the debit amounts will equal the total of the credit amounts.

Accounting period The period of time over which the earnings of a business are measured. *Same as* Fiscal period.

Accounts payable The money that a business owes to its trade creditors. This money is a liability of the business.

Accounts payable ledger A book or file containing all the accounts of ordinary creditors representing amounts owed to them by the business.

Accounts receivable The money that is owed to a business by its customers. This money is considered an asset of the business.

Accounts receivable ledger A book or file containing all the accounts of debtors (customers) representing amounts owed by them to the business.

Account title The name of the item for which an account is prepared, entered at the top of the account page.

Acid-test ratio The ratio of current assets, excluding inventory, to current liabilities. *Same as* Quick ratio.

Adjusting entry An entry made before finalizing the books for the period to apportion amounts of revenue or expense to the proper accounting periods or operating divisions. For example, the apportioning of wages between accounting periods when the current period ends between two paydays.

Asset Anything owned that has a dollar value. *Contrast* Liability.

677

Audit An examination of the accounting records and internal controls of a business in order to be able to express an opinion about the business's financial position and results of operation.

Auditing The process of conducting an audit. *See* Audit.

Audit strip In a cash register, a paper tape that provides a continuous record of all transactions that occur on a business day and which can be accessed only by authorized persons. *Same as* Detailed audit tape.

B

Balance column account The most commonly used type of account, in which there are three money columns, one for the debit amounts, one for the credit amounts, and one for the amount of the balance. *Same as* Three-column account.

Balance sheet A statement showing the financial position (the assets, liabilities, and capital) of an individual, company, or other organization on a certain date.

Bank credit advice A business form by means of which a bank informs a depositor that an increase has been made in the bank account and the reason for the increase.

Bank debit advice A business form by means of which a bank informs a depositor that a decrease has been made in the bank account and the reason for the decrease.

Bank deposit An amount of money or its equivalent placed in a bank account.

Bank reconciliation A routine procedure to find out the reasons for a discrepancy between the balance on deposit as shown by the bank and the balance on deposit as shown by the depositor.

Bank reconciliation statement A statement accounting for the differences between a bank account as reflected in the books of the bank and the same account as reflected in the books of the depositor.

Book of original entry Any journal; that is, the book that contains the first, or original, record of each transaction. *Same as* Journal.

Business transaction A financial event that changes the values in certain accounts and that therefore affects the financial position of the business.

C

Capital The difference between the total assets and total liabilities of a business. *Same as* Net worth, Owner's equity.

Cash discount A reduction that may be taken in the amount of a bill provided that the full amount is paid within the discount period shown on the bill.

Cash payments journal A special columnar journal used to record all transactions that directly cause a decrease in the bank balance.

Cash receipts list A business paper, prepared daily, that lists the monies received by a business from customers on account and other sources.

Cash refund The return of money to the buyer by the seller in respect to deficient goods that were paid for.

Cash sales slip A business form showing the details of a transaction in which goods or services are sold to a customer for cash.

Cash short or over The amount of money by which the business's cash receipts for the day are more or less than what they should be.

Certified cheque A cheque for which the bank takes the funds out of the payer's account in advance, and puts them aside to honour the cheque when it is presented by the payee.

Change fund A small quantity of bills and coins, usually between fifty and one hundred dollars, placed in the drawer of a cash register at the beginning of the day for the purpose of making change for customers. *Same as* Float.

Chart of accounts A list of the accounts of a business and their numbers, arranged according to their order in the ledger.

Cheque copy A copy of a cheque, used as the source document for a payment made by cheque.

Classified financial statement A financial statement in which data are grouped according to major categories.

Closing an account To cause an account to have a nil balance by means of a journal entry.

C.O.D. (Cash on delivery) A term of sale whereby goods must be paid for at the time they are delivered.

Collection period The ratio of accounts receivable to charge sales for the year, multiplied by 365. It indicates the average number of days it takes the business to collect an account receivable.

Commission An amount paid periodically to a salesperson or an agent calculated as a percentage of the amount of goods or services sold by that person.

Common-size statements Financial statements that show individual items as percentages of a selected figure, known as the base figure.

Comparative financial statements Financial statements that present the figures for successive years side by side, along with the amount of change.

Contra account An account that must be considered along with a given asset account to show the true book value of the asset account. *Same as* Valuation account.

Control account A general ledger account, the balance of which represents the sum of the balances in the accounts contained in a subsidiary ledger.

Corporation A legal entity as determined by statute, separate and distinct from its owners, with a capital divided into shares which, when issued, are held by shareholders. The liability of the shareholders is limited to the amount of the capital for which they have subscribed. *Same as* Limited company.

Correcting journal entry An accounting entry to rectify the effect of an error.

Cost of goods sold The total cost of goods sold during an accounting period.

Credit To record an amount on the right-hand side of an account. *Contrast* Debit.

Credit invoice A business form issued by a vendor to reverse a charge that has been made on a regular sales invoice. The reason for the reversal is explained in detail on the invoice. *Same as* Credit note.

Credit note A business form issued by a vendor to reverse a charge that has been made on a regular sales invoice. The reason for the reversal is explained in detail on the note. *Same as* Credit invoice.

Creditor Anyone who is owed money by the business. *Contrast* Debtor.

Cross balancing The procedure whereby the total of all the debts in a journal is checked against the total of all the credits in the journal to make sure that the two totals agree.

Cross-referencing Part of the posting sequence in which the journal page number for a given entry is recorded in the appropriate account, and the account number, in turn, is recorded on the journal page.

Current asset Unrestricted cash, an asset that will be converted into cash within one year, or an asset that will be used up within one year.

Current bank account A type of deposit account offered by the bank specifically to meet the needs of businesses.

Current liability A short-term debt, payment of which is expected to occur within one year.

Current ratio The ratio of current assets to current liabilities.

Customer's statement of account A record of customer's account for a one-month period, showing purchases made during the period, payments received during the period, and the unpaid balance remaining. Statements of account are usually sent out each month by a business to its customers.

D

Daily interest savings account A bank account that offers fairly high interest, calculated on a daily basis, on fluctuating savings. Cheques cannot be used with this account.

Debit To record an amount on the left-hand side of an account. *Contrast* Credit.

Debit ratio The ratio of the total liabilities of a business to the total assets. This measures the proportion of total assets acquired through borrowed money. The debt ratio is complementary to the equity ratio. *See* Equity ratio.

Debtor Anyone who owes money to the business. *Contrast* Creditor.

Declining-balance method of depreciation A method of calculating the annual depreciation of an asset as a fixed percentage of the remaining value of the asset. Under this method, the asset's annual depreciation becomes progressively smaller. The percentages to be used are determined by government regulation. *Contrast* Straight-line method of depreciation.

Delivery expense Transportation charges on outgoing merchandise. *Contrast* Freight-in.

Depreciation The decrease in value of a fixed asset over time. For accounting purposes, this decrease is calculated according to a mathematical formula.

Detailed audit tape In a cash register, a paper tape that provides a continuous record of all transactions that occur on a business day and which can be accessed only by authorized persons. *Same as* Audit strip.

Discrepancy item An item arising out of a transaction that has not been recorded equally in both the bank statement and the records of the depositor. *See* Bank reconciliation.

Double entry system of accounting The system of accounting in general use in which every transaction is recorded both as a debit in one or more accounts and as a credit in one or more accounts. Under this system, the total of the debit entries equals the total of the credit entries.

Drawings A decrease in owner's equity resulting from a personal withdrawal of funds or other assets by the owner.

Duty Special charges imposed by the government of a country on certain goods imported from a foreign country.

E

Employee's earnings record A form used to provide a cumulative record of all the payroll data during a calendar year for a particular employee. One is prepared for each employee.

Equity ratio The ratio of the total equity to the total assets of a business. This measures the proportion of total assets acquired by invested capital. The equity ratio is complementary to the debt ratio. *See* Debt ratio.

Expense A decrease in equity resulting from the costs of the materials and services used to produce the revenue. *Contrast* Income, Revenue.

F

Financial position The status of a business, as represented by the assets, liabilities, and owner's equity.

Fiscal period The period of time over which earnings are measured. *Same as* Accounting period.

Five-journal system An accounting system in which five journals are kept in process at the same time, each one recording transactions of a particular type.

Fixed asset A long-term asset held for its

usefulness in producing goods or services. *Same as* Plant and equipment.

Float A small quantity of bills and coins, usually between fifty and one hundred dollars, placed in the drawer of a cash register at the beginning of the day for the purpose of making change for customers. *Same as* Change fund.

Forwarding The process of continuing an account or journal on a new page by carrying forward all relevant information from the completed page.

Freight-in Transportation charges on incoming merchandise. *Contrast* Delivery expense.

Fundamental accounting equation The equation that states that total assets minus total liabilities are equal to owner's equity. A − L = OE.

G

GAAP *See* Generally accepted accounting principles.

General ledger A book or file containing all the accounts of the business other than those in the subsidiary ledgers. The general ledger accounts represent the complete financial position of the business.

Generally accepted accounting principles Guidelines established by professional accountants to be followed in the preparation of accounting records and financial statements.

Gross pay Earnings before deductions.

Gross profit In a trading business, the excess of net sales over the cost of goods sold.

I

Imprest method The method of handling petty cash in which the removal of monies is only recorded in the accounts at the time when the fund is replenished.

In balance A state in which the total value of all the accounts (or columns in a journal) with debit balances is equal to the total value of all the accounts (or columns in a journal) with credit balances. *Contrast* Out of balance.

Income An increase in equity resulting from the proceeds of the sale of goods or services. *Same as* Revenue. *Contrast* Expense.

Income statement A financial statement that summarizes the items of revenue and expense, and shows the net income or net loss of a business, for a given fiscal year.

Income summary account The temporary account to which the total revenues and the total expenses are transferred during the closing process. The balance of the account represents the net income or the net loss for the period and is transferred to the owner's capital account as part of the closing process.

Insiders The owners, managers, and executive group of a company who have access to company information not available to others. *Contrast* Outsiders.

Internal control The plan of organization and all the coordinated methods used to protect assets, ensure accurate, reliable accounting data, encourage efficiency, and adhere to company policies.

Inventory turnover For a trading business, the cost of goods sold figure divided by the average merchandise inventory. This represents the number of times the business has been able to sell its inventory in a year.

J

Journal A specially ruled book in which accounting entries are recorded in the order in which they occur. A transaction is recorded in the journal before it is recorded in the ledger. *Same as* Book of original entry.

Journal entry An accounting entry in the journal.

Journalizing The process of recording entries in the journal.

L

Late deposit A deposit that is made on the last day (usually) of the period covered by the bank statement but which does not appear on the bank statement until the following period.

Ledger A group or file of accounts that can be stored as pages in a book, as cards in a tray, as tape on a reel, or magnetically on disk. *See* Account.

Liability A debt of an individual, business, or other organization. *Contrast* Asset.

Limited company A legal entity as determined by statute, separate and distinct from its owners, with a capital divided into shares which, when issued, are held by shareholders. The liability of the shareholders is limited to the amount of the capital for which they have subscribed. *Same as* Corporation.

Liquidity The ease with which an asset can be converted into cash.

Liquidity ratio One of a number of ratios or numbers calculated by formula and used to help assess the ability of a company to pay its debts. *Same as* Solvency ratio.

Long-term liability A liability which, in the ordinary course of business, will not be liquidated within one year.

M

Manufacturing business A business that buys raw materials which it converts into new products and sells to earn a profit.

Merchandise inventory The goods handled by a merchandising business. *Same as* Stock-in-trade.

Merchandising business A business that buys goods to resell them at a profit. *Same as* Trading business.

Multi-columnar journal A journal containing a number of columns in which items of a similar nature are grouped during the recording phase. Its purpose is to reduce the labour of posting.

N

Net income The difference between total revenues and total expenses if the revenues are greater than the expenses. *Contrast* Net loss.

Net loss The difference between total revenues and total expenses if the expenses are greater than the revenues. *Contrast* Net income.

Net pay Earnings after deductions.

Net worth The difference between the total assets and total liabilities of a business. *Same as* Capital, Owner's equity.

Nominal account An account that accumulates data for only one fiscal period at a time. Revenue, expense, and drawings accounts are nominal. *Same as* Temporary accounts.

NSF cheque A cheque that was not cashed when presented to the issuer's bank because there were not sufficient funds in the issuer's bank account to cover the amount of the cheque.

O

Opening an account The process of setting up a new account in the ledger.

Opening entry The first accounting entry in the general journal, the entry that records the beginning financial position of a business, thereby opening the books of account.

Out of balance A state in which the total value of all the accounts (or columns in a journal) with debit balances does not equal the total value of all the accounts (or columns in a journal) with credit balances. *Contrast* In balance.

Outsiders A company's bankers and other creditors, prospective investors, shareholders, government agencies such as

Revenue Canada, and others who do not have access to company information as do insiders. *Contrast* Insiders.

Outstanding cheque A cheque that is issued and recorded, but not cashed, during the period covered by a bank statement, and that therefore does not appear on the bank statement. *See* Discrepancy item.

Owner's equity The difference between the total assets and total liabilities of a business. *Same as* Capital, Net worth.

P

Partnership The relationship that exists between persons carrying on a business in common for shared profits. Does not apply to the members of a corporation.

Payment on account Money paid to a creditor to reduce the balance owed to that creditor.

Payroll The total process of calculating and preparing the employees' earnings.

Payroll journal A sheet of columnar paper on which are recorded the details for calculating individual net pays of employees as well as the total payroll figures for the period. *Same as* Payroll register.

Payroll register A sheet of columnar paper on which are recorded the details for calculating individual net pays of employees as well as the total payroll figures for the period. *Same as* Payroll journal.

Pencil footings Tiny pencil-figure totals used in accounts and journals. *Same as* Pin totals.

Periodic inventory method A method of accounting for merchandise inventory in which the record of items in stock is updated only at the end of an accounting period. *Contrast* Perpetual inventory method.

Perpetual inventory method A method of accounting for merchandise inventory in which the record of items in stock is kept up to date on a daily basis. *Contrast* Periodic inventory method.

Personal chequing account A bank account that pays no interest on savings and is designed for those who write a lot of personal cheques.

Petty cash fund A small quantity of cash, usually no more than $200, that is kept in the office for small expenditures.

Petty cash voucher A form that is filled out when money is removed from the petty cash fund and no bill for the expenditure is available.

Physical inventory The procedure by which the unsold goods of a merchandising business are counted and valued at the end of a fiscal period.

Pin totals Tiny pencil-figure totals used in accounts and journals. *Same as* Pencil footings.

Plant and equipment Long-term assets such as trucks, held for their usefulness in producing goods or services, and which are not normally for sale. *Same as* Fixed assets.

Point-of-sale terminal A sophisticated electronic cash register that is connected to and is able to interact with a central computer.

Post-closing trial balance The trial balance that is taken after the closing entries have been posted.

Post-dated cheque A cheque that is dated for some time in the future and that cannot be cashed until that date arrives.

Posting The process of transferring the accounting entries from the journal to the ledger.

Prepaid expense An expense, other than for inventory or capital, with benefits that extend into the future and that is paid for in advance.

Profitability percentage One of a number of percentages calculated by formula and used to help assess the company's ability to earn a profit.

Proving the cash The process of counting the cash receipts at the end of the day and comparing the total to the book figure for total cash receipts for the day as determined by the company records.

Public accountant An accountant who offers services professionally to the general public.

Public accounting The profession of the public accountant who offers a variety of accounting services to the public for a fee.

Purchase invoice The name given to a supplier's sales invoice in the office of the purchaser. *See* Sales invoice.

Purchase on account A purchase that is not paid for at the time it is made; also called a purchase on credit.

Purchases journal A special columnar journal in which are recorded the accounting entries for all transactions involving the buying of goods or services on account.

Q

Quick ratio The ratio of current assets, excluding inventory, to current liabilities. *Same as* Acid-test ratio.

R

Rate of return on net sales The ratio of net earnings to net sales, expressed as a percentage, used comparatively to measure the net income performance of a company.

Rate of return on owner's equity The ratio of net earnings to average owner's equity, expressed as a percentage, used to evaluate the company's performance relative to other investment opportunities such as government bonds.

Real accounts An account the balance of which is not closed out at the end of the fiscal period but which is carried forward into the succeeding period.

Receipt on account Money received from a debtor to reduce the balance owed by that debtor.

Registered pension plan A private pension plan, registered and approved by the government, for which contributions, up to a given maximum, are tax-free. *Same as* Registered retirement savings plan.

Registered retirement savings plan (R.R.S.P.) A private pension plan, registered and approved by the government, for which contributions, up to a given maximum, may be deducted when calculating taxable income. *Same as* Registered pension plan.

Remittance advice The tear-off portion of a cheque, or a separate business form accompanying a cheque, which explains what the cheque is for.

Replenishing petty cash The procedure whereby the petty cash fund is renewed when it reaches a lower limit.

Report form of balance sheet A balance sheet which presents the information in a vertical format, the assets section being presented above the liabilities and equity section. *Contrast* Account form of balance sheet.

Restrictive endorsement One that places a condition on the cashing or depositing of a cheque.

Retail sales tax A percentage tax based on and added to the price of goods sold to a customer.

Retailer A merchandising business that buys goods from wholesalers and manufacturers and sells them to the general public with a view to making a profit.

Revenue An increase in equity resulting from the proceeds of the sale of goods or services. *Same as* Income. *Contrast* Expense.

S

Salary A fixed amount paid regularly to an employee for services, regardless of the number of hours worked. Salary is usually set at a certain amount per week, per month, or per year, and is paid weekly, half-monthly, or monthly.

Sale on account A sale for which no money is received at the time it is made; also known as a sale for credit.

Sales invoice A business form, prepared whenever goods or services are sold on account, showing a description of goods or services, the price, and other information. *See* Purchase invoice.

Sales journal A special columnar journal in which are recorded the accounting entries for all sales of merchandise on account.

Service business A business that sells a service, not a product.

Sole proprietorship A business enterprise the equity of which belongs entirely to one person.

Solvency ratio One of a number of ratios or numbers calculated by formula and used to help assess the company's ability to pay its debts. *Same as* Liquidity ratio.

Source document A business paper, such as an invoice, that is the original record of a transaction and that provides the information needed when accounting for the transaction.

Statement of account A detailed record of a customer's account usually for a period of one month.

Stock-in-trade The goods handled by a merchandising business. *Same as* Merchandise inventory.

Straight-line method of depreciation A method of calculating the depreciation of an asset whereby the depreciation is apportioned equally to each year of the asset's life. *Contrast* Declining-balance method of depreciation.

Subsidiary ledger A separate ledger that contains a number of accounts of a similar type, such as the accounts receivable ledger or the accounts payable ledger. The accounts in a subsidiary ledger make up the detailed information in respect to one particular control account in the general ledger.

Synoptic journal A multi-columned journal with a number of selected special columns and two general columns. The special columns are used to record the more frequently occurring items; the two general columns are used to record the less frequently occurring items. Each of the special columns is reserved for a specific type of entry as indicated in the column heading. At posting time, the totals of the special columns are posted to the general journal, and not the individual items contained in the columns.

T

T4 slip A formal document prepared by employers for all employees showing payroll data for the year, such as total gross pay and total income tax deducted, which is used to work out an individual's income tax return.

Taking off a trial balance The process of comparing the total value of the debit accounts in a ledger with the total value of the credit accounts in a ledger. *See* Trial balance.

Taxable earnings These equal the employee's gross pay after the premiums for Canada Pension Plan, unemployment insurance, and any registered pension plan have been deducted.

Temporary account An account that accumulates data for only one fiscal period at a time. Revenue, expense, and drawings accounts are temporary. *Same as* Nominal account.

Terms of sale The conditions agreed to at the time of sale, between the buyer and the seller, in respect to the length of time allowed for payment and whether a cash discount can be taken.

Three-column account The most commonly used type of account, in which there are three money columns, one for the debit amounts, one for the credit amounts, and one for the amount of the balance. *Same as* Balance column account.

Timecard A card that records the times that an employee starts and finishes work each day. A timecard is usually for a one- or two-week period.

Times interest earned ratio The number arrived at by formula to show the company's ability to cover its interest expense out of net earnings.

Total personal exemptions An amount made up of several items, limited by regulation, the total of which may be deducted from earnings for income tax purposes.

Trading business A business that buys goods in order to sell them at a higher price for profit. *Same as* Merchandising business.

Transaction *See* Business transaction.

Transposition error A mistake caused by the interchanging of digits when transferring figures from one place to another. The trial balance difference that results from such an error is always exactly divisible by 9.

Trend analysis A document that presents financial data in percentages, for a number of periods, so that tendencies can be seen that are not evident when looking at the dollar figures alone.

Trial balance A special listing of all the accounts balances in a ledger, the purpose of which is to see if the dollar value of the accounts with debit balances is equal to the dollar value of the accounts with credit balances. *See* Taking off a trial balance.

Two-column general journal A simple journal with two money columns, one for the debit amounts and one for the credit amounts.

V

Valuation account An account that must be considered along with a given asset account to show the true value of the asset account. *Same as* Contra account.

W

Wages An amount paid periodically to an employee based on the number of hours worked or the quantity of goods produced. Wages are usually paid on a weekly basis.

Wholesaler A merchandising business that buys goods from manufacturers and other suppliers and sells them to retailers with a view to making a profit.

Work sheet An informal business form prepared in pencil on columnar bookkeeping paper, used to organize and plan the information for the financial statements.

Working capital The difference between the current assets and the current liabilities of a business.

Index

A

Abbreviations, on financial statements, 22
Account, defined, 68
Accountability, 282–284
    defined, 282
Account balances, 83–84
    calculating, 83
    exceptional, 84
    interpreting, 84
Account form of balance sheet, 18–22, 256
Accounting
    careers in, *see* Careers in accounting
    objectives of, 1
    professional accountancy, 4, 8–9
    study of, 3–4, 8–9
    usefulness to business, 2
    vs. bookkeeping, 169–170
Accounting controls, 221, 510–516
Accounting cycle, 6–7, 186–187, 265–266
    steps in the complete accounting cycle, 330, 331
Accounting department of a business, 5–6
Accounting entry, defined, 75
Accounting equation, fundamental, 15–16
Accounting organizations, 8
Accounting package (computerized accounting), 154–157
Accounting period, 106
Accounting tasks, 5–6
Accounting terms, 10, 35, 59, 92, 123, 159, 200, 238, 271, 315, 347, 395, 451, 522, 593, 660
Accounts payable, 16
    procedures for maintaining, 222–223
    subsidiary ledger for, 213
Accounts receivable, 16
    subsidiary ledger for, 213
        flowcharts on procedures, 217–220
Accounts receivable turnover, 579
Account title, 180
Acid-test ratio, 578

Adjusting entries
    adjustment process, 285–286
    computer exercises, 313–315
    defined, 286
    for depreciation, 296–302
    effect on financial statements, 308–309
    and the eight-column work sheet, 286
    for insurance used, 289–291
    journalizing and posting, 337
    for late purchase invoices, 291–293
    for supplies used, 287–289
Analyzing financial statements
    common-size statements, 568–571
    comparative statements, 564–568
    key ratios and statistics, 576–583
    trend analysis, 571–572
    users of financial statements, 563–564
Analyzing transactions, 53–54
Assets, 14
    claims against, 26–27
Audit, defined, 283
Auditing, 4
Audit strip (detailed audit tape), 500–501

B

Balance column account, 178
    compared with T-account, 179
Balance sheet, 18–22
    account form, 256
    classified, 256, 257
    common-size, 570–571
    equity section of, 262–264
    important features of, 21–22
    report form, 256
    steps in preparing, 19–21
    in three-ledger system, 215
    updating, 51
Bank accounts, business, 107, 649–650
Bank accounts, personal, 482–486

687

Bank advices, 142
Bank credit cards, 488–492
    accounting for bank credit card transactions, 490–491
    advantages and disadvantages of, 489–490
    common features of, 489
    the role of the bank and the credit card centre, 491–492
Bank deposit, defined, 484
Banking, personal, 482–486
Banking for a business, 496–506
Bank reconciliation, 512–516
    bringing the accounts up-to-date, 515
    defined, 513
    locating the discrepancy items, 514–515
    personal bank reconciliation, 516
    recording the discrepancy items, 515
Bank reconciliation statement, 513
Bank statements
    for a personal chequing account, 483
Bookkeeping
    manually or by computer, 170
    vs. accounting, 169–170
Book of original entry, 172. *See also* Journal
Business entity concept, 29, 672
Business ownership, forms of, 3
Business transactions, 43

C

C.O.D. (cash on delivery), 443
Canada Pension Plan, 622–623
    employee contributions, 622–623
    employer's contribution to, 623, 642
Canadian Institute of Chartered Accountants (CICA), 28
Capital, 14, 15
Careers in accounting, 12–13, 41–42, 66–67, 101–102, 132–133, 166–168, 208–210, 247–248, 280–281, 327–328, 359–360, 409–410, 468–469, 537–538, 611–612, 670–671
Case studies, 38–40, 63–65, 98–100, 128–132, 165–166, 205–207, 244–246, 275–279, 323–326, 353–358, 403–408, 463–467, 532–536, 603–610, 665–669
Cash
    payment of payroll by, 648–649, 653
    procedures for control of, 511–512
Cash discounts, 442–447
    accounting for, 443–446
    defined, 442–443
    on the income statement, 447
    terms of sale, 443
Cash payments journal, 435–436
Cash receipts journal, 433–434
Cash receipts list, 141
Cash receipts of a business, 496–498
Cash refunds, 385
Cash registers, 512
    point-of-sale terminals, 498
    stand-alone electronic cash registers, 498, 499
Cash sale
    sales tax on, 150–151
Cash sales slip, 135
Cash short or over, 504
Certified cheques, 485–486
Certified General Accountants (CGAs), 8, 9
Certified Management Accountants (CMAs), 8, 9
Change fund (float), 498, 500
Charge sale, 443
    sales tax on, 151–152
Chartered Accountants (CAs), 8, 9
Chart of accounts, 116–117
Cheque copies, 140
Cheques, 482, 484
    certified, 485–486
    NSF, 484–485
    payroll, 649–650, 653
    post-dated, 486
Claims against the assets, 26–27
Classified financial statements, 256–257
Closing an account, 330, 339–343
Closing entries
    four-step procedure for recording, 339–341
    for a merchandising business, 376–378
    summary of purposes, 342–343
Collection period, 579
Columnar journal. *See* Synoptic journal
Columnar paper, use of, 22
Commission, 616
Common-size financial statements, 568–571
    computer exercise, 592
    defined, 569
Comparative financial statements, 564–568
Computerized accounting
    accounting for a merchandising business, 392–393
    accounting package, 154–155, 157
    accounting spreadsheet, 31–34, 57–59
    adjusting entries (exercises), 313–315
    computer menu, 155–157
    data entry, 196–198
    income statement, 122
    payroll packages, 656–659
    six-column work sheet, 269–270
    subsidiary ledgers, 235–236
    trend analysis and key ratios and statistics (exercises), 590–592
Computers in accounting, 9
Conservatism, principle of, 29, 672
Consistency principle, 283–284, 673–674
Continuing concern concept, 29, 672
Contra account, 300
Control accounts, 214–215
    balancing subsidiary ledger with, 220, 221
Controls, accounting, 510–516
Corporation, 3
Correcting journal entry, 185

Cost of goods sold, 362–363
    formula, 367
    revised formula, 389
Cost principle, 144, 673
Credit, 73. *See also* Debit and credit
    buying and selling on, 118
    in general journal, 174
Credit cards, 488–492. *See* Bank credit cards
Credit invoice (credit note), 382–384
    defined, 383
Creditors, 16
    creditors' claims first, 26–27
    as users of financial statements, 283
Cross balancing, 418–419
Cross-referencing, 182–183
    in the five-journal system, 438
    in the synoptic journal, 421, 424–425
Current bank account, 504
Current ratio, 577–578

D

Daily interest savings account, 482
Data entry, 196–198
Date, recording in journal, 173, 174
Debit, 73
    in general journal, 174
Debit and credit
    applying the rules of, 74–80
    in the expanded ledger, 117
Debtors, 16
Debt ratio, 580, 581
Declining-balance method of depreciation, 298–299
Deposit: preparing receipts for, 504–506
Depreciation
    adjusting entry for, 300–302
    declining-balance method, 298–299
    defined, 296
    straight-line method, 297–298
Discounts allowed, 446, 447
Discounts earned, 446, 447
Double-entry system of accounting, 80–81
Drawings, 113–114
Dual purpose sales slip, 137
Duty, 371

E

Employee's earnings record, 654
End-of-period procedure, 330
Equation analysis sheet, 44–45
    updating, 45–50
Equity. *See* Owner's equity
Equity ratio, 580, 581
Equity section
    of balance sheet, 262–264
Errors
    correcting, 184–185
    in subsidiary ledger balance, locating, 223
    in trial balance, detecting, 188–190
Expense, 103, 112

F

Financial position of a business, 14
Financial statements
    analyzing. *See* Analyzing financial statements
    classified, 256–257
    effect of adjusting entries, 308–309
    quality of, 283
    typed or printed, 264, 265
    users of, 282–283
    work sheet and, 259–266
Fiscal period, 106
Five-journal system, 432–438
    cash payments journal, 435–436
    cash receipts journal, 433–434
    cross-referencing, 438
    posting in, 438
    purchases journal, 436–437
    sales journal, 434–435
Fixed assets, 296
Float, 498, 500
Forwarding, 186
Freight-in account, 371
Full disclosure principle, 284, 674
Fundamental accounting equation, 15–16

G

GAAPs. *See* Generally accepted accounting principles
General ledger, 213
Generally accepted accounting principles, 28–29, 672–674
    business entity concept, 29, 672
    conservatism, principle of, 29, 672
    consistency principle, 283–284, 673–674
    continuing concern concept, 29, 672
    cost principle, 144, 673
    full disclosure principle, 284, 674
    matching principle, 113, 673
    materiality principle, 284, 674
    objectivity principle, 55, 672–673
    revenue recognition convention, 111–112, 673
    time period concept, 107, 673
Going concern concept, 29, 672
Gross pay, 613–616
Gross profit, 363
Group life insurance, payroll deductions for, 631

H

Health insurance
    employer's contribution to, 643
    payroll deduction for, 630

I

Imprest method of handling petty cash, 477–479
"In balance", 87
Income statement, 103–107
    classified, 257
    common-size, 568–570
    computerized accounting, 122
    cost of goods sold on, 362–363
    defined, 103
    for a merchandising business, 375–376
    returns and allowances on, 388–389
Income Summary account, 341
Income tax, payroll deduction for, 625–629
    employee contributions, 628–629
    taxable earnings, 628
    total personal exemption, 625, 628
Industrial accountants, 4
Insiders of a company, 563
Institute of Chartered Accountants, 9
Institutional accountants, 4
Internal control, 510–511
Inventory. *See* Merchandise inventory
Inventory control. *See* Periodic inventory method; Perpetual inventory method
Inventory turnover, 579–580
Investors, as users of financial statements, 283

J

Journal
    defined, 172
    synoptic. *See* Synoptic journal
    two-column general, 172–175
Journal entries, steps in recording, 174
Journalizing, 172, 173–174
    in the five-journal system, 432–437
    in the synoptic journal, 411–417, 426–427

L

Late deposit, 514
Late discounts, 446
Ledger
    balance column account compared with T-account, 178, 179
    balancing, 86–90
    completing, 116–119
    defined, 68
    expanded, 109–114
    forms of, 69
Ledger accounts, 68–71
    important features of, 71
Liabilities, 14
Limited company. *See* Corporation
Liquidity, 21
Liquidity ratios, 577–582

M

Mail receipts, 496
Managers, as users of financial statements, 282
Manufacturing business, 3
Matching principle, 113, 673
Materiality principle, 284, 674
Menu (computer), 155–157
Merchandise inventory, 361–362
    account, 370
    balance sheet presentation for, 362
    inventory cycle, 365, 366
    two aspects of, 363, 364
Merchandising business, 3, 361
    computerized accounting for, 392–393
    income statement for, 375–376
    new accounts for, 373, 374
Multi-columnar journal. *See* Synoptic journal

N

Neatness, importance of, 23
"Net 30", 443
"Net 60", 443
Net income, 103, 253
Net loss, 103, 253
Net pay, calculating, 632
Net worth, 14
Nominal accounts
    closing out, 330
    defined, 329–330
Non-routine entries
    to subsidiary ledgers, 222–223
    in the synoptic journal, 426–427
NSF cheques, 484–485

O

Objectivity principle, 55, 672–673
"On account", 119, 443
"1/15, N/60", 443
Opening an account, 180
Opening entry, 175
"Out of balance", 87
Outsiders of a company, 564
Outstanding cheque, 514
Over-the-counter sales, 496–498
Owner's equity, 14, 15
Owners, as users of financial statements, 283

P

Particulars column, 174
Partnership, 3
Payment on account, 119
Payroll
    defined, 613
    payment to employees, 648–650
    recording, 641–646, 653–654
Payroll deductions, 620–632
    calculating net pay, 632
Payroll journal, 620–621
    completing, 633

proving the accuracy of, 633
using as a book of original entry, 653
Payroll liabilities, employer's remittance of, 645–646
Payroll package (computerized accounting), 656–659
Pencil footings, 83
Periodic inventory method, 364, 365–367, 369–371
    limitation of, 367
    list of words and phrases, 373
Perpetual inventory method, 364, 365
Personal chequing accounts, 482, 483, 484–486
Personal exemption from income tax, 625, 628
Petty cash fund, 476–479
    defined, 476
Petty cash voucher, 477–478
Physical inventory, 367
Pin totals, 83
Point-of-sale terminals, 498
Post-closing trial balance, 330, 343
Post-dated cheques, 486
Posting, 178–187
    in the five journal system, 438
    six steps in, 180, 181
    the synoptic journal, 420–425
Posting reference, 172
Prepaid expenses, adjusting for, 289–291
Profitability percentages, 582–583
Proving the cash, 497–498, 502–503
Public accountant, 4
Purchase invoice, 138–139
    late-arriving, 291–293
Purchase on account, 119
Purchases account, 370
Purchases journal, 436–437
Pure savings account, 482

Q

Quick ratio, 578

R

Rate of return on net sales, 582–583
Ratios and statistics, in financial analysis, 576–583
    computer exercise, 591
Real accounts, defined, 329
Receipt on account, 119
Recordkeeping, basic practices in, 22–23
Registered pension plans, 625
    employer's contribution to, 642–643
Registered retirement savings plans, 625
Remittance advice, 141
Replenishing petty cash, 478–479
Report form of balance sheet, 256
Restrictive endorsement, 505
Retailer, 361
Retail sales tax, 149–152
Return on owner's equity, 583

Returns and allowances, 382–389
    on the income statement, 388–389
    purchases returns and allowances accounts, 386
    sales returns and allowances accounts, 385–386
Revenue, 103, 110–111
Revenue recognition convention, 111–112, 673
Ruled lines, use of, 23

S

Salaries, 614
Sale on account, 119
Sales account, 370–371
Sales invoice, 136
Sales journal, 434–435
Sales tax, 149–152
    accounting for, 150–152
    remitting, 152
Savings accounts, 482
Service business, 3
Shareholders, as users of financial statements, 283
"60 days", 443
Social Insurance Number, 621
Sole-proprietorship, 3
Solvency ratios, 577–582
Source documents, 54–57, 134–149
    defined, 134
    number of copies of, 144
    summary of, and related accounting entries, 143
Spreadsheet, accounting, 31–34
    recording transactions on, 57–59
Statement of account, 229–233
    automated system, 230–232
    and the customer, 232–233
    defined, 229
    manual system, 230
Stock brokers, as users of financial statements, 283
Stock-in-trade. See Merchandise inventory
Straight-line method of calculating depreciation, 297–298, 299
Subsidiary ledger
    balancing, 220, 221
    defined, 214
    keeping up-to-date, 223
    locating errors in, 223
    non-routine entries to, 222–223
Subsidiary ledger accounting, 211–237
    computerized accounting, 235–236
    customer's statement of account, 229–233
    subsidiary ledger systems, 217–223
    subsidiary ledger theory, 212–215
Summary exercise, 470–475
Supplementary exercises, 539–562
Synoptic journal, 411–427
    cross balancing, 418–419
    forwarding in, 419

journalizing in, 411–417
    variations, 426–427
  posting, 420–425
  two-journal system, 426

T

T4 slip, 654
T-account, compared with balance column account, 179
Terms of sale, 443
"30 days", 443
Three-ledger system, 213–215
Timecards, 614–616
Time period concept, 107, 673
Times interest earned ratio, 581–582
Transactions, analyzing, 53–54
Transposition error, 190
Trend analysis, 571–572
  computer exercise, 590
Trial balance, 86–90
  out of balance, 89–90
  detecting errors in, 188–190
  importance of, 89
  post-closing, 343
  procedure unchanged in expanded ledger, 118
  taking off, 87–88
Two-column general journal, 172–175
Two-journal system, 426
"2/10, N/30", 443

U

Unemployment insurance, 623–624
  employee contributions, 623–624
  employer's contribution, 624
  employer's contribution to, 642
Union dues, payroll deduction for, 630–631
Universal Product Code (UPC), 393

W

Wages, 614–616
Wholesaler, 361
Women in accounting, 8–9
Work habits, developing good, 54
Working capital, 578
Working capital ratio, 577–578
Work sheet
  balancing, 303
  defined, 249
  eight-column
    balancing, 303
    extending, 302–303
  extending, 302, 303
  finalizing for a loss situation, 253
  and financial statements, 259–266
  for a merchandising business, 373–378
  six-column work sheet (computerized accounting), 269–270
  steps in balancing, 252
  steps in preparing, 249–252
  uses of, 343

EveryWoman's® Health

The Complete Guide to Body and Mind

EveryWoman's®
Health

The Complete Guide to Body and Mind

FOURTH EDITION

By 15 Women Doctors

JUNE JACKSON CHRISTMAS, M.D. • ELIZABETH B. CONNELL, M.D. • KATHRYN SCHROTENBOER COX, M.D. • FRANCES DREW, M.D. • BARBARA GASTEL, M.D. • ANNE GELLER, M.D. • TOBY OREM GRAHAM, M.D. • MARY JANE GRAY, M.D. • MARGARET NELSEN HARKER, M.D. • CHRISTINE E. HAYCOCK, M.D. • DOROTHY HICKS, M.D. • FRANCES M. LOVE, M.D. • HELENE MACLEAN • LONNY MYERS, M.D. • MAUREEN MYLANDER • KATHRYN LYLE STEPHENSON, M.D. • LOUISE TYRER, M.D.

DOUGLASS S. THOMPSON, M.D., CONSULTING EDITOR

Edited by Helene MacLean

Illustrated by Leonard D. Dank

GUILDAMERICA
B O O K S™

DOUBLEDAY BOOK & MUSIC CLUBS, INC.
GARDEN CITY, NEW YORK

Copyright © 1980, 1982, 1985, 1990 by Doubleday Book & Music Clubs, Inc.
All Rights Reserved
Printed in the United States of America
EveryWoman's® and EveryWoman's Library® are trademarks of Doubleday
Book & Music Clubs, Inc.

GuildAmerica Books™ is a trademark registration pending on behalf of
Doubleday Book & Music Clubs, Inc.

Although the information and guidance in this book are appropriate
in most cases, and may supplement your physician's advice, it is recommended
that you consult your own physician concerning your personal medical
condition.

Book design by Robert Aulicino
Art direction by Diana Klemin

Quality Printing and Binding by:
Berryville Graphics
P.O. Box 272
Berryville, VA 22611 U.S.A.

CONTRIBUTORS

Consulting Editor DOUGLASS S. THOMPSON, M.D.
Clinical Professor of Health Services Administration, University of Pittsburgh Graduate School of Public Health; formerly Clinical Professor of Obstetrics and Gynecology and Clinical Associate Professor of Community Medicine, University of Pittsburgh School of Medicine

Illustrator LEONARD D. DANK
Consultant Medical Illustrator, St. Luke's–Roosevelt Hospital Center and Women's Hospital, New York City

Authors

JUNE JACKSON CHRISTMAS, M.D., Past President, American Public Health Association; Professor Emeritus of Behavioral Science, City University of New York Medical School, New York City

ELIZABETH B. CONNELL, M.D., Professor, Department of Gynecology and Obstetrics, Emory University School of Medicine, Atlanta, Georgia

KATHRYN SCHROTENBOER COX, M.D., Assistant Attending Physician, Obstetrics and Gynecology, New York Hospital–Cornell Medical Center; Clinical Instructor, Cornell University Medical College, New York City

FRANCES DREW, M.D., M.P.H., Professor of Community Medicine, University of Pittsburgh School of Medicine, Pittsburgh, Pennsylvania

BARBARA GASTEL, M.D., M.P.H., Formerly of National Institutes on Aging, Bethesda, Maryland

ANNE GELLER, M.D., Chief, Smithers Alcoholism Treatment and Training Center, St. Luke's–Roosevelt Hospital Center, New York City; Assistant Professor of Social Medicine, College of Physicians and Surgeons, Columbia University, New York City

TOBY OREM GRAHAM, M.D., Associate Professor of Medicine, University of Pittsburgh School of Medicine, Pittsburgh, Pennsylvania

MARY JANE GRAY, M.D., Professor of Obstetrics and Gynecology, University of North Carolina Medical School, Chapel Hill

CONTRIBUTORS

MARGARET NELSEN HARKER, M.D., Adult General Medicine, Morehead City, North Carolina; Electronics Data Systems (1979–1982), Raleigh, North Carolina; Assistant Professor of Surgery (1975–1979), University of North Carolina Medical School, Chapel Hill

CHRISTINE E. HAYCOCK, M.D., Professor of Surgery, University of Medicine and Dentistry of New Jersey, New Jersey Medical School, Newark; Fellow, American College of Sports Medicine

DOROTHY HICKS, M.D., Professor of Obstetrics and Gynecology, University of Miami School of Medicine; Director, Rape Treatment Center, Jackson Memorial Hospital, Miami, Florida

FRANCES M. LOVE, M.D. (deceased), Specialist in Occupational Medicine; Retired Southwestern Regional Medical Director, Gulf Oil Corporation

HELENE MACLEAN, Medical Writer and Editor; Author, *Caring for Your Parents*

LONNY MYERS, M.D., American College of Sexologists, Chicago, Illinois

MAUREEN MYLANDER, National Institutes of Health, Bethesda, Maryland

KATHRYN LYLE STEPHENSON, M.D., Santa Barbara Cottage Hospital, Santa Barbara, California

LOUISE TYRER, M.D., Vice-President for Medical Affairs, Planned Parenthood Federation of America, Inc.

CONTENTS

Part One   GUIDE TO TOTAL HEALTH

THE HEALTHY WOMAN   21
June Jackson Christmas, M.D.

KNOW HOW YOUR BODY FUNCTIONS

The Skeletal Muscular System: The Framework   The Circulatory System: Movement of Blood   The Respiratory System: Supply of Oxygen   The Digestive System: Nourishment   The Urinary System: Removal of Waste   The Nervous System: Communication and Control   The Endocrine System: Internal Control and Balance   The Reproductive System: Perpetuation of the Species

THE RELATIONSHIP BETWEEN PHYSICAL AND MENTAL HEALTH

TAKE RESPONSIBILITY FOR YOUR OWN HEALTH

Primary Prevention: Prevention of Illness   Secondary Prevention: Early Diagnosis and Treatment   Tertiary Prevention: Rehabilitation

BE AN ACTIVE WELL-INFORMED PARTNER IN HEALTH CARE

Holistic Health   Self-Care   Health Services

NUTRITION, WEIGHT, AND GENERAL WELL-BEING   55
Toby Orem Graham, M.D., and Helene MacLean

THE NUTRIENT CONTENT OF FOOD

Protein   Carbohydrates   Fat   Vitamins   Minerals   Water and Fiber   Balanced Nutrition

SELECTION OF FOODS FOR BALANCED NUTRITION

Food Groups   Food Labeling   Food Additives   The Importance of Breakfast   Fast Foods

NUTRITIONAL NEEDS AT SPECIAL AGES AND STAGES

Nutrition in Pregnancy   Nutrition When Breast Feeding
Nutrition for the Older Woman

WEIGHT
Desirable Weight   Overweight and Obesity   Dieting
Exercise   Drugs   Group Therapy and Behavior Modification
Underweight

TWO MAJOR EATING DISORDERS
Anorexia Nervosa   Bulimia

FRAUDS

FITNESS   Christine E. Haycock, M.D.   109

BENEFITS OF PHYSICAL FITNESS

YOUR BODY'S ENERGY

THE FIRST STEP—A PHYSICAL EXAMINATION

SUITABLE CLOTHES AND PROPER EQUIPMENT

INJURIES

DEVELOPING A FITNESS PROGRAM TO CONDITION YOUR BODY

SEXUAL HEALTH   Lonny Myers, M.D.   125

SEXUAL STAGES
Infancy and Childhood   Adolescence   Adulthood

SEX AND HEALTH CARE

LOVE

SELF-RESPECT

FEMALE SEXUAL RESPONSE
Physiological Response   Questions Often Asked About Orgasm

SEXUAL ENRICHMENT FOR COUPLES

SEXUAL THERAPY

CONTENTS 9

Sexual Dysfunction—Physical Conditions   Sexual Dysfunction—Psychological Causes

SEX AND SINGLE WOMEN

EXTRAMARITAL SEX

SEXUAL ADDICTION

ALTERNATIVES IN SEXUAL EXPRESSION

Masturbation   Sexual Fantasies   Lesbianism and Bisexuality

SEX AND EDUCATION FOR PARENTHOOD BY CHOICE

CONTRACEPTION AND ABORTION 159
Elizabeth B. Connell, M.D.

RISK-BENEFIT RATIO

SELECTION OF METHOD

HORMONAL METHODS—FEMALE: "THE PILL"

Major Severe Side Effects   Contraindications   Minor Adverse Side Effects   Beneficial Side Effects   Injectables   Implants   "Morning After" Pill

HORMONAL METHODS—MALE

INTRAUTERINE DEVICES

Adverse Side Effects   Contraindications

BARRIER CONTRACEPTIVES

Diaphragm   Cervical Cap   Vaginal Sponge   Condom   Barrier Methods in Combination

NATURAL FAMILY PLANNING—PERIODIC ABSTINENCE

FEMALE STERILIZATION

MALE STERILIZATION

INDUCED ABORTION

Menstrual Extraction   Dilatation and Evacuation (D&E)

Dilatation and Curettage (D&C)   Intra-Amniotic Infusion
Hysterotomy and Hysterectomy   Drugs   Counseling

AVAILABILITY OF EFFECTIVE CONTRACEPTION AND SAFE ABORTION

PREGNANCY AND CHILDBIRTH 191
Kathryn Schrotenboer Cox, M.D.

CONCEPTION AND EARLY DEVELOPMENT

DIAGNOSIS OF PREGNANCY
Signs and Symptoms   Pregnancy Tests

WHO WILL DELIVER YOUR BABY?
Obstetrician-Gynecologist   Family Practitioner   Nurse-Midwife   Lay Midwife

WHERE WILL YOU HAVE YOUR BABY?
Hospital Delivery   Home Delivery   Childbearing Center Delivery

HEALTH CARE DURING NORMAL PREGNANCY
Emotional Changes   Diet   Smoking, Alcohol, and Drugs   Activity

COMPLICATIONS OF PREGNANCY
Bleeding and Spontaneous Abortion (Miscarriage)   Bleeding in Later Pregnancy   Ectopic Pregnancy   Pre-eclampsia and Eclampsia (formerly called toxemia of pregnancy)   Chronic and Genetic Diseases   Infections   Rh Disease   Intrauterine Fetal Death   Hydatidiform Mole

EVALUATING FETAL HEALTH
Sonography   Amniocentesis   Chorionic Villi Sampling   Alpha-Feto Protein Assessment   Prenatal DNA Studies   Other Procedures for Prenatal Diagnosis   Fetal Monitors

LABOR AND DELIVERY
Natural Childbirth   First Stage of Labor—Dilatation of the Cervix   Anesthesia   Second Stage of Labor—Delivery   Third Stage of Labor—Afterbirth

CESARIAN SECTION

CONTENTS 11

AFTER THE DELIVERY
Rooming-In   Hospital Visitors   The "Baby Blues"   Physical Recovery   Breast-Feeding

INFERTILITY Kathryn Schrotenboer Cox, M.D.   247

MALE INFERTILITY
Causes of Male Infertility   Tests for Male Infertility   Treatment for Male Infertility

FEMALE INFERTILITY
Causes of Female Infertility   Tests for Female Infertility   Treatment for Female Infertility

ARTIFICIAL INSEMINATION

NEW DEVELOPMENTS IN INFERTILITY

GYNECOLOGIC DISEASES AND TREATMENT   267
Mary Jane Gray, M.D.

FINDING CAUSES OF COMMON PROBLEMS
Doctor/Patient Relationship   Pelvic Examination   Pap Smear   X-ray, Sonography, Laparoscopy, Colposcopy, and Hysteroscopy   Biopsy

PROBLEMS AND DISEASES
Menstrual Problems   Other Vaginal Bleeding   Lower Abdominal Pain   Vaginal Discharge   Incontinence   Prolapse of the Uterus   Infections   Tumors   Endocrine Problems

TYPES OF GYNECOLOGIC TREATMENT
Treatment of Infection   Hormone Therapy   Cautery   Surgery   Radiation Therapy   Chemotherapy   Counseling

SEXUALLY TRANSMISSIBLE DISEASES   305
Louise Tyrer, M.D.

WHAT WOMEN NEED TO KNOW ABOUT STD

DESCRIPTION OF SPECIFIC STDS
AIDS (Acquired Immune Deficiency Syndrome)   Chancroid

Chlamydial Infections   Gonorrhea   Granuloma Inguinale
Hemophilus Vaginalis (HV) and Corynebacterium Vaginale
Hepatitis B   Herpes Simplex Virus Infection (Genital Herpes)
Molluscum Contagiosum   Pelvic Inflammatory Disease (PID)
Pubic Lice ("Crabs")   Scabies   Syphilis   Trichomoniasis
Urethritis   Vaginitis (Nonspecific)   Venereal or Genital Warts
(Condyloma Acuminata)   Yeast Infections (Monilia)

OTHER STDS AND SEXUAL PRACTICES

Amebiasis   Giardiasis

BREAST CARE   Margaret Nelsen Harker, M.D.   329

GROWTH AND DEVELOPMENT OF THE BREAST

POSTMENOPAUSAL ESTROGENS AND THE BREAST

BREAST SELF-EXAMINATION

EVERYDAY BREAST CARE

BREAST DISORDERS

Anatomical Abnormalities and Endocrine Dysfunction   Normal
Physiologic Changes   Benign Cysts and Tumors   Infections
Malignant Disease

TREATMENT

Nonmalignant Disorders   Breast Cancer

COSMETIC SURGERY   361
Kathryn Lyle Stephenson, M.D.

DECIDING TO UNDERGO COSMETIC SURGERY

CONSULTATION WITH THE COSMETIC SURGEON

SURGICAL PROCEDURES

Rhinoplasty (Nose Alteration)   Rhytidoplasty (Face Lift)
Abrasion and Chemosurgery   Removing Scars and Deep
Wrinkles   Maxilloplasty, Mandibuloplasty, Mentoplasty, and
Malarplasty   Blepharoplasty (Eyelid Lift)   Eyebrow Lift
Otoplasty   Mammaplasty   Plastic Surgery Procedures
Following Mastectomy   Lipectomy   Liposuction   Spider
Hemangioma and Capillary Varicosities

YOU DECIDED TO HAVE COSMETIC SURGERY

SUBSTANCE ABUSE 395
Helene MacLean and Anne Geller, M.D.

MOOD-ALTERING DRUGS

ALCOHOL

Women and Drinking Problems   Alcohol Dependence (Alcoholism)   Alcoholism as a Family Problem   Alcohol and Pregnancy

PRESCRIPTION DRUGS

Tranquilizers   Sleeping Pills   Amphetamines

NON-PRESCRIPTION DRUGS

Weight-Loss Drugs   Nicotine (Cigarette Smoking)   Caffeine

ILLEGAL DRUGS

Cocaine   Heroin   Marijuana   LSD

CONCLUSION

RAPE AND FAMILY ABUSE   Dorothy Hicks, M.D. 427

SEXUAL ASSAULT: RAPE

History   Myths About Rape   Current Statistics   Updating the Law   Marital Rape   Date Rape   Protecting Yourself   What You Should Do If Attacked   Treatment

FAMILY ABUSE AND VIOLENCE

Battering   Child Abuse and Neglect   Abuse of the Elderly

INCEST

HEALTH ON THE JOB 463
Frances M. Love, M.D. and Helene MacLean

WELL-BEING IN THE WORKPLACE

Noise   Bad Air   Aches and Pains   Eyestrain and Irritation   Photocopiers   VDTs

THE HEALTH-RELATED PROFESSIONS

STRESS

FOOD AND DRINK ON THE JOB

SEXUAL HARASSMENT

Sexual Harassment and the Law   Some Practical Suggestions

PREGNANCY

OTHER BENEFITS

AGING HEALTHFULLY—YOUR BODY   485
Helene MacLean and Barbara Gastel, M.D., M.P.H.

AGE-RELATED CHANGES IN PARTS OF THE BODY

Skin   Eyes   Ears   Teeth and Gums   Nervous System
Heart and Blood Vessels   Lungs   Digestive System   Urinary
and Reproductive Systems   Sexual Response   Bones and Joints
Feet   Diabetes   Infection

GOOD MEDICAL CARE

MEDICATION

EXERCISE

SAFETY

AGING HEALTHFULLY—YOUR MIND AND   519
SPIRIT   Maureen Mylander

PROBLEMS FACING OLDER WOMEN

Income   Housing and Transportation   Crime   Widowhood
Social Supports   Sex and Sensuality   Self-Image
Depression   Sleep Problems   Drugs and Alcohol   Suicide
Psychotherapy and Personal Growth

ADAPTATION

Earning Power   Learning Power   Networking   Loving
Pets   Shared Living   Exercise   Life Work   Political Clout

LOOKING AHEAD

YOU, YOUR DOCTORS, AND THE HEALTH   545
CARE SYSTEM   Frances Drew, M.D., M.P.H.

CONTENTS 15

CHOOSING YOUR DOCTORS
Geography   Qualifications   Fees   Style of Practice   Age, Personality, and Subculture   Sex of Physician   The First Visit   Changing Doctors   Hospital Outpatient Departments   Choosing a Specialist   Getting a Second Opinion

PAYMENT PLANS
Health Maintenance Organizations (HMOs)   Blue Cross/Blue Shield   Medicare   Medicaid

BEING A WOMAN AND A PATIENT

EMERGENCY CARE

HOSPITALS
Your Rights as a Patient   Additional Safeguards   Your Comfort as a Patient   Cooperative Care Units

YOU AND YOUR PHYSICIAN
What You Have a Right to Expect from Your Physician   What You Should Not Expect from Your Physician   What Your Physician Has a Right to Expect from You

THE COMMUNITY OF HEALTH CARE

Part Two   ENCYCLOPEDIA OF HEALTH AND MEDICAL TERMS   585

APPENDIXES   797
SUGGESTED HEALTH EXAMINATIONS FOR WOMEN

IMMUNIZATION GUIDE

COMMON MEDICAL TERMS

HOW TO READ A PRESCRIPTION

BRAND AND GENERIC NAMES OF COMMONLY PRESCRIBED DRUGS

HEALTH CARE PERSONNEL

DIRECTORY OF HEALTH INFORMATION

INDEX   827

LIST OF ILLUSTRATIONS

Part One

Skeletal System 23–24
Voluntary Muscular System 25
Circulatory System 27–28
Respiratory System 31
Digestive System 32–33
Urinary System 35
Nervous System 37
Endocrine System 40
Female Reproductive System 43–44
Male Reproductive System 46
Menstrual Cycle 47
Common Contraceptive Methods 161
Laparoscopic Tubal Sterilization 183
Vasectomy 183
Dilatation and Evacuation 186
Female Genital Tract: Ovulation, Fertilization, and Implantation 194
Uterine-Fetal Relationship 197
Weight Gain During Pregnancy 208
Amniocentesis 226
Stages of Labor 231
Positions of the Fetus 238
Causes of Male Infertility 251
Causes of Female Infertility 252, 255
Tests for Infertility 258–259
Vaginal Examination 270
Bimanual Examination of Uterus 271
Abdominal and Vaginal Hysterectomy 297
Pelvis After Hysterectomy 299
Development of the Breast 331
Cross-Section of the Breast 333
How to Examine Your Breasts 336–337
Cystic Disease 344
Signs of Breast Cancer 349
Growth of Breast Cancer 350
The Types of Mastectomies 357
Cosmetic Surgery of the Nose 370
Cosmetic Surgery of the Face 373
Cosmetic Surgery of the Breast 383
Nicotine and the Body 417

A WOMAN'S BODY: STRUCTURE AND FUNCTIONS
A 16-page full-color portfolio after page 432

Part Two

Angina Pectoris 599
Appendicitis 604
Atherosclerosis 609
Biopsy 614
Blood Composition 616
Bursitis 622
Chest Pains 629
Heredity 632
Colostomy 634
Slipped Disc 654
Ear 658
Ectopic Pregnancy 660
Endometriosis 663
Eye 666
Gallbladder 676
Glaucoma 680
Gonorrhea 683
Heart Attack 690
Heimlich Maneuver 693

Hemorrhoids 694
Hernias 696
Hymen 700
Kidney 710
Knee Disorders 711
Mouth and Larynx 713
Liver 717
Lymph Node 719
Medic Alert 723
Pap Smear 739
Prolapse of Uterus 751
Sex-Linked Abnormalities 763
Skin 767
Stroke 776
Ulcer 786
Urinary Tract Infections:
   Cystitis 787
Vocal Cords 792

Part One
Guide to Total Health

THE HEALTHY WOMAN

June Jackson Christmas, M.D.

Past President, American Public Health Association; Clinical Professor of Psychiatry, Columbia University College of Physicians & Surgeons; Professor Emeritus of Behavioral Science, City University of New York Medical School

Health is a positive state—not merely the absence of disease. Yet, we often describe health in a negative way. We may consider ourselves healthy because, at the moment, we have no aches or pains and are not under the care of a doctor. But health is a condition of wellness, a state of physical, mental, and emotional well-being. It is too valuable to be described by what it is not. It is too important to be left entirely in the hands of others, whether they are doctors, advertisers, druggists, neighbors, or friends.

There are three things *you* can do for your health:

- Know how your body functions and be aware of the factors that affect your well-being.
- Take responsibility for making wise decisions that promote good health.
- Be an active, well-informed partner in health care.

KNOW HOW YOUR BODY FUNCTIONS

The body is a living, dynamic organism, one that is constantly replacing or repairing its old or damaged parts. It consists of many systems that are interrelated and dependent on each other for effective functioning. A weakness in one system frequently leads to malfunction in others. For example, the function of the brain and nervous system affects all parts of the body; the pituitary gland influences growth, reproduction, metabolism, and a number of other activities, including uterine contractions at childbirth.

The descriptions and illustrations that follow summarize how the systems of your body work.

THE SKELETAL MUSCULAR SYSTEM: THE FRAMEWORK

Your skeletal muscular system forms the framework of your body. It consists of bones, muscles, tendons, ligaments, and joints. The skin can also be considered part of this system in that it constitutes part of the framework. These elements give the body its shape, enable the body to move, and protect the vital organs.

Muscles are attached to bones by tendons. The bones are held together by ligaments of connective tissue that enable the bones to move when the muscles contract. Joints are the points at which two bones meet. They are classified as hinge, pivot, or ball-and-socket, according to the kind of motion their structure allows. Joints of the skull are fixed, or nonmovable.

Muscles are composed of bundles of fibers that have the ability to contract in response to a complex system of electrochemical signals transmitted from the brain through the nervous system. All muscle fibers store fuel for activity in the form of glycogen, a sugar created by the body's metabolic process.

The approximately 600 muscles of the human body make up about half its total weight. They are divided into three types. The voluntary muscles normally are controlled by the conscious mind. The involuntary muscles control the functions of internal organs, such as the caliber of the arteries and the size of the pupils, via impulses arising automati-

SKELETAL SYSTEM

- Clavicle
- Scapula
- Sternum
- Rib
- Humerus
- Vertebral column
- Elbow joint
- Ulna
- Pelvis
- Sacrum
- Coccyx
- Radius
- Carpals
- Metacarpals
- Phalanges
- Femur
- Patella
- Tibia
- Fibula
- Tarsals
- Metatarsals

BONES OF SKULL

1. Frontal
2. Parietal
3. Temporal
4. Zygomatic
5. Eye orbit
6. Maxilla
7. Mandible

FUNCTIONS OF SKELETAL SYSTEM

Body's weight

Cancellous bone — supports weight

Articular cartilage

Space within cancellous bone — manufactures red blood cells

Calcium and phosphorus storage in the body

Marrow cavity

Compact bone

Fat storage

ELBOW JOINT (Typical synovial joint)

Ligament

Humerus

Joint cavity

Synovial membrane

Articular cartilage

Radius

Ulna

VOLUNTARY MUSCULAR SYSTEM

- Sternocleidomastoid
- Trapezius
- Deltoid
- Pectoralis major
- Biceps
- Triceps
- External oblique
- Rectus abdominis
- Brachioradialis
- Flexors of hand
- Extensor tendons of fingers
- Patella
- Tibialis anterior
- Tibia

- Scapula
- Biceps
- Radius
- Ulna
- Elbow joint
- Triceps
- Humerus
- Muscle
- Tendon
- Outer covering
- Bone
- Pectineus
- Adductor longus
- Sartorius
- Quadriceps femoris
- Gastrocnemius
- Soleus
- Extensor tendons of toes

DANK

cally in the brain. The cardiac, or heart muscle (myocardium), is a third, distinct type.

The voluntary muscles move the skeletal and other parts of the body and maintain posture. When seen under a microscope the fibers of these muscles appear to be striped; thus they are referred to as striated muscles. These are the muscles we use for walking, speaking, gesturing. The state of partial contraction in which the voluntary muscles are held is called muscle tone. Exercise and proper nutrition are necessary to maintain tone and condition. If these muscles are not used regularly, they may atrophy and become slack. They are also subject to fatigue if extended use depletes their supply of stored glycogen and causes a build-up of lactic acid.

The involuntary muscles function continually during respiration, digestion, and circulation. These muscles are not striated and are called smooth muscles. They do not atrophy when not used regularly. For example, the uterine muscle maintains the capacity to contract even if it is never used or is used only once or twice in a lifetime.

The cardiac muscle is unique in its composition. It is made up of partially striated fibers that contract and relax continuously throughout a lifetime. This muscle has its own "built-in" nerve conduction system.

The skin, the largest organ of the body, completes the body framework. It contains the sense of touch, keeps fluids in and foreign bodies out, and helps to regulate temperature. Changes in the condition of the body and in emotional states are reflected in skin temperature, moisture and color, as may be seen, for example, in the flush of fever or embarrassment.

THE CIRCULATORY SYSTEM: MOVEMENT OF BLOOD

The circulatory system consists of the heart and a network of blood vessels throughout the body. As the pumping action of the heart moves the blood through the network, oxygen, nutrients, and other substances are distributed to all parts of the body. Perhaps the most surprising thing about the heart is not that it fails but that it works as hard and as long as it does. It weighs only about a pound. If the pathways through which the blood circulates were laid out end to end, they would cover a distance of about 75,000 miles. In order to keep approximately 5 quarts of blood circulating through these pathways, the heart pumps about

8,000 quarts of blood every 24 hours and continues to do so over a life span—on average 27,000 days or 75 years.

The heart, essentially a muscular pump, consists of four chambers:

BLOOD FLOW IN THE HEART

the left and right atria and left and right ventricles. Blood from each atrium flows into its corresponding ventricle. There is a valve between each atrium and ventricle (the tricuspid valve on the right and the mitral valve on the left) that prevents blood from flowing from the ventricle back to the atrium. The right atrium receives blood from the entire body except the lungs and contracts to pump it into the right ventricle. The right ventricle pumps blood into the pulmonary artery and then to the lungs. The left atrium receives blood from the lungs and pumps it into the left ventricle. The left ventricle pumps blood into the aorta and then to the rest of the body. There is a heart valve (pulmonic) at the junction of the right ventricle and the pulmonary artery and another (aortic) at the junction of the left ventricle and the aorta. These valves prevent the blood from flowing backward. Automatic nervous system impulses from the brain to a part of the heart called the sinoauricular node (the heart's pacemaker) control the rate at which the

CIRCULATORY SYSTEM

ARTERIES
- Common carotid
- Axillary
- Aortic arch
- Pulmonary
- Coronary
- Aorta
- Brachial
- Renal
- Radial
- Ulnar
- External iliac
- Descending lateral circumflex
- Palmar

VEINS
- Jugular
- Superior vena cava
- Pulmonary
- Cephalic
- Basilic
- Inferior vena cava
- Renal
- External iliac
- Femoral artery and vein
- Greater saphenous
- Anterior tibial artery and vein
- Peroneal artery and vein
- Lesser saphenous

Small artery

Capillaries

CO_2 and waste from tissues

Small vein

Nutrients and O_2 to tissues

heart contracts, normally 60 to 100 times a minute when an individual is not exercising.

The pulse is caused by the flow of blood through the arteries as the heart contracts. Blood pressure in the arteries is the force exerted against the walls of these vessels as blood flows through them. As the ventricles contract there is a spurt of blood into the arteries, and blood pressure increases. This is systolic pressure. The pressure when the ventricles are relaxed and filling with blood is diastolic pressure.

The circulatory system consists of three separate but interrelated divisions: coronary, pulmonary, and systemic. The heart has its own circulatory system made up of the coronary arteries that originate in the aorta. The pulmonary circulation carries blood from the right ventricle through the lungs via its arterial system and back via its venous system to the left atrium. In the lungs carbon dioxide is removed and oxygen is picked up. The systemic circulation carries this reoxygenated blood via its arterial system from the left ventricle throughout the body and then carries deoxygenated blood via its venous system back to the right atrium.

The arteries in this system branch into arterioles and become smaller and smaller until they become capillaries that are as fine as hairs and form a network throughout all the tissues. It is at the capillary level that oxygen and other substances seep out to the tissue cells and waste products and carbon dioxide are absorbed. The waste products are removed from the blood as it passes through the liver, kidneys, and lungs. The blood returns to the heart via the venous system, from capillaries to venules to the larger veins and finally to the right atrium.

THE RESPIRATORY SYSTEM: SUPPLY OF OXYGEN

Through the respiratory system, air moves into and out of the body. Air is inhaled through the nose and mouth; it moves into the trachea (windpipe) and its divisions (bronchi), then into the bronchioles of the lungs, and finally into the alveoli, the very thin sacs of the lung. The thin membranes of the alveoli are in contact with this air on one side and blood on the other. The oxygen in the inhaled air passes across the membranes and unites with the hemoglobin in the red blood cells. The oxygenated blood is then carried to the tissues. Carbon dioxide is transferred from the blood across the membranes to the air to be exhaled.

The entire process of air moving into and out of the body and the exchange between the blood and air is called respiration.

When breathing occurs, the size of the chest cavity changes. Muscular contractions, which may be either automatic or voluntary, flatten the diaphragm and move the ribs upward to expand the chest cavity. With this expansion, air pressure around the lungs is decreased below that of the atmosphere and air enters the lungs (inhalation). Exhalation occurs because the opposite happens: the diaphragm and chest wall contract, the pressure on the lungs increases, and air is expelled.

THE DIGESTIVE SYSTEM: NOURISHMENT

Digestion is the conversion of food into energy and into the various substances that can be assimilated by the body cells. The digestive, or gastrointestinal system, includes the gastrointestinal (GI) tract and other organs related to the digestive process such as the pancreas, liver, and gall bladder. Food progresses through the body in the GI tract, a continuous hollow tube about 30 feet in length that begins at the mouth, includes the esophagus, stomach, small intestine, and large intestine (colon), and ends at the anus.

The mechanical and chemical breakdown of food begins in the mouth. Chewing grinds it into small pulpy pieces, and enzymes in saliva, mainly ptyalin, begin the chemical conversion of some starches into sugar. The saliva also lubricates the food as it passes into the esophagus.

No chemical action takes place in the esophagus, but its rhythmic contractions (peristalsis) propel the food into the stomach. Peristaltic action continues to push the food along, helps to liquify it, and mixes it with gastric juices.

The stomach contains glands that secrete gastric juices containing enzymes, chiefly pepsin, and hydrochloric acid that further break down the food into a semiliquid and accelerate the digestive process. Carbohydrates pass through the stomach quickly; proteins move through more slowly because they take longer to digest. Some fats are split up in the stomach, but most are digested farther on. The only substances absorbed directly from the stomach into the blood are moderate quantities of alcohol and some other drugs. Activity in the stomach reaches its maximum about two hours after a meal. A comparatively light meal

RESPIRATORY SYSTEM

ENLARGED ALVEOLI

- CO_2 from body to alveoli in veins
- Muscle
- O_2 to body in arteries
- CO_2
- O_2

- Larynx
- Trachea
- Alveoli
- Bronchial tree
- Right lung (3 lobes)
- Diaphragm
- Nasal cavity
- Pharynx
- Bronchiole
- Bronchus
- Space for heart
- Left lung (2 lobes)

DIGESTIVE SYSTEM

CROSS-SECTION OF INTESTINE

- Outer covering
- Involuntary muscle layer
- Layer of glands
- Secretory and absorptive layer
- Esophagus
- Diaphragm
- Liver
- Stomach
- Gallbladder
- Spleen
- Pancreas
- Large intestine
- Small intestine
- Pelvic bone
- Appendix
- Rectum
- Anus

FUNCTIONS OF DIGESTIVE SYSTEM

- **Esophagus** — food passage
- **Stomach** — mechanical and chemical digestion
- **Liver** — among many functions, the production of bile
- **Gallbladder** — storage of bile
- **Pancreas** — secretion of digestive enzymes
- **Duodenum** — secretion of enzymes, reception of bile and pancreatic enzymes, chemical digestion, and absorption of digested material
- **Small intestine** — chemical digestion and absorption of digested material
- **Large intestine** — absorption of digested material and water
- **Waste material**
- **Appendix**
- **Large intestine** — storage of waste prior to elimination
- **Rectum and anus** — elimination of waste material

DANK

may pass through in three to four hours, while a heavy meal may take as long as six.

The end of the stomach opens into the duodenum, the first section of the small intestine. As food enters the duodenum it is mixed with secretions from the liver, gall bladder, and pancreas. Pancreatic juices and bile from the liver or gall bladder begin to break down proteins into amino acids, convert starch and complex sugars into simple sugars, and metabolize fats into fatty acids and glycerine. The diameter of the small intestine is approximately 1/2 inch, its length about 22 feet, and its total internal surface area about 100 square feet. Through the length of the small intestine these processes continue until the food is completely broken down into its nutrient compounds. These nutrients are absorbed through the intestinal lining into the blood and then transported throughout the body, particularly to the liver. This stage of digestion takes from four to five hours.

Substances that are indigestible and any remaining water proceed into the large intestine, which is about 51/2 feet long. Digestion in the sense of conversion of food into nutrient compounds is completed in the small intestine, but the first part of the large intestine absorbs some remaining nutrients. Liquid waste is absorbed through the lining of the large intestine into the blood. The remaining solids, or feces, reach the final segment of the large intestine, the rectum, and are evacuated through the anus. This final aspect of digestion may take from five to twenty-four hours.

THE URINARY SYSTEM: REMOVAL OF WASTE

Your body must not only build up the substance of its tissues and gain energy from the food you eat; it must also get rid of the end products of body metabolism. These waste products continuously reach the blood and are carried to various places for excretion: carbon dioxide and water (in the form of water vapor) are exhaled from the lungs; salts and other water are exuded through sweat; other wastes such as urea, uric acid, and creatinine are removed by the kidneys and excreted in urine.

The kidneys are the main filtering organ of the body. They also help to maintain the balance between salts and fluid in the body and to keep body minerals in balance. The kidneys filter blood plasma and thus form urine. While the amount of urine produced from hour to hour can vary

URINARY SYSTEM

- Vena cava
- Aorta
- Renal artery and vein
- Right kidney
- Urine flow
- Pelvic bone
- Ureter
- Urinary bladder
- Urethra

ENLARGED NEPHRON

considerably, the daily total is 2 to 3 pints. Many factors account for the varying rate of urine formation. The ingestion of alcohol, tea, and coffee, all of which are diuretics, increases the amount as does cold weather. Conversely, stress, perspiration due to hot weather or strenuous exercise, and limited intake of fluid decrease the amount.

The ureter leads from each kidney to the urinary bladder. The urethra leads from the bladder to the external opening, called the meatus, through which urination occurs.

THE NERVOUS SYSTEM: COMMUNICATION AND CONTROL

The nervous system is a complex organization of integrated structures that control an individual's reaction and adjustment to both internal and external environments. These reactions and adjustments include the rapid actions of the body such as muscular contractions, various visceral activities such as peristalsis, and the secretory activity of some endocrine glands.

The nervous system is composed of special cells called neurons, each of which contains fibers that reach out toward, but do not touch, other neurons. An electrochemical contact between them, called a synapse, transmits the impulse. The nervous system functions primarily through a vast number of reflexes and reflex arcs. This reflex system starts with the stimulation of a receptor organ, such as the skin. This stimulation initiates an impulse that is transmitted by a conduction system to an effector organ such as a skeletal or a smooth muscle that responds to the initial stimulus. This conduction system is composed solely of nerves or of nerves plus hormones secreted by endocrine glands.

The nervous system is essentially separated into two large segments: the central and the peripheral nervous systems. The former is made up of the brain and the spinal cord. The brain is in the cranium and has many parts, the major one being the right and left occipital lobes or hemispheres. These lobes are linked together on their lower surfaces, thus forming several structures including the medulla oblongata (bulb) that is also the beginning of the spinal cord. Another major part of the brain is the cerebellum, which also has two linked hemispheres. Memory, intellectual processes, perceptions of emotion, sensory perception, and both voluntary and involuntary motor functions are controlled and integrated with each other by the brain. The major parts of the brain

NERVOUS SYSTEM

- Brain
- Brachial plexus
- Spinal cord
- Intercostal
- Radial
- Median
- Ulnar
- Lumbo-sacral plexus
- Sciatic
- Saphenous
- Common peroneal
- Superficial peroneal
- Deep peroneal
- Tibial
- Lumbar plexus
- Femoral

SIDE VIEW OF BRAIN

- Frontal lobe
- Parietal lobe
- Occipital lobe
- Temporal lobe
- Cerebellum
- Spinal cord

CROSS-SECTION OF NERVE

- Motor nerve from brain to muscle
- Outer covering
- Inner covering
- Sensory nerve from sensory organ to brain
- Nerve fiber

make up what is called the cerebrum; hence such words as "cerebral" and "cerebration" are used to describe the brain/mind function. The brain also produces a group of proteins with analgesic capabilities many times more powerful than morphine. These substances, called endorphins, are thought to play an important role not only in relieving pain but also in such brain/mind functions as memory and behavior modification.

The spinal cord extends from the base of the brain downward through the vertebral canal. In an adult it is about 18 inches in length and 1/2 inch in diameter. It contains both motor and sensory nerve tracts that traverse its entire length. The spinal cord and the brain are covered by three layers of protective membranes (meninges) between two of which the cerebrospinal fluid circulates.

The peripheral nervous system consists of many paired nerves that conduct impulses to and from the brain and spinal cord. Twelve of them originate in the brain and are referred to as the cranial nerves. They control the muscles of the face, eyes, tongue, etc. They also serve as the nerves for the special senses of sight, hearing, smell, and taste. The 31 pairs of spinal nerves along the entire length of the spinal cord course through the bony spinal column and reach the muscles, blood vessels, organs, and skin surface of the entire body except the face. These nerves group together at several points and form plexi such as the sacral plexus.

A special group of peripheral nerves makes up the autonomic (involuntary) nervous system that has two divisions, the sympathetic and parasympathetic. The sympathetic group arises from the middle portions of the spinal cord; the parasympathetic from the brain and lowest portion of the spinal cord. In general both divisions supply nerves to the same structures including the eyes, heart, lungs, blood vessels, gastrointestinal tract, adrenal and other glands, and liver. Each division is physiologically antagonistic to the other. Thus, the sympathetic system serves to mobilize energy for sudden activity—dilates the pupils, increases the heart rate, etc.—while the parasympathetic system acts to slow such activities to conserve energy. Ordinarily, however, they balance each other to maintain all the body's vital functions in a state of equilibrium or homeostasis.

THE ENDOCRINE SYSTEM:
INTERNAL CONTROL AND BALANCE

The endocrine system, often referred to as a master control system, consists of nine interconnected ductless glands that secrete chemicals (hormones) directly into the bloodstream. These hormones affect and are affected by the entire nervous system, and they are the major regulators of growth, sexual development, secretion of other glands, metabolism of sugar and protein, and emotional states.

The hypothalamus is the master gland of endocrine activity. Located in the base of the brain, it secretes at least ten substances that trigger or block the release of specific hormones by the pituitary gland, which is attached to it by a stalk. The hypothalamus is the center in which the activities of the central nervous and endocrine systems are integrated.

The pituitary gland has an anterior portion and a posterior portion. The anterior pituitary secretes tropic hormones and stimulating hormones. The latter stimulate hormone secretions in several other endocrine glands. The anterior pituitary also secretes prolactin which, among other things, initiates and maintains lactation after pregnancy, and growth hormone (GH), which is essential for cell growth and proliferation. Overproduction of GH prior to full growth causes gigantism and after full growth, acromegaly. Underproduction prior to full growth results in pituitary dwarfism. The posterior pituitary secretes vasopressin, which conserves body water. Another of its secretions (oxytocin) stimulates smooth muscles, including those of the uterus at the time of childbirth, and contributes to the ejection of breast milk.

The thyroid gland regulates the rate at which the body utilizes oxygen and food through the production of thyroxin. Underproduction of this hormone (hypothyroidism) produces cretinism in infants and the listlessness and drowsiness of myxedema in adults. Overproduction causes hyperthyroidism.

The paired parathyroid glands secrete parathyroid hormone (PTH), which controls the blood levels of calcium and phosphate in the body. Underproduction results in low levels of calcium and can cause muscle cramps, even convulsions; overproduction drains the bones of calcium and can produce kidney stones.

The islets of Langerhans, thousands of cell clusters scattered through-

ENDOCRINE SYSTEM

Pineal

Hypothalamus
Secretions which control release of pituitary hormones

Pituitary
Adrenocorticotropic Hormone (ACTH)
Thyroid Stimulating Hormone (TSH)
Melanocyte Stimulating Hormone (MSH)
Follicle Stimulating Hormone (FSH)
Prolactin
Growth Hormone (GH)
Vasopressin
Oxytocin

Thyroid
Thyroxin

Parathyroid
Parathyroid hormone

Thymus

Adrenal
Epinephrine
Norepinephrine
Aldosterone
Cortisol
Corticosterone
Androgen
Estrogen

Pancreas
Islets of Langerhans
Insulin
Glucagon

Ovary
Estrogen
Progesterone

out the pancreas, regulate the body's use of carbohydrates through the production of insulin and glucagon. Underproduction of insulin is associated with diabetes mellitus; overproduction causes hypoglycemia (low blood sugar). Glucagon acts in the opposite way.

The paired adrenal glands have a cortex or outer portion and a medulla or inner portion. The cortex produces steroid hormones—glucocorticoids (cortisone and several others), which control the metabolism of protein and sugar; mineralocorticoids (aldosterone), which control the balance of mineral substances and fluids; and sex hormones (androgen, mainly testosterone, and estrogen). Underproduction of both groups of corticoids produces a rare condition called Addison's disease. Overproduction causes Cushing's syndrome. Excess androgen production can induce the development of masculine secondary sex characteristics in females and young boys. Excess estrogen production has little effect on mature women. In young girls it can lead to enlargement of the breasts and early maturation of the uterus and vagina. In males it can lead to breast enlargement (gynecomastia). The medulla produces catecholamines (epinephrine, or adrenaline, and norepinephrine). These are produced also in the endings of the sympathetic nerves. They normally contribute to the maintenance of homeostasis, but they also enable the body to respond to danger, fright, anger, or sudden physical stress with an increased heart rate and faster breathing.

The male sex glands, the testes, produce sperm and the male sex hormone testosterone, which is responsible for the development of male secondary sex characteristics such as voice change and facial hair. Overproduction of testosterone produces virilism; underproduction produces eunuchism. The female sex glands, the ovaries, produce ova or eggs. They also secrete estrogen and progesterone, hormones needed for menstruation, reproduction, feminine secondary sex characteristics, and skeletal development, plus androgens. Excessive production of these hormones occurs very rarely and then only with certain ovarian tumors. Absence of them early in life causes female eunuchism. Underproduction of them later in life causes menstrual irregularities and, ultimately, menopause.

The thymus gland appears to play a role in the body's resistance to disease, metabolism of calcium, and development of the skeleton and sex glands. Prior to puberty, the pineal gland secretes a hormone called melatonin, which inhibits the biochemical process of sexual maturation.

THE REPRODUCTIVE SYSTEM:
PERPETUATION OF THE SPECIES

The female reproductive system consists of internal and external sex organs. The external sex organs are called the vulva. The mons pubis (mons veneris) is a pad of fatty tissue in front of the pubic bone that from puberty on is covered with pubic hair. Two folds of fatty tissue covered with skin, the labia majora (outer lips) and the labia minora (inner lips), protect the vaginal and urethral openings that lie between them. The labia minora are sensitive to touch and sexual arousal. Just below the mons, the labia minora join to form a hood over the clitoris. The clitoris, the most sexually responsive female organ, is composed of erectile tissue that becomes engorged with blood during sexual activity. It is homologous to the penis.

Below the clitoris is the urethral meatus, the external opening of the urethra. Below that is the vaginal opening or introitus. The hymen is a thin fold of mucous membrane across the introitus, partially blocking it. After being stretched by ordinary physical activity, insertion of tampons, or intercourse, only a ridge of tissue usually remains around the introitus. Beyond the hymen on each side of the vaginal opening is a mucus-secreting gland (Bartholin's gland). The perineum is the area between the external genitals and the anus.

The internal sex organs include the vagina, the uterus, the fallopian tubes, and the ovaries. The vagina is a tubular, muscular structure covered with skin that extends from the vulva upward and backward to the uterus. The vaginal walls stretch and contract during intercourse; during childbirth, they expand greatly. Continuous secretions from the vaginal wall keep the vagina clean, maintain acidity to prevent infection, and provide lubrication for intercourse.

The uterus (womb) is a hollow, pear-shaped organ about the size of a lemon. In a nonpregnant state, its walls (myometrium) are one of the strongest muscles in the body. The cervix, the base or neck of the uterus, projects into the vagina and has a small opening (cervical os) in its center through which sperm can travel upward and through which menstrual blood flows down.

The fallopian tubes (oviducts) are paired muscular narrow canals that extend from each side of the top of the uterus to the ovaries. In an adult

FEMALE REPRODUCTIVE SYSTEM

- Pelvic bone
- Ovary
- Fallopian tube
- Round ligament
- Pubic bone
- Uterus
- Vagina
- Shaft
- Hood
- Clitoris
- Urethral meatus
- Labia majora
- Labia minora
- Interior of vagina
- Remnant of hymen
- Bartholin's gland
- Perineum

SIDE VIEW OF EXTERNAL AND INTERNAL GENITALIA

- Fallopian tube — ovum and sperm pathways; fertilization site
- Ovary — ovum and hormone production
- Uterus — sperm pathway; implantation and development of fetus
- Round ligament
- Mons pubis
- Bladder
- Clitoris — sensory organ
- Urethral meatus
- Labia majora and minora — protection
- Sacrum
- Cervix
- Rectum
- Anus
- Perineum
- Vagina — organ of intercourse and birth canal

they are about 5 inches long. The end near the ovary is open and enlarged so that an ovum, when released from the ovary, can be "trapped" by, enter, and travel along the tube.

The ovaries, organs about the size of an almond, are located on either side of the uterus. The breasts (discussed in detail in the "Breast Care" chapter) produce milk following the birth of a baby.

The Male Reproductive System

The male reproductive system consists of the penis, urethra, scrotum, testes, and some glands. The penis contains erectile tissue which on sexual arousal is engorged with blood and becomes erect, thus facilitating sexual intercourse. The urethra is the tube in the center of the penis through which urine and semen leave the body. The prostate gland and Cowper's glands, located at the junction of the bladder and urethra, produce the seminal fluid in which sperm cells are mixed, thereby forming semen.

The Menstrual Cycle

The menstrual cycle is a dramatic example of the delicate balance and interactions maintained by your body. A series of complex feedback interactions among several organs and glands stimulate ovulation (production of the reproductive cell, the egg), prepare the uterus for pregnancy, and, if conception does not occur, make adjustments so that the process can begin again. Menstruation is the process by which tissue, built up in the uterus in readiness for the implantation of a fertilized ovum, is discharged through the vagina if conception does not occur.

The cycle is repeated throughout the reproductive years of a woman's life from menarche, the onset of menstruation, to menopause, the cessation of menstruation. Menarche occurs between the ages of 10 and 16, when certain secretions from the hypothalamus begin to stimulate the pituitary. Menopause occurs between the ages of 45 and 55 when ovarian follicular function ceases. Its onset is gradual.

The complete menstrual cycle takes approximately a month. That is, the time from the beginning of one menstrual period to the beginning of the next ranges from 25 to 35 days. The menstrual flow or period lasts

MALE REPRODUCTIVE SYSTEM

UNCIRCUMCISED PENIS
- Shaft of penis
- Urethra
- Foreskin
- Left testis

CIRCUMCISED PENIS
- Glans

- Bladder
- Pubic bone
- Suspensory ligament of penis
- Urethra — semen and urine pathway
- Penis — erectile copulatory organ
- Glans — sensory stimulation
- Urethral meatus
- Prostate — secretes seminal fluid
- Seminal vesicle — secretes seminal fluid
- Rectum
- Cowper's gland — secretes seminal fluid
- Anus
- Perineum
- Vas deferens — sperm pathway
- Epididymis — storage of mature sperm
- Testis — sperm and hormone production
- Scrotum

MENSTRUAL CYCLE

Pituitary initiates follicle growth with FSH

Pituitary causes ovulation with FSH and LH

Follicle
Ovum
Ovulation
Corpus luteum

The growing follicle secretes estrogen

Estrogen repairs and rebuilds the endometrial lining of the uterus

After ovulation the follicle becomes the corpus luteum which secretes progesterone

Progesterone completes the endometrial buildup

The corpus luteum degenerates and a new follicle grows

The endometrium is shed in the flow or period

ENDOMETRIUM (Lining of uterus)

Menstruation 2-7 days
Ovulation 7th-21st day
14 days
21-35 day menstrual cycle
Menstruation

Ovary
Ovulation
Ovum
Fallopian tube
Endometrium
Uterine muscle
Cervix

from 2 to 7 days. The length of the cycle and of the menstrual period varies from woman to woman and in any one woman from time to time.

There are three phases in each menstrual cycle and the primary organs involved are the hypothalamus/pituitary, ovary, and uterus.

We consider the first day of the menstrual phase to be the day menstruation begins. As the estrogen and progesterone levels fall (see postovulatory phase below) the functional layers of the endometrium (the lining of the uterus) begin to shed and appear as menstrual flow. As menstruation continues, estrogen and progesterone levels drop further and follicle-stimulating hormone (FSH) from the pituitary increases. FSH stimulates the proliferation, usually only in one ovary, of masses of cells called follicles that secrete estrogen. FSH also stimulates the enlargement of the ovum in a follicle. The estrogen stimulates further development of the ovum, a drop, via a negative feedback system, in FSH, and, via a positive feedback system, an increase in LH that stimulates further follicle development and with it an increase in estrogen secretion. This additional estrogen stimulates the start of the "rebuilding" of the endometrium, which causes menstruation to end and marks the beginning of the preovulatory phase.

During the preovulatory (proliferative or follicular) phase, estrogen levels continue to increase, FSH to decrease, and LH to increase slightly. The endometrium further thickens and its glands and blood vessels increase. One of the follicles (the dominant follicle) and its ovum continue to mature, while the others shrink. Finally, there is a surge of LH from the pituitary that triggers the dominant follicle to rupture.

Ovulation is not a phase of the menstrual cycle but an event that more or less marks the change from one phase to another. After the follicle ruptures, the ovum is expelled from it (ovulation), and the follicle is transformed into a corpus luteum (yellow body) that secretes increasing amounts of progesterone and estrogen. Some women sense a little pain with the rupturing of the follicle. The progesterone causes a rise in body temperature shortly after ovulation. The high level of estrogen induces temporary chemical changes in the vagina, cervical mucus, uterus, and tubes that facilitate sperm penetration of the uterus and their survival and upward movement in the uterus and tube. It also causes anatomical changes that bring the end of the tube and the ovary closer together. The ovulatory effects last for only a few days.

During the postovulatory (secretory or luteal) phase, the increasingly high levels of estrogen and progesterone from the corpus luteum stimulate the endometrium to form secretory glands that prepare it for the implantation (about 7 days after conception) of a fertilized ovum if conception occurs. Some women experience breast thickening and tenderness as well as other changes such as premenstrual tension and fluid retention during the post-ovulatory phase.

If the ovum is not fertilized—a process that normally occurs in a fallopian tube—the corpus luteum begins to degenerate about 14 days after ovulation and its production of progesterone and estrogen decreases. When this happens, the arteries and veins in the thickened lining of the uterus become constricted; deprived of their rich blood supply, the top layers of endometrium are shed, and menstruation occurs.

THE RELATIONSHIP BETWEEN PHYSICAL AND MENTAL HEALTH

Important relationships exist between physical health and mental health. On the one hand, an emotional state is reflected in physical responses. When you are worried or frustrated, you may have feelings of tension in your neck, a headache, or a feeling of tightness in your stomach. On the other hand, emotional or mental disorders may be caused by physical problems or diseases. Severe myxedema (thyroid malfunction) may result in mental abnormalities. Some illnesses reflect the interaction between the body and emotions, especially illnesses of the skin and digestive, respiratory, cardiovascular, and urinary systems. These parts of the body are under the control of the involuntary nervous system. Family tensions can contribute to such disorders as dermatitis, colitis, ulcers, asthma, changes in heart rate and rhythm, hypertension, and urinary frequency. Stress on the job may contribute to arthritis and rheumatism.

TAKE RESPONSIBILITY FOR YOUR OWN HEALTH

An important aspect of health is an awareness of the sources of potential illness. Promoting your own well-being involves prevention of illness, early treatment of symptoms, and minimizing disability.

PRIMARY PREVENTION: PREVENTION OF ILLNESS

There are three levels of prevention. Primary prevention is directed toward keeping a disorder from occurring. Immunization is the classic example of primary prevention. Today, primary prevention includes the vaccinations that children receive against whooping cough, diphtheria, tetanus, German measles, measles, and polio. As an adult, you may have been immunized against influenza or, when you were planning to travel, against hepatitis, yellow fever, or other infectious diseases. Environmental health controls are another form of primary prevention: fluoridation of water to prevent dental cavities, proper sewage disposal, purification of water, and pollution control, including the elimination of hazardous air pollutants in the workplace.

The term primary prevention also refers to choices you make in behavior and activities that may affect your health. Do you smoke? How much sleep do you usually get? Do you eat a nourishing breakfast? Do you practice daily oral hygiene? Do you use seat belts? Would you be in better shape if you drank less? Do you protect yourself against sexually transmissible diseases?

Clearly, eating a well-balanced diet, not smoking, and drinking in moderation if at all are activities that have a major effect on your health and are within your power to control. Also, although you may not be able to eliminate stress in your life, you can take a good look at how you handle it. Are you quick to rely on sleeping pills in order to get a good night's sleep, to seek (and to receive) tranquilizers because some of the problems of everyday living seem to be too difficult? Some women become dependent on alcohol, the most serious drug abuse problem in our country. Others smoke or eat too much. These activities are not conducive to promoting your health. If any of these habits continues, you may be placing yourself at a greater risk of hypertension; of heart, liver, or lung disease; or cancer.

In recent years, more and more women have been learning to deal with stress in ways that are not self-destructive: planning a regular exercise routine or attending a weekly dance class, setting aside a few hours for uninterrupted activities that are pure pleasure, saving money in order to have a regular session with a good masseuse.

SECONDARY PREVENTION: EARLY DIAGNOSIS AND TREATMENT

Secondary prevention refers to early diagnosis, detection, and treatment of a disease in order to reduce its consequences, duration, and severity. Breast self-examination, an annual visit to a gynecologist for professional breast examination, a mammography as recommended, a Pap smear to detect signs of cervical cancer, blood pressure measurements to keep track of hypertension risk, blood analysis for signs of anemia or dangerous cholesterol levels, eye examinations to check on the onset of glaucoma are among the things you can do to facilitate secondary prevention.

TERTIARY PREVENTION: REHABILITATION

Finally, there is a third level of prevention—rehabilitation. Rehabilitation is directed toward minimizing disability, deterioration, or the limitations that might result from a stroke or a serious accident. If help is sought early in the course of a chronic illness such as arthritis, rehabilitation can prevent further deterioration and improve the chances for social, psychological, and physical adjustment.

BE AN ACTIVE WELL-INFORMED PARTNER IN HEALTH CARE

In order to take greater responsibility for your own health and well-being, it is important to become as knowledgeable as possible about the various approaches to health care.

HOLISTIC HEALTH

There is an increasing interest in looking at people as whole human beings living in their family, community, and social environments, rather than as isolated organs or systems. New attention to holistic health reflects this orientation.

The concern with the whole person is the essential element of the holistic approach. It does not compartmentalize you into the various parts of your body or even according to kinds of specialists that you might see. Because there is an overemphasis on specialization in medical care, interest has recently been expressed in a return to the family physician, to the primary care physician, to that person who can deal with the individual on many levels.

SELF-CARE

While holistic medicine attempts to reduce overreliance on specialists, self-care is directed toward reducing overreliance on medical services in general. Self-care as a concept may be considered to be enlightened self-interest. This means that you as a woman do a regular monthly breast examination, so that you are able to detect any suspicious findings and bring them to the attention of your health care provider. It also means an emphasis on a more health-promoting life style. For some people it also means turning from total reliance on medical care.

To take full advantage of the benefits of self-care you should approach it with the same sense of responsibility you apply to medical services. The most extreme self-care advocates avoid all doctors and actively reject any kind of medical intervention. However, although the body has wonderful curative abilities and many ailments and disorders will respond to home remedies, rest, and tender loving care, there are also many that will not. Your knowledge of when to turn to a doctor for professional diagnosis and treatment is part of enlightened health care.

Like so many aspects of life in the United States, the self-care concept has been widely exploited by quacks and promoters of questionable remedies. Manuals of self-knowledge and health care flood the bookshops, presenting a challenge to you as a discriminating reader. Can you differentiate between sound practical advice and a simple-minded panacea for a complicated problem that requires professional expertise and advanced diagnostic tools?

One of the innovative approaches related to the increasing interest in self-care has been the development of self-help groups. You are probably aware of Weight Watchers, Overeaters Anonymous, and Alcoholics

Anonymous. Now there are self-help groups for people coping with diabetes, hypertension, muscular dystrophy or chronic depression. Self-help groups have been organized to provide information, to clarify the role of medical care in dealing with problems, and to help people through serious physical and emotional problems or through life crises such as bereavement and loneliness.

The benefit of self-help groups comes from the fact that when you are with someone who has some of the same problems you have, you tend to share positive experiences as well as burdens, and to generalize or universalize your experiences. In doing this you gain some insight and understanding. Self-help groups provide both the knowledge and the emotional support that membership in any group gives.

Some of these self-help groups have led to the establishment of clinical services for women, including medical services provided by women health practitioners, counseling programs, and educational and consciousness-raising discussion groups. These are consistent with the increased participation of consumers in making decisions.

With increased awareness of health care, it is hoped that changes and reform may come in the ways in which all services are organized and provided. The consumer movement has caused consternation, resentment, and anger among many people in medicine whose attitudes and approaches had never before been questioned by the people who used their services. This is particularly true of physicians who have occupied a sacrosanct position. The desire for change, especially by women whose emotional and intellectual needs have not been met, is very much related to becoming an equal participant in the health care partnership.

HEALTH SERVICES

Citizen participation in health service now extends to the establishment of alternative health care services, particularly those in which potential patients carry on health care activities themselves. In some instances women's groups have banded together for education—to understand how their bodies function; to learn what to expect during an examination by a gynecologist, during childbirth, during sexual intercourse; to become informed regarding all aspects of sexuality and reproduction about which women as patients have been kept ignorant. Other groups seek to ensure less sexist behavior on the part of physicians, generally males, or to demand their rights as patients to accept or not to accept a doctor's recommendation for medication as the only solution to a health problem or for proceeding with a radical mastectomy or a hysterectomy before other options are seriously evaluated. Still others are concerned with abortion rights and reproductive freedom.

Even if you feel that the medical care you personally receive is adequate, you might consider that active participation in a women's health group (to whatever degree seems best for you) can have an effect in the long run on the health care system. Your participation will help to influence those within the medical community to be more attuned to the needs of the individual patient. Your participation can help to demonstrate that the patient can be an equal in a process that depends on persons on both sides of the relationship. The progress of treatment and rehabilitation can be influenced by your attitude, knowledge, and involvement in the health care partnership. Already, there have been many influential forces. The patients' rights movement, the women's movement, the public's increased concern with elitism in medical practice, and the demands for more citizen participation in the affairs of hospitals, clinics, and health centers have already affected the attitudes of health care providers.

This exchange of information gives those in the field of health care a better sense of what helps you accept their guidance and follow their recommendations. This issue has sometimes been referred to as "patient compliance," a misnomer. Ideally it should be a more active process, in which a knowledgeable person (1) understands her role in the process of becoming or staying well, (2) asks pertinent questions, and (3) knows to whom to turn for further information or help. Unfortunately when knowledge and understanding are lacking, you may often find yourself misunderstanding directions, confused as to what the problem is, and reluctant to follow instructions.

Alternative health services may be effective in dealing with such issues, but there is a need for real reform in the way health care is organized and provided. Health care should emphasize health rather than sickness, partnership rather than hierarchy, and quality health care as the right of all women—and of all people.

NUTRITION, WEIGHT, AND GENERAL WELL-BEING

Toby Orem Graham, M.D.
Associate Professor of Medicine, University of Pittsburgh School of Medicine, Pittsburgh, Pennsylvania

Helene MacLean
Medical Writer and Editor; Author, *Caring for Your Parents*

We are what we eat! Our food choices affect our health, energy, appearance, and disposition. Eating the right amounts and kinds of foods supplies us with energy and stamina for work and play, provides for our growth, maintains our bodies in good health, and helps to keep us mentally alert. That's what nutrition is all about. It is unfortunate, but too often true, that many women become interested in nutrition only because of some specific circumstance: when they are pregnant or breast-feeding, or are overweight and want to diet, or have children with a weight problem, or develop symptoms stemming from inadequate nutrition such as fatigue resulting from iron-deficiency anemia. It is the purpose of this chapter to encourage increased attention to good nutrition at all times, not only as treatment for a problem but as the basis for good health and well-being.

THE NUTRIENT CONTENT OF FOOD

Nutrition is the process whereby our bodies use food to supply us with energy; build, maintain, and repair body tissues; and regulate body processes. Nutrients, those chemical substances obtained from food during digestion, are usually grouped into five classes—protein, carbohydrate, fat, vitamins, and minerals. Two other substances, water and fiber, although not technically considered nutrients, are also essential in the diet. Nutritional needs generally are expressed in two ways: (1) as the amount needed for an individual to avoid deficiency (daily requirement) and (2) as the average daily amount that entire population groups should consume to prevent deficiency (recommended daily dietary allowance, or RDA). Because statistically the RDAs are set two standard deviations above the mean requirement (the mean requirement defines the needs of 97 percent of normal persons), the RDAs exceed the needs of many people and, furthermore, are established for healthy persons (Table 1). The RDA takes into account the dietary form of the nutrient, the efficiency of absorption, and other factors in addition to the estimated daily requirement for the nutrient. The United States Recommended Daily Allowances (U.S. RDA) are a simplified form of the RDA devised for use in nutrition labeling. These standardized recommendations may be changed from time to time on the basis of new scientific evidence.

The amount of energy a nutrient can supply is measured in calories. Sometimes the type of food is homogeneous, and the caloric content can be estimated from the volume (see Table 1).

Table 1

Nutrient	Kilocalories/gram
Protein	4
Carbohydrate	4
Fat	9

PROTEIN

Protein is the basic substance of all living cells and is, therefore, vital in the diet for cellular growth, replacement, and repair. Protein is composed of combinations of amino acids, which are organic compounds containing nitrogen and hydrogen. The material needed for different types of body cells, including enzymes, hormones, red blood cells, and antibodies, is provided by different combinations of the amino acids. The protein derived from such animal foods as meat, fish, eggs, and dairy products, contains all of the amino acids we need to construct proteins in our body (essential amino acids) and is, therefore, known as complete protein. The protein derived from plant food, such as nuts, legumes, and grains, usually lacks some essential amino acids in the amounts needed and is, therefore, incomplete. However, complete protein can be obtained by eating plant foods if they are combined to complement one another, that is, to supply in combination all the required amino acids. Examples of such complementary foods are dried beans and corn, peanuts and wheat, and soy bean products and rice. These combinations are the basis for healthful vegetarianism, and they also form an essential part of a nutritious diet in parts of the world where meat and fish are either unavailable or too expensive for the majority of the population. At least one-third of one's daily protein requirement should be eaten at the first meal of the day to assure maximum energy during the day.

CARBOHYDRATES

Carbohydrates, the sugars and starches, supply most of the body's energy needs. They are also necessary for protein digestion and certain brain functions. Some forms are rapidly absorbed into the bloodstream unchanged to provide energy immediately. Others are converted by digestion into a form that can be stored for later use. Their presence in adequate amounts allows the body to preserve protein, which also supplies energy, primarily for body building and maintenance functions. Carbohydrates are obtained from fruits, vegetables, and grains.

FAT

Fats and oils (fats that are liquid at room temperature) are composed mainly of fatty acids. Fats are an excellent source of energy, providing more calories per gram than do protein or carbohydrates. Fatty acids contain or are involved in the digestion of the fat-soluble vitamins—A, D, E, and K. Stored body fat helps to maintain body temperature by providing insulation and also protects body structures and organs. Fats are found in abundance in animal and plant products, including meats, dairy products, nuts, and some vegetables.

Both the quantity and quality of fat in the diet should be considered. Obviously, eating more than the body needs leads to excess body fat. While it is usually assumed that calories are calories no matter what their source, a significant study conducted at the Stanford Center for Research in Disease Prevention and published in the July, 1988 *American Journal of Clinical Nutrition* points to a different conclusion. From this study, it appears that the percentage of body fat is directly related to the proportion of daily caloric intake that comes specifically from fat. The more fat and the fewer sugars and starches consumed by the subjects, the more of their total body weight consisted of fat. This may explain why Americans eat less but weigh more than they did 50 to 75 years ago. In spite of all warnings to reduce this amount, about 40 percent of today's typical American diet comes from fat. This amount is about one-third more in fat calories than were consumed in the past when a much greater proportion of starchy foods were part of the normal diet. This conclusion is consistent with an extensive study of the Chinese diet. On a pound for pound basis, Chinese consume 20 percent more calories than Americans, but they derive only 15 percent of their calories from fat. Because their diet is rich in starchy and fibrous carbohydrates that offer protection against clogged arteries, both heart disease and clinical overweight is quite rare among the Chinese.

Cholesterol

The *type* of fat consumed is equally important. Fatty acids differ in their chemical structure. If one additional hydrogen atom can be incorporated into the carbon chain, the fatty acid is called an unsaturated fat.

If the hydrogen cannot be incorporated, it is a saturated fat. If two or more hydrogen ions can be added, it is known as a polyunsaturated fat. The polyunsaturates are almost exclusively vegetable in origin: corn oil, safflower oil, soybean oil, and the like. Practically all animal fats are saturated. The fats found in milk and cream substitutes as well as those that are in solid white shortenings derived from palm oil or coconut oil are also saturated. Excess consumption of saturated fats is known to raise the amount of cholesterol, a lipid, in the bloodstream. A great deal of attention is currently being given to the relationship between excessively high blood/cholesterol levels and arterial disease (atherosclerosis).

Cholesterol is a waxy type of animal compound present in all animal tissues and essential to many body processes. It is manufactured by the body and stored in the liver. Cholesterol also comes from the food we eat, and a high level in the blood (called serum cholesterol) is a danger to health because it encourages the formation of fatty plaque in the arterial walls, causing them to narrow and lose their elasticity.

Because cholesterol is a fatty substance, fatty proteins are required to transport it to the liver for storage or eventual secretion. These proteins, known as high density lipids (HDLs), perform a beneficial function in removing cholesterol from the arterial walls. Low density lipids (LDLs) have the opposite effect, adding to the amount of accumulated cholesterol instead of diminishing it. Thus, the *nature* of the fats in the diet plays a critical role.

It is generally agreed that the level of cholesterol should be approximately 200 milligrams per deciliter of blood, and that a measurement above 225 is considered somewhat risky. It is also agreed that when the measurement appears to be suspect in terms of the patient's general health and dietary precautions, the measurements should be taken again, preferably by a different laboratory. Lab technicians can and do make mistakes.

Because blood cholesterol levels tend to increase with age and arterial health is diminished not only by a natural loss of elasticity but more dangerously by clogged walls, any measures that decrease cholesterol are important. The usual recommendations include weight control, reduction of salt intake, increased exercise, abstention from smoking, cutting down on alcoholic beverages, and above all, attention to diet.

Cholesterol and Diet

In July 1988, Dr. C. Everett Koop, Surgeon General of the United States, issued the most comprehensive report on nutrition and health ever prepared by the government. While it presented no new findings but essentially corroborated recommendations of the past decade, one of its major pieces of dietary advice was that most people should reduce total fat in the diet but particularly saturated fats, defined as animal or vegetable fats that remain solid at room temperature. Especially to be avoided are butter, untrimmed meat, and palm oil.

The American Heart Association has recommended that fats should make up no more than 25 percent of the total daily caloric intake, an amount that can be measured as two tablespoons of polyunsaturated fats.

Here are some guidelines:

- Beef, lamb, pork, and ham contain more fat than veal, turkey, chicken, and fish.
- Bacon, sausages, and all cold cuts are high in fat.
- Removing the skin from chicken and turkey considerably reduces the fat.
- Hard cheeses contain more fat than cooked meat.
- Yogurt is an excellent substitute for sour cream, and yogurt spread is an excellent substitute for cream cheese.
- Barley, oatmeal, rice, pasta, and bulgur are low in fat.
- Examine the color of ground meat. The lighter it is, the more fat it contains.
- To be avoided: too many egg yolks, butter, cream, vegetable shortening.
- Trim all fat from beef and poultry; skim off all fat from stews and soups.
- Examine labels on packaged breakfast cereals, crackers, and snack foods and avoid those containing oils derived from palm and coconut.
- Eat more low fat dairy products such as low fat cheeses, skim milk, and buttermilk.
- Eat fatty ocean fish and shellfish in moderation.

- Olive oil and peanut oil are the preferred vegetable oils for cooking and salad dressings.

The following menus, each of which adds up to less than 2100 calories, should also be helpful in showing you how to plan satisfying meals that are low in fat:

BETTER DIETS GRAM BY GRAM

30 Percent Menu
(Most desirable diet)

BREAKFAST

40% Bran Flakes, 1 ounce	90	0.4 grams
Milk, 1 percent, 1/2 cup	50	1.5 grams
Orange juice, 6 ounces	83	0 grams
Coffee, decaffeinated	0	0 grams
Milk, 1 percent, 1 tablespoon	6	0.2 grams

LUNCH

Minestrone soup, 1 cup	80	3 grams
Tuna, 3 ounces	111	4.7 grams
Mayonnaise, 2 tablespoons	200	22 grams
Lettuce, tomato	7	0 grams
Whole-wheat bread, 2 slices	140	2 grams

SNACK

Swiss cheese, 1 ounce	105	8 grams
Apple, 1	80	0.2 grams

DINNER

Spaghetti, 2 cups, plus 6 ounces tomato sauce and 3 ounces cooked lean ground beef	619	13.6 grams
Grated Parmesan cheese, 1 tablespoon	25	2 grams
French bread, 1 slice	100	1 gram
Butter, 1 pat, and garlic	50	4 grams
Green salad	14	0.1 grams
Oil and vinegar dressing, 1 tablespoon	63	7 grams
Frozen fruit-flavored yogurt, 8 ounces	210	2 grams

20 Percent Menu
(Most desirable diet)

BREAKFAST

Cheerios, 1 ounce	110	2 grams
Raisins, 2 tablespoons	52	0.1 gram
Banana, 1/2 cup	70	0.5 grams
Milk, 1 percent, 1/2 cup	50	1.5 grams
Orange juice, 6 ounces	83	0 grams

LUNCH

Split-pea soup, 1 bowl	240	5 grams
Turkey breast, 3 ounces, with lettuce and mustard	106	3 grams
Rye bread, 2 slices	130	2 grams

SNACK

Pear, 1	100	1 gram
Toasted corn tortilla with skim-milk mozzarella cheese, 1 ounce	145	6 grams

DINNER

Spaghetti, 2 cups, plus 6 ounces tomato and mushroom sauce	432	5 grams
Grated Parmesan cheese, 2 tablespoons	50	4 grams
Spinach salad, 1 cup, plus 1/2 cup orange sections	38	0.1 grams
Oil and vinegar dressing, 1 tablespoon	63	7 grams
French bread, 2 slices	200	2 grams
Parmesan cheese and garlic, 1 tablespoon	30	2 grams
Sherbet, 2/3 cup	181	2.7 grams

SOURCE: Center for Science in the Public Interest

Fish Oil Supplements and Cholesterol

Some women have been convinced that capsules of fish oil are an essential dietary supplement. These capsules, which can cost as much as 25¢ each, contain a concentrate high in substances known as omega 3 fatty acids. These fatty acids are the polyunsaturated fat found in great concentration in fatty cold water fish.

Relevant studies investigated the fact that Eskimos have practically no heart disease, and in 1985, *The New England Journal of Medicine* published data indicating that eating as little as one ounce of fish a week reduced risks of death from heart disease. Data was also presented that linked fish oil with the prevention of arthritis and cancer. However, there is considerable disagreement about these findings on the part of the scientific community and the Food and Drug Administration.

Because the studies are considered inconclusive, fish oil is neither an approved food additive nor an approved drug, nor is it on the FDA list of foods "generally regarded as safe." Because no official agency is monitoring the quality of fish oil supplements, they could be contaminated with hazardous chemicals. Also, the fish livers from which they are derived might contain toxic levels of vitamins A and D.

It should also be taken into account that not only can excessive amounts of fish oil interfere with blood clotting but they are also known to stimulate the body's production of prostaglandin E_3, a substance that increases bone loss and thereby raises the risk of osteoporosis, a disease common among Eskimos. Thus, it is probably safer, more effective, and certainly cheaper to eat fish for these necessary oils, especially salmon, sardines, tuna, bluefish, mackerel, oysters, squid, rainbow trout, and American eel.

VITAMINS

Vitamins, sometimes referred to as micronutrients, are organic substances that are present in foods and are needed in very small amounts (a few micrograms or milligrams) to enable specific metabolic reactions to occur. They generally serve as coenzyme catalysts for intracellular enzyme system reactions. Each vitamin has a specific function. Because only small amounts of vitamins are needed to trigger and control these reactions and because they are used again and again, only small amounts are needed daily for replenishment. Although some vitamins can be synthesized by humans, all vitamins should be supplied in essential amounts by the food we eat each day (see Table 2).

A woman in normal health who is eating properly prepared and adequately balanced meals does not need supplemental vitamins (see Table 3). However, women over 55 or 60 years of age may need them because their diets are inadequate or because, as some clinicians believe, their gastrointestinal absorption mechanisms are impaired. Women on special or restricted diets should discuss the advisability of vitamin supplements with their doctors. When a situation exists that increases tissue requirements for vitamins, such as hyperthyroidism, pregnancy, lactation, or postoperative convalescence, or when there is disturbance in vitamin absorption as occurs in hypothyroidism, the

TABLE 2

RECOMMENDED DAILY DIETARY ALLOWANCES (RDA) FOR VITAMINS AND MINERALS[a]

Minerals

	AGE (years)	CALCIUM (mg)	PHOSPHORUS (mg)	MAGNESIUM (mg)	IRON (mg)	ZINC (mg)	IODINE (µg)
Infants	0.0–0.5	360	240	50	10	3	40
	0.5–1.0	540	360	70	15	5	50
Children	1–3	800	800	150	15	10	70
	4–6	800	800	200	10	10	90
	7–10	800	800	250	10	10	120
Males	11–14	1200	1200	350	18	15	150
	15–18	1200	1200	400	18	15	150
	19–22	1200	800	350	10	15	150
	23–50	800[c]	800	350	10	15	150
	51+	800	800	350	10	15	150
Females	11–14	1200	1200	300	18	15	150
	15–18	1200	1200	300	18	15	150
	19–22	1200	800	280	18	12	150
	23–50	800[c]	800	280	18	12	150
	51+	800	800	280	15	12	150
Pregnant		+400	+400	+150	+10[h]	+5	+25
Lactating		+400	+400	+150	h	+10	+50

doctor usually prescribes any necessary vitamin supplements. In addition, some women who regularly take certain medications such as anticonvulsants (e.g., Dilantin, barbiturates), isoniazid, antibiotics, and oral contraceptives may need supplemental vitamins.

A diet deficient in necessary vitamin content leads to clinically identifiable deficiency states that can be successfully treated with therapeutic doses of the appropriate vitamins. The efficacy of small doses of vitamins in deficiency diseases led to the hypothesis that large doses may cure other diseases, sharpen natural functions, and prevent illness. High-dose vitamin therapy is touted as useful in a broad range of illnesses, from the common cold to schizophrenia. The use of vitamins in doses many times the RDA for the cure or prevention of disease is termed *megavitamin therapy*. A single multivitamin each day is not likely to provide any nutrients not provided by a balanced diet, but it is also not likely to cause any harm. However, those who take vitamins in doses many times the RDA are exposing themselves to the dangers of vitamin toxicity as described below.

Fat-Soluble Vitamins			*Water-Soluble Vitamins*						
VITAMIN A (μg RE)	VITAMIN D (μg)	VITAMIN E (mg α-TE)	VITAMIN C (mg)	THIAMIN (mg)	RIBOFLAVIN (mg)	NIACIN (mg NE)	VITAMIN B-6 (mg)	FOLACIN (μg)	VITAMIN B-12 (μg)
420	10	3	35	0.3	0.4	6	0.3	30	0.5
400	10	4	35	0.5	0.6	8	0.6	45	1.5
400	10	5	45	0.7	0.8	9	0.9	100	2.0
500	10	6	45	0.9	1.0	11	1.3	200	2.5
700	10	7	45	1.2	1.4	16	1.6	300	3.0
1000	10	8	50	1.4	1.6	18	1.8	400	3.0
1000	10	10	60	1.4	1.7	18	2.0	400	3.0
1000	7.5	10	60	1.5	1.7	19	2.0	240	2.0
1000	5	10	60	1.4	1.6	18	2.0	240	2.0
1000	5	10	60	1.2	1.4	16	2.0	240	2.0
800	10	8	50	1.1	1.3	15	1.8	400	3.0
800	10	8	60	1.1	1.3	14	2.0	400	3.0
800	7.5	8	60	1.1	1.3	14	1.6	190	2.0
800	5	8	60	1.0	1.2	13	1.6	190	2.0
800	5	8	60	1.0	1.2	13	1.6	190	2.0
+200	+5	+2	+20	+0.4	+0.3	+2	+0.6	+400	+1.0
+400	+5	+3	+40	+0.5	+0.5	+5	+0.5	+100	+1.0

[a]The allowances are intended to provide for individual variations among most normal persons as they live in the United States under usual environmental stresses. Diets should be based on a variety of common foods in order to provide other nutrients for which human requirements have been less well defined.
[c]Until age 25, the calcium allowance should be 1200 mg.
[b]The increased requirement during pregnancy cannot be met by the iron content of habitual American diets nor by the existing iron stores of many women; therefore the use of 30–60 mg of supplemental iron is recommended. Iron needs during lactation are not substantially different from those of nonpregnant women, but continued supplementation of the mother for 2–3 months after parturition is advisable in order to replenish stores depleted by pregnancy.
SOURCE: *Recommended Daily Dietary Allowances, Revised 1989,* adapted from the National Academy of Sciences–National Research Council, Washington, D.C.

Vitamin Supplements

As a result of a heightened concern for good nutrition, food fads on which "health food" stores have been able to capitalize and widespread human gullibility to the extravagant claims of pharmaceutical advertising, the vitamin business grew from $500 million in 1972 to $3.5 billion in 1988. This has come about because 45 percent of the American population swallow one or more vitamin or vitamin and mineral pills every day, a statistic without equal in the Western world.

Here are some facts and fables about vitamin and mineral supplements:

- It needs saying over and over that a balanced diet composed of foods containing the essential nutrients normally provides the necessary daily amounts of vitamins and minerals.
- While some nutrients are lost in shipping, storing, and processing, far more are lost in the kitchen because of inappropriate refrigeration and overcooking.
- Women whose eating patterns do not meet all nutritional needs because they are constantly on one or another trendy diet should accept the fact that pills and capsules cannot take the place of food on a permanent basis.
- Supplements are in order for the many Americans who consume significantly less than the recommended levels of vitamins A, B_6, and C as well as calcium, iron, and magnesium.
- Women concerned about the advantages of organically grown food —and there *are* advantages—should be aware that the vitamin content of food is a function of its genes and not of the soil in which it is grown.
- On stress and vitamins: megadoses are needed only for the major stress of surgery, serious burns, fractures, or advanced cancer and not for the stresses of daily life.
- On supplements of vitamin A: if your diet is rich in betacarotene, a nutrient transformed by the body into vitamin A, you are at lower risk for lung and colon cancer. (One medium-sized carrot supplies a full four days worth of betacarotene.)
- Pregnant women should not take any vitamin A supplements with-

out a physician's advice because excessive doses are highly toxic and can cause malformations of the fetus.
- Too much vitamin B_6 can lead to numbness and irreversible damage to peripheral nerves.
- The dangers of self-medication with large doses of vitamin C are discussed under water-soluble vitamins.

Terminology in vitamin science is confusing because over the years some vitamins have been assigned letters, some have been given names, and some are referred to by both a letter and a name. Names are used on food packages. Vitamins can be divided into two main groups—fat soluble and water soluble.

Fat-Soluble Vitamins

The fat-soluble vitamins are A, D, E, and K. Because dietary excesses can be stored in the body, they are not absolutely necessary in the diet every day and evidence of deficiencies is slow to develop.

Vitamin A is essential to keep healthy the skin and the mucous membranes that line the eyes and respiratory, gastrointestinal, and urinary tracts. Also it keeps our tear ducts functioning, makes night vision possible by combining with a protein to form visual purple, seems to be involved in reducing susceptibility to general infection, and contributes to bone growth. Carotene, a substance that the body converts to vitamin A, is present in fruits and vegetables, particularly those that are yellow, green, or orange. Vitamin A itself is present only in animal products, particularly liver, and to a lesser extent in milk, eggs, butter, and margarine.

The only unequivocal signs of vitamin A deficiency in humans occur in the eye. In the United States only night blindness is usually encountered and that is seen most frequently in chronic alcoholics.

Because vitamin A is readily stored in the body, toxic levels can accumulate if intake is excessive. At levels of intake over 2,000 IU/kg/day, toxic symptoms can occur. Those at risk for developing vitamin A toxicity include not only food faddists purposefully taking large amounts but also pregnant women and children taking or being given excessive amounts of vitamin A inadvertently as a vitamin supplement. High-potency vitamin supplements, containing potentially toxic amounts of vitamin A, are available without prescription, so consumers

TABLE 3 A GUIDE TO THE VITAMINS

Vitamin	Best Sources
A	liver; eggs, cheese, butter, fortified margarine and milk; yellow, orange, and dark green vegetables (e.g., carrots, broccoli, squash, spinach)
B_1 (thiamin)	pork (especially ham), liver, oysters; whole grain and enriched cereals, pasta and bread, wheat germ; brewers yeast; green peas
B_2 (riboflavin)	liver, meat; milk; dark green vegetables; whole grain and enriched cereals, pasta and bread; mushrooms
B_3 (niacin)	liver, poultry, meat, tuna; whole grain and enriched cereals, pasta and bread; nuts, dried beans, and peas; made in body from amino acid tryptophan
B_6 (pyridoxine)	whole grain (but not enriched) cereals and bread; liver; avocados, spinach, green beans; bananas
B_{12} (cobalamin)	liver, kidneys, meat, fish, oysters; eggs; milk
Folic acid (folacin)	liver, kidneys; dark green leafy vegetables; wheat germ; brewers yeast
Pantothenic acid	liver, kidneys; whole grain bread and cereal; nuts; eggs; dark green vegetables; yeast
Biotin	egg yolk; liver, kidneys; dark green vegetables, green beans; made in intestinal tract
C (ascorbic acid)	many fruits and vegetables, including citrus, tomato, strawberries, melon, green pepper, potato, dark green vegetables
D	milk; egg yolk; liver, tuna, salmon; made on skin in sunlight
E	vegetable oils; margarine; whole grain cereal and bread, wheat germ; liver; dried beans; green leafy vegetables
K	green leafy vegetables; vegetables in cabbage family; milk; made in intestinal tract

Main Roles	Deficiency Symptoms
formation and maintenance of skin and mucous membranes, bone growth, vision, reproduction, teeth	night blindness, rough skin and mucous membranes, no bone growth, cracked or decayed teeth, drying of eyes
release of energy from carbohydrates, synthesis of nerve-regulating substance	beriberi, mental confusion, muscular weakness, swelling of heart, leg cramps
release of energy to cells from carbohydrates, proteins, and fats; maintenance of mucous membranes	skin disorders, especially around nose and lips; cracks at mouth corners; eyes very sensitive to light
works with thiamin and riboflavin in energy-producing reactions in cells	pellagra; skin disorders, especially parts exposed to sun; smooth tongue; diarrhea; mental confusion; irritability
absorption and metabolism of proteins, use of fats, formation of red blood cells	skin disorders, cracks at mouth corners, smooth tongue, convulsions, dizziness, nausea, anemia, kidney stones
building of genetic material, formation of red blood cells, functioning of nervous system	pernicious anemia, anemia, degeneration of peripheral nerves
assists in forming body proteins and genetic material, formation of hemoglobin	anemia with large red blood cells, smooth tongue, diarrhea
metabolism of carbohydrates, proteins and fats; formation of hormones and nerve-regulating substances	not know except experimentally in man: vomiting, abdominal pain, fatigue, sleep problems
formation of fatty acids, release of energy from carbohydrates	not known except experimentally in man: fatigue, depression, nausea, pains, loss of appetite
maintenance of health of bones, teeth, blood vessels; formation of collagen, which supports body structure; antioxidant	scurvy; gums bleed; muscles degenerate; wounds don't heal; skin rough, brown, and dry; teeth loosen
essential for normal bone growth and maintenance of strong bones	rickets (in children): retarded growth, bowed legs, malformed teeth, protruding abdomen; osteomalacia (in adults): bones soften, deform, and fracture easily, muscular twitching and spasms
formation of red blood cells, muscle, and other tissues; prevents oxidation of vitamin A and fats	breakdown of red blood cells; symptoms in animals (reproductive failure, liver degeneration, muscular dystrophy, etc.) not seen in man
essential for normal blood clotting	hemorrhage (especially in newborns)

SOURCE: © 1979 by The New York Times Company. Reprinted by permission.

and physicians must exercise caution and check the vitamin A content of supplements they purchase or recommend. There is no evidence that high doses improve night vision.

Vitamin D helps to regulate the absorption and utilization of calcium and phosphorus, which are needed to form strong bones and teeth. It is found naturally in a few foods of animal origin, primarily eggs, milk, and butter, but only in small amounts. Generally, therefore, these foods, and particularly milk, are enriched with vitamin D. In the presence of sunlight, the skin synthesizes vitamin D.

Doses far in excess of the recommended amounts may produce abnormally high levels of blood calcium, which can cause kidney damage, high blood pressure, and depression of brain function. Deficiencies cause rickets in children and bone softening in adults.

Vitamin E (tocopherol) is an antioxidant and thus serves as a food preservative. In the body it is involved in cellular respiration and in muscle and red blood cell formation. It is found in a wide variety of foods including green leafy vegetables, whole grains, liver, and dried beans. Deficiencies are almost never seen in humans but can reduce the stability of red blood cells. High doses of vitamin E have been recommended for the cure and prevention of an amazing spectrum of problems or illnesses including impotence, heart disease, cancer, and mental retardation. However, there is no evidence to support the claims of those who promote vitamin E supplements for the prevention and treatment of these conditions. High doses of vitamin E interfere with vitamin K metabolism, may lengthen the prothrombin time—one measure of the clotting ability of blood—and may cause easy bruising or bleeding from the nose, gums, intestine, or kidney. Claims that vitamin E will ward off the effects of aging, enhance fertility, and restore or improve libido (sexual drive) and potency have not been substantiated.

Vitamin K is needed to form the prothrombin factor that must be present for blood to clot (coagulate). Its name derives from the Danish word *Koagulation*. It is present in green leafy vegetables and cabbage and is synthesized by bacteria in the digestive tract. Deficiencies characterized by diffuse internal bleeding are sometimes seen in adults with liver disease that impairs absorption capacities because of insufficient bile. Deficiencies may also occur in persons on antibiotic therapy, which causes changes in intestinal bacteria, and in newborn infants. They are treated by injections of vitamin K.

Water-Soluble Vitamins

The water-soluble vitamins are the so-called B complex vitamins and vitamin C. (Two additional substances, choline and inositol, are sometimes considered to be B vitamins, but they are actually not vitamins.) Each B vitamin is unique and there is now no functional justification for continuing to refer to them as a group. Dietary excesses of water-soluble vitamins can be stored only in limited amounts. Ascorbic acid can be stored for longer periods. Therefore, they must be supplied every day and deficiencies often develop rapidly.

Thiamin (B_1) is necessary as an oxidizing agent in the release of energy from carbohydrates and in the synthesis of certain nerve regulating substances. Because no one food is exceptionally high in thiamin, we must eat a selection of foods to get our daily supply. Good sources are whole grains, dried beans, leafy vegetables, milk, and liver and other meats, especially pork. It is important to note that some thiamin is lost when foods are cooked in water or at high temperatures.

Severe thiamin deficiency causes beriberi, one of the first deficiency diseases to be recognized. Its major signs and symptoms are those of peripheral neuritis with weakness, aching, and burning, especially in the legs; central nervous system manifestations such as irritability and confusion; cardiovascular problems such as rapid heart beat and enlarged heart; and gastrointestinal symptoms such as loss of appetite and constipation.

Riboflavin (B_2) is essential in hydrogenation processes that release energy from carbohydrates, proteins, and fats. It also is essential for healthy skin and mucous membranes and for good vision in bright light. Milk and cheese are the best sources, and liver, eggs, and yeast are also rich in riboflavin. Although not affected by heat in cooking, riboflavin is soluble in water, and some of it can be lost when foods are cooked in water. Riboflavin deficiency causes cracks around the corners of the mouth (cheilosis), inflammation of the lips, and tongue changes (glossitis).

Niacin (nicotinic acid, nicotinamide, B_3) works with thiamin and riboflavin to produce energy in cells. It is needed to change glucose to glycogen, our only storage form of carbohydrate, and has a role in the synthesis of fat and cholesterol. Liver and yeast are the most concentrated sources of niacin, but the best commonly eaten food sources are meats, poultry, fish, and legumes. It also is synthesized in the body from tryptophan, an amino acid. A lack of it causes pellagra with skin eruptions, sore and swollen tongue, diarrhea, and impaired brain function. Niacin has recently been prescribed on an experimental basis as therapy for high levels of blood cholesterol that do not respond to other, more established treatments.

Pyridoxine (B_6) facilitates reactions in which amino acids (the building blocks for protein) are absorbed and metabolized, and it plays a role in the formation of red blood cells. The list of chemical reactions that require pyridoxine is enlarging continually as research efforts progress. The best sources are those containing the other B vitamins—liver, whole grain cereals and bread, green beans, spinach, and bananas. When wheat is made into white flour, most of this vitamin is lost, and food processing also has a destructive effect on it. Requirements for pyridoxine increase when the protein of the diet is increased, as in pregnancy. Old age and medications such as birth control pills and hormones may also increase requirements. The main signs of pyridoxine deficiency are secretory and weepy lesions of the skin around the nose and mouth, and mouth and tongue soreness.

Pantothenic acid, another of the B vitamins, is essential for the metabolism of carbohydrates, proteins, and fats. It is also involved in hormone formation. Its physiologically active form is known as coenzyme A. A deficiency of pantothenic acid has almost never been seen in humans, possibly because it is present in ordinary foods, particularly liver, eggs, and wheat germ.

Folacin (folic acid, folate, pteroylglutamic acid or PGA) is essential for the formation of new cells, the production of red blood cells, and protein synthesis. Liver, yeast, and fresh green vegetables are rich sources, but it is present in nearly all foods. However, because 50 to 90 percent of folacin may be destroyed by prolonged cooking or by canning, some people have a deficiency, particularly those on very marginal diets, many of whom are alcoholics. Pregnant and nursing women generally are thought to need extra folacin. Deficiency leads to megoblastic (large red blood cells) anemia, inflammation of the tongue, and diarrhea. Antifolic acid preparations are used to treat some types of cancer because folacin is essential for cells to divide and multiply.

Cobalamin (cyanocobalamin, B_{12}) is essential for the normal functioning of all cells in the body, particularly the blood-producing cells in the bone marrow and the cells of the nervous system and digestive tract. It is found only in foods of animal origin. Plants, including yeast, which are good sources of other B vitamins, provide no cobalamin. Beef, liver, lamb, cheese, and oysters are exceptionally good sources. A lack of cobalamin generally results from malabsorption rather than from a dietary inadequacy. Deficiency causes pernicious anemia, a rare but once fatal disease, now effectively treated with periodic injections of this vitamin.

Biotin, another B vitamin, is involved in the metabolism of carbon dioxide. It is present in egg yolk, dark green vegetables, liver, and green beans. It is synthesized in the gastrointestinal tract. Deficiency of it is unknown except when it is induced experimentally.

Ascorbic acid (vitamin C) is needed to form collagen, the protein that binds our cells together. It promotes wound and bone healing and normal blood clotting. By maintaining the elasticity and strength of blood vessels, vitamin C prevents easy bruising. It is also needed for the absorption of iron. The best sources are fruits including strawberries, oranges, and grapefruit. Vegetable sources include broccoli, tomatoes, cauliflower, and green pepper.

Scurvy, which results from ascorbic acid deficiency, has been known since early Egyptian times. It is the subject of much of the fiction and nonfiction written about the British Navy, where in 1753 a Scottish doctor discovered that sailors who got lemon juice during long voyages at sea remained healthy and those who did not developed extreme lassitude, bleeding gums, and skin bruises.

High doses of vitamin C have been recommended by Nobel-laureate Linus Pauling and others for the prevention and treatment of the common cold. While there is some evidence that chronic vitamin C supplementation results in a slight decrease in the duration and severity of cold symptoms, there is no evidence that large supplements are more effective than more modest supplements (50–100 mg/day). *However, there is considerable cause for concern about potential harmful consequences of high doses of vitamin C* that (1) acidify the urine and may lead to the development of kidney stones in people with gout, (2) are metabolized to oxalate and may contribute to the development of calcium oxalate kidney stones, (3) may condition the body so that a reduction of vitamin C intake to normal levels may cause abnormally low blood levels of vitamin C, (4) interfere with the guaiac test for blood in the stool (a test that is widely used in screening people for colon and rectal cancer) making it falsely negative, and (5) may result in scurvy when infants born to mothers who took high doses of vitamin C during pregnancy are placed on formula containing normal levels of vitamin C.

MINERALS

The minerals important in human nutrition can be classified into three categories: those which the body stores in large quantities (sodium, potassium, calcium, magnesium, phosphorus); the trace minerals whose importance is known (iron, zinc, copper, iodine, fluoride, selenium, chromium); and other trace minerals (cobalt, molybdenum, manganese, cadmium, arsenic, nickel) whose role in human nutrition is uncertain (see Table 2). Of the latter group, it is only manganese for which some evidence of deficiency in humans has appeared.

Many minerals are widely available in foods. Moreover, they are easy to provide as supplements. Because of these facts and because it is difficult to assess body stores, it is not surprising that overload syndromes occur more frequently for minerals than for vitamins. Sodium (Na), potassium (K), calcium (Ca), iron (Fe), and fluoride (F) are most commonly involved in overload syndromes.

Sodium as salt or NaCl can be harmful even under common conditions of use. Sodium and chloride, along with potassium, are the regulators for the passage of nutrients in and out of cells. Although the process is complicated, the most important factor is balance. Too much or too little salt upsets this balance. While the average daily intake of salt is between 8 and 12 grams, the amount needed to stay healthy is less than 200 milligrams a day. One teaspoon of salt contains 2 grams of sodium. It's the sodium that concerns us most: in excess, sodium can cause fluid retention and contributes to hypertension in susceptible individuals.

Sodium needs in normal persons can be met by an intake of 92–184 mg per day. This requirement will vary with increased sweating or increased losses in the urine or stool due to disease. In Western societies an adult with free access to salt may consume from 2.3 to 6.9 g of sodium (100–300 mEq) per day, or from 8 to 12 g of salt, and much more is added in the form of condiments, fats, and salad dressings. Some of the most commonly used products are listed in Table 4.

In food preparation a number of compounds are added in addition to salt (NaCl). Those that increase the sodium content of most prepared foods are listed below as they appear on package labels.

1. Monosodium glutamate (MSG)—in packaged and frozen foods
2. Baking powder—in breads and cakes

NUTRITION, WEIGHT, AND GENERAL WELL-BEING

3. Baking soda (sodium bicarbonate)—in breads and cakes
4. Brine—in processed foods (e.g., pickles)
5. Disodium phosphate—in cereals and cheeses
6. Sodium alginate or caseinate—as thickener and binder
7. Sodium benzoate or nitrite—as preservative
8. Sodium hydroxide—to soften skins of fruits and olives
9. Sodium propionate—to inhibit mold in cheeses
10. Sodium sulfate—as preservative in dried fruit
11. Sodium citrate—as buffer for canned and bottled citrus drinks

In addition to food, sodium is present in drinking water and in medications. Water that is softened may contain as much as 1,500 mg of sodium per liter. Most medications do not contain enough sodium to present a problem, but a few are very high in sodium—for example, antibiotic suspensions, Rolaids, Di-Gel liquid, Alka-Seltzer, Bromo-Seltzer, Metamucil, and Sal Hepatica. Recently, however, a special promotional point is being made about the low-sodium or no-sodium versions of some of these over-the-counter products. In general, liquid formulas contain more sodium than do capsules or tablets.

Sodium is usually restricted in the diets of people with high blood pressure, congestive heart failure, kidney failure, liver failure, and high blood cholesterol levels.

Because of a growing demand on the part of consumers for salt-free processed foods, the availability of canned and frozen soups and vegetables in this category has increased, simplifying meal-planning for millions of concerned women. Low-sodium additions to food that give zest and appeal to foods prepared and served without salt are listed in Table 5. Commercially available salt substitutes and packaged salt containing as much as one-third less sodium than the usual product are now to be found on supermarket shelves. If significant amounts of these salt substitutes are used, they may contribute a major supplementary source of potassium and provide that potassium in a form that is ten times cheaper than potassium chloride solutions or powders. Many cookbooks and government pamphlets are available in local libraries for those who require low-sodium diets.

Potassium (K), the major mineral within the body's cells, along with sodium and calcium, regulates the passage of nutrients into and out of cells. It also regulates the heart and may provide protection against stroke. Good sources of potassium are meat, fish, citrus fruits, dairy products, nuts, leafy green vegetables, potatoes, bananas, and water-

TABLE 4

SODIUM CONTENT OF VARIOUS CONDIMENTS

Product	Portion	Representative Na Content (mg)
Baking powder	1 tsp	339
Baking soda	1 tsp	821
Catsup	1 tsp	156
Meat tenderizer	1 tsp	1,750
Monosodium glutamate	1 tsp	492
Mustard, prepared	1 tsp	65
Pickle, dill	one	928
Pickle, sweet	one	128
Salt	1 tsp	1,938
Sauce, A-1	1 tbs	275
barbecue	1 tbs	130
soy	1 tbs	1,029
Worcestershire	1 tbs	206
Butter, regular	1 tbs	116
Margarine	1 tbs	140
Salad dressing, bottled	1 tbs	109–224

melon. Those taking diuretics for high blood pressure, heart failure, or fluid retention lose significant amounts of potassium in the urine and often require additional potassium as a supplement or in the diet. Some salt substitutes that are rich in potassium are an inexpensive way to provide extra amounts of this mineral. Symptoms of potassium deficiency include lethargy, muscle weakness, and abnormal heart rhythm.

Calcium circulating in the bloodstream helps blood to clot, is required for muscle contraction and relaxation, and helps to regulate nerve activity. The most important muscle of all, the heart, contracts and relaxes in large measure because of an adequate and controlled level of calcium. Combined with phosphorus as calcium phosphate, it forms the hard material of bones and teeth. Calcium in bone is absorbed and replaced continually to maintain the proper level in the blood. Calcium absorbed from the teeth, however, cannot be replaced. Therefore, broken bones heal but teeth cannot repair themselves. (see Table 8, p. 95 for foods high in calcium.) Vitamin D is essential in the diet for the proper metabolism of calcium from food sources. Important sources are milk, milk products, and egg yolk.

Self-medication with calcium supplements can have undesirable ef-

NUTRITION, WEIGHT, AND GENERAL WELL-BEING

TABLE 5

NATURAL LOW-SODIUM SEASONINGS THAT CAN SUBSTITUTE FOR SALT

Uses	Alternate Seasonings
General cooking	Lemon juice, garlic, onion, and yogurt are the most useful; pepper and chili powder are good if tolerated
Meat	Lemon, garlic, onion, pepper, oregano, curry powder, rosemary, thyme, paprika, ginger
Fish and poultry	Lemon, garlic, onion, pepper, ginger, oregano, paprika, parsley, sesame seed, savory, tarragon, thyme
Egg dishes	Pepper (red or black), basil, marjoram, onion, oregano, tarragon, thyme
Vegetables	Pepper, basil (especially for tomatoes), dill, thyme, oregano, chervil, rosemary, yogurt (potatoes especially)
Soups	Garlic, onion, pepper, bay leaf, basil, thyme

fects. Three or four times the recommended daily amount can lead to the formation of kidney stones and might also interfere with iron absorption. In some cases, excess calcium can be deposited in soft tissues and be confused with cancer. Excess supplements can also cause constipation and may increase the release of excess stomach acid, possibly heightening the risk of ulcers. There is no definitive evidence that calcium supplements retard bone loss in older women and prevent osteoporosis or compensate for a lifelong diet deficient in calcium.

Other minerals required by the body include magnesium and phosphorus. Some foods rich in the former are meats, seafood, green vegetables, dairy products, and cereals. Phosphorus is found in all foods, but some of its major dietary sources are milk, grains, and cereals.

Trace minerals of importance in human nutrition include iron (FE), zinc (Zn), iodine (I), and fluoride (F).

Iron is the constituent of hemoglobin that enables the red blood cells to transport oxygen to all parts of the body. Only 15 milligrams of dietary iron are needed each day to replace the red blood cells that are destroyed in the body's processes. During menstruation a woman needs an additional 3 milligrams to compensate for the blood loss. These daily requirements are easily obtained in a diet containing such foods as eggs, lean meat, liver, peanut butter, molasses, kidney beans, raisins, and green leafy vegetables. In those cases when heavy menstrual bleeding over a period of months results in iron-deficiency anemia, a prescribed supplement is indicated.

Zinc is a cofactor for nearly 100 of the body's essential enzymes. Eye tissues, especially those involved in dark adaptation, contain high concentrations of zinc. Also, it speeds the healing of wounds and is necessary for the proper functioning of the immune system. (If zinc is insufficient, the disease-fighting cells—the T-lymphocytes—may be inadequately produced. The average zinc content of the diet in adults ranges from 10 to 15 mg per day and is just adequate to provide the RDA. During growth, pregnancy, and lactation, an additional 5–10 mg per day are required. Muscle meats and seafood, especially oysters, are rich in zinc. Conditions that compromise the body's zinc supply include excessive alcohol intake, cirrhosis of the liver, and gastrointestinal diseases, especially Crohn's disease.

Iodine is required to prevent thyroid goiter in adults. The RDA is 150 mg per day, and the requirement during pregnancy and lactation is somewhat higher. Seafood is an excellent and consistent source. Iodized table salt, which contains 76 mg of iodine per gram of salt, is the usual supplement for dietary iodine in the United States. One teaspoon of iodized salt contains 260 mg of iodine and 2 grams of sodium.

Fluoride is concentrated in bones and teeth and results in increased resistance to tooth decay. Recommended intake is 1.5–4.0 mg per day for adults, 2.0–2.5 mg per day for children, and 0.1–1.0 mg per day for infants. These recommendations are based on prevention of dental caries not on total body requirement. Water is the major source of fluoride, and it is recommended that water supplies contain at least 1 mg/liter, a level that will ensure adequate fluoride intake to decrease the incidence of caries. Other foods naturally high in fluoride include ocean fish and tea.

WATER AND FIBER

Two substances that are technically not nutrients but are essential to healthy function and structure are water and fiber. Water, the most abundant substance in our bodies, carries all nutrients and wastes to and from our cells and regulates body temperature. Fiber (cellulose in plant food) speeds and stimulates the digestive process and the elimination of unused and indigestible foods. Dietary fiber is plant cell wall polysaccharides and lignin that resist digestion by enzymes of the human intestine. The fiber content of foods is usually described on the basis of crude fiber, the residue of food after sequential acid and alkali treatment. The three major classes of dietary fiber are cellulose, noncellulose polysaccharides, and lignin. A high-fiber diet increases stool bulk, produces more frequent stools, and decreases transit time through the intestine. There is compelling evidence that high-fiber diets reduce the likelihood of diverticulosis, irritable bowel syndrome, and colon cancer. Table 6 lists total dietary fiber per average serving and can be used as a guide to design a high-fiber diet. In addition, many non-prescription psyllium preparations such as Metamucil, which add bulk to the diet, are available.

TABLE 6

FIBER IN FOODS

Portion	*Fiber (in grams)*
Apple, 1 small	3.1
Banana, 1 medium	1.8
Beans, green, 1/2 cup	1.2
Beets, cooked, 2/3 cup	2.1
Bran, 1 cup	2.3
Bread, rye, 1 slice	2.0
Bread, whole wheat, 1 slice	2.4
Bulgur, dry, 1/3 cup	5.6
Carrots, cooked, 3/4 cup	2.1
Celery, raw, 2 1/2 stalks	3.0
Grapefruit, 1/2	2.6
Grape-Nuts, 1/3 cup	5.0
Orange, 1 small	1.8
Pear, 1 medium	2.8
Peas, green, 1/2 cup	3.8
Potatoes, cooked, 2/3 cup	3.1
Rice, brown, cooked, 1 cup	1.1
Rice, white, cooked, 1 cup	.4
Rolled oats, dry, 1/2 cup	4.5
Shredded wheat biscuit, 1	.3
Strawberries, fresh, 1/2 cup	2.6

BALANCED NUTRITION

Nutrients work together. Each nutrient has specific functions, several may be necessary for a particular function, and one may affect how another operates in the body. For example, vitamin A cannot be absorbed unless the right amount of vitamin D is present. A sudden increase in the amount of phosphorus without a proportionate increase in calcium makes the unchanged amount of calcium inadequate for the body's needs. An extra supply of one nutrient cannot make up for the deficiency of another. Therefore, good nutrition means balanced nutrition, with all the necessary nutrients supplied in the right proportions.

SELECTION OF FOODS FOR BALANCED NUTRITION

All the required nutrients cannot be obtained from any single food. In order to be sure of balanced nutrition we must select our nourishment from a variety of food products. For convenience in making that selection, foods with similar nutrient content are grouped together.

FOOD GROUPS

Foods in the milk group supply us with calcium, protein, and riboflavin (B_2). The group includes all types of milk and milk products, such as cheese and yogurt.

Foods in the meat group supply protein, niacin, iron, and thiamine (B_1). It includes meats (pork, veal, lamb, beef), fish and shellfish, poultry, eggs, and certain plant foods that supply large amounts of protein, such as legumes and nuts.

The fruit-vegetable group supplies vitamin A, vitamin C, some minerals, carbohydrates, and fiber.

Foods in the grain group supply carbohydrates, B vitamins, iron, and fiber. The group includes all grains and cereals, such as barley, buckwheat, corn, oats, rice, rye, and wheat.

Table 7 lists the four basic food groups and gives specific examples of foods for each, the amount in each serving, and the recommended number of servings per day based on age and whether women are pregnant or breast-feeding.

Approximately 10 million Americans now call themselves vegetarians, and the ranks continue to grow. A large number eat fish, a smaller number also eat chicken, and most eat dairy products that strict vegetarians (called vegans) do not. Some women who eliminate meat from their diet do so out of strong convictions about unnecessary cruelty to animals; others are convinced of the health benefits of abstaining from red meat.

A properly planned vegetarian diet contains all the necessary nutrients. Proteins are supplied by combining complementary proteins, especially legumes, with grains or with nuts and seeds. The most frequently used legumes fall into two categories: peas (lentils, split peas, chick peas, black-eyed peas) and beans (kidney, lima, navy, pinto, fava, soy, also used as tofu). Dairy products, such as eggs, milk, yogurt, and cheese, need not be combined with other nutrients to supply protein. Many delicious ethnic dishes that originated with cooks who had to economize at the same time that they were concerned with proper nourishment for their families have become great favorites with vegetarians: mushroom and barley soup, all meatless pasta recipes, grape leaves stuffed with rice and pine nuts, scallion and beansprout omelets, and the like. Augmented with fruit and vegetables, such meals can be comparatively inexpensive and rich in vitamins, minerals, and fiber, high in complex carbohydrates, and very low in fats.

While there is no conclusive evidence that a vegetarian diet can cure various ailments (there are many such claims, ranging from relief for arthritis sufferers to prevention of vaginal infections), obvious health benefits abound. Here are a few:

- lower blood levels of cholesterol and triglycerides
- lower risk of heart attack
- less likelihood of high blood pressure
- lower prevalence of serious overweight
- lower prevalence of breast and colon cancer.

Whereas vegetarians were once considered "cranks," they are among the factors responsible for the widespread popularity of salad bars and the availability of fish dishes on many restaurant menus.

FOOD LABELING

The Food and Drug Administration (FDA) has set standards for food labeling that are designed to help consumers know what they are buying and to provide information on the nutritional content of food products.

The FDA requirements for food labels include:
1. Name and address of the manufacturer.
2. Name of the product. The FDA divides foods into two groups: those for which a "standard of identity" has been described and those for which there is no standard of identity.
   a. A standard of identity is basically a definition consisting of a list of ingredients that a product must contain. The FDA has such standards of identity for hundreds of products including mayonnaise, fruit pies, jams and jellies, margarine, canned fruits, and frozen vegetables.
   b. The standard of identity may be quantitative. For example, fruit preserve cannot be called "jam" or "jelly" unless it contains 60 percent fruit by weight.
   c. Some foods must be labeled "imitations" when they are nutritionally inferior to the products they resemble. Jam that contains less than 60 percent fruit must be labeled "imitation."
   d. If a product is not covered by a standard of identity, it must bear its common or usual name or an appropriate descriptive term. Although there is no standard of identity for sausage, it is generally accepted that sausage contains meat, and a product that does not contain meat cannot be called sausage.
3. The quantity of the contents in weight, measure, or count. This must be displayed on the front of the box.
4. Ingredient listing. Foods for which there is no standard of identity must have their ingredients listed on the label in order of their predominance by weight. If there is a standard of identity for a product then the ingredients need not be listed. The list of ingredients on the labels of foods that contain artificial flavoring or coloring or a chemical preservative must specifically indicate that the food is artificially flavored or colored or that it contains artificial preservatives.
5. Number of servings. The label need not state the number of servings in the package, but if it does state the number of servings it must also state the size of the serving.
6. Nutrition labeling. Only a small number of products are required by law to have nutrition labels. These products fall into two groups:
   a. Foods advertised for their nutritional properties, e.g., "low calorie," "low fat," "high in vitamin C."

TABLE 7

RECOMMENDED SERVINGS OF BASIC FOOD GROUPS TO SUPPLY ESSENTIAL NUTRIENTS

Number of Servings per Day		*Food Group/Serving Size*
Child	3	MILK
Adolescent	4	1 cup (8 oz) of yogurt; 1 1/2 slices (1 1/2 oz)
Adult	3	cheddar cheese; 1 cup pudding; 1 3/4 cups
Pregnant woman	4	ice cream; 2 cups cottage cheese
Breast-feeding woman	4	
Child	2	MEAT
Adolescent	2	2–3 oz cooked, lean meat, fish, poultry; 2
Adult	2	eggs; 2 slices (2 oz) cheddar cheese, 1/2
Pregnant woman	3	cup cottage cheese; 1 cup dried beans,
Breast-feeding woman	2	peas; 4 tbsp peanut butter
Child	4	FRUIT-VEGETABLE
Adolescent	4	1 cup raw fruit or vegetable; 1/2 cup
Adult	4	cooked fruit or vegetable; 1 medium
Pregnant woman	4	fruit, esp. citrus; 1/2 cup juice
Breast-feeding woman	4	
Child	4	GRAIN (Whole grain, fortified, or
Adolescent	4	enriched)
Adult	4	1 slice bread; 1 cup ready-to-eat cereal;
Pregnant woman	4	1/2–3/4 cup cooked cereal, pasta, cornmeal,
Breast-feeding woman	4	rice, or grits; 1 small muffin or biscuit; 5
		saltines; 2 graham crackers

SOURCE: Adapted from recommendations of National Dairy Council, Rosemont, Ill., 1978 and the American Dietetic Association, 1986.

    b. Foods that have been enriched or fortified with nutrients, such as cereals to which vitamins have been added.

Nutrition labels must include the following information:

    a. The content of eight nutrients (protein, calcium, iron, vitamin A, vitamin C, thiamin, riboflavin, and niacin). This must be listed in terms of a percentage of the U.S. Recommended Daily Allowance (U.S. RDA), which differs from the Recommended Dietary Allowance (RDA) discussed earlier. The U.S. RDA used on nutrition labels applies to people over age 4 who are not pregnant or lactating. In almost all cases this is the same as the 1968 RDA for adult males, but for iron the RDA for adult females is used.

    b. Serving sizes. (Designated serving sizes may be larger than most people

would eat. This is done to make the nutritional content of the product appear larger than it is.)
7. Warnings. If a food contains saccharin, the label must state: "Use of this product may be hazardous to your health. This product contains saccharin, which has been found to cause cancer in laboratory animals."

Other information given (but not required by the FDA) includes:
1. Department of Agriculture grades that are based on physical properties such as texture, color, size, and uniformity of appearance. For the most part, these grades have nothing to do with nutritional quality.
2. Dating to help the consumer judge food freshness.

FOOD ADDITIVES

Food additives have received much publicity in the recent scientific and lay press. The FDA defines food additives as "substances added directly to food, or substances which may reasonably be expected to become components of food through surface contact with equipment or packaging materials, or even substances that may otherwise affect food without becoming part of it."

Food additives are divided into two groups. One consists of newly developed additives regulated by the FDA and the other includes substances in use for a long time and called the Generally Recognized as Safe List (GRAS).

Most intentional additives, such as spices, herbs, flavorings, and oil extracts, are added for flavor. Some, such as monosodium glutamate, are flavor enhancers. Foods lose quality or become unsafe to eat because of chemical changes within the food or because bacteria or molds develop. Antioxidants, such as butylated-hydroxy anisole (BHA), prevent fats from becoming rancid and are added to oils, salad dressings, fried foods, potato chips, margarines, and baked goods or cake mixes that contain shortening. Ascorbic acid (vitamin C) is added to keep peeled and cut fruits from turning brown. Sugar, the oldest additive, is used to prevent molds from growing in bread, baked goods, cheese, syrup, candy, and jams and jellies. Additives such as salt, sodium nitrate, and sodium nitrite are used to cure meat, thus preventing harmful bacteria from developing.

Mineral and vitamin additives are used to enrich the nutritive value of foods, most commonly bread and flour. Milk is enriched with vitamin D while margarine, skim milk, and nonfat dry milk are enriched with vitamin A. Potassium iodide is added to table salt to prevent thyroid

NUTRITION, WEIGHT, AND GENERAL WELL-BEING

goiter, and fluoride is added to water because of its preventive action against tooth decay.

Additives that are used to give or maintain texture include emulsifiers, stabilizers, and thickeners that give body or greater consistency. Emulsifiers keep chocolate candy from changing color if it becomes warm and keep ice cream smooth and creamy by helping fats and other liquids to mix and stay mixed. Stabilizers keep solids and liquids from separating, as in chocolate milk, and prevent flavor loss from cake and pudding mixes.

Chemical substances such as citric acid (lemon juice) and acetic acid (vinegar) are used to give flavor and texture to foods such as jellies and jams, pickles, and salad dressings. Sodium hydroxide provides the glaze on pretzels.

While food colors were once derived from plants, 90 percent of all colors now in use are synthetic and are obvious in such foods as ice cream, soft drinks, pudding mixes, and gelatin desserts. Many of the synthetic dyes used to color foods, especially dyes prepared from aromatic compounds, were banned several years ago as a result of toxicity tests. Recent tests indicate that excessively high levels of colors violet 1, red 2, and red 4 produce tumors in rats and mice. As a result of the Federal law's "Delaney clause," which bars from use any food additive that induces cancer in man or animals, the number of permitted food colorings has decreased.

There are additives to keep foods moist called humectants and others to keep salt and powdered sugar free-flowing. Firming agents help canned tomatoes hold their shape, and sequestrants keep soft drinks clear by removing trace metals that cloud the water. Sodium nitrite, sodium nitrate, which is converted to nitrite in the body, and sodium chloride (table salt) have been used for centuries to keep meat from spoiling. Before the advent of refrigeration and freezing, salting was the only way to keep meat. The formation of botulism toxin, the most deadly of all food poisons, can be prevented by the sodium nitrite in the salting mixture used to cure meats. In addition, sodium nitrite prevents fat from becoming rancid, produces the popular cured flavor, and gives the meat a pleasant pink color. These substances are added to all cured and smoked meats (bacon, bologna, ham, frankfurter, corned beef, and so forth).

During the last decade there has been a great deal of research on factors in food and the environment that might cause cancer. Among the compounds found to produce cancer in rats were nitrite and its precursor, nitrate. Although cancers occurred only when the intake of either was high, the results cast suspicion on the safety of cured meats. Harmful compounds are more easily formed at a high temperature. For instance, nitrosamines, which are derivatives of nitrate and nitrite, are carcinogenic agents formed when bacon, which has been cured with nitrate or nitrite, is cooked. The nitrosamines then are present in the bacon and also are released into the air. As a result neither nitrate nor nitrite is used now in many cured meats such as bacon, and when they are used, the amount has been reduced to the minimum needed to preserve the product.

The leading food additive used in the United States is sugar. The prejudice against sugar is conspicuous in the supermarket where an increasing number of foods are labeled "natural," "no sugar added," or "in natural juice." The concern about sugar stems not only from a preoccupation with overweight and tooth decay but also from an accumulation of evidence that for some women, sugar is a powerful mood-altering substance that can undermine emotional stability.

The concern about excess sugar in food has prompted the development of artificial, non-nutritive sweeteners, such as saccharin and aspartame, which taste sweet because they stimulate taste receptors in the same way but which cannot be oxidized by the body to yield energy. Links between saccharin and bladder cancer in rats have been an important factor in efforts by the FDA to restrict its use. While new studies do not prove that saccharin is entirely harmless, they show *no* evidence that it has played a significant role in cancer of the urinary tract, including the bladder. The risk for children, especially those exposed in utero, and for older people with lifelong heavy use has yet to be determined.

Aspartame (NutraSweet), a synthetic combination of two amino acids, is now available in the United States for use as a sweetener in breakfast cereals, powdered beverages, gelatins, puddings, fillings, whipped toppings, and chewing gum. It is also available under the trade name Equal as a tablet or powder for table use. It is 180 times as sweet as sugar (sucrose) and the amount of aspartame equivalent in sweetness to one teaspoonful of sugar (16 calories) contains only 0.1 calorie. Studies in rats indicate that unlike sugar (sucrose), aspartame does not promote dental caries. Aspartame was kept off the market for many years because one study suggested that rats fed aspartame might have a higher incidence of brain tumors. Other studies did not show a higher incidence, and the U.S. Food and Drug Administration has concluded with "reasonable certainty" that aspartame does not cause brain tumors. Its long-term safety remains to be determined.

In July, 1988, a new artificial sweetener was approved by the FDA for use in dry food products and for sale, like saccharin, in powder and tablet form for consumer use. Marketed under the brand name Sunette, the chemical compound acesulfame potassium is said to be 200 times sweeter than sugar and has no caloric content. It is also said to be more stable than aspartame. Already, however, consumer advocates are concerned that two animal studies indicate that this latest artificial sweetener has toxic effects. The FDA counters these charges by pointing to four long-term studies showing that no toxic effects could be attributed to this latest entry into the artificial sweetener market, a market that represents $1 billion in the United States.

THE IMPORTANCE OF BREAKFAST

Too many working women skip breakfast and then gobble down the wrong foods after they've checked in with the boss. Takeout breakfasts from fast food establishments are very high in fat, salt, sugar, and cholesterol—typically eggs, croissants, doughnuts, sweet rolls, fried ham, sausages, or bacon. Commercial bran muffins are likely to be high in sugar and saturated fats. Fruited yogurt contains 140 calories of heavily sugared preserves and 140 calories of yogurt. Watch out for bagels with cream cheese and for commercial granola, usually high in fat and sugar. Nondairy creamers are a bad idea because they're made of corn syrup and coconut oil.

If you can possibly take the time to do so, have breakfast at home. Prepare a dish of hot cereal in the microwave oven. Blend yogurt, buttermilk, or liquefied powdered milk with banana, peaches, or fruit juice.

If you don't have to hurry, sit down to a proper breakfast of fresh fruit or juice and whole grain cereal or whole wheat toast or prepare something untraditional such as brown rice with yogurt and raisins or a chicken sandwich on whole wheat pita bread. Remember that eating a good breakfast means eating less and spending less on lunch, breakfast can supply nutrients such as vitamins C and D and calcium and iron that may be missing in other meals of the day, and eating a nourishing breakfast can reduce impatience and irritability and improve late morning concentration span.

FAST FOODS

Because many of us eat more than half our meals away from home, fast-food chains have thrived and the industry continues to grow. Women are attracted to the foods they offer because they are filling, inexpensive, attractive to children, and sometimes even taste quite good. While not synonymous with "junk," which provides little or no nutrients other than sugar and calories, fast foods are not nutritionally balanced. For the number of calories they provide, fast-food meals oversupply us with fats and salt while undersupplying us with vitamins. The meals at fast-food chains may be low in sugar, but the beverages (soft drinks and shakes) and desserts are not. In terms of food groups, these meals are severely deficient in vegetables (except potatoes) and fruit. However, in response to a growing demand, some chains are offering salads in addition to their usual menus. But the salads are likely to have their "freshness" preserved with sulfites and may not contain a sufficient variety of fresh greens. In any case, fast-food meals should not be eaten regularly and, on days when they are, they should be augmented at other times of the day with a good assortment of fresh fruit, vegetables, and grains.

A word about those french fries, which are always a nutritional booby-trap. Potatoes when baked or steamed are an excellent food because in proportion to their calories they provide relatively large amounts of protein, vitamins, and minerals. But when fried in deep fat, they become a high-fat, high-calorie food, and when doused with salt and ketchup, their sodium content is very high.

NUTRITIONAL NEEDS AT SPECIAL AGES AND STAGES

The general information presented on calorie requirements and balanced nutrition applies to the healthy woman age 23–50 who is not

NUTRITION, WEIGHT, AND GENERAL WELL-BEING

pregnant and not lactating. Older women and those who are pregnant or lactating have special nutritional needs.

NUTRITION IN PREGNANCY

Pregnancy is a unique and special time in the life of a woman. All women want their babies to be healthy. The main reason some babies die or are not healthy is that they weigh 2,500 grams (5.5 pounds) or less at birth. While smoking and excessive alcohol consumption are two leading causes of the low birth weight problem, the major cause is inadequate maternal nutrition during the pregnancy and even before conception.

Adequate nutrition is needed not only to provide the caloric energy and the essential nutrients such as proteins, vitamins, and minerals required by the growing fetus but also to sustain the many physiologic and metabolic changes that occur in the mother. A healthy, well-nourished woman who is not underweight during pregnancy requires about 300 extra calories each day over the nonpregnant diet of approximately 2,100 calories (see table 7). These ideally should be provided from food in the following ratios: 50 to 60 percent from carbohydrates (preferably complex starch), 15 to 20 percent from protein (animal and vegetable), and 25 to 30 percent from fat. Such a 2,400 to 2,500 calorie daily diet will provide all her energy needs.

Equally important, however, is attention to other essential nutrients and the variety of sources that supply them. It is also preferable to eat smaller meals more frequently than to stick with the three "square meals" that may cause a certain amount of discomfort as the pregnancy progresses.

Here are some guidelines for daily essentials:

- *Protein and iron.* 4 servings chosen from lean meat; poultry; organ meats such as liver, kidney, sweetbreads; fish; eggs; nuts; and for vegetarians, legumes combined with whole grains.
- *Calcium and protein.* 4 servings chosen from whole milk, buttermilk, yogurt, cottage cheese, farmer cheese, low fat hard cheeses, ice cream.
- *Vitamins A and C.* 5 servings chosen from green leafy vegetables, carrots, tomatoes, citrus and other fruits, red and green peppers, potatoes (white and sweet).

- *B vitamins.* 4 servings chosen from whole grains and enriched grains in brown rice, pasta, breads, muffins, oatmeal and other cereals (preferably cooked and sweetened with fruit juice rather than packaged products processed with too much salt, sugar, and saturated fats).
- *Lots of fluids.* water, natural fruit juices, 3 cups of tea or coffee (preferably decaffeinated), salt-free seltzer (an alcoholic beverage only on special occasions).

Of the essential nutrients, protein is most important because it is vital to the formation and growth of the fetal brain, which is more fully developed at birth than the rest of the body. A healthy woman needs approximately 76 grams of protein each day, particularly in the last three months of pregnancy. This is 30 grams more than an acceptable nonpregnant daily protein diet of 46 grams. A quart of milk contains 32 grams of protein. Vegetarian diets are often deficient in certain types of amino acids and special care must be taken to eat the complementary foods to get complete proteins.

Another essential nutrient is iron, used by the body to make the needed additional maternal hemoglobin that carries oxygen to all the tissues including the fetus. Because many women have insufficient stored iron and no diet can supply the increased amounts necessary, ferrous sulfate is often prescribed—one 5-grain tablet a day is sufficient—starting as early in pregnancy as possible and continuing for about a month after birth. Daily folic acid is often prescribed, too, to prevent both folate deficiency and a rare kind of anemia called megaloblastic anemia. Accumulating evidence suggests that supplements of other vitamins are also important during pregnancy. These supplements can be critical if the daily diet is not sufficiently varied and nutritious enough to contain the amounts of vitamins A, C, D, and several of the B vitamins that are required to meet the needs both of the mother-to-be and the growing fetus. This safeguard is especially important for those vegetarians who don't eat dairy products.

Because individual eating habits vary so much and because only 20 to 30 percent of women in the United States begin pregnancy in a good nutritional state, it is crucial for every pregnant woman to discuss her nutritional needs with her health care provider early in her pregnancy or even before pregnancy if possible. Women with poor or marginal diets, adolescents, women underweight, and women carrying twins, for

NUTRITION, WEIGHT, AND GENERAL WELL-BEING

example, need more calories and protein than the amounts noted above.

As pregnancy continues the most convenient way to assess nutritional status is by observing weight changes from week to week. This should be about 2–4 pounds of tissue, not fluid (edema), during the first trimester, and then a little less than 1 pound a week thereafter for a total gain of around 27 pounds. Such a gain suggests good nutritional intake. Lesser gains usually indicate inadequate nutrition and the possibility of a resultant low birth-weight baby. Most obese women also should gain this amount. Slightly greater gains ordinarily are not a problem for the baby or mother.

In the past salt restriction was invariably suggested if not demanded. We now know that salt restriction is unnecessary and unwise except when pregnant women have certain chronic diseases such as congestive heart failure or high blood pressure, which are often treated by restricting salt. One problem with excessive salt is that it tends to be associated with empty calorie foods such as potato chips, which may replace foods containing other essential nutrients.

NUTRITION WHEN BREAST FEEDING

Proper nutrition is essential for successful breast feeding. The energy and nutritional costs to the nursing mother are high. Compared to her pre-pregnancy needs, she needs as much as an extra 1,000 calories per day for the first three months and more from the fourth month on if breast feeding continues. She needs an extra 20 grams of protein daily. Needs for vitamins A and C are modestly increased. The high calcium content of breast milk requires an extra 400 milligrams per day in the diet. The extra calcium, vitamin A, and protein can be supplied by drinking an extra 1 1/4 pints of milk each day; the extra vitamin C can be supplied by two additional servings of citrus fruit or tomatoes.

During a normal full-term pregnancy, about 3 kilograms of nutrients (fat and protein) are stored in the body. These provide 200 to 300 calories of energy a day for three months. Women who breast feed their babies lose most of this extra tissue by six months unless they maintain a very high intake of food. Women who do not breast feed but wish to lose weight must restrict their caloric intake or increase their activity to get rid of the additional fat gained during pregnancy. Regular eating and drinking habits and responding to thirst usually assure an appropriate amount of fluid.

NUTRITION FOR THE OLDER WOMAN

Older women who live alone are at special risk of being undernourished or poorly nourished because they can't be bothered preparing proper meals for themselves; or because they snack and then have no appetite; or because they smoke too much, drink too much, and get too little exercise.

If mealtime is a chore rather than a pleasure, alter your mealtime habits. Instead of the standard three "squares" a day, have two meals—a late breakfast or brunch and an early dinner when you are most hungry or, if you're an early riser, have four smaller meals arranged somewhat as follows: at 7 a.m.—fruit juice or a piece of fresh fruit and a hot cereal with milk; "elevenses"—a boiled or coddled egg, whole wheat toast with margarine or a muffin with peanut butter, and tea or coffee; lunch at 2—tuna or salmon salad with watercress, sliced tomato, shredded carrot, stewed fruit, tea or coffee; dinner at 6—steamed vegetables and pasta, yogurt with fresh fruit; before bedtime—crisp rye crackers and hot cocoa.

If you find you're not very hungry most of the time, the best thing to do for working up an appetite is to schedule some form of exercise on a regular basis, such as swimming at the local "Y", joining an exercise class especially designed for older women, finding a senior folk dance group, taking a brisk two-mile walk every day with a friend, and you'll find that food takes on a new importance.

Food should appeal to the eye too. Make meals that look appetizing by including colorful vegetables and garnishing with a parsley sprig. If your sense of taste has become less acute, and food seems bland and unappealing, don't add large and potentially harmful amounts of salt and sugar to your meals. Use lemon, herbs, and spices to enhance flavor. Be realistic about your chewing ability. If your teeth are not up to the rigors of chewing a steak or if you wear dentures, you will find cubed or chopped foods easier to deal with. A few fresh flowers on the table or candlelight can make mealtime an event rather than a bore, even when you eat alone. Books about "cooking for one" can give you new ideas for attractive meals. When possible, invite a friend, a relative, or a conge-

TABLE 8

FOODS THAT ARE GOOD SOURCES OF CALCIUM

	Serving Size	*Calcium Content* (milligrams)	*Calories*
Skim milk	1 cup	302	86
Low-fat milk (2%)	1 cup	297	121
Whole milk	1 cup	291	150
Buttermilk	1 cup	285	99
Low-fat yogurt:			
Plain	1 cup	415	144
Fruited	1 cup	314	225
Low-fat cottage cheese	1 cup	138	164
Swiss cheese	1 ounce	272	107
Cheddar cheese	1 ounce	204	114
American cheese	1 ounce	174	106
Ice cream	1 cup	176	296
Frozen yogurt	1 cup	200	290
Sardines (with bones)	3 ounces	372	175
Salmon (canned)	3 ounces	285	188
Shrimp	1 cup	147	148
Oysters	1 cup	226	158
Bean curd (tofu)	4 ounces	154	86
Bok choy	1 cup	116	11
Collard greens	1 cup	357	63
Dandelion greens	1 cup	147	35
Kale	1 cup	206	43
Mustard greens	1 cup	193	32
Turnip greens	1 cup	267	29
Broccoli	1 cup	136	40

Certain dark green, leafy vegetables are rich in calcium but also contain oxalic acid, which binds with calcium and blocks its absorption. These include spinach, Swiss chard, sorrel, parsley and beet greens.

nial neighbor for dinner and use this as an occasion to try out a new recipe.

Fruits, vegetables, and grains high in fiber are especially important to help counter several common problems among the elderly, especially constipation and diverticular disease.

Excess phosphorus tends to enhance the loss of bone as we get older, yet the typical American diet contains proportionately more phosphorus than calcium in foods such as meats, soft drinks, snacks, and cheeses, especially processed cheeses that contain phosphorus in the form of phosphates used as additives. Snack foods that are just as tasty include unsalted nuts, pumpkin seeds toasted in a little bit of olive oil flavored with garlic, yogurt with fresh fruit, and whole grain crackers with some homemade applesauce dressed up with cinnamon and nutmeg instead of sugar.

Many older women require special diets for their chronic health problems. For example, if you have heart disease or high blood pressure you may need to restrict your intake of salt. Diet is the main way to control many cases of diabetes that begin in the later years of life. Women taking blood pressure medication often require foods rich in potassium. Some medications may interfere with nutrients in food and thereby create the need for dietary supplements. Supplements in no matter what category should not be taken without discussing them with your primary care doctor who prescribed the medication rather than with a nutritionist or with a salesperson in a health food store.

In addition to the many special diet cookbooks to be found in public libraries and bookshops, such diets are also available on request from the American Diabetes Association, the American Heart Association, and the American Cancer Society (see the Directory of Health Information for addresses).

Geriatric specialists point out that many older women suffering from memory loss, depression, and apathy may be assumed by family members and sometimes even by doctors to be showing signs of senile dementia when, in fact, the symptoms are attributable to nutritional deficiencies. (And when these deficiencies are combined with overmedication with tranquilizers, the results can be quite distressing.) If in fact faulty and insufficient diet accounts for the symptoms, they are likely to vanish when dietary essentials are provided.

When illness and disability occur, shopping for and preparing nutritious foods can become difficult. Check your phone book for agencies that deliver meals and that can refer you to group meal programs, and homemaker services. For information about community facilities and all your entitlements as a senior citizen, get in touch with your local area agency on aging.

WEIGHT

When the Metropolitan Life Insurance Company issued a table in 1942 headed "Ideal Weights," it did not include a breakdown by age, and the weight ranges prescribed for healthy men and women were indicated according to height only. When the table was revised and reissued in 1959, it was headed "Desirable Weights." The 1983 version, in which the weight goals are several pounds higher than before, appears in Table 9. It has not been superseded (as of 1988) and it was issued without a descriptive adjective.

These recommendations continue to be the standard used by countless doctors and health experts, and to millions of women they represent a tyranny that has caused a great deal of misery and aberrational behavior. Controversy over these recommendations was initiated in 1985 by a government researcher who maintains that "the lowest death rates are associated with leanness in the 20s followed by moderate weight gain into middle age and beyond." Table 10 represents the recommendations of Dr. Reubin Andres, clinical director of the Gerontology Research Center of the National Institute of Health. He recommends the same weight goals for men and women of the same height, and in arguing against the notion that individuals ought to maintain the same weight throughout their adult lives, he points out that there is overwhelming evidence that "as you go through life, it's in your best interests to lay down some fat."

While a majority of specialists on cardiovascular diseases disagree with him, Dr. Andres has many highly respected allies. The director of Johns Hopkins University Center on Aging, Dr. William R. Hazzard, believes that a little extra fat appears to help aged people endure illness and that those gaining about one pound a year seem to do better, even though prevailing opinion disagrees.

As is usually the case with statistical studies, they are rarely the last word because of the impossibility of accounting for all variables. While there appears to be a direct link between middle-aged overweight and many diseases, no account is taken of genetic background, the dangers of childhood obesity, and where the extra weight is carried. On this latter subject, it is generally agreed by all specialists that a big belly represents a greater health hazard than big hips, thighs, and buttocks.

TABLE 9

1983 METROPOLITAN HEIGHT AND WEIGHT TABLES

MEN

Height Feet	Inches	Small Frame	Medium Frame	Large Frame
5	2	128-134	131-141	138-150
5	3	130-136	133-143	140-153
5	4	132-138	135-145	142-156
5	5	134-140	137-148	144-160
5	6	136-142	139-151	146-164
5	7	138-145	142-154	149-168
5	8	140-148	145-157	152-172
5	9	142-151	148-160	155-176
5	10	144-154	151-163	158-180
5	11	146-157	154-166	161-184
6	0	149-160	157-170	164-188
6	1	152-164	160-174	168-192
6	2	155-168	164-178	172-197
6	3	158-172	167-182	176-202
6	4	162-176	171-187	181-207

WOMEN

Height Feet	Inches	Small Frame	Medium Frame	Large Frame
4	10	102-111	109-121	118-131
4	11	103-113	111-123	120-134
5	0	104-115	113-126	122-137
5	1	106-118	115-129	125-140
5	2	108-121	118-132	128-143
5	3	111-124	121-135	131-147
5	4	114-127	124-138	134-151
5	5	117-130	127-141	137-155
5	6	120-133	130-144	140-159
5	7	123-136	133-147	143-163
5	8	126-139	136-150	146-167
5	9	129-142	139-153	149-170
5	10	132-145	142-156	152-173
5	11	135-148	145-159	155-176
6	0	138-151	148-162	158-179

Weights at ages 25-59 based on lowest mortality. Weight in pounds according to frame (in indoor clothing weighing 5 lbs. for men and 3 lbs. for women; shoes with 1" heels).

What isn't usually pointed out in this discussion of "haunch versus paunch" is that individuals have no control over where the fat goes first because this pattern is determined by heredity rather than by preference. And while health experts never cease stressing the dangers of overweight, they rarely give the same prominence to the dangers of constant dieting and the negative results of waging a constant battle with one's body. This battle not only consumes psychic energy that could more profitably be spent in other ways but is also responsible for the recent psychiatric category known as "eating disorders."

There is some irony in the fact that at the same time that authorities believe overweight to be one of the major health problems facing American men and women, Americans have been getting a little fatter each year and their life expectancy is increasing too.

TABLE 10

GERONTOLOGY RESEARCH CENTER
(Men and Women)

Height	20-29	30-39	AGE RANGE 40-49	50-59	60-69	Height
4'10"	84-111	92-119	99-127	107-135	115-142	4'10"
4'11"	87-115	95-123	103-131	111-139	119-147	4'11"
5'0"	90-119	98-127	106-135	114-143	123-152	5'0"
5'1"	93-123	101-131	110-140	118-148	127-157	5'1"
5'2"	96-127	105-136	113-144	122-153	131-163	5'2"
5'3"	99-131	108-140	117-149	126-158	135-168	5'3"
5'4"	102-135	112-145	121-154	130-163	140-173	5'4"
5'5"	106-140	115-149	125-159	134-168	144-179	5'5"
5'6"	109-144	119-154	129-164	138-174	148-184	5'6"
5'7"	112-148	122-159	133-169	143-179	153-190	5'7"
5'8"	116-153	126-163	137-174	147-184	158-196	5'8"
5'9"	119-157	130-168	141-179	151-190	162-201	5'9"
5'10"	122-162	134-173	145-184	156-195	167-207	5'10"
5'11"	126-167	137-178	149-190	160-201	172-213	5'11"
6'0"	129-171	141-183	153-195	165-207	177-219	6'0"
6'1"	133-176	145-188	157-200	169-213	182-225	6'1"
6'2"	137-181	149-194	162-206	174-219	187-232	6'2"
6'3"	141-186	153-199	166-212	179-225	192-238	6'3"
6'4"	144-191	157-205	171-218	184-231	197-244	6'4"

All heights without shoes, weights in pounds without clothes.

"DESIRABLE" WEIGHT

While it may be true that in the abstract, there is a physiologically "desirable" weight for each of us, the weight that we "desire" depends on many factors: the dictates of our doctor, the dictates of fashion, the demands of a spouse or companion, peer pressure, what feels "comfortable," how we order our priorities in terms of expending psychological effort.

Too many young women are smoking because they're afraid of getting "fat" if they stop, by which they mean they might have to wear a size 10 instead of a size 8. In an article in *Cosmopolitan* (January, 1985), Jane Fonda revealed that she had been bingeing and purging as often as 20 times a day from the time she was 12 until she was 35 when she decided to overcome this eating disorder known as bulimia. Many health experts now believe that the chronic unhappiness associated with repeated and unsuccessful efforts at weight control may in itself shorten life.

At its simplest, a "desirable" weight is one that is more or less within the range of either table and can be maintained without constant worry and thought while eating a nutritious diet with occasional treats and occasional deprivations and keeping fit through regular exercise.

OVERWEIGHT AND OBESITY

Whether you think you're overweight according to the tables, according to your mirror, or in comparison with your two best friends, the National Institute of Health has put 1/6 of the American population—about 34 million people—in this category. A much smaller number would be considered clinically obese. In any case, the condition results from an imbalance between calories consumed and calories used as energy. When calories consumed are greater than those needed and burned for energy, the excess is stored primarily as fat. The factors known to be involved in keeping body weight normal include learned behaviors associated with eating, physiologic factors implicated in the regulation of food intake, change in hormonal status, effects of early nutritional status, genetic endowment, level of activity, and differences in fat cell number and size. The limitations of space preclude reviewing all of these, but we should review factors involved in the early onset of obesity, nutrition and eating patterns during infancy and adolescence, and the impact of fat cell number and size.

There is some evidence that fat infants may become fat children who then become fat adults. While it is possible that heredity has some influence on why a child becomes fat, most physicians and students of nutrition are convinced that the most important factor in childhood obesity is how a child is fed during the early years. Children become fat because they are overfed and stay fat because (1) eating patterns and attitudes formed in early life continue and (2) fat infants develop more fat cells than do those of normal weight. Once excess fat cells are acquired, they are not lost through dieting. When an excess number of fat cells is present, the obese child, and later the obese adult, can become thinner only by reducing the fat cell size to smaller than normal. Prospective studies have shown that 60 to 80 percent of infants who are overweight during the first year of life will be of normal weight by 4 to 7 years of age, but a significant proportion, up to 20 percent, will remain overweight and probably be obese. The chance of becoming an obese child and an obese adult is definitely greater for an obese infant than for one of normal weight. Consequently, prevention of obesity in infancy by educating parents in sound nutritional principles and closely monitoring weight during infancy is important.

The initial onset of obesity is not as common during adolescence as it is during the preadolescent period. Many obese teenagers were obese children. The typical obese teenager has exogenous obesity, that is, the excess weight results simply from an excessive caloric intake in relation to body energy needs and expenditure. Primary glandular or endocrinologic abnormalities, such as thyroid or adrenal malfunction, are rare.

In general, controlling obesity is difficult and frustrating. The statistics on treatment leave no doubt that treatment rarely produces a permanent and sustained weight reduction. While any method of weight reduction (and there are more than 17,000 such methods published to date) will produce some degree of weight loss in almost all motivated obese women, maintenance of the reduced body weight occurs in something less than 10 percent. After reviewing most studies on obesity and treatment programs, one must conclude that one of the surest ways to reduce the prevalence of obesity is to prevent its occurrence!

It should be noted, however, that Dr. Jules Hirsch of the Rockefeller University has for 20 years promoted the view that fat people are biochemically different from thin ones. His research indicates that many women are obese not because they eat too much or move around too little but because they burn calories too slowly. Another study has shown that there exists a strong genetic tendency to gain weight easily. In this category, only one dieter in 10 achieved lasting success, and those who were able to lose significant amounts of weight had to survive in a state of semi-starvation. Some researchers are therefore convinced that there are many women who are 30 percent overweight according to stringent health standards who would be better off, all things considered, if they stayed fat because they suffer too much medically, physically, and psychologically when they attempt to meet what is for them an unachievable goal. But even for these women, losing the first 10 percent of overweight is critical for correcting a tendency to diabetes and high blood pressure.

In typical cases of overweight, the goals of treatment are basically to decrease calorie intake and to increase calorie expenditure (negative calorie balance). Although the biologic and physiologic mechanisms leading to a positive calorie balance are often unclear, the fact remains that for a woman to add fat to her body stores, she must eat more calories than she is using in her daily activities. This can occur because her food intake is excessive, her calorie expenditure (physical activity) or basal metabolic needs are lower than normal, or because her absorption of food from her gastrointestinal tract is greater than normal.

Motivation is the fundamental factor for the success of any weight reduction program. The obese woman must want to lose weight. An impending marriage is a most potent factor motivating weight loss. Short-term but significant weight loss often accompanies the desire to fit into that formal dress for a special event. In most instances weight loss is a matter of personal pride and vanity augmented by the present fashion. Pregnancy, as noted before, is an inappropriate time to diet because the nutritional needs of pregnancy are high.

Basically, there are four major areas of treatment: going on a diet, exercise, drugs, and group therapy including behavior modification. Before discussing these in detail, it should be pointed out that:

- Very thin isn't as "in" as it used to be. Fashion models now weigh about 8 pounds more than they did 15 years ago.
- Women with visibly extra pounds aren't the pariahs they used to be. Very attractive distinctly overweight models appear regularly on television ads promoting extra large pantyhose and extra size clothes.
- Americans, mostly women, spend more than $20 billion on diets and diet products, mostly without permanent success.
- More and more young women are risking impaired growth and maturity by substituting soft drinks for milk, which results in fragile bones.

- The risks of being overweight are greatly exaggerated, while the risks of constant dieting are largely ignored.
- There is an increase in the number of young women on college campuses suffering from serious eating disorders.
- Years of yo-yo dieting can induce strong self-dislike.
- Brisk walking for one hour a day can result in a loss of 25 pounds a year as well as an improvement in physical fitness.
- We are not all the same metabolically. No one should try to stay on a diet of less than 1,500 calories a day, especially because such a diet would be impossible to maintain over a lifetime.

DIETING

Trendy diets aren't following each other with the speed they once did. One of the reasons is that it has become increasingly apparent that they don't work over the long term. Another is that many women are reordering their priorities: between going to work, taking care of children without a husband to help, wanting to be physically fit rather than faddish, and making good health an important consideration, they are less likely to fall for "miracle" ways of losing weight. Who remembers Dr. Herman Taller's "calories don't count" diet of the 60s? Or the Mayo Diet that recommended eating grapefruit with every meal because it "burned fat"? Within more recent memory are Dr. Atkin's Revolutionary Diet and the late Dr. Tarnower's Scarsdale Diet, two popular versions of the low-carbohydrate, high-protein diet that proposes an unlimited consumption of proteins and fats while severely limiting carbohydrates. Women on such a diet often lose up to 8 pounds in the first week, but because carbohydrate restriction has a diuretic effect, the weight lost is mostly water. The severe restriction on carbohydrates, below 60 grams a day, can also result in ketosis as fat is used as an alternative fuel. When the breakdown products of fat, called ketone bodies, build up in the blood, the breath smells fruity and women may complain of an unpleasant taste and nausea. The end result is usually a loss of appetite, so food intake is curbed. If this type of diet is maintained for only a short time, say, one or two weeks, the ketosis is short-term and probably not harmful. However, any episode of ketosis may have harmful effects on an unborn child, so none of the low-carbohydrate, high-protein diets is recommended for pregnant women. Also, the high protein consumed in such diets can be harmful to patients with kidney disease.

Dr. Stillman captured the interest of many diet-conscious readers with his Quick Inches-Off Diet that proposed high-carbohydrate, low-protein meals, specifically forbidding meat, seafood, poultry, milk, and cheese. His magic formula was supposed to allow women to lose inches wherever wanted or needed. It is true that if a woman has abnormal fat deposits and loses weight, these deposits, like all of her body fat, will get smaller. However, disproportionately large thighs will remain disproportionately large!

I will mention the simple "starvation" diet to decry its use, except under the careful direction and supervision of a physician. Its principles are simple—do not drink or eat anything but water and lose 1 pound a day. The hazards of starvation or fasting are many including ketosis, dehydration, nausea, fatigue, and loss of minerals, such as potassium, calcium, and magnesium. The weight loss is due to loss of muscle mass and water, the latter quickly regained when the period of starvation, short-term for obvious reasons, is over.

The large variety of diets as well as the transience of their popularity indicates that none can guarantee long-term success. Of course, any diet that results in a negative calorie balance, meaning that fewer calories are consumed than are burned for energy, will allow the obese woman to lose weight. However, no single diet is good for everyone, and there is no real evidence that any particular dietary mixture accelerates the rate of weight loss. The main reasons for the failure of these fashionable diets are that they do little to educate the woman with a serious and chronic weight problem in the basic and sound nutritional principles necessary to achieve and maintain the weight that is best for her, nor do they address either the underlying emotional issues or behavior patterns that cause overeating.

EXERCISE

Physical activity is an important factor in determining caloric needs and, clearly, inactivity promotes obesity. Obese adults, by and large, are less active than normal weight individuals. Not only do they spend less time in physical activity but even when they participate, their time is spent less vigorously.

While exercise can be an important factor in any weight reduction program, the use of exercise in the treatment of obesity is surrounded by faddism. Despite the advertisements of reducing salons, there is no evidence to support the claims that by mechanical means you can selectively mobilize fat from one part of the body. In studies done with tennis players, the greater amount of exercise in the playing arm was not accompanied by any decrease in fat deposits in that arm.

Without a reduction in calorie consumption, exercise is not an effective way to reduce weight because it takes far too much activity to burn up a significant number of calories. Would you walk 3 to 4 miles for a piece of cake? That's the distance it takes to burn up the energy in the cake's calories.

It is important to point out, however, that exercise is often accompanied by a reduction in excessive food intake, apparently by reducing appetite. Not only can exercise decrease food intake but it can also decrease body fat. Studies involving college students have shown that a program of mild to moderate jogging or walking on a treadmill reduced body fat, increased lean body mass, and decreased body weight without other dietary control.

With grossly obese patients, although it is harder to achieve effective levels of exercise, more weight is lost through exercise than in patients of normal weight. In a study of 12 massively obese patients all maintained on the same liquid formula diet, 6 had an exercise program and 6 did not. In the 6 who exercised the rate of fat loss and weight loss was clearly increased.

In summary, exercise in combination with diet produces greater weight loss than diet alone. If you are trying to lose weight, drive less and walk more. On public transportation signal for a stop before you reach home and walk the rest of the way. Climb stairs instead of pushing the elevator button, especially when you must negotiate three or fewer flights. Walking daily is the easiest form of exercise and 1 mile a day costs your body more than 500 calories a week. In a year that's 8 pounds walked away. By reducing food intake by 100 calories each day, you will take off another 10 pounds.

DRUGS

Drugs are not an effective treatment of obesity and many, in fact, are harmful. Used not only to suppress appetite but supposedly to break down fat, their effectiveness, if any, is short term. And there are inherent side effects and potential dangers associated with the use of thyroid hormone, amphetamines, diuretics, and starch blockers (see "Substance Abuse").

GROUP THERAPY AND BEHAVIOR MODIFICATION

A number of successful weight reduction organizations administer their programs in a group setting. Weight-Watchers, TOPS (Take Off Pounds Safely), and Overeaters Anonymous are the best-known self-help organizations for the obese. In general, the cost to the individual is modest and less than that of standard medical therapies. Studies evaluating the effectiveness of group treatment compared to standard medical treatment in achieving weight loss suggest that patients in group programs stay in treatment longer and are more successful in losing weight. Presumably, this is because people with a similar problem reinforce and encourage one another.

Behavior modification in a group setting appears to be the most effective method to date for treating obesity. The basic principle of this approach is the assumption that eating is a learned behavior. If a woman is obese, then her eating behavior is maladapted and should be unlearned. Appropriate behavior conducive to achieving and maintaining a normal body weight can be substituted. The following are some simple suggestions for changing eating patterns. Eat only while seated at a proper eating place and using proper utensils. Eliminate eating in front of the television or snacking by the kitchen sink. Concentrate solely on eating, not on the television, a magazine article, or the conversation around you. Be aware of every bite.

Eat slowly, chew slowly, and pause between bites. Overeaters are frequently fast eaters who are unaware of how much they eat.

Plan menus for the week in advance and count calories *every* time you eat. Compulsive women may find that careful records of meals and snacks prevent splurging and spontaneous eating. Shop for groceries after you have planned your menu and after you have eaten a meal. Never grocery shop when you are hungry!

Eat because you are hungry and stop when you are no longer hungry; don't eat because you are depressed, it is a holiday, you need a reward, or you are anxious to please your hostess.

These changes in eating habits can aid you in losing weight, and when such learned behaviors become automatic, they will help you maintain the weight that is best for you.

I remind you that what I have offered here is no "magic," no mysterious combination of special foods assuring instant, painless weight reduction. Instead, I have presented basic information about nutrition so you can plan meals that are well balanced and provide calories that are appropriate for your metabolic needs and activity level. Dieting becomes necessary only when these basic guidelines are not followed and overweight results.

UNDERWEIGHT

While most women who are concerned about their weight want to lose, or at least not add, pounds, some want to gain weight. Usually the reason is to have a better figure, occasionally to be "healthier," though in general an underweight person who achieves ideal body weight will not be healthier. However, women who are 10 or more percent below ideal body weight when they become pregnant are more likely to have low birth-weight babies. The approach to gaining weight is the opposite, of course, to that used for losing weight. Caloric intake must exceed caloric expenditure. In theory at least, a pound will be gained for every 3,500 calories of intake in excess of expenditure. Women who have been underweight for a long time rarely have a disease that makes them underweight, though some may have a "genetic predisposition" to being slim or lean. Many of them smoke and get too little sleep and too little exercise. Almost all of them simply do not eat enough. To eat more and gain weight they usually need to reorganize their eating styles: three meals a day (some suggest that six smaller meals are better) of proper quality. If you want to gain weight without stuffing yourself with the wrong foods, here are some suggestions:

- Instead of eating foods high in animal fats such as heavy cream, cold cuts, and hard cheeses, choose high fat vegetable foods such as peanut butter, avocado, nuts, and olive oil salad dressing.
- Eat plenty of high calorie vegetables, especially potatoes, corn, winter squash, peas, and beans.
- Have a daily serving of pasta, rice, cracked wheat, or kasha.
- Cut down on coffee, tea, and cola drinks, and drink milk instead.

A change in exercise activity usually is necessary too. Some exercise is essential to develop abdominal muscle tone, to enhance digestion, and to assure that the weight gained will be pleasingly distributed and not just "blubber." Moderate exercise may stimulate appetite. I do not recommend any other appetite enhancers or high-calorie preparations. Stopping smoking will help gain weight. None of this will be easy, because you almost certainly will be attempting to alter long-standing eating and exercise patterns.

TWO MAJOR EATING DISORDERS

ANOREXIA NERVOSA

Anorexia nervosa, which afflicts adolescent and young women, is the relentless pursuit of thinness through self-starvation. Basically, anorexia nervosa is a psychiatric disorder with the main issue a struggle for control and a sense of identity. Many young women affected with this disorder have struggled for years to make themselves over and to be "perfect" in the eyes of others, usually of parents with extremely high expectations. Their concept of their own body image becomes distorted, and even when they are less than ideal body weight for their age, height, and body frame, they see themselves as fat when looking in a mirror.

The outstanding characteristic of this disorder is reduced calorie intake. Not only is the amount of food rigidly restricted, but the whole pattern of eating becomes disorganized in bizarre ways. In many cases, the absence or denial of hunger alternates with an uncontrollable impulse to gorge oneself. After gorging, the anorectic may induce vomiting or take laxatives to purge herself (see section on bulimia). Paradoxically, anorexia nervosa is often preceded by obesity and usually begins or becomes overt with dieting. However, in contrast to the ordinary dieter, who makes the supreme sacrifice each time she rejects an ice cream sundae or suffers every time she declines her hostess' offer of chocolate cake, the anorectic adolescent will insist that she is not hungry, does not need to eat, and that not wanting to eat is "normal." In contrast to her emaciated appearance, she is overly active, often exercising religiously for many hours each day or increasing her participation in sports. She is an overachiever and her parents will describe her as "a real perfectionist." Secondary amenorrhea, the cessation of menstrual periods, though a characteristic feature of anorexia nervosa, is not an essential part of the disorder. Because the menstrual cycle is so easily affected by emotional disturbances, loss of periods is commonly observed in women under severe stress, and the psychological as well as nutritional stresses on the anorectic are indeed severe. In advanced stages of emaciation, which these young women often reach, true loss of appetite may result from severe nutritional deficiency, similar to the complete lack of interest in food that occurs in the late stages of starvation during a famine. If such becomes the case, hospitalization may be recommended. Before such an advanced stage of the illness is reached, it is essential that the condition be approached by psychotherapists who specialize in the treatment of eating disorders. Therapy usually involves the family as well as the young woman herself.

BULIMIA

A severe eating disorder often associated with anorexia nervosa, bulimia is characterized by compulsively eating large amounts of food very quickly and then getting rid of it by vomiting or using strong laxatives. Popularly known as "bingeing and purging," bulimia together with anorexia nervosa are recognized by the American Psychiatric Association as obsessive illnesses. The association's criteria for identifying the bulimia syndrome are the following:

- Recurrent episodes of binge eating over periods of about two hours.
- Feeling a lack of control over eating behavior during the binges.
- Engaging in self-induced vomiting, use of laxatives, and/or fasting to counteract the effects of bingeing.
- A minimum average of two binge-eating episodes per week for at least 3 months.

Most binges take place in secret and typically consist in eating a dozen brownies or a quart of ice cream and a pound of fudge at one sitting. Some bulimics may steal both food and money to support their "habit."

The health risks can be devastating, and where signs of the disorder exist, treatment should be sought as promptly as possible. All specialists agree that early treatment of this disorder is essential to recovery because the aberration cannot only become a lifelong pattern but can do irreversible bodily harm if permitted to continue. (See Directory of Health Information for list of support groups and associations.)

FRAUDS

With an increased interest in nutrition and its relation to such matters as emotional well-being, disease prevention, and general health, many women are being victimized by quacks who claim to have all the answers—usually at a substantial fee.

- Watch out for self-styled "nutritionists" who say that MDs, the FDA, and the entire medical establishment don't know the latest facts about nutrition and health.
- Be suspicious of anyone who claims to have a special diet that can *prevent* certain diseases.
- If you're consulting a nutritionist, ask to see credentials from an accredited institution of higher learning that confers academic degrees.
- Stay away from anyone who recommends hair analysis and other unproved diagnostic methods as a way of creating a special diet "just for you."
- Suspect anyone who claims that a balanced diet won't keep you healthy and that you *must* buy an assortment of vitamin and mineral supplements.

Fitness

Christine E. Haycock, M.D.
Professor of Surgery, University of Medicine and Dentistry of New Jersey, New Jersey Medical School, Newark, New Jersey; Fellow, American College of Sports Medicine

Serious interest in physical fitness and a more than casual involvement in sports for women have become increasingly widespread since the late 1960s. Even before this period, health authorities were placing more and more emphasis on the relationship between physical fitness and improved health. And for the rapidly growing ranks of women who were self-supporting or who were the sole support of their families, good health had become more than a matter of good looks: it was a top priority for compelling economic reasons.

Since the 1970s, ads for sturdy hiking boots and sneakers for women have displaced those for "spectator" sports shoes, and jogging clothes have joined "dressy" dresses in the wardrobe. Across the United States more and more girls and women are spurred on to athletic achievement by the accomplishments of such women as Martina Navratilova, Chris Evert, Steffi Graf, Nancy Lopez, and Evelyn Ashford, and those who are not especially motivated by the competitive spirit are making a commitment to the goal of good health through fitness. Women of all ages are hiking, playing tennis, dancing, swimming, and playing team sports. Women have discovered that the bicycle is a blessing, for exercise, economy, and getting from one place to another conveniently. More and more women are joining physical fitness classes at the Y, spending their vacations at health spas, and banding together to organize community sports programs. And everywhere—in city streets, local gyms, athletic clubs, suburban roads—women are jogging. It is estimated that more than 6 million American women ranging from adolescents to those over 70 have adopted this sport as their chief means of maintaining physical fitness.

Much publicity has been given to that aspect of the women's movement that has focused on equal access to athletic facilities for school children of both sexes, on allowing young girls to participate in traditional male sports, and on breaking down sexist barriers to achievement for girls who would prefer to pitch in Little League than go to social dancing class. What is sometimes not emphasized is how physical activity relates to changing the overall stereotype of the female as nonphysical, helpless, and weak. Increased attention to physical activity can allow a young girl to develop the habit of thinking in terms of physical fitness, to acquire an awareness of the capabilities of her body, and to experience the satisfaction that can be derived from achieving competence in any area.

Perhaps only a few women have the ability or the interest to become star athletes or even participants in competitive sports. Many see little connection between their overall image of themselves and their attitude toward the condition of their body. You live with your body all the time and feeling awkward, helpless, and weak about such an important aspect of yourself cannot help but affect your total self-image. In more positive terms, to know that your body functions well and to realize that with proper training and discipline you can become competent in physical activity cannot help but contribute to a good self-image, to the habit of thinking of yourself as able to *do.*

There is no question that physical fitness is related to improved health and that specific types of exercise improve the function of specific parts of the body (these will be discussed later). However, in terms of total fitness, the benefits of activity seem to derive from more than just the direct relationship between exercise and improved tissue function. Exercise per se is not the automatic key to fitness. Studies have shown that people who exercise do not need less sleep, eat less, smoke less, or lose weight. But, studies have shown that the percentage of people who score positively on indexes of psychological well-being is higher among those who are highly active than among those who are inactive. The more active report increased self-confidence, better self-image, improved coordination, increased stamina and strength, and fewer illnesses. They feel less tense, more disciplined, less tired, and more productive. Clearly, we cannot separate the physical and psychological aspects of physical activity: they interact and enhance one another in contributing to good health and well-being.

BENEFITS OF PHYSICAL FITNESS

The term physical fitness is defined as the ability to exercise or carry on daily activities without undue distress or fatigue and to be able to respond effectively to occasions requiring physical exertion. A fit individual usually feels good and functions well.

There are two general rewards from exercise: the physical and physiological improvement of the body itself and the achievement of greater psychological or emotional well-being. Of course, the other requirements of good health, including proper nutrition and rest, must be met.

The benefits of exercise are not confined to any particular age group, and it is beyond doubt that exercise is a more critical health factor for women than for men because women are more likely to suffer from obesity and from the disabilities resulting from osteoporosis. Recent studies have provided evidence that a suitably designed exercise program for postmenopausal women, combined with supplemental calcium, can retard the development of bone-thinning osteoporosis. This devastating condition is responsible for most of the large numbers of hip and spinal fractures, resulting from even minor falls, in elderly women and appears related to changes in calcium metabolism and low estrogen hormone levels in this group. For this reason the administration of estrogen and progesterone under careful supervision also assists these women, along with a diet and exercise regimen.

We also now know that women who do weight lifting will not develop the bulging muscles seen in their male counterparts because they have much less of the male hormone testosterone. Exercise using weights or resistance apparatus is a valuable tool for women to develop the upper limb strength they otherwise may lack.

Exercise contributes to the physiological improvement of the body by increasing muscle strength, flexibility of the joints, and cardiovascular endurance. Exercise, along with suitable diet, also heightens muscle tone and reduces the amount of fat in the body. Exercise that strengthens the muscles can also improve cardiac and respiratory function and circulation. The heart muscle is strengthened, and the reduction of the general proportion of fat in the body aids in lowering blood pressure and lessening the amount of cholesterol. Healthier muscle tone makes it possible to perform daily tasks at home or in the office with much less fatigue.

An improvement in flexibility enables women to bend and stoop and reach without undue risk of muscle strains and pulls. Women tend to be more flexible than men because they generally have looser joints. Because of this flexibility and because their muscles are smaller, they can bend their backs and touch their toes more easily than most men. Flexibility exercises involve stretching muscles and maintaining the mobility of joints. These are the exercises that have traditionally been encouraged more for women than for men, not only because they are consistent with the woman's physique but also because they do not produce the muscular development that was assumed would result from other types of exercises. This supposition is gradually changing: men are working to develop more flexibility, while women are lifting weights to become stronger.

Endurance is the ability to persist in an exercise: for example, to engage in long distance running, to play a game for an extended period of time, or, in nonsports terms, to be able to complete or remain at a task that requires physical exertion. Endurance depends in part on cardiovascular function, the ability of the heart to pump blood efficiently through the lungs and the circulatory system, thereby supplying plenty of oxygen to muscles. Cardiovascular endurance can be measured by how far a woman can run, how long she can exercise on her bicycle, or how far she can swim in a specified time, all depending on her age.

One of the most highly publicized aspects of jogging has been its role in improving cardiovascular endurance. It is believed that vigorous exercise increases the rate of circulation, makes the body more efficient at delivering oxygen to the heart and other body tissue, widens the coronary arteries, and perhaps increases the level of high density lipoprotein, a substance thought to remove cholesterol from the arteries. Even mild exercise, such as brisk walks several times a week, wards off cardiovascular disease as well as hypertension. Whatever else research proves about the relationship between a strong heart and regular exercise, it unambiguously indicates that the *absence* of exercise and a sedentary life style go hand in hand with cardiovascular disease.

In addition to muscle strength, flexibility, and endurance, there are secondary aspects of physical improvement through exercise: power, agility, and speed. *Power* determines how far you can throw an object, how far you can jump, or how much you can lift or push. *Agility* enables you to change directions quickly as you chase a tennis ball, skip a rope, or climb a ladder. *Speed* enables you to win the race, chase a ball, or run after a child. These three assets are obviously critical for excellence in a particular sport, and, although they are not critical for general physical fitness, they certainly do contribute to the ability to do everyday activities that anyone might be called on to perform.

Exercise affects other body processes as well. It enhances the digestive function: it is a reliable and effective aid to normal bowel movements and thereby reduces the incidence of conditions and complaints resulting from constipation. Doing exercises that produce muscle fatigue also helps us to sleep. Exercise reduces muscle tension caused by stress and is, therefore, an invaluable and comparatively simple way to achieve relaxation. Women who are experiencing anxiety, depression, and other emotional disorders benefit from exercise programs that provide an outward release from their repressed frustrations and tensions. Because exercise improves you by conditioning your body, it helps make you aware of your good health, which produces a general feeling of well-being and personal contentment.

Strenuous exercise programs such as jogging, gymnastics, and other highly competitive sports may produce amenorrhea (absence of menstrual periods). However, it should never be assumed that exercise is in and of itself the cause of disruption or cessation of the menstrual cycle unless all other causes, particularly anorectic behavior in adolescents, have been ruled out. When in fact strenuous exercise does prove to be the cause, the amenorrhea is likely to be temporary, and menstruation returns when stressful training has been reduced. As for the effect of exercise on menstruation itself, women who engage regularly in physical activity such as brisk walking or daily jogging report less premenstrual tension, less discomfort, shorter periods, and less bleeding.

Nor does strenuous exercise have adverse effects on a later pregnancy. Indeed, pregnant women may also benefit from proper exercise programs by improving their muscle tone for delivery. The results of an advanced study published recently in the *Journal of the American Medical Association* indicated that only when pregnant women were pushed to exercise at maximum level did the heart rate of the fetus appear to be affected. While the American College of Obstetricians and Gynecologists recommends that when exercising pregnant women should not exceed a pulse rate of 140 beats per minute, the new study points out that even at pulse rates of 150 per minute, the fetal heart rate remained unaffected. This applies primarily to well-trained athletes. Most pregnant women who exercise should probably not exceed the 140 per minute pulse rate. Thus, the long-term results of a woman's participation in sports and exercise are usually beneficial for her health and well-being at all stages of her life.

YOUR BODY'S ENERGY

When we work or play we need energy. That energy is produced by our bodies from fuel in the form of the foods we eat. (The importance of proper diet is emphasized in the chapter "Nutrition, Weight, and General Well-Being.") Here it should be pointed out that many firmly held opinions about the right food and drink for high energy have been discredited. Muscle cells depend mainly on carbohydrates for fuel: thus, a high protein diet is a poor choice. Most Americans consume about twice as much protein as their bodies need, and they would be in better condition if they ate more food containing the slow-burning starches found in grains, beans, breads, and pastas made with unrefined flour. The fast-burning carbohydrates, especially the sugars found in candy bars, are effective for a quick energy spurt, but they are burned up too quickly to provide a steady source of fuel.

An essential component for all energy production is oxygen. Oxygen is obtained from the air through our lungs. It is absorbed into the bloodstream and carried by our red cells (in hemoglobin) to all parts of the body. In addition, our hormones, such as thyroid, parathyroid, and insulin, play necessary roles in energy production and availability for use. For example, a woman with an over- or underactive thyroid gland would have difficulty exercising. An underactive gland slows down all of

FITNESS

her metabolic processes to reduce the role of energy production, while an overactive thyroid speeds up the body processes to the degree that energy is used up even when she is not exercising.

Energy is measured in the form of calories. We know that the body requires a certain number of calories per day in order to maintain itself and to carry on normal activities. The number of calories consumed during exercise is variable. Vigorous activity such as jogging, jumping rope, or bicycling obviously will consume more calories than team sports such as softball, and these in turn more calories than less active sports such as golf or bowling.

There are calorie guides available in most book stores as well as texts on nutrition and exercise that indicate just how many calories are produced from different foods and how many are burned in different activities. One handy device is a small slide calculator available from Universal Fitness Products, which indicates how many calories are burned per hour for most sports and daily activities according to weight. (See Tables 1 and 2 listing calories burned during exercise.)

TABLE 1

CALORIES BURNED PER HOUR IN VARIOUS ACTIVITIES (BODY WEIGHT, 125 LB)

Daily Activities

Class-work, lecture	84	House painting	176
Cleaning windows	207	Housework	203
Conversing	92	Kneeling	60
Chopping wood	367	Making bed	196
Dancing (moderate)	209	Mowing grass	
(vigorous)	284	(power, self-propelled)	203
(fox trot)	222	(power, not self-propelled)	222
(rhumba)	347	Office work	150
(square)	342	Personal toilet	95
(waltz)	257	Resting in bed	59
Dressing or showering	160	Sawing wood	391
Driving	150	Shining shoes	149
Eating	70	Shoveling snow	389
Farm chores or carpentry	193	Sleeping	59
Floor (mopping)	227	Standing (no activity)	71
(sweeping)	183	(light activity)	122
Gardening	178	Watching television	60
Gardening and weeding	295	Working in yard	177
Hoeing, raking and planting	235	Writing	92

TABLE 2

EXERCISE AND CALORIE EXPENDITURE (BODY WEIGHT, 150 LB)

Activity (for one hour)	Calories
Bicycling 6 mph	240
Bicycling 12 mph	410
Cross-country skiing	700
Jogging 5 1/2 mph	740
Jogging 7 mph	920
Jumping rope	750
Running in place	650
Running 10 mph	1,280
Swimming 25 yds/min.	275
Swimming 50 yds/min.	500
Tennis—singles	400
Walking 2 mph	240
Walking 3 mph	320
Walking 4 1/2 mph	440

SOURCE: Exercise and Your Heart; *NIH Publication No. 83-1677*
A lighter person will burn fewer calories and a heavier one will burn more. For example, a 100-pound person would burn about one-third fewer calories than shown in the chart, and a 200-pound person would burn about one-third more calories. Exercising *harder* or *faster* for a given activity will only slightly increase the calories spent. A better way to burn more calories, says NIH, is to exercise *longer* and cover more distance.

THE FIRST STEP—A PHYSICAL EXAMINATION

Before embarking on an active exercise program of any kind, a woman of any age who has been leading a sedentary life or who has been exercising only mildly or sporadically should have a thorough physical examination. It is worth noting that until the introduction of the specialty known as sports medicine, medical schools did not teach doctors-to-be about the negative effects of exercise. This is, therefore, an area that most doctors know very little about. However, a checkup is especially important for women who suffer from hypertension, backaches, or bursitis, or who have had major surgery or a reset limb. Also health problems may exist that a woman is not aware of. For this reason, in addition to the routine general physical, she should have a pap smear, a chemical analysis of the blood that includes a blood count and a basic thyroid screening test, a cardiac evaluation, and a pulmonary evaluation.

Mild cases of iron deficiency anemia (low hemoglobin) are common, due in some cases to poor dietary habits but more often to the fact that some women lose more iron during menstruation than they get in their diets. An anemic woman is handicapped in exercises requiring endurance or strenuous exertion. When the oxygen-carrying capacity in the bloodstream is reduced, the ability to produce energy is also reduced. Iron deficiency anemia is quickly corrected by taking iron tablets daily.

An electrocardiogram can reveal certain malfunctions of the heart, and if the woman is over 35, a stress cardiac test may be done but only on a highly selective basis. In this test electrocardiograph leads are attached to the subject's chest while she runs on a treadmill. The result gives a good indication of the heart's reaction to the extra stress of exercise. It must be done under strict medical supervision at a center properly equipped with the necessary instruments.

Where special conditions such as heart disease, hypertension, diabetes, or pregnancy exist, medical monitoring is a must, but this does not mean you cannot participate. Quite the contrary, exercise can be very beneficial and actually lead to physical improvement.

SUITABLE CLOTHES AND PROPER EQUIPMENT

Clothing and equipment for the exercise of your choice should be selected carefully. Clothing in general should be loosefitting, have a high cotton content for absorbency, and an open weave to permit sweat to evaporate. These characteristics are especially important in both underclothing and uniforms worn in warm climates or for indoor sports. Underpants should have soft inside seams and should not rub, bind, rise up, or cause overheating. Leotards and tights are unsuitable wear for intense exercise, and especially ill-advised are rubber suits or pants that do not allow body heat to be dissipated and, therefore, prevent the body from cooling off naturally. In outer garments a higher percentage of synthetic materials is acceptable, but they should be lined with cotton.

Studies indicate that the considerable force involved in breast motion during vigorous exercises can result in chafing, sore breasts, and irritated, bleeding nipples. A properly made bra restricts this abrasive motion and prevents chafing or discomfort caused by bra straps that slip off the shoulders. While a small-breasted woman seldom has problems related to her bra, large-breasted women often do. A bra that is well made and correctly fitted will not slip up over the breast no matter how strenuous the exercise. Bras specifically designed for wear by women engaged in active sports are available.

Shoes and socks should always be selected with care because improperly fitted footwear will result in blisters, foot strains, and sprains. It should not be assumed that one type of footwear is suitable for all purposes. Sports experts make the following recommendations:

- For brisk walking, shoes should be lightweight, well-cushioned, especially under the toes, with flexible patterned soles, uppers of "breathable" material, and a reinforced area at the toe to protect against stubbing.
- For running, shoes should have soles that curve upward front and back and a heel that is slightly raised.
- For tennis, shoes should be sturdy, with flat soles, a reinforced front, and hard squared-off edges. On clay courts, shoes should be soled in open-treaded rubber to accommodate sliding; on hard courts, rubbed or patterned polyurethane soles are recommended.

Shoes for active sports should be bought in a store with an experienced, knowledgeable staff. The size of the shoe is irrelevant and the fit all important. Shoes should feel right in the store because they are made of materials that can't be "broken in," nor will they stretch when you get them home. It is not appropriate to buy men's shoes even though they may feel more "comfortable" at first try: women's feet have higher arches and narrower heels, and their footwear is designed to take these differences into account. It is also advisable to shop for shoes at the end of the day (and especially at the end of a warm day) when the feet are largest.

In caring for sports shoes, wear them only for the purpose for which they were bought and not for casual street wear. If they get wet, dry them away from direct sun and heat.

In addition to absorbing moisture, socks should be thicker at points of greatest stress so that they provide added cushioning. They should be roomy enough to enable the toes to wiggle easily but not so large that they bunch into wrinkles and folds inside the shoe. Socks should be changed at least once a day or more often if feet perspire heavily.

Foot care is critical to the enjoyment of an active life. To prevent blisters, calluses, and ingrown toenails, the following procedures are recommended:

- Wash your feet with soap and lukewarm water every day and dry them thoroughly, especially between the toes.
- If your feet perspire heavily, sprinkle them each day with cornstarch or medicated foot powder.
- For protection against fungal infections, use an antifungal powder or spray.
- About twice a week, soak your feet in warm soapy water for ten minutes and, after drying them, rub away dried or thickened skin surfaces with a pumice stone.
- Cut toenails straight across.
- Do not cut corns away with a razor blade. Treat yourself to a visit to a podiatrist for treatment of corns and discard the ill-fitting footwear responsible for causing the corns.

Equipment such as tennis racquets and golf clubs should be chosen with the advice of a professional or at least with the help of a knowledgeable clerk in a well-equipped sporting goods store. Equipment that is the wrong size or weight or is poorly made may lead to injuries such as tennis elbow (an inflammation of the tendons in the elbow).

INJURIES

Injuries to women in sports are basically no different from those sustained by men. Injuries seemed more prevalent among women when they first began their active involvement in sports in large numbers, but their vulnerability was due primarily to poor physical fitness before beginning to participate, lack of conditioning, and poor training and coaching. Inadequate preparation caused more accidents not only among women playing on teams but among individuals who jogged, played tennis, or went skiing before they knew how to handle themselves and their equipment.

Even though it now appears that women in general are no more susceptible to injury than men, it is still true that any individual in poor condition beginning a new activity is especially vulnerable. If no other help is available, read a good book on the sport that interests you. A knowledgeable friend can be a good guide. It is often worth the expense of joining a sports club or taking a few private or group lessons before dashing off into a disaster on the tennis court or ski slope.

In general most injuries sustained by women involve the lower limbs. Ankle and knee strains and sprains are especially common, and shin splints (pain in the anterior shin area of the lower leg) and chondromalacia (cartilage inflammation of the knees) occur more frequently in women than in men.

Women do not suffer severe injuries to the breast, and the idea that a blow to the breast will cause cancer has no foundation in fact. Injuries to the reproductive organs of the nonpregnant female are rare. After the first trimester of pregnancy, when the uterus rises up out of the protective bony pelvis, there is a danger of injury as a result of a severe blow. Therefore, after the third month the pregnant woman should avoid sports in which there is any possibility of a blow to the abdomen, but other activities, such as swimming, dancing, tennis, may be continued as long as the woman desires. Certainly a woman's menstrual period is no reason to discontinue any sport, even swimming.

Whatever exercises or sports are chosen, be alert to signals from your body indicating that you should stop at once to rest and, if the symptoms continue, have them evaluated by a doctor. Watch out especially for sharp pains, marked shortness of breath, dizziness or lightheadedness, chest pressure, and pressure in the throat.

DEVELOPING A FITNESS PROGRAM TO CONDITION YOUR BODY

You can develop your own fitness program to suit your available time, your activity preferences, and available facilities. It might consist of an exercise routine or sports activities alone or a combination of exercises and any other vigorous activity, such as jogging, swimming, or whatever you like to do. However, there are certain requirements that your program should meet. First, it should include activities to develop all the components of fitness—flexibility, strength, and cardiovascular endurance. Second, it must be done regularly. Third, it must include adequate warm-up and cool-down periods. Fourth, it must involve a high enough level of exertion of long enough duration to achieve its intended benefits.

If you work for a company that has initiated an employee fitness program or if you belong to a union that has a special membership arrangement with a health club, be sure to investigate the advantages of participation. Following the lead of Japan and Scandinavia, many corporations in this country now permit employees to work out on company time, thereby achieving big savings in health insurance costs, cutting down absenteeism, and increasing production by raising employee morale.

An increasing number of women whose main job is running a household and caring for children are following an exercise program at home. This alternative is less boring if one or two friends or neighbors get together on a regular basis and also share the cost of some of the home equipment, which can range from a few dollars for a jump rope to several thousand for a well-equipped home gym. In comparison shopping, keep in mind that price is not necessarily an indication of sturdiness. This is especially true of exercise bicycles. Also, a rowing machine or a ski machine provides a more complete workout than a bicycle does.

Special attention should be given to the hazards of unsupervised exercise at home, especially neglecting to do the necessary warm-ups, wearing the wrong shoes, and doing aerobic dance routines on a nonresilient floor.

In many communities it is possible to find a "mobile" health club that makes house calls for women on tight schedules, for those who wish to avoid the embarrassment of performing in public, or for those who want more personalized attention than would be possible at a conventional health club. Prices range from about $25 for a 20-minute workout to as much as $100 for a one-hour session.

Whatever arrangements are made, it should be noted that different types of activities develop different components of fitness. Sports also vary in the aspect of fitness they develop. For example, softball is good for strength but not for endurance. Jogging and bike riding are excellent for endurance and for strengthening pelvic and leg muscles but do not increase flexibility or exercise the arms. Walking contributes to muscle strength and grace of motion as well as improving blood circulation in the legs and reducing foot tiredness. When done frequently and briskly, it can equal the physical fitness achieved by jogging with less risk of injury. Further, it can be done almost anywhere and anytime over a variety of interesting routes.

A special note for walkers, runners, and cyclists: to avoid attacks, especially sexual attacks, the following rules should be observed:

- Don't go into areas that are completely deserted.
- Don't take short-cuts through unknown territory.
- Avoid being out before dawn or after dark.
- Don't run with unknown men and, if possible, use the buddy system.
- Be alert and figure out an escape route if you sense trouble.
- Know where the phones are.
- Change direction suddenly if it seems sensible to do so.
- Don't carry mace or a weapon that can be taken away from you and used against you.
- The best defense against unexpected attacts is running or cycling in groups.

Yoga is excellent for flexibility and relaxation but does little for strength and endurance. Dancing, particularly aerobic dancing, develops all components and uses all parts of the body. Swimming is considered by many experts to be the perfect exercise because it involves all the muscles, relieves tension, and conditions the cardiovascular system. It is often prescribed for back or joint problems or injuries incurred in jogging or racquet sports. The backstroke is particularly helpful for those who suffer from chronic backaches, and it is ideal for arthritics. In addition to providing a feeling of relaxation and exhilaration, it is much less boring than jogging, and working women can usually find a conveniently located pool where they can swim during their lunch hour or before or after work.

Swimmers should be alert to such risks as swimmer's ear (infection caused by the retention of polluted water in the ear canal) and leg or foot cramps resulting from overexertion, cold, or insufficient warm-up. To be on the safe side:

- Don't swim alone for long distances in a lake or any body of water where no lifeguard can see you.
- Don't take a sudden dive into very cold water.
- Don't swim when overly tired or after a heavy meal or after alcohol consumption.

When you've chosen the activity most congenial to you, be sure to combine it with other activities to achieve a total conditioning program.

Maintaining a regular routine may be the hardest part of conditioning. Plan the time you intend to devote to it and stick to your schedule. Studies have shown that effective results will not be derived from less

TABLE 3

ACTIVITIES RATED ACCORDING TO PHYSICAL FITNESS BENEFITS (FLEXIBILITY, STRENGTH, CARDIOVASCULAR ENDURANCE)

	Flexibility	Upper Body Strength	Lower Body Strength	Cardiovascular Endurance	RATING 1 *Poor* 2 *Fair* 3 *Average* 4 *Good* 5 *Excellent*
Walking, slowly			x		1
briskly			x	x	2
Running			x	x	3
Running program*	x	x	x	x	5
Bicycling			x	x	3
Swimming (all basic strokes)	x	x	x	x	5
Kayaking		x			2
Canoeing		x			2
Sailing, small boats	x	x	x		3
large boats					1
Rowing	x	x			2
Horseback riding			x	x	3
Karate (martial arts)	x	x	x	x	5
Bowling		x	x		1
Ballet	x		x		4
Folk dance			x	x	3
Square dance			x	x	3
Modern dance	x	x	x	x	5
Aerobic dance	x	x	x	x	5
Gymnastics	x	x	x	x	5
Backpacking			x	x	2
Golf, walking			x	x	2
cart			x		1
Snow skiing, Alpine	x		x	x	4
Nordic	x	x	x	x	5
Water skiing		x	x		3
Mountain climbing	x	x	x	x	5
Yoga	x				2
Weight lifting		x	x		2
Tennis, singles	x	x	x	x	4
doubles	x	x	x		3
Badminton	x	x	x	x	4
Racquetball	x	x	x	x	5
Field hockey	x	x	x	x	4
Basketball	x	x	x	x	4
Soccer	x	x	x	x	5
Softball	x	x	x	x	3
Volleyball	x	x	x	x	4

*Running combined with upper body flexibility and strength exercises.

SOURCE: *Total Woman's Fitness Guide,* © 1979 by Gail Shierman and Christine Haycock. World Publications, Inc., Mountain View, California. Reprinted with permission.

than three periods of activity each week. If you find it hard to carry out an exercise routine at home or on your own, try to interest your neighbors or friends in forming a group. Exercises done with a group are generally more pleasurable than those done alone. Some women are too self-conscious to join a group until they have achieved some competence, but eventually they find that the social benefits of the group include many psychological advantages. Join the local Y, see if a local university has an open sports program, or find a community center with exercise classes. Health clubs can be good, but check with members to find out whether the privileges are worth the price. You should also check on the staff to find out whether they are properly trained in the use of the equipment and in handling any medical emergencies that might arise. Find out if the club requires a physical examination prior to admission and what types of exercise programs it has. Don't commit yourself to a year's membership until you have visited the premises as a guest once or twice. Unless you participate regularly in its programs, you will probably waste money. On the other hand, if investing the money in a membership will discipline you into regular participation, it might be money well spent.

Remember that you cannot plunge into vigorous activity directly. If you are just beginning your routine, you must work into it gradually. Even after you are in condition to sustain strenuous activity, your body needs a warm-up and cool-down period of moderate exertion to avoid undue stress. Ten minutes of some of the stretching exercises described below would provide the necessary transition.

The question of how long each period of activity should be depends on the kind of activity. The most fitness benefit is derived from activity that maintains the heart beat at 70 percent of its maximum rate for 30 minutes, producing what is called the "training effect." For the average woman the maximum is about 180 to 190 beats per minute. If you can maintain your rate at about 125 to 135, you will be achieving fitness. You can measure your heart rate by counting the pulse at the neck (carotid artery) or wrist (radial artery). The less stress your activity places on the heart and muscles, the longer you have to do it to achieve fitness. Movements that bring the pulse up to achieve a training effect are commonly called "aerobic" exercises. For example, running produces a steady stress that can sustain the 70 percent heart rate, so that 30 minutes of running is sufficient exercise for one period of activity. Sports that produce less or more sporadic stress have to be done longer to achieve the same results.

SEXUAL HEALTH

Lonny Myers, M.D.
American College of Sexologists, Chicago, Illinois

SEXUAL STAGES

You were born a sexual being, but as you grow older, sexual activity may play an important part in your life, its role may be minor, or it may be completely absent.

INFANCY AND CHILDHOOD

Infants include their genitals as they explore their bodies. We are just beginning to realize how sexual infants are. Orgasms have been observed in babies of 3 months and are common in childhood before puberty.

Unfortunately, too many infants soon learn that "down there" is "dirty." Many mothers who smile while they play with other parts of their babies' bodies frown as they change diapers and wash the genital area. Very early in life infants get the message that genitalia are off limits for playful fondling. Attitudes toward masturbation vary greatly; too many mothers slap infants' hands with a stern "No! No!" Some simply ignore masturbation in their babies, and a small but growing number smile at the activity.

Sexual activity that comes so naturally to children has been condemned by many religions, creating much guilt and anxiety. Rational discussions of sex are rare, especially in the presence of children. The simplest questions may evoke such negative responses from adults that children may not ask again, and this negativism becomes a significant part of their sex education. Avoidance, too, plays a major part. When the subject of sex is avoided, children receive a strong message that there is something mysterious, exciting, wrong, and upsetting about it. However, an ever-increasing number of young parents seem to be able to talk comfortably about sex with their children, and following official mandates about sex education, schools are including formal instruction as well as informal conversations about various aspects of sex.

Children get sex messages from other sources, too. A popular message that comes through the media is, "Be sexy; don't have sex!" Radio, television, billboards, magazines, comics, all encourage girls to have sexy eyes, sexy hair, sexy teeth, sexy breath, while the official rules of behavior dictate no sex. Girls are trained to tease men. Traditionally, they are taught to hold out for marriage. That is less common now, but many are still encouraged to extract a price—don't give it away.

Another contradictory message is, "Sex is dirty; save it for the one you love!" Individually, fewer and fewer people seriously regard sex as dirty, yet sexy pictures are dirty pictures, a sexy joke is a dirty joke, and "Don't be dirty" means don't do anything sexual, even tell a sexy story. Why one should save this "dirty" thing for a loved one is a logical question with no good answer.

ADOLESCENCE

Although parental negatives may drastically limit children's awareness of sex, by adolescence they are keenly aware of sexual changes in the body. At this sensitive time the relationship with parents usually changes. There is a sudden lack of intimacy: hugging and kissing and most forms of physical contact are greatly diminished. Sometimes children feel guilty, thinking they have done something to displease their parents. On the other hand, incest, one of the most poignant problems of family life, has recently come out of the shadows for public inspection. (This sexual aberration that usually takes the form of abuse by the father of his daughter, is discussed in detail in "Rape and Family Abuse.")

Our society provides few acceptable means for close physical contact during adolescence, and actually encourages unacceptable means. In addition to the media messages that to "Be sexy" is one of the most important standards by which people are judged and also the key to happiness, society provides leisure time, proximity, and highly suggestive books, pictures, music, and dancing. The results are predictable: millions of sexual contacts among adolescents and an epidemic of adolescent pregnancies.

Only a generation ago fear of pregnancy kept many girls virgins. Now, not only are contraception and abortion available to many, but out-of-wedlock pregnancy is no longer the horrible worse-than-death consequence of sex that it used to be. The status of motherhood may get the adolescent immediate attention, but all too soon adolescent mothers become far more harassed by the burdens and responsibilities of parenthood than impressed with the new status. Strong feminist beliefs often create an incentive to avoid motherhood.

Although the education and awareness programs launched nationwide exaggerate the danger of penis/vagina and oral sex, certain groups of responsible teen-agers have reduced the numbers of sex partners and increased their use of condoms because of their fear of AIDS. However, there has been no drastic reduction in teenage sexual activity as measured by pregnancies and sexually transmitted diseases. Except among gay males, there has been no significant reduction in cases of gonorrhea and chlamydia among adolescents.

ADULTHOOD

Each individual has distinct and unique experiences. You approached your adult sexuality in your own special way. You may have read manuals with explicit pictures and detailed information about sex. You may have seen pornography often. You may be knowledgeable about the details of human sexual response. You may have friends who choose alternative life styles such as swinging singles, gay world, open relationships, group marriage. On the other hand, you may have chosen to avoid dealing with explicit sex material and nontraditional sexual relationships, preferring to retain a sense of privacy and some mystery about the subject of sex. All variations are found in large groups of women with similar socioeconomic and marital status.

You may have a set of moral values and standards that work well for you, or you may be somewhat confused about what is right and wrong about sex for yourself and for teenagers. Clearly, setting standards in a free and contraceptive society is far more difficult than accepting established standards based on a concept of wrong-doing, a fear of pregnancy, and a feeling that AIDS and other sexually transmissible diseases are a form of punishment for breaking the rules set down in time-honored sacred texts.

There are no simple answers and we need to think through this highly complex and fascinating aspect of human living. We may be born sexually free, but how much freedom is compatible with responsible adulthood? with intimate marriage? with sensitive parenthood? with safeguarding physical and mental health? We have dealt only with the tip of the sexual iceberg.

SEX AND HEALTH CARE

Some relevant statistics:

- Most American women in their 20s who have never been married are sexually active.
- For the first time since the '60s, more than half of all American adults consider premarital sex acceptable, but people over 50 and a majority of those whose education ended with grade school still disapprove.
- More than one American in 10 lives alone.
- The median age of women marrying for the first time is 23.3 years, the oldest since the government began to keep these figures in 1890. Of women 20 to 24 years of age, 58.5 percent are unmarried, the largest number since figures began to be kept.

Your response to the contradictory and confusing influences in your past, sexual activity or lack of it, the type of relationships you have, and your feelings about yourself are factors that contribute to your overall health and well-being as much as what you eat, what you breathe, and how you exercise.

What makes sex different from other factors involved in health are society's proscriptions. Although we live in a society in which unhealthful eating habits and environments are not only acceptable, but in many ways encouraged, there is no stigma to seeking healthy alternatives: you may move to a less polluted area or choose to be a vegetarian or abstain from smoking. But when you experiment sexually, the resultant stigma may create more anxiety than the new sexual experience can relieve.

A woman who recognizes her sexual needs and seeks to satisfy them, even within the bounds of what is considered conventional sex, may be regarded with some suspicion by her partner. And a woman who has any ideas about unconventional sex, such as acting out a fantasy of having sex with another woman, had better keep them a secret. Few of her friends would understand and, most probably, her family physician would be shocked. (Doctors whose medical credentials were completed before 1967 never were expected to learn anything about human sexuality in medical school. Despite the success of Masters and Johnson's work and the proliferation of sex therapy clinics, courses in human sexuality remain grossly inadequate in most medical school curricula.)

However, there are those outspoken physicians who believe that sexual activity, including sexual experimentation, may be very beneficial to your health—whether within marriage or not, whether with the opposite gender or not, whether with one person or several, whether with love and commitment or not. There is general consensus that many people do not enjoy the health aspects of sex largely because of the condemnation of sex-for-pleasure they experienced as children and its reinforcement in religion. Unfortunately, most people do not even think of sexual satisfaction in terms of health benefits or consider possible ill effects of sexual deprivation. And this approach is confirmed by many doctors. Certainly, they would not prescribe sex even if the history of the patient suggested that sexual frustration was contributing to the physical symptoms presented. Suppose you go to your primary care physician complaining of vague symptoms such as headaches, insomnia, or indigestion, and the routine physical examination and laboratory tests are normal. Your complaints will probably be dismissed with a prescription for medication to relieve the symptoms, but it is not likely that the physician will explore or even discuss sexual deprivation as a contributing factor. If your mild symptoms develop into severe and demonstrable problems, such as hypertension or a gastric ulcer, your doctor will then take you seriously and treat your worsened condition with respect and professionalism. The chances are that even after you have developed a serious medical problem, the doctor will not investigate the psychosexual difficulties that may have contributed to it, that may slow or prevent recovery, and that may contribute to recurrence. Doctors' training and the way they practice medicine work against their having time or ability to recognize and deal with the role of sexual deprivation in physical diseases.

Now suppose you go to an enlightened doctor who suspects that sexual deprivation is a significant factor in your health problem. Obviously a doctor cannot write a prescription for a lover for you, for some inventive variation in sex with a monogamous partner, or for experimentation with more unconventional sexual expression. But he or she will probably not even discuss this remedy as first choice and go on to second-best treatments. If your problem were arthritis, and a change of climate were the treatment of choice, your doctor would be equally powerless to change the climate or arrange for your whole family to move, but the advantages of a warm, dry climate would be presented as a possible first option and then a second-best option would be considered.

Regarding the needs for touching, the situation is quite different. How often do patients and doctors discuss such matters as the role of physical embracing in emotional health? Actually, the deprivation may be more of a touch deprivation than a lack of sexual stimulation and response. Unfortunately, there are very few ways in which to enjoy skin-to-skin contact except during sex and satisfactory sex partners are not always available to fulfill needs. Some sophisticated, assertive adults might be able to communicate their need to cuddle naked without sex, but for most people it is difficult to find such contact outside a pair-bond relationship where the two sleep together often. Fear of sex denies many people many opportunities to touch warmly, with or without clothes. We have only recently learned how important "stroking" is for our psychological and physical good health. It has been proven that babies do not thrive without adequate tender touching, and almost all adults need tender touching too. Sexual deprivation usually means touch deprivation. The number of orgasms reached per unit time is usually less important. Orgasms reached by masturbation may be highly gratifying "sexually" in one sense and still leave you feeling "sexually" deprived.

So far only the ill effects of sexual inactivity have been discussed. There are possible ill effects from sexual activity as well. It may not only be a contributing factor to physical disease but may also cause it directly. The dynamics of its indirect effect are the same as for inactivity: that is, sexual relationships may cause anxiety, frustration, hostility, and other negative emotions that contribute to physical disease. Its direct effect is clear: sexual activity is the means by which the sexually transmissible diseases (STD) are contracted.

There is a middle ground between being hysterical about STD and pretending that they do not exist. Every effort should be made to minimize the risks, but contracting STD should not stigmatize a person nor should the fear of STD be used as an excuse to impose religious restrictions on sexual behavior.

AIDS

Some recent developments:

- The scientific community strongly disagrees with Masters' and Johnson's publicized estimates of AIDS in the heterosexual population and the ease with which it might be transmitted.
- The fear of AIDS, herpes, and other STDs has brought about the end of the sexual revolution and the indulgence in recreational sex for many concerned adults.
- Where the incidence of AIDS is highest—on the East and West Coasts—gay men are changing their sexual behavior for reasons of health rather than for reasons of morality. The result is a new ethic based on restraint and abstinence from anal intercourse.
- According to statistics, at least 10% of gay men are married, and a recent survey of bisexuals indicates that 90% of these remain sexually active with their wives. It is this fact that has raised the problem of whether doctors should breach doctor-patient confidentiality in the interest of the wife's wellbeing when it is discovered that the husband is infected with the AIDS virus.
- There is no doubt that the prevailing fear of AIDS is increasingly affecting the libido of single women and of men who worry that a woman of their choice might have been sexually involved with a bisexual man.

(For a more detailed discussion of AIDS and other STDs, see "Sexually Transmissible Diseases.")

LOVE

Some people insist that a romantic relationship, a pair-bond, is the form of love that is essential to good health. In my opinion, that reflects a limited concept of love. We all know fascinating people who thrive on various forms of nonromantic love. We also know the sad plight of women who are shattered when an exclusive romantic relationship comes to an end. It is certainly advisable to recognize that the role played in one's life by romantic love changes over the years. Priorities are reassessed. Deep emotional attachments to friends and family can remain constant, and both are accessible to all women except for the totally self-involved narcissists. Loyalty and caring, the foundation of all forms of love, can be exchanged between lovers, friends, and relatives. There are many overlaps with all three types of love.

In general it is not regarded as healthy to have sex with friends or co-workers, that is, with anyone outside the pair-bond. The theory is that sex will change the relationship either because a pair-bond will develop or because the ego complications that are involved with sex will interfere with the relationship. However, I know of many cases in which people who have been friends for more than ten years report that their relationship included sex during some periods and not during others, depending on circumstances, other commitments, or the mood of one or both of the friends, and that sex never interfered with their healthy on-going friendship. I know of a few cases where persons who were working together had sex only once and went right back to a normal working relationship without any of the complications so-called experts would predict.

SELF-RESPECT

Everyone needs self-respect for good health. At the basis of self-respect is a complex system of standards of behavior and expectations we set for ourselves and society sets for us. It is generally accepted that self-respect is enhanced by giving and receiving love, whether it be romantic, friendship, or family love. The relationship of sex to self-respect is much more variable, because it involves so many social and religious proscriptions. At one end of the spectrum are women who need to limit sex to one lifelong partner for self-respect. At the other end are women who need to feel respect for their partner(s) but to whom the number or gender of sexual partners is unimportant. In between is a full range of conditions different women need to nurture their self-respect: monogamous marriage, including serial marriages; love and commitment but not necessarily involving the sanctioned commitment of marriage; relationships only with a partner who is also single; no homosexuality; no group sex, and so on.

Sex, love, and self-respect have a profound influence on our overall health and well-being. A loving sex relationship is somewhat like a strong body constitution: both contribute to an exuberant sense of good health but neither can guarantee anything. Remember that whereas you can be healthy, even thrive, without sex adventures, you cannot thrive without love and self-respect. Also I would like to add that the need for love and self-respect lasts a lifetime, whereas the need for sex varies during your lifetime and is likely to decrease later in life, despite the highly publicized exceptions to this general rule.

FEMALE SEXUAL RESPONSE

Although Masters and Johnson have described physiological response to direct sexual stimulation in great detail, they do not deal with the sudden desire to kiss or hug someone who turns you on. This is also a "sexual response." Having dinner, walking along the beach, washing dishes—almost any common activity may be sexual, depending on whom you are with or depending on your fantasies! Your sexual response can be a way of looking, a way of moving your body, a way of touching, a dream.

In common parlance, "female sexual response" means how your body responds to genital stimulation. Masters and Johnson effected a gigantic breakthrough by making these responses legitimate concerns. It is clear that they emphasize variety and that no two persons react in exactly the same way, but by publishing charts and describing standards they have inadvertently created goals for many who read their material. Remember that all the charts and descriptions are a compilation of many, many different variations. They should not be taken as a statement of how you should respond, nor should they be interpreted as limitations to your response.

PHYSIOLOGICAL RESPONSE

The basic female sexual response described by Masters and Johnson consists of a period of arousal, a plateau phase, one or more orgasms, and a resolution to the resting state. But that is not necessarily true for all women at all times. You may enjoy arousal and resolution without a need for the intermediate phase. You may jump to the plateau stage without a slow gradual arousal.

You may have a slow arousal and a long plateau with a gradual release of tension that could never be classified as orgasm but still leaves you relaxed in your resolution stage. My definition of "good sex" is to be aroused, have a good time, and end up feeling warm, glowing, and contented.

Following is a detailed description of basic physiologic responses. During arousal the vagina becomes lubricated. This lubrication is a seepage from the walls of the vagina, not an actual secretion, because structured glands are not involved. This response is considered analogous to the erection of the penis in the male. As stimulation continues (whether direct or indirect), there is generalized vascular engorgement of the entire pelvic area. The swelling includes the clitoris, the labia, and the expansion of the vaginal barrel. Also the nipples become erect and both the areola and breasts themselves enlarge. The uterus begins to elevate.

During the plateau phase the uterus continues to be elevated and may double in size due to vasocongestion. While the deeper vagina continues to expand, the lower third of the vagina decreases in circumference. Color changes occur and may include a flush on the chest and deepening of color of the vulva. In women who have given birth, sometimes the vulva reaches a purplish hue. In very dark-complexioned females this will not be recognized.

Although most of us think of orgasm as a total body response, the female orgasm, as described by Masters and Johnson, consists solely of a series of contractions of the orgasmic platform, a group of muscles located in the lower third of the vagina. These contractions are 0.7 to 0.8 seconds apart and are usually from 3 to 12 in number. During orgasm, pulse, blood pressure, and respiration are significantly increased, often accompanied by convulsive body movements. With continued stimulation orgasms may occur in succession. The orgasmic phase is followed by the resolution phase. During resolution the engorgement subsides, and breasts and genital area (including uterus) return to their usual state.

Voluntary movements range from minimal hip movements to total body involvement throughout arousal and plateau. During late plateau and orgasm, involuntary movements are added, sometimes overwhelming, sometimes small and specific. Individual responses cover a wide range. Some women are always silent, others routinely make gasping or grunting sounds, still others scream out. Also, the same woman may have very different responses (with the same or different partners) on different occasions.

The important thing to remember is that the cycle may take different forms. With direct stimulation of the clitoris an orgasm may occur with none of the ancillary changes, such as enlargement of breasts or color changes in the labia. The resolution phase may be complete within a few minutes of the beginning of stimulation. Or you may experience an arousal and plateau that may last a half hour or more with a very gradual return to complete resolution. It is quite possible to experience engorgement and resolution without ever recognizing a point of orgasm. Instead of a major peak experience you may have a series of small orgasmic releases, each one discharging some of the tension until gradually there is no tension and you feel relaxed and comfortable.

And you can enjoy all these responses without having intercourse. Masters and Johnson report that orgasms during manual and oral stimulation are more intense than orgasms during coitus. But remember that Masters and Johnson measure intensity with laboratory equipment, without regard for the woman's personal response, that is, how she experienced the orgasm.

"Did you come?" may be difficult to answer. How many of us count contractions of the orgasmic platform and check stopwatches to clock them at 0.7 seconds? Far more sensitive questions are "Did you enjoy yourself? Do you feel comfortable?" But if there is good communication, even these questions are usually unnecessary. Whatever your sexual experience, clinical or dramatic accounts of others need not cause anxiety or performance demands. Orgasms need to be put in perspective. Enjoy your sex life with mini-orgasms, the Big O, or just plain close, intimate pleasure.

Unfortunately, Masters and Johnson did not include descriptions of or comments about the G Spot or about female ejaculation. The G Spot, which is present in some women, is a small area of sensitive tissue on the upper anterior wall of the vagina near the urethra. Stimulation of this tissue produces, at least on some occasions, a distinctive pleasurable sexual response. Female ejaculation is the expulsion of fluid, not urine, from the urethra during orgasm. By not acknowledging these two sexual responses, Masters and Johnson have undoubtedly reinforced anxiety in thousands of women who experience them.

QUESTIONS OFTEN ASKED ABOUT ORGASM

What is the difference between a vaginal orgasm and a clitoral orgasm? The differences between vaginal and clitoral orgasms are basically twofold. First, vaginal orgasms result from vaginal stimulation, with or without G Spot stimulation, and clitoral orgasms result from clitoral stimulation, direct or indirect. Rarely, breast stimulation or even just a very erotic situation may elicit an orgasm. Second, vaginal orgasms always include intense sensations within the vagina, and clitoral orgasms always include intense sensations in the clitoral area. These sensations often occur together along with other body responses. I describe these differences only in response to the question, because I prefer to emphasize the similarities of the two orgasms rather than their differences. Either type of orgasm may be local and minimal or involve the entire body and be ecstatic.

The vaginal orgasm has come full circle in the last century. Freud described vaginal orgasm as being the "mature" orgasm and put down clitoral orgasms as "immature." Masters and Johnson, on the other hand, emphasized clitoral orgasms, describing the clitoris as the trigger to female orgasm. The fact that many women experience orgasm in positions of coitus where direct stimulation of the clitoris is impossible was explained by theorizing that the thrusting motion of the penis caused tension on the hood of the clitoris causing indirect clitoral stimulation. The G Spot may contribute to women having vaginal orgasms without direct or indirect stimulation of the clitoris.

Current thinking tends to give legitimacy to both vaginal and clitoral orgasms without diminishing the value of either. An orgasm, the response to stimulation, is similar whether or not the clitoris or G Spot is involved. It is somewhat like tearful weeping. The tears are the same whether produced by an onion or a tragedy, even though the emotional and body reactions may be very different. Similarly, the contractions of the orgasmic platform are the same, whether produced by stimulation of the clitoris or by a more unusual stimulus.

I can have an orgasm by direct stimulation when my husband uses his fingers, but I want to have an orgasm during intercourse. What can I do? First, try to understand *why* this is so important to you. Is this goal something you feel must be accomplished to be "sexually mature"? Are you seeking to experience what so many romantic novels describe, that is, the ecstasy the woman feels while her lover is thrusting within her? Or is it just a curiosity, something you expected and anticipated, but has never happened? If you conclude that it really isn't important, simply cross it off your list of things to worry about. It is possible to have an exciting, fulfilling sex life without having orgasms during intercourse. However, if you conclude this is a "must" for you, try different coital positions so that the penis can come in direct contact with your G Spot, if you have one. Use your imagination and/or sex manuals to discover different positions with which to experiment. If this doesn't work, try supplementing the penile thrusting with direct stimulation of the clitoris. This can be done by using your finger or your lover's finger, or by either of you applying a small vibrator to the clitoris during intercourse. Another technique is to stimulate your clitoris to a point close to orgasm just before intercourse. Different positions may facilitate indirect if not direct stimulation of the clitoris. I just hope you continue the pursuit only so long as it is fun for you and that you do not make the attainment of orgasm during intercourse a source of unnecessary frustration.

I have read about orgasm, but I have never reached the peaks others describe. Sometimes I wonder if I have ever had one. Can you help me understand? As I have said before, you should not attempt to measure your own responses against the reports of others. What is often omitted from descriptions of the orgasmic response is that it may be a rather dull experience with only the involuntary contractions of the vagina to confirm it. At the point of orgasm your body takes over the sexual response. Movements that had been partly involuntary and partly voluntary become entirely involuntary. But it need not be dramatic. The important part is this lack of control. There may be no waves of energy, no undulating movements of the hips, perhaps a gasp or two, and that's it. This has been proven in the laboratory. Masters and Johnson have recorded physiological orgasms manifested only by specific muscular contractions when the woman was unaware of a peak experience.

Romantic novels and stories often describe the ecstasy of simultaneous orgasm. I've never experienced this. Is it important or very different from non-simultaneous orgasm? In my opinion simultaneous orgasm has been overrated. It does give the satisfaction of cooperative good timing and a special joy that your partner is climaxing at the same time you are, but what is lost is the sharing of the other's orgasm. During climax your attention is directed to the sensations of your own body. There is no "attention" left to direct toward your partner, other than the general knowledge that he is experiencing his climax at the same time. Separate climaxes allow you to share each other's experience in a much more intimate way. When your partner climaxes, you can empathize, appreciate, almost live through the experience, and when you climax, you can completely abandon yourself to yourself without diverting any attention outside your own body. I am talking about only the few minutes of high plateau phase and climax itself; before and after these stages the feeling of intimacy may be exquisite. Whatever you like best is right for you. If you feel it is important, put your imagination to work figuring how, with your particular pattern of intercourse, this might be possible. But do not allow it to create anxiety. Simultaneous orgasm is not essential to a full and satisfying sex relationship.

SEXUAL ENRICHMENT FOR COUPLES

For some couples, sex improves with time. They report that after twenty or thirty years, the excitement and satisfaction they experience far exceeds the achievement of their earlier years. This increase in pleasure may be due to the elimination of all the stresses associated with raising children and building financial security. Often when women develop a new interest in sex after menopause, they realize that fear of pregnancy during all the previous years interfered with their ability to relax and enjoy sex free of anxiety.

However, this storybook crescendo of sexual enjoyment just isn't true for most couples. More common is a gradual decrease in excitement, with or without continued deep satisfaction. Most marriages sustain many ups and downs in the joy, comfort, and closeness that sex offers.

Whether you consider your sexual relationship good, mediocre, or bad depends a great deal on your expectations. Some women were taught that they were lucky if it didn't hurt and that "nice" women did not enjoy sex. Other women have been exposed to the fantastic joys possible during sex and are disappointed if each encounter is not "the greatest show on earth."

Fortunately, communication in this area is becoming less awkward. Thanks to the women's movement, women are becoming increasingly comfortable with their sexuality, with the result that they can talk about their needs and wants more freely. Gone are the days when large numbers of women would pretend to be sexually satisfied, would moan and writhe as if they were having an orgasm—all in order to please a husband who concentrated only on his own pleasure. (Many of these women were led to believe that it was entirely their fault that they weren't reaching climax, and so they never felt free to discuss the problem with their partners.)

If you'd like to enhance your marital sexual activities, you can certainly do so if the spark is still there and communication lines are open. Here is a list of suggestions (the list is by no means exhaustive and is meant to inspire you to improvise some of your own activities):

Create an atmosphere conducive to tenderness, sensitivity, and romance. When was the last time you really prepared for sex? Have you ever given it the amount of time and energy you devote to a dinner party? Do you provide incense, candlelight, your favorite music, and a suitable stretch of uninterrupted time? Too often sex is relegated to "after everything else" so that it inevitably becomes an afterthought rather than an occasion in its own right.

Try a sensuous massage with slightly scented oil, rent an erotic video that you can watch together; take time. Remember how sexy taking each other's clothes off can be. Perhaps a dance in your underwear or nude. Once in a while agree in advance not to have genital sex but spend time caressing and enjoying sensuality to the fullest. If one or both is experiencing a refractory period following an early orgasm, continue the gentle touching and cuddling, with or without more sex.

Experiment with new techniques. Perhaps you already have a large repertoire; perhaps not. Perhaps you already enjoy oral sex as an experience by itself; perhaps oral sex offends you. Too many people think of noncoital sex, such as oral sex, as foreplay only. But for many couples oral sex is a rewarding experience in and of itself, whether or not it leads to orgasm. Oral sex is very different when done simultaneously than when you take turns. Sometimes it feels good to caress your partner during oral sex; other times it may feel good just to lie back and receive. Treat yourself to some time when every iota of energy is directed fully to responding, to feeling the sensations all over your body as well as in your genitals. And you may be surprised at how much you enjoy changing roles, becoming the initiator instead of the receiver.

Explore the use of sexual aids. Two of the most common sexual aids are dildos and vibrators. They may be used in a variety of ways, including dildos during oral sex and vibrators during intercourse. Rejecting sexual aids is another example of an isolated standard of anything sexual. When a male friend pooh-poohed the use of a dildo, one female friend of mine retorted, "You may be talented and possess a magnificent penis, but I don't know any man who can perform oral sex on me when his penis is in my vagina, and I like that as a variation."

Occasionally emphasize humor, playfulness, and craziness. If you feel better making every sexual encounter a serious matter, skip this paragraph. But if you have suppressed harmless, crazy ideas because grown-ups "don't act like that," read on. I believe that too many times we live under restrictions that serve no purpose and prevent a lot of fun. Haven't you ever felt you wanted to just play like a puppy dog? Is there a law against going to the bedroom to change for dinner and arriving at the table in your birthday suit? Have you had sex at least once in every room in the house? How about a good roll on the living room floor? Do you have a favorite scene in a play you would like to act out? This is only scratching the surface of possibilities. Although someone said of sex, "I never knew you could have so much fun without laughing," you can laugh too!

Get away. There is something about entering a hotel room and closing the door that acts like magic for some couples. A bathroom you didn't clean; a bed you won't have to make up. If the prices in the dining rooms are exorbitant, bring a picnic of your favorite foods or send out for a pizza. Pick a hotel with the services you like, such as a sauna or swimming pool. It will be a change from a dinner and the theatre night and within the same price range.

Talk openly. For some this will be one of the hardest suggestions to follow. Sometimes it is easier just to do something different and not discuss it ahead of time. That's fine. By talking openly I mean discussing your expectations, your wants, and what feels good with your partner. I also mean asking and listening. One way to start is to recognize how difficult it is and question each other about why it is so awkward, always with a sense of perspective. You are only verbalizing about a basic human response!

Attend a sex workshop. Workshops are held in major cities throughout the country. Most show explicit films and use street language for desensitization and resensitization. To find out about workshops in your area, contact AASECT or the American College of Sexologists. Not everyone might enjoy or benefit from one, but I will never forget one couple who wrote to us after attending, "We've been married 35 years and never enjoyed sex so much as that weekend after the workshop; and it keeps getting better!"

Most of what I have said about married couples applies to living-together couples, although these relationships rarely last more than ten years. One of the biggest problems living-together couples have is how to deal with the expectation of marriage of one or the other partner. It is fairly easy for couples to ignore this problem when both are under 30, but when the woman's biological clock begins to tick more loudly and the question of parenthood becomes an issue, either the relationship ends or marriage and family follow.

And a dramatic change is likely to occur following the marriage no matter how autonomous each individual was before. Even if the wife is working, there is a strong tendency to revert to sex role stereotypes, with the woman doing more of the household tasks and the man taking on more financial responsibility. For some, sex may get better, but for others, it suffers greatly. What used to be exciting in a love-sex relationship may suddenly become less erotic after the marriage vows. Some couples report this happened when they moved in together, even before marriage.

In two-career marriages, fatigue, tension, and lack of time affect the quality of sex. Unspoken resentments may find their outlet in performance. A husband whose worldly success is increasingly overshadowed by his wife's may punish her by rejecting her in bed in the same way that once-powerless wives withheld or granted their sexual favors as the only leverage they had in their struggle for power in a relationship.

SEXUAL THERAPY

With sex out of the closet more people are becoming more aware of their sexual needs and more interested in sexual health. These new attitudes help explain the steady increase in the number of people seeking sexual therapy. Here again, more and more women have been liberated to the point where, if their husband's sex drive is too low, they will suggest that a few sessions of sex therapy may provide the solution.

Among sexual therapies there is a definite trend toward treating couples even though only one partner appears to have a problem. In females the usual complaint is lack of orgasm, especially orgasm during intercourse. In males the most common complaints are impotence and premature ejaculation.

In recent years, another phenomenon has emerged. Known as inhibited sexual desire, or absence of sexual desire, it is now one of the leading sexual disorders and is thought to be the direct cause of many marital breakups. Therapists don't believe this is a new problem but rather that more men and women are calling attention to it because they have higher expectations of what a good sex life means.

By now it is known worldwide that a little more than two decades ago, Masters and Johnson, the pioneering sex therapists from St. Louis, revolutionized the treatment of sexual malfunction. Since their original experiments, millions of Americans have undergone treatment for impotence, premature ejaculation, failure to achieve orgasm, and absence of sexual desire. And many couples have been "curing" themselves with the aid of books and articles that spell out tested therapeutic procedures.

While there is no doubt that among the thousands of sex therapy clinics many are staffed by incompetents and out-and-out charlatans offering "treatments" that can be dangerous to unsuspecting clients, reputable sex therapists have saved many marriages and helped many distraught individuals to enjoy the blessings of normal sexual performance. Reputable sex therapy clinics are usually connected with a teaching hospital and supervised by the department of psychiatry. Therapists with the training and credentials essential for professional standing screen potential clients very carefully and usually eliminate those whose marriages as such are beyond redemption. (People with serious personality disorders are also eliminated.)

A therapeutic program usually begins with a physical examination and the taking of a sex history. If no physical conditions are found to be the cause of the sexual dysfunction, the next step consists of educational counseling to dispel the myths and misunderstandings that may interfere with healthy functioning. The next goal is to open channels of communication so that verbal and nonverbal messages can be conveyed without embarrassment. (Inability to communicate likes and dislikes is one of the basic causes of sexual dissatisfaction and incompatibility.) The couple is given "pleasuring" exercises to practice at home.

These usually include overall tenderness with an initial proscription against touching the breasts or genital area. The couple discusses the exercises at the next session. This process is very helpful in encouraging the partners to express themselves about what pleases and does not please them. After several assignments, genitals may be caressed, but no intercourse is permitted. This is especially helpful to the male, as it allows for intimate, sensuous massage with no demand to perform. Because anxiety is a major cause of sexual problems, being relaxed and understanding goes a long way toward a satisfying sexual relationship. Throughout the treatment, which may consist of 15 to 20 sessions, special attention is given to the couple's differences in temperament and the emotional environment they generate together.

SEXUAL DYSFUNCTION—PHYSICAL CONDITIONS

Most sex therapists are not physicians, and most will ask you to be checked for any physical abnormality that might relate to your sexual problem. For example, a complaint of painful intercourse (dyspareunia) may be due to any number of physical conditions including an intact hymen, skin or mucous membrane irritations of the vulva, vaginitis (infectious or atrophic), adhesions of the clitoral hood, insufficient vaginal lubrication, a severely retroverted uterus (tipped way back), pelvic infection, ovarian tumor, endometriosis, and a disturbance in the lower bowel. If there seems to be no evidence of organic abnormality, psychological causes must be explored. For example, dyspareunia might be traced to religious proscriptions or sexual trauma in childhood, such as rape or incest.

One cause of dyspareunia is vaginismus, a severe spasm of the perineal muscles and lower third of the vagina. Vaginismus is a classic example of a psychosomatic disorder. It is a physical condition that has its origin in psychological trauma; the physical condition is entirely involuntary and no amount of will power can relax the muscles. The treatment consists of a combination of psychotherapy and dilation with Hegar dilators. Masters and Johnson send the couple home with dilators and instructions after the initial dilation in the clinic. It is essential that both partners understand both the physical condition and the psychological origin for the best therapeutic results. The spasticity of vaginismus is very distinct from the spasmodic contractions of the same muscles during orgasm. Vaginismus and various physical causes of dyspareunia generally can be diagnosed only by a careful pelvic examination.

Despite the general statements that vaginas accommodate to all sizes of penises, a significant number of cases of dyspareunia are due to the inability of a small vagina to receive a large penis comfortably. Some penises are simply too big for the woman's introitus (opening) or vaginal barrel. The dyspareunia may be caused by the penetration or by the thrusting. A short, very thick penis may cause pain only on penetration, whereas a long, moderately thick penis may cause no pain on penetration but be extremely painful on deep thrusting. Thrusting pain may be alleviated by trying positions that do not utilize the entire shaft of the penis within the vagina. Penetration pain may be relieved by lubrication and dilation or in rare cases surgery.

Some of the less common physical conditions that may influence sexual behavior are hormonal imbalances and nervous system disorders, which cause interference with the normal pathways between sensory and motor components of sexual response, and diabetes, which may cause impotence in the male and affect female response.

About a decade ago the vast majority of sexual dysfunction cases were attributed to psychological, not physical problems. In the past, some experts estimated the proportion of physical causes of sexual dysfunction to be as low as 3 percent. However, if we include the effects of prescription and other drugs, we know now that physical factors are responsible for a far greater proportion of sexual dysfunction cases. Exact figures are not known and vary considerably depending on what group is studied. For groups in which the routine use of prescription drugs is common, the incidence of sexual dysfunction due solely to psychological causes may fall below 50 percent.

The point is that we are now aware that scores of commonly prescribed drugs affect sexual function adversely. Among the worst culprits are antihypertensive drugs, mood-altering drugs, including nonprescription recreation drugs (alcohol, marijuana, heroin), drugs that regulate the heart, and drugs for sedation, including sleeping pills. And more and more evidence is accumulating that indicts an even wider range, including drugs to treat gastrointestinal disorders, arthritis . . . in fact, almost any ailment.

If you or your partner are having trouble with satisfactory sexual response, take a careful look at any and all drugs you are taking or have taken in the recent past. In most cases stopping the drug will bring about a reversal and sexual function will be restored. Unfortunately your doctor may have prescribed the drugs without the knowledge of this unpublicized side effect. Don't be shy. Ask your doctor about the drug's potential to interfere with good sexual response. Long lists of potentially harmful drugs have been compiled and published in both medical and lay publications. Of course, the mere announcement of a drug's *potential* to cause sexual dysfunction does not imply that the drug is necessarily responsible in any given case. A reasonable case must be made for a cause-and-effect relationship before permanently withholding a drug essential to your best health, but a suspicion of cause and effect should be enough to make you discontinue a drug that you may well be able to get along without. Do not underestimate the power of drugs, including alcohol, to have an adverse effect on sexual function. Do not hesitate or neglect to bring up this important issue with your doctor.

SEXUAL DYSFUNCTION—PSYCHOLOGICAL CAUSES

Traditionally, our sexual training has been one of restraint. To be "good" we had to train our bodies not to respond to sexual stimuli. Then, suddenly, this body, thoroughly conditioned over many years not to respond to sexual stimulation, is supposed to respond enthusiastically. Sexual restraint, which used to be good, is now bad, and sexual response, which used to be bad, is now good! Unfortunately, our nervous system is very complex, and we cannot compel our bodies to reverse their carefully developed patterns of restraint. Much of sex therapy is "unlearning" the proscriptions of the past.

Some of these proscriptions are sexist and restrict females to a lower status, thus diminishing self-respect. The nonphysical causes for inadequate sexual response in women include fear of consequences (pregnancy or disease), low self-esteem (self-depreciation), anxiety about doing the right thing (fear of failure), ignorance about what is healthy (fear of perversion), guilt about experimenting (feeling only penis-vagina penetration is proper), inability to communicate (silent sex and hope for the best), being unable to receive (trained only to nurture others), inability to accept sex-for-pleasure (cannot defy early proscriptions).

Sometimes these handicaps to sexual fulfillment exist when there is adequate libido; the woman wants to enjoy sex to the fullest but just can't. Other times the desire for sex is lacking. Loss of libido may be general, relating to all men, or specific, relating only to the spouse or partner. General loss of libido may be voluntary or involuntary. Some people make an effort to turn off sexual desire. They find the hassles of sex outweigh the joys and they intentionally train themselves not to respond to sexual stimuli. With disuse, the neural pathways will indeed become less responsive but still remain functional. An ideal situation with an ideal partner can almost always revitalize this basic human response.

Involuntary loss of libido may stem from a series of rejections, multiple unsatisfactory experiences, lack of opportunity, or some conflict with a partner. Within the pair-bond, boredom, hostility, and disappointment are common causes of loss of libido. You may be turned off at night because your partner was too critical, too flattering, or too dull during the day. You may have a feeling of distance because he doesn't understand you or your needs, and your desire for sex may depend on feeling intimate with someone who empathizes with you. Or you and your partner may have reduced sex to such a mechanical level that you just can't stand going through motions, once joyful and meaningful, now just dull routine.

Excitement is an important factor in libido. (I have suggested possible ways to inject excitement into a partnership in the section on sexual enrichment.) Often age is used as an excuse to allow libido to wane. Finding a partner may be difficult for an older woman, and rather than admit defeat, she may use the excuse, "I'm too old for that."

Many women are aware of the psychocultural source of their problems but are unable to get their emotions and bodies to catch up with their minds. They intellectually accept and understand but need and want help in overcoming old habits. These women are highly motivated and have a high success rate with modern couple therapy.

A recent study has yielded a composite picture of a specific type of nonorgasmic woman suffering from the "good girl" syndrome. She was an obedient child who did well at school, and, as an adult, although she is married (she does what's expected of her), she lives near her parents, in many cases in the same neighborhood, and she never argues with her mother. Such women may enter therapy after the death of the father. Therapy may be simple and take no more than about twelve sessions.

Because these women didn't masturbate as children, they are given exercises for stimulating the vaginal muscles as well as erotic literature to stimulate and feed their fantasies. The first goal is the achievement of arousal, and when this occurs, the next goal is the achievement of orgasm with the sexual partner.

In addition to individual and couple therapy, group therapy is also effective in solving dysfunctional problems of psychological origin. These groups stress both education and self-assertion. Women learn basic female anatomy and physiology and receive training in assertive behavior. Honesty and self-revelation are encouraged, but the dynamics are supportive rather than based on confrontation as in the encounter groups. Although groups directed at therapy are led by professionals, it is quite possible to start your own support group, if only to share experiences and gain confidence in the process.

For help in finding therapists in your area, I suggest consulting your local medical society, organizations dealing with marriage counseling, or professionals trained in various schools of humanistic psychology, such as transactional analysis, rational emotive therapy, gestalt. If you have difficulty finding someone locally, you might write to: American Association of Marriage and Family Counselors, American Association of Sex Educators, Counselors & Therapists (AASECT), or Association of Humanistic Psychology (see Directory of Health Information).

If you are just given a name or look in the classified section of your telephone book, be sure to get references. Be sure to find out the average length of therapy and the cost range. Find out about your health insurance coverage. There are many competent sex therapists, but there are also quacks, and, unfortunately, there is no uniform licensing process. Check credentials in terms of both training and current membership in reputable organizations such as those listed above. Help is available, even if hard to find.

SEX AND SINGLE WOMEN

The contemporary single woman of no matter what age has many options regarding her sex life but should always take into account the ways in which to handle the problem of sexually transmissible diseases now more complicated than the problem of contraception. What can you expect if you are single? Certainly a lot depends on your community. Your options may be very limited if you live in a very small town without access to a large city. In large cities it depends mostly on you. However mature or liberated you feel your views are, if your partner does not share the same views you may find yourself in an exploitative sexual situation. Thousands of single women are hurt every day and many become very frustrated: "Is there no such animal as a sensitive, decent man?" Many conclude that the price of sex is too high. They prefer to go without sex until they can enjoy a solid commitment on the man's part.

On the other hand, if you are single and want a more active sex life, I strongly suggest that you begin to talk openly about sex when you date, and I am including the grandmothers here too. One easy way to break into the subject of sexual values is by talking about role stereotypes: Do you believe women and men should continue to have different roles (the man taking the initiative, picking you up, paying for dinner)? What do you think of changing social roles over the last decade? Do you believe in the double standard? And don't be angry if your date is honest and says he wants sex. What is important is that he doesn't pressure you with his wants and that he is sensitive to your wants, whether that involves the opera, swimming, or sex.

Sensitivity means an acceptance of the fact that when you say "No" you mean NO and not yes. Too many men have been culturally conditioned to believe that women say "No" to sexual advances just to be coy and to tease and, therefore, are not to be taken at their word. This mistaken premise often ends up in what has come to be known as "date rape" and causes considerable anguish to the victim (see "Rape and Family Abuse").

Be as honest as possible about your feelings and what you want. And don't be afraid to say that you are confused, if that is true. Take some risks but always weigh what you are doing against the realistic alternatives. You may decide you would rather be home with a good book. If so, gently excuse yourself early and go home. However, if you've embarked on a program of risk-taking, always be sure that there's a condom in your purse when you leave for a new adventure. If the date turns out to be a possible sexual partner whose past is unknown to you, you'll have to make it clear that you're not risking your health (and if he's smart, there's no reason he should risk his in the event that you might have had some experiences with bisexual men). No condom; no sex.

Finally, there are those singles who want a vacation from sex, temporary or permanent, sometimes referred to as "the new celibacy." This implies celibacy by desire or design, not by fear or default. Sometimes it is much simpler to make a decision to abstain from sex than to weigh the pros and cons on each date or in each relationship. The declaration need only be to yourself. If a fantastic man appears on the scene, you can certainly change your mind. In the meantime you have avoided the decision-making process regarding the average man you will meet. Sex becomes nonnegotiable. You are temporarily choosing abstinence. You may or may not include masturbation in your pact with yourself. You may experience a sense of relief. No more struggling with, "Shall I or shall I not?" "If he takes me to dinner, will he expect me to go to bed with him?" "I wonder if he really likes me or just wants sex." "If I go to that party and do meet someone very attractive, do I want to have sex?" If sexual encounters have been troublesome for you, maybe a clean break will be more helpful than "I'll give it one more try." For some, one reason for experimenting with the new celibacy is political, a way of demonstrating independence. And as any young feminist will tell you, "It used to be liberated to say 'Yes' to sex, but now we're liberated enough to say 'No.'"

EXTRAMARITAL SEX

In a recent report on women and infidelity, the following facts emerged:

- 30% to 50% of married women have had extramarital affairs.
- Younger women freed by economic independence and the sexual revolution of the 60s are as likely as men to seek extramarital relationships. (When Kinsey did his studies in the late 40s and 50s, results showed that more than twice as many married men as married women had affairs: 56% to 26%.)
- Although awareness of AIDS has curtailed one-night stands, durable relationships continue to occur.
- In a 1986 survey by the American Psychiatric Association on family

patterns, only 8% of the respondents suspected their spouses of having illicit relationships.
- The general consensus is that adultery is wrong, but many people commit it anyway.
- Among the reasons given for extramarital affairs are:

  Women have more contact with men in the workplace. Common career goals and shared accomplishments have been described as powerful aphrodisiacs.

  Women who married young and went from the protection of their family to the protection of their husband feel they have missed the satisfactions of autonomy.

  Many women indicate that the two most important aspects of extramarital relationships are communication and companionship, not sex.

  A considerable number of women use an affair as a way of ending a bad marriage.
- It is generally agreed by therapists that infidelity is a *symptom* of a troubled marriage and not in itself the *cause* of the trouble.

SEXUAL ADDICTION

The concept of addiction has been expanded in recent years to include not only gambling and overeating but also sexual activity that has gone out of control. Therapists define sexual addicts as those men and women who treat sex the way other people abuse drugs: dependence on sex becomes a psychological narcotic. Women in this category get into a cycle similar to that of other addicts. The compulsive behavior pattern is characterized by a preoccupation with sex that interferes with normal relationships with a spouse or lover; an uncontrollable desire to have as many sexual experiences as possible in a short period of time; a compulsion to engage in sexual activities that leave feelings of shame, guilt, anxiety, and depression; taking time out from essential activities in order to seek out sexual adventures; and using sex as a way of escaping from the problems of daily living.

Sexual addiction surfaced as a clinical disorder in the 1970s when some members of Alcoholics Anonymous founded Sexaholics Anonymous in California. There are now hundreds of groups nationwide with slight variations in name and program. Many of the members are patients at sex therapy clinics associated with hospitals. Of the patients receiving treatment for sexual addiction, one in three is a woman.

If you identify with some or all of the behaviors attributed to sex addicts and you feel your life would be improved if you were in control of your sexual impulses rather than being at the mercy of them, you might want to contact a support group. Consult your phone book under Sexaholics Anonymous or Sexual Compulsives or if there are no such listings, you can receive information about the group nearest you by writing to one of the founders of the movement: Roy, PO Box 300, Simi, California 93062. Reputable sex therapy clinics can also put you in touch with similar groups. (See Directory of Health Information.)

ALTERNATIVES IN SEXUAL EXPRESSION

MASTURBATION

Sexual health can also mean an understanding of forms of expression that have been considered unconventional or that have been tabooed by our society. We should be able to consider in an objective and open way alternative forms that might be desirable for others or for ourselves.

Since the Kinsey Report in the 1940s and the many books on child care and development that guided parents through the baby boom following World War II, masturbation has shed the many taboos that surrounded it. More people have no trouble talking about it, and many more practice it without feelings of self-recrimination. The attitude of specialists in healthy sexual development point out that children use genital self-stimulation as a way of achieving pleasure, reassurance, and relief from anxiety. During adolescence, sexual pressures place masturbation in the role of relieving sexual tension and exploring one's body responses. In recent years, 70 percent to 80 percent of college women say that they masturbate regularly.

Dr. Helen Singer Kaplan, psychiatrist and sex therapist at New York Hospital–Cornell Medical Center has said that based on her clinical experience, those who masturbate during adolescence seem less likely to develop sex problems as adults. Other therapists point out that mutual masturbation plays an indispensable role in the repertory of love-making, and studies by Masters and Johnson found that although women preferred to have sex with a partner, the orgasms they achieved by masturbating were more intense.

There is little doubt that there is an increase in the number of women who masturbate regularly. This increase is accounted for by the growing number of divorced and widowed women, of young women living alone who find masturbation an acceptable form of safe sex in the age of AIDS, and of two-career marriages that require frequent and long separations.

However, women who are convinced that masturbation is wrong shouldn't be led to believe that they *must* practice it. In fact, many women aged 50 and over have a hard time transcending those childhood admonitions not only about the sinfulness of "self-abuse" but about the belief that masturbating would make them incapable of enjoying normal sex with their husband.

Maybe you don't want to re-examine attitudes. Perhaps what you have been taught seems right to you and you are comfortable sticking to the rules set down for you. No one is suggesting that anyone ought to change. But many do want to be free from old rules, including rules about touching and masturbation, especially because they may be very private and not involve anyone else. My approach is to apply to masturbation exactly the same standards for behavior one applies to other activities. Do you want to? Will it hurt someone? Will it interfere with your other obligations? Will it make you feel good? Will it cause guilt and anxiety?

Although this chapter is not designed to advocate any particular behavior but rather to give support to various options in human sexual expression, I cannot write about masturbation without defending the right of children to masturbate without guilt or physical punishment. I do not endorse the right of parents to punish children for masturbating: in my opinion it constitutes a form of child abuse.

SEXUAL FANTASIES

Sexual fantasy appears to be practically universal, and because 90 percent of sexuality is said to be in the mind, mental images play an indispensable role in arousal and enjoyment. Thus, an understanding of the nature of female sexuality is based on an understanding of female sexual fantasies. Recent reports affirm the propensity of females to have dramatic, exciting fantasies during sex, or while reading about sex, looking at sexy pictures, lounging on their couches, sunning at the beach, or whatever.

In my experience interviewing women and men, I find a definite difference in the incidence of male and female fantasy. Males fantasize more regularly than females. But among females the imagination and extent of the fantasies are comparable to those of males, except that the content is likely to be more romantic and more passive.

There is a tendency for some females to be anxious about the "wildness" of their fantasies or to feel guilty if they fantasize about someone else while making love to their partners. Feelings of guilt are most likely to occur if the fantasies involve situations that in real life would be considered degrading. In fact, some fantasies in this category can be so distressing that they shut off sexual feelings altogether.

Most professionals are supportive of fantasies. Let go! Enjoy whatever fantasies come into your head. Unfulfilled dreams acted out in fantasy can relieve tension and anxiety. It is understandable that some people might be judgmental about fantasizing about other people while making love, especially if sharing the fantasy would be upsetting to the partner. However, no matter how much honesty there is about physical activities, it is a rare person who can share every dream with her mate—not impossible, but rare.

It is important for most women to have a private, unshared segment of life. For some it may function as a boost toward independence, helping to get away from the total belonging to another person. For others, whose independence is more secure, fantasies can be shared as an option, what they *want* to do, not what they *need* to do.

LESBIANISM AND BISEXUALITY

We don't know how prevalent lesbianism is. Kinsey estimated that homosexual experiences to the point of orgasm occur in from 10 to 12 percent of women. The *Hite Report* indicates a slightly lower incidence. Lesbians who do not advertise the erotic aspect of their relationships are rarely distinguished from good friends. While many lesbians stay "in the closet" because of jobs, family, and neighbors, more and more feel free to reveal their sexual preference, especially since the passage of antidiscriminatory legislation as a result of gay activist political clout. However, there are probably thousands of secret lesbians who never act out their sexual preference and many who repress knowledge of that preference. These women get married (because they are supposed to), have children (because they are supposed to), and never find the right circumstances to express their true inclinations.

There are also those women who are heterosexual but have a curiosity about making love to another woman. Some interest in loving women is really quite logical in our society where "sexy" is equated with a provocative female body. Although the image of the sexy woman is meant to appeal to men, women are exposed to the same message. In addition, most female bodies are softer, more graceful, generally more conducive to caressing than male bodies. Women are allowed to have tender, warm feelings for each other, and the idea of making love could be construed as a reasonable extension of that. I am convinced that it is common for women to fantasize about having sex with a dearly loved female friend, but most may never make these feelings known because they do not want to risk offending or hurting the people they love.

In studying human sexuality, Kinsey did not categorize individuals as either homosexual or heterosexual. Rather, he tried to determine the proportion of each preference within the individual. He devised a scale to measure the proportion in a person's actual behavior and a person's inclinations. The scale ranges from 0 to 6 with 0 meaning 100 percent heterosexual and 6 meaning 100 percent homosexual. Thus, a woman with a strong homosexual preference who leads a completely heterosexual life would be rated 0 on the behavior scale and perhaps 5 on the inclination scale, assuming she did indeed have some inclination toward heterosexuality. A person who has an equal number of experiences with women and men and who has no preference between the genders would be a 3 on both scales. Double 3s are rare. Most people have a preference for one gender or another, although they may be active with both genders. The word bisexual loosely applies to all who even have fantasies about sex with both genders, even though their behavior is limited to one gender such as the secret lesbian rated 0-5. In a more restricted sense, the word bisexual would apply only to persons who, in adult life, have experienced sexual relations with both genders.

It seems to me illogical to consider a bisexual woman less mature in her sexual attitudes than an exclusive heterosexual. If she can make love the way heterosexuals do and also make love to another woman, in what way is she less good, less sexual, less of a person, and, most of all, less lovable?

Because little research has focused on female homosexuality, many myths about lesbians and bisexual women remain current. We can contribute to debunking a few of them.

In any lesbian couple, there is always a butch and a fem. Most lesbian couples do not consist of a masculine type (butch) and a feminine type (fem). They are commonly women without such specific characteristics who happen to be attracted to each other and enjoy satisfying each other sexually. Of course, as in any couple, there will be differences in assertiveness but generally couples do not follow the traditional male-female model of primary breadwinner and primary homemaker.

Women are lesbians because they can't get a man. Many men regard lesbians as making the best of second-best and express the belief that they would not be lesbians if they were able to find a man to love them. This is simply not true. Lesbians *prefer* women and would choose a woman rather than an equally attractive, compatible man. They have no trouble describing how much more effectively women make love.

Lesbians always use penis substitutes. Although some lesbians have experimented with dildos, few use these penis substitutes as a regular part of love making. Rather, they enjoy caressing each other, including oral stimulation.

All lesbians are unfit mothers. Few heterosexual mothers could pass the psychological tests given to lesbian mothers seeking custody of their children. Many of these mothers have been judged by professionals to be psychologically healthy and their homes described as loving, supportive environments for children, only to have the legal system deny them custody. This same legal system is far more hesitant to demand that children be separated from heterosexual women, even though they may be far less competent and less loving. With limited foster homes and other alternatives available, a heterosexual drug addict, alcoholic, or known childbeater has less chance of having her children taken away from her than a responsible out-of-the-closet lesbian. Only within the last decade are the courts finally beginning to consider the welfare of the child. Too often the "unfitness" of the lesbian mother exists only in the bias of the judge, without regard to the actual nurturing the child is receiving.

Lesbians and bisexual women are basically different. Lesbians and bisexual women have no special qualities that set them apart from other women except their choice of sex partners. Some are smart, some are dull; some extroverts, some introverts; some leaders, some followers; some creative, some not. Many women feel that heterosexual relationships are never equal, that an imbalance of power always exists, and that only through sex with another woman can they enjoy a truly equal partnership. For some, bisexuality seems to provide the best of both worlds.

SEX AND EDUCATION FOR PARENTHOOD BY CHOICE

Why don't we stress to children how important it is not to have a baby unless and until they are prepared for parenthood—intellectually, emotionally, socially, and financially? Although we cannot set up standards for adults without dangerous encroachment on individual freedom, we can generalize that girls under 18 years of age are not qualified to be independent mothers. Mothers 17 and under could be required to be supervised and to attend classes in nutrition, child care, etc. Details of such a program are beyond the scope of this chapter, but I believe that there is a real need to get out of our current paradox. Namely, girls who are denied birth control because they are too young for sex may become mothers with no education in either responsible sex or responsible parenthood.

Despite the fact that some teenagers get pregnant intentionally, grade school teachers would have no trouble convincing most pupils that the burdens of parenthood are great and that it is most important to avoid accidental pregnancy at a young age. Sounds so reasonable, so why not? I have concluded that the major reason is that teaching parenthood by choice validates recreational sex. Apparently this is so abhorrent to our mores that it is better to put up with ignorance and millions of accidental pregnancies among teenagers. All teenagers are sexually active: some in fantasy only, some in masturbation only, some in necking and petting, some in coitus, some in homosexual sex. Our need to ignore this reality and to continue to outlaw practical courses in responsible sexual behavior is basic to our problem of children having children.

And it's not just children. Many adults do not have adequate birth control information or services. True, many doctors provide contraception and Planned Parenthood has centers in all major cities, but birth control is still a taboo subject in television, radio, and newspaper ads. It is no small irony that it took the dangers of exposure to AIDS to put condoms on the media map, although it is still unacceptable to advertise them as a contraceptive device.

The desire to bolster the social directive that people ought to "get married and have children" in that order links parenthood more closely to marriage than to sex and makes us unwilling to deal with the problem of the thousands who do not follow that directive. We seem to ignore the fact that marriage does not cause parenthood, sex does!

One last point. The religious proscriptions against birth control are not really against birth control: they are against sex, especially sex for women. Babies that are denied birth because of abstinence are not lamented. It is all right not to have babies, as long as you do not have sex. We need to endorse nonprocreational sex in order to teach responsible sexual behavior. As long as we deny the right of women to be sexual except when they want to become pregnant, we are doomed to random reproduction, irresponsible parenthood, and all the social tragedies that follow. It is clear that our attitudes toward sexuality reach far beyond our personal lives into the realms of education, politics, and sociology.

One of the nation's most comprehensive resources for information and referrals relating to all aspects of human sexuality is SIECUS, the Sex Information and Education Council of the United States. This private, nonprofit organization was established in 1964 to promote healthy sexuality as an integral part of human life (see Directory of Health Information).

CONTRACEPTION AND ABORTION

Elizabeth B. Connell, M.D.
Professor, Department of Gynecology and Obstetrics, Emory University School of Medicine, Atlanta, Georgia

Throughout most of history, the continued existence of society—families, communities, nations—depended on producing enough children to survive against the great odds of infant mortality, famine and drought, pestilence, and war. But even in this struggle for survival, men and women had reasons for wanting to control fertility and devised methods by which to do so.

As human survival became less threatened, people were able to turn their attention to private reasons for family planning. Whereas in agrarian economies benefits were derived from the large family, modern cost factors encouraged fewer children as the Industrial Revolution advanced.

Added to these changing social and economic factors was the emergence at the beginning of this century of the women's movement—spearheading attempts to establish female roles beyond the limits of the home. Increased education, opportunities for employment, and development of role models outside the family tradition resulted from and further stimulated the movement. It was given additional impetus by the need for women in the work force during World War I. Soon it became clear that in order to pursue these expanded goals, women had to be able to control their fertility—to reduce the number of children they had and to be able to plan when they would have them.

Most recently, survival has again begun to influence ideas of family planning. Today the threat is *not* underpopulation but rather increased awareness of the many dangers associated with overpopulation. Because of environmental pollution and depletion of natural resources, we now recognize that our planet can suffer irreversible damage and that we may not find ways to replace the resources we are consuming at an ever-increasing rate. For these and many other reasons, people are concerned about the need to limit excessive reproduction of ourselves.

In recent years, many studies have been carried out in an attempt to understand the various steps involved in human reproduction in order to control unwanted pregnancy. As a result, old methods have been made safer and more effective and new ones have been developed.

RISK-BENEFIT RATIO

The question is often asked, "What is the best method of family planning?" At the present time there is no single "best" method, and there will be none until the "ideal contraceptive" is discovered, which will probably never happen. The attributes of the ideal contraceptive are that it be totally safe, effective, and reversible; that it be inexpensive, easy to distribute, and easy to use; and that its use be unrelated to the actual time of sexual relations.

With the development of oral contraceptives (OCs) and subsequently of IUDs, it was believed in each case that an ideal contraceptive method had been found. Unfortunately, with time and continued study, it has been discovered that neither of them is entirely safe or entirely effective. Therefore, we must continue to deal with what is known as the risk-benefit ratio.

We have learned that any medication that is powerful enough to have a desired effect on the human body will, almost of necessity, carry with its use a certain amount of risk. Today's medications, taken according to instructions, are generally safe and effective. The risk-benefit ratio of most drugs in proper dosages is heavily weighted on the side of the benefits. The level of risk that is acceptable varies with the intended use of a particular drug. For example, when we assess drugs to be given for

CONTRACEPTION AND ABORTION 161

the treatment of advanced cancer, we are willing to accept a relatively high degree of risk. However, when dealing with contraceptive methods to be used by essentially normal, healthy women, possibly for prolonged periods of time, to prevent a pregnancy, we insist that the risks be very low.

COMMON CONTRACEPTIVE METHODS

Vasectomy

Oral contraception

IUD

Tubal ligation

Condom

Spermicidal jelly/cream/foam/sponge/film

Diaphragm/Cervical cap

SELECTION OF METHODS

A woman should carefully consider several factors when deciding which birth control method she should use, after discussing all the options with her health care provider. First of all, medical factors must be considered. It has been shown that the risk of death for any woman in good health up to the age of 35 is lower using any of the currently available methods than becoming pregnant and carrying a child to term. After the age of 35, any method is much safer than becoming pregnant and having a baby, except for women who take oral contraceptives and smoke. In the current climate of great anxiety about the side effects of pills and IUDs, these two facts are often ignored. These comparisons are valid in developed countries where the health care is excellent; they are infinitely more important in developing countries. In areas of the world where health care is minimal or absent, the risks associated with pregnancy and childbirth far outweigh any possible danger associated with contraceptive use. When a woman is not in perfect health, it is necessary to look at the specific contraindications to the use of any particular form of family planning. These will be considered under the various methods.

In addition to purely physical factors, emotional, behavioral, and psychological factors must also be taken into consideration when selecting a contraceptive technique. Even though you may be perfectly capable of using a particular method from a purely medical point of view, if you have a distaste for that method or harbor undue concern or anxiety about its use, then it is not the method for you. If you know that you cannot remember to take pills properly or use a barrier method each time you have intercourse, you must take this into account.

Certain social and economic factors also come into play, including the cost of the contraceptive method, the availability of health care for the initiation of the technique and for the follow-up required, and numerous religious and cultural attitudes.

It must also be recognized that the method that is "best" for a woman may change a number of times during her lifetime. For example, a teenager who only has sexual relations infrequently should not take oral contraceptives but should use a male or female barrier method. However, when she begins to have intercourse frequently, she may well turn to the use of oral contraceptives. Barring any difficulties and if she does not smoke, she may continue with this method up to the time of her menopause. Once she has had a child, she may select an intrauterine device but only if she is in a mutually monogamous situation. As she approaches her perimenopausal years, she has several options. She may have an intrauterine device inserted, go back to a barrier method, or if she and her partner are convinced that they do not want any more children, consider sterilization of either one as a possible alternative.

HORMONAL METHODS—FEMALE: "THE PILL"

Women through the centuries have swallowed all sorts of concoctions made of plant and animal materials in their attempts to prevent or terminate unwanted pregnancies. During the Middle Ages many mercury, strychnine, and lead poisonings occurred, thousands of women dying when they used these agents to try to control their fertility. With the discovery of oral contraceptives, women for the first time had a technique that, if taken as directed, was virtually 100 percent effective.

The combined oral contraceptives (estrogen plus progestin) have been in use for more than a quarter of a century and the mini-pill (progestin alone) for more than ten years. These agents have been more widely studied than any medication in the history of humanity. At the present time it is estimated that 54 million women are using the pill, more than 10 million of them living in the United States. In addition, there are another 50 million women who have used an oral contraceptive at some time in the past.

The OCs of today are radically different from those developed 25–30 years ago. Although the specific hormones are essentially the same or similar, the dosages and formulations have undergone tremendous changes. There are two major types of OCs available in the United States today. One is the combined pill made in two different forms: estrogen and progestin in the same dose throughout the treatment cycle and the newer type, the multiphasic pill, with varying doses in different parts of the cycle to reduce the total hormone dose to the lowest possible levels consistent with effectiveness. The mini-pill contains only the progestin and is taken daily.

The combined estrogen and progestin pills prevent pregnancy by stopping ovulation, the monthly release of an egg by an ovary. Their use as a contraceptive method is based on the fact that during pregnancy these hormones, made by the ovaries and placenta, block the production of the hormones that are responsible for ovulation, thus preventing the establishment of an additional pregnancy. In the case of the minipill, the mechanism is somewhat more complicated. Studies have shown that not all women who use these pills stop ovulating. The mechanism (or mechanisms) of action in this instance appears to be the effects of the hormone on the cervical mucus, the lining of the uterus, the fallopian tubes, and other anatomical changes. While similar effects occur with the combined pills, their effectiveness is achieved mainly by the blocking of ovulation.

MAJOR SEVERE SIDE EFFECTS

Not long after widespread use of the pill began, it became clear that certain complications were occurring in a small number of women. Considerable unhappiness has been voiced over the years about the fact that these side effects were not recognized earlier. However, it must be remembered that when complications resulting from the use of a drug are so rare that they affect only say, one in every 250,000 to 500,000 users, as in the case of the pill, thousands of women must be carefully followed for a number of years in order to detect those complications.

In addition, because of the complexity of our daily lives, it is very difficult to be able to relate a particular adverse reaction to a particular medication. Given the number of drugs in common use, the various food additives, the multiple pollutants in our environment, not to mention the innumerable variables of individual responses, it takes wide usage of a particular drug over a considerable period of time to be able to make an accurate assessment of possible adverse side effects.

Cardiovascular

The first side effects noted (and the ones that are still the most serious) are related to the cardiovascular system. The first risk that was described in both British and American studies was the development of thromboembolic disease—the formation of blood clots, usually in the legs, some of which could break off and travel to the lungs or the brain producing serious damage and occasionally death. This complication was found to be related to the estrogen component and its frequency has progressively decreased as the dosage of estrogen in the pill has been reduced from 100–150 micrograms to 30–35 or less.

The next cardiovascular risk to be identified was stroke. Once again, the chances of having a stroke have decreased as the dosage of the estrogen and, more importantly, the progestin have been reduced.

The complication of heart attack is rare before the age of 35; prior to that age there is virtually no difference in the rate of heart attack between users and nonusers of the pill. It is essential to note that the risk of heart attack associated with the use of oral contraceptives is almost entirely limited to those women over 35 who smoke, particularly those who smoke heavily, and especially in those who have additional risk factors such as high blood pressure; diabetes; obesity, elevated blood cholesterol, or low density lipoproteins (LDL).

Women who have major surgery, particularly pelvic or abdominal surgery, also have been found to have a four- to sixfold increase in thromboembolic complications. Pills should be stopped at least four weeks prior to major elective surgery and another contraceptive prescribed. The alternative contraceptive should be continued after surgery until the woman is fully ambulatory. The same rules hold true for women who are immobilized, for example because of serious fractures, for a long period of time.

Metabolic

A number of metabolic changes have been observed in women taking oral contraceptives, related primarily to sugar and fat metabolism. These changes are primarily due to the progestin component. They lead to the elevation of blood sugar as seen in diabetics and to a pattern in blood lipids similar to those found in people with cardiovascular diseases. With the new low-dose pills, however, these alterations are either minimal or entirely absent. What this means from a clinical point of view, however, has yet to be determined.

A very few women have a profound elevation in their blood pressure when they first start taking oral contraceptives. This hypertension disappears promptly when the pill is stopped. A certain number of other women develop a mild increase of blood pressure as they continue to take oral contraceptives. However, their blood pressures usually remain within normal limits and usually return to pretreatment levels after stopping the pill.

It has been shown that certain of the liver function tests change during pill use, reverting quickly to normal after discontinuing its use. There is also a rare benign liver tumor that is apparently associated with the use of oral contraceptives. It regresses after the pill is stopped, but, because these tumors are vascular, bleeding occasionally occurs, necessitating emergency abdominal surgery.

Fetal

There have been many studies to determine whether oral contraceptives taken early in pregnancy have any adverse effect on an unborn baby. Early in the study of oral contraceptives, when higher dose pills were being used, it was noted that an occasional female baby showed signs of masculinization, but this is no longer observed with today's pills. The discovery of the serious effects on a small percentage of daughters of mothers who took large doses of the estrogen diethylstilbestrol (DES) during pregnancy (discussed below) raised many questions and considerable anxiety about possible, unknown fetal effects of regular doses of any form of estrogen.

Oral contraceptives have also been used as tests for pregnancy, but this is no longer an acceptable medical practice. First, they are not particularly reliable tests and, secondly, there has been, for many years, concern about possible fetal damage. Thus, women have been told not to use oral contraceptives when there is any question that they might be pregnant. It is important to note, however, that current studies do not show any relationship between fetal damage and use of OCs.

Malignancy

One of the major reasons given by women today for either not starting or for stopping the pill is the fear of cancer. Thousands of unplanned and unwanted pregnancies have occurred because of this fear, when women panicked and stopped using the pill but did not substitute any other method. Whereas a cause-and-effect relationship between smoking, cardiovascular complications and oral contraceptives has been established, there are still no data conclusively documenting that any such relationship exists between oral contraceptives and cancer of any part of the female reproductive tract or elsewhere.

Actually, it is now clear that quite the opposite is true. British and American studies have both shown that there is a lower incidence of benign and malignant ovarian tumors in women taking the pill. Moreover the combined pill exerts a protective effect against endometrial cancer. Even more important, some prolonged protection against both ovarian and endometrial cancers has been documented. This occurs once a woman has taken the pill for at least one year and lasts for over fifteen years. While one study suggested an association between pill use and melanoma of the skin, subsequent studies have failed to show such a relationship. The cause was probably unprotected over-exposure to sunlight.

Despite tremendous amounts of adverse publicity resulting in great anxiety, there is no proof today that oral contraceptives cause cancer. However, because we know that it takes a considerable period of time for cancer to develop, careful observation of women taking oral contraceptives is being continued, particularly regarding the possibility of cancer of the cervix.

Concern also continues to be expressed about the possibility of the pill producing breast cancer. Once again, all of the larger, well controlled studies to date have failed to show any association even in women considered to be at high risk because of factors such as a family history of this disease. Moreover, there is a significant reduction in the number of women who develop two very common benign tumors—fibroadenomas and fibrocystic disease. However, several smaller recent studies appear to suggest a possible association. Multiple reviews of these data have found that the risk, if present, is limited to specific sub groups, that the studies have a number of methodologic flaws, and that the results do not correlate with current epidemiologic data.

Drug Interactions

Studies have shown that interactions may occur between certain drugs. In the case of the pill several drugs can reduce the pill's contraceptive effectiveness and also may result in bleeding between periods. The most important of these agents include barbiturates (phenobarbital), phenytoin (Dilantin), and certain antibiotics, especially isoniazid, rifampin, and possibly tetracycline. Women who have to take these products on a long term basis should be given a 50 mcg. oral contraceptive.

CONTRAINDICATIONS

At the present time the U.S. Food and Drug Administration (FDA) lists a number of absolute contraindications to the use of the pill. The list is based on proven major adverse side effects, as in the case of the cardiovascular disorders, and on conditions for which a relationship is suspected but not necessarily proven.

1. Known cardiovascular conditions or a past history of these conditions, including thrombophlebitis and thromboembolic disorders (formation of blood clots and embolisms), cerebrovascular disease (stroke), myocardial infarction (type of heart attack), or coronary artery disease.
2. Markedly impaired liver function.
3. Known or suspected carcinoma of the breast.
4. Known or suspected estrogen-dependent neoplasia (abnormal tissue growth).
5. Undiagnosed abnormal genital bleeding.
6. Known or suspected pregnancy.

As we have mentioned, more and more evidence is being accumulated showing that the combination of increasing age and heavy smoking raises the risks of heart attack and stroke considerably higher than either age or smoking alone. In fact, current data indicate that the two factors have a synergistic effect—one in the presence of the other increases the risk that each could produce separately, that their combined effect is greater than the sum of their effects simply added together.

Therefore, women over 35 and particularly those with additional risk factors, should not take the pill if they smoke or not smoke if they take the pill. Obviously, as a general health measure, women should be encouraged not to smoke whether they take the pill or not. Indeed it has been suggested, not entirely facetiously, that, given the differences in relative risks, pills should be put in vending machines and cigarettes placed on prescription!

There is increasing concern about the use of Accutane for severe acne, because it is clearly associated with fetal damage. Women using this drug should not become pregnant and should always be protected by a highly effective method of contraception such as the pill.

MINOR ADVERSE SIDE EFFECTS

There are a number of side effects, most of which disappear by the end of the third cycle, that are annoying but not serious or life-threatening. Among the most frequent of these are alterations in the menstrual flow, most often a decrease (a change considered to be desirable by many women). There may also be irregular spotting and bleeding between periods, heavier bleeding at the time of the menses, and, on occasion, a total absence of menses. Breast tenderness may be observed, and there is often an increase in the amount of vaginal discharge. Nausea with occasional vomiting occurs but is usually seen early. Weight gain is noted by some women, but this is much more apt to be related to changes in food intake than to the pill. Pigmentation over the forehead and cheeks, the same type seen in pregnancy, may also occur with use of oral contraceptives.

BENEFICIAL SIDE EFFECTS

Too often only the adverse side effects of the pill are presented by all forms of media. The beneficial side effects of the pill are only rarely discussed in the same context, which is most unfortunate.

A number of salutary changes have been noted, such as decreases in breast, ovarian, and uterine tumors. In addition, certain very common benign breast tumors, fibroadenomas, and fibrocystic disease, are less common in women who use OCs. Women whose cycles are extremely irregular or who have heavy menstrual bleeding resulting in anemia may be virtually assured that these problems will be solved by the use of oral contraceptives. Premenstrual syndrome (PMS) and menstrual discomfort are also often relieved, and acne frequently diminishes markedly. Of major importance is the fact that women who take the pill have fewer ectopic pregnancies and ovarian retention cysts as well as less risk of developing rheumatoid arthritis and pelvic inflammatory disease (PID), toxic shock syndrome, uterine fibroids, osteoporosis, and endometriosis.

INJECTABLES

For a number of years researchers have sought a long-acting hormonal preparation that could be given by injection to block ovulation. Such a method would have its greatest application in certain areas of the world where medication is not felt to be significant or helpful unless it is given by injection, but it would also benefit any women who, because of medical, social, or psychological reasons, cannot cope with the demands of pill-taking or the use of barrier methods. Moreover, when health care personnel and facilities are limited, a technique that requires a single act of motivation on the part of the patient and infrequent professional follow-up is obviously highly desirable. At present there is no injectable contraceptive approved in the United States, despite the fact that an excellent product, Depo Provera, has been used safely and effectively by millions of women all over the world for many years.

IMPLANTS

Under development and in use in many foreign countries is an implantation procedure in which small capsules containing an ovulation-inhibiting hormone (progestin) are inserted just beneath the skin of the arm. One of the best-studied of these is known as Norplant; the implants steadily release progestin for up to five years. This contraceptive method is basically as effective as sterilization, with the additional advantage of reversibility because the implants can be removed at any time. Many clinical studies have been carried out on this implant, resulting in the accumulation of large amounts of data. These have been presented to the FDA, and, hopefully, approval will soon be obtained.

"MORNING AFTER" PILL

Considerable research has been directed toward finding a substance, a so-called "morning after" pill, that will prevent pregnancy after unprotected sexual relations at the time of ovulation. It was shown many years ago in monkeys and then in the human female that the use of sufficient doses of any estrogen at this time will prevent implantation. The synthetic estrogen DES (diethylstilbestrol) was previously implicated in genital abnormalities of the female offspring of women who took it to prevent impending miscarriage, so this use of the drug was discontinued. When estrogen or a combination OC is taken, it probably causes the lining of the uterus to reject the implantation of the fertilized egg. Again, these regimens are widely used, but still not approved by the FDA.

HORMONAL METHODS—MALE

Pressure to develop male contraceptive methods has increased in recent years, particularly by activist women's groups. But even an ideal male contraceptive would in no way replace female contraception. Although many women feel that men should share in the responsibility for preventing unwanted pregnancy, not all of them would be willing to surrender their own fertility control to their sexual partner, even in a monogamous situation. It is even more unlikely that women with multiple sex partners would want to depend entirely on the males to use contraceptives to protect them against pregnancy.

Male methods have been studied for many years. It has been found much more difficult to block completely male fertility than female. There is a growing body of evidence, based on some recent studies, that a man may produce a pregnancy even though his sperm count is very low by current standards.

A number of hormonal preparations have been tested as male contraceptives. Some of the earlier studies were done with estrogens. While these agents effectively depressed the development of sperm in the male, they were quickly abandoned when it was found that they also produced a number of side effects such as breast enlargement, impotence, and the lack of desire for sex.

In 1987, a worldwide study involving 400 men was begun, using injections of testosterone, the male hormone, as a form of birth control. Reports indicate that these injections reduce the sperm count to practically zero without affecting the male's sex drive. According to the World Health Organization (WHO), 75 percent of men everywhere would be interested in this method of contraception if it proves to be safe and effective. However, WHO has predicted that a male contraceptive is at least 20 years away.

INTRAUTERINE DEVICES

The second major form of female contraception, introduced more recently than the pill, is the intrauterine device (IUD). We know from history that the first intrauterine devices were pebbles placed in the uterus of a camel to keep her from getting pregnant on long trips across the desert. Metal devices have also been used by women in the past. However, because of concerns about infection, their use flourished briefly and then was abandoned.

In the 1970s and 80s, IUDs once again regained their popularity, being used by 2–3 million American women. Unfortunately, because of growing problems related to litigation and product liability insurance all but one IUD (Progestasert) were taken off the market. This occurred despite the fact that the devices removed from the market—the Saf-T-Coil, Lippes Loop, Cu-7, and Tatum-T—were still approved by the FDA as safe and effective. Fortunately for women for whom IUDs are the method of choice, the best of the copper-bearing IUDs, the Cu 380A (ParaGard), was introduced in mid-1988. When IUDs are compared with oral contraceptives, the older data suggested that IUDs cause fewer deaths but more illness, especially cases of pelvic inflammatory disease (PID). However, it is now recognized that there is no increased risk with copper devices for mutually monogamous women. In addition, the failure rates are less than 1%—comparable to OCs.

For a while it was felt that intrauterine devices prevented pregnancy either by speeding the egg through the tube so quickly that it could not be fertilized or by producing a mild and otherwise insignificant uterine infection that prevented implantation. Continued study has shown that neither of these mechanisms is the one that prevents pregnancy. Recently conducted studies have shown that IUDs exert their primary effects prior to fertilization. They interfere with the transportation of both sperm and egg with the end result that fertilization usually does not occur. This newer information should help to put to rest the idea that IUDs interfere with implantation, perceived by some as being abortions.

An intrauterine device is inserted through the cervix into the uterus by a trained specialist with the use of special instruments. All IUDs inserted today have one or two plastic strings that protrudes through the cervical os. These strings are used for identification and removal of the device. Following insertion, it is quite common to have cramping and spotting, but this usually disappears after a few hours or days. IUDs may be inserted at any time, but it is easier to do so around the time of ovulation because the cervix is dilated slightly if there is no chance of the woman's being pregnant. It has been shown that IUDs may be inserted immediately following early abortion without increasing the risk of side effects. Studies with existing devices have shown a high rate of expulsion when inserted immediately after delivery and there may be an increased risk of perforation of the uterus at that time. Therefore, it is usually advised that the insertion be postponed six to eight weeks after delivery. Newer devices, which look quite promising, are being studied for this particular use.

There are only two IUDs currently available in the US. The first of these is the Progestasert—a hormone-bearing device. While it is effective, it has the disadvantage of having to be changed each year. The new copper-bearing IUD (ParaGard) is effective for at least four years.

A woman who wants an IUD needs to be evaluated carefully. She needs to have a thorough medical evaluation including a pelvic examination, Pap smear, and any other indicated studies. Most important is an investigation of her personal history especially the number of sexual partners and sexually transmitted diseases. When her history and the results of the tests indicate that she is a suitable candidate for IUD use, an insertion may be carried out. The cervix is cleansed, and a tube containing the collapsed IUD is inserted through the cervix. When the tube is removed, the IUD unfolds in place. The strings that extend through the cervical opening should be used to check after each menstrual period that the IUD remains in its proper position. If the string is longer or shorter than usual or if it can no longer be felt, the doctor should be consulted promptly to find out whether the IUD has shifted to an improper place or if it has been expelled.

It is currently believed that the IUD is not the method of choice for women who have not yet had a child. Moreover, there is a clear risk of PID if either person has multiple sexual partners.

ADVERSE SIDE EFFECTS

Women who are considering an IUD should recognize that use of an IUD carries with it the risk of certain adverse effects.

Initial discomfort

For the first few days after insertion, women often experience cramps and bleeding. During the first few periods that follow, there may be heavier bleeding than usual, and the periods may last longer.

Expulsion

Any IUD may be expelled, most often during the first menses or the first three months of use. Although in most cases the expulsion is noted, some women are unaware that this has happened. Some physicians, therefore, recommend that a barrier method also be used during the first month or two.

Perforation of the uterus

One of the most compelling reasons for a medical checkup when the strings cannot be felt is the possibility that the IUD has perforated the uterus and has traveled into the abdomen. Although most perforations occur at the time of insertion, on occasion they may be noted later. Prompt location with special instruments, and if necessary, with ultrasound, enables the doctor to remove it and take any additional measures that are necessary.

Pelvic inflammatory disease

It is now well documented that the incidence of PID is highest among women who have multiple sex partners or whose partner(s) have multiple sexual partners, and in those who have had this disease before. The symptoms of PID can range from very mild to very severe. It can cause temporary or permanent infertility when there is extensive damage to the fallopian tubes. In some cases, it can be sufficiently life-threatening to require prompt hospitalization and, on occasion, extensive pelvic surgery that will leave the women permanently sterile. Any IUD wearer who experiences a heavy foul-smelling vaginal discharge, irregular bleeding, or pain in the lower abdomen, with or without fever, should see her doctor without delay.

Intrauterine pregnancy

If a pregnancy develops in the uterus even though the IUD is in place, there is a 50 percent chance that a miscarriage will occur. The possibility of a miscarriage is reduced by half if the IUD is removed as soon as the diagnosis of pregnancy is made. If this is not done, there is an increased risk of infection, stillbirth, and premature delivery. However, it is important to note that there is no risk of direct damage to the fetus if a pregnancy goes to term with the IUD still in place.

Ectopic pregnancy

Whereas it used to be believed that IUDs increased the risk of ectopic pregnancy, this is no longer felt to be the case. In fact, during the first three years of use, the risk is even lower than normal but then returns to the rate found in the general population.

Effects on fertility

In most instances a contraceptive method other than an IUD should be the choice of a woman who has not yet had a child but who is planning to become pregnant at some time in the future. However, there are occasional situations where the IUD is still the method of choice for such women when they are in a mutually monogamous relationship and have contraindications to other birth control methods.

Malignancy

Considerable concern has been expressed about whether or not the continued presence of an IUD can stimulate malignancy. Careful prolonged study of thousands of women wearing IUDs, some of them for many years, has failed to show a connection between the presence of this device and the subsequent development of a malignancy of the cervix or the uterus.

CONTRAINDICATIONS

At the present time the FDA lists the following contraindications to the use of the IUD.

1. Known or suspected pregnancy.
2. Acute, chronic, or recurring pelvic inflammatory disease.
3. Acute cervicitis.
4. Postpartum endometritis and infected abortion.
5. Abnormal genital bleeding.
6. Gynecologic malignancy.
7. Anomalies of the uterus that grossly distort the uterine cavity.
8. Submucosal or intramural leiomyomata (tumors beneath or within the wall of the uterus) that grossly distort the uterine cavity.
9. Known or suspected allergy to copper (for copper IUDs only).

BARRIER CONTRACEPTIVES

Barrier contraceptives, such as the condom and the diaphragm combined with spermicides, were discarded in favor of the pill and IUD because they were easier to use and didn't require application with each act of intercourse. The older methods were considered messy, unromantic, a nuisance, and the cause of diminished pleasure compared to the ease and unobtrusiveness with which the pill and IUD could provide close to 100 percent assurance against unwanted pregnancy. More recently, however, several factors have caused a reversal in attitudes.

The earliest return to the diaphragm and other barrier methods

CONTRACEPTION AND ABORTION 177

resulted from objections to the pill by many feminists and health advocates on the following grounds: that it introduced chemicals into the body whose long-term effects might not be known for decades, that the pill was an invasive factor contraindicated by a respect for the body's natural functioning and that it was an ongoing expensive procedure whose end result was the enrichment of the pharmaceutical companies. Particularly among educated women, ironically enough, the slogan was, "If the diaphragm was good enough for mother, it's good enough for me."

As for the condom, it has now emerged as a major form of protection against the transmission of AIDS as well as herpes, gonorrhea, and other sexually transmissible diseases. In addition, studies have shown that the various spermicides (foams, jellies, creams, suppositories, foaming tablets), diaphragms, cervical caps, and the contraceptive sponge and film, when used properly and consistently with each act of sexual intercourse, actually have a far higher rate of effectiveness than thought by the general public and, in fact, by many physicians. The key to this, of course, is absolute adherence to proper and consistent usage. Each barrier method has its own special instructions for use on the package, which must be followed carefully if these levels of effectiveness are to be attained.

A major compelling advantage of barrier methods is the fact that there are no health risks associated with them as such except for rare cases of allergic response or local irritation. The most vexing problem is the rate of unwanted pregnancies when these methods are used. A woman who relies on them through all the years of her childbearing capability may have an average of two or three unwanted pregnancies. However, from a statistical point of view, if they are terminated early by suction abortion, the health risks she faces are extremely low.

DIAPHRAGM

It has been shown recently that, despite widespread opinions to the contrary, the diaphragm can be used effectively by women who are young and inexperienced and who, for these and other reasons, would hardly be considered ideal candidates for the use of any sex related method. In one study, when such a group was properly instructed and constantly encouraged, they had a failure rate of less than 2 percent, which is in the general range of pills and intrauterine devices.

To fit properly, the size and type of diaphragm must be determined by the anatomy of the individual woman. If a diaphragm is too small, it may not stay in place and may slip off the cervix; if it is too large, it may press on the urethra and cause a urinary tract infection. It must always be used with a spermicidal agent and be left in place for six hours without douching. If intercourse occurs again during this time, more spermicide must be inserted. Because of the possibility of developing toxic shock syndrome, diaphragms should not be left in for more than six hours after the last act of intercourse and should not be used during menses.

CERVICAL CAP

The cervical cap was used in the U.S. but disappeared with the emergence of the pills and IUDs. It has been used by many women, especially by those in self-help groups, and was approved by the FDA in 1988. It is popular because it is smaller than a diaphragm and may be left in place for two days without having to add spermicide. The device, which is made of plastic, looks like a thimble. It fits over the cervix and is held in place by suction. When used correctly and combined with a spermicide, it has an effectiveness rate of approximately 94–95 percent. Not every woman who wants to use a cap can be fitted, and some women find their insertion and removal more difficult than the diaphragm.

VAGINAL SPONGE

A barrier method that is now available over the counter is a small disposable sponge made of polyurethane and permeated with a spermicide. The sponge need not be fitted by a physician, and one of its chief attractions is that it allows for more spontaneous sexual activity than the diaphragm. Its effectiveness is based on its action as a barrier, the inactivation of sperm by the spermicide, and the absorption by the sponge of the ejaculated semen. The sponge may be kept in place for 24 hours, during which time intercourse can take place repeatedly without any further preparation. It has approximately the same effectiveness as the diaphragm and the cervical cap.

CONDOM

While condoms have been used in one form or another since the time of the ancient Egyptians, it is only in recent years that they have been used not only for contraception, but also as protection against the transmission of sexually transmitted diseases (STDs) including the AIDS virus. In 1977 when the Supreme Court declared anti-condom laws unconstitutional, condoms came out of the druggists' hidden stock. They are now openly displayed and sold in vending machines nationwide.

According to a recent study by the National Center for Health Statistics, the condom remains the device most commonly used in the first sexual encounter. Nowadays, sales to women make up 40 percent or more of the total; condoms are advertised in women's magazines and displayed in drugstores next to feminine hygiene products. They are now being made in a variety of colors and are being manufactured out of materials that are thinner and therefore interfere less with sensation. Various textures are being used to increase the pleasurable sensations accompanying their use. Lubricants and spermicides are being applied to the condom for easier and more effective use.

It is important that the condom be put on before any contact is made with the vulva and that a half inch be left free at the end of the penis to catch the seminal fluid. The penis and condom should be removed together from the vagina shortly after ejaculation, holding on to the rim of the condom so that no spillage occurs. Furthermore, in the training of potential users, efforts are being made to involve the female in applying the condom to eliminate the serious objection many men have when they are forced to stop in the middle of foreplay to put on the condom. When putting on the condom is made part of foreplay, this sense of interruption is dispelled and the acceptability of the condom is proportionately increased.

Condom use should be recommended to women who are at risk for STD. This is true even for those who are using a highly effective contraceptive method such as the pill or IUD, inasmuch as they do not protect against all STD transmission, particularly the very dangerous and incurable viral diseases.

BARRIER METHODS IN COMBINATION

It is now being increasingly appreciated that the combination of a male and a female method such as, for example, condom plus spermicide, has a very high rate of effectiveness with a failure rate of approximately 1 percent. The lack of any serious side effects of the various barrier methods makes them extremely attractive for those individuals who have sexual relations very infrequently, who have contraindications to the pill and the IUD, and who are looking for maximum safety in the use of a form of contraception as well as for protection against AIDS and other STD.

NATURAL FAMILY PLANNING— PERIODIC ABSTINENCE

New attention is also being paid to methods of natural family planning—previously called rhythm and now often called ovulation detection and periodic abstinence—largely because these techniques are the only ones acceptable to the Roman Catholic church. They are all based on the premise that sexual intercourse must be avoided during that time span of each menstrual cycle when ovulation is occurring. Calculations of "safe" and "unsafe" days for intercourse can be made in different ways, all based on the fact that the unsafe days usually begin several days before ovulation and continue for three to five days thereafter. The time of ovulation may be determined in several different ways. 1. *The calendar method:* A precise record is compiled of the length of the menstrual cycle for one year. In typical cases, ovulation occurs 14 days before menstruation begins. Therefore, taking into account the four- to five-day life span of the sperm and the 24-hour life span of the egg, the unsafe days can be calculated. 2. *The temperature method:* Body temperature rises slightly following ovulation and stays elevated until the next onset of menstruation. A woman must take her temperature every morning before she gets out of bed. She must abstain from intercourse each month until three days after the temperature rise. 3. *The cervical mucus method:* In the course of the menstrual cycle, the consistency of the mucus varies greatly. At the time of ovulation it is clear, thin, copious, and watery. At all other times it is thick, gray, and sparse. 4. *The symptothermal method:* This is a combination of the temperature method plus the detection of a variety of a number of physical changes associated with ovulation.

All of these methods are especially unreliable if the menstrual cycles are short, and they suffer from the disadvantage of moderate to severe curtailment of the frequency of sexual relations. Furthermore, if a woman's cycles are grossly irregular, it is extremely difficult to predict the actual time of ovulation and, therefore, the number of days she must abstain from sexual intercourse is increased proportionately.

FEMALE STERILIZATION

Voluntary sterilization continues to be the most widely used method of birth control in the United States. Of the approximately 36.5 million women of childbearing age, 11.6 million depend on this method. The women who are themselves sterilized number 6.8 million, and an additional 4.9 million have spouses who have been sterilized. More than half of all women electing to use this method are over 35 years of age. They do not want to have any more children and do not wish to continue using the pill, an IUD, or a barrier contraceptive for the many remaining years of fertility during which they might have an unwanted pregnancy.

Sterilization of women has been made much easier in recent years by the development of new instruments and new techniques replacing the previously used laparotomy—the surgical opening of the abdomen—after which the fallopian tubes can be ligated in any number of ways, by tying, cutting, or clipping. It makes no difference how it is done provided that a segment of each tube is blocked. The tubes can also be occluded using the vaginal route (colpotomy), and, still experimentally, via the uterine route (hysteroscopy). Tissue adhesives can be introduced using the hysteroscope. Alternatively, silicone plugs may be placed into the tubal openings. The latter technique is theoretically reversible, but sufficient work has not yet been done to see if pregnancies will result after removal.

With the development of the laparoscope and other more sophisticated forms of equipment, the entire scene changed radically. Procedures may now be done at any time during a woman's reproductive life. Moreover, a steadily larger percentage of these procedures are now being carried out in hospital and free-standing outpatient clinics and often under local rather than general anesthesia. Many patients come in, have their procedures done, and go home the same day or, at most, stay one night in the hospital.

Most recently, the mini-lap procedure has been developed. This method is even simpler than the laparoscopic techniques. A small incision is made near the top of the pubic hair, the tubes are grasped under direct vision and ligated. The entire procedure takes only a few minutes and, after a few hours' rest, the patient is able to go home.

While some of the new techniques are much easier, faster, and less expensive than the older ones, no method has been developed to date that is completely effective and totally safe. The failure rate in most female sterilization procedures is extremely low, being less than 1 percent. Some of the failures involve ectopic pregnancies. However, because the tubes are intra-abdominal organs, even the simplest procedure involves opening the abdomen. This inevitably carries with it some degree of risk, though very small, of complications such as hemorrhage and infection. The chance of repairing the tubes for future pregnancies depends largely on the amount of the tube destroyed at the time of surgery.

MALE STERILIZATION

Male sterilization, or vasectomy, is now performed as often as female sterilization. It has always been and remains an extremely simple technique because the vas are in the scrotum. It is simple to identify the vas under local anesthesia and to perform either cauterization or removal of a piece of both of the vas. There are virtually no serious complications. The infrequent minor complications are related to immediate or delayed hemorrhage and occasionally the development of a postoperative wound infection. The procedure is almost 100 percent effective. However, contraception must be used for a period of time following vasectomy until the man's sperm count has dropped to zero, and the count should be checked from time to time. While the vas may be surgically repaired, this does not always result in the resumption of fertility.

LAPAROSCOPIC TUBAL STERILIZATION

Laparoscope through incision below umbilicus

Forceps grasping fallopian tube through second incision

Bladder

Vagina

Ring around tube

Uterus

VASECTOMY

Vas deferens exposed through small ¾" incision

Testicle

Small ½" segment is removed and ends tied

One stitch

INDUCED ABORTION

Abortion has been and continues to be one of the major forms of family planning throughout the world. This is true whether abortion is legal or illegal in any given country. It is estimated that 1.6 million abortions are currently performed each year in the United States. Of these, 99 percent are carried out within 20 weeks of conception, most of them in the early weeks of pregnancy.

The earlier an abortion is done, the safer it is and the simpler the procedure. If an unwanted pregnancy is suspected, pregnancy tests should be done as soon as possible. If a woman is pregnant, she should decide quickly whether she is going to terminate the pregnancy. Complication rates of even the simplest and safest procedures, which can be done vaginally, increase with each week, and the abdominal procedures necessary at later stages carry much greater risk and are psychologically and medically more traumatic.

The various suction techniques used for early abortion are extremely easy and safe. New instruments have been developed that can be inserted under local or no anesthesia, produce a minimum of trauma to the cervix, and are highly effective.

When suction abortion is no longer practical because of the advanced state of pregnancy, one must turn to the use of the more traditional D&C procedures. And, once pregnancy has advanced well into the second trimester, an entirely different approach must be used. The uterus may be emptied by the induction of labor, using one or more chemical agents such as prostaglandins, saline, or glucose, or the products of conception can be removed by surgical procedure, a hysterotomy or hysterectomy. In addition, the prior insertion of laminaria into the cervix may speed up the induction of labor.

MENSTRUAL EXTRACTION

Menstrual extraction is a term usually applied to abortions done within six weeks of the last menstrual period. It is also commonly referred to as menstrual regulation, endometrial aspiration, endometrial extraction, preemptive abortion, and a variety of other terms. The original menstrual regulation was carried out simply to cut down on the length of time a menstrual period took. It removed all of the tissue at one time rather than have it flow out over a period of several days. The same name and the same technique were subsequently applied to the termination of early pregnancy, usually before a positive diagnosis was made. The term has been maintained for several reasons. First, in those areas of the world where abortion is illegal, these procedures are carried out as therapy for the delayed onset of menses. Because pregnancy is not diagnosed, there can be no legal consequences. Secondly, women who find themselves in these situations very often do not wish to know whether or not they were pregnant.

DILATATION AND EVACUATION (D&E)

As more experience has been gained in doing early abortions, dilatation and evacuation (suction abortion, suction curettage, vacuum curettage) has come to be used for the majority of abortions done during the first fourteen or fifteen weeks of gestation. The instrument most frequently used is a suction curette (vacurette) made out of a soft material and inserted into the uterine cavity after dilatation of the cervix. This reduces the possibility of perforation of the uterus. The procedure is usually done under local anesthesia, the woman being given a tranquilizer or a short-acting intravenous barbiturate.

The advantages of these procedures are that they are relatively easy to do, the complication rates are very low, the amount of blood lost is minimal, and the effectiveness in totally removing the pregnancy is very high. The procedures can usually be done in less than one minute in early pregnancies but require somewhat more time when the pregnancies are more advanced.

Patients recover rapidly from these procedures; they usually return to their homes within a matter of hours and resume their normal activities almost immediately. Complications are rare including perforation of the uterus, excessive bleeding, postoperative infection, and, on occasion, leaving some tissue behind requiring a repeat procedure.

DILATATION AND EVACUATION
(SUCTION ABORTION)

- Enlarged vacurette
- Clamp steadies uterus
- Uterus
- Endometrium and fetal material
- Vacurette
- Retractor holds vagina open

DILATATION AND CURETTAGE (D&C)

This procedure has been carried out for the diagnosis and treatment of uterine conditions for many years and is also used for first and early (sometimes later) second-trimester abortions. In most instances, it is carried out under general anesthesia. However, dilatation and curettage can also be done using paracervical block, backed up with tranquilizers, sedatives, and other drugs.

Before doing the curettage, it is necessary to dilate the cervix in order to introduce the curette. This may be done by progressively enlarging the size of the endocervical canal using metal dilators. It may also be done by inserting laminaria (a form of seaweed) and leaving it for several hours, usually overnight. This technique allows for the gradual dilatation of the cervix. Studies are currently under way to see whether this gradual dilatation may produce less long-term damage such as premature delivery and spontaneous abortion than the more rapid dilatation with metal dilators.

Once the cervix has been dilated, a surgical curette, usually made of metal, is introduced into the uterus through the cervical canal. The entire surface of the uterine cavity is then scraped with the curette, removing all the fetal and placental tissues.

In this procedure, the complications are also rare. They include perforation of the uterus, excessive bleeding, and the development of postoperative infection.

INTRA-AMNIOTIC INFUSION

Abortion can also be induced by the introduction of various fluids into the amniotic sac. Preparations that have been used are hypertonic saline, hypertonic glucose, urea, and prostaglandins. These techniques are indicated when the pregnancy has advanced too far to do a D&E or D&C. The skin is sterilized, a local anesthetic is injected, a needle is put through the abdominal wall into the amniotic cavity, amniotic fluid is withdrawn, and then the solution is introduced into the cavity. Contractions generally begin twelve to twenty-four hours later, and the patient then proceeds to deliver the dead fetus and the placenta. Very very rarely is the infant born alive.

There are a number of complications that have been noticed with these techniques. With the use of saline, patients may develop abdominal pain, vomiting, hypertension, and a rapid heart rate. In rare instances they may develop problems with blood clotting. Patients receiving prostaglandins often have the side effects of lowering of blood pressure, nausea and vomiting, and diarrhea. Inasmuch as these are surgical procedures, there is always the risk of hemorrhage. Incomplete evacuation of the uterus, delayed hemorrhage, and infection may also occur although they are not frequently encountered.

HYSTEROTOMY AND HYSTERECTOMY

Hysterotomy (the surgical opening of the uterus) is also employed as a form of abortion but only in late pregnancy. The abdomen and the wall of the uterus are opened surgically, and the fetus and the placenta are removed. The uterine wall is sewed back together. On rare occasions the uterus and the fetus may be removed by hysterectomy, usually because of some uterine abnormality.

These two surgical techniques are much more complicated and, therefore, have a higher rate of complications than the simpler techniques described earlier.

DRUGS

A new drug, RU 486, has been developed in France and is currently being marketed there and in China. It blocks the production of a hormone (progesterone) essential to the maintenance of pregnancy. When used early in conjunction with a prostaglandin, it is highly effective and has lower rates of complications than standard operative procedures. This is true for first trimester abortions and particularly true when compared to the risks of second trimester procedures. RU 486 has been violently opposed by anti-abortion groups in the US, making it very unlikely, given the current political climate, that women will soon have this drug as a viable option. What is quite possible, as was the case of the IUDs, is that women who can afford it will travel to other countries, but this method will not be available to those less well informed and less well off financially.

COUNSELING

Effective counseling is one of the most important aspects of abortion services, and any facility that does not provide it must be viewed as inadequate. A counselor can explain and answer questions about the procedure to reduce fears and clear up any misunderstanding about what is about to happen. It is almost inevitable that the woman will have some feelings of guilt and anxiety; the counselor can give support for the decision to have the abortion and give the woman a chance to express these feelings. Given current knowledge about contraception and its wide availability, the question of why the pregnancy occurred can be explored. Perhaps the woman simply did not know enough about contraceptive methods, a situation that the counselor can remedy easily. Bringing out into the open more complex reasons for having an unwanted pregnancy—social factors, personal relationships, or even just lack of forethought—may not eliminate the reasons, but awareness of them may help her to avoid another unwanted pregnancy.

Whatever the reasons, a discussion of future contraception is essential, even though the abortion procedure is safe and most women overcome the psychological trauma associated with it.

Newer data now becoming available suggest, although the conclusions are still controversial, that women who have more than one abortion, regardless of the type of procedure that was performed, may in the future have higher rates of spontaneous abortion, fetal death in utero, and premature delivery than women who have had one abortion or none. Even if there is only a possibility that this medical conclusion is true, it is important to counsel women to use contraception to prevent future abortions.

It is becoming increasingly apparent through surveys that a majority of men want some type of counseling when an abortion is to terminate a pregnancy for which they are responsible. While some clinics are hostile to men and many women want to preserve total autonomy in every aspect of their decision, more and more family planning centers have inaugurated counseling for both partners.

AVAILABILITY OF EFFECTIVE CONTRACEPTION AND SAFE ABORTION

Despite the many developments in all forms of birth control, sterilization, and abortion procedures, the benefits of these advances are not uniformly available. There is a tremendous variation, particularly in the availability of sterilization and abortion, from one section of this country to another and from one area of the world to another. Society has placed varying degrees of emphasis on the importance of these techniques. In some areas their use has been facilitated, even encouraged; in others such services have been totally discouraged; and in still others they are impossible to obtain without breaking the law.

From a purely economic point of view, it is clear that effective contraception has every advantage over unwanted pregnancy. This is equally true of the health implications. When one views the medical problems wrought by large numbers of unwanted pregnancies in terms of illegal abortion, increased infant and maternal illness and death, and the increase in psychological problems (in both parents and children), there are compelling reasons for making contraceptives freely available to all those who need and wish to use them.

PREGNANCY AND CHILDBIRTH

Kathryn Schrotenboer Cox, M.D.

Assistant Attending Physician, Obstetrics and Gynecology, New York Hospital—Cornell Medical Center; Clinical Instructor, Cornell University Medical College

The birth of a first child is a major milestone in a woman's life: it marks the end of one stage and the beginning of a new one. Whether to have a child or not is a decision that must be weighed carefully. It is not uncommon today for a couple to decide that for them the burdens outweigh the rewards. On the other hand, a couple who wait until they know they are ready for the responsibilities of a child often find that the commitment that results from such a decision increases their enjoyment of parenthood. A conscious decision that now is the right time for you to have a baby will help you to see beyond the problems and permit you to focus on the joys of pregnancy and parenthood.

Having a baby before finishing high school can create difficult, and often lifetime, psychosocial and financial problems. Many women fear that having a first baby after age 35 will increase the risks. Older women face greater risks because they are more likely than younger ones to have a chronic disease, such as diabetes or hypertension. The fetal risks relate to these maternal risks and also to increased fetal genetic risks. However, healthy older women do well in pregnancy, and those with disease who get specialized modern clinical care generally do well also. Many genetic conditions can be diagnosed prior to birth, as noted later in this chapter.

If you plan to delay your first pregnancy for some time, you can do several things in the preceding years to help assure future fertility and good health. Find out from a doctor whether you ovulate regularly and, if not, be evaluated and treated. Also, you should have periodic pelvic examinations and pap tests; get immunized, if necessary, against rubella; get family genetic histories assembled and be evaluated for personal genetic diseases or traits; maintain a nutritious diet; keep your body in good shape by exercising regularly; stop smoking altogether; minimize alcohol intake; and get good medical care promptly when necessary.

About three months before trying to conceive:

- If there is even the slightest possibility of having contracted AIDS through past sexual intercourse with a bisexual man or an intravenous drug user, arrange to be tested for the AIDS virus.
- If you've been on the pill, stop taking it so that ovulation and your periods can return to their normal cycle.
- If you've been using an IUD, remove it so that the uterine lining can heal.
- If you haven't already, stop smoking and stop drinking.

One month before trying to conceive:

- Stop taking all over-the-counter medications, including aspirin, vitamins, and cough medicine.
- Have a session with your doctor about any and all your prescription medications and their potentially harmful effects on the fetus-to-be.

CONCEPTION AND EARLY DEVELOPMENT

The reproductive process begins as your body hormones make the necessary changes to ripen an egg (ovum) in one of your ovaries. If you have a 28-day menstrual cycle, this will take place in the first 14 days of the cycle. As the egg ripens, it moves to the outer surface of the ovary. On about the fourteenth day ovulation occurs—a surge of hormones causes the egg to burst forth from the ovary. In a woman with a shorter or longer cycle, the day of ovulation will be sooner or later, as described below.

The menstrual cycle may be divided into two parts by ovulation. From the first day of the menstrual period to ovulation is the preovulatory (also called the proliferative or follicular) phase. From ovulation until the next menstrual period is the postovulatory (also called the secretory or luteal) phase. Regardless of the length of the menstrual cycle, the postovulatory phase lasts approximately fourteen days. The variation in women with shorter or longer cycles takes place in the first part of the cycle. For example, in a woman with a 21-day cycle the first part of the cycle lasts 7 days, ovulation takes place on the seventh day, and the second part of the cycle lasts 14 days. In a woman with a 35-day cycle the preovulatory phase lasts 21 days, ovulation occurs on the twenty-first day, and the postovulatory phase lasts 14 days.

During sexual intercourse semen is deposited in the vagina, usually near the cervix. The sperm move first through the cervical canal and then through the uterus to the fallopian tubes. The sperm are best able to fertilize an egg in the first 48 hours after intercourse, although there are reports of sperm living as long as a week before fertilization.

After ovulation the egg begins traveling down the fallopian tube toward the uterus. The sperm usually meet the egg in the outer third of the fallopian tube where one sperm penetrates the egg to fertilize it. The egg is generally fertilized within 4 to 20 hours after ovulation, but there are exceptions to this as well. After the egg has been fertilized, no other sperm can enter it. The egg and the sperm each contribute to the child half of its genetic material.

Each egg carries an X chromosome. Half of the sperm carry Y chromosomes and the other half carry X chromosomes. If an X-bearing sperm fertilizes the egg, the resulting child is female (XX). If, instead, a Y-bearing sperm fertilizes the egg, the resulting child is male (XY). Therefore, the sex of the child is predetermined by the sperm. The anatomical differences develop early in gestation when something called the H-Y antigen, present only in XY embryos, stimulates the gonads to become testicles, which start producing hormones in proportions that cause the embryo to develop as a male. In the absence of the

FEMALE GENITAL TRACT
OVULATION, FERTILIZATION AND IMPLANTATION

CROSS-SECTION OF UTERUS

H-Y antigen the embryonic gonads will not become testicles and the resultant infant will be female.

Recent laboratory studies have shown that there are biochemical differences between the X-bearing and the Y-bearing sperm. These differences may allow either the X or Y sperm to survive longer or move faster in certain environments. Books and articles have been written that suggest using acid or alkaline douches or changing the position, frequency, or timing of intercourse to help alter the odds of having a boy or a girl. Unfortunately, the reproductive tract is more complex than the test tube, and many studies have given conflicting results.

There is a laboratory technique that is used to separate Y sperm (male) from X sperm, and the desired sex sperm can then be injected via artificial insemination into the woman's vagina. (The technique does not give an absolute separation.) It is about 75 percent successful in producing a male, less so in producing a female. Needless to say, many unanswered scientific, demographic, and ethical questions have arisen in this connection.

Medical ethicists are anticipating the problems that society will have to face when reproductive technology will provide parents with the means for accurate predetermination of the sex of their offspring. All surveys indicate that the overwhelming majority favor a male child as the firstborn, consigning female children to second place both literally and figuratively with all the negative consequences of that ordinal position.

Twinning may occur by two separate alterations in the reproductive process. Fraternal twins result when a woman produces two eggs during the same month and they are fertilized by two different sperm. Identical twins result when a single fertilized egg splits in half at an early stage of development. Identical twins are much less common than fraternal twins, occurring in about 1 out of 250 pregnancies. Fraternal twins occur in approximately 1 out of 90 pregnancies, but the percentage is increased with the use of fertility drugs or when certain racial or hereditary factors exist. For example, twins are more common in the United States than in Japan and are more common in black families in the United States than in white families. A woman who herself is a twin has an increased chance of having twins.

The endometrial lining of the uterus is prepared every month by hormonal changes to receive a fertilized egg. If no fertilized egg is received, the endometrium is shed as the monthly menstrual flow. During the cycle in which conception occurs, the fertilized egg continues to travel down the fallopian tube and implants in the endometrium. The implantation takes place about seven or eight days after the egg has been fertilized. The area on the ovary where the egg developed forms a small cyst (called the corpus luteum of pregnancy). This cyst produces a hormone (progesterone) that sustains the pregnancy in the early weeks until the placenta (afterbirth) has developed sufficiently to take over this function.

Nestled in the endometrial lining of the uterus, the cells divide. Some of the cells will develop into the fetus. Other cells begin forming the placenta. Besides producing hormones necessary to maintain a pregnancy, the normal placenta acts as an organ of exchange between mother and fetus. Oxygen and nutrients are removed from the mother's blood, absorbed by the fetal blood, and delivered to the developing fetus through the umbilical vein. The fetal waste products return to the placenta via the umbilical arteries and are then transferred into the mother's bloodstream.

In the early weeks of pregnancy the embryo is too small and underdeveloped to be recognizable as human. After 7 weeks have elapsed from the last menstrual period, the fetus is approximately 1 inch long. There is a recognizable head and body, but there are only thick buds where the arms and legs will form. By 10 weeks the fetus is about 2 1/2 inches long and is taking more recognizable human form as the arms and legs are lengthening. At 14 weeks the fetus is about 4 1/2 inches long and may weigh 3 ounces. By this time the placenta is normally well-developed. By 18 weeks the mother may feel slight movements. At 28 weeks the fetus weighs an average of 2 1/2 pounds and measures about 14 inches. In the last few months of pregnancy, the fetus grows rapidly. At 40 weeks, the end of the average pregnancy, the fetus is usually about 20 inches long and weighs 6 to 9 pounds.

Your doctor will measure your pregnancy in weeks from your last menstrual period. To make a quick calculation of the "due date," subtract three months and add one week to the first day of your last menstrual period.

UTERINE-FETAL RELATIONSHIP

- Uterine muscular wall
- Uterine lining (decidua)
- Uterine cavity
- Chorion
- Amnion
- Amniotic cavity
- Placenta
- Umbilical cord
- Fetus 12 weeks after conception (actual size)
- Cervix
- Vagina

DIAGNOSIS OF PREGNANCY

SIGNS AND SYMPTOMS

Many women think that a missed period, morning sickness, and fatigue are necessary signs of early pregnancy. However, even these classic symptoms may not always be present, and their presence does not always indicate pregnancy. There are other reasons for missing menstrual periods including emotional stress, excessive weight loss, intensive exercise schedule, illness, thyroid disease, and the recent use of birth control pills. For example, if you recently stopped taking birth control pills, it may be several months before your body readjusts and you resume having regular monthly periods. On the other hand, many women who are pregnant have a light "menstrual period" during the first month or two of pregnancy.

Nausea or inability to tolerate certain foods or tobacco smoke is common during early pregnancy. Often the nausea can be relieved by eating a few crackers in the morning before getting out of bed. Sometimes, however, vomiting is such a problem that medication is required to control it.

Breast tenderness is a reliable sign of pregnancy. The feeling of soreness usually starts about the time of the missed menstrual period or a week or two later. But because the feeling also occurs premenstrually, it is possible to be fooled by this sign. Some women begin producing excessive saliva; others experience fatigue. Some are constipated; others have diarrhea. Still others experience a large increase in appetite. Every person is slightly different. You may experience all of these symptoms or you may experience none of them.

PREGNANCY TESTS

There are several different tests which can tell you whether or not you are pregnant. Some are more accurate than others, and in recent years home pregnancy tests provide reliable results, but only if instructions are followed very carefully.

All pregnancy tests are based on the dectection in the blood or urine of the hormone called human chorionic gonadotropin (HCG). The levels of secretion of HCG double every two days in the first trimester.

Tests have been developed in which antibodies are used to detect HCG in the woman's blood or urine. The blood test, called radioimmuneassay or RIA, can detect HCG as early as 7 days after ovulation and fertilization, or about one week before a missed period. The urine test, which is older, has been improved to the point where it is almost as sensitive as the blood test. However, it cannot be relied on to detect pregnancy until almost two weeks following conception, or a few days before the missed period. While these tests are highly accurate, a lower than normal amount of HCG in the blood or urine may produce a false-negative result, and the test should therefore be repeated after a week if a pregnancy is suspected. An ectopic pregnancy, or an impending miscarriage, may result in lower than normal HCG values. (Higher than normal HCG levels are produced by a multiple pregnancy or some other anomaly that should be investigated further.)

Pregnancy tests are offered free of charge or at low cost by some family planning clinics. Your local health department or the county medical society can supply information of this kind.

HOME PREGNANCY TESTS

Many of these tests are essentially the same as the urine pregnancy tests performed professionally in clinics and in doctors' offices. The test kits are available in most drugstores and can be bought without a doctor's prescription. If you are planning to use a home test, make sure that the test uses monoclonal antibodies rather than hemagglutination, a process considered less reliable than the antibody technique. Instructions on how to take the test and how to read the results must be followed with extreme care.

If the results of the home test are positive, the results should be sent to the doctor for confirmation of the pregnancy. If the results are negative, you may still be pregnant. The test should be repeated in about 10 days if your period still has not begun. If the result is negative second time around, pregnancy has probably not occurred but a doctor should be consulted to find out why menstruation has been interrupted.

WHO WILL DELIVER YOUR BABY?

In the United States, babies are delivered every day by obstetrician-gynecologists, family practitioners, nurse-midwives, and lay midwives. Depending on the state in which you live and the size of your community, some or all of these choices may be available to you. Whichever type of professional you select, the most important thing is to find someone with whom you are comfortable and in whom you have confidence. If you have a special problem such as heart disease, hypertension, hyperthyroidism, etc., you should be cared for by an appropriate specialist as well.

OBSTETRICIAN-GYNECOLOGIST

To become an obstetrician-gynecologist, a physician who has already received a medical degree, must spend a minimum of three or four years in an approved residency program working in the field of obstetrics and gynecology under the supervision of specialists in that field. After completing this training, most become certified in obstetrics and gynecology by passing difficult examinations given by the American College of Obstetrics and Gynecology. Obstetrician-gynecologists and residents in obstetrics and gynecology deliver approximately 70 percent of the babies born in the United States. At the present time approximately one out of every six obstetrician-gynecologists in the United States is a woman. This percentage is increasing as more women are graduating from medical schools and selecting a career in this specialty.

Obstetricians vary in their attitudes toward childbirth as well as such specifics as medications during labor, breast feeding, role of the father, episiotomy, rooming-in, and length of hospital stay. If any of these things are important to you, discuss them with your obstetrician early in pregnancy.

FAMILY PRACTITIONER

Many babies are delivered by family practitioners, particularly in rural areas or small towns where such a doctor may be the only one available. Many women enjoy having the family doctor, who takes care of the entire family for all medical problems, care for them during pregnancy, labor, and delivery. Many family practitioners have had some advanced training in obstetrics. A family doctor trained in obstetrics can handle a normal pregnancy and childbirth, but he or she may refer you to an obstetrician or other specialist if you have serious complications at any time during pregnancy.

NURSE-MIDWIFE

Certified nurse-midwives deliver approximately 2.3 percent of the babies born in the United States. These midwives are registered nurses (RNs) who have had an additional one or two years of training in obstetrics. Almost all are women. There are approximately 3,000 certified nurse-midwives in clinical practice in all 50 states. The profession continues to grow, with up to 250 new practitioners certified annually. In a recent year (1985), of the approximately 85,000 births attended by nurse-midwives, 85 percent occurred in hospitals, 11 percent in birthing centers, and 4 percent in the mother's home.

According to the American College of Nurse-Midwives, the nurse-midwife's management of labor and delivery may differ from that of some physicians. Nurse-midwives are less likely to use fetal monitors or use forceps. They often prefer deliveries in a bed instead of on a delivery table. An episiotomy, an incision to enlarge the vaginal opening prior to delivery, is often not done by nurse-midwives. Many offer family planning and postpartum checkups. Typically, they try to encourage breast feeding and rooming-in. (Of course, many physicians are willing to deliver your baby and care for you in this manner.)

Because nurse-midwives generally have fewer patients than either obstetricians or family practitioners, they may have more time to spend with each patient during prenatal visits or during labor. Nurse-midwives handle uncomplicated pregnancies quite satisfactorily. However, if complications arise, the patient may have to be transferred to the care of a physician.

The licensing of medical personnel varies from state to state, and a few states still have very restrictive laws regarding nurse-midwives. By law in most states there must be an obstetrician available to the midwife in case of emergency. Most midwives today practice with obstetricians or use obstetricians as consultants. If you would like to know whether there are any nurse-midwives practicing in your area, contact the American College of Nurse-Midwives.

LAY MIDWIFE

Lay midwives are people without nursing degrees who are trained to deliver babies. As a group lay midwives are the most willing to perform home deliveries. Many states recognize only nurse-midwives and do not allow lay midwives to practice. Some states that permit lay midwives to practice have little or no regulation. Because of this wide variation in regulation by states, the level of training required of a lay midwife also varies enormously. Before you select a lay midwife, you should inquire thoroughly into the level of his or her training.

WHERE WILL YOU HAVE YOUR BABY?

The decision as to where to have your baby should only be made after you have carefully considered the alternatives.

HOSPITAL DELIVERY

Approximately 99 percent of all babies born in the United States today are born in hospitals. The birth of a baby is a normal physiological process and is usually uncomplicated. However, when complications do occur, they often happen very quickly and with little or no warning. Labor may be progressing well when vaginal bleeding begins and the baby's heartbeat starts to slow. Even a healthy mother with an uncomplicated pregnancy and a normal labor and delivery may have a baby that has difficulty breathing and needs to be given oxygen and receive immediate pediatric care. Similarly, a woman with a totally uncomplicated labor and delivery may have a postpartum hemorrhage ten minutes later. While these complications are not common, they can be catastrophic if proper medical care, including needed blood, oxygen, or medications, is not available. Most women opt for a hospital birth to have the assurance that any necessary treatment is immediately available if any complications do occur.

HOME DELIVERY

Some women choose to have their babies at home. They object to the cold and sometimes impersonal environment of the hospital and prefer to share the intimate joyous experience of birth with their families and friends rather than with doctors and nurses in masks and gowns. Labor and delivery are normal processes, not diseases.

If you are considering home delivery, discuss it thoroughly with the person who is overseeing your prenatal care and delivery (your clinician, whether it be physician, nurse-midwife, or lay midwife). During the course of your prenatal care the clinician can tell you if any condition indicates a likelihood of complication. In such a case you may be advised that hospital delivery would be much safer.

Even if it is assumed that delivery will be normal, arrangements must be made for emergency transportation and additional medical aid in case of unexpected difficulty. Even if arrangements have been made, there is still a risk that complications may develop too quickly to be treated adequately. In many European countries home delivery is safer than in the United States because of an extensive system of back-up ambulances and emergency teams that can be dispatched at a moment's notice. Here, comparable systems have been developed in only a few communities.

CHILDBEARING CENTER DELIVERY

A third and increasingly popular option for women who find hospital delivery too impersonal and expensive and home delivery too informal is an independent licensed childbearing center staffed by certified nurse-midwives. These centers are usually located in a suitably converted private dwelling where the mother-to-be goes for prenatal care and delivery after she has been evaluated by a physician who rules out the likelihood of complications. There are approximately 140 childbearing centers in 38 states, with 300 additional ones expected to open soon. An increasing number of states have enacted licensing requirements for the centers. Licensing is required for insurance coverage.

An important aspect of the appeal of this lying-in arrangement is the considerable saving it represents. On the average, with all services included, delivery in a childbearing center costs about half of a hospital delivery. Typical services include a preparation-for-parenthood program consisting of 10 to 14 weekly sessions of two hours each; prenatal care provided by a licensed nurse-midwife who also attends the mother during labor and birth; the services as necessary of a backup team of obstetricians, pediatricians, and nurse assistants; facilities for a 12-hour stay by the family after the baby is born; a complete examination of the baby by a pediatrician; home visits by public health nurses within 24 hours as well as on the third and fifth days; a checkup of the mother at the center a week after delivery and a final checkup 5 to 6 weeks later.

If you are interested in having your baby at such a center, be sure to investigate the arrangements for transfer to a hospital in case of an emergency. Information about a childbearing facility in your area is available from The Cooperative Birth Center Network.

HEALTH CARE DURING NORMAL PREGNANCY

As soon as you think or know you are pregnant, you should begin your prenatal care. Early visits to your doctor are important to identify any problems or potential problems. If you are healthy, such visits will probably occur only once a month. By the end of pregnancy your visits will probably be weekly.

The first visit is likely to be the longest. It should include a medical history, family history, and a physical examination. If you have a full-time job and intend working through most of your pregnancy, your doctor should be told about the nature of your work, the environmental risks, whether you're expected to stand all day, and other circumstances that might affect your well being and that of the fetus. Your personal habits will be reviewed in terms of smoking, alcohol consumption, coffee dependency, and the like, because anything that might reduce the blood supply to the fetus puts its healthy development at risk. Blood tests will be taken to determine your blood type, whether you are Rh-negative or Rh-positive, and whether you are anemic. Other tests will be taken to see if you have syphilis, gonorrhea, or a urinary tract infection. You may also be tested for immunity to German measles and toxoplasmosis, and you may be asked whether there is any reason to believe you should be tested for the AIDS virus.

If you are healthy and your pregnancy is uncomplicated, subsequent visits will include an examination of the size of the uterus, a measurement of your blood pressure and weight change, and perhaps a urine test. Blood tests may be repeated later in pregnancy. Although these checkups are simple, they can detect many of the problems that can occur during pregnancy. At the beginning of the third trimester, your doctor may review the demands of your job and will recommend when you should begin your maternity leave.

Now that you are pregnant you will undoubtedly want to learn as much as possible about the process that you are about to experience. Recently there has been an increase in the availability of "preparation for childbirth" classes. These classes may be given in hospitals, doctors' offices, prenatal clinics, community meeting places, or private homes. The classes sponsored by nurse-midwife associations are usually very good. Most courses of this kind include the father-to-be during the last few sessions, especially if one of the "natural" childbirth methods is your choice.

Although the format may vary, the basic goal of these classes is to educate a pregnant woman and her partner about what to expect during pregnancy, labor, and delivery. The more you understand about what is happening and why it is happening, the more comfortable you will feel. If tours of the labor and delivery area of your hospital are offered, take one. Such a tour will make your surroundings seem more familiar to you when you arrive for your delivery.

EMOTIONAL CHANGES

For many women pregnancy is a pleasant, happy time; it may also be a time of psychological stress and mixed emotions. Much of what a woman expects of pregnancy is a result of what she has heard over the years from her mother, sisters, friends, and relatives. A woman who has heard repeatedly of the horrors and terrible pain of labor may face childbirth with fear and apprehension. A woman who has grown up in a neighborhood where many families had five or six children may assume it must be easy.

An unplanned pregnancy, in or out of wedlock, may bring with it considerable emotional stress. Even a couple who has planned and waited for years for a family will probably have some doubt and ambivalence. You don't know in advance how the baby will affect your life and whether or not you will like the changes. You may worry about how much everything will cost. If you have been working, you may be concerned about how you will find a baby-sitter and may wonder how having a baby will affect your career.

Of course your appearance will change. The radiant glow that accompanies pregnancy may be attributable not only to the state of excitement and elation but also to the hormones of pregnancy that affect your skin. (In this connection, either avoid exposure to the sun, or, if you insist on sunbathing, be sure to use a sunblock with a protection factor of 15.) Don't be upset by the spidery veins that may suddenly appear on your upper body, arms, and legs. They are caused by blood vessel changes and normally disappear within three months of delivery. However, the stretch marks that turn whitish will remain.

Though often a time of closeness between a husband and wife, pregnancy can also be a time of friction in a marriage. Men's attitudes toward childbirth vary as much as women's. Some men cannot relate to the pregnancy at all, while others feel every wave of nausea and every contraction personally. The important thing to remember is that these attitudes don't make them better or worse as husbands or as fathers.

Most psychologists consider pregnancy a crisis time. Your feelings about your own parents, your childhood experiences, your relationship with the father of the child, your friends, and your job are all changing. Your body is going through rapid physical and hormonal changes and it is sometimes hard to believe that you will ever return to a nonpregnant size and shape. It is not at all surprising that there are times of emotional fluctuations during pregnancy.

DIET

If a woman is healthy and has good eating habits, it may be unnecessary for her to make any major diet changes during pregnancy. Many women are surprised that there is not a great increase in the amount of food required during pregnancy. Although a pregnant woman's caloric intake may not be greatly increased, it is important that the calories be obtained from foods that will provide the proper protein, vitamins, and minerals for her baby's development. If you have not been eating a well-balanced diet, it is essential that you correct that once you become pregnant. Your baby is totally dependent on you to supply it with the necessary nutrients for proper growth and development. You are feeding your baby! For advice on proper nutrition and weight gain during pregnancy, see "Nutrition, Weight, and General Well-Being."

SMOKING, ALCOHOL, AND DRUGS

Anytime is a good time to stop smoking, but pregnancy is an especially important time for you to stop. In women who smoke there is an increased likelihood of premature, low-birthweight, and stillborn babies. Complications of pregnancy including bleeding, placenta previa, and premature rupture of the membranes are also more frequent in smokers. Many of these complications are thought to be caused by higher levels of carbon monoxide and lower levels of oxygen in the blood of women who smoke. Nicotine and small amounts of carbon monoxide circulating in the mother's bloodstream also may have adverse effects.

The harmful effects of smoking on the baby do not end at the time of delivery. Nicotine is transmitted through breast milk and some of the undesirable consequences of this are known to produce a mild irritability. Also, bronchitis, pneumonia, and other types of respiratory distress are more common in children who live in a family where one or more family members smoke.

Alcohol also has been shown to affect the fetus adversely. Babies of alcoholic mothers are more likely to have birth defects including mental and growth retardation. The fetal alcohol syndrome consists of a

WEIGHT GAIN DURING PREGNANCY

AT 12 WEEKS   24 WEEKS   36 WEEKS

POUNDS GAINED

25, 20, 15, 10, 5 Pounds

¼, 1, 3, 5, 8, 11, 14, 17, 19-20, 24-30

Weeks after last normal menstrual period: 4, 8, 12, 16, 20, 24, 28, 32, 36, 40 small baby with a smaller than normal head, characteristic facial appearance, heart defects, and mental retardation. While these serious problems are associated with heavy drinkers, some medical researchers feel that no alcohol should be drunk during pregnancy because even small amounts can have a harmful effect on the fetus. The caffeine in coffee, tea, many soft drinks, chocolate, and a number of drugs, when consumed in large quantities (4 or more cups of coffee a day, for example) may possibly cause birth defects.

Studies have shown that very few women go through an entire pregnancy without taking a single drug. This, of course, includes such things as vitamins, iron, or an occasional aspirin. Unfortunately, in our society many drugs are used more from habit than actual need—a decongestant for every stuffy nose or a sleeping pill that is not always necessary. Pregnant women should avoid the use of any medications that are not truly essential, because no drug has been proven to be 100 percent safe for the unborn. Drugs taken by a woman during pregnancy can cross the placenta and reach the fetus, and unfortunately, most pregnant women use as many as four drugs during the early months, when the fetus is at greatest risk.

At least 80 percent of the drugs on the market have never been tested for safety during pregnancy because of FDA restrictions and the potential dangers of such testing. However, among those drugs known to be potentially harmful are: aspirin taken near the end of pregnancy (acetaminophen is a better choice); such antibiotics as tetracycline, streptomycin, and the sulfas (penicillin, ampicillin, and the cephalosporins are safer); the anti-inflammatory drugs nidomethacin and naproxen; the anticonvulsant Dilantin; the anticoagulant Warfarin; some high blood pressure medications; and excessive amounts of vitamins C, D, K, and of calcium and copper. Studies have also shown that Accutane, the drug widely prescribed for acne, if used during the first three months of pregnancy puts the mother at 25 times the normal risk of having a baby with a major malformation. In addition, the FDA has issued warnings on Valium and Librium, which may cause cleft lip and palate or other defects in a small percentage of babies if taken by the mother during the first three months of pregnancy. Lithium, a drug used in certain psychiatric conditions, is thought to cause a significant increase in congenital cardiovascular malformation if taken during early pregnancy. Hormones, including progesterones, estrogens, androgens, and birth control pills, if taken during early pregnancy perhaps may endanger the fetus and cause genital or limb abnormalities. The FDA recommends that all women discontinue birth control pills at least three months before becoming pregnant, though recent studies have challenged the necessity of this.

A pregnant woman must be concerned about other substances besides drugs. Artificial sweeteners cross the placenta and reach the developing fetus. Any live-virus vaccines should also be avoided. Chemicals, pesticides, and other toxic sprays may be absorbed into the mother's bloodstream. Because the effects of such substances on the fetus are unknown, it is best to limit contact with them.

ACTIVITY

Keeping active during your pregnancy is very important. However, because of cardiovascular, weight, and posture changes, many pregnant women find that they tire more quickly. Because there has been very little significant research on exercise during pregnancy, different doctors are likely to make different recommendations. A 1988 study indicates that participation in a physical fitness program designed especially for pregnant women had no negative effects on either mother or fetus. These mothers-to-be had shorter second stages of labor, perhaps because of increased cardiovascular fitness and increased ability to postpone fatigue.

If your pregnancy is proceeding normally, most of the activities you enjoyed before can be continued. Your guiding principle should be *moderation*. Swimming in unpolluted waters, bicycling, running, and walking are all safe. In fact, walking is one of the best exercises for a pregnant woman.

Do not do any exercise that raises your pulse rate above 160. Avoid saunas, hot tubs, steam rooms, or excessive heat in any form. Abstain from exercise in hot, humid weather, and if you must exert yourself to the point of heavy sweating, be sure to increase your liquid intake. Don't engage in exercises that necessitate lying on your back, because this posture may alter the blood flow to the fetus. Avoid workouts involving bouncy movements such as jumping rope and hard games of tennis requiring abrupt changes in direction. Other sports to be given up during pregnancy include horseback riding, downhill skiing, and scuba diving.

Anyone with a chronic condition such as diabetes, high blood pressure, or cardiac impairment should ask the doctor for advice about an exercise schedule.

Many women wonder if they should travel while they are pregnant. This question usually can be answered with a bit of common sense. It would normally be wise not to travel to any part of the world where primitive public sanitation conditions prevail or where there is an epidemic. In general, the greatest risk in traveling is that you could develop a complication in a place where it would be difficult to obtain adequate medical care. Because complications are fewest during the middle three months, that is the safest time to travel. During the first three months there is always a possibility of a spontaneous abortion (miscarriage), during the last three there is a chance of premature labor or of ruptured membranes.

Continuing or starting to work during pregnancy is a matter of great concern to a growing number of women. They ask how long they can work. The answer depends on their desires, their companies' pregnancy benefit policies, the type of work, whether their pregnancies are complicated in some way, how much energy they use getting to and from work and doing things at home, and other factors. A healthy woman with a normal pregnancy whose energy expenditure on the job and at other times is not more than minimally fatiguing can work until she is at least 36 weeks pregnant, maybe longer. Physically, a woman could return to work, if there have been no complications of great consequence, two weeks after delivery. However, specialists on early childhood development feel that the early weeks and months are important times for mother and baby to be together. Many women do not return to work until six weeks to three months after delivery, and many more choose to stay home longer or work on a part-time basis if these arrangements can be made. Every woman should know her employer's benefits and maternity policies and discuss her particular situation with her physician or other care provider (see "Health on the Job").

Many factors contribute to the change in sexual relations that most couples experience during pregnancy. A woman may feel extremely attractive during pregnancy or she may feel that she is totally undesirable. A man's feeling about the attractiveness of his pregnant lover may be just as variable. Some couples find that pregnancy is a time of increased sexual intimacy. Others find that their previously good sexual relationship has deteriorated. Some men express anxiety about possible trauma to the developing fetus during intercourse. Women often experience uterine cramping after orgasm, which may lead to fear of inducing abortion in early pregnancy or inducing labor later on. The pregnant woman's expanding shape may cause difficulty in finding comfortable positions.

Certain conditions may cause your doctor or midwife to recommend limitation of sexual relations during pregnancy. Among these conditions are a history of several early or midtrimester spontaneous abortions or of premature labor, multiple pregnancy, polyhydramnios (excess amniotic fluid causing overdistention of the uterus), low-lying placenta, or placenta previa. Sexual relations should be discontinued if you have been told that your cervix has started to dilate, if your membranes have ruptured, or if you are having vaginal bleeding.

If the pregnancy is uncomplicated, I have always advised my patients that they could continue sexual relations until I find, by vaginal examination, that the cervix has started to dilate. Because this often occurs during the last month of pregnancy many physicians routinely recommend discontinuance of sexual intercourse a month before the baby is due. Some recent studies have questioned the safety of intercourse in uncomplicated pregnancies, pointing to a small number of spontaneous abortions, infections, and premature deliveries occurring after sexual intercourse. More definitive studies need to be done in this area. In spite of the questions raised by these studies, the evidence doesn't seem conclusive enough to recommend limitation of sexual relations during the first eight months of a normal pregnancy.

COMPLICATIONS OF PREGNANCY

Although most pregnancies are uneventful and result in the birth of a normal healthy baby, complications sometimes arise. These complications include bleeding and spontaneous abortion, premature labor, ectopic pregnancy, pre-eclampsia and eclampsia, chronic and genetic disease, infections, Rh disease, intrauterine fetal death, and hydatidiform mole.

BLEEDING AND SPONTANEOUS ABORTION (MISCARRIAGE)

It is calculated that 15 to 20 percent of known pregnancies end in miscarriage (technically called spontaneous abortion) and that in 60 percent of all miscarriages the fetus is either anatomically or genetically abnormal. Thus, the phenomenon of spontaneous abortion can be viewed as a process of natural selection, because a healthy fetus is not easily dislodged. Most miscarriages occur during the first three months, and the increase in occurrence is attributed to many factors: the rising rate of sexually transmissible diseases, complications arising from the use of IUDs, and the postponement of pregnancy by more and more women into their late 30s when eggs are likely to develop chromosomal abnormalities.

Although the occurrence of a bloody vaginal discharge reminiscent of menstruation once or twice in early pregnancy is not uncommon, it is sufficient reason to contact your doctor promptly. Until consultation and examination, limit physical activity as much as possible and avoid sexual intercourse. Generally the bleeding stops spontaneously and is no further problem. In cases like these, usually no cause for the bleeding is found.

The bleeding, however, may be evidence of a threatened abortion—an indication that a spontaneous abortion (miscarriage) may occur. By definition, pregnancies that end before the completion of the twentieth week of gestation are called abortions. If the bleeding is heavy, persists for a number of days or weeks, and is accompanied by cramping pain, it is even more suggestive of a threatened abortion. An abortion may be, of course, either spontaneous or induced. A threatened abortion becomes an inevitable abortion if the cervix dilates and the membranes rupture. This progresses to a complete or an incomplete abortion according to whether or not all the tissue comes out of the uterus spontaneously. Any tissue or suspected tissue appearing with vaginal bleeding should be kept and shown to your physician. Any tissue remaining in the uterus must be removed by a D&C. Sometimes an abortion occurs without any bleeding or other symptoms. This is most commonly diagnosed when the uterus stops growing in early pregnancy and is confirmed by an ultrasound examination that reveals a shriveled sac instead of a live fetus. This is a missed abortion and a D&C is performed to remove the abnormal tissue.

A spontaneous abortion can be a very upsetting experience. It is important to realize that spontaneous abortions are very common and usually cannot be prevented. Furthermore, recent studies on the aborted tissue have shown that many of these pregnancies were not developing normally. Thus, spontaneous abortions help to assure that most pregnancies that reach the sixth month will result in normal, healthy babies. Having one spontaneous abortion does not mean that you will experience difficulty with your next pregnancy nor does it mean that there is anything wrong with you or your partner. However, if a woman has had one miscarriage or more than one, there is a 25 to 40 percent likelihood that she will have another. After the second one, she should have a complete workup to find out what accounts for the problem.

Recent research indicates that some women with a faulty or underactive immune system reject the fetus as a foreign body because they lack a type of antibody that normally fights against this rejection during pregnancy. It is thought that this circumstance may account for as many as half the miscarriages experienced by the 2 million women who have miscarriages of normal fetuses. An experimental treatment for this condition involves the use of donor transplant cells that stimulate the production of the essential antibodies in the recipient.

BLEEDING IN LATER PREGNANCY

One relatively uncommon problem that causes bleeding in later pregnancy is placenta previa. The placenta normally attaches to the side or the top of the uterine cavity. In placenta previa it attaches instead to the lowest part of the uterus and covers all or part of the cervix, thus possibly blocking the baby's exit through the birth canal. Bed rest will decrease the likelihood of bleeding, although extensive bleeding may nevertheless occur. The baby must be delivered by cesarean section if the placenta is blocking the entire cervix.

Another cause of bleeding in pregnancy is separation of a portion of the placenta from the uterine wall (placental abruption). If the detached portion is large, labor may begin. If the placenta detaches completely, the fetus will be unable to receive oxygen and nutrients from the mother and will die. Fortunately, the amount of separation is often small enough to allow the pregnancy to proceed normally.

If you have any bleeding during pregnancy, you should contact your physician. Keep in mind that not all bleeding during pregnancy means that something is wrong. Some women bleed during the first few months of pregnancy at the time they would have had their menstrual period. Sometimes an irritation on the cervix can cause bleeding after intercourse. During the last few weeks of pregnancy many women have some spotting after a vaginal examination. Also, a small amount of bleeding sometimes occurs near the end of pregnancy as the cervix begins to dilate.

ECTOPIC PREGNANCY

In some pregnancies the fertilized egg does not implant in the uterus but in an ectopic (abnormal) location. By far the most common type of ectopic pregnancy is the tubal pregnancy. Other types include abdominal, ovarian, and cervical pregnancy.

Some women with an ectopic pregnancy exhibit all of the normal symptoms of pregnancy; others have none because of the lower hormone levels associated with ectopic pregnancies. Spotting is quite common in tubal pregnancies. As the embryo grows and pushes on the walls of the fallopian tube, pain can develop. Because the diameter of the tube is small, the pregnancy may rupture through the side of the fallopian tube, causing extensive intra-abdominal bleeding. In some cases the first sign of an ectopic pregnancy is a fainting spell caused by this sudden loss of blood internally. Ectopic pregnancies almost always cause symptoms that differ from those of a normal pregnancy before 12 weeks. Occasionally, such pregnancies wither away, the woman remains well, and they are never diagnosed. They almost never result in a live birth.

The chances of developing an ectopic pregnancy are greater among women over 35, and among those who have had a history of pelvic infections, an infection after an abortion, an ectopic pregnancy in the past, or who use intrauterine contraceptive devices (see chapter on contraception for the relationship between IUDs and ectopic pregnancy). However, ectopic pregnancies often occur in the absence of any of these factors, and they are one of the four major causes of death during pregnancy, the other three being toxemia, infection, and hemorrhaging. It is a matter of concern that extrauterine pregnancies have increased dramatically in recent decades, the number tripling from 17,800 in the 1970s to 52,200 in 1980, and the rate doubling among total pregnancies. Some authorities attribute this rise to the increase in cases of gonorrhea, chlamydia, and inadequately treated pelvic inflammatory disease.

In many cases an early tubal pregnancy may be removed and the fallopian tube repaired, but frequently the tube is irreparably damaged and must be removed. However, if the other tube is normal, future pregnancies are possible. As more women are learning to recognize the symptoms of a possible ectopic pregnancy and seek earlier care, and with the development of more sophisticated diagnostic techniques such as laparoscopy and sonography, more surgery is being done before the tube is irreparably damaged. This, coupled with improved surgical techniques including laser surgery, means that it is becoming less and less necessary to remove the tube.

PRE-ECLAMPSIA AND ECLAMPSIA

(FORMERLY CALLED TOXEMIA OF PREGNANCY)

An abnormal elevation of blood pressure developing during the latter half of pregnancy (gestational hypertension) may occur in up to 5 percent of all pregnancies. A mild increase in blood pressure without any other symptoms is common. Though bleeding during pregnancy and placental abruption are more common in women with gestational hypertension, in most cases there is no ill effect. If the increase in blood pressure is significant, bed rest may be recommended in an attempt to prevent complications.

However, a rise in blood pressure when accompanied by edema (fluid retention) and protein in the urine, indicates the onset of a condition called pre-eclampsia. Rapid weight gain caused by the fluid retention, severe headaches, and visual disturbances may occur. Pre-eclampsia is more common with first pregnancies. When mild, it can be treated by bed rest and sedation. Severe cases may require large doses of sedatives and medications to lower the blood pressure. In its most severe form pre-eclampsia can be life threatening to both mother and baby, and delivery may be necessary even if the infant is premature. Severe pre-eclampsia is rare and with proper treatment is usually not a problem after delivery.

Eclampsia is an intensification of the symptoms designated as pre-eclampsia and is also characterized by convulsions. Eclampsia may develop from untreated pre-eclampsia or it may occur without preliminary milder symptoms. No matter when in pregnancy eclampsia occurs, the pregnancy must be terminated after appropriate anticonvulsive-antihypertensive medication has been given. In women without chronic high blood pressure or kidney disease, pre-eclampsia or eclampsia usually does not recur during subsequent pregnancies.

CHRONIC AND GENETIC DISEASES

Because of medical advances, successful pregnancy is now possible for women who in past years might not have been able to have children. This includes women under treatment for diabetes, high blood pressure, heart disease, epilepsy, and many other diseases. However, because proper treatment during pregnancy may be quite complicated, a woman with any of these problems should consult a doctor before she becomes pregnant.

If you have a mild form of diabetes, which is controlled by diet or by constant amounts of insulin, your diabetes probably will not prevent you from conceiving. However, pregnancy is not always easy for a diabetic woman. Blood sugar levels must be followed closely and the insulin dosage adjusted frequently during pregnancy. Hospitalization is often necessary, especially late in pregnancy. If your diabetes has been difficult to control or if it has affected your kidneys or vision, pregnancy could seriously worsen your diabetes and threaten your life. Some women develop diabetes during pregnancy. Many physicians now perform screening tests for diabetes on all women during pregnancy. If this test is *not* done routinely by your doctor, you should ask to have it performed.

Diabetic mothers have an increased chance of needing a cesarean section, because babies born to diabetic mothers may be large, sometimes over 10 pounds. Also, many babies of diabetic mothers are delivered early to avoid fetal complications during the last few weeks of pregnancy. A baby of a diabetic mother may have hypoglycemia (low blood sugar) for the first day or two of life, but this can usually be treated by prompt feeding or intravenous feeding of sugar solutions.

Medication for high blood pressure may have to be adjusted during pregnancy. Some drugs are safer than others during pregnancy, and you should be on the safest possible drugs in the lowest dosage that will control your blood pressure. Some complications, such as bleeding and separation of the placenta, are more common in patients with high blood pressure. Babies born to mothers with severe high blood pressure may be smaller than average.

There are many changes in your heart and circulatory system during pregnancy. Some, but not all, heart problems may be worsened.

Pregnancy may be complicated by epilepsy. The risk of having a baby with a serious congenital defect is three to four times higher in epileptic women. Many of these birth defects, including cardiac anomalies, facial anomalies, and cleft lip and palate, are thought to be caused by the drugs used to control epilepsy, yet studies have shown that epileptic mothers who did not take medications during pregnancy also had an increased incidence of birth defects. At present there is no test for these specific defects during pregnancy. However, even with these problems and despite the substantially greater risks, most babies born to epileptic mothers (whether they are taking medication or not) are completely normal.

If there is any history of congenital malformation, mental retardation, or known genetic disorders in your family, you should see a qualified genetic counselor before you become pregnant. Some birth defects are hereditary, while others are not, and a counselor can advise you in advance about your chances of having a normal child. Many of these conditions now are detectable in prospective parents and in the fetus.

INFECTIONS

A woman may be exposed to a variety of infections during pregnancy. The most frequent of these is the common cold. A cold is a viral infection, and the usual routine of adequate rest and fluids is also appropriate for a pregnant woman. In addition, your doctor may recommend small doses of an aspirin substitute such as Tylenol because aspirin itself is not considered safe at certain times, and some nonprescription cold remedies contain drugs that may not be safe during pregnancy. You should check with your physician before you take *any* medication.

If you have a bad cough or a fever, you should notify your doctor promptly. What begins as a cold may progress to a more serious infection such as tonsillitis, sinusitis, or pneumonia. These infections are often bacterial and should be treated with antibiotics. Some antibiotics, such as tetracycline and chloramphenicol, should be avoided during pregnancy, but others, such as penicillin and erythromycin, are commonly used without any known side effects to the baby.

Urinary tract infections, such as bladder and kidney infections, may also occur in pregnant women. The symptoms of a bladder infection are burning urination and foul-smelling urine. The symptoms of a kidney infection are low back pain and a high fever. If you have any of these symptoms, notify your doctor promptly. Your urine can be examined microscopically and cultured for bacteria to determine whether you have a urinary infection. A mild infection can usually be treated by an oral antibiotic, but a severe infection may require hospitalization and intravenous antibiotics.

Some infections during pregnancy can cause dangerous side effects to the fetus before birth or to the baby as it passes through the birth canal. These include rubella (German measles), syphilis, gonorrhea, genital herpes, and AIDS. The most serious disease that can be transmitted by an infected mother to her newborn infant is AIDS. (See "Sexually Transmissible Diseases.")

Rubella in a woman during the first three months of pregnancy can cross the placenta and cause congenital rubella syndrome, that is, fetal blindness, deafness, brain damage, growth retardation, or death. Although not every baby whose mother has German measles during early pregnancy develops these abnormalities, the percentage that show some damage is high, perhaps up to 50 percent. After the rubella epidemic of 1964 there were over 20,000 babies born in the United States with congenital rubella syndrome. Because of widespread vaccination against the disease and improved diagnostic techniques, the number of affected babies born has decreased to about 25 a year.

A simple blood test can confirm if a woman is immune to rubella. If she is not immune, she should have an immunization against the infection before she becomes pregnant. Because the vaccine contains a mild strain of live rubella virus, it should be given at least three months before a woman becomes pregnant; it should never be given to a woman who is already pregnant.

Unfortunately, it is not until they have become pregnant that many women realize that they are not immune to rubella. In this case exposure to anyone with the infection must be avoided. If you are not immune to rubella and think that you may have been exposed, notify your doctor so that the appropriate blood tests will be taken to see if you develop the disease. Postpartum rubella immunization should be given to prevent this problem during subsequent pregnancies.

If a pregnant woman is or becomes infected with syphilis, the bacteria can travel through her bloodstream and across the placenta to infect the baby. If she is treated promptly with antibiotics, the baby has a good chance of being completely normal. For this reason blood tests for syphilis are done routinely during pregnancy. If you think you may have been exposed to syphilis after your initial blood test, let your doctor know promptly in order that the test may be repeated and your baby protected.

In the early stages of gonorrhea a woman may notice a foul-smelling yellow vaginal discharge, although often there are no symptoms at all. In early pregnancy the infection may spread into the uterus and the fallopian tubes causing a generalized pelvic infection, which if not treated promptly can cause spontaneous abortion. During the second half of pregnancy, gonorrhea is less likely to spread but may remain in the cervix and infect the baby at delivery.

In the past, babies exposed to gonorrhea while passing through the birth canal often developed gonorrheal eye infections that caused blindness. Today the routine administration of silver nitrate eye drops or penicillin usually prevents blindness.

A third sexually transmitted infection is herpes genitalis. The initial symptoms of this disease may be painful blisters in the genital area, often accompanied by fever and swollen lymph nodes in the groin. Exposure to the virus as the baby passes through the birth canal can lead to severe infection and death. A woman who has herpes genitalis near the end of pregnancy should be delivered by cesarean section before the membranes rupture to prevent exposure of the infant to the infection.

RH DISEASE

Thanks to an immunization process developed in the mid-1960s that prevents an Rh-negative woman whose fetus is Rh-positive from developing Rh antibodies, Rh disease, which can severely affect a fetus, occurs very infrequently.

At your first prenatal visit your blood will be typed to determine whether you are Rh-negative (less than 14 percent of people are) or Rh-positive. If you are Rh-negative, another test will be done to see if you have Rh antibodies. These are rarely present in a first pregnancy. If you do have Rh antibodies, it is because at some time you have been exposed to Rh-positive blood, most likely when you previously had an Rh-positive baby and some of its blood leaked into your circulation when it was born. In medical terminology, if you have Rh antibodies you are said to be "sensitized." If you are sensitized and your fetus is Rh-positive, it is possible that your Rh antibodies can damage the fetus's blood cells, causing it to have hemolytic anemia, brain damage, and other serious problems. Sensitized Rh-negative women need to be tested periodically during pregnancy to see if there are changes in their Rh antibody titres. This can give some indication of whether the fetus has any degree of Rh disease. But periodic examination of the amniotic fluid, obtained by amniocentesis (see below), gives more accurate information about the fetus. If the fetus has Rh disease, intrauterine transfusions and/or early delivery may be necessary. Exchange transfusions may be needed after delivery.

The immunization process referred to above involves giving a blood product called Rhogam (Rh-immune globulin) intramuscularly to all unsensitized Rh-negative women who give birth to an Rh-positive infant. It must be given within 72 hours after delivery and almost always prevents sensitization. Thus, the possibility of Rh disease in subsequent pregnancies is virtually eliminated.

For the same reason, Rhogam is also given to unsensitized Rh-negative women after a spontaneous or induced abortion, an ectopic pregnancy, or an amniocentesis to prevent them from becoming sensitized because the fetal Rh type generally is unknown. Many physicians now give Rhogam to all unsensitized Rh-negative women between the 28th and 32nd week of pregnancy to prevent the rare case of sensitization during pregnancy. Once an Rh-negative woman has been sensitized, Rhogam is of no value.

INTRAUTERINE FETAL DEATH

Sometimes for no apparent reason in a normal, uncomplicated pregnancy the fetus will die. Fortunately, this is an uncommon occurrence. A mother may notice that the baby has stopped moving. An examination by her doctor will fail to detect a fetal heart beat, and other tests, such as X-rays or sonograms (see discussion of fetal health below), may confirm that an intrauterine fetal death has occurred.

In the past after such a diagnosis the woman was sent home to wait for labor to begin spontaneously, which might take as long as a month or two. With better labor-inducing medications available today, labor is often induced shortly after the diagnosis of intrauterine fetal death.

After delivery (stillbirth) the fetus is examined to determine the cause of death. The umbilical cord may be wrapped tightly around the fetus's neck or may be knotted. It may be abnormal or there may have been a problem with the placenta. However, in a significant number of cases no cause at all is found. You should ask your doctor if there is any evidence that the cause of death might be repeated if you become pregnant again. Fortunately, these problems usually do not recur and subsequent pregnancies generally result in normal healthy babies.

HYDATIDIFORM MOLE

Another complication of pregnancy is hydatidiform mole (also called molar pregnancy). It is not common in the United States, occurring in approximately 1 out of 2,000 pregnancies. It is more common elsewhere, for example occurring as frequently as 1 out of 125 pregnancies in Taiwan.

Early in pregnancy the placenta becomes a "tumor" with the appearance of a large cluster of grapes. Usually no fetus develops. Though usually benign, a hydatidiform mole has the potential for becoming malignant. In early pregnancy there may be no unusual symptoms. Eventually, it may be diagnosed by bleeding and passage of characteristic tissue, by an abnormally large or small uterus with no fetal heart beat, or by X-ray studies.

Hydatidiform mole is usually removed by a dilatation and curettage or a suction curettage. If it occurs in a woman who has completed her family, hysterectomy may be recommended. Because the hydatidiform mole produces pregnancy hormones, any remaining growth or a recurrence can be detected by blood or urine pregnancy tests. Such tests are taken on a regular basis for 9 to 12 months or longer following removal to make sure that the condition does not recur or become malignant. If frequent testing reveals a recurrence or a malignant change, it is treatable and almost always curable by chemotherapy. In many women future pregnancies are still possible even after chemotherapy and a suitable waiting period to ensure there is no recurrence.

EVALUATING FETAL HEALTH

Among the many advances that have occurred in the field of obstetrics over the past few decades are the techniques for studying the fetus before birth: amniocentesis, sonography, fetal monitoring, and the alpha protein test. More recent advances include chorionic villi sampling, detection of additional genetic flaws, and—the latest and most exciting —a technique first used in France in 1983 and now available in a few medical centers in the United States that enables doctors to evaluate, treat, and give blood transfusions to a fetus while it is still in the uterus.

SONOGRAPHY

A new technique that has been used with increasing frequency over the last few years is ultrasound, or sonography. This procedure produces an image on a screen (sonogram) by bouncing sound waves through the abdomen. It locates the fetus in a manner similar to radar locating a submarine. While this test is painless and does not expose the fetus to X-rays, it should not be performed routinely nor should it be used to satisfy curiosity about the sex of the offspring or merely to view the fetus. Sonography is appropriate when the doctor wishes to make an accurate diagnosis of an abnormality in the progress of the pregnancy. For that purpose, it might be recommended in about one-third of all cases.

About one-third of all obstetricians have sonography equipment in their offices, and it is also available in the radiology departments of most hospitals.

AMNIOCENTESIS

Various fetal chromosomal abnormalities and certain fetal diseases can be detected by testing amniotic fluid obtained by a procedure called amniocentesis. The procedure is fairly simple. A sonogram is obtained to determine the location of the placenta, and the lower abdomen is cleaned with an antiseptic solution. A local anesthetic is given, and a long, thin needle is inserted through the abdominal and uterine walls (avoiding the placenta) into the amniotic sac. Amniotic fluid is then removed with a syringe. This procedure can be done only by a specially trained person.

The risks of amniocentesis include infection, injury to the fetus or the placenta, Rh-sensitization, leakage of amniotic fluid, and bleeding. Some of these complications may lead to fetal death. In expert hands the overall complication rate of amniocentesis is less than 1 percent.

A common reason for doing an amniocentesis is to determine whether the fetus is genetically normal (genetic amniocentesis). This generally is done as soon as possible after the sixteenth week of pregnancy. Fetal cells that are in the fluid are cultured and then examined for chromosomal abnormalities, especially for Down syndrome. New data reveals that Down syndrome (technically called Trisomy 21 after the number assigned to the abnormal chromosome) increases steadily with age rather than rising dramatically at age 35. Because it is now known that the statistical curve is continuous, amniocentesis has become an accepted procedure. In New York State, for example, the number of pregnant women under 35 undergoing amniocentesis nearly tripled between 1979 and 1982. The role of the father's age in the Down syndrome statistics is uncertain, but it is possible that it is a factor as well. Amniocentesis should be considered by all pregnant women over 34 years of age, and perhaps younger, who would consider abortion if the fetus has this genetic defect.

Amniotic fluid is tested for other reasons too. These include managing pregnancies with Rh problems, diagnosing fetal open neural tube defects, and assessing fetal lung maturity when premature delivery is anticipated. A baby born with immature lungs requires very special pediatric care. Amniocentesis is done occasionally to remove part of amniotic fluid when, for some reason, there is an excessive amount of it.

CHORIONIC VILLI SAMPLING

A new method of early prenatal diagnosis that is simpler and quicker than amniocentesis and can be done as early as the 9th week of pregnancy is known as chorionic villi sampling. Whereas amniocentesis involves withdrawing of the amniotic fluid by way of a hollow needle that penetrates the mother's abdominal wall, this newer method withdraws a sample of the chorion villus (the membrane that surrounds the fetus and eventually becomes the placenta) and removes the sample through the cervix or through a needle stuck in the lower abdomen.

Ongoing research about the safety of this procedure is being conducted by the National Institute of Child Health and Human Development with the participation of major medical centers nationwide. Results are expected to be published in 1991, and if it should prove as safe as amniocentesis, chorionic villi sampling will replace the older method of prenatal assessment. The fact that it can be done so early in pregnancy means that if, because of genetic defects, abortion is the choice, abortion would be that much safer. Although this test is being chosen increasingly, it is still not FDA approved and, therefore, considered an experimental procedure.

ALPHA-FETO PROTEIN ASSESSMENT

Alpha-feto protein (AFP) is produced by every fetus and is present in both its amniotic fluid and its mother's blood. If the AFP level in the latter is abnormally high (positive test) around the fourth month of pregnancy and, when repeated, is also positive, it may mean that the fetus has an open neural tube defect (an incomplete closure of the neural tube around the spinal cord or brain). It may also mean that there are twins or that the fetus is older than it was thought to be. In any event, sonography is then done, and if it does not verify the possibility of an open neural tube defect, an amniocentesis is done, and its AFP measured. If it is positive (high), there is a 90 percent chance that the fetus has an open neural tube defect. In the United States, 1–2 out of 1,000 babies have a neural tube defect (NTD). Couples with a family or personal history of NTD are at some increased risk of having an NTD baby and certainly should have the AFP blood test. But, because only 5 percent of all NTD babies have a parent with such a history, couples without such a history also may desire the test that, although not conclusive, requires no more than a blood sample for assessment. Also, a very low AFP measurement may indicate an increased risk of chromosomal abnormality such as Down syndrome and may indicate the need for further testing to rule out such a disorder.

AMNIOCENTESIS IN EIGHTEENTH WEEK

- Needle withdrawing amniotic fluid
- Pubic bone
- Bladder (emptied)
- Uterus
- Fetus
- Amniotic sac

SELECTED CHROMOSOME PAIRS FROM AMNIOTIC FLUID

| NORMAL | SOME ABNORMAL CHROMOSOMES |

SEX CHROMOSOMES

Female XX

Turner's syndrome

Trisomy X

Male XY

Klinefelter's syndrome

AUTOSOMES

Pair 21

Trisomy 21 or mongolism

PRENATAL DNA STUDIES

Until comparatively recently, the genetic diseases detectable by DNA studies of the fetus numbered about 50, including sickle cell anemia, Tay Sachs, and Down syndrome. Since 1985 it has become possible through these studies to detect hemophilia, cystic fibrosis, and muscular dystrophy. The studies are not only very expensive, but the investigators must know in advance which disease is being looked for. Only a few laboratories nationwide are equipped to perform prenatal DNA tests, but those parents-to-be who can afford the expense and who want reassurance about the health of the fetus should know that this option exists.

OTHER PROCEDURES FOR PRENATAL DIAGNOSIS

Fetoscopy is still an experimental procedure, usable in the second trimester, to make prenatal diagnoses of hemoglobinopathies and coagulation defects. It involves passing a small-caliber fetoscope through the abdominal wall into the uterus.

One of the most promising developments in prenatal assessment enables doctors to thread a needle into the tiny blood vessels of the umbilical cord and use the needle to withdraw fetal blood samples as well as to inject drugs into the fetus or to supply blood transfusions. This procedure has already revolutionized the treatment of fetuses with Rh disease and is expected to find a way of testing fetuses for infection with the AIDS virus that occurs in about forty percent of the offspring of AIDS-infected mothers.

FETAL MONITORS

Many hospitals now have fetal monitors that record the fetal heartbeat and contractions of the uterus during labor. In some hospitals monitors are used for all patients in labor; others have monitors only for patients who have a higher than normal risk of developing complications.

Fetal monitors can be attached either externally or internally. In external monitoring the monitor is placed on the mother's abdomen by means of adjustable bands. In internal monitoring a wire is inserted through the vagina and attached to the fetal head. A catheter may also be inserted through the vagina into the amniotic sac adjacent to the fetus.

The use of a fetal monitor should not prevent the mother-to-be from finding a comfortable position in labor whether that be sitting or lying on her back or side. Although some women do not like the idea of being attached to a machine, it is important to realize that the valuable information obtained in this way may protect the life of the baby, and many women are reassured to be able to "see" the baby's heartbeat on the monitor during labor.

Monitors are used to test for, among other things, abnormalities in the fetal heart rate. For example, a drop in the fetal heart rate may signal that the fetus is not receiving adequate levels of oxygen because of an abnormal decrease in blood flowing to the baby during contractions. The decrease might be caused by a twisted or knotted umbilical cord. This problem can sometimes be improved by changing the position of the mother or by giving her oxygen.

Monitoring may also be used for patients who are not in labor if the pregnancy is complicated, if the baby is overdue, or if the mother has a medical problem. For example, a fetal monitor can be used to perform the nonstress test (NST), which determines whether the baby's heartbeat accelerates after the baby kicks or moves. A temporary increase in the fetal heart rate after movement is an indication that the baby is in satisfactory condition.

If this test is also nonreactive, a contraction stress test (CST) is done, again using a fetal monitor. Mild contractions are started by stimulation of the mother's nipples or by injection of a dilute intravenous solution of oxytocin, the hormone that is released by the body during labor. A healthy fetus will exhibit a stable heart rate during and after the contractions. On the other hand, a decrease in the fetal heart rate following the contractions may indicate that the fetus is not receiving sufficient oxygen.

Another fairly recent test now performed in some large medical centers finds out if a baby is receiving sufficient oxygen by actually taking a sample of the baby's blood. This test, called a scalp pH, is usually done only during labor and only if the membranes are ruptured. It may be performed if fetal heartbeat abnormalities are noted or if there are other reasons to believe that the baby may not be receiving adequate oxygen. In a manner similar to the way a blood sample is obtained by sticking a finger with a lance, a small puncture is made in the baby's scalp and a few drops of blood are drawn into a capillary tube. The pH of the blood indicates the amount of oxygen being received.

If these tests indicate that the baby is in jeopardy and delivery is not imminent, it will be necessary to induce labor or to deliver the baby by cesarean section. These tests have undoubtedly prevented the deaths of some babies who would not have lived if prompt action had not been taken.

LABOR AND DELIVERY

Normally labor and subsequent delivery occur 38 to 40 weeks (gestational age) after the start of the last normal menstrual period (a term birth). (This is 36–38 weeks after conception, but this time reference is rarely used.) Labor that occurs before 37 completed weeks of gestation is considered to be premature or pre-term labor. The mechanisms responsible for the onset of labor at any time are not well identified. Premature labor is more likely to occur when a woman has more than one fetus; has a serious obstetrical condition (pre-eclampsia, placental bleeding); has chronic liver, heart, or kidney disease; or has experienced a serious trauma, either physical or emotional. In most instances, however, there is no well-understood explanation. Premature delivery may also be caused by an incompetent or "weak" cervix, a relatively rare condition.

The problem about premature labor is that it may lead to the premature birth of an underdeveloped premature infant whose chance of survival or of being normal is reduced. The earlier the birth and the more underdeveloped the infant, the smaller the chance. These babies should be cared for in a hospital's intensive care nursery and if possible be born in that hospital rather than transported there after birth.

There is a great need to learn more about what causes premature-labor so that efforts can be made to prevent it. Sometimes it is possible, particularly if the membranes have not ruptured, to arrest it with various pharmacologic agents and to postpone the birth by days or weeks so that the fetus can develop further prior to birth. However, premature birth usually follows premature labor.

Labor that occurs after 42 or more completed weeks of gestation is postmature (post-term) labor. After this time, if the dates are certain, the fetus is usually better off in a nursery than in the uterus, and consideration may be given to inducing labor.

NATURAL CHILDBIRTH

Natural childbirth has become quite popular in the United States over the last few years. Its popularity began after Grantly Dick-Read wrote *Childbirth Without Fear* in 1944. He wrote that labor pain could be eliminated by education in the process of labor and delivery. Despite the substantial contribution of this new theory, it soon became apparent that Dick-Read was not entirely correct, because even with extensive knowledge about labor and delivery many women still felt pain.

The next step in the popularity of natural childbirth was the Lamaze or psychoprophylactic technique. Psychoprophylaxis is the psychological and physical preparation for childbirth. This technique originated in Russia and was brought to France by Dr. Ferdinand Lamaze in the early 1950s. Its popularity in the United States followed the publication in 1959 of *Thank You Dr. Lamaze* by Marjorie Karmel, an American woman who became familiar with the Lamaze technique during her pregnancy in France.

The Lamaze technique combines education about labor and delivery with breathing and relaxation exercises. The exercises must be practiced in the months and weeks prior to labor. The partner has an important role as coach. Using the Lamaze breathing techniques, many women are able to go through labor needing little or no medication. Though a purist may insist that a true Lamaze birth means no medication at all, many people believe that the concept is broad enough to include the use of a small amount of medication to relieve pain.

With my observations as an obstetrician and as a woman who has experienced labor, I feel that the Lamaze technique has something to offer to every pregnant woman. I believe that the knowledge of what is happening to your body in labor and delivery can reduce your apprehension and fear and, therefore, reduce the pain of your labor. I also feel that the Lamaze breathing and relaxation techniques reduce, though not necessarily eliminate, the need for medication in labor.

STAGES OF LABOR

MID-FIRST STAGE
- Placenta
- Bladder
- Pubic bone
- Birth canal (vagina)
- Cervix thinned out
- Rectum
- Uterine wall
- Sacral bone
- Coccyx

MID-SECOND STAGE
- Cervix
- Head in birth canal

MID-THIRD STAGE
- Contracting uterus
- Placenta
- Cord

FIRST STAGE OF LABOR—DILATATION OF THE CERVIX

No two labors are alike. Labor may be long and difficult or it may be short and uncomplicated. Unfortunately, there is no way to predict what your labor will be like or how you will respond to it. When labor begins, you may feel the contractions as mild cramps or they may be very uncomfortable. As labor progresses, the contractions become stronger and more frequent. In active labor the contractions usually occur about every 2 to 3 minutes and last from 45 to 90 seconds. Usually the membranes rupture spontaneously either before or during labor, but if they do not, they are ruptured artificially before the delivery.

The cervix, the lowermost portion of the uterus, must open so that the baby may be born. During most of pregnancy the cervix is firm, thick, and long, with only a very small opening in the center. Late in pregnancy the cervix becomes softer, thinner, and may begin to open before the onset of labor. When labor begins, the changes in the cervix take place much more rapidly. The contractions of the uterus push the baby's head against the cervix and cause it to open. In order for the baby to be born, the cervix must be fully dilated to 10 centimeters (about 4 inches).

The first stage of labor is the time from the onset of labor to the time when the cervix is fully dilated. The length of this stage of labor varies greatly from woman to woman. It averages 8 to 12 hours in most women having their first child, but it can be much shorter or much longer. In subsequent pregnancies it is usually shorter.

Near the end of the first stage of labor, when the cervix is almost fully dilated, the contractions are usually quite strong and the woman begins to feel the urge to push with them. This part of labor is called transition. After complete dilation, with pushing and the force of the contractions the baby descends in the pelvis, usually turning to the most favorable position as it descends.

It is sometimes necessary to induce labor instead of waiting for it to start spontaneously. For example, if the mother develops severe pre-eclampsia or has diabetes, if the baby is long overdue, if fetal monitoring indicates that the baby's life is in jeopardy, or if labor does not begin spontaneously after the membranes rupture, labor may have to be induced. In some cases it is induced by the artificial rupture of membranes. In most cases an infusion of a solution of pitocin (oxytocin), which causes the uterus to contract, is necessary. Intravenous pitocin may also be administered to stimulate spontaneous labor that is progressing very slowly. This solution is given intravenously in gradually increasing amounts. Induced labor may be both faster and stronger than spontaneous labor.

ANESTHESIA

A difficult and painful labor may require some anesthesia or analgesia. Anesthesia may also be required for medical reasons or for a forceps delivery.

The most commonly used medications for labor are pain-killing drugs such as Demerol. With small doses many women are less uncomfortable but still wide awake and able to participate in and enjoy the delivery of their child. However, some women find that even small doses of these medications make them drowsy or nauseated.

Epidural anesthesia involves the insertion of a needle in the mother's back and the injection of a novocaine-type drug into the space next to the spinal canal. An epidural will normally eliminate pain from approximately your waist to your toes and will make it difficult to move your legs. This technique allows you to be completely awake but free from pain. Caudal anesthesia is similar to an epidural but the needle is inserted at a point much lower on your back.

Epidural or caudal anesthesia requires a specially trained anesthesiologist and is not available at all hospitals. These anesthetics do not always work perfectly and they may have undesirable side effects. Some women are numbed on only one side of their body or not at all. Sometimes this type of anesthesia can cause the contractions to become less frequent and it often interferes with the mother's urge to push during the second stage of labor. By lowering the mother's blood pressure, epidural or caudal anesthesia can even cause a temporary slowing of the baby's heartbeat.

Unlike epidural or caudal anesthesia, which can be used to provide pain relief during labor, spinal anesthesia is used to provide relief only for delivery. Saddle block is a type of spinal anesthesia. A needle is inserted into the mother's back and the medication is injected into the space that contains the spinal fluid. Under spinal anesthesia most women are completely numbed from their waist to their toes. When spinal anesthesia is given for a cesarean section, the numbness usually extends to the lower part of the mother's ribcage. The numbness may last for several hours after delivery depending on the type of anesthetic used and the individual's sensitivity to it. A small percentage of women may have a severe headache for several days after spinal anesthesia.

Local anesthetics can be used in various ways during labor and delivery to provide pain relief. Paracervical block is the injection of local anesthetic into the tissue adjacent to the cervix during labor. Pudendal block involves the numbing of the nerves that supply the lower vagina and perineum (the space between the vagina and the rectum). This technique is often used in order to perform a forceps delivery. Finally, local anesthesia may be injected directly into an area where an episiotomy is to be cut or a tear is to be repaired.

SECOND STAGE OF LABOR—DELIVERY

The second stage of labor extends from full dilatation to the delivery of the baby. The length of this stage also varies. It may last two hours or more with the first baby but is usually much shorter in subsequent pregnancies.

In a typical United States hospital delivery you are taken from the labor room to the delivery room and put in the lithotomy position (on your back with your legs in stirrups as for a pelvic examination). In other countries the mother's normal position for delivery may be on her side or in a squatting position. The area around the vagina is washed off with an antiseptic solution and cloth or paper drapes are placed over your abdomen and legs.

If an episiotomy is necessary, it will be done after the top of the baby's head becomes visible. An episiotomy is an incision made in the perineum to expand the vaginal opening to allow the baby to be born without extensive stretching or tearing of the muscles and tissues in this area. Some physicians and midwives believe that an episiotomy should be performed as infrequently as possible because it's not always necessary and may be uncomfortable. Others believe that it should be done in most cases to avoid the stretching and tearing. In countries where episiotomies are seldom used, there is an increased incidence of protrusions of the bladder or rectum into the vagina in older women who have had several children. This problem is thought to be related to the damage to the tissues that sometimes occurs if no episiotomy is done. However, many women who deliver without an episiotomy do not have this problem. Much depends on the strength and flexibility of your muscles and tissues and the size of your baby. (The hormone relaxin, secreted by the corpus luteum and available in synthetic form, can facilitate delivery by causing the relaxation of the pelvic ligaments and widening the birth canal, thus playing a significant role in the avoidance of cesarean births.)

The first part of the baby to emerge is usually its head. Then the shoulders are delivered and the rest of the body slips out easily. After emerging, the baby will take a first breath and cry a first cry. When the baby begins breathing, oxygen is received through the lungs rather than through the placenta and the umbilical cord. At this time the cord is clamped and cut.

There is no need to become alarmed if forceps are used to assist in the delivery of your baby. Forceps are metal instruments, shaped somewhat like a pair of large spoons, which fit against the sides of the baby's head and are used to guide it through the birth canal. Marks commonly caused by the forceps may remain on the baby's cheeks for several days and are not indicative of any problem. Forceps are often used if an emergency delivery is necessary as in the case of "fetal distress" or bleeding. However, if these problems occur early in labor, before the cervix is fully dilated, a cesarean section may be necessary. Sometimes forceps are used because the mother is too exhausted to push the baby out or because the baby's head is tilted in a position that makes spontaneous delivery very difficult. Some doctors believe that premature babies should always be delivered with forceps to protect the head from the pressure of the birth canal.

A device sometimes used as a substitute for forceps is a vacuum extractor, a plastic or metal suction cup that is placed over the baby's head to guide it through the vagina. While a vacuum extractor does not leave marks on the baby's cheeks, it may leave a temporary swelling or bruising of the top of the head.

Recently some hospitals have modified the environment provided for labor and delivery. In some places routine deliveries may be done in a bed rather than on a delivery table. In other places the delivery room is darkened and soft music played. In still others an attempt is made to give the delivery room a more homelike atmosphere by the installation of curtains, carpeting, and pictures. Such rooms are called birthing rooms. Generally only women who have uncomplicated pregnancies and wish to deliver without anesthesia are permitted to give birth in a birthing room. One or two support persons (visitors) are encouraged to be with her through labor, delivery, and recovery. In many places, in fact, a support person is permitted to be present in a regular delivery room, even during a cesarean section. In a delivery technique called a Leboyer delivery, lights and noise are kept to a minimum, the child is placed on the mother's abdomen for several minutes before the umbilical cord is clamped, and the baby is promptly given a bath in warm water. This technique was devised to try to ease the trauma of the newborn's entry into the world. However, there is no scientific evidence that this approach has any beneficial effect.

THIRD STAGE OF LABOR—AFTERBIRTH

The third stage of labor involves the delivery of the placenta. Usually within a few minutes after the delivery of the baby the placenta separates itself from the wall of the uterus and is expelled. After this point the episiotomy or any tears are repaired. Dissolving sutures are usually used; there are no stitches to be removed.

CESAREAN SECTION

Cesarean section is the delivery of a baby through an incision in the abdominal and uterine walls. General anesthesia may be used or the mother may remain awake with either spinal or epidural anesthesia.

In recent years there has been a strong and outspoken reaction against the increase in cesarean deliveries. In 1986, approximately 906,000 such deliveries were performed, representing about 21.4 percent of total births. Many experts are convinced that at least half of these were unnecessary. (The United States stands first in the rate of cesarean deliveries.) Taking note of the fact that this rate has quadrupled since 1970, Dr. Warren Pearce, executive director of the American College of Obstetrics and Gynecology, agreed that the rate should be no higher than 12 to 16 births out of every hundred. He also noted that it was by no means always necessary to repeat the cesarean procedure if it was used once before. These repeat performances are among the main cause of the swelling in the statistics. Other contributing factors include an overdiagnosis of abnormal labor and fetal distress (an overdiagnosis partly caused by the ever-present possibility of a malpractice suit), and the fact that the procedure is more convenient and considerably more profitable both to doctor and hospital.

Informed critics point out that the substitution of cesarean sectioning for normal labor can increase the risk of illness or death for the mother in addition to leaving her with an incalculable psychological burden. As for the increase in cost, whereas a normal birth requires a hospital stay of no more than three days, a cesarean birth can involve a stay three times as long.

A woman who is told during pregnancy that a prenatal diagnosis indicates the need for cesarean delivery would be wise to seek a second opinion, and women who have had one such delivery should not assume or be led to believe that a second one is inevitable. In the considered opinion of the most informed members of the profession, this point of view is completely outdated.

There are two types of skin incisions used for cesarean deliveries: a vertical incision from the navel to the pubic hairline or a horizontal ("bikini") incision near the top of the pubic hairline. A vertical incision may be necessary if the cesarean delivery is an emergency, if the baby is very large or in an abnormal position, or if the patient is obese. In other cases either type may be used, although many physicians have been trained to use predominantly one type of skin incision or the other.

The various layers of the abdominal wall are carefully opened until the uterus is exposed. In most cases a horizontal incision is then made in the lower part of the uterus and the baby is delivered. The uterus is then carefully repaired and the abdominal wall is closed.

Cesarean section may be necessary if the baby is in a position that makes vaginal delivery difficult or potentially dangerous. For example, 4 percent of all babies are in the breech position (either buttocks or feet first) at the end of pregnancy. The baby's head is the largest part of the baby that must pass through the mother's pelvic bones. When a baby is born head first, the head has a chance to elongate and thus decrease in diameter in order to pass through the pelvic bones. When the baby is breech, the head does not have a chance to accommodate itself to the mother's pelvic bones, and some babies born breech suffer permanent damage. For this reason many doctors now advise a cesarean section in all cases of breech babies unless there is specific evidence that the mother's pelvic bones are large enough to accommodate the baby's

POSITIONS OF THE FETUS

VERTEX (95%)

BREECH (4%)

TRANSVERSE (1%).

head. The evidence of adequate pelvic bones could come either from the history of a previous delivery of a large baby, from a physician's examination of the mother and fetus, or from pelvic X-rays. Even if the pelvis is large, other factors involving the position of the breech baby's arms or legs may influence the physician to recommend a cesarean section.

A position that makes vaginal delivery impossible is a transverse lie (across the pelvic opening, neither the head nor buttocks down). Unless the baby can be turned into a normal position, it cannot be born vaginally and must be delivered by cesarean section.

Sometimes a cesarean section must be done for the safety of the mother. If the mother has severe pre-eclampsia, severe high blood pressure may be life-threatening to her. If labor cannot be quickly induced, a cesarean section may have to be done. Similarly, any danger to your baby, as evidenced by a drop in the baby's heart rate, may cause your doctor to recommend a cesarean section.

After a cesarean section, you will probably be in the hospital for at least a week. As with most abdominal operations, you will receive intravenous fluids for a few days. Moving around will be difficult, but forcing yourself to get up and walk will probably speed your recovery. You will need more rest than if you had a vaginal delivery. Not only is your body going through the adjustment of getting back to a nonpregnant state, but it must also recover from a major abdominal operation.

AFTER THE DELIVERY

Your baby has been born and you are probably elated. You hold your baby in amazement at this new life. But labor has been aptly named and you have been working very hard and are exhausted. You very likely have missed a night's sleep and you will probably sleep soundly for a few hours after the baby is born. Meanwhile your baby will be in a nursery being evaluated and cared for by a pediatrician and nurses. New babies should have a full physical examination to check for congenital or genetic problems and possible infections. A few days later babies should have a blood test to evaluate their thyroid function and to see if they have phenylketonuria (PKU). If either test is positive, proper treatment can prevent major future problems. Babies born to mothers with diseases such as diabetes or hepatitis B or who are taking certain medications need to be evaluated for any related problems.

ROOMING-IN

Many hospitals have made "rooming-in" available to mothers. Perhaps you have just had a baby girl. Rooming-in allows you to be with her, care for her, feed her, bathe her, and change her under the supervision of the hospital's nursing staff. Some hospitals offer a modified rooming-in where you can take your baby during the day but have her cared for in the nursery at night. Others allow you to rest for the first day or two before you take the baby both day and night. The baby is usually taken out of the room when you have visitors.

If you are at all apprehensive about caring for your new baby, rooming-in provides excellent practice with trained people to answer your questions and to give you assistance. Recent experimental evidence, mostly from animal studies, seems to show that prolonged early contact between mother and child (called bonding) may be beneficial to the health and well-being of both mother and child. Rooming-in allows more contact between mother and child during these important early days.

However, you should consider your feelings and physical condition after the delivery. When you leave the hospital, you will be returning to your care of the household with the additional attention and energy the baby requires. If you're very tired and want to take advantage of your days in the hospital to recover your strength, rooming-in is not essential.

HOSPITAL VISITORS

Well-meaning friends and relatives want to visit mother and baby as soon as possible, and if it weren't for hospital rules, the lying-in room would be mobbed from morning to night. A new mother should make sure there's a phone at her bedside not only so that she can keep in touch with the world but also to have a tactful way of discouraging unwanted visits and postponing them until after homecoming.

If you're pregnant with your second child, it's a good idea to find out in advance of delivery what policy the hospital imposes on visits by

PREGNANCY AND CHILDBIRTH 241

children who want to see the new family member. Many hospitals now allow young children to enter the maternity floor, but most don't permit them to get any closer than the glass partition outside the nursery.

THE "BABY BLUES"

After the first day or two of excitement, many women experience some form of postpartum depression, the "baby blues." Many things contribute to it—the letdown after nine months of anticipating the birth, hormonal changes accompanying the start of the flow of milk, fatigue from labor, anxiety about the realities of having a baby who needs taking care of. This depression is usually very short-lived—a few bouts of tears and you are on your way home.

However, this depression may recur periodically in the first few months after birth as your body continues to make major adjustments in returning to the nonpregnant state, as you deal with your new role and activities, especially if it is a first child, and as you simply go through the physical stress of not having an uninterrupted night's sleep. Again, the depression usually passes quickly. But if the depression persists or if you're increasingly upset by the constant crying and your nerves are ragged because of constant loss of sleep, it is extremely important for your well-being and the building of a satisfactory relationship with the baby *not* to deny your feelings of anger and frustration and *not* to keep trying to suppress your feelings of irritation with the baby because the feelings produce so much guilt. Better by far to deal with the negative feelings, air them, and accept the need for help and support. In such circumstances, don't let anyone make light of your anxieties. Speak to your doctor about your agitated state and ask for a recommendation of a therapist and a support group until you can face the day-in, day-out stress of parenting without feeling overwhelmed.

PHYSICAL RECOVERY

After delivery you will have vaginal bleeding. The blood comes from the uterus and is called lochia. Lochia will be heavy and bright red for the first few days after delivery. Thereafter, the flow decreases but may persist as a brown staining lasting for several weeks. If you are breast feeding, there may be an increase in bleeding at feeding time. You may also feel cramps during feedings. You may feel your uterus as a firm grapefruit-sized or larger mass in your lower abdomen. The uterus will return to almost normal size within a month.

If you do not nurse, your first menstrual period may come in six to eight weeks, although it may be delayed for several months. If you do nurse, your first menstrual period will normally be later. Some women have no menses while they nurse; others resume having menstrual periods after four to six months.

The return of fertility is also unpredictable. Some women ovulate within a month after delivery and before their first menstrual period; in others the return to the normal ovulating cycle takes much longer. Although breast feeding may reduce your chances of becoming pregnant, you should not count on this alone to prevent pregnancy. Many women ovulate and become pregnant while nursing. Whether you are nursing or not, if you do not wish to have another baby right away it is important to use some form of contraception as soon as you resume having sexual relations. Most physicians recommend waiting at least two weeks before resuming sexual relations. Some recommend waiting until after the postpartum checkup, four to six weeks after delivery. At this time most women who are not breast feeding are over any effects of their pregnancy.

If you have had an episiotomy you may find the stitches uncomfortable for the first day or two, and you may be given a mild pain medication. The pain gradually decreases, although it may last for several days or weeks. Pain with sexual intercourse may last for several months after the episiotomy is healed. Conscious tightening and relaxation of the perineal muscles surrounding the episiotomy will help healing and will also decrease the pain of the episiotomy. This exercise also helps a normal tone to return to these muscles.

Hemorrhoids are varicose veins in the rectal area and are very common in pregnant women, even those who have no evidence of varicose veins in any other place. They develop during pregnancy because of the pressure on the veins from the growing uterus and are aggravated by the constipation that is common in pregnancy. Hemorrhoids often worsen at the end of pregnancy and during labor. In the first few days after delivery you may need an anesthetic cream to help reduce the discomfort. Fortunately, in most women hemorrhoids disappear or become asymptomatic within a few months after delivery.

Some women experience difficulty in urination after delivery. The

PREGNANCY AND CHILDBIRTH

baby's head presses against the bladder while moving through the birth canal and this pressure can result in a decrease in the normal sensation in this area for a time after delivery. Anesthetics used in labor and delivery can also decrease the sensation of the bladder. The reduced sensation can cause difficulty in control of urination or difficulty in knowing when the bladder is full. Sensation and control gradually return to normal after delivery.

If you weigh yourself on the day after delivery, you will probably find that you have lost only about 12 to 16 pounds. The weight gained in pregnancy is more than just the weight of the baby, the placenta, and the amniotic fluid. For example, the breasts normally increase by about 1 pound, blood volume increase accounts for about $3^{1}/_{2}$ pounds, and the uterus increases by $2^{1}/_{2}$ pounds. The mother's body also retains fluid and a small amount of fat is deposited. Most mothers shed an additional 5 pounds in the first two weeks after delivery. Mothers who nurse use up some of the additional fat that has been deposited during pregnancy; mothers who do not nurse may have to go on a more restrictive diet than nursing mothers in order to return to their normal prepregnancy weight.

The stretch marks (striae) that may have developed on your abdomen or breasts will gradually fade but will not disappear completely. In spite of many available ointments and home remedies, there is no prevention or cure for a stretch mark.

BREAST-FEEDING

During pregnancy the glands in your breasts develop in order to produce milk after the baby is born. During the last few months there may be leakage of a small amount of colostrum, a thin yellow fluid. Shortly after delivery the amount of colostrum increases substantially, and colostrum is the only food that breast-fed babies receive during the first few days of their life. On the third or fourth postpartum day, production of milk begins. The amount of milk that is produced depends on the amount of stimulation and sucking by the baby. The repeated emptying of the breasts increases the milk supply to meet the needs of a growing baby.

Breast milk is the ideal food for a baby. The Committee on Nutrition of the American Academy of Pediatrics recommends that every mother breast-feed her baby unless there is a specific medical reason why she cannot. Among the many benefits are the following:

- The baby's nutritional needs are more closely satisfied by breast milk.
- Antibodies in the milk confer important immunities on the baby.
- Breast-fed babies are less likely to become overweight.
- Allergies are less likely to develop.
- Nursing contributes to better tooth and mouth development.
- The hormones produced in nursing help in the contraction of the uterus.
- Weight is lost more easily after the delivery.
- Bonding between mother and infant is achieved more naturally.

Every woman who thinks she might be interested in breast-feeding should give it a try. Almost all women who really want to can do so if given the proper support and encouragement. You can nail down this support in advance, if some time toward the end of pregnancy you arrange to meet the doctor who will be your baby's pediatrician and make sure that an understanding is reached *before* delivery about your intention to breast-feed the baby. If for one reason or another you sense the doctor's disapproval, find a more sympathetic pediatrician. It is also extremely important that you have a similar discussion with your obstetrician. The nursery nurses must be told in advance of delivery that you plan to breast-feed your baby, and, therefore, the baby will have to be brought to you regularly for this purpose as often as necessary during your hospital stay. The importance of establishing this understanding cannot be overemphasized. What happens in many nurseries is that new babies are routinely formula-fed, so that when the baby is brought to the mother for "feeding," it may not be at all interested because it is not at all hungry, thus defeating the mother's original intentions and causing considerable disappointment.

The good nutritional habits of pregnancy must be continued during breast-feeding. Most women require more calories each day during nursing than they did during pregnancy as well as an even higher liquid intake, especially of milk. Special caution must be exercised about the risks of various medications and the need to abstain from spicy foods whose flavors might come through in the milk causing it to be unpalatable to the infant (garlic is a known offender).

Breast infections are not uncommon in nursing mothers, but if promptly treated they need not be serious. A breast infection may result from a clogged milk duct or from a small crack in the nipple. The infected breast is hot and tender to touch, and the woman may have a fever or feel weak and generally ill. Notify your physician promptly if you have any evidence of a breast infection. Usually antibiotics can be given and nursing can continue when the infection improves. If the infection is not treated soon enough, an abscess may develop (a localized collection of pus in the breast). An abscess may respond to antibiotics or may require surgical drainage. Even after this complication breast-feeding may be continued if desired.

One of the most difficult problems for a breast-feeding mother is not knowing the amount of milk that her baby is receiving. In the early weeks of life babies often cry for unexplained reasons. The bottle-feeding mother knows how much formula the baby took at the last feeding and can feel with confidence that hunger is not the problem. A breast-feeding mother may worry that the baby is hungry and that her milk supply is inadequate. These doubts may lead her to substitute a bottle at the next feeding or give a supplementary bottle. The baby then nurses less and as a result her milk supply is decreased. If a mother's milk production is insufficient, continued stimulation by frequent nursing will usually increase the supply. It is important to remember that for thousands of years before infant formulas were available, all babies were raised on breast milk alone.

Alternatively, many women prefer and enjoy the many advantages of bottle-feeding their babies. Perhaps they are planning to return to work in a short time or they are afraid that they will be tied down. To some mothers the idea of breast-feeding is simply not appealing. If you feel this way, it is better to make your choice and abide with it. A woman who breast-feeds only because her friends or doctor have urged her to do so is rarely successful.

If you decide not to breast-feed, you will experience a few days of discomfort from about the third to sixth day after delivery. Your breasts may feel full and may leak a small amount of milk. Your breasts should be tightly bound to maintain pressure on them in order to decrease the production of milk and to relieve the discomfort that you may experience. If the breasts are not emptied, the production of milk ceases and the milk already in the breasts is eventually absorbed. Sometimes hormones are given after the birth to inhibit lactation in women who do not intend to breast-feed.

This, then, is the story of childbirth. Too often when I was pregnant, I thought of the labor and delivery as an endpoint. So many thoughts during pregnancy are directed toward that long-awaited day. Of course, I knew that I would go home from the hospital with a baby, but when I was pregnant it was difficult to think of the growing, kicking lump in my abdomen as a real person. I soon found that instead of being the end, delivery is only the beginning of much more. I'm continually amazed at how quickly a child grows and develops. To wait for the first smile, to listen for the first words, to look on breathlessly as the first independent steps are taken, these are some of the first rewards of motherhood. Whatever the frustrations and the sacrifices, enjoy every moment whenever you can!

INFERTILITY

Kathryn Schrotenboer Cox, M.D.

Assistant Attending Physician, Obstetrics and Gynecology, New York Hospital—Cornell Medical Center; Clinical Instructor, Cornell University Medical College

Infertility is usually defined as one year of frequent intercourse without contraception that does not result in pregnancy. Various studies have shown that from 65 to 90 percent of all couples who conceive spontaneously will do so within the first year of trying, and 90 to 95 percent will achieve pregnancy within the first two years. However, fertility and infertility are not always absolutes. "Reduced fertility" would be a better term than infertility in those cases where pregnancy is possible but takes longer than two years to achieve. About 40 percent of "infertile" couples conceive in 7 years, including those couples who are considered treatment "failures."

At least one couple out of ten will experience some difficulty in becoming pregnant. It can be a painful experience to enjoy the children of friends and neighbors and to fend off the well-meaning questions of relatives while month after month goes by without any sign of pregnancy. Unwanted infertility can put a tremendous strain on a marriage as well as on the individual partners.

A professional evaluation of infertility may add to the humiliation and sense of failure. The reproductive capacity of both partners will be examined and their sexual relations timed to comply with a doctor's suggestions. There is often an emotional toll when a man is told that his sperm count is below normal or a woman learns she does not produce enough of the necessary hormones. It may be particularly difficult for a woman to find herself infertile if she had a previous pregnancy voluntarily terminated because it was unplanned or inconvenient.

Great advances have been made in the study of infertility in the last twenty years. There are improved diagnostic techniques, such as blood hormone tests and laparoscopy. There are improved surgical techniques and better treatment for medical problems, chronic illnesses, and infections. And with the great advances in the technology of reproduction, there are new solutions too.

Because there are many causes of infertility, there are many tests to evaluate an infertile couple. Often there is more than one contributing factor. Most infertility problems in women are handled by obstetrician-gynecologists; the male partner may be referred to a urologist. Infertility was legitimized as a medical specialty as recently as the 1960s, and there are now many private clinics as well as infertility centers connected with major hospitals where treatment may be obtained, sperm banks are maintained, and donor eggs are available for transfer implantation. The American Fertility Society can supply the names of accredited physicians who practice in various parts of the United States.

MALE INFERTILITY

Male factors are estimated to cause about 30 percent of all infertility problems and to contribute to them in another 20 percent. Whatever traditional wisdom may have to say about whose "fault" the problem is, statistics indicate that the responsibility is divided about equally between the sexes.

CAUSES OF MALE INFERTILITY

The production or quality of sperm may be affected by congenital and genetic abnormalities, injuries to the genital tract, heat, age, sperm agglutination, acute and chronic infection (often sexually transmissible infections), malnutrition, previous surgery, allergies, chronic illness, radiation, varicocele, or certain medications. Among these medications are Tagamet used in ulcer treatment, and drugs used for treating cancer, some antibiotics (especially those used to treat tuberculosis). Also heavy smoking of marijuana and smoking generally, alcoholism, and stress may result in impotence or inability to ejaculate.

Varicocele, a varicose enlargement of the veins of the spermatic cord, is a potentially curable cause of male infertility. While this condition occurs in many men with normal fertility, it has been found to be present in as many as 40 percent of infertile men. Half of all men with varicoceles have decreased sperm count or sperm motility or other changes in the semen analysis. Theories of the cause of these changes include heat, pressure, and toxic substances from the dilated vessels.

Permanent or temporary damage to the male testis can occur as a result of a genital infection or a systemic infection. Gonorrhea may do enough damage to the male genital tract to result temporarily in a marked decrease in the sperm count. Mumps in an adult male may involve one or both testicles and may cause severe testicular damage. Fortunately, usually only one testicle suffers severe impairment and the sperm count, though possibly reduced, is usually compatible with fertility. Any systemic viral or bacterial infection may cause a temporary depression in the sperm count.

TESTS FOR MALE INFERTILITY

Because many of the infertility tests for women are more complicated and involve more risk than those for men, infertility testing often begins with the male. A semen analysis is a simple test that can provide a great deal of information. The male is asked to submit a recently ejaculated semen specimen to the physician or laboratory. This specimen is then examined microscopically to determine sperm count, their size and shape, and if they are able to move normally. There is no sharp line of demarcation between fertility and sterility in the sperm count. Counts of less than 20 to 40 million per cubic centimeter are often correlated with decreased fertility, although men with counts of 5 to 10 million have fathered children. A high percentage of sperm with abnormal shape, size, or decreased motility is also correlated with decreased fertility. The semen can be analyzed also for antibodies and cultured for various infections.

TREATMENT FOR MALE INFERTILITY

Some causes of male infertility are sometimes correctable. A varicocele may be surgically repaired to improve fertility. Treatment with antibiotics of a chronic infection can enable a previously infertile man to become fertile. In some situations, where substance abuse is a contributing factor, it may be essential for the male to abstain entirely from alcohol and/or other drugs and to join self-help groups in order to do so. Re-evaluation of medications prescribed to treat a chronic illness may produce positive results. A careful study of the man's exposure to occupational hazards such as radiation, lead, or dangerous pesticides may indicate a possible solution through change in employment.

In other cases administration of various hormones can increase a borderline sperm count or suppress sperm antibodies enough to make conception possible. These hormones include testosterone, thyroid hormone, and cortisone. In some situations clomiphene citrate or human menopausal gonadotropins (Pergonal), medications that are used to induce ovulation in infertile women, may also be given to a man whose pituitary deficiency is the cause of his inability to father an offspring.

FEMALE INFERTILITY

It is estimated that there are more than three million women in the United States who cannot become pregnant.

CAUSES OF FEMALE INFERTILITY

The problem of infertility appears to be confronting more women than ever before, and according to the National Centers for Disease Control, this increase is partially attributable to an increase in sterility-causing diseases. For example, between 1965 and 1976, reported cases of gonorrhea tripled, and during the same decade, there was a 600 percent increase in the number of women using IUDs, which put them

CAUSES OF MALE INFERTILITY

- Psychologic
- Pituitary imbalance
- Thyroid disease
- Severe illness and acute infection
- Adrenal imbalance
- Diabetes
- Infections
- Genital surgery and infections of:
  - Seminal vesicles
  - Prostate
  - Urethra
  - Vas deferens
- Varicocele
- Testicular radiation, heat, injuries, diseases and congenital abnormalities

CAUSES OF FEMALE INFERTILITY

at increased risk for pelvic inflammatory disease, a major cause of infertility. According to a 1985 infertility study, as many as 88,000 women may be unable to conceive because of infections that occurred while they were wearing an IUD. The drop in fertility has also been attributed to the postponement of pregnancy into the 30s because of career demands or because of uncertainty about the long-term stability of the spousal relationship.

Specifically, abnormalities of the fallopian tubes, including scarring from endometriosis or previous infections or surgery, or swelling from a current infection account for about 20 to 30 percent of all infertility problems. Problems with ovulation are thought to be the cause of infertility in about 10 to 15 percent of all cases. Chronic diseases such as thyroid disease, uncontrolled diabetes, or liver disease usually cause infertility by interfering with the complex mechanism of ovulation. In approximately 5 percent of the cases there is a problem with the cervix or cervical mucus. Other factors include on-the-job exposure to chemicals and radiation and sustained strenuous exercise, such as marathon running, which can cause temporary (that is, reversible) infertility in some women even though their menstrual cycles may continue to be normal.

Endometriosis is a condition where tissue that looks like endometrial tissue (the tissue that lines the uterus and is shed each month in menstruation) is located outside of the uterus. It is uncertain whether this develops from a backflow of endometrial tissue during menstruation into and beyond the fallopian tubes or from an "embryological mistake" whereby endometrial cells develop in an incorrect location is uncertain. Endometriosis is usually located only on the pelvic organs surrounding the uterus, but in rare instances it can be found in other places such as the upper abdomen or lung.

These areas of endometriosis may bleed at the time of the menstrual period just as the uterine endometrium does. This may cause pain, and because there is no way for the blood to escape, scarring may develop. This scarring may seal off the ovaries and prevent the egg from reaching the fallopian tube. Even if there are only small areas of endometriosis and the tubes and ovaries are not completely blocked, fertility may be reduced.

Infertility related to tubal blockage and pelvic adhesions is on the rise. An increase in sexually transmissible infections, widespread use of intrauterine contraceptive devices, and the increase in elective abortions are all thought to play a role. The infections include gonorrhea, mycoplasma, and chlamydia. Women with intrauterine contraceptive devices may have chronic low-grade infections and some may develop an acute severe infection or a pelvic abscess. Though severe pelvic infection was more common before abortions were legal, a mild infection is not unheard of after an elective abortion today. A ruptured appendix may also cause pelvic infection and scarring of the fallopian tubes. Pelvic adhesions may occur after surgery to remove ovarian cysts, fibroids, and tubal pregnancies or after any other lower abdominal or pelvic surgery.

Irregularities in the shape of the uterus can occasionally cause infertility, although they are more frequently associated with spontaneous abortions than with the inability to conceive. The most common cause of irregularity in the shape of the uterus is fibroids (benign fibrous growths of the uterus). Other causes are congenital or developmental abnormalities. Recently, some abnormalities in the shape of the uterus have been found in daughters of women who took the drug diethylstilbestrol (DES) during pregnancy.

Both hypothyroidism and hyperthyroidism and other hormonal abnormalities may cause infertility by unbalancing the delicate and complex regulation of the menstrual cycle. Severe illness of any sort (diabetes, liver disease) can also affect the normal cycle and cause infertility.

A vaginal infection may alter the cervical mucus and the pH of the vagina creating a hostile environment in which the sperm may be able to live for only a very short time.

The presence of sperm antibodies in cervical mucus or vaginal secretions may cause infertility. There is controversy among physicians about how often this may be a factor because these antibodies may be found in people with normal fertility. In some couples, however, these antibodies appear to kill or inactivate the sperm.

There is a significant number of infertile couples who complete all of the standard testing without any obvious cause of infertility. Many of these couples eventually conceive. Unfortunately, some remain infertile. However, with advances in infertility testing, fewer and fewer cases of infertility remain unexplained.

Timing of intercourse is important. A woman with a 28-day cycle should have intercourse every other day from the tenth to the eighteenth day of her menstrual cycle. These are the days of her maximum fertility. A male with a low sperm count should get special intercourse timing instructions, as should the woman with a shorter or longer cycle.

Position during intercourse may also be important. Sperm may reach

UTERINE, CERVICAL AND VAGINAL CAUSES OF INFERTILITY

- Congenital uterine abnormalities
- Endometrial infections
- Endometrial dysfunctions
- Uterine fibroids
- Cervical strictures and infections
- Vaginal Infections

OVARIAN AND TUBAL CAUSES

Tubal infections and diseases resulting in:
- Kinking and adhesions
- Scarring and narrowing
- Closure

Ovarian: infections, cysts, tumors, endometriosis, congenital, radiation the cervix more easily when the woman, lying on her back, draws her knees up to encircle her partner's hips. After his orgasm the woman should maintain this position for 10–15 minutes or relax with a pillow under her hips.

TESTS FOR FEMALE INFERTILITY

Basal Body Temperatures

Keeping a record of basal body temperatures can be helpful in establishing whether or not a woman ovulates. Every morning, immediately after waking up and before any activity, the woman takes her temperature. Special thermometers which are somewhat easier to read than regular thermometers are available for this purpose. Before ovulation morning oral temperatures usually range from 97.0 to 97.5° Fahrenheit (morning temperatures can be a degree lower than those taken later in the day). After ovulation, because of the effect of increased levels of progesterone, morning temperatures are usually 98.0° Fahrenheit or above until menstruation occurs. Ovulation usually occurs during the day before the temperature rise. Therefore, an accurately recorded temperature chart which shows low temperatures in the early part of the menstrual cycle and higher temperatures for the last 14 days is presumptive evidence that ovulation has occurred.

Endometrial Biopsy

Another test to help determine if ovulation is occurring is an endometrial biopsy. This test is usually performed on the first day of the period or in the week before a period is expected. An endometrial biopsy normally can be done in the physician's office without the use of anesthesia. A speculum is inserted into the vagina and the cervix is grasped with an instrument called a tenaculum, which may cause a slight pinching sensation. Then a small, thin instrument is inserted into the uterine cavity to take the biopsy. This procedure may cause a brief cramping sensation. The removed tissue is sent to a laboratory to be examined microscopically. In addition to confirming whether ovulation has occurred, this test sometimes can identify other causes of infertility such

INFERTILITY

as infection and certain rare causes of infertility. Though scarcely ever a problem, this test has the theoretical risk of interrupting an early pregnancy. Therefore, if there is any chance that the patient may be pregnant, it should not be done.

Hormone Tests

Measurement of blood and urinary hormone levels can help to give evidence whether or not a woman is ovulating. For example, because progesterone levels in the blood rise after ovulation a blood test taken after ovulation will reflect this. However, many authorities still consider the endometrial biopsy the most accurate proof that ovulation has occurred.

Measures of the level of other hormones may also yield information. For example, certain conditions that are associated with abnormally high male hormones such as testosterone or cortisonelike hormones can cause infertility. Also follicle-stimulating hormone (FSH) and luteinizing hormone (LH) are two messenger hormones that play essential roles in the delicate ovulation mechanism. If these are present in slightly reduced or elevated amounts or do not fluctuate appropriately during the month, infertility may result. The hormone prolactin (which plays an important role in breast milk production) may be abnormally elevated and be the cause of infertility. Treatment of this elevated hormone level with the drug bromocryptine will in many cases cure the infertility.

Cultures and Serologic Tests

Cervical mucus can be cultured for gonorrhea, chlamydia, mycoplasma, and other infectious agents. Serum can be tested for chlamydial antibodies that are suggestive of a chlamydial infection of the tubes.

Hysterosalpingogram

A hysterosalpingogram is a test used to study the uterus and fallopian tubes. It can be done in a hospital or in the office of a radiologist. A speculum is inserted into the vagina and the cervix is grasped with a

TESTS FOR INFERTILITY

1. MEDICAL, SOCIAL AND SEXUAL HISTORY
2. PHYSICAL EXAMINATION OF BOTH PARTNERS
3. COMPLETE PELVIC EXAMINATION
4. SEMEN ANALYSIS

Sperm

5. DAILY BASAL BODY TEMPERATURE

Ovulation

7. HORMONAL LEVEL TEST

6. ENDOMETRIAL BIOPSY

Uterus

Curette

8. HYSTEROSALPINGOGRAM AND/OR RUBIN TEST

9. POSTCOITAL TEST

Sperm-mucus pool

Speculum

10. LAPAROSCOPY

Inflated abdomen

tenaculum. A dye-injected apparatus is then attached to the cervix, the dye is slowly injected into the uterus, and X-rays are taken. Most women feel the injection of the dye to be about as uncomfortable as moderate menstrual cramps. The X-rays show the internal outlines of the uterus and fallopian tubes as the dye fills them. If there is any abnormality in the shape or size of the uterus or a blockage in the fallopian tubes, this may show up on the X-rays. This test also gives valuable information to a DES-exposed woman prior to a pregnancy. The degree of abnormality of the shape of the uterus is predictive of the chances of premature labor during the pregnancy and will help determine how closely such a woman needs to be monitored during pregnancy.

Rubin Test

Another test designed to determine if the fallopian tubes are blocked is the Rubin test. This test, which was developed in the early 1920s, was a breakthrough in infertility testing. The Rubin test is similar to the hysterosalpingogram except that it is done in a doctor's office and does not use X-rays. Instead of a dye, carbon dioxide gas is introduced through the cervix into the uterus and fallopian tubes. The physician places a stethoscope on the abdomen to listen for escaping gas. Hearing the gas within the abdominal cavity means that at least one of the fallopian tubes is open. Because of the shortcomings of this test many physicians now rely completely on the hysterosalpingogram for this information, although the test is still occasionnally performed. The gas may cause a tubal spasm and give a false impression of a permanently closed tube. Or, extensive pelvic adhesions may not be detected.

Postcoital Test

A postcoital test (PC test) is a painless, simple test that often can yield important information in the evaluation of an infertile couple. This test is done around the time of ovulation. You must come to the physician's office within a specified number of hours after intercourse. A speculum examination is done and a small sample of the cervical mucus and vaginal fluid are taken and examined microscopically. This examination will show if the cervical mucus is normal, if the sperm are active and alive, and if there is any evidence of sperm antibodies.

Laparoscopy

Laparoscopy is often the final step in an infertility workup. This is done in a hospital, usually with general anesthesia, although local anesthesia can be used. A small incision is made just below the navel and a long needle is inserted into the abdominal cavity. The abdominal cavity is filled with carbon dioxide gas. The laparoscope, a long, narrow, lighted tube, is inserted into the abdominal cavity and the pelvic organs can be seen. Dye is injected into the uterus. The physician can look through the laparoscope and see whether the dye spills out of the ends of the fallopian tubes, thus determining if the tubes are open or blocked. In addition, laparoscopy can diagnose endometriosis, pelvic adhesions, and previous pelvic infections.

TREATMENT FOR FEMALE INFERTILITY

Once the probable causes of infertility have been identified, treatment can begin. If irregular ovulation or lack of ovulation is the problem, ovulation may be induced with medication. These medications are the well-known fertility drugs. It is important to remember that these fertility drugs are helpful only if the infertility is caused by a problem with ovulation and cannot help at all if the infertility is caused by something else.

The most commonly used medication to induce ovulation is called Clomid (clomiphene citrate). Through its effect on the hypothalamus, clomiphene citrate stimulates a release of FSH and LH from the pituitary. FSH and LH are the hormones that act on the ovary to cause the ripening and release of eggs. The medication is taken in the form of a pill for five days during the month. Minor side effects include hot flashes and lower abdominal discomfort. Clomiphene citrate substantially increases the chances of having twins by stimulating two eggs to ripen instead of one. It increases the chances of having triplets and quadruplets only minimally.

In the rare cases when Clomid doesn't work, a second type of fertility medication must be used. This medication is called Pergonal (or human menopausal gonadotropin) and must be given by injection every day until ovulation occurs. This treatment is both costly and time consuming, and a woman must be closely watched for any adverse side effects. By causing several eggs to ripen at one time, the use of this medication can result in triplets or quadruplets. Ultrasound monitoring can detect how many eggs are ripening, and if more than three appear to be viable the woman is advised to refrain from sexual intercourse so that unwanted multiple births can be avoided. Serious side effects of Pergonal include large ovarian cysts and massive shifts in body fluids.

Problems with the fallopian tubes may be treated surgically. The fallopian tubes may have been blocked as a result of a congenital abnormality, of scarring subsequent to a previous pelvic infection or to endometriosis, or of previous pelvic surgery. Sometimes the fallopian tubes themselves are normal, but adhesions surrounding them prevent the egg and sperm from meeting.

There is a reasonable chance that the surgical removal of the adhesions will improve fertility. Unfortunately, when repairing the fallopian tube requires major reconstructive surgery (tuboplasty), the success rate is much lower. Even when it is possible to open the fallopian tubes, tubal function does not always return to normal, and the infertility may persist. Frequently operating microscopes, very fine instruments, and lasers are used to improve the success rate of tubal surgery.

An experimental procedure that may eliminate the need for surgery in some cases of blocked fallopian tubes has been adapted from a technique used to unclog coronary arteries. It consists in threading a catheter carrying a small balloon through the uterus into the blocked tube. When the balloon is inflated, the fallopian tube is stretched, and the obstructive tissue is washed out.

Treatment of endometriosis may improve fertility. In some cases the treatment is surgical: large areas of endometriosis are removed and adhesions that have formed by the scarring are opened. Lasers may be used at the time of laparotomy or through the smaller laparoscopy incision to remove endometriotic implants. In other cases the treatment is medical. Endometriosis is known to improve during pregnancy and after menopause, and medication may be given to induce a pseudopregnancy or pseudomenopause state. Female hormones, such as progesterone or combinations of estrogen and progesterone, can be given in high enough doses to prevent menstruation for six to nine months, causing a regression of the endometriosis over this period of time (pseudopregnancy). Alternatively, the regression can be caused by giving danazol, a drug that can prevent menstrual bleeding for six to seven months (pseudomenopause). After the medications are stopped, normal menstrual cycles begin again and pregnancy may occur. The causes of any hormonal abnormalities should be identified and appropriately treated.

Other treatments are available for other specific causes of infertility. For example, treatment of a vaginal infection may correct the infertility, especially if the partner is treated simultaneously. Sometimes problems with the cervical mucus may be treated by the administration of low doses of estrogen. Sperm antibodies may disappear if no sperm are present for six months, so the use of a condom or sexual abstinence may make future fertility possible. If there is a medical problem, such as thyroid disease, treatment of the medical problem may itself correct the infertility.

ARTIFICIAL INSEMINATION

When both partners are presumed to be fertile, artificial insemination (AI) can be attempted with sperm from the male partner (AIH—husband) if there is an anatomic defect in either partner that prevents the sperm from being deposited near the cervix. These defects include hypospadias (abnormal position of the urethral opening) in the man and an abnormal position of the cervix in the woman. Artificial insemination also may be necessary in certain types of sexual dysfunction. If the male partner is not fertile but the woman is presumed to be, artificial insemination is attempted using sperm from a donor, usually anonymous. The donor, generally matched to the partner in coloring and body build, is found by the woman's physician, either personally or through a sperm bank. The semen from a nonpartner, must be screened for a variety of sexually transmissible diseases including AIDS, gonorrhea, syphilis, herpes, hepatitis B, and chlamydia. Freezing of sperm decreases the likelihood of infection and allows more time for testing of the donor. This is being used increasingly. At the time of ovulation the sperm is injected into the woman's vagina at the opening of the cervix.

Artificial insemination, which has been practiced for about 200 years, was successfully used in the United States in 1884 for the first time. This method now accounts for approximately 10,000 births each year. It should be noted that there are fewer than 1 percent birth defects when donor sperm is used, compared to 6 percent in the general population.

With few children available for adoption today, artificial insemination is the simplest way that some couples can have a child. However, it is not something to be undertaken lightly because it raises countless psychological, moral, religious, and legal questions. Some men cannot cope with the fact that they are not the biologic father of their child, while other men feel that a child who has their wife's genes and whom they have raised is as much theirs as any child can be.

Couples who choose artificial insemination do not always have the support of others. In fact, because some major religious groups feel that artificial insemination with donor sperm is the equivalent of adultery, many couples who choose this procedure for achieving parenthood do not tell even their families or closest friends.

There are many legal questions about these children that have not yet been answered. Some courts in the United States, England, and Canada have held that they are illegitimate, while other courts have held that a husband who agrees to the artificial insemination of his wife has an obligation to support the child. A few states have passed laws to attempt to clarify the legal position of these children, but further legislation is sorely needed.

NEW DEVELOPMENTS IN INFERTILITY

In a new procedure, called in vitro fertilization, a woman's egg is removed surgically from one of her ovaries and fertilized in a glass dish ("test tube"). This fertilized egg is later placed back in her uterus. To date many women have had healthy babies by this method. It is used for women who have an obstruction of both fallopian tubes but have at least one normally functioning and surgically accessible ovary or in some other situations that cannot be corrected. These conditions exist in about 5 to 10 percent of infertile women. It is difficult to say what will be the ultimate impact of in vitro fertilization, but it is now being done at many medical centers.

Other new developments for overcoming infertility are even more controversial. One is implanting an in vitro fertilized egg in the uterus of a woman who did not produce the egg (a variant of the original in vitro fertilization approach). "Surrogate mothers" and "adoptive pregnancies" (donated embryos) are still other innovative developments. Because of the unanticipated complications and negative publicity surrounding the "Baby M." surrogacy situation, many states are beginning to pass legislation outlawing the entire procedure. As for the donated embryo transfer method in which the egg has been fertilized in the donor's body and then transferred to the womb of the mother-to-be, hospitals and fertility clinics nationwide are participating in it. Many questions remain unanswered. Should the donors be anonymous or should they be known to the recipient? Should the donating women be paid a standard fee for their time and trouble as well as for the donated egg? If sperm donors are paid by sperm banks, why shouldn't women sell their eggs? Who should establish guidelines for these third-party collaborations? The legal profession is waiting for medical ethicists to clarify the basis on which unambiguous laws can be formulated.

The most recent technological advance eliminates any need for third-party collaboration. Known as GIFT (*g*ametic *i*ntra*f*allopian *t*ransfer) and developed at the Health Science Center of the University of Texas, it proceeds in the following way: egg cells that are extracted from the woman by a laparoscope are mixed with about 100,000 sperm from the spouse and reinserted into the laparoscope for placement into the entrance of an oviduct from the ovary. In this way, the embryo can be fertilized inside the oviduct in its natural environment where cell division takes place without the need for laboratory culturing. When the procedure works as anticipated, the embryo descends into the uterus and develops into a normal fetus. The first birth to be accomplished in this way occurred in 1985 and yielded twins.

Although there have been major advances in solving some of the problems of infertility, much more is yet to be learned. There are still couples whose infertility is unexplained, and there are couples with known causes of infertility that cannot be cured.

Over the years, countless men and women have endured the indignities of testing and the difficulties of therapy, and they have spent great amounts of time and money in their efforts to overcome the problem of sterility. For the many fortunate couples who have been able to achieve parenthood, all efforts and expenses have been well rewarded.

GYNECOLOGIC DISEASES AND TREATMENT

Mary Jane Gray, M.D.
Professor of Obstetrics and Gynecology, University of North Carolina Medical School, Chapel Hill, North Carolina

Gynecologists are physicians who specialize in the care of women, with emphasis on matters relating to the reproductive system. Gynecological problems may have arisen for a few of us with the onset of menstruation. More complex problems concern most of us with the beginning of sexual activity, and for all women, regular examinations and cancer tests are a vital necessity.

FINDING CAUSES OF COMMON PROBLEMS

Most women would like to know more about their reproductive system and what may go wrong with it. Because of dissatisfaction with the care they have received, some women have left the mainstream of medical care for self-help groups. These groups are excellent for education in normal function and health maintenance and for emotional support. However, they are sometimes short on medical expertise and may be especially deficient in the use of advanced diagnostic tools and techniques. This chapter is intended to help women understand common gynecologic problems and their treatment (excluding contraception, STD and sexual dysfunction, discussed in other chapters) and to give women the knowledge they need to communicate more effectively with their physicians. A review of the anatomy of the female reproductive system and the physiology of normal menstruation will be helpful to the reader at this point.

DOCTOR/PATIENT RELATIONSHIP

The relationship between a woman and her gynecologist is likely to last a long time and cover many contingencies. Often the gynecologist becomes the woman's primary care physician. It is, therefore, important that the relationship should start out with mutual respect and should proceed in an atmosphere that encourages relaxed communication. Both participants may have an easier time if the first visit occurs when there is no need for crisis intervention but rather occurs because the patient wants to have a complete checkup for preventive purposes.

More and more, gynecologists are accepting a new patient's request to meet for the first time in the doctor's office, with the patient fully clothed, instead of in the examining room with the patient unclothed and about to assume a submissive posture.

The patient should be prepared to describe all problems in detail and be in command of all the facts of her personal and medical history. Remember that you can expect your gynecologist to help you with menstrual problems, infertility, contraception and abortion, pre-pregnancy counselling, prenatal care, childbirth, sexually transmissable diseases, hormone and breast problems, genitourinary infections, and the transitional difficulties of menopause. During the first discussion, the gynecologist will ask about the onset of periods, their previous and present character, pregnancies, abortions and a complete sexual history. It is essential to be honest in answering all questions. If the doctor seems uncomfortable with your life style, or if you feel that the doctor is not being thorough enough in taking your history because of the pressure of time and a crowded waiting room, find a different doctor.

PELVIC EXAMINATION

The patient should not douche for two or three days before the appointment and should empty her bladder beforehand to make the examination more comfortable for her and more accurate for the physician. The diagnosis of a gynecological problem is based on a thorough examination, which usually includes height, weight, and blood pressure measurements; feeling the thyroid gland; listening to the heart and lungs; and examining the breasts and abdomen before proceeding to the pelvic examination. Laboratory tests will be based on the patient's history and on whether the examiner is assuming primary responsibility for her health (*see* Suggested Health Examinations.

The first part of the pelvic examination is an inspection of the external genitals for lumps, sores, inflammation, and general hormonal status. The folds of skin forming the labia are separated in order to expose the urinary and vaginal openings. A woman who has had children may be asked to "bear down" or "strain as if moving your bowels" to demonstrate any weakness of the supporting tissues of the vagina.

Next comes the vaginal examination. After a finger locates the vaginal opening, a speculum is placed inside and opened. The speculum is a metal instrument a little like two shoe horns hinged together. When opened, it holds the vaginal walls apart and allows the examiner to see the vagina and cervix and check for inflammation or infection, scars or growths, and other abnormalities. A scraping of tissue and samples of discharge are taken for examination under a microscope and for cultures and a pap test. The woman may request a mirror to follow this part of the procedure.

After the speculum is removed, a bimanual pelvic examination follows. This consists of placing two fingers in the vagina and the other hand on the abdominal wall in such a way that the uterus and ovaries can be located between the two hands and the size, shape, consistency, and tenderness of these structures can be determined. Normal ovaries, like testes, exhibit a characteristic discomfort when examined in this way. Usually the examiner will then put a finger into the rectum to feel both the rectum itself and those structures lying near it in the pelvis.

VAGINAL EXAMINATION

INSERTION OF THE SPECULUM

Closed speculum inserted at angle to avoid causing pain

Speculum in open and closed positions

SPECULUM VIEW OF CERVIX AND VAGINA

Cervix — Cervical opening — Vagina

BIMANUAL EXAMINATION OF UTERUS AND ADJACENT TISSUES

PAP SMEAR

Named for Dr. Papanicolaou who developed this method for cancer screening, the pap smear has proved to be an inexpensive and accurate way to diagnose cervical cancer and malignant tumors of nearby organs such as the vagina and endometrium as well as potentially malignant changes. Cells from the surface of the cervix and vagina are placed on a glass slide and examined under a microscope by a technician trained in recognizing cancer cells and dysplastic cells. Dysplastic cells are cells showing evidence of changes that indicate they might at some time become malignant; dysplasia is the abnormal growth created by the aberrant cells. Recent evidence linking venereal warts and cervical cancer has caused increased attention to be given to cellular changes caused by the wart virus.

Because the pap smear selects a random sample of cells, false negative results are possible when abnormal cells are present but not sampled. Similarly, false positive readings are obtained when suspicious cells are seen which represent infection and not cancer. Abnormal pap smears must be confirmed by a repeat smear. An abnormal smear suggesting the possibility of cancer must be clarified by a colposcopy and biopsy.

Cytologists (professionals who specialize in detecting cancer cells under a microscope) often classify smears as follows. Some pathologists describe these categories without assigning classes.

Class I. Normal smear. Repeat at intervals suggested by your doctor.
Class II. Cells indicative of inflammatory changes, but no evidence of cancerous changes. Any infection should be treated and the pap smear repeated in six to twelve months.
Class III. "Suspicious" cells present indicating dysplasia with no evidence of cancer. Inflammation, if present, should be treated and the pap smear repeated after the next menstrual period.
Class IV. Cells strongly suggest cancer. A biopsy is always taken to confirm or rule out cancer.
Class V. Cancer cells present. Following biopsy, surgery or other treatment is carried out immediately.

A pap smear taken once a year is usually sufficient for early recognition of conditions that require treatment. However, certain conditions, such as previous dysplasia of the cervix, a history of prenatal estrogen medication, or a previous herpes infection, indicate the necessity for more frequent evaluation.

Considerable publicity has been given to the fact that the American Cancer Society and the American College of Obstetricians and Gynecologists recently recommended three annual pap tests after age 18 or when the woman has become sexually active. If all three tests are negative, the frequency of the tests is left to the discretion of the physician. If the women became sexually active before the age of 18, has had more than one sexual partner or has had herpes or warts she falls into a high risk category and should have smears at least annually.

These guidelines have also been adopted by the American Medical Association and the National Cancer Institute.

X-RAY, SONOGRAPHY, LAPAROSCOPY, COLPOSCOPY, AND HYSTEROSCOPY

If the examination or pap smear indicates the presence of a problem but further information is required for an accurate diagnosis, several other diagnostic procedures may be followed.

X-rays may be taken to study the structure and location of organs within the pelvic cavity. X-ray is most effective in showing hard tissue, such as bone, or in outlining the urinary and gastrointestinal tracts after the use of contrast material. The uterus and tubes can be outlined by injecting radio-opaque material through the cervix. The resulting X-ray is called a hysterosalpingogram.

Sonography or ultrasound is a technique in which sound waves are sent across the abdomen and their echoes recorded on a screen. The image on the screen is a sonogram. It provides a picture of soft tissue and can be used to determine the size and placement of organs and to detect any abnormal tissue mass, swelling, or fluid collection. The procedure is often done by a radiologist or in the radiology department of a hospital, but no radiation is involved.

Laparoscopy is a minor surgical procedure in which a lighted viewing tube (a laparoscope) is inserted into the abdomen through a small incision. It allows the visual examination of internal structures. Anesthesia is required, but the procedure can be done without an overnight stay in a hospital.

Colposcopy is the examination of the cervix and vagina with a magnifying device (a colposcope) in order to see details not visible with the naked eye. It is used to identify cervical or vaginal abnormalities, to examine abnormal surface areas, and to locate specific sites for biopsy if a pap smear indicates the presence of abnormal cells. Because the device enters only the vagina no anesthesia is required and the procedure can be done in a doctor's office.

Hysteroscopy involves putting a scope through the cervix and looking at the inside of the uterus.

BIOPSY

Biopsy is a surgical procedure that consists of taking a sample of tissue for examination under a microscope to determine whether the tissue is malignant or to identify an unusual growth or infection. In many cases the sample can be taken in the doctor's office with local anesthesia, but biopsies of internal structures or biopsies that involve the removal of a large amount of tissue require hospitalization and surgery. For example, an operating room is necessary for a biopsy of an ovary or for a cone biopsy of the cervix in which a large "cone" of tissue is removed for extensive evaluation. Endometrial biopsies and small "punch" biopsies of the cervix are office procedures.

PROBLEMS AND DISEASES

An understanding of the various gynecologic problems and diseases that may occur is important for every woman.

MENSTRUAL PROBLEMS

Too much has been made of the regularity of menstrual periods. No woman starts her first period at 12 and then menstruates every 28 days for 5 days until she reaches the menopause at 49. The numbers 12, 28, 5, and 49 are averages that are not indicative of the wide normal variation. An onset between 9 and 16, an interval from 25 to 35 days, a length from 2 to 7 days, and menopause from 45 to 55 are completely normal. Each woman has a pattern that is normal for her. It is also normal for an individual to skip periods in the early teens and again in the years just before the menopause. Periods will not necessarily be the same at 16 as at 26, 36, or 46. Nonetheless, periods can be too heavy, too light, too frequent, or too infrequent. Some of these deviations from normal will be considered.

Delayed Onset of Periods

Failure to start menstrual periods is termed primary amenorrhea. If a girl has not had a menstrual period by the age of 16, a medical investigation is warranted. A complete history of previous illness is important. The first point to be noted on physical examination is whether breast development shows that the ovaries are secreting estrogen. Then one must discover whether the hymen has an opening and if the vagina and uterus are normal. Other genetic and hormonal tests may follow in an effort to uncover and correct the cause.

Skipped or Delayed Periods

Skipped periods are common in the early teens before the complicated interactions between the hypothalamic area of the brain, the pituitary gland, the ovaries, and the uterus settle into the patterns that they maintain for almost 40 years. Usually nothing need be done unless these irregularities continue beyond the first year or two.

Pregnancy is one of the most common causes of secondary amenorrhea, the absence of periods after the initial onset of menstruation. Whenever a period is delayed a week in a sexually active woman whose periods follow a regular pattern, this possibility should be considered. Other symptoms of early pregnancy may include breast tenderness, nausea, and an increased frequency of urination. At such an early stage a pregnancy test is necessary for confirmation because examination is often inconclusive.

Stress, either physical or emotional, and excessive dieting (leading to a weight loss of 15 to 25 percent of body weight) can also cause skipped or delayed periods. Delayed onset or erratic menstrual patterns are associated with anorexia nervosa and with the excessive physical demands that lead to a low percentage of body fat in relation to total weight experienced by ballet dancers and young athletes.

Periods are often delayed one to six months in women discontinuing oral contraceptive pills. Problems with the pituitary, adrenals, thyroid, and ovaries also may delay periods. In the absence of pregnancy, it is usually reasonable to wait at least three months before seeking professional advice about the absence of periods.

Light Periods

The old wives' tale that a heavy period is necessary to rid the body of poisons runs against the facts that wastes are excreted through the kidney and the bowel and that menstrual discharge contains only old endometrium (the lining of the uterus) and a small quantity of blood. Light periods lasting one to three days are normal for many women. Most women on birth control pills have decreased blood loss and a shorter flow, regarded by most as beneficial side effects of the pill. However, a sudden change to a very light period may mean that the period has been skipped and that bleeding from some other cause is mistaken for a period. This sometimes occurs in early pregnancy.

Frequent Periods

Periods that come more often than every three weeks usually take place in the absence of ovulation. If they are regular and not heavy and if pregnancy is not desired, this condition is not serious. Periods without ovulation are most likely to occur during the early teens and premenopausal years.

Heavy Periods

Some women have heavy periods with clots lasting seven or eight days throughout their menstruating life. These heavier than average periods containing clots may be considered normal and not a medical problem. However, the blood lost each month with the menstrual period may lead to anemia in women who do not eat a diet containing sufficient iron. Most women between the onset of menstrual periods and the menopause have less hemoglobin in the blood than men. Heavy periods easily push a woman into iron-deficiency anemia, and such women require supplemental iron to be taken as pills.

Bleeding that requires a super tampon or pad that must be changed more than once an hour and continues for more than a few hours is considered unusually heavy and may indicate the presence of a medical problem.

Estrogen from the ovary stimulates growth of the lining of the uterus;

progesterone, produced by the ovary after ovulation, matures the endometrium so that breakdown and bleeding are controlled at the time of menstruation. Teenagers and premenopausal women, who often have periods without ovulation and therefore without progesterone, may have very heavy periods with serious blood loss and anemia. Even though women taking the oral contraceptive pill do not ovulate, the progesterone-type compound in the pill produces light, controlled periods. In young women heavy periods may be controlled by giving progesterone. In older women hormones can be used safely after cancer has been ruled out by curettage or biopsy.

Pregnancy may be a cause of heavy bleeding if it occurs after a period is delayed. At least one out of every ten pregnancies ends in spontaneous abortion or miscarriage accompanied by heavy bleeding, usually because of abnormal development of the fetus. Removal of the fragments of the pregnancy that are left in the uterus by suction or D&C (dilatation and curettage; see below) stops the bleeding.

In older women heavy periods are often caused by fibroids (benign muscle tumors of the uterus).

Midcycle Bleeding

At the time of ovulation, approximately midway between menstrual periods, there is a transient dip in estrogen levels. In some women this is enough to start the breakdown of the endometrium and consequent bleeding. If, as is usual, estrogen levels rise again, the bleeding stops. Careful attention to the timing of the bleeding usually clarifies this as the cause.

Premenstrual Syndrome (PMS)

For many years it has been recognized that most women experience some changes such as irritability, depression, mood swings, or headache just before the onset of their menstrual periods. For some women these symptoms last long enough and are severe enough to interfere with the normal functions of their lives. Distressing symptoms that occur 2 to 14 days before the beginning of menstruation and disappear after the period have come to be known as premenstrual syndrome (PMS). Almost all medical and psychological conditions become worse premenstrually, making it difficult to delineate true PMS.

Although PMS is clearly related to normal cyclic hormonal changes, the exact mechanism is not consistent. Measures that promote general health are useful. Decreasing caffeine and salt intake diminish irritability. Depression can sometimes be alleviated by vitamin B-6 in doses of not more than 100 mgs/day. Higher doses can cause nerve damage. Some women do better on oral contraceptive pills; others don't. Some clinics are using large doses of very expensive progesterone given in vaginal or rectal suppositories, but the effectiveness of the treatment is not established. Diuretics can reduce the puffiness, and an increase in exercise can stimulate the flow of endorphins.

According to Dr. Leslie Hartley Gise, director of the PMS Program at the Mt. Sinai Medical Center in New York, there are now more than 300 treatments for this condition, including vitamins, hormones, tranquilizers, and progesterone. In searching for a solution to their PMS problems, women should avoid being exploited by fly-by-night PMS clinics that offer "sure" cures. Your gynecologist is much likelier to offer dependable treatment, and if you can locate a PMS support group, participation in peer discussions can be very helpful.

Painful Periods

Pain with menstrual periods is termed dysmenorrhea. The most common type of dysmenorrhea starts within a year or two of the beginning of periods, is relatively constant, and tends to decrease with age and after pregnancies. This characteristic cramping pain is associated with cycles in which ovulation occurs, and it is considered normal if it is not incapacitating. Recent studies have shown that this primary dysmenorrhea is caused by substances called prostaglandins that are released when the endometrial tissue breaks down. They cause the uterine muscle to contract and can also stimulate the alimentary canal causing nausea and diarrhea. Mild menstrual discomfort can be relieved by aspirin, Tylenol, exercise, and a heating pad. More severe pain usually responds to compounds such as ibuprofin (Motrin, Nuprin, Advil), which function as antiprostaglandins. Women who are sexually active can often combine contraception with relief of dysmenorrhea by taking the oral contraceptive pill. Some women who are not having intercourse may also need the oral contraceptive pill for relief if the antiprostaglandins do not give adequate help.

Menstrual pain that begins after years of pain-free periods is usually due to gynecologic causes such as endometriosis, polyps, or fibroids. Dysmenorrhea is a frequent accompaniment of the IUD, making this method of contraception a poor choice for women who already have severe cramps. Whenever previously normal periods become painful, the doctor should be alerted.

Pain with Ovulation

Mittelschmerz, literally "middle pain," is pain that occurs when the egg breaks through the tiny cyst on the ovary where it has been growing. In most women this process is painless; in a few it is always painful; in many it is occasionally painful. At times the pain may be severe, mimicking the pain of appendicitis or other abdominal crises. The pain is characterized by an abrupt onset and usually clears within a few hours, although it may last a day or two. It is necessary to know when the last period occurred and what the woman's normal interval is between periods in order to label an episode of abdominal pain as mittelschmerz.

Menopausal Problems

The menopause, the cessation of menstruation, is the objective evidence that the ovaries are aging and secreting less estrogen. Hot flashes, frequently accompanied by sweating, and painful intercourse, which is the result of thinning of the vaginal lining and decreased lubrication, are the two clear-cut symptoms that respond to estrogen administration. Other symptoms such as emotional fluctuations and depression are not as readily explained by our current knowledge and may in part reflect the changing life patterns of middle age. Skipping periods near the menopause is normal, but when irregular or heavy bleeding occurs, the cause must be sought because cancer of the endometrium may occur in women of menopausal age. (Menopause is discussed in greater detail in the chapter "Aging Healthfully—Your Body".)

OTHER VAGINAL BLEEDING

Not all vaginal bleeding is related to menstruation but may be triggered by other events.

Bleeding After Intercourse

Bleeding that follows intercourse results either from injuries sustained during intercourse or, more commonly, from tissue made sensitive by inflammation or tumors of the vagina or cervix. Bleeding from tears in the hymen or vagina may occur in children who are sexually abused, in young women who are having intercourse for the first time, or in postmenopausal women who have not recently been sexually active. Sutures may be required to control heavy bleeding. An inflamed cervix or one with polyps or tumors is likely to bleed when touched by the thrusting penis. Such tumors can be either benign or malignant. Careful evaluation is always necessary.

Irregular Bleeding

Bleeding that occurs at random without regard to the menstrual cycle or is unrelated to sexual activity may be a symptom of endometrial cancer (cancer of the lining of the uterus), benign endometrial conditions, or hormonal fluctuations. Bleeding with an IUD in place is usually not serious but requires careful evaluation to distinguish it from other causes. Irregular bleeding in women on oral contraceptive pills is also sometimes hard to evaluate. Occasionally a D&C needs to be done to find the cause.

LOWER ABDOMINAL PAIN

In addition to menstruation and ovulation, other problems can cause acute or chronic pain. Pelvic infection or pelvic inflammatory disease, often abbreviated PID, is a frequent cause of pain. Gonorrhea, chlamydia, and other infectious organisms can cause PID. Such infections are more common in women using IUDs than in others. Whenever there is suspicion of PID, antibiotics should be used to minimize damage to the tubes and later sterility. (For further discussion of PID, see the chapter "Sexually Transmissible Diseases".)

Ovarian and uterine tumors, benign and malignant, may cause pain, as may the uterine contractions of an impending miscarriage. Many conditions of the intestinal and urinary tract are painful and must be considered among possible causes. Stress is another factor that may lead to abdominal pain, but organic causes should be eliminated by diagnostic tests before the pain is assumed to be psychological in origin.

VAGINAL DISCHARGE

The increased levels of female hormones that begin to circulate at puberty stimulate the glands of the cervix and increase the thickness and cellular activity of the vaginal wall. Together these changes cause increased vaginal moisture that collects at the vaginal opening as a completely normal "discharge." Observant women notice that this discharge is thickish and profuse about the time of ovulation. A marked increase in vaginal fluid also occurs as the first phase of sexual response and serves as a lubricant to facilitate intercourse. This reaction occurs whenever the woman is sexually aroused regardless of whether the source of stimulation is dreams, sexual fantasies, or actual touching of the genitals and regardless of whether or not further phases of sexual response are reached.

If the discharge increases, changes color or odor, and produces itching or irritation of the surrounding tissues, a vaginal infection is likely to be the cause.

INCONTINENCE

Women leak urine; men have trouble voiding. This generalization reflects the problems relating to the short urethra (tube from bladder to outside) in the female and the long urethra in the male. It is not unusual for a normal woman with a full bladder to lose a few drops of urine if she coughs or sneezes. The supporting tissue of the bladder is often damaged by childbirth so that, with stress, incontinence can become a major problem. The problem of incontinence may worsen when estrogen levels drop after the menopause. A variety of solutions should be considered before surgery is recommended. (See "Aging Healthfully—Your Body".)

The sphincter controlling the rectum and rectal supports can also be damaged by childbirth and may need surgical repair (see pelvic repair).

PROLAPSE OF THE UTERUS

During childbirth the ligaments that support the uterus may become so stretched and weakened that the uterus falls or drops into the vagina, often causing discomfort. Weakness of the bladder often occurs at the same time, causing difficulty holding urine, especially during the stress of coughing or sneezing or moving the bowels. Corrective surgery may be necessary. Prolapse should not be confused with a "tipped womb," which is a uterus that tips back toward the rectum. This is now known to be a normal position for the uterus in about one third of women.

INFECTIONS

Although not all infections of the female genital tract are sexually transmitted, a majority of them are. As with all infections, a search must be made for the organism responsible. Such a search involves cultures, smears that are stained for bacteria, and wet preparations in which a bit of discharge is placed on a slide and examined for organisms.

Cystitis and Urethritis

Increased frequency of urination coupled with pain on voiding usually means a bacterial infection of the bladder or urethra (cystitis or urethritis). Blood in the urine is a common symptom of infection. Often the bladder is so inflamed that the woman has difficulty holding her urine even briefly. If the infection originates in the kidneys (pyelonephritis), there is likely to be fever and pain in the side.

The diagnosis is made by obtaining the history, by a physical exam, and by a urine culture to find out which bacteria are present and to which antibiotic they are sensitive. If the discomfort is severe, the treatment may be started before the results of the culture are known and changed later if indicated. Treatment is usually continued for 10 days after the symptoms are gone, but shorter courses are almost as effective.

Sometimes infection is caused because organisms normally present in feces get into the urethra. To reduce this possibility, the wiping motion with toilet paper after a bowel movement should be from front to back only (away from your urethra).

"Honeymoon cystitis" is a term used for cystitis that occurs after intercourse. It is thought that intercourse and related sexual activity introduce bacteria into the urethra and bladder. Urination prior to beginning sex or, better, soon after coitus helps to "flush out" organisms from your urethra that can cause urethritis or cystitis.

In addition, the use of a diaphragm, especially one that is too large, may obstruct the urethra and predispose to cystitis.

Because antibiotics kill the normal vaginal bacteria as well as those causing infections in the bladder or elsewhere, a yeast or monilia infection often follows treatment. If these infections are a problem, antimonilial drugs can be used during antibiotic treatment.

Infected Bartholin's Glands

On either side of the vaginal opening, Bartholin's gland secretions contribute to sexual lubrication. If the opening of the gland is blocked, the gland becomes distended, cystic, and easily infected. An infected Bartholin's gland, called a Bartholin's abscess, is extremely painful. Treatment consists of heat, antibiotics, and cutting into the collection of pus so that it can drain. Often a catheter or drain is left in the gland for a few days so that the infection will not recur. Mere swelling of these glands without infection does not require treatment. Rarely, glands of the urethra or other glands in the vulvar area become infected.

Vaginitis

Vaginitis is an inflammation of the vagina that may cause pain and soreness of the vagina and vulva, burning (especially with urination and intercourse), itching, abnormal vaginal discharge, and odor. The discomfort may in some cases be severe enough to warrant emergency treatment.

Because there are so many different organisms and conditions that may result in vaginitis, it is necessary to find the cause by physical examination, cultures, and microscopic examination of the vaginal discharge before attempting treatment. Because the urethra and bladder are so close to the vulva and vagina, an infection in one area may cause symptoms in the other, making diagnosis difficult.

The most frequent vaginal infection, which is due to a yeastlike fungus commonly called monilia, is technically known as moniliasis or candidiasis. While not life-threatening nor the cause of permanent damage, this type of infection can be a great nuisance, especially to those who are vulnerable to it. There are some women who can be reinfected monthly, and during the infection, sexual intercourse becomes impossible. Even sitting causes great discomfort. Because the fungus flourishes when estrogen and progesterone levels are high, pregnant women and those receiving large doses of these hormones as replacement therapy are at higher risk. The organisms flourish in the warm moist environment of the vagina and are likely to take hold when antibiotics prescribed for a prior condition have killed the bacteria normally responsible for maintaining the acidity of the vagina. Other factors that encourage the fungal growth are tight pants, wet bathing suits, and nylon panty hose and underwear. Scented douches, bath oils, and bubble baths can be responsible for triggering the infection, and for diabetic women, the high sugar content of the vaginal secretions is an additional factor.

Itching, rash, and inflammation are symptoms of the infection, which is also characterized by a white, thick discharge with a yeasty odor. The diagnosis is made by examining a portion of this discharge under the microscope or by growing the organism in a tube. Candidiasis usually responds to treatment with antifungal creams or suppositories. A recent alternative is an oral medication, but because it can have undesirable side effects, its use should be closely monitored by the doctor. The use of this and other drugs by pregnant women or nursing mothers is contraindicated. When the infection has been cleared up, recurrences can sometimes be prevented by wearing loose cotton underpants and avoiding all pants that fit tightly in the crotch. It is also advisable to find out whether the infectious agent is being harbored by one's sexual partner.

The term nonspecific vaginitis is used to designate vaginal inflammation caused by miscellaneous abnormal bacteria. A foul-smelling discharge is often caused by the bacteria *Gardnerella vaginalis* together with organisms from the intestinal tract, but frequently the bacteria cannot be identified. Thinness of the lining of the vagina in a child or postmenopausal woman makes the vagina more susceptible to infection. The discharge with nonspecific vaginitis is usually white or yellow and may be streaked with blood. An unpleasant odor and swollen glands in the groin may be present. Nonspecific vaginitis is often treated with vaginal creams or suppositories. Oral antibiotics such as metronidazole may be used. Consideration must be given to treatment of sexual partners.

The vagina depends on a balance of normal hormone effects and normal bacteria to maintain its acidity and health. Strong douches can interfere with this balance. Some women are allergic to soaps, deodorants, and other preparations used around the vagina.

Not all organisms capable of producing vaginal irritations have been identified and, therefore, one should be careful about attributing symptoms to psychosomatic interactions. However, it has been found that for a number of reasons, including inadequate sexual lubrication, women with sexual and relationship problems have an increased incidence of vaginitis. Conversely, most women with vaginitis have dyspareunia.

Certain precautions can be taken to prevent vaginitis.

1. If the area is sore, don't attempt intercourse.
2. A condom can help prevent the spread of sexually transmissible diseases. Lubricate with a spermicidal cream or jelly and not with Vaseline, which can clog the pores of the tissues that line the vagina and weaken the latex of the condom.
3. Keep the genital area as dry as possible because organisms that cause vaginitis grow well in a moist environment. Cotton crotch underwear allows for more absorption and helps keep the genital area dry. Avoiding tight jeans or pantyhose may also help. Sitting for long periods of time in a wet bathing suit is conducive to yeast infections.
4. Practice good general hygiene. Washing the external genitalia thoroughly with soap and water is sufficient. Be sure to rinse thoroughly after bathing. Avoid bubble baths and perfumed soaps that may be irritating.
5. Avoid perfumed tampons, vaginal sprays, and frequent douching, especially with over-the-counter products, because they can be harsh and may kill normal bacteria and alter vaginal acidity.
6. An occasional douche (not more than twice a week) with mild vinegar solution (2 tablespoons to 1 quart water) can be used prophylactically if

recurrent vaginitis is a problem or if a woman feels the need for internal cleansing.
7. Do not douche during menstruation or pregnancy.
8. Do not use other people's towels.

Pelvic Inflammatory Disease (PID)

Pelvic inflammatory disease (PID) is increasing in incidence, in some cases because early symptoms are ignored, and in others because the symptoms are inadequately treated. The condition itself, which is bacterial in origin, is usually secondary to gonorrhea or chlamydia. (PID is discussed in detail in "Sexually Transmissable Diseases".)

Toxic Shock Syndrome (TSS)

Recently it was noted that healthy young women occasionally died of an illness that began during a menstrual period and was characterized by fever, severe diarrhea, aching, and rash. Eighty percent of these women used tampons. A toxic substance made by the bacterium *Staph. aureus*, occasionally found in the vagina, has been found to be responsible for the illness. "Super" tampons seem to be more dangerous, perhaps because they are retained for a longer time. A few cases have been associated with contraceptive diaphragms and sponges when these have been left in the vagina for more than 24 hours (see "Contraception and Abortion").

As women and their doctors have become aware of TSS, the number of cases and the mortality rates have fallen. Another factor that has contributed to the decline in infections is the redesign of sanitary napkins so that they are less cumbersome and easier to wear, no longer requiring belts, pins, and other paraphernalia. If you use tampons, do not leave them in place for more than four hours, do not use them to control vaginal discharges, and do not use them for more than five days during the month. If you use napkins, change them frequently.

TUMORS

The word tumor, which means growth or swelling, is used both for a malignant growth, cancer that can spread into surrounding tissues and from which pieces can break off and travel to other parts of the body, and for a benign or nonmalignant growth which may cause problems because of size or pressure but which does not spread.

Vulvar Tumors

Most lumps that women find on the external genitals or vulva are benign and may be warts, infections, or cysts. Sores or ulcers that do not heal in two to three weeks could be malignant and should be called to a doctor's attention.

Vaginal Tumors

Until the advent of a generation of women exposed before birth to high doses of estrogens such as DES, vaginal tumors were very rare. Now they are somewhat less rare. Most vaginal tumors consist of benign changes in the lining of the vagina, but cancer can occur. The colposcope is used to localize areas for biopsy.

Cervical Polyps

Small benign growths called polyps are the most common cervical tumors. These start in the cervical canal and appear at the cervical opening. Polyps are small, red, mushroomlike growths that bleed easily and irregularly. They are removed by a minor operation called a polypectomy, which usually can be done in the doctor's office. Cervical warts are also seen frequently.

Dysplasia

Early changes in the cells of the surface of the cervix that might become malignant are called dysplasia. These changes can be mild or severe, and sometimes disappear spontaneously. They are usually discovered by a pap smear and can best be evaluated by a combination of colposcopy and biopsy. Treatment consists of destroying the abnormal cells by means of hot cautery, freezing cryosurgery, or lasers.

Carcinoma-in-situ

More advanced changes in the cells covering the cervix are called carcinoma-in-situ (cancer in place). The term cervical intraepithelial neoplasia (CIN) is also used. While these cells appear malignant, they are confined to the covering layer of cells. Such cells may become malignant at any time, but on average they remain quiescent for about five years before spreading. Carcinoma-in-situ may be treated by cryosurgery, cautery, or excision biopsy. Follow-up with frequent pap smears is necessary to be sure all the abnormal areas have been removed.

Cancer of the Cervix

Invasive cancer of the cervix, one of the most common female malignancies, has dropped in frequency with the advent of pap smears. These smears permit detection and treatment of premalignant lesions. Cancer of the cervix can be treated by a radical hysterectomy or by radiation. A radical or Wertheim type of hysterectomy is one in which the tissue adjoining the uterus—the pelvic lymph nodes, tubes, and ovaries—are removed as well as the uterus. It is generally performed by specially trained gynecologic cancer surgeons.

Benign Uterine Conditions

Polyps may appear on the endometrium or lining of the uterus and are removed by D&C. Another type of irregular growth of the endometrium is called hyperplasia.

Endometrial Hyperplasia

Endometrial hyperplasia is a condition of the lining of the uterus that occurs when estrogen stimulates the endometrium continuously without the modifying effects of progesterone. Endometrial hyperplasia is reversible. However, if stimulation of the endometrium by estrogen (unopposed by progesterone), whether produced by the body (endogenous) or taken as medication (exogenous), continues uninterrupted for several years, cancer of the endometrium may result. The diagnosis is usually made by endometrial biopsy or D&C. Treatment is by the use of synthetic progesterones or, if severe, by hysterectomy.

Fibroids or Fibromyomata Uteri

Fibroids are very common benign tumors of the muscle of the uterus. Studies indicate that one woman in four aged 30 to 50 has fibroids. In most cases, they produce no symptoms. They are likely to increase in size when stimulated by estrogen, as happens during pregnancy. Following menopause, when hormone stimulation is reduced, the fibroids shrink. Fibroids can be felt during a manual examination of the pelvis. Even when they produce no symptoms, they should be checked twice a year to find out whether they have suddenly grown much larger.

Unless fibroids cause severe pain or pressure or grow to be larger than four inches in diameter, they need not be treated. However, even though they do not cause bleeding between periods, they can cause periods heavy or prolonged enough to result in anemia. Enlarged fibroids may press on the bladder, prompting a need for frequent urination. They may also cause back pain, and in some cases, they can interfere with conception by blocking the implantation of the fertilized egg.

Size, location, and complications produced by fibroids as well as the desire for continuing childbearing capability are all taken into consideration in deciding on treatment. Women approaching menopause can wait to see whether the fibroids will shrink when deprived of estrogen. If not, a hysterectomy may be recommended. Anti-estrogens can be used to temporarily reduce fibroid size. For women who wish to preserve their fertility, the recommended procedure may be a myomectomy, a more difficult operation, in which the fibroids are removed, leaving a scarred uterus. In deciding on treatment, women should be aware that in fewer than 3 cases per 1,000 do fibroids become cancerous.

Endometriosis

Endometriosis is a condition in which normal, benign cells of endometrial tissue break away from the uterus and start to grow in other locations in the pelvic cavity—the tubes, ovaries, and surface of the bladder and rectum. This condition is the third leading cause of infertility, affecting almost one-third of all infertile women. Recent research indicates that the disease often affects the bones as well as the genitourinary tissues and that the symptoms are caused by immune system hormones. During menstruation, women shed endometrial cells, but instead of leaving the body as part of menstrual waste, some of the cells move into the fallopian tubes and abdomen. Researchers believe that the reflux of the endometrial cells causes the body's white blood cells to secrete the immune system hormone interleuken 1. In women who have endometriosis, this hormone circulates in the bloodstream and suppresses bone growth. Thus, women with endometriosis are also at high risk for osteoporosis.

Endometriosis can produce many types of pelvic discomfort or none at all, but most typically causes pain that begins two or three days before the start of a menstrual period, possibly caused by changes in the endometrial tissue similar to those occurring in the uterus. The diagnosis can be made accurately by laparoscopy. Mild endometriosis, which produces no symptoms or effects, may not require treatment. Laser therapy has been used at the time of laparoscopy to heal early implants. Treatment with progestational agents and synthetic steroids such as danazol is based on the observed fact that endometriosis decreases when ovulation is prevented for three to six months. Other new approaches for treating endometriosis are being developed.

Cancer of the Endometrium

Malignant growth of the lining of the uterus is called carcinoma of the endometrium. It is one of the most common cancers in women and has been increasing in frequency. An association with estrogen stimulation, either that produced by the woman's own body or that taken in treatment, has been noted. If progesterone type drugs are given with estrogen, the rate of endometrial cancer is reduced to levels below those occurring without the use of any external hormones. The use of the oral contraceptive pill also reduces the rate of endometrial cancer. The chief symptom is irregular bleeding, usually during or after the menopause. Diagnosis is by endometrial biopsy or D&C. Treatment is primarily surgical removal of the uterus, often preceded or followed by radiation. The cure rate is excellent (80 to 90 percent) if diagnosed early.

Cancer of the Tube

Cancer of the fallopian tubes is very uncommon, hard to diagnose, and difficult to cure. The treatment is surgery.

Benign Ovarian Tumors

Because the ovary is a complex structure containing many types of cells including ova (which have the potential of making every type of cell), many different types of tumors can form in the ovary. The most common benign ovarian tumor is the simple cyst that occurs when the small cyst containing the ovum does not rupture at the proper time in the cycle to expel the ovum but continues to grow. Such cysts usually disappear in one or two months, but if they rupture, they may cause pain or internal bleeding and sometimes require surgery. Dermoid cysts, containing hair, fatty material, and often teeth, are common in young women and are thought to be embryonic remnants present before birth. Although benign, they require removal. Other benign ovarian tumors, both cystic and solid, may cause symptoms and require surgery. If an ovarian tumor persists, it must be removed to find out whether or not it is malignant.

Ovarian Cancer

There are many types of cancer of the ovary. The long-term outlook depends on the type, but all are difficult to diagnose early because symptoms do not occur early. Final diagnosis depends on removal of the tumor at the time of exploratory surgery for microscopic examination. Treatment consists of surgical removal of as much tumor as possible followed by chemotherapy. Women who have taken the oral contraceptive pill have a decreased incidence of ovarian cancer.

ENDOCRINE PROBLEMS

The gynecologic problems considered up to this point have been those for which a specific abnormal tissue has been responsible. Because of the complex interrelationship between the ovary, the hypothalamus, the pituitary gland, the thyroid, and the adrenal glands, many abnormalities of the menstrual cycle are caused by dysfunctions or malfunctions of these endocrine glands. These abnormalities include heavy, irregular menstrual periods, called dysfunctional uterine bleeding. Lack of periods and lack of ovulation may also be endocrine problems.

Unraveling the complexities of endocrine malfunction requires many expensive and complex hormone tests to discover the level of hormones in the body and to find out how one endocrine gland responds when hormones from another gland are administered.

Some pituitary malfunctions are caused by severe dieting or physical and emotional stress on the hypothalamus of the brain. Other problems are genetically determined. Treatment depends on the particular abnormality.

TYPES OF GYNECOLOGIC TREATMENT

Because of the number of treatment options available, it is important for women to become as knowledgeable as possible in order to make intelligent decisions.

TREATMENT OF INFECTION

Gynecologic infections may be caused by viruses, bacteria, fungi, spirochetes, and protozoan. Infection caused by each of these types of organisms requires a different type of treatment. Viruses, causing herpes and warts, are impossible to destroy effectively with current drugs. However, symptoms can be relieved and some effects of their presence can be treated. Warts, which are virally induced, can be removed by cautery, cryosurgery, or laser.

Different types of bacteria can be treated effectively with antibiotics.

Treatment becomes more difficult when bacteria become resistant to particular antibiotics. Specific agents are available to treat monilia and trichomonas, common causes of vaginal infections. Because effective treatment requires knowledge of the specific nature of the infectious agent, the telephone management of vaginitis and urinary tract infections is not dependable.

HORMONE THERAPY

The vast publicity given to problems associated with the use of the oral contraceptive pill has clouded the fact that the discovery of orally effective estrogen and progesterone compounds has revolutionized the treatment of bleeding problems in women, reduced the number of D&Cs required, and often permitted an alternative to hysterectomy for control of hemorrhage. Surgery is no longer the first therapy for heavy bleeding. The use of progesterones to bring on a period in women with infrequent periods reduces the likelihood of cancer of the endometrium.

Estrogens have been used successfully in menopausal women for many years to relieve hot flashes and painful intercourse due to the thinning of the vagina. No other treatment works so well. In addition, estrogen slows osteoporosis, the thinning of the bones that occurs with aging. The recent linking of the use of estrogen during and after menopause with an increased rate of cancer of the endometrium has reminded us that relative risks are always difficult to assess, but this risk is eliminated by the addition of synthetic progesterones. Recent studies show that women given estrogen have a decreased risk of heart disease.

Androgens, male hormones, are produced in small quantities in the female by the ovaries and the adrenal gland. Androgens are occasionally used in the treatment of endometriosis, but newer synthetic hormones, such as danazol and nafarelin, are proving more effective. Hormones of the thyroid, pituitary, and adrenal glands are used to treat problems related to these glands.

CAUTERY

Cautery refers to the limited destruction of diseased tissue by the use of chemicals, heat, or cold. The use of heat is termed electrocautery; the use of cold, cryosurgery. It is used to treat venereal warts and to destroy the abnormal cells of dysplasia and carcinoma-in-situ of the cervix. Lasers are a new form of cautery.

SURGERY

Despite the availability of drugs to treat many problems, surgery may be required for certain disorders.

Excision Biopsy

Cone biopsy or conization, described as a diagnostic technique, may also have therapeutic application. The removal of abnormal tissue for diagnosis may be treatment as well. Drawbacks include the need for hospitalization and anesthesia and the possibility of heavy bleeding and infection.

Incision and Drainage (I&D)

Antibiotics cannot get into the center of a cyst or cavity where blood vessels do not penetrate. Whenever there is a collection of pus that does not drain on its own, it is necessary to cut into the cavity to allow it to do so. This minor operation is called incision and drainage. If the abscess re-forms, the incision must sometimes be sewed open to insure long-term drainage. This procedure is frequently used to treat Bartholin's abscesses. Drainage of a major infection of the tubes and ovaries that does not respond to antibiotics requires abdominal surgery.

Vaginal Surgery

Vaginal surgery is involved in the repair operations carried out in those women whose vaginas and surrounding connective tissue have been stretched and damaged by childbirth. The supporting structures are reached through incisions in the lining of the vagina, excess tissue is removed, the supports strengthened, and the incisions closed. A vaginal hysterectomy can also be carried out in this way.

Polypectomy

The removal of a cervical or uterine polyp is called polypectomy. Cervical polyps can usually be removed in a doctor's office. Because the removal of endometrial polyps involves dilatation of the cervix, anesthesia may be required, either in an office or out-patient operating room or in the hospital.

Endometrial Biopsy

A narrow instrument can usually be fitted through the cervical opening into the cavity of the uterus in order to obtain endometrial tissue for study. Suction may be used to pull the tissue into a container. Although the biopsy is uncomfortable, anesthesia is usually not necessary and the procedure can be carried out in an out-patient clinic or office.

Dilatation and Curettage (D&C) and Dilatation and Evacuation (D&E)

The cervix can stretch wide enough to permit a 10-pound baby's head to pass through it, but at other times it is closed so that only a narrow tube 1/8 inch in diameter can be passed into the uterus. If larger instruments are required for an operation inside the uterus, the cervix is opened by passing metal tubes of increasing diameter through the opening until the cervix will allow the passage of the required instrument. This is called dilatation of the cervix. Alternate methods using dilators that gradually absorb fluid (laminarias) are available.

In order to remove tissue from the uterus, an instrument called a curette, a loop with a sharp edge, is used to scrape the endometrium off the muscular part of the uterus. This procedure is called curettage. The tissue may be removed for examination and diagnosis or it may be removed as part of treatment for heavy or irregular uterine bleeding.

Dilatation and curettage (D&C) may also be performed to terminate pregnancy, as may a similar procedure, dilatation and evacuation (D&E), which uses a suction curette, a hollow tube connected to a vacuum pump, to remove tissue by suction (see "Contraception and Abortion"). Usually local anesthesia suffices for these procedures.

Myomectomy

The removal of a smooth muscle tumor (fibromyoma or fibroid) of the uterus is called a myomectomy. Because fibroids are usually multiple and small ones may continue to grow even though the largest ones are removed and because a myomectomy is technically more difficult to perform and associated with more blood loss than a hysterectomy, these tumors are generally removed by a hysterectomy. Myomectomy is usually reserved for women who want future pregnancies.

Hysterectomy

Hysterectomy is an operation currently embroiled in controversy. Based on recent figures, more than half of the women in the United States will have a hysterectomy by age 65. The term hysterectomy refers to the removal of the uterus. A total, complete, or radical hysterectomy is the complete removal of the uterus including the cervix. A partial or subtotal hysterectomy is one in which the cervix is not removed. Most hysterectomies currently performed are complete.

As the most commonly performed operation in the United States in the 1970s, hysterectomies, the vast number of which were elective, became the focus of investigation by consumer advocates, feminists, and health care economists. The consensus among these groups is that one-third of all such operations are unnecessary, and in that regard, the following figures are of some significance: twice as many hysterectomies are performed in the South as in the Northeast; many more are performed in situations where the individual surgeon is paid a fee than if

ABDOMINAL HYSTERECTOMY

- Vertical incision
- or
- Transverse ("Bikini") incision

VAGINAL HYSTERECTOMY
(CROSS-SECTION OF PELVIS)

Bladder

Vaginal walls

Uterus

Incision

Incision

Uterus pulled into vagina — incision lines indicated

the surgery is done under a prepaid health plan. It is generally agreed that a hysterectomy is the necessary treatment for

1. Cancer or precancer of the uterus, fallopian tubes, or ovaries.
2. Irreversible or incapacitating damage caused by infection (Pelvic Inflammatory Disease).
3. Benign fibroids large enough to cause chronic pain and/or excessive bleeding.
4. Uterine bleeding of no matter what source that is unresponsive to hormone therapy or D&C.
5. Severe endometriosis that does not respond favorably to drug therapy.
6. A severely damaged uterus resulting from a mishandled childbirth or abortion.

The unresolved question is whether or not the operation should be performed on women near or past menopause who have heavy bleeding with no indication of uterine abnormality. Debate continues about the removal of the otherwise normal uterus either as a means of contraception or as a way of preventing future problems including the possibility of cancer.

Note that the term hysterectomy says nothing about the removal of the ovaries and tubes. Decisions regarding the removal of these organs must be made separately. Many gynecologists prefer to remove the ovaries whenever they are performing a pelvic operation on a woman at or near the menopause because the ovaries produce relatively little estrogen thereafter and ovarian cancer, which develops in 1 out of every 100 women, is hard to detect and hard to cure. Sometimes the ovaries must be removed before the menopause because of disease. In this circumstance estrogens should be given at least until the age of normal menopause.

The uterus can be removed through an abdominal incision, either vertical or crosswise, or through a vaginal incision around the cervix at the top of the vagina (see illustration). The operations are called abdominal and vaginal hysterectomies, respectively. Many factors influence the route chosen. The vaginal route is chosen if repair work is required for injuries to the bladder and rectum sustained in childbirth, and occasionally for other reasons. Frequently, with the patient's permission, the surgeon will take out the appendix at the time of an abdominal hysterectomy (it takes only five minutes longer) to prevent future appendicitis. Surgery for cancer is more extensive than other types and is always modified by the extent of the tumor found at the time of the

CROSS-SECTION OF PELVIS AFTER HYSTERECTOMY

surgery. Ovarian surgery and general exploration of the abdominal organs is easier with the abdominal incision.

A typical hysterectomy usually involves a three- to five-day hospital stay followed by three to five weeks of recovery time at home before resuming normal activities. For the woman previously engaged in a strenuous schedule, some curtailment of demands on energy should be made for at least three months. It is by no means unusual for some women to tire easily one year following surgery. In general, speed of recovery is affected by attitude, general health, and emotional support from family members, friends, and colleagues.

The loss of the uterus ends both childbearing and menstruation. The capacity to bear children has always been very important to women, and the loss of this potential may be threatening. Among the myths that have emerged regarding a hysterectomy is that sexual response is decreased. Actually, sexual response is usually unaffected. Some women anticipate the onset of obesity. The fact that physical activity is curtailed for a few weeks may confirm their fear and start them on an inactive, weight-gaining course. If the ovaries remain, estrogen production continues to the age of the expected menopause so that hot flashes and other menopausal symptoms do not occur until later, even though periods are absent.

The psychological aftermath of a hysterectomy depends on the degree to which the woman regards her uterus as her feminine identity. If she feels that her femininity resides in her womb, she may find the postoperative adjustment hard. If she understands and accepts the operation, she may welcome the relief of symptoms that the operation affords. The adjustment is hardest for the young childless woman; often counseling will be required to help her come to terms with this crisis in her life.

Tubal Surgery

The most common operation performed on the fallopian tubes is the tubal ligation for sterilization (discussed in "Contraception and Abortion"). Less common is the surgery (salpingectomy) necessitated by a tubal or ectopic pregnancy. If the other tube is normal, it is usual to remove both the tube and the pregnancy because a scarred tube, if left behind, may become the site of a second tubal pregnancy. However, the pregnancy often can be removed and the tube carefully repaired. Occasionally, women who have had tubal ligations for sterilization request reversal of the procedure. The tubes can be put back together using operating microscopes and microsurgical techniques, but such operations are difficult, expensive, and only about 50 percent effective.

Ovarian Surgery

Ovarian surgery involves removing part or all of an ovary because of cysts or tumors. Removal of an ovary is termed oophorectomy. In the case of benign cysts and tumors as much normal ovary is saved as possible. Pregnancies can occur in women with only half of one ovary. If an ovarian or uterine tumor is malignant, all of the reproductive organs are removed together because the cancer tends to spread to the nearby uterus and the opposite tube and ovary. Severe pelvic infections and abscesses involving the tubes and ovaries that do not respond adequately to antibiotics often require extensive surgery for cure.

Preparation for Surgery

Here are some ways to relieve the anxiety experienced before undergoing surgery:

1. Be sure you understand *why* the surgery is necessary.
2. Find out whether the person who will perform the surgery is a board-certified gynecological surgeon.
3. If you can choose the hospital, select the one associated with a large medical center rather than one that is privately owned.
4. Don't hesitate to ask any questions that occur to you at the last minute.
5. Check your health insurance coverage so that you'll know what to expect in terms of hospital bills, bills from the surgeon, the anesthetist, etc.
6. Organize your family life and your job responsibilities so that you don't have to worry about details when you're in the hospital.
7. If you have the time to do so, you can set up an emergency blood supply by donating your own blood and asking a friend or family member with the same blood type to make a donation on your behalf in case of need.

In addition, for any but minor office procedures, oral contraceptive pills should be discontinued one month in advance to help prevent postoperative blood clots. (But be sure to use some alternate method of contraception because an unplanned pregnancy can only complicate matters!) Aspirin increases bleeding time and blood loss and should not be used for two weeks before surgery.

A well-balanced diet with a minimum of caffeine and alcohol helps bring a woman to surgery in optimum condition. Each surgeon is likely to have other specific requests for the period immediately before the operation.

Surgical Complications

Fifty years ago surgery was so dangerous that no one needed to be told that there were risks involved. Now risks may be overlooked. This is a mistake. All anesthesia, whether general or local, involves a small risk of death. Hemorrhage and infection are potential hazards in almost all surgery, although blood banks and antibiotics have greatly reduced these risks. Adhesions, the attachment of one bit of injured tissue to another, occur after most abdominal surgery as part of the healing process and may cause pain or obstruct the bowel. This contingency is reduced by early ambulation.

RADIATION THERAPY

Radiotherapy involving X-rays or radioactive isotopes is reserved either for the treatment of malignancies in which the tumor has spread to areas that cannot be safely removed or for cases where experience has shown that the tumor responds better to radiation or to a combination of radiation and surgery than to surgery alone. Cells that are dividing rapidly are destroyed by irradiation more easily than are normal resting cells so that growing tumors can usually be treated with minimal damage to the surrounding tissue. Complications involving skin, bowel, bladder, and rectum do occur but have decreased with more powerful sources of radiation that can be more precisely directed to the involved area.

Cancer of the cervix, the endometrium, and the ovary all respond well to radiation, often with a high "cure" rate or 5-year survival rate.

CHEMOTHERAPY

The term applied to the use of a variety of drugs for cancer treatment is chemotherapy. Most of these drugs depend for their effectiveness on the susceptibility of rapidly growing tumor cells to toxic substances. The choice and use of these agents is a very complex, specialized field.

Cancer of the ovary and widespread cancer of the endometrium can occasionally be cured by chemotherapy. Many more tumors respond well to chemotherapy for months or years before recurring.

COUNSELING

Many problems presented to the gynecologist involve sexual functioning, interpersonal relationships, and questions concerning contraception and abortion. While a detailed discussion of the issues involved can take place during a regular visit, sometimes a more leisurely appointment needs to be scheduled. The physician may also feel that referral to another source of information or treatment would be in the patient's best interest. Such a referral, whether it be to a psychotherapist, an endocrinologist, a sex therapy clinic, or to one of the many support groups for cancer patients, should not be seen as a rejection but rather as evidence that the referring doctor is trying to find the person who can be most helpful in dealing with your personal area of concern.

SEXUALLY TRANSMISSIBLE DISEASES

Louise Tyrer, M.D.
Vice-President for Medical Affairs,
Planned Parenthood Federation of America, Inc.

The specter of venereal disease (VD), long kept in the closet, has emerged in epidemic proportions. In a typical year, over 6 million Americans are newly infected with a sexually contracted disease. As we learn more about diseases that can be transmitted from one sex partner to another, it has become apparent that the term VD is outmoded. VD used to be the "Big Five" diseases reported to most state health departments in the United States—gonorrhea, syphilis, chancroid, lymphogranuloma venereum, and granuloma inguinale. However, chlamydia, which affects 3 to 10 million Americans, is far more widespread than gonorrhea. As many as 50 million Americans are believed to be infected with genital herpes. Each year, there are one million new cases of genital warts, some of which are likely to be the forerunners of certain types of cancer. And the latest arrival in this somber litany as we all know is acquired immune deficiency syndrome, usually referred to as AIDS.

There are not only many diseases that are sexually transmitted; there are also diseases that may be contracted as a result of low systemic resistance, altered body metabolism, or other causes and are then transmitted to a sexual partner. Therefore, the term *sexually transmissible diseases* (STDs) has been adopted to cover this broad spectrum of conditions.

As long as people communicate through touching—and let's hope that this is forever—STD will be a potential problem. So, rather than deny ourselves sexual expression, we should learn about STDs, how to prevent them, and how to recognize their symptoms so that early treatment can be obtained. While we have antibiotics and other drugs that can cure or arrest many STDs, those that are caused by viruses, especially AIDS, continue to present a challenge to the scientific community and a major threat to the world at large.

There are at least 20 diseases that may be transmitted by sexual contact. Many ask why, with more knowledge about STD and readily available treatment, haven't STDs been eliminated or at least contained? As with other complex problems, there is no single simple answer. Some of the factors responsible are:

Increased sexual expression. All types of intimate contacts, including sexual, are increasing, particularly among the young. Changing sexual partners or having multiple partners greatly increases the risk of contracting an STD.

Contraceptive practices. Today the most effective methods of contraception are the pill, the IUD, and sterilization. However, none of these offers any protection against STD compared to the less effective barrier methods.

Social disgrace. Many people, including health professionals, still attach strong negative judgments to anyone with an STD. This person then reacts with shame and fear and delays diagnosis and treatment. Also, he or she may be unwilling to disclose his or her sexual contact(s), making it impossible to break the chain.

Asymptomatic carriers. Seven of the STDs, including chlamydia, syphilis, gonorrhea, and AIDs, may occur without any symptoms. People may be highly infectious and be completely unaware of their condition.

Resistant strains. Certain bacteria, particularly the one causing gonorrhea, may become resistant to the usual antibiotics. Because most people believe that one magic shot will cure them, they may not return for "tests of cure" and may still harbor the infection.

World travel. The mobility of our population today accounts for an increased rate of spread of STDs. Also, rare diseases, once indigenous to specific areas of the world, are now spreading globally.

Complacency. Public health agencies have not been spending enough time and money on identifying cases and contacts. This is coupled with an attitude held by many people that reporting of cases and tracing contacts is unimportant because treatment, except for AIDS, is so readily available.

Underreporting of cases. By law syphilis and gonorrhea (in most states), and recently AIDs and herpes type II (in some states), must be reported to health departments. However, only about one out of nine cases of these STDs in the United States is reported. This is frequently related to physician negligence, often because the professional is overly concerned about "protecting" the patient.

Education. There is insufficient education at all levels regarding STDs' frequency, prevention, recognition, diagnosis, and treatment. Also, educators need to dispel the stigma associated with STD so that it is considered with the same nonjudgmental attitude as other diseases requiring urgent treatment, such as appendicitis.

WHAT WOMEN NEED TO KNOW ABOUT STD

A woman has a built-in awareness of her bodily functions. Education about symptoms of the STDs can increase that level of sensitivity so that she can notice subtle changes that may indicate the onset of an STD. But what can she do to protect herself against infection and what should she know if she suspects she may have been infected?

There is no way to know in advance that a sexual partner is free of STD. Abstinence is the only guarantee against exposure. Of course, if it is apparent that the partner has a genital lesion or a discharge or admits exposure to an STD, avoidance of sex is the only safe course. A woman must not be bashful about querying her partner or even inspecting his genitals for lesions or urethral discharge, nor should she be offended if he wishes to do the same.

Assuming one is sexually active, the greatest protection against contracting an STD is to develop a monogamous relationship with a partner who is also monogamous. The general rule is: the more partners, the greater the risk of exposure and of contracting disease.

If either partner is not monogamous, insisting that the male use a latex condom affords a woman the best possible protection against her getting or giving STD. She would do well to carry condoms with her, in case her partner does not have one available, and should hold firm to the premise "no condom, no sex."

A woman can supplement this protection if she uses a vaginal barrier (for example, diaphragm with jelly or cream, the vaginal sponge, foam, or suppositories). The woman who takes the pill or has an IUD can, by the use of a barrier method not only slightly increase the protection her contraception affords but at the same time have some protection against STD.

If you are concerned that your partner may have a sexually transmissible disease, there are some things you should do to prevent becoming infected. It is important that your genital area be cleaned prior to and after sex. Also, urinating prior to beginning sex or, better soon after coitus helps to "flush out" organisms from your urethra that can cause urethritis or cystitis. This approach, however, will not reduce the occurrence of infection in the vagina or the cervix. Immediately wash the vulva with soap and water. Avoid strong medicated or highly perfumed soaps and deodorant sprays as they may be irritating. Insert an applicator or two of contraceptive foam, cream, or jelly high into the vagina and rub it on the external genitals as well. Although the protective effect of after-the-fact use of a vaginal contraceptive has not been documented, its prior use is known to be somewhat effective, so it couldn't hurt.

Douching is not effective and may even encourage bacteria to enter the cervical canal. Also, if you have a chemical vaginal contraceptive in place, douching would remove this effective barrier.

If there is a good possibility you have been exposed—say, your partner tells you of his prior exposure to someone with STD or you were raped—call a clinician (physician, hospital clinic, public health facility) and make an appointment to be seen right away. There are antibiotics that can be given that provide effective prophylaxis against gonorrhea, syphilis, and chlamydia when taken shortly after such sexual contact. (Antibiotics should be taken only after a known or possible exposure. They should never be taken before expected contact.) The clinician can recommend a plan of follow-up examinations to assure you of proper diagnosis and, if indicated, treatment.

Anxiety about having STD is common. Many people think they have STD when they do not. The only way to be sure is to have an examination and diagnostic tests. If the proper testing procedure is followed and the tests are negative, you can put the matter from your mind, while vowing to be more careful in the future. Some women, however, become so obsessed that they imagine all sorts of symptoms, such as itching and abnormal discharge. This is an unhealthy attitude, and if examination, testing, and reassurance does not solve the problem, psychological help may be necessary.

Certain important considerations are applicable to all STDs. The specific diseases are discussed in the next section.

1. A woman should ask her clinician to examine and test her for STDs at the time of her annual health checkup through whatever means are indicated (e.g., blood tests, pap smear, cultures, or examination of a "wet mount" of her discharge under the microscope).

2. A woman may have more than one STD. Therefore, it is important that tests to determine whether several diseases are present should also be considered and done if indicated.

3. In most instances, the sexual partner(s) require examination and treatment in conjunction with the woman to ensure a cure. The antibiotic used would usually be the same for both (presuming no allergy): however, dosages may vary based upon such variables as body weight, site of infection, or stage of disease. With some infections such as hemophilus vaginalis, use of a condom for about six weeks from the time the woman initiates treatment may be sufficient.

4. If a woman has recurring bouts of vaginal infection, with irritation of the surrounding skin, the local reaction can be reduced and sometimes virtually eliminated by not wearing restrictive and nonabsorptive clothing, such as tight pants or nylon panty hose. Dryness is a very important part of the healing process. During this phase it is best to wear skirts and cotton underpants, which should be changed daily, washed with a mild soap (avoid detergents), and thoroughly rinsed. Deodorant sprays should never be used on the sensitive vulvar skin. They can only cause problems.

5. If a woman masters the technique of internal vaginal and cervical examination, using a speculum, a good light source, and a mirror, and practices it routinely at least once a month (usually best done shortly after the menstrual period when the hormonal influences are at a low level), she may observe changes suggestive of the onset of STD. This will enable her to seek earlier diagnosis and treatment. For example, she may notice a change in the character of the vaginal discharge or an inflammation of the cervix.

6. Certain STDs or their treatment create a special risk for a fetus or a newborn. Therefore, a pregnant woman should familiarize herself with those STDs that may place her and her offspring at risk; she should talk with her obstetrician about the need for special tests and discuss appropriate options, if certain tests are positive. The type of therapy and the dosage of many medications must be made consistent with protection of the fetus. For example, pregnant women should not take tetracyclines as they can affect dental development in the fetus.

7. A woman must inform the clinician, prior to therapy, whether she has any drug allergies, particularly to penicillin or sulfa.

8. Follow-up examinations and tests to assure cure are mandatory after treatment of any STD. The return visit needs to be scheduled at the time of the initial visit.

DESCRIPTION OF SPECIFIC STDS

Each STD is discussed below alphabetically (not by frequency of occurrence) with symptoms, diagnosis, and treatment explained.

AIDS (ACQUIRED IMMUNE DEFICIENCY SYNDROME)

AIDS is characterized by a severe immune deficiency that leaves the body defenseless against "opportunistic infections." In the United States it occurs mainly among homosexual or bisexual males who have multiple male partners and among intravenous drug users. It usually is sexually transmitted by an affected male to a female partner but can be transmitted by an affected female to a male. A mounting number of AIDS-infected newborn babies are born to women who have AIDS as a result of sexual contact with others who have the disease including intravenous drug users, bisexual men or even heterosexual men who have multiple sexual partners.

To prevent the spread of AIDS, a woman should avoid sexual contact with persons known to have or suspected of having AIDS and be aware that having male sexual partners who are IV drug users or bisexual increases one's risks. Until the availability of a vaccine or a cure for this deadly disease, the only protection a woman can count on is the male use of a condom, preferably a latex condom, combined with a spermicide.

CHANCROID

The first symptom is a small, painful boil most commonly found on the external genitalia. It does not heal like the usual pimple and becomes a running sore. The causative organism, *Hemophilus ducreyi*, moves through the lymphatics into the groin and, if untreated, these infected glands break down and exude pus. It is fairly common in the tropics, rare in the United States. Often the diagnosis can be made by inspecting the lesion, but microscopic examination of the pus will reveal the causative organism. A microscopic examination to rule out syphilis must also be performed. Therapy usually consists of oral sulfa drugs or tetracycline combined with intensive compressing of the lesion(s).

CHLAMYDIAL INFECTIONS

Chlamydia are organisms that cause a variety of infections, some of which are sexually transmitted. The infections are difficult to diagnose. Chlamydia are neither viruses nor bacteria but are called elementary bodies. These bodies are incorporated in cells where they dwell and can be identified by microscopic examination of stained smears of the infected tissue.

Chlamydial infections are the most prevalent form of STD, far more widespread than genital herpes and gonorrhea. They can attack any part of the urogenital tract as well as the anus of both sexes. Chlamydia can cause sterility when it affects the fallopian tubes, and in young women, it is the major cause of pelvic inflammatory disease, which, if untreated, can lead to infertility. In males, it is a leading cause of nongonococcal urethritis that can result in male sterility. A woman who has had sexual intercourse with a man who has NGU often is treated as if she had chlamydial vaginitis.

Sixty percent of females and 25 percent of males show no serious symptoms until infection is quite advanced. Burning and frequency of urination occur most commonly in the male but can occur in females as well. Five to ten percent of pregnant women seen at prenatal clinics are

Heterosexuals and AIDS: Assessing the Risks

Based on data from several studies, researchers have roughly estimated the chance of becoming infected with the AIDS virus through heterosexual intercourse with partners of varying backgrounds. The true risk in individual cases may differ greatly from group averages. The scientists say that while even the group averages are only approximate, they accurately characterize the comparative risks. For all categories, the chance that the virus will be transmitted in a single sexual contact with a partner who is definitely infected is assumed to be 1 in 500; the condom failure rate is assumed to be 1 in 10.

Risk Category of Partner	Assumed Prevalence of Infection	One Sexual Encounter	500 Sexual Encounters
Infection Status Unknown			
Not in any high-risk group			
Using condoms	0.0001	1 in 50 million	1 in 110,000
Not using condoms	0.0001	1 in 5 million	1 in 16,000
High-Risk Groups[1]			
Using condoms	0.05 to 0.5	1 in 100,000 to 1 in 10,000	1 in 210 to 1 in 21
Not using condoms	0.05 to 0.5	1 in 10,000 to 1 in 1,000	1 in 32 to 1 in 3
Negative AIDS virus test[2]			
No history of high-risk behavior			
Using condoms	0.000001	1 in 5 billion	1 in 11 million
Not using condoms	0.000001	1 in 500 million	1 in 1.6 million
Continuing high-risk behavior[3]			
Using condoms	0.01	1 in 500,000	1 in 1,100
Not using condoms	0.01	1 in 50,000	1 in 160
Infected with AIDS virus			
Using condoms	1.0	1 in 5,000	1 in 11
Not using condoms	1.0	1 in 500	2 in 3

[1] A range is given because the extent of infection varies widely within the groups. The greatest risks involve homosexual or bisexual men and intravenous drug users from major metropolitan areas and hemophiliacs. The lower risks involve homosexual or bisexual men and drug users from other parts of the country, female prostitutes, heterosexuals from Haiti and certain African countries, and recipients in the early 1980's of multiple blood transfusions in areas where the virus is prevalent.

[2] A negative virus test could be misleading because of testing inaccuracy, because the person had not developed antibodies at the time of testing or because the person was infected after the test.

[3] Sexual intercourse or needle-sharing with a risk-group member.

SOURCE: Journal of the American Medical Association

Copyright © 1988 by The New York Times Company. Reprinted by permission.

infected at the time of delivery and there is considerable risk that chlamydial infection will be transmitted to the eyes of the newborn as it passes through the birth canal. It is estimated that each year, 70,000 infants are born with chlamydial conjunctivitis, a condition that requires prompt treatment if extensive scarring and blindness are to be prevented.

Chlamydial infections may be diagnosed by a recent test that takes only 30 minutes and is as good as or even better than the previous one that took four to six days. It is called MicroTrack and consists in taking a cell sample from the sexual organs and adding monoclonal antibodies to the sample. If chlamydial microorganisms are present, they combine with the antibodies, producing a radioactive signal that is visible in an ultraviolet microscope. However, there is still a considerable degree of inaccuracy with this test.

CYSTITIS

See "Gynecologic Diseases and Treatment"; URINARY TRACT INFECTIONS.

GONORRHEA

This common STD is caused by gonococcal bacteria *(Neisseria gonorrhoeae).* A symptom of uncomplicated gonorrhea is a green or yellow-green vaginal discharge, often with a distinctive mushroom-like odor not previously present. The infection may also occur primarily in the throat, producing pharyngitis, or in the rectum, causing proctitis. It has an average incubation period of 3 to 5 days. There is an 80 percent chance that a woman infected with gonorrhea will have no symptoms because the infection is located in the cervix, high up in the woman's vagina. In males the infection is in the urethra and causes a pus-like discharge. However, 10 to 20 percent of infected men have no discharge and no other symptoms. The fact that there are many asymptomatic carriers explains why this disease is almost impossible to eradicate. Complications of gonorrhea result from spread of the infection to other organs causing infection, inflammation, and any combination of the following conditions:

1. Lower abdominal pains.
2. Continuous low back pains.
3. Burning and frequency of urination, sometimes associated with a drop of pus or blood.
4. Swelling and tenderness (abscess) of the Bartholin's gland located near the opening of the vagina.
5. Pleurisy-type pains in the right upper abdomen (perihepatitis) or in the shoulder area.
6. Severe pain in the pelvic area as gonorrhea moves up into the fallopian tubes (pelvic inflammatory disease).
7. Severe generalized abdominal pain as the infection spreads from the tubes to the abdominal cavity (pelvic peritonitis).
8. Pelvic pain as abscesses develop in the pelvis.
9. Sterility, resulting from blocked tubes or surgery necessary to remove abscesses.
10. Other serious complications, such as gonorrheal arthritis and gonorrheal pericarditis.

The eyes of the newborn are particularly susceptible to gonorrheal infection. If prophylactic measures, such as instillation of silver nitrate solution or penicillin injection, are not taken at birth and the infection develops, blindness may result.

In women gonorrhea is diagnosed by a culture taken from the cervix. Other sites of possible infection such as the throat, urethra, or rectum need to be cultured as well if history and examination should indicate possible exposure at these sites. A positive culture provides a firm diagnosis of gonorrhea. However, a negative culture does not necessarily rule out the possibility, particularly if the infection has spread into the tubes or is at a site other than one that was cultured.

Injectable penicillin that is short-acting but gives a high blood level concentration is the preferred treatment for uncomplicated gonorrhea. It should be combined with the penicillin-enhancing drug probencid. Higher than usual doses of penicillin for longer periods are required when the infection is in the tubes or causing peritonitis. The Centers for Disease Control (CDC) now encourage combining tetracycline therapy with penicillin to treat chlamydia, a commonly associated infection, along with gonorrhea. All individuals undergoing treatment for gonorrhea must return at the appointed time for repeat cultures as a test of cure.

The presence of a strain of gonorrhea that is resistant to penicillin and tetracycline can be revealed by antibiotic sensitivity tests done on the cultured gonococci bacteria. In such cases, newer antibiotics, spectinomycin or ceftriaxone, are used for treatment.

The incidence of infertility (sterility) is higher following each tubal infection. If abscesses form in the tubes and ovaries, surgery may be required, frequently leaving a woman sterile. Early diagnosis and treatment can practically eliminate the need for surgical management.

Because there is now an effective vaccine against meningococcal bacteria that cause cerebrospinal meningitis, it is hoped that a vaccine against the related gonococcal bacteria will soon be available.

GRANULOMA INGUINALE

This disease, caused by an intracellular organism *(Donovania granulomatis)*, is rare in the United States. It is generally found in tropical climates and is usually associated with lack of personal cleanliness. A woman infected with this disease may note an unusual cyst, papule, or nodule in the genital area 3 to 8 days or as long as a few months after exposure. The cyst eventually breaks down, forming an ulcer with a granular base (a granulation is one of the tiny, red granules of new capillaries that form on the surface of an ulcer). Another type of early lesion is a clean, raised, velvety tuft of granulation tissue with a sharply defined margin that bleeds easily. These early lesions are not painful. They do not heal readily and they spread, so that if untreated they eventually may involve most of the vulva and even extend onto the buttocks or lower abdomen. Late in the course of the disease there is interference of lymphatic drainage and elephantiasis may occur.

Microscopic examination of tissue smears will reveal Donovan bodies included within the cell to confirm the diagnosis based on the appearance of the lesions.

The preferred treatment is tetracycline until all lesions are healed. Ampicillin, an oral penicillin derivative, is an alternative therapy. In the late stages, surgery may be necessary. However, if the disease is of long duration, it is often progressive, even with surgery.

HEMOPHILUS VAGINALIS (HV) AND CORYNEBACTERIUM VAGINALE

Heavy and unusual vaginal discharge, with or without irritation, is the most common symptom. Often, the discharge has an unpleasant fishy odor, is grayish, and may be frothy.

On a wet mount of vaginal secretions examined under the microscope, the causative organism will be seen, identified as "clue cells." It may also be identified in a pap smear or a stained smear examined under the microscope.

Oral antibiotics such as metronidazole or ampicillin should be curative. Use of sulfa creams vaginally may suppress symptoms.

HEPATITIS B

Symptoms of infection are often mild. Infected persons may report fatigue, loss of appetite, and some abdominal pain. In more severe cases, jaundice and enlargement and tenderness of the liver may occur. There is now scientific evidence linking HBV infection to liver cancer. The most common mode of sexual transmission is with anal intercourse. However it is now well recognized that this disease is a major occupational hazard for health care providers exposed to contaminated blood. Their infection rate is about six times that of the general public.

Currently there is no known effective treatment for chronic hepatitis B. There are two main approaches to prevention of hepatitis B infection using vaccines: pre-exposure and post-exposure immunizations. Pre-exposure immunization allows the body to produce antibodies to the virus in order to protect an individual against possible exposure. Post-exposure vaccination immediately after known exposure is also effective because of the long incubation period of the virus inside the liver cells, providing an opportunity for vaccine-induced antibodies to act before the infection spreads. Sexual transmission can be reduced by safer sexual practices including the use of condoms.

HERPES SIMPLEX VIRUS INFECTION (GENITAL HERPES)

Herpes simplex is a virus. Its two variants are herpes labialis, also known as herpes simplex virus type I (HSV-1), and herpes genitalis, or herpes simplex virus type II (HSV-2). Herpes labialis (type I) infection affects primarily the area of the head and neck where it causes what are commonly called cold sores or fever blisters. However, type I causes about 25 percent of herpes genital infections. Herpes genitalis (type II) is a distinctly different virus that affects primarily the genital area, often causing intensely painful lesions. However, of the 50 million Americans believed to be infected with genital herpes, only one quarter experience any symptoms even though they are capable of transmitting the infection to their sexual partners.

A woman infected in the genital area for the first time with herpes is usually asymptomatic (75 to 90 percent). The symptomatic woman generally will notice one or more small, painful, fluid-filled blisters on the external genitalia within 3 to 20 days after exposure. They may occur also or only in the vagina or on the cervix and may not be noticed, but they can be seen on examination or be identified by a pap smear. These soon rupture and, when located externally, form soft, extremely painful, open sores. Secondary infection with bacteria can further aggravate the situation. The lymph glands in the groin may become enlarged and tender.

The herpes viruses have a tendency to remain in the body without evidence of their presence and may reactivate (particularly type II) especially when stimulated by stress or illness. The initial infection usually heals in about 10 to 12 days. Recurrences heal faster and are less painful.

An acute herpes infection of the genital area (both types) during pregnancy may have adverse effects such as abortion, still birth, or infection of the newborn as it passes through the birth canal. It is estimated that neonatal herpes kills one-third of the newborns to whom it is transmitted and another one-third suffer from mental retardation. Therefore, when active infection is present at term, delivery by cesarean section may reduce the chance of infecting the baby. The additional concern that remains to be proven is the possible relationship between herpes type II infection and development, years later, of cancer of the cervix.

Herpes simplex infection is usually diagnosed clinically by inspection of the lesions or by pap smear where a typical giant cell is identified. In addition, viral cultures may be taken from the sores for positive identification or a fluorescein-conjugated monoclomal antibody test can be done to differentiate the type.

There is no specific treatment that cures herpes, and no vaccine against it is currently available. However, Zovirax (acyclovir), when taken orally for about five days at the time of an initial infection, is effective in reducing the symptoms of herpes and in shortening its duration. It also is effective, when taken for longer periods—perhaps four months or more—in reducing or preventing recurrences. Further, any recurrence usually is reduced in severity. While side effects from the acyclovir are infrequent, they may include nausea, vomiting, diarrhea, dizziness, and headache. A pregnant or breastfeeding woman should not take this medication unless her physician specifically approves of her doing so.

Additional therapy is directed toward further relief of discomfort and prevention of secondary bacterial infection of open genital lesions, usually with compresses and sitz baths; sometimes prescription pain medication is required. Acyclovir cream applied to the lesions of an initial herpes infection also may diminish its duration and discomfort. Avoidance of sexual intercourse when initial and recurrent lesions are present is best.

Although it is not known whether the use of a condom will with certainty prevent transmission of the virus from an infected male, its use is recommended. However, the virus may be transmitted from genital areas not covered by the condom.

MOLLUSCUM CONTAGIOSUM

The very large virus of molluscum contagiosum affects the skin. In addition to being an STD, it may be transmitted by other forms of close body contact. It causes a very small, pinkish-white, waxy-looking, polyplike growth appearing in the genital area and on the thighs. The incubation period varies from 3 weeks to 3 months.

Usually the diagnosis is made clinically. Microscopic examination of the stained contents of the lesion reveals the inclusion bodies of the virus contained within large ballooned cells.

Each lesion must be destroyed by hot or cold cautery or cauterizing chemicals. New lesions may occur 2 to 3 weeks following the initial therapy and require additional treatment.

PELVIC INFLAMMATORY DISEASE (PID)

PID is an infection of the tubes and ovaries and has multiple causes, some of which are STDs. The commonest pathogens that cause PID are chlamydia, *N. gonorrhea*, tuberculosis, streptococcus, and *E. coli*. It is now known to occur without the history or findings of an STD among some IUD users. In such cases, if the infection does not respond promptly to treatment, it is best to remove the IUD.

Infectious organisms travel up through the cervix and uterus and cause inflammation and even abscesses of the fallopian tubes, the ovaries, and the pelvis. Typically, a woman who has PID is acutely ill with fever and lower abdominal pain. About 13 percent of women are infertile after their first attack of PID. After three attacks, the proportion is as high as 75 percent. Ensuring that one's sexual partner is not an asymptomatic carrier of an STD can reduce one's risk of reinfection.

The diagnosis of PID is made by history, abdominal and pelvic examination, and laboratory testing. At times the interior of the abdomen is viewed with the laparoscope to differentiate between PID and appendicitis, ectopic pregnancy, or other intra-abdominal emergencies, these conditions being surgical emergencies while PID usually is not.

The treatment is a combination of antibiotics, orally or intravenously. If abscesses have formed that cannot be eliminated with antibiotics, surgery may be required. If so, the chance of sterility resulting is high, as often the uterus, both tubes, and the ovaries must be removed to effect a cure. However, laser surgery may preserve fertility in some instances.

PUBIC LICE ("CRABS")

An infestation with pubic lice (crab lice) is almost always sexually transmitted. However, lice or their eggs may be transmitted through infected clothing, bedding, and toilet seats. The adult organisms infest immediately, while their eggs hatch after 3 to 14 days. The most common symptom is intense itching in the pubic hair as a reaction to the bites of the lice.

The pubic louse is yellowish-gray in color, but after it is swollen with blood it becomes dark. It can be found attached to pubic hairs. The eggs are white and give the appearance of a "growth" near the base of the hair shaft.

An infestation of pubic lice can be cured readily with the application of gamma benezene hexachloride (not to be used during pregnancy), commonly known as Kwell, and other similar preparations. It is available as a cream, lotion, or shampoo. In order to prevent recurrence, the sexual partner(s) must also take treatment, and clothes and bed linen must be washed or dry cleaned.

SCABIES

Scabies may or may not be an STD and is readily transmitted by intimate contact. It is caused by a mite called *Sarcoptes scabies*. The characteristic lesion is the burrow of the mite under the skin. It appears initially as a small, wavy line, usually located between the fingers, on the wrists, armpits, breasts, buttocks, thighs, and rarely on the genitalia. The face is not usually involved. Itching is present wherever the burrowing parasite is found and is worse at night. Scratching can cause secondary infection of the lesions.

Scabies can be diagnosed by clinical history and the presence of characteristic lesions. Additionally, the burrow can be scraped to obtain the mite, eggs, and larvae, which can be identified under the microscope.

After a prolonged bath, with thorough cleansing of the affected areas, an emulsion of 25 percent benzyl benzoate, available without a prescription, is applied from the neck down. The treatment needs to be repeated in 24 hours. Often, the best way to diagnose scabies is to take the treatment. Continued itching after the treatment is related to secondary infection and should be treated symptomatically. Bedding and clothing must be washed or dry cleaned.

SYPHILIS

Syphilis and AIDS are the most serious of the STDs because both diseases are life-threatening, not only to the woman herself, but to her future children. Syphilis is caused by a spirochete organism known as *Treponema pallidum.* It dies very quickly outside the human body and is killed by soap and water if present on the skin—a good reason for thorough washing after sex. The organism passes from the chancre or skin of an infected individual who is in the primary or secondary stage to an uninfected person through the latter's mucous membranes or a break in the skin. Because symptoms can simulate many other disease conditions or the disease may be asymptomatic for many years, the discussion of symptoms will be divided into the stages of the disease—primary, secondary, latent, and late—and other special situations. The stages describe the *untreated* course of this disease.

The primary sore of syphilis is the chancre. It appears where the organism entered the body, usually on the genitals, and may appear as early as 10 days or as long as 3 months after infection. The chancre is usually a solitary, painless ulceration that feels firm and has a slightly elevated border. In the woman it is commonly located on the cervix or in the vagina hidden from view. The chancre exudes the spirochete and is highly infectious. Often the associated lymph glands are swollen. Even without treatment the chancre heals within 1 to 5 weeks, concluding the primary stage.

The onset of the secondary stage occurs anywhere from 6 to 24 weeks after the untreated primary phase. It is often heralded by a general feeling of ill health. This may include any combination of the following symptoms: headache, muscle or joint aches, pain in the long bones, loss of appetite, nausea, constipation, and a lowgrade, persistent fever. Swelling and tenderness of the lymph glands are often present, and the hair may fall out in patches.

The most classical visible symptom of a secondary infection is a nonirritating, highly infectious rash. It may appear anywhere on the body. If the extremities are involved, it is symmetrically distributed. It may also affect the mucous membranes of the body and in women is commonly found around the labia. On the mucous membranes it appears initially as a grayish-white surface that breaks down into sores with a dull red base that ooze a clear fluid loaded with the infectious spirochete. Syphilitic warts may also develop on the genitals. Unless secondary infection occurs, these lesions are not usually painful. Without treatment the secondary phase usually passes in 4 to 12 weeks.

Latent syphilis is asymptomatic, beginning at the conclusion of the secondary phase. It is not infectious to a sexual contact, but the spirochete can spread within a pregnant woman to her fetus. Early latent syphilis has a duration of less than 4 years, while late latent syphilis extends from 4 years to the development, if it occurs, of late syphilis.

Approximately one-third of individuals develop manifestations of late syphilis. The other two-thirds do not, but we do not yet know what determines into which group they will fall. The most common manifestations of late syphilis are gumma (syphilitic tumors) in any affected organ, cardiovascular syphilis, and neurosyphilis. Late syphilis can cause insanity and death.

The spirochete of the mother's untreated syphilis at whatever stage invades the placenta and eventually the fetus between the tenth and eighteenth week of pregnancy. If untreated, the risk of stillbirth or of congenital syphilis affecting the newborn is high. It is important for every pregnant woman to be tested for syphilis early in pregnancy so that the disease may be treated before it can damage the fetus.

Most children born to women who have untreated syphilis during their pregnancies will have congenital syphilis. Its effects include blindness, deafness, crippling bone disease, and facial abnormalities. Special blood tests combined with other diagnostic measures are essential when congenital syphilis is suspected.

There are several tests used to diagnose syphilis; their performance and accuracy are related to the phase of the disease. Part of the diagnostic process is a complete physical examination, not limited to the genitals. Diagnostic laboratory tests include:

1. Darkfield Microscopic Examination. Fluid obtained from a chancre or other open sores is examined under a microscope to identify the spirochete.

2. Serologic Tests for Syphilis (STS). A number of different tests are done on blood serum to see whether an individual has a pathologic level of antibodies to the spirochete *T. pallidum*. It takes about three weeks following the appearance of the chancre for STS to become positive. Certain tests measure antibodies that show a declining titre concentration in blood serum with treatment and are indicators of successful

therapy. Other tests measure antibodies that, when they remain permanently elevated, indicate whether a person has ever had the disease.

3. Spinal Fluid Examination. With latent or late syphilis it is necessary to have a serologic test done on the cerebrospinal fluid to determine whether the infection has invaded the central nervous system because neurosyphilis requires special treatment.

The treatment of choice is long-acting penicillin. The dosage and duration of treatment vary with the stage and manifestations of the disease. Follow-up to ensure cure or arrest is absolutely essential. In the event of penicillin allergy, alternative therapy is tetracycline or erythromycin.

TRICHOMONIASIS

This is one of the most common vaginal conditions. It is caused by a simple, one-celled, motile organism called *Trichomonas vaginalis*. The condition may be asymptomatic, and a woman may not know that she is infected until the organism is identified as part of the pap smear procedure. Usually, however, within 4 to 28 days after exposure, infected women will notice a greenish-yellow, often frothy, vaginal discharge associated with itching and an unpleasant musty odor. The discharge frequently causes irritation and redness of the vulva, and a spotting of blood may be mixed with the discharge. Inspection of the vaginal mucous membranes and cervix may reveal small red dots, commonly referred to as "strawberry marks." The lymph glands in the groin may become enlarged. The infection can spread to the urinary tract where it may be asymptomatic or may cause symptoms of urinary frequency and urgency. Trichomoniasis is frequently associated with other STDs and may mask their symptoms.

Clinical diagnosis can be made by identifying the strawberry marks on the vaginal wall and cervix. Microscopic examination of the vaginal discharge mixed with saline will reveal the presence of the organism.

Metronidazole is a specific cure for *T. vaginalis*. Alcoholic beverages must be avoided during therapy. Metronidazole must not be taken during the first four months of pregnancy. Sexual partner(s) also need to be treated simultaneously. Although vaginal creams, suppositories, and douches may relieve symptoms, they are seldom curative.

URETHRITIS

See "Gynecologic Diseases and Treatment"; URINARY TRACT INFECTIONS.

VAGINITIS (NONSPECIFIC)

Because a single causative organism or agent is seldom responsible for this condition, the symptoms vary widely. However, the condition is almost always associated with a vaginal discharge usually accompanied by itching or irritation of the vagina or vulva. Urinary symptoms of urgency and frequency may also be present. There are three general causative categories, two of which cannot be considered STD but must be considered in the differential diagnosis.

1. Chemical. Irritation often occurs from using products for "feminine hygiene" such as sprays, perfumed soaps, and douches. If the condition is chemically induced, it should subside when the use of such products is stopped.

2. Mechanical. A foreign body, such as a tampon, inserted in the vagina and "lost," frequently accounts for vaginitis with a particularly unpleasant odor. When the foreign body is removed and local antibiotic preparations are used, symptoms subside promptly.

3. Bacterial. Many bacteria that are not normal inhabitants of the vagina may cause vaginitis and be sexually transmitted. Those known to be responsible for causing vaginitis are: T-strain mycoplasmas, fusobacteria, *Escherichia coli,* and other coliform organisms (normal inhabitants of the bowel), clostridia, actinomycetes, and group B streptococci. Of these, the group B strep infection has the greatest potential of producing serious problems, particularly for a child born while a woman is harboring this infection as well as for post pregnancy infection for the woman.

A culture will usually reveal the causative organisms, while treatment varies with the diagnosis, the severity of the symptoms, the sensitivity of the organisms to antibiotic therapy, and whether the woman is pregnant. For such nonspecific bacterial infections, local vaginal therapy with creams or suppositories containing sulfa is generally the treatment of choice. This may be combined with antibiotic therapy if the infectious organism is group B strep and particularly if the woman is pregnant and near term.

VENEREAL OR GENITAL WARTS (CONDYLOMA ACUMINATA)

It is estimated that there are a million new cases each year of infection with one of the more than 50 known types of the human papilloma virus that causes genital warts. Increasingly strong evidence indicates that some of these are the cause of various kinds of cancer. In addition to cancer of the cervix, the papilloma virus has been found in cancers of the vulva, vagina, penis, and anus. One reason for the spread of the infection is the possible presence of the virus in genital areas not covered by a condom.

Soft, cauliflower-appearing warts, caused by a virus, develop anywhere from 6 weeks to 8 months after sexual exposure. In a woman these warts may be located in and around the vagina and rectum and may be single, multiple, or even confluent. They thrive in warm, moist areas. They grow even more rapidly when associated with vaginal infections and also with pregnancy. In some cases, they are extremely painful.

The diagnosis is usually made on the basis of appearance, and the virus may also be identified in a pap smear.

Because this is a viral infection, there is no specific cure. Two of the most important adjuncts to therapy are to treat any associated vaginitis and to keep the affected areas dry. Venereal warts usually can be treated successfully by applying a chemical called podophyllin. The medication must be used with care. Because it is very irritating to normal skin, it should be applied to the surface of the warts only, and within 6 to 8 hours after treatment a warm sitz bath should be taken to remove excess medication. This chemical is not recommended for use during pregnancy, because if too much is used and some is absorbed, it is toxic to the fetus. The warts can also be removed by cold or hot cautery, laser therapy, or surgical excision.

Injecting interferon directly into the warts has proved to be effective in more than 50 percent of the cases tested experimentally. However, no matter what method of removal is used, genital warts may recur.

YEAST INFECTIONS (MONILIA)

Monilial infections of the vagina and vulva are caused by a yeastlike fungus known as *Candida albicans*. This organism and other similar related organisms are, to some extent, normal inhabitants of the mouth, intestinal tract, and vagina of most healthy women. An upset of the normal symbiotic balance among these organisms can result in a marked overgrowth of the *Candida* organisms, leading to infection. Conditions that predispose to such an imbalance are diabetes, lowered systemic resistance, use of drugs such as antibiotics or cortisone, altered metabolic states such as pregnancy, use of birth control pills, and estrogen deficiency of the vaginal tissues in postmenopausal women. Acquiring monilia under such conditions is not considered an STD. However, once infection occurs, it can be transmitted to others through sexual contact.

The major symptoms in women consist of a white, cheesy vaginal discharge, vulvar itching and irritation, and a "yeasty" odor. If there is also associated yeast overgrowth in the gastrointestinal tract, it can produce symptoms of bloating, abdominal distress, and altered bowel patterns.

When the infection occurs in the mouth, it is known as thrush. White, cheesy patches appear on the tongue and then may spread inside the mouth and to the throat. Infants may acquire it following birth if the mother has the infection in her vagina.

The identification of the white, cheesy patches, adhering to the vaginal wall or in the mouth, is suggestive of a yeast infection. Microscopic examination will show the characteristic long chains of budding yeast organisms. Cultures can also be diagnostic.

Underlying causes, the conditions leading to the symbiotic imbalance, should be sought and treated if possible. Treatment is designed to reduce the number of causative organisms and restore a more normal vaginal flora. If the infection is not too severe, the use of a mild, acidic douche about 2 or 3 times a week may control it. A recommended douche is 2 tablespoons of white vinegar to 1 quart of warm water to which has been added 2 tablespoons of acidophilus culture. This culture (similar to normal vaginal flora) can be obtained from most health food stores; when kept refrigerated, the acidophilus bacteria survive for some time.

Specific therapy consists of vaginal and vulvar applications and of pills taken by mouth. Depending on the medication prescribed a course of treatment varies from 1 to 14 days and, if being re-treated, through a menstrual period. A male partner with symptoms of genital irritation or itching should be treated simultaneously.

If monilial infections are resistant or recurrent, a thorough medical evaluation should be done to determine appropriate steps most likely to effect a cure. For example, a course of oral medication may be instituted to reduce gastrointestinal moniliasis and its associated spread to the genital areas. Or, if oral contraceptive pills seem to be the aggravating factor, a different prescription or another method of contraception might be recommended, at least temporarily.

OTHER STDS AND SEXUAL PRACTICES

Because sexual practices other than vaginal intercourse are not uncommon, certain diseases not generally considered as STDs may be acquired through sexual contact. A woman who practices oral or anal sex as well as genital sex should let the clinician know this so that appropriate tests can be taken to evaluate the possibility of disease of the pharynx or gastrointestinal tract. Gastrointestinally transmitted STDs are much more common among homosexual and bisexual males and, through this route, their female partner(s) may contract any one of the following diseases.

AMEBIASIS

This infection is caused by a single-cell amoeba known as *Endamoeba histolytica.* Symptoms consist of diarrhea, often containing blood and mucus, associated with abdominal distress, low-grade fever, and a general feeling of illness. Infection can occur in the liver and other organs. Carriers of the disease, although asymptomatic, may have cysts in their stool or around their rectum that are highly infectious with oral contact. Microscopic examination of the stool reveals the organism or the cysts. Treatment is individually determined by a physician.

GIARDIASIS

This infection of the small intestine is caused by the protozoa *giardia lamblia* and is spread between sexual partners by the anal-oral route through fecal contamination with the organism. Symptoms include stomach cramps, bloating, and foul-smelling stools. Diagnosis is made through examination of a fresh stool specimen.

The drug of choice for treatment is metronidazole, which must be taken by both sexual partners.

Confronting this alarming array of diseases that may be sexually transmitted, one might be inclined to exclaim, "No more sex ever again!" However, the sex drive is a powerful part of human nature and so is a short memory for the unpleasant things described in this chapter. But to be forewarned is to be forearmed. Remember to take precautions to protect yourself against STD, have regular checks annually that include examinations to detect the presence of such diseases, be alert for unusual symptoms that may suggest the onset of a disease, and seek early diagnosis.

Breast Care

Margaret Nelsen Harker, M.D.

Adult General Medicine, Morehead City, North Carolina;
Electronics Data Systems (1979–1982), Raleigh, North Carolina;
Assistant Professor of Surgery (1975–1979), University of
North Carolina Medical School, Chapel Hill, North Carolina

Not only are a woman's breasts a graceful complement to her womanhood, but they are also symbols of her individualism and sexuality. It has been some time since the human breast was thought of as a mere milk gland, primarily useful for nourishing the species. The average woman, however, has little understanding of normal breast structure and function. Two facts are generally known: (1) breast cancer is a leading cause of death in women and (2) therapy often involves removal of the breast. Therefore, it is not surprising that the perception of any abnormality of the breast leads to anxiety and fear. Some women respond to this anxiety by seeking immediate attention for what often are normal physiologic changes. Other women respond by ignoring a significant abnormality that should be seen promptly for effective treatment.

It is the purpose of this chapter to alleviate unnecessary anxiety and fear and to encourage all women to participate in their own breast care. By becoming aware of the normal structure and function of your breasts, you can deal more confidently with any needed treatment. The attitudes of women patients and the capabilities of physicians are changing. No longer is the woman willing to be the ignorant recipient of treatment, and no longer are physicians limited to a single form of treatment.

GROWTH AND DEVELOPMENT OF THE BREAST

Throughout your life your breasts reflect changes in your endocrine system as well as changes related to age. Your breasts are formed during gestation and by the time of birth consist of a branching system of ducts that empty into the nipples. In the newborn, due to the influence of the hormones of pregnancy, there is often evidence of a clear milky secretion from the nipple. After a few days this secretion ceases. The breasts then remain dormant throughout the remainder of childhood, consisting chiefly of the nipples and rudimentary duct systems. Occasionally, a mass is noted during infancy or childhood that most often disappears. There is no cause for concern, although there is no satisfactory explanation for such masses.

At the time of puberty, as your ovaries begin to manufacture estrogen, several changes begin to take place. The first changes are noticeable between the ages of 9 and 15. At first the areola, the pigmented skin surrounding the nipple, begins to enlarge and darken. Beneath the nipple and the areola the previously quiescent duct system enlarges and grows. Branches also begin to form. Usually by the time of your first menstrual period, the normal, protuberant and firm adolescent breast is well developed. As the ovaries produce progesterone and the breast continues to develop, ducts begin to bud at the end of their branches, producing groups of glands. The essential components of the adult breast are now present.

Let us take a more detailed look at the normal adult breast. The breast normally extends from the second to the sixth or seventh rib and from the sternum (breast bone) to the side of the chest wall and into the axilla (arm pit). The average breast extends 1 to 2 inches out from the chest wall, is 4 to 5 inches in diameter and weights about 1/2 pound. The weight may almost double during lactation. It is very common to have one breast larger than the other, and most often it is the left breast that is larger. There is no explanation for this sometimes striking difference. The overall size of the breast is greatly influenced by the fat content.

DEVELOPMENT OF THE BREAST

Under the upper portion of the breasts are the muscles of the chest wall and some of the shoulder muscles that are attached to the chest wall. These muscles are the pectoral muscles. The breast itself normally glides smoothly over all of these muscles and is supported by ligaments called Cooper's ligaments, which rise from the deep portions of the breast to the skin, like guy wires.

The nipple and areola are covered by a modified membrane that is lubricated by special glands, which appear as little rough areas in the areola. These glands are called the glands of Montgomery and are similar to your other oil-producing glands. Situated in the center of the areola is the conically shaped nipple that has 15 to 25 tiny openings. These openings come from the ducts of the breasts and are very hard to see without magnification. Beneath the areola and nipple are tiny muscles responsible for erection of the nipple when stimulated. They are quite similar to the muscles that cause fine skin hairs to stand on end. The tiny openings on the nipple connect to the duct system of the breast, which radiates away from the nipple like the spokes of a wheel. Just underneath the nipple and areola, these ducts enlarge somewhat to serve as a reservoir for milk. As each duct extends toward the chest wall, it separates into multiple branches. At the end of these branches are the secretory glands of the breast. Each grouping of glands and duct tissue is called a lobe; the smaller branches and glands themselves are called lobules. Between the lobes and lobules is fat and connective tissue, including Cooper's ligaments. The lining of the ducts and glands consists of two layers of cells. Around the glands themselves are tiny cells that are like muscles and help to move milk toward the major duct system and nipple.

Blood is supplied to the breasts by arteries branching from beneath the sternum and between the ribs as well as branches from the large axillary artery. Blood is drained from the breast by veins that follow the same routes. Often the veins in and just under the skin of the breast are very visible. Lymph drains from the breast to five major lymph node areas. These areas are in the axilla, just above the collar bone, under the sternum, across to the opposite breast, and through passages that lead to the lymph nodes in the upper abdomen.

The nerve supply to the skin of the breast and the nipple-areola complex is generous and specialized at the microscopic level. The nerves are thought to play a role in stimulating milk production. They are also the explanation for the increased sensitivity of your breast, skin,

CROSS-SECTION OF THE BREAST

and nipple to stimulation of all sorts. These nerves originate low in the neck and from the nerve supply to the ribs.

During early pregnancy the first noted breast changes occur in the areola, which darkens and begins to enlarge. Subsequently there is increased budding and growth of the glands as well as the duct system. (For more detailed discussion of these changes, see "Pregnancy and Childbirth.")

With the onset of menopause your breasts will become less firm due to the regression of the glandular structures. Frequently, too, the supporting ligaments relax and the breasts become more pendulous. It is not unusual to be able to feel the breast ducts themselves in an elderly woman. If, however, a woman is taking estrogens after menopause, there may be less regression of the glandular and ductal structure. Such women will have breast tissue more like the younger adult, although there is still some relaxation and sagging due to lax ligaments and skin.

POSTMENOPAUSAL ESTROGENS AND THE BREAST

Because the need for postmenopausal estrogen varies, the individual's need must be carefully considered. Disability from symptoms such as "hot flashes," vaginal dryness, and bone changes should be weighed against the possible risk of endometrial carcinoma. This risk is not yet clearly identified but seems related to the dose given and duration of exposure. A woman who has menopausal problems should consult her physician, who may suggest referral to a specialist specifically knowledgeable in this complex and rapidly changing area.

Some women who take postmenopausal estrogen may find that their breasts seem to develop worrisome, relatively vague symptoms such as thickening, tenderness, or feelings of fullness. X-ray changes may show increased density more consistent with a younger age. In some cases estrogens must be discontinued or reduced greatly in dosage. Certainly if you are taking estrogens, you must examine your breasts regularly and see your physician for an examination at least once a year. You should also report any changes promptly. Such examinations should include a careful history, physical examination, and mammography when indicated. Mammograms should be performed only by a qualified radiologist who has access to the clinical information for interpretation. At present these are the best but not perfect diagnostic techniques and do not guarantee early detection of all problems. If you have concerns about your examination or the results, now is the time to be firmly assertive and ask for another opinion or referral to a specialist. These procedures should be followed by *all* women, whether or not they are taking estrogens.

BREAST SELF-EXAMINATION

Perhaps there is no better way you can safeguard your health than by regularly and carefully examining your breasts. You will come to know the subtle details of your breasts better than the most astute physician. With a good knowledge of your normal breasts you can detect any significant changes yourself. The illustration shows the proper technique and timing. Hormonal activity is minimal ten days after the start of your period, and self-examination is recommended at this time.

Any local unit of the American Cancer Society can put you in touch with further material, such as an excellent five-minute movie, demonstrating this technique. Also, your own doctor can help you learn and check your method. Your doctor or your local cancer society may have to help you to learn to find abnormalities, and you can practice on models of breasts with built-in lumps. These models are available at local units of the American Cancer Society and teaching hospitals. As outlined in the illustration, the timing of the examination is important, due to the variations that normally occur during each menstrual cycle. These variations will be discussed shortly.

What should you do if you find something? First, *be sensible!* Most problems are *not* cancer. Seek prompt attention from a competent physician. If you have found an early cancer, you have done yourself the biggest possible favor because these are highly curable.

EVERYDAY BREAST CARE

There are no mysteries regarding the care of your breasts. Good hygiene is important here as everywhere. The skin of the nipple and breast can be susceptible to dryness, particularly during the winter, and to allergic reactions to clothing. A cream or ointment that does not

HOW TO EXAMINE YOUR BREASTS

PART 1

When: Recommended time is ten days after period starts or same day every month for post-menopausal women
After hot bath, sitting before a well-lighted mirror

Arms at sides — become familiar with superficial blood vessel patterns; look for any unusual swelling, dimpling or puckering of skin

Stretch arms high — observe any changes

Press hands firmly on hips to flex chest muscles

PART 2

Lying down, one hand behind head, other hand examining breast; towel or pillow under inspected shoulder

Beginning at the X, examine "around the clock" by pressing gently in small circular motions; move in 1 inch toward nipple and repeat; examine every inch including the nipple

Finally, squeeze the nipple; any discharge should be reported at once.

contain alcohol can relieve such dryness. Some women prefer to remove the few dark hairs around the areola by plucking them. Care should be taken not to cause infection by doing so. You should not "dig" them out; pluck gently as you would in shaping your eyebrows. Electrolysis may be helpful in some instances. However, it is suggested that you first consult your physician. It is not unusual to have occasional scaling of the nipple, but crusting or bleeding is another matter and must be checked by your doctor.

Women with large breasts can be plagued with rashes and dryness under the breast fold, especially in the summer. Often such simple remedies as baby powder or cornstarch are effective in relieving the condition.

Most women, particularly those with large breasts, wear a brassiere for both support and comfort. The most important thing about a brassiere is fit. Any good department store can help with fitting. Women whose breasts change a great deal with their menstrual cycles may require more than one size brassiere. Many women find that their brassiere size changes after pregnancy and after menopause. It is not necessary to spend a lot of money for a brassiere that fits properly. A widely advertised brand name or features of decorations and luxury fabrics may enhance the cost but not the support.

A well-fitted brassiere is especially important for most athletic activities. This topic is discussed in "Fitness," the chapter on exercise. In general little breast injury has been noted in women athletes.

When should a young girl obtain her first brassiere? Often this is a matter of local social custom, and these customs have changed considerably since the days of the exaltation of the female as pinup girl wearing a tight sweater. If a young girl doesn't need a brassiere for breast support or to protect her nipples against abrasion during running or active sports, there's no reason for her to wear one. If on the other hand, an adolescent has heavy breasts and is self-conscious about them, a brassiere that provides support without binding in any way is a sensible investment. (Mothers should refrain from making *any* derogatory remarks about their daughters' breasts no matter what size they are.)

Once your breasts have developed, hormones have little to do with size, except during pregnancy and nursing. No amount of creams, ointments, or salves will affect your breast size. Exercises can only change the size of your pectoral muscles and rarely make a significant difference in your figure. Plastic surgery can increase or reduce your breast size and in some circumstances such surgery is indicated (see "Cosmetic Surgery").

It is usual for the nipples to become erect during sexual activity, but the absence of this response is not uncommon. It is not a sign of absence of arousal if sexual stimulation and foreplay produce only little change in the nipple. Other breast changes during sexual activity include venous engorgement, an increase in size of the breasts and later of the areolas (primarily in women who have not nursed), and a pink mottling. Injuries can be caused by overenthusiastic sex play. Vigorous sucking and chewing of the nipple can result in cracked nipples that may lead to infection, or painful, superficial ulcerations. While these conditions are not serious, it is sensible to consult your physician if they occur.

BREAST DISORDERS

The common disorders of the breast can be classified according to genetic or congenital abnormalities of anatomy, endocrine dysfunction, normal physiologic changes, benign cysts and tumors, infections, and malignant disease. Disorders in these groups are related to age (see Table 1). It is helpful to note, as shown in Table 2, that many adult complaints are not cancer.

TABLE 1

AGE AND COMMON BREAST PROBLEMS

Children and adolescents
abnormal or asymmetrical growth
fibroadenomas
Adolescents and young adults
fibroadenomas
benign duct tumors
cysts and cystic disease
physiologic changes
infections
Older adults
cysts and cystic disease
physiologic abnormalities
cancer

ANATOMICAL ABNORMALITIES AND ENDOCRINE DYSFUNCTION

There are several relatively common congenital anatomical disorders that do not become apparent until puberty. Failure to develop *any* breast tissue due to anatomical abnormality is exceedingly rare. However, "extra" breasts or parts of a breast occur in 1 to 2 percent of Caucasians and more frequently in Orientals. In all mammals, the breasts develop from an embryonic milk-line that extends on both sides of the body from the axilla to the groin. Breast tissue, nipples, or areolas in any combination may be present along this line and may be unilateral or bilateral. This is rudimentary tissue with no physiologic function. Even if enlarged during pregnancy these incompletely formed breasts will usually regress. A fully formed additional breast, however, may function normally and even provide satisfactory nursing. These more complete breasts are subject to the diseases affecting normal breasts.

TABLE 2

BREAST CONDITIONS—1,000 WOMEN SEEKING MEDICAL CONSULTATION

750	symptoms not requiring medical care
85	abnormal physiology, requiring medical care
80	benign, of physiologic origin, requiring medical care
30	tumors, not cancer, requiring medical care
55	cancer, requiring medical care
1,000	

SOURCE: C. D. Haagensen, *Diseases of the Breast,* rev. 2nd ed. Philadelphia: Saunders, 1974.

Another common problem that appears at puberty is a difference in the size of one breast compared with the other. This is not considered abnormal in most instances. However, because of the adolescent girl's intimate and excessively critical involvement with her body and its development, even a minor difference in breast sizes may give rise to anxiety. Parental reassurance can be helpful, but where the emotional disturbance is severe or the difference in breast size is conspicuous and is not satisfactorily adjusted by a custom-made brassiere, plastic surgery might be considered.

Like navels, some nipples are always "inners" rather than "outers." An inverted nipple that a woman has had all of her life is no cause for concern. But when a change occurs, an examination should be scheduled.

Abnormalities in the breasts that are associated with abnormal endocrine gland development or dysfunction are usually not noted until adolescence. Failure of the breasts to develop at all due to endocrine dysfunction is rare. However, this failure may be associated with the absence of ovaries or adrenal glands. Delayed or minimal breast development may be associated with ovaries that are functioning abnormally. Complex relationships between the pituitary, thyroid, and adrenal glands can produce numerous variations of delayed or minimal development. Failure of development of breasts by age 15, with or without associated onset of menstruation, should be investigated. Modern methods of evaluating gland function can usually pinpoint the precise problem. Replacement hormone therapy can often help to stimulate development of the nonadult breast. It should be noted that very small breasts may be completely normal. It is the function of the endocrine glands, not size of the breast, that determines the need for hormonal stimulation in adolescents. It should also be pointed out that hormonal medication will not increase the size of the normal adult breast and should never be considered for that purpose.

In some cases breast development begins early. If it begins before age 8, it is called precocious puberty. It is common for the other secondary sex characteristics, especially pubic hair, growth of the labia, and menstruation, to develop somewhat later than the onset of breast development. In the past it was thought that most of the problems of precocious puberty were related to a tumor of the ovary that caused increasing production of hormones. Because bone maturation and precocious growth often coexist, it now appears that precocious puberty is related to other or more general endocrine problems. A careful and complete endocrine evaluation is necessary to find the source of the disorder.

Children who develop breasts between 8 and 12 are considered to have early puberty not precocious puberty. Development may be unilateral and may be noted first as a soft, flat, 1 to 2 inch circular mass beneath the nipple. Because the opposite breast will begin to develop in several months, excision of this "mass" is not wise as the entire normal breast may be removed. It is not until about age 13 or later that some other common disorders such as cysts or fibroadenomas begin to occur.

NORMAL PHYSIOLOGIC CHANGES

During late adolescence and adult life normal physiologic changes in the breasts occur with each menstrual cycle. These changes do not represent disorders, and understanding them can relieve much unnecessary anxiety and concern. For three or four days before menstruation the breasts may become engorged, fuller and more sensitive. In some women there is quite a marked change. There may also be some increase in the nodularity or lumpiness of your breast. Less commonly, you may notice a more distinct lump or cystlike mass, which may be uncomfortable but which disappears with menstruation. The breast may become very tender. Other more general symptoms related to menstruation are fluid retention, mood changes, and pelvic cramps, together known as premenstrual syndrome.

Variability in symptoms is great. Such changes and complaints may not always occur with every cycle because there are times when, although the menstrual cycle is quite regular, you do not ovulate. The woman whose ovaries are intact after a hysterectomy should remember that menstrual symptoms, including breast changes, may be present, even though vaginal bleeding is absent. Awareness of your own pattern of symptoms and careful self-appraisal in these circumstances can be quite helpful.

Premenstrual breast complaints frequently require no therapy other than a good supporting brassiere and aspirin. Because caffeine has been implicated in the exacerbation of some of these symptoms (but not as their cause), it might be helpful to abstain from all beverages containing it. Physiologic changes in the breast associated with menstruation are sometimes described as cystic disease. To label such normal physiologic changes a "disease" is improper. (True cystic disease is discussed below.) Other premenstrual symptoms and their treatment are discussed in "Gynecologic Diseases and Treatment."

BENIGN CYSTS AND TUMORS

It is during young adulthood that problems of an enlarging mass or masses may begin to occur. Most often these masses are cysts, cystic disease, or fibroadenomas (see illustration). Cysts and cystic disease are a common problem in the adult woman. They rarely make their initial appearance after menopause, and indeed, menopause frequently "cures" the problem.

There is much confusion regarding this group of benign diseases. It is helpful to think of cysts as larger and less numerous in occurrence than the smaller multiple nodularities that characterize cystic disease. Other terms frequently used to describe cystic disease include chronic cystic mastitis, the fibrocystic syndrome, and fibroadenosis—a term used to describe some of the microscopic findings associated with cystic disease.

A cyst is a fluid-filled sac like a small balloon. The cause and significance of cysts and cystic disease is poorly understood and a source of controversy among medical experts. They are probably interrelated. At the present time no specific hormone imbalance has been identified, and the entire problem may be a normal result of the cyclic hormonal changes to which the breasts respond. The first general form of the problem is the presence of larger cysts containing fluid that can be withdrawn through a hollow needle. The second form is associated more often with nodularity and often the nodules are shown to be cysts only under microscopic magnification. There are other highly variable cellular changes noted under the microscope in both types of this disorder. Sometimes cysts and cystic disease follow the menstrual cycle. Occasionally a cyst may completely disappear as the menstrual cycle proceeds. In addition, it is common to have chronic and continuing difficulty with cysts or cystic disease. Whether or not there is an increased risk of cancer in a breast that has had cysts or cystic disease is not proven.

Continued monitoring by both you and your physician is advisable. No specific therapy is indicated. The influence of exogenous hormones, such as birth control pills, is not totally clear.

Another disorder of adult women is a form of benign tumor known as a fibroadenoma. Usually these tumors appear more commonly in young women than do cysts. Initial appearance after menopause is rare. Black

CYSTIC DISEASE

- Dense fibrous tissue
- Nodularity
- Small cysts

CYST

- Fluid-filled multiple cysts
- With or without bulge
- Solitary cyst

Tense, very movable rounded mass

FIBROADENOMA

Fibroadenoma causing skin bulge

Firm, encapsulated, nodular, very movable mass

adolescents seem more prone to develop fibroadenoma than white adolescents. This tumor, like a cyst, may produce a skin bulge. It is also movable and difficult to distinguish from a cyst. Unlike cysts, which are fluid-filled, fibroadenomas are solid masses. In general, there is little influence on these tumors by the menstrual cycle and they are seldom painful. Usually they grow very slowly, although in rare cases they grow rapidly during pregnancy. In some few cases, they spontaneously disappear or get smaller, particularly with onset of menopause. There is no nipple discharge and usually no pain. In younger women the diagnosis is often based on personal history and physical examination. Women over 25 should have the diagnosis confirmed microscopically, which means either excisional biopsy (removal of the whole mass) or needle biopsy (withdrawal of tissue sample). If the mass is not producing symptoms and is not enlarging, there is no compelling reason to remove it. However, if there is any doubt in the physician's mind or in yours regarding the diagnosis, surgical removal can be readily done. There is no known relationship between fibroadenoma and the development of subsequent cancer. The role of birth control pills in the natural history of fibroadenomas is not clear.

Less common in the young adult is another benign tumor, an intraductal papilloma. This is a growth of the cells lining the breast ducts, similar in some respects to a kind of wart. These growths can produce nipple discharge, which is often dark and contains traces of blood. The discharge may come from a single duct opening or from several duct openings in the nipple. You may become aware of the discharge because of a stain on your brassiere. Such symptoms, even without a palpable mass, require investigation by a physician. Intraductal papilloma has no known relationship to cancer but can mimic the symptoms of some cancers. There is no known specific relation to the menstrual cycle.

Another benign lesion that can produce nipple discharge is breast duct ectasia. Duct ectasia is the dilatation of the ducts just beneath the nipple with changes in the tissue surrounding the ducts. These changes are variable but can cause new nipple inversion. The lining cells of the ducts are thinned, rather than proliferating as in papillomas. Nipple discharge or discharge along with a slight suggestion of ropiness under the nipple may be the only symptom. Duct ectasia seems to be more common among women who have nursed for long periods of time. Duct ectasia is not malignant nor is there a known association with cancer. However, bloody nipple discharge and *new* nipple inversion are also signs associated with cancer. Usually, excision of the involved area is indicated for diagnostic purposes.

Copious nipple discharge that is clear or milky is called galactorrhea. Detailed endocrine studies can pinpoint the cause of this problem. Galactorrhea may be caused by antidepressant and antihypertensive drugs as well as oral contraceptives. Rarely the cause is a tumor in the pituitary gland.

Sometimes, there is a mild, clear nipple discharge for which there is no satisfactory explanation. As age increases and menopause ensues, this problem seems to decline.

Another relatively common breast disorder that makes its appearance in the adult woman and has signs similar to cancer is fat necrosis. Injury to the breast, such as a significant bruise, can cause scarring and damage to the fatty tissue. It can distort the skin and the damaged area may feel like a hard knot (a sign often associated with cancer). Such symptoms, which may occur long after any recalled injury, require prompt evaluation and usually biopsy to determine the specific diagnosis.

INFECTIONS

The breast and its overlying skin are subject to inflammation, infection, and possible abscess formation. Most infections are related to nursing. Infection of the mammary glands is called mastitis, which may begin with oversecretion or retention of milk. A fissure in the nipple may cause infection, usually with staphylococci bacteria. Symptoms of infection include diffuse redness, swelling of the skin or nipple, a tender painful mass appearing like a boil, fever, and general weakness. Breast infections require appropriate antibiotics. If the infection is not controlled soon enough, an abscess may develop that usually requires surgical drainage in addition to antibiotics.

Serious infections may cause residual thickening of the skin, scarring of breast tissue, and distortion of the nipple. However, most cases leave no residual change. Such infections are relatively infrequent today, except among women with diabetes, who are more prone to infections of all kinds.

It is rare, but possible, for a breast cancer to be associated with an infection, especially as age increases. Therefore, every effort must be made to investigate this possibility, particularly, in an older nonnursing woman who has a serious breast infection.

MALIGNANT DISEASE

Some relevant information:

- The most recent data presented by the American Cancer Institute indicates that new cases of breast cancer among American women are at the highest rate ever recorded reflecting a continuation of a trend of annual increases since 1980. Factors that contribute to this trend are an increase in early detection through self-examination and screening and the aging of the population.
- Breast cancer will strike one out of 11 women. Those whose mother *or* sister had breast cancer are at twice the normal risk; those whose mother *and* sister had breast cancer are at 14 times the risk of women with no family history of the disease.
- After lung cancer, breast cancer is the leading cause of death in women regardless of age.
- According to the Centers for Disease Control, one-half of all breast cancers spread beyond the breast before detection.
- On the relationship between alcohol and breast cancer:
  1. According to the New England Journal of Medicine April 7, 1987, as few as three alcoholic drinks a week place women at higher risk.
  2. According to a study conducted at Harvard Medical School of 89,000 women, those who had one drink or more every day had a 50 percent higher chance of getting breast cancer than nondrinkers.
  3. In a study by the National Cancer Institute of 7,000 women, those who had five drinks weekly were at 50 percent to 100 percent higher risk than nondrinkers.
  4. Studies indicate that the association between breast cancer and drinking is stronger among younger women than among older ones and among thinner women than among those who are overweight. A possible explanation for these statistics may be the effect of alcohol on the hormonal and/or immunological systems.

All studies stress the fact that early detection of breast cancer is of the greatest importance for ultimate cure. In order to be most effective in detecting breast cancer at an early and curable stage, breast self-examination should be practiced faithfully each month. Important signs that require investigation include:

- *Nipple discharge.*
- *Any change* such as the nipple drawing inward or pointing in a different direction.
- Any chronic *scaling* or *bloody secretion of the nipple.*
- Any *change in the contour or the symmetry* of the breast.
- Any breast *lump* or *thickening* that persists through a menstrual cycle.
- Any breast *skin dimpling.*
- Any *new* breast *lumps.*

Generally, there is a lead-time during which a cancer may be quite small and quite localized. The enlargement and spread may take many months or years. Cancers of the breast usually arise in the cells lining the ducts and glands and then progress outside the ducts (see illustration). There are rare forms of cancer arising from other tissues of the breasts and even more rare cancers that arise from other parts of the body and spread to the breast. Thus, any suspicious abnormality noted by a woman or her physician requires diagnosis by examination of the area. Usually this is done with a biopsy. Having a breast biopsy, however, is not equivalent to having cancer.

Most often breast cancer does not spread until after it has grown outside of the duct. Once outside the duct, spread is frequently first to the lymph nodes (primarily in the axilla). Almost any other area of the body can then be involved as subsequent metastases occur. It must be stressed that early detection and treatment can usually prevent this distant spread. The chance of long survival is greatly enhanced if the cancer is confined to the breast itself. Even when it has spread to the lymph nodes, the chance of survival is good. However, once the cancer has spread beyond the breast and local lymph nodes, complete cure is not possible although there may be several years of fairly comfortable life expectancy.

"Stage" of a breast cancer describes in shorthand the extent of spread. Survival is linked to these stages, as is treatment. Other factors also play an important role in survival and treatment. These can include age, menopausal status, hormone receptor presence or absence in the

SIGNS OF BREAST CANCER

DISTRIBUTION OF BREAST CANCERS

- Painless lump
- 47%
- 14%
- 22%
- 7%
- 2%

- Local pain
- Lump in axilla
- Lump enlarges
- Nipple changes
- Skin changes

FIRST SIGN OR EARLY SYMPTOM:

A painless lump is first symptom 80% of time

Outer upper quadrant is site about 50% of time

LATER SIGNS OR SYMPTOMS:

Local pain

Enlargement of the lump

Lump in axilla

Nipple changes:
soreness
discharge
retraction
ulceration

Skin changes:
dimpling
puckering

GROWTH OF BREAST CANCER

GROWTH RATE OF BREAST CANCERS IS EXTREMELY VARIABLE

Cancer arising in mammary ducts

Normal ducts

Cancer invading surrounding tissues

Axillary nodes

Cancer spread to adjacent lymph nodes (primarily axillary)

BREAST CARE

tumor tissue, specific microscopic type of cancer, and associated medical illnesses.

The anxiety a woman feels when some abnormality of the breast is detected is heightened as she tries to gather her courage and visit her physician. Indeed sometimes a woman will delay seeking diagnosis partly because of her anxiety regarding the "routine" examinations and procedures with which she is not familiar. It should be helpful for you, therefore, to know what to expect when you visit your doctor for a breast examination and evaluation. It should also be helpful in allowing you to judge for yourself if the evaluation of your problem is complete and reasonable. The following are only guidelines and may vary according to the age of the patient and to the specifics of the individual problem.

Prompt evaluation is essential. Telephone your physician immediately to describe your situation so that a decision can be made about how soon you need to be seen. At the time of your visit, your medical history as well as that of all the females in your family will be taken. You should bring with you all medications you are currently taking, both prescription and nonprescription. Attention will then be directed to your specific complaint and its relation to your menstrual cycle, duration, changes, and other associated symptoms.

Usually you will be asked to dress in a half-sheet or shawl-like garment for your examination. The first part of the examination is careful inspection of your breasts and nipples. A palpation of your breasts and examination of the nipples will be performed, first while you are sitting and then while you are lying down. You will be asked to put your hands on your hips and squeeze to tighten your pectoral muscles and to raise your arms above your head perhaps several times. These movements allow the doctor to examine the contour and symmetry of your breasts as well as their movement as you exercise your pectoral muscles. Sometimes very subtle but important changes can be seen in the skin with these techniques. The axillae and the areas above your collar bone will be examined.

Do not be embarrassed or concerned if the physician has some difficulty finding the abnormality you have found. After all, you have been checking yourself regularly and this may be your first visit to the doctor. You may have to help the physician when such a problem arises. Sometimes, however, a cyst or nodularity that may have been related to your menstrual cycle will have disappeared.

Your doctor may examine your nipple with a magnifying glass and you might be asked to help obtain a sample of the discharge. This may involve some discomfort, but it is necessary. The discharge may be tested for blood or smeared on a glass slide for microscopic study.

The remainder of the examination varies greatly. You may be asked to have a mammogram, a specialized type of X-ray for detecting small tumors and other tissue changes of the breast.

Mammography dates from the 1960s, and for the 20 years that followed, conflicting assessments and reports about the harmful effects of the radiation dose caused many women to be fearful about mammograms. Nowadays, the issue of exposure has been resolved in favor of the diagnostic value of the results. There is no doubt that low-dose mammography can detect tumors before they can be felt even by the most skilled fingers. This detection is possible because even the smallest tumors are likely to be denser than the tissue that surrounds them and they therefore show up as shadows on the film. (However, about 20 percent of tumors that can be felt do not show up in a mammogram because some women's breast tissue is as dense as a tumor.)

During mammography, each breast is placed on a small examination plate, and up to three different pictures made. Sometimes the radiologist may ask for other views or ask to examine your breasts. For nipple discharge complaints a tiny plastic tube may be inserted into the duct from which the discharge comes, and a small amount of special radiologic dye injected and additional mammograms taken.

Current controversy is focused not on radiation hazards but on cost effectiveness. While it is generally agreed by all health planners that annual screening of women over 50 can reduce breast cancer mortality rates by 30 percent through early detection, there are those reputable specialists who argue that routine mammography for younger women with no symptoms and no significant family history is not worth the tremendous expense. In the meantime, the guidelines of the American Cancer Society are:

- Age 35–39 Baseline mammogram
- Age 40–49 Yearly or every other year
- Age 50+ Yearly

Women with specific breast complaints may require a mammogram at any age. Individual specific recommendations can best be made by your own physician.

Breast examinations may include xerography (much like mammography but using a slightly different X-ray technique) and thermography (using heat detection). Thermograms are not recommended at this time and are still a research tool. Newer scanners such as CAT (computerized axial tomography) and ultrasound (like sonar) are also being investigated.

In addition to these techniques, the evaluation of a lump or mass in the breast quite often includes a needle aspiration. This aspiration is done using a small amount of local anesthetic in the skin so that a needle can be inserted into the mass. Sometimes several attempts may be needed to set the needle into a very movable mass. If fluid is present, it is removed through the needle. Those masses that are true cysts will collapse when the fluid is removed and usually do not recur. Normal breast cyst fluid varies in color from clear yellow to various shades of green or green-brown. As yet there is no known reason for these color differences. It is not always necessary to have normal appearing breast fluid examined because cell abnormalities are rarely noted. Abnormal fluid may be cloudy and/or contain blood or tiny tissue fragments. This fluid requires microscopic examination. Even if no fluid is obtained there may be enough cells in the needle for a pathologist to examine.

If the mass does not completely disappear with aspiration of the fluid, if a solid tumor is noted, or if a diagnosis cannot be made from the fluid or cells in the needle, a biopsy is indicated. The biopsy may be performed either with a much larger needle or through an incision, depending on individual circumstances. Such biopsies can frequently be performed in the office or clinic under a local anesthetic and have several advantages. They avoid the risk involved in general anesthesia. They do not require hospitalization, which is expensive, interrupts activities, and may be more anxiety-producing than outpatient treatment. There is no rush with pathological analysis as there is when the patient is under general anesthesia and the surgeon is waiting to proceed with treatment. If the results do indicate treatment is necessary, you and your physician have time to discuss all the therapeutic alternatives. There is no evidence that in the case of breast cancer (as in some other forms of cancer) proceeding in this manner will "spread the cancer."

After a needle aspiration, needle biopsy, or incisional biopsy there is some bruising. Sometimes after an incisional biopsy a small, thin, rubber drain may be left in place for one or two days. Generally, there is some discomfort that can be controlled by aspirin or other mild analgesics. It is very important to follow your doctor's instructions regarding activity and changing surgical dressings after such biopsies.

Hospitalization and a general anesthetic are indicated for the removal of intraductal papillomas, plastic surgery, extensive biopsy, and other major breast surgery. Fibroadenomas can usually be removed on an outpatient basis.

Any examination of fluid, tissues, or cells that have been removed may take several days. A "frozen section" is faster but not considered as final as a more detailed study requiring three to four days. The pathologist may have difficulty with some cases and require longer than several days for a specific diagnosis. The time it takes to do a careful examination of the tissue is time very well spent.

Most frequently now, a specific diagnosis is first established and the full extent of disease evaluated before definitive therapy is undertaken. Tissue studies, including hormone receptor tissue, can then be completed before treatment plans are finalized. Definitive treatment and various potential alternative treatments (including breast reconstruction) can then be discussed and clarified. The psychological benefit to the patient is obvious. No longer is it necessary to "go to sleep not knowing what will happen."

TREATMENT

Treatment of various disorders depends on the nature of the problem as well as numerous factors relating to the individual.

NONMALIGNANT DISORDERS

Congenital anatomic abnormalities rarely require specific treatment. Some of the developmental disorders described earlier can, if related to hormone imbalance, be helped with hormone treatment. Developmental disorders also may be helped with specific surgery, particularly if there is a great discrepancy in size between the two breasts. Cyclic changes in the breast related to the menstrual cycles often require no specific therapy, especially when the woman understands their nature. Cysts large enough to be aspirated successfully and that then disappear completely usually do not require further surgery. Cystic disease of the smaller cyst variety and with more nodularity may require closer follow-up and also a biopsy to be certain of the diagnosis. Women with this type of "lumpy" breasts need most of all to perform careful regular self-examination in addition to the regular follow-up by their physicians. No known medical therapy is at present indicated for cysts or cystic disease unless a specific hormonal imbalance can be identified and corrected. After menopause, most cystic disease regresses.

The benign masses such as fibroadenomas, papillomas, duct ectasia, and fat necrosis often require surgical excision either to confirm the diagnosis or to remove an annoying problem.

BREAST CANCER

Rapidly accumulating data from national and international studies make it imperative that any woman who has a diagnosis of breast cancer discuss her treatment plan with her physician on an individual basis. It is also advisable to seek a second opinion if there is reason for a well-informed patient to disagree with the first one.

Some historical background may be helpful. In 1894, Dr. William Halsted, a Baltimore surgeon, introduced the surgical procedure now called a radical mastectomy. That procedure, based on the theory that cancer began in the breast, slowly increased in size, traveled to the lymph nodes, and then spread, prevailed until the 1970s. It is now believed that by the time a tumor shows up on a mammogram or can be felt as a palpable mass, abnormal cells may already be growing outside the breast. Keep in mind that it takes from 8 to 10 years for one centimeter of breast cancer to grow and that it represents an accumulation of 100 billion cancer cells. It is assumed that in the meantime new clusters of atypical cells may be immobilized or destroyed by the healthy body's immune system. In 1985 the results were published of a 10-year study indicating that women with small malignant tumors 1 1/2 inches or less fared equally well if, instead of a mastectomy, the surgical procedure consisted of the removal of only the tumor and a small area of surrounding tissue, and the surgery was followed by radiation treatments. A study published in the New England Journal of Medicine in 1987 indicated that there was no difference in cancer recurrence survival between women who had a partial mastectomy followed by radiation therapy and those who underwent a radical mastectomy.

Surgery (mastectomy) is, and for many years has been, the cornerstone treatment of breast cancer that has not spread at all or at least has not spread beyond the axillary lymph nodes. If the cancer is found to have spread beyond the axillary nodes at the time of initial diagnosis, surgery will be of no or only limited benefit. The amount of tissue removed (type of mastectomy) depends on certain characteristics of the cancer such as its size and location, on the general health and age of the woman, and on her and her physician's personal preferences. There are eight surgical procedures used in the United States at the present time.

1. Supraradical or extended radical mastectomy. The breast, the pectoral muscles, which cover the chest, and the axillary and substernal lymph nodes are removed. To remove the latter, some sections of the rib must also be removed. Some surgeons also remove the supraclavicular lymph nodes (where the neck joins the shoulders). This procedure is rarely done now.
2. Classical or standard mastectomy (also called a radical mastectomy or the Halsted procedure). The breast, all the axillary nodes, and the pectoral muscles are removed.
3. Modified radical mastectomy. This is like the classical procedure except that the pectoral muscles are not removed.
4. Extended simple or extended total mastectomy. The breast is removed and a few axillary lymph nodes are removed for microscopic analysis to see if the cancer has spread to them. The pectoral muscles are not removed.
5. Simple or total mastectomy. This is like the extended simple mastectomy except that no, or only one, lymph node is removed.
6. Partial mastectomy, segmental resection, or wedge resection. The tumor and a fairly large amount of surrounding breast tissue are removed. The breast is not removed, but will be smaller. If the axillary nodes are also removed, the procedure is called a partial radical mastectomy.
7. Lumpectomy, tylectomy, or local excision. The breast lump is removed along with a small amount of surrounding tissue. The breast is not removed and may or may not be smaller. (Of the 500,000 women undergoing breast surgery in 1986, approximately 100,000 had lumpectomies, and it is assumed that by 1990, 40–50 percent will be treated the same way. However, according to the AMA Archives of Surgery, a lumpectomy is about 37 percent more expensive than a mastectomy because of the essential postoperative radiation treatments.
8. Subcutaneous mastectomy. Breast tissue is removed but overlying skin is not. The axillary nodes may or may not be removed. The nipple may be removed or left in place depending on the individual situation. The nipple may be temporarily grafted, usually in the groin. This procedure is not often used to treat carcinoma.

It must be stressed that the specific type of surgery is tailored to the individual circumstances. Surgery is *local treatment* and the type of surgery performed is greatly influenced by the specifics of location, size,

The Types of Mastectomies

Shaded areas indicate what is removed in each procedure. Cancer is designated by black spot.

Radical
Removal of breast, lymph nodes and underlying muscle.

Modified radical
Removal of breast, lymph nodes and nearby tissue. Option chosen by Nancy Reagan, if she has cancer.

Simple
Removal of breast, nipple and skin only.

Subcutaneous
Removal of interior breast tissue. Since procedure is usually done as a preventive measure, no tumor is shown.

Lumpectomy
Removal of cancer and nearby tissue.

SOURCE: American Cancer Society
Copyright © 1987 by The New York Times Company

and microscopic type of the cancer as well as other medical conditions. Also it is now common to consult with other oncologists (cancer specialists) regarding the complete treatment plans of which surgery may be one part. Should you require surgery for breast cancer you should be certain you understand the proposed treatment.

Depending again on your individual circumstances, treatment may include surgery, radiation therapy, endocrine (hormone) treatments, or chemotherapy. The presence of microscopic involvement of lymph nodes often indicates that such post-operative treatments are indicated.

Tumor tissue is now also analyzed for hormone (estrogen and progesterone) receptors. The presence or absence of these receptors indicates a great deal about the "behavior" of the particular tumor including the potential response to chemotherapy and hormone therapy. There is also some correlation with predicted survival (also of course taking into account the stage or extent of spread and other factors mentioned earlier). This is one of the most helpful applications of recent laboratory and clinical research.

Hormone treatments can be most helpful. These include adding hormones or blocking them. Female hormones (estrogens), male hormones (androgens), or blocking medications (anti-estrogens) can be utilized. At times surgical removal or radiation destruction of the ovaries is indicated. Other hormones (for example, prednisone) are also sometimes used.

Chemotherapy (drugs that poison cancer cells) is also used. Most chemotherapy is accompanied by side effects such as nausea and vomiting, hair loss, injury to the bone marrow, and generalized weakness. At present there are many drugs and combinations of drugs being used and no single regimen is clearly the best. If chemotherapy is recommended, you should have the risks and benefits explained to you before it is started. The National Institute of Health has made the following recommendations:

1. For premenopausal women (1/4 to 1/3 of breast cancer patients), a combination of drugs should be used depending on the woman's tolerance and response.
2. For women over 50 whose lymph nodes contain hormone-positive receptors the anti-estrogen agent tamoxifen can be used.
3. For postmenopausal women whose cancers were not linked to estrogen or progesterone combination chemotherapy is indicated.
4. For women of all ages whose cancer was confined to the breast and had not spread to the nodes, followup chemotherapy is not generally indicated.

BREAST CARE

Radiation therapy is also being used more frequently for certain kinds of breast cancer—usually in connection with surgical procedures that leave most of the breast tissue and chest muscles intact. Such treatment, if indicated, can be obtained at most major medical centers.

Immune treatment (immunotherapy) is also being studied. This treatment can stimulate your body's own defense mechanisms against cancer—much like a vaccine stimulates your defenses against polio and tetanus.

Other treatments are often discussed in medical literature, women's magazines, newspapers, television, and among friends. If you have any questions about their worth, you should consult your physician.

One further point must be made regarding breast cancer treatment. If, at the time of diagnosis, the cancer has spread to body parts beyond the lymph nodes, no form of mastectomy may be indicated. To determine this, you may be asked to undergo multiple tests. Some of these are blood tests, bone scans, liver scans, X-rays, and possibly biopsies of areas other than the breast.

Breast reconstruction following surgery is now becoming more common and is most often done by plastic surgeons. Reconstruction options should not be the major deciding factor in selecting the exact type of surgical procedure, as this selection depends on many individual factors and as the first purpose is to save your life. (Excellent booklets dealing with all aspects of breast surgery are available from the American Cancer Society. See also "Cosmetic Surgery.")

There are many myths regarding the psychosexual aftermath of breast surgery. It is clear that the most important goal is building and maintaining a positive self image. The fears that others will be repulsed by the new you are more easily put to rest when you face reality. There are no physiologic or sexual capabilities lost when a breast is lost, except the capacity to nurse. You are as fully capable of joyful sex and sexuality as you were prior to surgery. There are certainly severe stresses related to returning home, going back to work, and coping with the problems presented by a spouse's or a lover's reactions.

Support groups such as the Reach for Recovery Program of the American Cancer Society can help. The women volunteers in this organization have had mastectomies and will visit you in the hospital and help you when you return home. They have been trained to help other patients and understand the anxieties, fears, and problems accompanying breast surgery. Your doctor or nurse can readily contact them. The volunteer will usually bring you a temporary breast prosthesis to wear home and can accompany you when it is time to obtain a permanent one.

Relationships with your family, husband, lover, and friends will be affected as they would by any other serious and difficult problem in life. Seldom are sturdy relationships seriously harmed. Weak or difficult relationships are sometimes strengthened but can deteriorate. Unmarried or divorced women patients have told me that the true worth of a developing relationship with a man is strongly tested following breast surgery. Most physicians caring for cancer patients are now more aware and trained to discuss patients' psychosexual problems. Self-help groups can be a life-line during periods of depression, and if professional help is necessary, cognitive therapists can be especially effective in guiding you toward healthy new perceptions of your worth as a woman no matter what scars your body has sustained. The reassuring fact seems to be that love and communication—not breasts—are central to man-woman relationships.

Armed with more knowledge of the structure and function of your body, I urge you to be sensible regarding your breasts. Check your breasts once a month, tell your doctor about any changes, and insist on being fully and clearly informed about any suggested treatment.

COSMETIC SURGERY

Kathryn Lyle Stephenson, M.D.
Santa Barbara Cottage Hospital, Santa Barbara, California

There is nothing new about the desire to improve one's appearance —to look younger or more attractive. Surgery to help the individual change his or her self-image is not new. What is new is that cosmetic surgery has become accepted and sought not only by women but by men. There is no longer a stigma attached to seeking this assistance. Operations once considered the hush-hush prerogative of the rich and famous are now freely discussed and the "new" looks are launched at "coming-out" parties. The old look is discarded, sometimes along with old jobs, spouses, or psychiatrists.

Many factors account for the increasing popularity of cosmetic surgery. Contemporary culture in the United States is preoccupied with youth and with appearances. Women who feel threatened with the loss of a job at the age of 45 because they look too old (they are likely to have a life expectancy of 30 more years) are more and more determined to compete not only on the basis of skills and experience but on the basis of wrinkle-free faces. In the scale of values of many employers, years of experience and a mature sense of responsibility weigh less than the look of blooming good health associated with youth. Even though many young women are more conventional and conservative than some of their elders, a youthful appearance is usually associated with a "fresh point of view," "an active mind," and "up-to-the-minute attitudes."

Another factor that accounts for the recent increase in cosmetic surgery is the publicity given cosmetic surgery both in print and in the media. Prior to 1979, ethical plastic surgeons did not advertise. At that time, the Federal Trade Commission mandated that reputable trained plastic surgeons as an organized body could not have a proscription against advertising. As a result of advertising and publicity in the media, individuals seeking plastic surgery increased dramatically. Because this is elective surgery, the specialty has benefited more than any other specialty and the cost of the surgery has not decreased due to increased competition. So, also, have the qualified and unqualified practitioners proliferated.

The American Board of Medical Specialists recognizes as specialists in plastic surgery diplomates of the American Board of Plastic Surgery who have been trained in general surgery with additional years of plastic surgery and are qualified to operate on the entire body. Those individuals who have passed their board usually become members of the American Society of Plastic and Reconstructive Surgery. Also recognized to operate above the clavicle (collar bone) are those who have received their board in otorhinolaryngology and in their training received instruction in plastic surgery of the head and neck. These surgeons are identified as members of the American Academy of Facial Plastic Surgery and Reconstructive Surgery. No other surgeons or physicians are regarded as receiving adequate training to perform plastic surgery despite their representation to the public. This further confuses the patient who seeks a qualified plastic surgeon.

Improvements in instruments and refinements in technique, particularly in the technique of microsurgery, are constantly being made, and with the ongoing advances in medicine and anesthesia, operations can be undertaken with greater safety and more assurance of a successful result.

Where does the money come from for this surgery? Except for some ear alteration, breast reduction, and, increasingly, breast reconstruction after mastectomy, it is rarely paid for by any form of medical insurance: it is not covered by Medicare or Medicaid, although it is tax deductible. Secretaries, waitresses, executives, housewives, part-time parents who are reentering the job market are sufficiently motivated to make the necessary sacrifices in order to pay the bills. Some women forego vacations; others spend practically no money on clothes for years so that they can save up for the surgery. Some borrow money; others sell a valuable piece of jewelry. Girls in their teens are sometimes given the choice of money to spend on a nose job or on a sixteenth birthday party. Some conscientious surgeons are distressed by the number of women who repeatedly desire some additional procedure focusing on a new aspect of their appearance with which they are dissatisfied and who become dependent on plastic surgery.

DECIDING TO UNDERGO COSMETIC SURGERY

Cosmetic surgery is a specialty within the larger field of plastic surgery. Plastic surgery includes the repair of congenital defects (such as a cleft lip) and the restructuring of parts of the body damaged by disease (as in the case of breast cancer) or by injury (such as might be sustained in a fire, in war, or in an automobile accident). Cosmetic surgery as previously stated is usually elective. Its purpose is to improve an individual's appearance by changing the shape of the nose (rhinoplasty), removing wrinkles from the face (rhytidoplasty), correcting the wrinkles or bulge of the eyelids (blephaorplasty), altering the relation of the ear to the head (otoplasty), reducing or augmenting the size of the breast (mammaplasty), or removing excess fat by excision (lipectomy) or suction (lipoplasty).

Cosmetic surgery cannot perform miraculous changes in physical appearance or reconstruct basic personality defects such as self-rejection, incurable envy, the "if-only" syndrome, or hopelessly childish notions about "beauty and romance." Women with unrealistic expectations about results are almost certain to be disappointed. Women with specific and limited problems—whose livelihood is at stake because of premature wrinkles or bags under the eyes or who feels socially inadequate because she is flat chested or has localized areas of obesity that limit the type of clothes she desires to wear or who loathes her nose—are likely to be pleased with the solution cosmetic surgery can provide. When their impaired physical appearance, apparent to others or only to themselves, is corrected, they often develop more self-confidence as a result of their improved self-image, which carries over into their relationships with others.

While a face lift won't save a marriage that's on the rocks or guarantee a better job or a bigger salary, it can be helpful in building self-confidence and the assertiveness that can play a crucial role in many competitive situations. However, women whose obsession with looking young is profound and whose terror of aging is acute might benefit more from sustained soul-searching than from surgery. Any woman who wants to get the best return for a considerable investment of money and time should, therefore, be as honest with herself as possible about the motives that bring her to the surgeon's office.

Past or present therapy for unresolved emotional problems need not rule out the use of cosmetic surgery as one way, but never the only way, of dealing with psychological stress. The surgeon should be informed of the therapeutic situation and perhaps consult with the psychotherapist to evaluate the patient's suitability for the desired operation. Women who for many years have focused on some aspect of their appearance that is unsatisfactory to them as the reason for sexual or professional inadequacies should be gently guided toward what may be painful introspection about major flaws in their behavior and away from obsessive inspection of minor flaws they see in the mirror.

Surgery should not be undertaken when the patient's emotional stability has been threatened by a shocking experience. There is no doubt that some women who have experienced an unusually stressful crisis such as a divorce, a sudden death in the family, the unanticipated loss of a job, or the unexpected responsibility of taking care of an invalid child or parent, can benefit from the positive effects of a long-postponed improvement in appearance, but psychic stress has an adverse effect on the physiology of the body and in many cases can slow down the healing process.

Ideally, a person about to undergo elective surgery should be in the best possible physical and mental condition, always taking into account the fact that if the surgery is to be extensive, it will inevitably produce some feelings of anxiety in the patient about the outcome. A reputable surgeon will also ask the prospective patient a long list of questions to find out if she has had a recent severe illness, if she is addicted to alcohol, smoking, or any drugs such as tranquilizers or sleeping pills, and if she is a chronic user of any medication such as aspirin and antihistamines. Surgery may have to be delayed until she has ceased smoking or using alcohol or drugs for sufficient time so that they no longer affect the body. Some medications such as aspirin and antihistamines reduce the body's blood clotting efficiency, thereby increasing the potential hazard of postoperative bleeding. A patient addicted to certain types of drugs may require dangerously high doses of sedatives for adequate relief from pain. Estrogen medications may affect pigmentation following certain procedures. A patient who has been taking cortisone presents special problems and needs more than the usual amount of monitoring by an internist and an anesthesiologist before, during, and after the operation.

Before any woman goes to a cosmetic surgeon, she should attempt an honest assessment of her appearance and know precisely how she wishes it to be changed. Where exactly is the problem? Does the chin need strengthening? The nose need altering? Are the ears too outstanding? Does a body contour need to be changed? Take a good look in the nude. Perfect symmetry of either the face or the figure is usually out of the question. In fact, it is the slight asymmetry of the facial bones that gives most faces interest and individuality. Over time the concept of beauty has changed and is not unassociated with the position of women in society and their activities. Today, most females desire to be thin and full breasted and with the development of prosthesis and the relative simplicity of the operation, breast augmentation has been requested many times more frequently than breast reduction, which is a more major procedure. Probably the concept of the type of nose that is most desirable has changed most in the last fifty years; again that is a highly individual matter.

Advice from friends and family about cosmetic surgery should generally be avoided. Conflicting opinions of friends can be extremely confusing. Close relatives may be offended at the idea that a physical trait shared by the family is offensive to one member. While they may be as tactful as possible, their feelings or ethnic pride may be severely wounded. One or the other parent may refuse to permit a daughter to have her nose changed. In other cases a teenager may not have strong feelings one way or the other—in fact, may feel that her nose is exactly like a classic portrait—but her mother may want her to have her nose trimmed or straightened. With young people in particular, if those close to the patient take a negative view of prospective surgery, this attitude is likely to persist after the operation, causing the patient to be unhappy about the result. When the decision for surgery is finally taken, it should be taken as independently as circumstances permit.

CONSULTATION WITH THE COSMETIC SURGEON

Once the decision is made, the individual should seek a properly accredited surgeon. An inquiry to the Board of Medical Specialties will tell the caller whether the particular physician is board qualified in a specialty.

To have surgery undertaken by a physician who does not have the proper credentials not only adds to the risk of the surgery but may also lead to irreversible mutilation. The surgeon who has received the most publicity is not necessarily the most skilled or the most conscientious, and while more and more cosmetic surgeons are creating mini-hospitals in their own offices to lessen costs due to hospitalization, it is important to check on their conventional hospital association and if they are permitted in that hospital to perform the desired surgery. It is also important to check the facility. Is it accredited by the American Association for Accreditation of Ambulatory Surgery? Do they have cardiorespiratory equipment? Do they have a certified nurse or anesthesiologist to monitor the patient throughout the procedure who is also congenial to her and makes her feel confident rather than apprehensive?

When making an appointment with a surgeon for a first visit, the prospective patient should ask how much the fee will be for the consultation. The amount is collected at the time of the consultation and in some cases it may be deducted from the surgical fee. All questions relating to fees should be discussed in the greatest detail at the time of the first visit to avoid future misunderstandings. The patient would be well advised at the time to ask about the cost of the surgery, additional fees for possible x-rays, the anesthesia fee, laboratory fee, hospital or operating room fee, or any additional costs. She should take careful notes. She should also check her insurance policy to see if the anticipated surgery is covered. Few procedures are. However, some surgeries such as scar revision, outstanding ears in children, reduction mammaplasty, and surgery following amputation or partial loss of breast tissue are covered by many policies. While it may come as somewhat of a shock, most cosmetic surgeons expect to be paid in full in advance of an operation. The reason for this involves several practical considerations: unless the commitment to have the operation is made final by prepayment, cancellations and postponements can accumulate to the point where the surgeon cannot maintain any kind of schedule.

During the consultation, the surgeon will question the patient about her medical history and her physical condition. The woman who is not entirely honest or is evasive in her answers is asking for trouble and being unfair to herself and to the doctor. Special problems associated with previous surgery should be described in detail. Any bleeding tendencies should be mentioned. Drug dependencies and the use of any medication must be discussed. A history of hypertension, diabetes, asthma, kidney or heart disease, allergy, or mental illness must be mentioned.

Not only is it important for the patient to speak openly to the surgeon, but the patient should expect to get certain specific information from the surgeon. During the consultation, the prospective patient should be told about the following matters: problems ordinarily connected with the particular type of surgery requested, the patient's suitability or unsuitability for it, realistic limitations of the procedure and expectations of the results, potential complications, preparations essential before the surgery is performed, the actual technique by which the surgery is performed, the nature and length of postoperative recovery.

If, after this discussion, the patient wishes to proceed with the surgery and the surgeon feels she is a suitable candidate for it, photographs will be taken either during the first visit or during a subsequent pre-operative visit. Some surgeons think computerized imaging is helpful, but this is debatable. The surgeon evaluates the photographs with the patient at a subsequent visit prior to surgery. It is during this visit that the patient should feel free to ask any and all questions that remain unanswered in her own mind.

It must be especially emphasized that the patient should make a determined effort to hear what the surgeon says to her. If she doesn't trust her memory, she should write the responses down and have the accuracy of her transcription checked by the surgeon at the time or ask if the surgeon will permit tape recording of the conversation. If this is not permissible, it would be interesting to know the reason why it is not. Controlled studies of patients undergoing plastic surgery have shown that few patients remember postoperatively the statements made to them by the surgeon before the operation. The reason for this memory lapse appears to be the fact that in most instances patients have so firmly decided in advance to have the surgery that they are incapable of absorbing the information communicated to them by the surgeon.

There are also those patients whose anxiety about the procedure or the presence of a physician prevents their hearing anything that is said to them. They simply do not listen to the surgeon's recounting of the limitations of the procedure, the possibility of having to undergo secondary surgery, the immediate and delayed anticipated results, the time necessary for recuperation, or the potential complications.

While complications are not common, they do occur. There is no operation that is risk free. Hemorrhage may occur at the time of surgery or immediately following it; adverse response to anesthesia may occur despite all precautions and impeccable techniques; postoperative infection may complicate and delay healing and recovery. Incisions, although designed and sutured by the surgeon to be as inconspicuous as possible, do result in scars. Some individuals form elevated red scars termed bypertrophic or keloidal. Some scars stretch regardless of the physician's technique. How conspicuous the scars will be varies with the area of the body involved and with the patient's type of scar formation.

In recent years it has become increasingly popular to introduce foreign materials into the body. All patients should be aware of the normal response of the body to such substances as metal, glass, ivory, paraffin, silicone, and other synthetic materials. To protect itself from damage, the body's normal response is to extrude or to "wall off" these substances by the formation of scar tissue. Countless breasts have been lost or maimed by the injection of silicone, and there has been discoloration and loss of tissue in other parts of the body due to these injections. The substance migrates and can cause death if blood vessels are invaded and circulation is blocked.

All of these substances have been used in the past by both qualified surgeons and charlatans. However, qualified surgeons have discarded all but some silicone prosthesis. All surgeons agree that the most satisfactory substitute for missing tissue is autogenous tissue—similar tissue taken from the patient's body. For example, tissue needed for nasal reconstruction may be taken from a rib, ear, or septal cartilage.

SURGICAL PROCEDURES

There are several cosmetic surgery procedures that may be performed.

RHINOPLASTY (NOSE ALTERATION)

Rhinoplasty, alteration of the contour of the nose, is one of the most frequently requested cosmetic operations and one of the most difficult. It should not be done until after age 16, when bone development and cartilage growth are complete. Preferably, however, the surgery should not be postponed indefinitely. The overlying soft tissue on the bridge of the nose is not sufficient to conceal even the slightest irregularity and becomes less elastic and decreases in volume with advancing years. The development of excess scar tissue beneath the skin may alter the result desired by both the surgeon and the patient.

A nose may protrude too much or not enough. It may be hooked or depressed. The tip may be bulbous or pinched; it may turn up or turn down. The septum may deviate or it may be markedly crooked. The nose is rarely symmetrical: even the beauty queens of Hollywood constantly request that cameramen take their "best" side.

The patient who consults the surgeon about nose reconstruction often has many misconceptions about the problems involved. It is only after multiple photographs are taken from various angles, with the face in repose and smiling, that the problem can be analyzed and clarified. In a discussion that constantly uses the photographs as reference, the limitations of the alteration should be made as clear as possible to the patient. If the dorsum of the nose is to be augmented, there may be a limitation due to amount of soft tissue available. If the tip of the nose is to be reduced, there may be an excess of inelastic tissue that will not shrink adequately to drape over the reduced cartilaginous support. When this problem exists, it may be necessary to make an external incision that may result in a visible scar.

A reduction rhinoplasty is usually done under local anesthesia: the nerves are blocked with injections of xylocaine or procaine containing epinephrine, a synthetic hormone that limits bleeding. The surgeon can work without having his vision or his instruments obstructed by cumbersome anesthetic equipment. If general anesthesia is necessary because of the preference of the patient or the surgeon, endotracheal anesthesia is used: a breathing tube is inserted through the mouth into the trachea (the windpipe) to prevent the patient from getting blood into the lungs while unconscious. When general anesthesia is used, most

COSMETIC SURGERY OF THE NOSE

BASIC AREAS REMOVED

Bone and cartilage from hump

Bone

Cartilage from tip

BEFORE AFTER

All incisions inside the nostril

COSMETIC SURGERY

surgeons also inject local anesthesia containing epinephrine to limit bleeding that may obscure the operative field.

The surgery itself is performed through incisions within the nostrils unless the nostrils are to be decreased or otherwise reshaped. Through these incisions, the soft tissues are separated from the underlying bone cartilage. The cartilages of the tip are modified, the undesirable bony hump is removed by saw or chisel and filed for smoothness, and the lateral nasal bones are fractured to re-create the pyramidal form of the upper portion of the nose. If the dorsum of the nose needs to be augmented, the soft tissues from the dorsum will be elevated to insert the cartilage, bone, or silicone. Generally, the incision is made from within the nostril.

When the crookedness of the nose is caused by deviation of the septum (the cartilage that separates the two nostrils), a modification or resection of the septum is indicated. This is usually done before reducing the size of the nose. In many cases, only the tip needs to be modified. If the width of the nostrils is to be altered, it is necessary to make an incision at the margin of the ala (the wing of the nose) where it joins the upper lip and cheek.

Following the completion of the surgery, nasal packs are inserted and an external splint is applied to maintain the new position of the bones, limit postoperative swelling, and protect the operated sites. The packs are removed within a few days, but the external splint is likely to be retained for about a week. The postoperative pain is negligible, but the eyelids may become swollen and discolored, and while the nose is packed, mouth breathing causes the annoyance of dryness of the mouth. Some oozing of blood is common. The nose may feel stiff and numb. The numbness disappears gradually, and by the tenth day most of the swelling subsides. The appearance of the nose gradually improves, and usually by the sixth month the scar tissue has softened.

Following removal of the splint, the patient should not handle the nose, sneezing should be avoided, and all violent exercise should be eliminated for three weeks. Participation in contact sports should be discontinued for six months.

It is important to be aware of some of the most common complications that may follow this procedure. The formation of excessive scar tissue may result in distortion and a less delicate contour than anticipated. Asymmetry or deviation may occur. A flat arch and pinched nostrils or even partially occluded nostrils may present a postoperative problem. Profuse bleeding may occur with septal surgery. Following septal surgery, there may be a perforation of the septum or a collapse of the bridge of the nose. While most of these complications rarely occur, the patient embarking on a rhinoplasty should take these possible failures into account.

RHYTIDOPLASTY (FACE LIFT)

Rhytidoplasty is a major surgical procedure. For the best possible results it is essential that in addition to being in good health the patient be at her lowest normal weight. Any planned dieting should be done before rather than after the surgery so that the skin is slack and a maximum amount of tissue can be removed during the operation. The patient is usually advised to keep her hair long enough to cover the scars, which will be pink immediately after the surgery. Most surgeons do not shave the hair. Prior to surgery the patient will be told to wash her hair with antiseptic soap.

The procedure may include a forehead lift, cheek lift (meloplasty), and neck lift. Whether these operations are undertaken at the same time as the face lift or are done subsequently as separate procedures depends on the appearance of the patient and her overall physical condition.

While the surgery can be accomplished under local anesthesia with adequate premedication, many surgeons prefer to use supplemental intravenous or inhalation anesthesia as well.

A face lift consists of the separation of the skin and subcutaneous fat from the underlying muscles and fascia (fibrous connective tissue) and the pulling back and cutting away of the excess tissue. If a forehead lift is to be included, the incision extends across the forehead, usually behind the hairline where the scar will eventually be concealed and down into the area of the temples. Some surgeons prefer to make the incision below the hairline, and in an unusually high forehead this is preferable. In order to achieve improvement in the frown lines between the brows the muscles between the brows are cut and in some instances sections are removed. The incision goes in front of the ear, around the lobe, upward on the back of the ear or in the crease where it joins the head, and then as far as necessary into the hair-bearing area. While the incision may encircle the entire head, it usually extends only as far back as necessary to allow for the removal of an adequate amount of tissue.

COSMETIC SURGERY OF THE FACE

Incision for face lift

Incision and skin removed for eyebrow lift

Incisions and areas removed around eyelids

Inhalation anesthesia

Skin area within dotted outline is freed from underlying muscle

Mouth wrinkles dermabraded

Final incisions after face, eyebrow lift, eyelid and mouth corrections

Vertical incisions in the midline of the nape of the neck are sometimes used, but they are likely to produce unsightly scars. However, if such incisions are necessary, the scars can be partially hidden by wearing the hair longer in the back. Patients with a "turkey gobbler" neck may require an incision beneath the chin for the removal of excess skin and fat.

After the incisions are made and the skin and fat are separated from the tissue beneath them, they are retracted (pulled up and back) and the excess is cut away. Some surgeons think that they accomplish a better or more lasting correction if the fascia is retracted and firmly sutured. An additional procedure to improve the angulation beneath the chin is the removal of fat by excision or suction.

On completion of the surgery, many surgeons insert drains that are attached to suction to remove oozing blood and serum. The removal limits somewhat the extent of postoperative swelling, and monitoring the drains can alert personnel supervising the patient's condition to the onset of undue bleeding. Other surgeons prefer to rely on the around-the-head occlusive dressing.

For smoothing away fine lines in unoperated areas, usually just around the mouth but sometimes on the forehead, abrasion may be performed at the time of the face lift. Some surgeons advocate chemosurgery instead of abrasion (the two procedures are described later).

Postoperatively, there is surprisingly little discomfort or pain, although some patients become agitated by the comprehensive dressing that covers a large portion of the head, face, and neck. When there is pain, it should alert the surgeon to investigate the wound. Swelling and ecchymosis (black and blueness) are not uncommon. Each surgeon has a particular routine for the time of suture and bandage removal. The patient should usually allow three weeks as minimum recovery time because of possible swelling and discoloration. Better to be patient about revealing the "new look" than to present it prematurely, which sometimes leads to adverse criticism.

Of all possible postoperative complications, the most common one is the formation of a hematoma (a swelling containing blood). Persons at high risk for this complication are apprehensive patients whose blood pressure fluctuates after the surgery, individuals with abnormal and uncorrected blood clotting factors, and individuals whose physiology has been adversely affected by fatigue, smoking, or drugs. A large hematoma may lead to loss of tissue and infection. Smaller hematomas result in the development of heavier scar tissue, which may appear as a dimple or a lump that may take up to six months to soften.

Other complications involve injury to nerves and changes in pigmentation. Loss of skin sensitivity that may occur gradually diminishes. As the nerves regenerate, the patient may experience a tickling sensation similar to that which is produced by an insect crawling on the skin surface. The transection of a motor nerve may lead to permanent paralysis, but more often the immediate appearance of limited muscular activity is due to the swelling or compression of the nerve and when healing is complete, normal action returns spontaneously. When there is a change in skin pigmentation, it is most apt to occur in the neck.

Six months after surgery, recovery is usually complete and the maximum effect on appearance is attained. Of course there are individual variations due to heredity, age, quality of the skin, and general health. At that time additional minor surgical correction may be indicated in order to achieve optimum results. In the 40 to 50 age group, the time at which this surgery is most commonly undertaken, both the skin and the underlying adipose (fatty) tissue have already begun to lose their elasticity. The facial and cranial bones have begun to decrease in size. For these reasons, among others, not all wrinkles can be removed, and a face lift should not be undertaken with that expectation.

The length of time the improvement will last varies with the individual factors mentioned with regard to immediate recovery and also the amount of stress experienced; general health; maintenance of a constant weight; avoidance of excess exposure to the sun and overindulgence in alcohol, smoking, and drugs. There may be some relaxation at the end of six months that may be improved by minor surgery.

Mme. le Docteur Noel, a Parisian plastic surgeon of the 1920s with extensive experience in cosmetic surgery, observed, "We can set the clock back, but we cannot stop the disastrous ravages of time." Six to eight years after surgery is an average time at which the patient who recalls the original improvement is likely to wish to repeat the procedure. If it is not undertaken too frequently, repeat procedures will produce equally satisfactory results. And whether or not she does have repeat face lifts, the patient will continue to look younger than if she had not had the surgery in the first place.

I know of no procedure that produces such a high degree of euphoria in such a large number of patients. Some of this sense of well-being may be due to the character of the women who seek the improvement: usually they are energetic, determined to cope with life's more unpleasant realities, and eager to participate in the activities of the world around them.

ABRASION AND CHEMOSURGERY

Abrasion (or dermabrasion) is the removal of outer layers of the skin. Scars due to acne can be improved by beveling the edges of the scars if they are not the deep pitted "ice pick" type, although the abrasion may have to be repeated several times to achieve a skin surface that approaches the normal in appearance. Abrasion may also be done to smooth fine wrinkles. Because elevated levels of estrogen affect the pigmentation of the skin, the procedure should not be done on a woman who takes estrogens as replacement therapy or as a contraceptive. It should not be done on a woman who has a history of chloasma of pregnancy (pigmentary changes of the skin, primarily of the cheeks) or on a pregnant woman due to her altered endocrine function.

The procedure can be done under local anesthesia or by topical refrigeration (spraying on a solution that freezes the skin surface), but because dermabrasion takes a long time, many patients elect to have a general anesthetic or supplementary intravenous anesthesia. Most surgeons prefer to work on the entire face at one time in order to blend or feather out the margins at the hairline and beneath the jawline to get results as close as possible to the texture of the normal skin. At one time, sandpaper was used to remove the outer skin layers. Now most surgeons use a rotary diamond fraise, a revolving cylinder in which diamond dust is embedded. A rotary wire brush is also used by some surgeons.

Immediately following the surgery the face swells, as it would after a second-degree burn, and the swelling continues for at least two days. Pain is not acute after the first six hours, but the patient does suffer from a most disagreeable appearance caused by the accumulation of plasma that forms a crust. The crusting usually falls off within ten days, exposing rosy-colored tissue beneath. This color gradually fades and the skin takes on its normal coloration. It is absolutely essential that for six weeks the patient totally avoid any exposure to the sun and that for six months she protect her skin against the sun by wearing a large-brimmed hat and using a sun-blocking skin cream. If the face is exposed earlier, spotty pigmentation may occur. In individuals with darker skin, the exposed abraded area may become darker; in fair-skinned individuals it is usually lighter.

Occasionally there may be a difference in pigmentation even though the patient is not taking estrogens and was not exposed prematurely to the sun. Sometimes there is a formation of milia (white papules due to the retention of sebum). More rarely the procedure may result in red and elevated (hypertrophic) scarring.

Chemosurgery ("chemical peel"), the removal of the outer layer of skin by the application of chemicals, is preferred to abrasion by some surgeons treating fine wrinkles due to aging. It is not as satisfactory as surgical abrasion for acne and scars. Because the solution used contains phenol, individuals with kidney disease are not considered candidates for this procedure. The application of the chemical solution must be performed with extreme care to control the depth of penetration.

The patient's face is carefully cleaned and then the patient is heavily premedicated. As the surgeon applies the phenol solution with an applicator, the patient experiences a stinging sensation. The face is then blotted and a tape mask is applied unless the individual has very thin skin. The mask is left in place for 24 to 48 hours. During this time and for an additional 24 to 48 hours the face swells as it would following any burn, and often the pain requires narcotics. Following the removal of the tape, thymol iodide powder is applied to dry the weeping surface. Some surgeons prefer an application of vaseline. If the taping technique is used, usually within ten days to two weeks the powder is removed and cosmetics may be applied to the bright pink skin. This coloration gradually fades.

Complications following this procedure are similar to those following abrasion but are more apt to occur. The patient must protect her face from exposure to the sun for six months. The texture of the skin is more altered and hypo- or hyperpigmentation of the skin or a blotchy discoloration may occur. Although the improvement may be more prolonged following chemosurgery, some surgeons do not perform it because of the increased likelihood of complications.

REMOVING SCARS AND DEEP WRINKLES

Scars often may be made less conspicuous by redesign, by interdigitation of the tissue, or by using a different method of suturing. Elevated scars may be improved by the injection of cortisone or the application of pressure. These techniques may be used singly or in combination.

In the past for a depressed area surgeons have inserted various tissues of the body such as fat, fascia, derma (the deeper portion of the skin) or used silicone, sometimes with results that were difficult or impossible to correct later. At present efforts have been made to build up a depressed area by injection of other substances such as collagen Zymoderm (a purified cow skin derivative), the patient's own plasma, and more recently a solution of fat cells such as those obtained following liposuction. On a long-term basis the results have rarely been gratifying even if over-corrected or the substances subsequently reinjected.

MAXILLOPLASTY, MANDIBULOPLASTY, MENTOPLASTY, AND MALARPLASTY

The premaxillary portion of the facial bones (the upper jaw) just below the nose may protrude or recede too much for an attractive appearance. While some correction can be obtained from orthodontia, if the malocclusion is severe, maxilloplasty, the surgical recession or advancement of the bone itself, may be advisable. This is a major surgery that demands careful preoperative study, hospitalization, and longer postoperative care than most cosmetic surgery procedures. While it does in fact improve the patient's appearance, a maxilloplasty does not generally come under the heading of cosmetic surgery but rather is considered reconstructive surgery because function, namely, proper occlusion of the teeth, is always involved.

Severe malocclusion may also be corrected by mandibuloplasty, the resecting or advancing of the mandibular (lower jaw) bone. Frequently, the addition of bone, cartilage, or some type of silicone implant is used to bring the chin forward to achieve better facial balance. This surgery is often performed in conjunction with a rhinoplasty, making possible the use of the bone and cartilage removed from the nose for the reconstruction of the chin. As an additional procedure accompanying a face lift, it is especially valuable to the individual whose chin has receded excessively because of the premature loss of the lower teeth.

Chin surgery (mentoplasty) is undertaken under local anesthesia unless it is necessary to obtain bone from some other part of the body. The incision is made either inside the mouth or just beneath the chin, where the scar will be inconspicuous. The incision beneath the chin is used for the removal of excess bone to reduce an excessively long or prominent chin. After the operation the patient is limited to a soft diet for about ten days. While complications are rare, a nerve may be damaged, producing numbness and lack of mobility of the lower lip either temporarily or in rare instances permanently. Another postoperative complication may be the deviation (separation or slippage) of the material inserted. This is corrected by a secondary adjustment.

The appearance of some women is enhanced by malarplasty, the augmentation of the malar eminence or cheekbone. Bone or silicone is inserted to achieve greater prominence of the cheekbone. The incision may be made in the mouth, through the lower eyelid, or behind the hairline in the area above the ear. A pocket for the insertion of the bone or silicone is created by separating the overlying tissue from the bone beneath. The inserted material may angulate slightly or drift and give a grotesque facies. In thin individuals it may be apparent on close inspection.

BLEPHAROPLASTY (EYELID LIFT)

Blepharoplasty is the correction of puffy or wrinkled eyelids. Fullness or puffiness of the eyelids may occur even in young women, and it is usually a familial characteristic. In this condition the orbital fat that cushions the globe of the eye weakens the orbital muscle and a pseudohernia develops. The resulting puffiness becomes conspicuously wrinkled. In older women the wrinkling may occur without the puffiness. In some cases the overhang of the upper lid interferes with peripheral vision. The surgery can be and usually is performed under local anesthesia, but because most patients are nervous about surgery close to the eye, supplemental intravenous or inhalation anesthesia may be advisable. The additional anesthesia relaxes the patient who may suffer some pain when the fat is being removed. Vision is checked before the operation. Some surgeons insert plastic lenses for the protection of the eye. The surgeon also makes an estimate of the amount of tissue to be removed and usually draws an outline on the eyelid with a colored solution. The incision on the upper eyelid is ordinarily made in the fold of the lid where the eyeball meets the orbital bone. The scar is thus concealed when the patient's eye is open. The incision on the lower lid is usually made just beneath the lashes, where it will be hidden. The excess skin is removed, the muscles separated, and the fat gently extracted. Following the suturing of the skin, ice may be applied to limit swelling and discoloration. The sutures are removed by the fifth day following surgery. After the first week it is safe to stroke the eye horizontally, but not until the third week should it be rubbed vertically. By the tenth day after surgery, the patient generally is presentable without dark glasses.

In some cases excessive swelling may turn the eyelid out, or the lid may droop in a "hound dog" effect. These postoperative conditions almost always disappear with time. The eyelid tissue heals with practically no visible evidence of surgery. When scarring does occur, it is usually in the lateral area where the incision may have extended beyond the eyelid tissue and into the area of the "crow's feet." The patient should not anticipate the removal of all wrinkles. There is the occasional patient who may develop a persistent darker pigmentation of the lower eyelid. In others, if too much skin is removed, the lower eyelid may droop to the extent that the ability to close the eyes completely is lost. When this complication occurs, it has to be corrected by subsequent surgery. The muscular action of the upper eyelid is rarely damaged. While interference with the drainage of tears through the tear duct can occur, it rarely does. A few cases of blindness in one or both eyes, both temporary and permanent, have been recorded.

EYEBROW LIFT

There are some women whose eyebrows are so low that rather than perform an operation on the upper lid, the surgeon may suggest the excision of tissue above the eyebrow so that it can be repositioned. This improves the upper lid droop. While incisions in this area are likely to result in more conspicuous scars than those in eyelid tissue, the general total effect is likely to be more pleasing than before the eyebrows were elevated.

OTOPLASTY

Cosmetic surgery for the alteration of ear contour may involve reducing the size or form of the entire ear, the lobe, or the rim, but the most common operation is the correction of protruding ears. The protrusion results when the midportion of the ear (the concha) is too deep or the upper portion of the ear (the auricle) does not have as well-developed or acutely angulated folds as the normal ear. Making ears lie closer to the head can be accomplished only by surgery.

The surgery can be undertaken any time after the age of 6 when the ear has reached almost full development in most children. It should be done before the child has suffered psychological damage from taunts by thoughtless classmates and equally thoughtless relatives, but it can be done on adults.

The surgery is usually done in the doctor's office or on an outpatient basis in a hospital. With proper medication and a quiet reassuring environment, the operation can be performed on most children and adults under local anesthesia, although a restless or apprehensive child may require a general anesthetic. Most frequently the incision is made in the crease that separates the ear from the head. If the surgeon prefers to perform the operation from the front side, the incision is made just inside the rim. The soft tissue is elevated, and then the ear cartilage is revised by cutting the cartilage, excising an ellipse, or thinning it by abrasion or cross-hatching, and then suturing the tissue into the desired position. After the muscles and the skin are sutured, a bandage is applied around the head to splint the ear in the new position and to protect it.

The first dressing is often left in place for one week unless there is bleeding or the patient complains of pain. Pain may be caused by a bandage that is too tight or for some other reason that should be investigated. In most cases after the first day little medication is required because there is practically no pain. A head band may be substituted later and worn for about three weeks while the fractured cartilage is healing. The postoperative numbness or insensitivity of the ears usually disappears within a few months.

The scars are well hidden and complications minimal. The cartilage of the revised ear may not become reunited. If the cartilage does not reunite spontaneously, it may be necessary to resuture it. The gentle anterior curve may be too angular and necessitate a minor corrective procedure. While possible bleeding and infection can never be ruled out entirely, they occur infrequently.

MAMMAPLASTY

Mammaplasty may be performed either to augment or to decrease the size of the breasts.

Augmentation Mammaplasty

When augmentation mammaplasty was first done, breasts were increased in size by the transplantation of fat. In later operations fat and the dermal portion of the skin taken from the hip or abdominal area were used. Later still, glass balls and many synthetic prostheses of various materials were manufactured for the purpose of insertion. Then came the injection of silicone fluid. A silicone fluid or gel injected directly into the body migrates not only into the soft tissues in various parts of the body, but into the lymphatics and small blood vessels and thus can be transported to the liver, kidneys, lungs, heart, and brain. The use of this substance in mammaplasty resulted in the destruction and loss of otherwise healthy breast tissue and in some cases death caused by silicone embolism. At present, to prevent such disasters, the breast is augmented by the insertion of a silicone bag containing silicone gel or fluid and some prostheses have an additional covering of polyurethane. Some surgeons think that an additional covering of the bag with polyurethane lessens the postoperative problem of tissue contracture around the prosthesis. Instillation of cortisone has been explored, but at present there is no sure way to control the complication caused by the body's attempt to reject the foreign body.

Before augmentation is undertaken, preoperative mammograms are recommended to ascertain whether there is an unsuspected malignancy. As in all breast surgery, the patient is usually advised to use an antiseptic soap to wash her upper torso for several days before the operation. The surgery may be performed under local anesthesia or a combination of local and intravenous anesthetics. Many surgeons do this operation in their office or in the outpatient facilities of a hospital.

COSMETIC SURGERY OF THE BREAST

REDUCTION MAMMAPLASTY

Incision around areola | Stippled area to be removed | "Keyhole" pattern incision | Points **a** and **b** brought together | Transplanted nipple and areola

AUGMENTATION MAMMAPLASTY

Implant

Alternate incisions

Before the operation, the size and shape of the prosthesis is determined to be appropriate to the patient's thorax, the estimated recipient cavity, and the amount of tissue the patient has to cover it. The surgeon shows a sample prosthesis of the anticipated size to the patient. The surgeon may take two sizes to surgery to allow for variation in the actual cavity. The incision for the prosthesis may be below (submammary), at the armpit (axilla), or at the junction of the areola with the skin. The areolar and axillary incisions leave less conspicuous scars than the submammary incisions. The surgeon separates the breast and overlying tissue and inserts the prosthesis between two layers of fascia or beneath the chest muscles. When the submammary approach is used, there is less likelihood of transecting the breast tissue.

Although bleeding at the time of surgery is minimal, later oozing or bleeding from a large vessel may occur and result in a hematoma. This in turn can lead to necrosis (death) of the overlying skin or disruption of the wound. Visible scars can occur, but because the incision is small, they are a minor problem unless the patient forms keloids (raised red scars). Asymmetry is always a possibility, especially if the chest wall is asymmetrical. There may be an outpouring of a large amount of sera, with consequent swelling and the need for aspiration (removal of the liquid), unless drainage has been established at the time of surgery. The most common complication is the development of a firm fibrous capsule around the prosthesis, which occurs in 20 to 40 percent of the cases. This is a normal response of the body, which attempts to encapsulate a foreign object within itself, and it produces a breast that is firm, painful, protrudes abnormally, and is cold to the touch.

In an effort to keep the cavity in which the prosthesis was inserted as large as possible (to allow for scar tissue), many surgeons recommend frequent, firm rotary massage by the patient, extending over many months or for the duration of the patient's life. Also, whereas formerly the patient was requested not to use her arms and was practically swaddled in a firm garment, most surgeons now advise full use of the arms beginning on the third day. Sometimes a secondary procedure, either removing or splitting the capsule formed by the scar tissue, may be necessary, but it is not always effective. Surgeons have been attempting to rupture the capsule by manual compression. Unfortunately, when this is done, there have been cases of rupture not only of the scar tissue but of the silicone covering of the prosthesis resulting in the migration of the silicone gel.

Mammary implants may not last a lifetime. In 1988 the Maryland legislature passed a law—the first of its kind in the United States—that five days before undergoing breast implant surgery the patient must be given a brochure listing the potential risks and complications. More recently, because of the large percentage of contractures the Federal Drug Administration is investigating the use of silicone implants.

Reduction Mammaplasty

Large breasts not only interfere with a woman's ability to wear strapless clothes or other fashionable garments, but they may actually interfere with normal activities. By their excessive weight, the breasts become increasingly pendulous, alter posture, and may produce neck pain extending into the arms. Deep grooves are produced on the shoulder by the pressure of brassiere straps, and persistent uncomfortable dermatitis under the breasts is a common hot weather complaint. The possibility or even occurrence of complications after reduction mammaplasty is usually outweighed by the relief from daily discomfort and pain, the increased facility of body movement, and the improvement of the body's appearance both with and without clothing.

Reduction mammaplasty is a major surgical procedure performed in a hospital. Endotracheal anesthesia is preferred. In anticipation of possible blood loss, the surgeon may ask the patient to donate some of her blood two weeks before surgery so that it can be reserved for transfusion. This minimizes the possibility of an adverse reaction to the transfusion of someone else's blood. The patient should be in good health and should have refrained from smoking for at least two weeks before surgery to avoid pulmonary complications following the use of general anesthesia.

Before surgery the surgeon generally draws an outline of the anticipated incision on the breast, indicates the future site of the nipple, and estimates the amount of tissue that can be removed while still preserving the blood supply to the areola and the nipple. The incisions are usually made around the pigmented areola and extended either laterally or in the midline to the submammary area, where they are further extended horizontally. The skin, fat, excess breast tissue, and usually some of the oversized areola, are all excised. Some surgeons use liposuction to facilitate this surgery. The remaining breast tissue and fat are then fitted into the "skin brassiere" and the nipple is secured in its higher location. In some very oversized breasts it is necessary to separate the areola and nipple from the underlying tissue. After the tailoring of the breast tissue has been completed, the areola and nipple tissue are then applied as a free graft. Many surgeons insert drains attached to suctions for the removal of blood, sera, or liquified fat that might accumulate postoperatively and jeopardize the final results.

After the operation the patient wears a bandage around the chest or a special brassiere for approximately three weeks. During this postoperative period, physical activities involving the use of the upper arms are strictly limited.

The complications that can occur after this operation are bleeding, infection, prolonged drainage, loss of tissue, inversion of the nipple, and unsightly scars. Because of the large amount of fat in oversized breasts, there is a greater chance of infection than in most cosmetic surgery procedures. Tissue loss may occur because the blood supply is inadequate to the retained skin or areola and nipple complex, or the loss may result from infection or pressure. When such complications occur, a secondary procedure may be necessary. Follow-up surgery may also be necessary to correct asymmetry or depressed nipples. While the scars following breast reduction operations are more apparent than those resulting from other plastic surgery, they can usually be modified. Noticeable scarring is more likely to occur and to recur even after modifications in the submammary area.

The nipple may be hypersensitive for a period of time, and there may be some permanent decrease in sensitivity and erectility. With the passage of time the breasts will gradually become more pendulous than they were in the immediate postoperative period. Following a transposition procedure in which the nipple is secured into a higher position, a woman may breast-feed a baby, but she is not encouraged to do so. Future breast-feeding is impossible when the operation involves a free grafting of the nipple.

Mastopexy

Breasts naturally sag (ptosis) with the passage of time even when they are not abnormally large. The elevation of the ptotic breast is a much less complicated operation than the correction of oversized, dependent breasts. The designs of the incisions and the surgical procedure for lifting the sagging breast are similar to those of a reduction mammaplasty, but because the procedure is simpler and quicker the attendant risks are fewer and the scars are less conspicuous.

PLASTIC SURGERY PROCEDURES
FOLLOWING MASTECTOMY

After a simple mastectomy or a modified radical mastectomy, if enough subcutaneous fat remains, the contour of the breast can be recreated by the insertion of a prosthesis preferably under the musculature. When there is a shortage of tissue for coverage, some increase can be obtained by the insertion of a "tissue expander." This device is a silicone bag, the volume of which is increased gradually by the addition of fluid and thus stretches the overlying skin. Additional skin and fat for coverage of the prosthesis can be obtained from the adjacent abdominal area. If the areola and nipple have been removed, a portion of each from the remaining breast may be used as a free graft. If both breasts have been removed, it may be necessary to use tissue from the upper inner thigh to simulate the areola and nipple.

After a radical mastectomy, if extension of the cancer or of metastasis appears to be unlikely, consideration can be given to breast reconstruction. Following radical surgery that necessitated a skin graft for coverage or if irradiation was necessary, it is occasionally possible in a small-breasted individual to recreate a breast from an adjacent derma-fat "flap." If this is not possible, it is necessary to bring fat and skin tissue from a distance. Many surgeons use a musculacutaneous flap from the back or abdomen. In centers where they perform microvascular surgery the tissue may be obtained from the groin or buttocks. All of these procedures require several operations. The initial surgery requires four to six hours and the microvascular technique may require an additional two hours. The advocates of the latter technique maintain that it generally minimizes later surgery. Obviously these procedures are performed under general anesthesia in a hospital and require a longer period of hospitalization than other types of breast surgery. The nipple and areola can be simulated at later surgery as in a modified mastectomy.

In addition to the possible complications outlined relative to other breast procedures, there are other considerations involved in this surgery such as prolonged hospitalization, the inevitable scarring at the site from which the tissue was taken for reconstruction, the timing of the procedure, and finances. The timing of the procedure depends on the decision of the surgeon with regard to general suitability for the surgery and especially the degree to which the patient equates her breasts with her femininity. She must realize that although the goal is to recreate a normal breast, it cannot be totally achieved. In some instances a good simulation will be the result and at least the patient will look better in her clothes.

With increasing frequency the surgeon performing the mastectomy recommends that the patient consult a plastic surgeon prior to the surgery. Some surgeons in consultation with a plastic surgeon are of the opinion that there is no reason not to undertake the reconstruction at the time of the mastectomy. Others prefer to wait for six months after which time the scar tissue will be more pliable than if done a few weeks after the initial surgery. Delay does permit a period of observation for evidence of recurrence.

Another consideration with regard to this surgery is financial. This surgery has been recognized by most insurance companies as rehabilitative rather than strictly cosmetic and is covered by insurance. Nevertheless, each individual should check her policy because it is very costly and often there are several periods of hospitalization.

LIPECTOMY

There are two ways of removing fat from the body, either through a surgical incision or by the introduction of a blunt or sharp cannula through a small incision in the skin, which is termed lipolysis or liposuction. There are indications for each procedure and both are subject to many of the same complications. Lipectomy refers to the excision of skin and fat (dermoplasty) and lipolysis or liposuction refers to the removal of fat by the insertion of a blunt metal cannula through a small incision and attaching it to suction to remove fat.

Abdominal Lipectomy

Abdominal lipectomy was originally undertaken to correct extreme cases of obesity by removing some of the skin and subcutaneous tissue of a grotesquely pendulous lower abdomen. Today this surgery is also performed for the correction of the excessive flaccidity of the skin that may result from pregnancy or weight loss and for the improvement of the striae (stretch marks) caused by pregnancy. Often a lax, obese abdomen is associated with weakened or separated central abdominal muscles, and to obtain a good result in such cases it is necessary that the fascia surrounding these muscles be placated across the midline (folded over and sutured) to pull the muscles together.

The patient should be in excellent health before the surgery is scheduled because this is a major procedure performed under general anesthesia. The patient is usually requested to bathe with antiseptic soap for several days before entering the hospital. Preceding surgery, the pubic hair is shaved. The incision is usually made just above the pubic area and extends laterally across the area that would be covered by the lower part of a bikini. If there is an old midline scar, if improvement of the waistline is to be accomplished, or if the surgeon decides it would be more advantageous, a midline incision may be made instead of a horizontal incision. In some cases both incisions are made. The skin and subcutaneous tissue are separated from the underlying fascia as far up as the rib margin and sternum. The patient is placed in a flexed position, with knees and upper torso elevated so that the maximum amount of tissue can be removed. The excess is cut away, and the navel is relocated in a new opening made for this purpose. Blood loss is minimal. However, drains attached to suction may be inserted as there may be some postoperative ooze and liquefaction of fat as in a reduction mammaplasty. The flexed position is maintained as the wound is dressed. Various types of dressings are used, but most of them are designed to exert pressure and are similar to a panty girdle. The wearing of a supportive girdle for six weeks after the surgery is recommended. Ambulation usually begins on the third day and gradually increases as healing proceeds and the patient gradually becomes more upright in position.

Postoperative bleeding may occur and drainage may be excessive. Because the area is one of fatty tissue with a relatively small blood supply, infection may occur, but this is rare. Loss of tissue can occur because of a hematoma, excessive tension, or inadequate blood supply. When tissue loss does occur, a second procedure may be required for correction. Scars may be conspicuous. Rarely are all stretch marks removed. Those that were located in the excised skin are, of course, gone, but those in other areas remain. However, because the skin is more taut, the remaining striae are less conspicuous.

Thigh, Hip, and Arm Lipectomy

Excessive flabbiness of skin or excessive fat or both can also be removed from hips, thighs, and arms. The preoperative preparation and procedure are fundamentally similar to those required by the abdominal lipectomy, and potential complications are the same in all. The excision of arm tissue is the simplest.

The incision for the removal of excess tissue from the hip is usually made in the gluteal fold where the buttocks join the upper thigh. If the problem exists over the lateral portion of the upper thigh (trochanteric) area, the incision may extend around three-quarters of the thigh or at a slightly higher level where the scar will be hidden by a bikini.

For removal of excess skin from the inner thigh, a modified T incision is made extending vertically at the midline of the inner thigh and extending forward and backward for a limited distance at the groin.

To remove the excess skin and subcutaneous tissue of the upper arm, a modified T incision is made, with the vertical portion of the cut placed along the least visible portion of the arm and the horizontal cut extending into the armpit. The scar will be visible when the arm is raised. In deciding whether to have this surgery, the patient must choose between flabby arms and a visible scar.

For all these procedures, three weeks of disuse should be anticipated. After three weeks scars may increase in width but they also become paler and less conspicuous.

LIPOSUCTION

Liposuction (lipolysis) is used for the removal of localized fat and to facilitate other cosmetic procedures. At present it is a very popular procedure especially among young girls but is increasingly undertaken on middle-aged individuals who are suitable candidates. The development of several types of cannula in the past few years has permitted the surgery to be performed with deceptive ease and has resulted in many unqualified practitioners attempting the surgery. It is not without danger and has in some instances resulted in death for the patient. Therefore, special care should be exerted in the selection of a surgeon before the decision is made to undertake this procedure.

COSMETIC SURGERY

It is major surgery and the patient should realize that they should be in good health and not suffering from any kidney, cardiovascular, diabetic, or other disease. The same preoperative prohibitions as for other major plastic surgery procedures pertain. Preferably the patient is under forty because the overlying skin is more elastic and will adapt better to the new contour. It can be used for older persons who are not concerned with the appearance of the overlying skin after the surgery and are in better than average health for their age. Essentially, the operation is for the younger individual.

Preoperatively, the patient is prepared as for a lipectomy. The procedure is done under general anesthesia supplemented by local anesthesia. A small incision in the skin is made in an inconspicuous area. In the abdomen it is usually above the pubis or adjacent to the umbilicus (navel); for the hips or thighs, in the bikini area. The cannula (a blunt metal tube with perforations) is inserted approximately one inch below the skin and suction applied. It is reinserted at a different angle in a more or less radial fanlike pattern until the fat is removed from the previously designated area. Fat cells and fluid of disrupted fat cells as well as plasma and blood are removed with the suction. Limiting the amount to be removed at any one time to 2,000 c.c. is advisable. The risk of the operation increases with attempts to remove excessive amounts of fat at one time. The patient may go into irreversible shock.

Postoperatively, the involved area is strapped or an elastic pressure dressing is applied such as an elastic panty girdle on the abdomen or thighs. If there had been excessive bleeding, some surgeons may decide to insert drains, although this usually is not necessary unless a large vessel has been damaged. Overnight observation, preferably in a hospital, is essential. The patient is required to wear an elastic dressing or garment for three weeks, and activity is sometimes limited for longer depending on the area involved.

Liposuction is useful not only for limited amounts of fat localized in the abdomen or thigh and hip areas but also for fat at the inner knee, medial thigh, ankle, arm, breast, and beneath the chin. It is often used to facilitate lipectomy.

Essentially it is a blind procedure and complications such as blood and fluid loss can less easily and promptly be detected. Embolism (a clot) may enter a vessel and be carried to the lung, head, or heart and may be lethal. Venous stasis may lead to occlusion of a major vessel (thrombosis) and if it becomes infected (thrombophelitis) may result in a painful extremity. Vessels and nerves may be permanently damaged but immediately postoperatively a numbness or a burning sensation may be present which usually will gradually decrease. Skin loss may occur. Discoloration of the skin may occur and one of the most common problems is irregularity of the skin surface due to the skin not adapting to the decreased volume or to areas where there is increased scar formation beneath the skin. The use of smaller cannulas has helped reduce this corrugated appearance, but even with good technique there may be some wrinkling and dimpling. The patient does not display the large scars that are a real disadvantage in a lipectomy, but this surgery is for a different purpose—the removal of localized fat.

SPIDER HEMANGIOMA AND CAPILLARY VARICOSITIES

Spider hemangiomas, which appear on the face or the body as little red spots with tiny radiating blood vessels, and capillary varicosities, which usually appear on the thighs and legs, can be eliminated. This is accomplished by the injection of air and a chemically irritating (sclerosing) solution into the blood vessel through a very small needle. More than one visit to the physician may be required. It is imperative that the solution be injected directly into the vein so that it does not come in contact with adjacent skin. Contact with the skin may cause an alteration in pigment or even loss of the affected tissue. Some surgeons prefer to treat the little vascular lesions by touching them with an electric needle.

YOU DECIDED TO HAVE COSMETIC SURGERY

In this chapter I have presented a nontechnical survey of current procedures in cosmetic surgery. It is neither comprehensive nor definitive, but it is an attempt to explain what is involved in various operations as an aid to the women considering them.

During consultation, the patient should be told exactly what will take place before, during, and after the operation. All doubts and possible misunderstandings should be resolved before the operation. If the doubts remain, it is best not to schedule the surgery. To obtain the best results, the surgeon's instructions should be followed as closely as possible. A good postoperative result may well become a disaster because of the patient's lack of cooperation.

The criterion for the ultimate success of cosmetic surgery is the patient's greater pleasure in her appearance. Unfortunately, an operation that may be considered successful by the surgeon in terms of physical and esthetic results may not be viewed with the same enthusiasm by the patient. For those few women whose dreams of rejuvenation are so unrealistic as to be totally beyond the possibility of accomplishment, no improvement will ever be good enough. However, in spite of the limitations and the problems that must be taken into account, the vast majority of patients who have had surgery for the improvement of their appearance are happier for having done so.

The number of individuals having cosmetic surgery has increased tremendously since the newspaper ads and media have inundated the public and the number of physicians trained and untrained are performing these procedures. An unsatisfactory result that cannot be further corrected surgically may result in a gross deformity. Litigation is costly and for a number of reasons compensations are limited unless there is evidence of neglect or gross incompetence on the part of the person performing the operation. Therefore, it behooves the patient who is to undergo elective surgery to understand the procedure as completely as possible and to read with care preoperatively the permit that she signs. The qualifications and reputation of the surgeon and the environment in which he or she operates cannot be too carefully investigated. Is a certificate displayed in his or her office indicating certification by either of the recognized boards of plastic surgery? Does the surgeon have privileges to perform this specific operation in an accredited hospital?

The surgical set-up in the office should be the equivalent of a good hospital not only with regard to the physical situation but with regard to equipment and personnel. Is there equipment for monitoring the patient and cardiovascular resuscitation equipment? Are the personnel adequate and trained to operate the equipment? If the surgery demands general anesthesia is there a certified nurse or anesthesiologist to administer the anesthesia? These are questions to which the patient should have answers. A certificate by the American Association for Accreditation of Ambulatory Surgery displayed in the reception room or office gives the patient some assurance with regard to these questions. For careful investigation preoperatively, further help can be obtained from the sources listed in the Directory of Health Information.

SUBSTANCE ABUSE

Anne Geller, M.D.
Chief, Smithers Alcoholism Treatment and Training Center,
St. Luke's–Roosevelt Hospital Center, New York City;
Assistant Professor of Social Medicine,
College of Physicians and Surgeons, Columbia University

Helene MacLean,
Medical Writer and Editor; Author, *Caring for Your Parents*

Substances that alter mood and change perceptions and feelings have been used by humans since history was first recorded. They have been used in religious rituals to produce states of ecstasy or frenzy. They have been used to increase endurance and overcome fatigue. They have been used to lessen pain and suffering. They have been used in social gatherings. Recognizing the powerful effects of these substances, societies have developed rules and customs regulating their use.

In the United States attitudes and customs surrounding the use of mood-altering substances are extremely variable. They vary among ethnic and religious groups, they vary from region to region in the country, they vary according to age and to socioeconomic standing, and they vary from time to time depending on circumstances.

Today there are many points of view about how to define a mood-altering substance and about what standards to apply to "substance abuse." Is sugar a mood-altering substance? Is compulsive overeating "substance abuse"? Are smokers really drug addicts? Are you a drug addict if you can't get going in the morning unless you have a strong cup of coffee? Which drugs can legitimately be used by athletes?

On questions of substance abuse, there is not only a great deal of ambiguity; there is also considerable ambivalence. Take alcohol, for example. The so-called Prohibition Amendment to the United States Constitution is the only amendment that was ever repealed. Anger keeps mounting about drunk driving, but images of convivial gatherings almost always include beer, wine, or a bottle of hard liquor. Nor does the war on drugs or the war on crime ever spell out the role of alcohol in these plagues of society.

Consider the ambivalence about smoking. The addiction to nicotine is responsible for higher costs to the nation and more deaths than any other addiction. Yet in the interests of free enterprise and "free choice," cigarettes continue to be sold to whomever can afford to buy them including 12-year-olds with the money to put in a vending machine. And advertising campaigns continue to trap young women into believing it's a sign of "liberation" and high fashion to smoke.

Following are some figures to ponder when we talk about fighting the drug problem. They were presented in an article on addiction in the Sunday *New York Times Magazine*, March 20, 1988, by Joseph Califano, Jr., former secretary of the U.S. Department of Health, Education, and Welfare (now Health and Human Services):

- 54 million Americans are addicted to cigarettes.
- 18 million are addicted to or abuse alcohol.
- 1/2 million are addicted to heroin.
- 10 million abuse barbiturates and other sedative-hypnotic drugs.
- 60 million have used marijuana.
- 22 million have tried cocaine.

Somehow, in all this chaos, each woman, except for those whose religious beliefs determine every aspect of their daily lives, must determine her own attitudes and her own patterns of behavior. There is a tremendous mythology surrounding alcohol and drug use: for example, that you can't become an alcoholic if you only drink beer or that cocaine is not addicting or that smoking marijuana leads to using heroin. There is also a growing movement to reject all drugs, including those prescribed by physicians, in the quest for perfect health and well-being. And distressing as it may be, there has been considerable publicity about the high rate of substance abuse among physicians themselves. This professional problem has many consequences, not the least of which is a denial of the patient's addictions as a way of avoiding a confrontation with one's own.

Thus, a woman who wishes to make personal choices in terms of her physical and psychological well-being must inform herself and act in her own self-interest, free of social pressure and trendiness as well as of dependence on any single source as the final authority for what's good for her. As an autonomous adult, she can decide when to say "No," when to ask questions to get more information, when to contradict authority by presenting a body of facts, and, especially, when to seek help at the first sign of trouble.

It is hoped that the information that follows will enable you to meet the challenges of substance abuse. Also, if you are concerned about your own or someone else's alcohol or drug use, the sections on problem use and dependency should give you some guidelines. The section on obtaining help and information will enable you to take some action if necessary.

MOOD-ALTERING DRUGS

Drugs that alter mood fall into four major groups: sedatives, narcotics, stimulants, and hallucinogens (see Table 1). Each group has representatives that date back to antiquity: alcohol for the sedatives, opium for the narcotics, caffeine and nicotine for the stimulants, marijuana and peyote for the hallucinogens. These early drugs were extracted from plants, and some still are. Many modern drugs in these same categories are now synthesized in pharmaceutical laboratories. Manufactured drugs include the tranquilizers Valium and Librium and the various barbiturates for the sedatives, Demerol and methadone for the narcotics, Dexedrine and the various amphetamines for the stimulants, and phencyclidine (PCP) or lysergic acid diethylamine (LSD) for the hallucinogens.

Why are mood-altering drugs so powerful? Why have societies tried to regulate their use? In spite of their many differences, these drugs all seem to have some effect on systems in the brain responsible for pleasure, euphoria, or relief from pain. Animals in laboratories will work very hard, sometimes ignoring food, water, and sleep, to get injections of these drugs, and they will continue to inject themselves to the point of exhaustion and death. With sedative and narcotic drugs their self-injection is less extreme, but they will continue to the point where they become sick. Interestingly, laboratory animals are not very markedly turned on by hallucinogenic drugs. These seem to provide a uniquely human pleasure.

In medicine, potentially addictive drugs have been used for many purposes. Morphine, the opium derivative, has been used in the Western world for more than 150 years to alleviate pain and induce drowsiness. Barbiturates such as phenobarbital are prescribed as sedatives. Since the early 1950s when the chemical compounds were first discovered that led to the production of Librium and Valium, tranquilizers have been prescribed as an effective way to deal with anxiety and stress. Stimulants in the form of amphetamines were until comparatively recently prescribed for their appetite-suppressing effects. Even hallucinogens such as LSD were popular with some psychotherapists during the 1960s as a means of "unlocking" the buried material in the unconscious and making it accessible to the patient and the doctor for analytic inspection.

No matter whether these drugs were taken by women with or without medical sanction, the development of physical addiction, psychological dependence, and substance abuse in the broadest sense presents problems ranging from temporary disorientation to physical damage and, in extreme cases (sufficiently well publicized to need no further identification), to death. In medical use the loss of mental and physical efficiency and the development of tolerance have also been unwanted side effects. The fact that the pleasure-inducing effects can so easily lead to abuse and dependency, with disastrous consequences for the patient, has led to strict regulations regarding prescription of these drugs.

The effects of any drug depend on the drug itself, how it gets into the body, the amount taken, the individual, and the circumstances under which the drug is used. All drugs that change mood can be abused and can cause psychological or physical dependence. The risk of this happening increases with the strength of the drug, the amount, the rapidity with which it gets into the brain, and the frequency with which it is used. In order of increasing risk one can take a drug by mouth, by sniffing or snorting, by smoking, and by injecting into a vein. With a relatively weak drug such as marijuana, even smoking it does not result in a very high concentration in the brain. This is not to say that people cannot get into trouble with marijuana. They can and do, of course. But one is much more likely to get into trouble, indeed practically certain to

TABLE 1
COMMON DRUGS

Sedatives	Narcotics	Stimulants	Hallucinogens
Prescription Drugs			
SLEEPING PILLS	Codeine	Benzedrine	
Amytal	Darvon	Control	
Dalmane	Demerol	Dexedrine	
Doriden	Dilaudid	Dexatrim	
Halcion	Lomotil	Methedrine	
Nembutal	Methadone	Preludin	
Placidyl	Morphine	Ritalin	
Quaalude	Percodan	Tennate	
Seconal	Talwin		
TRANQUILIZERS			
Ativan			
Librium			
Miltown			
Serax			
Tranxene			
Valium			
Nonprescription Drugs		alcohol	
		caffeine	
		nicotine	
Street Drugs			
Blues	Heroin (skag,	Bennies	Marijuana
Downs	horse, junk,	Cocaine (crack,	(grass, pot,
Goofballs	stuff)	snow, flake,	weed)
Nembies	Methadone	coke)	Hash
Red devils	(dollies)	Crystal	LSD (acid,
Yellow jackets	Darvon (pinks	Dexies	cube, D)
	and greens)	Hearts	PCP (angel
		Speed	dust, hog,
			peace pill)

do so, if one snorts a very powerful drug such as cocaine or smokes it in the form of crack.

There are individual differences, too. The extremes of youth and age are more susceptible, and obviously the less you weigh the greater will be the effect of a given amount of drug. Some individuals, for reasons that are not yet known, seem to be more predisposed to problems with mood-altering drugs than others. Ongoing research that explores the predisposition to addiction indicates the presence of an aberration in brain neurophysiology that results in metabolic disease with a possible genetic base. Studies that concentrate on the addictive personality find common characteristics among those who indulge in compulsive self-destructive behavior (including not only substance abuse but overeating, gambling, and the like). Although there are many differences, the similarities include: impulsiveness, difficulty in delaying gratification, sensation-seeking, rebelliousness, weak commitment to social goals, sense of alienation, and low tolerance for stress. In defining the addictive personality, other specialists combine some of these characteristics with such factors as low self-esteem, vulnerability to anxiety and depression, and a history of conflicting parental expectations.

Finally, the circumstances in which drugs are used can profoundly affect how people feel and how they permit themselves to behave. Millions of women have used tranquilizers during the period for which they were prescribed in order to help them cope with a crisis and have never grown dependent on them as an easy way of dealing with the normal stresses of daily life. Others have become Valium "junkies" by collecting prescriptions from as many doctors as they could manipulate into writing them. If a woman has had practically nothing to eat because of compulsive dieting and then has two quick drinks at a party, the effect on her body and behavior will certainly differ from that of the woman who sips two glasses of wine while eating a business dinner.

ALCOHOL

It is not known when the special properties of fermented fruit and grain were discovered, but from mute testimony of archeological evidence it would seem that alcoholic beverages have been part of the human experience since before recorded history. Each society has had customs and rituals surrounding the use of alcohol. In some social and religious groups it is prohibited entirely; in others ritual use is permitted but intoxication proscribed. In our own pluralistic world, it is very difficult, perhaps impossible, to chart a course through the morass of conflicting views and to determine what is acceptable social drinking for a woman today. The problem has worsened as more and more women climb the corporate ladder or move into jobs where having a few drinks "with the guys" takes on the aura of a professional obligation. (At the same time that this problem has intensified, however, many more men and women are joining their colleagues for lunch and dinner and, without any embarrassment or fuss, ordering a nonalcoholic beverage without skipping a beat.)

For women who do drink moderately and would like some guidelines to help them determine what constitutes a safe drinking pattern over which they have total control, here are some helpful facts. Alcohol is metabolized at a constant rate of 3/4 oz. of absolute alcohol per hour. This is equivalent to one drink that contains 1 1/2 oz. of 100 proof hard liquor, 4 oz. of wine, or 8 oz. of beer. If you drink faster than this the blood and brain alcohol level will rise and you will experience some mood and behavior changes (see Table 2). Women generally weigh less than men and also have proportionally more body fat to water. If you match drink for drink with a man, you will have a higher level of alcohol in your blood than he will in his, unless he is much smaller than you are. You will, therefore, get drunk more quickly. Food in the stomach will delay the absorption of alcohol but it will not prevent you from becoming intoxicated if you drink enough to do so.

TABLE 2

Weight (lbs.) 100 125 150 175	*Blood Alcohol Level in Milligrams %*	*Behavior/Mood*
NO. DRINKS PER HOUR		
1–2 1–2 2–3 2–3	50–99	Euphoria, poor judgment
2–4 2–4 3–6 4–7	100–199	Poor coordination and thinking
4–6 5–7 6–9 7–10	200–299	Staggering, slurring, confusion
6–8 7–9 9+ 10+	300–399	Anesthesia, memory lapses

For women the effect of a given amount of alcohol, say three drinks in an hour, varies with the stage of the menstrual cycle. This is because the amount of body fluid changes. Just before menstruation, when fluid is retained, there is more water in the body for the alcohol to be distributed in. Therefore, the alcohol is present in a lower concentration and its effect on the central nervous system is reduced. Three drinks in one hour for a 130-pound premenstrual woman may make her happy, carefree, a little loquacious, impulsive, perhaps a bit clumsy. Taken in the middle of the menstrual cycle, the same amount is likely to cause stumbling, unfocused attention, uncontrolled giggling, and what can only be called socially inappropriate behavior.

Alcohol has a biphasic action. The initial effect is to stimulate thought, action, and social outgoingness and to induce a pleasant emotional state. If drinking continues, the depressant effects on the brain predominate with increasing disturbances in thinking and coordination. The pleasant mood evaporates, replaced by unpredictable mood swings, irritability, and depression. Because the initial effect is so pleasant, it is natural to try to recapture it or intensify it by drinking more. Alas, this cannot be done. Sensible social drinkers learn to bask in the evanescent glow provided by a drink or two, to sustain it by maintaining a low blood alcohol level, and then without regret to let it go.

The risks of drinking increase with the number of drinks you have. These include injuries from falls; inappropriate behavior; bumping into things; driving accidents; pedestrian accidents; being the victim of robbery, physical abuse, or date rape. And for women who have to go to work or have to meet the demands of small children at home, a hangover can cause serious problems.

WOMEN AND DRINKING PROBLEMS

Most people who drink do not consider themselves "problem drinkers." However, according to the National Council on Alcoholism, it is only since the 1970s that any research has been focused on women and alcohol. Here are some of the facts that have been emerging:

- 60 percent of adult women 18 and over drink; 40 percent are abstainers.
- Of the women who drink, 55 percent do so moderately (less than 60 drinks per month), while 5 percent are heavy drinkers.
- Women's drinking problems are often viewed as less serious than men's and their condition may be more frequently misdiagnosed.
- 34 percent of Alcoholics Anonymous membership is female.
- Regular drinking is common among high school girls, and a sizable number engage in heavy drinking.
- Women frequently engage in the high risk practice of abusing other drugs in combination with alcohol.
- Among alcoholic women, the incidence of suicide attempts exceeds

that of the female population as a whole as well as that of alcoholic men.
- Women are likely to develop liver disease with a lower alcohol consumption than men.
- Women are now heavily targeted for the marketing of alcoholic beverages. According to *Impact,* a liquor industry newsletter, women will spend $30 billion on alcoholic beverages in 1994 compared with $20 billion in 1984.

For women who deny they have any "problems" with drinking but often find themselves drinking more than they "intended" to, there are many warning signs along the way: having an auto accident after leaving a party in a state of intoxication, missing work, being late to work because of a hangover, not getting the housework done, having memory lapses, having intercourse with someone distasteful, fighting with friends or hitting one's children, being preoccupied with drinking, getting sick or throwing up, and spraining an ankle because of stumbling. The list is inexhaustible and covers damage to physical health, psychological well-being, social relationships, employment, and legal standing. Women who have a problem connected with alcohol use may be reluctant to think about it or to seek advice for fear of being labeled alcoholic. What is important is not the label "alcoholic" but what is happening to you when you drink. If you had a problem connected with the use of alcohol in the past year, what did you do about it? Were you able to change your drinking pattern so that the problem was resolved or have the same or other problems recurred?

The test below, which you can give to yourself, can help you determine your profile with regard to drinking.

(The Michigan Alcoholism Screening Test—"MAST")

Directions: If a statement says something true about you, put a check in the space under YES. If a statement says something not true about you, put a check in the space under NO. Please answer all the questions and add the total number of points scored.

		YES	NO
1.	Do you feel you are a normal drinker?		2
2.	Have you ever awakened the morning after some drinking the night before and found that you could not remember a part of the evening?	2	
3.	Does your wife/husband (or parents) ever worry or complain about your drinking?	1	

Questionnaire About Drinking Problems *(Continued)*

		YES	NO
4.	Can you stop drinking without a struggle after one or two drinks?		2
5.	Do you ever feel bad about your drinking?	1	
6.	Do friends or relatives think you are a normal drinker?		2
7.	Do you ever try to limit your drinking to certain times of the day or to certain places?	1	
8.	Are you always able to stop drinking when you want to?		2
9.	Have you ever attended a meeting of Alcoholics Anonymous (AA)?	5	
10.	Have you gotten into fights when drinking?	1	
11.	Has drinking ever created problems with you and your wife/husband?	2	
12.	Has your wife/husband (or other family member) ever gone to anyone for help about your drinking?	2	
13.	Have you ever lost friends (girlfriends or boyfriends) because of your drinking?	2	
14.	Have you ever gotten into trouble at work because of your drinking?	2	
15.	Have you ever lost a job because of your drinking?	2	
16.	Have you ever neglected your obligations, your family or your work for two or more days in a row because you were drinking?	2	
17.	Do you ever drink before noon?	1	
18.	Have you ever been told you have liver trouble?	2	
19.	Have you ever had delirium tremens (DTs), severe shaking, heard voices or seen things that weren't there after heavy drinking?	5	
20.	Have you ever gone to anyone for help about your drinking?	5	
21.	Have you ever been in a hospital because of your drinking?	5	
22.	Have you ever been a patient in a psychiatric hospital or on a psychiatric ward of a general hospital where drinking was part of the problem?	2	
23.	Have you ever been seen at a psychiatric or mental health clinic, or gone to a doctor, social worker, or clergy-		

Questionnaire About Drinking Problems *(Continued)*	YES	NO
man for help with an emotional problem in which drinking played a part?	2	
24. Have you ever been arrested, even for a few hours, because of drunk behavior?	2	
25. Have you ever been arrested for drunk driving or driving after drinking?	2	

If you score: 0-3 points   You are probably a social drinker
               4 points   You are borderline alcoholic
               5 points or over You are probably an alcoholic

Other good questions to ask:

Have you ever wondered whether you might be an alcoholic?
Have you ever felt you should cut down on your drinking?
Have you ever felt bad or guilty about your drinking?
Have people annoyed you by criticizing your drinking?
Have you ever had a drink first thing in the morning to steady your nerves or get rid of a hangover (eye-opener)?

ALCOHOL DEPENDENCE (ALCOHOLISM)

In the United States, alcohol dependence affects about 18 million adults and 4 million teenagers, and one arrest in 3 involves intoxication. For those who are alcohol-dependent, there is no consistent ability to control alcohol intake. Drinking takes place in response to intense internal psychological and physiological demands of which the drinker is often not consciously aware. Although an alcohol-dependent drinker may be able to control intake for a time, sooner or later she drinks outside her intention, either drinking when she intended to abstain or drinking more than the limit she had set for herself. Because women who become alcohol-dependent drink for all the reasons normal drinkers do and often do not know they are at risk and because the process of becoming addicted may take several years, it is not surprising that women deny to others and also to themselves the extent of their difficulties with alcohol. However, as more and more women enter the job market out of economic necessity and as the compelling need to be gainfully employed comes into conflict with the compelling need to drink, more women than ever before are seeking treatment for their alcoholism. Thus, one in every three members of Alcoholics Anonymous is female and many women are attending on-the-premises alcoholism treatment programs initiated by their employers. Also, women are becoming more aware of the need to take responsibility for their own health. Their consciousness has been raised by television programs and radio discussions that stress the negative effects of alcohol.

In addition to the personal misery and social distress suffered by the alcoholic woman, her life span is shorter by about 15 years than that of the average woman because of accidents while drinking as well as because of damage to organs in the body that can be fatal. Alcohol abuse eventually damages the heart, the liver, the ovaries, the brain, the nerves, the muscles, and the blood cells. It causes damage directly by attacking the delicate membranes surrounding cells and indirectly because of poor nutrition that usually accompanies heavy drinking. In addition to causing death from liver failure, fatal hemorrhage, or severe brain damage, alcohol causes illnesses such as inflammation of the liver (hepatitis), inflammation of the pancreas (pancreatitis), heart failure, damage to the bone marrow causing anemia, and severe memory loss. Alcoholic women may have irregular menstrual cycles, reduced fertility, and recurrent vaginal infections.

Coming from a family where there is alcoholism markedly increases the risk of developing the disease. If there are alcoholics in your family, you should be extra-vigilant about your alcohol use. Being in an environment where there is heavy drinking will increase your exposure and, therefore, the risk. As an example of sensible disease prevention, if your father was an alcoholic you would be wise to avoid working in a cocktail lounge or being part of an office clique that makes a ritual of getting drunk after work on Fridays.

You should also be aware of some drinking patterns that are risky and may signify trouble with alcohol. These include being intoxicated more than once or twice a year; drinking more than a glass of wine or an occasional beer when alone; drinking specifically to relieve stress; drinking to allay anxiety before meeting someone or doing something; drinking to relieve symptoms such as insomnia, tension, depression, or pain; drinking after the party is over; and, of course, drinking the next morning to relieve the hangover.

ALCOHOLISM AS A FAMILY PROBLEM

Late-onset alcoholism is a problem only recently researched and publicly discussed. It is estimated that from 10 to 15 percent of the elderly in this country abuse alcohol. Of the approximately 2 million men and women in this category, about two-thirds have a long history of alcoholism, but as many as 700,000 older Americans develop the dependency after the age of 60.

The condition is usually precipitated by an emotional upheaval or a family crisis over the death of a spouse, divorce, retirement, onset of a serious illness, and very often it is connected with a deepening depression caused by aging and the loss of independence.

If you spend time with your aging parents or relatives, be alert to the following symptoms and don't be quick to dismiss them as the inevitable consequence of aging: falling asleep in social situations, slurred speech, unsteady walk, deterioration in personal appearance or compulsive neatness, improvised explanations about reclusiveness or memory losses, black and blue marks resulting from falls, general hostility and paranoia. In many instances, it is a concerned family member who calls the condition to the doctor's attention rather than the other way around. It is also important to keep in mind that not only does the susceptibility to the effects of alcohol increase with age but that older women are frequently taking various medications whose interaction with even small amounts of alcohol can produce disastrous effects.

Alcohol treatment programs designed for the elderly are not easy to find, and it takes great tact to get an older person to admit that the problem exists. But help is available through social services for the elderly and through geriatric clinics in some hospitals. And of course you may get the support you need and some useful referrals from Al-Anon.

Leaving aside the specific problem discussed above, it is difficult to say whether it is more painful to be an alcoholic, to be a daughter of an alcoholic, to be married to one, or to watch a child in the throes of alcoholism. It is not uncommon for women to have suffered through all four conditions, because alcoholism does run in families and children of alcoholics themselves not infrequently marry alcoholics. In the course of a lifetime few of us are fortunate enough to be untouched by alcoholism. It is a prevalent disease. If not in ourselves or our immediate families, we may encounter it among our friends, our colleagues, our students, our employees. It does not spontaneously cure itself. If ignored it will continue. An alcoholic, like all addicted persons, is powerless to arrest the disease by herself. If it affects someone close to you, you will have to intervene.

First, find out where in your community an alcoholic can get help and also where you can get help if necessary. Information about this is in the next section. Next, confront the alcoholic person calmly and directly with your observations and concerns about his or her drinking behavior and with a list of the places where he or she can get help. You will be more effective if you intervene together with other people who are close to the alcoholic, but you can act alone as well. Then you have to set about changing your own behavior around the alcoholic's drinking, recognizing that you cannot control it by nagging or hiding the bottles; that you did not cause it, whatever the alcoholic person may imply; and that you cannot cure it. If, after your intervention, there is no significant change in the drinking, then you must consider what you have to do to improve the quality of your life. If the alcoholic is a spouse or a lover, you may decide that you must leave, but do not threaten to do so unless you intend to carry out your threat. Think of your own interest; paradoxically, this will be best for the alcoholic too. In the case of a friend you may say, with regret, that you cannot continue to see her while she is still drinking. Sometimes the actual loss of a spouse, lover, or friend will be the critical factor for recovery in an alcoholic. Al-Anon, an organization for the family and friends of alcoholics, can be a wonderful support during these crises.

In addition to and as an adjunct of Al-Anon several new organizations have been formed as a result of recent investigations into the special problems of children of alcoholics and the psychological warp caused by growing up in a home where family dysfunction is caused by alcoholism. While Al-Ateen maintains a schedule of self-help meetings for the younger offspring and Al-Anon conducts meetings for the adult offspring, The National Association for Children of Alcoholics (founded 1983) has a growing number of chapters nationwide, publishes literature, holds regional conventions, and supplies community guidance in the form of lectures and educational meetings and The Children of Alcoholics Foundation (founded in 1982) publishes pamphlets and acts as a clearinghouse for meetings of the various groups, including Al-

Anon, who conduct self-help sessions attended by the adult children of alcoholics in the greater New York area.

Since its small-scale beginnings in 1935, the pioneering organization known as Alcoholics Anonymous (AA) has led the way in demonstrating to the professional world how uniquely effective the concept of self-help can be. As a result, there are now similar organizations that attempt to duplicate its success in coping with the many problems confronting all of us nowadays.

In a little more than 50 years, it has grown to a worldwide membership of 2 million people who attend meetings in 73,000 groups on the 5 continents. The United States and Canada account for 43,000 meetings attended by 800,000 members with a common goal—to maintain their sobriety one day at a time.

If you want help with your addiction problems, look in your phone book. Make a call to find where and when the meeting is held, and go. All that will be asked of you will be your first name, a handshake at the door, and your attention when speakers tell their stories. You will soon learn that you are not alone if you have a drinking problem. There are thousands of people in AA who share this problem and are helping each other—as they can help you—to deal with it. There is one woman to every two men among new AA members now, compared to one to ten 20 years ago, and the gap is narrowing. Many larger cities have groups for women only.

For those who feel the need for professional treatment, there are physicians, psychologists, social workers, clinics, alcoholism units in hospitals, and rehabilitation centers where expert care can be found. Be careful, though. Not all health professionals are equally knowledgeable. Many have not had formal training in this area. The National Council on Alcoholism has affiliates in major cities that maintain a list of treatment sources. Finally, local hospitals usually have inpatient alcoholism units for detoxification and/or outpatient clinics that can be contacted for both treatment and information.

ALCOHOL AND PREGNANCY

Women who are dependent on alcohol during pregnancy are at risk of having a child with fetal alcohol syndrome (also known as FAS). It is the third leading cause of birth defects and the only one of the top three that is preventable. Newborns who suffer from the syndrome are characterized by gross distortion of facial features, misshapen heads, cardiac defects, and other malformations. Mental retardation is severe, and size is below normal. Where alcohol abuse during pregnancy is not so extensive, the effects on the fetus may be less dramatic but some abnormalities may be present nonetheless.

When FAS was first identified, information made its way through professional journals into prenatal clinics and obstetricians' offices. But it has taken about 20 years for official warnings about the dangers of alcohol to pregnant women to be posted in a few bars across the country. The National Council on Alcoholism and other interested groups are lobbying for a federal law that will require warnings about FAS to be as widespread as warnings about the dangers of smoking.

Most women want to know the risk of any drinking at all during pregnancy and what is a safe limit. My advice is that it is safest to abstain, although you shouldn't go through agonies of guilt if you have a glass of champagne to celebrate an important event, nor should you be filled with anxiety if you drank moderately before knowing you were pregnant. If you do have trouble abstaining, it would be a good idea to get some help.

PRESCRIPTION DRUGS

Because prescription tranquilizers, sleeping pills, and pain-killers have a high mood-altering potential, they are easily misused. Misuse unfortunately can become abuse, that is, using them in greater amounts or for purposes other than those for which they were prescribed and thereby developing a psychological and/or physical dependency.

Does this mean that sensible women should avoid these drugs altogether? No. Nothing so extreme is being suggested. However, *all* drugs should be given serious evaluation both by the doctor and the patient. It is the doctor's responsibility to explain what the drug will do, what side effects to expect, how its effects are changed in combination with other drugs (both prescription and nonprescription), whether it is safe to use during pregnancy, and how many times the prescription can be renewed without permission. The patient then has the responsibility of evaluating this information and deciding whether to take the drug or not.

Because these drugs, which are not life-saving in the same way that an antibiotic can prevent death from pneumonia, the benefits of relief from the symptom—anxiety, pain, or sleeplessness—have to be weighed against the side effects and hazards. The weighing process is different in each individual case. For example, for an alcoholic the risk of taking any mood-altering drug is very great. Not only is dependency on yet another substance an important consideration, but the combination of alcohol and sleeping pills has resulted in more than a few "accidental" deaths. In the case of an alcoholic, it becomes the physician's responsibility to withhold the drug in favor of recommending treatment for alcoholism. However, for a person undergoing surgery, the benefits of properly controlling pain postoperatively far outweigh the risk of becoming psychologically dependent on the drug.

TRANQUILIZERS

There are two kinds of tranquilizers: minor tranquilizers or antianxiety drugs and major tranquilizers or antipsychotic drugs. Because the latter, also called psychotropic drugs, are or should be prescribed only for severe mental illness, they will not be discussed here.

Minor tranquilizers are properly used for the temporary treatment of anxiety and the relief of stress caused by cumulative emotional conflict or a sudden trauma, such as the death of a spouse, parent, or child. They are best viewed as a bridge to other forms of therapy.

All of us feel anxious, tense, and excessively stressed from time to time. Unfortunately, there is a seductive philosophy that leads us to believe that a life free of any distress is desirable and possible rather than vacuous and meaningless. For those who are seduced into believing that one does not have to live through anxious moments in order to grow and develop, relief can be just a pill away. Many women, and many doctors, apparently do believe this, because 3.7 billion drugs in the class known as benzodiazepines (which includes minor tranquilizers such as Valium and some sleeping pills) are consumed each year in the United States. Increasingly, physicians, pharmaceutical companies, and patients themselves are recognizing that irresponsible pill popping creates new problems rather than solving old ones. Many women are, therefore, finding alternative ways of coping with the anxiety-producing events in their lives: behavior-modification therapy, exercise, marriage counseling, support groups, meditation and massage, assertiveness training.

If you are feeling apprehensive about going on a job interview, for example, there are several things you might do: you might talk with your friends about it, you might ask someone to rehearse with you, you might ask yourself what is the worst thing that could happen, and so on. You probably would still be anxious, but you could get through the interview and would discover several things: (1) you are still alive, (2) it wasn't so bad after all and the really terrible thing didn't happen, (3) there were some things you did quite well and some things that you could do better next time, and (4) you feel quite pleased with yourself for having done it. Next time you will feel less anxious. Now, suppose you pop a tranquilizer or two before the interview. You have not learned anything. You have not coped with anxiety. You have denied yourself the experience of being able to function even though anxious. The credit for getting through the experience belongs to the drug company. Next time you will feel just as anxious.

The effect of tranquilizers on the brain is similar to that of alcohol. Low doses will make you feel pleasantly relaxed and cheerful, while higher doses can make you intoxicated. Of the millions of women who have used tranquilizers since they appeared almost 40 years ago, the vast majority have used them quite safely, if perhaps often unnecessarily. Some, however, have found themselves using more and more and may have visited more than one doctor in order to obtain a sufficient supply to keep up with their growing need. A woman in this situation is very much like the woman dependent on alcohol. She is unable to control her use. She is frightened and ashamed of what is happening to her. She feels that she should be able to stop. She tries. She can't. She feels even more ashamed. When she does stop for a while she experiences severe anxiety, jitteriness, and insomnia, and she may even have a convulsion. She needs help desperately.

Even women who manage to kick the tranquilizer dependency after long use report withdrawal symptoms ranging from moderate to severe. Forty-three percent of the women in this category have had to deal with extreme emotional distress, dizziness, restlessness, headaches, and gastrointestinal upsets as well as heightened anxiety—all considerably more unpleasant and immobilizing than the symptoms for which they originally took the pills in the first place.

The risk factors for dependency on tranquilizers are similar to those for alcohol. If you are an alcoholic or have been dependent on other drugs, you should not use tranquilizers. If you have family members who have drug or alcohol problems, you should use them very cautiously if at all. Using more than prescribed, increasing the dose yourself, or using them to get intoxicated are patterns that place you at high risk.

When Betty Ford publicly announced her dependence on alcohol and tranquilizers and her determination to deal with her substance abuse problems, she not only saved her own life but also established a commendable precedent that enabled many women, both those in public life and those who are not well-known, to admit that they needed help. Nowadays there is no shame connected with taking time out for treatment at local hospital facilities or at the Betty Ford Center, a deserving monument to a brave woman.

SLEEPING PILLS

There is a vigorous debate among doctors specializing in sleep problems over whether sleeping pills are an effective way to treat insomnia. For short-term sleep problems where rest is essential—for example, in a hospital before and after surgery—they do have some limited use. For chronic, recurrent insomnia, there is general agreement that sleeping pills can do more harm than good.

Insomnia has a variety of causes, many of which can be eliminated by changes in diet, exercise, and sleep routines. If these changes fail, consultation with a sleep specialist may reveal some treatable medical cause. Sleeping pills act by chemically shutting down some areas of the brain. They work very effectively over the short haul. However because the brain adapts quite rapidly to the drug action, after a few days the same dose no longer has the same effect. Thus, the use of sleeping pills for longer than a few days causes three main problems.

The first and most common is that though the pill is no longer having any pharmacological effect, it becomes incorporated into the nighttime routine. For many of us, the behavior patterns involved in preparing for sleep are so unchanging as to be more of a ritual than a routine. Disturb one part of them and falling asleep becomes difficult. This is why people often experience insomnia when in strange places. It is not uncommon for a woman to take a sleeping pill each night for 30 years—29 years and 51 weeks after it has become neuro-chemically ineffective. Such a woman would be now absolutely unable to sleep without taking that pill. She is dependent on the pill not because of its pharmacological action but because of its place in the nightly ritual.

The second and quite dangerous problem is that of having to increase the dose to achieve the same effect. Increasing the dose of any mood-altering drug places you at risk for becoming dependent on it. As the dose goes up, the brain adapts to the new dose, so the next dose has to be higher. The third problem of long-term use occurring with some of the newer drugs, which are active over a longer period, is that of increased daytime effects. These can be fairly subtle disorders of thinking, judgment, and fine coordination as well as decreased attention and drowsiness—all of which can interfere with normal functioning on the job, at home, and, potentially most dangerous of all, behind the wheel of a car.

The problem of dependency on drugs prescribed for insomnia was more common in the past when sleeping pills were liberally prescribed and were in the form of barbiturates (Tuinal and Seconal), which seem to be more habit-forming than the benzodiazepines (Dalmane, Halcion). The pattern of dependency on sleeping pills is just like that described for tranquilizers: increasing dosage, attempts to control it, bewilderment, pain, and shame at what is happening. Withdrawal from barbiturates, however, can have much more disastrous consequences and, therefore, should never be attempted without close monitoring by a physician.

AMPHETAMINES

Amphetamines such as Benzedrine and Dexedrine used to be prescribed to induce loss of appetite and therefore loss of weight. They were not effective in this—nor are the current over-the-counter pills and for the same reason. There is an initial loss of appetite, then the body adapts, the appetite comes back, and the weight is regained. In addition to being useless they were also dangerous because of their tendency to produce psychological and physical dependence. Amphetamines have very sensibly been banned by the Food and Drug Administration for weight-reduction purposes.

Amphetamines are still used by students and long-distance drivers to stay awake, and some of these pill users get hooked too. Intravenous amphetamine users (speed freaks) are less common now than ten years ago. They have been succeeded by intravenous cocaine users.

NON-PRESCRIPTION DRUGS

WEIGHT-LOSS DRUGS

Recently there has been an increase in the abuse of over-the-counter "pseudo-speed" drugs, mainly by adolescents. They will give a "buzz" or a "rush" and are often consumed with alcohol. They are not harmless. They can cause symptoms ranging from mild anxiety to agitation and hallucination. They also can cause high blood pressure, and fatal brain hemorrhages have been reported in people consuming large amounts. Withdrawal symptoms when the drugs are stopped include headache and loss of energy.

NICOTINE (CIGARETTE SMOKING)

On May 16, 1988, the surgeon general of the United States issued the warning that nicotine is as addictive as heroin and cocaine. The warning, which was contained in his annual report, summarized the research of more than 50 scientists and 2,000 scientific articles indicating that smoking must be viewed as a life-threatening addiction and not merely as a dangerous habit. While the tobacco industry continues to maintain that "smoking is truly a personal choice," legislation has been introduced in the United States Senate calling for a label on tobacco products and the inclusion of text in all advertising that would read, "Warning: Smoking is addictive. Once you start, you may not be able to stop."

The problem of smoking is of great concern to the government because on a national scale this addiction is far more costly and deadly than the addiction to heroin, cocaine, or alcohol. As early as 1983, this concern was expressed by the government in a publication called "Why People Smoke" in which it was pointed out that cigarettes are addictive because nicotine "reinforces and strengthens the desire to smoke, thus causing users to keep on smoking." It has also been demonstrated that it takes at least ten cigarettes a day to maintain the addiction and prevent withdrawal symptoms.

What explains the nature of the addiction? Because most smokers know that smoking is extremely toxic, what exactly are the irresistible benefits? Here are some of the effects of nicotine on the brain and the mind:

- It alters the availability of important brain chemicals involved in feelings of reward and well-being.
- Smoking makes task performance easier, improves memory, reduces anxiety, increases pain tolerance, and reduces hunger.
- By taking short puffs or by inhaling deeply, the smoker can be either emotionally aroused or calmed.
- Because nicotine stimulates the release of the brain's opiates, the endorphins, smokers find activities pleasurable that might otherwise be boring.
- Smoking tends to reduce the desire for sweet-tasting high calorie foods.

Regarding women and smoking, a 1987 Report by The American Cancer Society revealed the following facts:

- Lung cancer now exceeds breast cancer as the leading cause of cancer deaths in women.
- The number of female smokers is almost the same as the number of male smokers because more men have stopped smoking.
- For women between ages 35 and 44 who smoke more than two packs a day, cigarette-related medical costs and lost work will add up to an average of $20,152 over a lifetime.
- Women who smoke heavily have nearly 3 times as much bronchitis and emphysema, 75 percent more chronic sinusitis, and 50 percent more peptic ulcers than women who don't smoke.
- After stopping smoking, the risk of a woman's developing lung and laryngeal cancer drops steadily, equaling that of nonsmokers after ten years.
- Among employed women, white collar workers smoke less than blue collar workers, and women who earn more than $25,000 a year smoke less than any other group of working women.

In addition to the threat of chronic diseases, women have to consider the effects of smoking during pregnancy: increased likelihood of miscar-

Nicotine and the Body

The report notes that nicotine is a powerful drug that acts in the brain and throughout the body.

Readily crosses blood-brain barrier and accumulates in brain. It is faster than heroin and caffeine, for instance, but not as fast as Valium.

Stimulates the brain's cortex.

Some effects on endocrine system are influenced by reaction of hyopothalamus, and pituitary gland.

Affects function of heart and lungs.

Relaxes some muscles.

SOURCE: American Cancer Society
Copyright © 1987 by The New York Times Company

riage and premature delivery and the probability of below normal weight of the newborn baby even if the delivery is at full term. In addition, if the mother and/or the father smokes, there is a significant increase in the possibility of Sudden Infant Death Syndrome. Also, according to several studies in the United States and elsewhere, smoking may impair a woman's ability to breast feed her baby. It has also been observed that women who smoke stop breast feeding their infants much earlier than nonsmokers because nicotine lowers the levels of prolactin, a pituitary hormone that stimulates the production of milk.

There are many explanations for the difficulties experienced by women who say they want to stop smoking but find it impossible to do so. To begin with, unlike abstaining from alcohol, which can be accomplished "one day at a time," abstaining from smoking has to be reaffirmed about five times every hour. And unlike alcohol or marijuana, its powerful benefits don't interfere with normal social intercourse; in fact, they are likely to enhance certain aspects of competence.

A psychiatrist specializing in nicotine research, Dr. Ovide Pomerleau at the University of Michigan, has said that the millions of people who are still smoking have more profound problems than the millions who have stopped. In a report in *The New York Times* (6/9/88), he pointed out that the addiction to smoking is a combination of physical *and* psychological dependence and that strongly addicted smokers are likely to fail if they attempt to give up both dependencies at once. He therefore recommends, as many other experts do, the use of nicotine-laced chewing gum to make the transition to total abstinence easier.

Nicotine-laced chewing gum was approved by the FDA in 1984 for sale by prescription only. It is most effective when used according to instructions and when the smoker is involved in an organized support program. Although its use seems to be trading one addiction for another, there is ample evidence that it is much easier to quit the gum than to quit smoking. In addition, the gum is less of a threat to health because it does not carry with it the dangers to the lungs of inhaling smoke and tars. Nor does it provide the powerful impediment to stopping that smoking does, namely, about 1/4 of the nicotine that enters the lungs when inhaling cigarette smoke reaches the receptor cells in the brain in 7 seconds whereas the nicotine in the gum is absorbed through the cheeks and takes almost one-half hour to reach peak level in the bloodstream. Thus, it provides the drug "fix" without providing the quick "rush" that cigarette smokers count on.

While a few women can go through all the withdrawal discomforts on their own, 95 percent of all smokers can kick the addiction when they are cheered on by a support group such as Smokers Anonymous or through attending such programs as those run by the American Cancer Society or the American Lung Association. Programs are also available through hospitals, community organizations, and corporate health efforts.

Some women have achieved success through treatment by an acupuncturist or a hypnotist. If you're contemplating either of these practitioners, be sure to check on licensing and credentials.

For most women who truly want to stop smoking, it may take several attempts over a period of three or four years. The more serious the intentions, the greater the likelihood of success. It is generally agreed that the most effective techniques are based on behavior modification

SUBSTANCE ABUSE

and self-monitoring of habitual reflexes. Here are some practical suggestions from the American Cancer Society:

- Throw away all your cigarettes at bedtime the night before you stop smoking.
- As soon as you wake up, take a cool shower and drink a glass of orange juice.
- Switch from coffee to tea or low-calorie chocolate milk at breakfast, don't linger over it, and leave the house fast.
- At your workplace, get busy at once, and if you must spend time on the phone, doodle on a scratch pad.
- Because smoking is forbidden in many places of employment but a cigarette break is allowed in restricted areas, use this time to stand up and take deep breaths.
- Drink at least six to eight glasses of water a day.
- When you return home, avoid alcoholic beverages including wine at dinner.
- Keep busy and change the chair in which you customarily watch television.
- Exercise as much as possible.

CAFFEINE

Caffeine and caffeinelike substances are present in coffee, tea, cocoa, cola drinks, and many medicines, both over-the-counter drugs (painkillers such as Anacin, Excedrin, Midol; many cold preparations; stimulants such as NoDoz) and prescription drugs (Migral, Cafergot, Fiorinal, Darvon compound). Because of its easy availability in leaves and beans that can be chewed as well as in processed beverages, caffeine may be the most widely used psychoactive drug in the world. Its effect on the central nervous system not only keeps people alert but, after only one cup of coffee, also provides an improvement in mood that may last for as long as two hours.

By triggering the release of adrenaline and increasing its presence in the bloodstream by a factor of 200 percent, caffeine speeds up the heart and stimulates the brain. However, there are some people on whom it acts like an amphetamine by producing a "high" and then letting them down. And while some women appear to suffer no mental or physical ill effects from absorbing large amounts of caffeine, others experience caffeine intoxication after drinking several cups of coffee at once, having two cups of strongly brewed tea on an empty stomach, drinking cola beverages throughout the day and evening, or drinking the beverages during the same period in which caffeine-containing medications are taken. Symptoms include rapid heartbeat, headache, sleep disturbances, heartburn, irritability, anxiety, and frequent urination. (Caffeine is a strong diuretic.) Heavy caffeine consumers should not mistake these feelings for the symptoms of anxiety and incorrectly treat them with a tranquilizer. The only sensible solution is to cut down caffeine consumption to the point where side effects are not troublesome or, in cases of extreme sensitivity to its effects, to abstain from caffeine altogether in all its forms.

For those women who have become addicted to caffeine, total abstinence can present problems, at least for a while. Withdrawal symptoms, which can last for several weeks, include drowsiness, an inability to concentrate, a disinclination to work, excessive yawning, and in more extreme cases, depression. The dependence need not be abandoned all at once if these symptoms are too upsetting. Transitional measures, usually successful, include one cup of morning coffee, a mix of regular and decaffeinated coffee later in the day, or a similar mix of soft drinks.

Because high caffeine intake can increase blood pressure by about 14 percent and is also suspected of raising blood cholesterol levels, women with hypertension or coronary problems should control their caffeine intake. Caffeine in large amounts also places the user at risks higher than the normal for pancreatic and bladder cancer. And because caffeine constricts the blood vessels, there is an association between heavy intake and nighttime leg cramps.

ILLEGAL DRUGS

The harm to health of the legal drugs alcohol, nicotine, and caffeine have been described in detail. And while some women have abused prescription drugs, the vast majority of users of these drugs are not taking them in order to get high, get a kick, get a rush, be sociable, or be in fashion. Street drugs or "recreational" drugs are quite different. No one is using them innocently as medication only to discover by accident that they have attractive and compelling mood-altering effects. They are being used specifically for these effects from the start. There is, however, a good deal of innocence and ignorance about the nature of these mood changes, the side effects, the dangers of addiction, and the hangover effects. The most sensible course for a woman concerned about her physical and psychological well-being is to turn down offers of illegal drugs of any kind. Nevertheless, the use of illegal drugs is so widespread that you should be aware of the significant effects of any drug so that you can make informed decisions.

COCAINE

Cocaine is found in the leaves of *Erythroxylon coca,* a shrub growing in the Andes. The natives of Peru have for centuries chewed these leaves for their stimulant effects, their suppression of hunger, and the euphoria that counteracts the demands of unremitting hard work. However, the amount of active drug extracted in this fashion is quite small, sufficient to produce a sense of well-being and increased energy but not enough to cause the devastating dependency resulting from the use of the highly concentrated drug available for the past century in Europe and the United States.

The United States is now in the midst of its second cocaine epidemic. The first occurred in the late 19th century when cocaine was hailed as the wonder drug by, among others, Sigmund Freud. It was widely used in patent medicines and, of course, was the prime ingredient in Coca Cola. It was not long before serious problems with intoxication and dependency began to surface. In 1914 its use was legally restricted by the U.S. government. Interestingly, its use declined when amphetamines became available, only to rise again 50 years later when amphetamines fell out of favor. (It has also been used as a local anesthetic since 1984.)

Cocaine is sold on the street as a fine, white powder sometimes called coke or snow. It can be snorted, smoked, or injected intravenously. The effects, which last for about 30 minutes, include a feeling of euphoria, heightened self-confidence, a rush of energy, and intensified sensuality. It is an effective appetite suppressant, and whatever the route by which it is taken, it gets into the bloodstream quickly, producing a more intense effect than amphetamines or other stimulants taken by mouth.

In 1987 it was estimated that 30 million men and women in the United States have tried cocaine and more than 5 million use it regularly. Because the high is so rapidly succeeded by the low as the effects wear off, there is a compelling desire to take it again as soon as it is available. When the drug becomes habitual, users suffer from increasingly damaged self-esteem, nervousness, insomnia, inability to concentrate, fatigue, anxiety, and depression. Women can become nonorgasmic and men impotent.

Cocaine carries with it the same risks whether it is snorted or injected into the skin, muscles, or veins. Eventually, in addition to risks of addiction, it can painlessly and permanently injure the heart muscle, leading to dangerously irregular heart beats that can result in sudden death. Convulsive seizures and hallucinations are not uncommon. Used during pregnancy, cocaine can cut off the supply of oxygen to the fetus and kill it or it can cause premature delivery of low weight babies who have tremors and are unusually irritable.

About one in every three cocaine-dependent people in the United States is a woman. It is estimated that 53 percent of the women referred for treatment are under 30, and of these a significant number are also addicted to alcohol and amphetamines, spending as much as $500 a week on their addictions. They are usually in middle- or upper-income brackets, well-educated, in competitive demanding jobs or dissatisfied with their lives.

An increasing number of women who enter AA are determined to put an end to their dependence on all drugs, both legal and illegal. Help is also available at many special treatment centers, both on an inpatient and outpatient basis.

Emergency information and referral can be obtained by dialing the 24-hour hot line 1-800-COCAINE (262-2463).

In the past few years, cocaine in its smokable form, known as *crack*, has become the street drug most closely associated with inner city crime. The use of crack is not only the quickest and most effective way to achieve the euphoria associated with cocaine, it is also, according to scientists who are researching drug dependence, the addiction almost impossible to give up permanently.

Dr. Charles P. O'Brien of the University of Pennsylvania School of Medicine has been quoted in *The New York Times* (6/25/88) as saying "Crack is the most addictive drug we've ever had to deal with. Most people who got started were addicted in six months to a year." (It can take as long as two to five years for heroin users to become addicted.) It is the hope of researchers that a more complete understanding of the biochemistry of this addiction will enable them to develop a medical treatment that can quiet the craving for the drug in the first few weeks of withdrawal.

HEROIN

Unlike cocaine, heroin is a narcotic substance that belongs in the category of opiates, a category that derives from the opium poppy and also includes morphine. The term *opiate* has come to be used interchangeably with the term *narcotic*, which is defined (in *Webster's Ninth New Collegiate Dictionary)* first as "a drug (as opium) that in moderate doses dulls the senses, relieves pain, and induces profound sleep, but in excessive doses causes stupor, coma, or convulsions." Thus, strictly speaking, although cocaine is *not* a narcotic but a stimulant, the term *narcotic* has come to be used generically to cover practically all illegal drugs.

During the 19th century and into the 20th, opiates were legal and widely used not only to alleviate pain but also, especially in the form of laudanum, to minimize the discomfort of headaches, menstrual cramps, and gastrointestinal distress. The widely advertised "little pink pills" and "magic elixirs" were innocently used as "nerve medicine" by millions of women who were quite literally drug addicts without anyone's especially noting the nature of their dependence. (Audiences have been made aware of one woman's descent into morphine dependence at the turn of the century in Eugene O'Neill's great play, *Long Day's Journey Into Night.)*

Heroin itself was considered a blessing when it first became available because it seemed a viable solution to the morphine addiction that had become so widespread among the wounded soldiers of the Civil War. Thus, heroin once stood in the same relation to morphine that methadone now stands to heroin.

Heroin can be used by skin-popping, snorting, injecting it under the skin, or injecting into a vein. The latter procedure is called "mainlining." Its effects are produced quickly, and they last from three to four hours. Heroin use goes all the way up the social scale, and many middle class users as well as entertainers and athletes are in methadone maintenance programs. Recent figures (6/25/88) indicate that 60 percent of the addicts in these programs can stay away from heroin for at least six months.

While only a limited number of susceptible women become alcoholics—and only after at least five years of heavy use—heroin addiction can develop more quickly and with chronic use comes a large number of serious physical disorders: lung abscesses, liver impairment, and brain/mind dysfunction. The result of injecting the drug with a contaminated needle is the AIDS death penalty. Death can also result from an overdose large enough to suppress the actions of the central nervous system to the point where heart and lungs cease functioning.

While withdrawal symptoms are difficult to endure—heavy sweating, tremors, hot and cold flashes, cramps, anxiety, and above all, a profound craving for the drug—none of these symptoms is life-threatening, and, in fact, some addicts who have kicked the habit "cold turkey" have survived to tell the tale with pride.

Treatment with the synthetic opiate methadone substitutes one addiction for another, but it enables those who participate in such programs in a disciplined way to function as productive members of society. Therapeutic residence communities have been attracting women who want to be rid of *all* drug dependencies. Information and referral for methadone programs and other types of treatment as well as support groups can be obtained through hospitals and social service groups in the community.

MARIJUANA

The source of this mildly hallucinogenic drug is the hemp plant *Cannabis sativa*, a common weed that has been used as an intoxicant for about 5,000 years, making its way from Asia to North Africa, and by 1800, to Europe. It has also been known for centuries in the Western hemisphere, but its use in the United States did not become popular until the 1920s, and it was not until the 1960s that marijuana peaked as the illegal drug of choice among the young. At the same time that marijuana smoking declined among high school and college students in 1986, cocaine use as well as the use of alcohol increased.

Like the tobacco leaf, the leaf of the marijuana plant is dried, crushed, and smoked in the form of a cigarette. It is estimated that approximately 60 million people in the United States have tried it, and about 25 million use it regularly because of the pleasurable state of relaxation it induces. It also causes some changes in perception: colors may appear to be brighter and the sense of time is lost. Because memory, logical thinking, and coordination are impaired, driving and smoking marijuana can be a deadly combination.

Unlike the intoxication produced by alcohol, which can produce hostility, aggressiveness, and generally offensive behavior, intoxication with marijuana produces a mood that is usually calm, reflective, and detached. While it is rare for hallucinations to occur, inexperienced users do experience them. Panic attacks may occur in inexperienced and experienced users, although more frequently in the former. Such attacks are characterized by anxiety, palpitations, and pains in the chest and are accompanied by fears of having a heart attack and losing one's mind. A calm atmosphere and reassurances that these feelings are only temporary and will vanish very soon can keep the problem from escalating.

There is no evidence that prolonged use causes permanent changes in the nervous system or impairment of brain function, nor is there evidence of permanent damage to the normal cardiovascular system. However, because it does cause changes in heart and circulation performance characteristic of stress, it poses a threat to anyone who suffers from hypertension, cerebrovascular disease, and coronary atherosclerosis. There is no clear connection between marijuana use and cancer.

According to a report issued by the Institute of Medicine of the National Academy of Sciences there is no evidence of marijuana's harmful effects on male or female fertility. There is evidence, however, that the active ingredient in the drug does pass into breast milk, producing undesirable effects in nursing infants.

A small proportion of marijuana users are heavy users. Chronic heavy use may result in loss of energy and drive, slow thinking, and apathy. Marijuana can certainly cause psychological dependence, where the user is preoccupied with the drug, experiences a craving for it, and is unable to do without it. Mild withdrawal symptoms with restlessness, irritability, and anxiety do occur when the drug use is stopped. Dependent users suffer from considerable emotional distress regarding their drug use as well as disorganization in their daily life and often loss of jobs and family. As with alcohol, signs of dependence include preoccupation with obtaining an adequate supply, unsuccessful attempts to cut down, guilt and unwillingness to talk about the drug, personality changes, increasing isolation, and social dysfunction.

LSD (LYSERGIC ACID DIETHYLAMIDE)

This most publicized and widely used of the synthesized hallucinogenic substances was created in 1943 by a Swiss scientist trying to find a remedy for migraine headaches. About 10 years later, the C.I.A. conducted experiments with it hoping to find a "mind-control" drug. Somewhat later still a few psychotherapists used LSD to induce "experimental psychosis" thinking that in this way they might be able to gain greater understanding of the biochemical basis of mental illness.

The use of LSD was eventually democratized at Harvard University by Timothy Leary who carried his offbeat messages far and wide. But by 1967, as a result of many unexpected and accidental deaths and many "bad trips" that left a large number of young people with permanent mental impairment, this vogue for the drug that offered "transcendental experiences" came to an end.

CONCLUSION

Understanding the hazards of substance abuse can be comparatively simple. The legal drug that can kill you before your time is nicotine. The legal drug that can lead to a dependency in which you have lost control over your life is alcohol. Legally prescribed drugs such as tranquilizers and sleeping pills can result in addiction unless they are used only for the period and the purpose for which they have been prescribed. And as for the whole range of illegal drugs, from comparatively harmless marijuana to life-threatening cocaine—saying "No" is the easiest way to ensure your well-being as a law-abiding citizen and as a woman who makes intelligent choices to safeguard her physical and mental health.

Rape and Family Abuse

Dorothy Hicks, M.D.
Professor of Obstetrics and Gynecology, University of Miami School of Medicine; Director, Rape Treatment Center, Jackson Memorial Hospital, Miami, Florida

The increasing violence in our society is reflected in the growing incidence within the family of sexual assault and the battering of children, women, and the elderly. Psychologists, sociologists, and other professionals point out that these crimes usually occur when an accumulation of frustration and rage can no longer be contained. The result in many cases may be an explosive assault so violent as to be life-threatening to the victim, who is always physically weaker than the perpetrator. While alcohol is a common factor in many of these occurrences, even more common is the fact that the perpetrators themselves have been victims of sexual abuse or repeated beatings in their own past.

The definitions of abuse and battering have also been expanded to include prolonged and unremitting psychological abuse and threats short of violence but completely demoralizing to the victims.

In recent years, many of these crimes have come out of the closet and onto the television screen in the form of documentaries about incest, docudramas about battered women who eventually murdered their husbands, and news stories about battered children brought to the hospital dead on arrival. The category known as "date rape" is becoming increasingly familiar, and the term "grannybashing" is heard in family courts to distinguish this particular crime from one in which an elderly person is attacked at home or mugged on the street by an unknown assailant.

Thus, the general public is being enlightened through films, plays, community forums, and newspaper editorials so that as activists, citizens, and potential jurors, they can achieve a better understanding of these crimes and as possible victims, they can know how to seek protection and help.

Equally important are the increasing efforts to broaden the awareness and deepen the sensitivity of lawmakers, the police, doctors, social workers, and hospital personnel to the widespread nature of assaultive and sexually aberrant behavior in the home. It is hoped that because of these efforts, problems of rape, incest, and domestic violence will be viewed not only in terms of the "sickness" of individuals or of the pathology of the family but from the point of view of the laxity and inadequacy of the legal and criminal justice system. Among the results of these efforts is the formation of advocacy groups and coalitions to lobby for legislation that takes reality into account rather than denying it. A major triumph has been the passage of laws in 22 states defining "marital rape" as a punishable crime.

Recently, *The New York Times* (August 25, 1988) headlined a story "Employers Act to Stop Family Violence." Here is the first paragraph: "Moving cautiously into a new area of corporate responsibility, a growing number of companies have begun to treat family violence as a sickness undermining the health and performance of their employees." A spokesperson for one of the treatment programs pointed out that "Family violence costs employers millions of dollars annually in lower productivity, turnover, absenteeism, and excessive use of medical benefits." The story was considered important enough to be given front-page prominence.

Whether because of a regard for human decency and dignity or because corporations find it cost effective to get involved, help is on the way and solutions are being sought for problems that were once considered a family matter rather than a matter for public concern.

We begin this chapter with the crime of rape because while not all women are actual or potential victims of domestic violence, every one of us, by virtue of being female, is a potential rape victim.

SEXUAL ASSAULT: RAPE

Rape is a violent crime, not an act done for sexual reasons, and it precipitates a crisis situation in the victim. The degree of the stress involved becomes more understandable if rape is viewed as a crime against one's person. This places it in the same category as other aggressive crimes such as robbery, assault, and the ultimate act of aggression, murder. In fact, as far as damage to the innermost self is concerned, rape is the most traumatic act short of murder.

HISTORY

The threat of rape has been a fear of women from prehistoric times to the present. It is interesting to research ancient laws and historical practice to see how they approached the problems posed by rape.

In ancient times, the Babylonian Code of Hammurabi and Mosaic laws allowed capture by force of women from outside the tribe. Such women were considered to be prizes of warfare. Acquisition of women within the tribe required payment of goods or money to the family. Perhaps this was a basis for the concept of criminal rape: to take the virginity of a maiden was equivalent to destroying property or stealing the goods and money she would have brought to the family.

Under the Code of Hammurabi a female had no independent status. She lived as a virgin daughter in the house of her father or as a wife in the house of her husband. A married woman who was raped shared the blame with her attacker and both were bound and thrown into the river, although her husband was permitted to rescue her if he chose to do so. A virgin who was defiled was held innocent and the rapist slain.

Hebrew laws were similar. The "offending" wife and her attacker were stoned to death. A virgin raped within the city walls was considered guilty because she could have screamed for help, but a maiden raped in the fields was considered guiltless: the rapist paid the girl's father a fine, and the two were forced to marry. If the virgin had been betrothed before the incident, the rapist was stoned to death.

Tales of rape and similar stories are found in the Bible and in the folklore of all peoples. Variations on the story of Potiphar's wife, the woman who unjustly accused Joseph of rape, are found in Moslem, Christian, and Hebrew folklore as well as in the myths of the Celts and the Egyptians as far back as 1300 B.C. The moral of the story is that a woman can cause a man a lot of problems by falsely crying rape.

The practice of forcible seizure of women for mates was for centuries considered acceptable. One way to obtain property in the Middle Ages was to abduct an heiress and marry her; it was not until the fifteenth century that this was considered a felony. Arranging marriages was a common method of acquiring property during these times, and in some forms this practice continues today.

In Europe in the eighteenth century an assault was not considered rape if a woman conceived, because it was believed that if she did not consent, she could not have conceived. The law was very vague about the rape of women who were not virgins. There are few records; apparently these victims were not taken seriously and the accusations quashed.

In the United States during the days of slavery it was accepted practice to use slave women as the owner desired, and it was common for them to be raped by the men in charge. There was no attempt to maintain a slave family, but instead the women were considered to be "breeders" and were valued as such.

During wars and occupations of conquered countries, women have always been considered a part of the spoils of war and were ravished by invading troops. The primary basis for the assaults was not sexual gratification but rather was part of the psychology of conquest—the right of the conqueror to overwhelm and humiliate his victims.

Old laws about rape and the attitudes about what was, and in many cultures still is, considered acceptable behavior, reflect the need to preserve social stability and to protect property. The protection of women as individuals against a criminal act is a comparatively recent and by no means universal concept.

MYTHS ABOUT RAPE

Many myths have persisted throughout the ages about the crime of rape, and they must be corrected if we are to make progress in dealing with this problem. Although we cannot deal with them all, here are some of the most prevalent.

1. *The rapist acts to satisfy sexual desires.* From the work that has been done with convicted sex offenders, it is now well known that sexual gratification is not the reason for sexual assault. The need of the attacker is to overpower, degrade, and humiliate. Violence, not sex, is expressed by the attack. The majority of rapists have a sexual partner with whom they identify and have a relationship and many have children.

2. *A woman cannot be raped if she doesn't want to be.* This is absolutely untrue. The primary reaction of a woman to a rapist is fear. Whether her attacker is a stranger or someone she knows, she is fearful of being maimed or killed.

3. *If women did not wear sexy clothes and act in a provocative manner, they would not get raped.* Because violence and not sexual gratification is the motive for the attack, what the woman wears and how she acts have nothing to do with it. Many are assaulted in their own homes; many are asleep in their own beds. Many victims are older women. A significant number are girls between the ages of 12 and 15.

4. *Rape is part of the sexual fantasies of women, or all women want to be raped.* It may be true that some women have sadomasochistic sexual fantasies in which varying degrees of force play a part and that some women at some time and for a variety of reasons want to take a submissive role in sexual relations. However, these thoughts are completely different from and are unrelated to fantasizing rape in the sense of wanting to be the unwilling victim of a violent, nonsexual criminal act.

5. *Most rapes are reported to the police.* Even the most optimistic observers feel that at best one in four attacks is reported to authorities; some think it is only one in ten. Rape situations that usually go unreported because the victims are convinced that no one will believe them include women known to be sexually promiscuous, women raped by a family friend or neighbor, women in mental hospitals, professors' students, doctors' patients, and lawyers' clients.

6. *You can tell a rapist by looking at him.* Rapists come in all shapes and sizes and from all socioeconomic and educational levels. Most rapists are attractive males and have no problem finding female companions. At least 50 percent have a steady sex partner, married or unmarried, and the partners have no idea that their men are sex offenders.

CURRENT STATISTICS

Rape is the fastest growing of the violent crimes. In 1977 there were 63,200 forcible rapes reported to the Federal Bureau of Investigation; in 1987, the figure rose to 90,400, and even the most conservative observers believe that only one in four rapes is reported to the authorities.

It is unfortunate that we have no clear picture of the actual numbers of rapes and sexual assaults. Many factors make the actual numbers difficult to determine. One is the misleading way in which crimes are categorized by law enforcement agencies. A rape is classified in one of three ways: forcible rape (includes attempted rape but does not include statutory rape or homosexual rape), child molestation, or rape-homicide. On the national average 15 percent of the rapes reported to the police are dismissed as unfounded, that is, the police establish to their satisfaction that neither forcible rape nor the attempt to rape occurred. Still another reason for the lack of accurate figures is that many accusations of rape are reduced via plea bargaining to a lesser charge such as breaking and entering or aggravated assault and, thus, are included in the figures for those crimes instead of being counted as rapes.

Victims also contribute to the inaccuracies in the known number of rapes. Most of the assaults are unreported because of the stigma attached to being a victim of sexual assault. Many people still have the attitude that the woman is responsible for tempting or teasing the attacker and is, therefore, at least partially to blame for the rape. Failure to report the assault is especially true in the case of the child victim. Parents are afraid of the reactions of family and friends and want to protect the child from any additional psychological trauma. Even in such cases the victim, the child, may be accused of being seductive and therefore responsible for the attack.

The following statistics reveal some rather startling facts about rape in the United States:

- 44 percent of women have been a victim of rape or attempted rape at some time in their lives.
- Only 12 percent of the time is the perpetrator a *total* stranger to the victim. That means that in 88 percent of all cases, the rapist was an acquaintance, neighbor, friend, family member, lover, or hus-

A Woman's Body

STRUCTURE AND FUNCTIONS IN FULL COLOR
Illustrated by Leonard D. Dank

SKELETAL SYSTEM

VOLUNTARY MUSCULAR SYSTEM · CIRCULATORY SYSTEM

ENDOCRINE SYSTEM · RESPIRATORY SYSTEM

DIGESTIVE SYSTEM

NERVOUS SYSTEM · URINARY SYSTEM

REPRODUCTIVE SYSTEM

THE BREAST

EMOTIONS AND THE BODY

SKELETAL SYSTEM

- Clavicle
- Scapula
- Sternum
- Rib
- Humerus
- Vertebral column
- Elbow joint
- Ulna
- Pelvis
- Sacrum
- Coccyx
- Radius
- Carpals
- Metacarpals
- Phalanges
- Femur
- Patella
- Tibia
- Fibula
- Tarsals
- Metatarsals

BONES OF SKULL

1. Frontal
2. Parietal
3. Temporal
4. Zygomatic
5. Eye orbit
6. Maxilla
7. Mandible

Body's weight

Cancellous bone — supports weight

Articular cartilage

Space within cancellous bone — manufactures red blood cells

Calcium and phosphorus storage in the body

Marrow cavity

Compact bone

Fat storage

Ligament

ELBOW JOINT
(Typical synovial joint)

Radius

Humerus

Joint cavity

Synovial membrane

Articular cartilage

Ulna

EMOTIONS AND THE BODY

Conscious and subconscious brain areas

Hypothalamus

Brain stem

Sensory impulses

Involuntary autonomic nerve impulses

Heart palpitations

TARGET ORGANS

Brain
 fatigue

Blood vessels
 headache
 flush

Scalp and neck muscles
 headache

Lungs
 asthma
 hyperventilation

Heart
 palpitations
 tachycardia

Nipples
 erection

Stomach
 nausea
 vomiting
 heartburn
 ulcer

Intestines
 diarrhea
 constipation
 gas
 mucous colitis

Uterus & vagina
 muscular spasm
 orgasm

Bladder
 frequent urination

Blood vessels
 hypertension

Palms of hands
 sweating

Muscles
 fatigue
 ache

Skin
 dryness
 scaliness
 itching
 hives
 flush

Emotions, whether pleasurable or stressful, activate brain areas which may send involuntary impulses to target organs. In the spot drawing (left) involuntary impulses make the heart beat rapidly and heavily. If this causes worry, the impulses are reinforced, thus perpetuating the cycle.

band. No matter what the relationship, if the woman did not consent to have sex, the act is defined as rape.
- More than 50 percent of all rapes occur in the victim's home.
- More than 70 percent of all rapes are planned.
- More than 90 percent are between people of the same race.

UPDATING THE LAW

The word "rape" comes from the Latin *rapere*, "to take by force." Other meanings are to plunder, to destroy, to seize and carry away by force. The traditional legal definition of rape is carnal knowledge (vaginal penetration) of a female through the use of force or the threat of force without her consent.

Although present laws vary from state to state, most states have changed or are in the process of changing their old rape laws so that they now speak of "sexual assault" or "involuntary sexual battery" and have degrees and penalties similar to those found in the laws for murder. Oral, rectal, and vaginal contact, as well as penetration, are grounds for conviction. A witness to the crime is no longer necessary. Because sexual assault is usually a one-on-one crime, requiring a witness is clearly ridiculous. There is a range of penalties for the offender. These newer statutes are far more realistic in terms of the nature of the crime and the effect on the victim. Women and girls can be damaged psychologically as much from an attempted rape as they are from an actual rape. Penetration of the oral and rectal cavities are often more humiliating than vaginal penetration and the effects more serious. The key concept in defining the crime of rape is the *absence of consent*. While the legal definition of rape may differ slightly from state to state, it is generally defined as forced sexual intercourse perpetrated against the will of the victim. It is by this definition that rape is a felony that can be characterized as a felonious assault. (The crime of *statutory* rape belongs in a different category. It is defined as "sexual intercourse with a female who is below the statutory age of consent." The age of consent differs from state to state.)

MARITAL RAPE

In this country, statistics indicate that more than 600,000 women are sexually assaulted by their husbands in any given year. While male judges have a hard time sympathizing with the wives in such cases, there is a growing number of states in which the spouse can be charged with rape. Oregon was the first state to pass a law making it illegal for a husband to rape his wife. In September, 1979 in Massachusetts a man was convicted of raping his wife at a time when the couple were living apart and in the process of getting a divorce. But because many lawmakers, mostly males, believe that by definition, a wife cannot be raped by her husband, marital rape is not a crime in 22 states (as of 1988). The assumption of the legislative bodies in these states is that when a woman gets married, she has conferred "conjugal rights" on her husband and given up her right to say "no."

Coalitions of human rights activists, women's groups, lawyers, and organizations concerned with reducing violence within the family present their position in more or less the same way: in whatever way the state law defines rape, no exception is to be made for a husband or a wife.

DATE RAPE

Many rapes in this category occur as a spur-of-the-moment event preceded by the male's consumption of a considerable amount of alcohol and growing out of the man's conditioning to believe that when a woman says *No,* she really means *Yes* and is using resistance as a teasing maneuver. About 20% are committed by 2 or more assailants (this is known as a gang rape, or colloquially, a gang bang) and can occur at a drunken party, in the back room of a bar, or in the back seat of a car.

The problem of date rape has become of increasing concern to corporations. In 1985, following the rape of a female employee by a company customer, Dupont established a rape prevention program, the first of its kind in the country. Primarily for the enlightenment and protection of Dupont's 22,000 female employees, the program also conducts workshops for male managers. The aim of these sessions is to overcome the male stereotyping of the female victims as having "asked for it." Career women, who don't like to think of themselves as vulnerable, are exposed to video tapes alerting them to where rape can occur: in the office after hours, in hotels during conferences, on business dates with colleagues. The videos indicate ways of fending off an attacker, whether it be a boss, an associate, or a business contact. The videos also make a special point of forms of protection when traveling in foreign countries on company business. In this pioneering program, which, it is hoped, is serving as a model for other corporations, employees who are raped can receive paid leave, counseling, legal aid, and if the case becomes public, help in dealing with the media.

Date rape has become so prevalent on college campuses, especially in fraternity houses, that special seminars are conducted to alert possible victims to the problem, to warn possible perpetrators of the unpleasant consequences, and to counsel the victimized. Unfortunately, there are some schools where attitudes can be said to reflect those of the general public. For example, the following responses resulted from a Midwestern campus survey in which men and women were asked, "Is it all right if a male holds a female down and forces her to engage in sexual intercourse if "he spends a lot of money on her?" (39 percent men and 12 percent women said, "Yes"); "she has had intercourse with others?" (39 percent men and 18 percent women answered, "Yes"); "she says she will have sex and then changes her mind?" (54 percent men and 31 percent women responded "Yes").

One of the reasons so many women—whether undergraduates, or working women—have been hesitant about going to court to accuse an acquaintance of rape—is that they have internalized some of these attitudes too. Instead of seeing themselves as a victim of a punishable crime, they are likely to blame themselves for what happened. They are also aware of how typical jurors are likely to view them. Even though most states now have "rape shield" laws that prohibit questions about the victim's sexual history, lawyers often ask such questions anyway, with the knowledge that they must be stricken from the record.

Unfortunately, jurors take more seriously the rape of a woman who appears chaste and conventional and are more likely to exonerate the man if the woman is known to be sexually active or if she knew her assailant. Thus, a majority of jurors nationwide are likely to make harsh judgments of a woman who keeps late hours, goes to bars, uses birth control pills, and has the same address as her boyfriend.

PROTECTING YOURSELF

What can you do to prevent being raped by a stranger? Most important is to recognize that you are a potential victim. Every female is vulnerable to attack regardless of her age. Sexual assaults occur in broad daylight as well as in darkness; in suburbs as well as in the downtown areas and ghettos; in homes as well as in parking lots, alleys, and automobiles.

Your home should be protected as well as possible. Use initials rather than your first name on the mailbox and in the telephone directory. If you live alone, add a fictitious name on your door so that the fact that you are alone is not apparent. Install good quality locks and dead-bolts. When you move into a new house or apartment, change or rekey the locks on the exterior doors so that the old keys will no longer work. Never leave an extra key in the mailbox, under the door mat, or over the door: these are the first places an intruder will look. Instead, give a key to a close friend or a trusted neighbor. Lock the door whenever you leave, even if you will be gone for only a moment; all a rapist needs is an opportunity.

Never open the door to strangers. The front door should be fitted with a peephole with a 180° angle so that you may see who is there without being seen yourself. In most states, a peephole is a legal requirement in multiple dwellings and is essential because a chain on the door is not likely to be strong enough to prevent forced entry. If there is any doubt about the identity of the person at the door, do not open it. Ask that utility men, repairmen, and servicemen of all kinds slip their identification under the door before you admit them. If you are satisfied with the authenticity of the ID, call the company to verify the identification. If a stranger wants to use the telephone because of an emergency, offer to make the call and ask him to wait outside. Fund raisers, poll takers, and the like should be told that their requests will be given your attention if they are submitted by mail. People with long questionnaires for political or product surveys should be told to phone you (but only if you wish to honor their requests).

Be alert to suspicious telephone calls. Never let the caller know you are alone and never give personal information about yourself, your family, or your neighbors. If you receive calls that are obscene or those in which the caller is silent or hangs up, notify the telephone company immediately. The police should be notified if threats are made. If you have a message-recording tape on your phone, the message to the caller should never indicate that "No one is home at this time" but rather that the caller has reached your phone number and can leave a message. Many women who live alone screen their calls via the answering machine before they pick up the phone and respond in person.

Walking alone, especially after dark, can be hazardous. Never stop to give directions to a stranger: just keep walking so that your questioner has to walk with you, and keep far enough away to avoid being grabbed. Some feminist groups suggest that when a woman is approached for information by a male stranger, she should say loudly over her shoulder, "Ask a man." Walk with a purpose, be aware, and don't wear shoes with very high heels, you may need to run. If you think you are being followed, check by crossing the street and reversing your direction. If there is any doubt, find a populated area and call the police.

Jogging alone in deserted areas day or night is inadvisable. Many women arrange to be accompanied regularly by a "buddy"—not only for safety but for human companionship.

Driving an automobile, especially when alone at night and/or in an isolated or unfamiliar location, can present special problems that necessitate precautions. Keep the car properly maintained so that breakdowns are less likely and keep the gas tank at least half full. Also keep a tire iron under the left front seat and telephone change in the glove compartment along with the number of a 24-hour towing service. Women who frequently travel by car on business or because of family responsibilities should have a telephone credit card or even a car phone. A traction mat, shovel, and bag of sand should be kept in the trunk in case you get stuck in snow or ice. Whenever you are in an unfamiliar area, lock the doors with the windows up. If possible, park your car in a central, well-lighted place and have your key out and ready to use when you return to it. Be sure that no one is crouched in the back seat before you enter the car. If your car becomes disabled, lock yourself in with the windows up, put on the four-way flasher, and wait until a uniformed police officer arrives. If strangers offer help, ask them to call the police for you. If you are in an isolated place and have a flat tire, drive slowly to a service station or public area. Sound your horn if you are in danger. Never pick up a hitchhiker. Never stop for a disabled vehicle or accident: go on to the nearest safe telephone and call the police.

These are some of the measures you can take to avoid becoming a victim. Above all, however, is the necessity to realize that you can be assaulted even though you do nothing to encourage the offender.

More and more women are enrolling in women's self-defense courses offered by community groups such as the local "Y" or the extension division of a local college. These courses usually discourage attempts to master the martial arts unless the woman is really serious about becoming a karate or tai chi expert, and if such is the case, she is directed elsewhere. Practical self defense courses emphasize the inadvisability of carrying a knife or Mace because such devices can be taken away by the attacker and used against the victim. A police whistle worn around the neck is recommended instead. In addition to these practical tips, such courses provide an increase in awareness of possible dangers, an increase in self-confidence, and a strong feeling of identification and fellowship with other women.

WHAT YOU SHOULD DO IF ATTACKED

No one knows how she will react when actually confronted by an attacker. Age, physical condition, previous experience and training, religious convictions, and basic personality traits all come into play in a crisis situation. Of considerable importance is whether the attacker is a total stranger, an acquaintance, or in any way known to the victim. It is also of some consequence if he is not only physically more powerful than she is but more powerful in other ways, that is, if the relationship is that of professor/student, psychiatrist/patient, or husband/wife.

One thing you must keep uppermost in your mind, however, is the fact that rape is a violent crime and that the need to humiliate and overpower, not sexual gratification, is the motivation for the attack. This will help you to prevent panic and to think clearly and make the best decisions possible.

If you are being threatened by attack, some of the following tactics may be used to try to avoid the attack. A loud noise such as that made by a police whistle or a Freon horn may be enough to frighten him off. Sometimes screaming will do the trick. Yell "call the police" or "fire." Do not yell "help": no one wants to help, but almost everyone wants to see a fire. Try to be sure there is someone near enough to hear the noise or your scream. Otherwise, you may infuriate the attacker, and if no one is there to respond, the problem may be intensified.

Stalling is another tactic that may help. Several ploys have proven to be useful. Among these is feigning a fainting attack or a convulsion. Pretending to have severe pains in the abdomen or chest may be effective. Vomiting or urinating on the attacker are other tricks that have aborted an attack.

Running to a safe place may be a successful tactic if the circumstances are favorable. However, you must be able to run fast and have a safe place within a reasonable distance to run to. If you are in an isolated area, any attempt to flee may make the situation worse by angering the rapist.

If it is impossible to avoid the attack, try not to do anything that will threaten the attacker. If you stay calm and do not antagonize him, it is usually possible to defuse his anger and prevent any serious physical injury. If he is a date who is drunk, stalling for time can be helpful because he may eventually pass out. (Also, a man who is drunk enough is not likely to be able to have an erection.)

Talking may be the best way to abort an attack if it is impossible to frighten him away or escape. It is necessary to talk calmly "with" him, not "to" him. Enhance his ego. Never cry, plead, moralize, or make small talk: this may be just what he is looking for and expects to hear. Although he may not have picked out a specific victim, the rapist has carefully planned the scenario for the rape and operates within this fantasy. Therefore, if the victim can talk with him and make him see her as a person, rather than as an object, and himself as a worthwhile individual, instead of some kind of monster, he may come to his senses and stop, ending the attack. Some women have talked about their families, religion, plans for the future: try anything to break his fantasy.

Fighting is the last tactic to use. All rapists are potentially violent and are capable of inflicting serious physical harm. If he has a weapon, he will not hesitate to use it. Many victims have been sprayed with their own Mace or shot with their own guns, and several "fighters" have had broken bones and other severe physical injuries in addition to genital trauma. Fighting is not the method of choice unless you have been well trained. Surprise and speed of reaction are necessary if you are to be successful. You must be able and willing to overpower and disable the attacker because the struggle itself may enrage him and increase his violence. The risk of serious injury is definitely increased when the victim responds with physical force. Remember the emotional stimulus for rape is anger and hostility not sex.

If an attack is inevitable, try to get it over with as easily and as quickly as possible. Submit and try to show no emotion. Although it is not necessary to cooperate, do not resist unless he is going to beat or maim you. Be alert to anything that may help to identify the man: height, weight, skin color, eye color, hair type and color, scars, language, odors, clothing. You can help the police immeasurably if you are alert and do not panic.

Remember rape is a crime and there is no more reason for you to feel embarrassed or ashamed than if you had been the victim of any other crime. You will need help because the psychological trauma of the attack, even if physical rape was not completed, can be destructive to you and others close to you. Some studies report that 50 percent of the victims are separated from the man in their life within two years after the rape.

The police should be called. (Unfortunately, because of persistent attitudes toward rape, there may be personal reasons for not wanting to call the police. For example, in one case a woman involved in a custody battle felt her husband might use the attack as evidence of her promiscuity.) Remember, rape is a violent crime; you are the victim of a crime. The police understand this and will be supportive and helpful. Rapists are repeaters, and the police may be able to identify the attacker just from your story. The victim can change her mind anytime, but unless the crime is reported, it will never be known how many rapes actually occur. It is not necessary to prosecute just because the crime is reported. The police will usually take the victim to a hospital or rape treatment facility for skilled care and will provide transportation in any case.

It is important to go "as is." No shower, bath, or douche should be taken, and the same clothes should be worn. Bed sheets, towels, and so forth should not be disturbed if the police are to be involved. The "scene" should be preserved, and all physical evidence of the attack saved.

If you do not want to call the police, call a rape crisis counselor (practically all phone books have such a listing), or you can ask the operator if there is a crime victim's hotline. Either source can recommend a physician who will examine you and give any medical treatment that is indicated. Either the counselor or the doctor will give you the psychological support and care you need. Do not underestimate the psychic trauma of sexual assault. Rape victims have special needs. Seek help from people who have been trained to counsel rape victims. This skilled care is necessary if you are to survive the attack successfully and have no permanent emotional damage.

TREATMENT

All victims of sexual attack need care and counseling. If the problem is not dealt with properly at the time, the effects may surface weeks, months, or even years after the attack and may take longer to resolve than if it had been taken care of at the time of the incident.

Comprehensive care, both medical and psychological, should be available to every victim of sexual assault. No one who does not understand the problems of these victims should be involved in their treatment. Trained specialists in this area must have empathy, not sympathy, for the patient. Understanding is essential; sympathy is degrading. Rape is a legal not a medical diagnosis; therefore, no judgments should be made by the medical team.

Today most areas have some kind of treatment facility available to the rape victim. Large cities have crisis centers, and many smaller communities have volunteers who are ready to counsel victims of sexual assault. This is especially true in university towns and those cities in which women's groups are well organized. A properly staffed rape treatment center is organized so that expert treatment is available at all hours. It may be connected with a hospital or be freestanding. The team consists of a gynecologist, a nurse, and a social worker, all of whom have been trained in crisis counseling and caring for the specific needs of the victim of sexual assault.

Because the victim has just been through an ordeal during which she felt completely powerless, it is absolutely necessary that the victim regain control of her life as soon as possible after the attack. One way to accomplish this quickly is to encourage her to make all necessary decisions. It is essential to explain to her that even if she does not wish to report the crime, she needs a medical examination and may need medication to prevent venereal disease and pregnancy. She must also face the possibility of having been infected with the AIDS virus. A test for AIDS may not be necessary at this time. Even if the test is negative at the time of initial examination, it should be repeated at 3, 6, and 12 months because it may turn positive later. She and those close to her will need professional counseling if they are to handle this crisis properly and go on with their lives. However, it is the victim who should have the decisive voice in determining what is to be done after all options and their possible consequences have been spelled out for her. In most cases, cooperation is forthcoming when this procedure is followed.

The examination of the patient should be done with only the physician and the nurse in the room unless the patient requests the presence of someone else. The police should never be in the room, even if they are involved.

The medical examination varies depending on the history of the attack. It is not only unnecessary but cruel to do procedures not indicated by the history. All examinations, however, should include careful documentation of injuries, tests for gonorrhea, chlamydia, drachomatias, syphilis, and AIDS (if the patient wishes), and tests to see if semen is present in the vaginal canal. If the police have been called into the case, specimens such as vaginal fluid, foreign bodies, pubic hair, venous blood, and saliva, are collected as evidence. Photographs of any injuries are essential because most bruises and abrasions are healed by the time the case goes to court; the patient has no visual evidence of the attack. Severe injuries should, of course, be treated before the routine examinations are done. In several instances in our experience the specimens to be used as evidence were collected in the operating room while the patient was under anesthesia.

Prophylactic medication should be offered for sexually transmissible disease (STD), and the patient should be encouraged to take it. Although the reported incidence of gonorrhea following rape is only 3 percent and of syphilis 0.1 percent, proper medical attention can ensure that neither is contracted because of a rape. If there has been abrasion of the skin, tetanus prevention may be indicated.

The incidence of pregnancy following a rape is reported as 1 percent. Despite this low risk, medication to prevent conception should be offered unless the victim is already pregnant or on a method of family planning or the assault occurred more than 72 hours before the examination. Pregnancy secondary to rape is not a pleasant prospect, and prevention is less traumatic than menstrual extraction or interruption of the pregnancy after conception has occurred. Several contraceptive methods may be offered, but the one most commonly used is Overal (two tablets at initial exam, two 12 hours later); the classical morning-after pill (diethylstilbestrol, or DES), or other forms of estrogen. If estrogen is used to prevent pregnancy, it must be given within 72 hours after the exposure. Insertion of an intrauterine device has been suggested, but this is questionable. Placing such a device is not always a simple procedure in women who have not been pregnant. In addition, any unnecessary manipulation in the vaginal area only adds to the trauma of the rape victim.

If the patient was treated with prophylactic or contraceptive medication, she should be reexamined and retested six weeks after the initial examination to be sure that she has not contracted a sexually transmissible disease or become pregnant in spite of the medication. If no antibiotics were given, the patient should be reexamined for gonorrhea two weeks after the attack.

The psychological assessment and counseling of the patient should begin as soon as the patient reaches a treatment center, although the formal counseling usually occurs after the physical examination. The doctor, nurse, and counselor evaluate the victim's mental state and her ability to cope with the situation as they talk with her.

The rape experience precipitates a crisis, and the trauma fits within the framework of the general crisis theory. A crisis is an event that produces stress and comes with suddenness: there is no opportunity to prepare for the emergency. The reaction of the rape victim is similar to that of grief. However, in addition to the deep sense of loss that the rape victim experiences, she must also deal with the emotions resulting from the threats to her safety and the invasion of her body. The loss of self-esteem and the threats to her relationships with others close to her only add to her difficulties. An inability to develop or recapture her sense of self-worth and realize that she is a worthwhile person is one of the long-term problems of a rape victim that can jeopardize her future success.

It is reassuring when the victim can talk with a counselor and find that the emotions and reactions that she is having are the same as those of other women who have been sexually assaulted and that she is not the only victim who has felt that way.

In the post-rape syndrome described by several investigators, the victim goes through three stages of recovery: the acute stage, the outward adjustment stage, and the integration stage. The length of time needed to pass through these stages may vary with the basic personality and previous experiences of the victim, but all rape victims go through these steps.

During the acute stage the woman experiences a gamut of emotions including shock, anger, fear, hostility, disbelief that it could happen to her, and often denial that it did happen. It is essential that she receive practical help as well as medical and psychological support during this time. Some of the practical problems that arise are whether she will tell her family or friends, where she will stay, if she needs money, whether she will report it to the police. All these things must be dealt with almost immediately after the attack.

She may have many physical complaints that will persist for weeks after the attack. Some of these are headaches due to the tension, inability to sleep, nightmares, abdominal pains, loss of appetite, and even nausea. Usually all these somatic complaints are the result of the psychological trauma she has experienced. It is important to make her realize that she is not to blame for the attack and that the offender is a criminal to be caught and punished.

It is during this first phase that it is so important for family and friends to provide adequate support and, if there is a special man in her life, for him to be understanding and realize the sexual fears she may have. If no one is available to understand and support her during this early phase, the victim may become disorganized and thus unable to regain a healthy self-image and unable to function or relate to others as she did before the attack.

The outward adjustment stage is the period during which the patient seems to be doing well, sometimes too well. She resumes her life, returns to work or school, and is apparently adjusting to and coping with the trauma. It is common during this phase for the patient to suppress her feelings, and she may be depressed. She may try to forget that the assault ever happened, and unless she is forced to, she may not face the problem and may stay in limbo for weeks. The longer this phase persists, the more difficult it is for the patient to begin the reorganization process.

Once the patient has faced the problem, she begins the integration stage. This is the period during which resolution of the rape experience takes place, and it may be several months or even years before this phase is completed. It is common for a patient to change her residence and telephone number in an effort to prevent the attacker from finding her and perhaps doing it again. She may seldom go out alone even during the daylight hours. The support of friends and family is again essential. The counselor encourages the victim to seek support, but at the same time expresses confidence that she will again be able to function at least as well as she did before the assault.

During this period the woman is willing to discuss her experience and can talk about it without becoming distraught. She may even be angry and be eager to punish the offender. However she reacts, she is ready to face her anxieties and verbalize her fears; she is ready to recover and return to her world.

If the woman decides to prosecute the offender, she will need ongoing support from her family and from the police and prosecutors. The court procedures are not easy, and it is difficult to win rape cases if the victim is young and pretty and has not had serious physical injuries. The police investigation is often long and tedious. The actual trial does not take place until months after the attack. It is impossible for the victim to resolve the experience and get on with her life until the trial is over. However, many victims, once they realize that the rapist is a criminal and repeats his crime over and over, are quite willing to prosecute and try to send him to jail "so he can't do this to another woman."

A woman raped by her husband or a family member (such as a stepfather or an uncle) or by a neighbor or friend has to deal with special problems. It will be no simple matter to establish and maintain her credibility and face the possibility of becoming a pariah in her family and her community because she is accusing an "innocent man who is a respected citizen." Support not only from legal counsel and a psychotherapist as well as from women's groups and self-help groups is indispensable during the period following the assault.

Women who decide to prosecute the rapist should look at themselves as trail blazers. Ten years ago the case would not have gone to court; twenty years ago no one would have listened to them at all.

FAMILY ABUSE AND VIOLENCE

According to a 1985 study by Dr. Murray Strauss of the University of New Hampshire Family Research Laboratory, spouse abuse occurs in about 32 percent of the nation's homes, and 22 percent of children are abused by their parents. If, in fact, the pattern of family violence is learned in childhood, it would appear that the problem is self-perpetuating unless strong measures are taken to break the chain of cause and effect.

There is also little doubt that early exposure to violence is reinforced by the outside world through stereotyped imagery in mass media and social interaction. The stereotyped masculine hero uses physical violence to achieve his objectives and is successful. Therefore, violence is not only acceptable but to be admired.

The data supports the theory that family violence is a learned response. Almost all the husbands came from homes in which there had been physical abuse between their fathers and mothers. Although the connection was not as common in the case of the wives, many of them did come from violent homes. Both husbands and wives in this group came from families in which physical punishment was used regularly to discipline the children. Because parents serve as powerful role models, this behavior teaches their children not only that violence is a useful and effective way to accomplish desired behavior but also that it is morally correct.

Another thing that the child learns from violence within the immediate family is that males are stronger than females and that if a battle is lost verbally, it may be won through the use of physical force. The male child learns from watching his mother's reaction that she is afraid of the father, even if they do not fight physically. He may apply this knowledge in adulthood by using violence or the threat of violence to maintain superiority over family members whose traditional rank is subordinate to his and to control those who challenge his authority.

Although the middle class tends to identify family violence with lower income status and ethnic minorities, family violence is not limited by economic class or social status. Perhaps violence within the family seems more common among the poor because more of these cases become police matters; the affluent are better able to keep the incidents from becoming public knowledge.

BATTERING

According to activists who have survived battering, legal specialists and advocates, and the National Coalition Against Domestic Violence battering is a pattern of behavior that results in establishing power and control over another person through fear and intimidation. It often includes the threat or the use of violence. It occurs when the batterers believe they are entitled to control their partners. Not all battering is physical. It can include a whole spectrum of behavior used to establish and maintain power, including economic abuse, sexual abuse, threats, intimidation, isolation, and exploitation of children. Whether physical or not, battering usually escalates. It may begin with threats and violent actions such as kicking a pet or smashing furniture, and then escalate to punching, sexual assault, beatings, and then proceed to life-threatening actions, such as breaking bones, choking, and brandishing weapons.

In answer to the question, "Who is battered?" the National Coalition Against Domestic Violence replies, "Rural and urban women of all religious, ethnic, racial, economic, and educational backgrounds and of varying ages, physical abilities and life styles. There is not a typical woman who would be battered."

Consider these facts:

- Although there are cases in which women have assaulted their spouses, men commit 95 percent of all assaults against spouses or ex-spouses according to a recent National Crime Survey.
- In 1986, 30 percent of female homicide victims were killed by their husbands or boyfriends according to the 1987 FBI Uniform Crime Reports.
- Battering is the single largest cause of injury to women in the United States according to a recent report by the Surgeon General.
- Each year, more than one million women seek medical help for injuries caused by battering.
- Over 50 percent of all women will experience physical violence in an intimate relationship in any given year, and for 24–30 percent the battering will be regular and ongoing.
- When the extent of the problem began to emerge in the mid-70s in the wake of the women's movement, feminists said, "Leave the relationship." But they didn't take into account that more than two million wives are trapped by their economic dependency, their fears, and their confusion about what is best for their children.
- Among the statistics presented by the TV documentary, "Battered Wives, Shattered Lives" (June 17, 1985), one in every five women hospitalized with serious injuries has been beaten, and 40 percent of serious injuries treated in hospital emergency rooms are suffered by battered women.

Next to acceptance of the learned response of violence, economic survival is perhaps the most important reason that the battered wife does not leave home. Many women have been conditioned since childhood to have no expectation for a career and therefore are not trained for employment. A woman still has fewer job opportunities than a man and often earns less holding a similar job. Because she is usually responsible for an unequal portion of the child care, her time is more limited and therefore her earning further restricted.

Even a court award of child support to the woman with children who does leave is no guarantee of economic stability. Fewer than half the husbands comply even during the first year, and efforts to make the fathers contribute are not only expensive but often futile. She, therefore, feels bound to stay for the economic good of the children. Wives who are fully dependent on their husbands for financial support often feel they cannot even call for help. They need some kind of job and strong psychological support before they can find the courage to break away.

While many researchers continue to focus on individual and family pathology as the basic causes of the abuse of women, feminist-oriented investigators of battering are asking quite different questions, questions concerned with social policies, community attitudes, and the norms that tolerate battering. The work of these researchers is extremely important because new findings and statistics are influential in the formulation of broad social policies affecting the definition of crime and the meting out of punishment.

For example, it has been the considered judgment of many investigators that the most effective way to end domestic violence is to arrest the perpetrator for a brief period and make arrangements for compulsory therapy and counseling when he is permitted to return home. But as recently as 1984, many members of the Attorney General's Task Force on Family Violence thought the problem was strictly a private family matter. However, when the Task Force concluded that physically abusive husbands should be arrested, police departments nationwide began to respond. (Evidence had already accumulated that domestic violence was twice as likely to recur in households when the police attempted to mediate the dispute rather than arresting the assaulter.)

The most dramatic change in the attitude of law enforcement agencies resulted from a New York City jury's decision in 1984 to award $2 million to a woman who sued the city for failure to protect her after she had begged repeatedly for police protection when her husband attacked her with a butcher knife. As a result of this case, assault arrests for domestic violence jumped 62 percent. In most such cases, when the police arrive, the assaulter says, "You can't arrest me; that's my wife," and is genuinely astonished when he is handcuffed and removed from the premises.

RAPE AND FAMILY ABUSE

In a landmark decision handed down in July, 1984, Chief Justice Robert N. Wilentz of the New Jersey State Supreme Court ruled that expert testimony on the behavior of women who have been subjected to sustained abuse from husbands or lovers is admissable to help establish claims of self-defense in murder cases. One purpose of this ruling was to negate the myths that battered women enjoy being abused, that they provoke their spouse's violent behavior, and that they are free to leave their abusers whenever they wish. When experts testify on the battered woman's circumstances, they emphasize that the syndrome is one of learned helplessness: she is convinced that she has nowhere to go and that if she tried to leave, the beatings would get worse. She is likely to believe that marriage is forever, that her husband is omnipotent, and that if she can figure out the magic formula, her husband will change.

Can domestic violence be predicted? Clues to the possible development of violence can be found in the affirmative answers to these questions:

- Did your partner grow up in a violent family?
- Does your partner have a nasty temper and does he overreact to small problems and the usual frustrations of daily life such as being deprived of a parking space or constantly getting a busy signal when trying to make an important call?
- Does your partner have low self-esteem?
- Are there frequent examples of cruelty to animals?
- Does your partner have rigid old-fashioned ideas about the place of women in the family and his role as undisputed dictator of the family's way of life?
- Are you and all women regarded as second-class citizens who should know their place?
- Does your partner want to know where you are and with whom at all times? Are you given any free time that is entirely your own?
- Does your partner constantly talk about "getting even" with others and play with weapons as a way of showing off?
- Does your partner show signs of rage if you can't figure out what is wanted or expected of you?
- Does your partner alternate between kindness and cruelty in an unpredictable way?
- Did your partner "rough you up" during dating or when you were living together? If he did, don't assume you'll be able to change abusive behavior when you're married.

It has also become increasingly clear that for many battered women, verbal and emotional abuse can be just as destructive as physical abuse. Because it is insidious in its cumulative effects, the victim may end up by doubting her own judgment and even her sanity. Here is a checklist compiled by the National Coalition Against Domestic Violence. How many of these things has your partner done to you?

1. Ignored your feelings.
2. Ridiculed and insulted women as a group.
3. Ridiculed your most cherished beliefs, your religion, your ethnic origins.
4. Withheld approval, affection, or appreciation as punishment.
5. Called you names, criticized you, shouted at you.
6. Humiliated you in front of the children or in public.
7. Refused to socialize with you.
8. Kept you from working or controlled all your money.
9. Took car keys or money away from you.
10. Regularly threatened to leave or told you to leave.
11. Threatened to hurt you or your family.
12. Punished or deprived the children when angry with you.
13. Threatened to kidnap the children if you left him.
14. Without any foundation in fact, harassed you or accused you of having illicit affairs.
15. Manipulated and confused you with lies and contradictions.
16. Destroyed furniture, punched holes in walls, smashed precious objects.

Rarely is there a close relationship in which none of this behavior is occasionally manifested or in which a spell of irritability doesn't produce actions and words that are later regretted. However, the critical questions for the victim of psychological abuse to ask herself are: Does she think she's going crazy? Is she really afraid of her partner? Is she constantly asking permission to do things and no longer making decisions on her own? Does she feel increasingly powerless?

A consequence of this type of abuse is that no positive messages get through to the battered woman because she is usually isolated by the batterer from family, friends, and neighbors. So what can a battered woman do?

Testimony from battered women in court cases, in interviews, and on TV talk shows emphasizes that the first step is to admit that the abuse exists as a real problem. The next step is to stop hoping and imagining that the problem will go away. Once an abused woman recognizes that she has every right to feel safe in her own home, free of physical harm and psychological impairment, she is on her way to finding a solution.

Here are some practical recommendations from "Plain Talk About Wife Abuse," a publication of the National Institute of Mental Health:

> A woman can do a number of things to protect herself. She can hide extra money, car keys, and important documents somewhere safe so that she can get to them in a hurry. The phone number of the police department should be handy. She should have a place to go, such as an emergency shelter, a social service agency, or the home of a trusted friend or relative.
>
> During an actual attack, the woman should defend herself as best she can. As soon as she is able, she should call the police and get their names and badge numbers in case she needs a record of the attack. Most importantly, she should leave the house and take her children with her. She may need medical attention, too, because she might be hurt more severely than she realizes. Having a record of her injuries, including photographs, can protect her legally should she decide to press charges.
>
> • • •
>
> A woman needs to talk to people who can help. Good friends can lend support and guidance. Organizations that are devoted to women's concerns and not bound by society's traditions can assist her. They might help her explore her options in new ways. Emergency shelters for women, hotlines, women's organizations, social service agencies, community mental health centers, and hospital emergency rooms are all possible sources of support.

Thanks to the efforts of the National Coalition Against Domestic Violence, there now exists a network of more than 1,200 shelters, safe homes, and counseling centers for battered women and their children. The network is known as SHELTER AID. It was created with corporate cooperation and is responsible for the establishment of the first nationwide toll-free domestic violence hotline, fully operational since 1987: 1-800-333-SAFE (7233).

The hotline is staffed 24 hours a day, seven days a week, by people trained to respond to requests for information, to spell out practical options, and to provide shelter referrals.

CHILD ABUSE AND NEGLECT

When 6-year-old Lisa Steinberg died in 1987 as a result of abuse, many people found it astonishing that this tragedy was acted out in an apartment on one of the most elegant streets in New York's Greenwich Village, that the child's adoptive parents (it turned out that the adoption was illegally accomplished) were a lawyer and a children's book editor (a battered woman whose face required extensive reconstructive surgery), that neighbors were disinclined to take the necessary steps to rescue the victimized child in spite of suspicious noises, and that no one at the child's school seemed to be aware of the physical abuse she was suffering.

This case provides a bitter lesson that contravenes many of the myths about batterers and their victims. It also alerts us to the fact that in spite of the pious lip service paid to the sanctity of the family, many social responsibilities remain unfulfilled because of overloaded services; lack of time; limited awareness on the part of the police, doctors, teachers, and social workers; and a tendency of the well-intentioned citizenry to look the other way.

It is often the case that in families where women are battered and abused, children are likely to be the victims of violence too or they are likely to become pawns in the power performance of the ascendant male. But there is a critical factor that differentiates child abuse from spouse abuse or from the sexual abuse of children by strangers. While these forms of behavior are indeed criminal, battering or psychological or sexual abuse within the family (as well as in a school or day care center) is performed by an adult with the moral duty and the legal responsibility to protect the child and, in the case of parents, whether a natural parent, single parent, step-parent, adoptive parent, or foster parent, to guide the child to normal adulthood.

In March, 1986, the National Center on Child Abuse and Neglect, a division of the Children's Bureau of the United States Department of Health and Human Services, published the results of an extended study by researchers and professionals in this field.

The study identifies four major kinds of child maltreatment:

Physical Abuse

This includes violent assault with an implement such as a strap or knife, burns, fractures, or other actions leading to possible injury. According to the study, this type of abuse, while the most dramatic and the most visible, is not typical. However, according to a 1987 report by the Chicago-based National Committee for the Prevention of Child Abuse, the death rates in a single year in this category showed a shocking increase of 29 percent in 24 states. The committee believes that nationwide, 1,300 children died in 1986 because of physical abuse compared to 925 in 1985.

Neglect

Neglect is divided into three categories: (1) physical neglect includes abandonment; refusing to seek, allow, or provide treatment for illness or impairment; inadequate physical supervision; disregard of health hazards in the home; and inadequate nutrition, clothing, or hygiene when the means for providing them are available; (2) medical neglect for disabled infants includes the withholding by hospitals of medically beneficial treatment from infants solely on the basis of present or future physical or mental impairments (many hospitals and doctors as well as parents feel that by "policing" the treatment of infants born with profoundly severe defects and limited life expectancy, the federal government is depriving professional experts as well as parents of their right to make autonomous decisions); (3) educational neglect includes knowingly permitting chronic truancy; keeping a child home from school repeatedly without cause; or failing to enroll a child in school.

Emotional Abuse

This includes verbal or emotional assault, close confinement such as tying up or locking in a closet, nurturance so inadequate that it results in a failure-to-thrive baby, knowingly permitting antisocial behavior such as delinquency or serious alcohol/drug abuse, or refusal to allow medical care for a diagnosed emotional problem.

Sexual Abuse

This includes sexual molestation, incest, and exploitation for prostitution or the production of pornographic materials. This remains the most under-reported form of abuse and neglect within the family. Although sexual abuse of children by nonfamily members and outside the home is beyond the province of this chapter, the following information is significant. In 1984, a three-year study was undertaken by the federal government because of several highly publicized sex abuse cases involving children's day care centers. The results, published in 1988, indicated that out of every 10,000 children enrolled in day care centers, reports were received each year that 5.5 percent were sexually abused. By contrast, for the same number of preschool children, according to confirmed cases reported to government agencies, 8.9 percent were molested in their own homes. This study also indicated that the day care abusers were often less likely to conform to the stereotype of the male pedophile: 40 percent were women, and 50 percent were college graduates.

The number of reported cases of abused and neglected children continues to grow. While preschool children to the age of 5 represented 34 percent of the population in 1984, this age group accounted for 43 percent of maltreated children. The highest risk of physical injury is found among the youngest children, while sexual maltreatment increases with age, occurring most frequently in the 12 to 17 age group. Recently available statistics also indicate that in 1984, 1,727,000 documented cases were reported, an increase of 17 percent over the previous year but an increase of 158 percent over the 669,000 cases reported in 1976. Whether this dramatic rise during the eight-year period represents an actual increase in the incidence of child abuse and neglect or whether it reflects a growing awareness of the problem and an improvement in data collection by state agencies, the sharp increase has become a matter for everyone's concern.

Because child abuse and neglect are found in all settings and in all income groups, it is often difficult to identify the families and children at risk. The incidence rates are the same for urban, suburban, and rural communities. However, the incidence of sexual abuse is higher in rural communities than elsewhere, while the incidence of emotional abuse and neglect is higher in suburban areas. In addition, families involved in child maltreatment are more likely to be headed by a female, reported families tend to have more children than the average family nationwide, and minorities are disproportionately represented in reported cases.

According to the extended federal study previously mentioned, a family is at risk if the parent is a loner and feels isolated, has no family or close friends, and does not get along well with neighbors; has no sense of the stages of child development and does not know what should be expected of a child at any given age; has a poor self-image and a pervading sense of worthlessness; feels unloved, unwanted, and has a deep fear of rejection; has severe problems with health, alcoholism, drug dependency; has been abused or neglected as a child and feels that violence can often solve life's problems; has not learned how to blow off steam and deal with frustration and anger in a socially acceptable way; and is experiencing severe stress because of a divorce or sudden unemployment without the availability of coping mechanisms or support systems. A family is also at risk if the child is "different" or "difficult"—sickly, disabled, unattractive—or was premature; reminds the parent in looks or behavior of a hated family member, a disappointing spouse, or a former loved one who walked out on the relationship; presents more problems than the other children in the family; and is seen as a mistake or a burden who destroyed the parent's career or chance for remarriage and is generally unwanted.

While there is still a great deal to be learned about preventing and treating child abuse and neglect, research into the changing nature of the family and clinical observations by professionals provide many helpful guidelines. It is important to initiate preventive help for troubled parents-to-be *before* the birth of a first child. After children are born, however, people should be alert to signs of escalating problems within the family so that counseling, parent education, and an emotional support network can be set up *before* children are harmed.

While services are essential for parents, children who have been abused or neglected must have prompt therapeutic attention in order to overcome physical and emotional traumas that may handicap them for life. Adolescents who frequently come to the attention of professionals as runaways, truants, or "behavior problems" must have special team treatment different from the protective services provided for younger children.

Studies of communities at the neighborhood level indicate that the incidence of child mistreatment is correlated with the *quality* of social cohesion, mutual support, and pride in the neighborhood not just with socioeconomic indicators alone. Whenever possible, efforts should be made to find direct service people, especially law enforcement personnel, teachers, social workers, and psychologists who share the family's culture, ethnicity, and background.

Because getting the right help is critical in preventing child abuse, there are some things you can do, depending on the situation.

- If you're a single parent suffering from stress, get supportive therapy and join a self-help group of parents with similar problems so that your frustrations don't lead you to "take it out on the kids."
- If your husband expects you to stand by while he beats the children, report his behavior to the proper child protection agency so that family therapy can prevent an eventual tragedy.
- If you're a new mother with signs of post-partum depression and anxieties that you'll harm your baby, don't permit family and friends to pooh-pooh your feelings. Talk to your pediatrician or to the baby care clinic personnel and arrange for supportive therapy or counseling.
- If you're a teacher, always be alert to signs of physical abuse and neglect of the children in your daily care. Investigate constant absences because of "illnesses" and insist on meetings with parents of young children who show signs of physical or emotional battering.
- If you're a friend or neighbor of a troubled family where children are at risk of being abused or are actually being mistreated, speak to the adults responsible for the well-being of the children and, if they tell you to mind your own business, report your suspicions to the local child protection agency.
- If you have the time to become a volunteer, seek out a child welfare agency and lighten the burden of overworked and underpaid professionals.
- If you're a concerned citizen, work for the election of legislators who understand that spending money on social services for children and needy or troubled families is a vital investment for the future health of the whole society.

ABUSE OF THE ELDERLY

It is only within recent years that the problem of elder abuse has come to public attention. The problem is not news to family court judges, social workers, neighbors, and relatives who have been dealing with it day in and day out. However, now that practically all states have passed laws requiring mandatory reporting of suspected cases of elder abuse as well as laws providing protective services to elderly victims, "grannybashing" is less of a secret than it used to be.

According to reports in *The New York Times* and *Modern Maturity*, the magazine of the American Association of Retired Persons (AARP), about one million older Americans—or one in five—are abused each year. Females are likelier victims than males, and 84 percent of reported physical abuse is perpetrated by sons. In cases of neglect and psychological abuse, daughters are the usual miscreants.

A typical case can be desribed as follows. The victim is a 75-year-old woman who may be ailing. She may be heavily sedated; her money is taken; essential medication and food are withheld; and she is locked in her room, denied visitors, and forbidden phone calls. Her complaints are met with a barrage of threats followed by beatings. Victims usually live with their abusers, and the problem cuts across racial, religious, social, and economic lines. The abuse is difficult to detect because the victims do not regularly spend time at centers where the bruises are noticed, or they are so vulnerable that they rarely go out at all.

Causes of the victimization are generally the same: a long history of poor interpersonal relationships, an adult child "repaying" an abusive parent, an impatient and greedy wish to gain control over the older person's money. Alcohol and drug dependence may play a significant role, and when women are the abusers of an aged parent, the cause is often unremitting caregiver stress.

There are many reasons for the victims' toleration of the abuse. In some cases, they feel guilty when attacked by their own offspring because, after all, it was they as parents who created these monsters. Or they remember that they themselves used to beat their children as a way of controlling them. Thus, the situation is one of transgenerational violence, with the abuser avenging an earlier history. Also, there are many older people who have been led to believe, or who imagine, that the alternative to their present misery is to be taken out of the family and forced to live among strangers or to be shipped off to a nursing home. With this possibility in mind, many victims have been disinclined to report their situation to any authorities.

With increasing awareness of the problem, however, most communities have established intervention services: elder abuse hotlines that operate around the clock can be contacted by concerned family members or neighbors whose fears about being sued for making false accusations are allayed by counselors. Where physical abuse is charged, the perpetrators are more likely than in the past to be charged with a crime punishable by incarceration followed by counseling. As in the case of the swift removal of the wife batterer from the premises, abusers of the elderly are likely to mend their ways when faced with a jail sentence.

At the request of the AARP, the Department of Family Medicine at Wayne State University undertook a comprehensive study of elder abuse. The study resulted in the following recommendations that could provide solutions to the problem. Raise the awareness of police, home health care workers, nurses, and doctors to signs of this aspect of family violence. Supply support services to relieve the stress of caregivers, especially such services as senior day care centers, chore helpers, and respite arrangements. Create neighborhood watch programs alert to the unexplained "disappearance" of elderly family members.

As a concerned citizen, you should report any instances of family abuse of the elderly to the relevant agencies—elder abuse hotline, protection services for the elderly, legal advocacy, and/or the social services division of the Area Agency on Aging. After you have made your complaint, follow through within a suitable time interval to find out whether any action has been taken. As the elderly victim of physical or psychological abuse, don't wait until the abuse escalates. If you feel you are being victimized, ask the proper authorities for protection. If you feel seriously threatened, consider alternative housing possibilities. Even though you may think yourself financially dependent on your children, you can achieve a certain amount of independence with the help of a good social worker. As a prime caregiver whose nerves are getting frazzled and who has trouble controlling her anger, try to find ways of lightening your load of responsibilities instead of permitting your enfeebled and demanding parent to become the target of your temper. Ask your local Area Agency on Aging about respite services. Look into adult day care centers that offer a broad spectrum of services to the elderly. Some are covered by Medicare, some by Medicaid, and most charge fees based on the ability to pay. Get in touch with the local Self-Help Clearing House and join the nearest group of CAPS (Children of Aging Parents) where you can share your frustrations, air your anger, and enjoy a feeling of solidarity with many others who are dealing with similar problems.

INCEST

Incest may be narrowly defined as coitus between blood relatives, although it has come to be extended to include any form of sexual contact—oral, anal, manual—between family members, including between stepparent and stepchild.

Unlike the other crimes discussed in this chapter, incest is not usually a crime of violence but rather a crime of seduction. The participants are most likely to be father or stepfather and daughter, although as more and more cases are brought to light, we hear about mother, or stepmother, and son, father and son, grandparent and granddaughter as well as sibling incest that may continue into adulthood.

Contrary to Freud's assumption that accounts by his Viennese patients about sexual molestation during childhood by a father or uncle were wish-fulfillment fantasies, incest is far more common than most people want to believe. Although it is extremely difficult to get the facts, therapists and lawgivers are inclined to believe that as many as one in ten families may be involved, although only one in twenty cases ever comes to the attention of authorities or health professionals. Perpetrators are usually ordinary citizens indistinguishable from other people and, as we know from several cases presented in television documentaries as well as from highly publicized murders, the men who seduce their daughters are likely to see themselves and be seen by the world at large as devoted and even devout family men.

In a typical case, wife and husband are sexually estranged for a variety of reasons (often the wife is "sickly"). The father is hungry for some form of physical contact; the daughter is resentful because her mother is not a nurturing mother. In such a situation, the driving force is not necessarily sex pure and simple but rather human closeness, which the father doesn't know how to achieve in a nonsexual way. The incestuous relationship is likely to begin as the daughter approaches puberty, but it may begin much earlier. Especially in custody situations where the father has weekend and vacation visiting rights, sexual abuse may begin when the child is a preschooler. Helen Singer Kaplan, M.D., Ph.D., director of the Human Sexuality Program at Payne Whitney Clinic of New York Hospital, has pointed out that rarely is incest a question of child rape but rather one of seduction. Children enjoy being sexually excited, and they have the capacity for arousal from about age four. Thus, they eventually feel guilty not only about disrupting normal family relationships but are likely to feel even guiltier because they enjoy the sexual arousal.

In a large number of cases, once the incest begins, it is likely to continue for several years, ending only when the daughter leaves home to go to college or to get married, or—increasingly common—when she runs away. In one study, it was noted that 50 percent of runaway girls left home because of sexual abuse by a family member.

While it is commonly assumed that there are usually three people involved in incest situations and that the mother is almost always aware on some deep level of what is going on, she will refuse to acknowledge the reality when confronted with it. In refusing to believe that such goings-on are happening in her own home, she makes no serious attempt to put an end to them. Dr. Kaplan, who is a well-known sexual therapist and an authority on nonorgasmic women, has also noted that such women are likely to have a history of sexual involvement with a father or older brother.

A significant number of incest survivors were seduced when prepubescent by a stepfather, possibly a pedophile who married the mother in order to gain access to the child, as in *Lolita*. It has been estimated by the American Psychiatric Association that from 12 to 15 million women nationwide have experienced incest in degrees of seriousness ranging from fondling to intercourse and that the number of cases involving stepfather and stepdaughter, previously put at 25 percent, is rising steadily because of increasing remarriage rates.

When such situations do come to light, it is not unusual for the mother to blame her daughter for seducing the stepfather and to force her to leave home. In those cases where the wife is entirely dependent economically on her husband, she must face the problem of the disruption of the family if she accepts the truth of the accusation. In one case that is not nearly so unusual as it might sound, a young woman who had been sexually molested by her grandfather since early childhood and for 20 years following finally made a formal accusation against him after she discovered that he had similarly abused her mother and was currently sexually exploiting a young cousin. What followed was the destruction of the grandparents' marriage, the censure of the mother, and the whistle-blower's pervasive guilt in the face of everyone's condemning her for ripping the family to pieces. Whatever punishment is meted out to the perpetrator, the incest survivor and the rest of the family must bear many burdens—social, economic, psychological, and spiritual.

Professionals are, therefore, inclined to recommend family counseling and supervision of the wrongdoer rather than a jail sentence, and many judges have been following these guidelines. There are, however, those men whose incestuous impulses are so strong that the prospect of jail is the only deterrent.

You can help prevent incest by being alert to some of the symptoms. In a young child, watch for nightmares, compulsive masturbation, and soreness in the genital area especially after visits with an estranged husband. In a preadolescent, be aware of withdrawal from friends, secretiveness, and depression. In a daughter who is entering adolescence, see if the father begins to behave like a suitor, is jealous of the daughter's male friends, and is hostile to her friends of both sexes. If any of these signs appear, it is important to seek appropriate help right away.

In addition, there are things you can do to prevent incest from emerging altogether. Be aware of any sensual fondling and kissing, so that such behavior can be discouraged in a casual but firm tone of voice. Never allow children to share their parents' bed nor witness sexual acts between parents. As parents, you should not make a habit of casual nudity and you should not shower or bathe with your children after they have reached the age of three years. If parents are sexually estranged, they should seek family counseling and, under the guidance of a counselor, consider embarking on sex therapy together.

Many women who have had to deal with the ineradicable psychosexual scars of incest have been able to achieve an adult equilibrium by confronting their anger and their guilt during one or another type of therapy. Participation in a local self-help group can be especially therapeutic for those women who have been unable to verbalize their feelings even, or especially, with those closest to them. If local mental health resources or community social services cannot supply the name and location of such an organization, get in touch with The Incest Survivors Resource Network, International.

In addition to the resources mentioned throughout this chapter, the following organizations can supply information, referrals, pamphlets, reading lists, and speakers for community forums: National Coalition Against Domestic Violence, Center for Women's Policy Studies, National Organization for Victim Assistance (NOVA), The Association of American Colleges' Project on the Status and Education of Women, National Center on Child Abuse and Neglect Information, and Women's Crisis Center (Rape).

HEALTH ON THE JOB

Frances M. Love, M.D.
Southwestern Regional Medical Specialist in Occupational Medicine, Retired Director, Gulf Oil Corporation (deceased)

Helene MacLean,
Medical Writer and Editor; Author, *Caring for Your Parents*

Here are some facts and figures of particular interest to gainfully employed women as well as women who work at home as housewives and mothers (many of whom may eventually enter or reenter the work force).

How many women in the United States are employed? More than 51 million women are part of the civilian labor force or 54.5 percent of all women 16 years old and older. By 1995, it is expected that this number will rise to 61.4 million, a participation rate of 60 percent.

Why do most women work? Most women work because of economic need. Seventy-five percent of working women are single mothers (widowed, divorced, or never married) or they are married to men earning less than $15,000 a year. One out of every five of all American households with children is maintained by a woman. Of all American women aged 20 to 30, 45 percent are still single and self-supporting, more than twice the number in 1960.

How many women become pregnant while working? From the highest professional levels, including doctors, lawyers, and corporate executives to office personnel and skilled and unskilled labor, 80 to 85 percent of women who work will become pregnant some time during their working years.

What is the job status of pregnant women who take maternity leave? In 1987, the U.S. Supreme Court upheld a California law that benefits pregnant workers by categorizing them as physically unable to work, thus entitling them to disability insurance as in cases of illness or injury. Under this ruling, employers are required to grant new mothers up to four months of *unpaid* leave and guaranteed job reinstatement.

How many working women have children of preschool age? Forty-eight percent have children less than one year old; 50 percent have children under three years old; 60 percent have children 3 to 5 years old.

Where do women work? Of the 51.1 million employed women, 69 percent are employed in service fields: offices, schools, libraries, wholesale and retail trade, health services, travel, beauty, and the creative and performing arts. The remaining 31 percent are employed in industry (a smaller part of this group are farm workers). The largest single occupational category, taking into account *all* male and female jobs and professions, is clerical work. There are 19 million workers in this category, and 80 percent are women. The category includes typists, file clerks, and operators of switchboards, keypunch machines, and video display terminals (VDTs).

Why are so many women seeking to hold jobs traditionally considered male strongholds? Workers in skilled crafts and trades, firefighters, and police officers earn more money than office workers. These jobs also offer union protection, good health and vacation benefits, and excellent pension plans. And not only are women moving into the corporate structure but, with increasing self-confidence, they are becoming doctors instead of nurses, lawyers instead of legal secretaries, and professors instead of librarians.

Do women have more job-related accidents than men? No. Studies indicate that gender differences are less important in job-related accidents than the level of job training, amount of experience, and the provision of suitable safety precautions. Furthermore, the relatively new science of ergonomics (sometimes called "human engineering") indicates that jobs need not necessarily be reserved for men because of their physical demands. Ergonomists base the design of equipment and work space on human characteristics so that people and things will interact most safely and effectively. Designers of office furniture and equipment as well as of tools and mechanical devices are only now beginning to take female body dimensions into account.

Do women stay home more often than men because of illness? Yes, but because of their children's illness rather than their own. The burdens of parenting fall almost entirely on working mothers rather than fathers, and women therefore take time off if a child is sick or has to go to the dentist or if a parent-teacher conference is scheduled. Also, in families where both parents work, it is less of an economic hardship if a woman loses a day's pay than if a man does.

How much organized day care is available for the young children of working mothers? Organized facilities outside the home are available for one out of every four children under the age of six. Of these, very few are licensed according to guidelines established by the individual states. Forty-four percent of the children of employed mothers are cared for by another woman in her own home.

How much do women earn? The gap between the earnings of men and women is steadily narrowing. In 1979 women earned 62.5 percent of what men earned and in 1987, the figure rose to 79 percent. However, sharp differences continue. In a recent year, only 13 percent of full-time women workers earned more than $25,000 compared to 46 percent of the men.

Are provisions being made for working women who are the prime caregiver of an aging parent? In increasing numbers, companies are devising special programs to accommodate the needs of valued employees who can only work part time or who need to take time off on a regular basis when the needs of an aging parent become a priority. Also, there is now a bill in Congress sponsored by Democrats and known as the Family and Medical Leave Act. This proposed legislation has a much broader application than the law that now covers maternity leave. Under its provisions, a male or female employee would be entitled to up to 18 months of unpaid leave not only for the birth, adoption, or serious illness of a child but also to care for the needs of an ailing dependent parent.

WELL-BEING IN THE WORKPLACE

In 1970 Congress passed the Occupational Safety & Health Act (OSHA). One of its provisions is that the employer is responsible for the safety and health of employees in the workplace. Another provision states that employees must be informed of known and suspected occupational health hazards. This "right to know" clause implies that those who have the information are obliged to communicate it to concerned employees.

The National Institute for Occupational Safety and Health (NIOSH) is the research and investigatory arm of OSHA. Any company, union, or committee of three employees may submit a formal request to NIOSH's Health Hazard Evaluation Program.

It is only in recent years that women's on-the-job health has become a matter of interest and concern to special groups. While it is true that many men face life-threatening occupational hazards, women are especially vulnerable, and in ever-increasing numbers, to the pervasive problems of stress-induced illnesses, and, more seriously, to the irreversible damage to childbearing capabilities caused by exposure to radiation and chemicals.

In hearings conducted on June 23, 1982 by the House of Representatives' Subcommittee on Education and Labor, testimony was given by a speaker on behalf of Nine to Five, the National Association of Working Women. Judith Gregory, Research Director of the Working Woman's Education Fund of the parent organization, pointed out that American management's idea of the office of the future means little more than a re-creation of the factory of the past. "Women office workers are on the front line of the new wave of automation," and women must therefore stress the need for more research on the cumulative negative effects of the new technology on their health.

By the end of 1986, a NIOSH report described in compelling detail the substantial health problems resulting from work overload, lack of control over one's job, limited job opportunities, and feelings of dehumanization attributable to technological "advances" in the workplace.

In addition to health problems caused by stress on the job, there are also some common complaints about the physical environment and its effects on health.

NOISE

An excessively noisy working environment is by no means limited to factories. Many women who work in offices, airports, and retail stores complain of the disastrous effects of ringing bells, clacking machines, loud voices, and the sound of piped-in music. Many unpleasant physical symptoms—rise in blood pressure, increase in sweating, "jumpy" stomach—are attributable to unacceptable noise levels. And when the sounds not only produce headaches but interfere with the ability to think straight, the secondary effects are likely to be general irritability and anxiety.

Because some of your coworkers may not know the extent to which the noise level is affecting their health and job performance, you might discuss the problem with them and try to present a list of practical suggestions for improvement: better soundproofing, phones that light up instead of ringing, sound-absorbing drapes and carpeting, and a lower sound level for the canned music.

BAD AIR

In the interests of energy conservation, most modern office buildings are designed with windows that can't be opened, and they are equipped with central air-conditioning that recirculates filtered air. The result in many workplaces is a combination of complaints known as *sick building syndrome.* This condition is characterized by irritation of the mucous membranes of the eyes, nose, and throat. While these symptoms seem to have much in common with an allergic response, they result not from an allergy but from indoor air pollution and inadequate ventilation. Typical irritants include asbestos and glass fibers from insulating materials, formaldehyde gases from foam and furniture (this slow exudation is known as "outgassing"), hydrocarbons from copying machines, dirt and detergent residues in floor coverings, and where legal restrictions have been slow to recognize the health hazards of exposure to secondary smoke—cigarette smoke.

Women who work in art departments or with arts and crafts materials should be especially aware of fumes and vapors from solvents and other necessary supplies that can have a harmful effect on the skin and respiratory system. It is especially important to read all labels carefully because they may contain warnings about contents linked to chronic diseases as well as to fetal damage. Especially toxic are solvents used in silk screening, which are associated with neurological damage, respiratory disease, and miscarriage. Ventilation requirements should be strictly observed in all cases.

After the source of Legionnaire's disease was identified in 1976, studies of the contents of air-conditioning mechanisms and humidifying ducts have indicated the presence of high levels of bacteria and other pathogens in many such systems.

Women who develop health problems attributable to faulty ventilation should find out whether women in other offices in the same building are having similar problems. If this is so, it should be possible to initiate an investigation of the entire system. It should be kept in mind that air should not be cleaned of pollutants by fans, which merely circulate the noxious substances, but by the installation of filters.

When new chemical substances are introduced or a process is changed, you should try to keep track of what appear to be coincidental illnesses and compare notes with your coworkers. Although manufacturers of harmful chemicals are required to provide a "Safety Data Sheet," these sheets may not be distributed to the people concerned. If you have any doubts about the toxicity of any substance you use regularly, call your local Poison Control Center. Also, NIOSH has conducted investigations into the cause and control of office air pollution and may offer guidance to your employer.

ACHES AND PAINS

If you spend most of your working day sitting down, the chair you use should be suitable for the body movements your job requires, and it should be adjustable to your own body dimensions. Unless these requirements are met, the result over a long period will be musculoskeletal aches and pains, especially in the shoulders and lower back. The first requirement of a chair is that it be sturdy and stable. Many accidents could be avoided if all office chairs, no matter what their other features, were designed so that the seat can swivel on a column that is set into a five-pronged base with casters that lock.

Whatever tasks you perform while seated, your hips and knees should be bent at right angles. If you have to operate a buzzer or a foot pedal, the seat height should be adjustable so that these movements can be accomplished comfortably. If you spend most of your time reading and writing at a desk and you don't operate a machine, your chair should have a firm straight back. If you work with your hands in a forward position on a keyboard, your chair should have a small flexible backrest that supports your lower back.

One of the most effective ways of reducing back problems is to develop and maintain good sitting posture. It's also helpful to set up a routine of exercises designed to strengthen the muscles that support your spine. Backaches can be reduced by varying your work posture from time to time, alternatively sitting and standing. Try not to stand in one position for too long, and be sure that your shoes are giving you proper support. Neither very high heels nor running shoes nor "barefoot" sandals are the right footwear for a job that requires hours of standing. Leather *(not* plastic) pumps or walking shoes with medium heels or low-heeled oxfords are the best choice.

If you have to lift heavy objects, be kind to your back by lifting them the right way. Don't bend over in a hairpin curve and hold the object at a distance from your body in order to keep your clothes clean. And don't try to prove your prowess as a weight lifter by attempting to pick up and carry anything that weighs more than about 25 pounds. That's just about the weight of a large plant, five reams of copying paper, or five encyclopedia volumes. Do bend from the knees, and when you raise the object, hold it close to your chest.

In addition to lower back discomfort, pains in the joints of the neck, lower arm, wrist, and fingers are associated with keyboard work, especially those operations during which your back moves very little and your wrist and fingers are constantly flexing and bending. These rapid repeated movements can lead to such disorders as tendinitis (inflammation of the fibrous tissue that connects the muscles to the bones), tenosynovitis (inflammation of the tendons and the membranes that line and lubricate the joints), "tennis elbow" (inflammation of the lateral muscles of the forearm), and carpal tunnel syndrome, which is caused by nerve damage in the fingers and is characterized by sharp pains as well as tingling sensations in the thumb and fingers. Some pains in the fingers and wrist, especially in the left hand, are attributable to the "q w e r t y" typewriter keyboard, in which the left hand does 60 percent of the work, and only 30 percent of the work is done on the easy-to-reach center keys. Unfortunately, and in spite of more sensibly designed keyboard arrangements, the old "q w e r t y" design was formally adopted as the international standard in 1971 and has since been built into the keyboards of the new technology. However, recent improvements in keyboard design have reduced the elevation between rows and sloped the key surfaces farther forward. Both these innovations have decreased the wear and tear on joints and tendons.

Sharp pains in the forearm (the catchall term is "tennis elbow") may be caused by constant flexing of the wrist or by maintaining an uncomfortable arm position at the desk. The latter problem may be solved by moving the chair closer to or farther from the desk at the same time that your back is correctly supported. Or try raising or lowering the chair seat to see whether the position of your arm on the desk is improved.

If pains interfere with work efficiency and/or with sleep, discuss the problem with your doctor and be sure to describe the nature of your job. If the doctor understands that the problem originates in your job, you may be advised to take anti-inflammatory medication at the same time that you try to alternate jobs with someone whose work doesn't require the same repetitive motions. In some cases of tenosynovitis, surgery can be helpful. The best treatment, however, is as much rest as possible for the affected joints.

EYESTRAIN AND IRRITATION

In a recent study of office workers' health problems (1980), 77 percent of all VDT operators listed serious eye complaints, and 56 percent of women engaged in other types of office work had similar complaints about irritation, including strain, tearing, and bloodshot appearance. Among the causes given were inadequate light; glare, both direct and reflected; cigarette smoke; and dusts and chemicals. If you and your colleagues have any control over the kind of light available in your work area, the ideal arrangement is a combination of natural and artificial light. If the light source is partially or entirely artificial, it should combine direct and indirect light. If you work at a desk for most of the day, ask for a desk lamp with a swinging arm so that light can be focused on or removed from particular desk and paper surfaces to keep glare at a minimum.

PHOTOCOPIERS

Almost all offices are equipped with photocopiers and, although a boon to modern business, care should be taken with their use.

- Don't try to save time by ignoring the manufacturer's recommendations for safe use.
- Always keep the document cover down, and never look directly at the light, even if you're only making a few copies.
- Make sure that the machine is installed in a well-ventilated area. No one should be expected to use a copier in an airless cubbyhole.
- If you handle quantities of electrosensitive paper, protect your hands and fingers with disposable surgical gloves.
- No one should be expected to sit in the path of the chemical exhaust from a copier. These fumes are a serious health hazard and should be properly vented.

VDTs

The automation of producing, transmitting, manipulating, and storing information is proceeding at a dizzying pace thanks to VDTs (video display terminals). These links between people and computers are also called word processors, VDUs (video display units), and CRTs (cathode ray tubes). It is predicted that by 1990, 50 percent of all women workers will be using the more than 38 million processors that are expected to be installed in offices, hospitals, factories, schools, and homes.

In the NIOSH study of 130 occupations, in which secretaries ranked second only to day laborers in the incidence of stress-related diseases, it was also found that the secretaries who operate VDTs face higher stress than all other groups, including air traffic controllers. There is not yet sufficient information about the cumulative threat of VDTs to women's health (occupational diseases often are not sudden and acute but slow and insidious). However, a recent Massachusetts survey indicates that VDT operators suffer from a higher rate of musculoskeletal discomfort, headaches, and fatigue than other clerical workers. In some parts of the country, and in many places of employment where office and professional workers are represented by unions, collective bargaining has resulted in special medical insurance coverage for VDT operators. Also, committees on occupational safety and health that are part of most state legislatures now have subcommittees whose special concern is the consequence of VDT work.

When NIOSH discovered that VDT workers had higher levels of complaints about aching and swollen joints than other office workers, it was found that musculoskeletal stresses could be decreased by adjusting as many parts of the work station as possible, particularly screens, lighting, and chairs, to the woman's needs. Problems of skin rashes from the static charge surrounding VDTs can be minimized by using an electrostatic shield.

For the reduction of psychological stress, an adjustable work schedule has been suggested. NIOSH also recommends job rotation and rest breaks for the reduction of fatigue, irritability, and anxiety: operators with moderate visual demands should take a 15-minute break every two hours; those with heavy demands, a similar break every hour. These recesses should be spent away from the work station with the option of resting, walking about, having refreshment in the cafeteria—whatever is most relaxing.

As for the cumulative effects of radiation emission from the VDT screens, current information is that the amount is minimal, far less than ambient sources, and that it offers no threat to a fetus. Manufacturers will supply the results of radiation emission testing for particular models.

THE HEALTH-RELATED PROFESSIONS

- Several unions of health workers have petitioned OSHA to issue standards for procedures involving patients with AIDS and hepatitis B. These guidelines are not yet complete. In the meantime workers abide by the directives of the National Centers for Disease Control.
- It has been found that the smoke plume given off by laser surgery may be contaminated with infectious agents such as the papilloma virus that causes genital warts, a possible precancerous condition.
- Because health professionals have to deal with unusually high levels of stress, the problem of legal and illegal substance abuse is widespread.
- Burnout is widespread too, especially among nurses who constantly experience a conflict between their responsibilities to their patients and the expectations of doctors and hospital administrators.
- Nurses and nurses' aides are at high risk for accidents and injuries because of the constant lifting of patients and moving of heavy equip-

ment. They are also at high risk for such infectious diseases as hepatitis.
- Health workers make up 50 percent of all workers exposed to ionizing radiation and its cumulative consequences.
- Radiologists are more likely to develop cancer and to have children with genetically determined diseases than the general population.
- Women workers routinely exposed to anesthetic gases not only suffer from headaches and depression but are at twice the normal risk for spontaneous abortions and birth defects.
- Nurses who prepare mixtures of cytotoxic drugs for cancer patients are themselves vulnerable to chromosome damage and cancer.

What is being done?

Union contracts for nurses contain specific clauses that spell out working conditions in terms of safety and health. On a broader scale, the American Nurses Association has resolved that "the ANA actively seek and support Rules and Standards which will ensure that employees have the right to know the identity of toxic substances and infectious agents to which the employee is exposed in the workplace; and further resolved that the ANA adopt a position that health care agencies should promote the basic health and safety of their employees by offering as a basic condition of employment periodic health assessment and screening, health and safety education, and prevention and treatment when exposure to hazardous condition occurs."

To alert the general population as well as nurses themselves to the latest findings, a national organization called the Nurses' Environmental Health Watch publishes a newsletter and runs a speakers' bureau.

STRESS

The previously mentioned NIOSH study found that in addition to secretaries and especially VDT operators, women's high-stress jobs are (listed alphabetically): bank teller, computer programmer, dental assistant, hairdresser, health technician, practical and registered nurse, social worker, teacher's aide, and telephone operator.

Health authorities are concerned about the increasing prevalence among working women of stress-induced aches and pains, sleep disorders, indigestion, eating problems, and loss of sex drive, not to mention the alarming rise in alcoholism and the abuse of legal and illegal drugs. One cardiologist (Dr. Robert S. Elliot at the University of Nebraska) has remarked on the growing number of heart attacks among the "superwomen," who are under more stress than their male counterparts.

However, on-the-job stress is not to be confused with challenge, especially the challenge that leads to accomplishment and recognition. No; the women most likely to suffer from stress and its related wear and tear on body and mind are those who

- feel locked into a job situation over which they have no control;
- get no respect or recognition from their superiors;
- have to deal with invasion of privacy and rudeness from men—either their peers, their superiors, or the company's customers;
- find their work boring *and* exacting;
- fear the prospect of unemployment because of increasing age;
- anticipate the negative aspects of automation;
- spend eight hours a day, five days a week, in an environment that is too noisy, badly ventilated, unsuitably illuminated, and too cramped for comfort.

Dealing with life's inevitable stresses is easier when you're in good health. While many of the stressful circumstances of your job may be out of your control, you *can* be in charge when it comes to eating the right foods, getting enough physical exercise, and setting your priorities so that you have some free time that belongs only to *you*.

If you have to do a lot of standing, be sure you're wearing shoes that fit properly. Have your eyes checked regularly, especially if your job makes special demands on your vision. If you feel that tinted glasses would reduce the discomfort of glare, see about getting them. If the job involves lots of bending and lifting, learn how to perform these tasks efficiently with a minimum of back strain. If you have to sit still for several hours at a time, do suitable stretching exercises during your midmorning and midafternoon breaks. At convenient intervals, practice some meditation techniques.

In many instances, solutions to job stress can be worked out by group action that is friendly rather than combative. Informal meetings with supervisors or with the boss can result in practical solutions to problems that actually interfere with efficiency and productivity. If you can take this point of view rather than proceeding from an adversary position, you may actually alert your employer to conditions that he or she wasn't even aware of.

More and more large organizations have inaugurated workshops in stress management. In some instances, these endeavors may have been an offshoot of an alcoholism treatment program; in others, they may be part of the company's overall employee health program. Companies both large and small are sponsoring Employee Wellness Programs that include dietary counseling, nutrition education, and physical fitness seminars. L.L. Bean in Maine has inaugurated an annual cholesterol and blood pressure check; other family-run enterprises are offering weight-control workshops and are making changes in the foods offered in employee cafeterias.

FOOD AND DRINK ON THE JOB

Many women find it difficult to maintain decent nutritional standards at work, especially if outside eating facilities are either unavailable or too expensive and the company cafeteria offers an unsatisfactory choice of food. Pregnant women may have to work out special solutions for the essential between-meal snacks and extra milk recommended by their doctors. Here are some ways in which *all* women can achieve a wholesome diet during working hours:

1. If the assortment of foods offered by the company cafeteria is inadequate when judged by current nutritional standards and if there is no access to outside eating facilities, bring your own lunch from home. This can include a thermos container of hot soup for a midmorning snack.
2. Instead of overloading on caffeine, sugar, and doughnuts or Danish pastry during your coffee break, choose milk, a bran muffin, fresh fruit, yogurt, or soup.
3. In workplaces that have vending machines offering only candy, junk food, and carbonated beverages, make a group request for machines that sell milk, pure fruit juice, bags of unsalted peanuts, boxes of raisins, and the like.
4. If there is no eating facility on the premises, ask the management to install a small refrigerator for storing food and a hot plate for preparing meals. In some offices, the preparation of "group soups" has become a standard procedure.
5. If you and some of your co-workers would like to have breakfast together, find out whether it's possible to have the company cafeteria open at least one hour before the workday begins.

6. Women who have been led to believe that "drinking with the men" is essential to getting ahead should give some serious thought to the negative aspects of this type of socializing, including the problem of alcohol addiction as it affects their male colleagues. Any woman can firmly and politely refuse to become an off-hours "drinking buddy."

SEXUAL HARASSMENT

Many misunderstandings and ambiguities complicate the relationship between the sexes in the workplace. Some are the result of differences in ethnic traditions; others are caused by socially conditioned generational differences. Many mixed messages are transmitted by people who are out of touch with their feelings. An increasing number of women, and especially women executives, are now involved in new situations that make both sexes uncomfortable. Many men in their 50s and older have the greatest difficulties in dealing with women who are their professional peers. Many men of all ages feel ill at ease about going to another city to attend a convention with a female co-worker. Many women aren't sure about how to entertain male customers or clients. And because no one wants to be accused of sexual bias or sexual harassment, it often becomes even more difficult to spell out the nature of the problem. But unless such problems are anticipated and aired for discussion, mutually satisfactory solutions can't be achieved.

What a woman perceives as sexual harassment depends to some extent on how she sees herself in relation to men. However, offensive, unwanted, and uninvited attention in the form of a day-in, day-out barrage of off-color jokes, sneaky pats and squeezes, and outright "propositions" can become so stressful as to affect a woman's health and competence. Such behavior becomes most threatening and difficult to deal with when it is an expression of power.

A typical traditional occurrence: in spite of appropriate behavior on your part, your superior takes advantage of his position and makes it clear that your work status, training, and advancement depend on the extent to which you grant sexual favors. A more recent scenario: with more and more women entering trades and professions previously considered male preserves, sexual harassment becomes an expression of hostility on the part of male peers. This form of angry aggressiveness is likely to be encountered in widely different groups—for example, among resident doctors in hospitals, among police officers and fire fighters, and in unionized skilled trades—where the message being conveyed is "No Women Wanted Here." In every occupation, when women become a competitive threat, sexual comments both verbal and visual become one of the power ploys for trivializing women and "putting them in their place" as no more than sex objects. An example of a situation now considered justifiable cause for complaint and corrective action: a secretary is expected to spend time in the mail room several times each day to instruct mail room employees on how to handle particular packages. The walls of the room are covered with obscene and pornographic pinups. An executive who has been properly indoctrinated by videos, consultants, and personnel directors in the more refined aspects of sexual harassment will see to it that the pinups are removed and other decorative materials substituted.

Many men have been raised in a tradition that has led them to believe that ogling, whistling, joshing, and patting are ways to flatter women, and they are truly astonished when they are told that many women find such behavior insulting and unacceptable. A department manager, male or female, can usually cool escalating antagonisms by having a talk session during which grievances are expressed and the perpetrators are made to understand the nature of the problem: not that *they* are objectionable, but that their behavior is. The essence of sexual harassment is that it is *unwanted*.

In its more extreme expression, sexual harassment usually consists of an escalating series of acts that can be grouped in one of two categories: the first consists of sexual actions that are an invasion of privacy, such as physical molesting, dirty jokes, and overt "propositions" that occur so frequently and are so unnerving that they interfere with the woman's competence and even her safety on the job. The second category of actions typically occurs as a form of revenge and retaliation for a rejection of the sexual offers, especially if the woman has complained. If the rejected person has the power to do so, he will proceed to undermine the woman's confidence by openly and severely criticizing everything she does and by depriving her of possibilities for adequate training and advancement.

As the stress grows, the woman may ask for a transfer, or she may be fired "because she can't handle interpersonal relationships." Or she may quit, knowing that she'll have to find another job without being able to get a recommendation from her former boss. One of the most destructive aspects of such situations is the victim's feelings of guilt—that she is somehow at fault for being a victim.

SEXUAL HARASSMENT AND THE LAW

Public attention began to focus on this problem in the 1970s, when investigations were conducted by various women's groups. Reports indicated that significant numbers of women who rejected sexual advances on the job not only were being deprived of advancement and raises but were also suffering from health problems induced by stress. In a 1976 survey of *Redbook* magazine readers, unwanted sexual attention in their work situations was reported by 88 percent of the 9,000 respondents. In a U.S. Merit Systems Protection Board report called *Sexual Harassment in the Federal Workplace*, it was estimated that this problem resulted in job turnover, absenteeism, and the use of health benefits that cost taxpayers $189 million over a two-year period.

Women who were denied job advancement or were fired because they rejected the sexual advances of a superior started to take legal action. Rulings by federal courts began to pile up in favor of the claimants, who based their cases on the view that sexual harassment was a violation of the antidiscrimination laws spelled out in Title VII of the 1964 Civil Rights Act. By 1980, the Equal Employment Opportunity Commission issued a series of guidelines that stated:

"Harassment on the basis of sex is a violation of Section 703 of Title VII. Unwelcome sexual advances, requests for sexual favors, and other verbal or physical conduct of a sexual nature constitute sexual harassment when (1) submission to such conduct is made either explicitly or implicitly a term or condition of an individual's employment, (2) submission to or rejection of such conduct by an individual is used as the basis of employment decisions affecting such individuals, or (3) such conduct has the purpose or effect of substantially interfering with an individual's work performance or creating an intimidating, hostile, or offensive working environment . . ."

The regulation holds the employer or its agents or supervisory employees responsible for acts of sexual harassment in the workplace and concludes: "Prevention is the best tool for the elimination of sexual harassment. An employer should take all steps necessary to prevent sexual harassment from occurring, such as affirmatively raising the subject, expressing strong disapproval, developing appropriate sanctions, informing employees of their right to raise and how to raise the issue of harassment under Title VII and developing methods to sensitize all concerned."

Six years later, in 1986, the U.S. Supreme Court handed down the decision that made sexual harassment in the workplace illegal. It was this decision that finally led many companies who had been somewhat remiss in handling the issue to hire consultants, show videos, and conduct workshops to generate discussion and clarification. What usually needs to be clarified is the difference between a warm, friendly environment and one in which sexual innuendos and pressure are making some people very uncomfortable. To implement the Supreme Court ruling further, large organizations have issued policy and procedural statements to supervisory personnel. In many cases, the company's guidelines are spelled out in employee handbooks.

In spite of these provisions, however, many women are reluctant to appear to be "troublemakers" or to take steps that seem to indicate that "they can't handle the situation on their own." Procedural red tape takes a long time to unwind, and besides, in smaller offices, a woman may be summarily fired. Also, women whose jobs involve direct contact with customers—waitresses, showroom personnel, and the like—may be flatly told that being nice to the customers goes with the territory.

SOME PRACTICAL SUGGESTIONS

Early in the 1980s, Dr. Mary Rowe, a labor economist at the Massachusetts Institute of Technology, wrote an article for the *Harvard Business Review* in which she proposed a letter-writing strategy for dealing with sexual harassment. She has since monitored more than 700 cases in which the letter produced the desired results. "The typical reaction was no reaction. It just stopped. In eleven years of working with the problem," said Dr. Rowe (in a *New York Times* interview, April 11, 1983), "I've found the letter to be the most effective way to get harassment stopped at no cost to the offended person."

Here's the kind of letter Dr. Rowe recommends:

1. The first paragraph describes the offensive conduct in detail. ("Dear Mr.____: Last month, your hand went from your lap to my lap to my knee and made its way under my skirt to the inside of my thigh. Several times since then, you put your arm around my shoulders and your hand ended

up on my breast. The other afternoon, you suggested we 'make a motel date for an evening fling.' ")
2. The second paragraph describes the writer's feelings about this behavior. ("I've been so upset by these unwarranted sexual advances that I haven't been able to sleep. My work is beginning to suffer because you've made me so nervous.")
3. The letter should conclude with an unambiguous statement about what the writer expects in the future. ("I would appreciate your treating me with professional courtesy and discontinuing all personal remarks from now on.")

Such a letter serves several purposes. First, it enables the woman to make a statement, thus giving her the feeling that she has some control over the situation. It also tells the perpetrator in no uncertain terms that the woman is serious in her rejection of the sexual advances. (This is no small matter. Many men have been socially conditioned to believe that when a woman says "No" she really means "Yes," and all they have to do is to keep trying.)

The letter should be brief, polite, and clear in its message. If possible, it should be hand-delivered by a messenger, with a signed receipt requested, or it should be sent by certified mail. A copy should be kept in the event that the harassment continues or escalates. If this should occur, the next step may be a meeting with the person in charge of hearing such grievances. Sometimes a transfer to another department can be arranged. If the recommended alternative is filing a formal complaint, the machinery for a hearing is then put in motion.

If your immediate boss or the personnel manager shrugs off your complaint and you're not sure of how to proceed, you can turn to other sources for practical help. A dependable counseling resource is the "Y," many of whose branches sponsor "rap" sessions and strategy guidance by professionals. The local office of the Equal Employment Opportunity Commission is the official agency for dealing with such complaints. And if you wish to get advice from your own lawyer, you can use the referral facilities of the Women's Bar Association of your city or state.

Women who belong to unions (not only those in industry but nurses, teachers, laboratory workers, and many secretaries) can press for clearly spelled-out clauses in their contracts.

If you are on the verge of quitting a job or have had to quit because of sexual harassment, you should find out promptly whether your state is one of the many that now guarantee unemployment benefits for such cases.

PREGNANCY

The Supreme Court decision of 1987 has established that from a legal point of view pregnancy leave be considered a right and not a privilege. However, this ruling is based on the concept that a woman's pregnancy is a "disability" comparable to a man's broken leg or some other temporarily incapacitating condition. It does not take into account either the pregnant woman's need for prenatal and postnatal care or hospital delivery costs, all of which should be, and now in many cases finally are, covered by medical insurance.

Working women have been slow to insist on their rights as they relate to reproduction, childbearing, breast feeding, and parenting, not to mention day care centers, provided free by the employer as they are in practically all industrially advanced countries. More and more concerned groups are pressing for the extension of maternal benefits, and in this connection it should be noted that forward-looking employers have been providing on-site day care facilities, while government employees on various levels, teachers, and workers with strong unions have achieved many parental benefits that are still out of reach for most women employees nationwide.

There was a time when women who became pregnant while they were working had to educate their doctors about some relevant circumstances. Nowadays, physicians are more knowledgeable about pregnancy and work and more involved in helping their patients resolve their interrelated work and pregnancy care needs. This is partly because employers are making it necessary for them to do so and partly because their patients are asking questions, just as we urge you to do. The American College of Obstetrics and Gynecology has published guidelines on this subject, and physicians are finding them to be helpful.

- After a consultation on the subject with your doctor, you and the father-to-be can make an informed decision about the most practical time to begin a maternity leave.
- If you stay on the job after your condition becomes obvious, you may have to deal with some good-natured and not so good-natured teasing from your male colleagues and/or customers, clients, etc. Keep your responses cool! "I happen to need the money." "I enjoy

my job as much as you enjoy yours." "The boss wants me to stay until the last minute because my work is essential." Write your own script and use it as necessary.
- If it's possible to do so, rearrange your working schedule so that you can avoid traveling during rush hours.
- Backaches are more common than ever, so be sure that your chair gives you the right support. Never sit on a chair that teeters or wobbles. If your usual chair is somewhat rickety, have it replaced.
- If your job normally requires long hours of standing (as it does for bank tellers, waitresses, saleswomen, and teachers, for example), request a stool of the right height so that you can sit occasionally without decreasing your efficiency. If you sit at a desk most of the time and your ankles are beginning to swell, provide yourself with a small footstool so that you can keep your feet raised under the desk.
- Don't feel embarrassed or apologetic about having to use the bathroom more often than usual.
- "Morning sickness" may strike at any time of the day, especially if you work in a poorly ventilated environment. For some women, an extra snack such as a dry biscuit is helpful.
- If you think air pollution is the problem, try to find out what the offending substance might be and discuss the situation with your doctor. Normally, the nausea that accompanies pregnancy subsides altogether by the eighteenth week.
- Be sure you're taking care of your extra nutritional needs by drinking milk during your "coffee break" and bringing chunks of cheese for midafternoon snacking.

OTHER BENEFITS

If your employer or your union offers a pension plan, examine the advantages of maximum participation and be sure you understand what happens to your contributions if and when you decide to leave the job before retirement. Income from a pension can eventually make the difference between economic independence and poverty.

If you haven't done so already, find out exactly what your medical benefits are. Your policy should spell this information out in detail, but if you still have questions, they can be answered by the personnel director, your union representative, or your boss.

If you're planning to quit your job, be sure that you know whether and for how long your medical coverage will continue between jobs. And when you start a new job, find out how soon your benefits begin.

When you're interviewed for a new job, find out what the health benefits are. (The variation from job to job and from state to state is very wide. Some benefits include abortion as well as all costs connected with pregnancy and delivery. What about psychiatrists' fees? What about dental surgery? Does your policy cover dependents?)

Do you have a doctor who is sympathetic about your on-the-job health complaints? Are you offered practical suggestions for how to deal with them? If Valium is prescribed as an all-purpose solution, don't think about changing jobs; consider changing doctors.

9 to 5: The National Association for Working Women publishes "The Working Woman's Guide to Office Survival," available to members, and the Women's Occupational Health Resource Center provides its members with newsletters and fact sheets covering all developments that affect women's well-being on the job.

AGING HEALTHFULLY— YOUR BODY

Helene MacLean,
Medical Writer and Editor; Author, *Caring for Your Parents*
Adapted from a chapter in an earlier edition by

Barbara Gastel, M.D., M.P.H.,
formerly of National Institute on Aging

Older people—and older women in particular—are far healthier than prevailing myths would have us believe. About eight in ten persons age 65 and older describe their health as "good" or "excellent" if asked to compare themselves with others of their own age, according to the U.S. Census Bureau. Death rates of the older population, especially of women, have fallen considerably over the past 40 years. Yet these decreases do not mean that all who live longer enjoy better health. In fact, hand in hand with women's increasing longevity goes the problem of increased and extended periods of chronic ailments. Unfortunately, not many doctors are trained in the health concerns that afflict older women. Mt. Sinai Medical Center in New York was the first and remains the only teaching hospital with a department of geriatric medicine. Nor is there any medical school nationwide that includes in its curriculum a course on the special health problems of a majority of the over-65 population, namely women.

Small wonder then that too many doctors are inclined to ascribe older women's complaints to the postmenopausal syndrome or to hypochondria or to the inevitable crankiness of old age. So, if there's a lot that doctors don't know about treating older women, the final responsibility for guarding one's health as one grows older is one's own. Aside from counting on a good genetic inheritance, the healthy aging woman should be able to depend on the accumulated benefits of long years of good habits and well-informed self-care.

AGE-RELATED CHANGES IN PARTS OF THE BODY

Healthful aging requires attention to the various parts of the body, to particular disorders, and to general well-being.

SKIN

Neither beauty nor health is skin deep, but healthy skin can contribute greatly to both appearance and comfort in the later years of life. With age the skin becomes less elastic, its glands lubricate less effectively, and cells controlling its color often start to malfunction. Thus, wrinkles and "age spots" frequently occur. Although some age-related changes in the skin seem to be inevitable, others can be prevented or delayed.

Long hours of exposure to the sun, often called "the skin's worst enemy," accelerate aging of the skin and increase the risk of skin cancer. To prevent sun damage it is necessary either to avoid the sun or to guard the skin. If properly applied, creams, oils, and lotions known as sunscreens help to protect the skin. The preparations that are most effective contain PABA (para-aminobenzoic acid) and sulisobenzone, the best sun-blocking agents now available. In choosing a sunscreen, look for the one with the highest sun protection factor (SPF). SPF 15 means that the skin will be guarded against the damaging effects of the sun for about seven hours. However, to achieve maximum protection, the sunscreen must be applied about one hour before exposure so that the active agents have enough time to penetrate the skin. Because sweat tends to wash the sunscreen away, it should be reapplied after wiping the skin. Reapplication during the same exposure period does not extend the time during which the sunscreen is effective.

Several other factors also can make the skin appear older. In winter, cold weather and freezing winds, dry and overheated rooms, and even the use of electric blankets can make the skin scaly and inelastic. In summer, air conditioning can have similar effects. Excessive alcohol intake, poor diet, and cigarette smoking also damage the skin.

Although nothing can completely arrest or reverse age-related changes in the skin, it is still possible to have attractive, healthy skin. One's own outlook is essential to others' perceptions. Aged skin does not mean lack of beauty. Many women feel that they are no longer attractive or even worthwhile once physical signs of aging begin to appear. However, attitudes are changing. As the population ages, so does our ideal of beauty. Among women now considered beautiful, many, for example Katharine Hepburn and Lena Horne, are in the later years of life. With women achieving more varied roles in society, other criteria are becoming more important than a youthful appearance.

Several mechanical procedures, including dermabrasion, chemical peel, collagen injections, and face lift, which can help to correct some types of age-associated skin damage, are discussed in the chapter on "Cosmetic Surgery." Simpler approaches, including the use of "wrinkle creams," skin lighteners and bleaches, make-up, and moisturizers can also improve or conceal the appearance of aged skin. Wrinkle creams generally contain both oil to smooth the skin and an irritant to cause slight swelling and thus fill out small lines and creases. Skin lighteners and bleaches can help to fade darkened areas of skin; as with medications, they must be used only as directed.

Moisturizers, among the most popular products for aging skin, temporarily improve the texture and appearance of skin and help to relieve dry, tight, itchy sensations. For moisturizers to be most effective, water should be patted onto the skin before their application. Generally, the effectiveness of a moisturizer is unrelated to its cost; many women find inexpensive products satisfactory, and moisturizers of different prices actually may contain similar ingredients.

Itching is a common problem in older persons. Several measures can help to relieve dry, itchy skin on the body. When bathing, use only mild soaps or cleansers, apply soap only to areas that need especially thorough cleansing (the underarms, pubic and anal areas, feet, hands), use warm rather than hot water, avoid long baths, and pat the skin dry gently instead of rubbing it briskly. After the bath, bath oil or another moisturizer should be applied to the moist skin. Addition of oil to the bath water is unwise, as the tub can become dangerously slippery. Humidification of the air, use of soft cotton flannel sheets, and addition of a small amount of bath oil to water used to rinse laundry also can be helpful.

Severe or persistent skin conditions such as rashes, sores, and unmanageable itching should be seen by a doctor. Some of the conditions may be relieved by locally applied measures, and others may be the first noticeable signs of a disease that affects the entire body and requires treatment. Growths on the skin should receive prompt attention to determine if they are malignant. The early removal of skin cancers almost always results in cure.

EYES

Visual impairment becomes more common with age. Of the estimated more than 500,000 Americans who are legally blind, nearly half are above age 65. However, conditions affecting the eyes of older persons often can be treated successfully, and many special aids and services are available to individuals with irreversible visual impairment.

Even before middle age, the lens of the eye starts to become less elastic. By age 40 the reduced elasticity produces in most people a condition called presbyopia, or difficulty in focusing on objects at close range. Most persons over 40 require reading glasses or bifocals. Trifocals are preferred by some women who don't want to keep changing glasses for their various visual needs, especially if they need correction for the middle distance—when playing the piano, looking at art on the walls of a museum, or viewing a computer screen. (Trifocals enable the viewer to see the painting clearly *and* to read the text that accompanies it *and* to recognize a friend from a distance of 20 feet who has just entered the gallery.) It takes some patience and practice to grow accustomed to wearing multifocal glasses, but in terms of eventual convenience, the time is well spent. Glasses in which the separation between the lenses is invisible are more attractive but may cause more difficulties during the early weeks of wear; persistence is usually rewarded.

Another condition affecting the eye is cataract, in which the lens becomes opaque or cloudy and thus vision becomes unclear. Although 95 percent of persons over 65 may have some degree of cataracts, in only a small proportion is the condition severe enough to interfere significantly with vision and require treatment. At present, surgery to remove the cataract is the only treatment available, and it is successful in 90 to 95 percent of cases. After surgery, replacement of the function of the individual's own lens is necessary, and special glasses or contact lenses are usually prescribed. A relatively new alternative to eyeglasses or contact lenses is the placement of a permanent plastic lens inside the eye during cataract surgery: the long-term safety and effectiveness of this procedure are still being evaluated.

Glaucoma, a condition characterized by increased pressure within the eye and loss of visual function, is the leading cause of blindness among the aged. In the most common type of glaucoma, medication can usually control the pressure and prevent visual loss if the condition is detected early. However, surgery may be needed in some cases. All adults aged 40 and over should, therefore, have a glaucoma check once a year and, if there is a family history of the condition, twice a year.

Diabetes, especially if present for many years, can damage the retina of the eye, so diabetics require careful, frequent eye examinations. A treatment called photocoagulation, which uses a laser beam, can help to destroy abnormal tissue and blood vessels in the retina and thus preserve sight in some patients.

Senile macular degeneration, a poorly understood deterioration of the part of the retina responsible for sharp, clear color vision, affects about 10 percent of persons over 70 years of age and appears to be more common in women than in men. Individuals with this condition generally retain some vision and thus can continue to care for themselves. However, as senile macular degeneration produces a large blind spot in the middle of the visual field, it interferes with such activities as reading, sewing, watching television, and driving. The condition is associated with abnormal blood circulation to the retina, and photocoagulation may prove useful in some early cases, although this treatment has not yet been fully evaluated. Special low vision aids, including magnifiers, telescopic lenses, and closed circuit television that projects printed matter onto a screen, can allow some people with macular degeneration to continue many normal activities.

Whatever the state of one's vision—and most older women can see very well if they are wearing the proper corrective lenses—the eyes should be treated with special consideration. Regular checkups by an ophthalmologist are essential. Any sudden variation in vision should be diagnosed at once because the condition of the optic nerve is an indicator of certain neurological problems. Tinted prescription lenses should protect aging eyes against strong sun, especially when driving on bright days.

Numerous public and private organizations assist the visually handicapped of all ages. The federal government and each state and territory have offices to provide and coordinate such services, and the American Foundation for the Blind is a major nongovernmental source of information. Aids available to the visually impaired include large-type books, magazines, and newspapers; recorded literature; counseling; at-home instruction; special Social Security benefits and income tax concessions; and devices to facilitate daily living.

EARS

Ability to hear declines with age. Although often the loss is too slight to interfere with ordinary activities, an estimated one-third of all persons over 65 have significant difficulty hearing. Hearing loss is more common in men, perhaps in part because of greater occupational exposure to noise. Although little is known about prevention of age-related hearing loss, avoidance of excessive noise is advisable.

A wide variety of hearing deficits occur in the aged, but certain features are especially common. The elderly often have the most difficulty perceiving high tones. In addition, speech can sound loud enough but nevertheless seem unclear. Thus, older persons may say that others are mumbling and may remark "I can hear you all right, but I can't understand what you're saying."

The first step in managing a hearing impairment is identification of the specific problem. A general physician can examine the ears, perform basic tests of hearing, and manage some hearing disorders. For additional evaluation and treatment, the patient may be referred to an otorhinolaryngologist (an ear, nose, and throat specialist), otologist (a physician specializing in the ear), or audiologist (a nonphysician specially trained to diagnose and manage hearing problems).

Often the diagnosis is presbycusis, which means hearing loss associated with aging. Although this condition cannot be cured, approaches such as hearing aids and special training can be very helpful. In other instances a reversible condition may be discovered. For example, treatment of an unsuspected ear infection or removal of wax clogging the ear canal can improve hearing.

Many older men and women find hearing aids helpful. Individuals are advised not to buy such devices without consulting a physician or audiologist, who can help select the most appropriate hearing aids and give advice as to their most effective use. Hearing aids make sounds louder, but they cannot correct hearing as precisely as glasses correct vision. A period of adjustment is often necessary, and sometimes a hearing specialist can help a patient to obtain hearing aids for trial periods of a few weeks each until a satisfactory device is found. Persons with conditions such as arthritis or stroke may find small parts of hearing aids difficult to handle: special hearing aids that compensate for some of these problems are available or are being developed.

Aids that may be especially helpful to hearing-impaired persons who live alone are attachments for telephones and televisions to amplify voices and devices that flash on a light when the doorbell or telephone rings. And now the American Humane Association is training "hearing dogs," which aid the deaf somewhat as seeing eye dogs help the blind.

Special training can help the hearing-impaired to make the most of their abilities. For example, "lip-reading," sensitivity to facial expressions and gestures, and use of appropriate questions can help the individual with a hearing loss to take an active part in conversation. Both individual instruction and classes in these skills are available in many communities. Family members, close friends, and employers may find attending such sessions along with the hearing-impaired individual useful in appreciating and dealing with the problem.

If you have difficulty hearing, the following suggestions may make communication easier.

- Ask people to face you.
- Keep background noise to a minimum.
- Ask people to speak clearly and loudly but not to shout.
- Suggest that someone addressing you get your attention, for example by a gentle tap on the shoulder, before speaking.
- Ask to be told what is being discussed if you join a conversation already in progress.
- If you do not understand what someone is saying, ask the speaker to repeat the statement using different words.
- When you are given important instructions, be sure you understand the message.

Effective management of hearing problems in the elderly has social and psychological benefits. It helps the individual to retain or regain an active role in the family and the community. Likewise, it aids in combating the loneliness, boredom, and depression that can befall those who are unable to take part in conversation and to enjoy fully radio, television, movies, and other popular forms of entertainment.

TEETH AND GUMS

For years being old meant being toothless, a condition detrimental to nutrition, speech, and appearance. Today, however, increasing numbers of older persons are retaining their teeth or obtaining satisfactory dentures. Lifelong care of the teeth and mouth is essential to general health in old age.

With age the mouth undergoes several changes. Although the risk of tooth decay decreases with increasing age, tooth loss because of periodontal disease (disease of the gums and other tissues surrounding the teeth) becomes more common with age. Gum recession may loosen teeth and expose tooth roots that are then more susceptible to decay and do not hold fillings well because their softer dentine is not covered by enamel. In addition, age-related changes and certain medications can cause the mouth to become rather dry. Dryness causes discomfort, fosters decay, and makes dentures more difficult to retain. Because of factors such as tooth loss and a diminished sense of taste, many older persons choose soft, sweet diets, which promote root decay. Age-related bone loss can make old dentures uncomfortable and new dentures difficult to fit.

Throughout life and particularly in old age, prevention of dental disease can be effective and more economical than treatment. Regular checkups, which should include detection of signs of local and systemic disease, prompt treatment of abnormal conditions of the teeth and mouth, and instruction in proper techniques of oral hygiene are essential although unfortunately not covered by many insurance programs. Daily mouth care, generally including both brushing and flossing, also is necessary. Devices such as electric toothbrushes and long-handled toothbrushes may help persons partially disabled by arthritis and other handicaps to maintain good oral hygiene. A well-balanced diet that provides plenty of chewing, is low in sugar, and includes sufficient fluid also promotes oral hygiene. As smoking is the prime cause not only of lung cancer but also of cancer of the mouth, avoidance of this habit is vitally important.

Proper management and suitable diets can help to reverse or arrest incipient conditions that affect the teeth and mouth in later life. For example, prompt replacement of missing teeth helps to preserve oral structures and aids in maintaining good nutrition. Sipping plenty of water with meals and in some cases rinsing with specially prescribed mouthwashes can relieve dryness of the mouth. Because of age-related changes in the mouth and elsewhere in the body, both the older patient and the dentist sometimes need extra patience and effort to achieve the desired results.

NERVOUS SYSTEM

Although mental impairment and other disorders of the nervous system are among the most feared conditions of old age, most people maintain a high level of mental competence and neurological function throughout life. Even after age 80 changes normally are slight and of little consequence. However, a significant minority suffer from disorders of the nervous system.

Any possible symptom of neurological disease, for example, partial paralysis, numbness, tremor, memory loss, or difficulty with speech, requires medical evaluation. In many cases examination will reveal a reversible condition such as depression, a vitamin deficiency, a side reaction from a drug, or overmedication with tranquilizers. In others, such as stroke, early diagnosis can help patient, family, and medical personnel cope more effectively with the condition. Unfortunately, many neurological problems are poorly understood, difficult to manage, and frustrating to all involved.

An estimated 4 to 5 percent of Americans over age 65 have some degree of serious intellectual impairment. Alzheimer's disease is the cause in about half of these cases, while a number of treatable conditions and stroke each cause about one-fourth. Impairment may be somewhat more common in women than in men, perhaps because women tend to live longer. Such impairment is commonly but rather imprecisely termed "senility," a label that does not denote a specific disease but rather stands for a wide variety of conditions.

Alzheimer's disease, a progressive, incurable degeneration of the brain of unknown cause, is believed to affect one to two million Americans and is the most prevalent cause of mental decline in old age. A common early symptom is severe difficulty with short-term memory (not the slight forgetfulness that many people exhibit). Later the individual may have difficulty thinking, undergo personality changes, and become confused. Eventually Alzheimer's disease renders its victims helpless and completely dependent on the care of others. Although much research is under way and several drugs have been reported to be promising in the treatment of Alzheimer's disease, effective treatment (or prevention) is probably years away. Physicians and other health personnel can help the individual to make the most of remaining abilities (for example, through the use of memory aids known as mnemonics) and can help the patient and family to cope with the condition. In both the United States and Canada families of patients with Alzheimer's disease are banding together to share support and information, and many communities have established "Alzheimer hotlines" to provide family caregivers with referrals.

Among the elderly, at least one-fourth of all dementia-like or pseudodementia symptoms are caused by over 100 other conditions, many of them treatable, even curable. Underlying treatable problems that can produce signs and symptoms mimicking those of Alzheimer's disease include depression, drug reactions, alcoholism, infections, heart disease, kidney failure, thyroid disease, head injury, and anemia. Mental impairment due to depression, for example, can be caused by such potentially correctable nonmedical problems as loss of family ties, anxiety over lack of money, and loss of physical independence. Certain medications, including small doses of tranquilizers and even over-the-counter antihistamines, can trigger Alzheimer-like symptoms. Blood clots in the brain, which could be treated by surgery, sometimes cause "pseudo-dementia." Elderly patients in nursing homes or similar institutions for more than three months are likely to have symptoms of dementia, as are some people with inadequate nutrition and fluid intake.

When these underlying problems can be discovered and remedied, normal mental function may return. Therefore, a thorough medical evaluation, including history, physical examination, and laboratory tests, is essential for anyone who seems to have become "senile."

Stroke occurs when part of the brain suffers damage because of insufficient blood supply: blood clots and broken blood vessels supplying the brain can be responsible. Although various symptoms can occur, the most common is paralysis of part of the body, either alone or combined with impaired speech. In time and with promptly instituted, vigorous rehabilitative therapy, improvement often occurs. Special devices can help persons with lasting disability to perform everyday tasks independently.

At least 2 million people now alive in the United States have suffered strokes. They affect approximately twice as many women as men and are the third most common cause of death in this country. However, particularly in the elderly, strokes have become considerably less common in recent years. The cause for this reduction is unknown, but recent strides in controlling high blood pressure, which strongly predisposes to stroke, may be playing an important role.

Although information on how to prevent strokes is incomplete, control of high blood pressure and adherence to the measures recommended in this chapter's section on the heart and blood vessels appear to be wise. "Little strokes" (short periods of partial blindness, speech difficulty, paralysis, or other impairment) warn of the possibility of major stroke and thus demand medical attention. Of course, anyone with symptoms that may result from stroke should seek medical attention promptly.

Parkinson's disease is estimated to affect only 1 person in 1,000 in the general population but 1 person in 40 over age 60. The three most common features of the disease are tremor, rigidity, and a bent posture. This condition's severity and rate of progression vary considerably from patient to patient.

Although the underlying cause of Parkinson's disease remains unknown, the condition is known to be associated with a shortage of dopamine in part of the brain. Since 1970 the drug levodopa, or L-dopa, which helps to replenish the supply of this substance, has been available by prescription. Although this medication has helped many patients, it is not totally and permanently effective, and often side effects eventually develop. Scientists are investigating several other agents in search of a medication that has fewer side effects and is more effective. Experimental brain tissue transplant surgery originated in Mexico City in 1987 and now being performed in the United States has not yet become standard procedure but has produced some promising results.

Most older persons escape the serious diseases just described, but the nervous system often becomes slightly less efficient with age. Generally, ingenuity and effort can overcome these limitations. For example, the use of lists and other reminders can compensate for minor difficulty with memory, attention to simple safety measures can prevent decreased balance and coordination from becoming hazardous, and a little extra time is often needed to learn complex new tasks. With patience and a positive attitude, knowledge and skills can continue to grow impressively throughout life.

Indeed, perhaps the best advice for keeping the normally aging nervous system healthy is to keep it active. The individual who remains interested in the world, who continues to use and develop mental and physical skills acquired throughout life, and who continues amassing knowledge is most likely to remain young at heart—and young at nerve and brain.

HEART AND BLOOD VESSELS

Cardiovascular diseases (diseases of the heart and blood vessels) remain the chief cause of death in the United States, as well as the cause of much suffering in the older population. With age the heart muscle thickens and narrowing of the arteries is likely to occur. The healthy aged heart can still perform satisfactorily under normal conditions but is less able to respond to extraordinary stresses. In addition, various cardiovascular disorders, including angina pectoris, myocardial infarction (heart attack), congestive heart failure, high blood pressure, and stroke, become more common with advancing age.

Research has suggested that the risk of cardiovascular disease is increased by smoking, high blood cholesterol levels, obesity, lack of regular exercise, high blood pressure, diabetes, and chronic excessive stress. Thus, not smoking, a well-balanced diet low in animal fat, maintenance of a normal weight, frequent and regular exercise, control of high blood pressure, and avoidance of unnecessary stress may help to prevent such conditions. These recommended preventive measures may also help to avoid further, more serious damage in persons who already have cardiovascular disease.

Angina pectoris, a temporary but recurring chest pain caused by an inadequate supply of oxygen to the heart muscle, is usually a sign that the blood vessels supplying the heart have become narrowed. It tends to occur during exercise, stress, and other situations in which the heart must perform extra work. Anyone with chest pain should consult a physician who may determine if the condition is angina and, if necessary, prescribe suitable medication. If corrective bypass surgery is recommended, at least one other opinion, if not two others, is indicated, because there is compelling evidence that for a significant number of patients nonsurgical treatment can be equally effective and considerably less costly and less traumatic. (Practically all health insurance plans, including Medicare, usually pay for second opinions when expensive procedures are involved.)

Heart attack, technically known as myocardial infarction, occurs when part of the heart muscle dies because the artery supplying blood to it becomes blocked. The nation's number one killer, it is much more common in young men than young women but rates in women increase considerably with age. Anyone experiencing symptoms of a possible heart attack—pain or pressure in the center of the chest that may spread to the shoulders, neck, or arms and sometimes dizziness, fainting, sweating, nausea, or breathlessness—should call for medical help immediately. With appropriate treatment most people can return to an active life after recovery from a heart attack.

Congestive heart failure, which occurs when the heart does not pump efficiently, can produce shortness of breath and swelling of the ankles. Medically prescribed measures including treatment of any associated heart conditions, drugs such as digitalis and diuretics, and a low-salt diet may provide relief of symptoms. Adjustments in life style to stay within the limits imposed by the condition can aid in coping with congestive heart failure. For example, a person who becomes breathless when climbing too many steps may wish to move to a one-story house, live in an apartment building with an elevator, or carry a magazine to read while pausing to rest at stair landings.

High blood pressure, or hypertension, especially essential (no known cause) hypertension, becomes more common with age. Among older persons it is found more frequently in women and tends to be especially common and severe among older black women. Although hypertension itself is painless and generally symptomless, it predisposes to heart attack, stroke, kidney damage, congestive heart failure, and other disorders. Every physical examination should include measurement of blood pressure. In treating hypertension a physician may suggest measures such as those described above in the discussion of prevention of cardiovascular disease, recommend a low-salt diet, and prescribe specific medications. Although vigorous treatment of hypertension is strongly recommended in youth and middle age, the benefits of treating some types of mild or moderate hypertension in those over 65 without heart disease are uncertain and, thus, less aggressive management may be considered.

Stroke, a cardiovascular disease resulting from insufficient blood supply to part of the brain, already has been discussed in the section on the nervous system.

Perhaps because more people are observing the measures described at the beginning of this section, death rates from cardiovascular disease, including heart attack and stroke, have decreased considerably in recent years.

Both being female and getting older increase the risk of developing varicose veins, enlarged or distorted veins often visible below the skin surface. Pregnancy leaves many women with this condition. With age the veins tend to become less elastic and the muscles supporting them generally weaken, thus predisposing to this disorder. Although many cases of varicose veins merely are unsightly, others can result in serious complications such as leg ulcers if not properly treated. Therefore, anyone who has this condition and experiences leg pain or discomfort should seek medical care. Doctors may recommend various measures, depending on the severity and type of varicose veins. The following suggestions for fostering good circulation are commonly made:

- Avoid round elastic garters, socks with tight elastic tops, and wearing elastic girdles for long periods of time.
- When possible, sit instead of stand. When sitting, do not cross your legs; instead elevate them on a chair or stool.
- Exercise your legs frequently. Walking and swimming are especially effective.
- When sitting for long periods of time, be sure to stretch your legs every hour or so.

To support the weakened veins, physicians sometimes prescribe elastic stockings or elastic bandages. In other cases, they suggest surgery, which may consist of such procedures as removing ("stripping") or tying off ("ligating") damaged veins.

LUNGS

Although respiratory function declines with age, the normally aging lung has sufficient reserve to function effectively under ordinary conditions. However, cigarette smoking increases the age-related changes, often to a dangerous extent. Chronic lung disease, especially that associated with smoking, makes activity and even breathing difficult for many older persons.

The chronic obstructive lung diseases, emphysema and chronic bronchitis, are considerably more common among smokers and tend to become evident between the ages of 45 and 65. In emphysema progressive damage to the smaller airways and to the air sacs may hinder the movement of air into and out of the lung and interfere with gas exchange. In chronic bronchitis the lung cannot obtain enough air because its passageways become blocked by swelling and by mucus and other fluids. These and other respiratory diseases, symptoms of which can include a persistent or recurring cough, "tightness" or pain in the chest, and a tendency to tire easily, require prompt medical attention. Measures such as stopping smoking, use of appropriate medications, good nutrition, sufficient rest, and practicing special pulmonary exercises (bending with head and chest down to promote lung drainage) can help to control chronic obstructive lung disease.

Lung cancer, mainly a disease of smokers and once largely a disease of men, has become so common among women that women's death rates from lung cancer have more than doubled in the last 15 years and since 1986 have superseded breast cancer as the leading type of cancer death in women.

The message of this section should be clear: avoidance of smoking is one of the most important factors in aging healthfully. Many harmful changes in the lungs, heart, blood vessels, and other parts of the body can be avoided or delayed by never smoking. Even in persons who have smoked heavily for many years, lung function often improves or its deterioration is halted or slowed after stopping smoking.

With the accumulated evidence of the dangers of secondary smoke, many states have enacted legislation compelling employers to set aside restricted areas for smokers. Women who themselves have never smoked but have had years of exposure to secondary smoke from family members' cigarettes, cigars, and pipes should urge the smokers to restrict their addiction to the out-of-doors, especially when children are part of the household.

DIGESTIVE SYSTEM

The digestive system usually ages successfully. Digestion of food generally remains adequate, but, as in other stages of life, upset and uncooperative stomachs are common.

In later life many factors can produce gastrointestinal distress. As at other ages, emotional stresses often produce abdominal discomfort and disturbances in bowel habits. Gallstones most frequently occur in women over 40, and cancers of the digestive tract generally become more common with age. Many other conditions, including ulcers, infections, and even back problems, can produce abdominal symptoms.

Because so many conditions can cause similar symptoms, self-diagnosis and self-treatment of digestive problems can be dangerous: self-medication with over-the-counter remedies can intensify some conditions rather than cure them.

"Heartburn" especially at bedtime is a common complaint of older women, often caused by the protrusion of part of the stomach above the diaphragm. Technically known as a hiatus or esophageal hernia, the discomfort of this condition may be eased by some minor dietary changes and by sleeping with the head raised. In cases of extreme discomfort where less drastic measures are ineffective, surgery may be recommended. An acid backflow or "reflux" into the mouth by way of the esophagus of some of the contents of the stomach is the result of the weakening of the muscular ring known as the esophageal sphincter. When this ring closes properly, it separates the bottom of the esophagus from the top of the stomach. Both the conditions described above are commonly linked together as "acid indigestion" and, in fact, both often respond positively to a change in eating and drinking habits, loss of weight if indicated, and avoidance of heavy meals in favor of more frequent "light" ones.

Constipation concerns many older people, often needlessly, because twice-a-day bowel movements may be as normal for one person as two a week are for others. Constipation is a problem *not* when one's bowels fail to move but when pain or discomfort occur *because* the bowels have not moved. Although constipation can result in part from age-related changes in the digestive system, life style seems to be a more important factor. Diets low in fiber and high in fats and refined sugars, anxiety and depression, lack of exercise, overuse of laxatives, inadequate fluid intake, skipping meals (especially breakfast), and repeated denial of the bowel reflex all can contribute to constipation. To prevent or treat this problem, eat a high-fiber diet that includes fruits, vegetables, whole grain cereals and breads, and bran. Make exercise (walking, bicycling, swimming) a part of your life style, avoid laxatives and enemas unless absolutely necessary, drink lots of fluids (six to eight glasses daily), eat breakfast, drink a warm beverage or prune juice in the morning, and respond to "nature's call" when it comes.

Fiber, a largely undigestible food component that is abundant in bran and in many fruits and vegetables, recently has received considerable attention. While fiber helps to control constipation, it remains unclear whether, as some claim, a diet high in fiber also aids in preventing hemorrhoids, bowel cancer, heart disease, and other disorders.

Anyone with symptoms such as abdominal pain, vomiting, change in bowel habits, or blood in the bowel movements should seek medical attention. In many instances the condition can be treated successfully. For most individuals "an apple a day" and *not* keeping the doctor away when he or she is needed are basic to successful, comfortable aging of the digestive system.

URINARY AND REPRODUCTIVE SYSTEMS

In part because of postmenopausal changes in the reproductive system, some types of urinary problems become more common with age. Low estrogen levels may predispose to infections of the urinary tract. Furthermore, weakening of pelvic structures, particularly in women who have borne several children, can produce "stress incontinence," a leakage of urine during such activities as coughing, sneezing, and straining. Special exercises often can help to control stress incontinence, and underwear is now available that has been especially designed to offer protection and assurance to women with this problem. (The fact that these garments are widely advertised on television by an attractive well-known older actress is a gratifying sign of the progress that has been made in openly talking about matters once considered too embarrassing to discuss even with one's close friends.) Where simple solutions are unsatisfactory, medication should be considered before resorting to surgery.

Menopause does not end the need for breast and pelvic examinations; their importance may even increase in the later years of life. Because older women no longer have the monthly menstrual reminder to do a breast self-examination, they should choose a specific date, for example, the first day or the day corresponding to one's birthday, on which to do it each month. The indications for special breast examinations, such as mammograms, are discussed in the chapter on "Breast Care," which also deals in detail with breast cancer and the progress that has been made in surgical treatment and reconstruction.

Regularly scheduled gynecologic checkups as well as consultation with a physician whenever problems such as bleeding arise continue to be important throughout life. Although in most cases of postmenopausal bleeding the underlying cause is benign, prompt medical attention is necessary to identify potentially serious conditions while they remain easily treatable. It should be kept in mind that unnecessary surgery is too often performed on older women (40 percent of the hysterectomies done in the United States are considered unnecessary by many reputable authorities). Therefore, second or even third opinions should be sought before proceeding with this operation.

SEXUAL RESPONSE

What actually happens to sexual functioning in old age? Basically, women and men experience a decrease in intensity and rapidity of sexual response. For a woman, this means that she may take as long as 5 minutes, compared to 15 or 30 seconds in younger years, to lubricate, but clitoral response remains the same. Between ages 50 and 70, the duration of her orgasm gradually declines from 8 to 12 contractions to 4 or 5. But there is no decrease in sexual arousability and frequently there is an increase. More important, women can still have multiple orgasms well into their eighties, an ability few men enjoy at any age.

As a man ages, the pattern is basically the same. Excitement builds more slowly; erection takes longer to attain. The plateau phase tends to last longer than during youth, making the older man better able to maintain erection without orgasm. When he does reach orgasm, it is usually briefer and less intense, and subsequent loss of erection may take just a few seconds compared to a younger man's minutes or hours. In other words, healthy men do not lose their ability to have erections and ejaculations as they age. But it takes longer to complete intercourse, which may be helpful, because older women also take longer to become sexually excited. Compared to women, men experience greater sexual changes with age and tend to desire sexual intercourse less often. When sexual response is less narrowly defined, however, both sexes can experience great physical satisfaction from caresses and cuddling at no matter what age.

BONES AND JOINTS

Brittle bones and stiff joints are common as our bodies age. One condition, osteoporosis, in which the bones become thin and brittle, is mainly seen in women who have passed the menopause. In the United States an estimated 15 million persons, at least 75 percent of them older women, have osteoporosis. At greatest risk are small-boned Caucasian and Asian women as well as those who are addicted to smoking, caffeine, and have been compulsive dieters for most of their lives. Osteoporosis may remain undetected until one of the weakened bones breaks. Fractures of the spine (vertebrae) and the hip (neck of the femur) are the most common. Or the condition may become apparent with the gradual compression of the spine, the loss of as much as two inches of stature, and the development of a conspicuous curvature of the spine that causes the head to fall forward.

Prevention of osteoporosis and the resulting fractures and deformities is an area of ongoing research. At a 1987 National Institutes of Health workshop sponsored by the National Osteoporosis Foundation, researchers agreed that the main cause of the condition is postmenopausal estrogen deficiency, and that smoking, heavy alcohol consumption, and physical inactivity are much more important factors in the development of osteoporosis than calcium deficiency. It would, therefore, appear that taking calcium supplements is effective only when combined with estrogen replacement therapy. If this form of treatment is undertaken, it should be combined with progestin (synthetic progesterone) to prevent endometrial cancer and should be closely monitored for the entire duration of the treatment. Postmenopausal estrogen replacement is contraindicated altogether for women who have had endometrial or breast cancer, stroke, liver disease, or who suffer from coronary artery disease or severe migraine headaches. A comparatively recent experimental treatment is the administration of the synthetic hormone calcitonin, which in its natural state in the body is thought to promote the storage of calcium in the bones. Originally given by injection, it is now used in the form of a nose spray that appears to cause fewer negative side effects.

About 10.6 million older Americans, most of them women, have arthritis, which is not a single disease but a class of several conditions affecting the joints. Pain, swelling, stiffness, and other joint symptoms demand medical attention because the various diseases in the arthritis family require different treatments. Often the physician can reassure the patient that the symptoms are likely to remain mild and require little or no treatment. In other cases, rest, medication (commonly including aspirin), exercise, physical therapy, and sometimes surgery may be necessary to relieve pain and preserve function. Persons with arthritis should be wary of quack remedies and devices that waste money and can cause permanent injury. Because arthritis generally comes and goes, these "cures" often are mistakenly considered effective. Devices such as long-handled combs and kitchen utensils, heightened chairs and toilet seats, and clothes without buttons or snaps can make daily activities easier and preserve independence for those partially disabled by arthritis.

When many people think of arthritis, they think of rheumatoid arthritis, a disease producing inflammation of the joints. This disease, most often seen in older people, affects about three times as many women as men.

Osteoarthritis, unlike rheumatoid arthritis, is not an inflammatory disease. It is much more common than rheumatoid arthritis, especially among the older population. Aging, irritation of the joints, and normal wear and tear all may contribute to this condition. Other risk factors include overweight, poor posture, injury, and physical strain at work or play. Generally, osteoarthritis is a slowly developing disease and is less severe than rheumatoid arthritis. In fact, most persons with X-ray evidence of the condition have no symptoms from it.

Gout is the best understood and most easily treated form of arthritis. Although most cases occur in men, some women develop gout after menopause. In this condition excess uric acid accumulates in joints, causing inflammation and pain. Specific drugs reduce the amount of uric acid in the body, thus preventing both the joint symptoms and the kidney damage that elevated levels of uric acid can produce.

FEET

Throughout life feet bear tremendous burdens. Year after year they support our weight; changing fashions, including towering heels, pointed toes, and tight shoes, create special stresses. Diseases such as diabetes and circulatory impairments increase the risk of serious foot problems.

Some foot conditions require the attention of a physician or a podiatrist (a specialist in foot care). For example, attempting to treat corns, calluses, and ingrown toenails oneself may be dangerous. Experts in foot care offer the following advice:

- Avoid decreasing the circulation to the feet. In particular, do not cross your legs thigh over thigh. Do not sit with one of your legs tucked under your bottom. Never wear a tight girdle, never use round elastic garters, and avoid socks with tight elasticized tops.
- Be kind to your feet by avoiding injuries and never placing them in very cold or very hot water. Test the temperature of the water with your hand before stepping into the bath; do not go barefoot, even at home; and do not apply hot water bottles or heating pads to your feet.
- Wash feet daily in warm, not hot, water and mild soap. Dry feet gently and thoroughly, especially between the toes.
- Inspect feet regularly for redness, rashes, injuries, and other abnormalities. Seek medical attention for such problems.
- Wear well-fitting hosiery and shoes. Shoes should be comfortable and provide both support and protection. In order to avoid irritation of the feet, new shoes should be worn at home for brief periods before keeping them on for longer intervals.
- Exercise your feet. Walking is the best exercise. In addition, doctors may prescribe specific exercises.

Manufacturers are now offering special walking shoes similar in construction to jogging shoes but taking into account the different foot muscles involved in the two activities. If custom-fitted inserts are necessary to balance the feet properly, they can be provided as well. In addition to walking, exercises may be recommended by a podiatrist or orthopedist if foot problems can be minimized by them.

Because diabetics are especially prone to serious foot disorders and must guard their feet carefully, they should obtain specific instructions from their physicians and podiatrists.

DIABETES

Diabetes, a condition in which excess sugar appears in the blood, is more common in later age and affects a greater proportion of older women than older men. Many new cases that occur in later life affect overweight persons, are relatively mild, and can be controlled by diet alone. Because diabetics are especially prone to foot disorders, eye problems, infections, diseases of the heart and blood vessels, and other conditions, both frequent medical care and attention to one's own health are important.

INFECTION

Infection is another threat to the older population. The usual signs and symptoms of infection may be absent in an older person. For example, an elderly individual with pneumonia may be tired and confused but lack fever or chest pain. Medical attention should be sought for any symptoms, not just the classic indications of infection.

Good general health practices, including sufficient rest, a balanced diet, and avoidance of unnecessary exposure to contagious disease are helpful in preventing infections. As the elderly are especially prone to serious or fatal complications of influenza, annual vaccination against this disease is commonly recommended for persons aged 65 and above: the newly developed "flu shots" are more effective and less likely to cause side reactions than those available years ago. The recently developed pneumococcal vaccine, which helps to protect against some types of pneumonia, also may be advisable for some older persons.

Travelers should take special precautions against gastrointestinal infections caused by bacteria in food and drinking water. Such precautions extend to insisting that bottled beverages be served without ice.

GOOD MEDICAL CARE

Care by health professionals becomes increasingly important in the later years of life. Finding appropriate physicians, home and community services, and nursing homes is of great importance.

Until recently, few doctors in the United States had any training in geriatrics. Today, however, more and more medical students, residents, and practicing physicians are studying the care of the aged. If a nearby medical school has a division of geriatrics, it may be able to recommend physicians who appreciate the needs of older patients. Friends, family, and colleagues also can provide useful recommendations. In choosing a primary care physician, inquire about his or her interest and training in geriatrics and knowledge of the facilities available for the aged. Because many older women are hospitalized at some time, information about the hospital to which the physician admits patients is also important.

Communication is basic to a good relationship with any health professional. A physician should show interest in understanding and helping the patient with her problems, explain illnesses and their treatment, and discuss the patient's role in guarding her own health and safety. A helpful physician must be someone a patient can and will talk to openly about symptoms and problems, who not only listens but really hears what's being said, who answers all questions as fully as possible, who doesn't reach for the prescription pad before the patient has finished talking, and who can be depended on to take complaints seriously rather than dismissing them as a bid for attention.

All patients have the right to be treated with respect and consideration regardless of age or economic circumstance. Unless a woman finds it congenial to be addressed by her first name by the doctor and the doctor's staff while she is expected to address them more formally, she should make it clear that she wishes to be addressed as "Miss" or "Mrs." or "Ms."

In addition to a main physician, older women often need the services of such specialists as cardiologists, neurologists, and rheumatologists. Also, routine care by ophthalmologists, gynecologists, dentists, and other specialists is important. Whether a patient can choose her own specialists depends on the nature of her health care and health insurance arrangements.

Nonphysician services for the ill and disabled also are of great importance to the aged, as they can enable an older person to continue living at home rather than to be prematurely institutionalized. Professional services include those offered by physical, occupational, and speech therapists, visiting nurses and a visiting case worker who evaluates the homebound person's needs on a continuing basis. Other services include Meals on Wheels, homemaker visits, and day-care arrangements. Sources of information about such assistance include physicians and other health professionals, local health departments, government and private agencies concerned with aging, religious and civic groups, and especially the local Area Agency on Aging, mandated by the federal government's Department of Health and Human Services to supply information and referrals to all older citizens and their families regardless of income.

Sometimes health problems become so severe or home services are so limited that nursing home care is the only feasible alternative. About 5 percent of the population over 65 resides in such institutions at any one time, and a much higher proportion of the population spends time in a nursing home at least temporarily during the later years of life. Almost three-quarters of elderly nursing home residents are women. For many older persons, the transition into a nursing home can be highly stressful. Likewise, many families and close friends experience feelings of guilt because they cannot care for an ill or disabled relative or lifelong friend. In many instances good nursing home care truly is in the best interests of the ill elderly individual, the spouse and the offspring as well as other family members and friends. Finding a satisfactory nursing home can alleviate much of the stress and guilt.

Concern about good nursing homes should begin early. Attention to the type of care that older or sicker friends and relatives are receiving can be helpful. Interest in and, if possible, volunteer work at nursing homes in one's community both improves the facilities and provides an inside view. Participation in local organizations concerned with the quality of nursing home care achieves similar goals.

The Federal Office of Nursing Home Affairs has prepared an informative booklet, "How to Select a Nursing Home," which concludes with a list of several dozen questions. Among items to consider in choosing a nursing home are:

- Is the atmosphere pleasant and friendly and do the current residents feel free to discuss their feelings about the staff?

- Are the mentally disabled residents separated from the others?
- Do the residents participate in planning activities and do they meet regularly with management and staff to air their complaints and offer their suggestions?
- Is the Patient's Bill of Rights conspicuously posted and is the name and telephone number of the state's Long Term Care Ombudsman (an officially designated functionary as required by federal law) known to the residents and their families?
- Does the nursing home seem to be a pleasant, friendly place to live? What do the current residents say about the home?
- Is the home clean, orderly, well-lighted, well-ventilated, and a comfortable temperature?
- Are residents' rooms attractive, conveniently furnished, safe, and sufficiently private?
- Does the nursing home have the required current license from the state or letter of approval from a licensing agency?
- Is the home certified to participate in the Medicare and Medicaid programs? Are you eligible for such coverage?
- Are necessary services, such as special diets and rehabilitative therapy, available?
- Is the nursing home safe for its residents, including the handicapped?
- What medical and dental services, including emergency care, are available?
- Does a qualified pharmacist supervise the pharmaceutical services?
- Is at least one registered nurse or licensed practical nurse on duty day and night?
- Are meals and snacks nutritious, appetizing, and sufficiently frequent?
- Is there a high-quality program of social and recreational activities?
- Does the nursing home have telephone service and indoor and outdoor recreational areas?
- Do the total estimated monthly costs and general financial policies compare favorably with those of other homes? Is the cost quoted inclusive, or are there extra charges for laundry, drugs, and special nursing procedures?
- Does the contract specify in detail such important aspects as costs, services, and standards?

MEDICATION

The 11 percent of the population over 65 uses approximately 25 percent of all prescription medication dispensed in this country, and the average older person receives 13 prescriptions, including renewals, each year. Drugs are the largest out-of-pocket medical expense for older persons.

Because the aging process and age-associated diseases can alter the body in various ways, reactions to certain medications can change with age. For example, age can affect the rates with which the body absorbs, processes, and eliminates certain drugs. Thus, the doses required can change, often in a downward direction. It is only recently and in response to considerable pressure from such advocacy groups as the Older Women's League that the FDA has begun to take the age factor into account when approving recommended doses of drugs. Women especially have been the inevitable guinea pigs in testing out the cumulative long-term effects of medicines prescribed for chronic illnesses because they live so much longer than men. Thus, many women have been taking drugs for heart disease, hypertension, and arthritis for as long as 30 years.

Older women can also experience side effects from drugs that differ from the side effects experienced by those who are younger. In addition, medications prescribed for one ailment can intensify or nullify the effects of a medication prescribed for a previous condition. It is especially important to contact one's doctor promptly if a drug produces any unfavorable effects, especially nausea, drowsiness, or mood swings, or if after taking it for the prescribed time, it fails to have any effect at all.

In order to prescribe the proper amount of the right medication, a doctor should ask all of the following questions:

- Have you ever had an allergic reaction to any medication? For example, did any drug ever give you hives or make you dizzy?
- Are you taking any medications? Which ones? In particular, are you taking any drugs prescribed by other doctors? Are you taking any nonprescription drugs such as vitamins, laxatives, antacids, or aspirin?

- Do you have any medical condition such as liver disease, kidney disease, or diabetes?
- Are you on a special diet, or do you have unusual eating habits?
- How much alcohol do you consume each day?

Likewise, it is essential for the patient to obtain information about any drug that a doctor prescribes. Among the questions that the Food and Drug Administration (FDA) suggests asking are:

- What is the name of the medication?
- What is the medicine supposed to do?
- What unwanted side effects might occur and should they be reported?
- Are there other medications that should be avoided while taking the medicine?
- How should the medication be taken? (How many times a day? Between, with, before, or after meals? At bedtime?)
- Is it necessary to take the medicine until it is all gone or just until the symptoms disappear?

It is also advisable to find out whether the medicine is necessary in the first place and whether the condition can be treated in some other way, such as through weight loss, a change in diet, or certain exercises. And the patient who is economy minded should always ask that the prescription be written in such a way that the pharmacist can supply the drug in generic form. This alternative, when possible, can represent substantial savings if the drug is to be taken over a long period.

Before visiting the doctor, you may wish to write out each of these questions and leave room to fill in the answers. Making several copies of the sheet (one for each drug) or a chart with room for information on several drugs can be helpful.

In spite of efforts to record the important information about each drug, questions can remain. For example, you may return home and think, "I forgot to tell the doctor that I sometimes take sleeping pills. Does that make a difference?" or "Is it safe to drive a car when I'm taking these capsules?" The best policy is to call the doctor's office for further information.

Your pharmacist can answer many questions about both prescription and nonprescription medications such as how to save money on medications and whether to store various drugs at room temperature or in the refrigerator. Some pharmacists keep lists (many are now computerized) of all drugs that a customer receives. This practice can prevent the filling of two prescriptions for the same drug or of prescriptions for medications that should not be taken together. When requested, pharmacists also can place medications in containers that are easy to open.

Older persons often take several medications simultaneously, and keeping track of them can be difficult. (The difficulty is compounded when one's spouse or housemate or the adult offspring with whom one lives is also taking several different medications.) The National Institute on Drug Abuse has prepared a booklet listing several approaches that may be helpful. It describes various types of charts on which to check off doses of medication. It also suggests placing the pills to be taken at each particular time of day in a separate container. For example, the compartments of an egg carton could be used to hold the pills to be taken together. However, before you store medications in other than their original containers, ask a physician or pharmacist whether it is safe to do so. Color-coding of medication bottles can help to prevent confusion.

It is important to remember that "drugs" include not only prescription but also over-the-counter (OTC) medicines. While drugs prescribed by a doctor are usually more powerful and have more side effects than OTC medicines, many of the latter contain strong agents and, when taken in large quantities, can equal a dose that would normally be available only by prescription. Aspirin can dangerously increase the effects of drugs taken by mouth to thin the blood (oral anticoagulants); the effects of cold remedies can combine with those of sleeping pills or tranquilizers to make an individual perilously groggy; antacids, laxatives, and alcohol can interact with many drugs in detrimental ways. Different medications can add to, distort, or cancel out each other's actions. Obviously, careful discussion of one's total drug profile—the use of nonprescription and prescription medications and alcohol—is necessary whenever a medication is added or discontinued.

In this connection, it is important to provide oneself with a magnifying glass so that it becomes possible to read the pharmaceutical company's informational enclosures (usually printed in a type face no larger than flyspecks) as well as the contents of the drug listed on the label. Some cough medicines, for example, contain as much as 25 percent alcohol, an undesirable combination with a sleeping pill or tranquilizer.

Vitamins and other dietary supplements can also lead to serious problems when taken in megadoses and/or in combination with certain drugs. Too many women are in the habit of self-medication with high dose supplements of various vitamins and minerals to prevent or cure a disease or to slow the aging process. This practice can be a waste of money or, worse, a threat to health. Large amounts of some of these nutrients usually pass out of the body, but sometimes they can build up to dangerous levels. For example, excess vitamin A can cause headaches, nausea, diarrhea, and eventually liver and bone damage. Other supplements such as vitamin B_{15} (pangamic acid) or the so-called "antiaging" pill, SOD (superoxide dismutase), are completely useless. Most older people can get the nutrients they need by eating a wide range of nutritious foods each day.

Foods and drugs can interact negatively as well. Some foods can distort the effects of drugs: the antibiotic tetracycline, for example, may not be well absorbed if taken with milk products. Conversely, long-term use of some medications can affect nutrition: frequent use of mineral oil as a laxative can hinder absorption of vitamin D and other nutrients. Diuretics, which are commonly prescribed for older patients, can cause loss of potassium, an essential mineral: potassium-rich foods such as tomatoes, oranges, raisins, prunes, and potatoes help to replenish this vital supply. Therefore, discussion of diet is also important when drugs are being prescribed.

Because drug costs also are of concern, especially to the many older persons with limited incomes, comparison shopping is a common practice. In choosing a pharmacy, other factors, such as convenience of location, delivery service, and the keeping of complete medication records for each customer, also deserve consideration. A large number of members of the American Association of Retired Persons forgo these advantages as a tradeoff for the savings made possible by ordering medications by mail from the organization's special service. However, many pharmacies have initiated special discount plans for Medicare recipients, and some enlightened state governments have enacted prescription payment assistance legislation to ease the burden for qualified fixed-income seniors.

In many instances the prescription of generic rather than brand name drugs can save money. In general brand name and generic drugs are equivalent to each other. The best approach is to ask one's physician whether the drug being prescribed is available in generic form and whether a particular brand has any advantage for a specific condition. Some states now have laws that allow pharmacists to substitute generic drugs or less expensive brands for the specified product unless the prescriber forbids it. Other states now require prescribers to state on all prescriptions whether they approve of such substitution.

Here are several final suggestions for drug safety:

- Be especially careful if you must take medications during the night. Be sure to turn on the light. In order to avoid accidental overdoses, keep only one dose of medication at the bedside.
- Never exchange medication with anyone else.
- Store medications separately from other substances (such as cleaning solutions and seasonings) in order to prevent accidental poisoning. Also, separate medications to be taken internally from those that are only for external use. Persons with poor vision may wish to glue bits of sandpaper on bottles of substances that should not be consumed.
- Unlike humans, medications often may not age healthfully. Therefore, dispose of old or expired drugs by flushing them down the toilet.

EXERCISE

Several years ago a friend wrote to me about a woman whom she had seen on the tennis court one hot, muggy August day. Impressed that a person who appeared to be past 60 remained so vigorous and skillful, my friend approached the older woman and introduced herself. During the conversation the woman mentioned that she was 82 years old.

Few women past 80 can or should chase tennis balls in 90 degree heat. But most older women can enjoy and benefit from frequent exercise. Many communities offer exercise classes for their older members. The decline in physical condition that occurs with age often results in part from lack of exercise. Appropriate exercise can help to prevent or reverse this process. It contributes to muscular function and to the health of the heart and blood vessels as well as to relieving tension and promoting a sense of well-being. Exercise also helps to maintain the figure and to decrease the risk of osteoporosis.

Certain types of exercise are specifically recommended for older women. Walking has been called the safest and best exercise for those both with and without heart disease. Because of the support that water provides, aquatic exercises often allow movement of joints and muscles in a manner impossible on land. In order to avoid potentially harmful changes in blood pressure, older women should enter and leave the water slowly. Physicians and physical therapists can prescribe special regimens for women with various disabilities, including exercises for rehabilitating muscles damaged by a stroke or slackened through long disuse following a fracture or for minimizing the crippling effects of arthritis.

Some women begin to participate in running for the first time after the age of 60 or even 70 to combat a disability or to overcome boredom and loneliness. Others engage in such vigorous activities as bicycling, long-distance hiking, and rowing. And countless others have joined health clubs that offer a large variety of activities ranging from modern dance classes to individually designed exercise programs. Before embarking on *any* program that makes unusual demands on one's body and stamina, it is essential to consult a physician. In addition to evaluating general physical condition, the doctor may perform tests that measure the heart's response to exercise. Instructions regarding such matters as the maximum amount of exercise to be performed daily and the highest heart rate to be reached should be followed carefully in order to maximize benefit and minimize risks.

SAFETY

As people age, accidents remain common and become more dangerous. Problems such as impaired eyesight and hearing, poor coordination, weakness, and stiffness from arthritis can increase the risk of accidents. Sleepiness from medications and worries about personal problems can lead to carelessness. Accidental injuries often are more serious in the elderly: a minor fall may only bruise a youngster but may break an older woman's hip. In addition, older persons often do not recover well from injuries such as severe burns.

Many simple measures can help to prevent accidents. Slowing the pace of our daily activities is one way. Another is to pay special attention to the safety features when moving to a new dwelling or to correcting the hazards in one's own. It's a well-established fact that there's no place like home—for serious accidents.

Falls are the most common cause of accidental death in those over age 65. To prevent the likelihood of their occurrence:

- Provide good, convenient lighting throughout and around the home.
- Place night lights in bedrooms and bathrooms or install remote-control switches that enable persons in bed and elsewhere to turn lights on and off.
- Light outdoor walkways and stairs.
- Wherever possible, place light fixtures and lamps so that bulbs can be changed without standing on a ladder.
- Pay special attention to stairways. Light steps well and provide light switches at both bottom and top of each flight.
- Have sturdy handrails—and use them.
- Use nonskid treads where possible.
- Tack down loose stairway carpeting and replace it if it is so worn out that holes or slipperiness present a hazard.
- Place a gate at the top of a stairway if you might walk near it at night.
- If moving, consider a house or apartment with few or no steps.
- Use nonslip floor waxes, avoid slippery throw rugs, and keep floors clear of objects over which a person could trip.
- Have grab bars over the bathtub and near the toilet, and place nonslip rubber mats or nonskid strips in the tub or shower.
- Keep outdoor walkways in good repair.
- Wear proper footwear. Well-fitting shoes with low, broad heels and nonslip soles and heels are best for everyday wear: keep them in good repair.
- Arise slowly from lying and sitting positions. Otherwise, faintness, dizziness, and falls can result. (Of course, anyone who becomes faint or dizzy often or for more than a moment should call a doctor.)

Burns are especially dangerous in later life. They are most likely to be avoided if you:

- Give up smoking entirely or, if you must smoke, never do so in bed or at any time when you're likely to be dosing off with a cigarette in your hand.
- Wear tailored, close-fitting clothes when cooking. (Loose long sleeves of housecoats, bathrobes, and nightgowns, are likely to catch on fire.)
- Use ranges that have controls that are easy to see, reach, and use and elements or signal lights that glow when burners are in use.
- Set controls on water heaters or faucets to prevent water from

AGING HEALTHFULLY—YOUR BODY

becoming hot enough to scald the skin, and check water temperature with the hand before entering the bath.
- Install smoke detectors throughout the house, test them regularly to make sure they're working, and have an emergency exit plan in case of fire.
- Use small, lightweight, easy-to-handle pots and pans for cooking, and discard or repair those with loose handles.

Motor vehicle accidents are the most common cause of accidental death in the 65 to 74 age group and the second most common in older persons in general. Nearly one-fourth of all deaths to pedestrians occur in those aged 65 and over. To reduce this risk:

- At night wear white, beige, or fluorescent clothing or carry a flashlight.
- Give yourself extra time to cross slippery streets in bad weather.
- To allow plenty of time to cross the street, wait for a new green light before starting.
- Always cross at designated pedestrian crosswalks, never cross between parked cars, and be especially careful in walking from your car to your destination after parking in a large shopping mall area.

Whether to continue driving a car and, if so, how to adjust driving habits, are important concerns. Age-related changes such as greater sensitivity to glare, poorer night vision, impaired hearing, diminished coordination, slower reaction time, and drowsiness induced by medications can make driving more difficult. Older drivers tend to compensate somewhat for these problems by driving less often and more slowly and by driving less at night, during rush hours, and in the winter. Those considering stopping or limiting their driving may wish to discuss the matter with their doctors. Because older women sometimes *must* stop driving, any plans to change one's residence should give consideration to easy access to public transportation, availability (and expense) of taxi services, and community travel companion chauffering for elderly nondrivers.

Several precautions should be taken to help prevent falls when using buses and other public transportation:

- Brace yourself when the vehicle is about to stop or turn.
- Because walking forward while the vehicle is slowing down is especially dangerous, move toward the door only when the vehicle has stopped or is moving at constant speed.

- Watch for slippery pavement and other hazards when entering and leaving the vehicle.
- Have fare ready in order to avoid losing your balance while fumbling for change.
- Use the vertical support bars when walking down the center aisle and if you must stand while the vehicle is moving.
- In order to keep one hand free to hold on to entrance and exit railings, don't overload yourself with bundles.

With age the body becomes less able to adjust to high and low temperatures. Therefore, care to avoid extremes of heat and cold is important. On hot days one should stay in a cool place and avoid strenuous exercise. In cold weather many older persons may be at risk of accidental hypothermia, a serious drop in body temperature. To avoid this condition:

- Keep the thermostat set at a temperature of at least 65° F. (Efforts to save energy by reducing room temperature can be a false economy for older persons.)
- Do not stay outdoors for long periods of time in cold weather.
- In cold weather wear plenty of clothing, including sweaters, robes, a cap or hat, and thick socks. Use enough blankets.

Don't allow vanity or inertia to stand in the way of maximizing your capabilities. Participate in life to the fullest in spite of any disabilities. Wear the right glasses, find an efficient hearing aid, use a cane if necessary, write things down to jog your memory, enjoy the gratification of reaching out to the less fortunate, and above all, unless you're a pampered guest or on vacation, don't let others do anything for you that you can do for yourself, unless you specifically ask them to.

AGING HEALTHFULLY— YOUR MIND AND SPIRIT

Maureen Mylander
National Institutes of Health, Bethesda, Maryland

We see—perhaps only in our imaginations—the older woman walking slowly along a busy city street, sitting in a doctor's waiting room, or endlessly rocking on a front porch in a small town. But these images capture little more than a stereotype, noting only the slowing of life. They do not convey the warmth that encircles a 72-year-old widow who lives with her daughter's family in her own wing of a farmhouse; or the companionship and activity shared by a 68-year-old woman and her husband as they live in a rent-free guide's house and show visitors the beauties of a national park; or the independence of an 81-year-old nurse who has never married and who, though legally blind, still often rides a bus 200 miles to spend the weekend with friends.

PROBLEMS FACING OLDER WOMEN

If, like the women described above, you are 65 years or older (society's rather arbitrary definition of "old age") you are, despite the stereotypes, probably leading an active, rewarding life. Still, you will face some difficult economic, social, and psychological problems. We will describe some of these problems and then talk about ways to adapt to them, so that you, in your seventies, eighties and even nineties, may be able to cope with adversities and to find new pleasures in old age.

INCOME

While many older women have adequate incomes and will enjoy even greater financial resources in the future, many of the country's current population of 18.3 million women over age 65 have to manage on limited incomes. Even those with substantial savings are apt to deplete their reserves if they live long enough, and studies indicate that a woman who reaches her 65th birthday in 1988 can expect to live to almost 84. Inflation, fewer years in the labor market, reluctance of employers to hire old people, and inequities in Social Security and retirement benefits all lighten an older woman's purse and threaten to place her among the nation's poor. Indeed, the 18,330,000 women aged 65 and older in 1987 had median incomes of about $6,400 when the poverty line was $5,255. It is also calculated that 73 percent of the elderly poor are women, many of whom live alone or with nonrelatives.

Women have, since World War II, increasingly entered the work force and have shifted from blue-collar to white-collar jobs. Yet their annual earnings are still only a little more than half as much as men's, and women constitute only 13 percent of all workers who earn over $25,000 a year. Most women work for minimum wages in what one author calls "pink-collar ghettos"—beauty shops, department stores, restaurants, and offices. Only 2.3 percent of women aged 65 and older are employed, even though age is a poor predictor of work performance. Numerous studies indicate that commitment, skill, and judgment are all very high for old people, men and women alike. Older women have been found more reliable than younger women at work, with lower rates of absenteeism and greater willingness to learn new tasks.

Because so many women have had and continue to have discontinuous employment histories and work at part-time jobs far more often than men do, about 5 million women between the ages of 40 and 65 have no health insurance coverage. Also, in the over-75 age group, where women outnumber men 2 to 1, health costs are highest.

The Social Security system also treats today's women inequitably. Founded when most women worked in the home and were considered lifelong dependents on their husbands, the system allowed no Social Security credit for their housework. Today at least 90 percent of the nation's aged receive Social Security benefits, but those paid to women are almost always lower than to men. Even when benefits are based on their own wages, women receive an average of $420 a month, compared to $550 for men.

Many industries employing women offer no pension coverage. In those that do, benefits are generally lower for women, and survivors' benefits are virtually nonexistent in private pension plans. Even under the Social Security system, a widow cannot draw 100 percent of her deceased husband's Social Security benefits unless she is age 65. Pressure is growing for changes in these policies both in government and in private industry, and proposals are before Congress to give men and women equally fair and adequate Social Security benefits. Local Social Security offices have the latest information about these proposals and about how much Social Security credit a worker has accumulated. For information about other federal programs to assist the elderly, contact a state or area agency on aging or the Administration on Aging.

The older woman's economic plight often is deepened by lack of formal education. In 1980 the average older woman had completed a median of 10.2 school years. This means half did not go beyond tenth grade. Some women in this age group have a poor knowledge of English, leaving them with few resources for coping with Medicare and Social Security forms, let alone jobs, mortgages, and higher finance. Farther along, this chapter describes how older women and men are continuing their formal education through adult programs and other courses in community colleges and universities.

HOUSING AND TRANSPORTATION

Inadequate income colors every facet of an older woman's life, especially a woman who lives alone. Her housing, for example, tends to be older and of lower market value than houses of elderly couples. Compared to what couples spend on housing, she has to allocate a larger part of her income for this basic need. Especially in rural areas, she is more likely to live in a house lacking complete plumbing (hot and cold water, flush toilet, and tub or shower). Often she is forced to give up her house and move to a small apartment, hotel, trailer, or retirement home or community. If she can afford the latter, it may offer a sense of security, companionship, and shared activities, but it also may be an age-segregated, largely female environment sequestered from the rest of society in what some critics call "golden ghettos."

Wherever she lives, housing costs will consume an increasingly large share of her income. In states where older women tend to congregate—California, New York, Florida, Pennsylvania, Ohio, Texas, Illinois, and Michigan—living costs are often high, making financial burdens even heavier. Yet women are finding ways to minimize such problems through group living arrangements, and these will be discussed later.

Transportation problems can be as vexing as housing. Most elderly women living alone do not have regular use of a private automobile because of expense or physical disability such as failing eyesight. Many never learned to drive and were unwilling or unable to assume this role when their husbands died. The consequences are especially severe in areas with inadequate public transportation systems. Unless there are reliable community networks for traveling assistance, a trip to the food store, the doctor's office, or a friend's home can be not only difficult but sometimes dangerous.

CRIME

Old people are victims of crime more than any other age group, but the crimes tend to be of a certain type: theft, including purse-snatching and pocket-picking; consumer fraud; and con games. Property crimes, or theft, are the most frequent kind and usually occur when the property is unoccupied. Many old people, especially women, live on income delivered at predictable times, and their shopping, banking, and other errands fall into fixed patterns that a criminal can observe easily. Older women are especially vulnerable to violent crime, including rape, if they live in inner-city and low-income neighborhoods.

Fear of victimization is a major reason many elderly people restrict their activities and become withdrawn and isolated. Those who become victims are left with a lasting sense of invasion and fear that can make them withdraw into virtual self-imprisonment. To prevent this outcome, some communities and states have established victim assistance programs, and many communities are using older volunteers as assistants to the criminal justice system.

WIDOWHOOD

The future aged population is growing steadily. Women age 65 and over outnumber older men 2 to 1, and no change in this statistic is envisioned for at least the next 50 years. Women generally outlive men by an average of 7 1/2 years, and the gap in life expectancy is expected to widen to at least 8—and perhaps as many as 12—years by the year 2000.

Thus, an overwhelming reality for women by their mid-fifties, most of whom married when they were younger, is widowhood. More than one-half of all American women will lose their mates by age 65, three-fourths by age 85, and the gap in male-female life expectancy will continue to widen. By the year 2000, given present mortality rates, there will be ten women for every five men over age 75, and most women will live into their eighties and nineties.

The male-female imbalance and the tendency for men to marry younger women means older women are not likely to find another husband. Although social taboos against older women marrying younger men are loosening somewhat, the average woman who marries a man two to three years older can expect about ten years of widowhood. Consider: if your husband is five years younger than you, your chances of widowhood are 6 in 12; if you and your husband are the same age, your chances of widowhood are 8 in 12; if your husband is five years older than you (most often the case), your chances of widowhood are 9 in 12.

Widowhood, from every standpoint, is one of the most difficult and demanding times in a woman's life. For many it follows a long period of caring for an ill and dying husband under incredible stress and threat to her own health. A woman whose husband has suffered a severe heart attack compared herself as she coped with his convalescence, took care of the household, and fulfilled her work obligations ". . . to one of those ducks you see swimming in a pond: their feathers are all in place and they're gliding around smoothly, but underneath, their feet are paddling like mad." And a 61-year-old woman whose husband is dying of cancer writes, "I have grown to depend upon my husband socially and emotionally and cannot make plans or face the thought of what the future will be without him."

The Holmes-Rahe stress scale, which measures the emotional toll of major life events, ranks loss of spouse first, far above the stresses of birth, marriage, moving, or job change. The bereaved, regardless of sex, loses someone to whom she or he is emotionally attached, and grief is the inevitable reaction. Some widows mourn longer and harder than others; some fall seriously ill. Mortality rates, too, are higher among the widowed, especially during the first six months.

How does a widow reduce the threat to health and happiness? "Give sorrow words," as William Shakespeare said in *Macbeth*. "The grief that does not speak knits up the o'erwrought heart and bids it break." Delayed or suppressed grief severely hampers adjustment to widowhood, a process that usually takes up to two years. Widows find various ways to endure it. Some turn to their children and family for solace; others to a trusted friend or psychiatrist. The Widow-to-Widow program, a nationwide network of self-help groups that lend support to widows through group meetings, phone calls, and visits, is helpful to many women.

One of the most progressive approaches to easing the pain of dying and death is the hospice, an organization that cares for and counsels the terminally ill and their immediate family. The first hospice was founded in New Haven, Connecticut, in the early 1970s and by 1987 there were more than 1,300 hospices nationwide, some of which are accredited for Medicare payment. They are affiliated with hospitals or are independent and most provide home care and psychiatric help to the families of the dying, sometimes for as long as a year after the relative's death. (Additional information is available from the National Hospice Organization.)

Widows often increase their stress and risk of illness by making rapid, major changes in their lives. They sell houses, change jobs, or move out of town soon after the funeral and only later realize the difficulty of making new friends and the pain of losing old ones. Some widows might be tempted to use tranquilizers or alcohol to numb the pain of loss, a "solution" that can become a major problem in itself.

Some researchers believe that anticipation of a spouse's death makes it easier to adjust to the loss, because there is time to grieve beforehand. One study of young widows and widowers under age 45 showed that good adjustment to widowhood was likely if the marriage was not critical to the widow's functioning and if she had adequate income, a satisfying career, and emotionally supportive friends. Indeed, many women report that they are happier, once they finish grieving, than when they were married. Their enjoyment stems from being, perhaps more so than at any other time in their lives, free and independent persons.

SOCIAL SUPPORTS

What about an older woman's inner, emotional resources? Regardless of sex or age, everyone needs a sense of security and belonging, nurturing, reassurance of worth, reliable assistance, emotional support, dependable access to others, and a network of social relationships. Indeed, people organize their lives around relationships that provide these emotional essentials. When death or other circumstances take one of these relationships away, people often turn to a social network or web of affiliations with kin, friends, friends of friends, co-workers, neighbors, and children. Neighbors and children, in particular, appear to play key roles in an older woman's network. They are important providers of social activities, personal assistance, and a sense that she is not alone in the world. But today's 70-year-olds belong to the famous "low fertility cohort" of women whose family size was limited by the Great Depression and who were too old for childbearing by the time their husbands returned from World War II. As a result, about a fourth of these women have no living children. Most of those who do have children see at least one on a regular basis, and these relationships remain an important source of continuity and support. By contrast, women reaching age 65 to 69 through the year 2000 will tend to have had more children, because they are the mothers of the post-World War II "baby boom."

Older women who have no husband, kin, or friends to meet their day-to-day needs stand a higher risk of becoming institutionalized. Families provide 80 percent of all home health care to older members needing such attention. Thus, despite the myth that families abandon their old, families, and especially children, remain the ultimate caregivers of old people in this society.

This helps explain the statistic, surprising to many, that only about 5 percent of the nation's old people live in nursing homes at any given time. Of these, about 75 percent are women, most of them widowed, divorced, or never married. A large proportion of these women could survive successfully in the community with friends or family to take care of them. Where social services are available through the assistance of federal, state, and community funding, increasing numbers of elderly "singles" can get needed care in their own homes.

SEX AND SENSUALITY

A sense of emotional well-being requires outlets of all kinds, including those for expressing sexuality. Because of low numbers of males their age, older women without mates are severely handicapped in finding such outlets. The widespread, but by no means universal, taboo against sex in old age does not help, nor do the many popular myths on which so many male comedians base their so-called humor. Older women who are interested in sex are typically presented as aggressive or as somewhat ludicrous. The message seems to be that women should not and do not seek sexual pleasure.

Some of these attitudes are relics of Victorian days, others stem from religious precepts that sexuality exists only for reproductive purposes. By this outmoded logic, sex after 60 is accepted for men, who can ostensibly still sire children, but not for postmenopausal women, who have no conceivable reason for indulging in sex. Some older women "lose" interest in sex to protect themselves against the probability that they will not find sex partners anyway. Others, who might have sexual opportunities, fear risking outright rejection should their lover be repulsed by their aging bodies.

Meanwhile, scientific evidence proves that sexual interest and ability can persist into the ninth decade for men and women alike. Indeed, data from a longitudinal study at the Duke University Center for the Study of Aging and Human Development indicate that some women's interest in sex increases as they grow older. Studies by Kinsey, Masters and Johnson, researchers at Duke, the National Institute of Mental Health, and National Institute on Aging indicate that people who are sexually active in their early years tend to remain sexually active. Past enjoyment, interest, and frequency are key determinants of sexuality in old age. Although sexual decline is often caused by poor physical health, including alcoholism, anemia, diabetes, malnutrition, and fatigue, some studies show that even the terminally ill often retain sexual desire. At times it even increases, perhaps to counteract anxiety over dying.

For most people, sex is important to well-being, identity, and a sense of control over one's body. Even more important is sensuality, which is broader than sexuality and involves all the body's senses in the enjoyment of a partner. Best of all are loving relationships marked by intimacy and affection, of which sex and sensuality are but a part. Thus sexual "neutering" of old people denies the human need for pleasure, tenderness, warmth, and the satisfaction of body contact. Full sexual expression, on the other hand, can provide intimacy, love, commitment, self-assertion—all psychological reinforcements at a time when people most need them.

SELF-IMAGE

The myth of sexlessness parallels other misconceptions that aging is a disease, as *Newsweek* once suggested in an article asking, "Can Aging Be Cured?" Contrary to such headlines, most older people are in basically good physical health and able to cope with the demands of daily living. So-called senility is not an inevitable consequence of growing old, nor are old people, according to yet another myth, unproductive, apathetic, withdrawn, crotchety, childish, inflexible, bound to the past, uninterested in the present, and afraid of the future. Women bear an additional burden of myths, the worst being that wrinkles, gray hair, and the like are ugly. The beauty industry capitalizes on these stereotypes and broadcasts that older women must remain youthful, no matter what the cost in cosmetics, creams, fad diets, reducing salons, exercisers, hair dressers, and plastic surgery. So ingrained is the equation of youth and beauty that many women agonize about growing old at age 30, a startling thought considering that they have lived considerably less than half their current life expectancies.

DEPRESSION

Susan Sontag has called growing old "a crisis that never exhausts itself." The crisis is mainly one of mind and emotions. While relatively little is known about emotional disorders in old age, it is known that the mental health of older people is affected by "cumulative deprivations," which involve an old person's ability to adapt to the stresses of aging. These, in turn, cause varying degrees of emotional distress.

Depression has not been studied adequately in older women, although it has been thought to be more prevalent among women than men, and this difference has been assumed to continue into old age. But recent studies suggest that rates of depression may equalize later in life.

Depressed people, regardless of age or sex, generally feel a strong sense of guilt, helplessness, sadness, low self-esteem, and hopelessness about the future. These feelings may be accompanied by frequent crying spells, loss of appetite and weight, constipation, sleep disturbances, fatigue, inability to concentrate, or other signs of physical distress. Depression in older people, especially those living alone, often is overlooked or mistaken for organic brain disease.

According to current theories, some depressions result mainly from external circumstances; others primarily from chemical changes in the brain. The major external causes of depression change with age. In young people they often relate to guilt and suppressed rage, while in old people depression commonly stems from loss—loss of youth, health, income, residence, status, and, worst of all, loved ones through death, relocation, or estrangement.

Women may be particularly predisposed to depression because of the psychological disadvantages of the traditional female role of "learned helplessness." Unlike men, women are taught that they cannot control what happens to them by any direct action, that they must be submissive to and dependent on men, and that they must find satisfaction through nurturing others rather than through their own accomplishments. Younger women are rejecting these assumptions, but many women in their seventies have been learning helplessness all their lives.

These are the women who have never written a check, have no idea how much money is in the bank, sell their property at a loss, and do not know what survivor benefits are due them. When they no longer have a husband, brother, or son to buffer them against the outside world, they fall apart. Many become depressed or succumb to a variety of other emotional impairments ranging from sleep problems to suicide.

SLEEP PROBLEMS

Many old people worry that lack of sleep will lead to serious illness, not realizing that what they see as a problem may be normal, age-related changes in sleep patterns. Sleep requirements change throughout life. A newborn infant needs 16 to 17 hours daily, while a healthy elderly woman may need 7 to 8 or even fewer hours.

Although sleep patterns and problems in old age are not well understood, it is known that sleep is lighter with more frequent awakenings. Some sleep problems in older people may result from physical illness such as degenerative diseases of the central nervous system. Other sleep disturbances stem from long-term dependence on hypnotics taken to relieve insomnia. Incompatible sleep schedules or physical illness of a bed partner may disrupt the sleep of both parties. And sleep disturbances may result from emotional conflicts and anxiety: a vague state of dread often accompanied by muscle tenseness, restlessness, rapid heart rate, and excessive sweating. In many cases sleep problems occur because older people anticipate sleeping problems or take little naps during the day and can't fall asleep at night. Some people suffer from the nightly anxiety that to close one's eyes means to invite death. Whatever the cause, continued difficulties with insomnia or sudden drastic changes in sleep patterns should be brought to a physician's attention.

DRUGS AND ALCOHOL

Sleeplessness by night and emotional distress by day cause many older people to turn to sleeping pills, mild tranquilizers, and other prescription and nonprescription drugs. These drugs can be of great benefit in relieving anxiety and other distressing symptoms when taken for a short time and, if necessary, combined with some form of counseling or psychotherapy. But when sleeping pills and other medications are used continuously over a long period, the result can be disastrous. Women are more likely than men to turn to drugs because they generally use more over-the-counter and prescription medications than men, who are more likely to turn to alcohol.

Nobody knows how many older women have become unwitting drug abusers, although the National Institute on Drug Abuse estimates that 1 to 2 million women of all ages have problems because of prescription drugs that, in too many cases, are supplied by doctors. For example, 60 percent of all drug-related emergency room visits involve women and are the result mainly of suicide attempts or drug dependency.

Alcohol abuse in the elderly is somewhat better documented: of the

14 million Americans who have alcohol problems, including alcoholism, more than 4 million are estimated to be women of all ages. It used to be assumed that there was relatively little alcoholism among women who were 65 or older because of the likelihood of alcohol-related death at an earlier age. In recent years, however, the problem of late-onset alcoholism has come out of the closet. With increased life expectancy, more and more elderly men and women are abusing alcohol late in life to relieve the pain of the death of a loved one, loss of health and income, loneliness, boredom, and feelings of inferiority. Many women who drink, young and old, are hidden abusers: they take alcohol or drugs at home where nobody will see them. The families know but ignore the problem because they feel ashamed or responsible. They also believe that men can drink and abuse drugs but not women. There is tragedy in this attitude because drug and alcohol abuse, if recognized, can, like many other diseases, be treated.

SUICIDE

Many people think about committing suicide at some point during their lives, but each year from 5,000 to 8,000 Americans over age 65 turn such thoughts into deeds. These suicides represent 25 percent of the total number reported, even though the elderly constitute only about 10 percent of the population. The number of suicides among the elderly, moreover, is probably underreported, with perhaps twice this many occurring among people over age 65. Among older men suicide is five times as frequent as it is among older women, but women *attempt* suicide far more often than men. Suicide rates are especially high among old people who lack spouses and jobs and who live alone in deteriorating neighborhoods.

Sometimes suicide takes subtle forms: accidental falls, overweight, heavy smoking, alcoholism, poor nutrition, neglect of routine medical examinations and treatment, failure to take life-saving medication, untreated vision and hearing problems, inadequate planning for possible medical emergencies, and uncontrolled psychological stresses. But the ultimate outcome—self-destruction—is the same.

PSYCHOTHERAPY AND PERSONAL GROWTH

An estimated 25 to 60 percent of the aged population may be in need of some form of psychotherapy. Yet, the aged receive very little psychiatric care on an outpatient basis. This occurs partly because members of this age group are not aware of the benefits of psychotherapy. They grew up in an era when mental illness was shameful and when talking openly about personal problems, even to friends, simply was not done. Older people tend, like much of society, to accept emotional distress and mental deterioration as normal parts of aging. In addition, many doctors are likely to treat emotional problems of older patients with tranquilizing drugs.

There is the myth that psychotherapy, a process in which a therapist helps a patient resolve mental distress, cannot benefit people over age 50 or 60. This attitude comes from numerous sources, among them Sigmund Freud, who maintained that old people are no longer educable, that treatment would continue indefinitely because of the mass of material to be covered in an old person's life, and that therapy for the young is more valuable because they have more years to live than older people.

Even today, many therapists cling to the misconception that the aged do not respond well to therapy. But not all. The American Association of Geriatric Psychiatry publishes a directory of more than 400 psychiatrists nationwide who specialize in treating older people. In addition, many social workers specialize in geriatric counseling.

When old people do receive help with emotional problems, they generally respond very well. Group therapy, in particular, succeeds with older patients because they become members of a social group that counteracts the effects of isolation. They learn to interact with others and to solve current problems, often with the help of another group member whose self-esteem is bolstered by being able to help. Rather than analyze childhood experiences or reconstruct personality as therapy often does for younger people, the focus is on immediate concerns. Family members often become part of the therapy counseling as well. Thus, the older patient might deal with grief, sexual and drug problems, fear of physical illness and disability, anxiety about death, and making new starts. One therapist has written that older people are better psychotherapy risks than the young, because the former can better postpone gratifications and acknowledge that one must perform to achieve.

Older women in therapy—and their families—should guard against overmedication with tranquilizers and especially with powerful psychotropic drugs such as Thorazine that may be inappropriate treatment for their emotional distress. Many women in their 60s and 70s who exhibit signs of memory loss or mental confusion may be suffering not from various forms of senile dementia but from the effects of having been drugged to the point of mental incompetence.

ADAPTATION

The emotional problems of the elderly and their response to the realities of aging are, in a sense, problems of adaptation. There is literally no end to what an older woman can do for her own well-being and for the needs of her community. How, then, can an older woman direct her efforts to adapt? How, more specifically, can she begin to lead a more rewarding life? The final section of this chapter will offer suggestions for income building, learning, networks, sexual needs, shared living, physical and mental fitness, and activism.

EARNING POWER

The older woman must first provide for her own basic needs, the most basic being money. To ensure an adequate income for old age, a woman cannot rely solely on Social Security income or retirement and pension plans. Paid work not only provides income, it provides a sense of accomplishment and worth when it relates to the needs of society. One 72-year-old woman has operated her husband's two-car taxi service since his death nine years ago. She is also treasurer for another cab company, is a notary public, and collects rent for several landlords. She teaches Sunday school, is a Cub Scout den mother, babysits, bakes cakes for friends, sews, and reads. Another woman, at age 68, drives a small tractor and works alongside her husband in their gardening and lawn-mowing business. A widow in Arlington, Virginia, started boarding dogs of neighbors in her home. Now she has a full-time pet hotel business and all the companionship, human and animal, that she needs. Another woman, lacking job market skills, decided at age 70 to put her culinary talents to commercial use. She cooks a week's worth of dinners at a time for customers' deep freezers.

These days when younger wives and single parents are working from 9 to 5, older women can augment their income and provide an essential lifeline in the form of responsible day care and outings, not only for children but for aged relatives who would like special attention while their family caregivers are away at work.

Older women who have retired on a pension or Social Security payments that scarcely cover necessities might take inventory of their marketable skills, especially those related to homemaking. A woman with an elegant handwriting can make posters and address invitations; talented needlewomen can create crafts and practical items; seamstresses can relieve women with full-time jobs of doing the family sewing. An ad placed in a local newspaper or a flyer posted in a laundromat can bring many responses to offers of house-sitting, cat-feeding, plant-watering, and mail-collecting for absent vacationers.

In 1974, Trish Sommers, cofounder of the Older Woman's League, designated as "displaced homemakers" women who lose their source of economic support through divorce or widowhood. According to a report issued in 1987 by the Displaced Homemakers Network, there are at least 11.5 million women of various ages for whom this organization speaks: 67 percent are widowed, 30 percent are divorced or separated, and the rest are abandoned. As of 1987, 22 states had enacted legislation establishing displaced homemaker centers that offer personal counseling, career planning, and workshops to teach job-hunting skills. The network itself is a national clearinghouse with more than 725 programs.

LEARNING POWER

To escape the trap of low-paying jobs, women need education and old age need be no barrier to receiving it. "Old men," T. S. Eliot once said, "should be explorers." This statement is even more true of old women, who are more numerous and who live more years in which to explore.

Freshmen already are getting older each year at colleges and universities throughout the United States. Fordham University in New York City has a College at 60 Program, Ohio State University has Program

60, and the University of San Francisco has the Fromm Institute of Lifelong Learning. Intellectual stimulation and adventure is also offered by Elderhostel, an international network of campuses and historic sites offering low-cost residential academic programs for older people. Courses range from computer programming to stress management and cross-country skiing and are offered at thousands of locations not only throughout the United States, Canada, and Mexico but also in England, Scotland, Israel, and Japan. Courses usually last one week, but Elderhostel has recently launched Intensive Studies programs lasting two weeks or more. The average age of participants is 68, and two-thirds are women. The growth of the program—from 200 Elderhostelers in 1975 to over 100,000 in 1987—attests to the need that it fills. Information is available from Elderhostel, and the Administration on Aging has information about other educational opportunities for older persons.

From around the country come stories about women in their seventies taking degrees and starting new careers afterward. One woman returned to school at age 50 to earn a master's degree in social welfare. She then directed the Gerontology Program at the State University of New York at Stony Brook and cofounded the National Action Forum for Older Women. At one small college in North Carolina, an English major was, at age 80, elected homecoming queen!

The field of gerontology is open to older people even if they have no experience. Universities with gerontology programs include Duke University, the University of Michigan, Columbia University, the New School for Social Research in New York City, and the University of Southern California, and the list grows longer each year.

Many women are learning self-sufficiency by taking adult education courses in car maintenance, household repairs, money management, and karate. Some find outlets for creativity at local colleges, senior centers, YWCAs, YMCAs, and other groups that encourage them to write, paint, draw, and sculpt, thereby fulfilling long-postponed desires to express themselves. The roster of women who published their first books or exhibited their first photographs or drawings after age 70 is long and distinguished.

NETWORKING

Many paths besides jobs and education lead to new life for the elderly. Old people, like young, need to replace the loss of loved ones. The distinguished psychiatrist Dr. Ewald W. Busse writes that living alone and losing loved ones do not in themselves produce the social isolation that afflicts so many older women. Instead, it is failure to develop any significant *new* relationships that saps life satisfaction. Thus, no woman need remain socially isolated because of widowhood or living alone.

One solution is to maintain close, emotionally supportive ties to others. The Unitarian Church's system of extended families, whose members act as one another's relatives, provide such ties. The American Association of Retired Persons sponsors Widowed Persons Service Programs in more than 175 communities nationwide. These programs offer practical help to bereaved men and women through a network of locally based religious, social service, mental health agencies, and educational institutions. The AARP also has compiled a comprehensive listing of resources in the United States and Canada for the widowed. A single copy of this directory, *On Being Alone,* is available without charge from the AARP Widowed Persons Service.

One of the most effective advocacy organizations is the Older Women's League (OWL) whose members meet regularly coast-to-coast to discuss ways to improve the lives of older women. OWL membership provides a special comfort to those who are isolated in rural areas as well as an agenda for better pay equity, health benefits, pension programs, job training for displaced homemakers, and decent housing for older women living alone. Older women also need to maintain networks of children, kin, friends, young people, and co-workers as well as members of the same organizations. Throughout life these networks can be an important source of support. They help members find jobs, housing, practical help, companionship, and emotional support. Because they offer so much, networks require much in return. They are a resource, like money in the bank, that women should maintain all their lives.

LOVING

An important source of emotional support and pleasure in old age is sexuality. One couple, after 35 years of marriage, moved to an isolated house in the country where they spend most of their time working the garden, swimming, and making love. The 68-year-old woman, in an article in *Ms.* magazine, wrote that she hopes the honeymoon will last forever. "We are always touching. I'm glad I'm not like Mama was—she slept downstairs, Daddy slept up, and they never gave each other a good word."

Maggie Kuhn, who at 65 launched an activist career that led to the founding of the Gray Panthers organization, includes maintaining an interest in sex and companionship with the opposite sex among her five new life styles for the elderly. She tells of a widow who for five years had been bedridden most of the time in her son's home. One day she received a letter from a man she had not seen in years. Next came a phone call. Shortly thereafter, she appeared downstairs fully dressed and carrying her suitcase. She told her astonished son and daughter-in-law that she was leaving to be married, gave them her love and a forwarding address, and left for a new life at age 82. She lived with her second husband until her death eight years later. In his book *Retirement Marriage,* Walter McKain wrote that marriage among older people is most likely to succeed when the bride and groom know each other well, when children and friends approve of the marriage, and when both bride and groom own a home, have sufficient income, and are reasonably well-adjusted individuals.

Unfortunately, few older women have opportunities to remarry. One solution to the shortage of older men is offered by author Anne Cumming in *The Love Habit: The Sexual Odyssey of an Older Woman.* Ms. Cumming advocates "intergenerational love" between older women and younger men—even men in their teens and twenties—and predicts that "my book will be required reading in the schools in 50 years' time."

More than 200 years ago Ben Franklin, who appreciated women until the end of his long life, offered similar advice. Franklin argued that older women (presumably, in those days, in their forties) and younger men (in their twenties) are ideally suited for one another, and that young men "in all (their) Amours . . . should *prefer old women to young ones.*"

Self-pleasuring is another sexual alternative, but many contemporary older women find it difficult to enjoy masturbation. Their generation tends to feel guilty about it and to believe that sexuality should be shared only with a husband or possibly a partner of long-standing commitment. They also tend to have a culturally induced difficulty accepting masturbation. An even more controversial sexual outlet for older women exists. In addition to those women who have maintained lesbian relationships for the better part of a lifetime, increasing numbers of women are finding physical and emotional fulfillment during their later years by establishing a mutually gratifying relationship with another woman. Such commitments often go beyond friendship into satisfying sexual and emotional bonds. Many women who create these relationships after a divorce or the death of a spouse have never thought of themselves as homosexual or bisexual. They may, if confronted, refuse to call themselves lesbians, but they will tell anyone who is curious about their way of life—that they have a companion whom they love and whose presence brings them great joy.

Women have other ways to find emotional fulfillment. For example, low income men and women over 60 can receive special training to spend 20 hours a week with children who have special needs such as those who are mentally or physically impaired and have been abandoned by their parents to foster homes and detention centers. Participants in the Foster Grandparents Program receive a small stipend and other benefits, and the time a child spends cuddling on the lap of a foster grandparent provides comfort, security, warmth, and the immeasurable benefits of loving and being loved to both.

Another program, the Retired Senior Volunteer Program (RSVP), is open to any retiree without regard to financial status. Participants can choose activities ranging from visiting the enfeebled homebound to acting as surrogate grandparents in day-care centers or children's hospital wards to reading to the visually impaired in nursing homes. Many women are enjoying new-found love and appreciation that gives their later years a deeper meaning.

PETS

Women who have always enjoyed involvement with a pet might consider having one as they grow older, especially if they live alone. Women who have not yet discovered the many blessings of pet ownership (which more than offset the responsibility and certain amount of inconvenience involved) could enter a world of new emotional experiences. Specialists studying the beneficial aspects of the interaction between pets and people conclude that "When older people withdraw from active participation in daily human affairs . . . animals can become increasingly important. [They] have boundless capacity for acceptance, adoration, attention, forgiveness, and unconditional love. . . . For the elderly, the bond with animal companions is stronger and more profound than at any other age." (Busted and Hines, *California Veterinarian,* August, 1982)

Involvement with a pet can help decrease the stress of depression, anxiety, and isolation as well as stress-related conditions such as coronary heart disease and high blood pressure. Taking care of a pet provides a built-in motivation for taking care of one's self. It is well-known that when pet-owners are hospitalized, their recovery is hastened by eagerness to get home to the animal who is being deprived of their loving care.

In choosing a pet for the first time, women should take their individual situation into account. Those who enjoy walking will find a dog an ideal companion. (A smaller breed can be paper-trained as well as house-broken should a spell of bad weather make walking difficult.) Cats are a great comfort and require less care, especially if there are two. Although cats tend to be more independent than dogs, they can give deep affection when treated affectionately. Finicky housekeepers can derive great satisfaction from birds or fish. Whatever the choice, sharing one's home with a pet can open up new worlds of love, companionship, and fun.

SHARED LIVING

Only about 15 percent of older people lived with their children in 1980, a reflection of the low birthrates of the Depression and fewer offspring to take care of aging parents. Yet most older people prefer the privacy and independence of living on their own. It is not surprising that group and age-integrated living arrangements are also becoming more popular. Challenging the notion expressed by the sixteenth-century poet that "Crabbed Age and Youth Cannot live together," one elderly woman shared her home with several young medical students who helped her maintain it. This kind of living arrangement redefines the family as a group of people united not by blood or marriage but by mutual needs and interests. Another woman, after her husband's death, subdivided their large old house into six apartments, lived in one, rented out the others to friends, and paid her mortgage and repair bills from the proceeds. Communal living arrangements of several people living together can provide companionship, mutual help, protection from crime, and an alternative to institutionalized living.

Some women live in accessory apartments in under-occupied single family residences. These apartments have their own kitchen and bathroom and offer total privacy without imposing a sense of isolation. Self-contained units known as "granny flats" are connected by a sheltered breezeway to the main family house. Information about match-up programs that help people locate shared housing is available from county and local agencies on aging, or from the Shared Housing Resource Center in Philadelphia, Pennsylvania, which publishes a directory of 400 shared housing programs titled "A Guide to Finding a House Mate," and a booklet on intergenerational living titled "A Consumer's Guide to Home Sharing." Both publications are free, if you send a stamped self-addressed envelope with your request.

Another alternative is retirement homes, which offer a continuum of care ranging from independent living apartments to skilled health care facilities such as those found in nursing homes. Additional information may be obtained from the AARP. Ask for "Consumer Housing Information for Seniors" when you write.

A recent development is for women to live together—on the move—in motor homes or trailers. Many who once enjoyed the freedom of the road with their late husbands are joining together for safety, companionship, and new experiences in sightseeing. Those with sufficient funds may share a luxury motor home. For women with limited incomes a trailer offers an economical way to see the USA and visit distant family members.

EXERCISE

Some people become convinced as they grow older that traveling and other exertions are bad for their health. But the human body is a marvelous machine that thrives on use. More than 2,000 years ago the physician Hippocrates suggested that functions that are not used become atrophied—"use it or lose it!" Several hundred years later Cicero listed four factors that adversely affect aging—being barred from useful activity, being weakened physically, being deprived of pleasure, and being aware of the nearness of death. More recent theories of successful aging add lack of proper sleep and diet, smoking, and heavy drinking to the list of harmful factors. Other studies confirm the importance of exercise, not only in maintaining physical health but in preventing or relieving depression, possibly because exercise increases one's sense of well-being by releasing the brain's endorphins, potent substances that act as analgesics and can produce a sense of euphoria.

It is never too late to start exercising, although the amount and type of exercise should depend on one's state of health—and nerve. One woman, described by author Jane Howard in her book *Families,* learned to swim at the age of 75 and before long was diving off the high board. Others are participating in special athletic events for Seniors—women's jogging competitions, bicycle races, and overnight hiking trips. Women who used to drive to destinations only a few blocks away are discovering the many pleasures of walking—in sturdy shoes. Many communities offer group walking tours that explore historic urban areas, and nature-lovers can join bird-watchers or wild life preservationists or mushroom hunters on seasonal outings. Physical fitness classes with the focus on the needs of older women are available in most communities, and a membership in a good health club is a rewarding gift to request from a spouse or an offspring.

LIFE WORK

Mental activity may be even more important than physical. Margaret Mead, who remained a working anthropologist until she died of cancer at age 76, used to say, "I know I can't live forever. I'm just not ready to go yet." She kept a journal of observations on the progress of her cancer and remained, until her death, passionately involved in life.

Simone de Beauvoir once said, "The only solution to the problems of old age is for each old person to go on pursuing ends that give existence meaning." One woman decided at age 70 to fulfill a lifelong dream of living in San Francisco. She invested her savings in a bus ticket and, despite limited social security income of $160 a month and a lame leg, successfully settled in a strange city where she had no friends or family. Today she plays in a band at a senior center and has walked across the Golden Gate Bridge six times. Another woman at age 72 founded an organization called Neighbors Helping Neighbors in which volunteers provide rides to doctors' offices, hospitals, and clinics for disabled people with no other means of transportation. For eight years she ran this enterprise from her small cottage in Sharon, New Hampshire before turning it over to a new manager. Looking back, she says, "Who would have thought my seventies would be the happiest years of my life?" In her nineties another woman began to write essays about aging. Asked why she took up writing, she replied, "I'd be bored to death if I didn't have something to do." After the better part of a lifetime devoted to classical Greek scholarship, Edith Hamilton wrote her first book at the age of 62 and continued to write and publish until 1957 when *The Echo of Greece* appeared to mark her 90th birthday.

Charles Schulz, creator of *Peanuts*, once suggested in cartoon form another way old people could remain assets to society. Lucy, while reading a composition to her class, concluded:

> "And so World War II came to an end. My grandmother left her job in the defense plant and went to work for the telephone company. We need to study the lives of great women like my grandmother. Talk to your own grandmother today. Ask her questions. You'll find she knows more than peanut butter cookies! Thank you!"*

* Text from PEANUTS by Charles M. Schulz; © 1976 United Features Syndicate, Inc.

Lucy, in effect, recommends "life review," an autobiographical process that allows an old person to take pride in the past by talking or writing about it, reading diaries or letters from an old lover, attending a reunion, or visiting one's birthplace. When an older person is encouraged to reminisce, perhaps by a grandchild with a notebook or tape recorder, the listener gains wisdom and experience, and the reminiscer discovers that somebody cares enough to listen.

POLITICAL CLOUT

Regardless of earnings or income, one of the most effective ways women can wield power is in the voting booth. In 1982, some 60 percent of the population 65 and over voted, the highest proportion of all age groups except the 45 to 64 group. Yet only rarely do older voters cast their ballots in a bloc. It is encouraging, however, that increasing numbers of old people are making themselves heard as members of such activist groups as the AARP, OWL, and Gray Panthers, a coalition of young and old who oppose age discrimination, age stereotyping, and other dehumanizing forces in our society.

Women in rural areas are beginning to join together to seek better solutions to problems of isolation, economic depression, and hard, underpaid work on the farm. They are holding statewide conferences to establish more effective networking and encourage political activism.

A final way of exercising power, in this case over yourself, is through living wills, which give you legal control over your own and your relatives' bodies. These documents enable you to decide, while you are still healthy and legally competent, whether you wish others to prolong your life by artificial means and heroic measures despite the indignity of deterioration, dependence, and hopeless pain. The growing movement toward hospice care, in the same vein, promises to provide a pain-free, humanistic environment in which to experience a terminal illness.

Society continues to view old people, even while they are still healthy, more as a problem than as a valued social, economic, and political resource. At a Conference on the Older Woman in September, 1978, Dr. Robert N. Butler, Director of the National Institute on Aging, commented on the survivorship of the old: "I for one am somewhat tired of hearing about the 'aging problem.' We are talking about a major human triumph in this century." Despite the litany of problems an older woman faces, she has great strengths and potentials. For example, she has the opportunity to:

- Become, perhaps for the first time in her life, an independent being, undominated by others and in full control of her life.
- Guard her physical and mental health.
- Fulfill her own expectations, not those imposed by society.
- Enjoy good friends and leisure pastimes.
- Exercise to keep physically fit.
- Continue to discover and use her talents.
- Remain curious and eager to learn.
- Remember that what is frowned upon in a girl of 20 is applauded as "character" in a woman of 80.
- Remain passionately involved with life, enjoying each day as it comes.

The older woman who does even a few of these things will begin to see a different person when she looks in the mirror—not a wrinkled facade but a successful individual who knows there still is work to be done, dreams to be dreamed, pleasures to be enjoyed. Older women who can view the aging process in this manner could serve as role models for women now in their fifties, forties, thirties, and even twenties. The women most likely to adapt successfully to the stresses of old age will be those who have adapted well to stresses of equal or greater severity throughout their lives. What is past is prologue.

LOOKING AHEAD

The 50-year-old woman of today has not been hardened to adversity like the 70-year-old who learned in the Great Depression to deal with problems similar to those encountered in old age. Yet these younger women have more education than ever before, and when they reach age 70, they will have more earned pensions and financial resources of their own. They will have more children and grandchildren to support them economically and emotionally in old age. Family ties will be extended, with parent-child bonds lasting 50 years or more, and grandparent-grandchild bonds 30 years or more. In sum, women now in their fifties and younger are likely to experience old age differently than the women who preceded them, and the experience will, on balance, be better.

If, to restate the proverb, "A woman resembles her times more than her mother," the prospects are even brighter for women now in their twenties, thirties, and forties. They will be even better educated, better paid, and healthier physically and mentally. They will have more models of accomplished women to emulate.

A study of three generations of women, aged 10 to 92, makes this final point. Grandmothers in the study had practically no formal education in their youth and had conventionally moral upbringings, although they had strong desires to be creative. Their granddaughters were less bound by conventional morals and more oriented toward achievement, control of their own destinies, and ability to influence others. This group, in every sense, represents changes in American womanhood over the last century. To return to an opening theme of this chapter, if women are to outlive men and, in that sense, inherit the earth, they might as well make the most of it. And, judging from those who are coming along, they will.

YOU, YOUR DOCTORS, AND THE HEALTH CARE SYSTEM

Frances Drew, M.D., M.P.H.
Professor of Community Medicine, University of Pittsburgh School of Medicine

The health care system today neither begins nor ends with physicians. The vastly improved health education offered daily in all media has drawn us, the patients, the public, the "consumer," into an awareness of and responsibility for our own health. Dr. Benjamin Spock's book on babies began an ever-expanding "do-it-yourself" movement. All of the women's magazines have columns about health maintenance and health problems, and their informational quality is generally high. Most newspapers have both a "Dear Abby" and a "Dear Doctor" letter-answering column, though here the information tends to be a bit more shopworn. Television has had some excellent documentaries, but its regular medical programs exploit the drama and the horrors. Many books have been written for the lay public, running the gamut from excellent and informative to tedious and overtechnical to downright quackery. Clearly, this torrent of information is responding to a perceived public interest, spurred on by the complexities, inadequacies, and above all, the costs of the health care system.

Not only have words tumbled forth. Numbers of self-help groups have arisen, whose goals are to alert people to their own ability to cope with illness. Women's cooperative clinics are one fine example; a group like Reach for Recovery for mastectomy patients is another. The patient is acquiring a growing sophistication about health, which is all to the good.

The result of all these trends is a new participation by the patient in a system that used to operate on a strictly authoritarian basis. Sensing a mounting backlash against the entire profession, doctors are responding (in many cases grudgingly) to the increasing independence of women so that a partnership is established in which both parties profit from the circumstance that the well-informed patient is healthier, recovers faster, and is more gratifying to treat.

Furthermore, this trend puts more pressure on women to accept responsibility for their own health. The list of life style-related diseases grows each year: cancer, heart disease, hypertension, alcoholism, obesity—all in some degree are under the control of the patient, who can prevent the disease or alter its outcome. More and more, physicians expect patients to take this responsibility rather than to ask for a magic medicine that will "do it for me." Roles are changing. The physician increasingly teaches as well as prescribes, and patients listen and learn.

Doctors have been listening and learning too. Thanks to pressures from consumer advocates, from the legal and counseling professions, and as a result of the rapid growth of specialists with credentials other than an M.D., physicians have been learning about subjects that were all but ignored in medical schools. Courses in human sexuality and sex therapy were not part of any medical school curriculum until the advent of Masters and Johnson. Except for a nod at deficiency diseases and special diets for particular gastrointestinal problems, nutrition was not seriously examined until more and more women concerned themselves with healthful diet rather than constant dieting. Interns can now recognize battered children when they are brought into the emergency room as "accident" cases. The concept of substance abuse is no longer limited to opium derivatives as doctors learn more about alcoholism, nicotine dependency, and addiction to some of the drugs they themselves prescribe. Death as a subject for discussion was ignored; now most reputable medical schools conduct seminars in dying, death, and bereavement, and they also examine the increasing number of questions that come under the heading of medical ethics, hoping to instill wisdom as well as knowledge in the men and women who play such a crucial role in all our lives.

As for our competence in caring for ourselves and others, there was a time when women shared a body of practical and useful information—how to deliver a baby, how to feed the family, how to raise the children, how to care for the sick. But male "specialists" undermined women's authority and competence in these matters. For good or ill, Dr. Spock replaced the wise grandmother; the male obstetrician replaced the female midwife. But women in our culture still usually plan the meals, make the major decisions about the life style of the household, and are, even when they work outside the home at a fulltime job, the custodians of the "nurturing" skills: nursing the sick and caring for the children and the elderly. In mastering this knowledge of preparing healthful meals, helping the helpless, recognizing the signals of substance abuse, women seek an ally they can trust.

How does the woman of today find a physician—for herself, her family, her child—who will both teach and treat her? How can she get the best available care? This chapter will attempt to serve as a guide to our present health care system.

CHOOSING YOUR DOCTORS

On the assumption that you are in a position to choose your own doctor (many women cannot do so because of the nature of their own or their spouse's health insurance coverage), it is important that you make your selection with care and enlightened concern. There are women who have lived to regret a decision to go to a particular physician because he was charming at a PTA meeting, or because she wrote a best seller, or because a friend found this wonderful M.D. who provided her with any number of amphetamines to help her lose weight. Keep in mind that the vigilance of patients is indispensable if the integrity of the medical profession as a whole is to be maintained. When Dr. Otis R. Bowman was secretary of the United States Department of Health and Human Services, he pointed out (*The New York Times,* June 6, 1986) that "Nowhere near enough doctors are being disciplined by state medical boards."

Not only is it estimated that as many as 28,000 people may be practicing medicine and treating tens of thousands of patients each year even though they hold no licenses and have had little or no medical training but also, when the Department of Health and Human Services conducted its first comprehensive survey (1986) of medical discipline and peer review, results indicated that although the majority of American doctors are well-qualified, 20,000 to 45,000 licensed physicians are likely candidates for some kind of discipline. These figures are derived from statistics on the prevalence in the profession of alcoholism, drug abuse, and mental illness. Other studies indicate that charges requiring some kind of disciplinary action include not only substance abuse but unnecessary surgery and sexual molestation of patients. Again, most doctors are honest, competent, hardworking, and uphold the standards of their profession. But it does no harm to be aware of the pitfalls in making your choice. There are some important considerations to review when deciding on a primary care physician.

GEOGRAPHY

While the doctor closest to your home may not be the top-of-the-list choice, it isn't practical to have to travel for more than an hour to reach the doctor you may have to visit regularly. If you live in a semirural or rural area, you may not have much choice. Know where your nearest hospital is located, and try to connect with a physician on the staff. While doctors on the staff of a teaching hospital (one attached to a university medical school) are usually well qualified, you can check out any doctor's background by calling the county medical society or by checking the medical directory at the reference desk of your local public library.

If you live in a metropolitan area, your choice widens considerably. You may wish to have a physician on the staff of a Catholic or Jewish hospital because of your religious beliefs; you may wish to get your care from a university complex; you may have strong preference for one or another hospital because of friends who have been there. The next step is to call either the hospital or a county medical society and ask them to give you the names of physicians in a given discipline on the staff of that hospital. You can then look them up in the telephone book and make inquiries about how soon you can have an appointment as a new patient.

QUALIFICATIONS

When you call a new doctor for the first time, you have every right to ask about his credentials if you haven't been able to find out about them on your own. Nearly every physician under 60 today is board certified in some discipline. Certification in either family practice or internal medicine indicates that the physician provides primary care rather than concentrating on the treatment of specific conditions.

FEES

Before you make your appointment, don't hesitate to ask about fees. If you have insurance coverage, ask whether you must pay the fee and wait for reimbursement or whether the doctor applies for reimbursement. If you're on Medicare, find out whether the doctor accepts assignment, and if the reply is "No," you'll have to decide whether you want to find a doctor who does.

When you ask about fees, find out if full payment for a first visit is expected before you leave the office, and, if it is, ask whether a personal check is acceptable. Above all, find out what the cost of a first visit will be and how long you can expect the visit to take.

STYLE OF PRACTICE

If you are satisfied with qualifications, the next question might be whether the office is a group or solo practice and, if it is a group, whether it is a group of physicians with the same types of practice (i.e., family practice, internal medicine, etc.) or a multispecialty group in which a large number of physicians representing a broad spectrum of practices work together (internal medicine, surgery, obstetrics, pediatrics, etc.). Group practice of the latter type is an outgrowth of the continuing trend toward specialization, a trend that has led to a growth in health care costs. It has been inevitable because the increased amount of information and the proliferation of technical procedures in all aspects of medical science can scarcely be mastered by a "general" practitioner, but at best, it is a mixed blessing for all concerned.

Most younger physicians, whatever the nature of their practice, are unwilling to go it alone for a number of reasons, one of which is the demanding nature of solo practice in terms of time and effort; another is the prohibitive cost of equipment and office staff.

The pattern of group practice, therefore, continues to grow. Practically all groups have a patient-admitting arrangement with a nearby hospital. The largest threat to continuing expansion of group practice is the rapid growth of health maintenance organizations.

Apart from the advantages to the physician, there are many to the patient. In an office with several physicians someone is always on call and always available. It may not be the person you see regularly, but your records are easily accessible when they are needed. If the group is a fairly large one, it is likely to include an internist who may be a subspecialist in cardiology or geriatrics, an ophthalmologist, an obstetrician/gynecologist, a pediatrician, and a general surgeon. There will be a contract with a radiologist, and there will be specific referrals to such other specialists as orthopedists, neurologists, and psychiatrists. Your records will be immediately available to all of them and you will be spared the time-consuming job of being a completely "new" patient over and over again.

AGE, PERSONALITY, AND SUBCULTURE

Patients are as varied as physicians, and no one is equally comfortable with everyone. Much has been written about why patients choose a particular physician and one of the most readable, accurate, and interesting studies is Earl Lomon Koos's *The Health of Regionville.* The author looked at a town in upper New York State in which five physicians practiced, asking patients of different backgrounds why they preferred a particular physician. The reasons given were that their physician (1) had served the family in the previous generation, and they saw no reason to change; (2) was known to them socially; (3) was recommended by a relative or friend; (4) was generally known in the community as a "good doctor"; (5) made home calls; (6) was "willing to spend time with you"; (7) didn't press for payment; (8) charged moderate fees;

(9) was "just liked as a person"; (10) was "the most available"; and (11) had "good equipment."

You will recognize many of these reasons as topics already discussed, but there is no gainsaying that past commonality of experience may make both the physician and the patient more comfortable and their interaction more effective, particularly if social or family pressures are contributing significantly to the ill health. You may need only technical expertise in a one-time visit to a specialist, but you should give extra weight to compatibility if your psychological as well as physical needs are to be met, which is usually the case. For example, a 60-year-old woman may be initially uncomfortable discussing her psyche or her sexuality with a 30-year-old man, and a teenager may be seriously mismatched on these same topics with a physician of grandfather's age. The physician's expertise and attitudes can sometimes overcome these initial obstacles, but time is lost in the process. As another example, the intelligent, informed patient is impatient with the physician who simply expects orders to be carried out and refuses to give answers of substance to questions, and the patient who expects authoritative treatment is equally put off by a physician who says, "I don't quite know what is wrong with you, but let's start here."

The only way to establish whether or not you trust and are comfortable with a physician is to try the relationship out. If you find yourself ill at ease or lacking in confidence, pay your bill and find someone else.

SEX OF PHYSICIAN

Some women prefer male physicians, some are indifferent, and some vastly prefer a woman. Preferences are apt to be particularly strong in seeking an obstetrician/gynecologist. While recent years have brought a sharp increase in the number of young women in all specialties and especially in family practice, the medical world is still predominantly male. If you feel strongly enough about finding a woman, the county medical society will give you names, but you may have to pay an extra price in convenience of location. With approximately one-third of each current class of graduates being women, this gap will close and the difficulties will lessen.

THE FIRST VISIT

Once you have selected a physician, there are several things you need to do and/or find out at your first visit.

- For your first visit, go when you're healthy and have a complete checkup so that the doctor has a norm against which to measure any future problems.
- Bring *all* your medications with you in a plastic bag. "All" means prescription *and* nonprescription drugs.
- Find out about office hours and whether any specific time is set aside for telephone consultation. Under what circumstances does the doctor make house calls, if ever?
- Who covers for the doctor during times of unavailability, especially on weekends and during vacations?
- More and more women who are meeting a doctor for the first time ask the staff to arrange that this meeting take place in the doctor's office when both doctor and patient are fully dressed *people* rather than in the examining room when the doctor is fully clothed as an authority figure and the woman is the disrobed powerless patient.
- When you see a physician for the first time, take a copy of your medical records and your family history with you. If you aren't asked for the following information in the first interview, be sure to provide facts about: the nature of your job if you work outside the home and how you feel about it, your current living situation, how often you exercise, how much leisure time you have and how you spend it, how much alcohol you consume regularly (this includes wine and beer as well as "hard" liquor), what your regular diet is like, and how much caffeine you consume.

If, after the first visit or even later, you are for any reason not comfortable or satisfied with the physician, you can and should look for someone else.

CHANGING DOCTORS

Everyone knows that marriage is easier than divorce and that many marriages are sustained on inertia rather than on compatibility or love. The same is true of doctor-patient relationships, and the techniques of "divorcing" your doctor are nearly as awkward as divorcing your husband. It can be done and in the long run should be, and, if we continue the analogy to marriage, annulment is easier than divorce. The sooner you get out, the better off you are.

If you are moving to another city, the situation is easy. The most comfortable solution is to choose a physician in your new locality (Dr. Y) and then write your former physician (Dr. X) asking to have all your records (which can be photocopied easily nowadays) as well as X-rays and other diagnostic materials sent to Dr. Y. If Dr. Y requests the record from Dr. X, you will be asked to sign a waiver. An even simpler way is to ask Dr. X for your records and take them with you to Dr. Y. Again, you will probably be asked to sign a release. This process is often facilitated by a conference with Dr. X before you move, in which you ask about physicians near your new residence. Each specialist is apt to have a list of all members of that specialty board in the United States, giving age, university, perhaps even residency training sites, and from this you can together cull some likely names.

If you want to change physicians within a group or go to a new office, embarrassment may glue you to the chair. Most people see the change as quite different than returning a dress to a department store, but while techniques differ, the motivation is the same—you are dissatisfied with your choice. If you are enrolled in a group practice, you are apt to have seen more than one primary physician over time because of vacations, on-call schedules, and the like. If Dr. A was your original physician, but the last time you had the flu you saw Dr. B with whom you felt more comfortable, you need only make your next appointment with Dr. B through the secretary. If you happen to be seeing Dr. B, you can easily say that you would really prefer to continue this relationship, and Dr. B can then manage the problem in the office with no fuss at all. Occasionally Dr. A may be upset and face you with your decision. Your only course then is to persevere with whatever diplomacy you can muster because your future comfort in your medical relationship is at stake.

You encounter only slightly more difficulty in changing completely to another office. Here the routine is exactly the same as when moving to another town. You choose your new physician, say that you have been seeing Dr. A who has your records, sign a waiver, and let Dr. B write requesting them from Dr. A. If your only contacts with Dr. A were for routine checkups or upper respiratory conditions, the record will contain very little important information and you can forget about asking for its transfer. On the other hand, if you have had any chronic or complicated condition or much laboratory data has accrued (the usual levels of some chemical values or what your chest X-ray looked like a year ago, etc.), your new physician needs and deserves to know all of these facts. No amount of embarrassment should prevent you from getting this information into the hands of your new physician.

HOSPITAL OUTPATIENT DEPARTMENTS

The word "clinic" (unless labeled Mayo, Menninger, Lahey, or Joslin) conjures up an image of crowded benches, offhand care, students as the only doctors—a medical Ellis Island. Today the facts are quite different.

Many university clinics are run in tandem with private doctors' offices and there is no way of telling who is the public patient and who the private. If you go to a clinic for your general medical care, it is certainly likely that you will have more than one physician over a five-year period, because much of the care is provided by residents. It is also true that you are apt to encounter an intern first. But a few facts should be taken into account before you panic.

Approximately 80 percent of visits to physicians are precipitated by either self-limiting illness (flu) or problems easily diagnosed and easily treated (rashes, sprains, headaches, ulcers, hypertension). Even when surgery is required (gallstones, appendixes, hernias, hemorrhoids), the procedure is usually a straightforward one. Appreciating this, recognize that the chairperson of medicine is as powerless to treat flu as is the medical student—aspirin and plenty of fluids to tide you through is still the best treatment. However, if you should acquire a complex disease such as leukemia, you can be certain that you will be seen by the chief of hematology in that institution and you can't improve on *that* quality of care. If you need surgery, you can sleep quietly through the anesthetic knowing that while the scalpel may be held by the chief resident in surgery, that resident has had five years of postgraduate training and a faculty member is scrubbed and standing by to supervise. In short, while it is difficult to consider a clinic as "your doctor," the care provided is of the highest quality. You have the advantage of continuity of records, and referrals are available to all specialties.

While a number of nonuniversity clinics are excellent, particularly in hospitals that have family practice programs or are situated in areas distant from an urban center, there is nonetheless a wide variation in quality. If you have a choice in a large, metropolitan area, choose a clinic associated with a medical school. You can then be confident that there is an approved residency training program, which means that there are an adequate number of appropriately trained faculty members to supervise. If you must choose between two community hospitals, phone and ask whether their residency training program is approved in medicine, surgery, or whatever. If it is not, go elsewhere, because the clinic is likely to be staffed by hospital personnel who will consider it a chore to treat you and will dispose of your problem as rapidly as possible.

In recent years the term *clinic* is frequently encountered in connection with outpatient services that require facilities, technological advances, and team treatment beyond the scope of the private practitioner. Among these outpatient clinics, many of them connected with prestigious medical centers, are Headache Clinics, Pain Clinics, Sex Therapy Clinics, Alcoholism Treatment Clinics, and Stroke Rehabilitation Clinics.

CHOOSING A SPECIALIST

A specialist is a physician who has had intensive training in one particular area of medicine and is usually certified by the national board of that specialty. Most are not in solo practice but share offices and facilities with others in the same specialty. Some accept self-referred patients, others accept patients only when referred by other physicians, and many are now associated with health maintenance organizations. If you are a member of such an organization, you are expected to use the specialist who is also a member.

Almost every primary physician establishes personal patterns of referral to known and trusted specialists. If you happen to have heard that Dr. Gray is a fine dermatologist and you ask to be referred, your physician has two choices: immediate agreement, even though this is not the usual pattern, or demurral with another suggestion. Many interpretations can be put on this latter action: your physician may know that although Dr. Gray is "nice," his competency level is not very high; Dr. Gray may simply be unknown, whereas other physicians in the usual office referral pattern are both known and competent; of course, your physician may be splitting fees, but that is both illegal and unlikely. What is fairly certain is that if your physician is competent and you have chosen well in the first place, your specialists will in turn be chosen well for you.

Your relationship to a specialist need not be as close as to your primary physician, unless you anticipate that your condition will require a great deal of interaction over a long period. We all would prefer dealing with congenial people at every turn of the medical road, but if you need a fracture set or a mole removed, you need technical skill more than congeniality. Your physician can, and should, be asked, "What kind of a person is Dr. Brown?" The honest reply may be something like, "Well, not very attractive, a little gruff, but superb in the operating room." If you know that much, you will accept a less than prepossessing manner because you are assured that this is the best person to deal with your problem. In short, if you are confident in your choice of primary physician, you can let the choice of specialists be part of your doctor's responsibility to you.

One primary care specialty area deserves particular comment—pediatrics. If your primary physician is in family practice, this may well include pediatrics. If you are receiving care from a group practice, there is probably a pediatrician in it. If you need to find a new doctor to care for children, recommended names will come from many sources—from your obstetrician, from your internist, from friends. Again, you need to know relationships to hospital staffs. All of the questions you asked before choosing your physician apply as well to the physician for your child, with some differences. You must feel confident that this person *likes* children, that your child will be comfortable, and that you can establish a cooperative relationship. More than any other specialist, the pediatrician relies on you to handle minor problems yourself while being instantly alert to danger. Young children can get very sick very quickly. You must feel comfortable about calling to raise any questions and to report symptoms you observe, but at the same time you must let yourself be educated in handling your own child, in learning to distinguish between the minor problems and signs of danger, and in understanding your child's pattern of response to illness.

Another area deserving comment is that of gynecology and obstetrics. While a woman might tolerate a patronizing physician in some limited specialties, such types (almost always men) represent a particular hazard in a specialty that by definition places a woman in a physically unique and dependent examination position that often includes discomfort as well. A pelvic examination should not be accompanied by small talk and should not be prefaced by "Now, honey, just relax." Enough indignity is associated with having one's legs in stirrups; you need not tolerate verbal indignity as well. Nowadays, most male gynecologists conduct their examinations in the presence of a female nurse as a guarantee against a possible charge of sexual molestation. In addition, the physician should spend time with you both before and after the examination when you are fully dressed. If you are not comfortable with your physician, seek comfort by discussing your concerns or change physicians.

GETTING A SECOND OPINION

Second and even third opinions are far more frequently sought when surgical intervention is an issue than when medical treatment alone suffices. In the surgical world, second opinions are either sought by patients for their own satisfaction or mandated by third-party payers. Some surgeons harbor a resentment toward the latter, regarding them as an abuse of their time.

The situation differs considerably when a patient asks for another opinion, or if the surgeon, sensing apprehension or discomfort on the part of the patient, suggests that she might be more comfortable if she saw someone else as well. If the patient has a particular physician in mind, the surgeon inevitably acquiesces and arranges for the consultation. If no name surfaces, the surgeon will suggest someone who is competent in the field. This may be another physician in the same group or it may be a physician in another group or another hospital (this is more frequently the case if the physician senses a distant relationship with the patient or senses suspicion on the part of the patient). Most surgeons admit to a tinge of resentment at being asked for another opinion, but they hide it with grace. On the other hand, all are flattered to be asked by another physician to give such an opinion. In the rare case of the patient suggesting a name that conjures up mistrust for whatever reason, the surgeon will agree but may add, "That's fine, but why don't you ask Dr. M as well?"

A referral is usually made when a physician who practices away from a metropolitan area has a patient with particular complications or a particularly difficult diagnosis. The patient is then referred to someone on the staff of a large medical center whose name is known to the referring physician because of articles read or papers heard. This is a combination consultation and second opinion. Occasionally such patients are self-referred because the physician in the larger area has seen one of their friends or has been featured in the press. In either of these cases the new physician is flattered to be asked and delighted to comply.

Finally, there is good and sufficient reason for getting more than one opinion about an impending operation, especially if it comes under the heading of elective surgery. Experts agree that a significant percentage of all gall bladder removals, hysterectomies, cesarians, and coronary bypasses are unnecessary, and that alternative treatments and less radical procedures can be just as effective. It would appear to be a basic assumption that where there are more surgeons, there is more surgery. In this connection, many corporations are asking the companies that provide health insurance for their employees to submit information that will make it possible to evaluate the competence of the doctors and hospitals with which it deals. Thus, it can determine which doctors are performing too many operations or are charging too much for them. It is also possible that some doctors don't order enough diagnostic tests. In any case, corporations want the medical community to conform to standards. They want to know, for instance, why hysterectomies are performed seven times more often in one community than in another and how this variation relates to the prevalence of uterine cancer where the operation is performed less frequently.

PAYMENT PLANS

There are various plans available to defray part or all of medical expenses. You should investigate which ones you may participate in.

HEALTH MAINTENANCE ORGANIZATIONS (HMOs)

HMOs are prepaid health care plans whose membership until recently was restricted to the gainfully employed and their families. Since 1985 Medicare recipients have also been included in their services. Basically HMOs combine the functions of an insurance company with those of a doctor/hospital by providing health care for a prepaid annual premium. There are two types of HMOs: the group practice that is connected to a particular hospital and is located in a central "service" area and the "individual practice" that includes doctors who enroll in the HMO and who limit their private practice so that they can accept patients assigned to them by the organization. In exchange for cutting down on their income from private fees, they receive a guaranteed amount of money each month for the patients assigned to them, and they also receive a share of the organization's profits.

You or your spouse may be a member of an employee group that offers prepaid medical care as a fringe benefit or you may live in a community that has a prepaid plan open to the public. You may even have a choice among groups offering such plans. About 15 years ago, there were only 39 HMOs nationwide. There are now more than 650, serving more than 27 million people, and about 70 percent of all U.S. doctors have HMO contracts either as part of the group itself or as private practitioners who treat HMO members. Many people prefer prepayment, assuming that the physicians offering it are of high quality, because it is easier to budget for a fixed sum each month than to worry about the cost of seeing a physician if a medical problem arises. A number of studies have shown that illnesses are seen earlier and treated more effectively when money is not an obstacle. Once you have joined such a plan, the group has the responsibility to care for you and the lag time to an appointment is shorter. However, because the primary care doctor in a health maintenance organization has the power to decide when a patient should see a specialist in the service group, the freedom of members to choose their own treatment is limited, unless they want to consult and pay for a specialist on their own. Another disadvantage is that the participating patients do not have any choice of hospital.

BLUE CROSS/BLUE SHIELD

If your employee benefits include or you have Blue Cross/Blue Shield or other health insurance coverage as an alternative to a prepaid plan, read the insurance contract carefully, compare the benefits, and estimate what your out-of-pocket costs would be for an ordinary illness. With any such insurance plan you are free to continue with your own physician, but many office charges may not be covered. For covered procedures the insurance carrier may be billed by your physician's office and its payment accepted as full payment. If you have a high income you may be charged an extra amount. If your physician does not participate in Blue Shield or has no mechanism for accepting third-party fees, you will be reimbursed directly by the insurance carrier and are then responsible for paying the bill. Be sure to check any insurance policy as to whether you are covered if traveling outside the United States. All carriers cover costs incurred within the United States.

If your health insurance contract includes "major medical," you have a bolster against catastrophe. If you or a family member is disabled, there are other sources of payment. The important point to remember is to read your contract carefully so you are not taken by surprise by deductible amounts or items not covered. Hospitals, clinics, and group practices all have someone available to explain the variations of coverage and will help you in wending your way through the complications. You can also consult your State Insurance Department for additional information and clarification.

Having established exactly what your coverage includes, you should discuss with your physician or someone in the office what additional charges may occur and under what circumstances. You must not be embarrassed to ask exactly what your care will cost you for a routine visit, for laboratory tests, for a house call. If you know these facts, you will avoid the irritation and dissatisfaction of receiving a "surprise" bill far higher than you expected, even though your expectation may have been unreasonable.

MEDICARE

If you are eligible for Medicare or if you are within a year of eligibility, inform yourself of the nature of your entitlements. As the result of an extensive study ordered by Congress in 1986, a new fee structure is to be based on the evaluation of the work done by a specialist, the costs of the particular practice, and the length of training involved. In the past, Medicare paid for doctors' services on the basis of "reasonable charges" but this system was not only deemed "irrational," it resulted in an annual increase of 15 percent in Medicare expenditures by the government. Thus, the study was ordered.

While the new "relative value" scale has been endorsed by the American Medical Association, there is a growing resistance on the part of individual doctors to accept the new fee structure, and Medicare patients are finding it increasingly difficult to locate physicians willing to accept them for treatment on the basis of assigned fees.

At the same time, however, a new bill had been passed in 1988 to protect Medicare beneficiaries from the expenses of "catastrophic illness," expenses covered only by private insurance referred to as "Medigap" coverage. This expansion in benefits, financed by a surtax on income taxes and a $4 additional monthly premium for Medicare coverage itself, was repealed before it took effect.

If you have any problems finding a doctor who accepts Medicare payments, consult your local Social Security office, and while you're there, be sure to pick up the brochures that are relevant to your particular situation so that you'll know exactly how the system works for you. And if you're traveling outside the United States, remember that Medicare does not cover any costs incurred abroad.

MEDICAID

If you are eligible for Medicaid because of your low income, in theory you are totally covered, but this coverage varies from state to state. In some areas private or community hospitals refuse to accept Medicaid patients and they are sent to a municipal or county facility. In general, Medicaid reimburses physicians at an even lower rate than Medicare and your best, perhaps only, recourse is to seek care in a hospital outpatient department. To check on your eligibility, consult your local Department of Social Services, and if you (or the person on whose behalf you are seeking the information) are over 65, consult the Area Agency on Aging in your vicinity.

BEING A WOMAN AND A PATIENT

The medical as well as lay literature has been exploding recently with objections about the ways male physicians treat (or mistreat) women. There is certainly much to what is said and a knowledgeable woman patient should be aware of the areas of danger.

A single case history will illustrate the problem better than any analysis. A friend, the mother of three daughters, two of whom were twins born 14 years before when she was 35, mentioned casually to me in a social setting that she had not menstruated since the twins were born, at which time she had bled profusely and been in serious condition for two days. A few more questions made it very clear to me that she had, at that time, suffered pituitary hemorrhage that had left her debilitated and chronically ill. Throughout the period she had seen both her internist and her obstetrician on many occasions and each had checked her blood count, listened to her symptoms of lassitude, weakness, lack of menses, and then said something like, "There, there, dear, you'll have that boy yet" or "It's just change of life" or "It's all your nerves." She was spending nearly a third of each day in bed, while still managing to get her children off to school and have dinner ready. She had been a vigorous and active woman before her illness but had been forced to be nearly a recluse after it. The most distressing part of the story came after my diagnosis.

For another three years she did nothing because she didn't want to offend her family physician by seeking other care and because by this time both doctors had indeed convinced her that it was in her head. When she finally went to a prestigious medical center in another city, she became a classic case presentation of serious pituitary deficiency. Her physician there told me later that she would forever be the paragon of a nonneurotic patient because, at the conclusion of the tests, he came into her hospital room, stupefied at the extent of her illness and the lag time to treatment, and said, "Mrs. S, I can't really understand how you have managed all these years." She replied, "Doctor, I couldn't have done it without coffee!"

While this may be an extreme instance, it has the virtue of being true and it illustrates all of the societal biases against women as well as the acceptance by a woman of a diagnosis of neurosis or menopause in the face of serious illness. Women are expected to be weak, are expected to complain of vague symptoms such as fatigue. Beyond that, there is always the menopause to blame. The best thing that could happen to women would be the abolition of the menopause, not because it is intolerable but because it's a catchall container into which all manner of unexplained symptoms are pitched. In contrast, were a man to complain of constant fatigue, he would probably be hospitalized instantly for a complete work-up and a diagnosis would be made within a week.

An excellent paper, "Alleged Psychogenic Disorders in Women" by K. J. Lennane, lists the complaints of women that physicians routinely impute to neurosis even in the face of ample evidence of organic cause. Nausea of pregnancy, premenstrual tension, and the menopause come readily to mind, but the list also includes infantile colic attributed to the mother's neurosis and carpal tunnel syndrome, which happens to occur most frequently in postmenopausal women. That these are reflections of a male-oriented society and a male-dominated profession is certainly clear to any woman. The pertinence of discussing them in this chapter rests with their warning value. If your physician murmurs that a symptom is psychosomatic, you should neither accept nor deny this suggestion until you have given it some thought. Look closely at your complaint, and ask yourself whether it is stress dependent. Question your life style and your sleeping and drinking habits; look yourself in the eye. Look particularly carefully at whether your complaint serves as an excuse for you at home or at work or whether it allows you to be treated differently, protected more or excused from unpleasant tasks. Such secondary gains frequently maintain symptoms in even well-adjusted, dynamic women. The body readily expresses the psyche's unconscious needs, and those "sick headaches" or recurrent fatigue or "bad colds" give many a woman a little more attention at home or a little more respite at work. After you have done all this and have come to the conclusion that you had the same stress last year and you didn't feel this way, go back to your physician and say so. Say you have looked at it, describe the factors you have considered, and then insist that you wish to explore further.

EMERGENCY CARE

Suppose that you are in a strange city and you suddenly become ill. Carry it further, and you are ill in a foreign country. What do you do? You know no one; you are unfamiliar with the hospitals and perhaps even the language. Most likely you will turn to the hotel manager who will supply the name of a physician. If your problem is a simple one, this may suffice, but if it is serious and requires hospitalization, you must be prepared to make your own choices. As a general rule you should ask to be taken to the university hospital if there is one, unless you have had the opportunity to call your personal physician long-distance and a better solution is forthcoming. This at least assures the highest quality of care in that community. Once in the emergency room, you will be seen first by a resident who will assess the situation and perhaps say that you need to be seen by a surgeon. Your next question should be, "If you needed a surgeon for your daughter in this hospital, whom would you call?" This question is entirely different from "Whom would you suggest?" because if the resident happens at that moment to be rotating through the service with Drs. A, B, and C, it is likely that one of them will be named. However, all residents know well who are the competent (and incompetent) physicians in that hospital in their discipline; each hospital has at least one "doctor's doctor" who somehow has all the medical and nursing staff families as patients because they know who is the best. If you ask the right question, you'll find that person and that's who you want.

But suppose you are in an automobile accident and find yourself in a hospital in a community alien to you. You are there not by your own choice, but because that is where the ambulance driver took you. Immediate care will lessen the urgency—bleeding will be stopped, intravenous fluids begun, some assessment of the gravity of the situation will be made. If the hospital is small and rural, it will be ill-prepared to deal with serious injury of the head, chest, or abdomen, and once your medical condition is stabilized, they will suggest and arrange for transfer to a more appropriate hospital. Here again, you will be offered some choices, and if you are too far away from your own physician and hospital, the wisest decision is to request transfer to the nearest university health center complex. Some hospitals other than university centers provide excellent care for the most complicated problems, but you have no way of knowing which they are, and you certainly wish to avoid a second transfer later.

If you have any condition that requires constant therapy, such as diabetes, allergies, or epilepsy, make sure that you *always* wear an identification tag, such as the Medic-Alert emblem, which gives the diagnosis and a collect call telephone number for additional information. (Write Medic-Alert, Turlock, California 95380 for further information.) An unconscious person cannot give a history, and your prior illness may be either the cause of your admission or may be seriously complicating it.

One last word about emergencies—they occur at home as well. If an accident happens or a family member suddenly becomes acutely ill, do not bother to telephone your physician. This will take costly minutes and the physician will almost certainly say, "Go immediately to the emergency room at the hospital." You should save the time of the call and go directly there, either by ambulance (call the local number, often 911) or in a private car or taxi. If possible, call or have someone call ahead to the emergency room to tell them you are coming and let them know the problem. Your physician knows, and you should know, that the little black bag and a medical presence are almost impotent in any true emergency and that a house call would do little except waste time. What is needed is immediate access to an X-ray machine, intravenous fluids, medications that a physician is unlikely to carry, and often sophisticated equipment housed only in a hospital.

Orders should be left in your house that specify exactly which hospital is to be used for which family member: the hospital(s) on which your pediatrician, internist, or general practitioner has staff privileges. The resident in the emergency room will phone the physician, but in the meanwhile the patient is being cared for in the best place with the best facilities and staff.

HOSPITALS

To most people, a hospital is a frightening place. It has unfamiliar machines and smells; it contains seriously ill and dying people; it is impersonal; it is above all mysterious. Processions of people in different uniforms troop through your room, each punching or poking or stabbing you for a different reason, until finally you lose track and simply submit. Once you submit, you have become "institutionalized"; you have accepted your own depersonalization. If you are seriously ill, this matters very little, but if you are comparatively well, it disturbs you. What are your defenses?

YOUR RIGHTS AS A PATIENT

In 1973, the American Hospital Association published a patient's bill of rights to which all accredited hospitals must accede. The following is an expanded updated version from Mt. Sinai Hospital in New York City, which is typical of those supplied to patients on admission to most hospitals across the country.

Quality care for all patients

You have the right to receive the best inpatient, outpatient or emergency treatment and access to programs that we can provide without regard to race, color, sex, age, religion, national origin, handicap, veteran status or source of payment.

Information

You have the right to know the name of the physician responsible for your care and to receive from your physician complete current information concerning your medical problems, the planned course of treatment, the probable length of hospitalization and the prognosis or medical outlook for the future, in terms you can be reasonably expected to understand. If your physician thinks that it is not medically advisable to give such information to you, it will be made available to an appropriate person on your behalf.

You have the right to participate in decisions that affect your care and treatment.

You have the right to consult with other physicians or specialists provided they have hospital staff privileges.

You have the right to know the name and function of each staff member who attends to you and who will perform any procedure or treatment.

Because this is a teaching institution, affiliated with a wide range of educational programs, you will meet doctors, nurses and students-in-training for other health care professions. Many of them will be involved in your care, assisting in the 24-hour, seven-day weekly services you need while hospitalized. They are taught to function as a team in patient care interests, and are under expert professional supervision. We believe that our patients benefit from the extra attention of these professionals and paraprofessionals in training.

Giving consent

You have the right to receive from your physician information necessary to give informed consent prior to the start of any operation, procedure and/or treatment. Except in emergencies, this explanation must include the risks that may be involved, the probable chance of success, the effects of the tests or treatment, the amount of pain or discomfort that may be entailed, and how long this may be expected to last. You must also be told if there is more than one medically acceptable way to treat your illness and the risks and benefits of alternative treatments.

You have the right to read and to be given a complete explanation of any consent form you are asked to sign, and to question and modify, with your physician, any part of the form that does not apply to your consent before you sign it.

Declining treatment

You have the right to decline further treatment. In taking such a step, consider your decision carefully and discuss it with your physician and family so that you understand the full extent of the consequences to your health.

Leaving against medical advice

You have the right to leave the hospital against your doctor's advice unless you cannot maintain your own safety, as defined by law, or have an infectious disease hazardous to others. If you do leave against your doctor's advice the hospital will not be responsible for any harm this may cause you, and you will be asked to sign an "Against Medical Advice" form.

Privacy

You have the right to every consideration of both your personal privacy and the privacy of your medical program. Case discussions and consultations are confidential. Your permission will be requested if you are to be presented at any conference or teaching exercise at which personnel other than those directly involved in your care is present.

Confidentiality

You have the right to confidential medical records.

No person or agency outside of those taking care of you can see them unless authorized by you, or by law. Under certain insurance programs, such as Medicare, your records may be reviewed before payment is approved.

If you are a minor, under 18 years of age, your rights pertaining to release of information differ from those of adults. Your doctor or nurse will explain these to you and to your parent or guardian.

Transfer to another institution

You have the right to expect that within its capacity the hospital will make reasonable response to your request for services. The hospital must provide diagnostic evaluation, necessary medical care, and, if necessary, arrangements for your transfer to another health facility when medically permissible. You have the right to receive information and explanation concerning the needs for and alternatives to such a transfer. The health facility to which you are to be transferred must first have accepted you for transfer.

Participation in research

You have the right to be told if the hospital plans to use experimental procedures or drugs during your care and to choose whether or not you will participate. You have the right to ask how your participation will help you and/or others. Your refusal to participate in research will not prejudice your continued medical treatment at the hospital.

Payment

You have the right to receive a bill itemizing hospital charges related to your care and are encouraged to examine it and to ask questions about any portion that you do not understand.

You have the right to ask for information and help in receiving financial benefits, for which you may be eligible, to help pay your hospital bills.

Complaints

You have the right to voice grievances to our staff, our governing body and the New York State Department of Health without fear of reprisal.

Participation in your health care

Your active participation will help us render better health care to you. Give accurate and complete information about your past illnesses, about other times you have been hospitalized, about medications you are taking, any allergies you may have, and other matters relating to your health.

Be sure to keep your appointments. If you cannot, notify the doctor, hospital or others who are concerned. Follow instructions carefully. Let the doctor or nurse know if you do not understand any part of them.

If you feel you cannot follow the instructions, say so. If you have any problems at home that may interfere with your carrying out your doctor's orders, a social worker may be able to help you. The nurse will call one for you. Follow your health care plan carefully once it has been agreed upon. Notify your doctor or nurse promptly of any sudden or unexpected change in your health.

Your responsibilities as a patient

Following hospital rules and regulations will help the hospital ensure your safety and comfort and that of other patients.

You are asked to respect your roommates' rights to privacy and quiet; to use radio, television and lights in a manner that will not disturb others. Remember, many patients need a lot of rest.

You are asked to limit your visitors to two at a time during visiting hours, and to ask them to maintain a quiet atmosphere and observe smoking regulations which are posted throughout the hospital. Smoking is not allowed in any patient room or bathroom. In addition, the New York State Health Code states that "priority" is to be given to the "rights of nonsmokers," so you and your visitors may be asked to refrain from smoking in the patient lounge.

You are responsible for using hospital supplies and equipment carefully in order to assure that they will be available for future patients.

You are requested to provide information for insurance processing of your bills, to pay them promptly, and to ask any questions you have about them as soon as possible.

ADDITIONAL SAFEGUARDS

In a growing number of states, patients now have the legal right to see their hospital records in spite of the opposition of many doctors who say that patients would not understand the meaning of the entries.

A recent development is the presence at about half the hospitals in the United States of patient advocates, also known as patient representatives or ombudsmen, who have nothing to do with caregiving. They are on the hospital payroll, in some cases assisted by a volunteer staff, to restore the personal touch, to bend some of the rules to accommodate a patient, to explain some of the doctor's orders and procedures when the doctor is too busy to do so, to arrange for special payment plans, and to provide emotional support for the family. (When you are admitted to a hospital, if you aren't given the patient representative's name along with the patient's bill of rights, ask whether the hospital has such a staff member and get the phone number.)

If your hospital is located in a state that has passed Living Will legislation and you have signed such a document, ask to have it attached to your hospital chart. If your state has *not* passed such legislation, make your wishes known and ask that they be honored to the full extent of the law.

According to an account in *The New York Times* (June 23, 1988) "about half of the nation's 6,000 hospitals now have ethics committees, most of them created . . . in response to a plea for better hospital policies following the celebrated Quinlan case." (Karen Ann Quinlan became comatose in 1975, but it took her family ten more years to win a court order permitting her to be removed from a respirator. She died in 1985.) Medical ethicists, also called bioethicists, are attempting to help resolve the moral and legal problems raised by technological advances in genetic engineering, third-party reproductive procedures, organ transplants, and the like. Robert M. Veatch, professor of religion and medical ethics at the Robert Kennedy Center for Bioethics at Georgetown University in Washington, D.C., has said, "Biophilosophers have chipped away at medical paternalism." Although the ethicists refrain from making decisions, their role is to analyze problems, clarify information, and suggest principles to be considered in arriving at a course of action. The positive results, according to Dr. Arthur Capalan, director of the Center for Biomedical Ethics at the University of Minnesota, is that physicians are more truthful in telling patients exactly what the diagnosis is and what to expect; they exercise more care in getting informed consent for treatment; and they have begun to see the patient not as a passive client but as an important participant in the healing process, a person who sets goals and can select different options.

If you and your family can profit from consultation with a medical ethicist because of confusion or conflict about treatment, be sure to ask whether such a specialist is available on the hospital staff, and, if not, find out how to reach one.

YOUR COMFORT AS A PATIENT

The cost of a private room in most hospitals is very high and is not covered by insurance, so your purse will favor your having a roommate.

By and large this contributes to your comfort and decreases your anxiety. You have someone to talk to; you have a mutual aid source; you have company. The drawbacks come when your roommate is a chronic complainer, entertains a constant parade of noisy guests, or keeps you awake at night by groaning or snoring. Under any of these circumstances you should speak with the head nurse and ask to be moved to another room. Discharges occur every day and within a reasonable time you should be relocated. Such requests are not unusual nor, if done with courtesy, are they interpreted as griping.

Both your phone and your visitors maintain your connections with the outside world; you will gradually sort out the staff and greet some of them with pleasure and enthusiasm; you will begin to understand the routines. All these lessen your anxiety and improve your state of well-being. Because most admissions are less than a week in duration, you will not have suffered inordinately and your next admission will be fraught with considerably less apprehension. If your condition or treatment requires a longer hospitalization, you will find that you adapt quite well to the restrictions imposed on you by the hospital, just as you adapted when you first went to camp or to college. The difference is that your psychic strength has been sapped by your illness and your flexibility does not compare with that of a healthy person.

At the time of admission for more serious conditions, many patients and families worry about whether they should engage a "special duty" nurse. Will the floor nurses come when one rings the bell or will they be too busy? Can the nursing station down the hall respond adequately to the patient's personal needs? The way to find this out at admission is to ask the nurses how they feel about the matter. The extent of nursing required will be a large factor; the number of patients on the floor another. In most situations there are enough nurses to meet all the needs of the patients, and they are highly skilled in dealing with the equipment and procedures required for the specialty clustered on that floor. If, for any reason, you feel that extra care is needed, the hospital has a roster of both registered nurses and licensed practical nurses who are available for special duty. The cost of a registered nurse is considerably greater than a practical nurse and in most situations there is no need for the former because the goal is largely to meet needs of creature comfort. Occasionally a physician feels that extra assistance is needed and has a particular nurse whose skills are appropriate to the case. You should accept this advice.

If you have worries about your convalescent period or if you will need further help or treatment at home, ask to see a member of the Social Service department. All of the community facilities are at their finger tips and they can be very helpful in arranging for the best post-hospital care.

The intensive care unit is far and away the most distressing hospital area. Patients are submerged under equipment, sleep is disturbed by constant monitoring, privacy is nonexistent, and relatives usually may visit only five minutes every hour. Families wait for each hourly visit wondering what they will find and what to say and often the patient is too ill to know or care whether someone visited an hour ago. The visiting rules were made to insure optimal care and to limit the number of people hovering around a bed when patient monitoring must be done repeatedly. If a member of your family is in such a unit and your life is being torn to tatters by these waits and unsatisfactory visits, do not be afraid to tell the nurse exactly what you intend to do—you will be back at six o'clock: you can be reached at such-and-such a number. Ask her to reassure the patient that you were there and will return. If the unit is comparatively quiet, she may allow you to stay longer than the five minutes if it will comfort the patient.

COOPERATIVE CARE UNITS

In April, 1979, University Hospital of the New York University Medical Center established the world's first cooperative care center, a facility combining patient education and family participation in medical care. Since that time, similar facilities have become available in a number of hospitals and medical centers nationwide. Typical units have the appearance of motel suites and provide accommodations for patients and partners of their choice—spouse, adult offspring, close friend. The partner, who is housed and fed without charge for the duration of the stay, agrees to spend from four to twenty-four hours a day with the patient and is taught to perform many tasks traditionally performed by nurses and nurses' aides. To qualify for such an arrangement where it is available, the patient must be able to walk independently or with a cane or to get around in a wheelchair. Typical patients are those who enter for chemotherapy or are sufficiently ambulatory to be transferred from another part of the hospital, or suffer from heart disease, vascular disorders, or have orthopedic problems.

Hospital services remain in place, and the patient does the walking, with or without the companion to the various treatment rooms, radiology department, nurses' station, dining room, and lounges. The patient is also given the prescribed supply of medication, and the companion is taught how to administer the drugs and how to keep a detailed chart.

This arrangement has many advantages, both for the hospital and the patient. The originator of the plan points out that the average cost is 40 to 45 percent lower than it would be for the same number of days in a traditional setting. As for the patients, by encouraging them to participate in their own care and maximizing their role and the family's role in recovery, everyone's dependence on the hospital is reduced. In addition, the creation of a "wellness" environment has a strong positive effect on the patient's morale, which in turn affects the progress of recovery.

YOU AND YOUR PHYSICIAN

Clearly, you expect your physician to provide good medical care, of which many facets have been covered above. But you have other expectations as well, some you may not consciously recognize and others may be unobtainable.

**WHAT YOU HAVE A RIGHT TO EXPECT
FROM YOUR PHYSICIAN**

Above all, you want *help*. If you are threatened with a serious illness, you not only want to be confident that you have been referred to the most competent specialists but you want some time to discuss the threat as well.

Let us assume that you have just discovered a lump in your neck and your doctor has confirmed that indeed it is a cause for further investigation, probably surgery. These are the facts, but many other things are whirling through your mind. Benign or malignant? How much surgery? How many hospital days? How much time off work? Who will look after the children? Will I have a disfiguring scar? Why do I have a lump at all? How much will it cost and how will we find the money? If I am hospitalized for a long time, what will it do to my marriage, my relationship? Who will look after me as I convalesce? If it is a malignancy, how will I face it? You may be tempted to play the courageous role and say nothing out loud, and unless your physician brings up the subject of your anxiety, you simply leave the office and continue to whirl at home, in bed, at work. You may not even wish to share this with your husband or best friend because you don't wish to "worry them." The result is a load of unnecessary anxiety piled on top of the realistic amount that the unsettling news brings you, and you may enter the hospital having lost both sleep and weight, with your blood pressure 20 points above its normal level.

Such courage is not only unnecessary but unwise. Your physician owes you help just as much as you are owed laboratory results, and you have every right to discuss all of these questions. It may well be that the schedule is too tight at that moment to cover the ground, but you should ask whether you can make another appointment in the very near future only to talk. Often you can be immediately reassured that the overwhelming odds are against malignancy and that, if it is benign, surgery is simple and hospitalization short. But, the "ifs" still lurk in the back of your mind and should be handled on top of the table.

Of course, many of your questions are not for the physician to answer. No matter how frankly you have discussed your marital situation, no other person can predict how your spouse will react or can tell you how to find money or a babysitter. But you can, and should, have every question answered about the medical situation. If and when surgery turns out to be agreed on, you can then be referred to a social worker or a community agency to help in arrangements for children and for convalescence.

Once you enter the hospital for surgery, the surgeon rather than your physician will probably be your "physician of record." Here the issue of informed consent will surface. The surgeon *must*, both legally and morally, describe to you the procedure anticipated, its probable outcome and complications, the period of convalescence you may have to anticipate, and possible alternatives, if any. Multi-syllable medical jargon should not be accepted. You have the right to understand exactly what will happen to you as far as the surgeon knows. The occasional rare complication naturally cannot be envisaged, but the usual procedure and its course can be. You should be quite clear that you understand as much as a layman can about what will happen to you. Your physician will undoubtedly come to see you frequently when making rounds and, because of personal knowledge, will be able to allay any new anxieties as well as interpret any findings that other physicians have left unexplained. It is possible that your doctor will also be in the operating room (whether you know it or not), anxious to find out what the status is, and will see you again the next day. There will have been discussions with the surgeon and a plan of action for the future will have begun to unroll.

Now let us suppose that you have a malignancy, that the surgery was far more radical than anticipated, the hospitalization longer, the cost greater, the scar wider, and the convalescence more stormy and fraught with new symptoms from X-ray or chemotherapy. The worst has happened and more decisions must be made. There will be conferences between your physician, the surgeon, and the radiologists and a plan of medical action will be formulated; the social service department will assist in sorting out the family and financial problems. Even so, your anxiety about *you* is high. What can you expect then?

You can expect, and should receive, comfort and honesty. Any question that you ask about your future should be answered. That last sentence is very carefully worded, and the appropriate analogy is to the sex education of a child. There is substantial agreement that in childhood, sexual questions should not be answered before they are asked because the child's unconscious or preconscious adapts the question to the amount of information that can be assimilated. Similarly, in questions of malignancy and death the patient virtually always asks the questions she wants answered, and no others. If your physician tells you that today most malignancies are treatable and many curable, you are not being conned: this is the truth. You should not dwell on all the frightening things that may or may not happen; you must participate actively in your own recovery. On the other hand, active participation depends on full information, so you will be told, for instance, that you should not return to work while getting radiation because you will probably be nauseated for a few weeks. The path of your immediate future can be accurately charted, but you cannot expect to be told what will happen in two years because no one knows. You and your doctor will be a team for that period, making decisions as you go in light of what is known about medicine and about you.

While one example does not cover all circumstances, it should indicate the dimensions of your physician's responsibility to you under the worst eventuality and you can then figure out what you should expect in other, less dire situations. Without question your physician should accept with grace any request for a second opinion; in difficult cases such a consultation usually is welcomed as either a new slant on the problem or confirmation. Any situation that offers a choice of therapies with different risks and side effects must be completely discussed: this is the essence of "informed consent." If a new approach to your problem is available only in another city, your physician should give you an objective evaluation of the treatment, refer you to lay literature in which it has been discussed, and, if you wish it, refer you to that site. Such a referral assumes that a complete record of your illness and laboratory findings will be sent prior to your appointment.

You also have every right to expect complete confidentiality from your physician, and this includes responsibility not to discuss anything in your record without your permission, even with your family. There will, however, be times when you will not only allow such a family discussion but will ask to have one. If, for instance, you will have to restrict your activities, it is important that your family understand why this is so and exactly what you can and cannot do. Their cooperation will be more complete if their information is first hand rather than through your interpretation. Furthermore, you may not be a reliable informant, because you may want to spare your family the extra tasks and responsibilities. However, it can't be said too often that successful treatment is the result of "team" participation. When those who are close to the patient become actively involved in performing the day to day chores that are part of the prescribed regimen, the probable outcome is vastly better.

You have a right to expect that the doctor or the doctor's nurse will return your phone call within a reasonable length of time when a message has been left with an answering service or on the telephone recording tape.

You have one further right—dignity. To be called "honey" or "dearie" is to be robbed of your identity by patronization. To be called by your first name without your permission is to establish a relationship in which you have been immediately cast as the meek, docile being who obeys orders. Some patients prefer being called Mary rather than Mrs. Brown, but the initiative should rest with the patient. State your preference but beware of an office in which first names are bandied around by physician and staff alike. You will never be treated as a colleague by such a group: you will always be the helpless little girl regardless of your age.

A word about doctors who overbook patients so that appointment times don't mean very much. If on several occasions (once is excusable) you arrive well in advance of your scheduled appointment time and have to spend the next two hours reading old magazines and listening to music not of your own choosing before you are directed to an examining room and then have to spend another half-hour waiting for the doctor, you have every right to inform the doctor that your time is valuable too and that you resent having to waste it in the waiting room. There are, in fact, some patients whose time is worth as much money as the doctor's, and a few of these have sent bills accompanied by letters explaining that they expect to be paid for time lost.

WHAT YOU SHOULD NOT EXPECT FROM YOUR PHYSICIAN

Your physician is neither your parent nor your best friend, even though you have often confided more intimate facts than you have to anyone else. To survive as a good physician objectivity must be maintained. You have no right to expect "love," in the sense of protection from all evil, nor should you ask advice on personal matters. Whether you should break off a relationship with your alcoholic lover or husband, whether you should buy a house instead of renting, or whether you should change your job—these are your decisions. Granted that each of these may cause you anxiety and be reflected in your physical condition, the physician has only two responsibilities: to advise you to see a psychotherapist or direct you to various community resources if your way of dealing with stress and conflict is to drink too much or hit the children or gobble pills, *and* in acute situations, such as death in the family, to prescribe a tranquilizer or a sleeping pill to tide you over, but you should not press to continue such drugs indefinitely. Supportive drugs not only postpone solutions but they can become problems in themselves.

Some patients feel that they have a right to manage their own illnesses and demand treatments that they have read about—multivitamins, laetrile, acupuncture, the newest diet. These therapies may be pharmacologically innocuous even though ineffective and costly, but they may, as well, be particularly contraindicated in your case. Your physician can and should explain to you why such treatment will not be prescribed for you whether because you wish to substitute it for more effective (but more discomfiting) medication or because you are using the medicine as a crutch to prevent yourself from facing reality. Even sophisticated patients may try to pressure a physician into prescribing antibiotics so that they can feel that something is being done, even when antibiotics are ineffective, as in viral infections. They also involve needless costs, and they may have unpleasant side effects, such as allergic reactions or digestive upset. Once you have trusted yourself to a physician's knowledge and judgment, you should accept advice without pressing for something else.

Nothing irritates and embarrasses a physician more than to be asked to play a collusive role in some questionable enterprise: to provide a medical excuse for an irresponsible child who played hookey, to improvise an acceptable reason for your having failed to show up at work when the truth was that you had a hangover, to lie on your behalf in filling out an insurance form. Responsible adults don't ask friends to lie for them, and you certainly shouldn't expect your doctor to do so.

Each physician has a few patients for whom "demands" are a way of life. Often they are rich enough to take the position that if they "pay" they can "demand." Implicit in this behavior is the assumption that the physician is their servant. These patients (more often women than men) have no insight into their infantile behavior, or that they are making a profession of being "ill" in order to manipulate their environment, whether this be the physician or the spouse or the children. They disrupt an office routine; they cause the physician to groan when their name is on the day's appointment list; they are the ones who take particular umbrage at being referred to a psychiatrist. When they have used up the tolerance of one physician, they move to the next. Their charts are thick; their bathroom cabinets full of pills; they frequently see more than one physician at a time without revealing this. Unwittingly, they are receiving the worst possible medical care because they will not accept good care.

WHAT YOUR PHYSICIAN HAS A RIGHT TO EXPECT FROM YOU

A doctor-patient relationship is most effective when responsibilities are shared. At its best, the relationship is between allies: you are partners in dealing with situations about which you have unequal information but in which you both have rights.

Patient responsibilities include a number of niceties that you would never ignore with a friend but are often ignored in physicians' offices. If you cannot keep an appointment, phone as far ahead as you can so that another patient can be scheduled for that time. If you must be late because the babysitter didn't come, phone the office before leaving home to find out if the doctor will still be able to see you or if it would be better to reschedule.

There was a time when it could be assumed that a doctor would send the patient a bill for services rendered and most of the time the bills got paid. Nowadays, it is usually expected that the fee for the visit be paid in cash or by check before the patient leaves the office. However, if you cannot muster the total amount at that moment, some offices will listen sympathetically and allow you to pay the bill in monthly installments. The important thing is to tell them your intentions so they know what to expect and plan their billing accordingly.

Another area of patient responsibility, rarely emphasized though exceedingly important to all physicians, is compliance to a therapeutic regimen. You should never lie to a physician about pills you have not taken or procedures you have failed to carry out. Nor should you withhold information about visits to another doctor who has made other recommendations and prescribed other medication or a nonmedical treatment such as a change in diet or acupuncture. Several things may result from such deception. The physician may assume that the regimen has failed and change course to a different, probably less appropriate one when you do not appear to be responding. Or, if you found that the medication produced unpleasant side effects and you stopped taking it without saying so, you have kept information to yourself that might be of use to another patient taking the same drug. It is also possible that, though the side effects are unpleasant, there are no other suitable options and the outcome of untreated disease is far worse. Any competent physician welcomes the truth and can, if necessary, explain to you why some unpleasantness is in your own best interest.

THE COMMUNITY OF HEALTH CARE

The physician is not the only source of health care: the network of health services stretches far beyond the physician's office and may provide as much as 90 percent of the total care. One good example is in the area of vision. You see an ophthalmologist who tells you that your child has amblyopia, a condition of muscle imbalance of the eyes that interferes with efficient focusing. If this condition is of moderate extent, surgery will not be suggested, but you will be referred to a clinic where special muscle exercises are taught and progress checked. The ophthalmologist will check the status of the condition in six months, but in the interim you will be receiving excellent and important health care continuously.

Take a more serious situation. You are a diabetic and your ophthalmologist has told you for a number of years that your retinae are deteriorating; you obviously know this because your vision is decreasing. There comes a point when you can no longer manage your job or your housekeeping or your transportation. The physician has done everything known and is powerless, but the resources of the community haven't yet been touched. Referral to a center whose entire purpose is the retraining of the blind should be made. Often physicians are ignorant of community facilities, and you may have to seek these out on your own or through a social service organization. Once you are appropriately linked up to a group, a program or an institution, you will embark on an educational experience of which your physician does not know the details or the techniques but only knows the results and the availability.

The number of paramedical services is so vast that it is the rare physician who is aware of them all. The accident or stroke victim who requires months of rehabilitation deals almost entirely with physical, occupational, and speech therapists under a doctor's supervision; a woman who has had a mastectomy gains more ongoing help from Reach for Recovery than from her surgeon; the multiple sclerosis victim is bolstered by the MS Society and its members though her physician is supervising her medications. The examples are innumerable, but almost all of these groups help to establish a way of dealing with a new problem or of minimizing difficulties with a long-standing one. In any of these areas your physician's responsibility rests with knowing what facilities relate to your problem and then referring you to the proper ones.

Another resource available in nearly every community is the Visiting Nurse Association. This group offers a variety of nursing services, from skilled nurse to homemaker, that may provide a much-needed respite for the family member responsible for a chronically ill patient. All too often physicians take for granted that if you are looking after your bedridden parent, no other caregiver is needed. If they have never had such a responsibility, they cannot conceive of the daily drain, of your need to get out of the house two or three times a week to walk in the park or go to a movie or visit a friend. (Many communities also offer respite services for long-term caregivers.)

The group whose responsibility it is to know *all* of these resources is the social service department of a hospital or community. If you are the victim of a chronic illness or the caregiver of a patient with one, it is well worth exploring with such a department some means of making the burden more tolerable. If the caregiver or the recipient of the care is over 62, the other source is the local Area Agency on Aging.

Over the past decade a number of new categories of health practitioners have appeared, and one, the nurse-midwife, has reappeared. She is the prototype for the others, a professional taught to deal competently with normal pregnancies and to recognize those abnormalities that should be referred to a physician. Physicians' assistants, pediatric and adult nurse practitioners, while doing different tasks, have the same orientation. Well-child care, monitoring of chronic disease, treatment of minor complaints, carrying out assigned tasks that they have been specially taught to perform—these are some of the ways in which they function as physician extenders. The school nurse, the industrial nurse, the "medic" are examples that come readily to mind. Many clinics and group practices include one or more such professionals and you should not feel that you have been cheated if you see them and not the physician during a routine visit. However, at times when you want to discuss a particular problem in detail with the doctor, you need not accept the services of an intermediary.

Other professionally trained people who use such procedures as biofeedback, hypnosis, acupuncture, and meditation are increasingly found to benefit certain patients and certain diseases, and physicians frequently refer suitable patients to such health care professionals. Osteopaths currently have very similar training to physicians and some excellent hospitals are staffed entirely by them. They can prescribe drugs; they can operate; they are fully licensed.

Dentists and podiatrists are examples of professions allied to medicine, sharing the same principles of belief and the same methods of treatment. They limit their practice to one area of the body and in these areas have a competence far exceeding physicians. They have comfortable relationships with the medical profession and referrals flow easily both ways.

Chiropractors have a limited area of skill—the manipulation of the musculoskeletal system, where, they believe, most disease originates.

Many a physician sends his patients with backaches to them after being assured that there is no underlying disease that should be treated surgically or by some other means, and many patients get a great deal of relief from pain. Nonetheless, the danger lies in the philosophic underpinnings of the profession. Medicine believes and teaches that there are multiple causes of disease and each should be treated in a particular fashion; chiropractic does not share this belief. A patient who deals first or exclusively with a chiropractor may get relief from pain for the moment but may harbor a disease that should be treated in quite another fashion.

Beyond these groups lie a wide range of "healers," and it is not uncommon to find patients dealing both with a physician and a nonmedical healer, particularly when the culture of the patient is alien to that of the physician. In many Third World countries, two-system healing exists. The patient goes to the clinic in the morning and to the herbalist, witch doctor, or medicine man in the evening as a way of hedging the bets! In our own society the same behavior often prevails. The patient, particularly if her disease is life threatening, will follow the physician's orders scrupulously while at the same time going to revival meetings or seeking an herbalist. The wise patient discusses this with her doctor who, it is hoped, can accommodate comfortably to such a dual track once assured there is no harm involved.

Many people are intimidated by physicians and the world of illness and hospitals and, thus, they forget that this territory is no different from any other. In a department store you have no hesitation in asking for directions or in pointing out inadequacies of merchandise or service. When you travel, you expect the maps to be accurate and the hotels as advertised; you assume (perhaps groundlessly) that trains and planes will be on schedule. The land of medicine should be no different. The maps should be as accurate and the directions as clear, and if you want to get from here to there, you should follow them. No worlds are without detours or accidents or frustrations, but one need not add to the vicissitudes by ignorance or false expectations. If you ask questions and follow directions carefully and intelligently, you have every right to get the best of medical care.

ic terms
Part Two
Encyclopedia of Health and Medical Terms

AA • *See* ALCOHOLICS ANONYMOUS.

Abdominal Pain • Acute pain or persistent ache in the region between the chest and the pelvis is a symptom that may be difficult to diagnose. Because the abdominal cavity contains the stomach, liver, spleen, gallbladder, kidneys, appendix, intestines, ovaries, and during pregnancy the expanding uterus, a disorder or infection of any of these organs may be the source of the discomfort.

Pain that disappears within a few hours and doesn't recur may be due to indigestion. If accompanied by nausea and diarrhea and subsides within a day or two, it may be due to a comparatively harmless virus infection of the intestinal tract.

Among possible causes of severe upper abdominal pain are the onset of a heart attack or food poisoning, both of which require emergency medical treatment. The formation of gallstones leading to gallbladder inflammation will produce pain ranging from mild and recurrent to acute enough to require hospitalization. When gallbladder inflammation affects the liver, symptoms of jaundice and hepatitis may produce pain when pressure is applied to the upper right side of the abdomen.

Colitis is likely to produce abdominal cramps and attacks of diarrhea; a peptic ulcer manifests itself in a burning pain a few hours after meals. Gastritis, an inflammation of the stomach wall, may be a temporary condition caused by tension, too much spicy food, caffeine, and/or alcohol. Its characteristically severe pain may subside when a new regimen is established.

Cramps in the lower abdomen sometimes occur immediately before or during the first day of menstruation, and for some women menstrual pain may spread to the back and down the leg. Among other causes of lower abdominal pain are endometriosis or endometritis (disorders of the uterus), infection of the fallopian tubes, ectopic pregnancy, and intestinal obstruction.

Persistent pain localized in the lower right part of the abdomen is a characteristic signal of the onset of appendicitis.

Abortion • The expulsion of a fetus through medical intervention or spontaneously.

Induced abortion (often called therapeutic) abortion is still one of the most common methods of birth control worldwide, with an estimated one pregnancy in three deliberately terminated. Since January, 1973, when the U.S. Supreme Court declared the antiabortion laws of two states to be unconstitutional, the decision to terminate a pregnancy during its first trimester (up to 12 weeks) has been a private matter between a woman and her doctor. Abortion is now the most frequently performed operation in the United States and one of the safest.

Spontaneous abortion is the expulsion of a dead embryo or fetus from the body of a pregnant woman before 20 completed weeks of gestation; also known as miscarriage. Because many miscarriages are not recognized, it is difficult to estimate the number of pregnancies that terminate in this way. Doctors, however, estimate the figures at one in ten. Of these, most occur between the sixth and tenth week of pregnancy. *See* "Contraception and Abortion," "Pregnancy and Childbirth," and "Directory of Health Information."

Abscess • An accumulation of pus in an area where healthy tissue has been invaded and broken down by bacteria. An abscess may form anywhere in the body that might be vulnerable to bacterial infection—around a hangnail or splinter, around an infected tooth, in the breast, in the middle ear, in the lung. Many abscesses can be cured with antibiotics, but some require surgical incision and draining.

When harmful bacteria begin to destroy tissue, blood rushes to the spot to provide the white blood cells and antibodies necessary for fighting off the infection. The resulting mixture of blood cells, bacteria, and dead tissue is called pus. Pain is caused by the inflammation of adjacent tissues and the accumulation of pus pressing against the adjoining nerves. The blood concentration causes redness.

A simple abscess beneath the skin may break through the surface, drain, and heal itself. A skin abscess should never be squeezed or cut open by an untrained person. A doctor or the emergency services of the nearest hospital must be consulted at once if the redness that surrounds an abscess begins to travel in a visible line towards a gland.

A tooth abscess is not only the cause of pain, but can also lead to a serious systemic infection if the bacteria get into the bloodstream. Prompt surgical treatment combined with antibiotics is essential.

Abuse • *See* "Rape and Family Abuse."

Acetaminophen • The generic name of a nonprescription drug that relieves pain and reduces temperature. It is widely available in such products as Tylenol and Datril. It is especially useful for those with a low tolerance for aspirin, but, unlike aspirin, acetaminophen is not an anti-inflammatory drug and, therefore, is not effective in treating arthritis. Research indicates that when acetaminophen is combined with alcohol, Valium, Librium, or barbiturates, liver damage can result.

Acidity and Alkalinity • Acids and alkalies are produced by the body for various metabolic purposes. The stomach produces hydrochloric acid, which is essential in protein digestion; the kidneys produce the alkali ammonia to neutralize body chemistry. Small amounts of the alkali sodium bicarbonate (bicarbonate of soda, baking soda) can remedy mild hyperacidity of the stomach, but an overdose can cause metabolic alkalosis. The overuse of diuretics as a way of losing weight may result in excessive loss of acids through the urine. An overdose of aspirin may cause salicylate (acid) poisoning.

Like most body tissues, the lining of the vagina is normally acid. It becomes alkaline at the time of ovulation in order to keep the alkaline sperm alive. In cases of infertility caused by an invariable acid environment of the vagina, chemicals are prescribed to produce vaginal alkalinity.

Acne • A skin disorder occurring mainly in association with the hormonal changes of adolescence, although women may experience it for the first time when they are in their 20s or 30s. The increased amounts of androgen produced by both the male and female sex glands stimulate the sebaceous (oil) glands of the hair follicles to produce an increased amount of the fatty substance called *sebum* that is normally discharged through the pores to lubricate the skin. The overproduction of sebum results in oily skin. The characteristic pimples, pustules, and blackheads of acne are formed when the pores become plugged by the sebum that has backed up, mixed with the skin pigments, and leaked into surrounding areas.

Acne is not caused by junk food or faulty hygiene: the chief cause is the onset of puberty combined with the hereditary factors that govern the oiliness of the skin. Mild cases usually clear up by themselves, especially when the affected areas are kept free of oil by regular cleansing. Nonprescription products containing benzoyl peroxide are helpful, and, for more stubborn cases, vitamin A acid cream (resorcinol), sun lamp treatments, and tetracycline pills may be beneficial. Current experiments indicate that Accutane (isotretinoin) a synthetic derivative of vitamin A administered in pill form over several months drastically reduces the amount of sebum produced in acne patients, thus controlling the chief cause of acne lesions. This treatment must be administered and monitored by a doctor so that the onset of negative side effects can be taken into account. For many cases unresponsive to all other medication, the benefits of Accutane continue for years after the treatment has been discontinued. A word of warning: because the drug is known to cause birth defects, women of childbearing age should avoid pregnancy during treatment.

If acne has left scars and blemishes, a dermatologist can be consulted about the advisability of removing them by the skin-planing technique known as dermabrasion. *See* "Cosmetic Surgery."

Acquired Immune Deficiency Syndrome (AIDS) • A condition, usually fatal, recognized in 1979 in the United States but present for many years in Africa, in which the body's immune system becomes incapable of warding off diseases and infections that would normally be overcome. AIDS is caused by a virus that is sexually transmissable. At greatest risk have been homosexual males and intravenous drug abusers who spread the disease through contaminated needles. The latter group of AIDS victims is spreading the disease to women who in turn infect their newborn infants. Also at risk are hemophiliacs requiring frequent blood transfusions and women who have sexual intercourse with bisexual men. In parts of Africa, AIDS is becoming endemic in the heterosexual population. Not all those who carry the virus get the disease in its virulent form, and a significant number have developed antibodies to it. Major efforts are being made worldwide to develop a vaccine against AIDS, but until such protection becomes available, the condom is promoted as the most practical safeguard against sexually transmitted infection. AIDS has raised moral, ethical, professional, political, personal, and religious problems for which few universally acceptable solutions have been formulated. See KAPOSI'S SARCOMA, PNEUMOCYSTIC PNEUMONIA, MENINGITIS, "Sexual Health," and "Sexually Transmissable Diseases."

ACTH • Adrenocorticotropic hormone, a hormone secreted by the anterior lobe of the pituitary gland and carried by the blood to the adrenal glands whose outer layer or cortex is stimulated to produce cortisone and aldosterone, the steroid hormones. Since the development of adrenal steroids that can be taken orally and have fewer side effects, ACTH is rarely used for treatment but is sometimes used in a diagnostic test of adrenal function.

Acupuncture • A therapeutic technique developed in ancient China and based on the assumption that the stimulation of various parts of the body by rotating needles or finger pressure can alleviate pain and cure disease. While western scientists reject the explanation that this technique influences the flow of "vital energy" at critical points throughout the body, the anesthetic and analgesic effects of acupuncture are being explored with varying degrees of success, in many hospitals in the United States and Europe, especially in pain-control experiments. An innovative use of acupuncture has been undertaken to relieve addicts of the agitation and discomfort that accompanies withdrawal from crack, heroin, or alcohol. According to some authorities, acupuncture stimulates the release of the body's endorphins, the natural pain killers that resemble morphine in their chemical composition.

Before embarking on acupuncture treatment for any disorder, it is advisable to examine the practitioner's medical credentials and legal status. State-chartered acupuncture centers in various parts of the United States will provide detailed information about their activities on request.

Acute Symptom • A symptom of a disorder that has a sudden onset and runs a comparatively brief course such as an "acute" asthma attack as opposed to a persistent, or chronic, manifestation of a disorder. "Acute" should not be confused with "life-threatening."

Acyclovir • An antiviral drug used in the treatment of genital herpes. Introduced as an ointment and then for intravenous injection, acyclovir is now available in pill form under the trade name Zovirax. While it does not eliminate the herpes virus, it prevents the spread of infection to healthy cells. Definitive studies have not yet been made on cumulative side effects nor on how the drug affects pregnant women. See HERPES and "Sexually Transmissable Diseases."

Addiction • A compelling physical need for or psychological dependence on a drug or chemical substance such that its habitual use must be maintained no matter how self-destructive the results. In recent years, the term has been more loosely applied to certain types of compulsive behavior such as overeating, gambling, and overspending so that the techniques successfully used by Alcoholics Anonymous can be duplicated by other self-help groups. See "Substance Abuse."

Addison's Disease • (adrenal insufficiency) A rare disorder whose immediate cause is failure of the adrenal gland cortex. The glandular underfunction is sometimes the result of tuberculosis. Other causes may be a tumor, hemorrhage, or any injury that interferes with hormone production. Addison's disease, once fatal, is now treated with cortisone and other forms of hormone replacement therapy in the same way that diabetes is treated with insulin.

Adenoma • A usually benign tumor composed of glandular tissue.

Adhesion • The union of two internal body surfaces that are normally separate and the formation of the fibrous, or scar, tissue that connects them. The scar tissue that forms around a surgical wound during the healing process may cling to adjoining areas causing them to fuse. Lung adhesions may occur after inflammation and scarring of the pleural membrane; abdominal adhesions may occur following peritonitis. Although most adhesions are painless and without consequence, they may occasionally cause an obstruction or malfunction that requires surgical correction. The incidence of postoperative adhesions has dramatically diminished as a result of early ambulation after surgery.

Adoptive Pregnancy • (donated embryo or embryo transfer) The transfer of an embryo, a few days after conception, (or a month or two if frozen after conception) from the uterus of a fertile woman to the uterus of an infertile woman with a synchronous menstrual cycle so that the pregnancy can continue in the infertile woman. The conception is achieved by artificially inseminating the fertile woman, usually with sperm from the partner of the infertile woman. See "Infertility" and Directory of Health Information.

Adrenalin • One of the hormones produced by the medulla or inner core of the adrenal glands; also known as epinephrine. This hormone maximizes the body's physiologic response to stress by increasing heart rate and blood pressure. By transforming the glycogen in the liver into glucose, adrenalin also provides the muscles with a quick source of energy so that they can perform effectively without suffering fatigue. Adrenalin dilates the pupils of the eyes for more effective vision and expands the bronchial tubes for more effective respiration. When the body sustains a wound, adrenalin increases the clotting capacity of the blood.

Aerobic Exercise • In common usage, an activity that maintains the heart beat at 70 percent of its maximum rate for 12 minutes or longer. Unlike anaerobic exercise, in which muscles are the source of energy, aerobics depend on oxygen to fuel the cardiovascular system, increasing the efficiency of the heart. Swimming, jogging, and walking briskly are effective aerobic activities. See "Fitness."

Afterbirth • See PLACENTA.

Agoraphobia • Literally, "fear of the marketplace." For those who suffer from this phobia, a panic attack occurs when they venture into public places or open spaces. This distress causes the victim to circumscribe activities and to refuse to leave the safety of home. Anxiety in this form is likely to be accompanied by hyperventilation, which in turn produces dizziness, sweating, weakness, and a sense of impending disaster. Agoraphobia, even in a mild manifestation, should be treated by a professional therapist.

AIDS • See ACQUIRED IMMUNE DEFICIENCY SYNDROME.

Air Pollution • See POLLUTION.

Air Sickness • See MOTION SICKNESS.

Al-Anon • An organization that, though separate from Alcoholics Anonymous, provides the same kind of help, support, and therapy for the family of the alcoholic that AA provides for the alcoholic. Alcoholism is considered a family disease because the alcoholic affects the mental and physical health of other members and their response in turn affects the alcoholic.

A person who suspects that any member of the household, including teenage children, is an alcoholic may find that going to Al-Anon meetings is an effective first step toward recognizing the illness for what it is and beginning to deal with it in a realistic way.

Al-A-Teen, a subsidiary of Al-Anon, is a fellowship for the adolescent children of alcoholics. See "Substance Abuse."

Alcohol • Any of a group of related chemical compounds derived from hydrocarbons. Ethyl alcohol, also called ethanol or grain alcohol, is the intoxicating ingredient of fermented and distilled beverages. Methyl alcohol, also known as wood alcohol or methanol, is widely used in industry as a solvent and a fuel. Taken internally, it is a poison that can lead to blindness and death. Rubbing alcohol, used on the skin as a cooling agent or disinfectant, may be ethyl alcohol made unfit for consumption by the addition of chemicals known as denaturants (denatured alcohol) or it may be another compound called isopropyl alcohol.

Alcoholic Beverages • Drinks that contain ethyl alcohol, the substance that results naturally from the fermentation of carbohydrates (sugars, such as those in grape mash, molasses, and apples, or starches, such as those in wheat, rice, barley, and other grains). Hard cider, beer, and ale contain about 3 to 5 percent alcohol; table wines about 10 percent; fortified wines like sherry about 20 percent. Beverages of higher alcoholic content, such as vodka, bourbon, and brandy, are called liquors or "hard" liquors and are produced by distilling the alcohol from the fermented mash. Liqueurs like Benedictine or Cointreau may contain as much as 35 percent alcohol, and whiskey and rum as much as 50 percent. The concentration of alcohol in a beverage is usually given in terms of "proof." Half of the proof number is the percentage of alcohol by volume; thus a 90-proof vodka is 45 percent alcohol, with the remainder made up of water, flavoring, and other ingredients. In assessing alcohol intake, it should be kept in mind that a 12-ounce can of beer contains four-fifths as much alcohol as a 1 1/2-ounce jigger of 80-proof whiskey, 6 ounces of wine equal 1 1/2 ounces of vodka, and 6 ounces of sherry contains almost twice as much alcohol as a 1 1/2-ounce jigger of whiskey.

Alcohol is a depressant and sedative that has a marked effect on the central nervous system. Intoxication occurs when the alcohol concentration in the blood is about 1/10 of 1 percent. A concentration of twice that amount results in marked intoxication. At 4/10 of 1 percent the drinker usually passes out.

All states have a law defining the minimal age for drinking alcohol legally, whether in a bar or at home. Driving when intoxicated (DWI), especially by teenagers, is a major cause of automobile accidents, many of them fatal.

While ongoing studies indicate that no more than one or two drinks a day lead to longer life expectancy than total abstinence, the consequences of chronic heavy drinking include irreversible brain damage (especially in the young), liver damage, and various cancers and lung diseases, especially when combined with smoking. Most recently, the U.S. Surgeon General has warned that pregnant women should abstain from all alcoholic beverages because there is no definitive information about a safe level of alcohol in the blood that would not cause damage to the fetus. It is now also known that the consumption of two drinks a day every day will cause a rise in blood pressure.

Anyone on a weight reduction diet should cut down on or eliminate alcohol: a glass of whiskey contains 120 calories with no nutritional value, and alcoholic beverages simultaneously increase the appetite and weaken the will to diet. Alcohol in any form generally should not be given as a first aid measure or as emergency treatment unless a doctor has issued the instruction. *See* "Substance Abuse."

Alcoholics Anonymous • A worldwide community resource for dealing with the problem of alcoholism. AA is a fellowship of men and women who help each other stay sober and who share their recovery experience freely with all those who have the desire to stop drinking. It is an integral part of the tradition that no member may violate another member's anonymity. Although its members may cooperate with other organizations that help alcoholics, AA is not affiliated with any sect, denomination, political group, or institution. Membership is estimated at more than 1 million men and women worldwide, with approximately 73,000 groups meeting in 92 countries. In the United States, since 1971 one out of every 3 new members is a woman. Each group is self-supporting through voluntary contributions. *See* "Substance Abuse" and "Directory of Health Information."

Alcoholism • Compulsive drinking, now recognized as a disease not a moral disorder by the American Medical Association, the U.S. Public Health Service, and the World Health Organization. Experts agree that the qualitative difference between the "heavy" or "hard" drinkers and alcoholics is that the former, unlike alcoholics, can control their drinking if and when they choose to. Social and heavy drinkers like alcohol but can do without it; alcoholics need alcohol, and their addiction becomes progressively worse. *See* "Substance Abuse."

Allergy • Hypersensitivity to a substance such as food, pollen, cosmetics, animal dander, or medicine or to a climatic condition such as sunshine or low temperature that in similar amounts is harmless to most people. An allergic response can occur anywhere on or in the body: on the skin, in the eyes, lungs, gastrointestinal tract. While an allergy may develop at any age, symptoms experienced in childhood have a tendency to abate with time, and some disappear altogether. A tendency to allergic response is inherited, although the nature of the allergy itself may differ from one generation to another. Why a particular allergy develops remains a medical mystery.

Allergies are essentially the result of a faulty response by the body's immune system, which reacts to an allergen by manufacturing antibodies as if the substance were a dangerous invader. In this process chemicals known as histamines are released into the bloodstream, and these chemicals are the immediate cause of the allergic symptoms. Histamine can produce two main effects: first, by increasing the permeability of the small blood vessels, it causes the fluid portion of the blood or serum to leak into the tissues; second, it causes spasm of particular muscles, especially in the bronchial tubes. The first condition produces swelling, blisters, and irritation of some tissues such as the eyes, nose, and skin; the second produces labored breathing and asthmatic episodes. In extreme cases hypersensitivity to penicillin or nonhuman antitoxin serum or to the venom in an insect sting produces sudden shock (anaphylactic reaction) that can be fatal.

Most allergies are treated by identifying the offending substance and avoiding it. This is relatively simple in the case of a cosmetic that causes a rash or a cantaloupe that brings on diarrhea or a pet whose dander produces an asthma attack. In many instances, however, identification can be extremely difficult. Specialists have evolved various scratch tests and patch tests that are painless, time-consuming, and not always helpful.

For cases in which avoidance is not possible and relief from symptoms is necessary there are desensitizing treatments that can build up a resistance to the allergen once it is identified. Medicines such as antihistamines, cortisone, ephedrine, and aminophylline, alone or in combination, may be effective in controlling the symptoms and reducing discomfort. Self-medication with any of these drugs prior to identifying the problem is always inadvisable. *See* ANTIHISTAMINE.

Alopecia • *See* BALDNESS.

Alzheimer's Disease • The most common cause of irreversible loss of total function in the elderly. This form of senile dementia affects about 1 million and perhaps as many as 2 million Americans, and of these it is estimated that about 10 percent have inherited it through a faulty gene. The basic cause in typical cases is unknown, but the course of the disease follows a pattern in which the memory deteriorates, the ability to communicate diminishes, and the patient becomes increasingly incapable of coping with the simple tasks of daily life.

In searching for the cause of Alzheimer's disease, it has been discovered that the "thinking" part of the patient's brain, the cerebral cortex, is clogged with tangled nerve cells that have degenerated because of what appears to be an aberration in the enzyme that enables the neurons to connect with each other. While there is no test for the onset of the condition, family members are usually alert to early symptoms of speech impairment and memory loss. In some milder cases, deterioration can be slowed down by suitable interaction therapy.

In recent years, practically every state has mandated the establishment of agencies that help families handle the financial and emotional burdens of dealing with this disease. See "Directory of Health Information."

Amebiasis • An infection caused by an ameba that invades the colon, resulting in diarrhea and bloody, mucoid stools. Amebiasis is one type of "traveler's diarrhea" and is also sexually transmissable. See "Sexually Transmissible Diseases."

Amenorrhea • The absence of the menstrual flow. Primary amenorrhea is the failure of menstrual periods to begin by the age of 18. The cause is usually endocrine (glandular) in nature. Secondary amenorrhea is the cessation of menstrual periods after they have begun. It occurs normally during pregnancy, nursing, and following the menopause. It may occur with weight loss and with certain physical activities such as long-distance running. When none of these circumstances accounts for the interruption of menstruation, it may be a symptom of malnutrition, alcoholism, glandular disturbance, or tumors. It may also be psychogenic in origin and related to a severe emotional disturbance, to a prolonged psychotic episode, or to an emotional condition such as anorexia nervosa. When there is no obvious explanation for either primary or secondary amenorrhea, a doctor should be consulted. See "Gynecologic Diseases and Treatment."

Amnesia • Loss of memory. Amnesia may be partial or extensive, temporary or permanent. With total amnesia (very rare), practically all mental functions would necessarily cease. Memory loss may result from brain damage caused by injury, tumor, arteriosclerosis, stroke, Alzheimer's disease, or alcoholism. It may also be caused by the psychological mechanism of repression. Amnesia following an accident or acute emotional shock may cause the victim to black out and forget the event itself but remember all details leading up to it. Except for the amnesia associated with senility, memory loss that wipes out past identity occurs more frequently in fiction than in fact.

Amniocentesis • A diagnostic procedure in which a small amount of the amniotic fluid that surrounds the fetus during pregnancy is withdrawn and examined to assess genetic and other disorders. The technique, developed in the 1960s, is accurate and relatively safe and requires only a local anesthetic. A needle similar to a hypodermic needle is inserted through the abdomen into the womb. The extracted fluid contains cells shed by the fetus, and when these cells are grown in laboratory cultures, it is possible to detect fetal sex as well as fetal chromosomal abnormalities. *See* "Pregnancy and Childbirth."

Amnion • The tough-walled membrane that forms the protective sac in which the embryo is contained within the uterus during pregnancy. The amnion and its contents (amniotic fluid) are commonly known as the bag of waters. During labor contractions the bag generally breaks and the fluid leaks out. *See* "Pregnancy and Childbirth."

Amphetamine • A category of drugs, including Benzedrine, Dexedrine, and Methedrine, that act as stimulants to the central nervous system. The somewhat indiscriminate use of amphetamines as antidepressants and aids in overcoming obesity; the widespread abuse of amphetamines in the form of "pep" pills and diet pills; the increased tolerance developed by some users; and the freak aftereffects experienced by athletes, dancers, students, and others who seek to perform at the peak of their powers through amphetamine intake have led to a greater control over the use and availability of these drugs. Their therapeutic use should be limited to cases of narcolepsy and to counteracting the effects of an overdose of sedatives. *See* "Substance Abuse."

Amyotrophic Lateral Sclerosis • (also called Lou Gehrig's disease) A progressive and eventually fatal disease of the nervous system characterized by muscular weakness of the extremities and increasing loss of function and mobility. Typical victims of this neuromuscular disorder are males over the age of 40. Physical therapy on a regular basis can slow down muscle atrophy.

Analgesic • Substance that temporarily reduces or eliminates the sensation of pain without producing unconsciousness. The most common over-the-counter analgesics are aspirin and acetaminophen (such as Tylenol). Narcotic analgesics derived from opium, such as codeine and morphine, as well as similar synthetic substances should be prescribed with caution because they are habit-forming. Analgesia may be produced by other means such as hypnosis and acupuncture. *See* ANESTHESIA.

Analysis • *See* PSYCHOANALYSIS.

Androgens • The male sex hormones that determine the secondary sex characteristics of men. Androgens are also called male steroids. Although the two chief androgens, testosterone and androsterone, are manufactured mainly by the male testes, they are also produced to a lesser extent by the adrenal glands of both sexes and by the female ovaries. In males they are responsible for the deepening of the voice and the development of the beard at puberty. They also account in part for the greater size and muscular development of men because they also stimulate the growth of muscles and bones. It is for this latter effect that they are used by some athletes. Androgens also control the oil glands and stimulate the manufacture of sebum, which lubricates the skin.

Androgynous • Having both male and female sex characteristics. True androgyny is extremely rare and can be corrected in part by a combination of hormone therapy and surgery.

Anemia • A condition in which there is a deficiency in the number of red blood cells, hemoglobin, or the total amount of blood. Anemia, whether acute or chronic, is not a disease in itself but rather the result of an underlying disorder: chronic malnutrition, industrial poisoning, bone marrow disease, heavy bleeding, intestinal parasites, kidney disease, or a defect in the body's ability to absorb iron. Because treatment varies according to the cause, accurate diagnosis is extremely important. The symptoms of a mild deficiency may be vague: listlessness, general lack of vitality, and fatigue following little effort. When the condition is more severe, the inability of the anemic blood to supply oxygen to body tissues can result in shortness of breath, rapid pulse, and the sensation that the heart is working harder or faster. Visible indications are the paleness of the lining of the eyelids and of the area under the fingernails. When the blood has sufficient hemoglobin, these parts of the body are a healthy pink.

Anemia should never be self-diagnosed for the purpose of self-treatment with tonics, vitamins, pills, or herbal remedies. It is a specific condition that can be diagnosed accurately only by laboratory analysis of blood samples.

There are several types of anemia. The most common form, iron deficiency anemia, is a deficiency of iron essential for the body's manufacture of hemoglobin. It may result from insufficient iron in the diet or from chronic blood loss from excessive menstrual flow or internal bleeding due to an ulcer or some other gastrointestinal disorder.

Pernicious anemia, also known as Addison's anemia, is a serious disease characterized by a breakdown in the mechanism of red blood cell formation, usually traceable to a deficiency of vitamin B_{12}, although this is rare because the amount required by the body is easily obtained from small amounts of animal products. It may sometimes occur among the strictest vegetarians unless their diet is supplemented by the vitamin in capsule form.

Hemolytic anemia results from the destruction of red blood cells, which may occur because of Rh incompatibility, mismatched blood transfusions, industrial poisons, or hypersensitivity to certain chemicals and medicines.

Aplastic anemia is caused by a disease of the bone marrow, the part of the body where red blood cells are manufactured. While some cases result from bone marrow cancer, others follow excessive radiation exposure or contact with a long list of substances that have the same destructive effect (the chemicals in certain insecticides, antibiotics, medicines containing bismuth and other heavy metals).

Hemoglobinopathies are forms of anemia of genetic origin. Included in this category are sickle-cell trait and anemia, thalassemia (Cooley's anemia), and hemoglobin C disease. When such a congenital trait is known to exist, genetic counseling is advised before pregnancy. *See* "Nutrition, Weight, and General Well-Being."

Anesthesia • Partial or total loss of sensation or feelings. Analgesia, one category of anesthesia, refers specifically to loss of sensation of pain. The great advances in surgery have gone hand in hand with modern methods of anesthesia and the discovery of a variety of anesthetics. The study of these substances and their application is known as anesthesiology. An anesthesiologist is a doctor who specializes in this branch of medical science. An anesthetist is not a doctor but usually a nurse with advanced training.

The following are among the procedures that produce anesthesia and analgesia. They may be used separately or in combination. Intravenous injection of sleep-producing drugs such as sodium pentothal produces light anesthesia. The injection of light anesthetics often precedes the use of longer-lasting methods when major surgery is involved. Inhalation of gases is used to anesthetize the whole body. Spinal injection of one of the cocaine derivatives deadens the nerves in a specific part of the body. Rectal administration by a light enema or paraldehyde, a sleep-inducing drug that is quickly absorbed by the body, is used for patients who are especially difficult to deal with, such as alcoholics, psychotics, or those who are extremely apprehensive. More limited procedures are local freezing, nerve block, such as the injection of procaine for dental surgery, and surface or topical analgesia, such as the use of cocaine-related drugs for eye surgery. Hypnosis is being used successfully in situations such as childbirth and pediatric dentistry. Acupuncture is being evaluated scientifically for its analgesic applications.

Aneurysm • An abnormal widening or distension of an artery or vein, forming a sac that is filled with blood. Aneurysms may be congenitally caused by a deficiency in the vessel walls or they may be acquired through injury or disease, especially atherosclerosis. The condition may exist for many years without any symptoms and may be detected only as a result of an X-ray taken for some other reason. Aneurysms in the arteries of the brain or in the aorta may make themselves known by pressure in the surrounding area, for example on the optic nerve or on an organ in the chest.

When the swelling is detected in a small artery or vein, the vessel can be tied off so that the flow of blood is redirected to healthier channels. The repair of larger vessels has recently been made possible by organ banks that provide vascular replacements, both plastic and those available from smaller mammals. Rupture of an aneurysm requires emergency hospitalization and treatment.

Angina Pectoris • Literally, pain in the chest and the signal of an interference (generally reversible) with the supply of oxygen to the heart muscle. The pain is rarely confused with any other; it characteristically produces a feeling of tightness and suffocation beginning under the left side of the breastbone and sometimes spreading to the neck, throat, and down the left arm. Angina pectoris is more common among men than women, but women, especially in their late fifties and sixties, may suffer from the condition, especially if they smoke or are overweight, hypertensive, or diabetic.

The onset of an angina attack is likely to follow strenuous exercise, exposure to cold and wind, eating and digesting a heavy meal, or the emotional stress of a quarrel or a frightening dream. In such circumstances the heart works harder and pumps faster and therefore needs an extra supply of blood and oxygen. When circulation is impaired in any way, especially by atherosclerosis, the blood supply does not reach the heart muscle cells quickly enough. The resulting lack of oxygen is the immediate cause of the pain.

An angina attack is usually brief and subsides after resting.

ANGINA PECTORIS

- Substernal pain
- Pain radiates to neck and down inner left arm
- Feeling of tightness and constriction

The traditional treatment when an attack occurs is to place a nitroglycerin (trinitroglycerol) tablet under the tongue. More recently, this drug is used in ointment form or in medicated discs and applied to the skin, or in tablet form to prevent occurrence. Nitroglycerin is effective because it dilates coronary arteries. Other medical treatments include: beta blockers that regulate the stimulation of the heart by the autonomic nervous system or calcium channel blockers that prevent spasms of arterial walls that choke off the supply of blood to the heart. Coronary bypass surgery, which replaces damaged coronary arteries, does not necessarily guarantee greater longevity than treatment by other means.

Angiography • A diagnostic procedure in which radiopaque substances are injected into the blood vessels so that any abnormalities or displacements are visible on an X-ray film. This type of radiological picture is called an angiogram.

Animal Bites • Any animal bite, even by a family pet, that breaks the surface of the skin requires attention. It should be washed at once with soap under running water. Medical attention should be sought for deep or severe bites and for any bite by a wild animal. Although rabies and tetanus are comparatively rare, they should never be excluded. Not only dogs and cats but squirrels, horses, mice, bats, foxes, and other warm-blooded animals are capable of spreading diseases through bites. For any bite that breaks the skin, the victim should go at once to a local doctor or hospital emergency room so that antibiotics can be administered and damaged tissue can be repaired as necessary. If the offending animal can be caught, it should not be killed but rather turned over to a veterinarian or a health authority. *See* RABIES.

Ankles, Swollen • The tissues around the ankle may swell for various reasons: heart disease, kidney or liver malfunction, pregnancy, or an injury. Women who spend lots of time on their feet, such as salespeople, artists, waitresses, housewives, are especially susceptible to this complaint in hot weather, not because of disease but because of insufficient venous return. When the puffy condition persists in spite of sitting with the feet extended and raised or a warm bath before bedtime, a doctor should be consulted.

Anorexia • Lack of or loss of an interest in eating food.

Anorexia Nervosa • A disorder of eating patterns involving severe weight loss to the point of malnutrition, cessation of menstruation, and a distorted perception of the body. Typical anorectics are adolescent girls in middle- or upper-class families with strong parental controls and high expectations for behavior and accomplishment. If not correctly diagnosed and treated effectively, this condition is fatal in about 5 percent of all cases.

Symptoms of obsessional involvement with food, bizarre eating and dieting patterns, conspicuous weight loss, and constant complaints about being "fat" should be evaluated by a physician who may recommend family therapy by an experienced specialist. It is assumed that the patient finds that dieting is one way of controlling her life in the face of overdemanding parents or that by fending off the body development and sexual implications of puberty she can remain a "little girl" indefinitely.

When malnutrition begins to affect the heart, blood pressure, and gastrointestinal function and is accompanied by signs of depression, hospitalization may be advised so that systematic therapy can be initiated and closely monitored. See BULIMIA, a related disorder, and "Directory of Health Information."

Antacid • A substance that, by neutralizing the acidity of stomach juice, relieves heartburn and gastric distress and is the safest treatment for ulcers. In choosing a nonprescription antacid among the different types on the market, keep the following in mind: some have significantly more salt than others, those in liquid form may be more effective even though less convenient, and the calcium contained in others may be responsible for stimulating the stomach to secrete additional acid. Ulcer patients should discuss medication with their physicians so that their conditions can be properly monitored.

Antibiotic • A chemical substance produced during the growth of various fungi and bacteria that has the capacity to kill or inhibit the growth of other bacteria or fungi. Since the discovery of penicillin in 1929 and its mass application during World War II, literally thousands of antibiotic substances have been isolated and studied. As disease-causing bacteria develop strains that are resistant to a particular antibiotic, new drugs are developed to counteract the adaptation.

While antibiotics have saved many lives, there is increasing concern about their indiscriminate prescription by doctors who rely on drug advertising rather than the more objective information in scientific journals. Surveys indicate that doctors most up-to-date about how to prescribe antibiotics are those most recently graduated from medical school and those who see only a few patients a day. Authorities agree that antibiotics are overprescribed and incorrectly prescribed to an alarming degree in the United States and that one of the best correctives to this situation is the informed self-interest of the patient. The correct application of antibiotics is the treatment of bacterial and certain fungal infections. They are ineffective against viral infections. They should not be prescribed as a preventive medicine, except for a few special conditions.

The following is a list by their generic names of the more commonly prescribed antibiotics and their application. You have every right as a patient to ask the physician if there is any reason not to prescribe a generic drug and if there are differences in effects among brands. Generic drugs are likely to be less expensive than brand-name products.

The penicillin group of antibiotics includes among others penicillin G potassium, penicillin V, and ampicillin. The first two are most frequently prescribed for streptococcus infections of the ear and throat, sinus infections, gonorrhea, syphilis, pneumococcal pneumonia. Ampicillin is prescribed for middle ear and urinary infections. Allergic reactions to penicillin may range from a mild rash, diarrhea, or nausea to severe shock. Any history of adverse reactions to penicillin in any form should be pointed out to a doctor, especially in an emergency situation involving a possible injection.

The tetracycline group includes tetracycline HCL (hydrochloride), chlortetracycline, oxytetracycline, and some new drugs in the same family. These are commonly prescribed under various brand names for bronchitis, acne, pneumonia, and, in cases of penicillin allergy, for syphilis and gonorrhea, also for Rocky Mountain spotted fever and other rickettsial diseases, some urinary tract infections, and amebiasis.

Erythromycin is an antibiotic developed for those patients who are allergic to penicillin or who should not be given tetracycline because of pregnancy or possible side effects on bone development. Erythromycin is the drug of choice for treating Legionnaire's disease.

Chloramphenicol is sold under the brand name of Chloromycetin. It should be prescribed only for typhoid fever, very severe cases of salmonella poisoning, and a few other major infections because it has been found in some cases to interfere with the production of blood cells in the bone marrow.

The sulfonamides are antimicrobial drugs that do not kill bacteria but effectively inhibit their growth. They are prescribed for urinary tract infections, bacillary dysentery, and as a prophylaxis against strep infections for patients who have had rheumatic fever.

A more recent class of antibiotics, the cephalosporins, may be prescribed when the precise nature of the bacterial infection is unknown because these drugs have a broad spectrum of effectiveness. The latest antibiotic group, called quinolones, can be used to treat bacterial infections that previously may have required hospitalization. Among the first two drugs in this category to receive FDA approval are ciprofloxacin and norfloxacin.

When given an antibiotic prescription, be sure to ask what side effects the drug might produce and how and when it should be taken. For example, the penicillins, tetracyclines, and erythromycin should be taken on an empty stomach either before meals or two hours after meals. Oral antibiotics should not be taken with fruit juices. Tetracycline should not be taken with milk or milk products. Prolonged exposure to the sun should be avoided when taking sulfa drugs. The sulfonamides should be taken with large quantities of fluids to prevent negative effects on the kidneys.

A useful nonprescription antibiotic ointment is Bacitracin, which inhibits bacterial growth in a cut or other skin lesion such as a nicked cuticle.

Antibody • A component of the immune system produced by cells called plasmocytes in the presence of an antigen (any substance foreign to the body) to destroy or neutralize that antigen: a specific monoclonal antibody is produced for each antigen. This specificity is the basis of immunization by vaccination: the introduction of a controlled amount or variety of a disease-producing organism stimulates the plasmocytes to develop the antibodies necessary to fight the organism in advance of an uncontrolled invasion of the body.

Antidepressant • A class of mood-changing drugs that counteract some of the immobilizing effects of depressive illness. While antidepressants do not cure mental illness, they have largely replaced electroshock therapy as a means of helping certain withdrawn or hysterical patients benefit from psychotherapy. In cases of agitated depression or hysteria, antidepressants may be combined with tranquilizers. They may also be prescribed to stabilize a suicidal patient. See "Substance Abuse."

Antidote • Any substance natural or synthetic that counteracts the effect of another substance, usually a poison. There are very few specific antidotes, and because ridding the body of a poison is a complicated matter, a local poison control center should be consulted immediately for emergency care.

Antigen • Any substance that stimulates the production of antibodies. Antigens are present in bacterial toxins, pollens, immunizing agents, blood, and other substances.

Antihistamine • Any of various drugs that minimize the discomfort of hay fever, hives, and other allergic reactions caused by the body's release of chemicals known as histamines. Depending on the nature of the allergy, antihistamines may be prescribed in the form of drops for the nose or eyes, a salve or topical ointment to be used on the skin, or pills to be taken orally. They may also be a remedy for motion sickness and are helpful in relieving the symptoms of a cold. However, they may reduce the effectiveness of birth control pills, and they should not be used by pregnant women to relieve the discomfort of "morning sickness."

Continuous and indiscriminate use of these drugs may have unpleasant effects and should be avoided. Because many antihistamines produce drowsiness, caution is advisable while driving a car and when alertness at a job or at household tasks is essential for safety. Abstaining from alcohol in any form is advisable when taking antihistamines.

Some of the over-the-counter antihistamines that produce relatively low levels of drowsiness are Dimetane, Contac, and Chlor-Trimeton. Benadryl is an antihistamine sometimes recommended as a "sleeping pill" because it presents none of the serious addictive problems of barbiturates. Nonprescription "daytime sedatives," widely advertised for their effectiveness in diminishing tension and anxiety, actually contain little more than an antihistamine that causes drowsiness.

Antiperspirant • A mixture of chemicals including aluminum chlorohydrate that diminish the amount of perspiration that reaches the skin and reduce the rate of growth of the odor-creating bacteria. (Deodorants only reduce the speed with which bacteria multiply). Because antiperspirants are considered drugs, their ingredients must be listed on their containers, and because they may contain irritants to the skin, it may be necessary to experiment with different brands to find one that does not produce a rash. Those packaged in spray cans may contain propellants harmful to the lungs and should be rejected in favor of a cream or roll-on product.

Antiseptic • A substance that inhibits or slows down the growth of microorganisms; in more recent usage the term means a substance that kills bacteria. Disinfectants are included under the general heading of antiseptics, although they are too strong to be applied to body tissues and are meant to make surfaces germ-free in kitchens, bathrooms, and sickrooms.

Antitoxin • A type of antibody that neutralizes the specific toxin released by a disease-causing agent. Antitoxins may be manufactured by the body's immune system or they may be injected as a defense against diseases such as tetanus, diphtheria, or botulism.

Anxiety Attack (also called panic attack) • In the clinical sense, an abnormal feeling of apprehension and fear in which the threat is not easy to identify. This condition of internally generated stress is typically accompanied by hyperventilation, rapid heartbeat, and sweating. An alcoholic hangover can be accompanied by such an attack; an excessive intake of caffeine can trigger an anxiety attack. Frequent episodes of this kind can lead to agoraphobia resulting in immobilization. Anti-anxiety anxiety drugs (Librium, Valium, Xanax) are recommended for short-term use only in order to reduce agitation and make psychotherapy possible. *See* "Substance Abuse."

Aorta • The largest and most important artery carrying blood from the heart to be distributed throughout the body. The aorta begins at the left ventricle of the heart, curves over and downward into the chest, and then penetrates the diaphragm for entry into the abdomen where it ends opposite the fourth lumbar vertebra. The branches of the aorta supply arterial blood to all parts of the body.

Apoplexy • *See* STROKE.

Appendicitis • Inflammation of the appendix, the 3- to 6-inch appendage or sac that lies in the lower right portion of the abdominal cavity at the junction of the small and large intestine. Appendicitis accounts for at least half the abdominal emergencies that occur between the ages of 10 and 30. The critical aspect of an attack of acute appendicitis is that the inflammation may result in a rupture leading to peritonitis (infection of the abdominal lining). When some undetermined element plugs up the tubelike appendix and hinders normal drainage the likelihood of bacterial infection increases. If the body's defenses do not stop the multiplication of colon bacilli and streptococci, inflammation results, causing three main symptoms: pain in the lower right side, nausea or vomiting, and fever. If one or all of these symptoms persist, see a doctor promptly.

If no doctor is available, call an ambulance to take you to the nearest hospital's emergency room. Under no circumstances should anything be taken by mouth without professional instructions: no food, no fluid, no medicines, and especially *no laxative or cathartic.* Self-treatment with an enema or a hot-water bottle is equally ill-advised.

An appendectomy performed under the best medical conditions has a very low mortality rate. Even when postoperative complications occur, they can be overcome with antibiotics.

So-called chronic appendicitis is a designation with little medical validity. Constant complaints of discomfort in the lower right part of the abdomen should be investigated for the correct cause.

Appetite • The natural desire for food, usually conditioned by psychological factors such as eating habits, pleasant memories, and the stimuli of the sight and smell of particular foods. Hunger, on the other hand, is a physiological phenomenon resulting from the contractions of an empty stomach. An infant's cries for food are an expression of hunger not appetite.

When appetite is active and intense beyond the apparent physical needs of the body, diabetes or a thyroid disorder may be responsible. More frequently, an insatiable appetite that leads to compulsive overeating may originate in an emotional problem that requires attention. Widely advertised appetite suppressants should be used according to label instructions and should not be considered a permanent substitute for changing one's eating habits.

People occasionally experience a loss of appetite in the presence of unattractive surroundings or uncongenial company. Emotions such as fear, anger, or anxiety affect the flow of stomach juices and diminish the appetite. A continuing loss of appetite, technically known as chronic anorexia (not to be confused with anorexia nervosa), may indicate kidney malfunction or cancer. When a lack of interest in food occurs in old age, it may be related to depression and withdrawal from life. *See* "Nutrition, Weight, and General Well-Being."

Arrhythmias • Abnormalities in the rhythm of the heartbeat due to disturbances in the electrical impulses that trigger the pumping of the heart muscle. The most common of these disturbances is a rapidly racing and pounding heart, called palpitations. Other abnormalities include excessively slow rate (below 60 beats a minute) called bradycardia, premature contractions of one or the other heart chambers sometimes caused by anxiety or too much caffeine or heavy smoking, and ventricular tachycardia in which an excessively rapid beat is accompanied by dizziness and chest pain.

Treatment depends on the circumstance. Artificial pacemakers correct a sluggish beat that deprives the heart of sufficient oxygen; medications such as digitalis and quinidine slow the heartbeat and reestablish a normal rhythm when fibrillation occurs. When stress and/or alcohol, coffee, and cigarettes are the obvious cause of arrhythmia, a change in life style is recommended.

Arteriosclerosis • A disease of aging, also called hardening of the arteries, in which the walls of the arteries thicken and lose their elasticity. It is more prevalent among men than women. *See* ATHEROSCLEROSIS.

Arthritis • Inflammation of a joint. The term is broadly used to cover almost 100 different conditions many of which do not necessarily involve inflammation but do result in aches and pains in the joints and connective tissues all over the body. The designation rheumatism is often incorrectly used for such aches and pains. The Arthritis Foundation estimates that about 20 million Americans suffer from some form of arthritis severe enough to require medical attention and that among the sufferers women far outnumber men.

Arthritis is a chronic condition, but it may be less of a problem if its symptoms are recognized early enough for prompt and proper treatment. The typical warning signs of the onset of one of the arthritic diseases are: stiffness and pain in the joints on getting up in the morning; tenderness, soreness, and swelling in one or several joints; tingling sensations in the fingers and toes; fatigue and weakness unconnected with any other disorder. Authorities emphasize that the mountain of misinformation about arthritis has been the cause of a great deal of unnecessary suffering and mismanagement of the various arthritic diseases. It is *not* true that most women have arthritis as they get older and there's nothing to be done about it. It is *not* true (loud and persistent claims to the contrary) that diet is an important factor in arthritis. It is *not* true that home treatments are just as effective as professional medical care. This last misconception is the most dangerous of all because it can lead to a delay in getting an accurate diagnosis and effective treatment early enough to avoid irreversible joint damage.

Rheumatoid arthritis is the most serious—and the most mysterious—of the arthritic diseases. Although no one is immune to it, 80 percent of all cases occur between the ages of 25 and 50, with three times as many women affected as men. There is no clear understanding about what triggers the disease, but it has been discovered that 80 percent of all patients have what is called the "rheumatoid factor" in their blood. This factor is an antibody that attacks the body's own gamma globulin setting up a circular interaction that causes the body's immune system to go awry and destroy its own tissues. In this destructive process, the cartilage that connects the joints is eroded and the joints themselves are attacked. No two cases are the same: in some the symptoms become progressively worse and disabling while in many others the pain and swelling are severe for several months and then vanish forever.

The disease chiefly affects the joints of the hands, arms, hips, legs, and feet, although the inflammation may attack connective tissue anywhere in the body. Because rheumatoid arthritis has so many variations, it must be treated on an individual basis by a specialist who is aware of all the possible forms of therapy: medication, rest, exercise, heat, surgery, and any combination of treatments to keep the inflammation from spreading, to eliminate as much pain as possible, to prevent the occurrence of irreversible deformities, and to maintain as much joint movement and function as possible.

For those patients who can tolerate the side effects, megadoses of aspirin remain the most effective treatment for pain and inflammation. Acetaminophen (Tylenol) is a substitute analgesic, but it lacks the anti-inflammatory strength of aspirin. A recent category of medicines known as nonsteroidal anti-inflammatory drugs (NSAIDS) has broadened treatment possibilities. Corticosteroid injections are used with caution and only for short-term therapy because of serious adverse side effects. Gold injections have produced positive results in some patients who can tolerate their cumulative toxicity.

Physical therapy is an indispensable aspect of treatment in all cases, and recent developments in surgical techniques—plastic surgery, fusions, and artificial implants—are achieving good results in overcoming deformities and disabilities.

Osteoarthritis, also known as degenerative joint disease, is the most common form of arthritis, usually an accompaniment to aging and rarely disabling. Mild aches and stiffness are likely to settle in those joints that have received the most use and weight stress; women are especially vulnerable to osteoarthritis of the hip, knee, big toe, and the end (or distal) joints of the fingers. Overweight is clearly a contributing cause because it places an added burden on the hip and knee joints. Joints that have been injured in falls or have taken constant abuse in athletics may be the source of arthritic discomfort. Heredity seems to be a factor that predisposes some women to osteoarthritis in the small joints of the fingers and toes. Tension that takes its toll in muscle fatigue is one of the factors that has led some specialists to call osteoarthritis one of the self-punishing diseases.

In many cases the disorder will show up in an X-ray before it has caused much discomfort. Typically, the symptoms are localized soreness, a constant pain of varying intensity resulting from pressure on nerve endings, or some difficulty in moving the joint easily, for example, a stiff knee or pains in the hip ("creaking joints"). While there is no cure for osteoarthritis, a doctor can recommend various procedures to ease the discomfort and to prevent further deterioration of tissue. See LYME DISEASE, GOUT, NONSTEROIDAL ANTI-INFLAMMATORY DRUGS, GOLD TREATMENT, PHYSICAL THERAPY, and the "Directory of Health Information."

Artificial Insemination • The transfer of semen into the vagina by artificial means for the purpose of conception. See "Infertility."

Artificial Respiration • Any of several techniques whereby air is forced into and out of the lungs when natural breathing has ceased. Because none of the techniques requires special equipment, they are first aid measures that almost anyone can master. Brain death occurs four to six minutes after breathing has stopped. Therefore, artificial respiration must be administered at once in such circumstances as a near-drowning, an almost lethal electric shock, and suffocation from smoke inhalation. It is therefore crucial to learn the techniques *before* the need arises in order to function swiftly and competently. Local Red Cross chapters or other community organizations should be contacted for information about courses that cover instruction in first aid for common emergencies.

Asbestos • A group of fibrous minerals of unusual strength, flexibility, and durability, characterized by resistance to heat and corrosion. Asbestos has been widely used to insulate buildings, as a fire-retarding component in construction materials, and as a protective covering against electrical damage. It is now known to be as deadly as it is useful if it is inhaled or (less likely) swallowed.

The submicroscopic silica-like fibers are responsible for the lung disease asbestosis and where exposure is combined with smoking, the result is almost always a fatal lung cancer. Other types of cancer, especially mesothelioma, a deadly malignancy of the lining of the chest and abdominal cavity, have been traced to inhalation or swallowing of asbestos dust more than 40 years after the exposure. Government regulations and rigorous inspections controlling the use of asbestos in industry remain unsatisfactory. Vigilant parents have increasingly refused to send their children to schools in which faulty repairs or negligence put them at great risk of inhaling the harmful dust.

Ascorbic Acid • Chemical designation of vitamin C. See "Nutrition, Weight, and General Well-Being."

Aspartame • A low-calorie sweetening ingredient (marketed as NutraSweet) widely used as a food and carbonated beverage additive. See "Nutrition, Weight, and General Well-Being."

Aspirin • Common name for the pure chemical acetylsalicylic acid; originally the brand name invented by the Bayer Drug Company but now a generic term. Aspirin is always aspirin no matter what company packages it. Therefore, there's no reason not to buy the least expensive brand. Aspirin is one of the greatest discoveries of all times because of its many benefits. It is a painkiller (analgesic); it lowers fever (antipyretic); it reduces some of the destructive consequences of arthritis (anti-inflammatory); and recently it has been reported to play a role in controlling the mechanism that causes blood to form clots (anti-coagulant).

The addition of certain chemicals to aspirin may be profitable to the manufacturer but of questionable value to the consumer. Aspirin combined with caffeine? It probably costs less to have plain aspirin with a cup of coffee. With phenacetin? In large doses this is an ingredient likely to produce stomach upsets and kidney problems.

Aspirin itself can be a stomach irritant and should be avoided by anyone with ulcers or gastritis. It can be "buffered" by combining it with an alkalizer such as a bicarbonate of soda pill or a half glass of milk. When aspirin causes an allergic response, acetaminophen (Tylenol or other aspirinlike analgesics) should be substituted.

Headaches, ringing in the ears, and drowsiness are signs of aspirin overdose. Severe cases of aspirin poisoning, with symptoms of vomiting and delirium, require emergency treatment.

There is compelling evidence that aspirin can increase the risk of Reye's syndrome, a little-understood, life-threatening disease associated with some viral infections of childhood, especially chicken pox. A child with a high fever, particularly a very young child, should not be medicated with aspirin except on the recommendation of a physician. Acetaminophen combined with aspirin is likely to be safer and just as effective.

Asthma • A respiratory disorder in which the air tubes of the lungs are constricted by tightened muscles, mucous plugs, and inflamed tissue, causing breathing to be mildly or severely labored; technically known as bronchial asthma. While most asthma victims are children, it is also common among adults, with men and women affected in equal numbers. Asthma is a disease that occurs in "attacks" or "episodes." Asthmatics are said to have lungs that are abnormally sensitive to certain stimuli, ranging from cat dander to chemicals to mold, to sudden changes in temperature to virus infections. The offending stimulus (in most cases an allergen that causes the body to produce histamines) triggers muscle tightening, mucous secretion, and tissue swelling in the bronchial passages that transport oxygen into the lungs. The victim of the attack begins to wheeze, cough, and gasp for air. An attack may subside in a few minutes or it may continue intermittently for hours.

A substance recently implicated in asthma and allergy attacks serious enough to be life-threatening is metabisulfite, used as a preservative in dried fruits, pickled foods, and the fresh vegetables served in salad bars. It is not the sulfite that is so dangerous but the small quantities of sulfur dioxide it gives off. In people sensitive to this gas, asthma symptoms can occur within minutes of inhaling it.

Asthmatics who know exactly what substances or circumstances precipitate an attack but cannot easily avoid the stimulus should be desensitized. If the episodes are of mysterious origin, the American Lung Association recommends that a doctor be consulted before taking any medicines.

Purse-size hand-held bronchodilators in aerosol or measured dose form are available in varying strength and are useful for relieving an emergency attack. Cortisone may be prescribed as an aerosol spray or in liquid or tablet form. It is usually carefully supervised because of negative side effects.

Because no environment is pollen-free, pollutant-free, dust-free, or mold-free year round, moving is rarely a final solution. For some the answer is as simple as avoiding other people's cigarette smoke; for others it is as difficult as giving up smoking themselves.

Attacks that are triggered by tension or anxiety may be eliminated after a period of productive psychotherapy.

Astigmatism • A defect in the curved surface of the lens or the cornea that results in blurred vision. When the refracting surface is not truly spherical, rays of light coming from a single spot are not brought into sharp focus. Astigmatism is a common disorder of vision that is easily corrected with properly fitted eyeglasses or hard contact lenses.

Atherosclerosis • A thickening and decreased elasticity of the arteries combined with the formation of fatty deposits (plaques) on or beneath their inner walls. When these plaques become large enough to block the flow of blood, the tissue beyond the block dies (infarcts). This blockage of blood flow is what causes the brain damage in most strokes and the heart muscle damage (myocardial infarction) in most heart attacks. Similar blockage may occur in other blood vessels, resulting in such conditions as kidney failure and gangrene in the legs. Atherosclerosis is the major cause of cardiovascular disease, which is the immediate cause of about half of the deaths in the United States each year.

ATHEROSCLEROSIS

Plaque narrowing coronary artery

The heart

The causes of atherosclerosis are not sharply defined. Because the disease is rare in undernourished populations, some specialists blame overeating, especially of animal fats. Because the disorder is not a major problem in agricultural countries, other specialists blame the stresses of industrial society, especially because its incidence is greatest among male business executives. Because between the ages of 35 and 40 the death rate from atherosclerosis is almost 500 percent higher for men than for women, researchers have begun to explore the role of sex hormones in its development.

Smokers of both sexes are at higher risk for developing cardiovascular disease because the tars and nicotine as well as the gases in the smoke itself combine to increase the plaque deposits within the arterial walls.

Although simple hardening of the arteries (arteriosclerosis) is a concomitant of aging, the fatty deposits (atheromas) are not. Medical science has discovered special constituents, known as HDL (high density lipoproteins), in the blood of certain people that seem to break down cholesterol instead of allowing it to remain and clog the arteries.

One of the recently developed diagnostic procedures for assessing arterial disease is phonoangiography. This procedure records the noise produced by the blood flow in a constricted artery and feeds the sound into a small computer for analysis. The loudness and pitch indicate the degree of narrowing caused by the fatty deposits. Phonoangiography can be conducted on an out-patient basis as a screening test when dangerous degrees of atherosclerosis are suspected.

Athlete's Foot • *See* FUNGAL INFECTIONS.

Autoimmune Responses • The body's production of antibodies against its own tissues. The autoimmune mechanism is one of the most important areas of present-day medical research because it is thought to be responsible for such diseases as lupus erythematosus, Crohn's disease, rheumatoid arthritis, thyroiditis, multiple sclerosis, and probably many other diseases and phenomena.

Autopsy • Examination of a body after death. Tissues and fluids are examined grossly, microscopically, and chemically. Autopsies permit precise identification of the cause of death and can sometimes identify genetic disease, which it is important for surviving family members to know about.

Backache • The discomfort of backache, sometimes called lumbago, can in most cases be reduced by appropriate exercises and by rectifying such causes of the problem as poor posture, overweight, ill-fitting shoes, or an improper mattress. Upper back pain can often be traced to stress and anxiety and to osteoporosis of the spine in older women. Lower back pain may be caused by arthritis, diseased kidneys, premenstrual pressures, or a sedentary job during which too many hours are spent in an improperly designed desk chair. Most cases are caused by strain on the muscles and connective tissues surrounding the spinal column. With increasing age, these muscles need to be strengthened by exercises so that the back is properly supported. Good posture when sitting and standing as well as a firm mattress when sleeping can minimize lower back problems. Weight loss, especially if the abdomen is too heavy, relieves extra strain on back muscles. High heels should be worn only for those special occasions when very little walking is required. Heavy objects should be lifted not by bending from the waist but by squatting in a deep knee-bend position. *See* "Fitness" and "Health on the Job."

Bacteria • Single-cell microscopic organisms, essentially a form of plant life without chlorophyl, that occur everywhere in nature. Some bacteria are harmless, many are useful, and some cause disease. Bacteria are classified by their shape: bacilli are rod-shaped, spirochetes spiral, vibrios hooklike, and cocci round. Cocci are also classified by the way they are grouped: diplococci occur in pairs, streptococci run together in a chain, and staphylococci are clustered.

The development of antibiotics was based on the observation that there are substances in nature, produced by microorganisms and fungi, that can destroy disease-producing bacteria.

Bacterial Endocarditis • A serious infection of the lining of the heart. The internal chambers and valves of the heart are lined with a delicate tissue called the endocardium. Normal endocardium is usually resistant to bacterial infection, but where valve abnormalities exist, either congenital or caused by rheumatic fever, valve replacement, or mitral prolapse, the danger of endocarditis is a particularly serious threat. Women with such a heart disability should discuss prophylactic antibiotic therapy with their oral surgeon before a tooth extraction and with other surgeons before any procedure. Otherwise the bacteria, usually streptococci, that escape into the bloodstream may cause bacterial endocarditis, which can be fatal.

Bag of Waters • See AMNION.

Baldness • Loss or absence of hair; technically called alopecia. Although women may temporarily lose hair as a result of an acute fever, anticancer chemotherapy, tuberculosis, thyroid disorder, or pregnancy, they are spared the characteristically male baldness that is permanent. When women's hair begins to thin, estrogen or steroid treatment may be effective. Although chemicals in hair dyes or constant "permanents" may cause hair to break off, it will grow back unless the root is destroyed.

Barbiturate • A class of sedative and hypnotic medicines derived from barbituric acid that have a depressant effect on the central nervous system. Depending on the type and amount prescribed, barbiturates produce sedation, sleep, or anesthesia. An overdose may result in coma, respiratory failure, and death.

Short-action barbiturates such as sodium pentothal are injected intravenously as anesthetics. Sodium pentobarbital (Nembutal) and sodium secobarbital (Seconal) are slower acting; an oral dose of 100 mg produces about six hours of sleep. Phenobarbital, one of the slowest acting barbiturates, may be prescribed with other drugs for the control of epileptic seizures.

The indiscriminate prescribing of barbiturates and their consequent overuse have come under severe criticism. Sedatives and sleeping pills that contain no barbiturates have become available in recent years. Barbiturates should be used only when and as prescribed and should be prescribed only when there is an authentic need for them. These drugs not only can be physically and psychologically addictive but can produce the kind of confusion responsible for accidental overdose. The combination of alcohol and barbiturates can be lethal. Sudden and total withdrawal can also be lethal and should *never* be attempted without medical supervision. *See* "Substance Abuse."

Barium Test • A diagnostic test for the exploration of gastrointestinal disorders by X-ray. Barium sulfate, a harmless chalky substance, is administered to the patient. The opacity of the barium causes the gastrointestinal (GI) tract to stand out in a white silhouette on the fluoroscope or X-ray plate, making visible to the diagnostician ulcers, tumors, and various other disorders of the stomach, duodenum, or intestines. The barium, mixed with water and a drop of flavoring, is taken orally for an examination of the upper tract. A barium enema is administered for an X-ray examination of the lower bowel and colon.

Bed Sore • Patch of degenerating skin tissue, technically called decubitus ulcer, caused by prolonged and uninterrupted pressure of the bedding on the skin of a patient immobilized during an illness or postoperative convalescence. Elderly women and women with diabetes or heart disease are especially susceptible. The parts of the body most vulnerable are the area over the heels, the shoulders, the elbows, the buttocks, and the ankles. The first symptom of the sore is redness of the skin; continued interference with circulation produces a blue appearance of the affected area and then the formation of ulcers. Preventive measures are advisable as bed sores heal with great difficulty and are susceptible to infection. Bed linens should be soft, smooth, and dry. The patient's skin should be washed and powdered each day and the vulnerable areas cushioned with cotton pads. If possible, the bedridden patient should change body position every few hours.

Bee Stings • *See* INSECT STINGS AND BITES.

Bell's Palsy • Paralysis of the muscles of one side of the face caused by pressure on the facial nerve that consequently becomes incapable of transmitting impulses. The cause is assumed to be a virus infection of the ear canal with resultant pressure on the facial nerve. The condition causes loss of the blink reflex, inability to close the eyelids, a flow of tears from the affected eye, and the dribbling of saliva from the immobilized side of the mouth. Recovery occurs without treatment in practically all cases. Electrical stimulation of the damaged nerve is recommended by some doctors; others prescribe cortisone to reduce inflammation. Until the blink reflex is restored, the eye must be protected from excessive dryness and foreign particles. In most cases the condition subsides in a few weeks. At its very worst the deformity caused by Bell's palsy can be partially corrected by cosmetic surgery.

Beta Blockers • Certain drugs that reduce the activity of the heart and narrow the bronchial tubes by blocking the body's natural flow of epinephrine, the substance that normally increases the heartbeat and relaxes the muscles of the bronchi. Introduced in 1967, the first of these drugs, Inderal (propranolol), became the most prescribed pill of the next decade because of its effectiveness in treating arrhythmias and angina disorders as well as high blood pressure. It has also been successfully prescribed for migraine headaches and even for patients prone to anxiety attacks. Similar drugs such as Lopressor (metoprolol) and Tenormin (atenolol) are more selective in their blocking effect. By being "cardioselective" they do not narrow the bronchial tubes and are, therefore, more suitable for patients predisposed to asthma. Other beta blockers are available that differ in the frequency with which they must be taken and that have different side effects. Because they interfere with the normal functioning of the hormone system, some beta blockers can cause impotence, and they have also been known to cause depression, especially in older patients.

Anyone who depends on a beta blocker medication should report negative side effects promptly and should inform the prescribing physician about all other medications being taken at the same time, both prescription and nonprescription, if dangerous drug interactions are to be avoided. Anyone who has been taking Inderal or a similar drug on a long-term basis should not discontinue its use abruptly. Monitoring by a physician is essential during withdrawal.

Bifocals • *See* EYEGLASSES.

Bile • A yellow-brown fluid with a greenish tinge secreted by the liver and concentrated and stored in the gallbladder until needed for the digestive process, especially for the digestion of fats. The channel known as the biliary duct carries bile into the small intestine for this purpose. When the gallbladder has been removed, bile passes directly from the liver into the duodenum through the biliary duct. Among the constituents of bile are cholesterol, bile salts, some proteins, and the emulsifier lecithin. When the balance of these contents is upset, a common type of gallstones, which are actually a precipitate of cholesterol, may form. In some instances such gallstones can be treated medically by dissolution rather than surgically. *See* JAUNDICE.

Biofeedback • A technique whereby a person learns how to achieve a state of relaxation that minimizes arteriolar constriction in her body in order to ward off headaches, particularly vascular headaches, and other symptoms of stress. Biofeedback training has been helpful for some cancer patients in dealing with pain, and positive results have been achieved in lowering blood pressure.

A sensitive device that measures skin temperature, which in turn reflects blood flow, is used in biofeedback training. Training should be supervised by a practitioner connected with an accredited hospital, clinic, pain treatment center, or by referral through a reliable physician or psychotherapist. *See* "Directory of Health Information."

Biopsy • The microscopic examination of small fragments of tissue cut from an organ of the body.

Most biopsies are performed under local anesthesia in the physician's office. While the procedure is considered essential in order to confirm or rule out a diagnosis of cancer, it may also be scheduled for exploratory purposes when such conditions as infertility or arterial inflammation are involved. *See* "Gynecologic Diseases and Treatment," "Breast Care," and "Infertility," and illustration on next page.

Birth Control • *See* "Contraception and Abortion."

METHODS OF BIOPSY

INCISION

ASPIRATION

CURETTAGE

Birth Defect • Any disorder or disease that is either genetically determined (inborn or inherited) or congenitally caused by drugs, including alcohol, caffeine, prescribed medications; occupational, residential, or environmental exposure to chemicals or radiation; or virus infection, injury, or malnutrition that affect the normal physical and mental development of the fetus before birth. See "Pregnancy and Childbirth" and "Substance Abuse."

Birthmarks • Congenital skin blemishes visible from birth. The most frequent type of birthmark, commonly called a strawberry mark and technically known as a hemangioma, is a collection of small red or purplish blood vessels appearing on the skin surface. Most of these marks disappear by the time a child is 3 or 4. If they do not or if they grow and ulcerate, they can be removed by radiotherapy or surgery. The mark known as a port wine stain is formed by a combination of blood vessel clusters and erratic pigmentation. This blemish does not disappear spontaneously, but it may be effectively hidden under cosmetics prepared for this purpose.

Bisexuality • Sexual attraction to both men and women. An increase in the number of people who consider themselves bisexual may be due to the fact that more men and women feel free to acknowledge their bisexual feelings. However, the problem of AIDS raises many questions about the vulnerability of women who have sexual relationships with bisexual men. See "Sexually Transmissible Diseases."

Black Eye • Discoloration, swelling, and pain of the tissues around the eye, usually caused by a bruise that has ruptured tiny blood vessels under the skin. An icepack or cold compress applied immediately after the blow will slow subcutaneous bleeding, thus reducing the symptoms. A warm, wet compress applied on the following day will help absorb the discoloring fluids. If a blow to the eye is followed by persistent blurring of vision or severe pain, an ophthalmologist should be consulted promptly. If the black eye is the result of physical abuse by one's spouse or some other member of the household, prompt steps should be taken to avoid more serious injuries and indignities. See "Rape and Family Abuse."

Blackhead • A skin pore in which fatty material secreted by the sebaceous glands has accumulated and darkened, not because of dirt, but because of the effect of oxygen on the secretion itself. Blackheads usually accompany the acne of adolescence and may occasionally trouble older women whose skin is oily. Their occurrence may be reduced by keeping the skin clean and dry. When blackheads do appear, the temptation to squeeze them should be resisted in order to avoid infection. *See* ACNE.

Bladder Disorders • *See* URINARY TRACT INFECTIONS.

Bleeding • *See* HEMORRHAGE.

Blister • A collection of fluid (lymph), usually colorless, that forms a raised sac under the skin surface. A common cause of blisters is friction on the skin. Improperly fitted shoes should be stretched or discarded and gloves should be worn when using tools that may blister the hands. Minor injuries that do not break the skin may rupture a tiny blood vessel beneath the skin and cause a blood blister. Blisters are also associated with allergic reactions to poison ivy, with infections caused by the herpes simplex virus (fever blisters or cold sores), and with fungus invasions such as ringworm.

A large and painful blister may be drained in the following way: sterilize a needle by placing it in a flame, swab the area with soap and water, prick the outer margin of the blister, press the inflated skin surface gently with a sterile gauze to remove the fluid, and apply Bacitracin ointment and a sterile bandage. Any inflammation or accumulation of pus around a blister that has ruptured is a sign of bacterial infection and should be examined by a doctor.

Blood • The principal fluid of life: the medium in which oxygen and nutrients are transported to all tissues and carbon dioxide and other wastes are removed from tissues. Blood maintains the body's fluid balance by carrying water and salts to and from the tissues. It contains antibodies that fight infection, delivers hormones from the endocrine glands to the organs they influence, and regulates body temperature by dispersing heat in the form of perspiration. Every adult body contains about 1 quart (1,000 cc) of blood for every 25 pounds of weight. About 45 percent of blood composition consists of red cells that contain hemoglobin, white cells that fight infection, and platelets essential for the clotting process. The remaining 55 percent of blood composition is plasma. Blood plasma consists of water (over 90 percent) and proteins, hormones, enzymes, and other organic substances. Dissolved in the plasma are such proteins as globulins, fibrinogen, and albumen. *See* BLOOD SERUM, HEMOGLOBIN and illustration on next page. Blood diseases are discussed under the specific headings: ANEMIA, HEMOPHILIA, LEUKEMIA.

Blood Clotting • The coagulation or solidification of blood during which blood proteins and platelets combine to seal a break in the circulatory system. One of the plasma proteins indispensable in the clotting process, AHF (the *anti*hemophilic *f*actor), is missing from the blood of hemophiliacs. Medicines known as coagulants are available to hasten clotting in the case of hemorrhaging; vitamin therapy may be necessary in those cases where diet

Blood Pressure • The amount of pressure exerted against the arterial walls when the heart contracts (systolic pressure) and when it relaxes between beats (diastolic pressure). These measurements vary according to changes in the rate at which the heart beats and changes in the dilation or constriction of the blood vessels. The pumping action of the heart and the efficiency of the arteries in circulating the body's five quarts of blood are affected by many factors: general health of the heart muscle, elasticity and smoothness of the arterial walls, emotional stress, overweight, smoking, ingestion of drugs, alcoholic intake, time of day, and so on.

Blood pressure is measured by a device called a sphygmomanometer. It consists of a rubber cuff that can be blown up by squeezing an attached rubber bulb. The cuff is connected to a mercury-filled glass tube or to a gauge calibrated in millimeters. The cuff is wrapped around the brachial artery of the upper arm and inflated. As the cuff begins to put pressure on the artery, the mercury indicator rises. The doctor or nurse places a stethoscope on the crook of the elbow where the sound of the arterial pulse can be heard while continuing to inflate the cuff until the arterial blood flow is momentarily halted. The air pressure in the cuff is then released so that the blood flow resumes, producing a rhythmic tap. As soon as this tap is heard, the pressure registered on the gauge is recorded. This number is the systolic pressure. The cuff is then deflated slowly until the sound becomes so faint that it can scarcely be heard. The number registered by the gauge

deficiencies or faulty metabolism interfere with normal clotting.

Blood clots that form within the cardiovascular system are a major hazard because they impede circulation and can deprive vital organs of oxygen necessary for survival. Anticoagulants are used to counteract the formation of dangerous blood clots that may accompany diseases of the veins (phlebitis) or arteries (atherosclerosis). Heparin, a drug until recently used only in high doses to reduce the possibility of clotting in high-risk patients after surgery, injury, or childbirth, is now being used preoperatively in low doses by some surgeons. In addition to its many other properties, aspirin is an anticoagulant because it depresses platelet activity.

at this moment is the diastolic pressure.

The figures 120/80 are sometimes called an average reading, but they should not be considered a rigid norm. Normal readings for age ranges are: 17 to 40 years, up to 140/90; 41 to 60 years, up to 150/90; 61 years and older, 160/90. Lower limits of both systolic and diastolic pressures vary and their significance, if any, must be individually determined.

Blood Pressure, High • *See* HYPERTENSION.

Blood Serum • The clear, yellowish liquid that separates from whole blood when it clots. It contains proteins, enzymes, hormones, and chemicals such as glucose and sodium—all the constituents of whole blood except hemoglobin and fibrinogen. Protein antibodies (gamma globulins) present in the blood naturally or subsequent to active immunization can be fractionated out from serum, concentrated, and injected intramuscularly into another person to provide passive (short-lived, not more than 6 months) immunization against such diseases as hepatitis and measles. *See* GAMMA GLOBULIN

Blood Test • Laboratory analysis of the blood that provides information for the diagnosis of a disorder or disease. If only a small amount of blood is required, it is taken from the fleshy cushion of a finger. When a large amount is needed for several different laboratory tests, blood is usually taken from a vein in the crook of the arm.

A patient entering the hospital for surgery is often given several blood tests. These are necessary for diagnostic purposes as well as to establish the patient's blood type in the event a transfusion is required. Blood tests for hemoglobin, cholesterol, and glucose are among the routine procedures of a comprehensive annual checkup. Such tests can indicate the presence of diabetes, anemia, kidney disorder, glandular disorder, hepatitis, and the presence of antibodies indicating the exposure to such diseases as AIDS. *See* "Suggested Health Examinations."

Blood Transfusion • The infusion of blood into the veins of a patient from an outside source. Transfusions had unpredictable results until the beginning of the twentieth century when blood groups were discovered. The accurate matching of blood is necessary for a successful transfusion.

The replenishment of blood is a lifesaving measure in such circumstances as hemorrhage resulting from accident, tissue injuries caused by severe burns, or blood loss attendant on surgery. While whole blood may be desirable in most cases, it may not be essential in instances of shock when the crucial requirement is blood plasma or serum. These components can be accumulated without regard to type because they are universally compatible. They can be stored frozen in large amounts and drawn on in emergencies involving large numbers of victims such as a plane crash.

Among the recent developments in blood transfusion are two techniques with broad application. *Plateletpheresis* involves taking blood from a healthy donor, removing the platelets that are the component essential for clotting, and immediately returning the remainder—the red cells, white cells, and plasma—to the donor. The transfusion of platelets can extend the lives of patients with certain types of anemia, leukemia, and other malignant diseases for whom bleeding episodes might otherwise be fatal. This procedure in no way endangers the donor's blood supply because platelets in the body of a healthy person are automatically replaced within two days. The second innovation in transfusion is a technique whereby white blood cells can be supplied to cancer patients who are receiving drugs that temporarily suppress the ability of the bone marrow to manufacture them. In this way patients undergoing anticancer chemotherapy are provided with the white cells necessary for fighting infection.

The risk of contracting AIDS or hepatitis has led to the recommendation by some hospitals that patients preparing for elective surgery should bank their own blood in advance should a transfusion be necessary.

Blood Types • For many years it had been observed that some blood transfusions were successful and some were not, but it was not until the twentieth century that the riddle of incompatibility was solved. It is now known that the blood of all humans, regardless of skin color, race, country of origin, or sex, can be classified under four main groupings: A, B, AB, and O. Blood type O (the "O" stands for zero) is composed of red cells that can blend with any type of plasma. Because of this compatibility, a person with O type blood is a universal donor. Conversely, anyone with AB type blood is a universal recipient. Of each 100 individuals, approximately 45 will be type O, 40 will be type A, 10 will be type B, and 5 will be type AB. There are many minor subtypes that are inconsequential for most people. *See also* RH FACTOR.

Body Odors • Natural odors associated with the human body. Fresh perspiration from a healthy body is practically odorless. Most unpleasant body odors are caused by the presence of bacteria or fungi that multiply in areas where perspiration can accumulate, such as the genital area, the armpits, and between the toes, and by stale perspiration absorbed by clothing. Regular scrubbing with soap and water and regular changes of clothes should keep the body clean and odorless. It should be noted that vaginal sprays can be quite harmful to the delicate membranes they are supposed to deodorize. *See* ANTIPERSPIRANT and DEODORANT.

Boil • A painful bacterial infection, usually staphylococcal, of a hair follicle or sweat gland, occurring on the face, scalp, neck, shoulders, breast, or buttocks. The infected lump, technically called a furuncle, may be as small as a cherry pit or quite large. Because the infection can easily spread, a boil should be treated promptly. Moist, hot compresses should be applied several times a day. The boil should then be covered with an antibiotic salve such as bacitracin ointment and protected by a sterile gauze bandage. A boil should never be squeezed, especially one on the nose, ear, or upper lip, because some of the bacteria may invade the bloodstream instead of going to the lymph glands or being exuded to the skin surface leading to possible blood poisoning. Boils that do not drain naturally following the application of heat and moisture may have to be incised surgically. Those that occur in groups (carbuncles) or that recur may be the result of faulty habits of personal hygiene, low resistance, diabetes, or a strain of bacteria requiring a newer antibiotic. Such cases should be treated by a doctor.

Bone • The hard tissue that forms the major part of the skeleton. The 206 bones in the human body are connected by ligaments at the joints and are activated into movement by muscles secured to the bones by tendons. Bones are covered by a thin fibrous membrane called periosteum that sheathes and protects them and supports the adjacent tendons. The periosteum stops at the joints that are covered by a layer of cartilage. The fibrous layer of tissue directly under the periosteum gives bones their elasticity. Next are the dense hard layers called compact tissue within which are encased the porous materials known as spongy tissue. The innermost cavity of bone contains the marrow, which is the source of red blood cell production. Every layer of bone is criss-crossed by blood vessels. Bone tissue also contains a large number of nerves.

The hardness and strength of the skeleton result from the mineral content—calcium phosphate. This mineral, plentiful in milk, is essential for the transformation of cartilage into the calcified part of bone during childhood and adolescence. Bone tissue, even when fully formed in adulthood, constantly renews itself, but because the rate of renewal slows with age, the bones of the elderly become more brittle as they become more porous and less elastic. Known as osteoporosis, this condition when it occurs in women is caused by the decreasing flow of estrogen that characterizes the menopause.

The health of bones may be impaired by dietary deficiency of the mother during pregnancy or of the child during the years of growth, by infectious diseases (osteomyelitis), degenerative diseases (osteoporosis, osteoarthritis), tumors, and a rare form of primary cancer (sarcoma). The most common bone injury is a fracture, and bones may also bleed internally after sustaining a severe bruise. *See* "Aging Healthfully—Your Body."

Botulism • A form of food poisoning caused by bacteria that produce a toxin that attacks the nervous system. The causative bacterium, *Clostridium botulinum*, thrives in low-acid, low-sugar substances where there is no oxygen. It is typically found in improperly preserved foods, such as canned vegetables, meat, or smoked fish, and the contaminated food rarely smells, tastes, or looks spoiled. Faulty procedures in home canning are responsible for a significant number of cases, as many as half of which are fatal. Diagnosis is simplified by the fact that several people, including household pets, are likely to be affected at the same time.

Nausea and vomiting occur generally in less than 24 hours and may or may not precede the central nervous system symptoms that are caused by the toxin and whose onset usually is from 12 to 36 hours after eating. These symptoms are double vision, puffy or drooping eyelids, and paralysis that impedes swallowing and breathing. The victim must be hospitalized at once for treatment to nullify the toxin and to prevent respiratory failure. Anyone who has eaten the spoiled food must be treated without delay with botulinus antitoxin.

Bowel Disease • *See* COLITIS, COLON CANCER, CHOHN'S DISEASE, DI-

VERTICULOSIS, IRRITABLE BOWEL SYNDROME.

Brain • The central organ of the nervous system, interpreting all sense impressions, controlling the activities of over 600 of the body's voluntary muscles, regulating the autonomic nervous system, and through its capacity for storing and recalling the messages received by its billions of cells, functioning as the memory bank that we call the mind.

The human brain is made of soft, convoluted, pinkish-gray tissue that weighs about 3 pounds and fits within the confines of the skull. Enveloping the brain and separating it from its bony encasement are three tough membranes, collectively called the meninges, which also sheathe the spinal cord. Between two of these membranous layers is the cerebrospinal fluid that may be tapped for accurate diagnosis of such diseases as cerebrospinal meningitis. The portion of the brain that has come to be synonymous with the mind is the cerebrum whose outer layer, the cerebral cortex, is fissured, furrowed, and wrinkled into "gray matter." The deepest fissure divides this part of the brain into two distinct halves: the nerves in the right hemisphere control the left side of the body and vice versa. Emerging from the cerebrum at the middle of the skull and extending down the back of the neck into the spinal cord is the brain stem; on either side of the brain stem are the two halves of the cerebellum. The cerebellum is the portion of the brain whose essential function is the coordination of muscular activities.

Because the activities of the brain are manifested by the transmission of electrical impulses, normal and abnormal brain wave patterns can be charted by an instrument called an encephalograph. This enables neurologists to diagnose such disorders as epilepsy and tumors and to explore the various stages of sleep by the different brain wave patterns they produce. The brain responds to electrical stimulation from the outside, thus revealing the particular function of different areas.

The brain also functions as a gland, manufacturing substances similar in chemical composition to morphine that have the same effect on the body as synthetic painkillers. These hormonelike substances are called endorphins and enkephalins. The amounts in which they are produced and released are presumed to define the body's sensations of pain and pleasure as well as to account for the symptoms of some forms of mental illness.

Many brain tumors that were previously untreatable or inoperable can now be reduced by radiation or completely removed due to advances in the techniques of hypothermia and microsurgery. Legal death is now defined not by the cessation of the heartbeat, but by the death of the brain resulting from oxygen deprivation. *See* ALZHEIMER'S DISEASE, EPILEPSY, and PARKINSONISM.

Breast Examination • *See* "Breast Care." *See* "Suggested Health Examinations."

Breech Delivery • Childbirth in which the baby emerges buttocks or feet first instead of head first. *See* "Pregnancy and Childbirth."

Bronchitis • Inflammation of the lining of the bronchial tubes, the air passages that connect the windpipe and the lungs. In its acute form the inflammation may be an extension of an upper respiratory viral infection or may be caused by a bacterial infection following an upper respiratory illness. Such an attack is accompanied by fever and coughing up of the excess mucus secreted by the inflamed membranes. Bed rest and an expectorant medicine that loosens the sputum rather than one that suppresses the cough are the standard treatment. Antibiotics are used if the infection is diagnosed as bacterial. Chronic bronchitis is a much more serious matter because the recurrent or persistent coughing and spitting up can lead to irreversible lung injury and an increased vulnerability to emphysema and heart disease. In chronic bronchitis, the victim coughs and spits up yellow mucus, especially in the morning and evening, and eventually the condition becomes irreversible. Too many patients take early symptoms for granted and wait until the disease approaches a disabling stage before seeing a doctor. The first and indispensable aspect of treatment is to stop smoking. In some cases rehabilitation may involve a change of job. In others the symptoms may gradually disappear after strict adherence to a wholesome regimen: proper diet, mild exercise, rest and relaxation, and avoidance of lung irritants. See EMPHYSEMA.

Bruise • An injury in which small subcutaneous blood vessels are damaged but the skin surface remains intact; also called a contusion. When the skin is broken, the injury is called an abrasion or a laceration. In a bruise the escape of blood into the surrounding tissues causes pain and swelling as well as the characteristic discoloration of the skin. The effects of a bruise may not be visible when a blow is sustained by a muscle, a bone, or an ear. Healing is usually hastened and pain reduced by the use of cold compresses just after the injury to slow down the bleeding. An injured arm or leg will cause less discomfort and mend more quickly if it is elevated. The application of heat to the bruised area the following day is likely to hasten the reabsorption of the blood. If symptoms increase rather than abate, a doctor should be consulted, especially where deeper internal bruises are suspected. See BLACK EYE.

Bulimia • An eating disorder characterized by binge eating followed by induced vomiting, repeated up to four or more times a day. Some victims take multiple laxatives. Most victims are women who are perfectionists and begin this binge-purge behavior in their late teens. The problem often begins after losing weight by dieting. Binging appears to be a stress relief and purging is done to avoid obesity. Many victims manage to hide their problem from others for years. It is difficult to treat, and there can be serious, even fatal, complications. The cause is unknown. See ANOREXIA NERVOSA, a related disorder, and "Directory of Health Information."

Bunion • A deformity of the foot that occurs when the big toe deviates from its natural position because of inflammation at the joint connecting the toe to the foot. Continuing pressure results in the hard swelling at the base of the toe and the development of the bunion. Discomfort is best relieved by correcting the footwear that causes the problem. In mild cases, with shoes that fit properly, the condition may be eliminated without further treatment. When the pain is severe enough to interfere with normal functioning even when wearing shoes with an orthopedic correction, surgery may be the only practical solution.

Burns • Injuries resulting from contact with dry heat (fire), moist heat (scalding by steam or liquid), electricity, chemicals, or the ultraviolet rays of the sun or a sunlamp. Whatever the cause, the injury is classified according to the extent of tissue damage. A first-degree burn is one in which the skin turns visibly red; a second-degree burn causes the skin to blister; a third-degree burn damages the deeper skin layers and may destroy the growth cells in the subcutaneous tissues. Even a first-degree burn is potentially dangerous if a large area of the body has been affected, especially if the victim is very young or very old. Until professional help is available a person who has sustained a serious burn should lie down and liquids should be administered but only if they can be consciously swallowed. Ice cold water can be gently applied to the burned area. *Do not* give any alcoholic beverage. *Do not* disturb blisters. *Do not* attempt to remove clothing adhering to burnt skin. *Do not* apply oily salves or ointments or antiseptic sprays except in cases of superficial burns involving a small area. More and more hospitals are establishing special burn treatment centers where new techniques are applied to save lives and reduce suffering.

Bursitis • Inflammation of a bursa, one of the small fluid-filled sacs located at various joints throughout the body for the purpose of minimizing friction. Bursitis most commonly oc-

BURSITIS OF THE SHOULDER

Bursa is swollen and filled with calcium deposits

Normal joint capsule

Muscle Humerus (upper arm)

Scapula (shoulder blade)

curs at the joints receiving the most wear and tear: at the hip, shoulder, knee, and elbow. "Housemaid's knee" and "tennis elbow" are the result of bursa inflammation. A bunion is the result of inflammation of the bursa that lubricates the joint between the big toe and the foot. An acute, and acutely painful, attack of bursitis may occur after an accident, following unusual exertion connected with moving heavy objects, or as a concomitant of a systemic infection. Although such an attack may be self-healing within a week or ten days, the process can be eased and hastened by taking aspirin or some other analgesic and immobilizing the affected joint in a sling or a flexible bandage.

Caffeine • A widely ingested drug found in coffee, tea, and cola drinks, and in many over-the-counter medicines. It stimulates the central nervous system, the heart, and the kidneys. Some people are especially sensitive to caffeine and should keep their consumption to a minimum, especially if it interferes with sleep and is the obvious cause of arrhythmias. Studies of caffeine as a cancer-causing agent have not yielded definitive results, nor has it been unambiguously linked to birth defects, premenstrual syndrome, or painful periods. While women prone to the formation of the spongy lumps that characterize the fibrocystic breast syndrome may feel more comfortable if they eliminate all caffeine from their diet, it is not the *cause* of the condition. It has been established, however, that although only small amounts of caffeine pass into breast milk, such amounts are sufficient to result in wakefulness and irritability in nursing babies. See "Substance Abuse" and "Pregnancy and Childbirth."

Calcium • A metallic element essential to life. See "Nutrition, Weight, and General Well-Being."

Improper metabolism of calcium during the growing years may result in osteoporosis, a disorder in which the bones are excessively brittle and weaker than normal. This condition commonly occurs during aging, especially in women, and is caused by the loss of calcium associated with the cessation of estrogen production. A diet deficient in calcium and vitamin D during pregnancy or at other times may cause muscle cramps, especially in the legs. If the symptom persists in spite of proper nutrition, it may indicate faulty calcium metabolism, necessitating the injection of the calcium or the vitamin directly into the bloodstream. This particular malfunction may be due to underactivity of the parathyroid glands. Overactivity of the glands may cause excessive amounts of calcium in the bloodstream, which in turn may encourage the formation of kidney stones and increase the likelihood of bone fractures. No connection has been established between the consumption of large amounts of calcium-containing dairy products and the formation of kidney stones.

Calculus • Technical term for stone formation in the body. Calculi may develop in the gallbladder or in the kidneys. See GALLSTONES and KIDNEYS AND KIDNEY DISORDERS.

Calendar Rhythm Method • A means of contraception based on the avoidance of sexual intercourse during those days of the month when a woman is most likely to conceive. See "Contraception and Abortion."

Callus • An area of the skin that has thickened as a protection against repeated friction; also an irregular bump on a bone that has formed when the recalcification process closes a fracture. The calluses that form on the hands as a result of constant friction or repeated pressures can best be prevented by wearing protective gloves. Most of those that form on the soles of the feet or around the outer rim of the heels can be eliminated by wearing proper footwear. Calluses of this type become painful when they are thick enough to transfer pressure exerted on them to a bone. Calluses can be reduced by rubbing them with pumice or an emery board.

Calorie • A unit of energy measurement used in both physics and in the study of nutrition. Food is the fuel that provides the body with the energy essential for carrying on the life processes. The potential energy provided by various foods as they are metabolized by the body is measured in calories. See "Nutrition, Weight, and General Well-Being."

Cancer • The general term for a disease process in which the cells in a particular part of the body grow and reproduce with abnormal rapidity. This defect in the controls that govern normal cell growth characterizes about 200 different diseases known as cancers, most of which are also called malignancies or malignant tumors. Cancers that are created by disordered epithelial cells and arise on the surface of the lining of a tissue or within a duct are *carcinomas*. Malignancies that originate in bones and muscles are known as *sarcomas*. Those that originated in the blood-forming organs are called *leukemias*. Those that start in the lymphatics are called *lymphomas*. Malignancies created by the cells that carry the dark pigment melanin are called *melanomas*.

A cancer is said to be localized when the diseased cells remain clumped together even if the group of cells grows into a visible mass large enough to invade underlying or surrounding tissue. When some of the diseased cells break away and make their way into the bloodstream or the lymphatics eventually reaching other parts of the body, the cancer is said to have metastasized. See also CARCINOMA, SARCOMA, LEUKEMIA, MELANOMA, METASTASIS.

Candidiasis • A yeastlike fungus, also called moniliasis or thrush. See "Sexually Transmissible Diseases."

Canker Sore • An ulceration of the mucous membrane at the corner of the mouth or inside the lips or cheeks. While not attributable to a single cause, canker sores may result from a deficiency of vitamin B_{12} or iron, or their onset may be triggered by stress, viral infection, menstruation, sensitivity to particular foods, or mechanical irritation by a rough-edged tooth or filling or ill-fitting dentures. Most canker sores are occasional and self-healing. Recurrent canker sores so painful that they interfere with talking or eating should be treated by a physician.

Car Sickness • See MOTION SICKNESS.

Carbohydrates • Any of a number of chemical substances, including starches, sugars, cellulose, and gums, containing only carbon, hydrogen, and oxygen in varying amounts with the ratio of hydrogen to oxygen usually being two to one as in water. Carbohydrates are present in many foods, primarily in grains and potatoes as starch and in fruits and vegetables as sugar. They are an indispensable source of animal (human) energy. Dietary starch and polysaccharide (complex) sugars—maltose, sucrose, and lactose—are converted into glucose in the digestive tract and are absorbed in that form into the bloodstream. Monosaccharide (simple) sugars—glucose, fructose, and galactose—are absorbed into the blood unchanged. Some of these absorbed monosaccharides are used immediately to provide energy.

The rest are converted into glycogen by the liver and stored primarily in the liver and muscles for later energy or are converted into fat. Many factors, including diseases, influence the rate and amount that is absorbed. The most common disease that interferes with normal carbohydrate metabolism is diabetes mellitus. *See* DIABETES, GLUCOSE, SUGAR, and "Nutrition, Weight, and General Well-Being."

Carcinogen • Any agent (tobacco smoke, X-rays, asbestos fibers, food additives, drugs) capable of causing changes in cell structure (mutagenesis) and therefore a potential cause of cancer.

Carcinoma • One of the two main groups of cancers; the other is sarcoma. A carcinoma originates in epithelial cells located in glandular structures, mucous membranes, and skin. Practically all malignancies of the skin, tongue, stomach, uterus, and breast come under this heading.

Cardiopulmonary Resuscitation (CPR) • An emergency lifesaving technique in which oxygenated blood is sent to the brain and other tissues of the victim of cardiac arrest by the simultaneous administration of artificial respiration and external manipulation of the heart. CPR must be initiated at once following a heart attack, electric shock, or any other circumstance in which the lack of circulation has begun to deprive the brain of oxygen. Because of its proven effectiveness when administered by a properly trained individual, the Red Cross and the American Heart Association are encouraging ordinary citizens, including teenagers, to take the six- to twelve-hour CPR courses being offered under their auspices.

Carotene • A plant pigment especially plentiful in carrots and also found in yellow, orange, and red fruits and vegetables in smaller amounts. Carotene is essential in the diet because it is converted into vitamin A in the body. It is also one of the weaker pigments in human skin. Its yellowish tone is generally masked by the melanin pigment in dark-complexioned women, but a fair complexion will take on an orange hue if the diet contains an excessive amount of carrots.

Carpal Tunnel Syndrome • Inflammation of a median nerve at the point where it travels from the forearm through the tunnel formed by the wrist bones ("carpus" is Latin for "wrist") in order to reach the fingers. Because the tunnel is covered by a tight band of fibrous tissue, the nerve is pinched when the surrounding tendons and ligaments swell. Swelling occurs because of irritation brought about by an injury or constant wear and tear associated with occupations in which the wrist is constantly flexed as it must be in hitting keys all day long—the common lot of office workers, pianists, and certain kinds of machine operators.

When the pain is mild, a molded splint can be worn, which reduces pressure by preventing the wrist from flexing. If the pain is severe, a simple surgical procedure cuts open a part of the fibrous tissue, thereby reducing pressure on the nerve. *See* "Health on the Job."

Cartilage • The tough, whitish elastic tissue that, together with bone, forms the skeleton. There are three different types of cartilage. Hyaline cartilage forms the extremely strong slippery surface of the ends of the bones at the joints, acting as a shock absorber. It is also the material of which the nose and the rings of the trachea are made. Fibrocartilage is densely packed with fibers and forms the disks between the spinal vertebrae. Elastic cartilage is the most flexible, forming the external ear and the larynx. The stiffness in the joints that characterizes osteoarthritis is associated with a deterioration of cartilage.

CAT • *See* COMPUTERIZED AXIAL TOMOGRAPHY.

Cataract • Opacity or cloudiness that develops in the crystalline lens of the eye. When the lens becomes so opaque that light can no longer reach the retina, loss of vision results. Fortunately, restoration of eyesight is accomplished safely and successfully in 95 percent of the hundreds of thousands of cataract operations performed every year in the United States. Although a few types of cataracts are congenital or are caused by injury, infection, or radiation exposure, the largest number by far are senile or degenerative cataracts—those that develop after the age of 60. They are one of the leading causes of blindness among the aged. Diabetics should be especially vigilant about changes in vision. In addition to other problems affecting their eyes, they are likelier to develop cataracts earlier and faster than is normally the case and should, therefore, schedule visits to an ophthalmologist several times a year.

In most instances the cloudiness develops so slowly that no significant change in vision is detectable. Annual visits to an ophthalmologist for a glaucoma check after the age of 40 are the best way to find out about incipient cataracts and to plan ahead for their removal. However, for most people the first awareness of a cataract comes with blurred or dimmed vision, double images, and a scattering of light beams when looking directly at a street lamp or at the headlights of an approaching car. As soon as any of these symptoms occur, an ophthalmologist should be consulted. *The only effective treatment for the condition is surgery.* Because there is as yet no magical method for "dissolving" cataracts with "special medicines" nor can they be treated by a "special" diet, all such claims should be regarded as quackery and, if possible, reported to the proper authorities for investigation.

A cataract operation consists of the removal of the degenerated lens and its replacement with an artificial lens in the form of eyeglasses, contact lens, or more recently, for certain patients, an intraocular lens. Whether the surgery is the conventional method that removes the cataract by lifting it out in one piece or the newer method that pulverizes the lens with an ultrasonic probe, recovery is considerably faster today than in the past. Even in cases where there is some difficulty in adjusting to the artificial lens, it rarely takes more than a few months for the transition to occur.

Because people who develop a cataract in one eye are likely to have the same problem with the other eye, it is considered advisable to schedule early treatment of the damaged eye without waiting for the cataract to develop fully or "ripen," so that the unaffected eye can provide unimpaired vision following the operation.

Catheterization • The procedure in which a tube is inserted through a passage in the body for the purpose of withdrawing or introducing fluids or other materials. Catheters have been used for centuries, but since the introduction of plastics they are less costly to manufacture and give minimal discomfort to the patient. In the more common applications, a catheter is introduced into the urethra for draining urine from the bladder; an intravenous catheter is used for "tube-feeding" following surgery; a nasogastric tube is used for withdrawing samples of material from the stomach as a diagnostic clue. Catheterization is essential in the administration of oxygen through the nose, and it can effectively remove stones lodged in the ureter, the passageway connecting the kidney and the bladder. Cardiac catheterization is routinely used to detect and measure critical abnormalities caused by circulatory disorders.

Cauterization • The burning away of infected, unwanted, or dead tissue by the application of caustic chemicals or electrically heated instruments. Cryosurgery used in the treatment of certain types of tumors is a form of cauterization; the removal of surface moles with an electrical needle is another. Cauterization of cervical tissue to prevent the spread of erosion is a common gynecological practice, and it is also used to remove a small, localized cervical cancer.

Cavities • *See* DENTAL CARIES.

Cell • The structural unit of which all body tissues are formed. The human body is composed of billions of cells differing in size and structure depending on their function. In spite of these differences every cell includes the same basic components: an outer limiting membrane that regulates the transport of chemical substances into and out of the cell, a mass of cytoplasm containing substances involved in metabolism and genetic transmission, a nucleus whose membrane contains the concentration of RNA and encloses the DNA that determines the hereditary transmission of genetic characteristics. The study of normal cell structure and behavior is basic to cancer research, because all cancers are characterized by aberrational cell growth and reproduction.

Cerebral Palsy • A neuromuscular disorder of unknown cause and varying degrees of severity whose symptoms usually appear by age 3. Cerebral palsy is characterized by an inability to control the muscles of the arms and legs, by mild or serious speech impairment, and by jerky movements of the head and torso. Intellectual disability is not necessarily associated with this disorder, but emotional problems are likely to become deep-rooted unless the child receives strong familial support and understanding treatment in school. Physical and speech therapy as well as medication to reduce spasticity are aspects of treatment. Factors placing the child at higher risk include extreme prematurity and mental retardation of the mother. *See* "Directory of Health Information."

Cerebrovascular Accident • *See* STROKE.

Cervical Cap • A contraceptive device made of plastic and individually fitted so that it can be placed snugly over the cervix. It is about as effective as a diaphragm. *See* "Contraception and Abortion."

Cervix • The neck or narrow portion of any organ but generally used to refer to the hollow end of the uterus that forms the passageway into the vaginal canal. The cervix is approximately 2 inches in length. Under normal circumstances it has the diameter of a quarter with an opening *(os)* that has the diameter of a drinking straw. At the time of delivery, the cervix dilates to a diameter usually given as 10 centimeters or five fingers.

Women who use a diaphragm should be aware of the position of the opening of the cervix, because the diaphragm is inserted across this opening as a barrier against the passage of sperm toward the ovum.

During pregnancy natural processes deposit a thick layer of mucus across the cervical entrance, sealing off the womb against invasion by infectious organisms.

The first symptom of infection of the cervix (cervicitis) is likely to be a vaginal discharge that becomes more abundant immediately following menstruation. Other signs may be bleeding, pain during intercourse, a burning sensation during urination, or lower back pain. Such symptoms should be brought to the attention of a gynecologist. A culture of the discharge may be necessary to identify the infectious agent, especially if the infection does not respond to antibiotic medicines or fungicides. Where tissue erosion has occurred, cauterization by electricity, chemical application, or freezing may be necessary.

Another cause of bleeding, especially in middle-aged women with a history of cervical infections, is the presence of fleshy growths called polyps. Although these growths are easily removed and generally benign, a tissue biopsy is performed to rule out the possibility of cancer. The best safeguard against cervical cancer, one of the leading causes of cancer deaths in women over 40, is an annual pap test. *See* "Contraception and Abortion," "Pregnancy and Childbirth," "Infertility," and "Gynecologic Diseases and Treatment."

Cesarean Section • A surgical procedure in which an incision is made into the uterus through the front of the abdominal wall to deliver a baby when vaginal delivery is difficult or impossible or presents a risk to the mother or the baby. The fact that a first child was delivered by cesarian section does not preclude a vaginal delivery for births that follow. The mother should be given the option whenever possible. At a time when many women feel that conscious participation in the birth experience is an inalienable right and when many fathers want to share as much of the experience as the hospital will allow, cesarean deliveries sometimes cause feelings of deprivation, depression, and guilt. Fortunately, support groups are now available to deal with this contingency. *See* "Pregnancy and Childbirth" and "Directory of Health Information."

Chancre • An ulcerated sore in the area of bacterial invasion that is the first sign of the primary stage of syphilis. *See* "Sexually Transmissible Diseases."

Chemotherapy • The treatment of illness by the use of specific chemicals. One of the earliest such treatments was the use of quinine against the malarial parasite. This was followed by Dr. Paul Ehrlich's discovery in 1910 that salvarsan effectively destroyed the spirochete that causes syphilis and by later development of sulfa drugs and antibiotics. More recently, the term has been expanded to include the application of such drugs as chlorpromazine (Thorazine) in controlling some of the symptoms of mental illness.

At present, treatment of various cancers by chemotherapy has increased survival rate in a significant number of cases. Upwards of 50 drugs used in various combinations for specific cancers are now available. Not all of these have undesirable side effects, and in 90 percent of all cases, they are administered on an outpatient basis, often in the physician's office. Surgery and radiation have been producing more and more positive results, but the greatest advances have been made in chemotherapy, especially when the cancer is diagnosed and treated in its earliest stage. As cancer research progresses, more drugs are found that can kill diseased cells without damaging the healthy ones.

Chest Pains • Discomfort in any part of the thorax, usually caused by a disorder of one of the organs within the thoracic cavity enclosed by the rib cage, by an injury to a rib, or by a strained muscle. The site of a disorder may be the heart, lungs, large blood vessels, esophagus, or part of the trachea. Any viral or bacterial infection of the respiratory system may be accompanied by pain that may become acute when constant coughing is involved. Various allergies to mold, dust, animal dander, chemical pollutants may be another cause. Pain might be referred to the chest by the nervous system from areas outside the thoracic cavity. For example, certain types of indigestion produce a pain that may be mistaken for a heart attack. In most cases, however, the pain resulting from cardiovascular problems is the feeling of tightness and suffocation characteristic of angina pectoris. Almost all chest pains that originate in respiratory or circulatory disorders are intensified by smoking. Persistent chest pains should always be diagnosed and treated by a doctor.

ORIGINS OF CHEST PAINS

Inflammation of esophagus

Inflammation of lung, bronchi, or pleura

Injured rib

Inflammation of diaphragm

Coronary artery disease or spasm

Chilblains • Inflammation of the skin, accompanied by burning and itching, usually caused by exposure to cold. Special vulnerability to chilblains may result from poor circulation, inadequate diet, or an allergic response to low temperatures.

The condition is easier to prevent than to treat. Anyone sensitive to the cold should always wear warm clothes, especially woolen or partly woolen socks (never 100 percent synthetic), fleece-lined boots, and woolen gloves.

When chilblains have occurred, no attempts should be made to "stimulate" circulation by applying extreme heat or cold to the affected areas. In most cases a warm dry environment will bring about a return to normal. If the symptoms persist or if blisters form on the skin surface, a doctor should be consulted for further instructions.

Chlamydia • A frequently misdiagnosed bacterial disease of the reproductive system that infects upward of 5 million men and women each year. While sometimes presenting only mild symptoms, chlamydia is believed to cause pelvic inflammatory disease, infertility, and miscarriage. It can be identified by a specific laboratory test and is successfully treated with antibiotics. *See* "Sexually Transmissible Diseases."

Chlorine • A chemical element widely used to purify public water supplies and disinfect swimming pools because it is cheap, easily manufactured, and effective against bacteria, viruses, and fungi. An excessively chlorinated swimming pool will cause temporary eye discomfort, and skin contact with chlorine in household bleaches will produce an itching and burning rash as an allergic reaction where sensitivity exists to this chemical.

Chloromycetin • Brand name of the antibiotic chloramphenicol. *See also* ANTIBIOTICS.

Chlorpromazine • The first of the major tranquilizers, chlorpromazine (brand name Thorazine) has been used since 1952 to forestall the onset of acute psychotic episodes in schizophrenic and manic-depressive patients. In the treatment of the mentally ill, this drug is prescribed not as a cure but to control their disturbances in perception. This application of chemotherapy has largely replaced electroshock treatments, previously used for the same purpose.

A patient taking this drug should be advised of some of the possible side effects: dry mouth, drowsiness, blurred vision, and photosensitivity. Long-term use may lead to the condition called tardive dyskinesia characterized by jerky movements of the facial muscles. All side effects abate when the drug is discontinued.

Chlorpromazine should not be prescribed for mild anxiety or depression, especially when the patient is elderly. Other more suitable and less disorienting medications are available for these conditions.

Choking • Obstruction of the air passage in the throat by a swallowed object that has gone into the windpipe instead of into the esophagus. When food is being swallowed, an automatic mechanism closes the flap at the top of the trachea (windpipe). It is not unusual, however, for a morsel of food or, in the case of a small child, a foreign object such as a button to "go down the wrong way." This is apt to happen when a sudden intake of breath caused by laughing, talking, or coughing occurs while a person has food in her mouth. The immediate signs of choking are an inability to speak or breathe. In minutes the skin turns bluish, and unless emergency assistance is prompt, the results can be fatal.

If an infant is choking, hold the

body upside down by the torso and strike its back lightly several times between the shoulder blades. For an older child or an adult use the Heimlich maneuver, a life-saving technique illustrated in entry under HEIMLICH MANEUVER.

Cholesterol • A crystalline fatty alcohol found in animal fats, blood, bile, and nerve tissue. Cholesterol is synthesized in the liver and is the material from which the body's steroids, including the sex hormones, are manufactured. It is also one of the chief constituents of biliary gallstones that can now be dissolved by a drug that reduces the liver's synthesis and secretion of cholesterol. Because high levels of cholesterol in the blood serum increase the likelihood of atherosclerotic disease and the possibility of heart attack and because about 20 million Americans are considered at high risk, specialists recommend that all adults should have a blood cholesterol checkup as part of a routine physical examination. For those with higher than acceptable levels (more than 240 milligrams per deciliter of blood), a strict diet is advised. If diet doesn't improve the condition, medication is now available that inhibits cholesterol production.

In addition to abstaining from foods that are high in cholesterol, such as butter, cheese, whole milk, egg yolk, and liver as well as hydrogenated fats such as solid vegetable shortenings and solid margarines, specialists recommend that fish, such as tuna, salmon, mackerel, and herring be consumed at least twice a week instead of red meat. The consumption of supplementary fish oil should be discussed with a physician, and eggs and cheese need not be eliminated from the diet unless the results of the cholesterol blood test indicate the advisability of doing so.

Chromosomes • Stringlike structures within the cell nucleus that contain the genetic information governing each person's inherited characteristics. Normal human body cells contain 46 paired chromosomes composed of DNA (deoxyribonucleic acid). An ovum contains 22 autosome and 1 sex (X) chromosomes. A sperm contains 22 autosome and 1 sex (X or Y) chromosomes so that when they combine during reproduction the offspring cell receives its full complement of 46 "message carriers."

The sex of an offspring is determined by the combination of the sex chromosomes designated as X and Y. If an egg is fertilized by a sperm carrying the X chromosome, the offspring will have two X chromosomes and will therefore be female (XX). If an egg is fertilized by a Y-bearing sperm, the offspring will have one of each and will be male (XY).

Chromosomal abnormalities vary in significance, the more serious ones being responsible for birth defects, mental retardation, and spontaneous abortion.

The possibility of abnormalities severe enough to warrant abortion can be determined through prenatal genetic counseling. Research in recent years indicates that environmental and occupational exposure to various chemicals can cause irreversible damage to chromosomes, leading to genetic mutations in the offspring. Possible effects of various drugs are discussed in the chapter "Substance Abuse." *See* AMNIOCENTESIS SEX-LINKED ABNORMALITIES and illustration on next page.

HEREDITY

Gene for specific characteristic on pairs of chromosomes

Baby receives one chromosome from each parent for each pair

Chronic Symptom • Symptom of a disorder that lasts over a long period of time, sometimes for the remainder of the patient's life, such as the joint pains characteristic of rheumatoid arthritis or the cough associated with emphysema.

Cimetidine • A drug (Tagamet) that lowers the acid secretion of the stomach and is, therefore, widely prescribed for gastritis and ulcers when changes in diet and more traditional nonprescription antacids are ineffective. Nursing mothers should not take this drug because the amounts that end up in breast milk are sufficient to affect the baby adversely.

Cirrhosis • Degenerative disease especially of the liver in which the development of fibrous tissue with consequent hardening and scarring causes the loss of normal function. Cirrhosis of the liver is most frequently associated with chronic alcoholism, affecting 15 percent of all heavy drinkers. However, the condition may also occur after infectious hepatitis or, more rarely, as a consequence of toxic hepatitis in which liver cells are damaged because of sensitivity to such drugs as chlorpromazine (Thorazine) or chloramphenicol (Chloromycetin). Overconsumption of salt is also a contributing factor.

Cirrhosis is insidious because it may be asymptomatic until it has resulted in irreversible damage. When symptoms are manifest, they include abdominal swelling with fluid, soreness under the rib cage, swollen ankles, weight loss, and general fatigue. In advanced cases the signs are jaundice and possible vomiting of blood leading to collapse. When alcoholic cirrhosis is treated promptly at an early stage, the liver may repair and rehabilitate itself. Total abstention from alcohol and a diet rich in proteins and supplementary vitamins are essential to recovery. *See* LIVER.

Claudication • *See* INTERMITTENT CLAUDICATION.

Claustrophobia • An irrational, persistent, and often insurmountable fear of enclosed places such as elevators, windowless rooms, and the like.

Climacteric • The time in a woman's life when her childbearing capabilities come to an end; the menopause. The so-called male climacteric is characterized by the psychological stresses that accompany aging rather than the loss of reproductive potential. See "Aging Healthfully—Your Mind and Spirit."

Clinics • Medical establishments that offer treatment on an outpatient basis. A clinic may be publicly supported or privately owned; it may be free-standing or part of a hospital's many services. Special clinics exist for special functions such as prenatal and baby care, eye and ear, abortion, psychiatric. See "You, Your Doctors, and the Health Care System."

Clitoris • The female genital organ located at the upper end of the vulva. The clitoris is the counterpart of the male penis and although it may vary in size and placement, it is a direct source of orgasm for most women. See "Sexual Health."

Coagulation • See BLOOD CLOTTING.

Cocaine • A drug with stimulating properties derived from an alkaloid found in the coca tree's leaves. See "Substance Abuse."

Codeine • A mild narcotic drug derived from opium. Codeine is prescribed in tablet form as a painkiller, especially by dentists after a tooth extraction or periodontal surgery. A federal law requires that pharmacists keep records of their sales of codeine-containing medicines including cough syrups to prevent their being bought in large quantities for narcotic purposes. Some women find codeine the most effective analgesic for premenstrual pain; others find that it produces side effects of nausea and constipation. Because codeine can pass into breast milk, mothers should postpone nursing for 4 hours after taking it.

Coffee • A beverage containing varying amounts of caffeine and producing such side effects as insomnia and heartburn and, in some people, withdrawal symptoms such as headaches, irritability, and fatigue. Decaffeinated coffee produces less of these side effects. See also CAFFEINE, "Substance Abuse," and "Pregnancy and Childbirth."

Coitus Interruptus • The withdrawal of the penis before ejaculation as a means of preventing pregnancy. As a contraceptive method its failure rate is high. See "Contraception and Abortion."

Cold Sores • See HERPES.

Colitis • Inflammation of the colon (large intestine). The type most frequently encountered is mucous colitis, also known as irritable bowel, a condition in which the lower bowel goes into spasms with or without cramps accompanied by an alteration of diarrhea and constipation. A far more serious condition is ulcerative colitis in which there is tissue impairment. A mucus and blood mixture is often found in the feces of persons with ulcerative colitis, the onset of which typically occurs among young adults of both sexes, eventually producing disabling attacks of diarrhea. Cancer of the colon or rectum develops in up to 10 percent of those who have had colitis for ten years or more.

The cause of colitis in any of its manifestations is presumed to be emotional stress produced by anxiety. Unfortunately, it is an illness in which cause and effect produce a vicious circle, making it difficult to treat medically. In practically all cases of ulcerative colitis psychotherapy in one form or another is indispensable to the abatement of the more disturbing symptoms. Because patterns of remission and relapse are usual, the disease must be treated with patience and care, including supervision of diet, bed rest, and elimination of as many tension-producing factors as possible. Where complications of weight loss, anemia, or infections develop, medicines with the least number of adverse side effects must be administered. In extreme cases removal of the diseased portion of the bowel is essential as a life-saving measure. See IRRITABLE BOWEL SYNDROME.

Colon Cancer • Fifteen percent of all cancers occur in the colon and rectum; in women, this cancer is the most common after breast cancer, and, in men, it follows lung cancer in frequency. Fortunately, there is a high success rate in curing it following early detection.

The last word is not yet in on the relationship between a high fiber diet and the reduction of colon cancer. Evidence indicates that a low fat diet is equally important. It also appears that people with a family history of this disease are at higher risk and should, therefore, schedule the screening tests necessary for prompt detection. Kits have recently become available for home use that test stool samples for hidden (occult) blood, but positive results are by no means reliable and can be unnecessarily distressing. The American Cancer Society recommends the following procedures on a periodic basis: after age 40, a digital rectal examination, and after age 50, laboratory analysis of a stool sample; examinations every three years of the lower colon and rectum with a sigmoidoscope. The latter procedure should be scheduled more frequently when the patient has a history of rectal polyp removal.

Colostomy • A surgical procedure by which an artificial anal opening is created in the abdominal wall. A colostomy may be performed as a temporary measure after bowel surgery or it may have to be a permanent procedure. Patients who have undergone a colostomy usually must regulate their diets to control the character of their stool. An important aspect of colostomy management is participation in a mutual support group where people who are experienced in coping with the physical, psychological, and

COLOSTOMY

Temporary artificial opening

social problems associated with this procedure help the new patient to adjust to it with a minimum of anxiety and embarrassment. *See* "Directory of Health Information."

Colostrum • The thin, pale yellow substance exuded by the breasts late in pregnancy and immediately following delivery. Colostrum contains proteins, minerals, and antibodies and provides adequate nourishment for the newborn baby before breast milk becomes available, usually about the third day after birth. Mothers who do not wish to breast-feed their babies should discuss with their doctor the importance of providing them with colostrum for the two days following delivery. *See* "Pregnancy and Childbirth."

Colposcopy • A diagnostic procedure in which a magnifying device (colposcope) is used to examine the cervix and vagina. Colposcopy requires no anesthesia and can be done in a doctor's office.

Coma • Deep unconsciousness resulting from, among other circumstances, injury to the brain, stroke, poisoning by barbiturates or alcohol, overdose or underdose of insulin, coronary thrombosis, or shock. Expert care should be obtained without delay, and if the victim is suffering cardiac arrest, cardiopulmonary resuscitation should be initiated.

Common Cold • The designation for any of a large number of brief and relatively mild virus infections of the upper respiratory tract that may produce uncomfortable symptoms in the nose (rhinitis), throat (pharyngitis), or voice box (laryngitis). Because allergies to grasses and pollens produce certain overlapping symptoms, they are often mistakenly labeled "summer colds." The development of a cold vaccine has so far proved impractical because the symptoms are caused by more than 200 different viruses.

An ordinary cold should *not* be treated with antibiotics. These medicines are ineffective against viruses and may cause undesired side effects such as changes in normal bacteria. However, a cold accompanied by a cough, a fever of over 100°, or a painful sore throat can be more than a common cold and should be diagnosed by a doctor. The ordinary upper respiratory viral infection may produce any or all of the following symptoms in combination: stuffed or running nose, mildly scratchy throat, teary eyes, heavy breathing, fits of sneezing, some impairment of the sense of taste and smell, mild headache, and a general feeling of lassitude. Many healthy adults do not bother to treat these symptoms and go about their business until the cold goes away, usually within three or four days. Others buy over-the-counter medicines containing antihistamines, often exchanging drowsiness for unclogged nostrils and dry eyes. Such medicines can neither prevent nor cure a cold, but they do relieve some of the symptoms. The occasional use of nasal decongestants may be harmless and somewhat helpful, but overuse can have a destructive effect on delicate mucous membranes. While there is no unambiguous evidence that vitamin C can prevent or cure a cold, it is argued by some enthusiasts that its action is similar to that of interferon, a substance produced in the body that suppresses virus growth. It is this protein substance that scientists hope to synthesize eventually as the most generalized and effective method of fighting the many viruses that produce common cold symptoms.

Computerized Axial Tomography (also called a CAT scan) • A radiographic process in which a computer constructs a three-dimensional image of an interior body structure from a series of cross-sectional images created along an axis. Since its introduction in the early 1970s, CAT scanning has become an indispensable and reliable tool in the diagnosis of brain disorders, cancers, and other conditions previously inaccessible to conventional X-rays. A CAT scan is quick, painless, and can be accomplished in about half an hour on an outpatient basis.

Concussion, Cerebral • Impairment of brain function resulting from a blow to the cranium or jaw. Concussion is the mildest form of head injury causing a temporary loss of consciousness. Recovery may be accompanied by dizziness, headache, and amnesia about the events preceding the injury. Any head injury resulting in a loss of consciousness should be evaluated by a physician.

Condom • A protective sheath, generally made of thin rubber, that is used to cover the penis during sexual intercourse as a way of preventing sperm from entering the vagina and also as protection against venereal disease. It is the only contraceptive device that can be used by the male sexual partner, and since the crucial importance of halting the spread of AIDS, it is being widely promoted as the dependable barrier that makes "safe sex" possible. *See* "Contraception and Abortion" and "Sexually Transmissible Diseases."

Conjunctivitis • Inflammation of the conjunctiva, the thin membrane that lines the eyelid and covers the front of the eye. The disorder is commonly called pink eye. Conjunctivitis may be caused by bacteria or a virus or it may be an allergic response to a new brand of eye makeup, a reaction to a chemical pollutant in the air or water or to radiation on the job or in the environment, or the result of irritation from an ingrown eyelash in the lower lid. An inflammation caused by bacteria or a virus is highly contagious, and precautions should be taken to prevent its spread to others and to minimize self-reinfection. In such cases, an ophthalmic antibiotic ointment is usually the effective treatment. When dandruff in the eyebrows and eyelashes is the cause of conjunctivitis, a non-prescription steroid ointment is the preferred treatment. An eye doctor should be consulted about the negative aspects of continued use.

Consent Laws • State legislation that covers the following circumstances. (1) *The age of consent:* the age of a woman before which sexual intercourse with her is considered statutory rape whether or not she has given her consent to the act. (2) *Treatment or diagnostic test consent:* a patient undergoing surgery or some other potentially hazardous procedure must sign a statement consenting to the operation. In the case of a child (defined differently in different states) or an incapacitated or incompetent adult, the form must be signed by a responsible member of the family. In an emergency, responsibility is assumed by the physician.

Constipation • A condition in which the fecal matter contained in the bowels is too hard to eliminate easily or in which bowel movements are so infrequent as to cause physical discomfort. The body may take from 24 to 48 hours to transform food into waste matter, and the frequency with which this waste is normally eliminated may vary from once a day to once a week, depending among other things on age, diet, amount of exercise, medication, emotional health, and general personality traits.

The most common causes of chronic constipation unaccompanied by any organic disorder are faulty diet, insufficient exercise, emotional tension, chronic dependence on laxatives, and heavy use of certain drugs. Most antacids contain active chemicals that are constipating (aluminum hydroxide and calcium carbonate); tricyclic antidepressants (Elavil) and certain painkillers (codeine and Demerol) have a similar effect. Older people and pregnant women are often constipated, and so are diabetics and people with an underactive thyroid.

In most cases, an increase in the consumption of fruit and vegetables as well as dietary fiber plus a regimen of daily exercise will solve the problem. When constipation alternates with diarrhea (as in colitis and irritable bowel syndrome), a recommended treatment is the use of Metamucil or similar products that increase the bulk content of the stools. In all cases, the regular use of enemas or laxatives is self-defeating because it causes the bowel to depend on artificial stimulation rather than on natural signals.

The feelings of bloat and general malaise that usually accompany constipation have nothing to do with the body's absorption of "poisons"; they are caused by messages from the nervous system reacting to a distended rectum. When these symptoms persist after elimination or when constipation itself persists in spite of all common-sense treatments, the possibility of an organic disease or obstruction should be investigated by a doctor. *See* FIBER.

Contact Dermatitis • An inflammation of the skin caused by external contact with any substance that acts as an irritant, produces an allergic response, or sensitizes the skin when exposed to sunlight. Symptoms include an itchy rash, dry cracked patches, hives, blisters, and in severe cases, soreness and general malaise.

The more common irritants include strong soaps and detergents that produce "dishpan hands" and chemicals such as turpentine, paint thinners, and strippers used by artists, housepainters, and furniture restorers. The culprit widely known to produce allergic contact dermatitis is poison ivy (also poison oak and sumac). Other substances in this category include certain metals, dyes, or fibers worn next to the skin.

Phototoxic substances include some sunscreening products and the fragrant oils and essences in certain lotions and cosmetics. Dermatologists increasingly report that they treat rashes caused by face makeup and hair preparations. Patients report that they suddenly develop allergic responses to topical medications they have been using over a long period to treat contact dermatitis, medications containing antibiotics or topical anesthetics.

Another self-defeating reaction occurs when the lanolin in skin softeners used to counteract the drying effect of exposure to cold or chemical irritants ends up by clogging the pores and causing a rash.

Where the dermatitis can be traced to a particular source, the condition usually subsides when the substance is removed. The discomfort of an allergic response to poison ivy can be minimized by washing the exposed areas at once with strong soap, swabbing the skin with alcohol, and rinsing with water. If and when a rash appears, a drying lotion containing calamine, such as Caladryl, can be applied. If large blisters appear together with areas of severe inflammation, a physician may prescribe an ointment containing steroids as well as a steroid medicine to be taken by mouth.

Contact Lenses • Plastic lenses that are measured so that they fit on the cornea and are ground to individual prescription so that they correct defects in vision. Contact lenses are worn by an estimated 14 million people, both young and old, and are especially popular with performers, athletes, and all those who associate eyeglasses with a negative self-image. In addition to their cosmetic advantages, contact lenses afford the wearer increased peripheral and side vision. Elderly people who have undergone cataract surgery are pleased to have contact lenses that provide almost perfect vision as an alternative to the thick-lensed glasses that used to be the only corrective for their visual impairment.

There are four different types of contact lenses, each with special advantages and disadvantages: *hard lenses* are the oldest kind and remain the most popular because they are the least expensive, the easiest to care for, and they offer the most accurate correction of vision defects. They last longer but take longer to become accustomed to. Hard lenses are preferred by those who need bifocals. They are available in various tints for use as sunglasses, and they also offer the option of eye color change. A recent development that makes hard lenses a possible choice for women previously too sensitive to tolerate them is the use of Teflon coating on the lens. This coating eliminates the irritation on the cornea and produces no other negative reactions. *Gas permeable lenses* have openings that enable the cornea to "breathe," thus making them more comfortable to wear and reducing the incidence of irritation and infection. *Soft lenses* mold to the cornea like a second skin, thereby reducing the likelihood of trapped foreign objects, dust, and the like. While they are easier to insert into the eye, they cost more than hard lenses and are more trouble to keep clean because they have to be sterilized every night. Soft lenses have to be replaced more often than hard ones, and some people find them uncomfortable because they "dry out" in a low humidity environment. Bifocals and various tints are available in the soft lens category. *Extended wear* lenses are the only type that can be left in the eyes for as long as two weeks and can therefore be worn during sleep. They are especially preferred by those who want clear and near-perfect vision on awakening.

Anyone contemplating the switch to contact lenses or who needs vision correction for the first time and would prefer not to wear traditional eyeglasses should discuss the options with an ophthalmologist. Frequent checkups are recommended, especially during the first year of contact lens use so that any problems of irritation and inflammation can be treated at once if the cornea is not to be scarred. Instructions about cleaning lenses should be followed carefully to avoid the possibility of infection. It has been noted that some cleaning agents that contain the chemical thimerosal are responsible for a contact dermatitis on the hands. Should this occur, other cleansers can be substituted.

Contraception • The prevention of conception following coitus; birth control. *See* "Contraception and Abortion."

Convulsions • Violent and abnormal muscular contractions or spasms that seize the body suddenly and spontaneously, usually ending with unconsciousness. Convulsions are almost always a symptom of a serious disorder and they are the classic manifestation of the grand mal seizures of epilepsy. They are not uncommon among children during infections of the nervous system, during generalized infections that cause a very high fever, or as a sign of Reye's syndrome, which is associated with several viral diseases, especially with chicken pox. Convulsions are one of the critical consequences of withdrawal from barbiturates and alcohol following heavy and habitual use. They may also occur in adulthood from a tumor or from diseases that attack the brain and central nervous system, especially encephalitis and meningitis.

At first sign of seizure, the victim should be placed lying down, with the head turned to one side. The mouth should be opened (forced open if necessary) and something (a knotted handkerchief, a wadded piece of sheet, or a smooth stick) put between the upper and lower teeth to keep the mouth open so that an airway can be maintained and to keep the patient from biting his tongue. If the tongue is swallowed, keep the mouth wide open and free the tongue with a finger. Then seek medical attention.

Cornea • The transparent tissue that forms the outer layer of the eyeball, covering the iris and the lens through which vision is achieved. The most serious disease that affects the cornea is herpes simplex keratitis; it causes more loss of vision in the Western world than any other corneal infection. When this virus attacks the tissues, painful ulcers form and to date there is no successful cure for the condition. The infection may recur frequently causing progressive impairment each time.

One of the hazards of wearing contact lenses is inflammation of the cornea, which must be treated promptly to avoid irreversible scarring. Any soreness or redness of the cornea, whether caused by the presence of a foreign particle or an infection should be called to an ophthalmologist's attention.

Corneal dystrophy is an inherited disease in which there is a progressive loss of vision resulting from an increasing cloudiness of the tissue. Corneal dystrophy as well as vision impairment caused by damage to the cornea can be corrected by a corneal transplant.

Corns • An area of thickened skin (callus) that occurs on or between the toes. There are two types of corns: hard corns that are usually located on the small toe or on the upper ridge of one of the other toes and soft and white corns that are likely to develop between the fourth and fifth toe. The hard core of both types of callus points inward and when pressed against the surrounding tissue causes pain. Corns are the result of wearing shoes that are too tight, and unless proper footwear is worn they will recur.

Treating corns at home with razor blades or with strongly medicated "removers" can injure surrounding tissues, resulting in additional discomfort and sometimes in serious infection. The sensible course is a visit to a podiatrist.

Coronary Artery Disease • *See* HEART ATTACK, ATHEROSCLEROSIS.

Coronary Bypass Surgery • A procedure in which a healthy vein is removed from the patient's leg and inserted between clogged and blocked coronary arteries and the aorta. By increasing the supply of blood to the heart, this type of surgery minimizes or eliminates severe angina attacks and other disabling coronary conditions. There is considerable controversy about the need for surgery in cases that can be effectively treated in less radical ways. Studies indicate that survival rate for patients who have undergone bypass surgery is not dramatically different from that of patients whose symptoms have been controlled with drug therapy.

While the operation is comparatively simple, it can cost as much as $30,000, and it is not suitable for all cases of diseased coronary arteries. Anyone contemplating a bypass operation would be well advised to get more than one opinion before proceeding.

Corpus Luteum • The ovarian follicle after it releases its ovum. The corpus luteum produces the hormone progesterone that prepares the lining of the uterus for possible implantation of a fertilized ovum and is essential to the maintenance of pregnancy. If conception occurs, the corpus luteum continues to produce progesterone for a short time until the placenta takes over this function. If conception does not occur, the progesterone level drops, the corpus luteum degenerates, and menstruation starts. *See* "Pregnancy and Childbirth."

Corticosteroids • *See* STEROIDS.

Cosmetic Surgery • *See* PLASTIC SURGERY and "Cosmetic Surgery."

Cosmetics • Unlike drugs, cosmetic preparations are not required to provide the user with a detailed list of contents. Although vitamins, hormones, preservatives, floral essences, and root oils may produce adverse reactions in individual cases, they are not considered "dangerous." When an accumulation of evidence causes justifiable concern as in the case of a red dye that might be cancer-causing or unsafe levels of asbestos dust in an expensive talcum powder, the FDA steps in and rules that the offensive substance must be eliminated.

The price of many overpriced cosmetics is determined not by the cost of the ingredients but by the cost of packaging and promotion. Those products that claim to be based on a "secret formula" would have to be designated as a drug if they could in fact have a basic effect on the function or structure of any part of the body. Mysterious skin rashes often turn out to be the result of contact dermatitis produced by an ingredient in a hair preparation or facial cosmetic. Allergic reactions such as puffy eyelids or itchy patches of skin are a signal that hypoallergenic preparations should be substituted.

Because infections are easily spread by powder puffs, lipsticks, or mascara brushes, these articles should not be borrowed or lent. *See* CONTACT DERMATITIS.

Coughing • A reflex action for the purpose of clearing the lining of the air passages of an excessive accumulation of mucus or disturbing foreign matter. The air expulsed carries with it foreign irritants such as dust, industrial pollutants, particles of food, or abnormal secretions that are irritating the larynx, trachea, or bronchial tubes. Coughing may also be a psychological manifestation of boredom or a means of attracting attention. A so-called "smoker's cough" is associated with chronic bronchitis; persistent coughing and hoarseness may be a sign of cancer.

Medicines that loosen the secretions resulting from an inflammatory condition of the mucous membranes and make it easier to cough them up are called expectorants. The congestion may also be loosened and coughed up by a high fluid intake, especially hot tea or hot lemonade with honey. Steam inhalation is another helpful treatment. It is important to rid the air passages of the accumulated mucus by coughing it up, but if a "dry" cough interferes with sleep, the doctor may recommend a cough suppressant. Suppressant medicines may contain codeine or some other opiate that requires a prescription. Over-the-counter cough medicines that contain alcohol (and practically all of them do) should not be given to children, nor should they be used by anyone taking sleeping pills or tranquilizers.

Coughs associated with common colds may last two to three weeks after all other symptoms have disappeared. A cough that lasts longer or causes pain in the chest should be discussed with a doctor.

CPR • *See* CARDIOPULMONARY RESUSCITATION.

Crabs • Parasites, also known as pubic lice, that infest the genital and anal hairs, causing extreme itching and irritation. *See* "Sexually Transmissible Diseases."

Cramps • The pains associated with involuntary muscle spasms. Heat cramps are caused by the body's loss of water and salt during heavy sweating. Leg cramps may occur during strenuous exercise, and especially in the lower leg and foot during the night. When they occur early in pregnancy, the leg should be stretched as far as possible; later in pregnancy, the knee should be raised to the chest. Leg cramps may also be a sign of diabetes when accompanied by other characteristics of this disorder. Menstrual cramps (dysmenorrhea) are caused by the body's production of prostaglandins. The discomfort can be treated with prostaglandin-inhibitors such as Motrin. Stomach cramps may be the result of overeating and the habit of swallowing air, by metabolic intolerance to certain food substances such as milk or gluten products, by food allergies, by the onset of "traveler's diarrhea." Severe stomach cramps may be a sign of food poisoning, not only of food tainted by bacterial toxins but by a poison inherent in the food itself as in certain mushrooms.

Cramps that persist even when practical measures are taken to eliminate the cause should be diagnosed by a doctor.

Crib Death • *See* SUDDEN INFANT DEATH SYNDROME.

Crohn's Disease • Also called inflammatory bowel disease and regional ileitis because it is associated with chronic inflammation of the small intestine (ileitis) and/or parts of the large intestine. No specific cause of Crohn's disease has been identified, although stress appears to be involved in all cases. Onset usually occurs in young adulthood and may be accompanied by such disorders as rashes, pains in the joints, and the formation of kidney stones. People with Crohn's disease have attacks of diarrhea, severe abdominal cramps, nausea, and fever. Weight loss is common and the consequences of malabsorption of vitamin B12 and calcium may also occur. The disease can be correctly diagnosed by barium X-rays of the upper and lower gastrointestinal tract and by inspection with a sigmoidoscope and colonoscope. Medical treatment on an outpatient basis consists of prescribing a drug in pill form that combines an aspirin derivative and a sulfa antibiotic. Dietary supplements are part of ongoing treatment. Psychological support by family members, supplemented when necessary with therapy for the patient, makes a significant difference in the patient's morale.

Cryosurgery • Operations in which tissues are destroyed by freezing them, usually with supercold liquid nitrogen or carbon dioxide. Cryosurgery is frequently used for the removal of hemorrhoids, warts, and moles and for treatment of cervical erosion. Cryosurgical instruments are also used successfully in certain types of delicate brain surgery, in correcting retinal detachments, and removing cataracts.

Curettage • A procedure in which an instrument called a curette scrapes a part of the body in order to remove a tissue sample for examination or to remove unwanted tissue.

Cushing's Syndrome • A group of symptoms caused by the presence in the body of an excess of corticosteroid hormones. Formerly, Cushing's syndrome was a rare disorder resulting in most cases from overactivity of the adrenal cortex because of a glandular tumor or from hyperfunction of the pituitary gland. It has become more common, now resulting from the side effects of medication containing steroids prescribed as long-term therapy for chronic diseases of the kidneys, the joints, etc.

Early symptoms include weakness, facial puffiness ("moon" face), and fluid retention, followed by general obesity and an interruption of menstruation.

When Cushing's syndrome is attributable to glandular malfunction caused by a tumor, surgery is essential. If total removal of the gland is indicated, replacement therapy of the corticosteroid hormones is necessary for the remainder of one's life.

Cuts • *See* FIRST AID.

Cyanosis • A blue appearance of the blood and mucous membranes caused by an inadequate amount of oxygen in the arterial blood. A cyanotic appearance is one of the first signs of a number of respiratory diseases in which lung function is so impaired that the blood cannot take up a sufficient amount of oxygen. Cyanosis is also a characteristic of certain heart diseases characterized by abnormal shunting of blood. The cyanotic characteristic of the so-called blue baby is due to a congenital heart defect that leads to an excess of unoxygenated arterial blood. Surgery often is helpful in correcting such defects.

Cyst • An abnormal cavity filled with a fluid or semifluid substance. While some cysts do become malignant, most are harmless and are often reabsorbed by the surrounding tissues, leaving no trace of their existence. A benign cyst that interferes with the proper functioning of an adjacent organ, such as a gland, is removed in an operation called a cystectomy.

There are several categories of cysts. Retention cysts occur when the opening of a secreting gland is blocked, causing the secretion to back up and form a swelling. In this category are several different types. Sebaceous cysts cause a lump to appear under the skin. Mucous cysts are commonly found in the mucous membranes of the mouth, nose, genitals, or inside the lips or cheeks. Breast cysts may result from a chronic mastitis that causes the ducts leading to the nipples to be blocked by the development of fibrous tissue. Kidney cysts are a congenital defect eventually proliferating to the point where they interfere with kidney function.

Pilonidal cysts form in the cleft between the buttocks. They are called "pilonidal," which means literally resembling a "nest of hair," because the folding over of the skin in the cleft between the buttocks results in ingrown hairs that block the pores of the ducts leading outward from the sebaceous glands. When the retained secretions accumulate and back up, the affected area becomes swollen and painfully inflamed. When the cyst is small, treatment need be no more complicated than warm sitz baths to open and drain the abscess. The open cyst is covered with an antibiotic ointment to prevent the complication of bacterial invasion. A pilonidal cyst that becomes chronic and recurs with uncomfortable frequency may require surgical removal.

Ovarian, cervical, vaginal, and endometrial cysts are discussed in "Gynecologic Diseases and Treatment."

Cystic Fibrosis • An inherited, disabling respiratory disease of early childhood. The disease is genetically transmitted to offspring when both parents are carriers; when only one parent is a carrier, some of the offspring may also be carriers. Although there is no known cure for cystic fibrosis, new treatments have increased the life expectancy of patients with the disease. *See* "Directory of Health Information."

Cystitis • *See* URINARY TRACT INFECTIONS.

Cystocele • A hernia in which part of the bladder protrudes into the vagina. A cystocele causes a feeling of discomfort in the lower abdomen and may produce bladder incontinence. The abnormal position of the bladder results in an accumulation of residual urine that increases the possibility of bacterial infection. Surgical correction is therefore advisable.

Cystoscopy • A diagnostic procedure in which the inner surface of the bladder is examined by an optical instrument called a cystoscope. The procedure, usually performed by a urologist, consists of passing the cystoscope through the opening of the urethra into the bladder. Inflammation, tumors, or stones can be detected by means of an illuminated system of mirrors and lenses and tissue samples can be obtained. If diagnostic X-rays are to be taken during a cystoscopy, a catheter may be passed through the hollow tube of the instrument in order to inject radiopaque substances into the bladder.

D & C • *See* DILATATION AND CURETTAGE.

D & E • *See* DILATATION AND EVACUATION.

D, E & C • *See* DILATATION AND EVACUATION.

DTs • *See* DELIRIUM TREMENS.

Dalmane • An antianxiety drug (flurazepam) chemically related to Valium and Librium and widely prescribed as a sleeping pill, especially because its side effects are preferable to those of barbiturates used for the same purpose. Total abstention from alcohol is recommended. Dalmane should not be used over an extended period if dependence is to be avoided. Doses for elderly patients should be adjusted downward to prevent overmedication.

Dandruff • A scalp disorder characterized by the abnormal flaking of dead skin. The underlying cause of the condition is not known, but it is directly related to the way in which the sebaceous glands function. There is no evidence that dandruff is triggered by an infectious organism.

Normal skin constantly renews itself as dead skin cells are shed. Oily dandruff is the result of overactivity of the tiny oil glands at the base of the hair roots, accelerating the shedding process. The hair becomes greasy and the skin flakings are yellowish and crusty, similar to the flakings that characterize "cradle cap" in infants. This condition can be especially troublesome when it affects the eyelashes.

A dry type of dandruff occurs when the sebaceous glands are plugged, causing the hair to lose its natural gloss and the flaking to be dry and grayish. In either type of dandruff it is important not to scratch the scalp, as broken skin may lead to infection.

There are several medicines that can control dandruff and sometimes eliminate it. If over-the-counter shampoos containing tar or zinc pyrithione prove ineffective, treatment by prescribed medications such as shampoo containing silenium sulfide may be necessary.

Deafness • *See* HEARING LOSS.

Death • Traditionally, the end of life was presumed to have occurred when breathing ceased and the heart was still. However, the increasing technological means for prolonging life and the concern of the medical profession as to precisely when a donor's organs should be removed for transplantation created a compelling need for a "redefinition" of death in terms acceptable to both the legal and medical professions. State legislatures now have statutes in which death is equated with the irreversible cessation of brain function. The criteria for brain-death are generally accepted by the medical profession throughout the world.

Following the lead of California in 1976, 41 states have enacted a "right-to-die" law that gives people the opportunity to make out living wills prohibiting the use of unusual or artificial devices to prolong their lives if they become terminally ill.

Most medical schools have introduced courses in dying and death as part of the curriculum, and doctors now discuss these previously taboo subjects not only among themselves but also with their patients and the families of those who are terminally ill. Also, a new respect for the natural and essential process of grieving has resulted in an increase in the number of therapists who specialize in bereavement counseling. Such counseling can provide supportive understanding following the death of a family member or a beloved friend. *See* HOSPICE.

Deficiency Disease • A disorder caused by the absence of an essential nutrient in the diet. Not until the twentieth-century discovery of the vital role of vitamins was this category of disease understood, although before that time people had discovered through trial and error what foods or extracts appeared to prevent particular disabilities such as the control of rickets with cod liver oil (rich in vitamin D) and the control of scurvy with citrus juice (rich in vitamin C). Pellagra was once prevalent in areas where meat, eggs, or other foods containing niacin were not part of the diet because of poverty. Through the use of synthesized niacin as an additive in commercially processed foods, this deficiency disease has practically disappeared.

Certain types of blindness and skin ulcers, once thought to be infectious ailments, were discovered to be the result of diets deficient in liver, eggs, and other foods rich in vitamin A. Margarine and many other widely used items are now fortified with this vitamin. Beriberi, a deficiency disease that produces gastrointestinal and neurological disturbances, is caused by a lack of fresh vegetables, whole grains, and certain meats, all of which contain vitamin B^1 (thiamine). Mild beriberi symptoms are likely to appear among people on restricted diets, among alcoholics, and among crash dieters who fail to take supplementary doses of this essential nutriment. All of these deficiency diseases, however, are rare in the United States, in large part due to the multivitamin fortification of bread. *See* "Nutrition, Weight, and General Well-Being."

Degenerative Disease • A category of disorders having in common the progressive deterioration of a part or parts of the body leading to increasing interference with normal function. Among the more common of the degenerative diseases are the various forms of arthritis, cerebrovascular disabilities caused by the dystrophy diseases that impair neuromuscular function, arteriosclerosis, and the many disorders connected with progressive malfunction of the heart and lungs.

Dehydration • An abnormal loss of body fluids. Deprivation of water and essential electrolytes (sodium and potassium) for a prolonged period can lead to shock, acidosis, acute uremia, and, especially in the case of infants and the aged, to death. Under normal circumstances water accounts for well over half the total body weight. The adult woman loses about 3 pints of fluid a day in urine; the amount of water in feces is variable but may account for another 3 or 4 ounces; vaporization through the skin (perspiration) and the lungs (breath expiration) account for another 2 pints. Normal consumption of food and water generally replaces this loss. A temporary increase in the loss of body fluid due to heat, exertion, or mild diarrhea is usually accompanied by extreme thirst or a dry tongue and can be rectified simply by drinking an additional amount of liquid. Salt pills are not always necessary as an aid to fluid retention. Dehydration that accompanies the acidosis signaling the onset of diabetic coma or of certain kidney diseases requires prompt hospitalization and treatment.

Delirium Tremens (DTs) • Literally, a trembling delirium; a psychotic state observed in chronic alcoholics as a result of withdrawal of alcohol. Withdrawal from barbiturates after long use will produce the same condition, which is characterized by confusion, nausea, vivid hallucinations, and uncontrollable tremors. The victim of delirium tremens may become obstreperous and therefore should be hospitalized for self-protection as well as for the treatment of chronic alcoholism or drug dependence. See "Substance Abuse."

Delusions • False and persistent beliefs contrary to or unsubstantiated by facts or objective circumstance; one of the symptoms of severe mental illness and also associated with overdoses of certain addictive drugs. Delusions are false beliefs, as differentiated from hallucinations, which are false sense impressions. As an example, an individual suffering from paranoid schizophrenia may have delusions of being destroyed by people who are thought to be enemies. In true paranoia the delusion becomes the focus of all activity. Some delusions are difficult to recognize and the person is merely thought of as an eccentric. When a delusion takes the form of ordering the individual to commit an illegal act or one destructive to himself or others, hospitalization is mandatory.

Dental Care • The strength or weakness of one's teeth begins with one's genetic inheritance combined with the prenatal health and diet of one's mother. (Pregnant women please note.) However, good health, good habits of oral hygiene, and periodic dental checkups are the most important factors in preventing the decay of teeth. Tooth decay is incurable and irreversible, and prompt treatment of cavities is essential. A cavity should be filled before decay advances beyond the enamel. Otherwise bacteria may penetrate the dentin and attack the pulp chamber of the tooth. This may produce an infection that not only kills the tooth but, in extreme cases, may spread throughout the body causing bacteremia and possibly bacterial endocarditis, a serious inflammation of the lining of the heart.

A vaccine immunizing against tooth

decay is one of the long-range goals of the National Institute of Dental Research. Until such a vaccine is available, the most effective means of preventing dental caries is through regular visits to the dentist for checkups and cleanings and proper home hygiene. X-rays should be taken only when absolutely necessary.

Some dentists recommend the application of a plastic sealant on the biting surfaces of the teeth to prevent the destructive consequences of plaque formation. All agree that the consumption of sweets should be kept to a minimum and, if possible, restricted to mealtimes. Dietary considerations include eating foods known to protect tooth surfaces, especially cheddar cheese, which seems to neutralize mouth acids. Basic oral hygiene consists in using a toothpaste that contains fluoride and a brush with bristles that are resilient rather than stiff. Unwaxed floss should be used to remove accumulations between the teeth. A recent mouthwash called Peridex sold only by prescription appears to be effective in reducing plaque.

Health insurance policies should be read carefully for information about dental coverage, and if it is included, the dentist should indicate what payment procedure is to be followed.

Because dental fees vary considerably, not only in different parts of the country but in the same city or town, it is wise to discuss fees with the dentist prior to treatment. Medicaid covers a major part of dental bills, but Medicare provides no dental coverage at all.

Dental Caries • Tooth decay, in particular cavities caused by bacteria. *Streptococcus mutans,* a microorganism that induces cavities, is related to the bacterial agent that causes strep throat. Some people appear to inherit an immunity to caries. The decay results from bacteria feeding on sugar and producing a corrosive acid. There are billions of bacteria in the saliva, but only *S. mutans* appears capable of creating an adhesive out of sucrose that adheres to the enamel tooth surface gradually destroying it. *See* DENTAL CARE.

Dental Plaque • A deposit of materials on the surface of the teeth that becomes the medium in which destructive bacteria feed on sugar and produce the toxins that eventually destroy tooth enamel. *See* DENTAL CARE and DENTAL CARIES.

Dentin • The hard calcified tissue that forms the body of a tooth under the enamel surface. When bacterial decay spreads from the enamel into the dentin, a toothache is likely to occur. If this symptom is ignored, the bacteria will eventually invade the pulp and increase the probability of the death of the tooth.

Dentures • Artificial teeth used to replace some or all natural teeth. Dentures may be removable or permanently attached to adjacent teeth. While preventive dentistry has reduced the number of women who need dentures at an early age, the loss of some teeth is almost inevitable with advancing age. Teeth should be replaced promptly to avoid the possibility of a chewing impairment, which can lead to a digestion problem, speech impediment, or the collapse of facial structure caused by the empty spaces. In addition, missing teeth imperil the health of the adjacent natural ones. Dental materials and techniques used today make it virtually impossible to distinguish between a person's artificial and natural teeth.

A recent development, known as dental implantation, has become increasingly popular with those who can afford it or whose medical insurance provides partial coverage. In this procedure, artificial teeth are permanently attached to the jaw. Several different techniques are used, but it is not yet known how well any of them will withstand the test of time. *See* "Directory of Health Information."

Deodorants • Over-the-counter products containing chemicals that slow down the bacterial growth in perspiration, thus diminishing the likelihood of unpleasant body odor. Unlike antiperspirants, deodorants do not inhibit the amount of perspiration itself. Vaginal deodorants advertised for "feminine daintiness" should be avoided because of their irritating effect on tissue. Daily use of a pleasantly scented mild soap is a safer, cheaper, and sufficiently effective way of keeping the genital area clean. *See* ANTIPERSPIRANT.

Deoxyribonucleic Acid • *See* DNA.

Depilatory • *See* HAIR REMOVAL.

Depressant • A category of drugs (also called sedative-hypnotic drugs) that produce a calming, sedative effect by reducing the functional activity of the central nervous system. The two main groups are the barbiturates (Nembutal, Seconal, and the like) and the minor tranquilizers (Valium, Librium, Xanax). These drugs, which are widely prescribed as anti-anxiety medications and sleeping pills, can result in physical and psychological dependency when used regularly over a long period. *See* "Substance Abuse."

Depression • A feeling that life has no meaning and that no activity is worth the effort; profound feelings of hopelessness and self-deprecation. *See* "Aging Healthfully—Your Mind and Spirit."

Dermabrasion • A procedure in which the outermost layers of the skin are removed by planing the skin with an abrasive device. *See* "Cosmetic Surgery."

Dermatitis • Inflammation of the skin, often accompanied by redness, itching, swelling, and a rash. Inflammation caused by direct contact with an irritant is called contact dermatitis; inflammation caused by psychological stress is called neurodermatitis. Types caused by viruses, bacteria, fungi, or parasites are called infectious dermatitis; they are discussed under entries entitled BOIL, FUNGAL INFECTIONS and HIVES. Other forms appear under the headings CHILBLAINS, FROSTBITE, and HIVES. *See also* CONTACT DERMATITIS, RASHES.

DES (diethylstilbestrol) • A synthetic nonsteroidal estrogen hormone. DES was first prescribed in the 1950s to prevent miscarriage. In 1971 it was discovered to be the specific cause of a rare type of vaginal cancer found at a young age in a few female offspring of women who took the hormone. This cancer, previously rare in women under 50, is called adenocarcinoma; it is an *iatrogenic* cancer, that is, a cancer inadvertently caused by prescribed medication.

DES daughters should be examined periodically by a gynecologist. For

DES mothers, there is a suspected risk of breast and gynecologic cancers. *See* "Directory of Health Information."

Desensitization • A process whereby an individual allergic to a particular substance is periodically injected with a diluted extract of the allergen in order to build up a tolerance to it. *See allergy.*

Detoxification • A form of therapy, usually conducted in a hospital, whereby the patient is deprived of an addictive drug and given a substitute one in diminishing doses. Alcohol, heroin, and barbiturate detoxification produces severe withdrawal symptoms that can be eased by the use of sedatives on a transitional basis. When detoxification has been accomplished, a program of physical and psychological rehabilitation is essential. *See* "Substance Abuse."

Dextrose • A variant of glucose. *See* GLUCOSE.

Diabetes • A chronic disease characterized by the presence of an excess of glucose in the blood and urine. In juvenile diabetes, this condition prevails as a result of an insufficient production of insulin by the pancreas. In most cases of adult onset diabetes the amount of insulin produced is normal, but the body's ability to use it is not. Insulin is the hormone essential for converting carbohydrates (sugars and starches) into glucose, the body's most important fuel.

Although the basic cause of diabetes is still unknown, the condition can be controlled if treated correctly. The full name of the disease is diabetes mellitus, roughly translatable from the Greek and Latin as "a passing through of honey."

According to the American Diabetes Association, the number of diabetics is increasing, with approximately 14 million Americans being affected at this time. Of this number, 10 million are aware of having the disease and are under treatment; the other 4 million are unaware of their diabetic condition or are not being treated for it. Adult onset diabetes is the direct cause of at least 40,000 deaths a year and is considered to be the indirect cause of an additional 300,000 deaths because of cardiovascular and kidney complications. Thus, it can be considered the third highest cause of death in the United States.

Symptoms of the disease are easily recognized and once the diagnosis has been confirmed, most diabetics, given the proper treatment, are able to live normal lives. The increased life expectancy of diabetics, particularly in the case of women over 30, is largely due to the discovery of insulin by two Canadian scientists in 1921–22. This hormone, produced by the pancreas, regulates the body's use of sugar by metabolizing glucose and turning it into energy or into glycogen for storage for future use. An insufficiency of insulin or other abnormalities not fully understood results in the diabetic's inability to metabolize or store glucose, thus leading to its accumulation in the bloodstream in amounts large enough to spill over into the urine. This metabolic aberration causes the characteristic symptoms of diabetes: frequent urination due to the abnormal amount of urine produced to accommodate the excess glucose that the kidneys filters out of the blood, chronic thirst, an excessive hunger. Dramatic weight loss occurs because, being unable to use glucose, the diabetic must use body fat and protein as a source of energy. In order to reach the proper balance of insulin production and glucose conversion, which is constantly being regulated by the normal body, each diabetic must be individually stabilized through a controlled regimen of medication, diet, and energy output.

In addition to the previously mentioned symptoms, other symptoms that indicate the possibility of diabetes are drowsiness and fatigue; changes in vision; repeated infections of the kidneys, gums, or skin; intense itching without a known cause; and cramps in the extremities. Any woman with symptoms suggesting diabetes should have a urine and blood sugar test. There is also a simple laboratory procedure, the glucose tolerance test, that can identify prediabetics, thus alerting the doctor and patient to the possible onset of the disease.

When medication is essential to maintain normal blood sugar levels, the amount of insulin needed is determined initially by the level of glucose in the blood. Thereafter it usually can be determined by the level of glucose in the urine, which is tested regularly by the patient. Variations in the results of the urine tests are the guide to necessary adjustments in diet, medication, and exercise. The use of oral drugs that stimulate the pancreas to produce its own insulin may be recommended with or without an insulin supplement. This procedure requires constant monitoring by the physician.

With the combined efforts of patient and doctor, satisfactory control can be attained and is reflected in the patient's general feeling of well-being, the maintenance of normal blood sugar and negative urine tests, and a minimal fluctuation of weight. Less severe cases of diabetes can be controlled successfully by diet and exercise alone.

Control is essential in order to avoid two specific reactions: hypoglycemia, a condition in which the blood sugar level is too low, and hyperglycemia, in which it is too high.

Hypoglycemia is likely to occur if the diabetic does not eat additional food to compensate for physical exertion, skips a meal, or takes too much insulin. Onset is sudden, the symptoms being nervous irritability, moist skin, and a tingling tongue. The situation can be corrected quickly by promptly eating or drinking anything containing sugar—a spoonful of honey, a glass of orange juice, a piece of candy, or a lump of sugar.

Hyperglycemia accompanied by acidosis and diabetic coma was the chief cause of early death in diabetics before the discovery of insulin. While rare today, hyperglycemic reaction does occur when the diabetic fails to take the necessary amount of insulin. Blood sugar builds up to a point at which the body begins to burn proteins and fats, a process that ends in the formation of chemicals known as ketones. When the accumulation of ketones leads to a critical imbalance in the body's acid concentration, the result can be a diabetic coma. This condition is characterized by a hot dry skin, labored breathing, abdominal pain, and drowsiness. The patient should be hospitalized immediately so that the correct doses of insulin can be administered. A diabetic should carry cubes of sugar and wear a diabetic identification tag or bracelet at all times. *See* MEDIC ALERT.

A woman with diabetes should use a contraceptive method other than the pill, because the pill can increase the already existing hormonal imbalance. Should she wish to become pregnant, her chronic condition will not affect her fertility, but once conception occurs, the blood sugar level of a diabetic woman may rise precipitously and behave erratically throughout the pregnancy. It is therefore essential that urine tests be made three or four times a day and that the blood sugar level be checked during prenatal visits as a guide to adjusting the dose of insulin. If the mother-to-be takes proper care of herself, there is every reason to expect a normal, healthy baby.

Diabetes that develops after having a baby or at middle age may not present the usual symptoms of urine frequency, thirst, and excessive appetite, but may be discovered because of a persistent skin infection or in some other way. In women over 60 a comparatively asymptomatic diabetes may lead to arteriosclerosis and in turn to a stroke or heart attack. Related disorders of vision, kidney function, and the nervous system may also develop in cases of delayed or improper control of diabetes.

Most diabetics lead a productive and fulfilling life, both on a personal and professional level. Women applying for jobs are protected by a federal law that prevents employers from discriminating against applicants solely on the basis of this disorder. Diabetics should be in touch with their local chapter of the American Diabetes Association. This organization provides information on current research, job options, travel possibilities, summer camps, and international affiliations. It publishes a magazine that contains practical material on menu planning and medical equipment and provides a forum for an exchange of ideas on living as a diabetic or with one. *See* "Directory of Health Information."

Diabetic Retinopathy • An abnormal condition in the retina occurring among diabetics who have had the disease for a prolonged period of time. Diabetic retinopathy was practically unknown until the lives of diabetics were extended by the use of insulin. Leakage of blood and fluid from the retina's tiny blood vessels is the cause of the condition and the degree of vision impairment depends on the extent of the leakage. If the retinal hemorrhage is extensive and leads to a proliferation of "new" vessels and obstructive fibrous tissue, surgery is essential to prevent sight deterioration. Photocoagulation is the treatment in which a laser beam is directed at the diseased retinal tissue in an attempt to destroy it and prevent it from activating new obstructive tissue growth.

Dialysis • The separation of waste matter and water from the bloodstream by mechanical means, usually used in cases of loss of kidney function through temporary or permanent impairment. The dialysis machine, which may be installed in the home of the patient or used at a hospital or special clinic, is connected to the body by a complex arrangement of tubes. Blood containing impurities and wastes, which would normally be filtered out by healthy kidneys, runs through one set of tubes past a thin membrane. On the other side of the membrane is a solution that extracts salt wastes, excess water, and other substances from the blood by osmotic pressure. The cleansed blood is then returned to the body through another set of tubes. This procedure is routinely followed at least three times a week and takes about four hours per treatment.

Kidney dialysis may be essential for a limited period following complications caused by bacterial (streptococcus) infection or a viral disease such as hepatitis. However, permanent dialysis is a lifetime support for about 60,000 Americans. They may have to cope with other conditions because of their dependence on this process, but none is as life-threatening as the loss of kidney function.

For many years after the invention of the machine in 1946, it was in short supply. Thanks to advances in technology, the supply is now unlimited. The number of users increased considerably after Congress passed a law in 1973 amending the Social Security Act to extend Medicare funds to anyone under 65 suffering from kidney failure.

Diaphragm • A rubber, dome-shaped cap inserted over the cervix to prevent conception. *See* "Contraception and Abortion."

Diaphragm • The large muscle that lies across the middle of the body, separating the thoracic and abdominal cavities. The diaphragm is convex in shape when relaxed. Approximately 20 times a minute, on receiving signals from the area of the brain that controls the respiratory process, it tenses and flattens so that the thoracic cavity enlarges, thus enabling the lungs to expand each time a breath is taken.

Many nerves pass through this muscle and it also contains large openings to accommodate the aorta, the thoracic duct, and the esophagus. When there is a weakening of the muscle structure that surrounds the esophagus, the stomach may push upward into the hole, causing the disorder known as a diaphragmatic or hiatus hernia. Involuntary spasms of the diaphragm are the cause of hiccups.

Diarrhea • Abnormally frequent and watery bowel movements usually related to an inflammation of the intestinal wall. The inflammation may follow infection caused by microorganisms that produce food poisoning or dysentery. Causes of diarrhea may be a particular food, caffeine, alcohol, a new medication, the regular use of certain antacids, too strong a cathartic, an allergy, excitement, or emotional stress. Diarrhea is also associated with toxic shock syndrome. Some women have mild diarrhea with the onset of menopause, and practically all women have diarrhea before the onset of labor. At times it is accompanied by stomach cramps, nausea, vomiting, and a feeling of debility due to loss of body fluids and salt.

Chronic diarrhea may be a symptom of any of the following: thyroid disturbance especially hyperthyroidism, nonspecific ulcerative colitis, a cyst or tumor of the bowel, low level chemical poisoning, and alcoholism. Diarrhea alternating with constipation is characteristic of ileitis and Crohn's disease.

The weakening effects of a brief siege of diarrhea can be remedied by the replacement of lost fluids and a bland diet. If the condition persists, the doctor may request a stool sample for laboratory analysis. If no infectious agent is discovered, diagnosis may involve internal examination with a proctoscope (a lighted tube that is passed into the rectum) or sigmoidoscope (a similar device for examining the sigmoid colon), blood tests, or a barium test.

What has come to be known as traveler's diarrhea is the sudden onset of cramps and loose stools caused by infection with a strain of the bacterium *E. coli*, which produces a toxin that damages the colon's fluid-absorbing function. The nonprescription medicine that works the fastest is Pepto-Bismol, now available in tablets that come in purse-size packages. If the cramps and diarrhea continue in spite of this treatment, a doctor should be consulted.

Diethystilbestrol • *See* DES.

Dieting • The systematic attempt to lose weight by cutting down on caloric intake. *See* "Nutrition, Weight, and General Well-Being."

Digitalis (Digoxin) • A substance derived from the dried leaves of the foxglove flower (*Digitalis purpurea*) and used in the treatment of heart disease. For several hundred years digitalis has been used effectively as a means of stimulating the action of the failing heart muscle, while at the same time slowing down the heartbeat.

Because digitalis is potentially poisonous, the amount prescribed may have to be adjusted from time to time to strike a balance between a dose large enough to be effective but not so large as to be dangerous. Continuing supervision by the doctor is, therefore, mandatory. Symptoms suggestive of toxicity such as nausea, loss of appetite, headache, diarrhea, and irregular pulse should be reported to the doctor promptly.

Dilantin • An anticonvulsant drug (phenytoin) used in treating epilepsy. Unpleasant side effects should be discussed with the physician. Dilantin has been promoted for other conditions, but its effectiveness has not been substantiated beyond its prime use.

Dilatation and Curettage (D&C) • The expansion of the cervix by the use of surgical dilators and the removal of tissue from the lining of the uterus with a curette. The D & C procedure is used in early pregnancy as an abortion method; following a miscarriage to remove unexpelled tissue; in diagnosing uterine cancer, abnormal bleeding, or other discharge; and in certain cases of infertility to improve the general condition of the uterus. *See* "Contraception and Abortion," "Gynecologic Diseases and Treatment."

Dilatation and Evacuation (D&E) • The expansion of the cervix with surgical dilators and the removal of the contents of the uterus by suction. Sometimes curettage is done after the suction (D,E,&C). *See* "Contraception and Abortion."

Disc, Slipped • The dislocation or herniation of one of the cartilaginous rings that separate the spinal vertebrae from each other. The column of 33 bones that make up the spine bears much of the body's weight above the hips. The vertebrae themselves are constantly being subjected to stress and sudden shock due to lifting, bending, and performing other activities that are part of one's daily routine. The discs between the vertebrae are the built-in shock absorbers held in place by rings of tough, fibrous tissue.

As the tissue degenerates with age, it compresses more and more, result-

SLIPPED DISC

Vertebral body
Spinal cord
Spine of vertebra
Herniated disc
Normal disc

ing in the feeling of occasional stiffness. When a disc slips out of position because of this compression, it presses on a spinal nerve—most commonly the sciatic nerve—causing pain to radiate along its path. In severe cases, the pain radiates from the lower back into the buttocks, through the thighs and calves, and into the feet. When the pressure on the nerve is not so intense, discomfort may be restricted to the lower back. In either case, whether mild or immobilizing, the condition is called sciatica. If the pain is thought to originate along the path of a nerve higher up, an X-ray of the spine may be necessary.

Before more radical measures are taken, treatment consists of bed rest on a firm mattress, aspirin or equivalent pain killers, and for people who want to remain as active as possible, a back support. When such measures fail to bring relief, some doctors recommend traction. Some patients are helped by acupuncture followed by a program of exercises that strengthen the back muscles. Most cases of slipped disc recover without surgery.

A recent nonsurgical treatment whose long term benefits have yet to be evaluated is the injection of an enzyme (chymopapain) that dissolves the central portion of the disc. The procedure, called chemonucleolysis, is performed under local or general anesthesia in only a few hospitals. In a small number of slipped disc cases relief sufficient to make mobility possible can be achieved only by an operation known as a laminectomy: a piece of the vertebra is removed and the protruding piece of the disc that is causing the pressure is eliminated. Recovery is usually complete in a couple of weeks.

Prevention of the slipped disc problem is best achieved by: participating in an exercise program directed towards strengthening the muscles that support the back, maintaining proper body weight, wearing high heels only for special occasions, and lifting heavy objects (including one's children) not by bending from the waist but by bending the knees.

Dislocation • Specifically, the displacement of a bone from its normal position in the joint; also called subluxation. Dislocations most commonly occur in the fingers and shoulder and less frequently in the elbow, knee, hip, and jaw. A dislocation does not necessarily involve a break in the bone, but it almost always involves some damage, either slight or serious, to the surrounding ligaments and muscles. Anyone may experience a dislocation as a result of a fall or a blow, but it is a routine hazard among dancers and athletes.

Once the displacement occurs, particularly if the site is the shoulder or elbow, it is likely to recur because of the stretching of the sac and the ligaments that hold the joint in place. After several recurrences surgery is usually recommended to tighten the tissues.

A sudden dislocation can be extremely painful, and because the possibility of fracture as well as injury to surrounding nerves and blood vessels must be taken into consideration, prompt medical attention is essential to ensure restoring normal function. To minimize pain and swelling, cold compresses should be applied to the injured area. The injured joint should be immobilized while transporting the victim to the doctor or hospital.

Diuretic • Any drug that increases urinary output, thereby decreasing the body's sodium and water volume. Diuretics, also called water pills, are indispensable in the treatment of heart failure, and they are often used in treating high blood pressure and certain kidney and liver disorders. Patients receiving a daily dose of this type of medication are advised to consume extra potassium to compensate for possible excretion of this essential mineral. When there is uncertainty about the need for compensatory potassium, a simple blood test can provide the answer.

Anyone who takes diuretics on a daily basis should exercise caution about spending prolonged periods in the sun because of an increased likelihood getting sunburned. Older people also run the risk of heat stroke because of dehydration. Diuretics should not be combined with such substances as prostaglandin inhibitors or calcium supplements. Physicians have observed the development of secondary gout symptoms in patients who have been taking diuretics over a long period as treatment for heart disease and/or high blood pressure.

Common substances such as caffeine and alcohol have a diuretic effect.

Diverticulosis • The presence of diverticula, an abnormal mucous membrane pouch, in any part of the gastrointestinal tract but especially in the colon. Diverticulosis may be entirely without symptoms and is most commonly found in middle-aged and elderly women with a history of chronic constipation. Because the diverticula formations are visible in X-rays following a barium enema, accurate diagnosis of diverticulosis is comparatively simple.

Diverticulitis is the inflammation of diverticula and it may produce cramps and muscle spasms in the lower left side of the abdomen. Treatment should be prompt to prevent the serious consequences of fistula development or complete intestinal obstruction. Bed rest, a bland low-residue diet, and antibiotics are usually successful therapy. In severe cases of diverticulitis, where a rupture of the colon may lead to peritonitis, surgery should be performed without delay.

Dizziness • *See* VERTIGO.

DNA • One of the basic components of all living matter; the molecular material in the nuclear chromosome of the cell responsible for the transmission of the hereditary genetic code. The designation DNA stands for the chemical compound deoxyribonucleic acid, the molecules of which are connected in an arrangement known as the double helix. The discovery in 1962 of the molecular composition of DNA is the foundation on which the comparatively new field of genetic medicine is based. *See* GENETIC ENGINEERING.

Dog Bites • *See* ANIMAL BITES.

Dopamine • A substance in the brain that is essential to the normal functioning of the nervous system. A decreased concentration of dopamine is assumed to be the underlying cause of Parkinsonism. Symptoms of this disorder are dramatically alleviated by chemotherapy with dopamine in the synthesized form known as L-dopa.

Down Syndrome (previously called Down's Syndrome) • This most common form of inherited mental retardation is caused by defective chromosomal development in the embryo. It was formerly referred to as mongolism because of the downward curve of the affected offspring's inner eyelids. In addition to retardation, these children may suffer eye disorders and have a tendency to develop leukemia. However, as a result of the recent and ongoing reassessment of the capabilities of Down syndrome children, expectations have expanded to the point where language skills are being taught with computers. Institutionalization, which offered minimal stimulation, is no longer the prevailing option. It is increasingly ruled out in favor of home care and enrollment in special programs.

The incidence of Down syndrome increases with the age of the mother from 1 birth in 1,000 among women between 20 and 25 years of age, to 1 birth in 100 among 40-year-olds, to 3 births in 100 among women 45 years old or older. The role of the father is uncertain. *See* AMMIOCENTESIS, "Pregnancy and Childbirth," and "Directory of Health Information."

Dramamine • Brand name of the chemical dimenhydrinate, an antihistamine effective against motion sickness and vertigo. Because it induces drowsiness, it should never be taken before driving or engaging in any activity requiring mental alertness.

Duodenal Ulcer • An open sore in the mucous membrane lining of the duodenum, the portion of the small intestine nearest to the stomach. *See also* ULCER.

Dying • *See* HOSPICE.

Dysentery • An infectious inflammation of the lining of the large intestine characterized by diarrhea, the passage of mucus and blood, and severe abdominal cramps and fever. There are two types: bacillary dysentery is caused by several different types of bacterial strains; amebic dysentery is caused by amebae. Both types are endemic in parts of the world where public sanitation is primitive. Dysentery is spread from person to person by food or water that is contaminated by infected human feces and by houseflies that feed on human excrement containing the infectious agent. It may also be spread by food handlers who transmit the disease by way of unwashed hands.

When bacillary dysentery is diagnosed in the very young or very old or in anyone with diabetes or some other chronic condition, hospitalization is usually recommended so that dehydration can be prevented or treated.

In milder forms of dysentery, rest combined with a prescribed dose of an antibiotic or other medication is a common course of treatment. Close supervision is important in the case of amebic dysentery because the infection can become chronic if amebic abscesses are formed in the liver.

Travelers to parts of the world where infection is an everpresent hazard should take the necessary precautions against dysentery by drinking only bottled water or other bottled beverages *(never* with ice), avoiding raw fruit and vegetables, and, if possible, inspecting the facilities where food is prepared to make sure that the premises are screened against flies. If traveler's diarrhea or "La Turista" does occur, the first treatment of choice is Pepto-Bismol. *See* DIARRHEA.

Dysmenorrhea • Painful and crampy menstruation. The discomfort is usually felt in the lower abdomen, extending into the lower back, and in some cases into the lower part of the legs. Dysmenorrhea may occur with or without headaches and may be the result of tension. *See* "Gynecologic Diseases and Treatment," PREMENSTRUAL SYNDROME, and PROSTAGLANDIN.

Dyspareunia • Painful sexual intercourse caused by physical or psychogenic factors or a combination of both. Women for whom intercourse is so painful that it interferes with their sexual life should consult a gynecologist. *See* "Sexual Health."

Dyspepsia • *See* INDIGESTION.

Dysplasia • An aberration of cellular development that may occur in the cervix, lung, and other places. In the cervix it is diagnosed by a pap smear. Although cervical dysplasia usually does not progress to cancer, women in whom it has been diagnosed need to be examined regularly. Some cases of dysplasia clear up without treatment; others require cauterization or other treatment.

Dyspnea • Labored breathing; the feeling of being "out of breath." Dyspnea is a symptom or sign of insufficiently oxygenated blood resulting from an obstruction in the air passages such as occurs in chronic respiratory diseases; a reduction in the capacity of the lungs to carry on the normal oxygen-carbon dioxide exchange because of areas of scar tissue; certain forms of heart failure in which the lungs fill with fluid; chronic anemia. An acute breathlessness may accompany asthma, bronchial pneumonia, the sudden onset of an allergic response that causes the swelling of the windpipe, and myocardial infarction. It is also one of the most distressing manifestations of an anxiety attack. Shortness of breath that often accompanies obesity can be rectified by loss of weight. When dyspnea is accompanied by chest pain or when it is chronic, medical evaluation is indicated.

Ear • The organ of hearing and equilibrium. The ear is divided into three parts: the outer ear consists of the visible fleshy auricle that collects the sound waves, which are then transmitted through the ear canal; the middle ear contains the three bones of hearing; the inner ear is the site of the organ of hearing and the organ of balance. The thin layer of tissue known as the eardrum, also called the tympanus or tympanic membrane, forms the barrier between the outer ear and the middle ear. The bones of hearing in the middle ear, called the ossicles, are named for their respective shapes—the hammer, anvil, and stirrup. They are connected to the bone surrounding the middle ear by ligaments. When loud noises strike the eardrum, tiny muscles attached to the ossicles limit the vibrations of the eardrum by contracting, thus protecting it and the inner ear from damage. Equal pressure is maintained on both sides of the eardrum because the eustachian tube connects the middle ear to the upper rear part of the throat. The organ of hearing within the inner ear is called the cochlea, a spiral-shaped organ whose name means "snail" in Latin. The cochlea covers the nerves that sort out various sound messages and sends them on to the auditory center of the brain. The organ of balance, made up of the three semicircular canals situated in three different planes of space within the inner ear, maintains the body's equilibrium in relation to gravitational forces. Any disturbance or infection of the semicircular canals results in vertigo and imbalance.

The hearing process works in the following way. Any vibrating object that pushes air molecules at a rate ranging from 15 to 15,000 vibrations per second (the range of human audibility) causes waves to enter the ear canal and strike the eardrum. The vibrations are transmitted by the eardrum to the middle ear where their intensity is magnified by the ossicles. The waves are then sent through a membranous window behind the third bone and are transmitted through the fluid within the cochlea. Hairlike structures within the cochlea communicate with the auditory nerves in such a way that a sound of a particular pitch and volume is perceived by the brain.

Ear Disorders • Diseases, infections, mechanical difficulties, and pressure problems that affect the ears. The disorders directly responsible for the onset of deafness are discussed under the headings HEARING LOSS and OTOSCLEROSIS. The irreversible effects of exposure to occupational, recreational, or environmental sound that is excessively loud are discussed under NOISE.

Discomfort within the ear may range from irritation due to dermatitis of the outer ear to a feeling of pressure caused by congestion in the eustachian tube to acute pain resulting from bacterial infection of the middle ear. Until the discomfort is diagnosed, it may be temporarily relieved with aspirin and the application of heat. Any sharp pain in the ear, an earache that lasts more than a day, an earache accompanied by a discharge, or chronic pain resulting from exposure to dangerous sound levels should be investigated by a doctor immediately.

Because the ears are directly connected to the nose and throat by the eustachian tube, a head cold is likely to cause the ears to feel "stuffed." The symptom may be remedied by the supervised use of nosedrops. Nostrils should not be held closed when blowing the nose, because closing both at once may force infectious material into the ear. Similar precautions should be taken while swimming. Air should be breathed in through the mouth and exhaled through the nose; if the mouth or nose fills with water, it should not be swallowed but rather sniffed into the back of the throat and spat out. Earplugs may be worn. If water enters the ear, it can usually be drained by the force of gravity when lying down with the ear to the ground.

Otomycosis, a fungus infection of the outer ear, results from swimming in polluted waters and causes itching, swelling, and pain. It is often accompanied by crusted sores that must be kept dry in order to cure the condition. Fungicidal ointments and antibiotic salves are usually effective treatment.

Infections of the middle ear, more common in childhood than in later years, can be brought under control by antibiotics.

Echogram • A recording produced on an oscilloscopic screen that shows the difference between the wave patterns of healthy and diseased tissue, a difference that cannot be distinguished by X-rays. Echocardiograms provide tracings of the ultrasonic waves reflected from the internal heart tissues. The echoencephalogram provides similar material for the diagnosis of brain disorders.

Eclampsia • An acute condition occurring during pregnancy characterized by elevated blood pressure, convulsions, and coma; also known as toxemia of pregnancy. *See* "Pregnancy and Childbirth."

Ectopic Pregnancy • The implantation of the fertilized ovum in a fallopian tube, the cervix, or the abdomen instead of within the uterus. *See* "Pregnancy and Childbirth."

Eczema • A skin disorder, also called atopic dermatitis, characterized by redness, swelling, blistering, and scaling and accompanied by itching. The tendency to eczema is inherited, and onset at any age may be triggered by stress, extremes of temperature, allergy, medication, or skin contact with silk or wool.

Eczema is treated by eliminating the underlying cause and by topical creams that reduce discomfort and hasten healing. Medicated creams are most effective when applied immediately after bathing. An effort should be made to avoid excessively humid environments, and swimmers who are eczema-prone should always wear earplugs to avert the unpleasant consequences of ear infections. When flareups are traced to stress, psychotherapy might be helpful.

Edema • Swelling caused by the abnormal accumulation of fluid in the tissues. The archaic term for edema is dropsy, derived from the Greek word *hydrops* from *hydros,* meaning "water." Edema is a symptom of various disorders, many of which require immediate treatment. The edema that accompanies heart failure or circulatory impairments usually takes the form of swollen ankles, but it may occur in the more serious form of accumulation of fluid in the lungs. Edema may also be caused by impairment of kidney and liver function.

Puffy eyelids and ankles are among the symptoms of pre-eclampsia, a condition that afflicts pregnant women. Fluid retention and a bloated feeling are associated with premenstrual syndrome. Under normal circumstances, the edema and other discomforts vanish with the onset of menstrual flow. If the edema persists between periods, it should be checked by a doctor.

EEG • *See* ELECTROENCEPHALOGRAM.

Ejaculation • The reflex action by which semen is expelled during the male orgasm. Premature ejaculation, the most widespread sexual dysfunction, occurs because the male cannot control his level of sexual arousal and therefore reaches orgasm sooner than he or his partner desires.

The disorder is not associated with any physical abnormalities, and sex therapy techniques have a high success rate when both partners participate in a series of prescribed exercises over a period of several weeks. *See* "Sexual Health."

EKG • *See* ELECTROCARDIOGRAM.

Elective Surgery • *See* SURGERY and "You, Your Doctors, and the Health Care System."

Electrocardiogram (EKG) • A tracing that represents the electrical impulses generated by the heart as measured by an instrument called an electrocardiograph. The resulting pattern indicates the rate of the heart rhythm, tissue damage that may have occurred following a heart attack, the effect of various medications on the heart muscle, and other valuable information for the diagnosis of cardiac disorders. A recent application is the recording of variations in the behavior of the heart at the same time that increasing demands are made on it by the patient's participation in the Treadmill Test, which involves walking and jogging at progressively faster speeds.

Electroencephalogram (EEG) • A tracing by an electroencephalograph of the electrical potential produced by the brain. Electrical impulses picked up by electrodes attached to the scalp surface are amplified so that they are strong enough to move an electromagnetic pen to make a record of brain wave patterns. This procedure is quick and painless. It is used routinely to diagnose tumors, brain damage resulting from an accident or injury to the head, and neurological disorders such as epilepsy.

Electrolysis • *See* HAIR REMOVAL.

Electroshock Therapy (ECT) • Also called electroconvulsive therapy, and generally referred to as "shock treatment." A procedure in which a controlled amount of electric current is passed through the frontal area of the brain of a mentally ill patient. The physical response is convulsions and unconsciousness. The treatments may be administered on an outpatient basis, or, if a suicide attempt has been made or is anticipated, during hospitalization. Some specialists believe that ECT may yield insights into the relationship between the brain's biochemical and electrochemical behavior and the patient's severe depression; others agree with the patient advocacy movement that wants to outlaw the procedure altogether.

Electroshock is not a cure for any form of mental illness, but when treatments are given in series, they may temporarily relieve some of the more anguishing emotional symptoms and thereby make the patient accessible to other forms of psychotherapy. While it has largely been replaced by antidepressant drugs and tranquilizers, it may be the therapy of last resort for those mentally ill patients categorized as "treatment resistant" to all medication.

Embolism • Obstruction of a blood vessel by material carried in the bloodstream from another part of the body. The material, or embolus, is most often a blood clot, but it may also be a fat globule, air bubble, segment of a tumor, or clump of bacteria. *See* PHLEBITIS, THROMBOSIS.

Embryo • The term by which the developing human organism is known from conception to the end of the eighth week of pregnancy. After that time and until delivery, it is known as the fetus.

Emphysema • A severe respiratory disease, incurable but treatable, characterized by the air-filled expansion of the lungs. Emphysema is more prevalent among men than women and is most commonly observed in heavy cigarette smokers living in an area with a high level of air pollution. The disease develops gradually and is usually preceded by a chronic cough and intermittent bouts of bronchitis. Its progress is insidious, especially because in its early stages the damage is not detectable by X-rays. However, when there is reason to suspect that the disease exists, early diagnosis of respiratory obstruction can be verified by a simple breathing test in which an instrument called a spirometer measures the time taken by the patient to empty her lungs of the deepest possible intake of air.

More obvious symptoms may not

become apparent until after age 50, by which time the lung's functioning surface area is progressively diminished by the destruction of the walls that separate the air spaces. The loss in resiliency in these walls disrupts the exchange of oxygen and carbon dioxide so that the lungs become inflated by an accumulation of stale air. At this stage, breathing is difficult after a minimum amount of exertion. As breathing becomes more labored, the heart is forced to work harder to increase the blood supply to the lungs.

To counteract the debilitating effect of emphysema, proper breathing techniques must be established in order to enhance lung capacity. Other aspects of treatment include a proper diet to counteract weight loss, supplementary oxygen, elimination of environmental irritants, immunization against respiratory infections, and medications that dilate the bronchial passages. Although other pollutants play a role in the development of emphysema, the most significant cause is the chronic inhalation of tobacco smoke.

Encephalitis • Inflammation of the tissues covering the brain associated with such viral infections as measles, herpes simplex, chicken pox, and AIDS. In comparatively rare cases, it may also occur following vaccination against polio and other forms of immunization against viral disease. It may be produced by lead poisoning, or it may follow the infectious bite of certain ticks and mosquitos. The disease may occur at any age. Typical symptoms are fever, vomiting, headache, and in some cases convulsions. Correct diagnosis is made by laboratory tests of the blood, spinal fluid, and stools and by an electroencephalogram, and in some cases by examination of a sample of brain tissue. Where the cause is the herpes simplex Type I virus, specific medicines can be effective. In other cases, treatment consists of bed rest and medication to keep the fever down.

Endocrine System • A physiological system that includes the ductless glands whose secretions, the hormones, are delivered directly into the bloodstream. *See* "The Healthy Woman."

Endometrial Aspiration • A technique in which suction is applied to remove the lining of the uterus (the endometrium). *See* "Contraception and Abortion."

Endometriosis • A condition in which tissue normally found in the lining of the uterus (the endometrium) begins to grow in the ovaries, fallopian tubes, bladder, or between the rectum and vagina. *See* "Gynecologic Diseases and Treatment."

Endometritis • Inflammation of the endometrium (the lining of the uterus), caused by bacterial infection that may follow a normal delivery, a cesarean section, an induced or spontaneous abortion, or irritation resulting from an IUD. Symptoms include pain in the lower abdomen, discharge, and fever. Acute endometritis is usually treated with antibiotics. Where the condition is caused by an IUD, a reevaluation of birth control methods should be considered. Chronic cases that do not respond to medication may require curettage.

Endorphins • A group of morphine-like chemicals produced by the

COMMON SITES OF ENDOMETRIOSIS

brain and found in large quantities in the spinal fluid and in various parts of the endocrine system, especially the pituitary gland. The endorphins in the brain appear to regulate the pain receptors, and they may also affect memory, learning, and the hormonal changes involved in puberty and the sexual drive. Because endorphins are released by exercise, they may account for the euphoria experienced by runners. *See* PAIN.

Endoscopy • Examination of a hollow cavity or an internal organ with an illuminated optical instrument (endoscope). Among the more commonly used instruments are the cystoscope for examining the bladder, the proctoscope for examining the lower portion of the intestine and rectum, and the bronchoscope for locating the origin and extent of respiratory disorders.

Enema • The injection of a fluid into the lower bowel by means of a tube inserted into the rectum; also, the fluid injected. A barium enema is administered prior to X-rays of the lower gastrointestinal tract, a sedative enema may be used for a calming effect, and a warm water or special solution enema is often recommended in special cases of constipation. The habitual use of enemas as a means of bowel evacuation is not recommended because they are apt to impair the natural responses involved in the normal process of elimination. Disposable enema units are a convenient substitute for the more traditional equipment that must be washed and stored.

Energy • The capacity for activity. Energy may take mechanical, electrical, chemical, or thermal form. All fuel is stored energy, and the body's fuel is food. The chemical energy stored in food is transformed by the metabolic process. The three essential sources of human energy are proteins, fats, and carbohydrates. "Lack of energy" may be traced to faulty diet, chronic illness, or stress. *See* "Fitness."

Enterocele • A hernia in which a loop of the small intestine protrudes into the vaginal wall. The condition may reveal itself when X-rays are taken to diagnose pain. Surgical correction is the usual treatment.

Enuresis • Involuntary bedwetting while sleeping; more specifically, by a child past the age at which bladder sphincter control is expected.

Enzyme • An organic substance, usually protein, manufactured by the cells of all living things and acting as a catalyst in the transformation of a complex chemical compound into a simple or different one. The human body produces hundreds of different enzymes, each with a specific function: some ward off invasive microbes; some are related to the chemistry of muscle function; three main groups of digestive enzymes are essential for the normal metabolic processing of proteins, fats, and carbohydrates; and particular enzymes are involved in maintaining normal respiratory function.

An inherited liver enzyme disease has been identified as the underlying cause of phenylketonuria (PKU disease), which can result in mental retardation unless diagnosed early and treated through special diet.

Epiglottis • The leaf-shaped flap of cartilage covered with mucous membrane that lies between the back of the tongue and the entrance to the larynx and the trachea (windpipe). In the act of swallowing, the epiglottis folds back over the opening of the larynx, which contains the vocal apparatus (in the glottis), and channels the food from the back of the tongue to the esophagus. The disruption of this mechanism, such as by a person's laughing while eating, may allow food to enter the windpipe, leading to a coughing spell and in more serious cases to choking.

Epilepsy • The general term for a category of symptoms characterized by overactive electrical discharge of the brain cells. This imbalance leads to seizures that vary in magnitude and duration. Petit mal seizures are brief, may recur many times a day, and are scarcely perceptible to the onlooker. They involve a sudden and short loss of consciousness and may be accompanied by twitching eye and face muscles. Grand mal seizures involve convulsive spasms, loss of consciousness, stiffening of the arms and legs, and sometimes, a loss of bowel control. The unconscious state may last for several minutes. On regaining consciousness, the victim of the seizure may be disorientated for as long as a few minutes or a few hours.

There are as many as 4 million people in the United States who suffer from one or another form of epilepsy; in half these cases, the cause is unknown. The others can be explained by an injury to the brain, a stroke, tumor, or hereditary predisposition.

The seizures can be controlled in approximately 80 percent of all cases with anticonvulsant medicines. It often subsides completely, particularly in younger people, and medication can be discontinued.

An unambiguous diagnosis of epilepsy is based on an electroencephalogram, a CAT scan, as well as a complete physical examination, a medical history, and a family history.

Temporal-lobe epilepsy is a form of the disorder that may cause abnormal behavior without the characteristic seizures. When this form of the disease exists, it is important that the cause of the aberrant behavior be properly diagnosed as physical rather than psychological so that it can be treated medically or surgically rather than with psychotherapy.

Because anticonvulsant medications are thought to reduce the effectiveness of birth control pills, women with epilepsy who are using this form of contraception should investigate alternative methods. *See* "Directory of Health Information."

Epinephrine • *See* ADRENALINE

Episiotomy • An incision made in the perineum from the vagina downward toward the anus during the final stage of labor. *See* "Pregnancy and Childbirth."

Epstein-Barr Virus • *See* MONONUCLEOSIS, INFECTIOUS.

Erection • The swelling and stiffening of the penis or increase in length, diameter, and firmness of the clitoris resulting from sexual arousal. The stimulus may be psychological (sexual fantasies), visual (the sight of a sexually appealing person), or physical (touch).

There is no correlation between the size of the flaccid penis and the same penis in erection, which may range on the average from 5 to 7 inches. There is no correlation between body size and the size of the erect penis nor between the size of the erect penis and sexual prowess. Inability to have an erection is called impotence.

Erogenous Zone • Any area of the body, especially the oral, genital, and anal, that is the source of sexual arousal when stimulated by touch.

Erythromycin • Generic name for an antibiotic commonly prescribed to patients with a penicillin allergy and to pregnant women and young children when the tetracycline antibiotics are considered inadvisable. Erythromycin is the specific medication for Legionnaire's disease, and as a topical ointment, it is helpful in treating acne. In tablet form, this antibiotic should be taken on an empty stomach, either one hour before meals or two hours after meals. Its effectiveness is increased when accompanied by an 8-ounce glass of water.

Esophagus • The muscular tube that transmits food from the mouth to the stomach; the gullet. This portion of the alimentary canal is approximately 10 inches long; it extends from the pharynx through the chest and connects with the stomach just below the diaphragm. Between the esophagus and the stomach is a muscular ring, the esophageal sphincter, that opens to permit food to leave the esophagus and descend into the stomach. Weakening of this sphincter muscle to the point where it does not close properly results in the back flow or reflux of some of the acid contents of the stomach. When this esophageal reflux occurs, the result is the sensation of "heartburn" or acid indigestion. Conditions that contribute to the malfunctioning of the esophageal sphincter include overweight and pregnancy.

Estrogen • A sex hormone, primarily a female hormone, that is produced in the ovary, adrenal gland, and placenta. Males also produce estrogen in much smaller amounts in their adrenals. Estrogen regulates the development of the secondary sex characteristics in women and is involved in the menstrual cycle and the implantation and nourishment of a fertilized ovum. Synthetic estrogen is widely used in birth control pills and in estrogen replacement therapy to treat symptoms of menopause including osteoporosis. *See* "Contraception and Abortion," "The Healthy Woman," "Aging Healthfully—Your Body," and DES.

Eustachian Tube • The canal that connects the middle ear with the back of the throat and equalizes the pressure on either side of the eardrum. Swallowing is the mechanism by which air is forced into the tube, correcting the stuffy sensation in the ears produced by a change in air pressure as occurs in an elevator or airplane. The eustachian tube is also the pathway through which infection may travel from the nasal passages into the middle ear.

Eye • The organ of vision. The eyes are contained in bony sockets of the skull. The extent of their movements depends on six delicate muscles attached to the top, sides, and bottom of each eyeball. The movements of the lids, which serve to protect the eyes, are controlled by other muscles that are both voluntary and involuntary.

The front of the eyeball is covered by the translucent tissue called the cornea. It is a continuation of the tough fibrous sclera, the white of the eye that protects the delicate structures within. Under the cornea is a middle, pigmented layer that forms the iris, which is responsible for the color of the eyes and which is densely supplied with blood vessels. The iris functions in much the same way as the diaphragm of a camera, narrowing or widening in response to varying light conditions to expand or contract the pupil, the opening through which light enters the eye. The dilation of the pupil is influenced by various chemicals as well as by light intensity.

The light that passes through the pupil is focused on the retina, the expanded end of the optic nerve extending into the middle of the brain. Within the retina are the nerve cells, the light- and color-sensitive rods and cones, and the many connections that supply information to the occipital lobes of the brain where stimuli are transformed into the images called "seeing." The information the eyes continuously send to the brain may be acted on immediately or may be stored away as memory for future recall.

The main part of the eyeball is filled with a transparent jelly called the vitreous humor, and the area in front of the lens is filled with a watery substance called the aqueous humor. The eyes are constantly lubricated, cleansed, and protected from infection by the tears secreted through the lacrimal ducts.

Among the more common disorders of vision are astigmatism, farsightedness, and nearsightedness, all of which can be corrected by prescribed lenses.

Because many disorders of the eye progress slowly and insidiously, regular examinations should be scheduled *before* dramatic changes in vision occur. Cataracts and glaucoma, the two main causes of blindness in this country, can be treated surgically. Diabetic retinopathy, the leading cause of new blindness in the United States, can be treated effectively when diagnosed early. Macular degeneration is a condition in which poor circulation associated with aging progressively impairs the macula, the part of the retina responsible for clear central vision. This condition has no cure. However, because peripheral vision remains unimpaired, macular degeneration does not prevent independent functioning with the use of special visual aids.

Cornea scarring by contact lenses can be avoided if irritation is promptly reported and corrected. A cornea damaged by disease or accident can now be replaced by a transplant.

Aging is responsible for the discomfort caused by "dry" eyes. This condition results from the gradual diminishment of the natural flow of moisture from the tear ducts. When the eye is deprived of this lubrication, the dryness creates the sensation of the presence of grains of sand under the lid. Many varieties of nonprescription artificial tears are available to deal with this problem.

Blurred vision is associated with various medications, especially the tricyclic antidepressants, such as Elavil and Tofranil, and antipsychotic drugs, such as Thorazine, Stelazine, and Haldol. This side effect disappears when the drugs are discontinued.

Eyes that burn and itch may be reacting to an allergy or to indoor on-the-job pollution. Unpleasant eye symptoms may develop because of constant use of Video Display Terminals. (*See* "Health on the Job").

Foreign objects in the eye should be dealt with by an eye doctor. Eye makeup and especially the brushes used to apply it should never be borrowed or lent as a precaution against the spread of infection. Women engaged in racquet sports should *always* wear protective glasses.

Eye Examination • Any variation of vision, no matter how minor, should be evaluated. An ophthalmologist, a physician specializing in the eye, can diagnose or treat any disorder that might be affecting vision. Optometrists can check visual acuity and prescribe corrective lenses but cannot diagnose organic eye disease. (An optician makes the prescription lens.) Women over forty should schedule a routine checkup for glaucoma once a year. Anyone whose diabetes is insulin-regulated should have regularly scheduled examinations by an ophthalmologist familiar with the problem of diabetic retinopathy.

Eyeglasses • Lenses, made of glass or plastic, ground to individual prescription for the correction of defects in vision, such as nearsightedness, farsightedness, and astigmatism. Bifocals are worn when both short-range and long-range vision require correction. If vision is impaired at the middle distance as well, a second pair of glasses or trifocals may be necessary. For women whose distance vision is normal but who need reading glasses, half-lenses are often a satisfactory solution. Tinted glasses or sunglasses ground to individual prescription are both practical and useful for outdoor purposes. Women engaged in active sports should wear shatterproof glasses, and those who travel should carry an extra pair of glasses or the prescription for their corrective lenses. As changes in vision occur, the eyes should be checked for a new prescription. In order to decide whether to wear conventional glasses or contact lenses it is wise to consult an ophthalmologist. *See* CONTACT LENSES.

Eyestrain • A feeling of tiredness in the eyes often accompanied by headache. The problem may exist with no apparent impairment of vision and is commonly the result of using one's eyes under poor lighting conditions. Eyestrain is an increasingly common complaint of women who use Video Display Terminals for the better part of their working day. In general, it is important that the illumination come from the side and the rear in such a way that no shadow is cast on the object on which the eye is focused. It is also recommended that 60 or 75 watt light bulbs be used for reading. Office workers who suffer from chronic eyestrain due to poor lighting should make every effort to see that the condition is corrected. If the eyes tire before the completion of a task, they can be rested by closing the lids or by gazing into the distance. Television will not cause eyestrain if the set is properly adjusted and the viewer at a distance of approximately 6 feet from the picture. While it is advisable to have light in the room, it is important that it does not bounce off the TV screen into the viewer's eyes. *See* "Health on the Job."

Facial Tic • *See* TIC.

Fainting • A brief loss of consciousness caused by a temporary lack of oxygen to the brain; technically called syncope. (Fainting should not be confused with shock, which is an emergency situation resulting from a critical loss of body fluids.) Fainting is usually preceded by lightheadedness, weakness, pallor, and a cold sweat. Circumstances that may reduce the brain's oxygen supply are a sudden emotional trauma, an excess intake of alcohol, and standing up for the first time after an illness. Standing still increases the chances of fainting because the blood supply to the brain is temporarily diminished. When one feels faint it is best to lie down or sit down with one's head lowered between the knees until the dizziness subsides. To help someone who has fainted, loosen all clothing and make certain that there is an adequate amount of fresh air to be breathed. Alcohol should not be administered as a means of reviving someone who has fainted. If consciousness is not regained within a minute or two, a doctor should be summoned.

Recurrent fainting spells should be reported to a physician to determine the cause. Heart disease, anemia, or diabetes may be a contributing factor.

Fallopian Tubes • Two tubes, each approximately 4 inches long, extending from the ovaries to the uterus. *See* "The Healthy Woman," "Pregnancy and Childbirth," "Infertility," and ECTOPIC PREGNANCY.

Family History • Facts concerning the health conditions, both mental and physical, of a patient's blood relatives. Some diseases are clearly inherited; others that do not necessarily have a genetic foundation may run in the family. With the increasing recognition of inheritance and predisposition as determinants of many diseases, every woman should be aware of her family's past and present medical history and should give this information to her doctor in detail. It can be useful to collect the family's medical history while the older members are still living even though they may be geographically scattered. Especially relevant is information about asthma and allergies, breast cancer, glaucoma, severe mental illness, Alzheimer's disease, alcoholism, and carriers of recessive genes related to inherited diseases. In describing a grandfather's diabetes or another relative's Duchenne muscular dystrophy, for example, the patient is providing the doctor with information that may be a clue for the early diagnosis of a condition. *See* HEREDITY and "You, Your Doctors, and The Health Care System."

Farsightedness • A disorder of vision in which only distant objects are seen clearly; technically called hyperopia. Farsightedness occurs when the lens of the eye focuses the image behind the retina rather than directly on it because the eyeball is shorter than normal from front to back. This disorder is corrected by wearing a convex lens that bends the light rays to the center of the retina.

Fasting • *See* "Nutrition, Weight, and General Well-Being."

Fats • An essential nutrient, found in both plant and animal food, composed of fatty acids (organic compounds of chains of carbon atoms with many hydrogen and some oxygen atoms added on). *See* "Nutrition, Weight, and General Well-Being."

Feet • The underlying cause of most foot problems is often improperly fitted shoes. Shoes and hosiery should be selected carefully for proper fit, comfort, and support. Natural leather is preferred over other shoe materials because it allows the feet to "breathe" and has flexibility. Extremely high heels are inadvisable for those who walk a great deal because they place a strain on the foot and calf muscles and often cause posture problems that result in back pain. Support hosiery is helpful in cases where constant standing places extra pressure on the blood vessels of the feet and legs. When a blister occurs, it must be given prompt attention to avoid the possibility of infection.

Feet can be pampered by elevating them for short periods; circulation problems can be helped by immersing the feet in hot water and then rinsing with cold water. Exercises may keep feet limber and counteract the effects of poor circulation. These exercises may be simple ones such as wriggling the toes or picking up small objects with the toes. Walking barefoot on lawns or beaches is also helpful in keeping feet in good condition.

Runners and long distance walkers should have their footwear checked to find out about the advisability of installing a custom-made orthotic device in one or both shoes to compensate for bone or muscle irregularities.

For chronic foot problems, consult a podiatrist (formerly called a chiropodist). *See* "Fitness."

Fellatio • *See* ORAL SEX.

Fetal Monitoring • *See* "Pregnancy and Childbirth."

Fetus • The organism in the uterus after the eighth week of pregnancy. Prior to that time it is called an embryo. Some time around the eighteenth week the fetal heartbeat can be detected by placing an ear or a stethoscope against the mother's abdomen, and "quickening" or fetal movement also begins at about this time. By the twenty-fourth to twenty-seventh week a fetus is considered viable and, if born, may be kept alive with special hospital equipment and intensive care.

Fever • Body temperature that rises significantly above 98.6°F or 37°C, presumably due to a change in metabolic processes. A 1-degree variation is well within the normal range, because temperature rises this much after exercise, after a heavy meal, during hot weather when the body must work harder to rid itself of heat, or during ovulation when the increase in the secretion of progesterone affects the body processes.

A high fever usually results from a bacterial or viral infection: a woman who experiences a high fever of sudden onset should consult a physician about the possibility of toxic shock syndrome. Any high fever accompanied by vomiting and/or diarrhea, by pains in the neck, throat, muscles, joints, and by severe headaches, requires a doctor's prompt attention. Some other circumstances that should receive professional diagnosis include onset of fever and abdominal cramps during pregnancy, and a persistent low-grade fever accompanied by a cough or general malaise.

Chills often precede or alternate with a high fever. As the temperature rises, the patient feels achy and thirsty, skin becomes hot and dry, urine is scant, and, depending on the cause, vomiting may take place. Until a doctor is consulted, a person with a high fever should stay in bed, drink lots of liquids, and take two aspirin or Tylenol tablets every four hours while awake.

Note that the temperature reading on a rectal thermometer is usually 1 degree higher than the reading on a mouth thermometer. It should also be kept in mind that the seriousness of an illness cannot be judged by the presence or absence of fever. *See* RHEUMATIC FEVER, ROCKY MOUNTAIN SPOTTED FEVER, TYPHOID FEVER, UNDULANT FEVER.

Fever Sores • *See* HERPES.

Fiber • Cellulose or roughage in food. Fiber cannot be digested by humans. However, in small amounts it has a stimulating effect on the peristaltic action of the intestines and thus is useful in preventing sluggish digestive action and constipation. In larger amounts it acts as an irritant and can lead to unpleasant gastrointestinal disturbances. A balanced diet containing whole grain breads and cereals and cooked and raw vegetables provides sufficient fiber. *See* "Nutrition, Weight, and General Well-Being."

Fibrillation • A condition in which the fibers of a muscle contract in groups or singly rather than in unison, thus causing parts of the muscle to twitch in rapid succession. When fibrillation occurs in the ventricles of the heart, the muscle cannot contract in a coordinated way, and the heart stops beating. A patient in the intensive coronary care unit of a hospital who experiences ventricular fibrillation after a heart attack has a 90 percent chance of survival if treatment begins within one minute. Treatment consists of the use of a machine called a defibrillator, which attempts to jolt the heart back into its proper rhythmic pattern by means of electric current. Monitoring equipment in coronary care units can anticipate the onset of fibrillation by the characteristic EKG pattern of skipped ventricular beats. This monitoring system enables the doctor to prescribe medication that helps to prevent impending danger. Ventricular fibrillation is thought to be a major cause of sudden cardiac death in nonhospitalized women with no previous history of heart disease. Attempts are, therefore, being made to identify likely victims of fibrillation *before* onset.

Fibroadenoma • A benign tumor composed of fibrous tissue. *See* "Breast Care."

Fibrocystic Disease • *See* "Breast Care."

Fibroid Tumor • *See* "Gynecological Diseases and Treatment."

First Aid • Emergency treatment administered to the victim of an accident or unexpected illness prior to the arrival of medical assistance. Instruction in the fundamentals of first aid are available under the auspices of local Red Cross chapters, hospitals, or community organizations. Such instruction enables the potential rescuer to provide emergency treatment in the event of a crisis. First aid can be effectively and promptly administered if the proper supplies are on hand. Every home should have the following first aid supplies available:

roll of 2-inch wide sterile gauze
individually packaged gauze squares
cotton-tipped swabs
aspirin or Tylenol tablets
antihistamine tablets
oral and rectal thermometers
adhesive strip bandages, assorted sizes
sterile absorbent cotton
roll of adhesive bandage tape
paper tissues
tongue depressors
hydrogen peroxide
antiseptic spray
Bacitracin ointment
Pepto-Bismol
baking soda (bicarbonate of soda)
rubbing alcohol
surgical scissors and tweezers

Fish Oil • A nutritional supplement promoted for its effectiveness in lowering the risk of heart disease. It is presumed that the inclusion of the oilier fish in the diet serves the same purpose. *See* "Nutrition, Weight, and General Well-Being."

Fissure • A crack in a mucous membrane. Fissures at the corner of the mouth are called cheilosis and result from a riboflavin (vitamin) deficiency. An anal fissure caused by chronic constipation may lead to the further inhibition of bowel movements due to the severity of pain accompanying the passage of stools. Another type of fissure, cracked nipples, is often found in nursing mothers. It can best be prevented by the use of lubricating cream. Because fissures may be a source of infection, a doctor should be consulted for proper treatment.

Fistula • An abnormal opening leading from a cavity or a hollow organ within the body to an adjacent part of the body or to the skin surface. Anal fistulas that occur because of a lesion or abscess in the anal canal or the rectum eventually become painful enough to require surgical removal. A fistula between the urethra and the vagina that results from damage to the organs during childbirth or during surgery may cause incomplete bladder control and urinary incontinence. A fistula between the vagina and the rectum may also occur after an operation. Both conditions should be evaluated for surgical correction.

Flu • *See* INFLUENZA.

Fluids • The maintenance of proper fluid balance within the body is essential. An excessive loss through diarrhea, vomiting, hemorrhage, or perspiration leads to dehydration. Fluid intake should be increased to offset the effects of a fever and to hasten recovery from a cold.

The presence of salt and potassium and other electrolytes is essential for normal cellular use of fluids. People using diuretics must have regular tests to determine whether the salt and potassium levels are maintained or whether a potassium supplement is necessary.

The condition of edema, or the abnormal fluid retention manifested in puffiness or swelling of the eyelids, ankles, or other parts of the body, is a symptom of an underlying condition that should be diagnosed by a doctor and corrected.

Fluid accumulation is one of the chief causes of the discomfort associated with premenstrual syndrome, and fluid retention is one of the negative side effects experienced by some women who take birth control pills.

Fluoridation • The addition of a fluoride (a chemical salt containing fluorine) to public drinking water. There are still some pockets of resistance to this practice, but health authorities, including the U.S. Public Health Service, the American Dental Association, the American Medical Association, and the World Health Organization, have found no compelling evidence of harmful effects and have found that fluoridation is responsible for a significant decrease in dental decay among children. There is no question that the incidence of cavities is much lower where fluorides occur naturally in the water supply than elsewhere.

The benefits of fluoridation are increased by the use of a toothpaste containing fluoride, and many dentists recommend the added protection of applying fluoride directly to the teeth of young children.

Studies have produced evidence that older people profit from the benefits of fluoridated water by having less fragile bones and thereby sustaining fewer fractures. This advantage appears to be especially significant for older women.

Fluoroscope • An X-ray machine that projects images of various organs as well as bones of the body in motion when the patient is placed between the X-ray tube and a fluorescent screen. While the image is not as sharp as that produced by an X-ray on film, fluoroscopy can provide the doctor with an immediate picture of a functional disturbance of the heart, an incipient sign of respiratory distress (as the patient breathes), the exact location of a foreign object lodged in the windpipe, an obstruction in an organ that interferes with circulation, and other information that increases the possibility of achieving an accurate diagnosis. Most fluoroscopic procedures are done on an outpatient basis unless the symptoms being diagnosed required previous hospitalization.

Folic Acid • One of the B-complex vitamins. *See* "Nutrition, Weight, and General Well-Being."

Food Additives • Chemicals intentionally or unintentionally combined with foods during the growth of the products themselves and/or when they are being processed for distribution and consumption. Among the earliest intentional additives were preservatives that kept bread fresh, and in the 1920s, putting iodine in table salt as a cheap, safe way to prevent goiter. Many deficiency diseases such as rickets, anemia, and pellagra, once endemic in parts of the United States and among the urban and rural poor, have all but disappeared thanks to the addition of such nutrients as vitamin D to milk; vitamin A to margarine; and niacin, riboflavin, thiamine, and iron to bread. Under the regulations of the FDA *intentional* additives are permissible if: they upgrade the nutritional value of food, improve its quality, prolong its freshness, make it more readily available and more easily prepared, and enhance its appearance for consumer acceptability. This latter aspect of additives has led to an ongoing 30-year bureaucratic battle over the safety of certain artificial colorings used for everything from baby food to the skin of citrus fruits, not to mention ice cream and soft drinks. More recently, scientists and consumer advocates have urged food processors to reduce the amount of salt added to a long list of edibles. Elimination of salt altogether would help from 10 percent to 30 percent of the population in dealing with a genetic tendency to high blood pressure. With more and more working women eating in restaurants, salad bars, and company cafeterias, the dangers of such additives as sulfites (to preserve freshness) and monosodium glutenate (to enhance flavor) are becoming an increasing cause for concern.

Unintentional additives include pesticide contamination, plant growth regulators, antibiotics given to cattle and poultry in large doses, and industrial wastes that pollute the waters from which many food fish come to the dining table.

Both intentional and unintentional additives are the subject not only of cancer studies but of the cumulative effect on the central nervous system and the possible dangers to the fetus during pregnancy. Women concerned with the problems presented by food additives should scan newspapers and magazines for any results of food tests conducted by the FDA. Local libraries often provide consumer action pamphlets and reference material on this subject. *See* "Nutrition, Weight, and General Well-Being."

Food Poisoning (Food-Borne Illness) • The general term for any acute illness, usually gastrointestinal, which is caused by the ingestion of contaminated food or of uncontaminated food that is poisonous in and of itself. The term "ptomaine poisoning" is incorrect. The most common symptoms include nausea, vomiting, abdominal cramps, and diarrhea. Food can be contaminated by bacteria (salmonella, staphylococci, and *Clostridium botulinum* which causes botulism, among others), viruses (hepatitis and the Norwalk virus carried mainly by uncooked shellfish taken from waters contaminated by raw sewage), chemicals (such as sodium fluoride, monosodium gluconate), parasites, plankton, and poisonous plants eaten by milk-producing cows. Salmonella and staphylococci are the most common contaminants. Salmonella are the usual contaminants of meat and poultry but are killed by proper cooking. When not killed and if present in sufficient numbers, they infect the eater and cause abdominal cramps and diarrhea some eight or more hours after ingestion. Staphylococci, if present, produce a toxin that multiplies rapidly in high protein foods, especially those containing eggs, such as salads, mayonnaise, and custards, when exposed to warm temperatures for several hours. This toxin causes nausea and vomiting three to six hours after the foods containing it are eaten.

Proper cooking and refrigeration are the best ways to prevent disease from these two bacteria. Fortunately, most victims recover quickly and spontaneously from illnesses caused by both of these bacteria, although for infants and elderly people they can be life-threatening because of the danger of dehydration.

Poisonous foods include certain mushrooms, berries, nuts, and fish. Many authorities recommend that raw fish in any form, whether shellfish or sushi, should be avoided, especially by those who have liver problems, diabetes, or gastrointestinal disorders.

Food poisoning can produce serious illness and death especially if the central nervous system is affected as happens in botulism and mushroom poisoning. Any one believed to be ill from food poisoning (usually recognized because several people become ill simultaneously), who has symptoms other than mild nausea, vomiting, abdominal cramps, and diarrhea, should seek medical attention promptly as should those who possibly have been exposed to botulism or poisonous plants. *See also* BOTULISM.

Fracture • A crack or complete break in a bone. A closed or simple fracture is one in which the skin remains intact. An open or compound fracture is one in which the skin is ruptured because the broken bone has penetrated it or because whatever caused the fracture also opened the skin. A complex or comminuted fracture is one in which the bone has been broken into many pieces or part of it has been shattered. Fractures often involve damage to surrounding ligaments and blood vessels. Immobilization, preferably by splinting, is the safest way to manage a fracture until professional treatment is available. In many cases a simple fracture may be indistinguishable from a sprain except by X-ray.

Frigidity • The term, now considered scientifically inaccurate and unacceptable, previously used to describe a form of female sexual dysfunction characterized by the absence or inhibition of erotic pleasure and sexual responsiveness. *See* "Sexual Health."

Frostbite • Injury to a part of the body resulting from exposure to subfreezing temperature or wind-chill factor. Because the affected tissue can be irreversibly destroyed, frostbite is an emergency situation. The first signs are a tingling sensation and then numbness and a bluish-red appearance of the skin. If countermeasures are not taken at this stage, the affected areas begin to burn and itch as in chilblains, there is a total loss of sensation, and the skin turns dead white. Because the frostbitten area is extremely vulnerable to further injury, any clothing that may be an additional constraint to circulation, such as boots, socks, or tight gloves, should be removed as gently as possible. If circumstances permit, the injured parts of the body should be immersed quickly in warm—not hot—water. If this is not practical, the patient should be wrapped in blankets. If the feet are involved, walking should be forbidden. If an arm or a leg is involved, the victim should be encouraged to elevate it. Absolutely no attempt should be made to massage the affected parts, rub them with snow, or apply heat. Keep the victim comfortable by offering hot beverages, a sedative, and a painkiller. Smoking is forbidden because the nicotine will constrict the already impaired circulation. A dry sterile dressing should be used to prevent infection. If there is no visible return of circulation after these measures have been taken and the person's condition appears to be deteriorating, medical care should be obtained without further delay.

Fungal Infections • Diseases caused by fungi and their spores that invade the skin, finger and toenails, mucous membranes, and lungs and may even attack the bones and the brain. These diseases are known as mycoses. Fungi are parasites that may feed on dead organic matter or on live organisms. Fungi and their airborne spores or seeds are everywhere. Of the countless varieties, some cause mold and mildew, some are indispensable in the formation of alcohol and yeast, and a small number cause infection.

The more common fungal disorders are those confined to the skin, such as ringworm that results in red, scaly patches that itch and may form into blisters. Ringworm is highly contagious and can be passed on by household pets as well as by contaminated towels and bed linens. To prevent its spread from person to person and from one part of the body to another, ringworm should be treated promptly with suitable antifungicides. Athlete's foot (tinea pedis) is a form of ringworm that can be difficult to cure once it takes hold. The fungus usually lodges between the toes, multiplying rapidly in the warm, damp, dark environment and eventually causing the skin to crack and blister. To control a chronic case, feet should be kept meticulously clean and as dry as possible, a fungicidal powder should be sprinkled in the shoes, and a medicated ointment should be spread between the toes. If athlete's foot persists despite these measures, professional attention should be sought. The same fungus sometimes affects the nails (onychomycosis) and usually requires professional care.

Thrush is an oral fungus infection that attacks the mucous membranes of the mouth and tongue, and where resistance to infection is low, especially where the diet is deficient in vitamin B, it may spread into the pharynx. It is characterized by the formation of white patches that feel highly sensitive. Similar patches may also appear in the vagina and rectum (moniliasis or candidiasis). Where only the mouth is involved, mouthwashes containing gentian violet may be recommended. In cases of moniliasis, medicated suppositories are usually prescribed.

It is thought that a regimen of certain antibiotics increases vulnerability to various fungus infections, because the medicines kill off not only the bacteria causing a particular disease but also the benign ones whose presence guards against the growth of fungi. In recent years the medical profession and public health authorities have been concerned with a group of fungus infections that attack the lungs and can eventually invade other organs. Of these, histoplasmosis and "cocci" or coccidioidomycosis (also known as desert fever) are the result of breathing in certain spores that float freely in clouds of dust. The spores are harmless if swallowed, but those that find their way into the air sacs of the lungs begin to grow and multiply, spreading inflammation through the respiratory system and eventually into other parts of the body. Typical symptoms include a chronic cough, fever, and other manifestations that may be confused with pneumonia or tuberculosis. When tests produce the correct diagnosis, hospitalization may be required for the administration of a specific medication called Amphotericin-B.

G Spot • A small area of sensitive tissue that some women identify on the anterior wall of the vagina near the urethra. It is sometimes called the female homologue of the male prostate.

Gallbladder • A membranous sac, approximately 3 inches long, situated below the liver. The gallbladder drains bile from the liver, stores and concentrates it, and eventually sends it on to the duodenum. The alkalinity of the bile is essential for neutralizing the acidity of the digested material leaving the stomach. Its component juices transform fatty compounds into simpler nutrients that can be absorbed by the intestines. A system of ducts controlled by sphincters releases bile when it is needed and forces the excess back into the gallbladder for storage.

GALLBLADDER

POSSIBLE SITES OF OBSTRUCTION BY GALLSTONES

When the gallbladder has been surgically removed because of infection or blockage, bile goes directly from the liver to the intestine without any ill effects on digestion.

In some cases the concentrated bile in the gallbladder forms into gallstones. Inflammation of the gallbladder, technically called cholecystitis, may be acute or chronic. In its acute form it usually follows bacterial infection or a sudden blockage of one of the ducts by a tumor or a large stone. Symptoms of an attack are nausea, vomiting, sweating, and sharp pain in the upper right part of the abdomen under the ribs, possibly extending to the shoulder. Jaundice may also be present. If the acute phase of the attack does not subside, emergency surgery may be necessary to prevent the danger of a rupture. The gallbladder should not be removed unless X-rays indicate that the condition cannot be cured by routine medical treatment. Chronic gallbladder disease may cause gassiness and discomfort following a meal containing fatty foods. Abdominal pain may be brief but recurrent. In many cases the condition can be alleviated by a low-fat diet. When a low-grade infection of the bile ducts is the source of the discomfort, antibiotics may be prescribed. *See* GALLSTONES.

Gallstones • Solid masses that form within the gallbladder or bile ducts. The stone-forming tendency of bile results in three different types of stones: those composed of a combination of calcium, bile pigments, and cholesterol; those that are pure cholesterol; and those rare formations that are made of bile pigments only. Gallstones of the first two types are especially prevalent following pregnancy and also appear to be connected with estrogen replacement. Overweight is another possible factor.

Cholesterol gallstones can be dissolved medically with a chemical compound similar in composition to natural human bile acid, thus eliminating the necessity for surgery to remove them if they cause an acute gallbladder attack. Because simple X-ray procedures are not definitive in locating the presence of gallstones, other tests are administered before surgery is scheduled. Among these are contrast dye X-ray for intravenous cholangiography and an oral gallbladder test that takes less than an hour on an outpatient basis.

Gamma Globulin • The portion of the blood richest in antibodies. It is produced mainly by the lymphocytes in the lymphoid tissues and is one of the body's strongest defenses against infectious disease. Gamma globulin in one of two forms may be injected to confer passive (temporary) immunity to certain diseases such as hepatitis. Immune serum globulin is derived from blood taken from donors who have an immunity to a specific disease either naturally or subsequent to active immunization. A specific preparation, such as measles immune globulin, is derived from donors who are convalescing from the disease or who have been recently immunized against it. Gamma globulin shots are also recommended for visitors to countries where attention to public sanitation is dangerously inadequate.

Gangrene • A condition in which tissue dies primarily due to loss of blood supply. Gangrene usually involves the extremities but may occur in any part of the body where circulation has been cut off or in which massive infection has caused the affected tissue to putrefy. Among the circumstances leading to most gangrene are severe burns, frostbite, accidents involving contact with corrosive chemicals, untreated ulcerated bedsores, a carelessly applied and improperly attended tourniquet, or any other condition that cuts off circulation. The gangrenous condition that occurs due to atherosclerosis, whether or not diabetes is present, most commonly affects the extremities. In such cases a toe or finger will shrink and turn black, and there will be a distinct line of demarcation between the healthy and gangrenous tissues.

In one form of the circulatory disturbance known as Raynaud's phenomenon, spasms in the arteries of the fingers and toes cut off blood supply and leave the extremities vulnerable to tissue damage. This damage begins as ulcers but, if untreated, can progress to gangrene.

It is now possible to prevent the spread of gangrene with antibiotics and surgery. Should circumstances indicate the possibility of tissue death, particularly if numbness and discoloration of the extremities are apparent in a diabetic, emergency treatment is essential.

Gastrointestinal Disorders • Any number of conditions affecting the normal functions of digestion and elimination of food as it passes through the alimentary canal. Disorders may result from an infection caused by bacteria, viruses, or parasites; an obstruction due to a tumor; ulcers; hernias; allergies; food-borne illnesses; metabolic defects; or stress. Symptoms may include mild to severe abdominal pain, constipation, diarrhea, rectal bleeding, jaundice, weight loss, nausea, vomiting, loss of appetite. Diagnosis of many disorders of the esophagus, stomach, small intestines, lower bowel, and rectum is based on X-rays. The diagnosis of other gastrointestinal disorders may require laboratory tests of blood and stools. Depending on the findings, treatment may involve a specific medication, a special diet, or surgery.

Generic Drugs • See "Brand and Generic Names of Commonly Prescribed Drugs."

Gene Splicing • See GENETIC ENGINEERING.

Genetic Counseling • The National Institute of General Medical Sciences estimates that some 12 million Americans bear the risk of transmitting hereditary disorders. For this group of people genetic counseling has become a vital medical service. There are more than 100 medical genetics counseling services nationwide. The greater majority are attached to university hospitals that can administer the tests for genetic abnormalities. In addition to Down syndrome detectable by amniocentesis, there are upward of 2,000 diseases known to be caused by one or another single faulty gene. For those parents-to-be who are alert to a family history of such disorders as Tay-Sachs disease, muscular dystrophy, or cystic fibrosis (among others), genetic counseling provides information about the factors associated with the particular disease, including diagnosis, the usual course of the disorder, and the risk of its occurrence or recurrence. Counseling also explores alternatives that take these factors into account and at the same time conform with the individuals' ethical principles and religious convictions. See AMNIOCENTESIS, HEREDITY, "Pregnancy and Childbirth," and "Directory of Health Information."

Genetic Diseases • See HEREDITY.

Genetic Engineering (Gene Splicing) • Since the genetic code was discovered in 1953 and completely deciphered in 1966, genetic engineering has become a major area of biotechnical advance. By splicing genes, the genetic structure of micro-organisms, yeasts, foods, and potentially any biologic entity including humans, can be altered to produce changes in structure and function. By now, recombinant DNA methods applied to bacteria and yeasts have yielded insulin and other hormones, human serum albumin, various toxins, vaccines, and interferon. These techniques have tremendous implications for treating disease, repairing genetic defects, and improving nutrition. However, there are definite possibilities of abuses. Several countries have moved in the direction of banning research on modifying human genes in ways that could be transmitted from generation to generation. In the United States, while universities and research organizations that receive money from federal sources are regulated by guidelines established by the Recombinant DNA Committee of the National Institutes of Health, such regulatory constraints on private industry are difficult to achieve. Biotechnical manufacturers have been competing in the race that takes advantage of advances in genetic engineering to produce vaccines and other highly profitable products, and, as with many previous advances in science and technology, regulatory laws will eventually evolve through courtroom battles.

Genital Herpes • *See* HERPES and "Sexually Transmissible Diseases."

Geriatrics • The branch of medical science that deals with the diseases and the health maintenance of the aged. It is related to gerontology, which studies not just medical problems but all aspects of aging—biological processes, environmental factors, and social problems. *See* "Aging Healthfully—Your Body" and "Aging Healthfully—Your Mind and Spirit."

German Measles • *See* RUBELLA.

Giardiasis • A disease of the upper small intestine caused by the giardia protozoan. The infestation is spread by contaminated food or water or in oral/anal sexual activity. Symptoms include abdominal cramps and diarrhea. Diagnosis is based on laboratory examination of a stool sample. Flagyl is the treatment of choice.

Gingivitis • Inflammation of the gums caused by an enzyme released by the bacteria that flourish in the plaque that accumulates on improperly cleaned teeth. This same circumstance is also the cause of cavity formation. Inflammation usually starts in the gingival crevice, a groove between the gum and the tooth.

Gingivitis is most prevalent in women who smoke, whose diet is deficient in a particular nutrient, and who have been negligent in practicing proper oral hygiene methods. When gingivitis is associated with pregnancy, it is usually temporary and associated with hormonal changes.

Because untreated gingivitis results in the destruction of bone tissue and the loosening or loss of teeth, gum inflammation should be treated promptly by a periodontist. *See* PLAQUE, PERIODONTAL DISEASE.

Gland • Any organ that produces and secretes a specific chemical substance. There are two categories of glands: the ductless or endocrine glands, whose secretions are delivered directly into the bloodstream, and the exocrine glands, whose ducts transport their secretions to a precise location. The major endocrine glands are discussed and illustrated in the "The Healthy Woman."

The most important exocrines are: the salivary glands, which produce the saliva that moisturizes the food in the mouth at the beginning of the digestive process; the sebaceous glands, found under the skin, which produce an oil essential for its health; the sweat glands, which maintain the body's temperature and are part of the excretory system. The pancreas, liver, stomach, and small intestines secrete vital digestive juices. The lachrymal or tear glands are closely involved with emotional response and are essential for the cleansing and lubrication of the eyes. The female exocrine glands include the vestibular glands (Bartholin's glands) located on either side of the vaginal opening and Skene's glands, located on either side of the urethral opening. The mammary glands in the breasts supply milk for offspring. The prostate gland in men produces a secretion related to the reproductive process.

The structures sometimes referred to as lymph glands are not glands and are properly called lymph nodes. *See* LYMPH NODES.

Glaucoma • An eye disease that leads to progressive impairment of vision due to increased fluid pressure within the eyeball to the point where it damages the optic nerve. Glaucoma is the leading cause of loss of vision in the United States. It is the cause of blindness in 60,000 people; two million are afflicted with glaucoma to some extent, and of these, about one quarter are unaware of its insidious progression. In its most common form, there are no signals until some irreversible loss of vision has occurred.

The rare form of the disorder is acute or closed angle glaucoma. Onset is sudden, accompanied by severe pain, redness, and blurring. The condition may be worsened by tricyclic antidepressant drugs. Closed angle glaucoma is a serious emergency requiring prompt treatment by an ophthalmologist.

GLAUCOMA

Cornea
Canal of Schlemm
FLUID FLOW IN NORMAL EYE
Ciliary body
Lens

Blocked canal of Schlemm
Increased pressure from fluid build-up

Onset of open angle or chronic glaucoma is verifiable only by means of a test that can diagnose the disease in its earliest stages. The pressure within the eye is measured by a noncontact device called a tonometer, and if any aberration is detected, further tests may be administered. These tests, which can be done by an optometrist as well as by a physician, should be scheduled once a year after age 40, and beginning at an earlier age if there is a family history of the disorder. Symptoms, which persist even after many changes in eyeglass prescriptions, are blurring of vision, difficulty in focusing, loss of peripheral sight, and slow adaptation to darkness. This more common form of the disease can also be precipitated or aggravated by medications, especially by antihypertensive drugs and cortisone.

While the glaucoma test can be administered by an optometrist, only an ophthalmologist can treat the symptoms. In most cases, irreversible damage to vision can be halted by the daily use of prescription eyedrops. The drug of choice is Timoptic (timolol maleate), a beta blocker believed to decrease eye fluid production. Because the eyedrops are absorbed into the circulatory system, this drug may produce negative side effects in patients with certain types of coronary or pulmonary disease. When prescribing Timoptic, the doctor should take this eventuality into account. For the 10 percent of glaucoma cases unresponsive to treatment with eyedrops, drainage can be accomplished by surgery. See "Directory of Health Information."

Glomerulonephritis • A kidney disease that affects the coiled clusters of capillary vessels, the glomeruli, through which the fluid content of the blood is partially filtered before it turns into urine. Each kidney consists of approximately a million of these filters. The capillaries may become inflamed following several varieties of bacterial infection, especially following a strep infection in the throat or elsewhere. Because acute nephritis may develop if the initial infection is not successfully treated with antibiotics, it is extremely important to consult a doctor immediately about any painful sore throat accompanied by a high fever. Postinfectious glomerulonephritis may also follow such viral infections as measles, mumps, chicken pox, hepatitis, and AIDS as well as syphilis and malaria. When glomerulonephritis occurs, the body retains fluid due to a collapse in the kidney's filtering capacity. Typical symptoms of the condition are puffy eyelids, swollen ankles, headaches, and decrease in urinary output.

Treatment for the underlying infection is combined with measures that prevent additional complications including limited salt and fluid intake followed by diuretics. If kidney failure is imminent, dialysis may be necessary for a short period. Practically all cases of postinfectious glomerulonephritis subside without further treatment when the underlying cause has been eliminated.

Glucose • A sugar that occurs naturally in honey and in most fruit and the one into which starches and polysaccharide (complex) sugars are converted by the digestive process. Glucose is a major source of body fuel. Because it can be absorbed from the stomach, it is one of the quickest sources of energy. Glucose, or its variant dextrose, is also the nutrient usually administered intravenously when a patient cannot eat normally.

Glucose is normally not present in the urine; its presence there may indicate diabetes. The glucose tolerance test (GTT) measures the rate at which the body removes glucose from the blood. After the patient drinks a sugar solution or glucose is given intravenously, a series of blood and urine sugar tests are made during the next three to four hours. The GTT is a more refined screening technique than a single test for glucose in urine or blood and is used to identify disease when these tests provide ambiguous or inconclusive results. See HYPOGLYCEMIA.

Glycogen • A starchlike substance derived largely from glucose and stored in various organs of the body. It is converted back to glucose by various enzymes under hormonal influence, including insulin, when needed for body fuel.

Goiter • An enlargement of the thyroid gland. This endocrine gland, located at the base of the neck, extracts the iodine absorbed by the blood from food and drinking water and uses it for the production of the hormone thyroxin. Thyroxin is stored in the glandular follicles and released into the bloodstream as needed for the regulation of the metabolic rate. The body's iodine requirements are no more than a few millionths of an ounce, and because iodine is generally present in the soil, in most areas the requisite amounts occur naturally in food and water. Certain inland regions of the United States, deficient in iodine were known as the goiter belt before the deficiency was compensated for by the use of iodized salt. The enlargement occurs because the thyroid's cells increase in number in order to satisfy the body's demand for thyroxin. Eventually the gland may develop nodules or lumps. The danger of goiter is that it may press on the surrounding organs, leading to difficulty in swallowing or breathing.

When properly treated with iodine or with thyroxin itself, the goiter usually subsides. Goiter is much more common among women than men because their bodies require considerably more thyroxin during puberty, the menstrual cycle, and pregnancy. A pregnant woman must be sure that her diet contains the iodine essential for the baby's healthy prenatal development.

Gold Treatments • Injectable gold in the form of water soluble salts or a gold compound taken orally as treatment for rheumatoid arthritis. While gold therapy (chrysotherapy) is not a cure, it is proving effective in halting inflammation, reducing pain, and in some cases it may even prevent further bone destruction in the joints. The oral gold preparation Ridaura (auranofin) appears to have fewer unpleasant side effects than gold injections. In either form, the therapy must be administered over an extended period before benefits become apparent. Close monitoring is essential to guard against liver and kidney damage. Gold treatments are an option for those rheumatoid arthritis patients who do not respond favorably to aspirin or the newer nonsteroidal anti-inflammatory drugs. See ARTHRITIS.

Gonads • The reproductive glands that in the female produce the ovum and in the male, the sperm cells. See OVARY and TESTICLE.

Gonorrhea • A widespread disease of the genitourinary system transmitted mainly through sexual intercourse. Two and a half million cases are reported annually, and of these, most are under the age of 30. When the disease is transmitted through anal or oral sex, it infects the mouth, throat, and rectum. A significant number of women infected with gonorrhea eventually suffer from pelvic inflammatory disease, a leading cause of infertility. *See* "Sexually Transmissible Diseases."

GONORRHEA

Gonorrhea has widespread effects one of which may result in infection and closing of fallopian tube

Gout • A form of arthritis resulting from a change in uric acid metabolism. This metabolic aberration may be inherited or may arise from the use of diuretics. It causes the uric acid naturally produced by the body to accumulate in the joints in the form of crystals, leading to acute inflammation and swelling. Joints affected by gout include those in the big toe and fingers and the ankle, elbow, and wrist. Pain in the big toe is most common because of the pressure of body weight on the foot. Two types of drugs are available that control rather than cure the condition: those that stimulate the elimination of uric acid and those that reduce its production. While the victims of gout are usually men, the disease sometimes attacks women, typically after the menopause. Where symptoms are ambiguous, a simple blood test can confirm the diagnosis.

Granuloma Inguinale • A sexually transmissible disease most commonly found in southern or tropical regions and caused by a specific organism, the bacillus *Donovania granulomatis*. *See* "Sexually Transmissible Diseases."

Guillain-Barré Syndrome • A neurological illness that attacks the peripheral nerves, beginning with a loss of sensation in the extremities and, in severe cases, extending to the face, neck, and torso, thereby endangering the ability to swallow and to breathe. The syndrome may follow a virus infection of the throat or the flu, and, in rare cases, is triggered by a flu vaccination. Accurate diagnosis is based on analysis of cerebrospinal fluid (spinal tap) for differentiation from polio or from the consequences of ingesting poisonous substances that might produce similar symptoms. Severe cases require hospitalization and monitoring for failure of vital functions. In most instances, recovery is complete with few residual effects. In a small number of cases, rehabilitation therapy is necessary for restoration of muscle function.

Gums • The fleshy fibrous tissue that covers the areas of the upper and lower jaw in which teeth are anchored. The mucous membrane that covers the gums forms a network of vessels that carry blood and lymph from the jaws to the face. Healthy gums are pink, firm, somewhat stippled, and form a collar around the neck of each tooth.

Practically all gum inflammation, or gingivitis, starts between the gum and the tooth in a shallow groove called the gingival crevice. It must be treated promptly by a dentist. A gum disease, commonly known as trench mouth and technically called Vincent's angina, is an infection of the mucous membrane. If permitted to spread, it may reach the lips and tongue. It is caused by a particular strain of bacteria, *Borrelia vincentii,* normally present in the mouth. When general health is good the bacteria are usually inactive, but when resistance is low and dental hygiene poor, these organisms, combined with other bacteria, often cause the disease. Its symptoms are inflamed gums, foul breath, and painful ulcers that not only bleed easily but may interfere with swallowing. It may be accompanied by swollen glands, sore throat, and fever. The disease usually clears up when treated with an antibiotic and can best be prevented from recurring by maintaining good health and proper oral hygiene.

The gums can be kept in good condition by brushing the teeth slowly from the gumline upward for the bottom teeth and from the gumline downward for the top teeth. Brushing the teeth horizontally is not correct because it does not stimulate the gums. Food particles lodged between the teeth and at the gumline should be dislodged by unwaxed floss, and tartar deposits should be scraped off by a dentist twice a year. Because improperly fitted dentures may affect gums adversely, dentures should be checked for necessary adjustments from time to time. *See* GINGIVITIS and PERIODONTAL DISEASE.

Hair • A specialized body growth consisting of dead skin cells that are filled with a tough protein material called keratin, which is also the main constituent of the nails. Aside from the palms of the hand and the soles of the feet, hair covers almost the entire body surface to help to retain heat. Conservation of heat is accomplished by the reflex response whereby individual hairs stand erect and diminish the loss of body warmth ("gooseflesh").

Color, texture, and distribution of hair are inherited. Color depends on the amount of the pigment melanin contained in the hair core: the less melanin, the lighter the color. Curly hair is oval in cross-section; straight hair is cylindrical. The average woman's head may contain as many as 125,000 hairs. Each hair root is encased and nourished by a follicle buried under the skin. The growing shaft is lubricated by the oily secretions from a sebaceous gland opening into each follicle. Hair grows at an average rate of approximately half an inch a month.

Hair gradually turns gray as the melanin pigment is depleted. The age at which this occurs is a factor of inheritance. The growth and nourishment of hair are controlled by hormone secretions and the general state of one's health. The application of creams, lotions, vitamins or minerals does not affect the growth and thickness of hair in a healthy individual.

Products used on the hair should be selected carefully to avoid any which irritate the skin, contain chemicals that might damage hair or skin, or might clog the pores of the scalp. Hair sprays should not be inhaled. Chemical hair dyes have been subjected to increasingly close scrutiny because of their potentially carcinogenic contents. Warnings in beauty shops and on home products should be evaluated carefully before deciding whether to dye one's hair.

The notion that hair can be analyzed to provide information about nutritional imbalances has yet to receive confirmation from the scientific community.

Hair Loss • *See* BALDNESS.

Hair Removal • Temporary or permanent elimination of unwanted hair, technically called depilation. The simplest and least expensive method for removal of unwanted hair from the legs and underarms is shaving after applying cream or a lather of soap. This method does not cause the hair to grow back in increasing amounts, as the number of hair follicles one is born with remains constant unless the hairs are removed by electrolysis. Sparse face hair or unwanted hair between the breasts can be removed with tweezers. While somewhat painful, waxing has become increasingly popular as a hair removal method and with proper training can be done at home. Hair may also be removed by a depilatory containing chemicals that dissolve the hair at the surface of the skin. A patch test should precede the use of a depilatory to rule out the possibility of an allergic response to the product. Depilatories should be used with caution on the face and never applied immediately after a bath or shower while skin pores are still open. For the same reason they should be removed with cool rather than warm water.

Permanent hair removal is achieved when each hair bulb is destroyed electrically. The procedure is expensive and time-consuming and must be performed by a trained operator.

Hallucination • The perception of a sound, sight, smell, or other sensory experience without the presence of an external physical stimulus. Hallucinations are produced by certain drugs. Hallucinatory episodes may be associated with such organic conditions as hardening of the arteries of the brain (cerebral arteriosclerosis) or brain tumor and with exhaustion, sleep deprivation, or prolonged solitary confinement or isolation from normal stimuli. Such experiences are also characteristic of delirium tremens, some forms of mental illness, and psychotic interludes following sudden withdrawal from barbiturates.

Hallucinogens • A category of consciousness-altering substances chemically related to each other; more popularly known as psychedelic drugs. *See* "Substance Abuse."

Hangover • Symptoms of headache, queasiness, thirst, or nausea occurring the morning after drinking alcohol; also feelings of disorientation and befuddlement following the use of sleeping pills containing barbiturates. The amount of alcohol that will create a hangover varies from person to person and from time to time for the same person. It may result after having had very little to drink if one was tense, angry, tired, or hungry.

The physiological mechanisms that

cause the symptoms originate in the disruptive effects of alcohol on body chemistry. Its diuretic properties result in thirst, irritation of the lining of the gastrointestinal tract causes nausea, and dilation of blood vessels leads to throbbing headache. If a remedy is necessary, aspirin will help a headache and an alkalizer may soothe the queasiness.

Hay Fever • *See* ALLERGIES.

Headache • Any pain or discomfort in the head; one of the most common complaints and a symptom for which medical science has itemized upwards of 200 possible causes. While it may be difficult to pinpoint a cause in a particular case, it should be comforting to know that very few headaches are serious.

Some familiarity with the structures of the head is helpful in understanding why headaches occur. The bony structure of the skull contains the orbits of the eyes, the nasal cavities, the eight nasal accessory cavities, known as sinuses, and the teeth. Two of the sinuses are in the cheekbone (the antra), two above the eyebrows (the frontal sinuses), and four more at the base of the skull. Within the skull and protected by its rigid bony surface is the brain, which itself has no pain receptors but which is surrounded by extremely sensitive tissues. It is covered by membranes known as meninges and by the cerebrospinal fluid that acts as a cushion between the brain and the skull and also circulates between the brain and its membranous layers as well as around and within the spinal cord. A network of blood vessels interlace the coverings of the brain to supply oxygen and other essential nutrients to the brain and to transport the depleted blood back to the heart. It is not difficult to imagine how many chemical, physical, psychological, neurological, bacteriological, viral, and other variables can lead to changes, usually temporary, in the structures just described, most of which are sensitive to pain. For example, swelling of the blood vessels, inflammation of the nerve endings, or muscular contractions at the base of the skull, will cause the head to pound, throb, or ache.

Simple headaches occur at varying intervals and may be annoying or mildly disabling. Most simple recurring headaches are generally known as tension headaches. The immediate cause of the pain is the stiffening of the muscles at the base of the skull, which sets up a cycle of contraction in response to pain and causes further pain because of the contractions. The usual reason for the stiffening of the muscles is emotional stress. In some cases, a muscle contraction headache may originate in a simple physical circumstance: a draft from a fan or air-conditioner, straining to see or hear, or a response to pain elsewhere in the body. Such headaches may be mild or severe. If they occur only rarely and respond favorably to over-the-counter analgesics and/or massage of the tightened muscles, they can be viewed as one of life's minor nuisances.

When headaches recur with debilitating frequency, further exploration into their cause is essential. They may be caused by injuries to the head or neck; reactions to certain pharmacologic agents including alcohol, incorrect refraction of vision, or a variety of diseases such as high blood pressure, diabetes mellitus, and hyper- or hypothyroidism. In trying to identify the cause of these headaches, women should not overlook the possibility that they might be triggered by a response to the chemicals in hairsprays, perfumes, room deodorizers, cleaning fluids, insecticides, and the like.

On-the-job headaches may occur not only because of tension but from exposure to noise, pollutants, and because of eyestrain resulting from long hours in front of a video display terminal. Headaches may also be part of premenstrual syndrome. In the elderly, when a headache is accompanied by dizziness, it may be a sign of overmedication. And medication itself may cause a headache as a side effect or because it triggers an allergic response. It is useful to discard certain myths. Constipation does not cause headaches; both conditions are caused by tension, anxiety, or suppressed feelings. Worrying about high blood pressure is a more common cause of headaches than high blood pressure itself. Menopausal headaches are likelier to result from anxieties about aging than from a drop in estrogen levels.

Treatment must be directed primarily toward the underlying cause, but, as an interim measure, some relief may be achieved by the injection of drugs that act as muscle-relaxants or local anesthetics. One of the most recent developments in the treatment of certain kinds of chronic headaches is biofeedback. Many hospitals now have established centers that use biofeedback techniques based on the patients' awareness of tension and relaxation mechanisms and how to control them.

Nonsimple recurring headaches differ from simple ones in several ways. They cause more severe symptoms and they generally are caused by dilation of the blood vessels in the brain. The most widely known of these vascular headaches are the classic migraine headache and the common migraine headache. The classic migraine tends to be familial, is pulsating in nature, affects only one side of the head at a time, may be preceded more or less immediately by loss of vision, flashing lights, or varying neurological symptoms, and is often accompanied by nausea and vomiting. The pain is most severe during the first hour and then subsides. Frequency tends to increase during stress and to decrease with age. Treatment varies and is varyingly successful. The common migraine headache is more common. Symptoms are less specific than those of classic migraine. Mood changes usually precede it and may last several hours or days before the headache starts. The headache, also on one side of the head, may last several days. Again treatment varies and is varyingly successful. A third type of vascular headache is called the cluster headache. It is a series of closely spaced headaches, each of 20 to 90 minutes duration, continuing for several days, and then often followed by months or years of no such attacks. It may be triggered by certain foods and chemicals, such as caffeine in coffee, tea, and cola drinks; nicotine in cigarettes; monosodium glutamate in various cooked and processed foods; nitrites added to smoked meats; congeners in certain alcoholic beverages; and estrogen in certain contraceptive pills. Treatment for vascular headaches includes drugs such as ergotamine, various analgesics including narcotics, and biofeedback techniques.

The acute nonrecurring headache usually has a sudden onset. It may be caused by a specific disease or condition that may or may not be serious or it may represent a change in the individual's pattern of simple recurring headaches. It may accompany a generalized infection, such as influenza, toxic shock syndrome, infectious mononucleosis, gastritis, sinusitis, otitis media (middle ear), or abscessed tooth, or it may be part of an infection of the central nervous system such as meningitis, encephalitis, poliomyelitis, or brain abscess. It may also be caused by a brain tumor, aneurysm, or hemorrhage. The hemorrhage may be caused by an injury (contusion, concussion, or skull fracture) or be unrelated to injury. One particular type of headache is associated with a medical procedure called a lumbar puncture or spinal tap. It can be extremely severe, is usually worse when standing or sitting up, and subsides in several days. Unless the headache subsides in a few hours a medical diagnosis should be sought so that the proper therapy can be initiated.

Severe recurrent headaches should never be dismissed as psychogenic in origin until *all* diagnostic tests, including a CAT scan, have ruled out the possibility of a brain tumor.

Health Maintenance Organization • *See* "You, Your Doctors, and the Health Care System."

Hearing Aids • Electronic instruments that amplify sounds. The instrument may be built into the temple piece of eyeglasses, fit inside the ear, or have a microphone behind the ear. In a once-popular model still preferred by many people because it is easy to shut off, the receiver is placed in the ear and the amplifier on the chest on top of the clothing. The most recent development is known as a cochlear implant in which the electrodes are inserted within the cochlea, the part of the inner ear connected with the auditory nerve.

A hearing aid must be fitted and regularly adjusted by a trained specialist (audiologist) after an ear specialist (otologist) has determined that some of the hearing loss can be restored in this way. Under no circumstances should a hearing aid be bought directly from a retail dealer. Community health centers or a doctor can supply the address of a nonprofit hearing aid clinic where the degree and type of deafness is accurately determined, recommendations are made for the type of instrument, if any, best suited to individual needs, and instruction is given in the most effective way to use the aid, including courses in lipreading if that skill might contribute to optimum results. All hearing aids take getting used to, and it may be necessary to try several different types and go back and forth for many readjustments before the instrument performs satisfactorily. Patience is required on the part of the wearer and the audiologist, and the wearer should not be discouraged too early in the adjustment process.

Hearing Loss • Interruption at any point along the path traveled by sound vibrations before the information can reach the brain for processing. Hearing loss may be partial or total, temporary or permanent, congenital or acquired. The two major causes are disorders of conduction, which generally result in a loss of low-pitched sounds, and nerve defects, which generally result in a loss of high-pitched sounds. When both conditions are present, the disability is called mixed deafness. Conduction deafness may be a consequence of any of the following: obstruction by wax accumulation, inflammation of the middle ear, fluid accumulation, damaged eardrum, infection of the eustachian tube, and otosclerosis. Otosclerosis, most common among the elderly, is a progressive disease that freezes one of the three bones of hearing (the stapes) into immobility by imbedding it in a bony growth, thus preventing the soundwaves from being transmitted to the inner ear.

Nerve deafness may be caused by severe head injury, chronic infection that disables the auditory nerve, tumor, drugs taken for some other condition, or prolonged exposure to damaging noise levels such as occurs when working close to noisy machinery, living near an airport, or listening constantly to very loud music either at rock concerts or through earphones with the volume turned up. Gradual nerve deafness may also be a factor of increasing age during which the neuroreceptor cells in the inner ear slowly deteriorate.

Sudden hearing loss, more likely to occur in one ear rather than in both simultaneously, may be caused by a virus infection or by the presence of a small blood clot that impedes the transmission of sensory messages along the blood vessels leading to the auditory nerve. In either case, treatment with drugs is usually effective in restoring normal hearing.

Ringing in the ears (tinnitus) that interferes with hearing may be caused by arteriosclerosis, hypertension, or medicines containing quinine. It may also be a symptom of Menière's disease.

Any indications of the onset of hearing loss should be investigated by an ear specialist. Conductive hearing loss is more susceptible to correction than nerve impairment and may be treated medically and surgically. New techniques of microsurgery have enabled specialists to restore hearing by a procedure called fenestration, which opens up a new path at the inner end of the middle ear along which sound waves can travel when the normal one is obstructed. Another ingenious operation is the stapedectomy in which the otosclerotic growth and the immobilized stapes are removed and replaced by plastic and wire that conduct the sound vibrations. *See* EAR DISORDERS, and "Directory of Health Information."

Heart Attack • A condition ranging from mild to severe in which one or more of the arteries that supply blood to the heart are blocked or occluded by a clot; also called myocardial infarction, coronary occlusion, or coronary thrombosis. The chief cause of a heart attack is the cardiovascular condition known as atherosclerosis. The blockage causes varying degrees of damage to that part of the heart that ordinarily gets its blood supply from the blocked vessel. The deprivation of blood supply results in a sudden and severe pain in the center of the chest. In some cases the chest pain radiates into the shoulders, back, and arms and is accompanied by pallor, nausea, and sweating, followed by shortness of breath. When these symptoms occur, particularly in the case of an angina patient, and do not disappear with the administration of nitroglycerin or other prescribed medication, an ambulance should be summoned immediately because the first hour after the attack is the period of greatest danger. Most doctors feel that if a heart attack victim reaches a hospital quickly, the therapeutic measures taken in the intensive coronary care unit can be effective. These measures combine the use of electronic monitoring and nuclear scanning with chemotherapy to reduce pain, decrease clotting, and strengthen the heart muscle. Whether or not coronary bypass surgery should be undertaken, or the damaged coronary vessel be "cleaned out" by a balloon-catheter device, an enzyme, or a laser beam is decided later on the basis of the patient's age, general health, and other individual factors.

HEART ATTACK

Dead tissue Obstructed coronary artery

A heart attack may occur at any time under a variety of physical or emotional circumstances. While men are more vulnerable to heart attacks than women, the risk increases in women after the menopause. Women over 40 who use the contraceptive pill bear a risk five times greater than women of the same age who do not use the pill. In the 30 to 40 age group the risk is three times greater. However, it should be kept in mind that in these age ranges, the pregnancy death rate is higher than the heart attack death rate. Widespread attention has been given to the warnings issued by the FDA that there is a substantial increase in the risk of heart attack or stroke in women on the pill who smoke. Women who fall into this category are ten times likelier to die because of a cardiovascular disability than women who neither smoke nor use the pill.

On a statistical basis and especially in men, the following conditions in one or another combination are responsible for most coronary attacks: obesity, diabetes, high blood-cholesterol, hypertension, sedentary life style, smoking, and emotional stress in the form of suppressed anger, perfectionism, and anxiety. One of the variables that acts as a powerful counterforce against heart attacks is a blood component known as HDL (high density lipoprotein), which appears to remove cholesterol from the arteries and transmit it to the liver for excretion. This component is likely to be higher in women than in men. It is also higher in nonsmokers than in smokers and in those who weigh too little rather than too much. The role of heredity is uncertain.

Heart Disease, Hypertensive • A heart muscle condition in which chronic hypertension impairs the functioning of the heart by causing it to pump with increased force. The abnormal demands cause the heart muscle to enlarge and increase the likelihood of heart failure.

Heart Failure • Weakening of the heart muscle to the point where it is unable to pump efficiently enough to maintain a normal circulation of the blood; also called cardiac insufficiency or congestive heart failure. This does not mean that the heart has stopped beating. Heart failure causes the blood reentering the heart to slow down and back up into the veins. The consequent congestion in the blood vessels results in the expulsion of some of the fluid through the vessels' walls into the tissues. This seepage produces edema, which in turn leads to swollen ankles, fluid in the lungs, and other signs of excess fluid retention. Many women who have had heart failure can recover and lead relatively normal lives with proper medical supervision, a salt-restricted diet, the use of diuretics supplemented with potassium where necessary, and suitable amounts of digitalis. Where obesity, diabetes, or hypertension exist as an underlying cause, they must be treated simultaneously.

Heart-lung Machine • A device that takes over the job of circulating and oxygenating the blood so that the heart can be bypassed and opened for surgical repair while it is relatively bloodless. The machine also facilitates operations on the lungs and major blood vessels as well as other types of surgery for high-risk patients.

Heartburn • A burning sensation in the lower esophagus. The discomfort, which may be concentrated below the breastbone, has nothing to do with the heart. It is the consequence of regurgitation by the stomach of a part of its contents upward into the esophagus. Because this partially digested matter contains gastric acid, it acts as an irritant. Heartburn may be associated with eating spicy foods, a hangover, a hiatus hernia, or emotional stress. It is not uncommon during the late stages of pregnancy. The catchall explanation of "hyperacidity" is far from correct and has caused many women to consume vast amounts of alkalizers in self-treatment. Where a hernia is the underlying cause and the heartburn is accompanied by spitting up food, surgical correction may be advisable. Most cases of occasional heartburn can be minimized by a sodium bicarbonate tablet and avoided by cutting down on rich, highly seasoned food, alcohol consumption, and tension-producing circumstances during and after mealtime. See ESOPHAGUS, and HERNIA.

Heat Exhaustion • The accumulation of abnormally large amounts of blood close to the skin in an attempt to cool the surface of the body during exposure to high temperature and humidity. This disturbance of normal circulation deprives the vital organs of their necessary blood supply. The smaller vessels constrict, causing the victim to become pale and eventually to perspire heavily. Pulse and breathing may be rapid, and dizziness and vomiting may follow, but the body temperature remains normal. Fainting may be forestalled by lowering the head to increase blood circulation to the brain. First aid consists of placing the victim in the shade if possible and providing sips of salt water in the amount of half a cup every quarter of an hour for an hour (the solution should consist of 1 teaspoon of salt per 1 cup of water or 0.25 grams salt per 8 ounces water). Feet should be elevated, clothing loosened, and as soon as it is practical to do so, cool wet compresses should be applied. If the condition does not improve or if the victim is elderly, has diabetes, or has a heart condition, emergency hospital treatment is necessary.

Heat Stroke • A grave emergency in which there is a blockage of the sweating mechanism that results in extremely high body temperature; also known (mistakenly) as sunstroke and not to be confused with heat exhaustion. The victim of heat stroke is more likely to be male than female, old rather than young, and, not infrequently, an alcoholic. The condition is often precipitated by high humidity and may follow unusual physical exertion. Because fever may go as high as 106°F, irreversible damage may be done to the brain, kidneys, and other organs if treatment is not initiated immediately. The skin will be hot, red, and dry. If the face turns ashen, circulatory collapse is imminent. An ambulance must be summoned and in the meantime efforts must be made to bring the victim's temperature down. All clothes should be removed, and the bare skin sponged with cool water. If possible, the victim should be placed in a tub of cold (not iced) water until there are indications of recovery. No stimulants of any kind should be given. Drying off and further cooling with fans should follow the immersion. Because return to normal is likely to be slow and require close medical supervision, hospitalization after emergency treatment is usually recommended.

Height • The growth hormone of the pituitary gland controls growth during childhood and adolescence. When maximum adult height is reached during adolescence, at about age 16 for girls and 18 for boys, this mechanism stops. Although heredity and hormones determine body build, eventual height may be influenced to a degree by environmental factors such as diet, disease, and activity. With improvements in diet and immunization against many childhood diseases, the average height of Americans increased steadily for about 100 years until around 1914 and since then has remained relatively stable. *See* "Nutrition, Weight, and General Well-Being."

Heimlich Maneuver • A lifesaving technique used in cases of choking to dislodge whatever is blocking the air passages. An obstruction that cannot be loosened and coughed up following a few sharp blows on the back is likely to be ejected by the Heimlich maneuver. This is accomplished by squeezing the victim's body in such a way that the volume of air trapped in the lungs acts as a propulsive force against the obstruction, causing it to pop out of the throat. The rescuer stands behind the victim and places both hands just above the victim's abdomen. A fist made with one hand is grasped by the other hand and quickly and firmly pressed inward and upward against the victim's diaphragm. The pressure on the diaphragm compresses the lungs and expels the air. If you are choking and no one else is present, you may perform the maneuver on yourself by making a quick upward jab at the diaphragm with your fist or pushing forcefully under your rib cage against a table edge or chair back. *See* CHOKING.

HEIMLICH MANEUVER

Hemoglobin • The red pigment in red blood cells; a combination of the iron-containing *heme* and the protein-containing *globin*. This substance carries oxygen to the tissues and removes carbon dioxide from them. The amount of hemoglobin in the blood can be determined by a simple test. A less than normal amount indicates anemia; excess indicates polycythemia.

Hemophilia • An inherited blood disorder characterized by a deficiency of those chemical factors in blood plasma involved in the clotting mechanism; also known as bleeders' disease. It is a sex-linked genetic disorder; the gene is carried by the female, but only male offspring have the disease. The sons of hemophiliacs are normal (assuming marriage is with a noncarrying female). Transmission occurs through one of the mother's two sex chromosomes: 50 percent of her sons will be hemophiliacs and 50 percent of her daughters will be carriers. Thus, while the disease runs in families, the pattern of transmission may cause it to skip several generations. Hemophilia varies in severity. It is not curable, but when bleeding occurs, it can be treated by the infusion of clotting components that are separated out from normal blood plasma. Such transfusions may also be used prior to surgery and may be administered regularly as a preventive measure against hemorrhaging.

Hemophiliacs are at special risk for the transmission of the hepatitis B virus and the AIDS virus in transfusions in spite of efforts to screen all blood donors and the highly refined techniques used in screening the blood itself.

Hemophiliacs must avoid the use of aspirin for any purpose because this drug's anticoagulant properties act adversely on the blood platelets that are essential for the clotting process.

Carrier screening and genetic counseling are available to those women who wish to be checked for the chromosomal defect that causes this hereditary disease. *See* GENETIC COUNSELING.

Hemorrhage • Abnormal bleeding following the rupture of a blood vessel. Hemorrhage may be internal or external; it may come from a vein, artery, or capillary. Subcutaneous hemorrhage follows a bruise or a fracture; blood may appear in the sputum, urine, stools, or vomit. When its source is arterial, it is bright red and spurts forth with the heartbeat; when it is venous, it is wine-colored and oozes out in a steady stream. Any untoward bleeding or signs of blood in the body's discharges should be called to a doctor's attention. Other than the bleeding that results from an accident, hemorrhaging may also follow surgery, even a simple tooth extraction; it may occur during childbirth; it may also be a sign of a disorder that ruptured a blood vessel, such as an ulcer, tumor, kidney stone, or tuberculosis. Any diseases that affect the clotting mechanism, especially leukemia or hemophilia, are characterized by hemorrhage.

Hemorrhoids • Varicose veins in the area of the anus and the rectum; also called piles. External hemorrhoids are located outside the anus and are covered with skin; internal hemorrhoids develop at the junction of the rectum and the anal canal and are covered with mucous membrane. Among the causes are chronic constipation, obesity, pregnancy, and, less commonly, a rectal tumor. Typical symptoms are intermittent bleeding during the passage of stools, itching, and when thrombosis (clotting) occurs, acute pain. The hemorrhoids that develop during pregnancy are caused by the increased pressure on the veins of the lower part of the body and are likely to diminish and disappear soon after delivery if other causative factors, such as overweight and especially constipation, are not also present. Treatment depends on severity: warm sitz baths are soothing, medication can reduce itching, injections of chemicals can control bleeding and shrink the swollen veins, and, if necessary, an operation can remove the diseased veins by cryosurgery. Any frequent discharge of bright red blood from the anus, even when unaccompanied by pain, should be brought to a doctor's attention.

Heparin • An anticoagulant found in the mucosal linings of the liver and other tissues. In synthetic form it is used medically and surgically to prevent clotting and to treat clotting disorders.

Hepatitis • Inflammation of the liver, generally a viral infection. Two related but somewhat different viruses have been identified: A (hepatitis A virus, or HAV)—formerly referred to as infectious hepatitis) and B (hepatitis B virus, or HBV)—formerly referred to as serum hepatitis. A third infectious agent, probably a virus but not yet proven to be, is called non A

HEMORRHOIDS

Internal hemorrhoid
External hemorrhoid
Anal opening

non B. It resembles hepatitis B in most respects.

Victims of hepatitis A excrete the virus in their feces for a week or two before becoming clinically ill and for a few days thereafter. Mild and subclinical infections are common. The disease is transmitted to others from fecal bacteria entering the mouth either directly (via contaminated water) or indirectly by seafoods such as raw clams and oysters. The incubation period is about a month. It is twice as common as HBV, occurring in about 15 per 100,000 people in the United States each year. It is most common among younger persons and is a major problem in day-care centers and institutions for retarded children. Victims are sick (jaundice, fever, anorexia, fatigue) for several weeks or months and generally recover completely, acquiring immunity to HAV in the process.

A small number of victims develop chronic hepatitis. A vaccine to provide active immunization is under investigation. Passive immunization with human immune globulin is recommended for those having intimate (sexual and other) contacts with known cases and for persons who will be working in day-care centers or visiting rural places where sanitation is poor (endemic areas).

Victims of hepatitis B carry the infectious virus (antigen) in blood, saliva, and semen for many weeks before becoming ill as well as during their acute illness. Some victims, as with HAV, never become ill. About 5 percent of the United States population has had HBV and is immune. Some 0.3 percent of persons in the United States are chronic carriers of the disease. Transmission is mainly via blood, either directly into another's blood (transfusions of contaminated whole blood or blood products, needle injections, etc.) or less directly via mucous membranes or breaks in the skin. Transmission also occurs from mother to fetus and via semen. The incubation period is 2–3 months. The disease is most common among health personnel who work with blood, male homosexuals, intravenous drug abusers, persons having intimate (sexual and other) contacts with HBV carriers, and newborn infants whose mothers have HBV or are carriers. An effective vaccine against hepatitis B is now available.

Other forms of hepatitis can occur without direct infection of the liver. Diffuse bacterial infections (septicemia) can cause a toxic hepatitis. Certain chemicals, such as carbon tetrachloride, can cause hepatitis in anyone who is exposed sufficiently, and certain medications, such as phenylbutazone, cincophen, and halothane, can cause hepatitis in those who, for unknown reasons, are sensitive to them. *See* "Sexually Transmissible Diseases" and "Immunization Guide."

Heredity • The transmission of characteristics from one generation to another, from parents to offspring, through the genetic information carried in the chromosomes. Geneticists are providing medical researchers with the tools for exploring the role of heredity in sickness and in resistance to disease. It is hoped that the dissemination of information about genetic disorders and the availability of genetic counseling will bring about a dramatic reduction in the medical, psychological, and economic problems created by hereditary diseases.

Among the more prevalent inherited diseases are: Tay-Sachs, Niemann-Pick, and Gaucher's disease, all three caused by faulty enzyme function and commonly associated with families of middle European Jewish ancestry; sickle-cell anemia, a blood disorder most common among blacks; Cooley's anemia, a more acute blood disease formerly called thalassemia; Huntington's chorea, a degenerative disorder of the central nervous system; hemophilia; several types of muscular dystrophy; galactosemia; phenylketonuria (PKU); cystic fibrosis, the most common genetic disease among Anglo-Saxons, carried by 1 in 20 whites or approximately 10 million Americans. Research on inherited immunities that seem to make some families immune to certain diseases is expected to yield information about resistance to disease in general. This research is still in an early stage of development. *See* CHROMOSOMES, GENETIC COUNSELING and FAMILY HISTORY.

Hernia • The protrusion of all or part of an organ, most commonly, an intestinal loop or abdominal organ, through a weak spot in the wall of the surrounding structure. A hernia, which may be acquired or congenital, is classified according to the part of the body in which it occurs. The *inguinal hernia,* occurring in the groin, accounts for about 75 percent of all hernias and is much more common among men than women. The *umbilical hernia* is more common among infants than among adults; some cases are self-correcting and some require surgery. *Incisional* or *ventral hernias* may develop after abdominal surgery in cases of unsatisfactory healing or because a chronic cough or obesity subjects the weakened tissue to extra strain. The *esophageal* or *hiatus hernia* is more common among the middle-aged than the young. In this condition a portion of the stomach protrudes through the opening for the esophagus in the diaphragm, producing symptoms that range from mild indigestion and heartburn to serious breathing difficulties and regurgitation of food after each meal. In less severe cases the discomfort can be eased by eating small and frequent meals of bland food and sleeping with the body propped up by extra pillows. Most hernias can be corrected by surgical repair of the weakened tissue.

THREE COMMON TYPES OF HERNIAS IN WOMEN

Hiatal portion of stomach protrudes through diaphragm

Diaphragm

Incisional

Inguinal

Heroin • A narcotic drug derived from opium by altering the chemical formula of morphine. *See* "Substance Abuse."

Herpes • Any of a group of related virus diseases characterized by the eruption of blisters and ranging from

mild to life-threatening. The herpes viruses share the capability of lying dormant in the body unless or until they are triggered into causing reinfection. There is no specific cure for any herpes disease, but drugs do exist that, when used early in the infection, can limit its course. The herpes virus types and the diseases they cause are:
Herpes simplex type 1 (HSV1) causes "cold sores" or "fever blisters" that erupt on or inside the mouth. They can be treated with the drug acyclovir in ointment form. HSV1 also causes ulceration of the cornea (herpes keratitis), which can result in irreversible damage to vision unless controlled from the outset with the hourly use of antiviral drops. The same virus causes herpes encephalitis, a serious inflammation of the brain characterized by sudden onset, high fever, and violent seizures. Previously almost always fatal, this form of herpes is now controllable with intravenous injections of the antiviral drug vidarabine (Vira-A).
Herpes simplex type 2 (HSV2) causes genital herpes, a sexually transmitted infection of the mucous membranes of the genital and anal area. No cure is available, but there are several drugs that can be taken to speed healing and limit recurrent attacks. *See* "Sexually Transmissible Diseases" and "Pregnancy and Childbirth."
Herpes zoster, the cause of chicken pox, is also the virus that causes shingles, a painful infection of the sensory nerves that results in inflammation of the skin along the pathway of the nerve. Herpes zoster, which means "blister girdle," is not contagious in this form. What activates the virus is not clearly understood. Inflammation typically occurs above the abdomen and less often along the path of the cranial nerve on the face and near the eye, with a potential for damage to the cornea. Sensitivity of the involved nerves (neuritis) and blisters may take several weeks to disappear, and in stubborn cases the patient may be left with acute neuralgia. There is no specific cure, but various medicines are available to reduce pain. Related to the herpes zoster virus are the Epstein-Barr virus that causes infectious mononucleosis and the cytomegalovirus (CMV) that causes a type of pneumonia in patients with AIDS.

High Altitude Sickness • A condition associated with the ascent to altitudes of 8,000 feet above sea level or higher, where the reduced concentration of oxygen in the air (rarefied air) leads to oxygen deprivation in the blood. When the red blood cells are unable to absorb a full supply of oxygen as they pass through the lungs, breathing becomes increasingly quick and labored. Giddiness, headache, nausea, and disorientation are among the warning signals of high altitude sickness. Tourists who plan to visit high altitudes and mountain climbers or skiers who intend to reach higher altitudes than customary should have a medical checkup to make sure that their heart and lungs can tolerate the stress. Tourists in high altitudes should eliminate smoking and drinking for the first two days and keep physical exertion to a minimum until the body has adjusted to the environment.

High Blood Pressure • *See* HYPERTENSION.

Histamine • A chemical compound found in all body tissues, normally released as a stimulant for the production of the gastric juices during digestion and for the dilation of the smaller blood vessels in response to the body's adaptive needs. Under certain conditions some people produce excessive amounts of histamine as an allergic reaction, causing the surrounding tissues to become swollen and inflamed. For such allergic responses, antihistamine medicines are available.

Hives • Irregularly shaped red or white elevations of the skin accompanied by itching and burning, usually caused by an allergic response involving the release of histamine; technically called urticaria. Hives may occur on any part of the body or in the gastrointestinal tract, and in some cases the weals may be as large as an inch in diameter. A topical anesthetic ointment or lotion may provide relief, but an antihistamine drug is usually prescribed to prevent additional eruptions. When hives occur for the first time, an effort should be made to identify the cause, especially if some medication is suspected so that a more serious recurrence can be avoided.

Hodgkin's Disease • A disorder of the lymphatic system characterized by the progressive enlargement of the lymph nodes throughout the body, especially of the spleen. It is a type of cancer that typically attacks young adults; men are twice as vulnerable as women. If the disease is localized, a 95 percent cure rate can be achieved by radiation treatment. If the disease spreads to the point where vital organs are endangered, various types of chemotherapy have proved effective.

Holistic Medicine • An approach to health and healing that views each patient as a psychobiological unit in a particular physical and psychosocial environment. This approach has been an attempt to counteract the dehumanizing results of medical specialization—one doctor for the heart, another for the skin, yet another for the psyche. The term *holistic* conveys the sense that each individual has a reality that is more important than and independent of the sum of his or her parts. Similar views have been propounded in the past, especially by doctors who focus on psychosomatic medicine on the assumption that the mental and physical aspects of a patient are inextricably bound together. The holistic attitude also takes into account the role played by the person's environment, family history, interpersonal situation, occupational factors, exposure to potential carcinogens, and the like.

Practitioners of holistic medicine stress the importance of patient involvement in the healing process, pointing out that passivity on the part of the patient encourages the view that "medicine is magic." The form that this involvement takes includes self-help wherever possible, self-awareness in recognizing messages from one's feelings and one's body, and openmindedness about the validity of types of therapy other than those that are part of conventional medical practice in the Western world.

Homosexuality • Sexual and emotional attraction to a member of one's own sex; called lesbianism among women. Extensive research on the subject of homosexuality still has not provided a concrete explanation of its cause. Today, many people consider homosexuality to be as natural to some people as heterosexuality is to most people. See "Sexual Health."

Hormone • Chemical product mainly of endocrine glands but also of other organs such as the placenta secreted directly into the bloodstream for transport to various organs for the regulation of life processes. Hormones normally control growth and sexual maturation and affect emotional response, digestion, metabolism, and other vital functions. Many hormones have been synthesized or extracted from other mammals. Their availability has made replacement treatment possible for certain types of hormone deficiencies.

Endorphins are the most recently identified hormone group. Their full range of effects is not yet clear, but, in addition to their morphine-like ability to relieve pain, they may also be the regulatory factor in growth and sexual development. See ENDOCRINE SYSTEM.

Hospice • A live-in facility that may or may not be part of a hospital or an organized program in which nurses, physicians, or lay persons care for, or make home visits to, people who are terminally ill, primarily with cancer, and have an anticipated six or less months to live. The purpose is to provide a more comfortable and more pleasant experience than the person would have in a hospital and to do this more economically. When an attending physician attests to the fact that the patient's condition is terminal, with death anticipated within six months, most medical insurance policies, including Medicare for those entitled to this coverage, will pay the cost of a hospice arrangement. See "Directory of Health Information."

Hot Flash • The most commonly reported symptom of the menopause; a disturbance of temperature regulation connected with the decrease in the body's supply of estrogen. See "Aging Healthfully—Your Body."

Hymen • The membrane that partially closes the entry to the vagina. The hymen varies in size, shape, and toughness. The opening in the hymen allows for the discharge of menstrual flow. While it may remain intact until penetration during the first sexual intercourse, it is by no means unusual for it to be stretched or ruptured by athletic activities or by tampons before any intercourse. In cases where the membrane is so thick or tough that intercourse cannot be accomplished without severe pain or in rare cases in which it completely seals the vaginal opening, it can be cut under a local anesthetic in the gynecologist's office.

Hyperglycemia • Excess amounts of sugar in the blood. This condition is one of the chief signs of diabetes. Milder cases that develop after the age of 50 may be treated by one of the oral hyperglycemic drugs. See DIABETES.

Hypertension • High blood pressure. Hypertension occurs more frequently among women, but it is more deadly to the male. Where hypertension exists, the smallest arteries (arterioles) constrict, causing the heart to have to pump harder in order to distribute blood throughout the body. Because the heart is a muscle, the harder it works, the bigger it gets. An enlarged heart in a hypertensive person is, therefore, a result, not a cause, of high blood pressure.

The causes of what is technically called organic hypertension are de-

UNBROKEN HYMEN
Clitoris
Urethral opening
Vagina
Hymen
Anus

tectable, and if they are corrected, hypertension is reduced. Common causes are arteriosclerosis and atherosclerosis, glomerulonephritis, and hyperthyroidism. The more widespread and insidious type of high blood pressure is called essential hypertension and is of unknown origin. Organic hypertension tends to progress unless treated, eventually attacking a vulnerable organ: the blood vessels of the brain (stroke), the kidneys (uremia), the coronary arteries (heart attack), the organs of vision (eye hemorrhage). Essential hypertension may have no noticeable symptoms, but the increasing blood pressure can gradually damage the heart, blood vessels, and kidneys. Ninety percent of all cases of hypertension are of the essential type,

and while there is no cure, control is possible for a significant number without medication. Recommendations include weight loss if necessary, regular exercise, a low salt diet, no smoking, moderate alcohol intake (any more than two drinks on a regular basis will increase risks), and a contraceptive other than the pill. It is considered normal for blood pressure to rise somewhat during the menopause and with advancing age.

When medication is necessary to bring blood pressure down to acceptable levels, there are many antihypertensive drugs available, including diuretics, beta blockers, and vasodilators. Because the drug of choice will probably be taken for a lifetime, careful monitoring by the doctor is important. Anyone taking such medications should consult with her doctor before deciding to discontinue it all at once. See BLOOD PRESSURE.

Hyperthyroidism • Overactivity of the thyroid gland. Typical symptoms include restlessness and weight loss in spite of overeating. In some cases goiter is present. Diagnosis of the condition is based on blood tests and other clinical procedures. Treatment usually consists of medicine or radioactive iodine that reduces the gland's excess secretion of thyroxin and its size, or, less frequently, surgery.

Hyperventilation • Loss of carbon dioxide from the blood caused by abnormally rapid or deep breathing. Hyperventilation produces symptoms of dizziness, muscle spasms, and chest pains and is one of the most common signs of an anxiety attack. Because the symptoms are an additional cause of anxiety, the condition may worsen to the point where it appears to be an emergency. Effective treatment consists of breathing into and out of a paper or plastic bag so that the exhaled carbon dioxide is reinhaled until the proper blood level is achieved, at which point the symptoms vanish.

Hypnosis • A trancelike state psychically induced by another person or by concentration on an object during which the subject's consciousness is altered for purposes of responding to the suggestions of the hypnotist. The trance may be so shallow that the subject is scarcely aware of a change in mental state, or it may be so deep as to have all the appearances of sleep. Approximately one person in five may be successfully hypnotized, and practically no one can be a successful subject without prior consent and trust in the hypnotist. The mechanism by which the hypnotic state is achieved is not precisely understood, but the technique has accepted medical applications when used by trained and reputable practitioners. Freud's theory of the unconscious evolved from the successful use of hypnosis for the treatment of hysteria. Hypnosis is now used instead of or together with mild anesthesia to facilitate childbirth; it is being taught to pediatric dentists (hypnodontia); and it has been used with some success by psychiatrists to get patients to stop smoking or nail-biting.

Hypochondria • An obsessive preoccupation with the symptoms of illness and supposed ill health. Any suggestion that physical checkups indicate normal organic health is greeted with resentment and disbelief. It is a malady in itself, because it is usually an expression of psychic distress. Hypochondria can sometimes be relieved by psychotherapy.

Hypoglycemia • An abnormally low level of sugar in the blood; a clinical condition of sudden onset characteristic of pre-diabetes and other diseases. It also occurs in diabetics when they have too much insulin or too large a dose of a hypoglycemic agent. Untreated, it can lead to confusion, sleepiness, or in extreme cases unconsciousness. "Low blood sugar" is not a common condition, and no one should embark on a special diet before consulting a doctor and arranging for blood tests. The confusion about hypoglycemia is partially due to the fact that its symptoms—sweating, palpitations, trembling hands—are similar to those produced by an anxiety attack.

Hypothalamus • The master gland of endocrine activity located in the base of the brain directly above the pituitary gland. *See* "The Healthy Woman."

Hypothermia • Abnormally low body temperature. Hypothermia may occur naturally as a consequence of prolonged exposure to extreme cold, especially when temperature regulation is affected by aging, disease such as pneumonia, or the ingestion of certain drugs and alcohol. The symptoms of hypothermia in such cases are slow breathing, weak pulse, and semiconsciousness. Body heat can be slowly restored by covering the patient. No other treatment should be administered without instructions from a doctor. Those who travel by car in severe winter conditions should keep several blankets in the trunk, especially if older people and children are aboard. See FROSTBITE.

Hypothermia can also be artificially induced in order to reduce the tissues' oxygen needs and to slow down the circulation of the blood, thus making certain types of operations possible. Hypothermia allows the surgeon to reach parts of the body that might otherwise be inaccessible in the performance of delicate operations on the brain and heart.

Hysterectomy • Surgical opening of the uterus, similar to a cesarean section. A hysterectomy is done to remove foreign bodies such as IUDs, occasionally to remove a mole, and for abortion only when other methods are contraindicated because of the age of the fetus. See "Gynecologic Diseases and Treatment."

Hysteria • In the psychiatric sense, a condition of uncontrolled excitability, intense anxiety sometimes accompanied by sensory disturbances (such as hallucinations), and general disorientation.

Iatrogenic Disease • Any disorder or disease caused by a physician's medical treatment. Among the less serious examples of iatrogenic disturbances due to side effects of medication are rashes, cramps, dizziness, itching; among the more serious are birth defects (Thalidomide), cancer (DES), shock (penicillin), hemolytic anemia (chloramphenicol), liver damage (Thorazine). It has been estimated that approximately 300,000 people are hospitalized each year in the United States because of an adverse drug reaction. Iatrogenic conditions are therefore one of the ten leading causes of hospitalization in this country. Women can partially protect themselves by questioning the doctor about the possible side effects of any prescribed medication, by keeping records of any unusual responses (such as allergic reactions) to particular drugs so that drug can be avoided if possible, and by avoiding the use of any antibiotic for a virus infection except under special conditions. In cases where a particular treatment carries with it a risk potentially equal to the condition being treated, the patient has a right to have this explained so that she can make a responsible choice.

Ibuprofen • The generic name of the analgesic drug marketed in prescription strength as Motrin and Rufen, and in over-the-counter lower dosage as Nuprin and Advil. These medicines are widely used as pain killers by people who cannot tolerate aspirin and who find them more effective than Tylenol for certain conditions such as menstrual cramps and arthritis. Drugs containing ibuprofen should not be taken by women who are on a regimen of diuretics for some other problem because the combination can lead to kidney damage.

Ileitis • Inflammation of the lower portion of the small intestine. See CROHN'S DISEASE.

Ileostomy • A surgical procedure to create an artificial anus to bypass the colon by bringing the ileum (the lowest part of the small intestine) through an opening made in the abdominal wall. An ileostomy is performed when ulcerative colitis, cancer, or other disease requires the removal of the colon (large intestine). It may also be performed as a temporary measure so that an obstruction in the colon can be removed without removing the colon itself.

Immunity and Immunization • Immunity is a biologic state of being resistant to or not susceptible to a disease or condition, usually, and here specifically, due to the presence of antibodies against the causative agent (antigen). The immunity may be congenital (acquired from the mother and present at birth but not long lasting), natural (resulting from an infectious disease that produces antibodies), or induced by immunization (vaccination).

Active immunization against some diseases may require periodic boosters to maintain the immunity; against others, the initial immunization may last a lifetime.

Passive immunization is achieved by introducing antibodies rather than antigens into the body. Antibodies are introduced by the injection of blood serum obtained from humans who have a natural immunity, have been actively immunized, or are convalescing from a particular disease. Individuals differ greatly in the efficiency of their immune responses depending on genetic inheritance and exposure to antibody formation. Some women may have a single experience with a genital herpes infection and never another because the virus is kept dormant. In other cases, the immune system is incapable of fighting off the recurrent attacks of infection. It is thought that a damaged immune system is responsible for some types of cancer, and in AIDS the immune system has been undermined to the point where the body is mortally vulnerable to infection and disease. *See* "Immunization Guide."

Impotence • Inability of the male to achieve and maintain an erection (erectile impotence); also, inability to achieve orgasm following erection (ejaculating impotence). Almost all men experience impotence at some time in their lives. It may be occasional and temporary or it may be chronic. The cause in over 80 percent of cases is psychological, resulting from conflicts that may arise from guilt, unacknowledged homosexuality, anxiety, distrust of women, or self-punishment. It may also be related to physical causes of fatigue, general poor health, and organic conditions such as diabetes, hormonal aberration, or inherited disorders of the genitals. Occupational exposure to radiation or certain chemicals, alcoholism, drug addiction, and certain prescribed drugs and tranquilizers are other causes. When impotence exists, psychiatric counseling or a professionally accredited sex therapy clinic should be considered only after a complete medical checkup has been conducted. *See* "Sexual Health" and "Infertility."

Incest • Sexual intercourse between a male and female who are not permitted by their society to marry; the proscription may be based on consanguinity (close blood relationship) or affinity (relationship by marriage). The problem of incest has come out of the closet only recently. It is much more common than previously assumed and cuts across race, religion, social class, and economic status. *See* "Rape and Family Abuse."

Inderal (Propranolol) • The first of the beta blocking drugs and the most widely prescribed drug in this category. *See* BETA BLOCKERS.

Indigestion • Any disturbance in the digestive process that results in discomfort; also called dyspepsia. An acute attack of indigestion may be sufficiently severe and disabling to require treatment by a doctor. Alkalizers are often ineffective and potentially damaging, particularly if the condition is caused by emotional stress. In most cases of indigestion the cause is not organic and can be corrected without medication. Digestive complaints are often due to eating too much too quickly, failure to chew food properly, poorly prepared food, excessive drinking of iced or carbonated beverages including beer, eating while one is upset or angry, overuse of such medications as aspirin or tranquilizers, eating too much raw food, or changing to a new diet. When indigestion persists in spite of corrective measures, a gastrointestinal study known as a barium X-ray or blood tests should be administered to determine the underlying cause.

Indocin (Indomethacin) • An aspirin substitute widely prescribed for the treatment of arthritis. It is especially useful for those who cannot tolerate large doses of aspirin. Indocin belongs to the recently developed category of nonsteroidal anti-inflammatory drugs (NSAIDs) that, unlike the steroids, can be taken over an indefinitely extended period without causing undesirable side effects. Indocin and similar drugs are effective because they inhibit the body's production of prostaglandins, some of which are implicated in inflammation of the joints.

Patients taking diuretics for a prior condition should report this to the physician who prescribes any of the NSAIDs because the combination can cause serious kidney damage.

The fact that Indocin is now available in generic form represents an important saving to users.

Induced Labor • Artificial stimulation of the birth process; often referred to as programmed labor or elective induction. Labor may be induced either by the injection of a synthetic hormone (oxytocin) that stimulates, speeds up, and intensifies uterine contractions or by a surgical procedure called amniotomy, the artificial rupture of the amniotic sac below the fetus. Labor should be induced only for medical, not convenience, indications. *See* "Pregnancy and Childbirth."

Infantile Paralysis • *See* POLIOMYELITIS.

Influenza • A contagious respiratory disease caused by a Type A or B virus; generally known as the flu and previously called the grippe. All strains of the flu virus are airborne, and the infection is spread in the coughs, sneezes, and exhaled breath of the affected person. The disease may reach epidemic proportions rapidly, especially because natural or artificially acquired immunity against one particular strain of the virus provides no guaranteed protection against another strain.

Symptoms may range from mild to severe. Typical manifestations are inflammation of the membranes that line the respiratory tract causing a running nose, scratchy throat, and mucous congestion that causes coughing. Fever may not be present or temperature may go as high as 104°F. Aching joints, appetite loss, and general malaise characterize even the mildest cases. Even when symptoms clear up, usually within ten days, the flu patient may feel weak and tired for some time. The cough may be persistent, and relapses may occur as a result of lowered resistance and premature resumption of normal activities. Lowered resistance to bacterial infection is the most serious complication of the flu. When a healthy adult has the illness, the usual treatment is bed rest, aspirin or Tylenol, lots of fluids, and as much sleep as possible. A cough medicine containing an expectorant may be prescribed to facilitate the hawking up of the accumulated phlegm. Amantadine, an antiviral drug, is effective in reducing the duration of Type A influenza. For flu patients who may be vulnerable to complications, such as people over 65, diabetics, very young children, or anyone with a heart, lung, or kidney disorder, antibiotics may be prescribed in addition.

Many doctors believe that people who are highly susceptible to serious complications should be vaccinated each year with a vaccine made from the killed viruses of the current strains responsible for the disease. Adverse responses to this form of immunization range from a slightly sore and swollen spot in the area of the vaccination, to a low fever and headache of several days' duration, to an uncomfortable response presumed to be allergic, to a 1 in 100,000 risk of severe reaction that affects the nervous system. It is likely that a new and better vaccine, given by nose drops, will be available in the next five years. See "Immunization Guide."

Inguinal Glands • A group of lymph nodes located in the groin. Any painful swelling or persistent soreness in this area should be brought to a doctor's attention.

Inner Ear • *See* EAR.

Insect Stings and Bites • While usually no more than a nuisance, the bite of an insect can at times cause disease or life-threatening emergencies. The stinging insects—hornets, wasps, yellow jackets, and bees—do not transmit disease, but the venom they inject may cause a severe allergic response known as anaphylactic shock. Ordinarily, however, the sting results in no more than swelling, redness, and localized pain. In the case of a bee sting the skin should never be squeezed in order to extricate the stinger, because this only forces the venom farther into the tissues. Instead, the stinger should be removed with a pair of tweezers held flat against the skin. Any sign of a systemic response to a sting, such as body swelling or respiratory distress, indicates the need for immediate professional attention. Women who are extremely hypersensitive to the venom should be desensitized by an allergist and continue the maintenance treatments usually necessary four or five times a year. Even after desensitization emergency adrenalin should be carried when there is the threat of a sting.

Biting and bloodsucking flies and mosquitos can transmit serious diseases. The common housefly does not bite but may be a carrier of infection. Aside from diseases endemic to the tropics, such as yellow fever and malaria, encephalitis can be transmitted by certain local mosquitos. Horseflies are also harmful because they can transmit rabbit fever (tularemia). Among dangerous parasites found in several parts of the world are fleas that transmit bubonic plague and typhus. It should be noted that the ticks that cause Rocky Mountain spotted fever are not indigenous to the West and may be found in other parts of the country. Immunization is available against all the above infections and should be taken into consideration by anyone planning a trip to an area of high-risk exposure. A parasite common in the rural South, known as the chigger, is the larval stage of the mite that causes scabies. While chiggers are not disease-bearing, their bite irritates the skin thereby leading the way toward a secondary infection. Once bitten, the victim can be relieved of the itching by the application of a paste of baking soda and water or calamine lotion.

Lyme disease, also called Lyme arthritis, is the most recently identified disease known to be caused by a tick bite. In this instance, the bite injects a disease-bearing organism called a spirochete, into the skin. Early treatment with tetracycline averts the possibility of the eventual onset of generalized arthritis. *See* LYME DISEASE.

While most spiders and other arachnids are harmless, there are three or four that inflict bites that must receive prompt attention: the scorpion found in the Southwest, the black widow spider (identifiable by its shiny black body whose underside is marked with a red hourglass shape), and a species of hairy tarantula found near the Mexican border. The aggressive fire ant is a more recent menace that is spreading its way through the Southern states. Its attack can be easily identified because it inflicts multiple stings around the original bite. The bite of a fire ant can cause severe systemic response in certain people. Anyone living in an area where fire ants exist should consider the advisability of desensitization.

Certain practical measures can reduce the hazards and discomforts of bites and stings without the use of insecticides that pollute the environment with dangerous chemicals. A few suggestions are the application of insect-repellent lotions containing such effective chemicals as diethylmetatoluamide, dimethyl phthalate, or dimethylearbate on exposed parts of the body several times a day; wearing protective clothing during walks in the country; avoiding the use of perfumes, lotions, sprays, and jewelry because scents and colors attract stinging insects; burning insect-repellent candles or incense sticks at picnics when food is exposed; keeping foods covered; and using screens for indoor protection. Women who own or rent vacation houses in the country should heed the warnings of local health authorities as to insect-borne diseases and the precautions one can take to combat them.

Insomnia • Sleeplessness, either chronic or occasional. Because it is generally believed that dependence on sleeping pills will only intensify insomnia, anyone trying to cope with the problem should try to find another solution for it.

Sleeplessness may be caused by any one of many factors that are easily corrected, such as eating rich food or drinking beverages containing caffeine within two hours of bedtime, watching overly exciting television programs, sleeping in a poorly ventilated room or on an uncomfortable mattress. When snoring and other noises interfere with sleep, ear plugs can often relieve the problem. Daytime exercise, a hot bath in the evening, and a glass of warm milk before retiring require little effort but are helpful. Scientists have found that an amino acid, L-triptophane, contained in certain foods, including milk, seems to act as a sedative. When insomnia is a result of depression or anxiety, the cause of the emotional distress should be explored before resorting to medication. See SLEEP, and "Substance Abuse."

Insulin • A hormone secreted by the groups of cells in the pancreas called the islets of Langerhans. Insulin performs several vital functions and is especially critical in stabilizing the body's metabolism of sugars and starches. The isolation of insulin by Canadian scientists in 1921–22 inaugurated the successful treatment of diabetes using insulin derived from the pancreas of pigs and cows, and, very recently from genetically engineered bacteria. See GENETIC ENGINEERING.

Intercourse • See SEXUAL INTERCOURSE.

Interferon • A cellular protein produced by white blood cells and fibroblasts that suppresses viral DNA reproduction. This antiviral substance is available as a genetically engineered drug but only for investigational purposes at this time. If its production is not prohibitively expensive, it may prove to be the cure for the common cold, and it may eventually be used to treat other viral diseases such as herpes and AIDS. Promising experimental results have also been achieved in the use of interferon for treatment of some cancers.

Intermittent Claudication • In simple language, occasional limping caused by an inadequate supply of blood to the lower leg during exercise because of partial blockage of a major artery in the upper leg by fatty deposits. This causative condition is called arteriosclerosis obliterans. The pain in the lower leg that causes limping subsides after a period of rest. The condition is not life-threatening, but the unexpected and sudden onset of pain can be immobilizing. Short of surgery to bypass or clean out the diseased artery, other measures that can be effective are total abstention from smoking, weight loss as necessary, and participation in a walking-for-exercise program.

Intrauterine Device • See "Contraception and Abortion."

In Vitro Fertilization • Fertilization of one ovum or several ova surgically removed from a woman's ovary and placed in a glass Petri dish ("test tube"), using her husband's or another man's sperm. The fertilized ovum is then implanted in the woman's uterus. It may also by prearrangement be implanted in the uterus of another woman who cannot produce an ovum, usually because her ovaries have been removed surgically or are no longer functioning. See "Infertility," and "Directory of Health Information."

Iron • One of the minerals that is an essential micronutrient. A deficiency of iron in the diet is the direct cause of the most common type of anemia, iron-deficiency anemia. An iron deficiency may occur temporarily if surgery or other conditions make a restricted diet necessary or during pregnancy when iron stored in the body is depleted by the demands of fetal development. Among the signs of borderline iron deficiency are canker sores and loss of hair. Where supplemental iron is considered advisable, ferrous sulfate pills are considered therapeutically superior to tonics advertised for "tired blood"; they are also less expensive. Iron pills or tonics should never be taken unless prescribed by a doctor after a blood test, because excessive amounts may be damaging in the absence of anemia. Only where there is a need to obtain a rapid response or where oral preparations cause gastric upset is iron given by injection. See "Nutrition, Weight, and General Well-Being" and ANEMIA.

Irritable Bowel Syndrome • A common condition, usually attributable to stress, in which an abnormal pattern of bowel contractions results in diarrhea alternating with constipation, bloat, and pain. Irritable bowel syndrome, also called spastic colon, is experienced by many young adults who avoid seeking medical advice for the condition, which is likely to be more responsive to a few months of psychotherapy than to medication. The purpose of the therapy is to guide the patient in finding more positive methods of handling tension and stress. Because many of the symptoms are similar to those of Crohn's disease and because the likelihood of cancer is an overriding fear of those who do seek a physician's advice, tests are usually given to rule out these more serious possibilities.

Itching • An irritation of the skin; technically called pruritis. Among the most common causes are insect bites, fungus infections, allergies, or contact dermatitis. Itching in the anal region may be caused by worms or hemorrhoids; in the vaginal area it may occur spontaneously or follow the use of certain antibiotics. Severe itching around the pubic hair may indicate the presence of crabs. Among other causes are an accumulation of dried body secretions under the arms, in the crotch, on the scalp, or between the toes; vaginal discharges; the drying out of the vaginal mucous membranes that occurs during menopause; exposure to cold temperatures; new skin growth following sunburn or scar healing; chafing by one body surface against another (e.g., under the breasts) or by tight clothing; emotional stress. A doctor may refer to local or generalized itching as neurodermatitis if no specific cause can be found. Certain serious disorders are accompanied by itching: diabetes, anemia, leukemia, jaundice, gout, liver malfunction, and cancer. Diseases in which an itching rash is a characteristic symptom include chickenpox, measles, and rubella.

The impulse to relieve itching by energetic scratching should be controlled because the irritation will only become more intense and the nails may cause breaks in the skin leading to secondary bacterial infection. Sometimes it is necessary to wear gloves. If topical medication provides no relief, medication taken orally or by injection may be necessary to relieve the itching until the underlying cause can be diagnosed and eliminated. The disorder that has the distinction of being called "the itch" is discussed under scabies.

IUD • Intrauterine device. *See* "Contraception and Abortion."

Jaundice • A yellowish appearance of the skin and the whites of the eyes resulting from an excessive amount of bile in the blood. As a sign of a disorder of the liver or the biliary tract, jaundice may be accompanied by diarrhea, abdominal pain caused by liver enlargement, bitter-tasting greenish vomit, and itching in various parts of the body. Among the usual underlying causes, the most common is infectious hepatitis; others are gallstones, cirrhosis, hemolytic anemia, and tumors that obstruct the normal circulation of bile. The treatment of jaundice depends on the diagnosis of the condition.

Joint Diseases • *See* ARTHRITIS, BURSITIS, etc.

Kaposi's Sarcoma • A malignant disease, primarily of the skin, which has a high prevalence in people with the acquired immune deficiency syndrome known as AIDS. *See* ACQUIRED IMMUNE DEFICIENCY SYNDROME.

Kidneys and Kidney Disorders • The kidneys are twin organs, each about 4 inches long, located on either side of the spinal column at the back wall of the abdomen approximately at waist level. As the lungs expand and contract during respiration, the kidneys move up and down. Examined in cross-section under a microscope, the functional units of the organ—the nephrons—are seen to consist of clusters of blood vessels, the glomeruli, that act as filters. The vital process in which the kidneys are indispensable is the continuous filtering of the blood to remove wastes and excess fluid while retaining or reabsorbing other materials. The kidneys also secrete hormones involved in the regulation of blood pressure and the red blood cell count. In order to understand how certain disorders originate, it is helpful to have some idea of how the kidneys work. As arterial blood enters the kidneys from the heart, it passes through the millions of nephrons. The waste materials go by way of the ureter into the bladder for eventual elimination through the urethra in the form of urine. The cleansed and filtered blood goes back into circulation through the veins, returning to the heart for recirculation. With a combined weight of only about 2/3 of a pound, the kidneys process more than 18 gallons of blood every hour and filter about 60 percent of all the fluid taken into the body, excreting as much as 2 quarts of urine each day.

The kidneys are subject to a number of disorders, some merely temporary, others potentially fatal. The most common problem is infection and the most common infection is pyelonephritis, an infection of the kidney's urine-collecting ducts. It may occur with no significant symptoms or it may be accompanied by back pain, fever, and chills. An acute attack of pyelonephritis occurs in about 5 percent of all pregnancies and usually requires antibiotic treatment. Kidney obstructions in the form of stones (usually calcium), cysts, or other abnormalities can lead to improper drainage, inflammation, and damage to surrounding tissues. Nephrosis, also known as the nephrotic syndrome, is a group of symptoms frequently accompanying some other condition. It is characterized by the leakage of large amounts of protein into the urine and leads to generalized swelling, especially a marked puffiness under the eyes. Kidney disease may also result from untreated hypertension, gout, and diabetes or as a consequence of chemical poisoning or prolonged shock. Chemical poisoning by certain drugs, individually or in combination, results in acute interstitial nephritis. This toxic reaction occurs especially when a combination of drugs doubles the negative side effects of each one. For example, anyone on a regular regimen of diuretics for hypertension should be aware of the potential hazard of taking some other medication in addition prescribed by a different doctor for a different condition. When any disorder reaches the point where the kidneys can no longer function, uremia (accumulation of urea nitrogen in the blood) occurs. Acute kidney failure may be helped by short-term dialysis. When irreversible damage to both kidneys has occurred, long-term dialysis or tissue transplant can prevent fatal consequences.

Any signs of kidney disease should be taken seriously, especially during pregnancy. Symptoms may include back pain below the rib cage, a change in the color or composition of urine or discomfort during urination, puffiness of any part of the body especially the area around the eye. Treatment depends on the specific diagnoses and may only require changes in the diet and the use of diuretics. Antibiotics are often prescribed for bacterial infection. In the case of an obstruction, surgery may be necessary. A recent experimental treatment for stones involves crushing them with shock waves while the patient is in a water bath. See DIALYSIS, GLOMERULONEPHRITIS and "Directory of Health Information."

Knee Disorders • The knee is one of the largest and strongest joints in the body, formed by the junction of the tibia (shinbone), the femur (thighbone), and the patella (kneecap). The bones are bound by ligaments and tendons and cushioned by cartilage and fluid-filled sacs called bursas. "Housemaid's knee," so called because it usually results from frequent kneeling on hard surfaces, is a form of bursitis. "Water on the knee" is a condition in which there is an excessive accumulation of the lubricating fluid secreted by the membranous lining of the ligaments that bind the knee joints together. This oversecretion, which may follow an injury or infection or may accompany arthritis, causes the kneecap to be raised and the surrounding tissue to become painful. Keeping the knee raised and rested is usually sufficient treatment. Chronic inflammation of the joint that occurs during arthritis can be relieved by therapeutic doses of aspirin or other nonsteroidal anti-inflammatory drugs. In severe cases, injections of steroids into the joint may be recommended for short-term therapy. Damage to the knee joint by rheumatic disease or athletic injury resulting in torn cartilage can be restored by a recent type of surgery made possible by the use of an arthroscope. This instrument can "see" disorders in the joint not easily made visible by X-ray or more traditional means. Other instruments that are attached to the arthroscope are manipulated by the surgeon in order to remove the damaged cartilage. This operation requires special skill and experience for the achievement of good results. It is not usually performed by a general orthopedic surgeon but rather by a specialist in handling sports injuries.

With the advancement in prosthetic devices, replacement of knee (and hip) joints has enabled those suffering from crippling joint disease to enjoy a greater degree of mobility than previously possible.

Scrapes, minor bruises, or superficial cuts that do not damage anything except the skin around the knee are not usually a problem of any magnitude. A fall or athletic injury that results in soreness and swelling will benefit from the prompt application of ice to minimize internal bleeding and an elastic bandage for support against further strain. The application of heat on the day following the injury can hasten healing. If the pain and swelling increases, the knee should be examined and probably X-rayed.

KNEE DISORDERS

Femur — Muscle
Cartilage may be worn — Kneecap
Meniscus may be torn — Swollen bursa of "housemaid's" knee

Lacrimal Ducts • Three sets of ducts involved in the flow of tears: 6 to 12 tiny openings that lead from the lacrimal (tear) gland at the upper, outside rim of the eye to the lacrimal sac; the lacrimal duct that leads from the inner corner of the eye to the conjunctival sac; and the nasolacrimal duct that leads from the lacrimal sac to the nose. When these ducts are overloaded by an abnormally heavy flow of tears, caused by strong feelings or by chemical or mechanical irritants, the excess liquid runs down the cheeks or through the nose. When the duct in the nose is blocked or swollen by allergy or inflammation during a respiratory infection, the eyes become watery. The dry, itchy eyes that may afflict the elderly result from a partial drying up of the lacrimal glands and a consequent decrease in the fluid that keeps the eye surface moist. The discomfort of this condition can be relieved by preparations known as artificial tears available without prescription. There are several different brands that can be tried in order to find the one that is most effective.

Lactation • The production of milk in the mother's breasts, beginning about three days following childbirth; also, the period of weeks or months during which the baby is breast-fed. See "Pregnancy and Childbirth."

Lactose Intolerance • An inability to metabolize milk and milk products without discomfort because of low levels of the enzyme lactase in the surface of the small intestines. Lactase is the enzyme essential for the proper absorption of the major sugar in milk, lactose. This malabsorption problem results in symptoms similar to those of spastic colon or colitis: diarrhea, cramps, and gassiness. When these discomforts occur after eating any and all dairy products, a simple blood test can diagnose the problem correctly so that suitable changes can be made in the diet.

Lamaze Method • A system of preparation for childbirth named after its originator, Dr. Ferdinand Lamaze. See "Pregnancy and Childbirth."

Laparoscope • An instrument consisting of an illuminated tube with an optical system that is inserted into an anesthetized patient's abdomen for visualization of its contents for diagnostic purposes (as in cases of ectopic pregnancy) and therapeutic purposes (e.g., tubal ligation). A similar instrument, a hysteroscope, can be inserted into the uterus for diagnostic and therapeutic purposes. See "Infertility," and "Gynecologic Diseases and Treatment."

Laryngitis • Inflammation of the mucous lining of the larynx, affecting both breathing and voice production. The condition may be chronic or acute; occurring because of a virus or bacterial infection; an allergic response; an irritation of the membrane by chemicals, dusts, or pollens; or recurrent misuse of the voice. The symptoms of milder cases usually include a dry cough, a tickling sensation in the throat, and hoarseness or a complete loss of voice, all of which result from swelling of the vocal cords. Fever may be present when laryngitis is produced by bacterial infection. The most effective treatment is silence. The condition is also helped by a day or so of bed rest in a room where the temperature is warm and the humidity is high enough to prevent irritating dryness, if necessary through the use of a humidifier or a vaporizer. Spicy foods, hot soups, smoking, or any other irritants should be eliminated. Chronic laryngitis may be the result of longtime exposure to such irritants as alcohol, smoking, or industrial fumes. Because hoarseness may also accompany the development of tuberculosis or cancer, it should be investigated by a doctor if it persists for more than a few weeks.

Larynx • A cartilaginous structure that contains the vocal cords and is held together by ligaments and moved by attached muscles; also called the voice box. It is located in front of the throat and is lined with mucous membrane continuous with the pharynx and the trachea. The larynx is the source of sound that emanates in speech and is also part of the respiratory system, being the passageway for air between the pharynx and the lungs. The largest ring of laryngeal cartilage characteristically protrudes in the male throat as the Adam's apple. The epiglottis at the base of the tongue forms the lid that closes the larynx during swallowing, thus preventing food and drink from going down "the wrong way" and causing choking. Obstruction of the larynx may occur because of an abscess in the cartilage lining or because of an injury. Tumors are not uncommon and are removed surgically, even if benign. Singers and politicians, due to the professional use of their voices, are more likely to develop nodes on their vocal cords than other people. Such growths may also be eliminated by surgery. Cancer of the larynx, which is more common in men than women, is associated with smoking. Smokers are six times more likely to develop cancer of the larynx than nonsmokers, and the risk is greater still for heavy drinkers.

If examination with a laryngoscope and various laboratory tests including a biopsy verify the presence of an obstructive malignancy unresponsive to radiation treatment, a laryngectomy, the surgical removal of part or all of the larynx, is performed. The surgery itself is not complicated, but because it involves removal of the voice box, the patient must undergo postoperative rehabilitation in order to learn a new speech process.

Laser • A device containing a gas such as carbon dioxide or other substance that amplifies and concentrates light waves into a tiny beam of immense heat and power. Called a

CROSS-SECTION OF MOUTH AND LARYNX

Nasal cavity
Hard palate
Soft palate
Tongue
Epiglottis
Vocal cords
Thyroid cartilage
Esophagus
Trachea

"bloodless scalpel," the laser permits pinpoint (1/160 of a human hair's width) surgery by vaporizing tissue layer by layer without affecting adjacent tissue only a few cell widths away. It has many uses in gynecologic treatment: removing ectopic pregnancies and the scars and adhesions of pelvic inflammatory disease and treating venereal warts, various diseases of the cervix such as noninvasive cancer, and perhaps herpes. It also is used in eye- and neurosurgery, to unclog blocked coronary artery and other blood vessels, and for diagnostic purposes. Laser surgery is especially useful in correcting such eye disorders as diabetic retinopathy, macular degeneration, and in some few cases, glaucoma.

Laxative • Preparation that encourages evacuation by loosening the contents of the bowel. A dependence on laxatives for the treatment of constipation is likely to worsen the condition because it deprives the colon of its natural muscle tone. Under no circumstances should a laxative be taken if there is cause to believe that the abdominal pain is due to an inflamed appendix. *See* CONSTIPATION.

L-dopa (Sinamet) • The most effective medication for parkinsonism; also called levodopa. When taken orally in carefully supervised doses, it increases the brain's amount of dopamine, the natural substance essential for the normal transmission of nerve messages. The loss of this substance causes the tremors and rigidity characteristic of the disease. L-dopa compensates for this loss in approximately 75 percent of all cases. *See* PARKINSONISM.

Legionnaire's Disease • A form of pneumonia ranging from mild to life-threatening caused by the bacterium *Legionella pneumophila*. This microorganism may be found in soil and especially in the stagnant water that accumulates in the air ducts of air conditioning systems in public buildings, in the workplace, and in hotels. The disease is airborne (person-to-person contamination is not known to occur) and is characterized by severe general malaise followed by high fever, chills, and a cough. When untreated at this stage, Legionnaire's disease has been fatal in more than 15 percent of all cases. There have also been many instances when symptoms are so mild as to go unnoticed and unidentified. When this occurs, the infection runs a course similar to that of a cold. For the serious cases, the effective treatment is erythromycin.

Lesbian • Woman whose emotional and sexual needs are directed toward other members of their own sex. *See* "Sexual Health."

Leukemia • A group of neoplastic diseases characterized by a proliferation in the bone marrow and lymphoid tissue of white blood cells whose excessive production interferes with the manufacturing of normal red cells. Different types of white cells are involved in the various forms taken by the disease. Acute lymphocytic leukemia, the most common form of childhood cancer and at one time almost always fatal, is now being controlled by a combination of radiation and chemotherapy. One type of acute granulocytic leukemia can occur at any age; the chronic leukemias (myeloid and lymphocytic among others) are unlikely to occur before middle age with men contracting the disease more frequently than women. While there is no accepted theory about the cause of leukemia, it is assumed that its rising incidence results from increased exposure to radioactivity in its many manifestations: industrial pollution, food contamination, too many diagnostic X-rays over too short a period, or radiation therapy for some other disease. It is also a likely concommitant of a breakdown in the body's immune defenses as occurs in AIDS.

Whatever the age and circumstances of the victim, leukemic symptoms are generally the same: unexplained weight loss, low energy, fever, subcutaneous hemorrhaging, various signs of anemia, and lowered resistance to infection because of the destruction of normal cells. As the disease progresses, especially in its myeloid form, the spleen becomes visibly enlarged and in chronic lymphatic leukemia the lymph nodes swell and become sore. Diagnosis of all leukemias is based on microscopic examination of blood samples, bone marrow, or lymph tissue. Treatment consists of a combination of anticancer drugs, corticosteroids, radiation, antibiotics, and transfusions of hemoglobin and platelets. Several of the leukemias, which were formerly fatal, have gone into remission as a result of the effectiveness of the new drugs, the use of generalized radiation, and the transplanting of healthy bone marrow.

Leukorrhea • An abnormal vaginal discharge. When the discharge is heavy, when it contains pus and has an unpleasant odor, or when it causes itching or burning of the vagina or the vulva, a diagnosis of the underlying condition should be made. Among the circumstances leading to leukorrhea are: mechanical irritation by a diaphragm, tampon, or IUD; chemical irritation by excessive douching or the use of vaginal deodorant sprays; vaginal infection by bacteria or fungi, especially candidiasis or trichomoniasis; venereal disease, especially gonorrhea; benign growths such as polyps or fibroid tumors. Heavy discharge may also be a sign of diabetes or cervical cancer. In most cases it can be cleared up by finding the cause and initiating proper treatment. See "Gynecologic Diseases and Treatment" and "Sexually Transmissible Diseases."

Librium • The first minor tranquilizer of the benzodiazepine family, introduced in the late 1950s, and followed by Valium in the early 1960s. These overprescribed drugs are for the temporary treatment of anxiety and should be discontinued when the patient is sufficiently in command of herself to explore the source of her anxiety so that she can find suitable ways of coping with it. Although smoking and drinking are considerably more dangerous and more addictive, long-term use of Librium can become a crutch difficult to discard. Pregnant women are advised against its use. Because Librium can cause drowsiness, anyone taking it should arrange to have someone else take the wheel. Alcoholic beverages should be avoided. Librium is now available in generic form at a considerable saving to the purchaser. See TRANQUILIZERS; "Substance Abuse."

Life Expectancy • The number of years a person of a given age may be expected to live, based on statistical averages. Current calculations for the life expectancy in the United States of white females at birth is 78.2 years. This is 25 years longer than life expectancy for the same group born in 1900. However, there has been little change in the life expectancy of women over 60—an adult woman of 65 in 1900 had a life expectancy of 13 more years and a woman of 65 today can expect to live 15 more years. This lack of improvement is balanced by the fact that more and more women live to be 60, thanks to progress in the prevention of death during childbirth, the control of infectious diseases, and improvements in public health. These advances also account in some measure for the fact that while the average length of life for women born in 1900 exceeded that of males by only two years, in our own time women live at least eight years longer than men on the average. Studies by the World Health Organization on this differential indicate that urban life lowers life expectancy for men and raises it for women. In underdeveloped countries, where women are often overworked, underfed, and frequently pregnant and where there is an age-old prejudice against female children typical of agrarian societies, the death rates for women are much higher than they are for men. It is anticipated that in the United States, if more men stop smoking and if women continue to smoke at present rates, the comparable life expectancy of the sexes will change.

Ligament • Band of tough fibrous tissue that connects and stabilizes bones at the joints. An injury resulting in the stretching or tearing of ligaments is called a sprain.

Lithium Carbonate • A chemical compound of the element lithium used in the treatment of manic-depressive illness; not to be confused with lithium chloride, another of the salts of lithium and no longer available for patients on low-sodium diets because of its dangerous side effects. Lithium carbonate is considered by specialists to be the first drug effective against a major psychosis. It is also being used increasingly for patients whose lives are disrupted by unaccountable mood swings originating in one of the depressive illnesses. Properly administered in supervised doses, it results in the emotional stabilization of many patients who have not responded well to treatments combining heavy sedation with tranquilizers, electroshock, and antidepressants. See MANIC-DEPRESSIVE ILLNESS.

Liver • The body's largest internal organ, dark red, wedge-shaped, weighing from 3 to 4 pounds, and located underneath the lower right side of the rib cage. Among its many vital functions are: the production of bile essential for fat digestion; the production and storage of glycogen for conversion to glucose; the synthesis of protein and the formation of urea; the storage of vitamins A, D, E, and K; the production of several blood components including the clotting factors; the inactivation of nicotine ingested during smoking before it can reach the stomach; the neutralization of poisons such as carbon tetrachloride, arsenic, and others that may enter the body from without as well as of those created from within. Inflammation of the liver (hepatitis) may be caused by chemical poisons, by sensitivity to drugs such as Thorazine and Chloromycetin, and by disease agents especially the viruses that cause the several types of hepatitis. If the infection is severe, the cells that are affected may be replaced by scar tissue, causing cirrhosis of the liver. Tumors of the liver, usually benign, are in some cases associated with contraceptive pills and estrogen replacement therapy.

A nourished liver that contains stored amounts of vitamins, proteins, and other nutrients is less likely to suffer irreversible harm from alcohol than a liver that is undernourished. The liver may also be adversely affected by disorders of the gallbladder, especially by gallstones. The signs and symptoms of liver disorder may include the following depending on the severity of the disease: a gradual swelling of the abdomen and sensitivity to pressure below the rib cage, clay colored stools, dark urine, and vomiting of blood. When disorders are treated promptly and a wholesome

LIVER

[Diagram of liver with labels: Liver cells, Bile duct, Gallbladder, Common bile duct, Portal vein, Duodenum, Small intestine]

regimen is followed, recovery is usually complete. *See* CIRRHOSIS and HEPATITIS.

Liver Spots • Irregularly shaped reddish brown skin blemishes once mistakenly attributed to malfunctioning of the liver. The spots, which are concentrations of melanin pigment similar to but larger than freckles, are not due to aging as such but rather to long exposure to sun and wind, to minor metabolic disturbances, and in some women to systemic changes that occur during pregnancy. The spots are generally harmless and can either be covered with a special cosmetic preparation or caused to fade by the use of an ointment that inhibits melanin production. If such a blemish suddenly thickens and hardens or if the surrounding tissue feels sore, a dermatologist should be consulted.

Longevity • *See* LIFE EXPECTANCY.

Lou Gehrig's Disease • *See* AMYOTROPHIC LATERAL SCLEROSIS.

Low Blood Sugar • See HYPOGLYCEMIA.

Lower Back Pain • *See* BACKACHE.

LSD • *Lysergic acid diethylamide, a hallucinogenic drug. See* "Substance Abuse."

Lumpectomy • The minimal surgical procedure for treating a small, localized cancer of the breast. When the removal of the lump and surrounding tissue is followed by radiation and chemotherapy, the recovery statistics are said to compare favorably with those cases in which the entire breast is removed. *See* "Breast Care."

Lung • One of two spongelike structures, each enclosed in a pleural sac, that together with the bronchial tree make up the lower respiratory system. Each lung is divided into lobes —three in the right lung and two in the left. Each lobe is divided into segments that have their own segmental bronchi and their own blood supply. The lungs are the organs in which the respiratory exchange of gases takes place. Under normal circumstances a signal reaches the brain approximately 16 to 20 times a minute indicating the need for an adjustment of the oxygen-carbon monoxide balance within the body. At this signal the diaphragm is thrust downward, increasing the chest capacity, making negative pressure and causing air to rush in to fill the pressure void, leading to the expansion of the lungs. This oxygen-laden atmospheric air travels through the airway passages until it reaches the alveoli. It is through the delicate membranes of the alveoli that the carbon dioxide in the blood of the pulmonary capillaries is exchanged for oxygen. The freshened blood then recirculates, a signal from the brain causes the diaphragm to relax, the negative pressure is reduced, the carbon dioxide is exhaled, and the lungs compress.

While some lung disorders can be diagnosed accurately by listening to the breathing sounds through a stethoscope or by sounding the chest wall by tapping one finger against it and hearing the effects of the percussion, the state of the lungs can best be assessed by more refined techniques. Ordinary X-rays and those taken after radiopaque materials have been instilled in the bronchial tree can disclose many different types of lung tissue damage. With the use of a bronchoscope, foreign bodies, parts of tumors, or even an entire growth can be localized and removed. Other laboratory procedures for defining lung disorders involve sputum examinations that can identify a bacterial invader, fungus, or industrial dust that may be causing progressive lung damage and examination of pleural fluid.

Chronic lung diseases such as bronchitis and emphysema are caused by smoking; exposure to occupational dusts, fumes, and molds; and by air pollution. According to the American Cancer Society, 75 percent of all lung cancers are caused by smoking. Lung cancer, which has long been the most frequent cause of cancer deaths for men, has become the most frequent cause of cancer deaths for women, having replaced breast cancer that until recent years was the Number 1 killer of women. Collapse of a lung (pneumothorax) may be partial and may occur because of bronchial obstruction by a blood clot, tumor, or plug of mucus, or it may be complete, affecting a lobe or an entire lung damaged by a bullet wound, tuberculosis, or cancer. *See* ASTHMA, BRONCHITIS, EMPHYSEMA, PNEUMONIA, SMOKING, TUBERCULOSIS, and "The Healthy Woman."

Lupus Erythematosus • An inflammatory disease that may involve various parts of the body and cause permanent tissue damage. Typical victims are women of childbearing age. In its milder discoid form it affects the skin only, producing a butterfly-shaped rash that spreads across the nose to both sides of the face. The rash may be accompanied by fever and weight loss as well as by arthritic pains in the joints. In its more serious form systemic lupus erythematosus involves the kidneys and the blood vessels. The cause is unknown and the disease may flare up unexpectedly, leaving the patient exhausted and weak. Recent research indicates that the disorder may occur or worsen when a latent virus is activated by overexposure to sunlight, emotional stress, or an unrelated infection. The symptoms have been explained as an aberration in the body's autoimmune system during which disease-fighting cells go awry and devour healthy tissue.

Lupus is a condition requiring long-term supervision. Special medications that control the disorder, especially heavy therapeutic doses of anti-inflammatory drugs, corticosteroids, and other drugs, may produce adverse side effects. The prescribed regimen must be carefully followed and readjusted from time to time depending on individual reactions. Patients with this disease should use a contraceptive other than the pill; if they do become pregnant, special management is needed. In all cases including the mildest, exposure to extreme sunlight should be avoided. *See* "Directory of Health Information."

Lyme Disease (also called Lyme Arthritis) • This disease, named for the town in Connecticut where it made its first known appearance in 1975, is caused by the bite of a tick usually found on deer in the wooded areas of the Northeast. The tick transmits a disease-bearing organism called a spirochete. A week after infection, a characteristic rash appears at the site of the bite. Red spots may appear elsewhere on the body, combined with symptoms similar to those of the flu: fatigue, headache, aching joints, sore throat, and fever. These symptoms are likely to disappear on their own (as they do with the flu), but about 50 percent of the victims eventually develop arthritis with attacks ranging from mild to immobilizing that occur at unpredictable intervals. In most cases, even these complications vanish, but some few people are left with flare-ups of pain and inflammation similar to those of rheumatoid arthritis. Lyme disease is most effectively treated at early onset with antibiotics. The earlier the treatment, the less likely the eventual complications.

Lymph Nodes • Glandlike organs located throughout the body that manufacture the disease-fighting cells known as lymphocytes. These cells are collected in the lymphatic vessels and delivered to the circulatory system in the fluid called lymph. Lymph is part of the blood's plasma. Among the most important lymph nodes and the ones that are superficially located are those found behind the ears, at the angle of the jaw in the neck, in the armpit, and in the groin. When reference is made to "swollen glands," a condition characteristic of such diseases as infectious mononucleosis, it is the nodes that are involved, because in addition to their providing the system with protective lymphocytes, they also filter foreign bodies and bacteria out of the lymphatic fluid. Other masses of lymphatic tissue that produce specialized white cells for counteracting infection are the tonsils, thymus gland, and spleen. The general term for inflammation of lymphatic tissue, of which

LYMPH DRAINAGE OF ARM AND BREAST

LYMPH NODE

Lymph returns to blood system

Lymphocyte production

Filtration of lymph

Tissue fluid enters lymphatic vessels

tonsillitis is an example, is lymphadenitis: a tumor of this tissue is a lymphoma, and a malignancy of the lymph nodes is a lymphosarcoma. Hodgkin's disease is a cancer of the lymphatic system, and in lymphocytic leukemia, the proliferation of defective lymphocytes leads to invasion of the bone marrow.

Until comparatively recently, most mastectomies involved the removal of all the lymph nodes under the arm.

Lymphogranuloma Venereum • A sexually transmissible disease caused by a parasite. *See* "Sexually Transmissible Diseases."

Macular Degeneration • An eye disorder in which gradual degeneration of a part of the retina leads to loss of central vision and eventually to legal blindness. *See* EYE.

Magnetic Resonance Scanner • *See* NUCLEAR MAGNETIC RESONANCE SCANNER.

Malaria • An infectious disease caused by several species of protozoa (parasites) that are transmitted by a mosquito that has bitten a diseased person, become infected, and then bitten another person. Occasionally it is transmitted by a blood transfusion. The natural disease occurs almost exclusively in underdeveloped tropical areas where mosquitos are prevalent, afflicting several hundred million Africans, Asians, and Latin Americans, and resulting in about 2 million deaths annually. It destroys red blood cells and causes bouts of severe chills, fever, and sweating daily, on alternate days, or at two-day intervals, depending on the particular parasite involved. The powerful drug chloroquine has successfully treated most strains of the disease, but in recent years, new strains of malaria parasites resistant to this drug present a new challenge to epidemiologists. Because of the seeming impossibility of eliminating the mosquito population in tropical areas, malaria continues to be the most widespread disease in the world and the most serious of the parasitic diseases as well.

Malignant • A term used to describe a tumor or growth that spreads to surrounding tissues or migrates through the lymphatics or bloodstream to more distant tissues and whose natural course is usually fatal. In common parlance, a malignancy is synonymous with cancer.

Malnutrition • Inadequate nourishment resulting from a substandard diet or a metabolic defect. Among common causes unrelated to the availability of adequate food are alcoholism, unnecessary vitamins substituted for essential foods, and crash dieting. Symptoms of malnutrition depend on the missing nutrients. In rare cases where a metabolic aberration such as abnormal enzyme production or glandular malfunction is the underlying cause, replacement therapy is usually effective. *See* DEFICIENCY DISEASE, ANEMIA, "Nutrition, Weight, and General Well-Being."

Malocclusion • Failure of the teeth of the upper and lower jaw to come together properly when the jaws are closed. A bite that is out of alignment should be corrected not only for esthetic reasons but also because, by achieving an even distribution of the pressures on the teeth, orthodontic correction contributes to the health of the gums. Maloccluded teeth are much more difficult to clean, and the faulty condition also subjects facial muscles to an abnormal stress that may lead to earaches and headaches. Even though orthodontia is a slow and costly process, an increasing number of adult women are finding the time and money well spent in terms of improvements in appearance and oral health.

Mammography • Specialized X-ray examination of the breasts to detect abnormal growths, especially cancer, at an early stage. *See* "Breast Care" and "Suggested Health Examinations."

Manic-depressive Illness • A mental disturbance characterized by periods of overenergized and overconfident elation followed by profound depression; also known as bipolar depression. Attacks may be severe and cyclic, with varying periods of normalcy occurring between onsets of the illness. Lithium carbonate administered at the beginning of the manic phase has a stabilizing effect on many people suffering from this disorder. *See* LITHIUM CARBONATE.

Marijuana • A mild hallucinogenic drug derived from the hemp plant (*Cannabis sativa*). Following the discovery that the active chemical ingredient in marijuana, tetrahydrocannabinol, known as THC, dramatically reduces the nausea caused by chemotherapy in most cancer patients, many states have passed laws legalizing the use of the drug for therapeutic purposes. *See* "Substance Abuse."

Massage • Kneading, rubbing, pressing, stroking various parts of the body with the hands or with special instruments for the purpose of stimulating circulation, relaxing muscles, relieving pain, reducing tension, and improving general well-being. Massage does not cause weight loss. It is one of the most ancient forms of therapy and continues to play an indispensable role in the rehabilitation program for victims of stroke, disabling arthritis, and other conditions in which muscle health has been impaired by disuse. In such cases a trained physical therapist works under the supervision of a doctor. While massage is most commonly done with the hands, electric vibrators and whirlpool baths (hydrotherapy) may be recommended for certain purposes. Family members can learn how to be helpful in relieving a tension headache or an aching shoulder by kneading the affected area rhythmically. An alcohol rubdown or massage can provide comfort following prolonged athletic exertion. Women who wish a body massage should locate a licensed masseuse through their doctor or a nurse.

Mastectomy • The surgical removal of breast tissue. *See* "Breast Care."

Mastitis • Inflammation of the breast. Mastitis may be mild or severe, chronic or acute, and is usually the result of infection or of a hormonal change. Acute mastitis may occur after delivery and during nursing when it is called puerperal mastitis. This is usually caused by bacterial infection introduced by way of the cracked skin of the nipples. Antibiotics normally cure this condition. If nursing is not to be continued, the breast must be emptied manually and lactation reduced by other medication. In rare instances chronic mastitis may follow an acute inflammation, and in still rarer cases the condition is caused by tuberculosis. *See* "Breast Care" and "Pregnancy and Childbirth."

Mastoid • Relating to the cells in the temporal bone that forms the part of the skull situated directly behind the ear. Inflammation of these cells, known as mastoiditis, usually results from an untreated infection of the middle ear. Antibiotics usually clear up an ear infection before it reaches the mastoid area.

Masturbation • Manipulation of the genitals exclusive of intercourse for the achievement of sexual gratification. Children masturbate as a means of exploring their bodies and sexual responses. Neither physical nor psychological harm results from masturbation, although guilt and anxiety are sometimes associated with the act because of the punitive measures inflicted by misinformed adults and the horror stories circulated by them. Mutual masturbation is commonly practiced as a form of foreplay preceding sexual intercourse. *See* "Sexual Health."

Measles • A childhood disease, also called rubeola, against which there is an effective immunizing vaccine. It should not be confused with German measles, called rubella, and discussed under that heading.

Medic Alert • A three-part system for emergency medical protection consisting of a metal emblem worn on the wrist or around the neck that identifies otherwise hidden medical problems, a wallet card with additional information, and an emergency, 24-hour, toll-free telephone answering service to provide still further information about the wearer's physical condition and medical needs in the event of collapse. For women with diabetes, a life-threatening allergy to insect stings, or other problems that could lead to the need for prompt professional attention, the Medic Alert identification can prevent potential disaster. The lifetime membership fee of $15 covers the cost of the engraved bracelet, the wallet card that is reissued each year, and the central record of the member's disabilities. The fee is tax deductible. Further information is available from the Medic Alert Foundation (a voluntary nonprofit organization). *See* "Directory of Health Information."

Medical Records • While it is assumed that physicians keep detailed records about their patients and that these records are made available when requested by another physician, every woman should keep her own medical records, and they should be kept up-to-date. Information should be compiled in a notebook set aside for the purpose and should consist of relevant family history, immunization shots and dates, pertinent facts about hospitalization, X-ray and other test reports when results are other than normal, allergies, and current medications. Side effects should also be noted. The records should be cumulative; past pages should not be discarded. Entries about surgery ten years before or a siege of pneumonia years before that may turn out to be unexpectedly helpful to the physician of the mo-

MEDIC ALERT FOR EMERGENCY MEDICAL IDENTIFICATION

ment. See FAMILY HISTORY and "You, Your Doctors, and the Health Care System."

Melanin • The pigment that determines the color of a person's skin, hair, and eyes. The main function of melanin is to provide protection against the sun's ultraviolet rays. It is produced by specialized cells called melanocytes whose number is the same in all races. Color differences are caused by the quantity of melanin produced and how it is distributed. See HAIR.

Melanoma • A tumor composed of cells heavily pigmented with melanin. A malignant melanoma, also known as black cancer, has the appearance of a mole, but it is the rarest and most treacherous type of skin cancer and the leading cause of death from skin disease. Melanomas, which do not usually develop before middle age, are more prevalent among women than among men, especially among blondes who are blue eyed and fair skinned. It is assumed that the increase in this cancer in the last few decades is due to overexposure to the sun in spite of warnings about how dangerous this practice can be. Because melanomas can develop on any skin surface, changes in the size or appearance of a mole or any bleeding or itching in the tissues that surround it should be diagnosed by a doctor immediately. The sudden appearance of a black spot on the white portion of the eyeball should be checked promptly as well.

Menarche • The first menstrual period, occurring usually in U.S. women between ages 12 and 13, with a range from ages 10 through 16. See PUBERTY.

Ménière's Disease • A disturbance of the labyrinth of the inner ear resulting in vertigo, nausea, hearing loss, and tinnitus (ringing in the ears). While the basic cause is not known, the symptoms arise because an increase in the amount of fluid in the labyrinth creates an abnormal pressure on the membrane of the labyrinth wall leading to loss of hearing and impairment of the sense of balance. These symptoms may recur frequently or as seldom as every three months. An attack may be mild and last for only a few minutes, or it may be severe, with disabling vomiting and dizziness lasting for several hours. Ménière's disease, which characteristically affects one ear, is more common among women than among men. Treatment is varied and includes the use of diuretics, antihistamines, drugs that dilate the blood vessels and speed up the circulatory flow, dietary changes that reduce cholesterol blood levels, lithium carbonate, and various tranquilizers. When all else fails and the condition seriously interferes with normal functioning, an operation on the labyrinth of the inner ear may be the only way to provide relief. Because this operation may result in a degree of permanent hearing loss, all other combinations of treatment are usually tried first.

Meningitis • Inflammation of the meninges, the membranes that surround the brain and spinal cord; also known as cerebrospinal meningitis. The inflammation may be caused by a virus or bacteria. Children are more susceptible than adults, but both sexes and all ages are vulnerable. The most acute and the most contagious forms of the disease are meningococcal meningitis and pneumococcal meningitis. In both of these diseases, the bacteria reach the meninges by way of the bloodstream from some other systemic infection.

Viral meningitis, also called aseptic, may accompany other virus infections, especially mumps, measles, herpes simplex, and AIDS. Whatever the source of the inflammation, the symptoms are the same: severe and persistent headaches accompanied by vomiting, high fever, sensitivity to light, and confusion.

Where the swelling of the meninges causes critical pressure on the brain, delirium and convulsions may also occur. It is characteristic for the patient to hold the neck stiff, because movements of the head intensify the already acute pain. Any signs that indicate the onset of meningitis should be checked immediately by a doctor who can make a definitive diagnosis following laboratory examination of a sample of cerebrospinal fluid. Treatment with one of the newer antibiotics, the cephalosporins, usually brings about recovery in bacterial meningitis if the diagnosis is made early. In the case of tubercular meningitis a longer course of therapy is necessary using the newer antitubercular drugs. The outcome of viral meningitis is varied depending on the underlying cause. A low-grade chronic meningitis may follow a simple pneumonia caused by a fungus (Cryptococcus) found in pigeon droppings. This fungal meningitis, which is characterized by fluctuating fever and chronic headaches, is diagnosed by an examination of cerebrospinal fluid and is successfully treated with amphotericin B, an antifungal drug.

Menopause • The span of time during which the menstrual cycle gradually wanes and finally ceases; also called the female climacteric or change of life. *See* "Aging Healthfully —Your Body."

Menorrhagia • The excessive loss of blood during menstruation. Among the causes are local or general infection, benign or malignant tumors of the uterus, hormonal imbalance, emotional stress, and hematologic disease. The condition may be said to exist when the amount of blood is excessive compared to usual periods. A thorough gynecological examination should be scheduled so that any abnormalities may be ruled out or treated. If menorrhagia goes untreated for several months, it is likely to be the direct cause of anemia.

Menstruation • The periodic discharge through the vagina of blood and sloughed off tissue from the uterus; the discharged matter is technically known as the menses. See "The Healthy Woman."

Mental Illness • Any of a group of psychobiological disturbances, generally categorized as psychoses (as distinct from neuroses) and characterized by such symptoms as severe and pervasive mood alterations, disorganization of thought, withdrawal from social interaction into fantasy, personality deterioration, hallucinations and delusions, bizarre behavior often without a loss of intellectual competence. While there is disagreement about the basic causes and mechanisms of severe mental disorders, one of the greatest advances in treating them has been the use of drugs that make seriously disturbed patients more accessible to other forms of therapy. In evolving current chemotherapy, basic research in the biochemistry of the brain has yielded important evidence to support the theory that psychotic disorders have a physiological foundation in errors of brain metabolism. There is also accumulating evidence that some mental illnesses, especially the syndrome known as schizophrenia, has a genetic basis. See DEPRESSION, MANIC DEPRESSIVE ILLNESS, PSYCHOSIS, SCHIZOPHRENIA, SENILE DEMENTIA, "Aging Healthfully—Your Mind and Spirit."

Mercury • A silver-white metallic element that remains fluid at ordinary temperatures; also called quicksilver. It is used as the medium of measurement in fever thermometers because of its response to heat and in sphygmomanometers, the instruments that measure blood pressure, because of its weight.

The dumping of industrial wastes containing mercury has irreversibly polluted many bodies of water in the United States and has so contaminated the fish in them that they are dangerous to eat. Occupational exposure to industrial fumes containing mercury is responsible for irreversible damage to kidneys, lungs, and the nervous system. According to the U.S. Environmental Protection Agency, *any* exposure to mercury is a health hazard.

Metabolism • The combined processes involved in the production and maintenance of the substances essential for carrying on the body's vital functions. Metabolism occurs within each cell where groups of enzymes catalyze and control the chemical reactions that must occur during the normal absorption of oxygen and nutrients and their transformation into energy. The basal metabolic rate is an important diagnostic aid that measures the rapidity of the metabolic processes when the body is at rest. The rate is abnormally high or abnormally low in certain glandular disorders. Many diseases, previously mysterious, are now known to be caused by genetically determined enzymatic aberrations in the metabolic process.

With the realization that drugs are metabolized at different rates depending on sex and age, manufacturers are adjusting recommended doses to conform with these variables, especially for patients over 60 who may have to take a maintenance medication for the next 20 years of their lives.

Metastasis • The spreading of a cancerous growth by extension to surrounding tissue (direct metastasis) or by the breaking away of clumps of diseased cells that invade other parts of the body (blood borne or lymphatic metastasis) where they settle and form secondary tumors. The invasive tumors are called metastatic growths.

Methadone • A synthetic narcotic used as a substitute for morphine and in the United States as a substitute for heroin in supervised centers for the treatment of heroin addiction. See "Substance Abuse."

Microsurgery • Meticulous surgery done under magnification using a special microscope. It is done when operating on small organs such as eyes, fallopian tubes, and ovaries; when reconnecting tiny blood vessels; and to minimize scarring.

Middle Ear • See EAR.

Midwife • See NURSE-MIDWIFE.

Migraine • See HEADACHE.

Milk • An essential food containing a good balance of fats, carbohydrates, and proteins as well as a major source of essential minerals and vitamins A and B_2. Because pasteurization destroys the vitamin C content, other sources for this nutrient, such as citrus fruits and juices, are recommended. Practically all processed milk is enriched with vitamin D and is homogenized for uniform fat distribution. An adult woman should include the equivalent of two cups of milk in her daily diet (this amount may take the form of yogurt or cottage cheese). It is inadvisable for any person to drink raw unpasteurized milk because it may cause undulant fever (brucellosis). See "Pregnancy and Childbirth," "Nutrition, Weight, and General Well-Being," UNDULANT FEVER, and LACTOSE INTOLERANCE.

Minerals • See "Nutrition, Weight, and General Well-Being."

Miscarriage • See "Pregnancy and Childbirth" and ABORTION, SPONTANEOUS.

Mole • A raised pigmented spot on the upper layers of the skin, usually brown and sometimes hairy. Moles may also have a blue appearance when buried more deeply, although the pigmentation is still brown. Yellowish rough-textured bumps produced by an abnormally active oil-secreting gland are called sebaceous moles. Any of these may be present from birth or they may appear early and disappear spontaneously. When such a blemish suddenly begins to change shape, itch, grow, or to bleed, it should be examined by a dermatologist. See MELANOMA.

Mongolism • See DOWN SYNDROME.

Moniliasis • Infection caused by a yeast-like fungus, *Candida albicans;* also known as monilia, candidiasis. See "Sexually Transmissible Diseases."

Mononucleosis, Infectious • A virus infection that causes an abnormality of and increase in the number of white blood cells containing a single nucleus; also called glandular fever. The symptoms are somewhat similar to those of the flu: fever, very sore throat, general malaise, and swollen lymph nodes. The infection is diagnosed by simple blood tests. Because the infectious agent, known as the EB virus (Epstein-Barr), is present in the throat and saliva, it is perhaps transmitted by mouth-to-mouth contact, explaining why younger people call mononucleosis the "kissing disease." The swelling of the lymph nodes is caused by the fact that the virus stimulates the number and size of the white blood cells (lymphocytes) which then become ineffective in carrying out their disease-fighting function. While the patient may suffer from extreme fatigue and complications such as a jaundiced liver, enlargement of the spleen, inflammation of the joints, or a secondary infection of the throat, hospitalization generally is not necessary.

The treatment is usually no more than bed rest, but it is important that a doctor be in charge of the patient so that medication can be prescribed if secondary conditions develop. While most patients fully recover, a small percentage are plagued with a lingering form of the illness, with general malaise, low fever, and fatigue persisting intermittently over a period of years. Instead of assuming that the patient is malingering, the continuing presence of high levels of Epstein-Barr antibodies in a blood sample can verify the fact that the virus, and not the patient's imagination, is producing the symptoms.

Mons Veneris • The mount of Venus; the triangular pad of fatty tissue and skin that covers the pubic bone; also known as the mons pubis or pubic mount. It is covered with hair from puberty onward. Following the hormonal changes of menopause, the hair may thin out and turn gray.

Morning Sickness • A feeling of queasiness and nausea experienced by about half of all pregnant women during the first few months of pregnancy. This queasiness may occur at any time during the day and for some women it may last all day long with or without vomiting, but it rarely continues beyond the twelfth week. *See* "Pregnancy and Childbirth."

Morphine • The active constituent in opium and the basis of the painkilling effects of all opiates, of which codeine (methyl morphine) is the weakest. The application of morphine in current practice is largely restricted to terminal patients and severe accident cases, but the use in these cases may eventually be superseded by other drugs. It has recently been discovered that pain-killing substances far more powerful than morphine occur naturally in the brain. *See* ENDORPHIN and "Substance Abuse."

Motion Sickness • Nausea and vomiting resulting from a disturbance in the balancing mechanism of the inner ear. The discomfort may occur in a car, train, airplane, or elevator, but it is most common on a ship that is simultaneously pitching and rolling. There are various antinauseant medications that can be taken in advance of a trip. A doctor can advise on which medicine might be most suitable for the particular circumstance and what the possible side effects might be. Car sickness is rarely experienced by the driver and is less likely to occur to a passenger sitting in the front seat with the window open.

Motrin • *See* IBUPROFEN.

Mucous Membrane • Thin layers of tissue that line a body cavity, separate adjacent cavities, or envelop an organ and contain glands that secrete mucus. The membrane is actually a mixture of epithelial tissue and its underlying connective tissue. The mucus, a watery exudate or slimy secretion, keeps the tissue moist. It may change in quantity and quality with disease, especially infections.

Multiple Sclerosis • A chronic degenerative disease of the central nervous system and the brain. The cause is not known, although evidence indicates that a factor such as an allergy or a virus triggers an autoimmune response in which the body's defense system turns against its own tissues. In this disease, the category of disease-fighting cells called lymphocytes bring about the progressive destruction of the fatty material known as myelin that sheathes the nerves. The designation "multiple" is used because, while the disease attacks mainly the nerves of the spinal cord and the brain, there is no special order or pattern to the destruction. In some people the first symptom may be eye dysfunction; in others a coronary disorder or a locomotion problem. When the nerve endings of the brain are attacked, symptoms include speech changes and emotional swings.

Multiple sclerosis is prevalent mainly in temperate climates: an estimated 1 in 5,000 persons living in northern United States and 1 in 20,000 living in southern United States are affected by it. The disease commonly appears between the ages of 20 and 40, with women twice as susceptible as men. Because the symptoms are easily confused with other disorders, multiple sclerosis is often very difficult to diagnose. Research has, therefore, been directed not only toward finding the specific cause but to developing an accurate blood test that would unequivocally identify the disease and rule out all other possibilities. Treatment must be adjusted to individual cases and continually supervised, because one of the characteristics of multiple sclerosis is that it may subside for months or even years and then flare up suddenly with serious effects. Relief is usually provided by anti-inflammatory medication, corticosteroids, antispasmodics, and muscle relaxant drugs. Physical therapy, bed rest, and special diets are other forms of treatment. *See* "Directory of Health Information."

Mumps • A contagious virus disease once common in childhood and now practically eradicated thanks to long-term immunization conferred at about 15 months of age. The virus affects the salivary glands, primarily the parotids (in front of and under each ear), and often the submaxillary (at the lower jaw) and the sublingual (under the tongue) glands. It may also affect the gonads. In a typical case the glands swell and become painful; when inflammation of the joints is also present, the condition is always temporary. In many instances, however, symptoms are so mild as to go undetected. Mumps is a serious matter only when secondary complications develop. These are primarily meningoencephalitis in children, a viral infection of the nervous system, and mumps orchitis in postpubescent males, an inflammation of the testicles that is rarely serious and rarely results in sterility. *See* "Immunization Guide."

Muscular Dystrophy • Any of a group of chronic genetic diseases characterized by the progressive deterioration of the muscles. The particular designation of the dystrophy is based on the muscle groups first affected, the age of the patient at the onset of symptoms, and the rate at which the degeneration proceeds. While a dystrophic disease may affect anyone at any time, it occurs five times more often among males than females. No form of the disorder is contagious, and while no cure has yet been found, various types of treatment, including special orthopedic devices, can relieve the debilitating symptoms.

The most common and most crippling of the dystrophic diseases is Duchenne muscular dystrophy, the only one known to be transmitted entirely by female carriers, with sons having a 50 percent likelihood of being affected by the disease and daughters a 50 percent chance of becoming carriers. Fortunately for women who are aware of the presence of the disease in their family, there is a blood test for the detection of carriers of Duchenne MD. *See* GENETIC COUNSELING and "Directory of Health Information."

Myasthenia Gravis • A comparatively rare neuromuscular disease characterized by abnormal weakness and fatigue following normal exertion. Depending on the muscles affected, symptoms include drooping eyelids, double vision, difficulty in locomotion, incapacity in chewing and swallowing, and, in the most threatening cases, inability of the muscles controlling respiration to function. The disease may be triggered by an infection, pregnancy, or a tumor of the thymus gland or it may be due to an inherited fault in the body's autoimmune system. Whatever the basic reason for the disturbance, the immediate cause appears to be an aberration in the neuromuscular production of the chemical acetylcholine, essential for stimulating the muscle fibers to contract. Successful treatment for some patients has consisted of medicines that help transmit nerve impulses to the muscles; others have been helped by surgical removal of the thymus gland (thymectomy); most recently still others have been treated with plasmapheresis. This procedure involves the pumping out of the patient's blood so that it can be cleansed of destructive antibodies (such as would exist in cases of faulty immunologic response). *See* "Directory of Health Information."

Mycoses • *See* FUNGAL INFECTIONS.

Myocardial Infarction • *See* HEART ATTACK.

Myopia • *See* NEARSIGHTEDNESS.

Nail • Extension of the outermost skin layer of the fingers and toes. Nails are formed from the fibrous protein substance called keratin that also forms the hair that grows outward from the scalp. This elastic horny tissue (actually made up of dead cells) is pushed upward from the softer living matrix of the nail below the cuticle. It takes about six months for a nail to be replaced from the base of the cuticle to the tip of the finger. The general well-being of nails is best maintained by good hygiene and diet. No special supplement is necessary, nor does eating gelatin toughen the nails.

Healthy nails should be pale pink, smooth, and shiny. Variations in their appearance may be indications not only of local disorders but of serious diseases. When nails are bluish and the fingertips clubbed, they are a sign of a circulatory or respiratory disorder; spoon-shaped nails are a sign of anemia; split or deformed nails may occur when there is arthritic inflammation of the finger joints; bitten nails indicate a response to emotional stress or simply a habit. White spots on the nails may develop after a nail has been bruised or injured or when too much pressure is exerted at the cuticle during manicuring. A more serious injury may lead to severe pain and the loss of the nail. Unless the nail bed from which the nail grows has been crushed, the new nail that grows back will be normal in all ways.

Fingernails and toenails are vulnerable to fungal infections, particularly to ringworm that can spread quickly into the nails from their free edge, causing discoloration and deformity. The most effective treatment consists in keeping the fingers and toes as clean and dry as possible and using the fungicide griseofulvin over a period of many months or until the diseased nail has been replaced by a healthy one. Peeling or splitting may be a sign of poor nutrition or a reaction to a particular brand of detergent or nail polish; the use of nail-hardening preparations may have an adverse effect, especially in chronic or extreme cases. Brittle nails that split often are a common problem of aging related to poor circulation. Splitting is also the result of constant immersion in water. Because nails swell when they are wet and shrink when they are dry, the repeated change in their condition makes them vulnerable at the tips.

Ingrown toenails are common among women whose shoes are too tight. It is usually the nail of the big toe that is forced to grow forward into the toe's nail bed at one or both corners. This distorted growth can be extremely painful, and it can also lead to infection. Self-treatment is possible, if undertaken early, by inserting a tiny cotton swab under the nail edge, thus lifting up the nail so that it is less painful and can grow forward more easily. During treatment comfortable low-heeled shoes should be worn, because high heels throw body weight against the toes. If there is any sign of redness or pain in the area, a podiatrist or medical doctor should be consulted without further delay. Ingrown toenails are best prevented by cutting the nails straight across rather than in an oval arch and by wearing shoes that fit properly.

Manicuring and pedicuring too often is likely to be damaging, and if nail lacquer is regularly used, it should not extend to the base of the nail because the live tissue there should be exposed rather than constantly covered.

Among the more common diseases associated with the nails are infections of the fingers or toes resulting from cuts, hangnails, or any lesions that permit bacterial invasion. The application of a softening cream will decrease the likelihood of cracked cuticles and hangnails. Such infections, called paronychia, can be extremely painful because of the pus and inflammation at the side of the nail. When soaking does not lead to drainage, it may be necessary to have the infected area lanced. Antibiotics are usually prescribed, especially if there is any danger of the spread of the infection.

Narcolepsy • A neurological abnormality characterized by four symptoms that may occur singly or in any combination. The most common symptom is constant fatigue combined with attacks of sleep at inappropriate times. The second is a loss of muscle tone (catalepsy) triggered by a strong emotional response such as anger, laughter, or astonishment. The onset of catalepsy causes total body paralysis even though the mind is alert and awake. The other symptoms are the occurrence of frighteningly real hallucinations immediately before falling asleep or immediately after arising and the experience of complete momentary paralysis at the same times. Anyone who suspects he or she has the illness should arrange for a simple and accurate laboratory test in which brain wave patterns and eye movements are monitored during sleep. While narcolepsy is not yet curable, various treatments are available for the different symptoms. The disease is under continuing study at sleep disorder clinics that are a part of hospital research centers. See "Directory of Health Information."

Narcotic • A drug characterized by its ability to alleviate pain, calm anxiety, and induce sleep, such as opium and its derivatives or synthesized chemicals. See "Substance Abuse."

National Institute for Occupational Safety and Health • A federal agency that monitors working conditions as they relate to health and safety and conducts an ongoing Health Hazard Evaluation Program. A formal request for such an evaluation may be made to the agency by any three employees, by a union, or by the employer. See "Health on the Job."

Natural Childbirth • See "Pregnancy and Childbirth."

Nausea • The feeling that signals the possible onset of vomiting. Nausea occurs when the nerve endings in the stomach and in various other parts of the body are irritated. This irritation is transmitted to the part of the brain that controls the vomiting reflex, and when the signals are strong enough, vomiting does occur. Nausea may be triggered by psychological as well as physical conditions. Many people are nauseated by the sight of blood, unattractive sights and smells, strong feelings of fear or excitement, severe pain, or nervous tension. Nausea may accompany physical problems such as infectious disease, gallbladder inflammation, ulcer, appendicitis, the early months of pregnancy, and, most typically, indigestion, motion sickness, and irritation of the inner ear. The nausea caused by anticancer drugs is treated by the active chemical (THC) in marijuana, available through the National Cancer Institute. In some women nausea is a side effect of contraceptive pills. The symptom may be relieved by taking the pill at bedtime rather than in the morning. When nausea is chronic and unrelated to any specific condition, stress is a likely cause that might be explored and alleviated by psychotherapy.

Nearsightedness • A structural defect of the eye in which the lens brings the image into focus in front of rather than directly on the retina so that objects at a distance are not seen clearly; also called myopia. This aberration of vision is usually inherited and occurs when the eyeball is deeper than normal from front to back. Nearsightedness manifests itself in childhood, becoming worse until adulthood, when it stabilizes at approximately age 40. Corrective glasses or contact lenses prescribed by an ophthalmologist or an optometrist should, therefore, be checked regularly for necessary adjustments.

Correction by a surgical procedure called radial keratomy was introduced in 1980, and although some patients are satisfied with the results, the long-term effects of this expensive operation have yet to be definitely evaluated.

Neck, Stiff • Absolute or relative inability to move one's head without experiencing neck pain. The immediate cause in severe cases is inflammation of the nerve endings related to the spinal vertebrae. In less acute cases it may be muscle fatigue, tension, or intermittent exposure to blasts of cold air. It may follow a whiplash injury or it may be an early symptom of a bacterial or viral infection of the meninges such as polio, meningitis, and other diseases affecting the nervous system. It also can be a symptom of cervical osteoarthritis. When the pain is no more than a "crick" in the neck, it usually can be alleviated by aspirin and a heating pad or by skillful massage.

Neoplasm • The general term for any new and abnormal tissue growth; a tumor, either malignant or benign.

Nephritis • *See* GLOMERULONEPHRITIS.

Nephrosis • *See* KIDNEY DISORDERS.

Nervous Breakdown • *See* DEPRESSION.

Nervous System • The brain, spinal cord, and nerves—the parts of the body that control and coordinate all activities of the body. *See* "The Healthy Woman."

Neuralgia • Pain in the form of a sharp intermittent spasm along the path of a nerve, usually associated with neuritis. The term is considered imprecise except when it designates the disorder trigeminal neuralgia or the condition known as post-herpetic neuralgia that may follow a case of herpes zoster or shingles, especially when the disorder occurs during one's later years.

Neuritis • Inflammation of a nerve or a group of nerves. The symptoms vary widely from decreased sensitivity or paralysis of a particular part of the body to excruciating pain. Treatment varies with the cause of the inflammation. Generalized neuritis may result from toxic levels of lead, arsenic, or alcohol, from particular deficiency diseases, from bacterial infections such as syphilis, or from a severe allergy response. Among the disorders that are caused by neuritis in a particular group of nerves are Bell's palsy, herpes zoster, sciatica, and trigeminal neuralgia.

Neuromuscular Diseases • A category of disorders affecting those parts of the nervous system that control muscle function. *See* CEREBRAL PALSY, PARKINSONISM, BELL'S PALSY,

NOISE

MULTIPLE SCLEROSIS, and MYASTHENIA GRAVIS.

Neurosis • A form of maladjustment in relationship to oneself and to others; usually a manifestation of anxiety that may or may not be expressed in chronic or occasional physical symptoms; also called psychoneurosis.

Nicotine • The powerful drug in tobacco that causes people to become addicted to smoking and to experience withdrawal symptoms when the drug dependency is overcome. *See* SMOKING and "Substance Abuse."

NIOSH • *See* NATIONAL INSTITUTE FOR OCCUPATIONAL SAFETY AND HEALTH.

Nipples • *See* "Fitness," "Sexual Health," and "Breast Care."

Nitrate, Nitrite • *See* "Nutrition, Weight, and General Well-Being."

Noise • Strictly speaking, any unwanted sound. The unit that expresses the relative intensity of sound is the decibel. On the decibel scale 0 represents absolute silence and 130 is the sound level that causes physical pain to the ear. A civilized two-way conversation measures about 50 decibels. The background noises in major American cities measure more than 70 decibels. Rock and disco music are usually played at about 110 decibels.

High intensity sounds cause physiological damage. The cells that make up the organ of Corti in the cochlea, which transmits sound vibrations to the auditory nerve, are hairlike structures that break down either partially or totally when subjected to abnormally strong sound vibrations. In the cochlea of retired steelworkers, for example, these hair cells are almost totally collapsed, and it is estimated that 60 percent of workers exposed to high intensity on-the-job noise will have suffered significant hearing loss by age 65 in spite of such safety precautions as ear plugs, ear muffs, "soundproofed" enclosures, and the like.

The Environmental Protection Agency estimates that more than 16 million people in the United States suffer from hearing loss caused by sonic pollution and another 40 million are exposed to potential health hazards without knowing it. The dangers to the emotional and physical well-being of individuals, families, and communities are in many cases obvious, but in even more instances they are insidious and cumulative. Here are some facts that trouble environmentalists and health experts. According to the National Institute for Occupational Safety and Health, two or three years of daily exposure to 90 decibel sounds will result in some loss of hearing. Constant exposure to moderately loud noise (over 75 decibels) increases the pulse rate and respiration and may eventually cause tinnitus, ulcers, high blood pressure, and mental problems associated with stress. A daylong ride in a snowmobile can irreversibly damage the organ of hearing. Many young people who regularly attend rock concerts where the sound is amplified to ear-splitting levels and who wear earphones when they listen to loud music have already sustained some permanent hearing loss; according to an extensive survey of students entering college, 60 percent have some impairment of hearing. Steady, moderately loud noise (power mowers, dishwashers, washing machines, vacuum cleaners, power tools, garbage disposal units) can cause the equivalent in housewives of battle fatigue in soldiers: constricted blood vessels, increased activity of the adrenal glands, irritability, dizziness, and distorted vision. People who are subjected to or subject themselves to high intensity sound are nastier and more aggressive than those who live and work in quiet surroundings. Children who live within earshot of the acoustical overload produced by the traffic on a superhighway are found to have more learning problems than a similar sampling of children whose nervous systems do not have to cope with constant background noise.

If exposure to noise is occasionally unavoidable, the use of ear plugs is recommended. If these are not available in an unexpected situation imperiling one's hearing, the ears should be covered with one's hands or fingers. Elements in the immediate environment that make unnecessary noise should be eliminated or toned down wherever possible. In addition, the Environmental Protection Agency encourages local community groups to establish noise complaint centers empowered to investigate and eliminate all sources of unnecessary noise.

Nonspecific Urethritis • *See* "Sexually Transmissible Diseases."

Nonsteroidal Anti-inflammatory Drugs (NSAIDs) • A new category of drugs as powerful as aspirin in controlling inflammation of the joints but which do not irritate the stomach or potentially cause internal bleeding when taken in the large doses necessary for long-term treatment of arthritis. Among these drugs are: clinoral (Sulindac), tolmetin (Tolectin), indomethacin (Indocin), phenylbutazone (Butazolidin), ibuprofen (Motrin and Rufen), and piroxicam (Feldene). This latter is the most recent NSAID and is preferred by many patients because it needs to be taken only once a day and is said to produce very few negative side effects.

Nosebleed • Bleeding, either mild or profuse, from the rupture of blood vessels inside the nose; technically called epistaxis. Nosebleeds may be caused by injury, disease, blowing one's nose too energetically, strenuous exercise, sudden ascent to high altitudes, or constantly breathing in dry air that causes the mucous membranes to crack. Other causes are hypertension, tumors, and excessive alcoholic intake. Many women experience nosebleeds during pregnancy. They may also occur for no discernible reason and with no ill effect. Bleeding can usually be controlled by sitting up (not standing or lying down), tilting the head forward (tilting the head back can cause the blood to obstruct the trachea), and pressing the soft flesh directly above the nostril against the bone for a few minutes. If this method is ineffective, the nostril may be packed with sterile cotton gauze that should remain in place for several hours. If the bleeding cannot be stopped promptly, emergency hospital treatment is advisable. If nosebleeds occur so frequently that they interfere with normal routines, it may be necessary to tie or cauterize the bleeding vessel. Any bleeding from the nose or mouth following an accident or a bad fall requires immediate medical attention.

Nuclear Magnetic Resonance (NMR) Scanner • A diagnostic technique that can provide more detailed cross-sectional images than X-rays or CAT scanners. In spite of its name, this device uses no nuclear power and has no significant radiation side effects.

Nuclear Medicine • A special branch of radiology that applies the advances in nuclear physics to the diagnosis and treatment of disease. One of the most important applications is the use of radioactive isotopes to irradiate abnormalities within the body so that they become visible on scanning machines. Radioactive chemicals are widely used in nuclear cardiology to diagnose abnormalities in coronary arteries and heart function, and in treating certain cancers and hyperthyroidism. Radioactive needles have made delicate nerve surgery possible.

Nuprin • *See* IBUPROFEN.

Nutrition • *See* "Nutrition, Weight, and General Well-Being."

Obesity • Overweight in excess of 20 percent more than the average for one's age, height, and skeletal structure. *See* "Nutrition, Weight, and General Well-Being."

Occupational Hazards • *See* NATIONAL INSTITUTE FOR OCCUPATIONAL SAFETY AND HEALTH and "Health on the Job."

Occupational Therapy • Formerly associated only with the use of arts and crafts for the rehabilitation of the mentally ill or the psychological well-being of the elderly, occupational therapy is now an indispensable aspect of the team approach to patients who have to learn new ways of coping with the mechanics and logistics of daily living as a result of temporary or permanent impairment. An occupational therapist teaches the victim of a stroke how to get dressed and undressed and how to get things done in the kitchen. A patient progressively crippled by arthritis is taught new ways of getting into and out of an automobile. When irreversible disablement occurs because of a spinal injury, an occupational therapist trains the patient to accomplish essential tasks in alternative ways so that the greatest degree of independence can be achieved. Professionals in this category are licensed and usually work under the supervision of an attending doctor in a hospital or clinic, providing services on an inpatient or outpatient basis, or, following a hospital stay, in the patient's home. *See* PHYSICAL THERAPY.

Opiate • Any drug derived from opium, the dried juice of the unripened seed pods of the poppy known as *Papaver somniferum*. All opiates have the effect of depressing the central nervous system to a greater or lesser degree, acting as a painkiller, producing euphoria, and inducing sleep. Morphine is the strongest of the naturally derived opiates; heroin is one of its semisynthetic derivatives; codeine, the weakest of the opiates, is derived from morphine or may be produced directly from gum opium. Paregoric, once widely used as a tranquilizer for babies, is an anise-flavored tincture of opium similar to laudanum, another opiate more widely used in the nineteenth century than aspirin is now. All opium derivatives are addictive and their use is strictly controlled by law. *See* "Substance Abuse."

Oral Contraceptives • *See* "Contraception and Abortion."

Oral Sex • Sexual stimulation by mouth and tongue of the female genitals, called cunnilingus, and sexual stimulation by mouth and tongue of the male genitals, called fellatio. Oral-genital contact is widely practiced as part of sexual foreplay and as a way of achieving orgasm. While it is a guaranteed method of avoiding pregnancy, it by no means eliminates the possibility of communicating sexually transmissible diseases.

Orgasm • The climax of sexual excitement, accompanied in women by vaginal contractions and in men by the ejaculation of semen. *See* "Sexual Health."

Orthodontia • The branch of dentistry that specializes in the correction of irregularities in the way upper and lower teeth come together when the jaw is closed. Irregularities causing the malocclusion range from teeth that overlap because of crowding, teeth that protrude forward from the upper jaw and tilt inward from the lower jaw because of thumbsucking, conspicuously wide spaces between teeth, and other problems such as inherited jawbone structure requiring minor surgery.

Although orthodontia is often undertaken for cosmetic reasons, dentists agree that gross malocclusions should be corrected for reasons of health: chewing is improved, cleaning is simplified, and gum disease is less likely to occur. Corrections in adults are slower and more painful to achieve than in children and adolescents, but in some cases they may be worthwhile to improve the health of the mouth.

The orthodontist takes a series of X-rays of the mouth and jaw and studies them to determine the extent and nature of the correction advisable. Plaster casts are made, and then various appliances for repositioning the teeth are selected to achieve the correction. These include braces, wires, plastic or metal brackets, neckbraces, rubber bands, and retainer plates. The appliances are readjusted regularly to keep pace with the slow shifting of the teeth. Wearing the retainer plate, which is scarcely visible because it is molded of transparent plastic, is essential during this period so that the straightened teeth do not drift back to their former position.

Before embarking on extensive orthodontia, a prospective patient should, in discussion with the family dentists and the orthodontist, compare the relative benefits of the treatment with any disadvantages, such as adverse effects on teeth, discomfort, time, and expense. *See* MALOCCLUSION, TEMPOROMANDIBULAR JOINT.

Orthotics • A specialty of medical science and mechanics that deals with the support of weak muscles and/or joints. Orthotists design custom-made devices to insert into shoes in cases where correction increases efficiency and reduces pain during jogging and other athletic activities. Orthotists also provide specially fitted braces and other supports made of molded plastic or lightweight metal to be worn as recommended by doctors for patients with potentially deforming diseases of the joints or spine.

Osteoarthritis • A chronic degenerative disease affecting the joints of men and women equally, in most cases after the age of 40; also called degenerative joint disease. See ARTHRITIS.

Osteopathy • A type of therapy practiced by osteopaths (Doctors of Osteopathy), which utilizes generally accepted principles of medicine and surgery but which emphasizes the importance of normal body mechanics and manipulation of the body to correct faulty body structure. In the United States today there actually is little difference between the way doctors of osteopathy and of medicine diagnose and treat disease.

Osteoporosis • Degenerative porousness of the bones, causing them to fracture more easily and to heal more slowly. Osteoporosis is a more common ailment of aging women than of aging men and is assumed to be related to the decrease in estrogen production following the menopause. See "Aging Healthfully—Your Body."

Ostomy • An operation in which an artificial opening is formed between two hollow organs or between a hollow organ and the abdominal wall, enabling a diseased organ to be "bypassed." Examples are: ileostomy (between ileum and abdominal wall) and ureterostomy (between ureter(s) and abdominal wall). See COLOSTOMY and "Directory of Health Information."

Otosclerosis • A condition in which one of the three bones of hearing, the stirrup, becomes immobilized by abnormal bony deposits. Otosclerosis, a more common cause of deafness among women than among men, can sometimes be corrected by surgery. See HEARING LOSS.

Ovarian Cysts and Tumors • See "Gynecologic Diseases and Treatment."

Ovary • The female sex organ whose function is the production of eggs and the female sex hormones estrogen and progesterone. See "The Healthy Woman" and "Gynecologic Diseases and Treatment."

Overweight • See "Nutrition, Weight, and General Well-Being."

Ovulation • The process by which an egg cell or ovum is released from the surface of the ovary to travel through the fallopian tube for possible fertilization. See "The Healthy Woman."

Oxytocin • A pituitary hormone naturally secreted under the normal circumstances of delivery for the stimulation of uterine contractions and of the secretion of milk. Synthetic oxytocin (Pitocin) may be given by injection or in pills to induce labor or to speed up contractions in a prolonged and painful labor. See "Pregnancy and Childbirth."

Pacemaker, Artificial • A transistorized device implanted under the skin in the area of the shoulder and connected by wires to electrodes implanted in heart tissue for the purpose of supplying a normal beat when the natural pacemaker has been irreversibly damaged or destroyed by disease. The effectiveness of artificial pacemakers is based on the fact that the heart naturally generates electrical impulses that cause the normal contractions of the blood-pumping mechanism. The implantation operation is safe and simple. The device with all its components weighs less than half a pound, and recent models last for about eight years. Pacemakers are tested regularly by telemetry so that operational defects can be corrected.

Pain • A distress signal from some part of the body, usually of brief duration and originating in the largest number of cases in a traceable disorder. Pain—throbbing, aching, pulsating, stabbing—arises in two different ways. Peripheral pain resulting from a cut finger or an abscessed tooth begins in nerve fibers located in the extremities or around the body organs; central pain, usually caused by injuries or disorders affecting the brain or central nervous system such as a tumor, stroke, or slipped disk, originates in the spinal cord or the brain itself. When this type of pain is chronic, it is the most difficult to assuage. Both types of impulses eventually reach the brain stem and thalamus where pain perception takes place.

It is now known that the brain produces chemical substances that are the body's own opiates against pain perception. These are known as endorphins and include the recently isolated dynorphin, which is 200 times more powerful than morphine in its action and 50 times more powerful than any previously known substance of its kind. It is hoped that with greater understanding of how these chemicals work, they will be used as powerful nonaddictive drugs for the control of pain as well as to produce other important effects on the brain for those suffering from mental illness and seizure disorders.

In the meantime, where pain is chronic and severe or where the perception of pain has become a problem in itself separated from its possible source, treatment is available in pain clinics that have made this problem their specialty. Among the methods that provide relief, separately or in combination, are acupuncture, electrical stimulation, biofeedback, and hypnosis. The chief dangers connected with the use of chemicals for minimizing severe or persistent pain are serious adverse effects of a particular chemical itself or in combination with other drugs and the possibility of drug addiction.

Palpitations • *See* ARRHYTHMIAS.

Pancreas • The large, mixed gland situated below and in back of the stomach and the liver. The pancreas is about 6 inches long. Its function is two-fold. One is the secretion of pancreatic juice, which contains the enzymes that flow into the digestive tract and are essential for the continuing breakdown in the duodenum and small intestine of fats, carbohydrates, and proteins. The second function is the secretion of insulin produced by almost a million clusters of specialized cells called the islets of Langerhans.

When these cells produce insufficient insulin for the body's needs, the result is diabetes. Other disorders of the pancreas include the formation of stones and of benign and malignant tumors, both treated surgically. Inflammation of the pancreas, pancreatitis, may be acute or chronic. Acute pancreatitis is a grave condition in which one of the enzymes begins to devour the tissue itself, leading to hemorrhage, vomiting, severe abdominal pain, and collapse. It may be associated with overdrinking, gallbladder infection, gallstones, or trauma. Chronic pancreatitis may be the result of recurrent acute pancreatitis. It is characterized by abdominal and back pain, diarrhea, and jaundice. When these symptoms exist, exploratory surgery is usually recommended to rule out the possibility of cancer.

Pantothenic Acid • One of the B complex vitamins. *See* "Nutrition, Weight, and General Well-Being."

Pap Test • A diagnostic procedure used chiefly for detecting the first signs of cancer of the cervix and sometimes the uterus. The test is named for Dr. George Papanicolaou, the American anatomist who discovered that cancerous cells are shed by uterine tumors into the surrounding vaginal fluid and can, therefore, be detected when a sample is examined microscopically. *See* "Gynecologic Diseases and Treatment."

Paranoia • A mental disturbance characterized by delusions of persecution and sometimes accompanied by feelings of power and grandeur. A clinically paranoiac person may not suffer from personality disintegration and may appear to be living a normal life, but it is not unusual for the disturbance to erupt into psychotic behavior. Antipsychotic drugs such as Thorazine and Compazine are often prescribed for clinical paranoia. The term "paranoid" may also be used to describe a general mental state that is not psychotic but is characterized by distrustfulness, suspiciousness, and a tendency toward persecution of others. This mental state frequently accompanies amphetamine and cocaine abuse and may also result from the intermittent use of marijuana. *See* "Substance Abuse."

Parkinsonism • A mild or severe disorder of body movement characterized by slow mobility, stiffness, and tremor; also known as Parkinson's disease. Most of the estimated million and a half victims of the disorder are over 60. Symptoms similar to those of Parkinson's disease may set in after encephalitis lethargica (once called "sleeping sickness"), may result from a stroke or a brain tumor, or may be a reversible side effect of tranquilizers such as Thorazine or antihypertensives such as Serpasil. True parkinsonism is a disorder of a particular group of brain cells that normally release a substance called dopamine that is essential to the regulation of normal body movement. In most cases the debilitating aspects of the disease are now controlled by dopamine medications in combination with other drugs. Surgery, physical therapy, and supportive psychotherapy are additional forms of treatment that can reduce the damaging effects on the body as well as on the personality of victims. Because patients over 60 are likely to be on medication for some other condition, the supervising doctor should be expected to make a regular check of all prescriptions being filled so that a dangerous combination of drugs can be avoided.

The most positive advances in treatment have been achieved by Mexican scientists who transplanted tissue from the adrenal glands into an appropriate part of the brain. Because these glands produce a hormone chemically akin to dopamine, the transplanted cells increase the brain's dopamine production. This experimental surgery, first performed in Mexico City in 1987 and now increasingly performed in the United States, has resulted in dramatic improvement in the physical and psychological well-being of victims of this disabling disease.

Patch Test • A diagnostic procedure for determining hypersensitivity to a particular allergen by applying it to the surface of the skin in a diluted solution or suspension. A positive allergic response is indicated by the appearance of a raised welt or hive caused by the body's histamine production. A similar test injects the attenuated allergen between the layers of the skin.

Pelvic Inflammatory Disease • A potentially dangerous condition in which infectious bacteria attack the uterus and other reproductive organs. The infection has been traced to the use of the contraceptive device known as the Dalkon Shield, and it may also be sexually transmitted. If it is not promptly and successfully treated with antibiotics, it can cause sterility. See "Gynecologic Diseases and Treatment," and "Sexually Transmissible Diseases."

Penicillin • The first of the antibiotics, discovered in 1929 by Sir Alexander Fleming in its natural form in the mold *Penicillium notatum;* now used to designate a group of related chemicals obtained from several molds or produced synthetically in various forms. The widespread application of penicillin is based on its ability to destroy bacteria harmful to humans without harming humans themselves. In some few cases, however, penicillin sensitivity rules out its use in favor of some other antibiotic. Any possibility of adverse effects should always be reported to the doctor and should especially be transmitted to hospital personnel in an emergency situation in which massive doses might create the greater emergency of anaphylactic shock.

Pep Pills • *See* AMPHETAMINE and "Substance Abuse."

Peptic Ulcer • *See* ULCER.

Perineum • The triangular layer of skin between the vulva and the anus in the female and between the scrotum and the anus in the male. Beneath the perineum in the female are the muscles and fibrous tissues that must stretch sufficiently to accommodate the passage of the baby during childbirth. To prevent the danger of tearing, a simple surgical incision called a perineal episiotomy is often performed. See "Pregnancy and Childbirth."

Periodontal Disease • The deteriorative process in which the tissues surrounding a tooth are destroyed by bacteria to the point where erosion of the bone results in the loosening and eventual loss of the tooth itself. While assiduous cleaning and flossing of teeth can keep cavities at a minimum and contribute to the health of the gums, periodontal disease is caused by a particular type of bacteria that thrive in the tartar that forms when some kinds of dental plaque become hardened. Pockets of infection gradually surround the tooth, and if they are not cleaned out by a periodontal specialist either by deep scaling or surgery (or a combination of both) they will eventually undermine the tooth. Until new preventive measures still in the experimental stage become a practical reality, the best protection against periodontal disease is frequent cleaning of the teeth by a dental hygienist, abstaining from smoking, and after age 35, regularly scheduled checkups by a periodontist as recommended by one's regular dentist. See GINGIVITIS.

Peritonitis • Inflammation of the peritoneum, the membrane that lines the abdominal cavity and covers the organs within it. Peritonitis may be chronic or acute. Chronic peritonitis is a comparatively rare condition associated with tuberculosis. The cause of acute peritonitis is usually the perforation or rupture of the appendix with a consequent spread of bacteria and interference of circulation. Symptoms are immobilizing abdominal pain, shallow breathing, and clammy skin. The condition is an emergency requiring prompt hospitalization and a more precise diagnosis on the basis of X-rays, blood tests, and physical exploration. Surgery is almost always inevitable.

Perspiration • The process by which the salty fluid (99 percent water and 1 percent urea and other wastes) is excreted by the sweat glands of the skin; also the fluid itself. The body has approximately 2 million sweat glands located in the lowest layers of the skin. They are connected with the outer skin layer, the epidermis, by tiny spiral-shaped tubes. The largest sweat glands are located in the groin and the armpit. The sweat glands normally produce about 1 1/2 pints of sweat a day in a temperate climate. The chief function of perspiration is to maintain constant body temperature despite variation in environmental conditions or energy output. Thus, when the internal or external temperature goes up, sweat can be seen on the skin surface where it cools the body by evaporation. The sweating process is controlled by the hypothalamus at the base of the brain. Because this gland is also responsive to emotional stress, fear and excitement will cause an increase in perspiration. "Breaking out in a cold sweat" is a common phenomenon.

Any disturbance in the functioning of the sweat glands is likely to be a symptom of some other disorder. Excessive perspiration may be due to a disease that also produces a high fever such as malaria or one that produces a chronic rise in temperature such as tuberculosis. Excessive sweating and urinating are possible symptoms of untreated diabetes. The hot flashes of the menopause are often accompanied by heavy sweating. Excessive sweating of the palms or soles of the feet is usually psychogenic in origin. Cold sweats accompany withdrawal from some addictive drugs, especially heroin.

While perspiration contains certain antibacterial chemicals that protect the skin surface, it can also be an irritant to tender skin. Prickly heat rash occurs when the sweat glands become blocked and the ducts leading to the skin surface rupture. The condition is usually a consequence of unaccustomed and profuse perspiration that keeps the skin damp. While prickly heat is more common among babies than among adults, clothing that chafes can cause it in adults as well. Fresh perspiration does not have an unpleasant odor. What is called "body odor" is caused by the bacteria that thrive in the damp sweaty areas of the skin that are not exposed to air, especially under the arms, in the folds of the genitals, and between the toes. *See* ANTIPERSPIRANTS.

Pessary • A device, often in the shape of a ring, worn inside the vagina to support a prolapsed uterus; also a vaginal suppository and sometimes another term for a contraceptive diaphragm.

pH • A measure of the degree of alkalinity or acidity of a given solution; the letters derive from *pouvoir Hydrogène* ("hydrogen power" in French), because the concentration of the hydrogen ion determines the pH number. Acidity is indicated by pH values from 0 to 7; pH 7.0 is neutral, and pH values above 7 indicate alkalinity.

Pharyngitis • Inflammation, either acute or chronic, of the pharynx, the tube of muscles and membranes that forms the throat cavity extending from the back of the mouth to the esophagus. Infection is most commonly viral, occurring as a minor sore throat. This type of infection usually runs its course in a few days and does not require treatment with antibiotics.

In more serious cases the cause is bacterial, as in streptococcus or strep throat, and results in high fever, severe discomfort when swallowing, and a stiff neck. It is extremely important that a sore throat or tonsillitis accompanied by fever over 100° F be checked by a doctor to prevent serious complications. A throat culture is usually taken to verify the diagnosis of bacterial infection so that treatment with penicillin or erythromycin can begin at once. A full course of the medicine must be taken even after symptoms have disappeared in order to guard against the possibility of post-infectious rheumatic fever. Chronic pharyngitis and hoarseness are usually the result of the misuse of the voice, regular exposure to irritating vapors or fumes, or heavy intake of alcohol. Even mild pharyngitis is aggravated by smoking.

Phenobarbital • An addictive drug of the barbiturate family prescribed in supervised doses as an anticonvulsant. Combinations with other medications must be carefully monitored. *See* "Substance Abuse."

Phlebitis • Inflammation of the vein walls, most commonly of the legs, and especially where varicosities exist. Phlebitis in a superficially located vein is usually accompanied by tenderness, redness, and swelling. Simple phlebitis may be caused by overweight, progressive arterio- or atherosclerosis, or it may follow an extended convalescence requiring bed rest. Phlebitis may also accompany pregnancy. Under these circumstances, the condition is not too serious and can be treated by elevating the leg, applying heat, and taking aspirin or some other anti-inflammatory medication to reduce pain and discomfort. Support stockings may be helpful if normal activities are to be pursued.

The inflammation is potentially more serious when it develops in a deep vein. Clotting may occur on the damaged wall, a condition known as thrombophlebitis, and it may impede circulation or may break away from the wall and circulate as an embolism. Deep thrombophlebitis may cause the entire leg to become swollen and very painful. When these symptoms occur, treatment with anticoagulants is initiated to keep clot formation at a minimum. Monitoring is mandatory when taking anticoagulants so that the possibility of excessive bleeding is anticipated and prevented. When phlebitis is so severe as to be disabling or if there is a strong possibility of clot formation, surgery may be recommended. Women with a tendency to diseases of the blood vessels should make every effort to refrain from smoking. *See* THROMBOSIS.

Phobia • An irrational and exaggerated fear of an object or situation usually related to an anxiety neurosis. Everyone experiences fear as a response to what each perceives as present or impending danger, but phobic response may be so encompassing as to be immobilizing. In severe anxiety or panic attacks the victim may experience dizziness, palpitations, profuse sweating, and in some cases a tendency toward suicide. Although almost any object or situation may elicit phobia in different individuals, several have been identified as common sources of phobic response: agoraphobia, the fear of being in open places; acrophobia, the fear of heights; ailurophobia, the fear of cats; and claustrophobia, the fear of being confined in small areas.

Phobias are a form of mental illness that is difficult to cure. In some cases the phobia may decrease as a result of life experiences that resolve the underlying conflict; in other cases, when the phobia is immobilizing (as in agoraphobia) or seriously interferes with one's career (as in fear of flying or of using an elevator), anti-anxiety medication combined with psychotherapy may produce positive results. Group therapy should be considered for mutual support in dealing with the same problem. *See* "Directory of Health Information."

Physical Examination • A part of a medical evaluation, the results of which provide information as to the general and specific condition of a person's health. In order to perform a comprehensive medical evaluation, the doctor must obtain the medical history, perform routine diagnostic tests, and do a careful physical examination of the various parts of the body, including an internal pelvic examination. It is extremely important to have periodic examinations so that any changes from previous evaluations can be recognized and treated if necessary. See "You, Your Doctor, and the Health Care System," and "Suggested Health Examinations."

Physical Therapy • Treatment of disease or disability by physical means, exercises, water, heat, massage, and electricity. Patients who benefit from this form of treatment are victims of stroke or polio, those who have neuromuscular or degenerative joint diseases, or those who have suffered a spinal injury or some other injury requiring the use of a cast and the eventual rehabilitation of muscles. Techniques and means depend on the patient's needs. Exercises designed to strengthen specific muscles or to coordinate the movements of a group of muscles may be active or passive. In passive exercise the therapist moves the affected parts until the patient is able to do so alone. In hydrotherapy the patient exercises in water which, because of its buoyancy, requires a smaller expenditure of energy. When patients are entirely immobilized as may occur in a stroke, physical therapy is begun in bed with massaging and applying heat. Physical therapists who are trained in schools approved by the American Medical Association usually work under the supervision of doctors in hospitals and clinics that have rehabilitation programs for both inpatients and outpatients. See OCCUPATIONAL THERAPY.

Pineal Gland • A small pinecone-shaped structure (pineal body) near the center of the brain but not a part of it. Prior to puberty it secretes a hormone called melatonin that inhibits the biochemical process of sexual maturation.

Pituitary Gland • The pituitary gland, no larger than a pea, is situated at the base of the brain directly above the back of the nose. It is controlled in part by the hypothalamus and in part by the hormones from the various endocrine glands (biofeedback), and it in turn controls the hormone production of all the other endocrine glands. See "The Healthy Woman."

Placebo • A preparation or procedure without pharmacologic or physiologic properties, which is administered for psychological benefit. Although placebos are no more than inert concoctions, they are known to cause a measurable difference in how many patients feel. Called "the placebo effect," this result is thought to be connected in some way with the brain's release of endorphins.

Placebos play an indispensable role in evaluating the effectiveness of new drugs. In a procedure known as the double bind test, half the participants are given the coded drug and the other half a coded placebo similar in appearance. When the test is completed, the code is deciphered and the results are tabulated and compared for assessment of the drug.

Placenta • The organ that attaches to the wall of the uterus during pregnancy and through which the developing fetus is nourished by the mother because it serves as an exchange between the mother's and the fetus's vascular systems; also known as afterbirth. See "Pregnancy and Childbirth."

Plantar Wart • A wart that develops in the sole of the foot. Such growths often are especially painful because they grow inward and thus interfere with walking. All warts are technically called verrucae and are caused by a virus. Treatment is surgical. Post-operative care involves several days of immobility to permit the tissue to heal before pressure is put on it.

Plaque • A flat patch; most commonly, dental plaque, which refers to a film of mucoid-like substance that adheres to tooth surfaces and provides the medium in which bacteria that liberate destructive acids thrive on the various forms of sugar that enter the mouth. The acids eventually destroy tooth enamel. Thus, dental plaque is largely responsible for cavities. It can be effectively removed by brushing the teeth, using unwaxed floss according to the dentist's instructions, and having a professional cleaning twice a year. There is recent evidence that some mouthwashes may provide additional protection against plaque formation. *See* GINGIVITIS and PERIODONTAL DISEASE.

Plastic Surgery • Operations in which damaged or abnormal tissue is repaired and rebuilt. Such damages or abnormalities may be congenital, as a hare lip, or they may be acquired, as disfiguring scars caused by burns or other injuries. Plastic surgeons also remove growths extensive enough to require skin grafting following the operation and they also specialize in the reconstruction of missing tissue with a prosthesis, a substitute manufactured of metals and plastics rather than of organic materials taken from another part of the body. Artificial limbs, jaws, breasts, and ears are some of the more customary prosthetic replacements. Change in appearance for esthetic reasons where no striking malformation exists, such as a face lift or nose reshaping, is called cosmetic surgery. *See* "Cosmetic Surgery."

Platelets • Round or oval disks in the blood that contain no hemoglobin and are essential to the clotting process; also called thrombocytes. This blood component is manufactured in the bone marrow. Platelet deficiencies occur in a number of diseases (leukemia, myeloma, lymphoma), as a result of certain drugs, and spontaneously (idiopathic thrombocytopenic purpura). Platelets can be transferred fresh or frozen for transfusion as needed.

Pleurisy • Inflammation of the pleura, the double membrane that lines the chest cavity and encloses the lungs. Pleurisy may be a consequence of pneumonia or a complication of tuberculosis. The pleural membrane consists of two layers of pleurae separated only by a lubricating fluid. Under normal conditions this double membranous structure permits the lungs to expand freely within the chest. However, under certain adverse circumstances two different disorders can occur: wet pleurisy, in which because of an inflammation of the pleura, abnormal fluid accumulates between the pleural layers; dry pleurisy, in which the pleura is inflamed, but there is no abnormal fluid. Pleurisy may or may not be acutely painful, but it always requires prompt treatment. Thanks to antibiotics, this disease has almost disappeared in the United States.

Pneumocystis Pneumonia • A lung disease caused by *Pneumocystis carinii*, an especially virulent protozoan. It is one of the complications, usually fatal, of the acquired immune deficiency syndrome known as AIDS and is considered an "opportunistic infection" because it primarily affects people, such as leukemia patients, whose immunity is compromised. See ACQUIRED IMMUNE DEFICIENCY SYNDROME.

Pneumonia • An acute infection or inflammation of one or both lungs, causing the lung tissues and spaces to be filled with liquid matter. Pneumonia, which may be a primary infection or a complication of another disorder, has three main causes: bacteria, viruses, and mycoplasmas. Inflammation may also be caused by fungus infections or by the aspiration of certain chemicals, of irritant dusts, or of food or liquids while unconscious due to anesthesia, intoxication, or other causes. The latter type is called aspiration pneumonia. Among the bacteria, the pneumococci are by far the most common cause; there are over 80 different types responsible for approximately 500,000 cases of the disease each year. Streptococcal pneumonia is less common; staphylococcal pneumonia usually is contracted in a hospital and has a high mortality rate; victims of pneumonia caused by the klebsiella bacteria also have poor chances of recovery. The pneumonias that are viral in origin account for about half of all cases. While in some cases recovery may be spontaneous without treatment or special precautions (many people have had "walking pneumonia" without realizing it), the disease known as primary influenza virus pneumonia is extremely serious, especially because the infectious organism multiplies with practically no accompanying sign of disease in the lung. Mycoplasmas, which were identified during World War II, are microorganisms smaller than bacteria, larger than viruses, and sharing characteristics of both. Mycoplasma pneumonia typically involves older children and young adults and is usually mild in its symptoms and brief in duration. Pneumonia that involves a major part or an entire lobe of a lung is known as lobar pneumonia, and when both lungs are involved, double pneumonia. Bronchopneumonia, which affects a smaller area, is slower to develop and is localized in the bronchial tubes with patches of infection reaching the lungs. While rarely fatal, bronchopneumonia is insidious because it may recur and resist conventional treatment.

In all cases of bacterial pneumonia, but especially in cases where resistance is low because of age, debility, or alcoholism, treatment with antibiotics must be initiated at once. In general, at the first sign of any of the following manifestations, a doctor's evaluation is mandatory: shaking chills, high fever, chest pains, dry cough, breathlessness, bluish cast to the lips and nail beds, and expectoration of rust-colored or greenish sputum when coughing. Some cases may require hospitalization, while others may be supervised at home. According to the American Lung Association, prompt treatment with antibiotics almost always cures bacterial and mycoplasma pneumonia. While there is as yet no effective treatment for viral pneumonia, adequate rest, proper diet, and sufficient time devoted to convalescence usually result in full recovery. Since 1977 an immunizing vaccine has been available that offers protection against some types of pneumococci. It is administered on an individual basis to those considered especially vulnerable to infection—people over 50, anyone in a nursing home, and anyone of any age suffering from chronic diseases of the heart, lungs, and kidneys and from diabetes and other metabolic disorders. It also is indicated for persons who have had their spleen removed. One injection of the vaccine is supposed to provide immunity for three years. The use of the vaccine is especially important because many strains of pneumococci have developed a resistance to previously effective antibiotics. *See* "Immunization Guide."

Poison • Any substance that can severely damage or destroy living tissue. Certain substances are harmful in any amount, while others, which are harmless or even beneficial in supervised doses, are poisonous in excessive amounts. Poisons can be absorbed through the skin, injected into the bloodstream, or inhaled, but most poisonings result from swallowing dangerous substances in small amounts or taking medications in overdoses. The most frequent victims are children under 5. Among adults the greatest numbers of poisonings are caused by an overdose of medicine, either swallowed accidentally or in a suicide attempt.

Because prompt action can make the difference between life and death, every member of the family, including children from the earliest possible age, should know that the number of the local poison control agency is posted next to the telephone with other emergency numbers. Local telephone directories usually list the number under poison control. When no such listing appears, efforts should be made *before* a crisis occurs to locate the closest agency by consulting the telephone operator, the nearest hospital, or the Red Cross chapter or by writing to the Division of Poison Control, U.S. Department of Health and Human Services, 5600 Fishers Lane, Room 18B-31, Rockville, Md. 20852.

Poison Control Center • A service organization on the community level that can be consulted 24 hours a day for information about the toxicity of a particular substance and the most effective countermeasures to take against it. The FDA provides these centers with up-to-date information on all potentially dangerous products. The centers are listed in telephone directories under Poison Control. The number of the nearest one should be immediately accessible at the home phone for quick use in a crisis.

Poison Ivy, Oak, and Sumac • Plants containing a poisonous chemical, urushiol, to which a majority of people in the United States eventually become sensitive. It is extremely unwise to assume that insensitivity to these plants is permanent. The chemical, which is contained in all parts of the plants—leaves, berries, roots, and bark—produces contact dermatitis in those allergic to it. In cases of hypersensitivity the itching and blistering rash may develop not only when the skin has touched the plant directly but also when a part of the body touches a piece of contaminated clothing or a dog or cat whose coat is contaminated by the allergen. Because the chemical can be spread by smoke from burning the plant, it should never be burned but destroyed by a suitable herbicide. When exposure does occur, contaminated clothing should be removed at once for laundering, and the potentially affected parts of the body washed with a strong, alkaline laundry soap. These preventive measures should be undertaken as soon as possible to limit the spread of the poison. When the rash appears, the discomfort can be reduced by the application of calamine lotion or a nonprescription hydrocortisone salve. Blisters that ooze and break should be covered with sterile gauze pads moistened with a baking soda solution. Milder cases are self-limiting and are likely to clear up in about a week without further attention. In severe cases cortisone may be prescribed as well as antihistamines to reduce the itching. The best way to prevent contact is to make a serious effort to learn what the plants look like so that they can be scrupulously avoided.

Polio • This acute infectious disease also known as poliomyelitis and infantile paralysis has been virtually eliminated thanks to effective immunization introduced in 1954. Polio is caused by a virus that attacks the nerve cells that control skeletal muscles. Mild cases are so slight as to go undetected; the most severe cases were fatal. Because polio epidemics are not uncommon where sanitation is primitive and public health measures practically nonexistent, travelers who plan to venture into the rural areas of Third World countries are advised by the U.S. Quarantine and Immunization Service to be reimmunized against the disease.

A phenomenon known as the "post polio" syndrome has been experienced by a significant number of the survivors of the disease. Progressive weakening of certain muscles occurs very slowly; if the original polio attack was a virulent one, the syndrome that sets in 40 or 50 years later may cause considerable discomfort. Doctors who know the history of these patients have been able to differentiate this muscle disability from the onset of other neuromuscular diseases.

Polyp • A smooth, tubelike growth, almost always benign, that projects from mucous membrane. Such growths are of two main types: pedunculate polyps that are attached to the membrane by a thin stalk and sessile polyps that have a broad base.

While polyps may occur in any body cavity with a membranous lining, they are most commonly found in the nose, uterus, cervix, and rectum. Those that develop in the nasal canal or sinuses may result from such irritations as frequent colds or allergies. While rarely dangerous, they can interfere with breathing and with the sense of smell; they may also be the cause of chronic headaches. Surgical removal is recommended in such cases, but there is no guarantee that the underlying irritation will not produce them again. Uterine polyps may cause irregular or excessive menstrual flow and may also be one of the causes of sterility. They can usually be removed without the need for hospitalization. The presence of cervical polyps may be manifested by bleeding between menstrual periods, after menopause, or with intercourse, or they may be "silent," only discovered during a routine gynecological checkup. Removal is considered advisable, with a biopsy to rule out the possibility of cancer. Polyps in the colon or the rectum are likely to cause discomfort in the lower abdomen and diarrhea as well as blood and mucus in the stools. A rectal polyp is usually removed as an office procedure by a proctologist. Annual postoperative checkups are recommended.

Polyunsaturated Fats • Nutrients that provide the body with the essential fatty acid linoleic acid and help maintain a low serum cholesterol level, thus reducing the likelihood of clogged arteries, a condition that is one of the main causes of heart attack. *See* "Nutrition, Weight, and General Well-Being."

Posture • The natural position or carriage of the body when sitting or standing. Good posture is the unconscious result of mental and physical health. While a rigidly held neck or a sunken chest may be second nature by the time adulthood arrives, poor posture can be improved by suitable exercise. Women who sit at a desk or typewriter for a large part of the day should have a posture chair that discourages slouching and supports the spine. For women who are on their feet a great deal, poor posture and attendant backaches may result from wearing ill-fitting shoes or shoes with heels that are too high or too low for comfort and healthy carriage. A critical review of footwear, office furniture, and posture when doing household chores may go a long way to eliminating back pain. Good posture during pregnancy is especially important, because the growth of the fetus and the enlarged abdomen place an extra strain on the spine. Standing against a wall several times a day with head up, shoulders back, belly sucked in, and buttocks tucked under can develop posture that will eliminate back discomfort before and after delivery. *See* "Fitness" and "Health on the Job."

Potassium • A chemical element that, in combination with other minerals, is essential for the body's acid-base balance and muscle function. Anyone taking a diuretic on a regular basis should find out whether potassium loss must be compensated for. *See* "Nutrition, Weight, and General Well-Being."

Pre-eclampsia • A condition of pregnancy characterized by abnormal retention of water, elevated blood pressure, and large amounts of protein in the urine, signaling the possible onset of convulsions (eclampsia). *See* "Pregnancy and Childbirth" and ECLAMPSIA.

Premature Ejaculation • *See* EJACULATION.

Premature Infant • An infant born before the completion of 37 weeks' (starting from the date of its mother's last normal menstrual period) gestation. Infants weighing less than 2,500 grams (five and a half pounds) at birth generally are also considered to be premature infants. *See* "Pregnancy and Childbirth."

Premenstrual Syndrome • A group of symptoms experienced by many women (perhaps 50 percent) that occur in a cyclic pattern but always in a particular phase of the woman's menstrual cycle. The symptoms generally develop a week or so before menstruation and include breast tenderness, abdominal bloating, fatigue, fluctuating emotions, and depression. *See* "Gynecologic Diseases and Treatment."

Proctoscopy • An internal examination with an instrument called a proctoscope, which enables the physician to see the rectum and the lower portion of the large intestine. The procedure may be performed by a proctologist or by one's prime care doctor. It is used in diagnosing hemorrhoids, in detecting polyps and cysts, and in routine screening for cancer in patients over 40.

Progesterone • The hormone secreted by the corpus luteum each month at the time of ovulation to prepare the lining of the uterus for embedding and nourishing of the fertilized egg. It is produced by the placenta during pregnancy and is important for the maintenance of pregnancy. Diminishing progesterone secretions is one of the changes that occurs during menopause. Progesterone may also be prescribed in replacement therapy when a deficiency is responsible for certain menstrual disorders connected with infertility. See "The Healthy Woman" and "Contraception and Abortion."

Prolapse • The downward or forward displacement of a part of the body; most commonly, the dropping of the uterus. A prolapsed womb is a consequence of impaired muscle support, which most often results from the stress of childbirth but is not unknown among women who have never had children. Dropping of the uterus may occur after menopause when muscle tone diminishes or when the cumulative effect of a lifetime of hard physical work takes its toll. The symptoms of uterine prolapse are frequent and painful urination, low backache, vaginal discharge, and a feeling of pressure on the vagina. Lying down provides relief from this last discomfort. When the prolapse is severe enough to cause the cervix to protrude through the vagina, special support in the form of a pessary may be a satisfactory alternative to surgery. See illustration on next page.

Propranolol • See INDERAL.

Prostaglandin • A hormonelike substance composed of unsaturated fatty acids and found in almost every tissue and body fluid. Prostaglandins are being identified in increasing numbers as indispensable for normalizing blood pressure, kidney processes, the reproductive system, gastrointestinal activity, and the release of sex hormones. Of those specifically isolated, the prostaglandins manufactured by the endometrium increase considerably just before the onset of the menstrual period. Because they cause strong uterine contractions, they are responsible for the premenstrual cramps suffered by some women. Antiprostaglandin drugs previously used only for treating arthritis because of their anti-inflammatory action are proving to be an effective treatment for painful menstrual periods. See DYSMENORRHEA and "Gynecologic Diseases and Treatment."

Prostate Gland • In the male genitourinary system, the gland surrounding the neck of the bladder and beginning of the urethra. As a sexual organ, its function is the manufacture of prostatic fluid, a component of seminal fluid in which the sperm cells are mixed to create semen.

Protein • One of several complex substances composed of combinations of amino acids; the basic substance of

PROLAPSE OF UTERUS

(Labels: Ovary, Bladder, Urethra, Everted vaginal wall, Cervix, Rectum, Uterus, Anus)

Correctional pessary holding cervix and uterus in proper position

which living cells are composed; essential nutrient in the diet of all animal life. See "Nutrition, Weight, and General Well-Being."

The symptoms of protein deficiency are physical weakness, poor resistance to disease, and fluid accumulation in the legs and abdomen. Liver disease and certain other disorders may interfere with normal protein metabolism. Over-the-counter medications for "tired blood" will not correct protein deficiencies.

The classification of *serum proteins* includes globulin and albumin. Globulin, which is divided into alpha, beta, and gamma globulin, is an essential component of the blood. Because gamma globulin is the richest in antibodies, it is often used to provide passive immunity to such infectious diseases as hepatitis. Albumins are serum proteins found in all living matter. Among the most important ones are egg albumin found in egg white, fibrinogen and hemoglobin in blood, myosin in meat, caseinogen in milk, casein in cheese, and gluten in flour. See LIPOPROTEIN, "Nutrition, Weight, and General Well-Being."

Pruritis • *See* ITCHING.

Psoriasis • A common skin disease of unknown cause, characterized by excessive production of cells of the outermost skin layer, which produces scaly red patches. As the new cells proliferate, they cover the patches with a silvery scale, and as the scales drop off, the area below is revealed as tiny red dots. Psoriasis is neither contagious nor dangerous. Symptoms may appear for the first time in early childhood, in adolescence, or not until later in life. The condition may be chronic or intermittent; it may be triggered by injury, illness, emotional stress, or exposure to excessive cold. The red patches may or may not be accompanied by itching. The parts of the body most often affected are the scalp, chest, elbows, knees, abdomen, palms, finger nails, and soles of the feet. About 10 percent of patients have an associated arthritis or gout.

In spite of advertising claims to the contrary, there is no cure for psoriasis. Professionally prescribed treatments that have been somewhat effective have had unfortunate side effects in many instances or have required weeks of hospitalization. A treatment that shows promising results is known as photochemotherapy. It combines oral medication with a photoactive drug followed by exposure to ultraviolet radiation. Recently, some patients treated with the anticancer drug methotrexate have experienced a reduction of psoriasis symptoms, but the negative side effects may be considered worse than the disease.

Psychedelic Drugs • *See* "Substance Abuse."

Psychiatry • The medical specialty that deals with the diagnosis and treatment of disorders of the mind and the emotions. *See* "Health Care Personnel."

Psychoanalysis • A method originated by Dr. Sigmund Freud for treating mental illness and emotional disturbances. The method is based on certain assumptions about the development from infancy onward of the human psyche or the mind as an entity with a life of its own that governs the total organism in all its relationships with others and with the environment. Psychoanalysts may be psychiatrists as Freud himself was, or they may be lay practitioners.

Psychoneurosis • *See* NEUROSIS.

Psychosis • Any mental illness characterized by disorganization of personality and a disordered contact with reality combined with bizarre behavior consisting of unpredictable mood swings and garbled speech and accompanied by hallucinations, delusions, and disconnected thoughts. Psychotic episodes may occur as a result of the use of addictive drugs, including the delusional episodes experienced by alcoholics. *See* "Substance Abuse."

Psychosomatic Illness • Any disorder that is functional in nature and that may be ascribed wholly or partly to emotional stress.

Psychotherapy • The treatment of mental illness or emotional disorders.

Psychotropic Drugs • Chemical agents that have an effect on the mind, thereby modifying emotions, perceptions, and behavior and alleviating some of the more acute symptoms of mental illness and psychological stress. The drugs used to treat the major psychoses are categorized as antipsychotic drugs and include (among others) Thorazine, Stelazine, Mellaril, and Haldol. The most widely prescribed category of mood-altering drugs comes under the general heading of "tranquilizers" and are more specifically known as anti-anxiety agents. These include (among others) Valium, Librium, Dalmane, Equanil, and Xamax. A third category includes the antidepressants. These are of two types: the tricyclics such as Tofranil, Triavil, and Elavil, and the MAO inhibitors such as Nardil and Parnate. *See* LITHIUM and "Substance Abuse."

Puberty • The period of development during which sex organs begin to function, becoming capable of reproduction, and secondary sex characteristics develop. In females it is marked by the onset of menstruation. See MENARCHE.

Puerperal • Relating to childbirth. See "Pregnancy and Childbirth."

Pulse • The beat of the heart as felt through the expansion and contraction of an artery, especially through the radial artery at the wrist below the fleshy mound of the thumb. The best way to take the pulse is to place the three middle fingers on this artery with sufficient pressure to detect the beat but not so heavily as to suppress it. Pulse rate is the term for the number of beats felt in 60 seconds. The normal adult rate ranges from 60 to 100 beats a minute. An abnormally slow pulse (brachycardia) may be caused by an overdose of digitalis, abnormal pressure within the skull, the onset of thyroid deficiency, or a crisis involving heart malfunction. An abnormally fast pulse (tachycardia) may result from high altitude sickness, congestive heart failure, hyperthyroidism, fever, excitement, or too much caffeine, alcohol, smoking, amphetamines, thyroid extract, or antispasmodics. The rhythm of the pulse in a normally healthy person is regular. Where perceptible irregularity exists, it may be associated with thyroid disease or it may be caused by auricular fibrillation, a symptom of chronic heart failure. If the pulse is not perceptible at the wrist, it may be felt through the carotid artery at the side of the neck.

Pus • The thick yellowish or greenish liquid that develops during certain infections. Pus is composed of white blood cells, tissue decomposed by bacteria or other microorganism, and the destroyed organism that caused the infection. It is often contained in an inflamed swelling called an abscess.

Quickening • The stage of pregnancy in which the mother becomes aware of fetal movements within the womb; also, the fetal movements themselves. See "Pregnancy and Childbirth."

Rabies • An almost always fatal disease of the central nervous system caused by the rabies virus. It occurs in warm-blooded mammals such as humans, foxes, dogs, bats, and skunks. It is transmitted by the bite of an infected animal because the virus is present in saliva.

The wound from any animal bite should be allowed to bleed and be scrubbed and flushed with soap and water. Then, if possible, it should be washed with zephiran chloride or some other substance (alcohol) of proven lethal effect on the virus. Suturing the wound is not advised. Whether the victim of the bite has been exposed to rabies depends, of course, on whether the biting animal is infected. This is more likely if the bite was not provoked and if the animal was wild. Further, the more severe the wound, especially if the bite was on bare skin, the more likely the victim is to get rabies if the animal was infected. The animal should be observed, caged if necessary, for approximately 10 days to see if it is sick, gets sick, or dies. If it has to be killed to be captured, care should be taken not to shoot it in the head because an examination of the brain is essential to determine if it is rabid. If the victim has been exposed or probably exposed to rabies, it is essential that rabies vaccine and probably antirabies serum be administered. Judgment must be used in deciding about the use of vaccine and serum because there are hazards associated with both.

The incubation period of rabies in humans varies from 10 days to 12 months, the average being about 42 days, and is characterized initially by fever, headache, and general malaise and then by a variety of central nervous system signs such as spasms of the muscles of the mouth, pharynx, and larynx on drinking. This symptom explains another name for rabies, hydrophobia (the fear of water). Death usually is caused by paralysis of the respiratory muscles. There is no specific treatment for the disease. *See* "Immunization Guide."

Radiation Therapy • The treatment of disease with X-rays and with rays from such radioactive substances as cobalt, iodine, and radium; also called irradiation. The effectiveness of this therapy, which is the special province of the radiologist, is constantly being increased by the invention of new machines and techniques that minimize the dangers of radiation exposure to healthy tissues at the same time that enough irradiation can be provided to benefit tissue already diseased. *See* X-RAY and NUCLEAR MEDICINE.

Radical Mastectomy • *See* "Breast Care."

Radium • A highly radioactive metal that spontaneously gives off rays affecting the growth of organic tissue. Body exposure, inhalation, or ingestion of radium may produce burns as well as several kinds of cancer, especially of the lungs, blood, and bones.

Rape • *See* "Rape and Family Abuse."

Rash • A skin eruption often accompanied by discoloration and itching and in most cases a temporary symptom of a particular infectious disease, allergy, or parasitic infestation. Rashes may be flat or raised, some run together into large blotches, and others turn into blisters. Many of the diseases of which rashes are a symptom, such as measles and rubella, are on the wane because of widespread immunization. Prickly heat, contact dermatitis, hives, and allergic responses to poison ivy, oak, and sumac are common causes of rashes. Rashlike symptoms usually accompany infections caused by funguses, parasites, and rickettsial organisms such as ticks. Virus diseases (mononucleosis) and sexually transmissible diseases, especially secondary stage syphilis, are characterized by rashes. Any skin eruption accompanied by fever or other acute symptoms such as a sore throat or tender swollen glands should be examined by a doctor.

Rectocele • The protrusion of the rectum into the vagina. This type of hernia causes difficulty in emptying the bowel and leads to constipation. It can be corrected by surgery.

Rectum • The lowest portion of the large intestine before the anal opening to the exterior of the body. It consists of the rectal canal, 5 to 6 inches long in crescent-shaped folds, and the anal canal, 1 to 1 1/2 inches long. When the rectum is filled with feces as the solid wastes of digestion are pushed downward by intestinal action, nerve impulses send messages to the brain signaling the need to defecate. The rectum may be affected by various disorders, most commonly hemorrhoids, polyps, prolapse, pruritis, and cancer. Proctitis (inflammation of the rectum) can be one of the consequences of gonorrhea. *See* PROCTOSCOPY.

Rehabilitation • *See* OCCUPATIONAL THERAPY, PHYSICAL THERAPY, and "Substance Abuse."

Remission • The decrease or disappearance of signs and symptoms during the course of a disease or a chronic disorder. The term spontaneous remission is used when there appears to be no therapeutic explanation for the abatement of the symptoms.

Resistance • The body's ability to ward off or minimize disease either through genetic capability, the presence of antibodies produced by immunization or environmental exposure, or a high enough level of physical and psychological health to combat infection without succumbing to it. The most efficient way to produce resistance to an increasing number of infectious diseases is by immunization. *See* "Immunization Guide."

Respiratory Disorders • *See* ASTHMA, BRONCHITIS, *etc.*

Retina • The innermost layer of cells at the rear of the eyeball; a membrane consisting of the light-sensitive rods and cones that receive the image formed by the lens and transmit it through the optic nerve to the brain. Retinal disease of one kind or another is the chief cause of blindness in the United States. With the extension in the life span of diabetics through the use of insulin a disease called diabetic retinopathy has come to the attention of medical science.

When a hole or tear develops in the retina or when an eye infection or tumor forces an excess of the vitreous fluid to seep between the retinal layers, the result can be a retinal detachment that can end up in a permanent loss of eyesight. There is an increased risk that this condition may occur in people with severe myopia. Thanks to photocoagulation and new microsurgical techniques, restoration of vision is accomplished in a large number of cases. *See* EYE and DIABETIC RETINOPATHY.

Reye's Syndrome • A childhood degenerative disease of the brain and liver, usually preceded by a virus disease such as chicken pox or flu. Because aspirin has been implicated in triggering this syndrome, doctors recommend acetaminophen for the control of fever and other symptoms of infections. The aspirin connection is under ongoing investigation. There is no specific treatment for Reye's syndrome.

Rh Factor • A group of genetically determined antigens found in the red blood cells of most people. The designation comes from the rhesus monkey involved in the original experiments. The 15 percent of the Caucasian population lacking this inherited blood substance, is known as Rh negative. Its absence in other races is much rarer. When the substance is missing, the blood is described as Rh negative, regardless of whether the major blood type is A, B, AB, or O. It is vitally important that Rh compatibility be established before a transfusion, especially when the recipient is a woman who may want children in future years. The reason for checking the Rh factor during pregnancy is to avoid the complications that ensue when the woman is Rh negative and the man is Rh positive. Because the mixing of the two bloods can have serious consequences, it is imperative to determine early in pregnancy if the Rh negative problem exists. See "Pregnancy and Childbirth."

Rheumatic Fever • A disease of the growing years usually triggered by an untreated hemolytic streptococcus infection and characterized by inflammation, swelling, and soreness of the joints. During rheumatic fever a condition known as rheumatic heart disease may develop. If the valves of the heart are affected and become so inflamed that they are distorted by the eventual formation of scar tissue, the efficiency with which they shut is permanently impaired. The impairment results in a backspill of blood that can be heard through a stethoscope as the so-called heart murmur. Anyone with this type of heart disability is especially vulnerable to further indirect valve damage subsequent to recurrence of rheumatic fever or to direct valve damage secondary to bacterial infection elsewhere (called subacute bacterial endocarditis). To avoid this complication, it is important that the proper precautions be taken against bacterial invasion of the bloodstream that may occur when a tooth is extracted, during urinary tract surgery, etc. Fortunately, antibiotics started prior to such procedures have eliminated this grave complication in most cases.

Rheumatism • A nonscientific designation for any painful disorder or disease of the joints, muscles, bones, ligaments, or nerves. See ARTHRITIS, BURSITIS, etc.

Rheumatoid Arthritis • *See* ARTHRITIS.

Rhinitis • Inflammation of the mucous membranes that line the nasal passages caused by viral or bacterial infection, allergy, or inhalation of irritants. Acute rhinitis, the technical medical term for the nasal disturbance of the common cold, is its most common form. In some cases viral rhinitis is complicated by bacterial invasion that may reach the ears and the throat. When streptococcus, staphylococcus, or pneumococcus bacteria are involved, the nasal discharge will be thick and yellowish with pus instead of being practically colorless, loose, and runny. Another form of inflammation is caused by an allergic reaction to grass, trees, dog hair, or other substances.

Rhinitis may become prolonged or chronic because of constant inhalation of noxious dusts, heavy smoking, constant exposure to excessively dry air, low resistance to infection by cold viruses, or constant bouts of sinusitis. Under these circumstances, the nasal membranes may thicken and swell to the point where breathing is impaired, headaches and postnasal drip are chronic, and the sense of smell is damaged. Also associated with chronic rhinitis is the development of polyps and of a separate disorder known as ozena in which the erosion of the mucous membrane results in a thick malodorous discharge that creates heavy crusts impeding proper breathing and attempts at nose-blowing.

Obvious symptoms of chronic rhinitis should be treated by a doctor. When rhinitis is associated with fever or other manifestation of bacterial infection, antibiotic therapy may be advisable. However, the typical stuffed or runny nose characteristic of an ordinary cold is likely to clear up as the cold runs its course. It has recently been observed that thousands of Americans abuse nasal sprays, especially those containing long-lasting vasoconstrictors that shrink the blood vessels in the nose and eliminate the symptom of "stuffed nose" associated with colds, allergies, and some sinus conditions. This dependence produces a "rebound" phenomenon in which the "cure" causes the symptoms to return in more acute form, so that more and stronger nasal decongestants are needed. Specialists therefore advise a careful reading of label warnings about dosage and continued application of all such medications.

Rhythm Method • *See* "Contraception and Abortion."

Riboflavin • A component of the vitamin B complex; also known as vitamin B$_2$. *See* "Nutrition, Weight, and General Well-Being."

Ribonucleic Acid • *See* RNA.

Rickettsial Diseases • A category of infectious diseases caused by microorganisms larger than viruses, smaller than bacteria but with characteristics of both, called rickettsiae after their discoverer, the pathologist H. T. Ricketts (1871–1910). Rickettsiae inhabit certain rodents as parasites and are transmitted to humans and animals by the bites of ticks, mites, fleas, and lice. The rickettsial diseases, which range from mild to extremely serious, commonly produce a rash, a fever, and a general feeling of malaise. When a particular rickettsial disease is accurately diagnosed on the basis of laboratory findings, it is usually treated with antibiotics. (This group of diseases should not be confused with rickets, a vitamin D deficiency disease.) *See* Q FEVER, ROCKY MOUNTAIN SPOTTED FEVER, and TYPHUS.

Ringworm • *See* FUNGAL INFECTIONS.

RNA • Ribonucleic Acid, the chemical compound contained in the cytoplasm of all cells and the carrier of genetic information provided by DNA to the ribosomes, the structures that synthesize amino acids into proteins. Through the information transmitted by RNA, inherited characteristics make their way from one generation to the next.

Rocky Mountain spotted fever • An infectious disease transmitted to humans by the bite of the American dog tick in the Eastern states and from rodents to humans by the wood tick in Western states; also called tick fever or Eastern spotted fever. In addition to a headache, fever, and aching muscles, one of the distinguishing characteristics is a rash that begins on the palms of the hands and the soles of the feet, spreading upward during the course of the illness. Other symptoms include sensitivity to light, abdominal cramps, and vomiting. Tetracycline halts the progress of the infection. Vacationers should find out if warnings of tick infestation have been issued in their location. Dogs should not be permitted to roam in tick-infested surroundings; where, in an attempt to eliminate ticks, areas have been sprayed with chemicals harmful to people and their pets, precautions should be taken against potentially dangerous contact. Another precaution is protective clothing. Anyone whose vacation plans or job requirements necessitate a prolonged stay in a tick-infested area should investigate the advisability of vaccination. *See* "Immunization Schedule."

Root Canal • The passageway through the root of a tooth for the nerve. When tooth decay has proceeded unchecked from the enamel into the dentin that surrounds the pulp chamber and the root canal, the only treatment that can prevent the loss of the tooth by extraction is known as root canal therapy. This consists in removing the nerve and the diseased pulp, sterilizing the chamber, and filling the area with an inert substance. The specialist who performs this type of treatment is called an endodontist.

Rubella • An acute virus infection accompanied by fever and a rash, a common contagious disease of childhood; also known as German measles. In spite of the fact that long-lasting immunization against this disease is available, many young women reach childbearing age without vaccination against it and without natural immunization from infection during childhood. Rubella immunity precludes the potentially harmful consequences to the fetus from exposure to the disease during the early months of pregnancy. Such consequences include brain damage, heart defects, blindness, and other deformities in as many as 50 percent of the affected offspring. If rubella is contracted during the first trimester of pregnancy, it is considered a valid reason for an abortion. Women of childbearing age who have never been vaccinated against German measles and who test antibody negative should receive a one-shot immunization against the disease. A three-month wait following the immunization should be scheduled before initiating a pregnancy so that the embryo's safety from contamination is ensured.

Rupture • A popular term for a hernia. *See* HERNIA.

Saccharin • A chemical coal tar derivative used as a sugar substitute and approximately 500 times sweeter than cane sugar by weight. Saccharin had been used routinely by diabetics and by people on low calorie diets until recent scientifically controlled experiments conducted with laboratory animals pointed to carcinogenic properties in saccharin. However, debate continues about the validity of these tests when applied to human consumption because no such controlled experiments can be duplicated with humans. A sugar substitute is by no means necessary for weight reduction; women concerned about controlling their weight might use sugar in small quantities or use no sweeteners at all.

Sacroiliac • The cartilaginous joint that connects the sacrum at the base of the spinal column to the ilium, the open section on either side of the hipbone. Low back pain can sometimes be ascribed to arthritis in this joint.

Saliva • The secretion of the salivary glands in the mouth. The largest of these, the parotids, are situated in front of and below each ear and discharge saliva through openings in the cheeks opposite the lower back teeth. Saliva not only keeps the mouth and tongue moist to facilitate speech and swallowing, it also softens food and through its enzymes initiates the digestive process by chemically changing the carbohydrates in the mouth into simpler sugars. Because the flow of saliva is activated by the nervous system, stimuli of sight, smell, taste, and even mental images of food will increase salivation. For the same reason, fear and anxiety will inhibit the flow, leading to the "dry mouth" sensation that accompanies some types of stress situations. Nutritional deficiencies and some medicines may also result in an uncomfortable decrease of saliva.

Salmonella • A group of rod-shaped bacteria especially irritating to the intestinal tract and responsible for most cases of acute food poisoning as well as for paratyphoid and typhoid fever. Abdominal cramps and diarrhea are the typical symptoms of salmonella infection. See FOOD POISONING.

Salpingectomy • Surgical removal of one or both of the fallopian tubes. This operation is usually necessary when surgery is done for a tubal ectopic pregnancy. See ECTOPIC PREGNANCY and "Gynecologic Diseases and Treatment."

Salpingitis • Inflammation of the fallopian tubes. It is usually caused by gonococci or other bacteria that ascend from the cervix but may also be caused by tuberculosis. Acute salpingitis, especially when it is recurrent, can result in scar tissue that obstructs the tubes (chronic salpingitis) thereby becoming a possible cause of sterility. Any acute pain on both sides of the lower abdomen accompanied by a vaginal discharge and frequent and uncomfortable urination should be diagnosed promptly for treatment with antibiotics. See "Infertility" and "Gynecologic Diseases and Treatment."

Salt • The chemical compound sodium chloride (NaCl); also called table salt. While a certain amount is essential for maintaining the body's chemical balance, it is advisable for people suffering from hypertension and certain types of heart or kidney disease to restrict their salt intake, because too much sodium may cause fluid retention.

Thanks to consumer efforts, it has become somewhat easier (but not easy enough) to find salt-free processed foods on market shelves. Several salt substitutes are also available, and especially helpful are the many cookbooks that specialize in low-salt recipes and menu planning.

When the body loses too much fluid, as in a long siege of diarrhea or heavy sweating, a salt deficiency may occur, manifested in muscle cramps, nausea, fatigue, and in extreme cases collapse. Prompt replenishment can be accomplished by eating salted crackers or nuts or by swallowing a sodium chloride tablet with some orange juice. However, salt tablets should not be taken routinely during hot and humid weather unless the recommendation is made by a doctor. How much salt, if any, a pregnant woman should eliminate from her diet to reduce the likelihood of edema is a matter to be discussed with the physician in charge of her prenatal regimen.

Sarcoma • A malignant tumor composed of connective tissue such as bone or of muscle, lymph, or blood vessel tissue; one of the two main groups of cancer, the more common being carcinoma (cancer of epithelial or gland cells). A sarcoma usually metastasizes rapidly, either through the bloodstream or through the lymphatics. While treatment is difficult, a combination of chemotherapy, radiation, and surgery can be effective in halting the progress of different types of sarcoma.

Saturated Fats • Those fats in the diet known to be responsible for raising the cholesterol content of the blood and thereby increasing the likelihood of arterial and coronary disease. *See* "Nutrition, Weight, and General Well-Being."

Scabies • *See* "Sexually Transmissible Diseases."

Scanning Machines • Diagnostic equipment by means of which parts of the body that cannot be examined by conventional X-ray can be seen and analyzed. *See* COMPUTERIZED AXIAL TOMOGRAPHY.

Schizophrenia • A category of psychosis, in which the victim suffers from severely disturbed patterns of thinking and feeling that lead to bizarre behavior. The schizophrenic syndrome, for which there is no known direct cause and no specific cure, is most likely to occur in early adulthood, although no age is immune. Common parlance has given the term the sense of a split personality, but this popular definition has nothing to do with the psychiatric diagnosis of mental illness. As with the manic-depressive psychosis, schizophrenic symptoms may be periodic and sometimes so immobilizing that hospitalization is necessary and at other times mild enough to liberate the patient for a comparatively normal life. Among the most striking symptoms of the condition are auditory hallucinations, delusions usually of grandeur or of persecution (paranoia), obsessive-compulsive behavior, distinct personality changes and mood swings without visible cause, and, above all, loss of control over fantasies. While there are many theories about the cause of the illness, circumstances that trigger its onset, and reasons for its remission, no single explanation is definitively convincing. Among the areas of ongoing research are constitutional predisposition in the form of an inherited recessive gene or a combination of genes; constitutional predisposition associated with oxygen deprivation of the brain during birth triggered by a metabolic aberration or related to a prenatal protein deficiency; environmental circumstances that create an atmosphere of anxiety and hostility and especially a conflict between parents or extreme parental disapproval and criticism.

When the disease is suspected, diagnosis is usually based on a complete physical examination, a series of psychiatric interviews, an electroencephalogram, and standard psychological tests. Conventional treatment may begin with one of the major psychotropic drugs such as Thorazine combined with psychotherapy, which may involve the family. Environmental therapy, involving residence in a halfway house rather than a hospital, is used in less severe cases, in those where symptoms have abated, or in those where living at home is out of the question because the family situation appears to be part of the problem rather than a possible solution. This form of therapy conditions or reconditions the schizophrenic for participation in the normal world even though some symptoms are ineradicable. Megavitamin therapy is used by some doctors, but conclusive evidence of its effectiveness has not yet been provided. In cases where the more immobilizing symptoms cannot be alleviated in any other way, electroshock may be used as a last resort.

Sciatica • Pain extending along the sciatic nerve, which is the largest nerve in the body and which supplies sensation from the back of the thigh, along the outer side of the leg, and into the foot and toes. The most common cause of sciatica is a slipped or herniated disk of the lower spine. Osteoarthritis is another cause. In some cases the pain is accompanied by a paralysis of some of the associated muscles of the thigh and leg. Inflammation of the sciatic nerve (sciatic neuritis), while rare, may be a consequence of diseases such as alcoholism or diabetes or of vitamin deficiencies. Sciatica may vanish unaccountably as it arrives, but in cases where it is persistently painful and immobilizing, efforts should be made to discover the underlying cause. Until the cause can be treated, relief may be provided by physical therapy, a girdle, and the application of wet heat combined with as much bed rest as possible.

Scopolamine • A chemical that depresses the central nervous system; also called hyoscine, and derived from a plant of the nightshade family. It was formerly widely used in obstetrics for its amnesiac and sedative properties to produce the stupified state known as "twilight sleep." Because of its potentially damaging effects on the newborn baby and the postpartum depression experienced by the mother, it has largely been abandoned in favor of other sedatives. Scopolamine is also an ingredient in nonprescription medications for the prevention of nausea associated with motion sickness.

Scrotum • *See* SEX ORGANS, MALE.

Scurvy • A deficiency disease resulting from an insufficiency of vitamin C in the diet. Vitamin C requirements are between 10 and 20 milligrams daily. Considerably more than that amount is provided by a conventional diet that contains citrus fruits and juices and various green vegetables both raw and gently cooked. *See* "Nutrition, Weight, and General Well-Being."

Sebaceous Glands • The oil-secreting glands situated in the epidermal layer of the skin, lubricating the surface and protecting it from the harmful effects of absorbing too much or too little moisture. The number of these glands, which may be as many as 12 to the square inch, varies from person to person and from one part of the body to another. The sebaceous glands secrete sebum that constantly seeps upward through the pores. Too little sebum production results in dry skin; too much in oily skin. During adolescence and pregnancy hormonal changes may affect the activity of the glands, leading to acne. Other conditions resulting from sebaceous disorders are dandruff and cysts.

Sedative • A category of drugs that in small doses reduce excitability, irritability, and nervousness by depressing the central nervous system and in larger doses induce sleep. This category includes barbiturates, tranquilizers, and bromides as well as chloral hydrate and alcohol. If used regularly or abused even over short periods, practically all sedatives produce dependencies of one kind or another that can lead to addiction. *See* "Substance Abuse."

Self-examination • *See* "Breast Care" and "Sexually Transmissible Diseases."

Self-help Group • People who meet on a regular basis to provide support for each other in dealing with a particular problem. Such groups, whose way of operating is patterned on Alcoholics Anonymous, are helpful to those who are coping with various types of addiction (to smoking, gambling, overeating; to parents coping with mentally ill children; to family members of victims of Alzheimer's disease). The proliferation of such groups testifies to their success in nonprofessional therapy and also as an adjunct to professional therapy. *See* "Directory of Health Information." "Nutrition, Weight, and General Well-Being," and "Substance Abuse."

Semen • The thick, whitish fluid produced and secreted by the male organs of reproduction and containing the sperm cells. A single ejaculation of semen normally contains 300 to 500 million spermatazoa in a little less than a teaspoon of fluid. One of the diagnostic procedures in infertility cases is analysis of semen to determine the shape, number, and motility of the sperm. *See* SPERM.

Seminal Vesicles • *See* SEX ORGANS, MALE.

Senile Dementia • Manifest and abnormal deterioration of mental function associated with aging and caused by physical or mental disease or a combination of both. While damage to brain function by arteriosclerosis and stroke are among the conspicuous causes of senility, psychological and social factors that lead to personality deterioration may be equally responsible. Among the most prominent of these factors are withdrawal from normal life, lack of interpersonal relationships, feelings of worthlessness aggravated by familial and social neglect, unrelieved anxieties about disease and death. From the diagnostic point of view, the correct designation of Alzheimer's disease is senile dementia of the Alzheimer type.

Symptoms that mimic senile dementia in the form of forgetfulness and wild mood swings have, in a significant number of cases, been traced to overmedication of older patients in hospitals and nursing homes. In all cases of seeming mental impairment, it is essential that a complete physical checkup, especially of vision and hearing be completed before assuming that the cause of the dementia is irreversible deterioration of brain/mind function. "Senile" is a clinical term and should never be used to describe anyone who is going through the normal aging process that may involve a slower rate of activity and response. *See* "Aging Healthfully—Your Mind and Spirit" and ALZHEIMER'S DISEASE.

SEX ORGANS, MALE

Serum • *See* BLOOD SERUM.

Sex-linked Abnormalities • Inherited disorders transmitted by a genetic defect in the X chromosome. Women have two X chromosomes and men have one X chromosome paired with a Y chromosome. Because the presence of a Y chromosome determines maleness, fathers always transmit their X chromosome to their daughters and their Y chromosome to their sons. Because of these factors, defective genes in the X chromosome follow a particular pattern of heredity. If in a female an inherited disordered X chromosome is balanced by a normal X chromosome, she will carry the disease trait without having the disease itself. If a male offspring of the female carrier inherits her genetically abnormal X chromosome, because it is his only X chromosome, he will have the disease. When a mother is a carrier, there is therefore a fifty-fifty chance that her male offspring will inherit her abnormal X chromosome and have the disease. Female offspring have a fifty-fifty chance of inheriting the abnormal chromosome and therefore a fifty-fifty chance of being carriers. Among the sex-linked abnormalities are such diseases as hemophilia, Duchenne muscular dystrophy, and the metabolic disorder known as the Lesch-Nyhan syndrome. *See* GENETIC COUNSELING.

SEX-LINKED ABNORMALITIES
(Carried by females and appear in males)

Sexual Abuse • *See* "Rape and Family Abuse."

Sex Organs, Female • *See* "The Healthy Woman."

Sex Organs, Male • The male reproductive organs. One of the most obvious differences between the reproductive organs of the male and the female is that whereas the scrotum and penis are visible, the female counterparts are hidden from view. Another major difference is that for the male, an erotic response in the form of an erection is generally essential for the reproductive role of the penis, but no such psychophysiological requirement exists for the procreative function of the female. The male sex organs consist of the penis, scrotum, testicles, and several glands, including the prostate. Within the testicles, which are loosely contained in the scrotum, are structures called the seminiferous tubules in which sperm cells are manufactured from puberty onward. The spermatozoa are conveyed from the tubules into the epididymis, part of the sperm conduction system, where they are stored temporarily until they make their way into the seminal duct (vas deferens) and from this duct into the seminal vesicles, which secrete a viscous material that keeps them viable. The urethra, which also carries urine from the bladder, is enveloped by the prostate gland. The prostate manufactures another fluid that mixes with the sperm and the seminal fluid to form the combination known as semen. The urethra passes through the length of the penis. When the penis is in a state of erection, muscular spasms send the semen through the urethra in the act of ejaculation that immediately follows the male orgasm. Any traces of urine that might be present in the urethra are neutralized during sexual excitation by an alkaline secretion from two tiny organs known as Cowper's glands. This chemical process is critical because spermatozoa cannot remain viable in an acid environment. Because of the dual role of the urethra and its location, the male reproductive channel is also called the genitourinary tract.

Sexual Intercourse • The entry of the penis into the vagina, usually preceded by sufficiently stimulating foreplay to cause an erection in the male and the flow of lubricating secretions in both partners; also called coitus. Extravaginal intercourse is also a common practice, involving anal entry and oral sex (fellatio and cunnilingus) that give satisfaction as foreplay or may be another means of achieving orgasm. Painful sexual intercourse for the female (dyspareunia) may result from inflammation of any part of the genitourinary system, prolapsed uterus, abnormal vaginal contractions, or psychogenic causes. See "Sexual Health."

Shingles • *See* HERPES.

Shock • A disruption of circulation that may be fatal if not promptly treated; not to be confused with electrical shock, insulin shock, or electroshock therapy. The immediate cause of circulatory shock is the sudden drop in blood pressure to the point where the blood can no longer be effectively pumped through the vital organs and tissues. Among the circumstances leading to this crisis are: low-volume shock following severe hemorrhage as occurs in multiple fractures, bleeding ulcers, major burns, or any accidents in which so much blood and plasma are lost that there is an insufficiency for satisfying vital needs; neurogenic shock in which the nervous system is traumatized by acute pain, fear, or other strong stimulus that deprives the brain of oxygen and results in a temporary loss of consciousness; allergic shock, also called anaphylactic shock, following the injection into the bloodstream of a substance to which the recipient may be fatally hypersensitive such as bee venom or penicillin; cardiac shock in which the pumping action of the heart is impeded by an infarction or by fibrillation; septic shock resulting from the toxins introduced into the circulatory system by various harmful bacteria as in toxic shock syndrome. Whatever the circumstances, shock produces similar symptoms in different degrees of swiftness: extreme pallor, profuse sweating combined with a feeling of chill, thirst, faint speedy pulse, and, as the condition intensifies, increasing weakness and labored breathing. Immediate hospitalization is mandatory. If shock is the result of a serious accident or of a heart attack, the patient should not

SINUSITIS

be moved except by people professionally trained to do so.

Shock Treatment • *See* ELECTROSHOCK.

Sickle-cell Anemia • An inherited disease characterized by the substitution of 90 to 100 percent of normal hemoglobin by an abnormal hemoglobin, called hemoglobin S. When exposed to normal but low oxygen tension, red blood cells containing this much hemoglobin S acquire the shape of a sickle. These red blood cells are destroyed more rapidly than normal red blood cells and a hemolytic anemia results. In addition, the sickled red blood cells occlude blood vessels, thus depriving various body cells of their oxygen supply causing them to die and producing rather widespread disease. There is as yet no cure.

A variant of sickle-cell disease is sickle-cell trait in which only 25 to 45 percent of normal hemoglobin is replaced by hemoglobin S. Persons with sickle-cell trait may have a mild anemia but only rarely have other problems. A simple blood test identifies the presence and quantity of hemoglobin S. Hemoglobin S is found almost exclusively in black persons of African origin. In the United States about 8 percent of Afro-Americans have the trait and about 0.2 percent have the disease. Because hemoglobin S is transmitted genetically, both parents must have either the disease or the trait for any of their children to have the disease. If only one parent has the disease or the trait, none of their children will have the disease, though some will have the trait. All sickle cell patients should take advantage of the recently available vaccination against pneumococcal pneumonia. *See* GENETIC COUNSELING, "Directory of Health Information," and "Immunization Guide."

Sinuses • Cavities within bones or other tissues; in ordinary usage, the paranasal sinuses, the eight hollow spaces within the skull that open into the nose. These cavities are symmetrically located in pairs. The maxillary sinuses are in the cheekbones, the frontal sinuses are above the eyebrows in the part of the skull that forms the forehead, the ethmoid sinuses are behind and below these, and the sphenoid sinuses are behind the nasal cavity. The sinuses act as resonating chambers for the voice, they help to filter dust and foreign materials from the air before it reaches the lower airway passages, and they lighten the weight of the skull on the vertebral bones of the neck that balance and support the head. Because all the sinuses are lined with mucous membrane, they are vulnerable to infection, to inflammation by allergens, and to the formation of polyps.

Sinusitis • Inflammation of the mucous membranes that line the sinuses. The passageway that connects the sinuses to the nasal cavity is narrow and therefore susceptible to obstruction because of colds, allergies, or the presence of polyps. Such obstruction prevents free drainage of the sinuses, causes an entrapment of air that cannot escape through the nostrils, and leads to an accumulation of mucus that can become a locus of viral or bacterial infection. Infectious organisms may be transported into the sinuses through the nose when an individual is swimming in contaminated water or may invade the maxillary sinuses by way of an abscessed tooth in the upper jaw. The characteristic symptom of sinusitis is a severe headache and face pain in the location of the affected sinus. Fever, swelling, discomfort in the neck, earache, and a stuffed nose are other symptoms.

Acute sinusitis usually clears up in a few days of bed rest; aspirin or other analgesic, limited use of nosedrops, steam inhalation, and air filters can make the recovery period more comfortable. If secondary bacterial infection develops in the sinuses the doctor may prescribe antibiotics.

When sinusitis becomes chronic, every effort should be made to find out the cause. If it can be traced to nasal polyps, consideration should be given to having them removed. When an allergy is responsible, precautions may require the use of an antihistamine combined with other medications that will keep the nasal passages clear. Heavy smoking is another cause as well as a contributing factor when other causes already exist. Irritation by the chlorinated water in swimming pools is yet another cause. Aside from the pain that accompanies chronic sinusitis, there is the remote danger of eventual complication in the form of osteomyelitis or meningitis. Because surgical drainage is advisable only in extreme cases, chronic sufferers should do what they can for themselves: smoking should be eliminated, air conditioners and humidifiers installed, and the environment indoors kept as free of dusts and pollens as possible by using air filters.

Skin • The body's outer surface and its largest organ, covering an area of approximately 25 square feet and weighing about 6 pounds. The skin envelops the body completely and is also a continuation of the mucous membranes of the mouth, nose, urethra, vagina, and anus. Among its many vital functions are the following: it provides a barrier against invasion by infectious agents; offers the delicate tissues beneath it a large measure of protection against injury from the outside; regulates body temperature by the expansion and contraction of its supply of capillaries and by the activities of the sweat glands; participates in the excretion of some of the body's wastes. Through its production of melanin, it wards off some of the damage of the sun's ultraviolet rays, and it also helps transform sunshine into essential vitamin D. In addition, the skin is one of the body's most delicate sense organs: through its vast network of nerve fibers, it transmits messages of pain, pleasure, pressure, and temperature.

What is commonly identified as "the skin" is merely its visible portion or the outermost layer of the epidermis. The epidermis is made of several layers of living cells and an outer horny layer of dead cells constantly being shed and requiring no nourishing blood supply from below. This is the comparatively tough layer that provides a shield against germs as long as it remains unbroken: the same nonliving skin cells form the hair and nails. Beneath the epidermis lies the dermis or true skin, bright red in appearance and containing the nerve endings and nerve fibers, sweat and sebaceous glands, and hair follicles. Beneath the dermis is a layer of fatty tissue, called subcutaneous tissue, which helps to insulate the body against heat and cold and which contains the fat globules that through a pattern of distribution give individuality to the features of the face and determine the contours of the body.

CROSS-SECTION OF SKIN

Labels: Pain receptor, Hair shaft, Sebaceous (oil) gland, Hair follicle, Blood vessel, Sweat gland pore, Epidermis, Hair muscle, Dermis, Touch receptor, Subcutaneous tissue, Sweat gland

Also within the subcutaneous tissue are the muscle fibers responsible for the subtle changes of facial expression.

Skin Care • For a healthy woman skin care need consist of rituals no more complicated or costly than cleansing with soap and water to remove accumulated grease, perspiration, dirt, and dead cells and maintaining a proper balance of the protective oils on the skin surface to prevent drying, scaling, and chapping. Medicated soaps are inadvisable unless recommended by a doctor, and when dryness is a chronic problem, detergent preparations may be less dehydrating and less irritating than true soap. Cleansing lotions, cleansing creams, or cold creams removed with tissues will never leave the skin as clean as rubbing a lather over it with a soft washcloth and removing the suds with warm water. All makeup should be removed before going to bed. The least expensive cleansing cream will do, followed by washing with soap and water.

Whether or not the skin is naturally oily or dry is an inherited factor. A vaporizer or humidifier is the best aid to counteracting the drying effects of central heating or air conditioning. Animal fat, especially lanolin that comes from sheep wool, is the oil closest to human sebum and is, therefore, the best thing to use when skin begins to flake or crack at the knees, elbows, or fingers. It is preferred to mineral oil or vegetable oil for the purpose of lubrication. A sensible regimen of diet, rest, exercise, and good habits of personal hygiene are all the care that the average woman's skin should require.

Skin Diseases • It cannot be repeated too often that most skin cancers are caused by overexposure to the sun. They are also the most common type of cancer, but, fortunately, with the exception of malignant melanoma that is fatal in one out of three cases, skin cancers are treatable with topical medication and/or surgery. Other skin diseases are discussed under individual headings. See ACNE, CONTACT DERMATITIS, ECZEMA, PSORIASIS, ETC.

Sleep • The period during which the body withdraws from wakeful participation in the environment but is by no means in a continuous state of rest and repose. Sleep and dream research has yielded the information that there are alternating stages of sleep during which the activities of body and brain vary greatly. Of special interest is the recurring stage known as REM (Rapid Eye Movement) sleep during which dreaming occurs. In the four stages of sleep leading up to the REM stage, the body becomes progressively more inert. With the onset of REM, the brain suddenly becomes alert and active, while the body, except for the perceptible movement of the eyes under the closed lids, is deeply "asleep." The brain chemistry of REM sleep can now be duplicated experimentally with drugs, and it is hoped that investigations of dreaming will provide information about the brain chemistry of mental illness.

What has been known for several decades is that all the phases of sleep are essential for well-being and that one of the dangers of barbiturate and alcohol addiction is that these drugs suppress REM sleep and thereby suppress dreaming.

Different individuals have different sleep needs, and these needs differ at various times in the same individual's life. Some women never need more than six hours; others need at least nine to function well. While it is true that older people need less sleep, they are also likely to take brief naps during the day.

A normal state of health is characterized by, as well as promoted by, good sleeping patterns, and when sleeping problems exist over a considerable period or when they arise suddenly without visible explanation, they should be investigated. Immediate recourse to hypnotics or barbiturates is no solution to the problem; rather, it creates a new problem in and of itself.

Unaccustomed sleepiness or drowsiness may be a temporary phenomenon resulting from a wide variety of causes: overexposure to the sun; too much alcohol, especially in an overheated room; poor ventilation; too many tranquilizers; antihistamines; hangover effects of sedatives, tranquilizers, or sleeping pills; and low-grade infection. Chronic sleepiness may be due to thyroid deficiency, anemia, hardening of the arteries of the brain, or in rare cases the disorder known as narcolepsy. See INSOMNIA and NARCOLEPSY.

Sleeping Pills • See BARBITURATES and "Substance Abuse."

Slipped Disc • See DISC, SLIPPED.

Smallpox • An acute, severe, highly infectious virus disease, eradicated throughout the world by enforced vaccination. While immunization is no longer relevant as a health measure (the last case was reported in 1977), laboratories in the United States and elsewhere maintain a stockpile of the smallpox virus in order to be able to produce the vaccine in the event of some future outbreak of the disease.

Smegma • A sebaceous secretion of a cheeselike consistency that accumulates near the clitoris and under the foreskin of the penis. Unless scrupulously washed off, it is likely to be retained and cause irritation under the foreskin of the uncircumcised male, leading to inflammation and pain.

Smoking • According to the U.S. Surgeon General, "Cigarette smoking is clearly defined as the chief cause of preventable death in our society. Thirty percent of all cancer deaths are attributable to smoking—not only cancer of the lung, larynx, and esophagus, but as a factor in bladder, kidney, and pancreatic cancer."

In a recent year, up to $35 billion was spent on smoking-related diseases in the United States. In 1985, lung cancer overtook breast cancer as the leading cause of cancer deaths in women.

Smoking is the principal cause of coronary heart disease in young and middle-aged women in the United States, and women who smoke as few as one to four cigarettes a day are two or three times more likely to have a heart attack as nonsmoking women. The combination of cigarette smoking and the contraceptive pill puts women at serious risk of stroke as well as of heart attack. Women who smoke more than one pack a day are four times as likely to develop Alzheimer's disease as nonsmokers.

In addition, it is well-documented that smokers suffer from chronic respiratory diseases, including bronchitis, emphysema, and asthma; have a higher rate of pneumonia; and face a greater risk in relation to anesthesia during surgery. They also experience more serious postoperative breathing problems.

Women who smoke are likely to suffer from headaches caused by the carbon dioxide in smoke, and for those who have ulcers, smoking is not only the greatest obstacle to healing even when ulcer drugs are used, it is also the greatest cause of ulcer recurrence following recovery.

Pregnant women who smoke diminish the supply of oxygen to the fetus, thereby upsetting fetal metabolism and the endocrine gland system and increasing the likelihood of prematurity, miscarriage, and fetal death. Infants born to smokers are likely to weigh less and to show slower rates of physical and mental growth. The nicotine transmitted in the milk of nursing mothers can cause vomiting, diarrhea, rapid heartbeat, and restlessness in the infant.

Parents who smoke are considered by health experts to be guilty of child abuse. A growing child constantly exposed to cigarette smoke is known to be more likely to suffer from ear, nose, and throat infections, bronchitis, asthma attacks, and decreased lung efficiency. And in terms of future damage, if the parent smokes, the offspring are likely to smoke too.

As a result of the well-documented health hazards of secondary smoke for the nonsmoker, many states have passed laws mandating smoke-free environments in public places as well as places of employment. Where such laws do not yet exist, corporate and small business employers are making their own regulations for the health protection of nonsmoking personnel. Recently, the arm of the law has reached into the home to guard vulnerable family members from the effects of secondary smoke.

Of the women who smoke, 4 out of 5 say they want to quit, but the addictive properties of nicotine make it hard to do so. In addition, most women who feel they might be strong enough to overcome their addiction are fearful that if they give up smoking, they will gain weight. In fact, 60 percent do gain from 10 to 20 pounds, which they find difficult to lose.

Among the reasons for the unwanted weight gain are the following: without the chemical interference of all aspects of smoking, the appetite increases, metabolism slows down, and food tastes better. It is also true that nicotine has its advantages: it makes performance easier, improves memory, reduces anxiety, reduces hunger, and increases tolerance for pain. However, smokers should consider other effects of nicotine as well.

Nicotine is absorbed into the bloodstream and has a variety of sometimes paradoxical effects. It may either increase or slow the heart rate; it may increase the breathing rate, raise blood pressure, and stimulate the body through the release of adrenalin yet inhibit muscle activity to the point of paralysis. (It is this latter effect that makes nicotine useful as a garden insecticide.) Nicotine is also a brain stimulant and in high doses can produce tremors and convulsions. Vomiting, intestinal cramps, and diarrhea may also occur. Obviously this is an extremely toxic drug, and while ordinary smoking is not associated with many of the above symptoms, subtle forms of intoxication are inevitable. Nicotine can also be fatal: death would result if the average adult were to swallow the contents of two high-tar cigarettes all at once. The lethal dose is in the range of 60 milligrams, and some brands contain 30 milligrams each. Cigarette smoke, however, contains 25 to 30 percent of this total amount. Chronic exposure to nicotine results in tolerance and habituation.

Appreciable amounts of carbon monoxide are also present in smoke. This gas is readily absorbed into the blood, where it combines with red blood cells and prevents them from performing their essential function of transporting oxygen from the lungs to the body's tissues. In regular smokers anywhere from 5 to 10 percent of the red blood cells are immobilized in this way. The immobilization produces a condition similar to anemia, even though the smoker appears to have sufficient red blood cells. This consequence may have particular implications for athletes, for individuals with heart impairment, and for pregnant women.

Finally, taking all variables into consideration, the facts clearly indicate that the death rate among smokers aged 45 to 65 years is 70 percent higher than for nonsmokers in the same age category. Another way of saying this is that a woman who smokes two packs a day at age 23 and who continues to smoke can expect to die 8.3 years sooner than her nonsmoking counterpart. These figures indicate that smoking is the major factor that wipes out the 8 years of additional life expectancy normally enjoyed by women in the United States. Is this the progress in terms of sexual equality implied in the cigarette advertising slogan that says "You've come a long way, baby!"?

For a detailed discussion of techniques that are recommended for overcoming the addiction to smoking without unwanted weight gain, *see* "Substance Abuse."

Soap • A substance compounded of fatty acids and alkali, usually with the addition of a pleasant scent. Although all soaps are antiseptic, some contain stronger chemicals than others and may cause contact dermatitis on sensitive skin. Women with fair skin and light eyes are likelier than others to be sensitive to highly perfumed soaps and should, therefore, choose those that are bland or hypoallergenic if they wish to avoid rashes. Deodorant soaps can effectively slow down the multiplication of bacteria, even though they do not kill them. Soaps containing lanolin are helpful in lubricating dry skin, and medicated soaps contain ingredients that can promote the healing of cracked skin. The vegetable fat in cocoa butter soap is not as effective a lubricant as lanolin.

Sodium Chloride • *See* SALT.

Sonogram • An image of interior portions of the body produced by high-frequency sound waves. This imaging is useful in locating gallstones; diagnosing heart impairment; and while not used for screening breast cancer, sonography is helpful in differentiating breast cysts and infections from malignancies. It is an especially important tool in evaluating a high-risk pregnancy. However, even though no adverse effect is connected with its use under these circumstances, it is not a routine procedure for checking on a normal pregnancy. *See* "Pregnancy and Childbirth."

Spasm • An involuntary contraction of a muscle or group of muscles, usually the consequence of irritation of a nerve. Coronary artery spasms, believed to be among the causes of angina and heart attack, have been traced to atherosclerosis, smoking, and/or stress. Spasms of the bladder, which result in the need to urinate even when the bladder is not full, may be the result of a urinary tract infection or some other condition that can be corrected by the right treatment. Spasms of the esophagus are so painful that they may be mistaken for angina attacks. Correct diagnosis is based on ruling out coronary artery disease and performing an esophageal motility study. Spasms in which there is an alternation of muscle contraction and relaxation, as occurs in hiccups, are called clonic spasms. When uncontrollable and repetitive spasms are without apparent cause, they are known as tics. Such tics, accompanied by pain, occur in trigeminal neuralgia. Any spasm that affects the entire body is called convulsive, as in the convulsions that accompany some epileptic seizures or that may occur when a high fever irritates the brain.

Spastic Colon • *See* IRRITABLE BOWEL SYNDROME.

Speculum • A metal or plastic instrument with rounded blades that dilate a body passage or cavity to facilitate examination. *See* "Gynecological Diseases and Treatment."

Speech Disorders • Abnormalities in spoken word formation that may be the result of organic anomalies, medication, disease, or emotional stress. For example, disordered speech may be caused by a cleft palate or severe malocclusion; overmedication with tranquilizers or an addictive use of barbiturates; diseases such as parkinsonism or cerebral palsy; conditions such as the aftermath of a stroke, and cumulative hearing loss, and normal occasions of emotional tension resulting in "stammering with embarrassment" or "sputtering with rage." Mild speech defects, such as a lisp or an inability to articulate the *r* or *l* sound correctly, may be a sufficient source of self-consciousness to require concentrated corrective therapy, especially if the defect causes a curtailment of such activities as speaking in public or produces difficulties during job interviews. A pronounced stutter can be agonizing. New audiovisual biofeedback techniques are being used in some speech therapy clinics with varying success depending on the seriousness of the disability. For adult stutterers corrective procedure may combine psychotherapy, medication, and disciplined reeducation of the tempo of word production as well as counseling for family members in how to help the stutterer.

Sperm • The male germ cell that must penetrate and fertilize the female ovum in order to accomplish conception. Sperm cells, technically called spermatozoa, are produced by the testicles under the stimulation of gonadotropins from the pituitary gland. The cells are carried in the semen, which is ejaculated during the climax of sexual intercourse (orgasm). Each sperm cell resembles a translucent tadpole and is about 1/5000 of an inch long, with a flat elliptical head containing a complete set of chromosomes and an elongated tail by which it propels itself through the cervical canal in the direction of the ovum. Of the millions that move upward into the uterus, only a few live long enough to reach the fallopian tubes. If an ovum is available, fertilization may occur. Only one sperm cell ordinarily penetrates. The single penetration barricades the ovum against further penetration, and the processes of reproduction are initiated. Where male infertility exists, the main cause is poor sperm production, either because of testicular disease, occupational exposure to certain pesticides and other industrial chemicals such as lead, general ill health, radiation exposure, dietary deficiency, alcohol, emotional stress, or overheated testicles. *See* "Infertility" and SEMEN.

Spermicide • Any substance that kills sperm. Spermicides are available in different forms: creams, foams, suppositories, and when combined with a condom, they are a highly effective contraceptive. This combination also provides excellent protection against sexually transmissible diseases.

Spleen • A flattened, oblong organ located behind the stomach in the lower left area of the rib cage. It is purplish red in color and weighs approximately 6 ounces. The spleen acts as a reservoir for red blood cells, which it supplies to the bloodstream in any emergencies that diminish oxygen content. Through a network of white cells called phagocytes, the spleen also cleanses the blood of parasites, foreign substances, and damaged red cells. In its paler lymphatic tissue it manufactures the white cells known as lymphocytes that ward off infection. When removal of the spleen is essential because of hemorrhage following an injury; because it is affected by malaria, tuberculosis, or other diseases; or to control thrombocytopenia (shortage of blood platelets) or other diseases, its functions are taken over by the liver and bone marrow. *See* PNEUMONIA.

Spotting • Irregular or recurrent nonmenstrual bleeding from the uterus, cervix, or vagina. The most common cause of spotting prior to menopause is hormonal imbalance, either natural or resulting from taking oral contraceptives. Causes after menopause are fibroids, endometrial cancer, excess synthetic estrogen. Spotting that occurs after strenuous exercise or sexual intercourse may indicate the presence of cervical polyps or erosions or small vaginal tears. Spotting should be investigated promptly with a pelvic examination, pap smear, and perhaps a D&C. When it occurs during pregnancy, it may signal the onset of a spontaneous abortion. The occurrence should be called to the doctor's attention at once, because a prompt regimen of bed rest may be all that is necessary to prevent the abortion.

Sprain • An injury to the soft tissues around a joint. Ligaments can be torn or stretched, with damage to associated tendons, blood vessels, and nerves. The severity of a sprain depends on how badly the joint was twisted or wrenched. In some cases the pain is immobilizing and there is considerable swelling accompanied by a large area of discoloration. Because the symptoms are practically indistinguishable from those of a simple fracture, it is sensible to have the injured part X-rayed. If this procedure must be delayed, the first-aid measures known as the RICE treatment should be observed: *R*est, *I*ce application, *C*ompression with an elasticized bandage, and *E*levation. If the site of the sprain (or possible fracture) is in the wrist or elbow, the arm should be supported by a neck sling improvised from a large scarf or a torn sheet. In milder injuries the healing process may be hastened by the application of heat the next day and the intermittent application of heat for short periods of time thereafter.

Staphylococcus Infection • A category of diseases caused by various strains of staphylococcus bacteria, so named for their tendency to grow in grapelike clusters (staphylo) and their round shape (coccus). They are responsible for toxic shock syndrome and for a life-threatening pneumonia that can follow an attack of viral flu; they cause some types of food poisoning; they produce skin disorders such as impetigo, boils, and sties; and they are also a cause of osteomyelitis, an inflammation of the bones, and of bacterial endocarditis, an inflammation of the inner lining of the heart. Staph infections present a particular problem in hospitals, where they are known to cause epidemics among the newborn. While many of these bacteria have developed strains resistant to penicillin and the older antibiotics, newer broad spectrum antibiotics are able to combat them effectively.

Sterility • *See* INFERTILITY.

Sterilization • Any process that removes the organs of reproduction or makes them incapable of functioning effectively. *See* "Contraception and Abortion."

Steroids • A group of hormones, also called corticosteroids, produced from cholesterol by the adrenal cortex and also available in synthesized form. At least 30 of these substances have been identified, of which the best-known and most widely used is cortisone. Among the many functions of the steroids are regulation of the water and salt balance of body fluids, assistance in protein metabolism, the formation of antibodies, and the repair of damaged tissues.

The fact that steroids suppress inflammation has provided helpful treatment for a large number of disorders formerly unresponsive to drug therapy such as lupus erythematosus, nephritis, and contact dermatitis as well as asthma, arthritis, and allergies. However, steroid therapy is usually scheduled on a short-term basis because of the unpleasant side effects. Monitoring is also required because of the dangers of sudden withdrawal after protracted use.

For people suffering from Addison's disease (nonfunction of the adrenal cortex), lifetime steroid replacement plays the same vital role as insulin does for the diabetic.

Stethoscope • A diagnostic instrument that amplifies the sounds produced by the lungs, heart, and other organs; used by doctors during the listening part of an examination known as auscultation.

Stillbirth • The delivery after twenty completed weeks of pregnancy of a baby that shows no sign of life. *See* MISCARRIAGE.

Stomach • The pouchlike digestive organ into which food is emptied from the esophagus. The stomach, which leads directly into the duodenum, lies below the diaphragm in the upper left portion of the abdomen, hanging more or less freely and moving with the intake and exhalation of breath. It is composed of three layers of different types of muscle fibers that respond to the need for expansion as the stomach fills with food and are responsible for the rhythmic contractions of peristalsis during which the digestive juices are mixed with the partially digested food and churned into a semiliquid consistency. The full stomach holds about $2^{1}/_{2}$ quarts; when empty, its walls lie flat against each other. The mucous membrane lining contains the glands that secrete hydrochloric acid and the digestive enzymes. The normal functioning of these glands is controlled by the actual presence of food in the stomach and by the neurological reflexes activated by the expectation or the sight of food. Like all glands, those of the stomach can be adversely affected by strong feelings. Anger especially increases the gastric secretion leading to a "churning" sensation, which, if chronic, may eventually be the cause of an ulcer. A sudden attack of anxiety or of acute fear may actually cause paralysis of the muscular wall of the stomach so that it dilates and drops to a lower part of the abdominal cavity resulting in a sinking sensation. Stomach disorders include mild indigestion, chronic or acute gastritis, ulcers (often the result of heavy drinking, smoking, and stress), and tumors both benign and malignant.

The decrease in the incidence of stomach cancer in the United States seems to be attributable to an improvement in eating habits.

Because aspirin is known to irritate the mucous lining of the stomach and in excess can cause gastrointestinal bleeding, it should be taken after a meal rather than when the stomach is empty. For those particularly sensitive to aspirin, medicines containing acetaminophen or ibuprofen are recommended. See HEARTBURN, INDIGESTION, and "The Healthy Woman."

Strain • A mild injury to a muscle, usually caused by subjecting it to unaccustomed tension, as occurs through overexertion or an accident; also called a pulled muscle. (A sprain is more serious, involving stretched or torn ligaments.) Among the most common are twisted ankles caused by a misstep and strained back muscles caused by lifting a heavy weight incorrectly. Wrist muscles may also be strained in various athletic endeavors. For treatment, see SPRAIN.

Streptococcus Infection • A category of diseases caused by strains of streptococcus bacteria, so named for their chainlike arrangement (strepto) and their round shape (coccus). Among the strep-caused disorders are pharyngitis (strep throat), scarlet fever, puerperal fever, and some pneumonias. Rheumatic fever or glomerulonephritis may follow a strep infection if it has not been definitively controlled by a full course of antibiotics.

The species *Streptococcus viridans*, which is normally present in the mouth and harmless for most people, is a cause of subacute bacterial endocarditis in people who have damaged heart valves. Because this species also surrounds the roots of abscessed teeth and because they may enter the bloodstream following the extraction of the tooth, a prophylactic dose of antibiotic medicine, usually penicillin, before a tooth is pulled is always advisable. *Streptococcus mutans* is a bacterial strain that causes cavities. An effective vaccine against this strain is expected to be available soon.

Stress • Physical, chemical, or emotional factors that constrain or exert pressure on body organs or processes and on mental processes; in contemporary, popular usage, psychological pressures. See "Health on the Job."

Stroke • A discontinuity or interruption of the flow of blood to the brain causing a loss of consciousness and, depending on the severity and length of the circulatory deprivation, resulting in partial or complete paralysis of such functions as speech and movement: also known as a cerebrovascular accident and sometimes still called apoplexy. The processes leading to a stroke are cerebral thrombosis, cerebral embolism, and cerebral hemorrhage. When the blood vessels of the brain have been damaged and constricted by atherosclerosis, the formation of a clot may completely block circulatory flow. A similar blockage may occur because an embolus of air, fat, or other foreign matter impedes blood flow to the brain. The chief underlying cause of cerebral hemorrhage is a preexisting condition of hypertension, especially in combination with arteriosclerosis or atherosclerosis. The consequences of a stroke, short of being fatal, depend on what part of the brain has been deprived of oxygen and for how long. The deprivation may be so brief as to be inconsequential, or an arm or a leg

STROKE

Arteries to brain

POSSIBLE CAUSES OF
INTERRUPTED BLOOD FLOW
TO BRAIN

Thrombosis   Embolism   Hemorrhage

may be paralyzed, speech may be impaired, or the victim may go into a coma. Hospitalization in an intensive care unit must be prompt, because the correct treatment immediately following the stroke and for the first few days afterward is crucial to the amount of recovery achieved by the patient. Physical therapy for the rehabilitation of the affected muscles should begin while the patient is still in bed. Team treatment by a speech therapist, occupational therapist, and continuing evaluation by medical experts, including a psychiatrist should inspire confidence in the patient and provide the motivation for maximum cooperation. Essential to rehabilitation is the involvement of family members and the establishment of an optimistic outlook in their minds as well. In the final analysis, the patient's determination to overcome the disabilities caused by the stroke is the most critical factor in the success of the treatment.

Stuttering • *See* SPEECH DISORDERS.

Sty • An infection of a sebaceous gland at the rim of the eyelid, usually at the root of an eyelash. The infection, which results in inflammation and abscess, is usually caused by staphylococcus bacteria. If it does not respond to home treatment of hot compresses applied for about fifteen minutes every two hours and the use of ophthalmic ointment that can be bought without prescription, a doctor should be consulted. The most likely causes of frequently recurring sties are a generally poor state of health with low resistance to everpresent germs and the careless habit of rubbing the eyes with unwashed hands. Unclean or borrowed articles of eye makeup may also carry infection resulting in sties.

Sudden Infant Death Syndrome (SIDS) • The sudden, unexpected, and inexplicable death during sleep of an infant who was well or almost well prior to death. For some unknown reason, breathing stops. In typical cases, the infants are 2 to 4 months old; very few are more than 6 months old. Disproportionate numbers are males who were born prematurely.

In the United States, SIDS is the largest single cause of infant deaths, claiming about 2 per 1,000 live births. Blacks are at the highest risk; Asians at the lowest. While the cause is unknown, the immediate circumstance is cessation of breathing during sleep (called sleep apnea). Low birth weight, prematurity, and drug/alcohol abuse by the mother during pregnancy appear to be contributing causes. See "Directory of Health Information."

Sugar • Any of the following sweet carbohydrates found in free form in various foods: sucrose (beets, cane, maple syrup); lactose (milk); maltose (malt products); glucose and dextrose (fruit, honey, corn syrup); fructose (honey, fruit juices). From a nutritional point of view, sugar is said to provide "empty" calories because it contains no vitamins or minerals.

It is known that the bacteria that flourish in dental plaque feed on sugar and produce the acids that destroy tooth surfaces. The use of a mouthwash or merely rinsing with warm water after eating sweets is, therefore, a practical defense against cavities. See CARBOHYDRATES, GLUCOSE, and "Nutrition, Weight, and General Well-Being."

Sulfonamides • A group of medicines, known as sulfa drugs, that inhibit the growth and reproduction of various bacteria. Because many of these drugs have negative side effects, they have largely been replaced by antibiotics. However, some sulfa drugs, especially sulfadiazine, may be prescribed, often in combination with other sulfa drugs, for meningococcal, E. Coli, and other infections.

A sulfa compound, sulfamethaxazole (Bactrim) is currently prescribed for infection by bacterial agents that have become resistant to penicillin. A related group known as sulfonylureal drugs are oral hypoglycemic medications prescribed for diabetic patients. One of the most frequently used in this category is Orinase (tolbutamide).

Because sulfa drugs may reduce the effectiveness of the contraceptive pill, a temporary shift to another form of birth control is advisable during the period of sulfa therapy.

Sunburn • Inflammation of the skin caused by overexposure to the ultraviolet rays of the sun or a sunlamp. The lighter the skin, the more quickly it burns. The condition may be limited to a reddening or it may be equivalent to a second-degree burn with blisters and a fever. The best treatment for a mild burn is to avoid the sun for a while and to leave the burned area alone or apply cold, wet dressings to reduce swelling and discomfort. A severe burn may require professional medical attention.

Excessive exposure to sun or a sunlamp does more harm than good for almost everyone. Irrefutable conclusions of medical research indicate that prolonged exposure increases the risks of skin cancer and of wrinkles. For the elderly and anyone with a heart condition, lupus erythematosus, or high blood pressure, the sun can be downright dangerous, especially if there is any possibility of the onset of heat stroke. Women taking certain medicines either for indefinite or short-term therapy should be aware of the fact that overexposure to the sun may produce skin eruptions. While reactions differ in individual cases, the following drugs should be suspected as a possible cause when a rash appears following a period of sitting or lying in the sun: birth-control pills, antihistamines, oral medication for diabetes, diuretics, antibiotics, fungicides, and tranquilizers.

Sunscreen • A light-absorbing chemical that protects the skin from the harmful effects of exposure to the sun. Most cosmetics contain one or another sunscreen, and it may be this very ingredient that causes the user to develop an allergic rash. As such, however, sunscreens are indispensable in reducing the likelihood of sunburn. The ointment or liquid should be applied an hour before exposure and reapplied after swimming or heavy perspiring. The strength of the protection is provided on the label by number, the highest number providing the maximum protection.

Surgery • *See* "Breast Care," "Cosmetic Surgery," "Gynecologic Diseases and Treatment," and "You, Your Doctors, and the Health Care System."

Surrogate Mother • A woman who contracts to bear a child for another woman who is sterile. The pregnancy is achieved by artificial insemination with sperm, usually from the partner of the sterile woman. The surrogate mother agrees to turn the baby over for adoption right after birth to the couple or sterile woman who pay for all the medical and legal expenses involved. In some cases, surrogate mothers act voluntarily; in others, they receive a large fee for their services. Most of the moral and legal questions raised by this procedure have yet to be resolved. In the meantime, many states have passed laws concerning surrogate motherhood so that the outright sale of babies can be prevented and the profiteering by intermediaries can be eliminated.

Syndrome • A group of signs and symptoms that occur together and characterize a particular disease or abnormal condition.

Syphilis • *See* "Sexually Transmissible Diseases."

Tagamet • *See* CIMETIDINE.

Tampon • A plug of absorbent cotton or similar material placed within a body cavity in order to soak up secretions and hemorrhagic blood, and especially to contain the menstrual flow. Tampons for this latter purpose are designed for easy insertion into the vaginal opening and for removal by an attached string. They can be used even if the hymen is still unbroken, although they may be difficult to insert until the hymen is stretched. Attention has focused on tampon use because of its connection with the severe and acute bacterial disease known as toxic shock syndrome. Following the adverse publicity about this connection, many women have switched to sanitary pads, now designed so that their use no longer involves the paraphernalia formerly associated with them. However, women who frequently suffer from urinary tract infections might be well advised to use tampons. All users of tampons should change them about 4 times each day.

Tay-Sachs Disease • An incurable and usually fatal genetic disease of fat metabolism found almost exclusively among Jews of central and eastern European origin. There is a statistical probability that in 1 of 900 marriages of these Ashkenazic Jews, both partners will be carriers of the gene. Genetic counseling in advance of a pregnancy is considered advisable for those who might be carriers. When the pregnancy already exists, amniocentesis can determine whether the fetus has the disease. Should this be the case, a therapeutic abortion usually is possible. *See* GENETIC COUNSELING.

TB • *See* TUBERCULOSIS.

Tear Glands • *See* LACRIMAL DUCTS.

Teeth • *See* DENTAL CARE, ORTHODONTIA, and PLAQUE.

Telemetry • The long-distance transmission by electronic signals of measurement data and other information. Telemetric devices, originally developed for rocketry and space science, have been adapted for attachment to telephones so that, for example, a doctor in a rural hospital can transmit a patient's electrocardiogram or electroencephalogram to medical specialists thousands of miles away for further evaluation. The technique is also widely used for testing artificial pacemaker competence by telephone.

Temperature • *See* FEVER.

Temporomandibular Joint (TMJ) • The joint in front of each ear where the skull connects with the lower jaw. The action of the joint, which is always bilateral, is controlled by a group of large muscles that enable the lower jaw to move up and down, and more rarely, sideways. When the jaw muscles are tensed unconsciously in tooth grinding, or consciously in clenching the teeth, or when they cannot function smoothly because of malocclusion, pains of seemingly mysterious origin are the result, especially pains in the ear or headache. A dentist who specializes in the diagnosis and treatment of the TMJ syndrome should be consulted when there is reason to believe that this irregularity is the source of chronic discomfort.

Terramycin • Brand name of oxytetracycline, one of the broad spectrum antibiotics. *See* TETRACYCLINE.

Test Tube Baby • *See* IN VITRO FERTILIZATION and "Infertility."

Testicles • The principal male organs of reproduction; the sex organs; also called testes. The testicles are located within the scrotum and produce the hormone testosterone, which determines the secondary sex characteristics of the male at puberty: deep voice, hair distribution, body build, and sexual drive. They also produce sperm cells. Each testis contains about 250 lobules in which tiny tubes produce the spermatozoa that leave the testicles at maturity by way of the convoluted passage called the epididymis. *See* "Infertility."

Tetanus • An acute infectious disease caused by the entrance into the body through a break in the skin of the microorganism *Clostridium tetani*. A tetanus-prone wound is one which is deep, has much tissue damage and necrosis (destruction), is uncleaned for four or more hours, and is contaminated by soil or street dirt. The exotoxin produced by the *C. tetani* bacteria affects the nervous system in such a way as to cause paralyzing muscle spasms, hence the term lockjaw to describe one of the early symptoms. The tetanus bacilli grow in the intestines of all mammals and are found in soil and dust contaminated by the feces of the carriers. Once a widespread and fatal disease, it affects fewer than 500 people a year in this country, thanks to routine immunization of infants and booster shots for children and adults. Any injury that might be a tetanus-prone wound is sufficient reason for consulting the closest doctor within 24 hours about proper immunization and antibiotic administration. See "Immunization Guide."

Tetracycline • A broad spectrum antibiotic prescribed, especially for patients with penicillin sensitivity for such bacterial infections as pneumonia, bronchitis, meningitis, for the rickettsial diseases, and for some sexually transmitted diseases. It is the antibiotic of choice for severe cases of acne, and some doctors prescribe it as a prophylactic measure against traveler's diarrhea. In such cases, the traveler must avoid exposure to the sun because tetracycline is photosensitive. Among other undesirable side effects are skin rashes and gastrointestinal irritation. Because it may discolor teeth and interfere with the bone development of a child whose mother took tetracycline in the last half of pregnancy, it is contraindicated after the fourth month of pregnancy. For similar reasons the American Medical Association recommends that other antibiotics be prescribed for children under 8 years of age. See "Brand and Generic Names of Commonly Prescribed Drugs."

Thermography • A technique for recording variations in skin temperature by the use of photographic film sensitive to the infrared radiation given off by the surface of the body. The result of the test is called a thermogram. Because tumor cells produce somewhat more heat than normal ones, this procedure can be helpful in the detection of incipient breast cancer. Thermography is noninvasive, but for purposes of diagnostic accuracy it is not as definitive as mammography.

Thiamin • One of the B complex vitamins; also known as vitamin B_1. See "Nutrition, Weight, and General Well-Being."

Thorazine • See CHLORPROMAZINE.

Thrombosis • The formation of a clot, technically called a thrombus, in a blood vessel, most commonly in a varicose vein in the leg or in any artery in which the interior walls are roughened by atherosclerosis. The blockage of a narrow blood vessel by a thrombus may have grave consequences: when the obstruction occurs in one of the coronary arteries (coronary thrombosis), the result may be a major heart attack; obstructive thrombosis in the brain is a cause of stroke. A complication of thrombosis is thromboembolism in which a part of the clot breaks off to form what is called an embolism, circulates to other parts of the body, and causes obstruction, as in pulmonary thromboembolism. The risks of thrombosis increase not only with age but with the use of the contraceptive pill, particularly among cigarette smokers. Two drugs used specifically to treat or prevent thrombosis are heparin, which is given intravenously or subcutaneously, and coumarin, which is taken orally. These drugs are called anticoagulants. There are also a number of drugs that have an anticoagulant effect especially when combined with coumarin. Included among these are steroids and salicylates (aspirin). *See* PHLEBITIS and "Contraception and Abortion."

Tic • Involuntary and repeated spasmodic contractions of a muscle or group of muscles; also called habit spasms or nervous tics. Such movements usually develop in childhood in response to emotional stress, and while they may subside from time to time during adulthood, they almost inevitably return during periods of fatigue or tension. Among the more common tics are blinking, clearing the throat, jerking the head, twitching the lips. Psychotherapy and tranquilizers can sometimes eliminate a tic, but the former treatment may be too time-consuming and too expensive and the latter may lead to problems more unpleasant than the tic itself. The specific instance in which involuntary spasms of facial muscles originate in a physical disorder is the symptom known as tic douloureux discussed under TRIGEMINAL NEURALGIA. *See* ALSO TOURETTE'S SYNDROME.

Ticks • Blood-sucking parasites. Some ticks are comparatively harmless, but others transmit disease. *See* RICKETTSIAL DISEASES, ROCKY MOUNTAIN SPOTTED FEVER, TYPHUS.

Tinnitus • The sensation of hearing sounds—humming, buzzing, ringing—that originate within the ear rather than as a result of an outside stimulus. Tinnitus should not be confused with the auditory hallucinations of some mental illnesses. The buzzing and ringing may be the temporary result of a blocked eustachian tube such as occurs during an upper respiratory infection or an allergic response. It may also occur after a head injury, following exposure to an extraordinarily loud noise, or as a side effect of certain medications, especially streptomycin. The diseases with which it is associated are Ménière's disease, otosclerosis, and brain tumor, but most cases are of mysterious origin. If the noises can be ignored, so much the better. When they are disturbingly intrusive at bedtime, they can be masked by soft music from a nearby radio. In recent years, ultrasonic irradiation of the inner ear has achieved some success. Where a hearing problem is also present, an electronic device that produces a sound that masks the noise of tinnitus can be fitted inside the casing of the ordinary hearing aid.

Tobacco • The three major components of tobacco smoking that cause medical concern are tars, nicotine, and carbon monoxide. Tars are not absorbed by the body, but because they are deposited in the cells lining the respiratory tract and lung air spaces, they act as cell irritants.

Nicotine is the powerful drug to which smokers become addicted. The carbon monoxide in inhaled smoke is absorbed into the blood where it impairs the red blood cells and prevents them from transporting oxygen from the lungs to the body tissues. *See* SMOKING, NICOTINE, and "Substance Abuse."

Tonsils • Two clumps of spongy lymphoid tissue lying one on each side of the throat, visible behind the back of the tongue between the folded membranes that lead to the soft palate. Together with the adenoids, which are located behind the nose at the opening of the eustachian tube, the tonsils function somewhat like filters, guarding the respiratory tract against foreign invasion. When they become infected, inflamed, or enlarged, they are the source of complications leading to difficulties in swallowing and to the spread of the infectious agents to surrounding tissues. When the infection is streptococcal (strep throat), antibiotic treatment must be prompt to prevent the further complication of kidney infection or heart involvement. When enlarged tonsils are a chronic cause of respiratory difficulties over several years or when the adenoids constantly transmit infection to the sinuses or the middle ear, removal by surgery should be considered. However, a tonsillectomy or adenoidectomy should not be undertaken without substantial indication that the operation is justifiable as a health measure.

Tourette's Syndrome • A disorder of unknown origin characterized by face and body tics, and eventually by vocal tics that include barking, squealing, and the compulsive use of obscene language and swearing. The disorder begins in childhood and at no point in its development is intellectual function impaired. Because the victim is incapable of controlling the antisocial behavior associated with the disorder, medication is considered advisable. The drug of choice is Haldol (haloperidol).

Toxemia • A condition in which the bloodstream has been invaded by toxic substances; similar to septicemia, and also called blood poisoning. The condition once known as the toxemia of pregnancy is now called eclampsia. See "Pregnancy and Childbirth."

Toxic Shock Syndrome (TSS) • A rare bacterial infection, fatal in some cases, characterized by high fever, diarrhea, vomiting, a dramatic drop in blood pressure, and a rash. The syndrome is associated in most reported instances with the use of menstrual tampons, especially highly absorbent ones. The infectious agent is a toxic substance made by a strain of staphylococcus bacteria. See TAMPON; "Gynecologic Diseases and Treatment," and "Contraception and Abortion."

Toxoplasmosis • A systemic infectious protozoal disease that may be serious and occasionally is fatal. A fetus whose mother is infected during pregnancy may become severely infected. The primary source of the infection is the feces of infected cats.

TPA (Tissue Plasminogen Activator) • A natural body substance known to dissolve small blood clots that routinely form in blood vessels. Thanks to genetic engineering, TPA, in short supply in its natural form, is now available as a medication for intravenous administration to unclog coronary arteries immediately after a heart attack so that the likelihood of a recurrent attack is minimized.

Tranquilizers • A category of drugs that suppress anxiety symptoms without effecting a cure. Tranquilizers are designated as minor if they have the effect of allaying stress and as major if they alter such psychotic manifestations as hysteria, hallucinations, extreme aggressiveness, or suicidal tendencies. The minor tranquilizers are the most commonly prescribed drugs in the United States, especially those that are members of the benzodiazepine group (Valium, Librium). The major tranquilizers (Stelazine, Thorazine) can be numbing and, in large doses, fatal. All tranquilizers have the potential of producing mild to extremely adverse side effects.

The anti-anxiety drugs are meant to be prescribed on a short-term basis and combined with psychotherapy so that eventually stress can be handled without medication. The major tranquilizers may enable some mentally ill patients to function more or less adequately, but adverse side effects may necessitate intermittent withdrawal of the medication. The use of all tranquilizers should be closely monitored by a physician. They should be avoided especially during the early months of pregnancy because they can cause irreversible damage to the fetus. See PSYCHOTROPIC DRUGS and "Substance Abuse."

Transfusion • See BLOOD TRANSFUSION.

Transvestite • An individual (usually a male) whose emotional and sexual gratification is achieved by dressing and behaving like a member of the opposite sex.

Traveler's Diarrhea • See DIARRHEA.

Tremor • Involuntary shaking or quivering, usually of the hands, but also of the head or other parts of the body. Tremors may be coarse or fine, depending on the amplitude of the oscillation. They may occur when the body is at rest, ceasing when intentional movement occurs, or they may occur only during acts of volition. The latter are called "intention tremors." Tremors may also accompany a chill or fever or may be one of the symptoms of withdrawal from alcohol, cocaine, barbiturates, and other drugs. Among the diseases with which tremor is associated are cerebral palsy, multiple sclerosis, parkinsonism, hyperthyroidism, arteriosclerosis of the brain, and late syphilis. The trembling that accompanies an anxiety attack or the onset of hysteria may be controlled by sedatives. When an organic disorder is the cause, the tremor usually diminishes with proper treatment of the disease.

Trench Mouth • See GUMS.

Trichomonas Vaginalis • A species of parasite that can cause vaginal inflammation in females and urethral inflammation in males; also called trichomoniasis. See "Sexually Transmissible Diseases."

Trigeminal Neuralgia • Intermittent and acute sensitivity of the fifth cranial nerve (the sensory nerve of the face); also known as tic douloureux. The condition is characterized by the sudden and unpredictable onset of paroxysms of extreme pain seemingly unaccompanied by any change in the nerve itself. The disorder is of unknown origin. It is more common among women than men and rarely occurs before middle age. The spasms of pain may be triggered by such random circumstances as a draft of cold air, blowing the nose, or an anxiety attack. Spontaneous remission may occur after a month of attacks, with recurrence months or years later. Drug therapy provides some pain relief. When recurrent attacks become so frequent and so painful that they interfere with eating and interrupt sleep, neurosurgery is recommended.

Tubal Ligation • Also called tubal occlusion. A method of sterilization in which the fallopian tubes are blocked in such a way that the ovum becomes inaccessible for fertilization. See "Contraception and Abortion."

Tuberculosis • A major infectious disease caused by the tubercle bacillus that usually attacks the lungs and less frequently the bones, joints, kidneys, or other parts of the body; once called phthisis and consumption, now commonly referred to as TB. The disease continues to flourish wherever poverty, poor diet, and crowded substandard living conditions prevail. The infectious organisms are spread through the air from person to person from the coughs and sneezes of anyone with the disease in an active stage. Public health authorities know that in the United States and especially in urban areas many millions have been infected with the bacillus and are carrying it in their bodies in latent form. If resistance is high, the bacilli may be killed by white blood cells or they may be walled up temporarily and immobilized in small masses called tubercles. Many people have gone through an active TB episode, mistaking the symptoms, if any, for those of a heavy cold: a cough, chest pains, and feelings of fatigue. Such an occurrence usually leaves a small area of scar tissue in the affected part of the lungs. It is not at all uncommon for a woman between the ages of 20 and 40 to take a tuberculin skin test as part of a thorough physical checkup and to be told that the results are positive. Under these circumstances a chest X-ray is suggested to find out if the lungs show any active disease. If the patient does not have active disease, prophylactic medication is often prescribed to suppress the possibility of later activation of the dormant disease. Antituberculosis drugs almost always are completely effective in treating the active disease. Witness to their effectiveness is the closing down of practically all TB sanitariums. Treatment for active cases may begin in a hospital, but as soon as the noninfectious stage is reached the patient is sent home to resume all normal activities while continuing to take the prescribed medications. The most important of these for prophylactic purposes is isoniazid. Several drugs exist for treating the disease. Anyone suffering from a chronic cough, chest pains, breathing difficulties, chronic feelings of fatigue, weight loss, heavy sweating at night, and irregularity in the menstrual cycle is advised to have these symptoms checked to rule out the possibility of TB.

Tumor • A swelling in or on a particular area of the body, usually created by the development of a mass of new tissue cells having no function. Tumors may be benign or malignant; benign tumors may, but usually do not, become malignant. The presence of a tumor within the body may be unsuspected until it grows large enough to produce symptoms of pain or to interfere with the normal function of an adjacent organ or nerve. Diagnosis by biopsy determines whether the growth is cancerous or not. A malignant tumor may be treated surgically or with radiotherapy and chemotherapy. A benign growth may or may not be removed surgically, depending on its location and its potential for becoming cancerous. See "Breast Care" and "Gynecologic Diseases and Treatment."

Typhoid Fever • An acute and highly contagious disease caused by the bacterial bacillus *Salmonella typhosa* (related to the bacteria that cause food poisoning); also called enteric fever. Typhoid and paratyphoid infections are endemic wherever the laxity of public health measures results in the contamination of the food and water supplies by urine and feces containing the disease-bearing organisms. Flies may transmit the disease; restaurant workers or food handlers who have had the disease may be carriers who spread the disease unless they are scrupulous in matters of personal hygiene. The infection may also be transmitted by shellfish from contaminated waters. In a case of typhoid fever, the bacteria attack the mucous membranes of the small intestine, producing stools and occasionally urine containing the typhoid bacteria. Symptoms begin after an incubation period of about two weeks and include fever, headache, vomiting, stomach cramps, fatigue, and mental disorientation. A rash of a few days' duration may erupt on the chest and abdomen. Milder cases subside spontaneously within a week or so. Antibiotics with or without corticosteroids will effect a complete cure when administered before major complications occur. Immunization against typhoid fever in adulthood is considerably less trouble than the infection and is at least moderately effective. Travelers to those parts of the world where the disease is endemic are, therefore, advised to get the necessary shots against it. Because three successive inoculations are necessary over a three-week period, the immunization or the booster shots should be planned well in advance of departure.

Typhus • An infectious rickettsial disease transmitted by the body louse. The disease is endemic in parts of Asia, Africa, and on the shores of the Mediterranean. In another form known as flea typhus it is common in the Far East and the Southwest Pacific. Typhus is not related to typhoid fever in any way. The onset of the disease begins with a headache, acute pains in the legs and back, and sieges of uncontrollable shivering. Within a few days a rash spreads from the torso to the arms and legs, and high fever may cause delirium. Antibiotic treatment is usually effective. Travelers to places where the disease is prevalent should have an antityphus vaccination provides immunity for about one year. *See* "Immunization Schedule."

Ulcer • A chronic lesion in the epithelial tissue either on the visible surface of the body or on the lining of an interior cavity such that the tissues below the skin or mucous membrane may be exposed. Ulcers may occur for many reasons: poor circulation (bedsores, ulcerated varicose veins), infections by microorganisms (ulcerated gums, syphilitic sores), and damage caused by extremes of heat, cold, malignant growths, or chemicals.

Peptic ulcers include gastric ulcers, which occur in the stomach itself, and duodenal ulcers, which occur in the upper portion of the small intestines and are ten times more common than gastric ulcers. Although it has long been assumed that the immediate cause of peptic ulcers is the secretion of hydrochloric acid when there is no food in the alimentary canal to neutralize its corrosive effects, there is now compelling evidence that some duodenal ulcers may be caused by a bacterial agent (campylobacter).

An ulcer that is diagnosed and treated when the symptoms first appear is more likely to heal quickly and less likely to recur than if it is ignored or treated with home remedies for indigestion. The first indication is a burning pain that recurs a few hours after eating. When the condition worsens to the point where the acid that has been burning a hole in the mucous membrane eventually eats into a blood vessel and causes a hemorrhage, the condition (bleeding ulcer) requires hospitalization and emergency treatment.

Considerable progress has been made in the diagnosis and treatment of ulcers thanks to the use of fiberoptic devices that look directly at the ulcer surface. Known as endoscopy, this technique provides much more accurate information than X-rays. It is now accepted that drugs rather than diet play the crucial role in treatment. (Ironically enough, the most recent evidence indicates that milk delays rather than hastens healing.)

Several categories of drugs are now available that limit tissue damage: those that neutralize acid after it has been secreted, including a wide selection of nonprescription antacids; those that treat ulcers by reducing the amount of acid secreted by the stomach, such as the acid-suppressors Tagamet (cimetidine) and a stronger compound Zantac (ranitidine) that needs to be taken only twice a day; and the third category of drugs which, like Sucralfate (carafate) create a coating of gel that adheres to the ulcerated area, providing a protective barrier against the acid secretion of the stomach.

While there is no doubt that stress plays some part in the ulcer problem, the one variable that postpones healing more than any other—more than coffee or spicy food—is smoking.

Ultrasonography • *See* SONOGRAM.

Umbilical Cord • The structure that connects the fetus to the placenta of the mother, functioning as a lifeline through which maternal blood is transmitted to the fetus and fetal blood is returned to the mother. At the time of birth the umbilical cord, which is approximately 2 feet long and is attached at what is to become the infant's navel, is tied at two points close to each other and cut in between them. The vestige dries out and falls

URINARY TRACT INFECTIONS

off naturally within less than a week. See "Pregnancy and Childbirth."

Undulant Fever • A disease caused by drinking unpasteurized milk taken from cows (also from sheep or goats) infected with Brucella microorganisms; also called brucellosis or Malta fever. In rare cases improperly cooked meat contaminated with these microorganisms also can be a source of the disease. Characteristic symptoms are pains in the joints, fatigue, chills, and a fever that may rise and fall at various times of the day or be low in the morning and rise slowly to 104°F by evening. These fluctuations in temperature account for the name of the disorder. If the disease goes untreated, the liver, spleen, and lymph nodes become swollen and sore. Because the symptoms may be confused with those of mononucleosis or rheumatic fever, a blood test should be made so that the nature of the infectious agent can be identified. The disease is curable with antibiotics.

Uremia • *See* KIDNEY DISORDERS.

Ureter • One of two tubes, each about 12 inches in length, connecting the kidney to the bladder. The urine produced in the kidney is transmitted by the muscular contractions of the ureters into the bladder, where it is stored until it passes through the urethra in the act of urination. Inflammation of the ureter (ureteritis) may result from the presence of a stone or cysts as well as from infection.

Urethra • The muscular tube, approximately 1½ inches long in women, that carries urine from the bladder to the exterior. Both sexes are vulnerable to urethritis (inflammation of the urethra) caused by gonorrhea infection. Contamination by other infectious organisms during catheterization or as a result of bladder infection is also common. *See* URINARY TRACT INFECTIONS.

Urinary Tract Infections • The urinary bladder is joined to the kidneys by tubes called ureters; the urethra is the vessel that leads from the bladder to the external opening through which urination occurs. Urinary tract infections can involve any of these organs, the most common being bladder infection, technically called cystitis.

CYSTITIS
- Ureters
- Bladder wall is red and swollen
- Urethra
- Vagina

This infection occurs as a result of the entry of bacteria during the formation of urine as it progresses from the kidneys outward. Urinary tract infections are rarely serious, but they can be very annoying. Cystitis has a tendency to recur intermittently, especially when it is transmitted sexually between partners. Symptoms are a burning sensation during urination and a frequent feeling of having to urinate when the bladder is practically empty. There may also be a nagging pain in the lower abdomen. It is important that the causative organism be identified by urinalysis and treated with the proper antibiotic.

Urination • The excretion through the urethra of liquid wastes stored in the bladder. The fluid secreted by the kidneys travels through the ureters into the bladder where it accumulates. The urine accumulated within the bladder is prevented from flowing into the urethra by the internal sphincter of the urethra (a sphincter is a circular muscle in a state of involuntary contraction). When the stimulus from a full bladder is transformed into a conscious effort to urinate, the bladder muscles are contracted and the sphincter is relaxed. The external sphincter of the urethra is also relaxed. These motor reflexes result in the deliberate discharge of accumulated urine through the urethra to the exterior. The act of passing urine is technically called micturition. Conscious sphincter control may be reduced temporarily in adults by acute fear or some other emotionally charged reaction. Loss or impairment of bladder control, technically called incontinence, may be a consequence of infection of the bladder or other part of the urinary tract, displaced pelvic organs, and, especially in aging men, disease of the prostate gland.

About 1 quart of urine is eliminated each day, somewhat more during cold weather and less during hot weather, because in warmer weather larger amounts of fluid wastes are eliminated through the skin in the form of sweat. On the average women urinate about four times daily, with frequency depending on the amount and type of liquid consumed, state of health, age, anxiety level, and other variables. The consumption of large amounts of tea or coffee may increase frequency of urination not only because of the extra fluid but also because caffeine is a mild diuretic. Frequency increases during pregnancy not only because the uterus presses on the bladder but also because nutritional demands require a greater intake of liquids, especially of milk. The need to urinate more frequently occurs in older women as a consequence of a natural loss of muscle tone.

Any persistent abnormal sensations during the act of urination or any sudden changes in frequency or color should be reported to a doctor. Painful urination accompanied by a burning sensation is symptomatic of infections that affect the bladder or urethra. The sudden onset of abnormally frequent urination may be caused by cystitis, diabetes, or incipient kidney failure. An inability to empty the bladder completely is usually related to interference by a stone, a tumor, or partial blockage by pressure from a prolapsed uterus or to neurological disease.

Urine Tests • The examination of a urine specimen by various laboratory procedures; also called urinalysis. Because normal urine is of constant composition within definite limits, changes in the color, consistency, clarity, or specific gravity are usually, but not always, a sign of disorder. Thus, every complete physical checkup, whether during health or illness and especially at frequent intervals during pregnancy, should always include a urine test as well as questions about urination. Any visible changes in the color of urine, which is normally a pale amber, might suggest disease. Laboratory tests check for several abnormalities. Albuminuria (proteinuria) is the presence in the urine of certain proteins (albumins) indicating the possibility of kidney disease, inflammations such as cystitis or urethritis, or, during pregnancy, preeclampsia. Albuminuria may also be a response to certain drugs. Glucosuria is the consistent presence in the urine of glucose (not the occasional presence of one of the other sugars) and is usually the indication of diabetes. Hematuria, or blood in the urine, warrants further examination by instruments (cystoscopy) or X-ray if the hematuria persists in order to discover what part of the urinary tract is the source of the bleeding. Among the more common causes are the presence of a kidney stone, a tumor, or some degree of kidney failure. Pyuria, or white blood cells in the urine, is an indication of an infection of the urinary tract, in most cases cystitis or urethritis. See URINARY TRACT INFECTIONS.

Uterus • The hollow, pear-shaped, muscular organ situated in the pelvis above the bladder; also called the womb. See "Contraception and Abortion," "Infertility," and "Pregnancy and Childbirth."

Vaccination • Inoculation with a preparation of dead or attenuated live germs for purposes of immunization against a specific disease. The word itself, which derives from the Latin word for cow, was created at the time that Jenner developed vaccine from cowpox as a method of immunizing humans against smallpox. Until very recently, vaccination has been used almost exclusively to mean smallpox vaccination. The word is now used synonymously with inoculation and immunization. See "Immunization Guide.".

Vaccine • A preparation of dead or weakened live microorganisms or of other effective agents injected into the body of humans or animals for the purpose of stimulating the production of antibodies against a particular disease without producing disease symptoms. The most important vaccines developed in recent years include those that provide protection against hepatitis B, pneumococcal pneumonia, and various strains of flu. Research continues on a vaccine against dental caries, and especially, against AIDS.

Vacuum Curettage • See DILATATION AND EVACUATION.

Vagina • The passageway that slopes upward and backward from the external genitals, the vulva, to the cervix; the female organ of sexual intercourse. See "The Healthy Woman," "Sexual Health," "Contraception and Abortion," "Pregnancy and Childbirth," "Gynecologic Diseases and Treatment," and "Sexually Transmissible Diseases."

Vaginal Discharge • Any emission from the vagina, including the menstrual flow, the secretion of a clear, slippery lubricating fluid during sexual intercourse, and between periods a mucoid secretion from the cervix. A vaginal discharge is abnormal if it has a bad odor, is thick and cheesy in consistency, is yellowish or greenish in color, or is tinged with blood between periods or after the menopause. A burning or itching sensation is another indication of abnormal discharge. When the disorder exists, it may be caused by mechanical irritation (IUD), chemical irritation (sprays and douches), or infection by fungi, bacteria, or other microorganisms. Blood-streaked discharge may be a symptom of fibroids, other tumors, cysts, or some other cervical or uterine disorder. While any abnormal discharge should be diagnosed and treated if it persists, prompt attention is especially indicated if there is any change in vaginal secretions during pregnancy, after an abortion, or during a regimen of estrogen replacement therapy. *See* "Gynecologic Diseases and Treatment" and "Sexually Transmissible Diseases."

Valium (Diazepam) • The most widely prescribed anti-anxiety drug belonging to the group of minor tranquilizers that includes Librium, Ativan, and Xanax. It is prescribed not only to relieve the distressing effects of anxiety but also for sleeplessness, and it may be combined with other drugs for ulcer therapy. Valium should not be recommended as an anti-depressant. In point of fact, it may itself cause depression if taken over a long period, and there has been considerable testimony about its addictive aspects. Thus, Valium is not intended for long-term use but rather as a means for arriving at sufficient emotional stability to benefit from psychotherapy so that the sources of stress can be handled in a positive way. Anyone who has been taking heavy doses of Valium should not discontinue its use abruptly; because of unpleasant withdrawal symptoms, professional monitoring is important. Taking Valium during pregnancy is contraindicated because of the possibility of fetal damage. Driving and other hazardous undertakings should not be engaged in when taking *any* tranquilizer. *See* "Substance Abuse."

Varicose Veins • Veins that are swollen and enlarged; also called varicosities. Varicosities include hemorrhoids (swollen anal veins), but the superficial veins of the legs, especially those located in the back and inner side of the calf, are the ones most frequently affected. Varicosities of smaller veins are visible through the skin as a bluish-red network of delicate lines going off in different directions from a particular source. A larger varicose vein is likely to have the appearance of a bumpy, purplish rope. Varicose veins are more common among women than among men, among people who spend a great deal of time standing in one place, and among the obese. They are a frequent development during pregnancy. Most women over 40 develop some varicosities. There seems to be an inherited predisposition to the condition.

Prevention, decreasing the likelihood of occurrence, and therapy for mild cases all involve relieving the pressure on the veins. Feet should be raised whenever possible. Constriction by crossing the legs or wearing tight girdles or garters should be eliminated. Symptoms such as swollen ankles and a general feeling of soreness in the legs can be alleviated by wearing individually fitted support stockings during the waking hours. Swimming, bicycling, and hiking as well as special leg exercises are effective therapy. Somewhat more drastic treatment consists of injections with medications that cause the swollen veins to harden and eventually wither so that the circulation is rerouted to healthier vessels. A more effective and permanent treatment for seriously distended veins is an operation that ties them or removes them completely. See PHLEBITIS.

Vasectomy • A surgical procedure that effectively sterilizes the male without impairing his hormone levels or his sexual performance. See "Contraception and Abortion."

Vegetarianism • A dietary regimen that at its strictest, includes no food of animal, bird, or fish origin and derives essential proteins from plant sources. Less rigid vegetarians may or may not eat eggs but include all other dairy products as well as fish and seafood. See "Nutrition, Weight, and General Well-Being" and "Directory of Health Information."

Vein • A blood vessel through which blood is transported back to the heart. Unlike arterial blood, which is bright red as a result of being freshly oxygenated, venous blood is dark, the only exception being the blood in the pulmonary veins that is being transported directly from the lungs to the heart. Because veins are less elastic and weaker than arteries they are more vulnerable to such disorders as varicosities and phlebitis. For a description of the circulatory system, see "The Healthy Woman."

Venereal Disease • See "Sexually Transmissible Diseases."

Vertebra • Any of the bones of the spine. The spinal column, which supports the body's weight and which provides the bony corridor through which the spinal cord passes, is comprised of 33 vertebrae, some of which are fused together. Depending on their location, they differ somewhat in structure and size: 7 cervical vertebrae are at the back of the neck; 12 thoracic vertebrae support the upper back; 5 lumbar vertebrae are in the lower back; 5 fused vertebrae make up the sacrum near the base of the spine; and 4 fused vertebrae form the coccyx. The vertebrae are separated from each other by fibrous tissue and cartilage discs that act as shock absorbers. When the displacement of one of these discs causes pressure on a nerve, the result may be acute pain. Osteoarthritis of the vertebral bones is one of the chronic diseases of aging responsible for backaches. Back discomfort may also originate in poor posture that affects vertebral position in relation to surrounding musculature. Osteoporosis of the vertebrae causes their collapse and the consequent loss of height seen in many older people. Tuberculosis of the spine is also a cause of vertebral collapse and deformity.

Vertigo • A sensation of irregular or whirling motion, either of oneself or of nearby objects; also called dizziness, although this latter term often is used incorrectly to describe a sensation of lightheadedness or feeling faint. There are many possible causes of vertigo. It can be brought on by rapid, continuous, whirling motion, such as riding a merry-go-round, or by watching objects in apparent rapid motion, such as telephone poles observed from a fast-moving car. It can be caused by various diseases that affect, directly or indirectly, the labyrinthine canals in the middle ear. *See* MENIÈRE'S DISEASE.

Vincent's Angina • *See* GUMS.

Virus • A submicroscopic disease-causing agent capable of reproducing only in the living cells of plants, animals, and humans. Among humans, viruses are responsible for a long list of otherwise unrelated communicable infections ranging from the common cold to a very rare and fatal brain disease (Creutzfeld-Jakob). When a viral strain responsible for a particular disease can be isolated and transformed into an effective immunizing vaccine, the disease itself can eventually be controlled. This has been the case with smallpox and to a large extent with such virus-caused infections as polio, measles, and rubella. Antibiotics are ineffective, and usually inappropriate, therapy for virus diseases except in cases where the patient might be critically vulnerable to secondary bacterial infection. Interferon, an antiviral substance naturally produced by the body, is being investigated as a possible treatment for colds and other viral infections. Widespread application depends on the ability to produce a genetically engineered substance at a practical price. *See* INTERFERON, HEPATITIS, FLU, HERPES, etc.

Vitamins • A number of unrelated organic substances that occur in minute quantities in food and are essential for life and health. Because the body cannot manufacture them, they must be supplied in the diet. *See* "Nutrition, Weight, and General Well-Being."

Vocal Cords • The two ligaments within the larynx that vibrate to create the extraordinary range of human sounds. Each reedlike cord is attached at one end to the front wall of the larynx (voice box) with the ends placed closely together. The other ends are connected to small rotating cartilage rings near the back wall of the larynx. These rotations cause the cords to separate or to close, thus controlling the amount of air that passes through the larynx. When the cords are open, the air passes through without producing sounds. When the cords are close together, the air that is forced through them causes them to vibrate like the reeds in a musical instrument. These vibrations create sound waves in the

VOCAL CORDS

Tongue
Epiglottis
Trachea
False vocal cord
True vocal cord
Esophagus

BREATHING

TALKING

form of a voice, and when the sound waves are articulated and controlled in a particular way, they produce speech and song. The pitch of the voice depends on the tension in the cords, and its depth depends on their length. Men's voices are deeper than women's because their vocal cords are longer. A common occurrence among singers and public speakers is the development of nodes on the vocal cords. These growths are usually removed by surgery. Sometimes they are malignant. See LARYNX.

Vomiting • The mechanism whereby the sudden contraction of the muscles of the stomach and the small intestine forces the partially digested contents of these organs upward and out of the mouth; technically called emesis. Vomiting and the feeling of nausea that characteristically precedes it may occur as a reflex response to tickling the inside of the throat, to an overfull stomach, to ingesting an emetic such as mustard or a poison, or to the presence of bacterial toxins acting as an irritant on the gastric membrane. It may also occur because of stimulation of the vomiting center of the brain. Motion sickness, overdoses of certain drugs and anesthetics, and emotional stress, such as strong feelings of revulsion or anxiety, can cause a reaction of vomiting. Medicines such as Dramamine and antiemetics prevent vomiting by depressing the response of this part of the nervous system. Vomiting may also occur because of obstructions in the intestines, uncontrolled paroxysms of coughing, the hormonal changes associated with pregnancy, and migraine headaches. Any recurrent or uncontrollable attacks of vomiting should be diagnosed by a doctor. In coming to the aid of someone who is vomiting following an accident, precautionary measures should be taken so that the patient does not inhale the vomitus and fatally obstruct breathing.

Vulva • The term for the external genital organs of the female. See "The Healthy Woman" and "Sexual Health."

Wart • An abnormal growth on the skin caused by a virus. Warts may occur at any age, but they appear less frequently as people grow older because an immunity to the virus may develop over the years. Because the virus can spread to lesions in the skin caused by scratching, shaving, or other factors, warts may appear in groups or in succession.

A wart on the sole of the foot is called a plantar wart. Because constant pressure causes it to grow inward, it may eventually press on a nerve and cause considerable pain. Because warts on other parts of the body are not sensitive or itchy, any sudden discomfort associated with them or any change in appearance or size should be called to a doctor's attention. Removal for cosmetic or other reasons is accomplished by various techniques including cauterization with chemicals or an electric needle, surgical incision, or by cryosurgery, a painless procedure that freezes the wart with liquid nitrogen. See PLANTAR WART.

Water Retention • See EDEMA, DIURETICS.

Weight • See "Nutrition, Weight, and General Well-Being."

Withdrawal Method • *See* COITUS INTERRUPTUS.

Womb • *See* UTERUS.

Wrinkles • The lines and furrows that mark the skin as it ages and loses elasticity. Heredity, hormonal interplay, emotional and physical health, and exposure to sun and wind are the chief factors that determine the age at which skin begins to wrinkle. Also, the skin of women who smoke seems to wrinkle earlier and more than of those who do not. Wrinkles cannot be removed or permanently delayed by creams or lotions; cosmetics can mask them, but those that claim to contain "magic" ingredients may do more harm than good. The technique of dermabrasion can temporarily erase the more superficial lines, but they will inevitably reappear as the sagging skin continues to move away from the supporting structures beneath. Cosmetic surgery can eliminate wrinkles for several years, but the decision to undergo such a procedure should be carefully considered. *See* "Cosmetic Surgery."

X-ray • Radiation of extremely short electromagnetic waves capable of penetrating certain matter opaque to ordinary light and producing images on photosensitive surfaces; also the image produced. Under ordinary circumstances, X-rays are more easily absorbed by bone than by flesh. By placing a fluorescent screen behind the body, the bones are delineated as shadows. This technique is called fluoroscopy. When permanent records are wanted, photographic plates that are sensitive to X-rays are used to produce images that can be dated and preserved as part of a patient's medical history. From its original application to injuries or disorders of the skeletal system, X-ray technology has been broadened by the technique of introducing radiopaque substances into the patient's body to provide information about nonskeletal disorders. For information about gastrointestinal problems, barium is introduced into the body either by mouth or by enema. Contrast dyes are administered intravenously to help in the location of kidney stones.

Within recent years, newer techniques have been rendering X-ray images obsolete. Scanning machines, magnetic resonance imaging, ultrasonography, and fiberoptic instruments enable the diagnostician to get information previously inaccessible by X-ray imaging. There is also a movement away from unnecessary "routine" X-rays of the chest and teeth. X-ray photos of the chest do not give any indication of the early phases of emphysema or bronchitis. However, breast X-rays (mammography) is considered a useful tool for discovering breast cancer as soon as signs appear in cellular anomalies.

Whether for diagnostic purposes or, more likely, as treatment *(see* RADIOTHERAPY), the danger of overexposure to X-rays has become a widespread problem. Among the consequences of overexposure are destruction of skin, loss of hair and nails, development of certain cancers, and damage to the genes, the reproductive organs, and fetuses. Pregnant women should avoid exposure to X-rays except in the greatest emergency. Under any circumstances a patient should always ask that a lead sheet cover those parts of her body not intended to show on the film. Because of the serious disabilities created by exposure, experts on radiation hazard advise patients to ask the following types of questions before X-rays are taken. Before having a complete set of 16 to 18 pictures as part of a routine dental checkup, ask the dentist what special problem exists that can be dealt with only in this way and why a whole series has to be taken if trouble is suspected in a particular area of the mouth. When a medical doctor suggests X-rays, ask what their purpose is, whether other tests do the same thing, whether the lowest possible radiation is being used to achieve the necessary result, and when the equipment was last inspected. Many states have no laws requiring that X-ray equipment be checked every year to make sure that it does, in fact, deliver intended doses rather than perilously higher ones and that it in no way exposes the patient to unnecessary hazards because it is incorrectly operated or outmoded. If X-ray pictures must be taken, it is advisable to have them done by a radiologist. While specialists are more expensive than general practitioners, they are more likely to have the most up-to-date equipment and the best-trained technicians operating it. Anyone who has undergone a series of X-rays and is moving to another city should ask the doctor or dentist for the films so that they can be turned over to whomever will be in charge of medical care in the new location. Unnecessary duplication with its attendant hazards, not to mention expense, is therefore avoided.

Yeast Infection • *See* "Sexually Transmissible Diseases."

Yoga Exercises • An ancient Hindu discipline, increasingly popular in the West, for the achievement of physical and mental relaxation. The exercises combine control of consciousness with various specific body positions coordinated with breathing patterns. While self-instruction is possible, beginners are likely to achieve greater proficiency in a group under the tutelage of an experienced teacher. The exercises can then be done at home or even at work at times convenient to one's own schedule. *See* "Fitness."

Yogurt • A food of custardlike consistency created by heating milk to produce the beneficial bacillus *Streptococcus thermophilus* and then fermenting the milk with an additional beneficial bacterial strain *(Lactobacillus bulgaricus)*. In the process of fermentation the milk sugar lactose is transformed into lactic acid, giving yogurt its characteristically tart flavor. In addition to its nutritional assets, yogurt is more easily digested than milk, and its bacteria have a beneficial effect on the intestinal tract, fighting off infectious bacteria and adding benign ones, especially those that might have been destroyed by antibiotics. It should be kept in mind that yogurt sold as a frozen solid may be a less fattening dessert than ice cream, but its beneficial bacteria are presumed to have been destroyed in the freezing process.

Zinc • One of the trace elements essential in the diet for the normal functioning of various enzyme systems. No one should take zinc supplements except on the recommendation of a doctor. While too little of this mineral can cause serious problems, too much will result in gastrointestinal disturbances and metabolic imbalances. See "Nutrition, Weight, and General Well-Being."

APPENDIXES

SUGGESTED HEALTH EXAMINATION SCHEDULES FOR WOMEN AT NORMAL RISK

*Interval Between Examinations (in months)**

	Age 18–40	Age 41–60	Age 61+
General physical examination and life-style counseling	36	12	12
Dental examination	6	6	6
Eye examination including glaucoma test	24	12	12
Breast examination	36	12	12
Breast self-examination	1	1	1
Pap smear	12 (36†)	12 (36†)	12 (36†)
Pelvic examination	36	12	12
Tests for sexually transmissible diseases	6–12‡	6–12‡	6–12‡

	Age 35–49	Age 50+
Mammography	Initial at age 35–39; thereafter yearly or every other year	12
Endometrial tissue sample	At menopause and periodically thereafter for women taking estrogens	

	Age 40+	Age 50+
Finger rectal examination	12	12
Test for blood in stool		12
Proctosigmoidoscopy		36–60

*Different intervals may be recommended for some women by their physicians.
†36-month interval (after two initial negative pap smears a year apart) recommended by the American Cancer Society. There are differences of opinion among professional groups and individuals regarding the ideal interval.
‡Intervals depend on individual sexual life styles.

IMMUNIZATION GUIDE

ACTIVE IMMUNIZATION

Recommended for routine use

Disease	Causative Agent	Type of Vaccine	Duration of Protection
Diphtheria	bacterium	toxoid	booster every 10 years and after exposure
Mumps	virus	live	probably lifetime
Pertussis (whooping cough)	bacterium	killed	several years; consider booster after exposure
Poliomyelitis	virus	live (Sabin) killed (Salk)	probably lifetime uncertain, possibly lifetime
Rubella (German measles)	virus	live	probably lifetime
Rubeola (measles)	virus	live	probably lifetime
Tetanus	bacterium	toxoid	booster every 10 years and after exposure

ACTIVE IMMUNIZATION

Recommended for special use for persons at high risk because of chronic illness, old age, occupational or natural exposure, or travel to certain foreign countries; duration of protection against each disease varies from a few months to years.

Disease	Causative Agent
IN CLINICAL USE	
Adenovirus infections	virus
Anthrax	bacterium
Botulism	bacterium
Cholera	bacterium
Hepatitis B	virus
Influenza	virus
Meningococcal meningitis	bacterium
Plague	bacterium
Pneumococcal infections	bacterium
Rabies	virus
Rocky Mountain spotted fever	rickettsia
Trachoma	*Chlamydia trachomatis*

APPENDIXES

Tuberculosis	bacterium
Tularemia	bacterium
Typhoid fever	bacterium
Typhus fever	bacterium
Variola (smallpox)	virus
Yellow fever	virus

NOT IN CLINICAL USE—experimental vaccines under investigation

Cytomegalovirus infections	virus
Dental caries	bacterium
Gonorrhea	bacterium
Hemophilus influenza	bacterium
Hepatitis A	virus
Herpes simplex	virus
Malaria	parasite
Varicella (chickenpox)	virus

PASSIVE IMMUNIZATION

Recommended for special use to provide temporary protection, 1 to 6 weeks, for nonimmune persons exposed, possibly exposed, or likely to be exposed to the disease; antitoxins are also used to treat the disease.

Disease	*Type of Vaccine*
Botulism	Antitoxin (animal)
Diphtheria	Antitoxin (animal)
Hepatitis A	Immune serum globulin (human)
Hepatitis B	Hepatitis B immune globulin (human) Immune serum globulin
Herpes zoster	Varicella-Zoster immune globulin (human)
Mumps	Mumps immune globulin (human); unproven value
Rabies	Rabies immune globulin (human) Antiserum (animal)
Rubella (German measles)	Immune serum globulin (human); unproven value
Rubeola (measles)	Immune serum globulin (human)
Tetanus	Tetanus immune globulin (human) Antitoxin (animal)

APPENDIXES

Varicella (chickenpox)	Varicella-Zoster immune globulin (human) Immune serum globulin (human); unproven value
Variola (smallpox)	Vaccinia immune globulin (human)

COMMON MEDICAL TERMS

Most of the words used by doctors are made up of two or three parts (prefixes, roots, suffixes) that come from Greek or Latin. Knowing the meaning of these word parts makes it easier to understand and use medical terminology.

PREFIXES

a-, an-	without (anesthesia)
ad-	toward or near (adhesions; adrenal)
anti-	against (antiseptic; antihistamine)
bi-	two (biceps; bisexual)
co-, con-	with, together (concussion; constipation)
cyano-	blue (cyanosis)
dys-	impaired, abnormal (dysmenorrhea; dysfunction)
ecto-	outer, outside (ectopic)
endo-	inner, within (endocardium; endometrium)
epi-	over, among (epiglottis; epidermis)
eu-	good, well (euphoria; euthanasia)
ex-	out, away from (expectorant)
hyper-	excessive (hyperacidity; hypertension)
hypo-	under, below (hypothyroid; hypothermia)
leuko-	white (leukocytes; leukorrhea)
ortho-	straight, correct (orthodontia; orthopedist)
pre-, pro-	before (premenstrual; prophylaxis)
re-, retro-	back, again (regression; retroperitoneal)
sub-	beneath, under (subconscious; subcutaneous)
super-	higher, above (superego)
sym-, syn-	together (symbiosis; synapse)
trans-	across (transfusion)

ROOTS RELATING TO MEDICINE AND THE BODY

aden-	gland (adenoma; adenoid)	haemo-	blood (hemangioma; hemoglobin)
angio-	blood vessel (angiography; hemangioma)	hepato-	liver (hepatitis)
		metro-	uterus (endometritis)
arthro-	Joint (arthritis)	myo-	muscle (myocardial; myoma)
bronchos-	throat (bronchitis; bronchoscopy)	narce-	numbness (narcotic; narcolepsy)
cardi-, coro-	heart (cardiogram; coronary)	nephros	kidney (nephritis)
cerebro-	brain (cerebral palsy)	osteo-	bone (osteoarthritis)
chole-	bile (cholesterol; chololith)	ophthalmos-	eye (ophthalmologist)
		otos-	ear (otitis)
colo-	colon (colostomy)	pepsis-	digestion (peptic ulcer; dyspepsia)
cyst-	sac; bladder (cystoscope)	pneuma-	lungs (pneumonia)
cyto-	cell (leukocyte)	proctos-	anus (proctoscope)
derma-	skin (dermatitis; epidermis)	rhinos-	nose (rhinitis)
		sarcos-	flesh (sarcoma)
diaeta-	regimen (diet)	sphygmos-	pulse (sphygmomanometer)
emetos-	vomit (emetic)		
enterion	intestines, gut (enteritis; dysentery)	soma-	body (psychosomatic medicine)
gastro-	stomach (gastric ulcer; gastritis)	phlebs-	vein (phlebitis)

SUFFIXES RELATED TO SYMPTOMS, DIAGNOSIS, SURGERY

-algia	pain (neuralgia)	-lysis	dissolving, separating (analysis; dialysis)
-ectomy	cutting out (appendectomy)	-oid	resembling (fibroid)
-genic	source (psychogenic)	-oma	tumor (lymphoma)
-graph	record, writing (electrocardiograph)	-osis	disease (tuberculosis)
		-ostomy	opening (colostomy)
-itis	inflammation (laryngitis)	-otomy	incision (episiotomy)

-pathy	disease (psychopathic)	-scopy	inspection (cystoscopy; microscopy)
-rhagia	overflow (hemorrhage)		
-rrhea	stream, discharge (dysmenorrhea; rhinorrhea)		

HOW TO READ A PRESCRIPTION

Rx	quantity	mg	milligrams
Sig	directions for taking	min	minim, a drop
aa	equal amounts of each	p.r.n.	as needed
ac	before meals	od	right eye
ad lib	whenever you want	os	left eye
bid	twice a day	pc	after meals
cc	cubic centimeter	qd	every day
dr	dram	qh	every hour
extr	extract	qid	four times a day
gm	gram	qs	as much as is sufficient
gr	grains	tid	three times a day
gt	drop		

BRAND AND GENERIC NAMES OF COMMONLY PRESCRIBED DRUGS

Every drug has a *generic name* which is derived from its chemical composition. Many drugs also have a manufacturer-assigned *brand name* under which they are sold and which is written on the prescription. Similar drugs may or may not be totally equivalent to each other pharmacologically. If a brand name drug is prescribed for you, you may wish to ask the prescriber if a less expensive but pharmacologically equivalent drug is available. If so, and if he or she is willing, ask to have the prescription marked "substitution permissible." You may then ask the pharmacist to fill the prescription with a drug that has only a generic name or with another brand name drug. This is known as generic equivalent substitution or brand name equivalent substitution. In some instances the pharmacist will offer spontaneously to make the substitution when the prescription

APPENDIXES

permits it. In some states, this is mandatory by law. The substituted drug generally is much less expensive.

Also, when you purchase an over-the-counter (OTC) drug, your pharmacist may be able to suggest a less expensive but pharmacologically equivalent drug.

Principles for drug substitution are described in the "Generic Drug Formulary" of the Pennsylvania Department of Health: "Generic substitutions are only permissible within a single dosage form category and must be of the same chemical entity and potency; for example, creams, ointments, and gels are not interchangeable and the generic product must be compounded with a vehicle having similar physical properties to the brand name drug; syrups are not interchangeable with elixirs; compressed tablets are not interchangeable with enteric-coated tablets, sublingual tablets, or capsules; erythromycin stearate is not interchangeable with erythromycin base or erythromycin estolate, and so on."

This table lists some frequently prescribed brand name prescription drugs for which equivalents exist, along with their generic names. The listings are grouped under headings which indicate the reason for which a drug most frequently is prescribed, although it also may be prescribed for other reasons.

This list is not all-inclusive, and, in addition, new generic equivalents come into existence from time to time as brand name patents expire and generic or brand name equivalents are approved by the Food and Drug Administration. Pharmacists have up-to-date information about what generic equivalents are available.

Inclusion in this list does not testify to the efficacy of any drug.

Brand Name	*Generic Name*
ANTIHISTAMINES	
Benadryl	diphenhydramine HCI
Chlortrimeton	chlorpheniramine
Periactin	cyproheptadine
Phenergan	promethazine
BRONCHIAL DILATORS	
Adrenaline	epinephrine
Brethine	terbutaline
Isuprel	isoproterenol
Theo-dur	theophylline
CARDIAC AGENTS	
Calan	verapamil
Lanoxin	digoxin

Nitro-bid	nitroglycerin
Nitrostat	nitroglycerin
Pavabid	papaverine
Persantine	dipyridamole
Pronestyl	procainamide

CHOLESTEROL

Nicotinex	niacin

DEPRESSION

Atarax	hydroxyzine
Elavil	amitriptyline
Tofranil	imipramine
Vistaril	hydroxyzine

DIABETES MELLITUS

Diabinese	chlorpropamide
Glucotrol	glipizide
Micronase	glipizide
Orinase	tolbutamide

DIARRHEA

Lomotil	diphenoxylate HCI

DIURETICS

Diuril	chlorothiazide
Esidrix	hydrochlorothiazide
Hydrodiuril	hydrochlorothiazide
Lasix	furosemide

HEADACHE, MIGRAINE

Gynergen	ergotamine
Sansert	methysergide
Wigrettes	ergotamine

HORMONES

Aristocort	triamcinolone
Deltasone	prednisone

Estinyl	ethinylestradiol
Hyprogest	hydroxyprogesterone
Kenacort	triamcinolone
Orasone	prednisone
Premarin	conjugated estrogen
Provera	medroxyprogesterone
Synthroid	levothyroxine

HYPERTENSION

Aldactone	spironolactone
Apresoline	hydralazine
Inderal	propranolol
Serpasil	reserpine

INFECTIONS

Achromycin	tetracycline
Amoxil	amoxicillin
Azulfidine	sulfasalazine
Chloromycetin	chloramphenicol
Erythocyn	cephalothin
Erythrocin	erythromycin
Flagyl	metronidazole
Fulvicin	griseofulvin
Furadantin	nitrofurantoin
Gantrisin	sulfisoxazole
Grisactin	griseofulvin
Ilotycin	erythromycin
Keflin	erythromycin
Korostatin	nystatin
Kwell	gamma benzine hydrochloride
Lotrimin	clotrimazole
Mandelamine	methenamine mandelate
Mycostatin	nystatin

Nilstat	nystatin
Nitrofan	nitrofurantoin
Nydrazid	isoniazid
Omnipen	ampicillin
Pen-Vee K	penicillin V (K)
Polycillin	ampicillin
Prostaphylin	oxacillin
Protostat	metronidazole
Tegopen	cloxacillin
V-Cillin K	penicillin V (K)
Vibramycin	doxycycline

INFLAMMATIONS

Aristocort	triamcinolone
Butazolidin	phenylbutazone
Indocin	indomethacin
Kenacort	triamcinolone

MENSTRUAL CRAMPS AND INFLAMMATIONS

Motrin	ibuprofen*
Rufen	ibuprofen*

MOTION SICKNESS

Antivert	meclizine
Bonine	meclizine
Dramamine	dimenhydrinate
Tigan	trimethobenzamide

MUSCLE RELAXANTS

Flexeril	cyclobenzaprine
Deloxin	methocarbamal
Robaxin	methocarbamal
Soma	corisoprodol

PAIN (ANALGESICS)

Darvon	propoxyphene
Demerol	meperidine
Sudoprin	acetaminophen
Tolwin	pentazocine
Tylenol	acetaminophen
Valorin	acetaminophen

SEDATIVES

Amytal	amobarbital sodium
Equanil	meprobamate
Miltown	meprobamate
Nembutal	pentobarbital
Seconal	secobarbital

SEIZURE DISORDERS

Dilantin	phenytoin
Mysoline	primidone

SPASMS OF THE GASTROINTESTINAL TRACT

Bentyl	dicyclomine
Pro-Banthine	propantheline

TRANQUILIZERS

Atarax	hydroxyzine
Compazine	prochlorperazine
Librium	chlordiazepoxide
Mellaril	thioridazine
Stelazine	trifluoperazine
Thorazine	chlorpromazine
Valium	diazepam

MISCELLANEOUS AGENTS

Antabuse	disulfiram
Benemid	probenecid

Eskalith	lithium carbonate
Retin-A	tretinoin
Ritalin	methylphenidate

HEALTH CARE PERSONNEL

PHYSICIAN

Doctor of Medicine (M.D.) Has received a degree from a school of medicine. Doctor of Osteopathic Medicine (D.O.) Has received a degree from a college of osteopathic medicine.

After graduating from one of the above schools or colleges all physicians must complete one year of post-graduate training (internship or first year of post-graduate training—P.G. 1) in an approved hospital to be eligible for a permanent medical license anywhere in the United States. Thereafter they may take additional years of post-graduate training (residency) in an approved hospital to become specialists. They also may spend additional time as research or clinical fellows at a medical school.

To practice medicine in the United States a physician must be licensed by the state in which he or she practices. When in practice, a physician will have a primary, and perhaps a secondary, field of practice or specialty and be referred to accordingly. He may be a family practitioner, internist, hematologist, surgeon, internist-cardiologist, etc. There are about 85 specialties recognized by the American Medical Association. Physicians are listed in the "Consumer Yellow Pages" of the telephone directory according to their specialty as well as by locality in the community in which they practice. Some of these specialties are:

ANESTHESIOLOGY. The anesthesiologist is responsible for choosing and administering the appropriate anesthesia for whatever surgery is planned. This choice is based on an assessment of the patient's medical history and present condition. *See* ANESTHESIA.

DERMATOLOGY. The dermatologist diagnoses and treats diseases of the skin, which is the largest body organ.

EMERGENCY MEDICINE. A physician who has specialized in this area is an expert in the split-second recognition, evaluation, stabilization, and care of trauma, acute illness, and emotional crisis. Most such physicians practice only in hospital or free-standing emergency departments.

FAMILY PRACTICE. The family practitioner (sometimes called general practitioner or primary care provider) offers basic and comprehensive medical care to any individual of any age. However, not all family practitioners do surgery or obstetrics.

INTERNAL MEDICINE. The internist (not to be confused with "intern") diagnoses most medical conditions but treats only those which do not require surgery. Many internists have a subspecialty, and some limit their practice to it. Among the better-known subspecialists are: allergist, endocrinologist (glandu-

---

* Advil and Nuprin, lower dosages, are available "over the counter."

lar and hormonal problems), hematologist (blood disorders), cardiologist (heart disease), and gastroenterologist (digestive disorders).

NEUROLOGY. The neurologist diagnoses and treats organic disorders and diseases of the nervous system which do not require surgery. See "Surgery" below.

OBSTETRICS AND GYNECOLOGY. The obstetrician is concerned with pregnancy and delivery; the gynecologist, with disorders and diseases of the female reproductive system and with birth control. Some obstetrician-gynecologists limit their practice to one of these two specialties. See "Contraception and Abortion," "Pregnancy and Childbirth," "Infertility," and "Gynecologic Diseases and Treatment."

OPHTHALMOLOGY. The ophthalmologist diagnoses and treats diseases of the eye and disorders of the structure and function of the eye such as myopia and presbyopia. See EYE EXAMINATION.

ORTHOPEDICS. The orthopedist diagnoses and treats all diseases and injuries affecting the skeletal system, including joints, muscles, ligaments, tendons, and bones.

OTOLARYNGOLOGY. The otolaryngologist (ENT specialist) diagnoses and treats diseases of the ear, nose, and throat and hearing disorders. See HEARING LOSS and HEARING TESTS.

PATHOLOGY. The pathologist is concerned with structural and functional changes in tissues and organs of the body which cause or are caused by disease. These changes are identified by examining, through various tests, blood, body fluids, tissue, feces, and other materials. See AUTOPSY, BLOOD TESTS, and URINE TESTS.

PEDIATRICS. The pediatrician diagnoses most medical conditions in children but treats only those which do not require surgery. Some pediatricians have a subspecialty to which they limit their practice. Among the better-known subspecialties are: cardiology, endocrinology, nephrology (kidney disease), and neonatology (care of premature or ill newborn infants).

PHYSICAL MEDICINE AND REHABILITATION. A physician specializing in this area is concerned with minimizing the disabilities of people who have had a disease such as a stroke or an injury that affects function of one or more parts of the body. See PHYSICAL THERAPY.

PLASTIC SURGERY. The plastic surgeon deals with the repair, restoration, or replacement of malformed, damaged, or missing parts of the body resulting from injury or from congenital defect—for example, repair of cleft palate, skin grafting after major burns, reconstruction of facial bones damaged in an accident, and replacement of a joint or limb with a prosthesis. Cosmetic surgery is that branch of plastic surgery concerned with changing appearance solely for esthetic reasons. See "Cosmetic Surgery" and PLASTIC SURGERY.

PREVENTIVE MEDICINE. A physician who practices preventive medicine is usually associated with community health programs and public health measures that aim to anticipate and prevent disease and injuries.

PROCTOLOGY. The proctologist specializes in medical and surgical treatment of disorders of the anus and rectum.

PSYCHIATRY. The psychiatrist is a licensed physician who specializes in the diagnosis, treatment, and prevention of mental and emotional disorders. *See* "Your Mind and Feelings."

RADIOLOGY. A radiologist uses X-rays, sonography, radioactive substances, and other forms of radiant energy in the diagnosis and treatment of disease. *See* RADIOTHERAPY and X-RAY.

SURGERY. A general surgeon performs any type of operation. Most surgeons specialize in a particular type of surgery. For example, the thoracic surgeon performs operations involving the lungs and heart. Neurosurgeons are called upon for the removal of brain tumors, repair of nerves following injury, and similar operations.

UROLOGY. A urologist specializes in medical and surgical treatment of disorders of the urinary tract.

About 300,000 physicians in the United States and Canada have been certified as Diplomates in a particular specialty by the American Board of Medical Specialties and hence are "Board Certified Specialists" rather than just "specialists." To be so certified a physician must have the minimal amount of postgraduate training required by a particular specialty board and must pass a written and sometimes an oral examination. Some boards offer subspecialty certification and some have voluntary recertification examinations. There currently are 23 specialty boards. A reference book containing the name, specialty, and geographic location of all Diplomates, as well as certain biographical information, is published annually and is available in many libraries. The specialty boards are: Allergy and Immunology, Anesthesiology, Colon and Rectal Surgery, Dermatology, Emergency Medicine, Family Practice, Internal Medicine, Neurological Surgery, Nuclear Medicine, Obstetrics and Gynecology, Ophthalmology, Orthopaedic Surgery, Otolaryngology, Pathology, Pediatrics, Physical Medicine and Rehabilitation, Plastic Surgery, Preventive Medicine, Psychiatry and Neurology, Radiology, Surgery, Thoracic Surgery, and Urology.

There also exist various "colleges" of physicians whose members have additional credentials. A member becomes a Fellow of the American College of Cardiology (F.A.C.C.), Gastroenterology (F.A.C.G.), Obstetrics and Gynecology (F.A.C.O.G.), Physicians (F.A.C.P.), Radiology (F.A.C.R.), or Surgeons (F.A.C.S.).

All physicians must devote a certain number of hours to graduate medical education activities each year to maintain their state medical licenses and hospital privileges. *See* "You, Your Doctors, and the Health Care System."

DENTIST

Doctor of Dental Medicine (D.M.D.) or of Dental Surgery (D.D.S.). Has received one of these degrees (which are one and the same) from a school of dentistry.

After graduating from dental school and obtaining a license to practice dentistry from the state in which they intend to practice, dentists may begin immediately to practice general dentistry. They also may take additional training at a dental school or approved hospital to become specialists.

The American Dental Association recognizes nine dental specialties. They are: Endodontics (root canal therapy); General Practice (also called family dentistry); Oral Pathology (laboratory activities); Oral Surgery; Orthodontics (correction of tooth irregularities); Pedodontics (children's dentistry); Periodontics (treatment of diseases of the gums); Prosthodontics (replacement and reconstruction of teeth); and Public Health.

About 15 percent of dentists in the United States have been certified by a Specialty Board of the American Dental Association. There are eight such boards: Dental Public Health; Endodontics; Oral and Maxillofacial Surgery; Oral Pathology; Orthodontics; Pedodontics; Peridontology; and Prosthodontics.

All dentists must complete a certain number of hours of graduate dental education each year to maintain their state medical licenses.

CHIROPRACTOR

Doctor of Chiropractic (D.C.) Has graduated from a chiropractic school or college.

After graduating from chiropractic school and obtaining a license to practice chiropractic from the state in which they intend to practice, chiropractors may begin to practice immediately. They use a therapeutic system based on the theory that disease is caused by subluxations—that is, partial dislocations—of the vertebral bones that cause pinching of the nerves emanating from them. The pinching of the nerves impairs the function of vital organs and is corrected by spinal adjustment.

OPTOMETRIST

Doctor of Optometry (O.D.) Has graduated from a school of optometry.

After graduating from optometry school and obtaining a license to practice optometry from the state in which they intend to practice, optometrists may begin to practice immediately. They do refractions to determine visual impairment and prescribe corrective lenses when indicated. They also do tests for glaucoma and certain other conditions but do not treat them.

PODIATRIST

Doctor of Podiatry Medicine (D.P.M.) Has graduated from a college of podiatry.

After graduating from a college of podiatry and obtaining a license to practice podiatry from the state in which they intend to practice, podiatrists may begin to practice immediately. They specialize in treating problems of the feet such as corns, warts, bunions, calluses, ingrown toenails, heel pain, hammer toes, and painful arches. Podiatrists formerly were called chiropodists. *See* "Fitness."

PROFESSIONAL HEALTH CARE WORKERS

There are many such professionals, and some of them work independently of doctors all or part of the time. A few have Ph.D. degrees and, therefore, are called "Doctor."

AUDIOLOGIST. A person with at least a master's degree who specializes in hearing testing and disorders. *See* HEARING LOSS and HEARING TESTS.

CLINICAL PSYCHOLOGIST. A person with either a master's or a Ph.D. degree who administers psychologic tests and treats mental and emotional problems. *See* "Your Mind and Feelings."

DENTAL ASSISTANT. A person who assists with the work in a dental office processing X-rays, preparing patients for examination, etc.

LAY MIDWIFE. A person with varying levels of training who delivers babies at home. The degree of state regulation of midwives is diverse. *See* "Pregnancy and Childbirth."

LICENSED PRACTICAL NURSE (L.P.N.). A person with brief training, usually a few weeks in a hospital program, in the nursing care of patients.

NURSE MIDWIFE. A registered nurse who has completed an organized program of study and clinical experience recognized by the American College of Nurse Midwives. This advanced study qualifies her to extend her practice to the care of pregnant women, to the supervision of labor and delivery, and to postnatal care in cases in which no abnormalities are present. *See* "Pregnancy and Childbirth." *See* REGISTERED NURSE below.

NURSE PRACTITIONER (N.P.) A registered nurse with advanced training in diagnosing and treating disease. Nurse practitioners take medical histories, do physical examinations, perform diagnostic tests, develop treatment programs, and counsel patients. State regulations regarding their duties vary greatly. Some nurse practitioners practice independently, others work in clinics, physicians' offices, or hospitals. *See* "Registered Nurse" below.

OCCUPATIONAL THERAPIST (O.T.) A person with at least a bachelor's degree and six months of specialized training. He or she teaches handicapped patients vocational and other necessary skills so that they may function as independently as possible.

OPTICIAN. A person who fits, supplies, and adjusts eyeglasses and contact lenses. Opticians are licensed in about half of the states.

PHYSICAL THERAPIST (P.T.). A person with at least a bachelor's degree and usually some specialized training in physical therapy. He or she provides special therapy for people who, because of disease or injury, have diminished strength, mobility, or range of motion. Exercise, heat, cold, and water are the major therapeutic methods. *See* PHYSICAL THERAPY.

PHYSICIAN ASSISTANT (P.A.). A person who, after at least two years of college, takes two years of specialized training to learn to do some of the things traditionally done by physicians. He or she takes medical histories, does physical examinations, performs diagnostic tests, and develops treatment plans. P.A.'s are always under the supervision of a physician either directly or, in some instances, by telephone. In some states they can prescribe certain medications.

REGISTERED DENTAL HYGIENIST (R.D.H.). A person with at least two years of formal training in examining, cleaning, and polishing teeth. Licensed by the state, he or she generally works under the direct supervision of a dentist.

REGISTERED DIETITIAN (R.D.). A person with at least a bachelor's degree and a dietetic internship or an approved coordinated undergraduate program in dietetics. He or she provides dietary counseling and nutritional care.

REGISTERED NURSE (R.N.). A person with a nursing diploma from a diploma school of nursing (hospital nursing school) or, as is more and more the trend, a bachelor's degree from a nursing school in a college. Nurses must be licensed by the state in which they practice. In addition to performing bedside nursing duties, R.N.'s often have administrative and teaching positions in hospitals and other health care facilities. This is particularly true of the degree nurses, some of whom also have master's degrees and Ph.D. degrees. Registered nurses also work in physicians' offices, clinics, and community health programs.

SOCIAL WORKER. A person with at least a bachelor's degree, but usually also a master's or Ph.D. degree in social work. Social workers in health care institutions help patients and their families in attempting to resolve various psycho-social-economic problems that are created by their illness.

SPEECH-LANGUAGE PATHOLOGIST. A person with at least a master's degree who assists persons whose speech is impaired by disease or injury to improve their verbal communication. *See* SPEECH DISORDERS.

DIRECTORY OF HEALTH INFORMATION*

ABORTION

National Abortion Federation
   900 Pennsylvania Avenue, SE, Washington, DC 20003
National Abortion Rights Action League (NARAL)
   1424 K Street, NW, Washington, DC 20005
National Right to Life Committee, Inc.
   419 Seventh Street, NW, Washington, DC 20004

AGING

ACTION
   Washington, DC 20525 (no street address needed)
Administration on Aging
   U.S. Department of Health and Human Services,
   330 Independence Avenue, SW, Washington, DC 30301
American Association of Geriatric Psychiatry
   PO Box 376A, Greenbelt, MD 20770
American Association of Retired Persons
   1909 K Street, NW, Washington, DC 20049
Children of Aging Parents
   2761 Trenton Road, Levittown, PA 19056
Displaced Homemakers Network, c/o Older Woman's League
   1010 Vermont Avenue, NW, Suite 817, Washington, DC 20005
Elderhostel
   100 Boylston Street, Boston, MA 02116
Foster Grandparents Program
   ACTION
   Washington, DC 20525
Gray Panthers Housing Task Force
   311 South Juniper Street, Suite 601, Philadelphia, PA 19107
National Association of Area Agencies on Aging

---

* A self-addressed, stamped business envelope often encourages a prompt reply.

600 Maryland Avenue, SW, Suite 208, Washington, DC 20024
National Council on the Aging, Inc.
    600 Maryland Avenue, SW, West Wing 100, Washington, DC 20024
National Caucus on the Black Aged
    1424 K Street, NW, Washington, DC 20005
National Council of Senior Citizens
    925 Fifteenth Street, NW, Washington, DC 20005
National Hospice Organization
    1901 N. Fort Myer Drive, Suite 402, Arlington, VA 22209
National Institutes on Aging
    U.S. Department of Health and Human Services
    National Institutes of Health
    9000 Rockville Pike, Bethesda, MD 20892
Older Women's League
    1010 Vermont Avenue, NW, Suite 817, Washington, DC 20005
Retired Senior Volunteer Program
    ACTION
    Washington, DC 20525
Widowed Persons Service (AARP)
    Box 199
    Long Beach, CA 90801

ALCOHOLISM

Al-Anon Family Group Headquarters, Inc.
    1372 Broadway, New York, NY 10019
Al-Anon Information Center,
    200 Park Avenue South, New York, NY 10003
The Children of Alcoholics Foundation
    200 Park Avenue, New York, NY 10166
National Association for Children of Alcoholics
    31706 Coast Highway, South Laguna, CA 92677
National Clearing House for Alcohol Information
    P.O. Box 2345, Rockville, MD 20852
A.A. Inc.
    175 Fifth Avenue, New York, NY 10010
National Council on Alcoholism, Inc.
    12 West 21st Street, New York, NY 10010

ALLERGY AND ASTHMA

Asthma & Allergy Foundation of America
    1707 North Street, NW, Washington, DC 20036
American Lung Association
    1740 Broadway, New York, NY 10019
National Institute of Allergy and Infectious Diseases
    U.S. Department of Health and Human Services
    National Institutes of Health
    9000 Rockville Pike, Bethesda, MD 20892

ALZHEIMER'S DISEASE

Alzheimer's Disease and Related Disorders Association
 70 E. Lake Street, Suite 600, Chicago, IL 60601
Geriatric Study and Treatment Program
 New York University Medical Center School of Medicine
 550 First Avenue, New York, NY 10016
National Institutes of Health
 Building 31, Room 8-A-16, Bethesda, MD 20892

ANOREXIA NERVOSA

American Anorexia/Bulimia Association
 133 Cedar Lane, Teaneck, NJ 07666
National Anorexic Aid Society, Inc.
 550 South Cleveland Avenue, Suite F, Westerville, OH 43081
National Association of Anorexia Nervosa and Associated Disorders
 Box 7, Highland Park, IL 60035

ARTHRITIS

The Arthritis Foundation
 1314 Spring Street, NW, Atlanta, GA 30309
National Institute of Arthritis, Metabolism, and Digestive Diseases
 U.S. Department of Health and Human Services
 National Institutes of Health
 9000 Rockville Pike, Bethesda, MD 20205

BIOFEEDBACK

Biofeedback Society of America
 4301 Owen Street, Wheatridge, CO 80033

BIRTH CONTROL

Family Life Information
 PO Box 10716, Rockville, MD 20852
Planned Parenthood Federation of America, Inc.
 810 Seventh Avenue, New York, NY 10019
Zero Population Growth, Inc.
 1346 Connecticut Avenue, NW, Washington, DC 20036

BIRTH DEFECTS

March of Dimes Birth Defects Foundation National Headquarters
 3035 Broadway, Tarrytown, NY 10591
National Down Syndrome Society
 411 Fifth Avenue, New York, NY 10010

BLOOD

American Association of Blood Banks
    1828 L Street, NW, Suite 608, Washington, DC 20036
American Red Cross National Headquarters
    17th & D Streets, NW, Washington, DC 20006

CANCER

American Cancer Society National Headquarters
    261 Madison Avenue, New York, NY 10016
Chemotherapy Foundation
    183 Madison Avenue, New York, NY 10016
Leukemia Society of America, Inc.
    733 Third Avenue, New York, NY 10017
National Hospice Organization
    1901 North Fort Myer Drive, Suite 307, Arlington, VA 22209
National Cancer Information Service
    9000 Rockville Pike, Bethesda, MD 20892
Reach to Recovery
    19 West 56th Street, New York, NY 10019

CEREBRAL PALSY

United Cerebral Palsy Associations, Inc.
    66 East 34th Street, New York, NY 10016

CHILD ABUSE

Clearinghouse on Child Abuse and Neglect Information
    PO Box 1182, Washington, DC 20013
National Center on Child Abuse and Neglect (NCCAN)
    400 6th Street, Washington, DC 20019

CYSTIC FIBROSIS

Cystic Fibrosis Foundation
    6000 Executive Boulevard, Suite 309, Rockville, MD 20852

DENTAL HEALTH

American Dental Association
    Bureau of Health Education & Audiovisual Services
        211 East Chicago Avenue, Chicago, IL 60611
Federation of Prosthodontic Organizations
    211 E. Chicago Avenue, Chicago, IL 60611
National Institute of Dental Research
    National Institutes of Health
    U.S. Public Health Service
    Building 31, Room 2C35, Bethesda, MD 20892

DES

National Cancer Information Service
   Department DES
   9000 Rockville Pike, Bethesda, MD 20892
DES Action
   Long Island Jewish Medical Center
   New Hyde Park, NY 11040

DIABETES

American Diabetes Association
   505 Eighth Avenue, New York, NY 10018
National Diabetes Information Clearinghouse
   Box: NDIC, Bethesda, MD 20205

DIGESTIVE DISEASES

American Digestive Disease Society
   7720 Wisconsin Avenue, Suite 217, Bethesda, MD 20014
National Digestive Diseases Education & Information Clearinghouse
   1555 Wilson Boulevard, Suite 600, Rosslyn, VA 22209
National Foundation for Ileitis and Colitis, Inc.
   444 Park Avenue South, New York, NY 10016

DRUGS

Food and Drug Administration (FDA)
   Office of Consumer Affairs, Public Inquiries
   5600 Fishers Lane, Rockville, MD 20857

DRUG ABUSE

Drug Enforcement Administration
   1405 I Street, NW, Washington, DC 20537
National Clearinghouse for Drug Abuse Information
   PO Box 416, Kensington, MD 20795
Pyramid East
   7101 Wisconsin Avenue, Suite 1006, Bethesda, MD 20814
Pyramid West
   3746 Mount Diablo Boulevard, Suite 200, Lafayette, CA 94549

ENVIRONMENT

Environmental Protection Agency
   Public Information Center
   PM 211-B, 401 M Street, SW, Washington, DC 20460

EPILEPSY

The Epilepsy Foundation of America
    4351 Garden City Drive, Suite 406, Landover, MD 20785

EXERCISE

American Alliance for Health, Physical Education, Recreation, and Dance
    1900 Association Drive, Reston, VA 22091
President's Council on Physical Fitness and Sports
    450 Fifth Street, NW, Room 7103, Washington, DC 20001

EYE DISEASES/BLINDNESS

National Library Service for the Blind and Physically Handicapped
    Library of Congress, 1291 Taylor Street, Washington, DC 20542
Recording for the Blind, Inc.
    20 Roszel Road, Princeton, NJ 08540
American Council of the Blind
    1010 Vermont Avenue, NW, Suite 1100, Washington, DC 20005
American Foundation for the Blind, Inc.
    15 West 16th Street, New York, NY 10011
American Optometric Association
    243 N. Lindbergh Boulevard, St. Louis, MO 63141
The National Society to Prevent Blindness
    79 Madison Avenue, New York, NY 10016
National Eye Institute
    National Institutes of Health
    Building 31, Bethesda, MD 20892
National Federation of the Blind
    1800 Johnson Street
    Baltimore, MD 21230
The National Braille Association
    1290 University Avenue
    Rochester, NY 14607

FAMILY ABUSE (see also CHILD ABUSE)

The Association of American Colleges' Project on the Status and Education of Women
    1818 R Street, NW, Washington, DC 20009
Center for Women's Policy Studies
    2000 P Street, NW, Suite 508, Washington, DC 20036-5997
The Incest Survivors Resource Network, International
    PO Box 911, Hickscille, NY 11802
National Coalition Against Domestic Violence
    PO Box 15127, Washington, DC 20003
National Organization for Victim Assistance (NOVA)
    717 D Street, NW, Suite 200, Washington, DC 20004

GENETIC COUNSELING *See* BIRTH DEFECTS

GYNECOLOGICAL DISORDERS

American College of Obstetricians and Gynecologists
    One East Wacker Drive, Suite 2700, Chicago, IL 60601

HANDICAPPED

American Coalition of Citizens with Disabilities
    1200–15th Street, NW, #201, Washington, DC 20036
Clearinghouse on the Handicapped
    400 Maryland Avenue, SW, Switzer Building, Washington, DC 20202
Federation of the Handicapped, Inc.
    211 West 14th Street, New York, NY 10011
ICD Rehabilitation & Research Center
    340 East 24th Street, New York, NY 10010
National Center for Handicapped Children and Youth
    PO Box 1492, Washington, DC 20013

HEALTH AND SAFETY

American Public Health Association
    1015 Fifteenth Street, NW, Washington, DC 20005
Center for Health Promotion and Education
    Centers for Disease Control
    1600 Clifton Road, Building 3, Room SSB 33A, Atlanta, GA 30333
Council on Family Health
    420 Lexington Avenue, New York, NY 10017
Medic Alert
    Turlock, CA 95380
National Highway Traffic Safety Administration, NTS-11
    U.S. Department of Transportation, 400 Seventh Street, SW, Washington, DC 20590
National Injury Information Clearinghouse
    5401 Westbard Avenue, Room 625, Washington, DC 20207
National Health Information Clearinghouse
    PO Box 1133, Washington, DC 20013-1133
National Institute for Occupational Safety and Health
    Technical Information Branch, 4676 Columbia Parkway, Cincinnati, OH 45226
National Self Help Clearinghouse
    25 West 43rd Street, Room 620, New York, NY 10036
Nurses' Environmental Health Watch
    33 Columbus Ave., Somerville, MA 02143
Product Safety
    Consumer Product Safety Commission, Washington, DC 20207

HEARING

American Speech-Language-Hearing Association
   10801 Rockville Pike, Rockville, MD 20852
The Deafness Research Foundation
   9 East 38th Street, New York, NY 10016

HEART DISEASE

American Heart Association
   7320 Greenville Avenue, Dallas, TX 75231
Association of Heart Patients Incorporated
   Box 54305
   Atlanta, GA 30308
National Heart, Lung, and Blood Institute
   National Institutes of Health
   9000 Rockville Pike, Bethesda, MD 20892
The Mended Hearts, Inc.
   7320 Greenville Avenue, Dallas, TX 75231

HEMOPHILIA

National Hemophilia Foundation
   110 Greene Street, Room 406, New York, NY 10012

HYPERTENSION

High Blood Pressure Information Center
   120/80 National Institutes of Health, Bethesda, MD 20892

INFERTILITY

American Fertility Society
   2131 Magnolia Avenue, Suite 201, Birmingham, AL 35256
Resolve, Inc.
   PO Box 474, Belmont, MA 02178

KIDNEY DISEASE

National Kidney Foundation
   Two Park Avenue, New York, NY 10016
Kidney, Urologic & Blood Diseases
   National Institute of Arthritis, Metabolism, and Digestive Diseases
   National Institutes of Health, Bethesda, MD 20892

LUNG DISEASE *See* RESPIRATORY DISEASES

MARRIAGE COUNSELING

American Association of Marriage & Family Therapy
   198 Broadway, New York, NY 10038

CONTACT Teleministries USA, Inc.
  Pouch A, Harrisburg, PA 17105

MENTAL HEALTH

Family Service Association of America, Inc.
  254 West 31st Street, New York, NY 10001
National Institute of Mental Health
  Alcohol, Drug Abuse and Mental Health Administration
  U.S. Department of Health and Human Services
  5600 Fishers Lane, Rockville, MD 20857
National Mental Health Association
  1800 North Kent Street, Arlington, VA 22209

MULTIPLE SCLEROSIS

National Multiple Sclerosis Society
  205 East 42nd Street, New York, NY 10017

MUSCULAR DYSTROPHY

Muscular Dystrophy Association, Inc.
  810 Seventh Avenue, New York, NY 10019

MYASTHENIA GRAVIS

Myasthenia Gravis Foundation National Office
  7–11 South Broadway, White Plains, NY 10605

NARCOLEPSY

The American Narcolepsy Association
  Box 5846, Stanford, CA 94305

NUTRITION

The American Dietetic Association
  430 North Michigan Avenue, Chicago, IL 60611
Community Nutrition Institute
  2001 S Street, NW, Suite 530, Washington, DC 20009
Department of Foods and Nutrition
  American Medical Association
  535 North Dearborn Street, Chicago, IL 60610
Food and Nutrition Information Center
  National Agricultural Library Building, Beltsville, MD 20705
Food and Drug Administration
  Office of Consumer Affairs, Public Inquiries, 5600 Fishers Lane
  (HFE-88) Rockville, MD 20857
North American Vegetarian Society
  PO Box 72
  Dolgeville, NY 13329

OSTOMY

United Ostomy Association
2001 West Beverly Boulevard, Los Angeles, CA 90057

PARKINSON'S DISEASE

American Parkinson Disease Association, Inc.
116 John Street, New York, NY 10038

PHOBIAS

Phobia Society of America
6181 Executive Boulevard, Dept. AL
Rockville, MD 20852

PLASTIC SURGERY

American Board of Plastic Surgery, Inc.
1617 J. F. Kennedy Boulevard, Suite 1561, Philadelphia, PA 19103
American Society of Plastic & Reconstructive Surgeons, Inc.
233 North Michigan Avenue, Suite 1900, Chicago, IL 60601

POISON CONTROL

Division of Poison Control, Food and Drug Administration
5600 Fishers Lane, Room 18B-31, Rockville, MD 20857

PREGNANCY

American College of Nurse-Midwives
1522 K Street, NW, Suite 1120, Washington, DC 20005. Telephone (202) 347-5445.
American College of Obstetricians and Gynecologists
One East Wacker Drive, Suite 2700, Chicago, IL 60601
Community Health Services
Health Service Administration, Parklawn Building
5600 Fishers Lane, Rockville, MD 20857
Cooperative Birth Center Network
Perkiomenville, PA 18074
National Clearinghouse for Family Planning Information
PO Box 2225, Rockville, MD 20852
National Center for Education in Maternal and Child Health
3520 Prospect Street, Washington, DC 20057
Office of Maternal and Child Health
U.S. Department of Health and Human Services
Room 7-39 Parklawn, Rockville, MD 20857

PREMENSTRUAL SYNDROME

The National PMS Society
   PO Box 11467, Durham, NC 27703
PMS Action, Inc.
   Box 9326, Madison, WI 53715

RAPE

Center for Women Policy Studies
   2000 P Street, NW, Suite 508, Washington, DC 20036
National Center for the Prevention and Control of Rape
   National Rape Information Clearinghouse
   National Institute of Mental Health
   5600 Fishers Lane, Parklawn Building, Room 13A-44
   Rockville, MD 20857
Women's Crisis Center, Rape
   306 North Division, Ann Arbor, MI 48104

REHABILITATION

National Rehabilitation Information Center
   4407 Eighth Street, NE, Washington, DC 20017-2299

RESPIRATORY DISEASES

American Lung Association
   1740 Broadway, New York, NY 10019
National Heart, Lung, and Blood Institute
   National Institutes of Health
   9000 Rockville Pike, Bethesda, MD 20892

RETARDATION

National Association for Retarded Citizens
   2501 Avenue J, PO Box 6109, Arlington, TX 76011
American Association on Mental Deficiency
   1719 Kalorama Road, NW, Washington, DC 20009

SEX ADDICTION

National Association on Sex Addiction Problems
   (800) 622-9494
S-Anon
   PO Box 5117, Sherman Oaks, CA 91413
Sex and Love Addicts Anonymous
   PO Box 88, New Town Branch, Boston, MA 02258
Twin Cities Sex Addicts Anonymous
   PO Box 3038, Minneapolis, MN 55403

SEX EDUCATION AND THERAPY

Association of Humanistic Psychology
   325 Ninth Street, San Francisco, CA 94103
Sex Information and Education Council of the United States/Resource Center and Library (SIECUS)
   32 Washington Place, New York, NY 10003
American Association of Sex Educators, Counselors & Therapists (AASECT)
   11 Dupont Circle, NW, Suite 220, Washington, DC 20036

SEXUALLY TRANSMISSIBLE DISEASES

AIDS National Hotline (ASHA)
   (800) 342-AIDS
American Social Health Association
   260 Sheridan Avenue, Suite B40, Palo Alto, CA 94306
Center for Disease Control, Venereal Disease Control Division
   Public Health Service
   Atlanta, GA 30333
National VD Hotline
   (800) 227-8922

SICKLE CELL DISEASE

Sickle Cell Disease Foundation of Greater New York
   209 West 125th Street, Room 108, New York, NY 10027

SMOKING

Office on Smoking and Health
   Technical Information Center
   5600 Fishers Lane, Park Building, Rockville, MD 20857

SPEECH

American Speech-Language-Hearing Association
   10801 Rockville Pike, Rockville, MD 20852
Speech and Hearing Institute
   ICD Rehabilitation and Research Center
   340 East 24th Street, New York, NY 10010

STERILIZATION

Association for Voluntary Sterilization, Inc.
   122 East 42nd Street, New York, NY 10168
Zero Population Growth, Inc.
   1346 Connecticut Avenue, NW, Washington, DC 20036

SUDDEN INFANT DEATH SYNDROME (SIDS)

Sudden Infant Death Syndrome Clearinghouse
   1555 Wilson Blvd., Suite 600, Rosslyn, VA 22209

SUICIDE

CONTACT Teleministries USA, Inc.
   Pouch A, Harrisburg, PA 17105
The Samaritans
   500 Commonwealth Avenue, Boston, MA 02215

TAY-SACHS DISEASE

National Tay-Sachs & Allied Disease Associations, Inc.
   92 Washington Avenue, Cedarhurst, NY 11516

WEIGHT CONTROL

Overeaters Anonymous
   2190 West 190th Street, Torrance, CA 90504
Weight Watchers International
   800 Community Drive, Manhasset, NY 11030

WORK

Committee/Coalition/Council on Occupational Safety and Health (COSH)
   Many cities have COSH groups listed in local directories.
The Women's Occupational Health Resource Center
   Columbia University School of Public Health
   117 St. John's Place, Brooklyn, NY 11217
The National Women's Health Network
   224 Seventh Street, SE, Washington, DC 20003
The Women's Alliance for Job Equity
   1422 Chestnut Street, Philadelphia, PA
The National Alliance of Home-based Business Women
   PO Box 95, Norwood, NJ 07648
National Institute for Occupational Safety and Health (NIOSH)
   200 Independence Avenue, SW, HHH Building, Washington, DC 20201
9 to 5: The National Association of Working Women
   614 Superior Avenue, NW, Cleveland, OH 44113

INDEX

Page references in italics refer to illustrations. Bold-faced references refer to the Encyclopedia of Health and Medical Terms.

AA. *See* Alcoholics Anonymous
AARP. *See* American Association of Retired Persons
Abdominal hysterectomy, *297, 342*
Abdominal lipectomy, 388–89
  postoperative conditions, 389
  surgical procedure, 389
Abdominal pain, **587**
Abortion, 213–14, **587–88**
  health information on, 813
  See also Induced abortion, Spontaneous abortion
Abrasion (dermabrasion), 376–77
Abscess, **588**
Abuse. *See* Child abuse, Elder abuse
Accidents, preventing, 515–18
Accutane, 168, **589**
Acesulfame potassium, 87
Acetaminophen, **588**
Acetylcholine, **729**
"Acid indigestion," 500
Acidity, **588–89**
Acne, **589**
Acquired immune deficiency syndrome (AIDS), 131–32, 310–11, **589–90**, **746**
  doctor-patient confidentiality, 131
  fear of, 131
  hemophiliacs and, **693**
  in heterosexuals, 131, 312
  Masters and Johnson on, 131
  pregnancy and, 192, 219
  preventing spread of, 310–11
  social effects of, 149
  testing for, after rape, 441–42
  transmission, 310
Acromegaly, 39
Acrophobia, **743**
ACTH (Adrenocorticotropic hormone), **590**
Acupuncture, **590**
Acute granulocytic leukemia, **714**
Acute lymphocytic leukemia, **714**
Acute pancreatitis, **738–39**

Acute rhinitis, **756**
Acute salpingitis, **759**
Acute sinusitis, **766**
Acute symptom, **590**
Acyclovir, 318, **590–91**
Addiction, **591**
Addictive personality, 399
Addison's disease, 41, **591, 774**
Adenocarcinoma, **648**
Adenoma, **591**
Adhesion, **591**
Adolescence, 126–27
  masturbation in, 151
  pregnancy in, 127, 156
  sexual activity in, 127, 156
Adoptive pregnancies, 264, **591**
Adrenal, *40*
Adrenalin, **591**
Adulthood, 127–28
Adult onset diabetes, **649**
Aerobic dancing, 122
Aerobic exercise, **591–92**
AFP. *See* Alpha-feto protein assessment
Afterbirth. *See* Placenta
Age of consent, **636**
Age-related changes
  in bones and joints, 503–4
  in digestive system, 500–1
  in ears, 490–92
  in eyes, 488–90
  in feet, 505–6
  in heart and blood vessels, 496–98
  in nervous system, 493–96
  in skin, 486–88
  in teeth and gums, 492–93
  in urinary and reproductive systems, 501–2
Aging
  common breast problems and, 339
  factors that adversely affect, 540
  health information on, 813–14
  safety and, 515–18
  smoking and, 168

Agoraphobia, **592**, **743**
AI. *See* Artificial insemination
AIDS. *See* Acquired immune deficiency syndrome
Ailurophobia, **743**
Air pollution. *See* Pollution
Air sickness. *See* Motion sickness
Albumin, **751**
Albuminuria (proteinuria), **789**
Al-Anon, 408, 409, **592**
Al-Ateen, 408, **592**
Alcohol, 400–2, **592**
  biphasic action of, 402
  breast cancer and, 347
  infertility and, 250
  pregnancy and, 207, 409–10
  Prohibition Amendment, 396
  risks of drinking, 402
  safe drinking patterns for women, 401–2
  women and drinking problems, 402–5, 529–30
Alcohol dependence. *See* Alcoholism
Alcoholic beverages, **592–93**
Alcoholics, children of, 406, 408–9
Alcoholics Anonymous (AA), 150, 405–6, 409, 422, **593**, **762**
  effectiveness of, 409
  membership and size of, 409
  women in, 402, 405–6, 409
Alcoholism, **593–94**
  denial of, 405
  drinking patterns that signify, 406
  in elderly, 407
  as family problem, 407–9
  family patterns of, 406
  incidence of, 405
  intervention, 408
  late-onset, 407
  physical damage caused by, 406
  professional help for, 409
  resources and information on, 813–14
  suicide in alcoholic women, 402–3
Alkalinity, **588–89**
Allergic shock, **705**, **764**
Allergy, **594**, **814**

Alopecia. *See* Baldness
Alpha-feto protein assessment (AFP), 225
Alzheimer's disease, 493–94, **594–95**, **762**
  resources and information on, 815
  smoking and, **769**
Amebiasis, 327, **595**
Amebic dysentery, **656**
Amenorrhea, **595**
  exercise as cause of, 113
American Association of Geriatric Psychiatry, 531
American Association of Retired Persons (AARP), 513, 542
  Widowed Persons Service Programs of, 535
American Board of Medical Specialties, certification by, 810
American Cancer Institute, 347
American Cancer Society, 335, 418, **634**
  on lung cancer, **718**
  mammography guidelines of, 352
  Reach for Recovery program of, 359–60
  suggestions for quitting smoking, 419
  on women and smoking, 416
American College of Obstetrics and Gynecology, 481
American Dental Association, **672**
American Diabetes Association, **649**, **651**
American Foundation for the Blind, 490
American Heart Association, **625**
American Hospital Association, 566
American Humane Association, 491
American Lung Association, 418, **608–9**, **746**
American Medical Association, **780**
  specialties recognized by, 808–10
American Nurses Association, 473
American Psychiatric Association, 460

INDEX

Amino acids, 57
Amnesia, **595**
Amniocentesis, 223–24, **595–96**
  in eighteenth week, *226*
Amnion, **596**
Amphetamines, 398, 411–15, **596**, 739
Amphotericin-B, **676**
Ampicillin, 315
Amyotrophic lateral sclerosis (Lou Gehrig's disease), **596**
Anaerobic exercise, **592**
Anal sex, 327
Analgesic, **596**
Analysis. *See* Psychoanalysis
Anaphylactic shock. *See* Allergic shock
Androgen, **589, 596**
  excess production of, 41
  in hormone therapy, 293
Androgynous, **596–97**
Androsterone, **596**
Angina pectoris, 496–97, **598–99**
Angiography, **599**
Animal bites, **599**
Ankles, swollen, **599–600**
Anemia, 117, **597**
  heavy periods due to, 276, 277
Anesthesia, **597–98**
  for labor, 233–34
Aneurysm, **598**
Anorexia nervosa, 106–7, **600**
  delayed or erratic menstrual patterns due to, 275
  resources and information on, 815
Antacid, **600**
Anterior pituitary, 39
Antibiotics, **600–2**
  oral contraceptives and, 167
Antibodies, **602**
Antidepressants, **602**, 752
Antidotes, **602**
Antigen, **602**
Antihistamine, **602–3**
Antiperspirant, **603**
Antiprostaglandins, 278
Antiseptic, **603**

Antitoxin, **603**
Anus, functions of, *33*
Anxiety attack (panic attack), **603**
Aorta, 27, **603**
Aplastic anemia, **597**
Appendicitis, **603–4**
Appendix removal, in hysterectomy, 298
Appetite, **604–5**
Area Agency on Aging, 508, 562, 582
Arm lipectomy, 390
Arrhythmias, **605**
Arteries, *28*, 29
Arteriosclerosis, **605**. *See also* Atherosclerosis
Arthritis, 504, **605–7**
  resources and information on, 815
Artificial insemination (AI), 263–64, **607**
  incidence of, 263
Artificial respiration, **607**
Asbestos, **607**
Aseptic meningitis, **724**
Aspartame, 86, **607**
Aspiration pneumonia, **746**
Aspirin, **606, 607–8**
  hemophiliacs and, **693**
  Reye's syndrome and, **755**
  stomach and, **775**
Asthma, **608–9**
  resources and information on, 814
Astigmatism, **609**
Atherosclerosis, 59, **609–10, 631, 689, 780**
Athlete's foot, **675**
Atopic dermatitis. *See* Eczema
Audiologist, 490
Augmentation mammaplasty, 382–85
  postoperative conditions, 384
  silicone in, 382
  surgical process, 382–84
Autoimmune responses, **610**
Autopsy, **610**

Bacillary dysentery, **656**
Backache, **610**

INDEX

Bacteria, **610–11**
Bacterial endocarditis, **611**
Bacterial pneumonia, **746**
Bag of waters. *See* Amnion
Baldness, **611**
Barbiturates, 398, 414, **611**
   oral contraceptives and, 167
Barium test, **612**
Barrier contraceptives, 176–80
   barrier methods in combination, 180
   cervical cap, 178
   condoms, 179
   diaphragm, 177–78
   vaginal sponge, 178–79
Bartholin's gland, 42
   infection of, 283
   treatment of abscesses of, 294
Basal body temperatures, 256
Battering, 446–51
   children of battered women, 452
   definition, 427
   economic dependence of women and, 447, 448
   practical recommendations for protection from, 451
   SHELTER AID telephone number, 451
   social policies on, 448
   statistics on, 447
Beauvoir, Simone de, 541
Bed sores, **612**
Bee stings. *See* Insect stings and bites
Bell's palsy, **612**
Benign cysts, 343–46
Benzodiazepines, 414
Beta blockers, **612–13**
Betacarotene, 66
BHA. *See* Butylated-hydroxy anisole
Bifocals. *See* Eyeglasses
Bile, **613**
Biofeedback, **613**
Biopsy, 274, **613**
   methods of, **614**
Biotin, 73
   guide to, 68–69

Birth control, **613**
   information on, 156–57
   religious proscriptions against, 157
Birth defects, **614**
Birthmarks, **614**
Bisexuality, 153–56, **614**
   AIDS and, 131
   attitudes toward, 154–55
   defining, 154
   myths about, 155–56
Black eye, **614**
Blackheads, **615**
Bladder, spasms of, **771**
Bladder disorders. *See* Urinary tract infections
Blepharoplasty (eyelid lift), 363, 379–80
   postoperative conditions, 380
Bleeding, irregular, 280. *See also* Hemorrhage, Menstrual problems
Blister, **615**
Blood, **615**
   clotting, **615–16**
   composition of, **616**
   flow of, in heart, *27*
   movement of, 26–29
Blood pressure, 29, **616–17**
   rise in, during pregnancy, 216
Blood serum, **617**
Blood test, **617**
Blood transfusion, **617–18**
Blood types, **618**
Blue Cross/Blue Shield, 560
Brachycardia, **753**
Brain, **620**
   parts of, 36–38
   side view of, *37*
Breakfast, importance of, 87–88
Breast cancer, 346–54
   alcohol and, 347
   biopsy for, 353
   chemotherapy for, 358–59
   growth of, *350*
   hormone treatments for, 358
   incidence of, 347
   lead-time in, 348

needle aspirations for, 353
oral contraceptives and, 167
signs of, 348, *349*
spread of, 348
"stage" of, 348
treatment for, 355–60
women at risk for, 347
Breast cysts, **643**
Breast examinations, by self, 52
Breast-feeding, 243–46
  benefits of, 243–44
  breast infections, 244–45
  colostrum, 243
  after delivery, 241, 242
  marijuana and, 425
  nutrition during, 91–92, 244
  support for, 245
  smoking and, 417
Breast reconstruction, 359, 387–88
Breasts, 45
  in adult, *331*
  age and common problems of, 339
  anatomical abnormalities of, 340
  benign cysts, 355
  blood supply to, 332
  brassieres for, 338
  caffeine and, 342
  cosmetic surgery for, 365, *383*
  cross-section of, *333*
  development of, *331*
  disorders of, 339–54
  estrogen and, 334
  everyday care for, 335–39
  in exercise, 117–18
  failure of development, 341
  growth and development of, 330–34
  how to examine, *336–37*
  infections of, 346–47
  in menopause, 334–35
  menstrual cycle and, 342
  nerve supply to, 332, 334
  nipples, 330, 332, 340
  nonmalignant disorders of, 354–55
  normal physiologic changes in, 342
  in pregnancy, 198, 334

  in pre-puberty, *331*
  postmenopausal estrogens and, 334–35
  in post-ovulatory phase of menstrual cycle, 49
  in puberty, 330, *331*
  in sexual arousal, 134
  in sexual resolution, 135
  size of, 330, 338–40
  silicone in augmentation of, 382
  structure of, 330–32
Breathing, 30
Breech delivery, **620**
Breech position, *238*
Bronchitis, **620–21**
Bronchopneumonia, **746**
Bruise, **621**
Body odors, **618**
Boils, **618–19**
Bones, **619**
  movement of, 22
  of skull, *23*
Botulism, **619**
Bowel disease, **619–20**
Bowman, Otis R., Dr., 547
Bulimia, 96, 107–8, **621**
Bunion, **621–22**
Burns, 516–17, **622**
Bursitis, **622**
Butler, Robert N., Dr., 542
Butylated-hydroxy anisole (BHA), 84
Bypertrophic scars, 368

Caffeine, 419–20, **622–23**, 633
  breasts and, 342
  in pregnancy, 209
  urination and, **788**
Calcitonin, in osteoporosis, 504
Calcium, 76–78, **623**
  foods that are good sources of, 93
  in osteoporosis, 111, 503
  phosphorus and, 80
  requirements for
    when breast feeding, 91
    in pregnancy, 89
Calculus, **623**
Calendar rhythm method, **623**

Callus, **623**
Calories, **624**
 burned per hour in activities, 115
 exercise and expenditure of, 116
 from fat, 58
 guidelines for fat in daily caloric intake, 60–61
 as measure of energy, 115
Cancellous bone, *24*
Cancer, **624**
 IUDs and, 176
 oral contraceptives and, 166–67
 smoking and, 492
Candidiasis, 284, **624**, 675
 treatment, 284
Canker sore, **624**
Capillaries, 29
Capillary viscosities, 392
CAPS (Children of Aging Parents), 458
Carbohydrates, 57, 114, **624–25**
Carbon monoxide, in smoking, **781**
Carcinogenic agents, 86
Carcinogens, **625**
Carcinoma-in-situ, 288
Carcinomas, **624**, **625**
Cardiac muscle, 26
Cardiac shock, **764**
Cardiovascular diseases, 496–99
Cardiopulmonary resuscitation (CPR), **625**
Cardiovascular system, oral contraceptives and, 164–65
Carotene, 67, **625**
Carpal tunnel syndrome, 469, 563, **625**
Car sickness. *See* Motion sickness
Cartilage, **625–26**
Catecholamines, 41
CAT. *See* Computerized axial tomography
Catalepsy, **731**
Cataracts, 488–89, **626**
 contact lenses and, **638–39**
Catheterization, **627**
Caudal anesthesia, 233
Cauterization, **627**

Cautery, 294
Cavities. *See* Dental caries
Ceftriaxone, 314
Celibacy, 149
Cell, **627**
Center for Biomedical Ethics, 571
Central nervous system, 36–38
Cephalosporins, **601**
Cerebellum, 36
Cerebral palsy, **627**
Cerebrovascular accident. *See* Stroke
Cerebrum, 38
Cervical cap, 178, **627–28**
Cervical intraepithelial neoplasia (CIN), 288
Cervical os, 42
Cervical polyps, 287, **748**
Cervicitis, **628**
Cervix, 42, **628**
 cancer of, 288
 dilatation of, 295–96
  in labor, 231–33
 infection of, **628**
 self-examination of, 309
Cesarean section, 217, 235, 236–37, 239, **628**
 indications for, 236–37, 239
 unnecessary cesarean deliveries, 237, 239
Chancre, **628**
Chancroid, 305, 311
Cheek lift. *See* Meloplasty
Cheilosis, 71, **671**
Chemosurgery ("chemical peel"), 377
Chemotherapy, 302–3, **628–29**
Chest pains, **629**
Chiggers, **706**
Chilblains, **629–30**
Child abuse, 452–56
 emotional abuse, 453
 four major kinds of, 452–54
 incidence of, 445
 National Center on Child Abuse and Neglect, 452
 National Committee for the

INDEX

Prevention of Child Abuse, 453
  neglect, 453
  physical abuse, 453
  sexual abuse, 454–56
  Steinberg, Lisa, 452
Childbirth
  men's attitudes toward, 206
  risks associated with, 162
Childbirth Without Fear, 230
Childhood. *See* Infancy and childhood
Children
  of alcoholics, 406, 408–9
  of battered women, 452
  tetracycline for, **780**
The Children of Alcoholics Foundation, 408
Chiropractors, 582–83
  role and function of, **811**
Chlamydia/Chlamydial infections, 311–13, **630**
  diagnosing, 311
  incidence of, 305
  symptoms, 311
Chloasma of pregnancy, 376
Chloramphenicol, 601, 630
Chlorine, **630**
Chloromycetin, **630, 716**
Chloroquine, **720**
Chlorpromazine (Thorazine), **629, 630**
Choking, **630–31**
Cholecystitis, **676–77**
Cholesterol, 58–59, **631**
  caffeine and, 420
  definition, 59
  desired level of, 59
  diet and, 60–62
  fish oil supplements and, 62–63
  HDLs, 59
  LDLs, 59
Choline, 71
Chorionic villi sampling, 224–25
Chromosomes, 193, **631**, *632*
Chronic bronchitis, 499, **621**
Chronic cystic mastitis, 343

Chronic diarrhea, **652**
Chronic lung disease, 498–99
Chronic meningitis, **724**
Chronic obstructive lung diseases, 499
Chronic pancreatitis, **739**
Chronic pharyngitis, **742**
Chronic rhinitis, **756–57**
Chronic sinusitis, **766**
Chronic symptoms, **632**
Chrysotherapy. *See* Gold treatments
Cicero, on aging, 540
Cigarettes. *See* Smoking
Cimetidine (Tagamet), **632, 786**
CIN. *See* Cervical intraepithelial neoplasia
Circulation, suggestions for, 498
Circulatory system, 26–29
  divisions of, 29
Cirrhosis, **632**
Claudication. *See* Intermittent claudication
Claustrophobia, **632, 743**
Climacteric, **632–33**
Clinics, 554–55, **633**
Clitoral orgasms, vaginal versus, 136–37
Clitoris, 42, *44*, **633**
Clomid (clomiphene citrate), 261
Clonic spasms, **771**
CMV. *See* Cytomegalovirus
Coagulation. *See* Blood coagulation
Cocaine, 421–23, **633, 739**
  effects of, 421, 422
  emergency telephone number for information on, 422
  19th century U.S. epidemic of use, 421
  use of, extent of, 421–22
  women dependent on, 422
Cochlear implant, **688**
Codeine, **633, 735**
Coffee, **633**
  urination and, **788**
  See also Caffeine
Coitus interruptus, **633**
Colds. *See* Common cold

Cold sores. *See* Herpes
Colitis, **587, 633–34**
Collagen, 73
Colon, polyps of, **748**
Colon cancer, **634**
Colostomy, **634–35**
Colostrum, 243, **635**
Colposcopy, 273, **635**
Colpotomy, 181
Coma, **635**
Combined oral contraceptives, 163–64
Common cold, **635–36**
  during pregnancy, 218
Compazine, **739**
Computerized axial tomography (CAT/CAT scan), **636**
Conception and early development, 192–93
Concussion, cerebral, **636**
Condoms, 148–49, 179, 307–8, **636**
  for AIDS, 310–11
  applying, 179
  for STDs, 177, 179
Confidentiality, between patient and physician, 577
Congestive heart failure, 497
Conjunctivitis (pink eye), **636**
Consent laws, **636–37**
Constipation, **637**
  age and, 500–1
Contact dermatitis, **637–38**
Contact lenses, **638–39**
Contraception/contraceptives, 156–57, 159–90, **639**
  availability of, 189–90
  barrier contraceptives, 176–80
  common contraceptive methods, 161
  female sterilization, 181–82
  implants, 170
  injectables, 170
  male hormonal methods, 171–72
  periodic abstinence, 180–81
  risk-benefit ratio and, 160–61
  selection of method of, 162–63
  See also Oral contraceptives

Contraction stress test (CST), 228
Convulsions, **639**
Cooley's anemia, **696**
Cooperative care units, 573–74
Cooper's ligaments, 332
Cornea, **639**
Corneal dystrophy, **639**
Corns, **639–40**
Coronary artery disease, **640**
Coronary artery spasms, **771**
Coronary bypass surgery, **640**
Coronary heart disease, **769**
Corporations
  date rape and, 434–35
  stress management programs of, 474–75
Corpus luteum, **640**
Cortex, 41
Cortisone, 365
Corynebacterium vaginale, 316
Cosmetics, **640–41**
Cosmetic surgery, 361–94, **640**
  acceptance of, 361
  advertising and publicity given to, 362
  advice from friends and family on, 365
  for breasts, 365
  collagen in, 378
  complications from, 368
  consultation with cosmetic surgeon, 366–68
  deciding to undergo, 363–65
  emotional state at time of surgery, 364
  expectations and success of, 363–64
  finding accredited surgeon, 366
  medical insurance for, 362
  physical and mental condition at time of surgery, 364–65
  psychological dependence on, 363
  qualifications for performing, 362
  silicone used in, 368
  surgical procedures in, 368–92
  synthetic materials used in, 368, 378

INDEX

Coughing, **641**
Coumarin, **780**
Counseling, for gynecologic problems, 303
Couples, sexual enrichment for, 138–41
Cowper's glands, 45, *46*, **764**
CPR. *See* Cardiopulmonary resuscitation
Crack, 422–23
Cramps, **641–42**
  in lower abdomen, **587**
Cranial nerves, 38
Creutzfeld-Jakob disease, **792**
Crib death. *See* Sudden infant death syndrome
Crime, older women and, 522–23
Crisis, definition, 443
Crohn's disease, 78, **642**, **652**
Cryosurgery, **642**
CST. *See* Contraction stress test
Cultures, for female infertility, 257
Cunnilingus, **764**
Curettage, **642**
Cushing's syndrome, 41, **642**
Cuts. *See* First aid
Cyanosis, **642–43**
Cyst, *See also* Benign cysts **643**.
Cystic fibrosis, **643**
Cystitis, 282–83, 313, **787**, **788**, **789**
  preventing, 308
  See also Urinary tract infections
Cystocele, **643–44**
Cystoscopy, **644**, **789**
Cytomegalovirus (CMV), **697**

D&C. *See* Dilatation and curettage
D&E. *See* Dilatation and evacuation
Dalmane (flurazepam), **644**
Dandruff, **644**
Darkfield Microscopic Examination, 322
Date rape, 148, 434–35
  corporate interest in, 434–35
  prevalency of, 435
Day care, 465
Deafness. *See* Hearing loss

Death, **644–45**
Deficiency disease, **645**
Degenerative disease, **645**
Dehydration, **646**
Delaney clause, 85
Delirium tremens (DTs), **646**
Delivery, 201, 229–36
  afterwards, 239–46
  at childbearing centers, 203–4
  episiotomy in, 234–35
  family practitioner for, 201
  forceps for, 235
  at home, 203
  in hospital, 202–3
  hospital visitors after, 240–41
  lay midwife for, 202
  Leboyer technique for, 236
  obstetrician-gynecologist for, 200
  physical recovery after, 241–43
  postpartum depression ("baby blues") after, 241
  professional help for, 200–2
  relaxing for, 234–36
  rooming-in after, 240
  sexual relations after, 242
  stretch marks after, 243
  vacuum extractor for, 235
Delusions, **646**
Dementia, 494
Dental care, **646–47**
Dental caries, **647**
Dental implantation, **648**
Dental plaque, **647**
Dentin, **647**
Dentistry, description of field, 810–11
Dentists, 582
Dentures, **647–48**
Deodorants, **648**
Deoxyribonucleic acid. *See* DNA
Depilatories. *See* Hair removal
Depo Provera, 170
Depressants, **648**
Depression, **648**
  correctable causes of, 494
  external causes of, 528
  older woman and, 527–28

Dermabrasion. *See* Abrasion
Dermatitis, **648**
Dermoid cysts, 291
DES. *See* Diethylstilbestrol
Desensitization, **649**
Detoxification, **649**
Dextrose, **649**
Diabetes, **649–51**
   cataracts and, **626**
   death due to, **649**
   eyes and, 489
   after having a baby or at middle age, **651**
   incidence of, **649**
   insulin for, **649**
   in old age, 506
   oral contraceptives and, **650–51**
   pregnancy and, 217
   symptoms and, **649–50**
   testing for, **650**
   treatment, **649, 650**
Diabetes mellitus, 41
Diabetic retinopathy, **651**
Diagnostic test consent, 636–37
Dialysis, **651–52**
Dick-Read, Grantly, 230
Diaphragm, 177–78, **652**
   cervix and, **628**
Diarrhea, **652–53**
Diet
   constipation and, 500–1
   fiber in, 500–1
   in pregnancy, 207
   study of, by physicians, 546
Diethylstilbestrol (DES), 166, 171, 254, **648–49**
Dieting, **653**
   for overweight, 100–1
   skipped or delayed periods due to, 275
Digestion
   definition, 30
   exercise and, 113
   process, 30–34
Digestive system, 30–34
   aging and, 500–1
   functions of, *33*

Digitalis (Digoxin), **653**
Dilantin (phenytoin), **653**
Dilatation and curettage (D&C), 186–87, 295, 96, **653**
Dilatation and evacuation (D&E), 185, *186*, 295–96, **653**
Dildos, 140
Directory of health information, 813–25
Disc, slipped, **653–54**
Dislocation (subluxation), **654–55**
Displaced Homemakers Network, 533
Diuretics, 513, **655**
Diverticulosis, **655**
Division of Poison Control, address, 747
Dizziness. *See* Vertigo
DNA (deoxyribonucleic acid), **655–56**
Dog bites. *See* Animal bites
Donated embryo transfer, 264–65
Dopamine, 495, **656, 740**
Double blind test, **744**
Double pneumonia, **746**
Douching, 308
Down syndrome, **656**
   AFP measurement for, 225
   amniocentesis testing for, 223–24
Dramamine, **656, 793**
Drugs
   abuse and dependency on, 398
   circumstances of use, 400
   common drugs, 399
   cost of, 513
   elderly and, 529–30
   foods and, interaction of, 513
   for overweight, 104
   in pregnancy, 207, 209–10
   prescribed drugs affecting sexual function, 144–45
   for weight-loss, 415
   See also Substance abuse
DTs. *See* Delirium tremens
Duchenne muscular dystrophy
Duct ectasia, 345–46
Duodenal ulcer, **656**

INDEX

Duodenum, 34
  functions of, *33*
Dying. *See* Death, Hospices
Dysentery, **656–57**
Dynorphin, **738**
Dysmenorrhea, 278–79, **641, 657**
Dyspareunia, 143, **657, 764**
  penis size as cause of, 144
Dysplasia, 272, 287, **657**
Dysplastic cells, 271–72
Dyspnea, **657**

Ear, **657–58**
  age-related changes in, 490–92
  diagnosis and evaluation of problems of, 490
  disorders of, **658–59**
  hearing aids for, 490–91
  hearing process, **658**
  management of hearing problems, 491–92
  middle and inner ear, *658*
  presbycusis of, 490
  suggestions for hearing impaired, 491
Eating disorders
  anorexia nervosa, 106–7
  bulimia, 96, 107–8
Ear alteration. *See* Otoplasty
Earning power, of older woman, 532–33
Ecchymosis, 374
Echogram, **659**
Eclampsia, 216–17, **659**
ECT. *See* Electroshock therapy
Ectopic pregnancy, 215–16, **659**
  HCG in, 199
  incidence of, 215
  IUD as cause of, 175
  signs of, 215
  sites of, **660**
  types of, 215–16
Eczema (atopic dermatitis), **659**
Edema, **660, 672**
EEG. *See* Electroencephalogram
Ehrlich, Paul, Dr., **629**
Ejaculation, **660**

EKG. *See* Electrocardiogram
Elbow joint (typical synovial joint), *24*
Elder abuse, 456–58
  Area Agency on Aging, 458
  causes of, 457
  Elder Abuse Hotline, 458
  incidence of, 457
  intervention services for, 457–58
  neighbors and, 457–58
  social agencies for, 458
  typical case of, 457
  victims' tolerance of, 457
Elderly
  abuse of, 456–58
  alcohol abuse in, 529–30
  alcoholism in, 407
  body temperature and, 518
  diabetes in, 506
  drugs and, 529–30
  exercise for, 514–15
  infection in, 506
  medication for, 510–14
  motor vehicle accidents by, 517
  psychotherapy and personal growth for, 531–32
  sex and sensuality of, 526–27
  sexual response in, 502–3
  sleep problems of, 528–29
  suicide in, 530
  survivorship of, 542
  vitamin supplements for, 512–13
  See also Medical care for elderly
Elective surgery, **660**
Electrocardiogram (EKG), 117, **660–61**
Electroconvulsive therapy. *See* Electroshock therapy (ECT)
Electroencephalogram (EEG), **661**
Electrolysis. *See* Hair removal
Electroshock therapy (ECT), **661**
Eliot, T.S., 533
Embolism, **661**
Embryo, **661**
Emergency care, 564–65
Emotional disorders, exercise for, 113

Emphysema, 499, **661–62**
Employment, women and, 520–21
Encephalitis, **662, 705**
Encephalitis lethargica, **739**
Encounter groups, 147
Endocrine dysfunction, 341
Endocrine glands, 36, **680**
Endocrine problems, 292
Endocrine system, 39–41, **662**
  hormones, 39
Endometrial aspiration, **662**
Endometrial biopsy, 256–57, 295
Endometrial cancer, 167
Endometrial hyperplasia, 288–89
Endometriosis, 253, 289–90, **662**
  common sites of, *663*
  treatment, 262–63, 290
Endometritis, **662**
Endometrium, 48
  cancer of, 290–91
Endorphins, 38, 542, **590, 662–63, 699, 738, 744**
Endoscopy, **663, 786**
Enema, 663
Energy, 663
Enteric fever. *See* Typhoid fever
Enterocele, 663
Enuresis, 663
Environmental Protection Agency, **733, 734**
Environmental therapy, **760–61**
Enzyme, **663–64**
Epididymis, *46*
Epidural anesthesia, 233
Epiglottis, **664, 713**
Epilepsy, **664**
  pregnancy and, 218
Epinephrine, 369
Episiotomy, 234, **665**
  pain with sexual intercourse after, 242
Epstein-Barr virus, **697**
Equal Employment Opportunity Commission, on sexual harassment, 478–79, 480
Erection, **665**
Erogenous zone, **665**

Erythromycin, **601, 665**
Esophageal hernia, 500, **696**
Esophagus, **665**
  functions of, *33*
  spasms of, 771
Essential hypertension, 497
Estrogen, 41, 276, **665**
  breasts and, 334–35
  cosmetic surgery and, 365
  dermabrasion and, 376
  endometrial cancer and, 290–91
  in endometrial hyperplasia, 288–89
  for endometriosis, 262
  excess production of, 41
  in hormone therapy, 293
  as male contraceptive, 171
  in menstrual cycle, 48
  osteoporosis and, 503
  for postmenopausal women, 111, 334–35, 503
  vaginitis and, 284
Ethics. *See* Medical ethics
Eunuchism, 41
Eustachian tube, **666**
Exercise
  activities rated according to physical fitness benefits, 123
  benefits of, 110–11
  calorie expenditure and, 116
  in digestive function, 113
  for elderly, 514–15
  for emotional disorders, 113
  health clubs for, 124
  length of activity period, 124
  menstruation and, 113
  for older women, 92, 540
  for osteoporosis, 111
  for overweight and obesity, 102–3
  physical examination before, 116–17
  physiological improvements from, 112–13
  pregnancy and, 113–14, 210
  regular routines, 122, 124
  suitable clothes and equipment for, 117–19

weight lifting for women, 111
Excision biopsy, 294
Exocrine glands, **679**
Extramarital sex, 149–50
Eyebrow lift, 380
Eyeglasses, **667–68**
Eyelid lift. *See* Blepharoplasty
Eyes, **666–67**
  age-related changes in, 488–90
  aids for visually impaired, 490
  cataracts of, 488–89
  diabetes and, 489
  examination of, **667**
  glaucoma of, 489
  senile macular degeneration of, 489
Eyestrain, **668**

Face lift. *See* Rhytidoplasty
Facial tic. *See* Tics
Fainting, **668**
Fallopian tubes (oviducts), 42–45, **668**
  cancer of, 291
  chlamydia of, 311
  in female infertility, 253, 254
  hysterosalpingogram for, 257, 260
  laparoscopy for, 261
  Rubin test for, 260
  salpingectomy, 300
  surgery for, in infertility, 262
  tubal ligation, 300
Falls, preventing, 515–16, 517–18
Family abuse, 445–58
  arrest of abusive husbands, 448
  battering, 446–51
  clues to development of violence, 449
  corporate interest in, 428
  incest, 459–62
  as learned response, 446
  media image of violence, 445–46
  National Coalition Against Domestic Violence, 450, 451
  psychological abuse, checklist of, 450
Family and Medical Leave Act, 465

Family history, **668–69**
Family planning, 159, 191–92
  periodic abstinence, 180–81
Family practitioner, for delivery, 201
Farsightedness, **669**
FAS. *See* Fetal alcohol syndrome
Fast foods, 88
Fat, 58–63, **669**
  cholesterol and diet, 58–63
  fish oil supplements and cholesterol, 62–63
  menus low in, 61–62
  polyunsaturated, 59
  saturated, 59, 60
  unsaturated, 58
Fat necrosis, 346
Fat-soluble vitamins, 67–70
  RDAs for, 65
FDA. *See* U.S. Food and Drug Administration
Feet, **669**
  age-related changes in, 505–6
  caring for, 118–19
Fellatio, *See also* Oral sex **764**.
Female ejaculation, 136
Female genital tract, *194*
Female infertility, 250–56
  causes of, 250–56
  cervical causes of, *255*
  ovarian causes of, *255*
  tests for, 256–61
  treatment, 261–63
  tubal causes of, *255*
  uterine causes of, *255*
  vaginal causes of, *255*
Female reproductive system, 42–45
  side view of external and internal genitalia, *44*
Female sexual response, 133–34
  defining, 133
  in old age, 502–3
  physiological response, 134–36
Fenestration, **689**
Fertility
  IUD and, 175–76
  marijuana and, 425

Fetal alcohol syndrome (FAS), 409–10
Fetal health, 223–29
  alpha-feto protein (AFP) assessment, 225
  amniocentesis in evaluating, 223–24
  chorionic villi sampling, 224–25
  prenatal DNA studies, 227
  sonography for, 223
Fetal monitors, 227–29
Fetoscopy, 227
Fetus, 669–70
  oral contraceptives and, 166
  smoking and, 769
Fever, 670
Fiber, 78–79, 670
  in diet, 79, 500–1
Fibrillation, 670–71
Fibroadenomas, 343, 345, 671
Fibrocystic syndrome, 343
Fibroids (fibromyomata uteri), 289
  heavy periods due to, 277
First aid, 671
Fish oil, 671
Fish oil supplements, 62–63
Fissure, 671
Fistula, 671–72
Fleming, Alexander, Sir, 740
Fluids, 672
Fluoridation, 672
Fluoride, 78
Fluoroscope, 672–73
Folacin. *See* Folic acid
Folate. *See* Folic acid
Folic acid (folacin/folate), 72, 673
  guide to, 68–69
  requirements of, in pregnancy, 90
Follicle-stimulating hormone (FSH), 48
  in female infertility, 257, 261
Food
  drugs and, interaction of, 513
  nutrient content of, 56–80
  good sources of calcium in, 93
Food additives, 84–87, 673
Food and Drug Administration (FDA). *See* U.S. Food and Drug Administration
Food groups, 80–81
  recommended servings of, 83
Food labeling, 82–84
Food poisoning, 673–74
Ford, Betty/Betty Ford Center, 413
Foster Grandparents Program, 537
Fracture, 674
Franklin, Ben, 536–37
Fraternal twins, 195
Freud, Sigmund, 421, 531
  on incest, 459
  on orgasm, 136
  theory of unconscious, 701
Frigidity, 674
Frostbite, 674–75
FSH. *See* Follicle-stimulating hormone
Fungal infections, 675–76

Galactorrhea, 346
Gallbladder, 676–77
Gallstones, 500, 677
  functions of, 33
  possible sites of obstruction by, 676
Gamma globulin, 677, 751
Gangrene, 677–78
Gastritis, 587
Gastrointestinal disorders, 678
  travel and, 506
Gastrointestinally transmitted STDs, 327
Gastrointestinal (GI) tract, 30, 32–34
Gay men, AIDS in, 131
Generally Recognized as Safe List (GRAS), 84
Generic drugs, 601, 802–8
Gene splicing. *See* Generic engineering
Genetic counseling, 678
Genetic engineering, 678–79
Genital herpes. *See* Herpes simplex virus
Genital warts (condyloma acuminata), 325

INDEX

Geriatric medicine, 507
Geriatrics, **679**
German measles. *See* Rubella
Gerontology, 534, **679**
Gestational hypertension, 216
GH. *See* Growth hormone
Giardiasis, 328, **679**
GIFT (gametic intrafallopian transfer), 265
Gingivitis, **679**
Gland, **679–80**
Glands of Montgomery, 332
Glaucoma, 489, **680–81**
Globulin, **751**
Glomerulonephritis, **681, 775**
Glossitis, 71
Glucagon, 41
Glucose, **681–82**
Glucose tolerance test (GTT), **650, 681–82**
Glucosuria, **789**
Glycogen, **682**
Goiter, **682**
Gold treatments (chrysotherapy), **682**
Gonads, **682**
Gonorrhea, 305, 313–15, **682–83,** 787
　complications of, 313–14
　diagnosing, in women, 314
　in female infertility, 250
　pregnancy and, 220
　prophylactic measures for, 314
　symptoms of, 313
　treatment, 314
Gout, 504, **683**
Granuloma inguinale, 305, 315, **683**
GRAS. *See* Generally Recognized as Safe List
Gray Panthers, 536, 542
Group medical practice, 549–50
Group therapy
　for elderly, 531
　for sexual dysfunction, 147
Growth hormone (GH), 39
G Spot, 136, 137, **676**
GTT. *See* Glucose tolerance test

Guillain-Barré syndrome, **683**
Gums, **683–84**
　age-related changes in, 492–93
Gynecologic checkups, 502
Gynecologic problems and diseases, 274–92
　cautery for, 294
　chemotherapy for, 302–3
　counseling for, 303
　endocrine problems, 292
　finding causes of, 267–74
　hormone therapy for, 293
　incontinence, 281–82
　infections, 282–86
　lower abdominal pain, 280–81
　menstrual problems, 274–79
　other vaginal bleeding, 280
　prolapse of uterus, 282
　radiation therapy for, 302
　surgery for, 294–302
　tumors, 286–91
　treatment of infection, 292–93
　vaginal discharge, 281
Gynecologist/obstetrician
　choosing, 557
　doctor/patient relationship, 268
Gynecomastia, 41

Hair, **684–85**
Hair removal, **648, 685**
Haldol (haloperidol), **782**
Hallucination, **685**
Hallucinogens, 398, 399, **685**
Halsted, William, Dr., 355
Hamilton, Edith, 541
Hangover, **685–86**
Harvard Medical School, on breast cancer, 347
Hay fever. *See* Allergy
HCG. *See* Human chorionic gonadotropin
HDLs. *See* High density lipids
Head, structure of, **686**
Headache, **686–88**
　causes of, **686**
　frequency of, **686–87**
　migraine, **687**

treatment, **687**
Health, as positive state, 21
Health care personnel, 808–13
Health care services, 580–83
Health care system, 545–83
 alternative therapies, 583
 being both woman and patient, 562–63
 emergency care, 564–65
 health care services, 580–83
 hospital outpatient departments, 554–55
 hospitals, 565–74
 patient's participation in, 546
 payment plans, 558–62
 physicians. *See* Physicians
Health care workers, types of, 811–13
Health examination, suggested schedules for, **797**
Health Hazard Evaluation Program, **731**
Health insurance, 558
 dental coverage, **647**
 Blue Cross/Blue Shield, 560
 HMOs, 559
 second opinions and, 497
Health maintenance organizations (HMOs), 559
Health on the job, 463–83
 aches and pains, 468–70
 bad air, 467–68
 day care, 465
 eyestrain and irritation, 470
 food and drink on the job, 475–76
 health-related professions, 472–73
 job-related accidents, 464–65
 medical benefits, 483
 9 to 5: The National Association for Working Women, 483
 noise, 466–67
 number of women employed, 463
 occupational hazards, 466
 photocopiers, 470–71
 posture, 468–69
 pregnancy, 481–82
 reasons for women working, 463

 sexual harassment, 476–80
 shoes, 469
 stress, 473–75
 VDTs, 471–72
 well-being in workplace, 465–72
 where women work, 464
 Women's Occupational Health Resource Center, 483
 women staying home for illness, 465
 workers with dependent parents, 465
Health-related professions, 472–73
Health services, 53–54
Hearing aids, 490–91, **688**
Hearing loss, **688–89**
Hearing process, **658**
Heart
 blood flow in, *27*
 blood vessels and, 496–98
 chambers of, 27–29
 description of, 26–27
Heart attack, **689–90**
 oral contraceptives and, 165
 See also Myocardial infarction
Heartburn, 500, **691**
Heart disease, hypertensive, **690**
Heart failure, **691**
Heart-lung machine, **691**
Heat exhaustion, **691–92**
Heat stroke, **692**
Height, **692**
Heimlich maneuver, **692**, *693*
Hemagglutination, 199
Hematoma, 374–75
Hematuria, **789**
Hemoglobin, **693**
 sickle-cell anemia and, **765**
Hemoglobinopathies, **597**
Hemolytic anemia, **597**, **765**
Hemophilia, **693**
Hemophilus vagialis (HV), 316
Hemorrhage, **693–94**
Hemorrhoids, **694**
 after delivery, 242
Heparin, **694**, **780**
Hepatitis, **694–95**

INDEX

Hepatitis B, 316
Heredity, **695–96**
Hernia, **696**
Heroin, 423–24, **696, 735**
   death from, 424
Herpes, **696–97**
Herpes simplex keratitis, **639**
Herpes genitalis, 220
Herpes simplex virus (genital herpes), 317–18
Heterosexuals, AIDS and, 312
Hiatus, 500
Hiatus hernia, **696**
High altitude sickness, **697**
High blood pressure. *See* Hypertension
High density lipids (HDLs), 59
Hip lipectomy, 390
Histamine, **697–98**
Hite Report, 153
Hives, **698**
HMOs. *See* Health maintenance organizations
Hodgkin's disease, **698**
Holistic health, 51–52
Holistic medicine, **698**
Holmes-Rahe stress scale, 524
Homosexuality, **698**
   AIDS and, 310
   as category, 154
   Kinsey Reports on, 153
"Honeymoon cystitis", 283
Hormones, **699**
   in energy production, 114–15
   role of, 39
Hormone tests, for female infertility, 257
Hormone therapy, 293
Hospices, 524, 542, **699**
Hospitals, 565–74
   cooperative care units, 573–74
   delivery in, 202–3
   intensive care units, 573
   outpatient departments, 554–55
   social service department, 582
   "special duty" nurses, 572
   your comfort as patient, 571–73

Hot flashes, 279, **699**
Housing and transportation, older woman and, 521–22
Human chorionic gonadotropin (HCG), 199
Huntington's chorea, **696**
Hydatidiform mole, 222
Hydrochloric acid, **588–89**
Hydrotherapy, **744**
Hymen, 42, **699**
   unbroken, *700*
Hyoscine. *See* Scopolamine
Hyperglycemia, **650, 699**
Hypertension, **699–700**
   aging and, 497
   caffeine and, 420
   oral contraceptives and, 165–66
   in pregnancy, 216
Hyperthyroidism, 39, **700**
   in female infertility, 254
Hypnodontia, **701**
Hypnosis, **701**
Hyperventilation, **700–1**
Hypochondria, **701**
Hypoglycemia, 41, **650, 701**
Hypospadias, 263
Hypothalamus, *40*, **701**, 741
Hypothermia, **701–2**
Hypothyroidism, 39, 64
   in female infertility, 254
Hysterectomy, 188, 288, 296–300, **702**
   abdominal, *297*
   cross-section of pelvis after, *299*
   incidence of, 302
   indications for, 296–98
   removal of ovaries and tubes in, 298
   typical hysterectomy, 299–300
   unnecessary examples of, 296, 298
   vaginal, *297*
Hysteria, **702**
Hysterosalpingogram, 257, 260
Hysteroscopy, 181, 273
Hysterotomy, 188

I&D. *See* Incision and drainage

Iatrogenic cancer, **648**
Iatrogenic disease, **702**
Ibuprofen, **702**
Ileitis, **652, 702**
Ileostomy, **702–3**
Illegal drugs, 420–26
Immune system, zinc for, 78
Immunity, **703**
Immunization, **703**
  guide to, 798–800
Immunotherapy, for breast cancer, 359
Impotence, **703**
Incest, 127, 459–62, **703**
  mother's role in, 460
  organizations for information and assistance, 461–62
  prevalence of, 459
  self-help groups for, 461
  stepfathers and, 460
  symptoms of, 461
Incisional hernia, **696**
Incision and drainage (I&D), 294
Income, of older woman, 520–21
Incontinence, 281–82, **788**
Inderal (propranolol), **703**
Indigestion, **704**
Indocin (indomethacin), **704**
Induced abortion, 184–88, **588, 704**
  availability of, 189–90
  counseling, 188–89
  dilatation and curettage (D&C), 186–87
  dilatation and evacuation (D&E), 185, *186*
  drugs for, 188
  hysterotomy and hysterectomy, 188
  intra-amniotic infusion, 187–88
  menstrual extraction, 184–85
Infancy and childhood, 125–26
Infertility, 247–65
  chlamydia as cause of, 311
  definition, 247
  new developments in treatment of, 264–65
  following gonorrhea infection, 314–15
  See also Female infertility, Male infertility
Influenza, **704–5**
"Informed consent," 577
Ingrown toenails, **730**
Inguinal glands, **705**
Inguinal hernia, **696**
Inositol, 71
Insect stings and bites, **705–6**
Insomnia, 413, **706–7**
Institute of Medicine of the National Academy of Sciences, on marijuana, 425
Insulin, 41, **707, 738**
  role of, **649**
"Intention tremors," **783**
Intercourse. *See* Sexual intercourse
Interferon, 325, **635–36, 707, 792**
Intermittent claudication, **707**
Intestine, cross-section of, *32*. *See also* Large intestine, Small intestine
Intra-amniotic infusion, 187–88
Intraductal papilloma, 345
Intrauterine devices (IUDs), 160, 172–76
  adverse side effects from, 174–76
  contraindications to, 176
  dysmenorrhea due to, 279
  endometritis caused by, **662**
  evaluation for, 173
  failure rate, 172
  in female infertility, 250–53, 254
  in history, 172
  insertion, 172–73
  mechanism of action, 172
  PID and, 172–75
  popularity and use of, 172
  pregnancy and use of, 192
  side effects of, 162
  types of, 173
Intrauterine fetal death, 221–222
Intrauterine pregnancy, 175
Introitus, 42

INDEX 845

In vitro fertilization, 264, **707**
Involuntary muscles, 22–26
Involuntary nervous system, 49
Iodine, 78
Irritable bowel syndrome, **708**
Iron, 77–78, **707–8**
  requirements for, in pregnancy, 90
Iron deficiency anemia, **597**
Islets of Langerhans, 39–41, **738**
Isoniazid, **784**
Itching, **708**
IUDs. *See* Intrauterine devices

Jaundice, **709**
Joints, 22
Juvenile onset diabetes, **649**

Kaplan, Helen Singer, 459
Kaposi's sarcoma, **709**
Keloidal scars, 368, 384
Ketones, 101, **650**
Ketosis, 101–2
Kidney cysts, **643**
Kidney dialysis. *See* Dialysis
Kidneys, 34–36
  disorders of, **709–10**
Kinsey Reports, on homosexuality, 153
Knee, disorders of, **710–11**

Labia majora and minora, 42, *44*
Labor
  inducing, 232–33
  stages of, *231*
Labor and delivery, 229–36
  anesthesia for, 233–34
  dilatation of cervix, 232–33
  natural childbirth, 230
  premature birth, 229
  See also Delivery
Lacrimal ducts, **711–12**
Lactation, **712**
Lactose intolerance, **712**
Lamaze method, 230, **712**
Laparoscope, **712**
Laparoscopy, *183*, 261, 273, 290

Laparotomy, 181
Large intestine, functions of, *33*
Laryngectomy, **713**
Laryngitis, **712**
Larynx, **712–13**
  cross-section of mouth and, *713*
Laser therapy, 290, **713**
Late-onset alcoholism, 407
Laudanum, **735**
Laxative, **713–14**
Lay midwife, for delivery, 202
LDLs. *See* Low density lipids
L-dopa (levodopa/Sinamet), 495, **714**
Leary, Timothy, 426
Leboyer delivery, 236
Legionnaire's disease, 468, **714**
Lesbianism, 153–56, **698, 714**
  butch and fem roles in, 155
  motherhood and, 155
  myths about, 155–56
  in older women, 537
  penis substitutes and, 155
  prevalence of, 153–54
Lesch-Nyhan syndrome, **763**
Leukemias, **624, 714–15**
Leukorrhea, **715**
LH. *See* Luteinizing hormone
Librium, 398, **715**
Life expectancy, **715–16**
"Life review," 542
Life-style-related disease, 546
Life work, of older women, 541–42
Ligament, **716**
Lipectomy, 388–90
  abdominal, 388–89
  for thigh, hip, and arm, 390
Lipolysis. *See* Liposuction
Lipoplasty, 363
Liposuction (lipolysis), 390–92
  complications from, 391–92
  surgical procedure, 391
Lithium carbonate, **716**
Lithotomy position, 234
Living wills, 542, 571, **645**
Liver, **716–17**
  disease of, 403
  disorders of, **716–17**

functions of, *33*
  oral contraceptives and, 166
  tumors of, **716**
Liver spots, **717**
Lobar pneumonia, **746**
Lochia, 241
Longevity. *See* Life expectancy
Lopressor (metoprolol), **613**
Lou Gehrig's disease. *See* Amyotrophic lateral sclerosis
Love, 132
  need for, 133
  in older woman, 536–37
Low density lipids (LDLs), 59
Lower abdominal pain, 280–81
Low-volume shock, **764**
LSD (Lysergic acid diethylamide), 398, 426, **717**
L-triptophane, **707**
Lumpectomy, 356, *357*, **717**
Lung cancer, **718**
  women's death rates from, 499
Lungs, 29, 498–99, **717–18**
Lupus erythematosus, **718–19**
Luteinizing hormone (LH)
  in female infertility, 257, 261
  in menstrual cycle, 48
Lyme disease, **706**, **719**
Lymphadenitis, **720**
Lymph nodes, **719–20**
Lymphogranuloma venereum, 305, **720**
Lymphomas, **624**
Lymphosarcoma, **720**

Macular degeneration, **720**
"Mainlining," 423
Malaria, **720**, **741**
Malarplasty, 379
Male hormonal contraceptive methods, 171–72
Male infertility, 248–50
  causes of, 248–49
  treatment for, 250
  tests for, 249–50
Male reproductive system, 45, *46*

Male sterilization (vasectomy), 182, *183*
Maxilloplasty, 378
Malignant, as term, **720**
Malnutrition, **720**
Malocclusion, **720–21**, **736**
Mammaplasty, 363, 382–86
  augmentation, 382–85
  reduction, 385–86
Mammograms/mammography, 334, 352, **721**
  American Cancer Society guidelines on, 352
  effectiveness of, 352
  process in, 352
Mandibuloplasty, 378
Manic-depressive illness, **721**
Marijuana, 398, 424–25, **721**, **739**
  cancer and, **731**
  effects of, 424–25
  in infertility, 249
  Institute of Medicine of the National Academy of Sciences on, 425
  use of, incidence of, 424
Marital rape, 434
Marriage
  among older people, 536
  sex roles after, 141
  sexual enjoyment in, 138
  statistics regarding, 128
  suggestions for sexual activities in, 139
Massage, **721**
Mastectomy, 355–58, **721**
  plastic surgery procedures following, 387–88
  Reach for Recovery self-help group for, 359–60, 546
  types of, 356, *357*
Masters and Johnson, 133, 546
  on AIDS, 131
  basic female sexual response described by, 134
  on female ejaculation, 136
  on intensity of orgasms, 135

INDEX

on masturbation, 152
on orgasm, 136, 138
revolution caused by, 142
Mastitis, **721–22**
Mastoid, **722**
Mastopexy, 386–87
Masturbation, 151–52, **722**
   in infancy and childhood, 125–26, 151
   mutual masturbation, 151–52
   older women and, 537
   orgasm from, 130
   for sexual dysfunction, 146
Mead, Margaret, 541
Measles, **722**
Medicaid, 561–62
Medical care for elderly, 507–9
   choosing physician, 507
   nonphysician services, 508
   nursing home care, 508
   role of physician, 507
   specialists, 507
Medic-Alert, 565, **722, 723**
Medical ethics, 571
Medical records, **722–23**
Medical school, changing role of, 546
Medical terms, 800–2
Medicare, 513, 521, 559, 561
   fee structure, 561
   "Medigap" coverage, 561
   second opinions and, 497
Medication for elderly, 510–14
   drugs taken simultaneously, 512
   generic drugs, 513–14
   keeping track of, 512
   over-the-counter (OTC) medicines, 512
   suggestions for drug safety, 514
Medulla, 41
Megaloblastic anemia, 90
Megavitamin therapy, 65
   for schizophrenia, **761**
Melanin, **723**
Melanomas, **624, 723**
Melatonin, 41
Meloplasty (cheek lift), 372

Men, sexual response of, 502–3
Menarche, 45, **723**
Menière's disease, **689, 723–24**
Meninges, 38, **620**
Meningitis, **724**
Menopause, 45, **724**
   breasts in, 334
   interest in sex after, 138
   problems in, 279
Menorrhagia, **724–25**
Menstrual cycle, 45–49
   estrogen in, 48
   length of, 45, 47–48
   LH in, 48
   ovulation and, 193
   postovulatory phase, 48–49
   preovulatory phase, 48
   progesterone in, 48
   secondary amenorrhea, 107
Menstrual extraction, 184–85
Menstrual periods
   oral contraceptives and, 169
   reasons for missing, 198
Menstrual problems, 274–79
   delayed onset of periods, 275
   frequent periods, 276
   heavy periods, 276–77
   light periods, 276
   menopausal problems, 279
   midcycle bleeding, 277
   mittelschmerz, 279
   painful periods, 278–79
   PMS, 277–78
Menstruation, **725**
   definition, 45
   exercise and, 113
Mental and physical health, relationship between, 49
Mental illness, **725**
Mentoplasty, 378–39
Mercury, **725**
Metabolism, **725**
   OCs and changes in, 166
Metastasis, **726**
Methadone, 423, 424, **726**
Metronidazole, 323, 328
Microsurgery, **726**

Migraine headache, **687**
Milk, **726**
Mineralocorticoids, 41
Minerals, 74–78
 categories, 74
 as food additives, 84
 RDAs for, 64–65
Mini-lap procedure, 182
Mini-pill, 163–64
Miscarriage. *See* Spontaneous abortion
Mittelschmerz, 279
Mole, **726**
Molluscum contagiosum, 318–19
Moniliasis, 284, **675, 726**
Monoclonal antibodies, 199
Mononucleosis, **726–27**
Monosaccharide (simple) sugars, **624–25**
Mons pubis (mons veneris), 42, **727**
Mood-altering drugs, 397–400
 categories of, 397
"Morning after" pill, 170–71
Morning sickness, **727**
Morphine, 398, **727, 735, 738**
 dependence on, 423
Motion sickness, **592, 727**
Motor vehicle accidents, 517
Mucous cysts, **643**
Mucous membrane, **728**
Multiphasic pill, 163
Multiple sclerosis, **728**
Mumps, **728–29**
Muscles
 definition, 22
 exercise and use of, 26
 types of, 22–26
Muscular dystrophy, **729**
Myasthenia gravis, **729**
Mycoplasma pneumonia, **746**
Mycoplasmas, **746**
Mycoses, **675**
Myocardial infarction, 497
Myomectomy, 289, 296
Myometrium, 42
Myxedema, 49

Nail, **729–31**
Narcolepsy, **731**
Narcotics, 399, **731**
 as term, 423
The National Association for Children of Alcoholics, 408
National Cancer Institute, **731**
 on breast cancer, 347
National Center on Child Abuse and Neglect, 452
National Coalition Against Domestic Violence, 446, 447, 450, 451
National Committee for the Prevention of Child Abuse, 453
The National Council on Alcoholism, 409, 410
 on women and alcohol, 402–3
National Hospice Organization, 524
National Institute of Dental Research, **647**
National Institute of General Medical Sciences, **678**
National Institute for Occupational Safety and Health (NIOSH), 466, **731**
 on poise, 733
National Institute on Aging, 542
National Institute on Drug Abuse, 512
National Institutes of Health, 503
 on chemotherapy, 358–59
 Recombinant DNA Committee of, **679**
National Osteoporosis Foundation, 503
Nausea, **731**
Nearsightedness, **731–32**
Neck, stiff, **732**
Needle aspiration, 353
Neighbors Helping Neighbors, 541
Neoplasm, **732**
Nephritis. *See* Glomerulonephritis
Nephrosis, **709–10**
Nerve, cross-section of, *37*
Nervous system, 36–38, **732**

INDEX 849

age-related changes in, 493–96
Networking, older woman and, 535
Neuralgia, **732**
Neural tube defect (NTD), 225
Neuritis, **732**
Neurons, 36
Neurogenic shock, **764**
Neuromuscular disease, **732–33**
Neurosis, **733**
New England Journal of Medicine, 347, 355
Nicotine, **733, 780, 781**
Nicotine-laced chewing gum, 418
9 to 5: The National Association for Working Women, 483
NIOSH. *See* National Institute for Occupational Safety and Health
Nitrites/nitrates, 85–86
Nitroglycerin, **599**
Nitrosamines, 86
Noise, **733–34**
Non-prescription drugs, 415–20
Nonspecific urethritis, **734**
Nonspecific vaginitis, 284–85
Nonsteroidal anti-inflammatory drugs (NSAIDs), **704, 734**
Nonstress test (NST), 228
Nose alteration. *See* Rhinoplasty
Nosebleed, **734**
NST. *See* Nonstress test
NTD. *See* Neural tube defect
Nuclear magnetic resonance (NMR) scanner, **734–35**
Nuclear medicine, **735**
Nuprin. *See* Ibuprofen
Nurse-midwifes, 201–2, 582
Nurses' Environmental Health Watch, 473
Nursing home care, 508
Nursing homes, selecting, 508–9
Nutrients
 caloric content, 56
 classes of, 56
 recommended servings of basic food groups, 83
Nutrition, 55

balance in, 80
when breast feeding, 91–92
definition, 56
frauds and, 108
on-the-job, 475–76
for older woman, 92–94
in pregnancy, 89–91
RDAs and, 56
study of, by physicians, 546
Nutritional needs, 56

Obesity. *See* Overweight and obesity
Obstetrician-gynecologist, 200
 description of field, 809
Occipital lobes, 36
Occupational Safety & Health Act (OSHA), 465–66
Occupational therapy, **735**
OCs. *See* Oral contraceptives
Older woman
 alcohol abuse in, 530
 children of, 525
 crime and, 522–23
 depression and, 527–28
 earning power of, 532–33
 emotional fulfillment and, 537
 exercise for, 92, 540
 of future, 543–44
 housing and transportation and, 521–22
 income of, 520–21
 learning and, 533–34
 as lesbian, 537
 life work of, 541–42
 loving and, 536–37
 masturbation and, 537
 networking and, 535
 nutrition and, 92–94
 pets for, 538
 political clout of, 542–43
 self-image of, 527
 sex and sensuality of, 526–27
 shared living for, 539–40
 social supports for, 525–26
 strengths and potentials of, 542–43
 suicide and, 530
 in therapy, 532

widowhood and, 523–25
Older Women's League (OWL), 533, 535, 542
Ombudsmen, 570–71
Omega 3 fatty acids, 62–63
Onychomycosis, **675**
Oophorectomy, 301
Opiate, **735**
  legal use of, 423
  as term, 423
Optometrist, role and function of, 811
Oral contraceptives (OCs), 160, 163–71, 275, 327
  assessing side effects of, 164
  beneficial side effects of, 169
  cancer and, 166–67
  cardiovascular side effects of, 164–65
  combined oral contraceptives, 163–64
  diabetes and use of, **650–51**
  drugs and, interaction with, 167–68
  in dysmenorrhea, 278–79
  fetal damage and use of, 166
  heart attacks and, **690**
  hormone therapy and, 293
  hypertension and, 165–66
  lupus erythematosus and, **718**
  metabolic changes due to, 165–66
  mini-pill, 163–64
  minor adverse side effects from, 169
  "morning after" pill, 170–71
  multiphasic pill, 163
  objections to, 177
  smoking and, 162, 163, 165, 168, **769**
  surgery and, 301
  as test for pregnancy, 166
  thrombosis and, **780**
  widespread use of, 163
Oral sex, 139–40, 327, **764**
Organ of Corti, **733**
Orgasm, **736**, **772**
  attainment of, during intercourse, 137
  Masters and Johnson on, 134–35
  description of, 137–38
  Freud on, 136
  in infancy and childhood, 125
  Masters and Johnson on, 130, 135, 136, 138
  in old age, 502–503
  simultaneous, 138
  vaginal versus clitoral, 136–37
Orinase (tolbutamide), **777**
Orthodontia, **736**
Orthotics, **736**
OSHA. *See* Occupational Safety & Health Act
Osteoarthritis, 606–7, **737**, **791**
Osteopathy, **737**
Osteoporosis, 63
  calcium for, 111
  endometriosis and, 290
  exercise for, 111
  incidence of, 503
  prevention of, 503
  of vertebrae, **791**
  women at risk for, 503
Ostomy, **737**
Otologist, 490
Otomycosis, **659**
Otoplasty, 363, 381–82
Otorhinolaryngologist, 490
Otosclerosis, **689**, **737**
Ovarian tumors, 167
Ovaries, *40*, 41, *44*, 45, **737**
  benign tumors of, 291
  cancer of, 291
Over-the-counter (OTC) medicines, 512
Overweight and obesity, 98–101, **735**, **737**
  dieting for, 101–2
  drugs for, 104
  exercise for, 102–3
  group therapy for, 104–5
  heredity versus nutrition in, 98–99
  treatment for, 99–100

INDEX 851

Ovulation, 45, 48–49, 237
  basal body temperatures, 256
  determining time of, 180–81
  endometrial biopsy for, 256–57
  hormone tests for, 257
  menstrual cycle and, 193
  pain with, 279
OWL. *See* Older Women's League
Oxytocin, **704, 737**
Oxygen
  in energy production, 114
  in respiratory system, 29–30

Pacemaker, artificial, **737–38**
Pancreas, *40*, **738–39**
  functions of, *33*
Pantothenic acid, 72, **739**
  guide to, 68–69
Papanicolaou, George, Dr., 271, **739**
Pap smear, 271–73, 288, **739**
  classification of, 272
  guidelines for, 272–73
Paramedical services, 581
Paranoia, **739**
Parasympathetic nervous system, 38
Parathyroid glands, 39, *40*
Parathyroid hormone (PTH), 39
Paregoric, **735**
Parenthood, education for, 156–57
Parkinson's disease, 495, **739–40**
Passive exercise, **744**
Patch test, **740**
Patient, responsibilities of, 579–80
Patient advocatepatient
  representative, 570–71
"Patient compliance," 54
Patient's bill of rights, 566–70
  complaints, 569
  confidentiality, 568
  declining treatment, 567
  giving consent, 567
  information, right to, 566–67
  leaving against medical advice,
    567–68
  participation in research, 569
  participation in your health care,
    569–70

payment, 569
privacy, 568
quality care for all patients, 566
transfer to another institution, 568
your responsibility as patient, 570
PC test. *See* Postcoital test
Pediatrician, choosing, 556–57
Pendunculate polyps, **748**
Pelvic examination, 269, 557
  after menopause, 502
Pelvic inflammatory disease (PID),
    253, 286, 311, 319, **740**
  causes of, 319
  diagnosis, 319
  IUDs and, 172–75
  lower abdominal pain due to,
    280–81
  treatment, 319
Penicillin, 310, 323, **600, 601, 740**
Penicillin allergy, 323
Penis, 45, *46*
  dyspareunia caused by, 144
Pep pills. *See* Amphetamines
Peptic ulcers, **785–86**
Perineum, 42, **740–41**
Periodontal disease, 492, **741**
Peripheral nervous system, 38
Peristalsis, 30
Peritonitis, **741**
Pernicious anemia, **597**
Perspiration, **741–42**
Pessary, **742**
pH, **742**
Pharyngitis, **742**
Phenobarbital, 398, **611, 742**
Phenylketonuria (PKU), 239, **664**
Phlebitis, **743**
Phobia, **743**
Phonoangiography, **610**
Phosphorus, 77
  calcium and, 80
  excess intake of, 93–94
Photochemotherapy, **752**
Photocoagulation, 489, **651**
Physical examination, **743–44**
Physical fitness, 109–24

activities rated according to
    benefits, 123
  benefits of, 111–14
  definition, 111
  developing personal fitness
    program, 120–24
  energy, 114–16
  See also Exercise
Physical therapy, **744**
Physician(s), **747–48**
  changing, 553–54
  "college" of, 810
  confidentiality from, 577
  dignity of patient and treatment
    by, 577
  disciplinary action for, 547–48
  fees, 549
  first visit to, 552
  getting second opinions, 557–58
  past commonality of experience
    between patient and, 550–52
  role of, 507
  selection of
    age in, 550–51
    for elderly patient, 507
    geography in, 548
    importance of, 547–48
    personality in, 550–51
  qualifications of, 549
  specialists, choosing, 553–55
  specialties of, 808–10
  study of diet and nutrition by, 546
  treatment of women by male
    physicians, 562–63
  what physicians have a right to
    expect from you, 579–80
  what you have a right to expect
    from, 574–78
  what you should not expect from,
    578–79
PID. *See* Pelvic inflammatory disease
"The Pill." *See* Oral contraceptives
Pilonidal cysts, **643**
Pineal, *40*, **744**
Pituitary deficiency, 562
Pituitary dwarfism, 39
Pituitary gland, 39, *40*, **744**

PKU. *See* Phenylketonuria
Placebo, **744**
Placenta, 196, 236, **744**
  delivery of, 236
Placental abruption, 214
Plantar wart, **744–45**
Plaque, **745**
Plastic surgery, 363, **745**, **809**. *See
    also* Cosmetic surgery
Plateletpheresis, **617–18**
Platelets, **745**
Pleura, **745**
Pleurisy, **745**
PMS. *See* Premenstrual syndrome
Pneumocystis pneumonia, **745–46**
Pneumonia, **746–47**
Pneumothorax, **718**
Podiatrists, 582, 811
Poison, **747**
Polio, **748**
Polypectomy, 295
Polyps, **628**, **748–49**
Polysaccharide (complex) sugars, **624**
Polyunsaturated fats, 59, **749**
Postcoital test (PC test), 260
"Post polio" syndrome, **748**
Posture, **749**
Potassium, 513, **749**
Pre-eclampsia, 216, **749**
  cesarean section and, 239
Pregnancy
  activity during, 210–12
  in adolescence, 127, 156
  alcohol and, 207, 209, 409–10
  bleeding during, 213–14, 277
  chloasma of, 376
  chronic diseases and, 217–18
  complications of, 212–22
  development of embryo, 196
  diabetes and, 217
  diagnosis, 198–99
  drugs in, 207–10
  emotional changes in, 205–6
  epilepsy and, 218
  exercise and, 113–14
  fetal positions in, *238*
  genetic diseases and, 217–18

INDEX

health care in normal pregnancy, 204–12
high blood pressure in, 217
home tests for, 199
infections in, 218–20
nutrition in, 88–91
after rape, 442–43
professional help for delivery, 200–2
sexual relations during, 211–12
signs and symptoms of, 198–99, 275
smoking during, 207, 416–17, **769**
STDs and, 310
tests for, 198–99
tetracycline in, 310, **780**
travel during, 211
weight gain during, *208*, 243
Premarital sex, 128
Premature birth, 229, 235
Premature ejaculation, **660**
Premature infant, **749**
Premenstrual syndrome (PMS), 277–78, **749**
Prenatal care in normal pregnancy, 204–12
diet, 207
first visit to doctor, 204
Prenatal DNA studies, 227
Prescription, how to read, 802
Prescription drugs, 410–11
Primary amenorrhea, 275, **595**
Primary influenza virus pneumonia, **746**
Primary prevention, 50
Proctoscope, **652**
Proctoscopy, **750**
Professional health care workers, types of, 811–13
Progesterone, 41, 48, 111, 262, 277, 278, 284, 290, 293, **640**, **750**
Progestin, 170, 503
Prolactin, 39, 257
Prolapse, **750**
Propranolol, **612**
Prostaglandins, 63, 187, 278, **641**, **750**

Prostate gland, 45, *46*, **750**
Protein, 91, **750–51**
requirements of, in pregnancy, 89–90
Psoriasis, **751–52**
Psychiatry, **752**
Psychoanalysis, **752**
Psychosis, **752**
Psychosomatic illness, **752**
Psychotherapy, **752**
Psychotropic drugs, **752**
PTH. *See* Parathyroid hormone
Ptosis, 386
Puberty, **752–53**
breasts in, 330
Pubic lice ("Crabs"), 319–20
Pulmonary artery, 27
Pulmonary circulation, 29
Pulse, 29, **753**
Pus, **753**
Pyelonephritis, 282, **709**
Pyuria, **789**

Quickening, **753**
Quinolones, **601**

Rabies, **753–54**
Radiation therapy, 302, 359, **754**
Radical mastectomy, 355–56, *357*
Radioimmuneassay (RIA), 199
Radium, **754**
Rape, 308, 429–45
current statistics on, 432–33
date rape, 428
dysparenia due to, 143
history, 429–30
legal definition, 433
marital rape, 428, 434
medical examination after, 442
myths about, 430–31
post-rape syndrome, 443
pregnancy after, 442–43
protecting yourself from, 436–38
rape crisis counselors, 440–41
rape treatment centers, 441
STDs after, 442, 443
stages of recovery after, 443–45

statutory, 433
testing for AIDS after, 441–42
treatment, 441–45
underreporting of, 431, 432
updating the law on, 433
what to do if attacked, 438–41
Rash, **754**
Raynaud's phenomenon, **678**
RDAs. *See* Recommended daily dietary allowances
Recommended daily dietary allowances (RDAs), 56, 64–65
Rectal polyps, **748**
Rectocele, **754**
Rectum, *33*, **754–55**
Red Cross, 625
Reduction mammaplasty, 385–86
REM (Rapid Eye Movement) sleep, 768
Remission, **755**
Resistance, **755**
Respiratory system, 29–30, *31*
Responsibility for health, 49–51
Retention cysts, **643**
Retina, **755**
Retired Senior Volunteer Program (RSVP), 537
Reye's syndrome, **608, 639, 755**
Rh disease, 220–21
Rheumatic fever, **756, 775**
Rheumatism, **756**
Rheumatoid arthritis, **606**
Rh factor, **755–56**
Rhinitis, **756–57**
Rhinoplasty (nose alteration), 363, 369–72
Rhytidoplasty (face lift), 363, 372–76
RIA. *See* Radioimmuneassay
Riboflavin, **757**
deficiency of, **671**
Ribonucleic acid. *See* RNA
RICE treatment, **773**
Rickettsial diseases, **757**
"Right-to-die" law, **645**
Ringworm, **675**
RNA (Ribonucleic acid), **757**

Robert Kennedy Center for Bioethics, 571
Rocky Mountain Spotted Fever, **757–58**
Root canal, **758**
RSVP. *See* Retired Senior Volunteer Program
RU 486, 188
Rubella, 219, **758**
Rubin test, 260
Rupture, **758**

Saccharin, 86–87, **758**
Sacroiliac, **758**
Salicylate (acid) poisoning, **589**
Saliva, **758–59**
Salmonella, **674, 759**
Salpingectomy, 300, **759**
Salpingitis, **759**
Salt (NaCl), 74–76, **673, 759–60**
for older woman, 94
in pregnancy, 91
sodium content, 76
substitutes for, 75
Salvarsan, **629**
Sarcomas, **624, 760**
Saturated fat, 59, 60, **760**
Scabies, 320
Scalp test, 228–29
Scanning machines, **760**
Scars, removing, 377–78
Schizophrenia, **760–61**
Sciatica, **761**
Scopolamine, **761**
Scurvy, 73, **761**
Sebaceous cysts, **643**
Sebaceous glands, **761**
Sebum, **589**
Secondary amenorrhea, 107, 275, **595**
Secondary prevention, 51
Second opinions, 557–58, 576–77
Sedatives, 399, **762**
Self-care, 52–53
Self-defense courses, for women, 438
Self-help groups, 52–53, 545–46, **762**

INDEX 855

Self-respect, 132–33
Semen, **762**
Seminal vesicles, *46*, **762**
Senile dementia, **762**
Senile macular degeneration, 489
"Senility," 493
Septic shock, **764**
Serologic tests, for infertility, 257
Serologic Tests for Syphilis (STS), 322
Serum cholesterol, 59
Sessile polyps, **748**
Sex
   "dirty" messages regarding, 125–26
   health care and, 128–32
   older woman and, 526–27
   single women and, 147–49
Sexaholics Anonymous, 150, 151
Sex education, 126
   in medical school curricula, 129
Sex-linked abnormalities, **763**
Sexual abuse of children, 454–56
Sexual activity
   in adolescence, 127
   after delivery, 242
   with friends or co-workers, 132
   getting away for, 140
   ill effects of, 131
   incidence of, in American women, 128
   new techniques for, 139–40
   in pregnancy, 211–12
   sexual freedom and responsibility, 128
   in single women, 148
Sexual addiction, 150–51
Sexual aids, 140
Sexual arousal, stages of, 133–34
Sexual attacks, avoiding, 121–22
Sexual communication, 140–43, 148
Sexual Compulsives, 151
Sexual deprivation, 129–30
Sexual dysfunction
   "good girl" syndrome, 146–47
   loss of libido, 146
   physical conditions, 143–45

   psychological causes of, 145–47
Sexual fantasies, 152–53
   rape and, 431
Sexual harassment, 476–80
   categories of, 477–78
   law and, 478–79
   practical suggestions for handling, 479–81
Sexual intercourse, **764**
   bleeding after, 280
   cystitis after, 283
   female infertility and, 254–56
Sexually transmissible diseases (STDs), 305–28
   avoiding, 307–8
   considerations applicable to, 309–10
   condoms for, 179
   description of specific diseases, 310–27
   exposure to, 308
   after rape, 442, 443
   self-examination for, 309
   testing for, 309–10
   treatment, 309–10
Sexual stages, 125–28
Sexual therapy, 141–43, 147
   Masters and Johnson and, 142
Shared Housing Resource Center, 539
Shared living, 539–40
Shock, **764–65**
Shoulder, bursitis of, *622*
Sick building syndrome, 467
Sickle-cell anemia, **696**, **765**
SIDS. *See* Sudden infant death syndrome
Sigmoidoscope, 652–53
Silicone, 382, 387
Single women, sex and, 147–49
Sinuses, **765**
Sinusitis, **765–66**
Skeletal muscular system, 22–26
   functions of, *24*
Skin, 26, **766–67**
   age-related changes in, 486–88
   care of, **767–68**

cross-section, *767*
diseases of, **768**
Sleep, **768**
Sleeping pills, 413–14
Small intestine, *33*
Smallpox, **768–69**
Smegma, **769**
Smokers Anonymous, 418
"Smoker's cough," **641**
Smoking, 396, 415–19, **769–71**, **781**
   age and, 168, 499
   The American Cancer Society on, 416
   breast feeding and, 417
   cancer due to, 492
   cardiovascular disease caused by, **610**
   in infertility, 249
   lung disease and, 498–99
   oral contraceptives and, 162, 163, 165, 168
   in pregnancy, 207, 209
   quitting, 417–19
   secondary smoke, 467
   ulcers and, **786**
   women and, 416–17
Smooth muscles, 26, 39
Soap, **771**
Social Security system, 521, **652**
Sodium, 74–76. *See also* Salt
Sonogram, **771**
Sonography, 223, 273
Sontag, Susan, 527
Spasm, **771**
Spectinomycin, 314
Speculum, 269, **771**
   insertion of, *270*
Speech disorders, **771–72**
Sperm, **772**
Spermicide, **772**
Specialists, 808–10
   certification of, 810
   choosing, 555–57
Sphygmomanometer, **616–17**
Spider hemangioma, 392
Spinal anesthesia, 233–34
Spinal cord, 38

Spinal Fluid Examination, 323
Spleen, **772–73**
Spontaneous abortion (miscarriage), 212–14, **588**
   HCG in, 199
   incidence of, 277
Sports
   aspects of fitness developed by, 121
   injuries from, 119–20
   women in, 109–10
Spotting, **773**
Sprain, **773**, **775**
Stapedectomy, **689**
Staphylococci, **674**
Staphylococcus infection, **773**
Statutory rape, 433
STDs. *See* Sexually transmissible diseases
Steinberg, Lisa, 452
Sterilization, 181–82, *183*, **773–74**
Steroids, **774**
Stethoscope, **774**
Stillbirth, 222, **774**
Stomach, **774–75**
   aspirin and, **775**
   functions of, *33*
Stomach cancer, **774**
Strain, **775**
Streptococcal pneumonia, **746**
Streptococcus infection, **775**
Streptomycin, **781**
Stress, **775**
   handling, 50
   lower abdominal pain due to, 281
   on-the-job, 473–74
   skipped or delayed periods due to, 275
   vitamins and, 66
Stroke, 494–95, 497–98, **775–76**
   causes of, **775–76**
   early diagnosis, 493
   incidence of, 495
   oral contraceptives and, 165
   prevention, 495
   symptoms, 494
Sty, **776**

INDEX 857

Subacute bacterial endocarditis, **756**
Subcutaneous mastectomy, 356, *357*
Subluxation. *See* Dislocation
Substance abuse, 395–426
 addictive personality and, 400
 alcohol, 400–10
 facts on, 396
 illegal drugs, 420–26
 mood-altering drugs, 397–400
 non-prescription drugs, 415–20
 prescription drugs, 410–11
 sleeping pills, 413–14
Suction curette, 185
Sudden infant death syndrome (SIDS), 417, **776–77**
Sugar, **777**
 as food additive, 86
Suicide
 in alcoholic women, 402–3
 in elderly, 530
Sulfamethaxazole (Bactrim), **777**
Sulfonamides, **601**, **602**, **777**
Sulfonylureal drugs, **777**
Sun, overexposure to, 486, **768**, **777**
Sunscreen, **778**
Surgery
 complications from, 302
 oral contraceptive use and, 165
 patient's fears about, 574–75
 preparation for, 301–2
Surrogate mothers, 264, **778**
Swimming, 122
Sympathetic nervous system, 38
Synapse, 36
Syndrome, **778**
Syphilis, 305, 321–23
 curing, **629**
 pregnancy and, 219–20
 tests for diagnosing, 322–23

Tachycardia, **753**
Tagamet. *See* Cimetidine
Tampon, **778**
Tay-Sachs disease, **778–79**
TB. *See* Tuberculosis
Teeth, **779**
 age-related changes in, 492–93

 malocclusion of, **720–21**
Telemetry, **779**
Temporal-lobe epilepsy, **664**
Temporomandibular joint (TMJ), **779**
Tenaculum, 256
"Tennis elbow," 469, 470
Tenormin (atenolol), **613**
Tenosynovitis, 469, 470
Terramycin, **779**
Term birth, 229
Testicles, **779**
Testis, *46*
Testosterone, 41, **596**
 as male contraceptive, 171
Test tube baby, **779**
Tetanus, **779–80**
Tetracycline, 310, 314, 315, **601**, **602**, **757**, **780**
Thermography, 353, **780**
Thiamin, **780**
Thigh lipectomy, 390
Thorazine, **716**, **739**
 for schizophrenia, **760**
Thrombocytes. *See* Platelets
Thrombocytopenia, **773**
Thromboembolic disease, 164–65
Thromboembolism, **780**
Thrombosis, **780–81**
Thrush, 326, **675**
Thyroid gland, 39, *40*
 in energy production, 114–15
 myxedema of, 49
 role of, 39
Thymectomy, **729**
Thymus gland, *40*, 41
Ticks, **781**
Tics, **771**, **781**
Timoptic (timolol maleate), **681**
Tinnitus, **689**, **781**
"Tipped womb," 282
Title VII of 1964 Civil Rights Act, 478
T-lymphocytes, 78
TMJ. *See* Temporomandibular joint
Tobacco, **781**
Tonsils, **781–82**
Touch deprivation, 130

Tourette's syndrome, **782**
Toxemia, **782**
Toxic shock syndrome (TSS), 178, 286, **652, 782**
Toxoplasmosis, **782**
TPA (tissue plasminogen activator), **782**
Trace minerals, 74
Tranquilizers, 398, 411–13, **752, 782–83**
  dependency on, 412–13
Transportation, elderly and, 522
Transverse lie, 237, 239
Transvestites, **783**
Traveler's diarrhea, **653, 657**
Treatment consent, **636–37**
Trichomonas vaginalis, **783**
Trichomoniasis, 323
Trigeminal neuralgia, **771, 783**
Tryptophan, 72
TSS. *See* Toxic shock syndrome
Tubal ligation, **784**
Tubal pregnancies, 215
Tubal surgery, 300
Tubercular meningitis, **724**
Tuberculosis (TB), **784**
  of spine, **791**
Tuboplasty, 262
Tularemia, **705**
Tumors, 286–91, **784**
  as term, 286–87
Twinning, 195
Tylectomy, 356
Typhoid fever, **785**
Typhus, **785**

Ulcer, **785–86**
Ultrasound, 273
Umbilical cord, **786–87**
Umbilical hernia, **696**
Underweight, 105–6
Undulant fever, **787**
U.S. Environmental Protection Agency, **725**
U.S. Food and Drug Administration (FDA), **747**
  age factor and recommended drug dosages, 510
  on contraindications to "pill," 168
  cosmetics and, **640**
  food additives and, 84, 86, 87, **673**
  requirements for food labeling, 82–84
U.S. Public Health Service, **672**
U.S. Quarantine and Immunization Service, **748**
U.S. Surgeon General, on smoking, **769**
University clinics, 554–55
University Hospital, NYU Medical Center, 573
University hospitals, 564–65
Unsaturated fat, 58
Ureter, **787**
Urethra, 45, *46*, **787**
Urethritis, 282–83, 324, **789**
  preventing, 308
Urinary system, 34–36
  age-related changes in, 501–2
Urinary tract infections, **787–88**
  in pregnancy, 218–19
Urination, **788**
  after delivery, 242–43
Urine, 34–36
Urine tests, **788–89**
  for pregnancy, 198–99
Uterine polyps, **748**
Uterine prolapse, 282, **750, 751**
Uterus, 42, *44*, **789**
  benign conditions of, 288
  bimanual examination of, *271*
  in conception, 195–96
  curettage of, 296
  in female infertility, 254
  fibroids of, 254
  hysterosalpingogram for, 257, 260
  IUD perforation of, 174

Vaccination, **789**
Vaccine, **789**
Vagina, *44*, **789**
  in conception, 193

INDEX

self-examination of, 309
   in sexual arousal, 134
Vaginal barriers, 308
Vaginal deodorants, **648**
Vaginal discharge, 281, **789–90**
Vaginal examination, 269, 270
Vaginal hysterectomy, 295, *297*
Vaginal orgasms, 136–37
Vaginal sponge, 178–79
Vaginal surgery, 295
Vaginal tumors, 287
Vaginismus, 143–44
Vaginitis, 283–86, 324–25
   causes of, 284
   nonspecific, 284, 324–25
   preventing, 285–86
   symptoms, 283–84
   treatment, 284
Valium (Diazepam), 398, 400, **715**
Varicose veins, 498, **790–91**
Vasectomy, 182, *183*, **791**
Vasopressin, 39
VD. *See* Venereal disease
VDTs (video display terminals), 471–72, **668**
Vegetarianism, 57, 81, **791**
Veins, *28*, **791**
Venereal disease (VD)
   factors in spread of, 306–7
   incidence of, 305
Venereal warts (condyloma acuminata), 272, 325
Ventral hernia, **696**
Vertebra, **791**
Vertex position, *238*
Vertigo, **791–92**

Vibrators, 140
Vincent's angina, **684**
Viral meningitis, **724**
Viral pneumonia, **746–47**
Virus, **792**
Vitamins, 63–73
   fat-soluble vitamins, 67–70
   guide to, 68–69
   RDAs for, 64
   vitamin supplements, 66–67
   water-soluble vitamins, 71–73
Vocal cords, **792**, **793**
Voluntary muscles, 25–26
Vomiting, **793**
Vulva, 42, **793**
   tumors of, 287

Wart, **793**
Weight, 95–106
   amphetamines for loss of, 414
   "desirable" weight, 97–98
   "Ideal Weights," 95–97
   oral contraceptives and, 169
   pregnancy and weight gain, *208*, 243
   underweight, 105–6
   See also Overweight and obesity
WHO. *See* World Health Organization
Widowhood, 523–25, 535
World Health Organization (WHO), 171, **672**, **715**
Wrinkles, 377–78, **794**

Yoga, 122, **795**
Yogurt, **795**